The Eurail Guide to World Train Travel
Twenty-sixth Edition 1996

DISCARD

Houghton Mifflin Company
Boston • New York 1996

Using the Eurail Guide

For those of you new to *The Eurail Guide*, welcome to the 26th edition! For those accustomed to the guide, welcome back! You'll be pleased to see that *The Eurail Guide*, like all good train systems, has been modernized. Not only has the guide been thoroughly updated and revised, it has been expanded in its descriptions of excursions and locations, and its travel tips and other helpful information have been amplified by people with experience. *The Eurail Guide*, as always, has been carefully designed to help train travelers move swiftly from city to city and capture both the pleasures and efficiency of rail travel in Europe and around the world. But, to make the most of this guide, there are **ten** key features of this book, and train travel in general, that you should always keep in mind.

• **Check and double-check departure and arrival times** *The Eurail Guide* offers you hundreds of precise timetables and schedules—in fact, the most complete, compact selection of schedules available to individuals. Train schedules have been selected to serve as model itineraries. Although all times listed here are accurate according to the published Thomas Cook schedules (the number appearing at the front of each schedule refers to the Thomas Cook Timetable number), precise times in all countries are subject to change and modification without notice. In addition to this, new trains and supplementary and seasonal trains are added and deleted all the time. This is normal and standard. In fact, train schedules undergo minor changes in Europe every three months. Thus it will always be necessary to check and double-check the departure and arrival times listed here and in all timetables. Most likely, changes will be slight and have little or no effect on the excursions described in this guide. However, a few minutes here and there might make the difference between a swift connection and a wasted afternoon.

• **Prices** Although the prices for train tickets and passes listed here were verified and accurate at printing, don't take them for gospel—all prices are subject to change. There are usually increases of 2%–5% in a given year, and certain trains require supplementary fares which, too, are subject to change. Note: Prices in this book are in U.S. dollars and British pounds based on December 1995 exchange rates. To calculate prices in other currencies, consult current exchange rates. Remember, the rate listed in the daily newspaper is the rate between banks. The rate you will get is usually at least 5% lower.

• **The 24-hour clock** International train schedules are almost always quoted according to the 24-hour clock, and thus the *Eurail Guide* maintains this practice.

You might not be used to seeing 6 P.M. written as 18:00 or midnight as 24:00. Between midnight and 1:00 A.M. time is depicted as 00:01 to 00:59. This might seem like the military, but it's standard fare around the world and good to get used to.

• **Travel days and dates** Unless designated otherwise, all schedules shown in this guide indicate daily departures. Likewise, schedules featured here are based on the prime travel season of late May to late September. That is when the majority of *Eurail Guide* users plan to travel. It's true that schedules tend to change slightly during the off-season and thus, as with the timetables, checking and re-checking schedules is highly recommended.

A note on certain schedules: British timetables differ from the Continental pattern. Summer timetables for British rail service begin on the first Monday of May. Changes occur on various dates—first in October and then again in January. Unless designated otherwise, the departure and arrival times given in this book are for the summer tourist season and apply to trips that will be made from late May to late September. In most cases these schedules change only slightly during September-May.

In most European countries, a summer timetable goes into effect on the last Sunday of May or the first Sunday of June, and remains in effect until and including the last Saturday in September. Winter schedules usually start on the Sunday following the last Saturday of September and run until and including the Saturday preceding the last Sunday of May of the following year.

• **Frequency** Highly traveled routes and lines between major cities are served by frequent train service. It is therefore not necessary in these cases to list all times of all trains. Train options from Paris to Lyon or London to Manchester are just too numerous to list. When the word "frequent" has been noted, you can count on a minimum of one train every hour in the period indicated.

• **Order of excursions listed** In the *Eurail Guide* you will find numerous suggestions of preselected roundtrip excursions or circle trips originating from key locations or base cities. The order in which these roundtrip excursions are listed is as follows:

(1) One-day excursions from a base city to an interesting destination, including practical travel information and information on what to see and do there. The schedules for one-day, roundtrip excursions, however, do not always reflect all the departure times from either the base city or the destination city. Only those departure times involved in making a one-day roundtrip are shown. On particular routes, there are frequently later departure times from the base city and earlier departure times from the destination city than those shown, although these clearly

would not be applicable to the one-day, roundtrip excursions.

(2) Scenic train rides, many of which can be made as a one-day roundtrip or circle trip.

(3) International rail service (trips to adjoining countries).

• **Stations** It is important to remember that many cities have more than one train station. In such cases, the name of the applicable train station is indicated (in parentheses) after the name of the city. In Austria, Germany, and Switzerland, train stations often do not have names, in which case the station is always indicated by the generic "Hauptbahnhof."

• **Before Leaving** Never plan to travel without finding out if the countries you are going to tour offer low-price train passes. And when those countries do provide train passes, make sure to inquire before you leave home if these passes need to be purchased in your country of origin or if they need to be bought in the country you will be visiting. There's nothing worse than a great deal you can't cash in on.

• **Reader Response** Information concerning international travel is constantly changing. The editors of the *Eurail Guide* wholeheartedly welcome correspondence from readers who have suggestions, tips, and pertinent information that can be verified and incorporated into the next annually revised edition. Thank you in advance for helping fellow rail travelers. Address all your letters to: Houghton Mifflin *Eurail Guide*, c/o Marnie Patterson, 222 Berkeley Street, Boston, MA 02116.

• **Table of Contents** The *Eurail Guide*—the most complete train guide on the market—includes train information from 119 countries around the world. See following page.

As international train travelers, you should know that information has not been included on train service in some 35 countries, either because they do not have rail systems or have drastically reduced their rail services due to governmental conditions.

Acknowledgments

Since that first slim (96-page) edition of *The Eurail Guide* appeared in 1971, train travel, especially in Europe, has continually improved and flourished. So has *The Eurail Guide*. For this, the 26th edition, there are many to thank.

This book could not have been made possible were it not for its parents, Marvin and Barbara Saltzman and Katharyn Ashe. They conceived of the idea and their creativity and love for the project will remain in its pages for many editions to come. Many thanks are also due David Applefield whose writing and research have brought new depth to the Central and Eastern European chapters and the book's introductory material, and Catharyn Tivy, who gave this edition of *The Eurail Guide* its new and improved look.

We are also grateful to the many railways and tourist commissions for providing us information, including extraordinary assistance from Cecile Campeau and Andrew Lazarus of Rail Europe; Michael Fox, Britrail Travel International; and Stephen Forsyth, Forsyth Travel Library.

The other important members of *The Eurail Guide* family are the scores of readers who have written to us over the years telling of their train travel experiences. Comments about your train journeys are welcome and appreciated.

- Marnie Patterson,
Editorial Director

Contents

Chapter 6 - Train Travel with a Eurailpass in Western Europe

Chapter 7 - Train Travel in Britain (England, Wales, and Scotland)

Table of Contents

Chapter 8 - Train Travel in Non-Eurailpass Europe

Chapter 9 - Train Travel in the Middle East

Chapter 10 - Train Travel in Africa

Chapter 11 - Train Travel in Asia

Chapter 12 - Train Travel in Australia

Chapter 13 - Train Travel in New Zealand

Chapter 14 - Train Travel in North America

Chapter 15 - Train Travel in Central America and the West Indies

Chapter 16 - Train Travel in South America

Chapter 17 - Accessing Useful Resources

CHAPTER 1

Appreciating the Pleasures of Train Travel

Since that first slim edition (96 pages) of the *Eurail Guide* appeared in 1971, train travel, especially in Europe, has continually improved and flourished. The 36 Trans Europ Express trains that were in service in 1980 have since been replaced by a fleet of more than 90 much faster and more frequent EuroCity trains. Dozens of those futuristic, high-profile, ultra-speed TGV trains (up to 238 miles per hour) now grace many European tracks.

In 1995 more than 60,000,000 passengers crossed the English Channel via the conventional train-plus-ferry. Today, the downtown-to-downtown London-Paris (or the opposite) journey has been reduced from the present seven hours to a mere three hours, and the London-Brussels trip from five hours to only three and a quarter hours. Time and distances are shrinking while the comfort and pleasure are increasing.

All EuroCity trains, in compliance with strict standards of speed, punctuality, safety, comfort, air-conditioning, and food and beverage services, have steadily improved train travel as an excellent means of touring. This tendency is not letting up as more inter-European TGV (train de grande vitesse) lines and services are opening up each year, and the visionary EuroStar high-speed service between London, Paris, and Brussels via the EuroTunnel which is revolutionizing train travel. As dry as statistics can be, those of the thirty-eight new trains - costing $40,000,000 a piece; each carrying six first-class cars, ten second-class cars, and two bar cars; a capacity of up to 800 passengers; and speeds close to 200 miles per hour - are undeniably impressive. It's a long way from the clunky way backpackers roughed it in the late sixties and early seventies! Train travel in much of Europe today challenges - and in some cases, surpasses - air travel in terms of speed, comfort, price, and certainly scenery.

For more than a quarter of a century the editors of the *Eurail Guide* have claimed that the most economical, safest, most convenient, interesting, and pleasant way to travel and really see the world is by train. Although it's doubtful you need convincing, consider the following:

• When traveling by train, departures are almost never delayed by weather, as is often the case with air or automobile travel.

• When traveling by train, departures and arrivals are in the center of cities, not in far-off suburbs, saving travelers lots of time, effort and expense. In fact, in Europe and Japan, many high-speed trains actually get you from a hotel in one city to a hotel in another city faster than by airplane when the distance is 250-350 miles.

• The cost of the least expensive, non-airconditioned compact car in Europe, for 350 miles-per-day travel, can easily come to more than $80 per day - with value-added taxes on rentals being wildly expensive (over 20% in Denmark, Hungary, Sweden, Norway, Austria, and Finland, and approaching that in Italy, France, and Britain). 1995 weekly rates for B-category automobiles with standard trans-mission and drop-off in the same country averaged $569 in Finland, $449 in Ireland, $389 in Sweden, $319 in Austria, and $299 in France. For an automatic transmission Mercedes Benz, typical prices in 1994 were: $1,429 in Britain, $1,279 in Ireland, $1,239 in Denmark, $1,099 in Austria and $1,059 in Norway. When you count the cost of insurance, servicing, overnight parking fees ($10-$20 per night at most hotels), substantial drop-off charges, and astronomical gasoline prices - sample prices-per-gallon for regular unleaded in 1994 were: $3.77 in Holland, $3.70 in Italy, $3.47 in France, and $3.34 in Germany - the case for train travel becomes increasingly clear. To add insult to injury, autoroute tolls can provoke cardiac arrest in travelers used to the New Jersey Turnpike or the Sunshine State Parkway. In 1992, motorists had to pay $43 in tolls for the 183-mile drive from Bilbao to Zaragoza. The 86-mile trip from Milan to Turin was $13. It was $14 to go 104 miles from Nice to Aix-en-Provence. *The Consumer Reports Travel Letter* stated in 1992 that extensive driving in France or Italy "will add $5-$15 to your daily cost."

Then, of course, there is the fatigue of driving, the exasperation of congested traffic, insane holiday patterns in many European countries, and the increasing nuisance and health risk of intense diesel fumes on major European roadways.

Now consider the train.

One can travel on high-speed, air-conditioned trains with any of more than 80 bargain European train passes for $10-$30 per day. The first-class, 15-day Eurailpass, the first-class Eurail Saverpass, and the first-class Eurail Flexipass all represent fantastic bargains in comparison to car rental or air travel, as do also the many European national and regional train passes listed throughout chapters 6 and 7.

By train travel you reach thousands of interesting destinations not accessible by air. Let's not talk about the worries, frustrations, and delays of socked-in airports, check-in requirements, baggage waits; or, by car, unexpected flat tires, the trauma of unfamiliar and congested arteries of foreign cities, strange traffic laws, and the many other problems, expenses, and inconveniences connected with airplane and auto travel. Let's focus on trains.

Whether in London or Tokyo, you will find food, information on local tours, assistance in obtaining lodging, money exchange, waiting rooms where you can relax, shoe repair, etc. at the principal rail stations. There is also the local flavor.

If you plan your itineraries well, you will see an array of visual delights that airplane passengers never see: indescribable seashores, vineyards tinted with afternoon sunlight, castles that have been straddling hilltops for centuries, raging rivers, breathtaking waterfalls, Alpine summits, remote villages founded before Christ, fjords, forests, lovely orchards and pastures - a feast of colorful scenes to enjoy long after the trip ends. You can take pictures or shoot video footage without having to pull over or take your eye from the road. You can meet strangers native to the country you're in or passengers also on their way somewhere new to you. You're free to read, to write, to drink, to flirt (this depends on your situation), to sleep, to daydream, to take a walk.

On a train you experience the sublime sensation of freedom, never losing your connection to the landscape around you, yet are detached from the trappings of daily life outside. You're a spectator and a participant all at once, and even at high speeds you come to understand another country through its changing terrain, land formations and distances between places. Traveling by train can elevate the act of travel from the banality of transportation to the poetic experience - all without sacrificing practicality!

As you approach your destination, you can feel the charge of excitement as people around you prepare their belongings and the train begins to brake. The new cityscape comes into focus and you feel energized, maybe even rested and refreshed. Perhaps you've even had time to shave or put on your makeup. A cup of local espresso or a glass of beer may await you at the end of the platform.

You say good-bye, maybe exchange addresses with those Amsterdam businessmen, students from Oslo or that Greek army officer, Croatian geologist, Uruguayan cardiologist, North Dakota farmer and his Chinese-Canadian wife, Emily, who gave you a bunch of Italian grapes, the family from Brazil with the twins, a Russian woman living in Frankfurt, the professor of French from Boston who knows your dentist. You get the picture. Your sense of the world and its people has grown overnight and you're glad to be alive. Welcome to train travel!

A Eurailpass must be validated at the
ticket office of your first departure. The
clerk will write on your pass the first
and last day it can be used, your
passport number, and he will stamp it
with his railroad office stamp.

You must start to use
your Eurailpass within
six months after the date
of purchase.

Your Eurailpass must be
kept in its cover at all times.
Without the cover, the pass
is invalid.

Note: If you fail to have your pass validated before your first departure, the train conductor can do this for you. However, there is a $3 fee for this kind of post-departure validation. Always be ready to present your passport. When a conductor checks or validates your pass, he will ask to see your passport too.

CHAPTER 2

Deciding How to Travel: Choosing a Eurailpass

Since 1959, that famous train travel bargain called the Eurailpass has been offered by Western European rail companies throughout the world, revolutionizing the scope of low-budget travel. This particularly came into mode during the sixties and seventies, when Europe instantly became accessible to young North Americans traveling by backpack and by train.

Currently there are twelve different Eurailpasses and options entitling one to unlimited first, or second-class train travel plus free or reduced fares on many bus and boat lines in the following 17 countries: Austria, Belgium, Denmark, Finland, France, Germany, Greece, Holland, Hungary, The Irish Republic, Italy, Luxembourg, Norway, Portugal, Spain, Sweden, and Switzerland. In addition, Eurailpasses are honored on those trains running to and from the airports of the following cities: Amsterdam, Barcelona, Bilbao, Brussels, Dusseldorf, Geneva, Frankfurt, Malaga, Paris, Pisa, Vienna, and Zurich.

Over 100,000 miles of European train travel is available to those in possession of a pass. Rest assured that despite the four main options open to train travelers over the age of twenty-six - first-class tickets, Eurailpasses, national passes, and second-class tickets - train travel with one or more of the Eurailpasses is the most economical and interesting way of experiencing international travel. But there are lots of distinctions, nuances, and tips you need to know in order to maximize the impact and enjoyment of your journey.

Eurailpass Rules and Pointers

• **Refunds** All Eurailpasses are non-refundable if lost or stolen. So be careful. It is forbidden to lend or borrow a Eurailpass. Treat your card like a passport. If you present an unused Eurailpass to a Eurailpass office before its validity begins, you are entitled to a refund of 85% of the purchase price. Otherwise, do not expect refunds for unused cards. Lost or stolen passes, though, can be replaced if the user can successfully produce the "proof-of-purchase" stub from the two-part pass issued at purchase.

• **Validity** All Eurailpasses become valid on the first day they are used, after first having been recorded at the ticket office of the station from where the first journey began. You must start to use your Eurailpass within six months after the date of purchase. Thus, a purchase on February 1 necessitates a first use prior to August 1. Longer delays invalidate the pass. It's a good idea to protect yourself from having your pass rendered partially or wholly invalid because the validity dates were entered incorrectly. The Eurailpass must be validated at the station ticket office at your first departure before you depart. At that time, the clerk writes on the pass both the first and last day it can be used. Before he does this, write a note with what you believe are the validity dates, show it to him, and ask him if he agrees with those dates. Only when he says your dates are correct, or explains why they are not, should you hand your pass to him for the dates to be entered on it. Once the clerk has written validity dates on the face of your Eurailpass, those dates cannot be changed, because any alteration of the dates invalidates the pass. If one fails to have the Eurailpass validated before boarding the first train ride, the train conductor can do so. However, there is a $3 fee for a post-departure validation. After your Eurailpass has been validated, remove the "proof-of-purchase" stub from the two-part pass. From then on, as you would do with traveler's checks, keep that stub separate from the pass. It is this stub that is required for a replacement in case the pass itself is lost or stolen.

• **Savings** Eurailpasses offer users unlimited travel, meaning precisely that: You can literally travel 24 hours a day for the entire period of validity. Countless travelers have used three and four times the price of their pass in train travel, saving hundreds of dollars from what their itinerary would have cost had they used ordinary tickets. The bargain does not end there. Tickets for the high-speed (EC), Inter-City (IC), and super-speed "TGV" trains cost more than an ordinary, slower train on the same route, with supplementary charges ranging from around $5 to over $18. Happily Eurailpasses include unlimited use of EC, IC, and TGV trains without having to pay anything extra.

On the other hand, not all Eurailpasses are wholly economical. Some European itineraries are less expensive using regular train tickets or using one or a combination of the many national and regional rail passes described elsewhere in this guide (see France Railpass, German Flexipass, Benelux Tourrail, etc.). The only way to find out if a Eurailpass or one of the numerous other passes will save you money is to compare their price with the total prices of tickets for particular itineraries.

• **Classes** Most train systems have first and second-class cars. If you have hesitations about second-class space in Europe, don't. Seats are completely acceptable, especially on trains in Austria, Belgium, Denmark, Finland, France, Germany, Holland, the Irish Republic, Luxembourg, Norway, Sweden, and Switzerland.

Although first-class is more comfortable and less crowded, it is of course more expensive. If you are considering traveling in the often crowded second-class, compute second-class fares at two-thirds of the first-class fares shown. This will give you the approximate price of a second-class ticket. While second-class is usually more crowded than first-class, often the disadvantage of having to stand because all the seats are occupied can be simply overcome by arriving early at the rail station. In Europe, first-class cars (and the first-class portion of mixed-class cars) are often marked by a yellow line running above the windows on the outside of the train. Note: Even though second-class tickets cost 66% of the first-class tickets, the cost of a typical itinerary using second-class tickets is often more expensive than when traveling first-class with a Eurailpass!

• **Reservations** Many of the EC, IC, and TGV trains require reservations, the price of which is often included in the supplement and the cost of the supplement is covered by the pass. However, Eurailpass travelers must still pay the small fee of usually $3 for each seat reservation.

• **Time savings** Eurailpasses add precious time to a travel schedule, in that travelers no longer need to stand in a ticket-selling line when in possession of a Eurailpass or Eurail Youthpass. Delays in line of up to 30 minutes are not uncommon.

     With or without a pass, if reserved seats are required or desired, it is necessary to allocate time for the separate seat reservation line when you have not made reservations before starting your trip. For more information about reservations see Chapter 3.

• **Itineraries** In addition to the 100,000 available miles of track, there are more than 700 train trips in and between the 17 Eurailpass countries listed in this guide for Eurailpass holders. See the Route Chart in Chapter 17. The first step in using the Route Chart is to make a list of your itinerary destinations. It is advisable to schedule any part of your trip that is not in the 17 Eurailpass countries (such as England, Yugoslavia, etc.) either before or after the days you are touring the countries in which your Eurailpass is valid, so as to avoid consuming Eurailpass days and thus be able to buy the shortest and least expensive Eurailpass necessary. Next, consult the Route Chart and note the first-class fare for each leg of your trip that can be covered by Eurailpass.

Eurail Guide Route Chart

Thanks to the unique and essential Route Chart found in Chapter 17, scheduling your train travel, matching your trips with validity periods of the available train passes, computing all ticket prices, and, perhaps most importantly, determining the most advantageous Eurailpass, national pass, or series of ordinary tickets to purchase has been made easy and accurate. The Route Chart is accurate enough to help you decide whether you want to make a particular trip in one day or break it up into two or more shorter trips. With the Route Chart you can quickly discover the least expensive way to complete your itinerary, and, if using one of the passes, how to coordinate timetables. Essentially you become your own, personalized travel agent!

How to Use the Route Chart

Travel time figures between two cities represent the longest or shortest possible time for each trip. The time stated for many routes when using a night train, can obviously be reduced significantly on a day train. Many night trains in Europe deliberately slow down or stop mid-journey so as not to arrive at major cities at an impractical, early time. Additionally there may be two or more trains running during the day, one of which is a fast express that makes the trip in less time than what is indicated on the Route Chart. So, take into consideration that the guide deliberately errs only on the long side. Despite this, the time shown in the *Eurail Guide* Route Chart, as a rule, is rarely more than 10% greater than the fastest time between two cities.

Eurailpass Prices

Prices quoted in this guide are based on current exchange rates and information and thus are subject to modification. Individual country pass (sold only in issuing countries) prices are shown in their respective currencies and are also subject to modification.

Most sources for Eurailpasses and ordinary tickets sold by individual European countries charge a non-refundable $10 handling fee per order (not "per pass"). Some travel agencies may also charge a handling fee. Be aware.

The Passes

••••• Eurailpass

Commentary: Depending on your itinerary, the least expensive formula can be buying a combination of Eurailpass and ordinary train tickets. For example, when traveling by train in excess of the 21-day period with the $90 Geneva-Zurich ride scheduled for the last day, you'll save $60 by buying a 21-day Eurailpass plus an ordinary ticket for the twenty-second day ($648 + $90 = $738) instead of buying a $798 one-month Eurailpass. On the other hand, if the trip on the twenty-second day is $151 or more, (Frankfurt-Copenhagen was $217 in 1994), you'll save money buying a one-month Eurailpass even though it is being used only 22 days. Calculate carefully before purchasing.

1996 Prices Per Person
• First-class, consecutive days:
    $522 for 15 days
    $678 for 21 days

$838 for 1 month
$1,148 for 2 months
$1,468 for 3 months
-There is a 50% discount for children between the ages of four and eleven.
-Note that children also count toward the minimum group number.
-Children under four travel free.

••••• Eurail Flexipass

This pass is the same as Eurailpass, but non-consecutive travel days within a 2-month period.

1995 Prices Per Person
$616 for any 10 days within a 2-month period
$812 for any 15 days within a 2-month period
-There is a 50% discount for children between the ages of four and eleven.
-Note that children also count toward the minimum group number.

••••• Eurail Saverpass

This pass for unlimited first-class travel allows three or more people to travel together between April 1 and September 30 with the same privileges as the consecutive-days Eurailpass described above, but with several (precise) advantages. Between October 1 and March 31, only two persons need to travel together.

1995 Prices Per Person
$452 for 15 days
$578 for 21 days
$712 for 1-month
-There is a 50% discount for children between the ages of four and eleven.
-Note that children also count toward the minimum group number.

••••• EurailDrive Pass

-Same privileges as the Eurailpass. Features four days of unlimited first-class train travel plus three days of a Hertz rental car with unlimited mileage, tax, basic liability insurance, and drop-off (providing that drop-off is within the same country as that in which the car is rented).

-There is also an option to buy up to five additional days of either train travel and/or car rental.

-This pass (up to 17 days of travel) must be used within two months.

Commentary: The 1996 per-person price for two or more persons when using the category of smallest car is $339. An option for single travelers is available at $419. Up to five additional rail days (at $55 per day) and up to five additional car days (at $55 per day for smallest car) are available.

Europass

-A flexible pass for unlimited first-class train travel in five of the 17 Eurailpass countries: France, Germany, Italy, Spain, and Switzerland.

-Sold worldwide outside Europe by travel agencies and Rail Europe (U.S. and Canadian offices listed under France).

-If only three or four countries are selected, they must border each other. For example, one cannot select Germany, Switzerland, and Spain.

1996 Prices Per Person

For three countries:	$316 for any five days
	$358 for any six days
	$400 for any seven days

For four countries:	$442 for any eight days
	$484 for any nine days
	$526 for any ten days

For five countries:	$568 for any eleven days
	$610 for any twelve days
	$652 for any thirteen days
	$694 for any fourteen days
	$736 for any fifteen days

Rail travel in any or all of four other countries can be added.

1995 Adult First-Class Prices:

	$45 for Austria
	$42 for Belgium
	$90 for Greece
	$29 for Portugal

-Half fare for children between the ages of four and eleven. Under four, free.

Europass for Couples

New: two people traveling together for five-seven days can take advantage of a new first-class Europass for four countries with costs only half for the second passenger

1996 Prices Per Couple

For three countries:	$474 for any five days
	$537 for any six days
	$600 for any seven days

- No discounts for children.

Europass Bonuses In addition to the regular rail routes, the following European transportation routes and services are included in the Europass:

France: the scenic Digne-Nice-Digne train route.

Germany: steamers operated by KD German Rhine Line (Cologne-Mainz-Cologne), and on the Mosel and Cochem Rivers. Also on the Mannheim-Nuremberg "Castle Road" and the Frankfurt/M-Fussen "Romantic Road" guided bus tours.

Switzerland: regular steamer service on the Rhine River (Schaffhausen-Kreuzliner-Schaffhausen), Aere River (Biel-Solothurn-Biel), and on the lakes of Biel, Brienz, Geneva, Lucerne, Murten, Neuchatel, Thun, and Zurich.

·····Euro Youthpass

This is a particularly advantageous pass limited to those under age twenty-six, offering unlimited second-class train travel with the same conditions as the Europass.

1995 Prices Per Person

For four countries:	$210 for any five days
	$239 for any six days
	$268 for any seven days
	$297 for any eight days
	$326 for any nine days
	$355 for any ten days
For five countries:	$384 for any eleven days
	$413 for any twelve days
	$442 for any thirteen days
	$471 for any fourteen days
	$500 for any fifteen days

·····Europass Drive

This pass lets you alternate the train - for longer distances, with the rental car for side trips. Car rental through Avis or Hertz in three categories of manual transmission. Train travel available for first-class travel only. This pass is good for any 8 days (5 rail, 3 car) within a two-month period plus 5 additional car days in the bordering Europass countries you choose.

1996 Prices for first-class trains, economy cars:

$610 for two adults, $55 for additional car day

$465 for one adult, $75 for additional car day

$31.50 for each additional rail day for two-adult package; $42 for additional rail day for one-adult package.

Eurail Youthpass

This pass is for unlimited second-class train travel in the same 17 countries which honor the first-class Eurailpass. It is often more advantageous for youths under twenty-six than the first-class Eurailpass. Compare and chose carefully. Note: the buyer of a Eurail Youthpass must prove that he or she is under twenty-six years of age on the first day of using the pass.

1996 Prices Per Person
$418 for fifteen days
($100+ less than the 15-day, first-class Eurailpass.)
$598 for one month
($240 less than the one-month, first-class Eurailpass.)
$798 for two months
($350 less than the two-month, first-class Eurailpass.)

Eurail Youth Flexipass

This pass allows for unlimited second-class train travel within a two-month period.

1996 Prices Per Person
$438 for any ten days
$588 for any fifteen days

Eurostar Channel Tunnel Tickets

In late 1994, the French, British and Belgian Railways received approval from the Intergovernmental Safety Commission to begin operation of trains through the Channel Tunnel. This service linked Paris to London in 3 hours and Brussels to London in 3 hours and 15 minutes. Since the innaugural trip, over two million passengers have used Eurostar between London-Paris and London-Brussels. Service between Paris-Brussels will begin in June 1996.

Eurostar links the three capitals with service almost every hour. Prices change frequently. At the time this book was printed, prices were as follows: London-Paris and London-Brussels (roundtrip, refundable): first class (with complimentary meal at you r seat for first class, buffet car for standard class) $344, standard class $242. There are also special fares for 26 and younger, Eurail passholders, and group rates.

Tickets are available in Britain, Belgium or France or from Rail Europe in the U.S. and Canada (call 1-800-EUROSTAR).

Eurailpass Bonuses

In addition to unlimited train travel, the Eurailpasses include numerous free bonuses or reduced prices for boat trips, buses and private railways. Many of these bonuses are not listed in the Eurailpass brochure, such as discounts on several Norwegian fjord boats and Swiss cable cars. It is always a good idea to show your Eurailpass before purchasing any bus, boat, cable car or train ticket in Europe. You have nothing to lose, and sometimes you'll be pleased to profit by an unexpected perk. In many cases, rides that are not covered completely with a Eurailpass will, however, include a discount. There is no reason to miss out on these. Here are the readily known discounts available to Eurailpass holders:

Austria
• Two track railways: (1) Puchberg am Schneeberg-Hochschneeberg and (2) St. Wolfgang-Schafbergspitze.
• Danube cruise between Passau and Vienna.
• Steamers on Lake Wolfgang.
• 50% Reduction on Lake Constance, Linz-Passau-Linz, and Vienna-Budapest ships.

Belgium
• 35% reduction on the Ostend-Dover ferry operated by Regie belgie des Transports Maritimes.

Denmark
• Ferry crossings: Aarhus-Kalundborg, Knudshoved-Halskov, Nyborg-Korsor, Fynshav-Bojden, Rodby Faerge-Puttgarden (Germany), Gedser-Warnemunde (Germany), Helsingor-Helsingborg (Sweden), and Frederikshavn-Goteborg (Sweden).
• 50% reduction on the Flyvebadene Company hydrofoil between Copenhagen and Malmo (25% for Eurail Youthpass).
• 20% reduction on the Steamship Company DFDS between Esbjerg and Harwich, New Castle and Faeroe Islands, and Copenhagen and Oslo.
• 30% reduction on the Color Line for the ship between Hirtshals and Kristiansand (Norway).

Finland
• Free passage on day sailings in both directions of the Silja Line Helsinki-Stockholm ferry. On night sailings, a bed in at least a four-bed cabin ($12) must be used. It can be upgraded to a higher cabin class at extra charge.
• 50% reduction on the Helsinki-Travemunde (Germany) ferry.
• Free rides on buses which operate on occasion as train substitutes.

France
• Irish Ferries ships between LeHavre-Rosslare, Cherbourg-Rosslare, and (late June to late August) LeHavre-Cork. (Port taxes are extra, payable in Irish Pounds. Reservations are required at all times for cabins, and during July and August for seats (Irish £5.20 including the port tax).
• Digne-Nice-Digne rail trip.

Germany
• Free sightseeing cruises on the Rhine, between Cologne and Mainz, and on the Mosel, between Koblenz and Cochem. (Eurail Youthpass holders pay an extra

charge on express-steamers. Everyone pays an extra charge on hydrofoils.)
• Three ferry crossings: Puttgarden-Rodby Faerge (Denmark), Warnemunde-Gedser (Denmark), and Sassnitz-Trelleborg (Sweden). Sassnitz is the most direct gateway from Berlin to Stockholm or Oslo, with both day and night trains operating on these routes.
• Two free bus rides: "Romantic Road" (Frankfurt-Munich-Frankfurt) and "Castle Road" (Mannheim-Nuremberg-Mannheim).
• Bus lines of Regionale Omnibus Verkehrsgesellschaften der Deutschen Bundesbahn.
• 50% reduction on three boat lines: Travemunde-Trelleborg (Sweden), Rostock-Trelleborg, and Travemunde-Helsinki ferries. Lake Constance cruises between Romanshorn and Rorschach and Lindau. Day trips by steamer: Passau-Linz-Passau.
• 25% reduction on two mountain railroads: Garmisch-Zugspitze (Schneeferner-haus) mountain railroad and selected cable cars in the summit area. Freiburg (Breisgau)-Schauinsland mountain railroad.

Greece
• The ferry crossing from Patras to Brindisi (see note under "Italy" Chapter 6).
• 30% reduction on Adriatica di Navagazione Line for ships Piraeus-Venice-Piraeus and Piraeus-Alexandria-Piraeus.

Italy
• The ferry crossing from Brindisi to Patras (see notes under "Italy" Chapter 6).
• 30% reduction on Adriatica di Navagazione's cruises Venice-Piraeus-Venice and Venice-Alexandria-Venice.
Warning: It's imperative to read notes under the Italy section before planning your itinerary! Don't let yourself be diverted to other ships at the Patras or Brindisi rail stations away from the Hellenic Mediterranean Line or Adriatica di Navagazione Line (the only ferries that honor Eurailpasses). Others make the voyage but charge large fees. Numerous cases have been cited of passengers deceived into believing these ships accept Eurailpasses. Steep charges were extorted after it was too late for passengers to leave departed ferries and return to the correct docks. The two proper lines charge pass holders $14 between June 10 and September 30. Reservations ($3 each) are advisable when using Eurailpass.

Hungary
• 50% reduction on Budapest-Vienna ships.

Ireland
• Irish Ferries ships: Rosslare-LeHavre, Rosslare-Cherbourg and (late June to late August) Cork-Le Havre. Port taxes are extra, payable in Irish pounds. Reservations are required at all times for cabins, and during July and August for seats (Irish £5.20 including the port tax).

Norway
• 30% reduction on the boat trip between Kristians and Hirtshals (Denmark) on Color Line steamships.

Sweden

• Five free boat trips: Stockholm-Helsinki. Note that passage is covered by Eurailpass only for those who reserve and pay for a bed on Silja Line. Stockholm-Aland Islands-Turku. Note that Eurailpass covers only a seat; payment is charged for a cabin. Helsingborg-Helsingor (Denmark). Goteborg-Frederikshavn (Denmark). Trelleborg-Sassnitz (Germany).

• 50% reduction (25% for Eurail Youthpass) on the Flyvebadene Company hydrofoil Malmo-Copenhagen.

• 50% reduction on the Trelleborg-Travemunde (Germany) and Trelleborg-Rostock ferries.

Switzerland

• Lake boats on the Biel, Brienz, Geneva, Lucerne, Murten, Neuchatel, Thun, and Zurich lakes.

• River boats on the Rhine (Schaffhausen-Kreuzlingen) and Aare (Biel-Solothurn) rivers.

• 50% reduction on Lake Constance boats between Romanshorn-Friedrichshafen and Rorschach-Lindau.

• 35% reduction on the Alpnachstad-Mt. Pilatus funicular and the Kriens-Mt. Pilatus cable car.

• 35% reduction on the entrance fee to Lucerne's Transport Museum, the largest of its kind in Europe.

••••• Rail Europ Senior (Senior Citizen Pass)

This senior-citizen pass offers senior citizens (age sixty and older) a 30% discount on first or second-class train tickets. Purchasers must buy a national senior pass from one of the issuing countries. That pass becomes a Rail Europ Senior Card. The pass is only sold to persons who can prove that they are permanent residents of one of the participating countries: Austria, Belgium, Croatia Serbie Slovenia, the Czech Republic, Denmark, Finland, France, Germany, Great Britain, Greece, Holland, Hungary, the Irish Republic, Italy, Luxembourg, Norway, Portugal, Slovakia, Spain, Sweden, and Switzerland. Valid for one year, these passes are sold at main rail stations of the issuing countries.

Use of Rail Europ Senior is limited by each of the participating countries. In France this pass is called the Carte Vermeil Plein Temps, which costs 265 FF and allows as much as a 50% discount on French trains (for "Blue Period" travel). A traveler using the Carte Vermeil Plein Temps or a Rail Europ Senior card issued by any other country cannot start a train ride between noon Friday and noon Saturday, from 15:00 Sunday to noon Monday, on certain holidays, or during various periods of heavy traffic. Few seats are allocated to holders of Carte Vermeil on some TGV trains, other high-speed trains, and EuroCity trains. Remember, the limitations on use of Rail Europ Senior can be significantly different in each of the participating countries.

••••• Inter Rail Cards

The famous Inter Rail Card offers unlimited, second-class train travel, but can be purchased only in Europe and Morocco, and is valid only for persons under twenty-six years old who can prove that they have resided at least six months in the issuing country. The bearer can travel half fare in the issuing country and free on the railways of the other countries purchased. This is very advantageous to young travelers already residing or studying in Europe.

The validity period begins on the first day the card is used, and that day must be within two months after the card is purchased. The card also allows discounts on ship services (Irish Sea, Spain-Morocco, France-Corsica, Italy-Greece), as well as on selected Swiss private railways.

The Inter Rail Card is sold at most rail stations in the following 28 countries and must be paid for in the currency of the country that issues it.

The price is more or less the same in the 28 participating countries, but does experience some fluctuation according to exchange rates. In France, the price is 2,142 FF. The 28 countries are divided into seven zones, and the pass is sold in four versions.

One-zone pass	Two weeks of unlimited travel	$210
Two-zone pass	One month of unlimited travel	$250
Three-zone pass	One month of unlimited travel	$280
Global seven-zone pass	One month of unlimited travel	$315

The Zones

Zone 1:	Great Britain, Northern Ireland, the Irish Republic
Zone 2:	Finland, Norway, Sweden
Zone 3:	Austria, Denmark, Germany, Switzerland
Zone 4:	Bulgaria, Croatia, the Czech Republic, Hungary, Poland, Romania, Slovakia
Zone 5:	Belgium, France, The Netherlands, Luxembourg
Zone 6:	Morocco, Portugal, Spain
Zone 7:	Greece, Italy, Slovenia, the European part of Turkey, and the Brindisi-Patras-Brindisi ferry

•••••EuroTrain Tickets

These tickets are discounted up to 40% on train and ship passage to over 2,000 destinations in all of Eastern and Western Europe (22 countries), including Turkey and Morocco, for anyone under twenty-six years old on the first day of travel, regardless of residence. A ticket is valid for two months and allows as many stopovers as desired.

Available in the U.K. from Eurotrain, Dept. E-93, 52 Grosvenor Gardens, London SW1W 0AG. In France, an equivalent discount service is called B.I.G.E.

Where to Purchase Eurailpasses

Many travel agents are equipped to sell most Eurailpasses, however, the following sources specialize in train passes and offer them directly to the public:

U.S.A. and CANADA

German Rail Inc.
3400 Peachtree Rd., NE
Atlanta, GA   30326

GermanRail Inc.
20 Park Plaza
Boston, MA 02116

Rail Europe
2100 Central Ave.
Boulder, CO 80301

CIT (Italian State Railways)
756 Route 83
Bennsenville, IL 60106

GermanRail Inc.
9501 W. Devon Ave.
Rosemont, IL 60018

CIT (Italian State Railways)
342 Madison Ave., #207
New York, NY 10173

German Rail Inc.
122 42nd St. 10168
New York, NY

Rail Europe
2087 Dundas East
Mississauga, Ont. Canada
L4X 1M2

GermanRail Inc.
222 W. Las Colinas
Irving, TX 75039

CIT (Italian State Railways)
6033 W. Century Blvd.,
Los Angeles, CA 90045

German Rail Inc.
11933 Wilshire Blvd.
Los Angeles, CA 90045

CIT (Italian State Railways)
1450 Cousillors
Montreal, P.Q., Canada (H3A 2E6)

CIT Tours, Inc.
80 Tiverton Court, #401
Marktown, Ont. Canada L3R OG4

German Rail Inc.
904 The East Mall
Etobicoke, Ont., L3R OG4 Canada

German Rail Inc.
240 Stockton St.
San Francisco, CA 94108

Rail Europe
226-230 Westchester Ave.
White Plains, NY 10604

Elsewhere in the World

AUSTRALIA: CIT-Australia Pty. Ltd.; Concorde International Travel; Thomas Cook Pty. Ltd.; Rail Plus

EGYPT: Thomas Cook Overseas Ltd.

HONG KONG: Hong Kong Student Travel Ltd.; Schenker Travel, Thomas Cook Overseas Ltd.

INDIA: Travel Corporation India Ltd.

INDONESIA: Pantravel Travel & Tourism Service

ISRAEL : European World Representatives

JAPAN: Japan Travel Bureau; Ohshu Express Ltd.; Recruit From A Inc.; Travel Plaza International Inc.

KOREA: Seoul Travel Service, Ltd.

MALAYSIA: Boustead Travel Services Sdn. Bhd.

NEW ZEALAND: Atlantic and Pacific Travel International, Ltd.; Thomas Cook Holidays

PAKISTAN: American Express International Banking Corp.

PHILIPPINES: PCI Travel Corporation; Thomas Cook Inc.

SAUDI ARABIA: Alrajhi Wings for Travel and Tourism; Orient Travel & Tours

SINGAPORE: American Express Travel Service; Thomas Cook Travel Services

SOUTH AFRICA: World Travel Agency Ltd.

SRI LANKA: Aitken Spence Travels Ltd.

TAIWAN: American Express International Ltd.; Federal Transportation Ltd.

THAILAND: DITS Travel (Diethelm International Transport Services, Ltd.)

UNITED ARAB EMIRATES: Thomas Cook A.L. Rostamani (Pvt) Ltd.

Other Passes and Discounts

Aside from the Eurailpass and Eurail Youthpass, there are alternative ways of saving money when traveling in Europe by train: special discount tickets, coupons, and special passes issued independently by various countries. Although details on all of them appear in this guide under the respective country listings, and most must be purchased in the respective country, the following is a listing of European train company offices and agents outside of Europe, other than the U.S. and Canadian offices listed on the previous pages, which handle special discount tickets.

Since regulations on discount tickets change frequently, it is suggested that you contact the office nearest you for information before leaving for Europe.

Austria
Austrian National Tourist Office
P.O. Box 491938
Los Angeles, CA 90049

1010 Ouest Rue Sherbrooke, Suite #1410
Montreal, Quebec, Canada H3A 2R7

P.O. Box 1142
New York, NY 10108-1142

2 Bloor Street East, Suite #3330
Toronto, Ontario, Canada M4W 1A8

Belgium

Reservations and tickets for Belgian trains are provided by the offices of Rail Europe, addresses for which appear under France.

780 Third Ave., Suite #1501
New York, NY 10017

Denmark

Scandinavian Tourist Boards
655 Third Ave.
New York, NY 10017

Finland

Finnish Tourist Board
1900 Avenue of the Stars, Suite #1070
Los Angeles, CA 90067

655 Third Ave.
New York, NY 10017

P.O. Box 246, Station "Q"
Toronto, Ontario, Canada M4T 2M1

France

Rail Europe
2100 Central Ave.
Boulder, CO 80301

11 East Adams St.
Chicago, IL 60603

800 Corporate Dr
Fort Lauderdale, FL 33334

2087 Dundas East
Mississauga, Ontario, Canada L4X 1M2

643 Notre Dame Ouest
Montreal, Canada H3C 1H8

360 Post St.
San Francisco, CA 94108

100 Wilshire Blvd.,
Santa Monica, CA 90401

409 Granville St.,
Vancouver, B.C., V6C 1T2, Canada

226–230 Westchester Ave.,
White Plains, NY 10604

Germany
German Rail Inc.
222 W. Las Colinas, Suite #1050
Irving, TX 75039

11933 Wilshire Blvd.
Los Angeles, CA 90025

9501 W. Devon Ave.
Rosemont, IL 60018-4832

904 The East Mall
Etobicoke, Ontario, Canada M9B 6K2

Great Britain
BritRail Travel International
1500 Broadway
New York, NY 10036-4015

Greece
Greek National Tourist Organization
168 No. Michigan Ave.
Chicago, IL 60601

611 W. 6th St.
Los Angeles, CA 90017

1233 Rue De la Montagne
Montreal, Canada H3G 1Z2

645 Fifth Ave.
New York, NY 10022

1300 Bay St.
Toronto, Ontario, Canada M5R 3K8

Holland
Netherlands Board of Tourism
225 No. Michigan Ave., Suite #326
Chicago, IL 60601

25 Adelaide St. East, Suite #710
Toronto, Ontario, Canada M5C 1Y2

Ireland
Irish Tourist Board
345 Park Ave.
New York, NY 10154

160 East Bloor St., Suite #1150
Toronto, Ontario, Canada M4W 1B9

Italy
Italian State Railways
6033 W. Century Blvd., Suite #980
Los Angeles, CA 90045

1450 Councillors St., Suite #750
Montreal, P.Q. Canada H3A 2E6

342 Madison Ave., #207
New York, NY 10173

80 Tiverton Court, #401
Markham, Ontario, Canada L3R 0G4

Luxembourg
Luxembourg National Tourist Office
17 Beekman Place
New York, NY 10022

Norway
Scandinavian Tourist Boards
655 Third Ave.
New York, NY 10017

Poland
Polish National Tourist Office
333 No. Michigan Ave.
Chicago, IL 60601

275 Madison Ave., Suite #1171
New York, NY 10016

Orbis Polish Travel Bureau, Inc. 3
42 Madison Ave.
New York, NY 10173

Portugal
Portuguese National Tourist Office
590 Fifth Ave.
New York, NY 10036

60 Bloor St. West, Suite #1005
Toronto, Ontario, Canada M4W 3B8

Spain
Tourist Office of Spain
8383 Wilshire Blvd., Suite #960
Beverly Hills, CA 90211

845 N. Michigan Ave., Suite #915E
Chicago, IL 60611

1221 Brickell Ave. , Suite #1850
Miami, FL 33131

665 Fifth Ave.
New York, NY 10022

102 Bloor St. West, Suite 1400
Toronto, Ontario, Canada M5S 1M8

Sweden
Scandinavian Tourist Boards
655 Third Ave.
New York, NY 10017

Switzerland
Swiss National Tourist Office
150 No. Michigan Ave., Suite 2930
Chicago, IL 60601

222 No. Sepulveda Blvd., Suite #1570
El Segundo, CA 90245

608 Fifth Ave.
New York, NY 10020

925 The East Mall
Etobicoke, Ontario, Canada M9B 6K1

Student Discount Cards

• International Student Identity Card (ISIC)

This well-recognized card (more than a million issued every year) is an international passport to low-cost travel for students over the age of twelve. Bearers of the ISI card are entitled to discounts on rail, air, bus, and ferry travel, as well as entrance fees to museums, theaters, cinemas, and other places of interest in approximately 60 countries.

Cards issued in the U.S. carry basic accident/sickness insurance, which includes emergency evacuation insurance coverage up to $10,000 and features a 24-hour, toll-free ISIC Help Line. The toll-free number helps students replace lost traveler's checks or passports, or locate English-speaking doctors and lawyers.

Although there is no maximum age limit for the card itself, some transportation companies (airlines, steamships, etc.) and other vendors have imposed their own age restrictions for the use of this card. If you're over thirty, some companies, movie houses, etc. don't like the idea of your profiting from student status. Try to insist.

Upon buying the card, students also receive the International Student Identity Handbook, which lists worldwide discounts and benefits. Even if a student discount is not posted, holders of the card should always ask about a discount before paying the full price.

Developed and regulated by the International Student Travel Confederation, the card carries the owner's full name, birth date, citizenship, school name, and photo. The official U.S. sponsor of the card is CIEE (Council on International Educational Exchange). The card is available from CIEE's Council Travel offices nationwide as well as from hundreds of university and college campus offices.

The 1996 card is valid September 1, 1995 through December 31, 1996 and costs $16. Applications must also include a passport-size photo (with name printed on back) and proof of current student status (copy of transcript, letter from registrar, or copy of bill showing payment of enrollment fees). For insurance purposes, applicants must provide the name, address, and telephone number of beneficiaries.

Student Travels, a free magazine that covers traveling, studying, and working abroad, and describes CIEE's products and services, is available by calling (212) 661-1414, extension 1108.

• Go 25: International Youth Travel Card

This card is not limited to students and is available to anyone regardless of nationality who is at least twelve but not over twenty-five at the time of purchase. Proof of age may be a passport (or photocopy of the data page from a passport), copy of a driver's license, or copy of a birth certificate. The benefits include significantly reduced fares on regularly scheduled airlines between the U.S. and Europe, Asia and Latin America, and also from Europe to Africa, Asia, and the Middle East.

The Go-25 Card also offers holders advantages concerning in-hospital health care and accident insurance while traveling outside the U.S. The card affords users access to the aid provided by the Traveler's Assistance Centers in case of medical, legal, and financial emergencies while abroad. Lastly, it provides certain discounts on transportation, tours, accommodations, restaurants, museums, theaters, cultural attractions, and historic sites.

The card is valid for one year and costs $16.

To Apply for Both Cards

For an application and the location of an issuing office nearest you in the U.S. or Canada, call (800) GET-AN-ID (438-2643) between 09:00 and 17:00 ET.

CHAPTER 3

How to Plan a Rail Itinerary

Every successful train trip contains three essential dimensions: the amount of time you have, the interesting destinations you choose, and the scenic routes you decide to take.

Amount of Time

When time and budget permit, it is recommended that the minimum length of a train trip through Europe should be 23 days, including your arrival and departure days. Of the 21 remaining days, when arriving in Europe from a great distance such as North America - especially the West Coast - you should not plan on much for your first day, other than getting settled into your hotel and recovering from the fatigue of the journey and, more importantly, the change of time zones. Very few people are immune to the temporary handicap of jet lag, and most travelers are well advised to go to bed and postpone any appreciable activity until the second day after the flight. That leaves only 20 active days for sightseeing, which is not really that much time if you plan on visiting numerous European countries.

Most travel writers recommend staying a minimum of two or three nights in most cities you visit, with only occasional one-nighters mixed in the itinerary. This, of course, depends a lot on you. You may opt for five nights in Paris and only two in Munich, or three in Vienna but one in Budapest. Even the sturdiest traveler, though, develops a psychosis when spending too many consecutive nights in different hotel rooms. Besides, if you travel mostly by day, as is suggested in order to see the countryside and meet and converse with fellow passengers, you will arrive in a city late in the day. And if you leave the next morning, you are certainly not going to see much in that city.

But on a two-night basis you can cover 10-11 different cities during your 21 full days in Europe. Reducing a trip to 14 days means reducing the number of cities to five or six. If 14 days is your limit, the 15-day Eurailpass and some fast footwork will still let you have a happy tour while covering a great deal of the continent. All this depends on your time restrictions.

Choosing Destinations

After deciding on the length of time one has to tour, the next step in itinerary planning is to pick the places to be visited, and most people usually have more cities in mind than time, energy and distance will allow. Unless you are indifferent to 15-hour journeys that bring you into a destination late at night, knowing the travel time between each point on your itinerary is essential. The timetables in this book give you that information on more than 9,000 different rail trips.

The common sense approach is to consult a map with a mileage scale and visualize what is practical and what is not while composing a list of places to see. Part of this narrowing-down process depends on what interests you the most. List destinations in order of your priority. Could you really spend three weeks in Europe and not visit the Sistine Chapel? Would your Aunt Olga forgive you if you passed up that invitation at her cousin's farm in Bergen? You decide. Obviously, if, for example, seeing the great art masterpieces is a priority, you'd want to select Paris and Florence over Avignon and Naples. If your interest is Alpine scenery, you are going to concentrate on Bern and Salzburg, not Barcelona and Copenhagen.

Selecting Routes

At this point, you have determined how many days you will be in Europe, where you want to go, and what's feasible in that time. You should now consider the most rewarding routes and the use of special trains.

The journey from Paris to Marseilles, for example, can be made on any one of a dozen ordinary, slower, and often more scenic trains instead of the high-speed TGV. If you'd like to stop for lunch in Dijon, don't take the TGV. However, if you'd like to get to Marseilles by noon and be on the beach by 2 P.M., you better opt for the faster train. A traveler has the same sort of choices of railway routes all over the world; the fastest train is not necessarily the most interesting, and yet the commonplace, slow train may be a real waste of time - or be an extraordinary experience. Be aware that there are choices, and then evaluate them.

Reservations—Train and Hotel

Train Reservations

Since 1989, it has become increasingly easy to make train reservations before arriving in Europe. Most travel agencies now can sell you all of your tickets and/or make all of both your seat and sleeper reservations. This does not mean that you must have seat reservations: they are required only on selected trains. However, anyone traveling on main routes during peak tourist months without reserved space will probably make the trip standing in the aisle and being brushed up against every 30 seconds by passengers ambling along the corridor. Keep in mind that Europeans can, and do, reserve train seats up to two months in advance. Don't be alarmed to see a very ordinary train from Bordeaux to Tours on an October Monday morning completely sold-out.

Reservation clerks in many European cities speak little or no English, although most train stations have multilingual information stands staffed with friendly workers. Writing out your request in clear and simple terms can save you much time in communicating and help insure against getting a less than perfect reservation. You should note on paper your destination, time and day of departure, and any other preferences. Be sure to follow the European custom of showing the day of the month first, followed by the number of the month. July 8 is "8/7." And use the 24-hour clock! If you wanted to take a train to Milan, leaving at 1:50 P.M. on July 8, your note should read "Milan -13:50- 8/7."

Eating and Seating

If you decide to dine at your seat or in your train compartment rather than in the restaurant car, you might want to request a window seat when making your train reservations. On most European trains - other than the TGVs - these are the only seats that have a full, fold out table. In some compartments, the seats next to the sliding door also have a fold out table. Other seats have airplane-style meal trays. Moreover, window seats, especially in train cars with six-seat compartments, afford you a better view of the scenery.

Smoking or non-smoking?

Another variation in seat reservations is that on nearly all European trains you can reserve seats in compartments where smoking is either prohibited or permitted. Depending on your preference, this can make a great deal of difference in either enjoying or detesting your trip. In Europe, smokers can be vehement about their habit and don't always understand or care about the arguments for not smoking. Carefully selecting your reserved seat is thus your guarantee to comfort.

Picking Sides

And still another reservation option to keep in mind is the side of the train you prefer to be seated on. Often there is a decided sightseeing advantage on one side and a corresponding disadvantage on the alternate side. Think of the Alps or the Mediterranean or Lake Como. Obviously if you are traveling along the Riviera, the view of the Mediterranean is possible only on the left side if you are traveling west, and on the right side when going east. After logic tells you which side of the train offers the best view, inquire while making your seat reservation if there is seating on that side.

Train Reservations: Pros and Cons

When reservations are made in Europe, the reservation charge ranges from $2 to $8 per ride. Reservations for seats on Europe's greatest trains can be made as much as two months in advance, and many Europeans grab spaces on them soon after they become available to be reserved. Casual tourists may discover a few days before they want to travel on a special train that it is completely sold-out.

While most European trains do not require reservations, many do: French TGVs, some of the Eurocity trains that go between countries, overnight trains, and the new ultramodern Euro Star. Such trains accept reservations two months in advance of your travel date. That is why it is wise to reserve seats even before you arrive in the countries you plan to travel in.

Reserving Before You Leave

For holders of Eurailpasses, French train tickets, French national passes, or the national passes for most other European countries, note that if you purchased your tickets or passes from a North American office of Rail Europe, train reservations (required and optional) for most European countries can be made for you by that same issuing office. This can be very helpful. Rail Europe charges $10 per person, per train reservation (including cable fee), plus a single $10 service charge for shipping and handling. Thus, two people reserving seats on three trains means six reservations or $60 plus $10, making a total of $70.

The North American offices of Italian State Railways listed in this guide also make reservations for train trips in Italy and most (but not all) other European countries, but only when a Eurailpass has been purchased from them. Note, though, that they do not make reservations in connection with Italian passes or ordinary train tickets. The maximum number of reservations they will make is three trips per pass. Their fee is $10 per train seat, which includes all communication fees. The cost for two people reserving seats on three trains, therefore, is $60. However, two people traveling together are not permitted to reserve six trains.

Holders of a Eurailpass who make seat reservations after arriving in Europe are exempt from the reservation fee. This does not apply to Italy's special "Pendolino" trains though for which a hefty supplement ranging from $6 to $28 is charged. Those supplements, however, include both a reservation fee and a meal!

If you have purchased your Eurailpass, German national pass, or tickets for German trains from one of the North American offices of German Rail (U.S. and Canadian offices listed in this guide), these offices will reserve any number of trains up to 10 days prior to each train's departure at a charge of $10 per person, per train, plus $7.50 per order for Federal Express charges.

It is always advisable to have the office that issues you the Eurailpass to telex or fax your reservation requests to Europe. This can result in your obtaining seats which might otherwise have been sold to someone else if your request had been slowed down by the mail.

Reserving on the Spot: Avoiding the Lines

If, on the other hand, you wait to reserve train space just before each departure, keep in mind that at most European stations you must get in one line for a ticket and in a different line for a seat reservation. Of course, if you have a Eurailpass you eliminate having to wait in the ticket line for a long time.

As a matter of fact, you can face long waits in as many as five different lines - and part of the trick of making the most of your limited time is to avoid standing in any. The lines include: information, ticket purchases, seat reservation, hotel accommodations, and baggage checkroom. There are tricks to eliminating line waiting for general information discussed in Chapter 4. Having a Eurailpass solves the ticket line wait. The solution to the hotel accommodation line, of course, is to make reservations before you leave home. The baggage check room problem is discussed in Chapter 5.

There is another way to reduce the amount of time spent in either the ticket or seat reservation lines. These lines are far shorter Monday to Thursday than they are on the weekend. Midmorning tends to be a better time to buy tickets or make reservations than during the lunch hours or in the early evening when it is the height of the commuter rush hours. During the mid-June to mid-September tourist season, it is often advantageous to have a hotel concierge or *pensione* owner obtain your reservations for you.

In any case, be sure to make reservations in the country you will be touring as much in advance as possible, preferably upon your arrival in the city you will be continuing your tour from. Requirements for reservations vary from country to country and, within a country, from city to city. In some Italian cities, for example, reservations cannot be made less than two hours before a departure. Milan requires three hours notice. Rome requires five hours notice! Let's say that your trip consisted of a New York-Paris flight, followed by a train trip to Geneva, and a second one from Geneva-Rome. Make the Paris-Geneva reservation on your first day in Paris, and make the Geneva-Rome reservation upon arriving at the Geneva station.

Five Simple Train Reservation Tips

1. When you leave your compartment to go to the W.C. (toilet), dining car, or merely to stretch your legs, leave some object on your seat — newspaper, hat, something to inhibit unreserved seat-grabbers from settling down in your space during your absence. While it is true that the conductor will aid you in removing an interloper, finding the conductor, explaining the problem and using his intervention is somewhat more bothersome than simply preventing the event.

2. Do not waste time trying to make a seat reservation for a train trip within Belgium, Holland, Luxembourg, or Switzerland. These countries sell seat reservations only for rides going into another country. However, finding a seat on trains of these countries is not a problem except on peak travel days.

3. On a normal working day, even though the reservation clerk claims all seats on a certain train are already reserved, you can often hop aboard and find an empty seat. Many European business people, when undecided as to which train they will be taking, make several advance reservations so as to cover all possibilities - and then forfeit the fee on unused reservations. This practice accounts for some unused seats being marked "reserved." If traveling without seat reservations, be careful not to waste time taking a reserved seat while the unreserved ones are being filled up. Check the seat chart outside each compartment or on each seat before you sit down. If you're ousted by the legitimate reservation holder, you may have to stand during the rest of the ride.

4. If the required advance time for making a seat reservation has run out, seek the conductor and, in your most charming manner, tell him (or her, although there are very few women conductors) your destination and seek his assistance in finding you a seat. As a brand of their own, train conductors are for the most part remarkably courteous, good humored, and cooperative and many, you will observe, welcome the opportunity of using their authority constructively.

5. Never, never discard a train ticket until after your trip has been fully completed and you have left the arrival station. You will frequently ride a train for hours without being asked to show a ticket or pass. Then, after you get off the train, you could discover that you are required to show your ticket or pass at the station exit, as is true in many London subway stations. If you have thrown your ticket away, you will undoubtedly end up having to buy a second one. Your best bet is to always hold onto your ticket, whether or not a conductor checks it.

Hotel Reservations

Once you have decided on the main elements, namely the amount of days, the specific cities, the trains and the routes, and train reservations you are ready to consider whether you want to reserve hotels in advance. There are pros and cons to both. In any case, all *Eurail Guide* recommendations are based on information recently verified by first-hand experience. The qualification "recently" is noteworthy, because quality of hotel and restaurant services are subject to periodic fluctuations. Management changes (and quality with it) faster than annually revised editions of any guide can wholly keep up with. When possible, consult competent travel agents, travel publications, and travel information sources that have current input from recent travelers. The best information comes from people who have just been there. To maximize your chances of landing great information, ask lots of questions.

In this guide, when faced with options, the preferences expressed tend to be oriented toward choices that maximize comfort and security. In most cases, this guide recommends its readers to reserve hotel accommodations well in advance, and, when possible, to reserve train seats whenever you are sure you want to be on a particular train on a certain date.

Some travelers object vehemently to such pre-planning tactics such as advanced reservations, claiming that you cannot be as footloose or carefree as you would like, linger where you have discovered unexpected attractions, or make impetuous detours or departures. There is no question that for those travelers forced to lead ordered routines, there are few activities that offer as much freedom as does train travel. The spontaneous choices you can make are vast. The feature that many people find irresistible about European trains is how easily one can, an hour after starting a ride going in one direction, abort at an approaching station and head elsewhere. Depending on how strongly this flexibility motivates you, and to what degree you are willing to endure the consequences of venturing into the unknown, advance hotel reservations may not be important to you.

On the other hand, if you ever have played an entire night of poker without holding one winning hand; or arrived in Copenhagen on the opening day of a World Bank Conference (no rooms within 20 miles); or traveled to Paris where the International Air Show opened on the day of your arrival, the most popular horse race on the Continent was being run the next day (no room within 30 miles), and your next stop was Dijon, where your first six choices of hotels were *complet*, even though nothing special was happening that week, you might want to re-think the advantages of advanced bookings.

From May through early October, European and non-European tourists pack all classes of hotels in leading European cities. Trade shows and business conventions pick up the slack instantly in September, October, March, and April. A hotel in Bordeaux (not Paris or Rome, mind you) responded to a request for reservations on July 13 that it was booked for the two nights needed in early October! Sometimes the difficulty of finding a room stems from a local holiday, a long weekend, a special event, or a large party that has booked all the rooms in a small region.

If you travel Europe without advance room reservations from March through October, it is wise to arrive in your destination city early in the day. Rooms available because of no-shows or last-minute cancellations frequently are taken before mid-afternoon. Otherwise you can spend a lot of time room hunting.

Upon arriving without a hotel reservation, go at once to the tourist accommodations desk in the train station. For a fee of $1 to $2, a host or hostess will telephone hotels, pensions, or bed and breakfasts to find you a room that comes close to your specifications. In certain cities (Amsterdam, Bergen, Brussels, etc.), this convenient service is not offered at the station but can be found at the city tourist office, often only across the road from the rail station, but sometimes quite a distance from it.

In the peak summer touring months you will find long lines and if, as is usually the case, your stay is brief, you will have to devote precious visiting time to obtain a room. When traveling in groups of two or more, it is effective for one person to remain at the station guarding the luggage while the other or others canvass the area near the station to find a room. All over Europe you will find many hotels within a radius of two or three blocks from the rail station. Many non-Europeans are unaware that stations even in the smallest cities have comfortable waiting rooms with upholstered chairs. If you follow this technique, be sure to use the shelter of these waiting rooms. Do not leave luggage unattended for even a few minutes. Aside from the risk of theft, Europeans are very sensitive to all potential risks of terrorism. In Paris and London train stations, the police tend to collect and blow-up all unattended bags.

Another housing solution used successfully by many is: get out of town immediately and stay in the suburbs, don't even attempt to battle the hustle and hassle of finding a hotel room downtown in a major city. This is possible, provided that the suburb is linked by train with the city you want to tour. Just pick a town of moderate size about 30–45 minutes train travel time away from a major metropolis and head there. On the plus side, you're more likely to find an affordable room. On the down side though, the town may be less interesting or downright dull and ugly and train service may be limited at night, forcing you to forego those theater tickets or late-night bar-hopping.

Preparing for an Autumn Tour

One thing that is nearly always overlooked in European, off-season itinerary planning is that after early September - and Fall is outstanding for touring Europe - English-language city sightseeing tours are often discontinued as the volume of tourists decline, particularly in important but smaller cities such as Avignon, Verona, Rouen, Tours, etc. If this poses a problem for you, in that you were counting on taking these city tours, there's no reason to despair. Nearly every city in Europe, even hamlets such as the charming port of Honfleur in Normandy, has a tourist office that supplies comprehensive folders in English. These folders include fine city maps, interesting descriptions of principal attractions and suggested walking tours which allow visitors to find on their own, and at their own pace, the most worthwhile historic sites, museums, churches, palaces, and other local high spots usually available in a motor coach sightseeing tour.

By early September, though, many city tourist offices run out of the current brochures. To insure against this disappointment there is a precaution you can take. Early in the year, write to the cities you plan to visit and request copies of literature and tourist maps in English. This can also help you decide what to visit and how long to spend at a destination.

Simply address your request to "Tourist Office" in each respective city or village. You'll be surprised how much this easy preparation will add to your travel enjoyment.

Documenting Yourself

It is more than useful, it is necessary, to arm yourself with a varied collection of up-to-date and informative guides, maps, and books if you want to be an informed and intelligent traveler. There are literally hundreds of sources of published information, ranging from great collections of general travel guides covering entire continents to highly specialized and thematic guides covering everything from restaurants and hotels to churches, cemeteries, wines, boutiques and even Paris *arrondissements*. You neither want to load yourself down, nor spend your whole trip with your nose in a book, but a carefully chosen selection of documentation is essential. As Alvin Toffler so poignantly documented in Powershift, it is information, even more so than cash, that opens doors in our contemporary world. This is equally true in the realm of individual travel, especially when it comes to destinations that are experiencing rapid change. Here are a few helpful suggestions on how to "document" yourself before venturing off.

Consumer Reports Travel Letter   Consumers Union produces a highly useful 24-page monthly newsletter on travel called the Consumer Reports Travel Letter (CRTL), in which worldwide travel services, money saving opportunities on major travel purchases, and astute tips on avoiding travel scams and overcharges are discussed. Throughout the year, CRTL presents annual country-by-country evaluations of train passes, company-by-company comparisons of rental car rates, ratings of major airline and hotel services, and a wide variety of strategies for finding the best travel values and keeping travel costs to a minimum. CRTL was one of the first consumer travel publications to highlight discount airline tickets from consolidators and to describe and compare half-price hotel programs. Like other Consumers Union publications, CRTL remains wholly unbiased and is careful about not accepting advertising or free travel services. For its $39 annual subscription, write to: CRTL, Dept. 'E', 101 Truman Avenue, Yonkers, NY 10703, or telephone (800) 234-1970.

Thomas Cook European Timetable   The venerable *Thomas Cook European Timetable* has been published in England consistently (under seven other titles) since 1873 with the sole interruption occurring during the war years. Its younger sibling, the *Overseas Timetable*, founded in 1981, was prompted by the increased interest in train travel outside of Europe. These publications have become the bibles of reliable and comprehensive train schedules for much of the world. The *European Timetable* (covering Britain and the Continent), scheduled for monthly publication on the first day of each month, comes out with great regularity although sometimes with slight delays. The *Overseas Timetable*, which covers the rest of the world, is issued every other month, beginning in January. Summer European train schedules appear in the June, July, August and September *European Timetable* issues. The latter contains an advance Winter Supplement. Similarly, the February through May issues contain advance Summer Service Supplements.

In addition to train, boat, and bus schedules, these publications, codified with an extensive array of symbols for services and other data, which are translated into ordinary language at the start of each edition, also provide information on available food services and sleeping accommodations.

The Thomas Cook publications are condensations of much more extensive national timetables published by all major countries. Inexpensive and complete national timetables can be purchased at rail stations in many countries.

Because some countries do not offer their own timetables, or run short of them, Thomas Cook's is valuable for carrying along on a trip as well as for studying at home while planning an itinerary. Numerous readers have reported that having a copy while touring allows them to make impromptu changes in travel plans. One flaw in Thomas Cook's system consists of its reliance at times on individuals of varying competence in underdeveloped countries where governments have not responded to pleas for "official information."

Caution: As Thomas Cook states in each edition, the services shown are subject to alteration, and travelers should recheck departure times upon arriving in each station.

Both publications can be obtained in North America from Forsyth Travel Library, P.O. Box 2975, Shawnee Mission, KS 66201, or by telephoning at 800-FORSYTH, Monday-Saturday, 09:00-16:30 Central Standard Time. Visa and Master-Card are accepted. Both cost $24.95, plus $4 for shipping. A combined purchase of the *European Timetable* and the Rail Map of Europe costs $33.95 plus shipping.

Eurail Timetable/Horaire Eurail/Eurail Fahrplan   The Eurail Timetable/ Horaire Eurail/Eurail Fahrplan contains most connections between important cities in Western Europe. It is sold at major European rail stations and is highly useful.

Horaires Lignes Affaires   There is another timetable, specialized and far more condensed than Thomas Cook's, that is free. Offered by the French National Railroads (see North American addresses), the very useful 32-page mini-folder is called *Horaires Lignes Affaires* (Business Route Timetable). Containing May-September schedules, it has timetables for many trains that connect French cities with each other and with foreign countries.

Other Useful Sources

Insight Guides   In total, there are over 200 titles in the *Insight Guide* series covering destinations large and small all around the globe. *Insight Guides* introduce a traveler to a destination with history, culture, and color photography. Read them before you go for "insight" in to the culture you're about to experience or peruse after you return from your trip to remind you of the sights you've just seen.

Insight Pocket Guides   Unlike most travel guides, Insight Pocket Guides are designed for those on a limited schedule, who need essential information in a format that is clear, concise and easy to access. In each Insight Pocket Guide, travelers will find practical and specific advice on what to do and where to go without the clutter and unnecessary detail found in many planning guides. As with the Insight Guides, Pocket Guides cover destinations all over the world and have brilliant color photography.

Insight Guides and Insight Pocket Guides are available in most travel and trade bookstores. To order by phone in the U.S.: 800-225-3362 or Canada: (416) 475-9126.

CHAPTER 4

Don't Miss The Train!

Cities with More than One Train Station

After arriving three days ago from London's Victoria Station at Paris's Gare du
Nord station, you've spent a few absolutely lovely days in the French City of Lights,
and now it's time to say au revoir and move on. Your train for Marseilles leaves in
an hour and you've properly taken the *Métro* across town, blew kisses to the Eiffel
Tower, and have returned in blissful innocence to the same station where you first
arrived. You look up at the board of departures and gasp; there are no trains to
Marseilles! "Impossible," you whelp, you've paid for secure reservations. You rush
to the information window ready to scream or sue somebody. There is a line - a
woman with lots of gold jewelry, a French poodle in each arm, and a cigarette
dangling from her lips, is inquiring about the car-train to Bezier over the Toussaint
long-weekend. There are now only ten minutes before your supposed departure time
and you are jumping out of your skin. Finally you reach the front of the line only to
learn from a SNCF clerk who keeps saying in his accented English, "Too bad, too
bad," that Paris has six major train stations, and you needed to be at the Gare de
Lyon, not the Gare du Nord, and now there's no time to make the departure. "Too
bad." You'll lose the TGV reservation fee and worse, the next TGV gets you to
Marseilles too late to attend the Prince concert you reserved tickets for on your
Amex card, and that cute hotel that you'd reserved four months earlier promised to
hold the room only until 6 P.M. And tomorrow you need time to visit the museum
before catching the train to Genoa. Everything is going wrong. Panic. Sniffle.

This cruel dramatization is just a friendly reminder that major cities have more
than one major train station. Determine beforehand whether your departure or transfer city has more than one station, and if so, make sure you know from which one
the train on which you are planning to continue your trip departs. Inquire at the
information booth upon arrival or simply consult the Thomas Cook European Timetable. Do not rely on getting that information an hour or so before your departure
from someone such as your hotel clerk or a taxi or bus driver. If you are making a
transfer, be certain that there is adequate time to get from one station to the other.

Here is a handy reference chart listing the 70 European cities with more than one rail
station.

Antwerp	Dublin	Lodz	Prague
Athens	Dunkerque	London	Ramsgate
Barcelona	Essen	Lyon	Rome

Basel	Exeter	Madrid	Rotterdam
Belfast	Folkestone	Malmo	San Sebastian
Belgrade	Geneva	Manchester	Seville
Berlin	Genoa	Marseilles	Southampton
Bilbao	Glasgow	Milan	Stockholm
Boulogne	Halsingborg	Moscow	Tilbury
Brussels	Hamburg	Munich	Tours
Bucharest	Harwich	Naples	Turin
Budapest	Hendaye	Newhaven	Venice
Calais	Irun	Oporto	Vienna
Casablanca	Le Havre	Orleans	Warsaw
Cologne	Leningrad	Oslo	Weymouth
Como	Liege	Paris	Wiesbaden
Copenhagen	Lisbon	Portsmouth	Zurich
Dover	Liverpool		

A Handy Vocabulary Chart for the Word "Train Station"

estacion	(Spain)
statione	(Italy)
Bahnhof	(Austria, Germany, and Switzerland)
la gare	(France)
Train station	(U.K. and Ireland)
Gare	(Belgium and Luxembourg)
Järnvägstation	(Sweden)
togstation (s-tog)	(Danish)

Finding Your Train Car: Train Splitting

How can one fail to admire the superhuman efficiency of Europe's vast international rail systems? Thousands of trains daily transport millions of people while achieving a dependability factor that is nearly perfect. An important part of this remarkable capacity is the technique of avoiding unnecessary duplication of personnel and equipment by switching cars, splitting trains, and calibrating transfer times between connections to a bare minimum.

There are a few simple things to remember when boarding your train. Before you leave the central hall of the station, ask if the car in which you will be starting your journey is going all the way to your destination. Often it is scheduled to be switched to another train or will at a particular city break from the rest of the train and join a piece of another train heading to a completely different destination. If this is the case, you must know at what point you must transfer from this train to another train en route to your destination or switch to another car on the initial train you've boarded. It's easier than it sounds.

If your car is to be switched to another train, note the name of the city where the switching will occur, the time it will take place, and the name of the stop just prior to the switching point. When you are on the correct track, and you are ready to board your train, your last step is to mount the correct car. Where a train originally consists of cars that are eventually going to different destinations, each car is clearly marked with the name of the city where it originated and the name of the city where it will terminate. Frequently, the sign will also designate some of the key cities where it makes stops. For example,

VENEZIA
Bologna — Firenze
ROMA

This sign shows that this train car originated in Venezia, makes stops at Bologna and Firenze, and terminates in Roma. If you're not versed in one or more foreign languages, you might find the names of certain cities to be less than obvious to you. Your mind will quickly learn to make the simple deduction that Venezia is Venice, Firenze is Florence, and Roma, of course, is Rome. It's a little trickier when, for example, you're boarding a French train headed for Prague via Germany. Or an Italian train heading to France. Did you know that Paris in Italian is Parigi or that Antwerp is the Flemish name for Anvers? Or that the German city of Aachen is Aix-la-Chapelle in French?

Next to the foldout steps that lead up into the train car you'll always see either the number "1" or "2" written on the side of the car or flashed on a digital panel, designating first-class or second-class seats. You may find a first-class car coupled to a second-class car, both marked with the same origin-destination sign. Or, a single car may be marked "1" at one end and "2" at the other end, indicating that one half is first-class and the other half is second-class. Although train cars are numbered, the order often gets shuffled. Generally, the first-class cars are found closest to the station hall and thus require less of a walk for the higher paying customers.

If you decide to sit in another car that will not be going all the way to your destination, what you must be careful about is that a car change or splitting doesn't occur while you are several cars away from your seat (and from your baggage, which usually is stowed either in your compartment or at the end of your car). You don't want to end up going in a direction that is not in your plans, and you certainly don't want to chug off to Luxembourg while your suitcases are heading to Munich or Vienna!

One U.S. Army colonel traveling with his family reported such an experience: while off to grab a sandwich in the bar car, the train split. "I got about as far as what had been the middle of the train…and there was no more train! I was heading off towards an unknown direction, without my family, at approximately 80 mph. with all of our money but without my passport or train ticket." The brave soldier who'd gone involuntarily AWOL finally circled back and met up with his worried wife and kids in Metz, "practically in a pool of tears."

Moral: Don't stray from your car while the train is stopped in a station. When traveling as a family or small group, each person should carry his or her own money, passport, and ticket or train pass.

Train Changing: The Connection Time

Frequently you will find that you cannot take a train directly to some point, and will need to change trains at a designated city. In many cases the connections are very convenient, so that you change from one train to another with only a short waiting period at the transfer station. For example, there is no direct train from Zurich to the popular location of Locarno, but the Zurich-Milan train arrives in Bellinzona at 12:33, and a train for Locarno departs Bellinzona just three minutes later at 12:36. This is completely normal and should not create too much stress. The track for the Bellinzona-Locarno train is next to the track on which you arrive from Zurich, making this change effortless. Even if the Zurich-Milan train is running a few minutes late - and you will be amazed how rarely trains in Western Europe are even slightly off schedule - your walk from one train to the other on this connection is about ten feet, and in the case of short delays the second train, or local train, will wait for the first train, or principal train.

On the other hand, international trains from Eastern countries (Turkey, Greece, etc.) usually arrive late due to delays at border-crossings. In these cases, and in the case of short transfer time in large city stations, the problem is the distance between tracks. Be ready to step off the first train as soon as it pulls into the transfer station. You may find you are arriving on Track #2 and departing from Track #21, a considerable distance and invariably involving first descending into the underground walkway that connects all tracks, and then climbing up the steps leading to your departure track. This transfer problem is compounded if your first train arrives late and the second train is an express train which cannot detain its scheduled departure time.

Normally your first train will arrive on schedule and you have more than enough time to make the change. However, it is best to inquire on board the first train with the conductor for the number of the track on which you are arriving and the number of the track from which your departing train leaves. You might have to make a mad dash for it. Sometimes you'll have to jump on the closest car of a train that is just about to pull out and then weave your way through the corridors a half a mile until you finally make it to your reserved seat or at least to a car that is heading to your destination. Such intense situations make for exciting stories, but do tend to be rather stressful.

One American expatriate from Boston writes about a harrowing experience worth sharing with other train travelers. Several years ago, he dropped off his wife and four-year-old son one Sunday in front of the Frankfurt main station, 30 minutes in advance of their train departure to Berlin, and then went off to return their car rental only to find that the Sunday drop-off point was two kilometers away. Unable to find a ride back or hail a taxi, he was forced to frantically hitchhike back to the station, and finally ran searching madly for the right track, noticing on the large clock overhead that it was exactly the time of departure! The right track eluded him and he rushed over to the train board and gleaned the schedule. Track 17. Off he dashed to the far end of the station only to spot that the Berlin train was already pulling out of *Gleis* 17! Warning bells were cautioning to keep away from the moving train. Sprinting behind and then alongside the last car in a scene reminiscent of the war film "Von Ryan's Express," he began slapping wildly at the glass panel of the already shut train door and screaming out of desperation in his broken German, "Mein Kind, mein Kind ist im Zug," (My child is on the train!). Adrenaline pumped, and, miraculously, the massive Bundesbahn locomotive - already half-way out of the station screeched to a halt. It was the first time in history that a tourist had ever stopped a passenger train in Germany; and the conductor, red with anger and ready to slap the obstructive traveler with a stiff fine, collared the man demanding that he quickly board the train and "produce the child." That is what he did, saving himself from prosecution and finally joining his family on the trip to Berlin.

Know your track number!

A Handy Vocabulary Chart for the Word "Track"

Anden	(Spain)
Binario	(Italy)
Gleis	(Austria, Germany, and Switzerland)
Perron	(Denmark)
Quai	(France)
Spår	(Sweden)
Spor	(Holland and Belgium)
Spor	(Norway)
Track	(U.K. and Ireland)
Voie	(Belgium and Luxembourg)

Most train stops in Europe are efficiently very brief: two or three minutes. Where a stop is fairly generous, say 20 minutes or more, it is often because some car on the train is being switched to another train and possibly also to another track in that station. You may be seated facing forward when you pull into a station and depart riding backwards!

Unwary passengers are apt to get out of the train at a stop and wander away, discovering too late that their train has left without them! When you have the urge to stretch your legs, get some fresh air, and check out the trackside attractions, try not to venture away more than a few feet away from the door of the train car. That way, if your car is being switched or the stop is shorter than you anticipated, you can jump back aboard.

Car-Sleeper Express Service

Europe's "Car-Sleeper Express Service" is one of the fastest growing train services in Europe today. Essentially you can sleep in a *couchette* or sleeping compartment on the same train that carries your auto. You can also ship your car ahead on an "Auto Express" while you ride on another train, and find your car waiting for you at your destination. Started by French Rail in 1957, this service is now offered in Austria, Belgium, Britain, Holland, Italy, Spain, and Germany, and links cities in those countries as well as in Portugal and Switzerland. The system annually moves more than 500,000 people and more than 160,000 cars. Inquire with the national rail offices or agents in your country. If you are buying a car in Europe with the idea of using it overseas and then shipping it home, this service might be very useful.

CHAPTER 5

Valuable Train and Travel Tips

Before Leaving Home: A Few Precautions

• It is always wise to make photocopies of your airline ticket, the identification page of your passport, your driver's license, and the credit cards you take with you. Leave one set of photocopies at home and take another set with you, storing it in a separate place from the originals.

• Leave a list of the serial numbers of your traveler's checks at home. Take a copy of that list on your trip, but keep separate from the checks. As you cash each check, tally the ones that remain unredeemed. This way you can spot if there is anything missing.

• If you wear glasses or contact lenses, pack an extra set. If there are any particular medicines you need, bring along an ample supply as well as a copy of prescriptions and generic names of those drugs. Keep these in your carry-on luggage. Leave medicines in their original labeled containers so as not to complicate customs processing. If any medications contain narcotics, carry a letter from your physician attesting to your need to take them. Leave a copy of your medical and dental records with a relative or friend.

• Include a tag or label with your name and address inside each piece of luggage, and lock your bags.

• Leave a copy of your itinerary with a relative or friend should it be necessary to contact you in case of an emergency. Some people contact their consulate when traveling in a foreign country. This can be particularly helpful when traveling in dangerous or unstable regions, but is otherwise unnecessary.

• Find out if your insurance policies cover you for theft, loss, accident, and illness while you are in another country. If yes, write down the procedures to follow in case an incident occurs.

What Weather to Expect

These general descriptions of seasonal weather patterns may be at least moderately helpful in your planning of where to go and when.

• North America and Europe
Spring: April-June, Summer: July-September, Fall: October-December. Winter: January-March.

• Mexico and Central America
Very rainy May-October.

• South America, Australia and New Zealand
Spring: October-December, Summer: January-March, Fall: April-June, Winter: July-September.

• Asia
Year-round tropical heat in Hong Kong, India, Indonesia, Malaysia, the Philippines, Singapore, Thailand, and the South Pacific islands. Typhoon season is June-September in Japan, August to mid-October in Taiwan. The monsoon months in India are June-August. The rainy season in most of Asia is May-September but is June-November in the Philippines.

• North Africa
Extremely hot, except December-February in Egypt.

• Middle East
Israel has mild Mediterranean temperatures year round. Iran, Iraq, Jordan, Lebanon, and Syria have four seasons similar to those in North America and Europe.

Customs Procedures and Duty-Free Shopping

It is good to know a few things about customs regulations before you begin your journey. Foreign-made articles taken abroad from the U.S. are subject to duty each time they are brought back into the U.S., unless you have acceptable proof of prior possession such as a bill of sale, insurance policy, jeweler's appraisal, or receipt of purchase. Watches, cameras, tape recorders, or articles identified by serial number or permanently affixed markings may be taken to the U.S. Customs office nearest you and registered before departure. The certificate of registration is valid for all future trips. This may be a slight hassle obtaining, but it is an effective way of being reassured if you travel with highly valuable or duty-susceptible items.

As for duty-free shopping, items in "duty-free" shops in major airports are not always the bargains they are played up to be. Only by comparison shopping can you be sure whether it is worthwhile buying that Hermés scarf, Mont Blanc pen, or Sony Walkman at the duty-free shop. Cigarettes and alcohol do tend to be well-priced. Remember that duty within EU countries has been erased. There is complete free trade. Furthermore, upon returning to your home country (non-EU) you may sometimes find that you must pay duty on your "duty-free" purchases. Duty-free means only that the airport store from which you made a purchase did not have to pay a duty when it bought the article.

To know what you can and cannot bring back to the country of your residence and what the duty tax (if any) will be when returning with articles purchased abroad, request a copy of the helpful booklet "Know Before You Go" published by the U.S. Customs Service, Custom Information Section, 6 World Trade Center, New York, N.Y. 10048.

Only a fool tries to smuggle through customs an article on which there is an embargo or outright ban or attempts to avoid paying duty for something that is subject to import tax. If caught, the penalty when entering the United States can be a combination of having the article seized, paying a fine on the amount of the U.S. value, and being subject to criminal prosecution. For example, if you buy a $1,000 piece of jade in Hong Kong and don't declare it, you'd be in violation of the 1993 law that stipulates that there is an exemption only on the first $400 of goods entering the U.S. which were purchased anywhere outside the U.S. other than the U.S. Virgin Islands, American Samoa, and Guam. After that first $400, the flat duty for the next $1,000 is 10%. Technically you would owe a duty of $60. In trying to avoid this $60 tax, you could lose the jade, be forced to pay a fine of $1,000, and face a jail sentence.

Another point: Do not try to bring home fruits, vegetables, plants, animal or fish products, or any perishable foods that cannot be cleared by your country's agriculture department. Without such clearance, it is a certainty such items will be confiscated and you may be subject to a fine. One traveler from Portland recently returned from Paris to the U.S. carrying the uneaten apple from his airline meal. He did not declare this food item and was fined $50 in Newark Airport. At Boston's Logan Airport, Agriculture Department officials use beagle dogs to sniff out smuggled foods and plants.

Overcoming Jet Lag

When your trip involves between a five- and nine-hour time change, those first few days of your overseas trip can be sluggish. There are ways, though, that you can greatly reduce the fatigue of jet lag and be more energetic sooner on your journey.

First, when traveling in a closed compartment such as airplanes or train compartments, drink as much water as you can to overcome dehydration resulting from lack of fresh air or from airconditioning. Remember that the more alcoholic beverages you absorb, the faster your body dehydrates. It's wiser to eat lightly or at least refrain from overeating if you want to feel better upon arriving. Dress comfortably by wearing loose clothing. Exercise as much as possible in flight or when in a closed compartment for a long time.

At one time SAS and Lufthansa published concise booklets describing exercises that can be performed by passengers while seated. Northwest Airlines shows an in-flight aerobics video on its overseas flights. If you don't mind seeming ridiculous, mimic the motions involved in rowing a boat and picking apples from an overhead branch. Rise up and sit down repeatedly. Alternately, raise your knees to your elbows. Nod your head and turn it vigorously from side to side. Turn your hands at the wrist while spreading and closing your fingers. Lift your heels up and then place them down firmly, while placing pressure on your toes. With toes up, rotate your feet in large circles. European travelers of course will think you've lost your marbles, but as the French are so fond of saying while shrugging shoulders and pursing lips, "Tant-pis" (What the heck!). You'll feel fine tomorrow.

Traveling by Night

There are some advantages to traveling by night train. You can hop from one place to another without sacrificing daytime activities in either the departure city or the arrival city. Also, by traveling at night in a regular sitting compartment, not in an extra-fare couchette or sleeping compartment, the holder of a Eurailpass can make a substantial contribution to a budget by dispensing with room rent. Attention: Even on comfortable trains, a night in a seat is not going to leave you in the best of moods in the morning. And, although you can wash in train bathrooms, the water is cold and not drinkable, the hygienic state of things is not always up to snuff, especially at the end of a long journey, and the movement of the speeding train makes it a bit tough to shave or put on or take off makeup.

On some trains the seats in the regular sitting compartments can be adjusted so that your seat and the one facing you to either come together or nearly meet, and many who are fortunate enough to be in a compartment that is not full are able to stretch out. This is one technique for eliminating hotel bills, which many students and other economy prone tourists have used successfully. However, if the seat opposite you is occupied, both you and the other passenger are going to spend the night sitting up. On a packed night train from Cairo to Luxor, a student from Philadelphia bragged of actually sleeping in the luggage rack above the seats. In the summer, be prepared to see everything.

The offsetting drawbacks of night trains are considerable. The pleasant act of meeting and conversing with Europeans and tourists from other parts of the world is reduced when you travel at night. And, of course, the scenery is severely dulled. If you are a light sleeper by nature, it's probable that you won't sleep well on trains, and certainly not while curled up in a seat.

Train sleeping accommodations vary from one European country to another, but generally they consist of *couchette* compartments (berths) or sleeping car compartments (beds). A blanket and a pillow are provided for each berth in a couchette compartment. There is no way to tuck the blanket in. It just slides around during the night. The sheet is often a fitted pouch which functions as top sheet and bottom sheet - you slip in between the halves. Some people undress fully or partially for bed, but a lot of this depends on your own sense of comfort in that each couchette in second class consists of six bunks, three on each side with a bottom, middle, and upper berth each. Privacy is thus minimal, yet dignity is never sacrificed.

The first-class *couchette* is a berth with four instead of six bunks (consisting of two rows of two bunks each). The 1995 price for each first-class bunk runs around $15 for holders of a first-class ticket or train pass. With either a first- or second-class ticket or with a train pass, the 1995 price per berth is around $23 in a four-berth compartment, $15 in a six-berth compartment.

Sleeping car compartments, called *wagon-lits* in French, and *schlafwagen* in German, are available in either a "small" or a "large" format. All are equipped with a power plug and a wash basin. The newer and faster trains have both 220- and 110- volt current, whereas the older trains only have the local 220. The small compartments convert to one, two, or three beds.

European rail authorities have stated repeatedly that specific prices for these sleeping car compartments (which vary in different areas of Europe) will not be available until the moment the reservation is confirmed. It is fair to estimate using the 1994 prices. For example, the Paris-Zurich night trip, with one bed in a small compartment, would cost about $105 plus the price of a first-class ticket ($117), thus a total of $222. For a large compartment with two beds, requiring two first-class tickets at $117, add about $70 per person for the compartment, thus $187 per person.

At those prices it might be better to sleep in a first-class hotel!

Note that neither *couchettes* nor compartments are included in the Eurailpass or any national train passes.

Don't worry about oversleeping or missing your early morning destination. You can always rely on being awakened, and not so gently, by the voice of a stationmaster bellowing over the public address system at stops along the way. Twenty minutes or so before you arrive at your destination, the train conductor will rap his knuckles on the door of your compartment and yell something like, "Leipzig, twenty minutes." When the train crosses international borders during the night, it is completely normal for the train conductor to collect passports before everyone goes to sleep. He will present the documents to the border police and return them to you in the morning. This avoids unnecessary disturbances. With the easing of internal European borders with the EU (European Union), border crossings have become extremely lax, although some routes in the summer are watched more closely for potential drug and terrorist movements.

Baggage

Karl Baedeker wrote in 1891, in the fourteenth edition of his Switzerland Handbook For Travelers: "The traveler will save both time and money by planning his tour carefully before leaving home. A super abundance of luggage infallibly increases the delays, annoyances, and expenses of travel. To be provided with enough luggage, and no more, may be considered the second golden rule for the traveler."

Criticism you will hear most about rail travel in Europe concerns the problems of storing and handling luggage. Don't count on being able to get a porter - many small cities don't have them. Nearly all the large cities with porters have too few. Some stations provide self-service carts, but the stations which do so often don't have enough of them at peak times.

An effective procedure if you travel in pairs is for one of you to guard your luggage while the other hurries toward the station to find a cart and returns to the track with it.

When boarding a train, you want to avoid the difficulty of hauling your luggage down the narrow corridors of several cars. Before your train arrives, examine the train diagram on the platform. The sequence of cars and the platform location for each car are indicated for all long-distance trains. Try to place yourself and your luggage at the correct site for boarding your car. This little procedure will simplify your life.

On many trains there is a storage area for luggage at one or at both ends of the car. On most trains you have to store your baggage on a rack above your seat, which tends to be very high. Lifting a 30-pound (or heavier) weight above one's head can be a physical strain for the elderly or those who have a physical disability.

On the whole, it is much better to travel with two small, relatively light-weight suitcases or duffel bags per person than with one monstrous case. The small ones are easier to lift, and there's a better chance of being able to store them under the seat or in station lockers.

Some trains have a baggage car, although the newer and faster trains have baggage services in which the luggage, bikes, etc. don't necessarily travel on the same train with you. Using the traditional baggage car is almost always inconvenient, and although the charge is reasonable - about $6 per piece, with a limit of 66 pounds each - it is more expensive than having your cases with you in your own car or in your compartment. Also, unless you verify that your luggage is to travel on the same train as you, it may go on another train - possibly arriving a day after your arrival. If you want luggage to arrive at your destination prior to your arrival, you can arrange to send it in advance and it will be held in the "checked luggage" room at your destination. Usually, no charge is made for the first two or three days of storage, however, after that, a small daily fee must be paid when claiming the bags.

Additionally when your bags are in the baggage car, you don't have access to them, and you may have to wait up to 30 minutes for your cases to be unloaded. In some countries, a well placed tip can help convince the porter to unload your gear surprisingly fast. Waiting for cases to be unloaded, in turn, delays you in getting to the room reservation desk at the tourist accommodation office inside the station - a delay that can cost you getting a decent room that night. Every minute counts in obtaining an available room during peak travel days in the high season. Waiting at the baggage car also delays you in getting into what can often be a very long line for taxis.

When you arrive in a city with more luggage than you need for that destination, savvy travelers opt to store excess stuff in a station locker. Others wisely return to the station the night before their departure so as to store luggage in a locker and facilitate the haul to the station the following morning.

Although there are baggage checkrooms at nearly all major rail stations, using a checkroom instead of a rental locker eats up precious time you could have used more pleasantly and productively. There are frequently long lines both when you leave your luggage and again when you are claiming it. If you use checkrooms instead of rental lockers, be sure to leave yourself adequate time prior to your train's departure to retrieve your suitcases. And, although these check-rooms are secure, it isn't all that reassuring leaving any valuables in unlocked luggage.

The most convenient and safest method of storing luggage is to place it in a 24-hour rental locker. Unfortunately the lockers present their own set of problems. Several European stations have too few lockers, have strict time limitations, and are too small for large bags. Again, small suitcases make better sense.

Another wise maneuver is to have small change on hand for each country you visit. It goes without saying, the lockers in each country work only with the local coins. You cannot use a *kroner* in France, or a *franc* in Denmark!

Eating on Trains

Food in the dining cars tends to be expensive, and the choice can be limited, although in the last few years the quality of food services has radically improved. In restaurant cars of *de luxe* trains, the lunch is a fixed menu, very tasty, and highly caloric. On ordinary trains, the restaurant car food is adequate…but still a bit pricey. On the French TGV, the bar cars are very comfortable and the choice and quality of the sandwiches is surprisingly good. Not only can you buy sandwiches and drinks, you can purchase newspapers and magazines, telephone cards for the phones onboard, cognac, and some gift items.

Dining in the restaurant car of a train speeding across Europe has to be one of the most graceful and elegant experiences in life. If you can manage to relax about the prices and not see the linen table cloth and heavy silverware as pretensions but as remnants of an old European style, you should have a jolly good time.

Here are a few examples of meals (with prices) on major European train routes. Amsterdam-Paris "Etoile du Nord" serves crayfish, duck or lamb chops, potatoes *Lyonnaise*, steamed vegetables, cheeses and rolls, and pastry for a cool $55. Dinner on the Oslo-Bergen trip may include salad, poached salmon with boiled potatoes, and beer for $42. Dinner on the Paris-Lisbon run of the "Sud Express" can be $36 for vegetable soup, wild turkey with rice, fava beans, flan and fruit, and coffee. Tuck in your napkin and enjoy. You can't do this between Albany and Buffalo! Note that on many trains, you must reserve a seat in the restaurant car for the entire trip if you want lunch or dinner.

Both budget travelers and many of those who can't afford the meals served on trains buy their food at a market or delicatessen or one of those great French charcuteries before they board a train. A hunk of cheese and some bread, salads, meats, patés, fruits, and wine can make for a copious and sensuous, yet informal eating experience.

Before making the 12-hour ride from Copenhagen to Amsterdam, try buying a dozen, delicious smorre-brod sandwiches in a shop just a block from the Copenhagen station. The variety includes shrimp, salmon, ham, chicken, and beef, all garnished with tasty cucumbers, asparagus, and tomatoes. For four meals for two people you can eat well at a total of $36. If you find the idea of "picnicking" attractive, you can ask your hotel or *pensione* to pack a lunch for you, or you can purchase food either at a store near the station, in a restaurant at the station, from a food market inside the station, or, along the way, from vendors that push carts up and down the platforms at many station stops.

You will find restaurants and food stores located in many principal rail stations. Food stores in the Copenhagen, Stuttgart, Vienna, and Zurich rail stations offer meat, cheeses, salads, breads, pastries, etc. that are excellent. In Germany, it is only in the main train station of a city that you can buy food after the traditional closing times of most shops: 6:30 P.M.

Remember in any case that it's always a good idea to bring along some food and a bottle of water on a long journey.

Airport-City Rail Connections
Here is a handy list of fast train travel times in minutes between major cities and their airports.
Amsterdam (18 minutes)
Barcelona (18)
Brussels (20)
Frankfurt (14)
London (50 minutes from Heathrow, 30 minutes from Gatwick)
Malaga (12)
Paris (37 minutes from De Gaulle, 35 minutes from Orly)
Rome (24)
Vienna (25)
Zurich (11)
(For a complete listing see Table #5 in Thomas Cook's *European Timetable*.)

Lost Money and Passports
Losing or having your money or passport stolen is a certain way to spoil at least a part of your trip. The best precaution is to carry a minimal amount of cash at one time. Traveler's checks and major credit cards are safer. Remember to record the numbers in a safe place. Also guard your return airplane ticket as closely as your cash, traveler's checks, and passport. Each year, approximately 3,000 U.S. pass-

ports are stolen and another 11,000 are lost. There is an increasingly aggressive market for American and European passports in Latin America and Asia. So take precautions.

If, despite all your precautions, you discover that your passport has been taken or is simply missing, don't panic. Here's what you do. First, notify the local police and obtain a signed copy of the police report. Take this document to the local office of your country's consulate. It is not necessary to go to your embassy: It is your consulate, not your embassy, that will assist you by issuing a replacement passport. Obtaining a replacement is expedited if you can provide the passport number. Otherwise, you might have a few days to wait. If, in addition to the passport number, you have a certified copy of your birth certificate or certificate of citizenship, the consulate usually can issue a new passport the same day without telexing or wiring the State Department back home. In order to issue a new passport, two ID photos are required. Note that U.S. passport requirements include very specific dimensions for photos, which are obtainable at only certain photographers or photo stores. Consulates always have a list of places that can make these photos in each foreign city.

Obviously, it's best not to lose your papers. The delay of missed connections, additional hotel bills, and taxis (to police, consulate, photographer, airline office, etc.) can amount to a terrible expense.

Day Rooms
Many non-Europeans are unfamiliar with an extremely convenient service called "day rooms" available at some rail stations. With this accommodation, the tenant has privacy, a place to change clothes, and sometimes even bathing facilities. Some day rooms have beds. The advantages of a rail station day room over a conventional hotel room are that it is usually cheaper and it is located at the station.

Last-Minute Checklist
Here are several important tips that can greatly increase the pleasure (or reduce the struggle) of your international travel.
• Carry as little luggage as possible. You will arrive at many rail stations where it is a long walk from the train to the taxis (often requiring walking up and down stairs) and will find that there are neither porters nor carts. If the luggage you take is a burden, bring along a lightweight folding luggage rack.
• Bring a bottle of mineral water on any long trip. Most trains only provide drinking water in the bar car.
• Pack soft-ply toilet paper, wash-and-dry packets, and plastic bags. The bags are useful for storing leftover food items, wet soap and damp or dirty laundry.

Signs—The International Language
What follows is a sampling of helpful signs you'll find in train stations all over the world.

Language. Don't worry. Europeans like to practice their conversational English, especially on trains. For detailed information, consult the English-speaking staff at tourist offices, information bureaus, and hotels. At the railroad stations, pictograms lead you not only to the information desk but to any other facility you may be looking for. There are also the highly visible and efficient time-tables posted inside the railroad station for get-it-yourself train information. Once you acquire the knack of reading them (and we shall tell you how, later on), they will get you on the right train at the right time on the right track.

Information

Temporary Luggage Storage. At almost every large station you'll find coin-operated lockers. Else, use the special baggage storage indicated by a pictogram and/or the legend: CONSIGNE DES BAGGAGES ... GEPAECKAUFBEWAHRUNG ... CONSIGNA DE EQUIPAJES ... DEPOSITO BAGAGLIO. You'll get a claim check which you have to present when you pick your luggage up again.

Baggage check room

Locker

Checking Your Luggage Through. Time and circumstances permitting, take your bulky luggage or bicycle along on your train, but not with you. Wherever inter-national border crossings and train regulations don't stand in your way, avoid the hassle by checking your extra pieces through to your destination, to ride in the luggage-car. The right counter for this service is indicated by a pictogram.

Luggage registration office

Door-to-Door Luggage Service. If you really want to travel light in France or Germany—with a claim check instead of luggage—find out whether your train station in the city you're in is one of those which pick up your luggage where you're staying and deliver it at your next stay. If that's the case, the small service fee is worth every penny of it.

Baggage Claim

Border and Customs Control. Be in your seat. Immigration officials will inspect your passport and whatever visa or other required documents right in your compartment, while the train moves across border points. You will be asked whether you have anything to declare, but as a foreign tourist in transit, especially with a EURAILPASS or STUDENT-RAIL-PASS, you will be given the appropri-ate considerations.

Customs

Changing Money. A railroad station is a good place to exchange the bills and coins of one currency for another. Look for the sign where the action is: BUREAU DE CHANGE...GELDWECHSEL...WECHSELSTUBE...OFICINA DE CAMBIO... OFFICIO CAMBEIO...UFFICIO CAMBIO ...or just follow the pertinent pictogram.

Currency exchange

Tickets

Which Ticket Window for What. At larger stations tickets for domestic and international travel are purchased at different windows. But as a EURAILPASS or STUDENT-RAILPASS holder, you have your ticket already. So all you'll really want is either the information or reservation window or desk—except in Spain, where you must get a boarding pass at the station before you can board a train.

Services for Businessmen. If you are combining pleasure with business, there are a number of TEE and Intercity trains on which you can hire a secretary, send telegrams or make telephone calls, make car-rental reservations ahead of arrival, or reserve a taxi to pick you up at your destination.

Rent-a-car

Taxi stand

Your Helpful Porter. You'll recognize him by his uniform or official badge. You can usually find one as your cab pulls up to the station. If not, look for him inside. Consult the proper pictogram to find the porters' room. You can rely on your porter to get you to the right track, train, and car. He will put you in a smoker or non-smoker, as you wish, will try his best to find a vacant window-seat, and will place your luggage into the overhead rack.

Call for porter

Washroom Facilities. You can freshen up in a "W.C." (Water Closet) at either end of your car. In most long distance trains next to the "WC" are separate Washrooms. And remember not to drink the tap water; it is not potable.

Rest rooms

A Seat Reservation. Even though you can travel on a European train in most cases without a seat reservation, it's always nice to have a reserved seat—at a window, if possible, or where you want your lunch or dinner served (yes, advance reservations can be made on some TEE trains for meals to be served in your seat). EURAILPASS and STUDENT-RAILPASS holders must pay for seat reservations, but it's very little for a lot of convenience.

Reservation

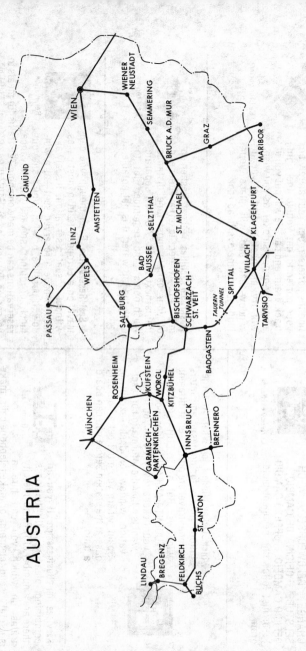

AUSTRIA

CHAPTER 6

EURAILPASS EUROPE

AUSTRIA

Overview

Trail travel in Austria promises to be not only an aesthetically exciting experience but an informative one as Austria has recently become a jumping off point for travel and trade with the rapidly evolving central and eastern European countries. When heading north, east, and south from Vienna, western travelers are destined to meet up with Hungarians, Czechs, Slovaks, Bulgarians, Romanians, and Russians, Europe's new travelers.

The Austrian Federal Railway, called the OBB (Osterreichische Bundesbahnen) is well-known for being on time and for providing clean and efficient service, although in the summer months the most popular routes can be overflowing with travelers attracted by the captivating Alps and enchanting music festivals. While travel between the major cities is swift and regular, the local mountain trains can be painfully slow although blissfully scenic. Train travel in Austria on the whole is a pleasant experience although in the words of one Viennese publisher, Austria can be tiring in that the Austrians tend to look inward as if the whole world were Austrian.

General Information

• Children under six travel free. Half-fare for children between the ages six and 14. Travelers over 15 must pay full fare.

• Special "through tickets" are required for "privileged trains," which cross German or Italian borders from one part of Austria to another without border formalities (customs, passport and currency control). These trains do not allow passengers to board or leave the train in Germany or Italy.

• The second-class couchette cars on most Austrian internal routes and on some international services have four berths per compartment instead of six. A supplement of 33% over the price of a couchette in a six-berth compartment is charged for them. Inquire about this when reserving a couchette.

The signs you will see at railstations in Austria are:

ABFAHRT	DEPARTURE
ANKUNFT	ARRIVAL
AUSGANG	EXIT
AUSKUNFT	INFORMATION
BAHNHOF	STATION
BAHNSTEIG	PLATFORM

DAMEN	WOMEN
EINGANG	ENTRANCE
FAHRKARTEN-SCHALTER	TICKET OFFICE
FAHRPLAN	TIMETABLE
GEPACKAUFBEWAHRUNG	BAGGAGE CHECKROOM
GLEIS	TRACK
HERREN	MEN
PLATZ RESERVIERUNG	SEAT RESERVATION
RAUCHER	SMOKING COMPARTMENT
SCHLAFWAGEN	SLEEPING CAR
SPEISEWAGEN	RESTAURANT CAR

Summer Time

Austria changes to Summer Time on the last Sunday of March and converts back to Standard Time on the last Sunday of September.

Austrian Holidays

Here is a list of Austrian holidays:

January 1: New Year's Day; **January 6**: Epiphany, Easter, Easter Monday; **May 1**: Labor Day, Ascension Day, Whit Monday, Corpus Christi Day; **August 15:** Assumption Day; October 26: National holiday; November 1: All Saints Day; **December 8:** Immaculate Conception; December 25: Christmas Day; **December 26**: St. Stephen's Day.

AUSTRIA'S TRAIN PASSES

European East Pass See Eastern Europe

Austrian Railpass Sold worldwide by travel agencies, by Rail Europe, and by DER Tours/GermanRail.

Also sold in Austria at travel agencies and railstations. Vouchers for this pass are sold at many major railstations near the Austrian border (such as Munich and Zurich), to be exchanged for Rabbit Card after entering Austria.

This pass is valid for unlimited travel on all Austrian Federal Railway lines and on state and private rail lines in Austria any 4 days within 10 days.

The 1996 prices for passengers 26 and older are: $165 for *first*-class, $111 for *second*-class. Children under 7 travel free.

Junior Railpass Same privileges as above. The 1996 prices for persons who are under 26 years old on the first day of travel: $95 for *first*-class, $64 for *second*-class.

Senior Citizen Half-Fare In 1996, women 60 and over and men who are 65 and older can buy train and bus tickets at half-price after purchasing a Senior Citizen's Identification for 240 Austrian schillings, available at all railstations and major post offices in Austria, and also at the Hauptbahnhof stations in Frankfurt, Munich and Zurich.

The ID (valid for one calendar year) can also be obtained by mail by sending a travelers check in the amount of $25 or equivalent, a photostat of the passport page which has a picture and states the holder's age, plus one passport-size photo to: OeBBVerkehrseinnahmen-und Reklamationsstelle, Mariannengasse 20, A-1090 Wien, Austria.

This discount is *not* valid on municipal transit lines (subway, trolley, bus).

Bundesnetzkarte (National Network Pass) Sold only in Austria. Unlimited train travel in all of Austria. The 1996 *first*-class prices are: 5,400 Austrian schillings for one month, AS-43,100 for one year. *Second*-class: AS-3,600 and AS-28,700.

Regional-Netzkarten (Regional Network Pass) Sold only in Austria. Unlimited train travel in any one of the country's 18 provinces for any 4 days within 10 days. The 1996 prices are: 630 Austrian schillings for *first*-class, AS-470 for *second*-class.

Kilometer Bank Sold only in Austria. Valid for *both* first and second-class seats. May be used by 1–6 persons traveling together on trips of over 70 km one way. Can be used in first or second-class. The conductor deducts trip distance for each passenger age 16 or older. Only half the distance is charged for each child age 6–15. No charge for children under age 6.

The 1996 prices are: 1,900 Austrian schillings for 2,000 km, AS-2,850 for 3,000 km, AS-3,800 for 4,000 km, and AS-4,750 for 5,000 km.

The maximum kilometers charged against this pass for any one trip are 600. Any number of kilometers above that are free.

For *first-class* use, one kilometer is counted as 1.5 kilometers.

EURAILPASS BONUSES IN AUSTRIA

Two track railways: (1) Puchberg am Schneeberg–Hochschneeberg and (2) St. Wolfgang–Schafbergspitze. The Danube cruise between Passau and Vienna. Steamers on Lake Wolfgang. Reduction of 50% on Lake Constance, Linz–Passau (and v.v), and Vienna–Budapest ships.

ONE-DAY EXCURSIONS AND CITY-SIGHTSEEING

Here are 31 one-day rail trips that can be made comfortably from Innsbruck, Linz, Salzburg and Vienna, returning to them in most cases before dinnertime. Notes are provided on what to see and do at each destination. The number after the name of each route is the Cook's timetable.

Innsbruck

Marvelous Winter resort. Gateway to many cable railway trips (Hungerburg, Hafelekar, Igls, Patscherkofel). See the 28 bronze statues around the enormous and magnificent tomb of Maximilian I in the 16th century Court Church and the effigy of King Arthur there. The silver altar at the Silver Chapel.

The roof (2,657 gold plated tiles) on Goldenes Dachl, built in 1500. The Museum of Tyrolean Folk Art, considered the most important collection of costumes and rustic furniture in Austria. The 18th century Roman-style Triumphal Arch. Reisenrundgemalde, a huge circular fresco depicting the Battle of Bergisel. The splendid views of the city and surrounding mountains from Bergisel Kaiserjager, containing the museum of the Tyrolean Imperial Light Infantry.

The excellent art collection of Archduke Ferdinand II at Schloss Ambras, open daily except Tuesday in Summer. The Alpen Zoo. The 18th century Imperial Palace. The paintings and furniture at the Tyrolean Regional Museum in the Arsenal of Emperor Maxmillian I.

Linz

Visit the schloss (castle) where Emperor Fredrich III lived, with its Upper Austrian Regional Museum collections of prehistoric and Roman antiquities, medieval armor and weapons, musical instruments and regional arts and crafts, open Tuesday-Saturday 10:00–18:00, Sunday 10:00–16:00.

Martinskirche, one of Austria's oldest churches. The medieval, Renaissance and Baroque exhibits in the City Museum at 7 Bethlehemstrasse, open Monday-Friday 09:00–18:00, Saturday and Sunday 15:00–17:00.

Take the 20-minute tram ride from the Urfahr section to Postlingberg, a hill on the south side of the Danube, to visit the Town Hall and see the view from there.

Kremsmunster, an enchanting small town established in 777, is a 30-minute drive south of Linz. Visit it in order to see the treasures in the monastery. It houses a fabulous library as well as an exceptional museum of natural history and early scientific instruments, a picture gallery, an art gallery, a fine collection of stained glass, and an armory.

Among its more than 100,000 rare books, 886 incunabula (books produced before movable type was invented in the 16th century), and 910 old manuscripts are the 2 famous "jewels" of the 230-foot-long library: the 8th and 9th century splendidly illuminated parchments called Codex Millenarius Major and Codex Minor. All 4 large rooms of the library are furnished with beautiful baroque bookcases.

Salzburg

Do not miss seeing the most amusing place in Europe, the 17th century Hellbrunn Palace. The 16th century 200-pipe barrel organ (played 3 times every day) in the 12th century fortress, 500 feet above the town (Festung Hohensalzburg) where 40-minute guided tours start every 15 minutes 09:00–17:30 daily in July and August. The traditional Music Festival (last week of July until the end of August).

Guided tours of the incredibly opulent rooms in The Residenz, the 17th century city palace of Salzburg's archbishops, start at 10:00, 10:30, 11:00, 11:30, 13:00, 13:30, 14:00, 14:30 and 15:00, Monday-Friday. The gallery of paintings in The Residenz (including Titian and Rembrandt) is open daily 10:00–17:00.

The painted ceilings in the 17th century Festspeilhaus. The collection of Mozart musical instruments and family memorabilia in the Mozart Museum, his birthplace (9 Getreidegasse), open daily 09:00–19:00. The vast musical library at Bibliotheca Mozartiana. St. Sebastian's Cemetery (Linzergasse 41). The 17th century Cathedral. The Universitatskirche. The Gothic cloister in the 9th century Benedictine Abbey of St. Peter.

The Glockenspiel Tower particularly at 07:00, 11:00 and 18:00 for the carillon concerts. The ancient marketplace, Alter Markt. The marble Angel Staircase and the Salzburger Barock-Museum in the 17th century Schloss Mirabell, and the marvelous gardens there. The superb collection of prehistoric objects, fossils and meteorites at the Natural History Museum.

Take the cable car to the top (5,800 feet) of Untersberg for a breathtaking view of Salzburg and the Alps. There are other good views of the city and river from Hettwer Bastion and also from the top of Monchsberg, Kapuzinerberg and Gaisberg.

Vienna (Wien)

The main tourist office (38 Kartnerstrasse) is open daily 09:00–19:00.

There is 30-minute train service [Table 835] from *Vienna (Nord) to the city's Schwechat Airport (Flughafen)* daily at 05:09, 05:47, 06:23 and hourly from 07:30 to 20:30, plus 10:07, 18:07 and 21:45. Also, daily except Sundays and holidays: at 06:47, 16:07 and 17:07.

Rail service *from the Airport to Vienna (Nord)* departs the Airport daily at 06:11, 06:34, 07:27 and hourly from 08:05 to 21:05, plus 11:26, 18:46 and 22:20. Also daily except Sundays and holidays: at 05:31, 07:05, 07:12 and 08:26.

For a glimpse at the world's most beautiful horses and extraordinary riding skill, see the Spanish Riding School. The view from the top of the south steeple of the 13th century Saint Stephen's Cathedral, reached by climbing 365 steps. That steeple is open daily 09:00–16:30.

Another great view is from the top of the Donauturm (Danube Tower). or from the hills in the Vienna Woods. Vienna's most elegant shopping streets are 2 pedestrian malls that run south and east from St. Stephen's: Karntnerstrasse and Graben. Three-hour boat trips on the Danube Canal operate daily except Monday at 10:00, 13:00 and 16:30 from Schwedenbrucke, a bridge that is a 15-minute walk from St. Stephen's.

See the Opera House. The Art Gallery. The Burgtheater. The Rathaus (City Hall). The gigantic Ferris Wheel and the miniature railway in the Prater amusement park.

Guided tours of some of the 1,400 rooms in Schonbrunn Castle, Vienna's Versailles, are offered daily 09:00–12:00 and 13:00–16:00. It is a 20-minute ride from Burgring on streetcar # 58.

Visit Tierpark, the zoo, in the Schonbrunner Schlosspark. The 2 museums of modern art, one in Palais Liechtensten, the other in Schweizer Garten. See the crown jewels of the Holy Roman Empire and the Austrian Empire, in the Imperial Apartments at the Hofburg (Imperial Palace), open Monday–Saturday 08:30–16:00 and Sunday 08:30–12:30.

The collection of great paintings (Titian, Rubens, Rembrandt) and Egyptian, Greek, Etruscan and Roman antiquities at the Museum of Art History on Ringstrasse, open Tuesday and

Friday 10:00–21:00, Wednesday and Thursday 09:00–18:00, Saturday and Sunday 09:00–18:00.

The many art museums in Belvedere Palace (medieval, baroque and modern art), open Tuesday-Saturday from 10:00 to varying afternoon hours, Sunday 09:00–12:00. The 20 centuries of memorabilia in the Historical Museum in the Karlsplatz, open Tuesday–Friday 10:00–16:00, Saturday 14:00–18:00, Sunday 09:00–17:00.

The Sigmund Freud Museum at 19 Berggasse, where the founder of psychoanalysis lived and practiced for many years, open Monday-Friday 09:00–13:00, Saturday and Sunday 09:00–15:00.

The many art museums in Belvedere Palace, open Tuesday–Sunday 10:00–16:00. The beautiful Austrian National Library at 1 Josefplatz. The great churches: Peterskirche and Karlskirche.

The finest collection of Durer paintings in the world and one of the world's largest graphics collections (1,000,000 prints from 5 centuries and 45,000 drawings) at the Albertina, 1 Augustinerstrasse, open Monday, Tuesday and Thursday 10:00–16:00, Wednesday 10:00–18:00, Friday 10:00–14:00, Saturday and Sunday 10:00–13:00.

The paintings of Kandinsky and other moderns at the Museum of the 20th Century in Schweizer Garten (near the Southeast Railroad Terminal), open daily except Wednesday 10:00–18:00. Works by Austrian painters and sculptors since World War II at the Museum of Modern Art in the Liechtenstein Palace, 1 Furstengasse, open daily except Tuesday 10:00–18:00.

The great paintings (Hieronymus, Bosch, Rubens, Titian, Van Dyck) at the Academy of Fine Arts, 3 Schillerplatz, open Tuesday, Thursday and Friday 10:00–14:00, Wednesday 10:00–13:00, Saturday and Sunday 09:00–13:00.

The treasures of the Holy Roman Empire, including the 10th century crown, at the Imperial Treasury, open Monday, Wednesday, Thursday and Friday 10:00–16:00, Saturday and Sunday 09:00–16:00 (November–March) or 09:00–18:00 (April–October).

Treasures collected by the Hapsburgs (including paintings by Pieter Bruegel the Elder and Rubens) at the Museum of Fine Arts on Maria-Theresien-Platz, open Tuesday–Friday 10:00–18:00, Saturday and Sunday 09:00–16:00 (November–March) or 09:00–18:00 (April–October).

The Austrian Baroque Museum and the Museum of Austrian Medieval art are located in the Lower Belvedere.

Vienna's largest outdoor food market (Naschmarkt) runs between Rechte Wienzeile and Linke Wienzeile.

Sightseeing flights over Vienna operate from the Schwechat Airport.

Take trolley car # 38 from Schottentor (in central Vienna) to **Grinzing**, the wine-tasting village. Continue from there on bus # 38A to the small Church of St. Joseph on the top of the 1,585-feet high **Kahlenberg**, from where Hungary and Czechoslovakia can be seen on clear days.

In the following timetables, where a city has more than one railstation we have designated the particular station after the name of the city (in parentheses). **Where no station is designated for cities in Austria, Switzerland and West Germany, the station is "Hauptbahnhof."**

Innsbruck - Bregenz - Innsbruck   800

Dep. Innsbruck	07:02 (1)	09:02 (1)	Dep. Bregenz	12:17 (1)	14:17 (1+2)
Arr. Bregenz	09:44	11:44	Arr. Innsbruck	14:58	16:58

(1) Restaurant car. (2) Plus other departures from Bregenz at 16:17 (1), 17:18 (1), 18:17 (1), 20:17 (1) and 21:38, arriving Innsbruck 18:58, 19:51, 20:58, 22:58 and 00:34.

Sights in **Bregenz**: Divided into 2 sections, features of the lower town include the lakeshore, the shopping district and the Voralberg Museum. The upper town has churches. Situated on the shore of the Bodensee (Lake Constance), easy day trips can be made from here to Innsbruck, Munich, Salzburg and Zurich.

The annual Music Festival (light opera and ballet on an unusual water stage in the lake) runs mid-July to mid-August. Take the funicular to the top (3,200 feet) of Pfander Mountain for a spectacular view of Bodensee, the Rhine River and the town of Lindau (see notes about Lindau under "Munich-Lindau"). The funicular runs 08:30–20:00 (until 22:00 in mid-Summer). Steamboats are operated on the lake from early April to early October.

Innsbruck - Igls - Innsbruck

Four miles from Innsbruck by suburban railway is the great ski resort of Igls.

Innsbruck - Kitzbuhel - Innsbruck   810

Dep. Innsbruck	07:20 (1)	09:20 (1)	11:20 (1)
Arr. Kitzbuhel	60 minutes later		

Sights in **Kitzbuhel**: This is one of the major winter resorts in the Alps. Cable cars take you from Kitzbuhel to many mountaintops. The city has one museum, some old churches.

Dep. Kitzbuhel	11:33	12:31 (2)	13:34 (1)	14:31 (2)	15:39 (1)	16:31 (2+3)
Arr. Innsbruck	60 minutes later					

(1) Light refreshments. (2) Restaurant car. (3) Plus other departures from Kitzbuhel at 17:26 (1), 18:23 (3), 19:33 (1), 20:32 (3) and 21:33 (1).

Innsbruck - Mayrhofen - Innsbruck   800

All of the Jenbach–Mayrhofen and v.v trains are second class only.

Dep. Innsbruck	09:02	13:02	15:02
Arr. Jenbach	09:20	13:20	15:20

Change from a standard-gauge train to a narrow-gauge train. Table 805

Dep. Jenbach	09:50	13:50	15:50
Arr. Mayrhofen	10:47	14:47	16:47

Sights in **Mayrhofen**: This is a popular Winter resort, with horse sleighs.

Dep. Mayrhofen	13:20	15:20	17:20	18:20
Arr. Jenbach	14:13	16:13	18:13	19:13

Change from a narrow-gauge train to a standard-gauge train. Table 800

Dep. Jenbach	14:38	16:38	18:38	20:38
Arr. Innsbruck	20 minutes later			

Innsbruck - Munich - Innsbruck   785

Dep. Innsbruck	07:07	09:07	09:43
Arr. Munich	09:52	11:52	12:39

Dep. Munich	14:00	15:00 (1)	17:00 (1)	18:00 (2)
Arr. Innsbruck	16:39	18:04	20:54	20:54

(1) Change trains in Mittenwald. (2) Change trains in Garmisch.

Innsbruck - St. Anton - Innsbruck   800

Dep. Innsbruck	07:02 (1)	09:02 (1)	11:02 (1)	11:53	12:44 (1)
Arr. St. Anton	08:20	10:20	12:20	13:33	13:54

Sights in **St. Anton:** A popular ski center since 1907, located at the eastern end of the 6-mile-long Arlberg Tunnel. The enormous number of ski lifts here offer a great variety of slopes.

Dep. St. Anton	11:37 (1)	12:03 (1)	13:37 (1)	14:00 (1)	15:37 (1)	16:03 (1+2)
Arr. Innsbruck	12:58	13:16	14:58	15:13	16:58	17:16

(1) Restaurant car. (2) Plus other departures from St. Anton at 17:37 (1), 18:39 (1), 19:37 (1), 21:37 (1) and 23:13.

Innsbruck - Salzburg - Innsbruck (via Zell am See)   800 + 810

The route via Zell-am-See is one of the most scenic rides in Austria, as well as a trip to an interesting destination. Exceptionally beautiful views of gorges, lakes, mountains and rivers.

All of these trains have a restaurant car.

Dep. Innsbruck	07:02 (3)	08:17 (1)	09:02 (3)	09:51 (1+4)
Dep. Zell-am-See	-0-	10:20	-0-	12:20
Arr. Salzburg	09:00	11:51	11:00	13:51

Sights in **Zell-am-See:** Minutes by bus from year-around glacier skiing.

Dep. Salzburg	13:00 (3)	14:08 (1+2)	15:00 (3)	16:08 (1+2)	17:00 (3+5)
Dep. Zell-am-See	-0-	15:41	-0-	17:41	-0-
Arr. Innsbruck	14:58	17:35	16:58	19:35	18:58

(1) Of the 2 routes between Innsbruck and Salzburg, this train takes the more interesting one (via Zell-am-See), one of the most scenic rail trips in Austria. (2) Operates late September to late May. (3) Via Kufstein. (4) Plus other departures from Innsbruck at 11:07 (3) and 13:02 (3), arriving Salzburg 13:00 and 15:00. (5) Plus other Salzburg departures at 18:14 (1+2), 19:00 (3) and 21:20 (3), arriving Innsbruck 21:35, 20:58 and 23:12.

Linz - Munich - Linz   67

All of these trains charge a supplement for first-class which includes seat reservation fee and have a restaurant car.

Dep. Linz	07:48	10:46		Dep. Munich	16:25	18:25
Arr. Munich	10:35	13:36		Arr. Linz	19:12	21:12

Linz - Salzburg - Linz   800

All of these trains have a restaurant car.

Dep. Linz	Frequent times from 05:34 to 23:30
Arr. Salzburg	1 to 2 hours later
Dep. Salzburg	Frequent times from 04:53 to 22:05
Arr. Linz	1 to 2 hours later

Linz - Vienna - Linz   800

Most of these trains have a restaurant car.

Dep. Linz	Frequent times from 04:30 to 23:15
Arr. Vienna (Westbf.)	1½ to 2 hours later
Dep. Vienna (Westbf.)	Frequent times from 04:40 to 23:30
Arr. Linz	1½ to 2 hours later

Salzburg - Zell am See - Innsbruck - Salzburg   800 + 810

The route via Zell-am-See is one of the most scenic rides in Austria, as well as a trip to an interesting destination. Exceptionally beautiful views of gorges, lakes, mountains and rivers.

These trains have a restaurant car, unless designated otherwise.

Dep. Salzburg	07:00 (1)	08:08 (2+3)	09:00 (1)	10:08 (2+3)	10:38 (1)
Dep. Zell-am-See	-0-	09:41	-0-	11:41	-0-
Arr. Innsbruck	08:58	12:12	10:58	14:09	12:36

Sights in **Zell-am-See**: Minutes by bus from year-around glacier skiing.

Dep. Innsbruck	11:51 (2+3)	13:02 (1)	13:20 (2+4)	13:51 (2+3)	15:02 (1+5)
Dep. Zell-am-See	14:20	-0-	15:16	16:20	-0-
Arr. Salzburg	15:51	15:00	16:53	17:51	17:00

(1) Via Kufstein. (2) Of the 2 routes between Salzburg and Innsbruck, this train takes the most interesting one (via Zell-am-See), one of the most scenic rail trips in Austria. (3) Operates late September to late May. (4) Change trains in Bischofshofen. Light refreshments on both trains. (5) Plus other departures from Innsbruck at frequent times from 15:20 to 21:14.

Salzburg - Kitzbuhel - Salzburg 810

All of these trains have a restaurant car.

| Dep. Salzburg | 06:11 | 08:08 | 10:08 | 12:08 |
| Arr. Kitzbuhel | 09:12 | 10:24 | 12:24 | 14:24 |

Sights in **Kitzbuhel**: See notes about Kitzbuhel under "Innsbruck–Kitzbuhe."

| Dep. Kitzbuhel | 13:29 | 15:29 | 17:29 | 02:22 |
| Arr. Salzburg | 15:51 | 17:51 | 19:51 | 02:40 |

Salzburg - Linz - Salzburg 800

Most of these trains have a restaurant car.

| Dep. Salzburg | Frequent times from 04:53 to 22:05 |
| Arr. Linz | 80 minutes later |

| Dep. Linz | Frequent times from 05:34 to 23:30 |
| Arr. Salzburg | 80 minutes later |

Salzburg - Munich - Salzburg 790

All of these trains charge a supplement for first-class which includes a reservtion fee and have a restaurant car, unless designated otherwise.

Dep. Salzburg	04:08 (1)	04:35 (2)	10:18	12:09	
Arr. Munich	06:03	06:13	12:07	13:36	
Dep. Munich	12:25 (3)	13:25	15:25	16:25	17:51 (2+4)
Arr. Salzburg	13:55	14:53	16:55	17:53	19:40

(1) No supplement charged. No restaurant car. (2) No supplement charged. Light refreshments. (3) Light refreshments. (4) Plus other Munich departures at 18:25, 19:51 (2), 20:50 (1), 21:51 (2) and 23:19 (1), arriving Salzburg 19:55, 21:40, 22:24, 23:40 and 01:01.

Salzburg - Schafbergspitze - Salzburg

A very scenic one-day trip that includes views of the 8-mile-long **Wolfgangsee (Lake Wolfgang)**, the warmest lake in Austria (79 degrees in Summer). The narrow gauge steam rack railway climbs 5,682 feet to the top of the **Schafberg**, from where there are glorious views of 13 lakes and many mountains. The ride from Schafbergspitze back to St. Wolfgang must be booked immediately on arrival at the summit. This railway operates May to October.

Bus. 812

Dep. Salzburg	06:45 (1)	08:15	09:15	11:25	12:15	13:15 (1)
Arr. Strobl	07:59	09:19	10:29	12:39	12:29	14:29

Change buses. 813

Dep. Strobl	08:15 (1)	09:40 (1)	10:40 (1)	12:40	13:40	14:40
Arr. St. Wolfgang	08:30	09:55	10:55	12:55	13:55	14:55

Change to steam rack railway. 813

Dep. St. Wolfgang	Train operates when it has at least 20 passengers.
Arr. Schafbergspitze	39 minutes after departing St. Wolfgang

• • •

Dep. Schafbergspitze	At random times
Arr. St. Wolfgang	39 minutes after departing Shafbergspitze

Change to bus. 813

Dep.St. Wolfgang	10:05 (6)	12:10	13:15	15:05	16:15 (5)
Arr. Strobl	10:18	12:23	13:28	15:18	16:30

Change buses. 812

Dep. Strobl	10:41 (2)	12:41	13:41 (3)	15:41	16:41
Arr. Salzburg	11:55	13:55	14:55	16:55	17:55

(1) Runs daily, except Sundays and holidays. (2) Runs Monday-Friday, except holidays. (3) Operates mid-July to mid-September. (4) Mid-July to late September: runs daily. Late September to mid-July: runs daily, except Sundays and holidays. (5) Plus other St. Wolfgang departures at 17:15 (4), 18:15 and 20:00 (3), arriving Salzburg 18:55, 19:55 and 21:40.(6) Sundays only.

Salzburg - Vienna - Salzburg   800

Marvelous views of the Alps and pretty farmland on this ride.

All of these trains have a restaurant car.

Dep. Salzburg	06:05	07:00 (1)	08:05	09:05 (1)	10:05	11:05 (1)
Arr. Vienna (Westbf.)	09:25	09:45	11:25	12:25	13:25	14:25

Dep. Vienna (Westbf.)	13:35 (1)	14:40	15:40	16:00 (1)	17:00 (1)
Arr. Salzburg	3 hours later				

(1) Supplement charged for first-class includes reservation fee. (2) Plus other Vienna departures at 18:40, 19:40, 20:40 and 21:25, arriving Salzburg 21:55, 22:55, 00:12 and 00:43.

Vienna - Baden - Vienna

A local tram runs at frequent time from the center of Vienna to Baden and v.v.

Sights in **Baden**: Only 16 miles from Vienna, Baden is an alternative to staying in Vienna.

Famous since the 1st century for the curative powers of its hot sulphur springs. Many of the rooms in hotels here have a faucet in the bathroom that carries mineral water. See the Baroque Trinity Column. Try your luck in the Casino in Kurpark.

Visit the house where Beethoven lived, at 10 Rathausgasse, open daily except Thursdays, May–September, 09:00–11:00 and 15:00–17:00.

Vienna - Budapest - Vienna 890

Dep. Vienna (Sud.)	07:14 (1)	08:03 (3)	Dep Budapest (Kel.)	17:25	18:30 (3+5)
Arr Budapest (Kel.)	10:03 (2)	11:08	Arr. Vienna (Sud.)	20:50 (4)	21:45

(1) Restaurant car. (2) Departs/arrives Budapest's Deli railstation. (3) Reservation required. Restaurant car. (4) Arrives Vienna's Westbahnhof railstation. (5) Plus other Budapest departures at 19:05(1+2) and 21:20, arriving Vienna 21:58 (Sud.) and 00:44 (Sud.).

Vienna - Graz - Vienna 830

All of these trains have light refreshments.

Dep. Vienna (Sudbf.)	06:22	07:22 (1)	08:22	09:22 (1)	10:22	12:22
Dep. Bruck a.d. Mur	08:20	09:36 (1)	10:20	11:36	12:20	14:20
Arr. Graz	08:55	10:10	10:55	12:10	12:55	14:55

• • •

Dep. Graz	13:05	13:50 (1)	15:05	15:50(1)	17:05	17:50 (1+2)
Dep. Bruck a.d. Mur	13:43	14:36 (1)	15:43	16:36	17:43	18:36 (1)
Arr. Vienna (Sudbf.)	15:33	16:33	17:33	18:33	19:33	20:33

(1) Change trains in Bruck an der Mur. (2) Plus other departures from Graz at 19:05 and 21:05 (1), arriving Vienna 21:33, and 23:33 .

Sights in **Graz**: A 2½-hour motorcoach sightseeing tour of Graz starts from in front of the Opera House weekdays at 10:00, June through September

From the main square (Hauptplatz) with its many markets of vegetables, fruits and flowers, go to the arcades with shops in the 17th century Luegghaus. Then to the City Hall (Rathaus) to see the city's symbol, a carved white panther.

Follow Neutorgasse to the Joanneum (state Museum of Styria), one of the world's oldest museums, to see its archaeological collection, library, paintings and exhibits of Styrian crafts (09:00–12:00 daily, 14:30–17:00 Monday, Wednesday and Friday).

Continue on Landhausgasse and Herrengasse to the splendid Renaissance Landhaus. Next door, in the 4-story, 17th century Styrian Armory (Zeughaus) is an exhibit of 17th century armor (for both men and horses) said to be the best and largest collection in Europe (same hours as the Joanneum). Its 32,000 weapons include complete suits of armor, guns, helmets, swords, lances, shields and breastplates.

Walk on Opernring to the outstanding Opera House and then through marvelous Stadtpark with its fantastic double-spiral Gothic staircase and cross the Glacis to visit the city's oldest church, 13th century Leekirche, the Church of the Teutonic Order.

Pass the castle and see the Diocesan Museum and Treasury in the 15th century Cathedral. Across a narrow street is the 17th century Mausoleum of Emperor Ferdinand II and his mother (Maria of Bavaria), open 11:00–12:00 and 14:00–15:00 from May to September, only 11:00–12:00 the rest of the year.

Don't miss the folk dance by carved wood figures performing at 11:00 and 18:00 on the 400-year-old clock in Glockenspielplatz. Nearby is the 116-foot-high belfry which has a 4-ton bell that the people here call "Liesl." See the exhibits of regional costumes, tools, folk art, etc. in the Volkskundemuseum (Folk Art Museum of Styria) open Monday, Wednesday and Friday 14:30–17:00.

Cable cars leave every 15 minutes from 38 Kaiser Franz Josef Kai for the 350 foot ascent to the top of Schlossberg (Castle Hill), from where there is a great view of Graz, its suburbs, the Mur Valley and the Alps.

Drink Schilcher (the local rose wine) and Steiermark beer. Local food specialties to sample are: Steierische Wurzelfleisch (pork shoulder), Sulmtaler Krainer (smoked pork sausage) and Steierische Brettljause (a dish of bacon, sausage, cheese, peppers and tomatoes served on a wooden platter).

Take the tram to **Eggenberg** to see the hunting museum in the 17th century castle there. Go to the top of Castle Hill (Schlossberg) by foot or funicular for a great view of Graz and tour the Bell Tower and Clock Tower, where the big hands show the hour and the small hands the minutes.

Take a local bus to nearby **Stubing**, which has the largest open-air museum in Austria (ancient wood churches, peasants' homes). Another tour goes to **Koflach**, where a stud farm that is an auxiliary of Vienna's Spanish Riding School has been breeding thoroughbred horses since 1798.

Vienna - Linz - Vienna   800

Most of these trains have a restaurant car.

Dep. Vienna (Westbf.)	Frequent times from 04:40 to 23:30.
Arr. Linz	2 hours later.
Dep. Linz	Frequent times from 04:30 to 23:15.
Arr. Vienna (Westbf.)	2 hours later.

Vienna - Melk - Vienna   Train Ride + Danube Boat Trip

The Melk-Vienna boat is covered by Eurailpass.

Train 800			*Danube Steamship 843*	
Dep. Vienna (Westbf.)	08:44 (1)	12:26	Dep. Melk	14:55 (2)
Arr. Melk	09:45	13:38	Arr. Vienna	20:15 (3)

(1) Light refreshments. (2) Operates from mid-May to late September (3) Arrives at Vienna's Reichs-brucke.

Sights in **Melk**: Walk from the railstation up the hill to the Abbey, built in 1133 but completely reconstructed 1702 to 1736. English-language guided tours are offered sometimes. There is a splendid view of the Danube from the terrace.

At the top of the stone Emperor's Stairway is the 644-foot-long Emperor's Corridor, off which are several rooms whose doors are made of highly decorated rare wood and in which many treasures are displayed. Also on this floor are the magnificently decorated Marble Hall (actually faux marble stucco), the gilded bookcases of inlaid wood in the Library (over 85,000 books and 1,200 manuscripts from the 9th to the 15th centuries), and the Abbey church with a pulpit made entirely of gold.

A restaurant at the Abbey serves a hearty lunch. For the return trip to Vienna by boat, go to the main river dock, not to the dock below the abbey.

Vienna - Salzburg - Vienna   800

All of these trains have a restaurant car.

Dep. Vienna (Westbf.)	06:00 (1)	06:40	07:35 (1)	07:40	08:40	09:00 (1+2)
Arr. Salzburg	09:00	09:55	10:35	10:55	11:52	11:58
Dep. Salzburg	14:05	15:05	15:25 (1)	16:05	17:05	18:00 (1+3)
Arr. Vienna (Westbf.)	17:25	18:25	18:30	19:25	20:25	21:05

(1) Supplement charged for first-class includes reservation fee. (2) Plus other departures from Vienna at 09:35 (1), 09:40 and 10:40, arriving Salzburg 12:35, 12:55 and 13:55. (3) Plus other Salzburg departures at 18:05, 19:05, 19:25 (1), 20:00 (1), 20:05, 21:05 and 21:57 (1), arriving Vienna 21:25, 22:25, 22:30, 23:05, 23:25, 00:25 and 00:58.

Vienna - Sopron - Vienna   830 + 833

A day-trip into Hungary.

Change trains in Wiener Neustadt.

Dep. Vienna (Sud)	07:52	10:52		Dep. Sopron	13:39	16:55 (1)
Arr. Sopron	09:11	12:11		Arr. Vienna (Sud)	15:05	18:33(2)

(1) Plus another Sopron departure at 19:39, arriving Vienna 21:05. (2) Monday -Friday except holidays.

Sights in **Sopron**: A 900-year-old architectural treasure, with 240 perfectly preserved historic buildings. The Castle has a Roman foundation and a Norman basement. Visit the 13th century Goat Church and Church of St. Michael. The 15th century synagogue. St. George Church. Holy Ghost Church. The 16th century Lyceum. The 18th century Trinity Statue. The rococo Erdody Palace. Many museums: Liszt, Stonework, Pharmacy, Guild History, and Fabricius House.

SCENIC RAIL TRIPS

Innsbruck - Brennero   380

The beautiful mountain scenery here can be seen either on an easy one-day roundtrip from Innsbruck or as a portion of the Innsbruck–Verona–Milan route.

Dep. Innsbruck	06:37 (1)	10:26 (2)	12:48	14:04 (3)	15:22 (4)
Arr. Brennero	07:38	11:08	13:20	14:45	16:12

• • •

Dep. Brennero	07:29	12:04 (4)	15:14 (5)	16:04	16:23
Arr. Innsbruck	08:10	12:27	15:55	16:37	16:59

(1) Second-class only. Light refreshments. (2) Light refreshments. (3) Runs daily, except Sundays and holidays. (4) Supplement charged for first-class includes reservation fee. Restaurant car. (5) Runs daily, except Sundays and holidays.

Innsbruck - Buchs   800

The excellent mountain scenery here can be seen either on an easy one-day roundtrip from Innsbruck or as a portion of the Innsbruck–Zurich route.

All of these trains have a restaurant car, unless designated otherwise.

Dep. Innsbruck	07:02	09:02 (2)	11:02 (2)	12:44 (3)	14:44(3)
Arr. Buchs	09:47(2)	11:50	13:51	15:08	17:08

• • •

Dep. Buchs	10:52 (3)	12:44 (3)	14:52 (3)	16:03 (2)	17:18 (2+4)
Arr. Innsbruck	13:16	15:13	17:16	18:58	19:51

(1) No restaurant car. (2) Change trains in Feldkirch. (3) Supplement charged for first-class includes resrvation fee. (4) Plus other Buchs departures at 18:19 (2), 20:18 (2) and 22:53, arriving Innsbruck 20:58, 22:58 and 01:37.

Innsbruck - Bruck an der Mur - Vienna

This indirect route from Innsbruck to Vienna, traveling south of the main line (via Linz), offers excellent mountain scenery. As the schedules below indicate, a stopover of up to 7 hours in Bruck an der Mur is possible.

All of the trains have light refreshments unless designated otherwise.

810

Dep. Innsbruck	05:20	07:20	09:20	11:20
Arr. Selzthal	09:28	11:28	13:28	15:28

Change trains. 825

Dep. Selzthal	09:32	11:32	13:32	15:32
Arr. Leoben	10:29	12:29	14:29	16:29

Change trains.
830

Dep. Leoben	10:25	12:25	15:20	17:20
Arr. Bruck an der Mur	10:36	12:36	15:33 (2)	17:33 (2)
Arr. Vienna (Sudbf.)	12:40	14:40 (1)	17:40	19:40

(1) Arrives at the Ost platforms. (2) Change trains in Bruck an der Mur.

Sights in **Bruck an der Mur**: Located in the Styrian Alps, at the meeting of the Mur and Murz rivers, on the main route between Vienna and Graz. See the 17th century Wrought Iron Well, the outstanding example of Styrian ironwork. The 15th and 16th century houses. The Parish Church.

Innsbruck - Feldkirch - Innsbruck   800

Very good mountain scenery. As the schedules shown below indicate, a stopover of 2-8 hours in Feldkirch is possible.

All of these trains have a restaurant car, unless designated otherwise.

Dep. Innsbruck	07:02	09:02	11:02	13:02	15:02	17:02
Arr. Feldkirch	09:14	11:15	13:14	15:14	17:14	19:14

Sights in **Feldkirch**: A medieval town, next to the Swiss border. See the Old Town and Marketplace. The 12-foot-thich walls at the 16th century Schattenburg Castle. The local museum, open daily except Wednesday afternoon.

Dep. Feldkirch	10:44	12:44	14:44	16:44	17:44 (1)	20:44
Arr. Innsbruck	12:58	14:58	16:58	18:58	19:51	22:50

(1) Supplement charged for first-class includes reservation fee.

Innsbruck - Garmisch - Zugspitze   785

The outstanding mountain scenery here can be seen either on an easy one-day roundtrip from Innsbruck or as a portion of the Innsbruck–Munich route.

For the first way:

Dep. Innsbruck	07:07	07:59	09:07 (1)	09:43 (2)	11:07	12:00
Arr. Garmisch	08:24	09:24	10:24	11:09 (3)	12:24 (3)	13:24
Change trains.						

The following schedule allows one to ride one cable route to the summit of Zugspitze and ride a different cable route back to Garmisch.

783

Dep. Garmisch	08:35	09:35	10:35	11:35	12:35	14:35
Arr. Eibsee	09:15	10:15	11:15	12:15	13:15	15:15

Change to cable railway.

Dep. Eibsee	Every 30 minutes from 08:00 to 17:30
Arr. Zugspitze	10 minutes later

(1) Change trains in Mittenwald. (2) Supplement charged. Restaurant car. (3) As the Garmisch departures show, there is time to lunch in Garmisch and take a later train to Eibsee and Zugspitze. See departures above.

Use a different cable railway in returning to Garmisch.

In 1994, all of the times Zugspitze-Schneefernerhaus and Schneefernerhaus-Garmisch were estimated.

787
| Dep. Zugspitze | Every 30 minutes from 08:15 to 16:45 |
| Arr. Schneefernerhaus | 4 minutes later |

• • •

787 Train
Dep. Schneefernerhaus	10:00	11:00	13:00	14:00	15:00	17:00
Arr. Garmisch	11:20 (1)	12:20 (1)	14:20	15:20	16:20	18:20

Change trains. 785
Dep. Garmisch	11:26 (2)	12:26	14:26	16:05 (3)	16:26 (2)
Arr. Innsbruck	12:41	13:48	15:47	17:40	18:04

(1) As the Garmisch departures show, there is time to lunch in Garmisch and take a later train to Innsbruck or Munich. (2) Change trains in Mittenwald. (3) Supplement charged. Restaurant car.

Here is the schedule for continuing on from Garmisch to Munich.

785
Dep. Garmisch	11:34	12:27	13:34	14:27	15:34	16:27 (1)
Arr. Munich	12:51	13:51	14:51	15:51	16:51	17:53

(1) Plus other departures from Garmisch at 17:34, 18:31, 19:34, 20:27 and 21:31.

Innsbruck - Salzburg - Innsbruck

The good canyon, lake, river and mountain scenery on this route can be seen either on an easy one-day roundtrip from Innsbruck (see details under "Innsbruck–Zell am See–Salzburg – Innsbruck"), or as a portion of the Innsbruck–Vienna route (see below).

Innsbruck - Vienna   800

Here are the schedules for going across Austria.

All of these trains have a restaurant car, unless designated otherwise.

Dep. Innsbruck	07:02	09:02	11:07	13:02	15:02	17:02 (1)
Arr. Vienna (Westbf.)	12:25	14:25	16:25	18:25	20:25	22:25

(1) Plus another departure from Innsbruck at 19:02, arriving Vienna 00:25.

Linz - Selzthal - Amstetten - Linz

The Selzthal–Amstetten portion of this easy one-day circle trip affords fine river, canyon and mountain scenery. There are good views of the colorful **Enns Valley**.

All of the Linz–Selzthal and v.v. trains have light refreshments. All of the Selzthal–Amstetten and v.v. trains are second-class only. All of the Amstetten–Linz and v.v. trains have a restaurant car.

825
Dep. Linz	08:40	10:40	12:40	14:40
Arr. Selzthal	10:16	12:16	14:16	16:16

Change trains.
826
Dep. Selzthal	10:19	12:19	14:19	16:19
Arr. Amstetten	12:50	14:50	16:50	18:50

Change trains.
800
Dep. Amstetten	12:54	14:54	16:54	18:54
Arr. Linz	13:32	15:32	17:32	19:32

The same trip can be made in reverse, using this schedule:

800
Dep. Linz	08:27	10:27	12:27	14:27
Arr. Amstetten	09:02	11:02	13:02	15:02

Change trains.
826
Dep. Amstetten	09:10	11:10	13:10	15:10
Arr. Selzthal	11:41	13:41	15:41	17:41

Change trains.
825
Dep. Selzthal	11:44	13:44	15:44	17:44
Arr. Linz	13:20	15:20	17:20	19:20

Salzburg - Zell am See - Innsbruck

There are exceptionally beautiful views of canyon, lakes, mountains and rivers on one of the most scenic rides in Austria. Schedules for this trip appear earlier in this section under both "Innsbruck–Salzburg" and "Salzburg–Innsbruck."

Salzburg - Gmunden - Stainach - Salzburg

There is fine mountain and lake scenery on the Gmunden–Stainach portion of this circle trip.

800

Dep. Salzburg	06:05 (1)	12:05 (1)
Arr. Attnang	06:50	12:50

Change trains.
815

Dep. Attnang	07:25 (2)	13:25 (2)
Dep. Gmunden	07:44	13:44
Dep. Bad Ischl	08:22	14:22
Dep. Hallstatt	08:46	14:46
Dep. Bad Aussee	09:06	15:06
Arr. Stainach	09:42	15:42

Change trains.
32

Dep. Stainach	09:55 (3)	20:49 (4)
Arr. Salzburg	12:04	22:48

(1) Restaurant car. (2) Second-class only. (3) Supplement charged for first-class includes seat reservation fee. Light refreshments. (4) Light refreshments.

Sights in **Gmunden**: A colorful little town. Artistic pottery has been made here since the 15th century. See the porcelain-tiled clocktower of the Renaissance Town Hall in the main square (Rathausplatz). Stroll from there along the beautiful flowerbeds and chestnut trees of the Esplanade to the yacht harbor and lakeshore beach. Walk on the breakwater to the Ort Chateau, built on a small island.

Sights in **Bad Ischl**: A popular mineral water spa since 1822. This is the center of the Salzkammergut resort region. Visit the home of composer Franz Lehar, now a museum. The Imperial Villa.

Sights in **Hallstaat**: One of Europe's oldest permanent settlements, it dates back to the 5th century B.C. The local museum traces the prehistoric stages of this region's culture.

See the colorful houses (blue, red, yellow or beige), every balcony and window festooned with flowers. It is a short walk to several waterfalls. Close to one that rushes through the town is a 16th century church that has a splendidly carved late Gothic altar.

You can see a unique collection of neatly piled, gaily decorated skulls of generations of villagers in the charnel house. There has never been enough land here for a cemetery.

Sights in **Bad Aussee**: This was the center of the salt region in the 15th century. Still popular for health-inducing brine baths. Both a Summer resort and Winter sports area. There are many picturesque lakes here.

Salzburg - Vienna

Marvelous views of the Alps and pretty farmland. See schedules for Vienna–Salzburg.

Salzburg - Villach - Salzburg   820

The excellent canyon and mountain scenery on this ride can be seen either on an easy one-day roundtrip from Salzburg or as a portion of the Salzburg–Venice route.

For the first way:

Dep. Salzburg	07:08 (1)	09:08 (1)	11:08 (1)	13:08 (1)	15:08 (2)
Arr. Villach	09:43	11:43	13:43	15:43	17:44

· · ·

Dep. Villach	10:19 (2)	12:18 (2)	14:19 (1)	16:19 (1)	18:19 (1)
Arr. Salzburg	12:53	14:53	16:53	18:53	20:53

(1) Light refreshments. (2) Supplement charged for first-class includes reservation fee. Restaurant car

Here is the schedule for going from Salzburg to Italy:

88		390	
Dep. Salzburg	09:08 (1)	Dep. Venice (Mestre)	15:31
Arr. Venice (Mestre)	15:18	Arr. Venice (S.L.)	15:40
Change trains.			

(1) Supplement charged. Restaurant car.

The very scenic Klagenfurt–Udine–Trieste portion of the Vienna–Trieste route is described under "Vienna–Trieste." A departure from Salzburg can connect with that trip at Villach.

Vienna - Puchberg am Schneeberg - Hochschneeberg - Vienna

The ride from Hoshschneeberg back to Puchberg must be booked immediately on arrival at the summit.

These schedules are Monday-Friday.

(Unsere Bahn)

Dep. Vienna (Sud)	06:52	07:52	09:52	10:52	11:52	13:52
Arr. Wiener Neustadt	07:30	08:30	10:30	11:30	12:30	14:30

Change trains.

Dep. Wiener Neustadt	07:36	08:36	10:36	11:36	12:36	14:36
Arr. Puchberg	08:26	09:26	11:26	12:26	13:26	15:26

Change to steam rack railway.

Dep. Puchberg   (Puchberg-Hochschneeberg services run May-October subject to demand.)

Arr. Hochschneeberg

Sights in **Puchberg**: Located at the foot of the mountain called Schneeberg, the eastern edge of the Alps. A Summer and Winter resort. Popular for water cures and weight-loss treatment.

Sights in **Hochschneeberg**: At 5,900 feet, there are good views and a restaurant at the peak.

Dep. Hochschneeberg

Arr. Puchberg   (Hochschneeberg-Puchberg services run May-October subject to demand.)

Change trains.

Dep. Puchberg	15:37	16:37	17:37	18:37	-0-	19:37
Arr. Wiener Neustadt	16:23	17:23	18:23	19:23	-0-	20:23

Change trains.

Dep. Wiener Neustadt	16:30	17:30	18:30	19:05	-0-	20:30
Arr. Vienna (Sud)	17:00	18:05	19:05	19:40	-0-	21:05

(1) Return journey to Puchberg must be booked *on arrival.*

Vienna - Bruck an der Mur - Innsbruck

This indirect route from Vienna to Innsbruck, traveling south of the main line (via Linz), offers excellent mountain scenery. The schedules allow a stopover in Bruck an der Mur.

820 + 830

Dep. Vienna (Sud)	09:22 (1)	11:22 (1)
Dep. Bruck an der Mur	11:24	13:24
Dep. Villach	14:19	16:10
Arr. Bischofshofen	16:09	18:09
Change trains. 810		
Dep. Bischofshofen	16:53 (2)	18:58 (2)
Arr. Innsbruck	19:35	22:09

(1) Light refreshments. (2) Restaurant car.

Sight in **Bruck an der Mur**: See "Innsbruck–Bruck an der Mur."

Vienna - Klagenfurt - Udine - Trieste

The marvelous farm and lake scenery on this route includes seeing **Worthersee**, a lake fed by warm springs that is very popular for swimming and boating, and the beautiful coastline from Udine to Trieste.

The great Worthersee resort area is open June through mid-September. The region around **Klagenfurt** has attractive lakes, rolling hills and wildlife parks.

Even if you don't stay there, at least watch for that area a few minutes before the stop at Klagenfurt. An early departure from Vienna is recommended in order to be able to see the Adriatic shore approaching Trieste in the afternoon sunlight, as we have done.

The comfortable local train from Udine hurtles downhill too fast to permit picture-taking, but you will have a memory of that truly beautiful scene forever. Have a seat on the right-hand side of the train for the best possible view.

Not only is Trieste a worthwhile one-day stopover, it is also ideal as a base for several short rail trips into Yugoslavia such as Villa Opicina, Sezana, Pivka, Postojna and Ljubljana. While staying in Trieste, it is also easy to make a one-day rail excursion to see the sights in Udine.

88				*378*		
Dep. Vienna (Sud.)	07:18 (1)	13:22 (2)		Dep. Udine	14:30 (3)	20:47
Dep. Klagenfurt	11:21	17:46		Arr. Trieste	15:36	21:56
Arr. Udine	13:58	20:40				
Change trains.						

(1) Supplement charged for first-class includes reservation fee. Restaurant car. (2) Restaurant car. (3) Second-class only. Runs Monday-Saturday.

Sights in **Trieste**: City buses go to Miramare Castle, Maximilian and Charlotte's lovely seaside palace. Constructed in 1856, it has been restored. The fine library and much of the original furniture are exhibited. Charlotte returned here after their tragic brief time as rulers of Mexico, made insane by Maximillan's death. The Piazza deli'Unita is reminiscent of Piazza San Marco in Venice. The 15th century Castello di San Giusto. The 14th century Cathedral of San Giusto. The ruins of a Roman amphitheater. The Civic Museum of History and Art. Take a taxi or bus from the railstation up to the 15th century Castello di San Giusto for views of the city and to see the collection of weapons and armor there. It is a scenic 30-minute bus trip (#45, from Piazza G. Oberdan) to visit **Grotta Gigante**, a cave large enough to contain St. Peter's Cathedral.

If you are starting from Salzburg, this is the schedule:

88		*378*	
Dep. Salzburg	09:08 (1)	Dep. Udine	14:30 (2)
Arr. Udine	13:58	Arr. Trieste	15:36
Change trains.			

(1) Supplement charged. Restaurant car. (2) Second-class only.

Now for the one-day excursion to Udine:

Trieste - Udine - Trieste   378

Dep. Trieste	07:00	07:42	08:35 (1)	09:05 (2)	10:55	12:27 (3)
Arr. Udine	08:17	08:53	10:03	10:33	12:12	13:37

Sights in **Udine**: The collection of paintings in the Civic Museum and Gallery, a 20-minute walk from the railstation.

Tiepolo's paintings are featured in both the Bishop's Palace and the Cathedral. Visit Piazza della Liberta.

Dep. Udine	12:35	13:03 (1)	13:42 (3)	14:30 (3)	15:35 (1)	16:56 (3+4)
Arr. Trieste	13:45	14:34	15:06	15:36	16:43	18:10

(1) Runs daily, except Sundays and holidays. (2) Runs Sunday only. (3) Second-class only. (4) Plus other departures from Udine at 17:35 (1), 18:02 (1), 18:32 (3), 19:35 (3) and 20:45, arriving Trieste 19:00, 19:12, 19:39, 20:54 and 21:53.

Danube Cruise

This service operates daily from mid-May to late September.

845

Dep. Vienna (Reich.)	08:00	Dep. Linz	09:15
Arr. Durnstein	13:35	Arr. Durnstein	16:10
Arr. Linz	22:55	Arr. Vienna (Schif.)	20:15

Sights in **Durnstein**: This small, fortified town is at the foot of a ridge surrounded by vineyards. Richard the Lion Hearted was held for for an enormous ransom in the Castle, from which there is a wonderful view of Durnstein and the valley below it.

The town's Parish Church and its main street are interesting.

INTERNATIONAL ROUTES
FROM AUSTRIA

The Austrian gateways for travel to Germany (and on to Copenhagen) are Innsbruck, Salzburg and Vienna. Vienna is also the access point for travel to Poland and Czechoslovakia (and on to Russia), Hungary, Romania and Yugoslavia (and on to Bulgaria, Greece and Turkey). Innsbruck, Salzburg and Vienna are also starting points for trips to Italy. Innsbruck is also the gateway to Switzerland (and on to Belgium, France, Holland and Luxembourg).

Innsbruck - Munich   785

Dep. Innsbruck	07:59	09:07	09:43 (3)	11:07 (4)	14:00	15:07 (5)
Arr. Mittenwald	08:39	09:43	10:37	11:54	14:44	15:59
Dep. Mittenwald	09:03	10:03 (2)	10:48	12:03	15:03	16:02
Arr. Garmisch	09:24	10:24	11:09	12:24	15:24	16:23 (1)
Dep. Garmisch	09:34	10:27	11:18	12:27	15:34	16:27
Arr. Munich	10:51	11:52	12:38	13:51	16:51	17:53

(1) All direct trains. (2) Restaurant car. (3) Direct train to Munich. No train changes. Supplement charged. Restaurant car. (4) Direct train to Munich. No train changes. (5) Plus other departures from Innsbruck at 16:00, 17:05 (5), 19:07 and 21:05, arriving Munich 18:53, 19:56, 21:52 and 23:52.

Vienna - Salzburg - Munich   67

If you are starting this trip in Salzburg, arrive at the Salzburg railstation sufficiently in advance of departure time to complete the German Customs clearance that takes place before boarding the train. There are departures fom Salzburg in addition to those shown here, at frequent times from 06:18 to 23:58 (Table 790).

Dep. Vienna (West)	06:00 (1)	09:00 (1)	09:40 (2)	10:40 (3)	11:40 (2+5)
Arr. Salzburg	09:00	12:04	12:55 (2)	13:55 (3)	14:55 (2)
Dep. Salzburg	09:05	12:09	13:05	14:18	15:05
Arr. Munich (Hbf.)	10:35	13:36	14:35	16:07	16:34

(1) Supplement charged for first-class includes reservation fee. Restaurant car. (2) Change trains in Salzburg. Restaurant car on both trains. Salzburg-Munich: supplement charged. (3) Change trains in Salzburg. Vienna-Salzburg: restaurant car. Salzburg-Munich: light refreshments. (4) Has first-class coach and second-class couchettes. (5) Plus other departures from Vienna at 16:00 (1), 18:40 (3) and 23:30 (4) and departing Salzburg at 19:05 (1), 20:18 (3), 21:55 (1), 22:15 (3) and 04:08 (4), arriving Munich 20:36, 22:00, 24:00 and 06:03.

Vienna - Prague - Berlin   60 + 96a

Dep. Vienna (Sud.)	07:39 (1)	11:39 (1)	20:25 (2)
Arr. Prague (Hole)	12:32	16:37	01:48
Arr. Berlin (Licht.)	-0-	21:26	07:14 (3)

(1) Supplement charged for first-class includes reservation fee. Restaurant car. (2) Carries a sleeping car. Also has second-class couchettes. Coach is second-class only. (3) Arrives at Berlin's Hauptbahnhof railstation.

Vienna - Warsaw (or Kiev) - Minsk - Moscow

Both of these trains carry only sleeping cars.

94 a

Dep. Vienna (Sudbahnhof)	21:50
Arr. Warsaw (Centralna)	10:22
Dep. Warsaw (Wschodnia)	11:11
Arr. Kiev	- 0 - (1)
Arr. Minsk	22:27
Arr. Moscow (Smolenskaya)	12:06

(1) Day 3.

Vienna - Budapest - Bucharest   61 + 890

Dep. Vienna (Westbf.)	10:05 (7)	13:20	08:30
Arr. Budapest (Keleti)	13:28	16:43	11:53
Arr. Bucharest (Nord)	-0-	-0-	-0-

Dep. Vienna (Westbf.)	18:20 (3+9)
Dep. Vienna (Sudbf.)	-0-
Arr. Budapest (Keleti)	21:38
Arr. Bucharest (Nord)	-0-

(1) Departs from Vienna's Hutteldorf railstation. Carries a sleeping car. Also has couchettes. (2) Arrives at Budapest's Ferencvaros railstation. (3) Supplement charged for first-class includes reservation fee. Restaurant car. (4) Arrives Budapest's Deli railstation. (5) Restaurant car. (6) Second-class only. (7) Restaurant car. Second-class only. (8) Carries a sleeping car. Also has couchettes. (9) Plus another Vienna (West.) departure at 19:08 (8), arriving Budapest (Keleti) 22:33 and Bucharest (Nord) 14:40 on Day 2.

Vienna - Belgrade and Athens

61

Dep. Vienna (Westbf.)	08:03 (1)	19:05 (2)	23:00 (4)
Arr. Belgrade	16:45	07:11 (2+3)	08:49 (3)
Change trains. 945			
Dep. Belgrade	22:00 (5)	07:40 (5)	18:00 (7)
Dep. Thessaloniki	-0-	21:38	07:41
Arr. Athens	-0-	06:33 (6)	-0- (6)

(1) Departs from Vienna's Sudbahnhof railstation. Restaurant car. (2) Direct train to Athens. No train change in Belgrade. Has couchettes. (3) Day 3 from Vienna. (4) Carries a sleeping car. Also has couchettes. Coaches are second-class only. (5) Carries a sleeping car. Also has couchettes. (6) Day 4 from Vienna. (7) Departs from Belgrade's Centar railstation. Carries a sleeping car. Also has couchettes.

Vienna - Belgrade - Istanbul   61 + 97 b

This train carries a sleeping car and has couchettes to Belgrade. The Vienna-Istanbul portion has couchettes and second-class coaches.

Dep. Vienna (West.)	23:00	Dep. Belgrade	22:00
During Summer Time,		*All year,*	
set your watch back one hour.		*set your watch forward 2 hours.*	
Arr. Belgrade	09:07 (1)	Arr. Istanbul	19:59 (2)

(1) Day 2 from Vienna. (2) Day 2 from Belgrade.

Innsbruck - **Verona** and **Milan** or **Venice** 76

Dep. Innsbruck	01:38 (1)	08:39 (2)	10:26 (3)	11:22 (3)
Arr. Verona (P.N.)	05:40 (1)	12:10 (2)	14:40	15:04(4+7)
Change trains.				
Dep. Verona (P.N.)	05:45 (1)	-0-	14:27 (4)	15:00 (3)
Arr. Milan (Cen.)	-0-	14:05	-0-	16:45
Arrive Venice (S.L.)	08:45	-0-	15:52	-0-

(1) Direct train to Venice. No train change in Verona. Has couchettes. Coach is second-class. (2) Direct train to Milan. No train change in Verona. Supplement charged for first-class includes reservation fee. Restaurant car. (3) Light refreshments. (4) Supplement charged for first-class includes reservation fee. Restaurant car or light refreshments. (5) Direct train to Venice. No train change in Verona. Supplement charged for first-class includes reservation fee. Restaurant car. (6) Direct train to Milan. No train change in Verona. Carries a sleeping car. Also has couchettes. Coach is second-class. (7) Plus other Innsbruck departures at 11:22 (4), 15:22 (5) and 17:22 (4), arriving *Venice* 17:15, 20:42 and 23:16. Also other Innsbruck departures at 15:22 (4) (terminates Venice SL at 20:35) 17:22 (2) (terminates in Milan 22:55) and 23:45 (6) (terminates in Verona at 03:35.)

Innsbruck - **Verona** - **Bologna** - **Florence** - **Rome** 76

Dep. Innsbruck	01:38 (1)	10:26 (2)	11:22 (3)	22:22 (1)	23:45 (4)
Arr. Verona (P.N.)	05:40	14:40	15:04	02:14	03:35
Arr. Bologna	07:47	16:14	17:16	04:08	05:32
Arr. Florence (S.M.N.)	09:06	-0-	18:23	-0-	-0-
Arr. Rome (Ter.)	-0-	-0-	20:30	08:15	-0-

(1) Carries a sleeping car. Also has couchettes. (2) Light refreshments. (3) Supplement charged for first-class includes reservation fee. Restaurant car. (4) Has couchettes. Coaches are second-class.

Vienna - **Nurnberg** - **Frankfurt** - **Cologne** 66

All of these trains charge a supplement and have a restaurant car, unless designated otherwise.

Dep. Vienna (Westbf.)	08:00	10:00	12:00	14:00	22:18 (1)
Arr. Nurnberg	13:14	15:14	17:14	19:14	03:54
Arr. Frankfurt	15:35	17:35	19:35	21:35	06:43
Arr. Cologne	18:05	20:05	22:05	00:07	09:21

(1) Carries a sleeping car. Also has couchettes. Light refreshments.

Vienna - Salzburg - Munich - Paris   32

Dep. Vienna (West.)	09:00 (1)	16:00 (2)	19:40 (3)	23:30 (4)
Dep. Salzburg	12:09	19:05	23:07	03:45
Arr. Munich (Hbf.)	13:38 (1)	20:36	-0- (3)	05:54
Change trains.				
Dep. Munich	13:48	21:06 (3)	-0-	07:48 (2)
Arr. Paris (Est.)	22:18	07:04	09:30	16:20

(1) Direct train to Paris. No train change in Munich. Restaurant car. (2) Supplement charged for first-class includes reservation fee. Restaurant car. (3) Direct train to Paris. Does not call on Munich. Carries a sleeping car. Also has couchettes. Coach is second-class. Light refreshments. (4) Has couchettes.

Vienna - Venice   88 + 391

Dep. Vienna (Sud.)	13:22 (1)	19:45 (1+2)	20:15 (2+3)	22:22 (4)
Arr. Venice (S.L.)	22:28	04:10 (5)	04:42	08:32

(1) Restaurant car. (2) Carries a sleeping car. Also has couchettes. (3) Late May to mid-June: runs daily. Mid-June to late Septermber: runs Friday, Saturday and Sunday. (4) Carries a sleeping car. Also has couchettes. Coach is second-class. (5) Runs Monday-Thursday.

Innsbruck - Zurich   86

There is marvelous Alpine scenery on this route. About 2½ hours before reaching Zurich, the train passes through one of Europe's longest rail tunnels, the 6.3-mile-long Arlberg.

Dep. Innsbruck	04:15 (1)	09:02 (2)	12:44 (3)	14:44 (4+5)
Arr. Zurich	08:26	13:26	16:26	18:26

(1) Carries a sleeping car. Also has couchettes. (2) Restaurant car Innsbruck to Feldkirch. Change trains in Feldkirch at 11:17. (3) Supplement charged for first-class includes reservation fee. Restaurant car. (4) Supplement charged for first-class includes reservation fee. Has a first-class Observation Car. Restaurant car. (5) Plus other departures from Innsbruck at 16:53 (4) and 18:44 (3), arriving Zurich 20:41 and 22:26.

BENELUX

BELGIUM, NETHERLANDS AND LUXEMBOURG

Overview

Although the term Benelux is still widely used to signify Belgium, The Netherlands, and Luxembourg, these three little nations cannot really be spoken about as one entity. It is true that in Flemish Belgium and The Netherlands the people speak more or less the same language and that the currency in Belgium and Luxembourg is interchangeable, but, nonetheless, train travel in these three countries and tourism in general are distinct. The Dutch Railways (Nederlandse Spoorwegen, NS) are highly dependable and although not as fancy or high-tech as the French or German trains, wholly efficient and pleasant. The Belgian National Railways, which like everything else in Belgium has a Flemish (Nationale Maatschappij der Belgishche Spoorwegen, NMBS) and French name (Société Nationale des Chemins de fer Belges, SNCB), runs mostly without incident, although has been known to halt services at times of national labor strikes.

GENERAL INFORMATION

Belgium

• Children under six travel free on Belgian trains, children ages 6 to 11 pay half-fare, children 12 and over must pay full fare.
• There is frequent 19-minute train service 05:39 to 23:14 from Brussels' (Central) and 15-minute train service between 05:43 and 23:18 from Brussels (Nord) to the National Airport [table 201] and from the Airport to Brussels: 05:24 to 23:46.

Holland

• Children under four travel free on Dutch trains, children ages 4 to 9 pay half-fare, children 10 and over must pay full fare.
• An 18-minute train ride between Amsterdam's Central rail station and Schipol Airport [table 238]runs frequently between 00:14 and 23:38.

Luxembourg

• Children under four travel free on Luxembourgois trains, children ages four to 11 pay

BENELUX

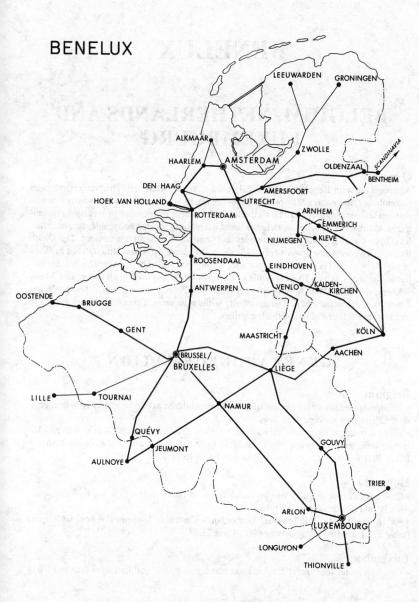

half-fare, children 12 and over must pay full fare.
• Between Luxembourg's Gare Centrale and Findel Airport [table 5] there are frequent buses.

The signs you will see at railstations in Belgium, Holland and Luxembourg are:

	BELGIUM and LUXEMBOURG	HOLLAND
Arrival	Arrivee	Aankomst
Departure	Depart	Vertrek
Exit	Sortie	Uitgang
Information	Renseignements	Inlichtingen
Luggage Check-Room	Consigne	Hetbagagedepot
Men	Messieurs	Heren
Restaurant Car	Wagon-Restaurant	Restauratie-Wagen
Sleeping Car	Wagon-Lit	Slaapcoupe
Smoking Compartment	Fumeurs	Rokers
Station	Gare	Station
Timetable	Horaire	Spoorboekje
Track	Quai	Spoor
Women	Dames	Dames

Summer Time

Belgium, Holland and Luxembourg change to Summer Time on the last Sunday of March and convert back to Standard Time on the last Sunday of September.

A list of holidays is helpful because some trains will be noted later in this section as not running on holidays. Also, those trains which operate on holidays are filled, and it is necessary to make reservations for them long in advance.

Belgium's Holidays

NOTE: When any holiday falls on Sunday, the following day is also a holiday.

January 1	New Year's Day	July 21	Independence Day
	Easter	August 15	Assumption Day
	Easter Monday	November 1	All Saints Day
May 1	Labor Day	November 11	Armistice Day (World War I)
	Ascension Day		
	Whit Sunday	December 25	Christmas Day
	Whit Monday		

Holland's Holidays

January 1	New Year's Day	May 1	Labor Day
	Good Friday		Ascension Day
	Easter		Whit Monday
	Easter Monday	December 25	Christmas Day
April 30	Queen's Birthday	December 26	Boxing Day

Luxembourg's Holidays

January 1	New Year's Day		Whit Monday
	Shrove Monday	June 23	National Holiday
	Easter	August 15	Assumption Day
	Easter Monday	December 25	Christmas Day
May 1	Labor Day	December 26	Boxing Day
	Ascension Day		

EURAILPASS BONUSES

A 35% reduction on the normal fare for the Ostend–Dover ferry operated by Regie belge des Transports Maritimes. Reduced fare tickets are available only in Ostend and Dover. There are no Eurailpass bonuses in Holland or Luxembourg.

BENELUX TOURRAIL PASS

This pass is for any 5 days of unlimited travel out of a one month period on all the rail lines of Belgium, Holland and Luxembourg, plus railway buses in Luxembourg. Sold at the railstations of all 3 countries and also by the U.S. and Canadian offices of the Netherlands Board of Tourism (800-598-8501) and Rail Europe (see "Holland" and "France"). The 1996 adult prices are: $217 for *first*-class, $155 for *second*-class. Junior Benelux, for persons under 26 on first day of travel, is for *second*-class seats and costs $104. Children under 4 travel free when not occupying a separate seat.

BELGIUM'S TRAIN PASSES

Tourrail Pass Sold at Belgian railstations. Unlimited train travel in Belgium for any 5 days out of a 17-day period.
   The 1996 *first*-class price is 2,825 Belgian francs. *Second*-class: Bf-2,020.
   Children under 6 travel free.

Half-Fare Card Sold at Belgian railstations. Entitles the traveler to unlimited first-class and second-class train travel at half-fare for one month. The 1996 price is 560 Belgian francs. Validity period starts on the day chosen by the holder of the card.

The Go Pass Provides 10 *second*-class trips for persons 6 to under 26 years old. The 1996 price is 1,316 Belgian francs.

HOLLAND'S TRAIN PASSES

The 7-Day Rail Pass, Public Transport Link and Domino passes are sold by U.S.A. and Canadian travel agencies and the office of Netherlands Board of Tourism at 225 No. Michigan Ave., Suite #326, Chicago, IL 60601.

7-Day Rail Pass Seven consecutive days of unlimited train travel. The 1996 prices: $134 for *first*-class, $90 for *second*-class.

Public Transport Link Available only in combination with the 7-Day Rail Pass (above). Provides unlimited use of city buses and streetcars throughout Holland. Price for children is the same as for adults: $14.

Domino Sold in the U.S.A. Canada by travel agencies and the offices of Netherlands Board of Tourism listed under "Holland." *Both versions of Domino (below) are valid for one month and cover unlimited train travel.*

Adult Domino The 1996 *first*-class prices are: $84 for 3 days, $135 for 5 days, and $250 for 10 days. For *second*-class: $64, $100 and $178.

Junior Domino For persons age 12 to 25. Available for *second*-class only. The 1996 prices are: $46 for 3 days, $71 for 5 days, and $124 for 10 days.

PASSES SOLD ONLY IN HOLLAND

These passes are sold at railstations and accredited travel agencies. A "Public Transport Link" that provides unlimited use of all city transit services throughout Holland (buses and streetcars) is available only in combination with all of the following passes, except "Multi Rover." Prices are the same for both adults and children.

One-Day Holland Tours Netherlands Railways offers during the Spring and Summer months 72 one-day excursions from Amsterdam to interesting destinations. Eurailpass holders pay only for the non-rail portions of these trips and for admission fees.

An example is the day that starts with a train ride from Amsterdam to Koog-Zaandijk to first see 17th and 18th century wood houses brought there from many parts of Holland and then a variety of windmills, some of which still operate. After you visit the Zaandam Clockwork Museum, where Dutch clocks from 1500 to 1850 are displayed, you take a 45-minute boat ride along other old houses and windmills. Coffee or a soft drink and a pancake at a restaurant are included in the price.

One-Day Rail Pass One day of unlimited train travel. The 1996 prices: 67 Dutch florins for first-class, Dfl-58 for second-class.

One Month Rail Pass Unlimited train travel for one month (expample: June 3–July 2). The 1996 prices: 765 Dutch florins for first-class, Dfl-510 for second-class.

Rail Rover One day of unlimited train travel. During June, July and August, it is valid all day, any day. From September through May: valid only after 09:00 on Monday–Friday, all day on Saturday and Sunday. Priced for 2–6 persons.

The 1996 first-class prices: 132 Dutch florins for 2 persons, Dfl-159 for 3, Dfl-180 for 4, Dfl-205 for 5, and Dfl-228 for 6. Second-class: Dfl-88, Dfl-105, Dfl-120,   Dfl-135, and Dfl-150.

Teenage Rover For people under age 18. Four days of unlimited second-class train travel. Sold only in June, July and August plus the Easter, fall and Christmas holidays. Proof of age (passport) and a passport photo are required. The 1996 price: 56 Dutch florins.

Summer Tour Unlimited train travel for any 3 days within 10 days during July and August. The 1996 first-class prices: 104 Dutch florins for one person, Dfl-149 for 2 persons. Second-class: Dfl-79 and Dfl-109.

LUXEMBOURG'S SPECIAL TICKETS

Valid on both trains and all public buses, including Luxembourg-City buses. Not valid for journeys departing from or arriving at border stations. Children under age 6 travel free.

All of the prices shown below are second-class. A supplement of 70 Luxemburg francs is charged for first-class.

Short-Distance Ticket Valid for a trip of up to one hour. The 1996 price is 35 Luxembourg francs. For a one-month ticket: 1996 price is 650 Luxembourg francs.

Book of 10 Short-Distance Tickets The 1996 price is 270 Luxembourg francs.

One-Day Network Ticket Valid for unlimited travel throughout the country from the time first used on one day until 08:00 the next morning. The 1996 price is 140 Luxembourg francs.

Book of 5 One-Day Network Tickets The 1996 price is 540 Luxembourg francs.

One-Month Network Ticket The 1996 price is 1,300 Luxembourg francs.

Group Pass For groups of 10 or more persons. If a roundtrip is in one day, the 1996 price is 70 Luxembourg francs per person. It is 140 Luxembourg francs per person if return takes place on the following day.

Senior Citizen Half-Fare A 50% reduction on both first and second-class train tickets for people over age 65. Presentation of identity card or passport required as proof of age. Not valid for journeys departing from or arriving at border stations.

ONE-DAY EXCURSIONS AND CITY-SIGHTSEEING

Here are 59 one-day rail trips that can be made comfortably from 3 major Benelux cities (Amsterdam, Brussels and Luxembourg City), returning to them in most cases before dinner time. (Five of these trips offer, in addition to interesting destinations, scenic fields of flowers in bloom mid-March through May.) Notes are provided on what to see and do at each destination. The number after the name of each route is the Cook's timetable. Three other one-day trips are recommended for exceptional scenery.

Schedules for international connections conclude this section.

Amsterdam

Trains depart Amsterdam's Central, RAI and Zuid railstations for Schipol (the airport) and from Schipol to Amsterdam at frequent times during all 24 hours. The journey takes 18 minutes.

The Tourist Office in the Central railstation is open daily 08:45–23:00 from Easter to September 30.

Your city sightseeing in Amsterdam should include the Rijkmuseum (State Museum) collection of Rembrandt, Rubens, Goya and El Greco paintings (42 Stadhouderskade). Also exhibited there are Dresden china, delftware, tapestries, prints, furniture, dollhouses and sculpture.

See the works of Chagall, Cezanne, Picasso, Calder, Pollack, Rodin, Braque and Warhol at the Stedelijkmuseum (Municipal Museum), 13 Paulus Potterstraat. A complete spectrum of Van Gogh paintings plus several by Gauguin and Toulouse-Lautrec at the Museum Vincent van Gogh (7–11 Paulus Potterstraat). The display of Indonesian and Far Eastern art and anthropology at the Tropical Museum.

The exhibit of 300 ship models, many atlases and charts, and 5,000 books in the National Shipping Museum (1–7 Kattenburgplein). Rembrandt's house (4–6 Jodenbreestraat). The Flea Market, near Rembrandt's house. Exhibits depicting the city's history since its founding in 1270, at the Amsterdam Historical Museum (92 Kalverstraat).

The history of Jews in Holland since 1590, at the Jewish Historical Museum (4

Nieumarkt). The altar and organ at the attic church of the 17th century Amstelkring Museum (40 Oudezijds Voorburgwal), the last of the "hidden" Catholic churches in Holland, with interesting 17th and 18th century furniture.

All 9 museums are open Tuesday-Saturday 10:00–17:00 and on Sundays and holidays 13:00–17:00.

Visit the Anne Frank House (263 Prinsengracht), open Monday-Saturday 9:00–17:00 and on Sundays and holidays 10:00–17:00. Take a 75-minute ride in a glass-roofed canal boat, starting at the piers in front of Central railstation or at Stadhouderskade, near the Rijksmuseum.

Royal Palace. The Tower of Tears. Nieuwe Kerk on the Dam, open Monday-Saturday 10:00–17:00, Sunday 12:00–15:00. Mint Tower. Free samples when ending the tour of Heineken Brewery, Monday–Friday starting at 09:30. The Flower Market (Bloemenmarkt), open Monday–Friday. Several diamond-cutting factories.

The Theater Museum (168 Herengracht), open Tuesday–Friday 10:00–17:00, Sundays and holidays 11:00–17:00. See Willet Holthuyen Museum (5 Herengracht), a classical 17th century canal house, elegantly furnished in the style of Holland's Golden Age. Open Monday-Saturday 09:30–17:00, Sundays and holidays 13:00–17:00.

Take an inexpensive half-day bus tour to the heart of the tulip district. It is near Aalsmeer, less than 45 minutes from Amsterdam. Visit the daily Aalsmeer Flower Auction, close to Amsterdam's Schipol Airport. The peak time at the auction is 08:00–10:00.

Brussels

Sightseeing starts in Grand Place, the ornate town square with many gilded buildings. Inside Hotel de Ville (Town Hall), there is a tapestry museum open daily in Summer, Monday–Friday in Winter. Next to it is a reproduction of a 17th century brewery. See the 15th century Notre Dame des Victoires church and the 17th century Flemish houses in nearby Place du Grand Sablon.

The marvelous Place Parc de Bruxeles gardens and lakes. The Royal Palace, at one end of this park, is open daily except Monday 09:30–16:00 for about 6 weeks during Summer. The Belgian Parliament is located at the other end of the park.

One of the world's best collections of 15th and 16th century Flemish and Dutch paintings (Rubens, Brueghel, Bosch) is exhibited at the Museum of Ancient Art & Modern Art on Rue de la Regence, open daily except Monday 10:00–17:00.

Nearby, the collection of rare musical instruments in the Royal Conservatory of Music at the Petit Sablon (also on Rue de la Regence), open Tuesday, Thursday and Saturday 14:30–16:30, Sunday 10:30-22:00, Wednesday 20:00–22:00.

The collection of paintings by both medieval masters (one section devoted entirely to Bruegel) and also those of later centuries through the 19th, in the Beaux Arts Museum at 3 Rue de la Regence. Then go through a short passageway to the new (1984) Modern Art Museum (Henry Moore, Dali, Magritte, Delvaux). Both museums are open daily except Monday 10:00–17:00.

See the impressive array of African art in The Royal Museum of Central Africa, 12km east, in Tervuren Park & Arboretum. The view from the Palais de Justice. The Law Courts.

The tapestries in the 13th century Cathedral of St. Michael.

The Brussels City Museum. The Museum of Arms and Armor. The museum of sculptures by Constantin Meunier, whose work depicts the dignity of laborers. The Postal Museum. The Royal Greenhouses. The Brueghel Museum, in the house where the painter lived his last 6 years.

The Railway Museum, on the mezzanine of Brussels' Nord railstation. The Art Nouveau pieces in the Horta Museum at 25 Rue Americaine, open daily except Mondays and holidays 14:00–17:30.

The most famous gourmet food emporium here is the Rob store at Boulevard de la Woluwe 28. (Take the subway from the center of town to the Tomberg stop and then bus #42, which stops in front of Rob.) Fruits from all over the world, an assortment of 25 ordinary and exotic pates (baby boar!), eel cooked in green sauce, snails marinated in wine sauce, numerous fish (live trout, Scotch salmon, Norwegian lobsters), 600 different wines, 35 types of mustard, chocolates galore.

A bus can be taken 10 miles to **Waterloo.**

Luxembourg City

The Citadel, with its 53 forts connected by 16 miles of tunnels. Fish Market, site of the city's oldest buildings. The State Museum, open daily except Monday 10:00–12:00 and 14:00–18:00. The Palais Grand-Ducal. The splendid view from the bridge that crosses the River Alzette. The Palais Municipal, on the Place d'Armes. The Municipal Art Gallery, open daily except Monday during Summer, only on Saturday and Sunday the rest of the year. City Hall. The old quarter, Pfaffenthal, with its medieval buildings. The Fort of Three Acorns. Malakoff Tower. The Church of St. Michael.

The Three Towers, marking the outer limits of the town in 1050. Notre Dame Cathedral. The 4th century Chapel of St. Quirinus, one of the oldest shrines in Christendom. The Museum of History and Art. General Patton's grave in the U.S. Military Cemetery, 3 miles away, at **Hamm.**

In the following timetables, where a city has more than one railstation we have designated the particular station after the name of the city (in parentheses).

On day trips from Amsterdam that we have designated "H-L," you will see in the area between Haarlem and Leiden, from mid-March through May, fields of tulips, narcissus, crocus and other bulb flowers in bloom. The region is known as the "Champs de Fleurs" (Fields of Flowers).

Amsterdam - Alkmaar - Amsterdam   225

Dep. Amsterdam   every 30 minutes from 07:22 to 23:22
Arr. Alkmaar   30 minutes later

Sights in **Alkmaar**: The Friday Cheese Market, from the end of April until the end of September, 10:00–12:00. The organ at St. Lawrence Church.

Dep. Alkmaar	every 30 minutes from 08:08 to 23:38
Arr. Amsterdam	30 minutes later

Amsterdam - Alkmaar - Haarlem - Amsterdam   225 + 224

It is easy to visit both Alkmaar and Haarlem in a single day-trip.

Dep Amsterdam	twice each hour		Dep. Haarlem	twice each hour.
Arr. Alkmaar	30 minutes later.		Arrive Amsterdam	19 minutes later.
Change trains.				
Dep. Alkmaar	twice each hour.			
Arr. Haarlem	28 minutes later.			

Amsterdam - Amersfoort - Amsterdam   230

Dep. Amsterdam	Frequent times from 06:32 to 23:32
Arr. Amersfoort	34 minutes later

Sights in **Amersfoort**: A beautiful citadel town with many canals and ancient streets. Popular among antique collectors and for taking side trips to **Spakenburg** (a quaint fishing village on the old Zuider Zee), **Laren** (to visit the Singer Museum), **Zeist** (to see the beautifully-furnished castle there), **Baarn** (to visit Palace Soestdijk, the residence of the former Queen Juliana, **Muiden** (to see the 15th century moated castle, Muiderslot).

Dep. Amersfoort	Frequent times from 07:24 to 23:23
Arr. Amsterdam	34 minutes later

Amsterdam - Antwerp - Amsterdam   18

Dep. Amsterdam	Frequent times from 06:23 to 21:25
Arr. Antwerp (Cen.)	2 hours and 20 minutes later

Sights in **Antwerp:** To the right of the railstation is one of the best zoos in the world, set in a beautiful garden. It is open daily 08:30–17:00. Walk through the maze of streets called Grote Markt (art galleries, bakeries, fruit stalls, antique shops).

You can watch diamonds being cut and polished at Diamond Land, 33 Appelmanstraat, open daily except Sunday 09:00–18:00. There is a good exhibit of the history of diamonds at the Provincial Museum of Safety, 28–30 Jezusstraat, open Wednesday-Saturday 10:00–17:00, with demonstrations on Saturday 14:00–17:00.

Visit the Cathedral, open April through mid-October: Monday-Friday 12:00–17:00, Saturday 12:00–15:00, Sunday 13:00–17:00. The rest of the year: Monday 14:00–17:00, Saturday 12:00–15:00, Sunday 13:00–17:00.

Flemish, Italian, French, Dutch and German masterpieces in the Gallery of Fine Arts, open daily except Monday 10:00–17:00. Rubens House, with many of his paintings, at 9–11 Wapper, open daily 10:00–17:00. The 16th century printing shop in the Plantin-Moretus Museum. The Marine Museum.

The Mayer van den Bergh Museum. The Folklore Museum. Town Hall. Guild Houses. Vieille Bourse (the Old Stock Exchange). The Rockox Mansion. The view of Antwerp from the 24th floor of Torengebouw.

Now a classy suburb of Antwerp, **Middelheim** was first settled in the 14th century. See there the more than 300 statues (by Henry Moore, Vic Gentil, Charles Leplae and many other great sculptors) in the 30-acre Middelheim Open-Air Museum of Sculpture, founded in 1950. It is 30 minutes by bus #17, #27 or #32, from Antwerp's Central railstation. The bus driver will tell you where to get off, and the walk to the sculpture park is 15 minutes from there, passing many splendid mansions.

One can begin circling the park-museum by starting either toward the left of the entrance (in the direction of the statue of Balzac) or to the right, along a tree-shaded stream and through a lawn that has many statues.

The park (admission free) is open daily 10:00 to sunset about 17:00 in Winter, 21:00 in Summer.

Dep. Antwerp (Cen.)	Frequent times from 07:54 to 22:00
Arr. Amsterdam	2 hours and 20 minutes later

Amsterdam - Apeldoorn   231

Dep. Amsterdam (Cen.)	2 minutes after every hour from 07:02 to 22:02
Arr. Apeldoorn	1 hour and 4 minutes later

Sights in **Apeldoorn:** From the railstation, take buses #102, #104 and #106 to the Het Loo Palace. Set in a 27,000-acre Royal Forest, the palace was a private residence for the Dutch royal family until it became a state museum in 1971.

Both the lavish, enormous palace and the geometric patterns of its extraordinary gardens are well worth visiting. Seventeenth century tapestries, magnificent furniture, exceptional Delft pottery and fine paintings (Rembrandt, Vermeer, van Ruisdael) are exhibited in the palace.

Dep. Apeldoorn	26 minutes after every hour from 07:26 to 23:26
Arr. Amsterdam (Cen.)	1 hour and 4 minutes later

Amsterdam - Arnhem - Amsterdam   240

| Dep. Amsterdam (Cent.) | Frequent times from 06:06 to 23:49 |
| Arr. Arnhem | 60–70 minutes later |

Sights in **Arnhem:** The nearly 3-square-mile Netherlands Open-Air Museum, a col- lection of several farm villages, depicting rural lifestyles from the 18th to early 20th centuries. Colored arrows direct visitors to one, 2 and 4-hour tours. Open April–October, Monday-Friday 09:00–17:00, Sunday 10:00–17:00. At the craft exhibits, wood shoes are chiseled, bread is baked, baskets and paper are made. See a blacksmith at his forge. Don't fail to try the little pancake balls called "poffertjes," and then eat some pannekoeken (traditional Dutch pancakes) and wafelen (waffles).

Also visit the 16th century Grootekerk (Ptotestant Church) and the extensively-restored Eusebiuskerk, a Gothic church. See the Duivelshuis (devil's house). The best collection of Van Gogh is at the Kroller-Muller Museum in the nearby National Park. Special buses go the several miles from the railstation to the museum and surrounding 13,300-acre national park during June, July and August. The museum is open Tuesday–Saturday 10:00–17:00, Sunday 11:00–17:00.

| Dep. Arnhem | Frequent times from 06:37 to 23:40 |
| Arr. Amsterdam (Cent.) | 60–70 minutes later |

Amsterdam - Bonn

All of the Amsterdam–Cologne and v.v trains charge a supplement.

28

| Dep. Amsterdam (Cen.) | 06:02 (1) | 07:06 (1) | 08:00 (3) | 09:00 (3) | 11:06 (1) |
| Arr. Cologne | 08:42 | 09:42 | 10:57 | 11:57 | 13:42 |

Change trains.

710 + 711

| Dep. Cologne | 09:19 | 10:19 | 11:19 | 12:19 | 14:19 |
| Arr. Bonn | 09:51 | 10:51 | 11:51 | 12:51 | 14:51 |

Sights in **Bonn**: See notes about Bonn under "Cologne–Bonn"

| Dep. Bonn | 12:12 | 14:12 | 16:12 | 18:12 | 20:12 |
| Arr. Cologne | 12:38 | 14:38 | 16:38 | 18:38 | 20:38 |

Change trains.

28

| Dep. Cologne | 13:17 (1) | 15:17 (1) | 17:17 (1) | 19:02 (3) | 21:17 (1) |
| Arr. Amsterdam | 15:51 | 17:51 | 19:51 | 21:51 | 23:51 |

(1) Light refreshments. (3) Restaurant car.

Amsterdam - Brussels - Amsterdam   205

Dep. Amsterdam	06:23	07:25	08:25	09:25	10:25	11:25
Arr. Brussels (Nord)	09:21	10:21	11:21	12:21	13:21	14:21
Arr. Brussels (Cen.)	09:26	10:26	11:26	12:26	13:26	14:26
Arr. Brussels (Midi)	09:30	10:30	11:30	12:30	13:30	14:30
Dep. Brussels (Midi)	13:10	14:10	15:10	16:10	17:10	18:10 (1)
Dep. Brussels (Cen.)	13:14	14:14	15:14	16:14	17:14	18:14
Dep. Brussels (Nord)	13:19	14:19	15:19	16:19	17:19	18:19
Arr. Amsterdam	16:08	17:08	18:08	19:08	20:08	21:08

(1) Plus other departures from Brussels (Midi) at 19:10, 20:10 and 21:10, arriving Amsterdam 22:08, 23:08 and 00:10.

Amsterdam - Cologne   28

All of these trains charge a supplement.

Amsterdam	06:02 (1)	07:06 (1)	08:00 (2)	09:00 (2)	11:06 (1)
Arr. Cologne	08:42	09:42	10:57	11:57	13:42
Dep. Cologne	13:17 (1)	15:17 (1)	17:17 (1)	18:02 (2)	19:02 (2)
Arr. Amsterdam	15:51	17:51	19:51	20:51	21:51

(1) Light refreshments. (2) Restaurant car.

Amsterdam - Delft - Amsterdam (H-L)   220

| Dep. Amsterdam (Cen.) | Frequent times from 00:18 to 23:43 |
| Arr. Delft | 60 minutes later |

Sights in **Delft**: The tourist information office (on the main square) provides a brochure that describes a walking tour which includes all of the city's principal sights.

See the 14th century New Church, where members of the Dutch royal family are buried. The Mausoleum of William the Silent at the 15th century New Church. The 17th century Prinsenhof (Princes Court), housing the Municipal Museum. Tetar van Elven Museum, containing the works of Vermeer and Pieter de Hoogh. Old Church. The Grain Market. Town Hall. The Old Delft Canal.

The Delft Pottery Factory ("De Porceleyne Fles") at 196 Rotterdamsweg is open May–September 09:00–17:00 Monday-Saturday and 13:00–18:00 on Sunday. It is open 09:00–17:00 Monday–Saturday from October through April. Its tour includes visiting a showroom, a shop and exhibits of antique tiles and mural ceramics.

| Dep. Delft | Frequent times from 00:25 to 23:58 |
| Arr. Amsterdam (Cen.) | 60 minutes later |

Amsterdam - Den Haag - Amsterdam (H-L)   220

| Dep. Amsterdam | 2–3 times each hour from 05:31 to 23:43 |
| Arr. Den Haag (H.S.) | 45–50 minutes later |

Sights in **Den Haag**: Binnenhof, a complex of palaces and courtyards, including the 13th century Hall of Knights (an 118-by-56-foot banquet hall where Holland's Parliament meets every September), and Gevangenpoort, Holland's 14th century prison.

Mauritshuis, a great art gallery (Rembrandt, Vermeers, Rubens) The finest collection in the world of 19th century Dutch art, at the Gemeente Museum. The collection of Rembrandts at the Bredius Museum. The Peace Palace. The Hidden Church, at 38 Molenstraat. The Mesdag Museum. The Costume Museum. Municipal Museum. The miniature city of Madurodam, with everything on a scale of 1/25th life size.

The marvelous paintings in the Johan de Witt Huis at Kneuterdijk 6, open Monday-Saturday 10:00–17:00, and on Sundays and holidays 11:00–17:00. The more than 1,000 puppets and marionettes at the Puppet Museum. The 5 miles of wide, beautiful beach.

| Dep. Den Haag (H.S.) | 2–3 times each hour from 05:39 to 00:38 |
| Arr. Amsterdam | 45–50 minutes later |

Amsterdam - Den Haag + Utrecht - Amsterdam (H-L)

It is possible to visit both Den Haag (see sightseeing notes above) and Utrecht in one day.

220
| Dep. Amsterdam | Frequent departures from 05:31 to 23:43 |
| Arr. Den Haag (**H.S.**) | 45–50 minutes later |

Change trains and railstations.
230
| Dep. Den Haag (**Cen.**) | Frequent times from 07:36 to 22:36 |
| Arr. Utrecht | 40 minutes later |

Change trains
240
| Dep. Utrecht | Frequent times from 07:15 to 00:20 |
| Arr. Amsterdam | 30 minutes later |

For those who prefer the direct trip to Utrecht and to have more time there, refer to notes under "Amsterdam–Utrecht"

Sights in **Utrecht**: The 13th century Dom Cathedral, and the view from the top of its 465 steps (300 feet high). In fall, winter and spring the tower is open only on weekends. Nearby is the Music Box and Street Organ Museum on Achter de Dom, open Tuesday-Saturday 11:00-16:00. Next door is the Museum of Contemporary Art at 14 Achter de Dom.

The museum of mechanical instruments, at 38 Lange Nieuwstraat. The Netherlands Railway Museum, at 6 Van Oldenberneveltlaan, open Tuesday–Saturday 10:00–17:00, Sundays 13:00–17:00. The 11th century St. Peter's Church. The paintings and Viking ship in the Centraal Museum at 1 Agnietenstraat, open Tuesday-Saturday 10:00–17:00, Sundays and holidays 14:00–17:00.

The ancient fish market, Vis Markt, an institution at the same location since the 12th century. The largest medieval art collection in Holland, at the Museum of Religious Art in Het Catherijneconvent (St. Catherine's Church and Convent).

The collection of 180 musical instruments ("from music box to barrel organ") displayed at the van Speeldos tot Pierement Museum. The Gold, Silver and Clock Museum. The Museum of Contemporary Art. The Museum of the Insurance Business.

Nearby interesting villages: **Breukelen**, for which New York's Brooklyn was named (castles, 17th century mansions), **Oudewater** (famous for its stork colony and 3-aisle church), and **Loenen** (known for its 18th century houses and their lovely gardens).

Amsterdam - Dusseldorf - Amsterdam 28

All of these trains charge a supplement.

Dep. Amsterdam (Cen.)	06:02 (1)	07:06 (1)	08:00 (2)	09:00 (2)	11:06 (1)
Arr. Dusseldorf	08:19	09:19	10:32	11:32	13:19

Sights in **Dusseldorf**: See notes about Dusseldorf under "Cologne–Dusseldorf"

Dep. Dusseldorf	13:39 (1)	15:39 (1)	17:39 (1)	18:26 (2)	19:26 (2+3)
Arr. Amsterdam (Cen.)	15:51	17:51	19:51	20:51	21:51

(1) Light refreshments. (2) Restaurant car. (3) Plus another Dusseldorf departure at 21:39 (1).

Amsterdam - Enkhuizen - Amsterdam 225

Local trains run every 30 minutes 07:19–23:19 for the 62-minute trip north from Amsterdam's Central railstation. Trains depart Enkhuizen every 30 minutes 08:09–23:09 for the 64-minute trip back to Amsterdam.

It is a 4-minute walk from the Enkhuizen railstation to its ferry dock. Boats depart every 15 minutes to the 700-acre Zuider Zee Open Air Museum, open summer months 10:00–17:00.

This museum consists of 130 houses, portraying life and work from 1880 to 1932. Allow at least 2 hours to tour it. Then take a 10-minute walk to the Binnenmuseum, an indoor complex of 15 exhibition halls displaying fine examples of furniture, fishing boats, toys and other items. It is open mid-February to December 31: Monday–Saturday 10:00-17:00, Sunday 12:00–17:00.

Amsterdam - Gouda - Amsterdam   239

Dep. Amsterdam	22 minutes after each hour, from 07:22 to 22:22
Arr. Gouda	50 minutes later

Sights in **Gouda**: Stained-glass in Sint Janskerk. The 15th century Town Hall. The famous Thursday cheese market.

Dep. Gouda	18 minutes after each hour, from 06:18 to 23:18
Arr. Amsterdam	50 minutes later

Amsterdam - Haarlem - Amsterdam   220

Dep. Amsterdam (Cen.)	Twice each hour, from 07:09 to 00:46
Arr. Haarlem	14 minutes later

Sights in **Haarlem**: It is only a few minutes' walk from the railstation to town center, Grote Markt, where jousting tournaments took place in the Middle Ages. Nearby is the 14th century Town Hall and many cafes.

Works by Franz Hals and many other great painters plus Delft tiles, Flemish wallpaper made of gilded and painted panels of leather, silver tankards and candlestands, pikes and swords, and stained and painted glass windows at the Frans Hals Museum at 62 Groot Heiligland (Note the address. That is the only mark outside the building!). This museum is only a 20-minute walk from the railstation, or take buses 1, 2, 3, 5, 6, 70 or 71.

In St. Bavo's, Holland's most beautiful church, hear the massive 5,000-pipe Baroque organ (ivory and tortoise shell keyboard) built in 1738 by Christiaan Muller. Mozart played it when he was 10 years old. It can be heard Sundays at 10:00 and 19:00, also at free concerts Tuesday at 20:15.

The World Clock at 88 Wagenweg. Teyler's Museum at 16 Spaarme (open Tuesday-Saturday 10:00–17:00), to see 16th to 20th century Dutch, Italian and French paintings as well as antique musical instruments, telescopes and globes.

Dep. Haarlem	Twice each hour, from 07:36 to 01:16
Arr. Amsterdam (Cen.)	14 minutes later

Amsterdam - Hoorn - Amsterdam 225

Dep. Amsterdam	Freq. times 07:19-00:31	Dep. Hoorn	Freq. times 06:33-23:35
Arr. Hoorn	40 minutes later	Arr. Amsterdam	40 minutes later

Sights in **Hoorn**: The full-scale enactment of 17th century trades and crafts in Hoorn's "Old Dutch Market" takes place in the Rodesteen Square on Wednesdays mid-June to mid-August: folk dances and stalls with basket weaving, net mending and the making of wood shoes. Daily from mid-June to mid-August (plus Saturdays and Sundays from mid-August through mid-September), a steam train with antique coaches operates between Hoorn and **Medemblik**.

See Hoorn's 17th century mansions and warehouses. The collection of paintings and antiques in the West Friesian Museum. The 17th century Weighhouse. The 16th century Hospital of St. John. The 2 medieval churches: Noorderkerk and Oosterkerk. The 16th century St. Mary Tower and East Gate, remains of the original fortification. The 17th century almshouse, St. Pietershof.

Amsterdam - Leiden - Amsterdam (H-L) 220

Dep. Amsterdam	Frequent times during all 24 hours
Arr. Leiden	33 minutes later

Sights in **Leiden**: Pieterskerk, the church where the Pilgrim fathers worshipped for 10 years before setting sail for America in 1620. The University. The Royal Arms Museum. The National Museum of Antiquities. The Municipal Museum. The National Ethnological Museum. The nearby flower center, called **Keukenhof**.

Dep. Leiden	Frequent times during all 24 hours
Arr. Amsterdam	33 minutes later

Amsterdam - Maastricht - Amsterdam 245

All of these trains have light refreshments.

Dep. Amsterdam	06:32 (1) Plus frequent times daily 07:32-22:02
Arr. Maastricht	2½ hours after departing Amsterdam

Sights in **Maastricht**: The 6th century St. Servatius Church, oldest church in Holland, where Charlemagne occasionally attended mass. There is a large statue of him in the rear of the church. Shoppers from not only nearby Dutch cities but even from Belgium, France and Germany come to the Market Day (produce and pastries) at Town Hall Square, Fridays 08:00–13:00.

See the carved wood columns of the choir in the 10th century Basilica of Our Gracious Lady. The many 17th and 18th century houses on the Stokstraat Quarter, each having a plaque that shows the construction date, the owner's name and his trade. Some of the old houses are now antique shops, art galleries and boutiques. Try the local Limburger cheese and gingerbread in one of the sidewalk cafes on famous Vrijthof Square.

A bus departs from the railstation for the short trip to the Mount St. Peter caves, consisting of 200 miles of labyrinths where people hid during a Spanish invasion in 1570. It was originally a sandstone quarry, worked from Roman times until the end of the 19th century. Since 1584, famous visitors (Napoleon, Archduke Ferdinand of Spain, Voltaire, Sir Walter Scott) have scratched their signatures on the walls of the very cold and very damp caves.

Dep. Maastricht	Frequent times from 07:31 to 21:31
Arr. Amsterdam	2½ hours later

(1) Runs Monday–Friday, except holidays.

Amsterdam - Paris - Amsterdam   18

Both of these trains charge a supplement.

Dep. Amsterdam (Cen.)	06:57 (1)	Dep. Paris (Nord)	18:38 (2)
Arr. Paris (Nord)	12:59	Arr. Amsterdam (Cen.)	23:59

(1) Runs daily. Light refreshments. (2) Reservation required. Runs daily, except Saturday. Restaurant car.

Amsterdam - Rotterdam - Amsterdam (H-L)   220 + 239

Dep. Amsterdam	Frequent times during all 24 hours
Arr. Rotterdam (Cent.)	60–70 minutes later

Sights in **Rotterdam**: The Netherlands Tourist Information Bureau has offices all over Holland. Look for its "VVV" sign.

Don't miss the view of the city and port from the top of the 340-foot high Euromast, open daily 09:00–22:00 March 15–October 14, and 09:00–18:00 October 15–March 14. Nearby, Heineken's Brewery (Crookswijksesingel 50).

The fantastic collection of 15th to 19th century Flemish and Dutch paintings and a wing of modern sculpture and art (Van Gogh and Kandinsky to the present day) as well as objects of glass, pewter, silver, lace, furniture and tiles in the Boymans-van Beuningen Museum (Mathenesserlaan 18–20).

Devices used by smugglers to defraud customs, at the Profesor van der Poel Tax Museum (Parklaan 14). The collection of globes, ships and atlases in the Maritime Museum (Leuvehaven 1). Many old vessels there can be visited.

The 75-minute boat trip in the harbor, one of the world's largest ports, departing every

45 minutes from Willemsplein Landing.

Stroll through the noteworthy Lijnbaan shopping center. Hear a free lunchtime concert every day at De Doelen, an enormous complex of music and congress halls, just across from Central railstation.

Unwind in the 10,000-acre Zuiderpark, Plaswijck Park, Zuiderparkgordel, Het Park, and the Kralingse Bos (woods). See the wide variety of trees in Arboretum Trompenburg.

Visit the collection of elephants, orangutans, tigers (Sumatran, Siberian and Bengal), great apes, reptiles and seals in the Blijdorp Zoo (open 09:00–17:00).

Enjoy many statues located throughout the city, particularly Mastroianni's "Kiss," at the Central Railroad Station. Visit "De Ster," a working windmill (spice and snuff grinding) near Kralingse Lake.

The collection of folk art of primitive cultures from the non-Western world at the Museum of Ethnology (Willemskade 25). Complete 17th, 18th and 19th-century interiors at the Rotterdam Historical Museum in the Schielands Huis (Korte Hoogstraat 31). Many art galleries, including Lijnbaan Centrum (Linjbaan 165) and Kunstzaal (Zuidplein 120). The Henrik Chabot Museum. The 14th century church, St. Laurenskerk.

Nearby **Delfshaven** is the port from which the Puritans started their voyage to the New World, sailing from there on July 22, 1620, before boarding the Mayflower off the English coast. That group spent its last night praying in Delfshaven's Reformed Church, now called Pelgrimvaderskerk (Pilgrim Fathers' Church). A stained-glass window and a plaque there commemorate the Pilgrims' sailing. Visit the "De Dubbelde Palmboom" Museum (with everyday objects used centuries ago in Rotterdam) and a pewter workshop in the Sack Carriers guildhouse.

The enormous hydraulic project of the Haringvliet sluices can be seen in nearby **Stellendam**.

Dep. Rotterdam (Cent.)	Frequent times during all 24 hours
Arr. Amsterdam	60–70 minutes later

Amsterdam - Rotterdam + Den Haag - Amsterdam (H-L)   220

This circle trip allows seeing only a few of the sights in Rotterdam (see notes in preceding listing) and in Den Haag (see notes earlier in this section), but one can see something of both Rotterdam and Den Haag in this one-day trip.

Dep. Amsterdam (Cen.)	Frequent times during all 24 hours
Arr. Rotterdam (Cen.)	65 minutes later
Dep. Rotterdam (Cen.)	Frequent times from 05:15 to 01:02
Arr. Den Haag (Hbf.)	16–24 minutes later
Dep. Den Haag	Frequent times from 05:39 to 00:38
Arr. Amsterdam (Cen.)	35–55 minutes later

Amsterdam - Utrecht - Amsterdam (H-L)   240 + 245

Dep. Amsterdam	Frequent times from 06:06 to 23:49
Arr. Utrecht	36–44 minutes later

Sights in **Utrecht**: see notes about sightseeing in Utrecht under "Amsterdam–Den Haag + Utrecht–Amsterdam"

Dep. Utrecht	3–4 times each hour from 06:37 until 00:20
Arr. Amsterdam	36–44 minutes later

Amsterdam - Zwolle - Amsterdam   230

All of these trains have light refreshments.

Dep. Amsterdam	Hourly, from 06:32 to 23:32
Arr. Zwolle	80 minutes later

Sights in **Zwolle**: Hear the famous Schnitger Organ in the magnificent St. Michael's Church. There are many beautiful buildings in this more than 700-year old town on the Ijssel River. This is a popular base for taking side trips to **Hattem** (great for local arts and crafts) and **Giethoorn** (the Venice of Holland, where everything moves on water).

Dep. Zwolle	Hourly, from 07:48 to 22:48
Arr. Amsterdam	80 minutes later

Brussels - Aachen - Brussels   200

All of these trains have light refreshments.

Dep. Brussels (Midi)	06:47	07:47	09:47 (1)	10:47	11:47 (1)
Dep. Brussels (Cen.)	06:52	07:52	09:52	10:47	11:52
Dep. Brussels (Nord)	06:57	07:57	09:57	10:52	11:57
Arr. Aachen	08:43	09:43	11:53	12:43	13:51

Sights in **Aachen**: Charlemagne's 8th century treasury at the Cathedral contains an extraordinary collection of German medieval ecclesiastical gold and silver, including the Shrine of the Virgin Mary, completed in 1236. The Grand Coronation Chamber in Town Hall.

Dep. Aachen	13:05	14:10 (1)	15:05	16:07 (1)	17:05	19:05 (2)
Arr. Brussels (Nord)	14:47	15:48	16:47	17:49	18:47	20:47
Arr. Brussels (Cen.)	14:52	-0-	16:52	-0-	18:52	20:52
Arr. Brussels (Midi)	14:55	15:56	16:56	18:01	18:56	20:56

(1) Restaurant car. (2) Plus another Aachen departure at 21:05, arriving Brussels (Nord) 22:47.

Brussels - Amsterdam - Brussels   18

Dep. Brussels (Midi)	Frequent times from 06:10 to 21:10
Dep. Brussels (Cen.)	4 minutes after departing Midi station
Dep. Brussels (Nord)	4 minutes after departing Central station
Arr. Amsterdam	3 hours after departing Brussels (Midi)

Sights in **Amsterdam**: See notes about sightseeing in Amsterdam.

Dep. Amsterdam	Frequent times from 06:23 to 20:25
Arr. Brussels (Nord)	3 hours later
Arr. Brussels (Cen.)	4 minutes after arriving Nord station
Arr. Brussels (Midi)	4 minutes after arriving Central station

Brussels - Antwerp - Brussels   205

Dep. Brussels (Midi)	Frequent times from 06:10 to 23:30
Dep. Brussels (Cen.)	4 minutes later
Dep. Brussels (Nord)	4 minutes after departing Central station
Arr. Antwerp (Cen.)	45 minutes after departing Brussels (Midi)

Sights in **Antwerp**: See notes about sightseeing in Antwerp under "Amsterdam–Antwerp–Amsterdam"

Dep. Antwerp (Cen.)	Frequent times from 06:19 to 23:19
Arr. Brussels (Nord)	40 minutes later
Arr. Brussels (Cen.)	4 minutes after arriving Nord station
Arr. Brussels (Midi)	4 minutes after departing Central station

Brussels - Brugge - Brussels   200

Dep. Brussels (Nord)	Frequent times from 05:47 to 22:47
Dep. Brussels (Cen.)	4 minutes after departing Nord station
Dep. Brussels (Midi)	7 minutes after departing Central station
Arr. Brugge	60 minutes after departing Brussels (Midi)

Sights in **Brugge**: The splendid view from the top of the 255-foot-high 13th century Belfry (365 steps), with its famous 47-bell carillon, in the city's main square, Markt. The Belfry's tower is closed 12:00–14:00. The interesting 15th century Town Hall and 15th century Recorders' House are on this square. The Tourist office is in the nearby Government Palace. (Many cafes are located in this area.)

At the 12th century Basilica of the Holy Blood, a phial said to contain a few drops of Christ's blood is displayed on Fridays. It was brought to Brugge in 1150 from the Second Crusade. Also there: a fine display of gold, silver and copper artwork. Open daily, except 12:00–14:30.

See the lace, pottery, gold pieces, musical instruments and weapons in the 15th century mansion that houses the Gruuthuse Museum. The small museum in the 13th century Saint Saviour's Cathedral. The black slate and gilded brass 16th century effigies and Michelangelo's white carrara marble Madonna with Child statue in the Church of Our Lady. Behind the Church, the Dutch masterpieces at the Groeninge Museum (open daily 09:30–12:00 and 14:00–17:00).

The collection of Old Flemish School paintings at the Hans Memling Museum, in a section of the 13th century Hospital of St. John (open 09:00–12:30 and 14:00–18:00 in Summer, 09:00–12:00 and 14:00–16:00 the rest of the year). Paintings and silverwork at the Archer's Guild of St. Sebastian. Ter Buerze, the world's first stock exchange, now a bank, on the corner of Acadamiesstraat and Vlamingstraat.

St. John's, the most beautiful of Belgium's 140 functioning windmills, built in 1770. Nearby is the beach resort **Knokke-Heist** (many hotels, shops and nightclubs).

Canal boats leave from several docks for half-hour cruises with English-language guides.

Dep. Brugge	Frequent times from 05:48 to 22:50
Arr. Brussles (Midi)	One hour later
Arr. Brussels (Cen.)	10 minutes after arriving Midi station
Arr. Brussels (Nord)	3 minutes after arriving Central station

Brussels - Cologne (Koln) - Brussels   200

Dep. Brussels (Midi)	06:47	07:47	09:47	10:47	12:03 (1)
Dep. Brussels (Cen.)	4 minutes after departing Midi station				
Dep. Brussels (Nord)	5 minutes after departing Central station				
Arr. Cologne	09:42	10:42	12:42	13:42	14:42
Dep. Cologne	13:14 (1)	14:14	15:14 (1)	16:14	18:14 (2)
Arr. Brussels (Nord)	15:46	16:45	17:45	18:45	20:45
Arr. Brussels (Cen.)	-0-	16:50	-0-	18:50	20:50
Arr. Brussels (Midi)	15:56	16:56	18:01	18:56	20:56

(1) Supplement charged. Restaurant car. (2) Plus another Cologne departure at 20:14, arriving Brussels (Nord) 22:45.

Brussels - Gent - Brussels 200

Dep. Brussels (Nord)	Frequent times from 05:47 to 23:17
Dep. Brussels (Cen.)	4 minutes after departing Nord station
Dep. Brussels (Midi)	5 minutes after departing Central station
Arr. Gent (St. Pieters)	40–50 minutes after departing Nord station

Sights in **Gent**: Located at the confluence of the Lys and Scheldt rivers. Flanked by many canals lined with 15th century gabled buildings.

The Tourist Office, located in the 14th century Town Hall, is near the 14th century Belfry and the 15th century Cloth Hall, where a 20-minute sound and light program commemorates ancient Gent. Two-hour walking tours start at the Tourist Office. A 30-minute boat tour on the canals gives a fine perspective of Gent's past.

See the superior collection of paintings at the Fine Arts Museum. The collection of furniture at the Museum of Decorative Arts. The reproductions of medieval Gent homes, ironwork, costumes and weapons at the Byloke Museum.

The fantastic altarpiece in St. Bavo's Cathedral. West from it is Graseli, the city's oldest port, lined by famous guild houses. Gent's other medieval harbor, Koornlei, is on the opposite bank from Graseli. Many of the old houses there were restored and reconstructed at the beginning of the 20th century.

See the foreboding dungeons and torture chambers in the 12th century Gravensteen (Castle of the Counts), modeled 8 centuries ago on forts visited by Philip of Alsace when he led Crusaders in Syria. Sint Jorishof, built in 1228 and operated as a hotel since the 15th century. It is believed to be the oldest hotel in Europe, with 70 rooms in the original building.

The largest indoor plant and flower show (nearly 7 acres) is held in Gent in April, every 5 years. The 31st show takes place in 1995.

Dep. Gent (St. Pieters)	Frequent times from 05:47 to 22:47
Arr. Brussels (Midi)	30–35 minutes later
Arr. Brussels (Cen.)	6 minutes after arriving Midi station
Arr. Brussels (Nord)	3 minutes after arriving Central station

Brussels - Liege - Brussels 200

Dep. Brussels (Midi)	Frequent times from 05:47 to 23:15
Dep. Brussels (Central)	4 minutes later
Dep. Brussels (Nord)	6 minutes after departing Brussels (Central)
Arr. Liege (Guillemins)	72 minutes after departing Brussels (Midi)

Sights in **Liege**: There are many museums on and near Rue Feronstree. The wonderful collection of illuminated manuscripts, ancient Roman pottery, tapestries, medieval sculpture and ancient coins in the Musee Curtius (do not miss seeing the enormous twin fireplaces in the large hall on the second floor). In a building at the rear of the Curtius is the Musee du Verre, which has an incredible collection of ancient Egyptian and Roman glassware.

See the exhibit of very beautiful guns in the Musee d'Armes, on nearby Quai de Maestricht. The clocks, tapestries, wood paneling, chandeliers, leather covered walls, porcelain, kitchen utensils and furniture in the Musee d'Ansembourg. The collection of impressionist and expressionist paintings (Courbet, Corot, Chagall, Gauguin and Picasso) at the Musee des Beaux-Arts. The Aquarium.

The columned courtyard at the Palais des Princes-Eveques. Stroll La Roture, the city's old quarter. Visit the colorful Sunday market at La Batte. Shop the boutiques on Rue Pont de I'lle and Rue Vinave de I'lle.

Dep. Liege (Guillemins)	Frequent times from 05:46 to 22:02
Arr. Brussels (Nord)	60–70 minutes later
Arr. Brussels (Central)	6 minutes after arriving Nord station
Arr. Brussels (Midi)	3 minutes after arriving Central station

Brussels - Luxembourg - Brussels   210

Dep. Brussels (Midi/Zuid)	22 minutes after each hour, from 05:22 (1) to 20:22
Dep. Brussels (Cen.)	6 minutes after departing Brussels Midi-Zuid
Dep. Brussels (Nord)	3 minutes after departing Brussels Central
Arr. Luxembourg	2½ hours after departing Brussels Midi/Zuid
Dep. Luxembourg	31 minutes after each hour, from 06:31 (2) to 20:31
Arr. Brussels (Nord)	2¼ hours later
Arr. Brussels (Cen.)	5 minutes after arriving Brussels Nord
Arr. Brussels (Midi/Zuid)	4 minutes after arriving Brussels Central

(1) The 05:22 departure runs Monday–Friday, except holidays. Additional departures from Midi/Zuid station at 07:15 and 12:20 (both charge a supplement and have a restaurant car) do not stop at Central station. (2) There are additional departures from Luxembourg at 08:14, 12:06, 16:59 and 20:06 which (except for ther 20:06) do not stop at Brussels Central. All have a restaurant car (except the 08:14). The 16:59 and 20:06 departures charge a supplement.

Brussels - Namur - Brussels   210

Dep. Brussels (Midi)	Frequent times from 06:21 to 22:47
Dep. Brussels (Central)	4 minutes later (1)
Dep. Brussels (Nord)	6 minutes after departing Brussels Central
Arr. Namur	One hour after departing Brussels Midi

Sights in **Namur**: The silver art in Sisters of Our Lady Convent. The fortress. The baroque 18th century Cathedral. The Diocesan Museum. The extremely elegant Casino, featuring gastronomic feasts.

Dep. Namur	Frequent times from 06:24 to 22:24
Arr. Brussels (Nord)	47 minutes later
Arr. Brussels (Central)	6 minutes after arriving Nord station (1)
Arr. BRussels (Midi)	4 minutes after arriving Central station

(1) A few trains do not stop at Brussels' Central railstation.

Brussels - Paris - Brussels 18

Dep. Brussels (Midi)	07:04 (1)	08:00	10:06 (2)	11:54 (3)
Arr. Paris (Nord)	09:37	11:11	12:55	14:25
Dep. Paris (Nord)	14:33 (2)	16:36 (2)	17:25	18:38 (4+7)
Arr. Brussels (Midi)	17:42	19:49	20:01 (1)	21:10

(1) Supplement charged. Restaurant car. Runs daily, except Saturday and Sunday. Early July to early September: runs Monday–Friday. (2) Light refreshments. (3) Reservation required. Supplement charged. Runs daily, except Sunday. Restaurant car. (4) Reservation required. Supplement charged. Runs daily, except Saturday. Restaurant car. (5) Restaurant car. (6) Has couchettes. (7) Plus other Paris departures at 19:29 and 23:22 (7), arriving Brussels 22:30 and 04:32.

Brussels - Tournai - Brussels 214

Dep. Brussels (Nord)	06:57	08:01	09:01	10:01	11:01	12:01
Dep. Brussels (Cen.)	4 minutes after departing Nord station					
Dep. Brussels (Midi)	6 minutes after departing Central station					
Arr. Tournai	08:03	09:06	10:06	11:06	12:06	13:06

Sights in **Tournai**: One of Belgium's leading art towns. Pick up a free map and brochure at the city tourism center, at Vieux-Marche-aux-Poteries 14, open Monday–Friday 09:00–19:00, Saturday and Sunday 10:00–13:00 and 15:00–18:00. English-speaking guides are available ($21 for a 2-hour tour in 1988).

Tournai is best seen on foot, and the place to start is at the Grand Place, a square that is lined with reconstructed medieval guild houses, of which the Cloth Hall is dominant. Nearby is the 236-foot-high 12th century Belfry. Its 16th century 43-bell carillon is played daily at 11:30.

Visit the 12th century 435-foot-long Romanesque Cathedral, particularly to see its 13th centuryIle-de-France Gothic choir and many fine paintings in several of its chapels. The remains of two 12th century murals there are extraordinary.

Also see the 13th century gilded copper Shrine of Our Lady, decorated with silver figures that depict scenes from the life of the Virgin...and a 7th century Byzantine cross studded with rubies, emeralds and pearls with what is said to be a fragment of the cross on which Jesus died imbedded in its back.

From Easter until the end of September, the Cathedral is open 08:30–18:00. The rest of the year: 08:30–16:30. Its Treasury is open from Easter until the end of September 10:00–12:00. Rest of the year: 10:00–12:00 and 14:30–16:30. Walk across the Scheldt River and see the earliest examples in Western Europe of bourgeois houses of the Romanesque period as well as 14th and 15th century Gothic houses. From the Pont des Trous (one of the oldest bridges in Europe), view the 5 mammoth Cathedral towers at dusk, silhouetted against the sky.

Dep. Tournai	Every hour 05:34 to 22:34
Arr. Brussels (Midi)	56 minutes later
Arr. Brussels (Cen.)	5 minutes after arriving Midi station
Arr. Brussels (Nord)	3 minutes after arriving Central station

Luxembourg - Basel - Luxembourg   176

Prior to 1991, departure at 05:28 from Luxembourg made this excursion more practical than it has been since then.

Both of these trains charge a supplement and have a restaurant car.

Dep. Luxembourg	10:01	Dep. Basel (SNCF)	16:26
Arr. Basel (SNCF)	13:39	Arr. Luxembourg	19:56

Sights in **Basel**: Superb Holbein, Delacroix, Gaugin, Matisse, Ingres, Courbet and Van Gogh paintings in the Kunstmuseum on St. Alban Graben. The collection of 18th century clothing, ceramics and watches in the Kirschgarten. The Historical Museum in the Franciscan church in Barfusserplatz. Shop on Freiestrasse.

See the 16th century Town Hall. The fishmarket. The 15th century New University. Take a boat excursion from the pier in the back of Hotel Three Kings. See the view of the city from the Wettstein Bridge. Visit Munsterplatz.

Luxembourg - Bonn - Luxembourg

720			*710*		
Dep. Luxembourg	05:37 (1)	09:40	Dep. Bonn (Hbf.)	15:53	20:46
Arr. Koblernz	07:40	11:56	Arr. Koblenz	16:38	21:41
Change trains. 710			*Change trains. 720*		
Dep. Koblenz	08:17	12:21	Dep. Koblenz	16:56	22:19 (2)
Arr. Bonn (Hbf.)	09:12	13:12	Arr. Luxembourg	19:10	00:23

(1) Runs daily, except Sunday. (2) Runs daily, except Saturday.

Luxembourg - Brussels - Luxembourg 210

Dep. Luxembourg	06:27	07:07 (1)	07:31 (1)	08:14 (2)	08:27	09:27
Arr. Brussels (Nord)	09:11	09:33	10:11	10:40	11:11	12:11
Arr. Brussels (Cen.)	5 minutes after arriving Brussels Nord					
Arr. Brussels (Midi)	4 minutes after arriving Brussels Central					

Dep. Brussels (Midi)	13:21	14:21	15:21	16:21 (3)	17:21	18:21 (4)
Dep. Brussels (Cen.)	4 minutes after departing Brussels Midi					
Dep. Brussels (Nord)	5 minutes after departing Brussels Central					
Arr. Luxembourg	16:11	17:11	18:11	18:15	20:11	21:11

(1) Runs Monday-Friday, except holidaays. (2) Second-class only. (3) Restaurant car. (4) Plus other Brussels (Midi) departures at 19:13 and 19:21, arriving Luxemburg 21:49 and 22:15.

Luxembourg - Clervaux - Luxembourg 219

The best view (from the viaduct) as you depart Luxembourg City is from the left-hand side of the train.

Dep. Luxembourg	08:10	10:10	12:10
Arr. Clervaux	08:55	10:55	12:57

Sights in **Clervaux**: This is the Ardennes area, where the Battle of the Bulge was fought in December, 1944. It is a 15-minute walk from the railstation, along the river, to the center of town. You cross a bridge over the river in order to get to the office of the miniature golf course. This is also the tourist information office, open from late March to late September 10:00–12:00 and 14:00–18:00.

You can obtain a copy of the description they provide about the "Family of Man" exhibition of Edward Steichen photos. This world-famous American photographer was born in Luxembourg. Then, go to see that collection at DeLannoi Castle, which also has the Battle of the Bulge Museum and its monument—one of General Patton's U.S. army tanks. It also has an exhibit of castle models.

The Castle is open 10:00–17:00 June through September (13:00–17:00 on Sundays and bank holidays the rest of the year). It is pleasant to lunch at the Castle's restaurant.

See the view from the Benedictine Abbey of St. Maurice.

Dep Clervaux	12:51	14:51	17:51	19:36	20:51
Arr. Luxembourg	13:38	15:38	18:34	20:25	21:36

Luxembourg - Cologne (Koln) - Luxembourg

720			710		
Dep. Luxembourg	08:30 (1)	09:40 (2)	Dep. Cologne	16:19 (2)	18:19
Arr. Koblenz	10:38	11:55 (2)	Arr. Koblenz	17:38 (2)	19:41
Change trains. 710			*Change trains. 720*		
Dep. Koblenz	11:21	12:21	Dep Koblenz	17:19	20:17
Arr. Cologne	12:38	13:38	Arr. Luxembourg	19:23	22:29

(1) Changes train in Trier, Arr. 09:10—Dep. 09:15. (2) Direct train. No train change in Koblenz.

Luxembourg - Dusseldorf - Luxembourg

720			650		
Dep. Luxemb'g	05:37 (1)	10:33 (2)	Dep. Dusseldorf	15:45 (4)	18:28 (3)
Arr. Koblenz	07:40	12:37	Arr. Koblenz	-0- (4)	19:45
Change trains. 650			*Change trains. 720*		
Dep. Koblenz	07:48 (3)	09:48 (3)	Dep. Koblenz	-0-	20:17 (5)
Arr. Dusseldorf	09:11	11:11	Arr. Luxemb'g	19:23	22:29

(1) Runs daily, except Sunday. (2) Runs daily, except Sundays and holidays. Change trains in Trier (arr. 07:25-dep. 08:19). (3) Light refreshments. (4) Direct train. No train change in Koblenz. (5) Change trains in Trier (arr. 21:38—dep. 21:43).

Luxembourg - Frankfurt - Luxembourg

720			650		
Dep. Luxemb'g	05:37 (1)	10:33 (2)	Dep. Frankfurt	13:51 (3)	14:51 (3+5)
Arr. Koblenz	07:40	12:37	Arr. Koblenz	15:11	16:11
Change trains. 650			*Change trains. 720*		
Dep. Koblenz	07:46 (3)	09:46 (3)	Dep. Koblenz	15:19 (4)	17:19
Arr. Frankfurt	09:08	11:08	Arr. Luxemb'g	17:33	19:23

(1) Runs daily, except Sunday. (2) Runs daily, except Sundays and holidays. Change trains in Trier (arr. 07:25-dep. 08:19). (3) Supplement charged includes reservation fee. Restaurant car. (4) Change trains in Trier (arr. 16:40-dep. 16:43). (5) Plus other Frankfurt departures at 17:51 (3) and 19:51 (3), arriving Koblenz 19:13 and 21:13.

Luxembourg - Koblenz - Luxembourg 720

These schedules show that a stopover in Trier is possible in both directions.

Dep. Luxembourg	05:37 (1)	06:37 (2)	08:30	09:40	10:33	12:30
Arr. Trier	06:18	07:25 (3)	09:10 (3)	10:26	11:15	13:10 (3)
Arr Koblenz	07:40	09:41	10:38	11:55	12:38	14:38

Sights in **Koblenz**: A pedestrian tunnel goes from the front of the railstation to the city tourist information office, open mid-June to mid-October Monday–Saturday 08:30–20:00, Sunday 13:30–19:00. For a small fee you can obtain; hotel reservations, a city map and a "Tour of the City" brochure. See where the Moselle and Rhine rivers meet. Visit the Old Town, St. Castor's Church and the Middle Rhine Museum.

Dep. Koblenz	12:17 (3)	15:19	16:56	17:19	20:17	22:19 (4)
Arr. Trier	13:36	16:38 (3)	18:10	18:38	21:37 (3)	23:40
Arr. Luxembourg	14:31	17:33	19:10	19:23	22:29	00:23

(1) Runs daily, except Sunday. (2) Runs daily, except Sundays and holidays. (3) Change trains in Trier. (4) Runs daily, except Saturday.

Luxembourg - Liege - Luxembourg 219

Dep. Luxembourg	08:10	10:10	12:10
Arr. Liege (Guillemins)	10:36	12:34	14:34

Dep Liege (Guillemins)	13:08	16:08	17:48	19:08
Arr. Luxembourg	15:38	18:34	20:25	21:36

Luxembourg - Mainz - Luxembourg

720

Dep. Luxembourg	05:37 (1)	06:37 (2+3)	08:30 (3)	09:40	10:33
Arr. Koblenz	07:40	09:41	10:38	11:55	12:38

Change trains. 650

Dep. Koblenz	07:52 (4)	09:52 (4)	10:52 (4)	12:22 (4)	12:52 (4)
Arr. Mainz	08:42	10:42	11:42	13:12	13:42

Sights in **Mainz**: The art collection in the Cathedral. The Museum of the Central Rhineland. The rare books in the World Museum of Printing in the Romischer Kaiser. The restored Baroque mansionns on the Schillerplatz and Schillerstrasse, in the Kirschgarten. Old Town. The sculptures in the Diocesan Museum.

Dep. Mainz	14:18 (4)	16:18 (4)	19:18 (4)	21:18 (4)
Arr. Koblenz	15:05	17:05	20:05	21:07
Change trains. 720				
Dep. Koblenz	15:19 (3)	17:19	20:17 (3)	22:19 (5)
Arr. Luxembourg	17:33	19:23	22:29	00:23

(1) Runs daily, except Sunday. (2) Runs daily, except Sundays and holidays. (3) Change trains in Trier. (4) Supplement charged includes reservation fee. Restaurant car. (5) Runs daily, except Saturday.

Luxembourg - Metz - Luxembourg   173 + 176

Dep. Luxembourg   05:26 (2)   07:11 (1)   07:44 (2)   10:01 (3)
Arr. Metz   45 minutes later

Sights in **Metz:** The fantastic railstation here looks like a castle because it was built for Kaiser Wilhelm II when he was Germanifying this region. The imperial apartments in the station were arranged for the Kaiser to enjoy his obsession with train-spotting.

See the oldest church in France, the 4th century Pierre-aux-Nonains.

The largest stained-glass windows in the world, in the 16th century Cathedral of Saint Etienne. The Cathedral was formed by the joining of two 12th century churches into a single building. Its contemporary Marc Chagall and Jacques Villon stained-glass are exceptional.

See the Gallo-Roman antiquities in the city's Museum. Walk across the 13th century Porte des Allemands (Gate of the Germans).

Dep. Metz   11:50 (1)   16:04 (5)   19:13 (3)   20:04 (4)   21:41 (6)   22:03
Arr. Luxembourg   45 minutes later

(1) Runs Sunday only. (2) Runs daily, except Sundays and holidays. Light refreshments. (3) Supplement charged. Restaurant car. (4) Supplement charged. (5) Restaurant car. (6) Runs daily, except Saturday. Supplement charged.

Luxembourg - Mulhouse - Luxembourg   176

Both of these trains charge a supplement and have a restaurant car.

| Dep. Luxembourg | 10:01 | Dep. Mulhouse | 16:50 |
| Arr. Mulhouse | 13:13 | Arr. Luxembourg | 19:56 |

Sights in **Mulhouse:** France's largest collection of antique cars, and one of the best collections in the world of old autos. The Musee Nationale de l'Automobile exhibits about 500 cars ranging from an 1878 steam-powered Jacquot to a magnificent 12-liter Bugati Royale. It is open daily except Tuesday 10:00–18:00.

The Museum of Fabric Printing (Musee de l'Impression sur Etoffes) has displays of textile arts (at 3 Rue des Bonnes-Gens). There are 8,000,000 fabric samples as well as drawings of printed and woven fabrics in its 1,700-volume library. April–December the museum is open daily 10:00–12:00 and 14:00–18:00. January–March: same hours, but closed on Tuesday.

Visit France's largest and best railroad museum, open daily at Rue Alfred de Glehn. Its exhibits include passenger cars, freight cars, and steam, diesel and electric locomotives.

Luxembourg - Paris - Luxembourg   173

Dep. Luxembourg	05:26 (1)	07:11 (2)	07:44 (3)
Arr. Paris (Est)	09:08	11:02	11:22
Dep. Paris (Est)	17:16 (4)	18:45 (5)	19:55
Arr. Luxembourg	20:45	22:31	23:54

(1) Supplement charged. Runs daily, except Sundays and holidays. Light refreshments. (2) Runs Sunday only. (3) Runs daily, except Sundays and holidays. Light refreshments. (4) Supplement charged. (5) Supplement charged. Runs daily, except Saturday.

Luxembourg - Saarbrucken - Luxembourg   — via Trier   720

These schedules allow stopping-over in Trier for sightseeing on the ride to/from Saarbrucken.

Dep. Luxembourg	06:37 (1)	08:30	09:40	10:33	12:30
Arr. Trier	07:25	09:10	10:26	11:15	13:10
Change trains.					
Dep. Trier	07:35 (2)	09:38	10:41	11:38	13:38
Arr. Saarbrucken	08:45	10:45 (4)	11:41	12:45	14:45

These schedules allow stopping-over in Trier for dinner en route back to Luxembourg:

Dep. Saarbrucken	11:12	12:15	15:12	17:12	20:10 (3)	22:10 (3)
Arr. Trier	12:19	13:15	16:19	18:19	21:10	23:12
Change trains.						
Dep. Trier	12:41	13:42	16:44	18:41	21:44	23:41 (5)
Arr. Luxembourg	13:23	14:31	17:33	19:23	22:29	00:23

(1) Runs daily, except Sundays and holidays. (2) Runs Monday-Friday except holidays.. (3) Light refreshments. (4) Runs Monday-Saturday (5) Runs daily, except Saturday.

Luxembourg - Saarbrucken — *via Metz* 173

These schedules allow stopping-over for sightseeing in Metz en route to/from Saar-brucken.

Dep. Luxembourg	05:26 (1)	07:11 (2)	07:44 (3)	10:01 (4)
Arr. Metz	06:11	07:58	08:31	10:43
Change trains.				
Dep. Metz	06:42 (5)	08:44 (6)	09:54 (7)	11:54 (8)
Arr. Saarbrucken	07:41	09:55	10:50	12:48

These schedules allow stopping-over in Metz for lunch or dinner en route back to Luxembourg:

Dep. Saarbrucken	13:10 (4)	17:09 (9)	18:18 (5)	19:15 (6)	
Arr. Metz	14:03	18:06	19:28	20:22	
Change trains.					
Dep. Metz	16:04 (10)	19:13 (4)	20:06 (12)	21:49 (11)	23:03
Arr. Luxembourg	16:49	19:56	20:45	22:31	

(1) Supplement charged. Runs daily, except Sunday and holidays. (2) Runs Sunday only. (3) Runs daily, except Sundays and holidays. Light refreshments. (4) Supplement charged. Restaurant car. (5) Runs Monday-Friday, except holidays. (6) Operates late June to early September. (7) Runs daily, except Sundays (8) Light refreshments.(9) Supplement charged. Light refreshments. (10) Restaurant car. (11) Supplement charged. Runs daily, except Saturday. (12) Supplement charged.

Luxembourg - Strasbourg - Luxembourg 176

Both of these trains charge a supplement and have a restaurant car.

Dep. Luxembourg	10:01		Dep. Strasbourg	17:48
Arr. Strasbourg	12:06		Arr. Luxembourg	19:56

Luxembourg - Trier - Luxembourg 720

Dep. Luxembourg	08:30	09:40	10:33	12:30	14:33
Arr. Trier	09:10	10:26	11:15	13:10	15:15

Sights in **Trier**: There are more Roman monuments here than in any other German city: the 4th century Porta Nigra (Black Gate), 2nd and 4th century baths, a 1st century amphitheater, and the 4th century Roman palace, Palastula (with its throne room of Roman emperors), now a Lutheran church. See the "Holy Coat of Trier," said to be Christ's robe, in the

Romanesque Cathedral, started in the 6th century.

Roman and medieval relics in the Municipal Museum. Peter's Fountain in the market square and, nearby, the 17th century Electoral Palace and 18th century Kasselstatt Palace.

Dep. Trier	13:42	16:44	18:41	21:44
Arr. Luxembourg	14:31	17:33	19:23	22:29

Luxembourg - Vianden - Luxembourg   217 + Government timetable

The Ettelbruck–Viandin bus leaves from the front of the Ettelbruck railstation. Re-check the bus schedules!!

Dep. Luxembourg	08:10	12:10	14:10
Arr. Ettelbruck	08:28	12:31	14:30
Change to bus.			
Dep. Ettelbruck	08:35	13:14	14:52
Arr. Vianden	09:03	13:38	15:15

Sights in **Vianden**: Leave the bus at the first stop, the Hotel Oranienburg. At the end of the day, don't fail to board the bus at Gare Routiere (the bus station) for the ride back to Ettelbruck. Most of the attractions in Vianden are closed 12:00–14:00.

Walk uphill from the Hotel Oranienburg to the large and very interesting castle, open daily March-December, only weekends in January and February.

Leave the castle at 12:00 and have lunch before visiting the home of Victor Hugo. Take the chairlift across the river to the top of a hill from which there are good views of the castle, dam and valley. After descending, walk across the top of the dam.

See the rococo altar in the 13th century Church of the Trinitarians. Visit the exhibits of folklore and ancient household items in the Museum of Rustic Arts.

Bus				
Dep. Vianden	14:34	16:26	18:10	20:31
Arr. Ettelbruck	15:05	16:55	18:38	21:01
Change to train.				
Dep. Ettelbruck	15:16	18:16	20:01	21:16
Arr. Luxembourg	15:38	18:34	20:25	21:38

SCENIC RAIL TRIPS

Most of the scenic rail trips of the Benelux countries are in Holland, and all of those are included in the list of one-day roundtrips from Amsterdam preceding this section. They are the train rides between Amsterdam and Delft, Den Haag, Leiden, Rotterdam and Utrecht.

The scenery on these trips is best from mid-March through May: fields of tulips, narcissus, crocus and other bulb flowers in bloom. The region is known as "Champs de Fleurs" (Fields of Flowers).

Three other scenic trips in the Benelux countries are listed in this section. All are noteworthy for beautiful river scenery.

Liege - Jemelle

This fine farm and river scenery can be seen by taking an indirect route from Brussels to Luxembourg.

200

Dep. Brussels (Midi)	10:18	11:18	12:18	13:18
Dep. Brussels (Cen.)	4 minutes after departing Midi station			
Dep. Brussels (Nord)	6 minutes after departing Central station			
Arr. Liege (Guill.)	11:40	12:40	13:40	14:40
Change trains. 215				
Dep. Liege (Guill.)	07:00	09:59	18:47	01:55 (1)
Arr. Namur	07:40	10:39	19:25	02:34
Change trains. 210				
Dep. Namur	13:12 (2)	14:22	15:22	16:22
Dep. Jemelle	-0-	15:00	16:00	17:00
Arr. Luxembourg	14:49	16:11	17:11	18:11

(1) Runs Monday–Friday, except holidays. (2) Supplement charged. Restaurant car. (3) Restaurant car.

Luxembourg - Liege 217

There is excellent farm and river scenery on this easy one-day roundtrip. See Luxembourg timetables above.

Namur - Dinant   210

This is a spur off the Brussels-Luxembourg route. The great farm and river scenery here can be seen either by breaking-up the ride from Brussels to Luxembourg (or vice versa) ...or as an easy one-day roundtrip from Brussels.

For the first way (showing both directions):

Dep. Brussels (Midi)	08:44 (1)	09:44 (1)	Dep. Luxembourg	08:27	09:27
Dep. Brussels (Cen.)	08:46	09:46	Arr. Namur	10:19	11:02
Dep. Brussels (Nord)	08:53	09:53	*Change trains.*		
Arr. Namur	09:42	10:42	Dep. Namur	10:47 (1)	11:47 (1)
Arr. Dinant	10:13	11:13	Arr. Dinant	11:13	12:13
Change trains.			*Change trains.*		
Dep. Dinant	10:25 (1)	11:25 (1)	Dep. Dinant	11:27 (1)	12:25 (1)
Arr. Namur	10:55	11:55	Dep. Namur	12:00	13:00
Change trains.			Arr. Brussels (Nord)	12:49	13:49
Dep. Namur	11:24	12:24	Arr. Brussels (Cen.)	12:56	13:56
Arr. Luxembrg	13:11	14:11	Arr. Brussels (Midi)	13:00	14:00

(1) Runs Monday–Friday, except holidays.

Here is the Brussels one-day roundtrip 210
All of these trains run Monday–Friday except holidays.

Dep. Brussels (Midi)	08:44	09:44	Dep. Dinant	14:25	16:25
Dep. Brussels (Cen.)	08:46	09:46	Arr. Namur	15:00	17:00
Dep. Brussels (Nord)	08:53	09:53	Arr. Brussels (Nord)	15:49	17:49
Arr. Namur	09:42	10:42	Arr. Brussels (Cen.)	15:56	17:56
Arr. Dinant	10:13	11:13	Arr. Brussels (Midi)	16:00	18:00

INTERNATIONAL ROUTES
FROM BELGIUM

The Belgian gateway for rail travel to London, Amsterdam, Basel (and on to Zurich and Milan), Cologne (and on to Hamburg and Copenhagen) and Paris (and on to Madrid) is Brussels.

Brussels - Amsterdam 205

Many of these trains have light refreshments.

Dep. Brussels (Midi)	10 minutes after each hour, from 06:10 to 23:10
Dep. Brussels (Cen.	4 minutes after departing Midi station
Dep. Brussels (Nord)	4 minutes after departing Central station
Arr. Amsterdam	3 hours later

Brussels - Basel - Milan   43

Dep. Brussels (Midi)	07:15 (1)	19:13 (2)
Dep. Brussels (Nord)	8 minutes after departing Midi station	
Arr. Basel (S.N.C.F.)	13:56	02:00
Arr. Milan (Cen.)	19:15	07:10

(1) Supplement charged. Restaurant car. (2) Coaches are second-class. Runs Friday and Saturday only.

Brussels - Cologne (Koln)   200

Dep. Brussels (Midi)	06:47	07:47	09:47	10:47	12:03 (1)	13:47
Dep. Brussels (Cen.)	06:52	07:52	09:52	10:52	-0-	13:52
Dep. Brussels (Nord)	06:57	07:57	09:57	10:57	12:12	13:57
Arr. Cologne	09:42	10:42	12:42	13:42	14:42	16:42

Dep. Brussels (Midi)	15:47	16:55 (1)	18:08 (1)	18:47	20:03 (1)	21:25 (2)
Dep. Brussels (Cen.)	15:52	-0-	18:12	18:52	-0-	-0-
Dep. Brussels (Nord)	15:57	17:03	18:18	18:57	20:12	21:34
Arr. Cologne	18:42	19:42	20:42	21:39	22:42	00:17

(1) Supplement charged. Restaurant car. (2) Coach is second-class.

Brussels - London via Oostende   (Jetfoil)   12

The schedules shown below are for late May to late September, unless designated otherwise. All of these ships require reservation, charge a supplement and have light refreshments.

Dep. Brussels (Nord)	09:47	11:47	14:47	17:47 (1)
Dep. Brussels (Midi)	09:59	11:59	14:59	17:59
Arr. Oostende	11:09	13:09	16:09	19:09
Change to boat.				
Dep. Oostende	11:45	13:45	16:45	19:30 (1)

Set your watch back one hour, except from late September to late October.

Arr. Dover (Western Docks)	-0-	-0-	-0-	-0- (2)
Arr. London (Vic.)	15:17	17:23	20:19	22:47

(1) The Oostende–London ship operates late June to late September. (2) Runs Sunday only.

Brussels - London via Oostende   (Regular Ferry)   12

All ferries require reservation and have a restaurant.

Dep. Brussels (Nord)	11:47	22:47
Dep. Brussels (Midi)	11:59	22:59
Arr. Oostende	13:09	23:54

Change to a boat.

Dep. Oostende	13:45	00:30

Set your watch back one hour, except from late September to late October.

Arr. Dover (Eastern Docks)	-0-	-0-

A free bus connects Eastern Docks with the railstation at Western Docks.

Dep. Dover (Western Docks)	-0-	-0-
Arr. London (Vic.)	17:23	06:30

Brussels - Luxembourg 218

See "Brussels-Luxembourg" under Luxembourg.

Brussels - Paris   18

Dep. Brussels (Nord)	01:27 (1)	-0-	07:44 (3)	09:45 (4)
Dep. Brussels (Midi)	01:53	07:04 (2)	08:00	10:04
Arr. Paris (Nord)	06:58	09:37	10:55	12:55
Dep Brussels (Nord)	11:32 (5)	13:46 (6)	15:50 (4)	16:23 (7)
Dep. Brussels (Midi)	11:54	14:13	16:00	17:10 (8)
Arr. Paris (Nord)	14:25	17:05	19:01	19:42
Dep. Brussels (Nord)	17:23 (7)	18:45 (10)	19:23 (7)	-0-
Dep. Brussels (Midi)	18:13 (9)	19:07	20:04 (6)	-0-
Arr. Paris (Nord)	20:43	22:05	23:01	-0-

(1) Has couchettes. (2) Runs Monday–Friday. Restaurant car. (3) Operates late August to late June. Runs Monday and Saturday. (4) Supplement charged. Restaurant car. (5) Reservation required. Supplement charged. Runs daily, except Sunday. Restaurant car. (6) Light refreshments. (7) Change trains at Midi railstation. (8)Supplement charged. Runs Monday-Friday. Restaurant car. (9) Runs daily. Supplement charged. Restaurant car. (10) Restaurant car.

INTERNATIONAL ROUTES
FROM HOLLAND

Amsterdam is the Dutch gateway for rail travel to London, Basel (and on to Zurich and Milan), Cologne, Hamburg (and on to Copenhagen) and Paris (and on to Madrid). Notes on the route to London appear under "London–Amsterdam" in Great Britain chapter.

Amsterdam - Brussels 205

Dep. Amsterdam	Frequent times from 06:23 to 22:15
Arr. Brussels (Nord)	3 hours later
Arr. Brussels (Cent.)	4 minutes after departing Nord station
Arr. Brussels (Midi)	4 minutes after departing Central station

Amsterdam - Cologne (Koln) - Mainz - Basel

Many castles are seen in the Koblenz–Mainz area as the train travels alongside the Rhine River. En route to Basel, sit on the left-hand side for the best views of marvelous Rhine River scenery.

All of these trains charge a supplement.

Dep. Amsterdam	06:02 (1)	07:06 (1)	08:00 (3)	09:00 (3)	11:06 (1+5)
Arr. Cologne	08:42 (2)	09:42 (2)	10:57	11:57	13:42 (2)
Dep. Cologne	09:00 (3)	09:50 (3)	11:07	12:07	14:00 (3)
Arr. Koblenz	09:51	10:51	11:51	12:51	14:51
Arr. Mainz	10:42	11:42	12:42	13:42	15:42
Arr. Basel (S.B.B.)	13:43	14:43	15:43	16:43	18:43

(1) Light refreshments. (2) Change trains in Cologne. (3) Restaurant car. (4) Carries a sleeping car. Also has couchettes. (5) Plus other Amsterdam departures at 13:06 (1+2), 15:06 (1+2) and 20:05 (4)…departing Cologne 16:00 (3), 18:00 (3) and 23:47…arriving Basel 20:43, 22:43 and 06:26.

Amsterdam - Osnabruck - Bremen - Hamburg - Copenhagen 22

Both of these trains have couchettes.

Dep. Amsterdam (Cen.)	20:09 (1)	19:06 (2)
Arr. Bremen	00:50	01:27
Arr. Hamburg (Hbf.)	01:54	02:35
Arr. Copenhagen	07:25	08:25

(1) Operates late June to early Sept. (2) Change trains in Duisburg.

Amsterdam - Luxembourg 38

Dep. Amsterdam	07:32 (1)
Arr. Maastricht	10:14
Change trains.	
Dep. Maastricht	10:14
Arr. Luxembourg	13:38

(1) Runs Saturday only June 4 - August 27.

Amsterdam - London via Hoek van Holland (regular ferry) 15

Dep. Amsterdam	09:32 (1)	19:48 (1)
Arr. Hoek van Holland	10:57	21:13
Change to ferry.		
Dep. Hoek van Holland	12:00	22:00 (2)
Set your watch back one hour.		
Arr. Harwich	18:00	07:00
Change to train		
Dep. Harwich	18:45	07:50
Arr. London (Liverpool)	20:00	09:00

(1) Light refreshments. (2) Reservation required.

Amsterdam - Brussels - Paris 18

Dep. Amsterdam (Cen.)	06:57 (1)	08:53 (2)	10:52 (3)	11:25 (3)	12:25 (3)
Dep. Antwerp (Berch.)	09:14	10:59	13:15	13:53	14:53
Dep. Brussels (Nord)	09:47	11:32	13:46	14:23	15:23
Arr. Brussels (Midi)	09:51	11:37	13:52	14:30 (4)	15:30 (4)
Dep. Brussels (Midi)	10:04	11:54	14:13	15:04 (5)	16:00 (5)
Arr. Paris (Nord)	12:55	14:25	17:05	17:43	19:01

Dep. Amsterdam (Cen.)	13:25 (3)	14:25 (3)	15:52 (8)	16:25 (3)	22:15 (9)
Dep. Antwerp (Berch.)	15:53	16:53	18:12	18:53	00:54
Dep. Brussels (Nord)	16:23	17:23	18:45	19:23	01:27
Arr. Brussels (Midi)	16:30 (4)	17:30 (4)	18:50	19:30 (4)	01:34
Dep. Brussels (Midi)	17:10 (6)	18:13 (7)	19:07	20:04 (3)	01:53
Arr. Paris (Nord)	19:42	20:43	22:05	23:01	06:58

(1) Supplement charged. Light refreshments. (2) Reservation required. Supplement charged. Runs daily, except Sunday. Restaurant car Brussels–Paris. (3) Light refreshments. (4) Change trains in Brussels--Midi. (5) Supplement charged. Restaurant car. (6) Supplement charged. Restaurant car. Early July to early

September: runs Monday–Friday. Early September to early July: runs daily, except Saturday. (7) Supplement charged. Restaurant car. (8) Restaurant car. (9) Has couchettes.

INTERNATIONAL ROUTES
FROM LUXEMBOURG

Luxembourg City is a gateway for rail travel to London, Amsterdam, Basel (and on to Zurich and Milan), Brussels, Cologne, Koblenz (and on to Frankfurt), and Paris. (Notes on the routes from Amsterdam, Brussels and Paris to London appear in Chapter 7.)

Luxembourg - Amsterdam   38

Dep. Luxembourg	16:10 (1)
Arr. Maastricht	19:21
Arr. Amsterdam	22:00

(1) Operates early June to late August. Runs Saturday only.

Luxembourg - Basel   40

Dep. Luxembourg	01:18 (1)	10:01 (2)	14:59 (2)	18:02 (3)
Arr. Basel (SBB)	05:16	13:39	18:25	21:30

(1) Carries a sleeping car. Also has couchettes. (2) Supplement charged. Restaurant car. (3) Restaurant car.

Luxembourg - Brussels   210

Dep. Luxembourg	04:09	05:27 (1)	06:27	07:07 (1)	08:14 (4)
Arr. Brussels (Nord)	6:40	08:11	09:11	09:33	10:40
Arr. Brussels (Cen.)	-0-	08:16	09:16	09:37	-0-
Arr. Brussels (Midi)	06:49	08:20	09:20	09:41	10:47

(1) Runs Monday–Friday, except holidays. (2) Second-class only. (3) Restaurant car. (4) Plus other departures from Luxembourg at 31 minutes after each hour from 08:31 to 20:31…also at 12:06 (3), 16:59 (3) and 20:06 (3).

Luxembourg - Cologne 720

Dep. Luxembourg	05:37 (1)	08:30	09:40 (2)	10:33 (3)	12:30 (4)
Arr. Trier	06:18	09:10	10:26 (2)	11:15 (3)	13:10
Change trains.					
Dep. Trier	07:17	09:15	10:36	11:17	13:17
Arr. Cologne	09:45	11:45	13:14	13:45	15:45

(1) Runs daily, except Sunday. (2) Direct train. No train change in Trier. Operates late June to mid-September. (3) Direct train. No train change in Trier. (4) Plus other departures from Luxembourg at 14:33 (3), 15:24 and 18:26, arriving Cologne 17:45, 19:45 and 21:45.

Luxembourg - Paris 173 *via Metz* 177 *via Rheims*

	173	*177*	*173*	*173*	*173*
Dep. Luxembourg	05:26 (1)	06:00 (2)	07:44 (3)	10:01 (4)	13:07 (5+9)
Dep. Rheims	-0-	10:01	-0-	-0-	-0-
Dep. Metz	06:11	-0-	08:35	10:53 (5)	14:15
Arr. Paris (Est)	09:08	11:27	11:22	13:40	17:10

(1) Supplement charged. Runs daily, except Sunday. Light refreshments. (2) Runs daily, except Sundays and holidays. Change trains in Longwy. (3) Runs daily, except Sundays and holidays. Light refreshments. (4) Supplement charged. Restaurant car. Change trains in Metz. (5) Supplement charged. Restaurant car. (6) Change trains in Longwy. (7) Runs daily, except Saturday. (8) Supplement charged. Light refreshments. (9) Plus other departures from Luxembourg at [173] 16:34 (7), [177] 17:18 (6) and [173] 17:25 (8), arriving Paris 20:22 (via Metz), 21:56 (via Rheims) and 21:04 (via Metz).

FRANCE

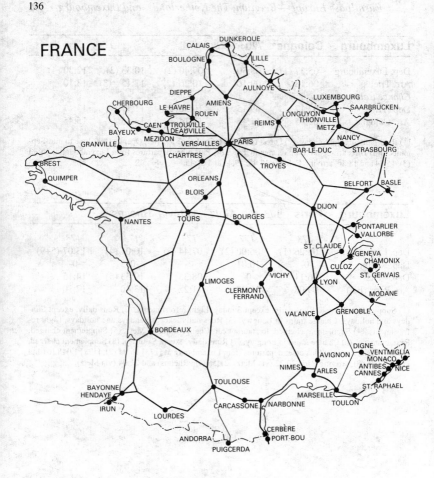

FRANCE

Overview

Travelers to Europe who return home without having ridden a French train are poorer for the experience. For over a decade the French State Railway, (Société Nationale de Chemins de Fer Français, SNCF) has been a leading force in international train travel, revolutionizing European rail with its streamline TGV (train à grande vitesse). The French high speed train has not only shrunk the country's borders, its cars are being exported and integrated into foreign rail systems as far and wide as China and Korea. The TGV has cut the traveling time in half between Paris and, for example, Marseilles, 900 kilometers away, to a little over four hours instead of eight. The TGV currently serves the Paris-Lyon-Marseilles line to the south with branches reaching Nice to the southeast and Perpignan to the southwest, Geneva and Lausanne in the east, Lille and Calais to the north, and the newer ultra high-speed Bordeaux Atlantic line to the southwest. High speed train travel is expanding rapidly in Europe with a network being prepared to tie in with London (via the EuroTunnel and Disneyland Paris) and several German, Belgian, and Dutch cities. The TGV requires reservations, which can be made in most travel agencies, all train stations, and at home with the Minitel, the home-style on-line computer that most French households and offices have perched in their hallways and desktops. Seat reservations for regular trains are also recommended during busy periods. Practically all French towns and cities and a large majority of even the rural villages are served by the SNCF. Although there has been a move away from Paris as the central transportation hub of France, the City of Lights still functions as the pivot point for much of French travel, especially internationally bound. New, smaller hubs are gaining importance, such as Lyon and Lille, which is particularly well situated for train traffic to the U.K., Belgium, Holland, and northern Germany. The Paris suburb to the south, Massy, now functions as a changing station for north-south passengers to avoid Paris. Marne la Vallée Chessy, TGV Hte Picardie, and Charles de Gaulle TGV, scheduled for opening in late 1994, have all been designed to move passengers across the country without having to transit in the already dense city of Paris.

In a nutshell, the train as a vehicle of transportation in France is both an excellent means of seeing some of the finest scenery in Europe and a model of contemporary European efficiency.

General Information

• Paris has nine main rail stations, six principal stations and three specialized stations designed for cars, etc., all of them connected to subway and commuter train (Métro and RER) lines. All offer a wide range of services: bars and restaurants, refreshment stands, lockers, business services, telephone and postal facilities, newsstands and information booths (sporadically staffed).

• SNCF Train Information

Information: 45.82.50.50

Reservations:

Grandes Lignes (national & international lines): 45.82.50.50

Ile de France (regional lines): 45.65.60.00
Minitel: 36 15 SNCF
Open daily from 8h-20h

• French rail tickets purchased in France are valid for travel any day within two months from the date of purchase. Train tickets obtained before arrival in France are valid for six months.

• Passengers using a French train ticket purchased in Europe must validate it (composter) in one of the many orange-colored machines located at the entrance to the platforms before boarding a train. Failure to do so may result in a stiff fine—train travel within France is essentially based on the honor system. In most cases a conductor will check your tickets anyway. You can purchase tickets onboard, but you pay a supplement. A person holding a non-validated European ticket is subject to a fine. All tickets purchased outside Europe are exempt from having to be validated.

• As for time changes, travelers should note that France turns its clocks ahead on the last Sunday of March and converts back to Standard Time on the last Sunday of September.

• French train travel is graced by scores of internal regulations and new specialized services stipulating tariffs and days and times for reduced-fare travel. Children under four travel free. Half-fare for children from 4 to 11. Children 12 and over must pay full fare. (See Prix Joker details listed below.)

• Semi-Couchettes. Some compartments on French trains have eight semi-inclined bunks (instead of seats) on these routes: Paris-Brest, Paris-Bordeaux, Paris-Hamburg, Paris-Quimper, Paris-Strasbourg, Paris-Ventimiglia, and Rheim-Nice. For reservation purposes, these "Cabine 8" bunks are treated as seats and no supplement is charged.

Signs you are likely to see at rail stations in France:

arrivée	ARRIVAL
consigne	BAGGAGE CHECKROOM
dames	WOMEN
départ	DEPARTURE
entrée	ENTRANCE
fumeurs	SMOKING COMPARTMENT
gare	STATION
horaire	TIMETABLE
location de place assise	SEAT RESERVATION OFFICE
messieurs	MEN
quai	PLATFORM
renseignement	INFORMATION
sortie	EXIT
voie	TRACK
voiture-lit	SLEEPER CAR
voiture-retsa	RESTAURANT CAR

Connections with Great Britain

With the opening of the EuroTunnel underneath the English Channel, which accomodates train cars as well as private vehicles, the war for the passengers is on, with the ferry boat companies and hydrofoil services battling to maintain market share by reducing prices, offering attractive specials, and increasing services. The EuroTunnel option is undoubtedly the fastest and easiest way to go between England and France, but for the time being the price remains an obstacle for many. As of late 1994, private cars were grouped on a special shuttle train car that is pulled through the tunnel in some thirty minutes. Passenger train service through the tunnel on "Eurostar" began in late 1994 and there are now trains leaving almost every hour. For more information on UK-France connections, see the chapter for Great Britain. For EuroTunnel information write to BP 69, 62231 COQUELLES or telephone (33) 21.00.60.00 in France. An information and reservation number in Paris is: 44.94.80.80. U.S. toll-free information: 1-800-EUROSTAR.

Another option is the **"UK-France Sampler:"**
For any 3 days within one month, unlimited rail travel in France plus 3 consecutive days car rental in the UK plus the Eurostar journey (Paris-London or London-Paris). 1996 *first*-class per person price for two adults traveling in an "economy" car: $304.50 (additional car day $30). *Second*-class: $241, additional car day $30.

French Holidays

In that train schedules differ between working days and holidays, and many trains do not run at all on holidays, a list of such days in France can be especially useful. Also, those trains which operate on holidays are often filled, and it is necessary to make reservations for them long in advance. When at all possible, avoid train travel in France on holidays, long week-ends, and the first and last day of the Paris-region's school vacations!

Public Holidays

January 1	Jour de l'An (New Year's Day)
Late March/April	Pâques (Easter)
Monday after Easter	Lundi de Pâques (Easter Monday)
May 8	Victoire 1945 (V.E. Day)
Sixth Thursday after Easter	Ascension (Ascension Day)
Second Monday after Ascension	Pentecôte (Pentecost)
July 14	Fête nationale/14 juillet (Bastille Day)
August 15	Fête de l'Assomption (Feast of the Assumption)
November 1	Toussaint (All Saints' Day), Halloween
November 11	Fête de l'Armistice (Veteran's Day)
December 25	Noël (Christmas)

DISCOUNT TRAIN TRAVEL IN FRANCE

Additionally, the SNCF publishes a color-coded calendar of travel days and times and prices. Here, in order of largest discount to smallest, the days are listed: Jour bleue: Saturday noon through Sunday 15h.Jour blanche: Friday noon through Saturday noon, and Sunday 15h through Monday noon. Plus holidays. Jour rouge: Principal days of departure.

As of the end of May 1994, this system is no longer used for TGV service. The SNCF also publishes a free Guide des prix Réduits, Guide to Reduced Priced Train Travel. Here are the principal reduced ticket possibilities for those traveling without a Eurailpass: Discounts depend on destinations, dates, and times.

• **Carrissimo and Joker**: youth fares, 12-25 years old, up to 50%.

• **Carte Kiwi and Joker**: When traveling with children (even one child) discounts can go to 60%.

• **Carte Vermeil and Joker**: Senior citizens discounts for the over-60 bracket.

• The Joker 30 fare offers travelers up to 60% off when reservations are made between 60 and 30 days before departure.

• **The Joker 8** fare offers a 40% discount when reservations are made between 60 and 8 days before departure.

• Multiple subscription options are also available to SNCF train users. The EuroDomino is a three, five, or ten day coupon for unlimited train travel during one month; the Modulopass is a six month or one year subscription for unlimited travel on a certain line or on the whole network depending on your needs; the Businesspass is a pass in the name of your company or organization enabling businesses to profit from a 15% discount when 25 or more round-trip tickets are purchased. Two new subscriptions are now available on the TGV Nord Europe line: The Temporis, which offers discounts to travelers making at least 16 trips within a 19 to 31 day period, and ABO 8, a special offer of up to 75% off for travelers making at least one round-trip journey per week.

• Children under four years old travel free, but a child is not entitled to a seat.

• Animals pay half fare of a 2nd class ticket or 28 FF if the animal is under six kilos and is carried in a bag measuring not more than 45 x 30 x 25 cm.

• If you want to travel with your car or motorcycle on the train, the SNCF has a complete list of destinations applicable to this service. Motorail is a European network of special trains, generally overnight, carrying passengers with vehicles on journeys up to 900 miles. In Paris, reservations can be made by calling 45.65.60.60. Otherwise, inquire at:

Gare Austerlitz (Tolbiac): 45.82.73.62.

Gare de Lyon (Bercy): 40.19.60.11.

Gare Montparnasse (Vaugirard): 40.48.14.72.

THE FRENCH TGV:
FASTEST TRAINS ON EARTH

Since 1981, France has operated the world's fastest trains, the train a grande vitesse, which can run up to 320 kilometers per hour and are operated at the top speed of 186 mph on the 126-mile Paris-LeMans line, making that trip in 55 minutes versus the one hour and fifty minutes needed by regular trains! In the nineties, one speaks more of the opening of new services and lines than the high speed, which has become as a given and banal detail in daily European travel. Seat reservations are required for practically all TGV trains—and are particularly essential on peak days and at peak hours. Standing is not allowed on TGVs. Currently, the SNCF has 136 direct TGV destinations from Paris, Lyon, and Lille, five ultra-modern stations opened or opening in late 1994, including a TGV station at Paris' Charles de Gaulle Airport, Lyon's Satolas Airport, and Lille's "Europe" station, through which the Paris-London three hour jaunt will pass. Essentially, this network is progressing faster than any annual guidebook can accurately report on!

Although certain supplements for certain trains may be in effect, pass holders should only count on the modest reservation fee of 30 FF.

The usual composition for a TGV is 386 seats: 111 in first-class, 275 in second-class. Each TGV has a bar car with snack and drink services as well as providing international press and telephone cards. Meals are brought to seats in some of the first-class cars, however, in most cases, those interested in dining should indicate such and proceed to the dining car at the set dinner hour.

The initial 1982 TGV service (Paris-Lyon, Paris-Dijon and Paris-Geneva) was expanded in 1983 to include Paris-Marseilles, Paris-Montpelier and Paris-Annecy-Grenoble. A TGV service Paris-Lausanne (with cross-platform transfer in Lausanne for trains to Milan) began in 1984. Service Paris-Grenoble started in 1985, Paris-LeMans and Paris-Tours in 1989. The nineties has brought an excellent TGV Atlantic line serving Poitier, La Rochelle, Bordeaux, and Nantes. The northern route, one of the most promising extensions to the system in that it connects Paris with the cities of northern Europe, boasts of an exceptionally rapid and regular Paris-Lille service in one hour.

FRENCH TRAIN PASSES

The French national passes are sold everywhere in the world, except in France—at travel agencies and offices of Rail Europe (U.S.A. and Canadian addresses listed in introduction). Here are the most widely used and advantageous passes available for France:

France Railpass Unlimited train travel for any three days within one month. The 1996 prices are: $198 for first-class and $160 for second-class. Up to six additional days may be added at $30 per day for first-class, $30 per day for second-class. Half-fare for children age 4-11. Both passes include the following bonuses:

• Free round-trip train service between Orly or Charles de Gaulle Roissy airports and downtown Paris.

• A one-day Metropass valid in second-class within the city limits on the Paris subway and bus systems.

• 50% discount on the Nice-Digne scenic private rail line.

• 15% discount on the Train + Auto car rental system (Avis) available at most rail stations and airports.

• 15-20% discount on the entrance fee to numerous national museums.

• A gift from the Printemps Department Store!

• Irish Ferries ships from Le Havre to Rosslare and Cherbourg to Rosslare (late June to late August). On arrival in Ireland, the bus service (taking passengers from Rosslare pier to the Rosslare rail station) accommodates all passengers, and at no charge.

• Le Havre-Cork. (Port taxes are extra, payable in Irish Pounds. Reservations are required for cabins at all times, and for seats during July and August.

• The bus (7FF charge) that transports passengers from le Havre rail station to the boat pier takes people on a first-come-first-served basis. When the bus is filled, people left at the rail station must take a taxi to the pier.

France Rail N Drive   Unlimited three days of train travel plus three days of car rental (any six days) within one month. Prices vary depending on number of passengers and the category of car. Note that the third and fourth passenger needs to pay only for a three-day France Railpass.

The 1996 prices per person for two persons with a compact size car is: $189 for first-class train and $159 for second-class. Up to six more days of train travel may be added at $30 per day for first-class, $30 per day for second-class. Up to six more days of car rental may be added at $44 per day for the compact size. All prices include the French sales tax TVA (Value Added Tax) which is 18.6%, unlimited mileage, and the basic legal liability insurance, as well as free drop-off anywhere within continental France. Note: the car may be driven in other countries but must be dropped-off in France. Avis has more than 500 rental locations in France. When possible reservations for cars should be made at least seven days in advance and in your country of origin. (In the U.S.A., the toll free telephone number is (800) 331-1084. For making reservation after arriving in France, phone 05-05-22-11 at least 24 hours in advance. Note: experience shows that car rentals booked in the US tend to me less expensive than the same rentals booked in France.

France Rail N Fly   Unlimited three days of train travel plus one day of air travel any-where in France (any four days) within one month.

The 1996 adult prices are: $295 for first-class, $255 for second-class. For children ages 2-11: $195 for first-class, $175 for second-class. Up to six more days of train travel may be added at $30 per day for first-class, $30 per day for second-class. For children age 2-11: $15 and $15. One additional day of air travel may be added at $99 for either first-class or second-class, for both adults and children.

Carte Vermeil Plein Temps   See Rail Europ Senior in the introduction.

Carte Vermeil Quatre Temps This senior citizen pass is available to persons aged 60 and older and may be purchased at major rail stations only in France. Those eligible for this card are able to purchase both first and second-class tickets at up to 50% discounts for travel on French trains. There are some restrictions though: travel cannot start between Noon Friday and Noon Saturday, from 15:00 Sunday to Noon Monday, and on certain holidays and periods of heavy train traffic. The Carte Vermeil Quatre Temps is valid for four rail trips within one year. The 1996 price of the card is 140 FF.

ONE DAY EXCURSIONS AND CITY TOURING

Here are 68 one-day round trip rail excursions that can be made comfortably from French cities, with return travel in most cases before dinner time. The comments provided on the major sites and events at each destination are designed to give travelers only a basic idea and a few suggestions of what to see. More specific guides are recommended for more in-depth and specialized discussion of these cities. Note that the number after the name of each route corresponds to the Thomas Cook Timetable of the same number.

Avignon

This walled city, the tourist capital of Province, can be entered through 14 different gates. You can obtain a city map or a personal guide at the Syndicat d'Initiative (41 Cours Jean-Jaurès). During the 14th century, Avignon was briefly the papal headquarters of the Roman Catholic Church when it was unsafe for a series of French popes to be in Rome. Take the one-hour tour of the Palace of the Popes, open daily January-March 09:00-12:45 and 14:00-18:00 April-late August 09:00-19:00 late August-September 09:00-20:00 October 09:00-19:00 November-December 09:00-12:45 and 14:00-18:00. Next to the Palace is the 12th century Cathedral of Notre-Dame-de-Doms. Outside the Palace you can board "Circuit #2" of a picturesque, 54-seater, trackless train pulled by a gasoline-powered locomotive that operates March through October, with daily departures every 15 minutes. This route is a climb to the top of a hill overlooking the Palace (a great view of the city and the Rhone Valley) and through the colorful Rocher Dom Gardens, where passengers can get off and return to the Palace by a later train. "Circuit #1" operates March through September and runs daily 10:00-19:00 for a 30-minute ride through the city's shopping streets and renovated old quarters. Initial boarding for this train (every 35 minutes) is at Palace Square. See the 13th to 16th century Italian-school religious paintings in the 14th century Petit Palais museum, open daily except Tuesday 9:30-11:30 and 14:00-18:00. Other medieval buildings worth seeing are the 12th century St. Ruff Church and the 14th century Gothic St. Didier Church. See the Roman sculptures and mosaics (some dating back 3,000 years) in the Lapidary Museum (housed in the 17th century Jesuit Church), open daily except Tuesday 10:00-11:55 and 14:00-18:00. Cross the Rhone River by walking or driving over the bridge to Villeneuve-les-Avignon and admire the view of Avignon from the other side of the river.

All-day bus tours from Avignon to many interesting places in this area can be taken from in front of the rail station. One tour includes Roman ruins at St. Remy, the village of Les Baux (sculptured during the Middle Ages from the top a stone hill), and the Roman theater in Arles. In nearby Orange, there is a Roman Triumphal Arch and an amphitheater built during the reign of Augustus. Don't forget that each summer in July and August Avignon hosts the most important theater festival in France. The population of the town multiply ten fold and its nearly impossible to find a room if you haven't booked in advance. But, the drama is excellent.

Bordeaux

Bordeaux turns its shoulders away from Paris and believes in its own supreme importance. A lively and wealthy port city, Bordeaux, of course, is one of the capitals of the French wine industry. Information about tours of the port and an excellent city map for making a walking tour of Bordeaux are available at the Tourist Office, 12 Cours du 30 Juillet. The opera, parks, hotels, Roman ruins and 18th century mansions are in the northern section of the city. Museums, churches and fine shops are in the southern part of Bordeaux. See the Maritime Museum, on the Quai de la Douane, the wonderful Louis XV houses on rue Fernand Philippart, and the modern stained-glass in the 14th century St. Michel Church on Place Dubourg. The view of Bordeaux from the top of that church's tower shouldn't be missed. The large 15th century bell tower, Grosse Cloche, the 13th century Gothic St. Andres Cathedral, and the Musée des Beaux Arts, open daily except Tuesday 10:00-12:00 and 14:00-18:00, are key sites. Many tourists admire the fans with mother of pearl, ivory and silver handles (plus Medieval furniture, costumes and ceramics) in the Musée des Arts Decoratifs (39 rue Bouffard), open daily except Tuesday 14:00-18:00.

Do not miss seeing the array of fruits, cheeses, wild game and many exotic foods at the market on Place des Grands Hommes. The fantastic carved plants and the swan boat in the Jardin Public provide an easy-going afternoon activity. The Maison des Vins at 1 Cours du 30 Juillet, where you can obtain information on visiting nearby famous wineries, is a useful stop. See the lovely 18th century Opera House, the Grand Theatre, the Museum of Painting and Sculpture, the Numismatic Museum, the Museum of Old Bordeaux, and the Bonie Museum of Far Eastern Art.

Lyon

France's culinary capital, Lyon, is second to Paris in size and importance in the country. Occasionally, two trains depart from the same track at Lyon's Perrache rail station standing in opposite directions. Be sure to stand at the correct end (North or South) of the track in order to board the train you want to ride. Check the departure signs at the underground passageway. Do not rely merely on a track number when departing from Perrache rail station!

Next to the North passageway of Track A is a take-out restaurant, handy for provisioning your trip. A metropolitan train connects Lyon's Brotteaux and Perrache rail stations. The ride is 15 minutes.

If you try to keep from eating at the spectacular Nouvelle Les Halles food market: 65 tantalizing stalls of meat, poultry, fish, produce, cheese, bread, pastry, coffee, tea, spices, wine and candy, you are certain to fail. Too tempting. Open 07:00-19:00 Monday-Saturday and 07:00-12:00 on Sunday. Here, you can buy pheasants in plumage, partridges, wild ducks, quail, snipe, frog legs, four varieties of oysters, shrimp, eel, cod and sole. There are goose, duck and game patés. Do not fail to sample the three Lyon specialties: Morteau de Jesu (pork meat in a pig's foot casing), the peppery pink and white salami, and the garlicky Lyon sausage. The wine here is magnificent. It has been said that Lyon has three rivers: the Rhone, the Saone, and the Beaujolais. You are in Burgundy country.

Stroll for a few hours through the winding streets of the three-block wide half-mile long ancient section (Vieux Lyon) and see the magnificent 15th century Renaissance mansions. Much information is available in the booklet Guide du Vieux Lyon sold everywhere in the city. Take the funicular to the 19th century Basilica of Notre Dame de la Fourviere to see the extraordinary mosaics on its floors, walls and nave. The view from either the terrace behind it or from the observatory above it is marvelous. Then walk downhill to the Gallo Roman Museum (open daily except Monday and Tuesday 09:30-12:00 and 14:00-18:00), built into the side of a hill next to several Roman ruins. Its exhibits include objects from prehistory to the end of the Roman Empire, as well as elaborate floor mosaics and scale models of ancient Lyons. Walking further downhill brings you to the Cathedral of St. Jean, which has 13th century stained glass and a 500-year-old astrological clock that performs a tableau at 12:00, 13:00, 14:00 and 15:00. The exhibits in the History Museum at the nearby Palais Gadagne cover the period from where the Gallo Roman Museum leaves off, including carved Renaissance furniture, prints, Nevers glazed pottery, and documents from the French Revolution. The adjoining Puppet Museum at 10-14 rue de Gadagne, honors Laurent Mourguet, a destitute weaver who, in seeking to attract customers with a puppet show, invented the character Guignol, whose name has come to symbolize children's afternoon puppet theater everywhere in France. Both museums are open daily except Tuesday 10:45-18:00.

In the more modern area of the city, grab the Bus #13 from the rail station, through the main shopping streets, to the Place de la Croix Rousse and then proceed by foot to Place des Terreaux to see the 17th century City Hall, the 19th century Opera House and The Fine Arts Museum. This museum, featuring works of Rodin, Renoir, Gauguin, Monet, Delacroix, Courbet and Corot, is open daily except Monday and Tuesday 10:30-18:00. Do not miss the Italian fountain with its four bronze horses, sculptured by the same Bartholdi who created the Statue of Liberty. The Musée des Tissus (34 rue de la Charite), open daily except Monday 10:00-17:30, houses a nearly 2,000-year-old collection of Oriental and European silks and velvets. It displays Persian carpets hung in a room that is 28-feet high. Next door, there is a fine collection of silver objects, kitchen utensils, Louis XIV furniture, tapestries and enamels in The Museum of Decorative Arts, open daily except Monday 10:00-12:00 and 14:00-17:30. Visit The Museum of Printing and Banking (13 rue de la Poullaillerie), open daily except Monday and Tuesday 09:30-12:00 and 14:00-18:00, and The Museum of Medicine in Hotel-Dieu on rue de l'Hopital, closed Monday. And, certainly treat yourself to a full and leisurely Lyonnais lunch and dinner.

Marseilles

If scenes from The French Connection flutter to mind, you'd not be wholly wrong. Marseilles is a Mediterranean sea port with a strong flavor of North Africa, Italy, and the middle East. Yet it can only be French. Enjoy the sun, the pastis, the mixture of southern laziness and Latin fervor. There are plenty of fancy shops on Canebiere, the main street. Visit the dungeon from which Monte Cristo escaped, at Chateau d'If, reached by launch from the Quai des Belges. Most of the museums in Marseilles are closed Tuesday. The Maritime Museum, on the ground floor of the Palais de la Bourse (Stock Exchange), the Fine Arts Museum and Natural History Museum in the Palais de Longchamps, the Roman Docks Museum, the Museum of Old Marseilles, the Museum of Mediterranean Archaeology, and the Lapidary Museum, both in the Park of Borely. There are fine views of the harbor from Fort St. Jean and Fort St. Nicolas. Don't neglect just sitting out on a terrace and ordering a Ricard with ice and watching the people as you eat olives. This is the south of France.

Nice

Aside from being France's retirement enclave, Nice has lots to offer travelers. See the price-less antiques, lavish carpets and exceptional paintings and sculptures in the Hotel Negresco at 37 Promenade des Anglais, the long and delightful avenue that follows the sea. Hotels and out-door restaurants dot the wide boulevards. The Jules Cheret Museum of Fine Arts, 33 Avenue des Baumettes (behind the Promenade des Anglais), has many of Cheret's paintings. The Matisse Museum, 164 Avenue des Arenes, has guided tours in English. Note that most of the museums in Nice are closed either Monday or Tuesday.

Visits might also want to take in the War Memorial. The view of the Bay of Angels from the Naval Museum, and the Bellanda Tower are memorable things to see. The Marc Chagall National Museum, a short walk down the hill from the Arenes station, the Roman Baths, the Terra Amata Prehistory Museum, and the 15,000 species of seashells at the Musée Inter-nationale de Malacologie are definitely worth your time. Take the lift to the Colline du Cha-teau fortress ruins. One drawback about the Nice area and the famed Cote d'Azur is the nerve-raacking traffic in the summer months.

Try the Nicoise cuisine: pissaladiere (the local pizza), socca (a pancake), ratatouile (sau-teed eggplant, onions, tomatoes and squash), le poulet farci aux figues (roast chicken stuffed with fresh figs), and of course salade nicoise.

Paris

For travelers arriving in Paris for the first time, a more in depth guide book is advised. Paris is one of the few destinations on earth that continues to mesmerize visitors. The myths that Paris generate are all true. Paris enchants and it annoys, it fulfills all expectations, and it demands that you return. It is welcoming and it is cold. It is a city to fall in love in and a city that nur-tures melancholia.

As for getting around, the city is particularly fortunate in that its famous Métro is ubiqui-tous. There is virtually nowhere you can't get to by metro, and the prices are reasonable. Buy a day pass or a three day pass if you plan to stay for a short time and use the metro a lot. Otherwise, a carnet of 10 metro tickets are about half the price of buying one ticket at a time (7 FF). There is also an elaborate commuter rail service called the RER, which serves both major airports approximately every 15 minutes (05:00-24:00) in both directions: From the Gare de Nord rail station north to Roissy Aeroport/Charles de Gaulle (26 minutes), and from Gare de Nord rail station south to Antony, where one picks up the OrlyVal train to Aeroport d'Orly (23 minutes). For a more detailed discussion of Paris and its transportation, consult *Paris Inside Out* (Houghton-Mifflin, 1995).

Paris Train Stations and the Directions They Serve

(Always double-check the station for any departure from Paris!)

Gare du Nord: Serves the north, including the Channel ports, where trains connect with ferries and hover crafts from Britain; also services Belgium, Holland and the Scandinavian countries.

Gare de l'Est: Serves the east, Nancy and Strasbourg, and Germany and eastern Europe, including ex-Yugoslavia and Moscow. (The former Paris-Frankfurt train now continues to Leipzig.)

Gare d'Austerlitz: Serves the southwest; Bordeaux, Toulouse, and Spain and Portugal via Orleans, Tours, Poitiers and Angouleme.

Gare St. Lazare: Serves Normandy and boat trains to/from Dieppe.

Gare Montparnasse: Serves western France, especially Brittany.

Gare de Lyon: Serves southwestern France, Switzerland, Italy and Greece.

Bus service connects these Paris rail stations:

Between Gare Austerlitz and Gare de l'Est, Gare du Nord and Gare Saint Lazare, Gare de Lyon and Gare de l'Est, Gare du Nord and Gare Saint Lazare, Gare du Nord and Gare de Lyon and Gare Austerlitz, Gare de l'Est and Austerlitz, Gare du Nord and Gare Saint Lazare.

Cultural Sightseeing

Here are a few basic idea of things to see in Paris. Use this list simply as a jumping off point.

• Musée d'Orsay, the converted train station on the Left Bank which served the Paris-Orleans line in the 19th century and became a museum in 1987, now houses much of the impressionists and early 20th century French collection, and should excite train travelers and art lovers alike. Its main attractions: works by Monet, Van Gogh, Renoir, Pissarro. A great place to start your Parisian visit.

• Louvre (open Monday and Wednesday 09:00-21:45, Thursday-Sunday 09:00-18:00). The Pyramid, designed by I.M. Pei has modernized the feel of this classic world-important museum. New wings opened in 1994.

• Montmartre area and the stunning Sacre Coeur church. Do this at night.

• Eiffel Tower, which needs no introduction.

• The obelisk at Place de la Concorde where Marie Antoinette was guillotined. • Arch of Triumph, from which an excellent rooftop view of Paris can be experienced. At the top of the Champs-Elysée.

• Grande Arch at La Defénse.

• Stained-glass windows at St. Chapelle.

• Deportation Monument behind Notre Dame Cathedral.

• Luxembourg Gardens. Go for a stroll or a jog or a pony ride. Paris at its most Parisian.

• Pompidou Center (closed Tuesday). France's most significant cultural center, library, and public meeting place.

• Musée of the Renaissance in the 16th century Chateau d'Ecouen Castle, with its antique tapestries, ceramics, arms, furniture, outstanding carved white fireplace and painted ceilings.

• Orangerie Museum, with its 150 works of impressionist painters including Renoir, Matisse, Cezanne, Picasso and Utrillo.

• Les Invalides and its Army Museum, where the preserved body of Napoleon is on exhibit. Enormous collection of uniforms, weapons, war trophies, flags, books, manuscripts and paintings. And, the Eglise du Dome (containing Napoleon's Tomb). Open daily 10:00-18:00 April-September and 10:00-17:00 October-March. A fine sound-and-light show is presented nightly, April-September.

• Rodin Museum, at Hotel Biron, closed Tuesday. The gardens are delightful. Don't miss "The Thinker." The Rodin Museum, 77 rue de Varenne, is open daily except Tuesday 10:00-17:00. (Visitors are not admitted after 16:30.)

• Tour Montparnasse offers an excellent view of Paris from its 650-foot high observation deck.

• Flower markets on the Ile de la Cite, the rue de Buci, and rue Mouffetard in the Latin Quarter

• Flea Markets (marché aux puces) on Saturdays, Sundays, and Mondays at Porte de Clignancourt, Porte de Vanves, and Porte de Montreuil.

• Eugene Delacroix Museum, 6 Place Furstenberg, is open daily except Tuesday 09:45-17:15.

• Jewish Art Museum, 42 rue des Saules, is open Monday-Thursday 15:00-18:00. The collection of naive art in the Le Halle St. Pierre Museum, 1 rue Ronsard, can be viewed daily 10:00-18:00.

• Museum of Mechanical Musical Instruments at Impasse Berthaud, open Saturdays, Sundays and holidays 14:00-19:00. Exhibit of 19th century player pianos, violins and banjos

• The Tobacco Museum, 12 rue Surcouf, is open daily except Sunday 11:00-18:00.

• The Pasteur Museum, 25 rue du Docteur-Roux, is open daily except Saturdays, Sundays and holidays 14:00-17:30.

• Honoré de Balzac Museum, 47 rue Raynouard, is open daily except Mondays and holidays 10:00-17:40.

• Galerie des Monnaies, Medailles et Antiques (in the National Library at 58 rue de Richelieu) there are exhibits from its collection of 400,000 historic coins.

• Other noteworthy museums include the Musée de la Mode et du Costume, 10 Ave. Pierre Premier de Serbie, the Archaeological Museum, electronic exhibits at the Musée Branly, Chinese and Japanese artifacts at the Musée Dennery, the Museum of French Bread, the Museum of Police History, the Musical Instruments Museum, the large poster collection in the Musée de l'Affiche et la Publicité (at the Decorative Arts Museum, 107 rue de Rivoli). 17th and 18th century furniture in the Musée Carnavalet, 23 rue de Sevigne, open daily except Monday 10:00-17:40. For flea market enthusiasts, check out the Marchés aux Puces at Porte de Clignancourt and Porte de Montreuil.

Other Attractions

• The Marais district, the oldest section of Paris, a maze of narrow 16th century streets, should not be overlooked. It can be examined by starting at the Pompidou Center and walking along rue Rambuteau to rue des Francs-Bourgeois, a street named in the 15th century, describing its poor residents who were exempt from paying taxes. Interesting documents (the order sending Marie Antoinette to the guillotine, the 1944 law giving French women the right to vote, etc.) can be seen in the History of France Museum at 60 rue des Francs-Bourgeois, open daily except Tuesdays and holidays 14:00-17:00.

Among the many elegant town mansions (called hotels in the 15th century) worth seeing in the Marais are Hotel d'Albret, Hotel de Fourcy, and Hotel de Lamignon (all on rue des Francs-Bourgeois). Then take note of the Hotel Merle and Hotel de Chatillon (along rue Payenne), and follow the signs leading to the Hotel Sale on rue de Thorigny, which housed in great elegance and perfect sophistication the Picasso Museum, open Wednesday 10:00-22:00, Thursday-Monday 10:00-17:15. There is an extraordinary collection of stuffed animals, furniture carved with animal figures, and silver encrusted riffles at the Hunting and Nature Museum, in the Hotel Gueneguad at 60 rue des Archives, open daily except Mondays and holidays 10:00-17:30. By walking down rue du Parc Royal, you pass the pink and white Hotel Duret de Chevry. Turn right to go down rue de Sevigne so as to pass by Hotel Le Peletier St. Fargeau and Hotel Carnavalet, now the Museum of French Interior design, open daily except Monday 10:00-17:40. Then visit the Maison de Victor Hugo (6 Place des Vosges), situated in the corner of one of Paris's most charming and elegant old world squares, open daily except Mondays and holidays 10:00-17:40. Next, walk down rue de Birague and onto rue St. Antoine in order to see Hotel Sully (at Number 62). By walking rue Mahler until it reaches rue des Rosiers, you arrive at the center of the Jewish district and the most famous delicatessen in Paris, Jo Goldbergs, at Number 7. Don't miss Chez Marianne, slightly further down the rue des Rossiers, for it is here that you'll experience the soul (and Tunisian deli delights) of the neighborhood, under the welcoming acceuil of owners Marianne and her philosopher/poet/grocer husband André. Nearby is the unusual Art Deco synagogue on the rue Pavee. The rue Simon-le-Franc will lead you back to the Pompidou Center.

• At the 14-acre Pere Lachaise Cemetery are the graves of Edith Piaf, Gertrude Stein, Alice B. Toklas, Colette, Sarah Bernhardt, Isadora Duncan, Simone Signoret, Frederick Chopin, Oscar Wilde, Honore de Balzac, Ferdinand de Lesseps (promoter of the Suez Canal), and Jean Francois Champollion (interpreter of the Rosetta stone). Upstaging them all though is the cult hangout and graffiti-sprawled grave of myth-making rock star Jim Morrison, who came to Paris to attempt to become an obscure philosophical poet and died there in 1971. Opened in 1804, it is the oldest of the four main cemeteries in Paris. It is open mid-March to mid-November Monday-Saturday 07:30-18:00, the rest of the year 08:30-17:30. On Sundays and holidays: mid-November to mid-January 09:00-18:00, the rest of the year 08:30-17:30. Other cemeteries of note include Montparnasse cemetery in which such notables as Jean-Paul Sartre, Simone de Beauvoir, and Samuel Beckett rest in peace.

• For the recreation-minded traveler, Paris offers some prime swimming pools. Swimmers can chose from a wide variety of pools in this city. The 50-meter Piscine Georges-Vallerey, located next to the Porte des Lilas metro station. built for the 1924 Olympic Games, has a transparent roof that is opened in sunny weather. The underground Piscine Suzanne Berlioux at Les Halles, near the Pompidou Center, is another modern 50-meter facility. Aquaboulevard de Paris is an indoor-outdoor amusement park (sand beaches, wave machines, slides. toboggans, mock tropical islands and lagoons) is near the metro Balard. The former Piscine Pontoise re-opened after renovations in 1990 with the new name Piscine du Quartier Latin. The famous Piscine Deligny located on a moored barge on the Left Bank of the Seine, burned down in 1993 and has yet to be restored. Joggers can practice their habit in the Jardin du Luxembourg, Parc Monceau, or—although on the edges of town—the expansive and verdant Bois de Vincennes or Bois de Boulogne, which doubles up after dark as a commercial meeting grounds for amorous encounters of every sort.

• As for cuisine, not only is Paris a feast of fine dining, its gourmet shops have the power of overwhelming visitors with the elegance and beauty of its window presentations. The prices will send you spinning, but there's no charge to look. The most famous of these fine shops is Fauchon on the Place de la Madeleine and its neighbor Hediard. Across the Place is La Maison de Truffe (19 Place de la Madeleine), where truffles, foie gras and caviar are the rule, and next door you'll be amazed by the Creplet-Brussol fromagerie featuring a cool 250 varieties of cheeses. Caviar Kaspia hosts fine caviar from Iran and Russia, with the Marquise de Sevigne specializing in sinfully rich and stunning fine chocolates for nearly 100 years. All this on Place de la Madeleine, which houses as well a kiosque for same-day half price theater tickets.

For additional information on Paris and its surroundings contact:
Office du Tourisme et des Congrès de Paris
127, av des Champs-Elysées
75008 PARIS
Tel: 49.52.53.54
Fax: 49.52.53.00

Strasbourg

An historical pawn, Strasbourg was French until 1872. German 1871-1918, French 1918-1940, German 1940-1944, and has been French since 1944. Currently the seat of the European parliment, Strasbourg has gained continental importance over the last ten years. On rue de la Rape, visitors can observe the city's majestic 13th century Cathedral of Notre-Dame. All of its windows are 12th, 13th and 14th century stained-glass. Its famous 60-foot high astronomical clock, which calculates eclipses, sunrises and sunsets into eternity, comes alive on the hour and quarter-hour, when figures appear from and return into its interior. The clock's major performance is at 12:30. It is then that the Four Ages of Man pass before Death, and the 12 Apostles move past the figure of Jesus. As he blesses them, a mechanical rooster flaps its wings and crows three times.

There is an extraordinary view of the city from a platform 217 feet above street level, at the top of the Cathedral's 328-step spiral staircase. From April-September, a fabulous sound-and-light show is presented inside the Cathedral: illuminated stained-glass windows, bells tolling, organ music, the whole works for an enchanting Alsatian evening.

There are three fine museums in the 18th century Chateau des Rohans (next to the Cathedral): a collection of Monet, Renoir, El Greco, Goya and Tintoretto in the Art Gallery; the relics in the Archaeological Museum; and a display of clocks, ironwork, earthenware and porcelain in the Museum of Decorative Arts. More recently, Strasbourg opened up a new museum of contemporary works.

Next to the Rohans is a 14th century building that houses wonderful 11th to 17th century Alsatian art in the Musée de lOeuvre Notre-Dame. Next to it is the Modern Art Museum. All of these museums are open daily except Tuesday 10:00-12:00 and 14:00-18:00.

You might want to take the one-hour sightseeing mini-train ride that starts at the south side of the Cathedral. It runs every half-hour, late March to the end of October. There are also cruises on the Rhine (90 minutes, three hours, and 11 hours) starting in front of the Palais des Rohans, and nearby Musée Alsacien, 23 Quai St. Nicholas, which houses impressive rooms dating from the early 17th century (furnished with marvelous utensils, stoves, wooden molds and pottery from the same era).

In all cases, treat yourself to a choucroute garni, an elaborate and copious Alsatian dish of sauerkraut, sausage, potatoes, and pork. Order an Alsatian white wine and you'll never regret stopping in Strasbourg.

Tours

Although much of the old city was destroyed in the 1944 bombings, Tour is worth a stop. One option is to take a 90-minute walk by departing the Tours rail station along Boulevard Heurteloup to rue Nationale, then turning right and going up one side of rue Nationale to the bridge that stretches over the Loire, and by returning along the opposite side of rue Nationale, crossing Boulevard Heurteloup, going one block further, turning left onto rue de Bordeaux, and following it directly back to the rail station. This will give you a fine overview of the city. Stop in and see the fine collection of paintings in the Musée des Beaux-Arts.

A pamphlet called "The Loire Valley by Train" may be obtained from the information desk at many French rail stations. It shows schedules of trains from Tours (not provided in Cook) that stop at stations near 12 different castles. The train to Azay-le-Rideau continues to Chinon. Another train goes to Amboise, Chaumont (Onzain), Blois and Beaugency. A third goes to Villandry (Savonnieres), Langeais, Samur and Angers. A fourth train goes to Loches and a fifth goes to Chenonceaux. These train rides range from 10 to 70 minutes in each direction. Most are less than 30 minutes. There are also bus tours from Tours to the castles.

TIMETABLES

In the following tables, when cities host more than one rail station, the name of the particular station has been designated in parentheses after the name of the city. Don't assume that the station from where you depart is the same as the station where you arrived. Doing so may cause you to miss your train.

Note: Renovation of Paris's Gare du Nord was completed in late 1993. Now it serves two functions: one station handles all long-distance trains (including TGVs) servicing Lille and the northern regions of France. The other, exclusively designed for traffic to the Channel Tunnel, includes a duty-free area and a customs baggage check for passengers traveling to Great Britain.

Avignon - Antibes - Avignon   79

Dep. Avignon	04:44 (1)	05:14 (2)	Dep. Antibes	20:08 (3)	20:23 (4)
Arr. Antibes	08:55	09:21	Arr. Avignon	00:05	00:04

(1) Runs daily, except Friday and Saturday. (2) Runs Friday and Saturday. (3) Runs daily, except Saturday and Sunday. (4) Runs Saturday and Sunday.

Sights in **Antibes**: The exhibit of 231 Picasso paintings at the special Picasso Museum in Grimaldi Castle, on Place Mariejol. Open daily except Tuesday 10:00–12:00 and 15:00–18:00.

Avignon - Arles - Avignon   151

Dep. Avignon	08:05 (1)	09:51	12:08	15:06
Arr. Arles	20 minutes later			

Sights in **Arles**: The ancient Roman cemetery, Alyscamps, that contains 400,000 sarcophagi, hand-carved granite caskets. The 21,000-seat Roman arena (open 08:30-19:00 in Summer, 09:00-12:00 and 14:00-18:00 the rest of the year). The museum of Pagan Art, in St. Anne Church on Place de la Republique (open 09:00-12:30 and 14:00-19:00 in Summer, 10:00-12:30 and 14:00-17:30 the rest of the year). The Roman Theater, open 08:30-12:00 and 14:00-18:00. The Forum, built during Augustus' rule. The Thermae, from Constantine's era. The 12th century Cloister in the marvelous Romanesque Church of Saint-Trophime.

Dep. Arles	12:05	13:36 (2)	14:46	17:53	20:13	22:33 (3)
Arr. Avignon	20 minutes later					

(1) Runs daily except Sundays and holidays. (2) Runs Monday-Friday, except holidays. (3) Second-class.

Avignon - Lyon - Avignon   151

Dep. Avignon	06:53	07:39 (1)	08:04 (2)	10:39
Arr. Lyon (Part Dieu)	09:02	09:26	10:18	12:44

Dep. Lyon (Part Dieu)	14:05 (3)	17:17 (3)	18:44 (3)	19:00 (4+6)
Arr. Avignon	16:01	19:17	20:41	20:49

(1) Operates late August to early July. Runs Monday-Friday, except holidays. TGV. Reservation required. Supplement charged. Light refreshments. (2) Runs daily, except Sundays and holidays. (3) Light refresh-

ments. (4) TGV. Reservation required. Supplement charged. Restaurant car. (5) Operates September through June. Runs daily, except Saturday. TGV. Reservation required. Supplement charged. Restaurant car. (6) Plus other departures from Lyon at 20:20 (3), 22:03 (5) and 23:43, arriving Avignon 23:09, 23:56 and 01:41.

Avignon - Marseille - Avignon   151

Dep. Avignon	08:05 (1)	09:51	10:52 (2)	11:45 (4)	12:08
Arr. Marseille (St. Ch.)	50–60 minutes later				

Dep. Marseille (St. Ch.)	14:01 (3)	14:39 (3)	16:50 (4)	17:10 (3)	17:31 (4)
Arr. Avignon	50–60 minutes later				

Dep. Marseille (St. Ch.)	18:17 (5)	19:25 (3)	21:45 (6)	22:59 (6)	23:21 (6)
Arr. Avignon	50–60 minutes later			

(1) Runs daily, except Sundays and holidays. (2) Runs Monday–Friday, except holidays. TGV. Reservation required. Supplement charged. Restaurant car. (3) Light refreshments. (4) TGV. Reservation required. Supplement charged. Restaurant car. (5) Runs daily, except Saturday. TGV. Reservation required. Supplement charged. Restaurant car. (6) Second-class.

Avignon - Monaco (Monte Carlo) - Avignon

151				*164*	
Dep. Avignon	08:05 (1)	09:51		Dep. Monaco	19:29
Arr. Marseille	09:06	10:54		Arr. Nice	19:46
Change trains. 164				*No train change.*	
Dep. Marseille	09:18	11:04		Dep Nice	20:00
Arr. Nice	11:43	13:36		Arr. Marseille	22:41
Change trains.				*Change trains. 151*	
Dep. Nice	11:57	14:15		Dep. Marseille	22:59
Arr. Monaco	12:13	14:34		Arr. Avignon	00:05

(1) Runs daily, except Sundays and holidays. (2) Second-class.

Avignon - Nimes - Avignon   163

Dep. Avignon	07:35 (8)	11:00	11:48 (1)	12:17 (2)	14:13
Arr. Nimes	25 minutes later				

Sights in **Nimes:** Many Roman ruins in excellent condition, such as the 1st century amphitheater (seating 24,000 people) in the center of the city, used in recent years for bullfights to entertain Spanish migrant workers. The construction of the arena was done by fitting large stones together without the use of mortar. The Arena is open 08:00-19:00 in Summer, 09:00-12:00 and 14:00-17:00 the rest of the year. Also see the beautiful 1st century rectangular temple, Maison Carree, and its collection of Roman sculptures, open 09:00-20:00 in Summer, 09:00-12:00 and 14:00-18:00 the rest of the year. The view of Nimes from the oldest Roman building, Tour Magne, on a hill outside the city. A few miles away is the enormous Pont du Gard Roman aqueduct. Visit the collection of Iron Age and Roman objects in the Archaeological Museum. Stroll through the 18th century Garden of the Fountain.

Dep. Nimes	11:55	12:47(1)	13:29 (3)	14:29 (1)	15:05	15:39 (4)
Arr. Avignon	25 minutes later					
Dep. Nimes	16:28 (5)	17:44	18:29	20:29 (5)	23:02 (7)	
Arr. Avignon	25 minutes later					

(1) TGV. Reservation required. Supplement charged. Light refreshments. (2) Runs daily, except Sundays and holidays. Light refresments. (3) Runs daily, except Sundays and holidays. (4) Runs Monday-Thursday. (5) Runs Monday-Friday, except holidays. (6) Runs daily, except Saturday. (7) Second-class. (8) Sunday only

Avignon - Orange - Avignon   151

Dep. Avignon	08:04	10:27	12:29	14:05	15:07
Arr. Orange	15 minutes later				

Sights in **Orange**: See the 10,000-seat Roman Theater (open 09:00-18:30 in Summer, 09:00-12:00 and 13:00-17:00 the rest of the year) and the ancient walls of the old city. The Roman Triumphal Arch.

Dep. Orange	11:51	14:48	15:55	17:21 (1)	19:40 (2)	21:04 (3)
Arr. Avignon	15 minutes later					

(1) Runs Monday–Friday, except holidays. (2) Runs daily, except Saturday. (3) Runs daily, except Fridays.

Bordeaux - Bayonne and Biarritz - Bordeaux   137

Dep. Bordeaux (St. Jean)	07:24	10:33 (1)	11:14 (1+2)	13:08 (1)
Arr. Bayonne	09:13	12:05	13:50 (3)	14:37
Arr. Biarritz	10 minutes after arriving Bayonne.			

Sights in **Bayonne**: This is the Cote Basque's leading port and private yacht harbor. Visit the cathedral, The Basque Museum, Chateau-Viex, The Museum Bonnat. Exhibits tracing Basque history and customs (farm tools, household objects, costumes) are in the Musee Basque, at 1 Rue Marengo.

Sights in **Biarritz**: France's snootiest beach resort since 1854. Golf, tennis and every type of water sport are popular here. There are many spas offering thalassotherapy. See the food market. A small grocery store called Maison Arosteguy stocks 120 types of Scotch whiskey and what has been described as "a dizzying array" of Armagnacs.

Dep. Biarritz	14:50 (1)	17:47 (1+2)	18:02 (4)	18:39 (2)	20:23 (4)
Dep. Bayonne	10 minutes after departing Biarritz.				
Arr. Bordeaux (St. Jean)	16:35	19:36	20:30	21:20	22:46

(1) TGV. Reservation required. Supplement charged. Light refreshments. (2) Runs daily, except Sundays and holidays. (3) Change trains in Bayonne. (4) Runs Sunday only. (5) Operates early July to late August. (6) Plus other departures from Biarritz at and 23:24 (5), arriving Bordeaux 01:57.

Bordeaux - Carcassonne - Bordeaux   139

Bordeaux (St. Jean)	06:39 (1)	08:23 (2)	11:47 (1)
Arr. Carcassonne	09:50	12:17	14:59

Sights in **Carcassonne:** The most interesting walled city (actually double-walled) in France and Europe's best preserved relic of the Middle Ages. The inner wall, built by the Romans in the 2nd century, bears 29 towers. The 13th century French outer wall has 17 towers and barbicans (fortified castles). It is a 30-minute walk from the railstation to the walled city. There is both bus and taxi service.

Nearby are the ruins of 5 other walls, to the South, erected by France in medieval days as additional protection from attack by the Spaniards. As you stand on the walkways at the top of the French wall, it is easy to imagine yourself shooting arrows through the narrow slits or dropping hot oil on the marauders below.

See the Narbonnaise Gate and drawbridge. Nearby is a bust of Dame Carcas, for whom the city is named. Carcassonne had been under siege by Charlemagne. She gathered the little grain the starving people had and scattered it to livestock in view of the soldiers who were by then weary of the months they had been waiting for the people inside the impregnable walls to capitulate.

Her bold act convinced the soldiers that the people could last much longer, and Charlemagne abandoned his attempt to starve-out the town.

Inside the Basilica of St. Nazare are many stone carvings depicting scenes from the fort's history, magnificent stained-glass windows regarded by many as the finest in southern France, and the rectangular tombstone of Bishop Radulph. Also see the 12th century Countal Castle.

Dep. Carcassonne	15:52	17:52 (4)	20:17 (1)
Arr. Bordeaux (St. Jean)	19:04	21:53	23:35

(1) Light Refreshments. (2) Light refreshments. Change trains in Toulouse (arr. 11:04–dep. 11:29). (3) Operates early September to early July. Change trains in Toulouse (arr. 18:36–dep. 19:16). Light refreshments Toulouse-Bordeaux. (4) Operates early July to early September. Change trains in Toulouse (Arr. 18:36-dep 19:16). Light refreshments Toulouse-Bordeaux.

Bordeaux - Limoges - Bordeaux   140

Dep. Bordeaux (St. Jean)	06:16 (1)	07:47 (2)	10:30 (3)	12:00
Arr. Limoges	08:30	10:39	13:59	14:34

Sights in **Limoges**: Tours of the famous porcelain and enamel factories are free, by applying to the Syndicat de la Porcelain, 7 Rue du General Cerez. Visit the Adrien Dubouche Museum, with its great collection of ceramics. The Municipal Museum, to see its display of china made in Limoges from the 12th century to the present. The Cathedral of Saint Etienne.

Dep. Limoges	14:39 (4)	17:37 (5)	21:05 (6)
Arr. Bordeaux (St. Jean)	17:37	20:34	23:23

(1) Operates early July to late August. (2) Runs daily except Sundays and holidays. Change trains in Perigueux (arr. 09:05–dep. 09:31). (3) Change trains in Perigueux (arr. 11:56–dep. 12:39). (4) Operates late August to early July. Runs daily, except Sundays and holidays. (5) Change trains in Perigueux (arr. 18:55–dep. 19:15). (6) Light refreshments.

Bordeaux - Lourdes - Bordeaux   137

Dep. Bordeaux (St. Jean)	07:24 (1)	11:06 (2)	13:12 (3)	17:06 (4)	19:05 (11)
Arr. Lourdes	10:17	13:32	15:53	19:25	21:49

Sights in **Lourdes**: A 14-year-old girl, Bernadette Soubirous, had numerous visions here in 1858, in the Massabielle grotto. The underground spring in the grotto is believed by many to have miraculous qualities. About 3,000,000 people come here every year, many of them disabled or diseased and hoping to be cured.

The immense underground church seating 20,000 was inaugurated in 1958.

On the other side of the torrent called Gave de Pau there is an interesting 14th century castle which was used as a prison from 1643 until the early 19th century.

Dep. Lourdes	15:02	16:44 (5)	17:40 (6)	19:00 (7)	19:40 (8+10)
Arr. Bordeaux (St. Jean)	17:27 (4)	19:36	20:04	22:05	22:46

(1) Operates early July–late August. (2) TGV. Reservation required. Supplement charged. Runs Monday-Friday except holidays. Light refreshments. (3) Light refreshments. (4) TGV. Reservation required. Supplement charged. Light refreshments. Runs daily except Friday and Sunday. (5) Runs daily, except Sun. and holidays. Change trains in Dax (arr. 18:12–dep. 18:29). (6) TGV. Reservation required. Supplement charged. Runs Sun. only. Light refreshments. (7) Runs daily. (8) Runs Sun. only. (9) Plus another Bordeaux departure at 20:53 (4), arriving Lourdes 23:22. (10) Plus another Lourdes departure at 22:52, arriving Bordeaux 01:57. For those overnighting in Lourdes, there are other departures from Lourdes at 07:52 (4), 10:21 (3) and 11:20 (3). (11) TGV runs Friday only.

Bordeaux - Nantes - Bordeaux   134

Dep.Bordeaux (St. J.)	06:53	10:27 (1)
Arr. Nantes	11:05	14:29

• • •

Dep. Nantes	13:51 (1)	18:13	19:35 (2)
Arr. Bordeaux (St. J.)	18:06	22:15	23:26

(1) Light refreshments. (2) Early July to early September: runs daily, except Friday. Early September to early July: runs Friday and Sunday.

Sights in **Nantes**: This was a commercial center under the Romans. The Normans pillaged the town in 834. After having been partly destroyed in World War II, its railway was placed underground.

This is an important seaport and shipbuilding center. See the extraordinary white marble Renaissance tomb of Francois II, duke of Brittany, in the Cathedral that was bombed during World War II. The church was restored, only to have its roof almost entirely destroyed by fire in 1972. The tomb was not harmed.

Tour the medieval castle that was rebuilt in 1466, Chateau des Ducs de Bretagne and its museums (entrance on the Rue des Etats). Guided tours are offered every half-hour, daily during July and August from 10:00–12:00 and 14:00–18:00. The rest of the year there are only 3 tours a day, and the castle is closed on Tuesday. The castle is surrounded by a moat and has a drawbridge at its entrance.

Visit the Jules Verne Museum (the author was born in Nantes in 1828), open daily except Tuesday 10:00–12:00 and 14:00–17:00. See the exceptional paintings in the Fine Arts Museum (10 Rue Georges Clemenceau), open daily except Tuesday and national holidays 10:00–12:00 and 13:00–17:45.

Stroll through the Passage Pommeraye, a decorative 3 level shopping arcade. Visit the Jardin des Plantes, a botanical garden and formal French park, with grottos, waterfalls, statues, ponds, 400 varieties of camelias, and 19th century greenhouses, containing many orchids.

There are 3-hour boat cruises on the **Erbe River**, leaving from 24 Quai de Versailles at 12:30 (Lunch), 14:30 and 20:00 (dinner).

Bordeaux - Narbonne - Bordeaux   139

All of these trains have light refreshments.

Dep. Bordeaux (St. Jean)	06:39	08:23 (1)	Dep. Narbonne	19:47
Arr. Narbonne	10:20	12:26	Arr. Bordeaux (St. Jean)	23:35

Sights in **Narbonne:** The Cloister adjacent to the Palace of the Archbishops. The choir of the incomplete Cathedral of Saint-Just.

(1) Change trains in Toulouse (arr. 11:04-dep. 11:13).

Bordeaux - Toulouse - Bordeaux   139

Dep. Bordeaux (St. Jean)	05:54 (1)	06:39 (2)	08:23 (2)	10:06 (3)	11:02 (4)
Arr. Toulouse (Matabiau)	08:49	08:57	11:04	12:12	13:01

Sights in **Toulouse:** The Basilica of Saint Sernin, displaying the remains of 128 saints, including 6 of the apostles and a thorn from the Crown of Thorns. It also has 7 extraordinary 11th century marble bas reliefs and the Meigeville Door, a 12th century sculpture of apostles watching Christ ascend to heaven surrounded by angels.

The museum on the history of art and an exceptional collection of busts of Roman emperors at Musee Saint Raymond on Place St. Sernin. The Roman and medieval sculptures in the Musee des Augustins, 21 Rue de Metz. The beautiful 14th century Church of the Jacobins.

Popular art of the region and the history of Toulouse, at the Musee du Vieux-Toulouse, 7 Rue du May.

Chinese, Japanese and Indian art at the Musee Georges Labit, 43 Rue des Martyrs de la Liberation. St. Etienne Cathedral. Two 16th century homes: Hotel de Bernuy and Hotel d'Assezat, and the view of the city from the tower of the latter.

The Office de Tourisme (Donjon du Capitole, Square Charles de Gaule, 31000 Toulouse) offered in 1992 a 2–hour walking tour at 09:30 and 15:00 for $7.50, as well as a $10 city bus tour at 15:00.

Obtain the tourist office's brochure describing 16 different one-day bus sightseeing excursions to nearby interesting places ($25.50 each in 1994). All of these trips start at 08:00 and arrive back in Toulouse between 19:00–20:30.

One of these tours goes to the 16th century Chateau de Saint-Genies-Bellevue; to Cordes, a 13th century walled town, to see marvelous Gothic houses and the quality arts and crafts sold at 14th Marketplace; to see more than 600 works of Toulouse-Lautrec in Albi, where he was born in 1864; then to Chateau de Latours for tasting Gaillac wine.

Every year, from the end of June to late September, both an international Piano Festival featuring noted soloists and a series of orchestral concerts (jazz to Beethoven) are presented in Toulouse.

Barges can be rented to tour the 17th century Canal du Midi all the way to the Mediterranean. Visitors can also rent motorboats and rowboats.

Dep. Toulouse (Matabiau)	13:46 (5)	16:24 (4)	16:48	17:17 (6)	19:16 (2+7)
Arr. Bordeaux (St. Jean)	15:55	18:24	19:04	19:25	21:53

(1) Runs daily, except Sundays and holidays. (2) Light refreshments. (3) TGV. Reservation required. Supplement charged. Runs daily, except Sundays and holidays. Restaurant car. (4) Restaurant car. (5) TGV. Reservation required. Supplement charged. Light refreshments. (6) TGV. Reservation required. Supplement charged. Runs daily, except Saturday. Light refreshments. (7) Plus another departure from Toulouse at 21:14 (2), arriving Bordeaux 23:36.

Bordeaux - Tours - Bordeaux   136

All of the Bordeaux–St. Pierre-des-Corps and v.v. trains, are TGV, require a reservation, charge a supplement and have light refreshments, unless designated otherwise.

Dep. Bordeaux (St. Jean)	07:14	10:24 (1)
Arr. St. Pierre-des-Corps	09:40	12:57
Change trains (cross-platform).		
Dep. St. Pierre-des-Corps	09:43	13:06
Arr. Tours	09:51	13:08

Dep. Tours	14:43	16:13	19:37 (2)
Arr. St. Pierre-des-Corps	14:50	16:20	19:45
Change trains (cross platform).			
Dep. St. Pierre-des-Corps	14:54	16:23	19:47 (2)
Arr. Bordeaux (St. Jean)	17:25	18:53	22:22

(1) Change trains in Poitiers (arr. 12:05-dep. 12:11). (2) Runs daily, except Fri. Light refreshments.

Dijon - Beaune - Dijon   149

Dep. Dijon	07:40	09:04	11:17	11:30	12:11	14:40 (1)
Arr. Beaune	20 minutes later					

Sights in **Beaune**: The wine capital of Burgundy. Popular for its old houses along narrow, cobbled streets. Famous for Burgundian food: coq au vin, game birds, terines of veal and pork, snails, salamis, sausages, terines of salmon and sole. Hotels and restaurants here are booked months in advance.

Visit the many great wineries in this locale, such as Chateau de Meursault, Marche aux Vins and Maison Patriarche. Persuade your hotel to sell you $100 tickets to one of the 17 "grand dinners" at the Clos de Vougeot, sponsored by the Confrerie des Chevaliers de Taste-vin. See the priceless art collection in the 15th century Hotel-Dieu. The other attractions there are the 28 red-canopied and red-curtained beds that were used 5 centuries ago, the original 15th century furnishings in the 160-foot-long Paupers' Room, the ancient pharmacy and kitchen, fantastic tapestries and rare pewter.

See the 15th century tapestries in the Notre Dame Church.

Many hot-air balloon trips are available in this area.

Dep. Beaune	13:30 (1)	14:03 (2)	14:22 (3)	15:23	17:17	17:56 (1)	18:44 (5)
Arr. Dijon	20 minutes later						

(1) Runs daily, except Sun. and holidays. (2) Runs Sunday only. (3) Runs Mon.-Fri., except holidays. (4) Runs Sat., Sun. and holidays. (5) Plus other Beaune departures at 19:36 (3), 21:08 and 22:52.

Dijon - St. Claude - Dijon 157

Dep. Dijon	06:35 (1)	16:43		Dep. St. Claude	16:32 (2)	16:52 (1)
Arr. St. Claude	09:31	20:03		Arr. Dijon	18:32	19:49

(1) Runs daily, except Sundays and holidays. (2) Runs Sunday only. Change trains in Dole (arr. 17:49–dep. 18:06).

Sights in **St. Claude**: The 15 manufacturers of smoking pipes who are located here have made this "the pipe capital of France." They produce 1,600,000 briar pipes annually. A walk down Rue du Pre and its extension, Rue du Marche, takes you past many pipe shops to the Pipe Museum, at 1 Rue Gambetta, visited by 35,000 people June–September (the only months the museum is open), 09:30–11:30 and 14:00–19:00.

Across from the Pipe Museum is St. Claude's Cathedral.

The Genod factory, at 13 Fauborg Marcel, allows visitors daily except Saturdays, Sundays and holidays 09:30–11:30 and 14:00–18:00. One of the pipe shops, La Tabatiere at 8 Rue du Pre, has pipes ranging in price from $5 to $1,400.

Limoges - Les Eyzies de Tayac 138

Dep. Limoges	13:34		Dep. Les Eyzies	22:55
Arr. Les Eyzies	15:33		Arr. Limoges	01:00

Sights in **Les Eyzies de Tayac:** This is the prehistoric capital of Europe. The tourist information office and the famous cave paintings are a short walk from the railstation.

Lyon - Annecy - Lyon 167

En route, the train splits. Some cars go to Annecy, others to Grenoble. Be sure to sit in a car marked "Annecy" (pronounced Ahn-see).

Dep. Lyon (Part-Dieu)	06:59	09:09
Arr. Annecy	09:00	11:09

Sights in **Annecy**: This is a beautiful lake resort. See the 12th century Island Palace. The shops in the old quarter.

Dep. Annecy	12:39 (1)	15:57	17:11
Arr. Lyon (Part-Dieu)	14:38	18:11	19:20

(1) Light refreshments.

Lyon - Dijon - Lyon 149

Dep. Lyon (Perrache)	05:35	06:43 (2)	08:16	-0-	-0-
Dep. Lyon (Part-Dieu)	05:44 (1)	06:52	-0-	09:34	12:49
Arr. Dijon	07:30	08:35	10:32	11:15	14:32

Sights in **Dijon**: Town Hall, formerly the palace of those swashbuckling dukes of Burgundy and now one of the richest museums in France. The Church of Notre Dame. The 13th century Cathedral of St. Benigne archaeological museum. The Palace of Justice. The Magnin Museum. The 14th century Chartreuse de Champmol, with its famous chapel portrait and Moses Fountain. Rude Museum.

Don't fail to have lunch in Dijon, France's food and wine capital.

Dep. Dijon	12:17 (3)	15:44	16:57	19:14	20:43 (4+5)
Arr. Lyon (Part-Dieu)	14:01	17:44	18:40	20:57	22:26
Arr. Lyon (Perrache)	-0-	17:56	-0-	-0-	22:36

(1) Runs Monday–Friday, except holidays. (2) Runs daily, except Sundays and holidays. (3) Light refreshments. (4) Runs daily, except Saturday. (5) Plus another Dijon departure at 23:24 (runs Sunday only), arriving Lyon-Perrache 01:06.

Lyon - Geneva 159

There are many scenic canyons on this ride.

Dep. Lyon (Perrache)	07:30(1)	09:24(1)	12:13 (1)
Dep. Lyon (Part-Dieu)	07:39	09:33	12:23
Arr. Geneva (Cornavin)	09:38	11:26	14:16

Dep. Geneva (Cornavin)	16:30	19:29(1)	21:54(1)
Arr. Lyon (Part-Dieu)	18:18	21:25	23:39
Arr. Lyon (Perrache)	18:27	21:34	-0-

(1) Light refreshments.

Lyon - Grenoble - Lyon 154

| Dep. Lyon (Part-Dieu) | 07:05 (1) | 08:18 (2) | 10:12 | 12:12 | 14:14 |
| Arr. Grenoble | 08:23 | 09:40 | 11:43 | 13:35 | 15:30 |

Sights in **Grenoble**: The information office outside the railstation offers maps, guides and city bus tickets. See the monumental Calder sculpture at the railstation. The very rich (Utrillo, Picasso, Ruben) art museum in the 16th century Palace of Justice. The contemporary art museum's collection of Delaunay, Picasso, Matisse and many surrealists.

Fine paintings in the Musee des Beaux Arts at Place de Verdun (Corot, Renoir, Monet, Roualt, Picasso, Utrillo). The Stendahl Museum, devoted to Grenoble's native son and greatest writer, whose real name was Henri Beyle. The Museum of the Resistance, in the house where Stendahl was born on Rue Jean-Jacques Rousseau. At the Municipal Library, the "Catholicon" (printed by Gutenburg in 1460), Stendahl's manuscripts, and more historic papers.

The geometrical gardens and 3 fountains in Place Victor Hugo, Grenoble's prettiest square, locale of expensive shops and sidewalk cafes. The Natural History Museum, in the Jardine des Plantes. The 17th century Church of St. Laurent. The City Gardens.

Take the cable car ride up to Guy Pape Park for a marvelous view of the city below and the fields surrounding Grenoble. While at the top, visit the military museum in the 19th century fort, the Bastille, and the Auto Museum.

Walk back to Grenoble, downhill, through the Jardine des Dauphines.

Another walk on the way down leads to a collection of Alpine artificats from the past (antique cradles, beds, chests, backpacks, school rooms) at the Musee Dauphinois, in a 17th century cloister.

Dep. Grenoble	13:02	16:00	16:58	17:23	17:55 (4)
Arr. Lyon (Part-Dieu)	14:28	17:26	18:16	19:06 (3)	19:10
Dep. Grenoble	19:16	21:06	21:55 (5)		
Arr. Lyon (Part-Dieu)	20:44	22:54 (3)	23:24		

(1) Runs Monday–Friday, except holidays. (2) Runs daily, except Sundays and holidays. (3) Arrives at Lyon's Perrache railstation. (4) Runs daily, except Saturday. (5) Runs Monday-Friday except holidays July 11- August 26.

Lyon - Marseille - Lyon   151

Dep. Lyon (Perrache)	07:26	-0-(1)	09:59	12:04 (2)
Dep. Lyon (Part Dieu)	-0-	09:03	-0-	-0-
Arr. Marseille (St. Ch.)	10:54	11:46	13:08	15:00
Dep. Marseille (St. Ch.)	14:39	17:10 (2)	18:17 (3)	19:25 (6+7)
Arr. Lyon (Part Dieu)	17:38	20:38	21:07	23:02
Arr. Lyon (Perrache)	-0-	-0-	-0-	-0-

(1) TGV. Reservation required. Supplement charged. Runs Monday-Friday, except holidays. Restaurant car. (2) Light refreshments. (3) TGV. Reservation required. Supplement charged. Runs daily, except Saturdays and July 14, 15 and August 14. Restaurant car. (4) Second-class. (5) Arrives at Lyon's Perrache railstation. (6) Plus another Marseille departure at 21:45 (4), arriving Lyon 01:11 (5). (7) Runs daily except Firday. Light refreshments.

Lyon - Paris - Lyon 150

All of these trains are TGV, require reservation, charge a supplement and have a restaurant car or light refreshments.

Dep. Lyon (Per.)	05:39 (1)	06:19 (2)	06:46 (7)	07:49 (3)	08:45 (4)
Dep. Lyon (P-D)	05:50	06:30	06:57	08:00	09:00
Arr. Paris (Lyon)	08:06	08:34	08:59	10:10	11:02
Dep. Paris (Lyon)	14:00 (3)	15:00 (3)	16:49 (8)	17:00 (3)	17:27 (2+6)
Arr. Lyon (P-D)	16:02	17:00	18:57	19:02	19:31
Arr. Lyon (Per.)	16:17	17:10	-0-	19:12	-0-

(1) Runs Monday–Friday, except holidays. (2) Operates early September to early July. Runs Monday–Friday, except holidays. (3) Runs daily. (4) Runs daily, except Sundays and holidays. (5) Runs daily, except Saturday. (6) Plus other departures from Paris at 19:00 (3), 20:00 (3) and 21:00 (5), arriving Lyon (P-D) 21:04, 22:00 and 23:14. (7) Operates early September to early June. Runs Saturday only. (8) Runs Saturdays, Sundays and holidays.

Lyon - Tours - Lyon 128

Dep. Lyon (Perrache)	06:36 (1)	-0-
Dep. Lyon (Part-Dieu)	06:46	09:12 (2)
Arr. Tours	11:40	14:10
Dep. Tours	15:51 (2)	18:21 (3)
Arr. Lyon (Part-Dieu)	20:49	23:16
Arr. Lyon (Perrache)	20:59	23:25

(1) Runs Monday and Saturday only. (2) Light refreshments. (3) Runs Friday and Sunday. Light refreshments.

Lyon - Vienne - Lyon 151

Dep Lyon (Perrache)	07:26	12:31
Arr. Vienne	18 minutes later	

Sights in **Vienne**: Many good Roman ruins. The Temple of Augustus and Livia, a large amphitheater, and the pyramid which once marked the center of a Roman coliseum. Ancient jewels and bronze and ceramic relics on exhibit at the Museum of Fine Arts. Try to dine at one of the world's most famous restaurants, Pyramide, open daily except Tuesday and closed November through mid-December.

| Dep. Vienne | 14:06 | 16:55 | 17:52 | 18:32 (1) | 21:19 (2) | 22:30(3) |
| Arr. Lyon (Perrache) | | 18 minutes later | | | | |

(1) Runs Monday–Friday, except holidays. (2) Runs Sunday only. (3) Runs Friday only.

Marseille to Aix-en-Provence 166

| Dep. Marseille (St. Ch.) | 07:49 | 12:28 |
| Arr. Aix-en-Provence | 35-40 minutes later | |

Sights in **Aix-en-Provence**: See the remarkable Vasarely Museum and the 18th century quarter of the city.

| Dep. Aix-en-Provence | 11:34 | 16:23 | 20:44 |
| Arr. Marseille (St. Ch.) | 35-40 minutes later | | |

Marseille - Antibes - Marseille 164

| Dep. Marseille | 09:18 | 11:04 | 13:17 |
| Arr. Antibes | 11:20 | 13:21 | 15:25 |

Sights in **Antibes**: See notes under "Avignon–Antibes"

| Dep. Antibes | 14:00 | 14:51 | 16:54 (1) | 18:47 (2) | 20:42 (2) |
| Arr. Marseille | 16:09 | 16:55 | 19:09 | 21:54 | 23:11 |

(1) Light refreshments. (2) Second-class.

Marseille - Cassis - Marseille SNCF timetable

| Dep. Marseille (St. Ch.) | 08:40 | 09:45 | 11:10 | 12:15 | 14:42 |
| Arr. Cassis | 30 minutes later | | | | |

Sights in **Cassis:** A fishing village and beach resort. There are many small restaurants here offering "the catch of the day" prepared so as to please any gourmand. The activities in Cassis are topless sunbathing, sailing, swimming, snorkeling, diving and fishing.

The municipal Casino is open daily 15:00-20:00. The "calanques" (coves) of **Port Miou**, **Port Pin** and **En-Vau** can be visited by foot or by boat.

| Dep. Cassis | 12:23 | 13:10 | 13:42 | 14:27 | 15:30 (1) |
| Arr. Marseille (St. Ch.) | 30 minutes later | | | | |

(1) Plus other departures from Cassis at 16:10, 17:34, 18:06, 19:07, 20:46 and 21:52.

Nice - Antibes - Nice 164

Dep. Nice	Frequent times from 05:05 to 00:20
Arr. Antibes	16–30 minutes later
Dep. Antibes	Frequent times from 05:35 to 23:45
Arr. Nice	16–30 minutes later

Nice - Cannes (and Grasse) - Nice 164

Dep. Nice	Frequent times from 05:05 to 00:20
Arr. Cannes	40 minutes later

Sights in **Cannes:** Stroll along Promenade de la Croisette to see the beautiful beach and splendid yachts, all the way to the Palm Beach Casino. Take boat rides on the Bay of Cannes or to the **St. Honorat** and **St. Marguerite** islands. On the latter, you can visit the prison that held the Man in the Iron Mask.

There is also a short boat trip to **Lerins**, where the 5th century Monastery of the Cistercians is located. It is said that St. Patrick began his evangelical tour of Europe from there. Visit the 10th century castle, Castrum Canois, on a mountain that overlooks Cannes. It houses the Museum of Mediterranean Civilization.

La Napoule is a few miles west of Cannes. The attraction there is the Chateau de la Napoule Art Foundation, one of the finest art galleries on the Riviera, open daily except Tuesday, with guided tours in the afternoon.

Sights in **Grasse:** Take the 50-minute bus ride from Cannes' railstation to nearby Grasse, the perfume capital of France. Many of the 35 perfume factories there are open to visitors. One of them, Parfumerie Fragonard, is only a 5-minute walk from the Grasse bus terminal. Near it is a Perfume Museum. The nearby hillsides are covered with wildflowers and jasmine every Spring.

Dep. Cannes	Frequent times from 05:20 to 00:15
Arr. Nice	40 minutes later

Nice - Marseille - Nice   164

These trains have light refreshments, unless designated otherwise.

Dep. Nice	06:00	06:37 (1)	08:25	09:10	10:38 (4)
Arr. Marseille (St. Ch.)	08:31	09:05	11:15	11:36	12:53
Dep. Marseille (St. Ch.)	13:17 (1)	15:20	15:52	16:39 (2)	17:25 (5)
Arr. Nice	15:40	17:55	18:30	19:05	20:10

(1) No light refreshments. (2) Restaurant car. (3) Supplement charged. Restaurant car. (4) Plus other Nice departures at 11:24 (3) and 11:59, arriving Marseille 13:43 and 14:29. (5) Plus other Marseille departures at 18:42, 20:35 and 22:03, arriving Nice 21:28, 23:02 and 00:25.

Nice - Monaco (Monte Carlo) - Nice   164

Dep. Nice	Frequent times from 06:05 to 00:35
Arr. Monaco	20–25 minutes later
	• • •
Dep. Monaco	Frequent times from 05:23 to 23:55
Arr. Nice	20–25 minutes later

Nice - Saint Raphael - Nice   164

Dep. Nice	Frequent times from 06:00 to 22:32
Arr. St. Raphael	60 minutes later

Sights in **Saint Raphael**: An excellent Riviera beach resort. Good golfing, hiking and sailing here. There is a gambling casino.

Dep. St. Raphael	Frequent times from 06:40 to 23:34
Arr. Nice	60 minutes later

Paris - Angers - Paris   123

All of these trains are TGV, require reservation, charge a supplement and have light refreshments, unless designated otherwise.

Dep. Paris (Mont.)	07:50 (1)	08:50	09:50	11:30
Arr. Angers (St. L.)	09:19	10:21	11:25	12:59

Sights in **Angers**: Located on Promenade du Bout du Monde (Walkway of the World's End), is the massive 13th century castle (Chateau d'Angers), with its 17 towers. It houses the world's finest collection of medieval and Renaissance tapestries. Don't fail to see the supreme tapestry, "The Apocalypse."

It was 430 feet long and about 20 feet high when it was woven in the 14th century, unbelievably produced in less than 7 years. What we can view today is 350 feet long and 15 feet high 8,600 square feet. What remains are 67 of the original 84 panels and 4 of the original 6 scenes showing a bearded figure sitting on a stone dais.

The Angers tapestry illustrates the text of the Book of Revelation, complete with the 4 horsemen (the last of which is death), followed by hell.

It is in the second half of the tapestry that we are shown the ultimate destruction (Judgment Day): shipwrecks, rains of fire, many-headed beasts (including a dragon that has 7 heads and 10 horns), the fall of Babylon, the extinction of both the sun and the moon, and the descent of Jerusalem from heaven to earth, where it becomes the eternal dwelling of those who are blessed. The miracle of the tapestry is its survival.

Dep. Angers (St. L.)	12:02	14:14	15:17	17:09 (2)	18:08 (3+6)
Arr. Paris (Mont.)	13:35	15:50	16:50	18:45	19:45

(1) Operates late August to mid-July. Runs daily, except Sundays and holidays. (2) Runs daily, except Saturday. (3) Early July to early September: runs daily, except Sundays and holidays. Early September to early July: runs daily. (4) Runs Sunday only. (5) Runs daily, except Sundays & holidays. (6) Plus other Angers departures at 19:24 (4), 19:49 (5), 20:55 (7) and 21:13 (4). (7) Runs Monday-Friday except holidays.

Paris - Basel - Paris 171

Dep. Paris (Est)	07:30 (1)	08:39 (2)	11:50 (3)	13:41 (4)	17:00 (5+7)
Arr. Basel (SNCF)	12:11	14:07	16:36	18:34	21:40
Dep. Basel (SNCF)	00:28 (6)	08:23 (5)	12:48 (2)	16:48 (8)	18:30 (2)
Arr. Paris (Est)	06:47	13:12	18:05	21:29	23:41

(1) Supplement charged. Runs daily, except Sunday. Light refreshments. (2) Light refreshments. (3) Light refreshments. Early July to Early September: runs daily. Early September to early July: runs Friday and Saturday. (4) Runs Monday-Friday, except holidays. Light refreshments. (5) Supplement charged. Restaurant car. (6) Has second-class couchettes. (7) Plus another Paris departure at 22:40 (6), arriving Basel 05:30. (8) Runs daily except Satrudays. Supplement charged. Restaurant car.

Paris - Bayeux - Paris 120

All of these trains have light refreshments, unless designated otherwise.

Dep. Paris (St. Laz.)	06:55 (1)	09:02 (2)	11:29 (3)	12:48 (4)
Arr. Bayeux	09:28	11:25	13:52	15:16

Sights in **Bayeux**: The world-famous 230-foot long, 20-inch wide embroidered tapestry, sewn by Queen Mathilda (wife of William the Conqueror) and her friends for 10 years after the 1066 Battle of Hastings, both to commemorate the Norman conquest of England and her husband becoming king of England.

On public view in Bayeux since 1077, it consists of 58 scenes that include 626 people, 37 ships, 33 buildings and 730 animals while also depicting 11th century life.

The battle waged by Duke William of Normandy involved transporting 10,000 Normans across the English Channel in 400 ships.

One of the world's greatest works of art, "Queen Mathilda's Tapestry" has been exhibited daily 09:00–19:00 (except Christmas and New Year's Day) in a museum which opened in 1983 after 2 years of construction. As many as 2,300 people enter the museum on some days, including hordes of schoolchildren that begin arriving at 10:00.

The tapestry is mounted on a horseshoe-shaped frame, sealed inside unbreakable glass. Its humidity and temperature are regulated. Except for the light directed at the tapestry, the rest of the hall is entirely dark. A 15-minute description can be heard over earphones in many languages.

Other local attractions are the World War II Battle of Normandy Museum (next to the British Military Cemetery) and the 3-spired Notre Dame Cathedral. There are views of a magnificent seascape from its high center tower.

Dep. Bayeux	15:05 (5)	18:04 (7)	18:51 (8)	20:21 (9)
Arr. Paris (St. Laz.)	17:45 (6)	20:40	22:02	23:09

(1) Early July to early September: runs daily except Saturday. Early September to early July: Tuesday-Saturday. (2) Late June to early September: runs daily, except Sundays and holidays. Early September to late June: runs daily. (3) Runs Saturday only. (4) Runs daily except Saturdays. (5) No light refreshments. (6) Arrives 30 minutes later from late June to early September. (7) Runs daily, except Sundays and holidays. Supplement charged. (8) Runs Sunday only. No light refreshments. (9) Runs daily, except Sunday and Friday. No light refreshments. (9) Runs daily except Sundays and holidays July 8-September 1.

Paris - Bayeux - Caen - Paris 120

As shown below, it is possible to combine a visit from Paris to both Bayeux and Caen in one day.

Dep. Paris (St. Lazare)	06:55 (1)	09:02 (2)	Dep. Bayeux	15:17 (2)
Arr. Bayeux	09:28	11:45	Arr. Caen	15:32

Sights in **Bayeux**: See notes above.

Sights in **Caen**: Although much was destroyed here during the 1944 Normandy invasion battle, numerous historical buildings have been preserved. Hotel d'Escoville, the "Chateau." The 11th century Abbaye aux Hommes and Abbaye aux Dames. The Museum. The church of Saint Sauveur. The Palace of Justice. Try these regional specialties: *tripes, berlingots, cider, Calvados.*

Take Bus #12 from the railstation 3 miles to the "Normandy Memorial and Museum for Peace." It documents both the 1944 Battle of Normandy and the resulting Allied march from here to Berlin with original war films, photos, huge animated maps and vivid re-creations of battle scenes. Open daily except the first 2 weeks of January. The hours during June, July and August are 09:00-22:00. During the rest of the year: 09:00-19:00. The last entry allowed is 75 minutes before closing time.

Dep. Caen	19:17 (3)	19:39 (4)	20:20 (5)	20:45 (6)	21:43 (3)
Arr. Paris (St. Laz.)	22:02	22:13	22:48	23:09	00:12

Here are schedules leaving more time in Caen.

Dep. Paris (St. Laz.)	06:55 (1)	08:06 (7)	09:02 (2)	10:31 (8)
Arr. Caen	09:14	10:42	11:11	13:01

• • •

Dep. Caen	14:15 (9)	15:47	16:37 (11)	18:30 (13+14)
Arr. Paris (St. Laz.)	16:37	18:22 (10)	19:07	20:40

(1) Early July to early September: runs daily, except Saturday. Early September to early July: runs Tuesday-Saturday. (2) Runs daily. (3) Runs Sunday only. (4) Runs Sunday and Monday. (5) Runs Friday. Light refreshments. (6) Runs daily, except Monday,Friday and Sunday. (7) Runs daily. Light refreshments. (8) Runs daily, except Saturday. Light refreshments. (9) Light refreshments. Early July to early September: runs daily. Early September to early July: runs daily, except Sundays and holidays. (10) Runs daily June 25-Sept. 4 (11) Operates early September to late June. Runs Sunday only. Supplement charged. (12) Runs Tuesday, Wednesday, Thursday and Saturday. (13) Plus other Caen departures at 19:17 (3), 19:39 (3), 20:20 (5), 20:45 (12) and 21:42 (3), arriving Paris (St. Laz.) 22:02, 22:13, 22:48, 23:09 and 00:12. (14) Supplement charged.

Paris - Blois - Paris   135 a

Dep. Paris (Aust.)	07:33 (1)	09:48 (5)	12:00
Arr. Blois	09:05	11:19	13:29

Sights in **Blois**: St. Louis Cathedral. Church of Saint Nicolas. Church of Saint Vincent. Church of Saint Saturin, and its curious cemetery. The Alluye Manor.

Visit the Castle of Blois, the palace of Catherine de Medici during the 16th century. From late March to late September, a sound-and-light show is presented there every evening. The other 2 fine Chateaux here are Chambord and Bracieux (Herbault-en-Sologne). For lunch in Blois, try the regional specialties: Rillettes, Loire fish, great local wines and cheeses.

Dep. Blois	13:33 (2)	15:51	17:14 (1)	19:41 (3)	20:10 (4)	20:34 (6)
Arr. Paris (Aust.)	15:14	17:37	18:46	21:43	21:52	22:04

(1) Light refreshments. (2) Runs daily, except Sundays and holidays. (3) Runs Sunday only. Operates early July to late August. Runs Sunday only. (4) Operates late August to early July. Runs daily, except Friday & Saturday. (5) Runs daily July 9-August 28. (6) Runs Sunday only from July 1 to August 29.

Paris - Tours - Paris   135

Here are schedules for having more time in Tours than when combining a trip from Paris to both Blois and Tours.

All of these trains are TGV, require reservation, charge a supplement and have light refreshments, unless designated otherwise. They travel at 186 miles per hour on some portions of this route.

Dep. Paris (Mont.)	06:55(4)	07:45 (1)	09:00(4)	10:45	12:15
Arr. Tours	08:06	08:55	10:07	11:51	13:25

• • •

Dep. Tours	12:59	14:44	16:07	17:14 (2)	17:47
Arr. Paris (Mont.)	14:05	15:55	17:15	18:25	18:55

Dep. Tours	19:47 (3)	20:23 (1)	20:59 (3)	21:51 (1)	22:07 (3)
Arr. Paris (Mont.)	20:55	21:35	22:10	23:00	23:15

(1) Runs daily, except Sundays and holidays. (2) Runs daily, except Saturday. (3) Runs Sunday only. (4) Runs Saturday and Sunday only.

Paris - Bordeaux - Bayonne - Biarritz - Paris   136 + 137

All of these trains are TGV, require reservation, charge a supplement and have light refreshments, unless designated otherwise..

Dep. Paris (Mont.)	06:55	08:10 (1)	10:00
Arr. Bordeaux (St. Jean)	10:28	11:08 (2)	13:02
Arr. Bayonne	12:06	-0-	14:38
Arr. Biarritz	12 minutes after arriving Bayonne		

Dep. Biarritz	14:50	-0-	16:37 (3)	17:47 (1)	18:54 (3)
Dep. Bayonne	15:02	-0-	16:50	18:00	19:06
Dep. Bordeaux (St. Jean)	16:33	17:27	18:28	19:41	20:44
Arr. Paris (Mont.)	19:55	20:30	21:30	23:00	23:45

(1) Runs daily, except Sundays and holidays. (2) Terminates in Bordeaux. (3) Runs Sunday only.

Paris - Bourges - Paris   141

Dep. Paris (Austerlitz)	07:18 (1)	09:33 (2)
Arr. Vierzon	08:43	11:11
Change trains.		
Dep. Vierzon	08:50	11:20
Arr. Bourges	09:11	11:45

Sights in **Bourges**: A key gateway to the chateau area of the Loire Valley. Bourges is a living history museum.

The beautifully preserved stained glass windows in the Cathedral of St.-Etienne are a dazzling play of red against magenta and deep blue, located in a narrow halll that is 387 feet long, 136 feet wide, and an amazing 130 feet high. "Spellbinding" is the only way to describe these windows that depict the Bible's great morality stories. The Cathedral's restored 17th century organ is the best one of France. The l'Archeveche Garden is near the Cathedral. See the medieval houses below the Cathedral on a stroll along the town's winding, cobbled streets.

Visit the 15th century Palace of Jacques Couer, open daily 9:00–12:00 and 14:00–18:00 (closes at 17:00 November–March). See the collection of Roman artifacts and antique ceramics at the Musee de Berry in the 15th century Hotel Cujas (4 Rue des Arenes), open daily except Tuesday 10:00–12:00 and 14:00–18:00 (Sunday: only 14:00–18:00).

The Museum of Decorative Arts in the 16th century Hotel Lallemant (6 Rue Bourbonnoux), open daily except Tuesday 10:00–11:30 and 14:00–16:30. The Municipal Garden and the garden at the City Hall, formerly the residence of a 17th century archbishop.

Dep. Bourges	17:50 (3)	18:53 (5)	19:15 (4)
Arr. Vierzon	18:10(3)	19:22	19:43
Change trains.			
Dep. Vierzon	18:29	19:46 (4)	20:36(5)
Arr. Paris (Austerlitz)	20:22	21:34	22:20

(1) Runs daily, except Sun. and holidays. (2) Operates early July to early Sept. (3) Direct train to Paris. No train change in Vierzon. (4) Runs Mon.–Fri., except holidays. (5) Runs Saturday, Sunday and Holidays

Paris - Brussels - Paris   18

Dep. Paris (Nord)	07:05 (1)	07:50 (2)	10:08 (3)	10:23 (4)
Arr. Brussels (Midi)	09:39	10:49	13:12	13:17

Dep. Brussels (Midi)	14:13 (2)	15:04	16:00 (5)	17:10 (6)	18:13 (7)	19:07 (4+8)
Arr. Paris (Nord)	17:05	17:43(1)	19:01	19:42	20:43	22:05

(1) Supplement charged. Runs Monday–Friday. Restaurant car. (2) Light refreshments. (3) Operates late June to late August. Restaurant car. (4) Restaurant car. (5) Supplement charged. Restaurant car. (6) Supple-

ment charged. Runs Monday–Friday. (7) Supplement charged. Runs daily, except Saturday. Restaurant car. (8) Plus another departure from Brussels (Midi) at 19:57 (2), arriving Paris 22:59.

Paris - Chantilly - Paris   SNCF Timetable

Dep. Paris (Nord)	Frequent times from 06:32 to 21:47
Arr. Chantilly	30–40 minutes later

Sights in **Chantilly:** (Pronounced "Shawnteeyee") The 16th century castle, actually 2 chateaux, has been called "the most beautiful house in France." It stands in a lake and is surrounded by magnificent gardens and a large forest.

Of the 2 routes from the railstation to the castle, the shortest distance (and most pleasant stroll) is to walk 30 minutes via a trail through tall trees and then across the large lawn infield of the racecourse, locale during the first 2 weeks of June every year for a very elegant horse-racing meet.

The 2 attractions are the chateau's Conde Museum and its Living Museum of the Horse. Among the fine objects exhibited in the Conde are priceless collections of art spanning 1,000 years; 13,000 books beginning with 10th century manuscripts, paintings (Delacroix, Fouquet, Ingres, Rembrandt, Clouet, Raphael, Rosselli, Greuze) and furniture; all on an estate of 17,000 acres that contain forests, farms, a racetrack with stadium, and a golf course.

Between April 1 and September 30, the chateau is open daily except Tuesday 10:30–18:00 (until 17:00 the rest of the year).

Between April 1 and October 31, the Grand Stables are open daily except Tuesday 10:30–17:00 (13:00–17:00 the rest of the year). Riders wearing 18th century costumes perform at 12:00, 15:00 and 17:00 April 1 to October 31 (at 14:30 and 16:00 the rest of the year).

See the spectacle of the Tuesday and Saturday fox hunts.

Dep. Chantilly	Frequent times from 05:53 to 23:19
Arr. Paris (Nord)	30–40 minutes later

Paris - Chartres - Paris   125

Dep. Paris (Montpar.)	07:00 (1) 08:56 (2) 09:29 (3) 09:58 (2) 11:14 12:59 (4)
Arr. Chartres	50–60 minutes later

Sights in **Chartres:** The main attraction is the magnificent 13th century Cathedral, third largest in the world, exceeded in size only by St. Peter's and Canterbury. Its stained-glass is unrivaled. Open daily 07:30–19:30, it is a short stroll from the railstation.

Also see the ancient process that was used to make the Cathedral's stained glass, at the Stained Glass Center, next to the Cathedral, open daily except Monday 10:00–18:00.

A city map and details on a self-guided walking tour of Chartres is available at the Tourist Office, across from the Cathedral. The Tourist Office is open Monday–Saturday 09:30–

12:30 and 14:00–18:30, and on Sunday 10:00–12:00 and 15:00–19:00 (closed Sundays, November–April).

Malcom Miller has conducted his world-renowned English-language tour of the Cathedral since 1958 (at 12:00 and 14:45). He usually offers 2 different tours.

Other sights: the Former Collegiate Church, the Church of St. Aignan, the Church of St. Aignan, the Church of St. Martin-au-Val and the Church of St. Foy.

Picassiete's Garden was built by a street sweeper out of pieces of garbage (broken bottles, enameled tiles, stones)...similar to Watts Tower in Los Angeles. A bus goes within a few blocks of it, 2 miles north from the center of Chartres.

Dep. Chartres	11:21	14:04	15:10 (2)	16:56 (2)	18:41(7)
Arr. Paris (Montpar.)	50–60 minutes later				

(1) Runs daily, except Saturday and holidays. (2) Operates early July to early September. (3) Runs Monday-Friday except holidays. (4) Runs daily, except Sundays and holidays. Early September to early july, runs daily. (5) TGV. Supplement charged. Light refreshments. (6) Runs Sundays only. Light refreshments. (7) Plus other departures from Chartres at 19:37, 21:10(2), and 21:33 (6).

Paris - Cologne (Koln) - Paris   25

Both of these trains charge a supplement and have a restaurant car.

Dep. Paris (Nord)	07:31	Dep. Cologne	17:08
Arr. Cologne	12:48	Arr. Paris (Nord)	22:10

Paris - Compiegne - Paris   101

Dep. Paris (Nord)	07:10 (1)	07:52 (2)	12:16
Arr. Compiegne	50–60 minutes later		

Sights in **Compiegne**: Town Hall. Vivenel Museum. Hotel Dieu. The 7th century Beauregard Tower. The "Clairere de l'Armistice" in Compeigne Forest, where Marshal Foch signed the 1918 armistice for France...and Adolph Hitler received the June 21, 1940 surrender of France.

Beautiful furnishings and decorations can be seen in the first drawing room, family drawing room, Emperor's library, music room, Empress's bedroom, a series of dining rooms, the hunting gallery, and the ornate ballroom at the Chateau built by Louis XV in the late 18th century.

Dep. Compeigne	10:28	13:12	19:10	20:11 (3)	21:57 (4)
Arr. Paris (Nord)	50–60 minutes later				

(1) Runs daily, except Sundays and holidays. (2) Daily to June 30 to September 1.(3) Runs Sunday only. (4) Runs daily, except Saturday.

Paris - Dijon - Paris   157

All of these trains are TGV, require reservation, charge a supplement and have a restaurant car or light refreshments, unless designated otherwise.

Dep. Paris (Lyon)	07:14 (5)	08:05	09:28 (1)	10:32 (2)	12:21
Arr. Dijon	08:51	09:47	12:04	12:10	14:00

Dep. Dijon	14:44	16:50 (3)	18:30	19:57	22:16 (4)
Arr. Paris (Lyon)	16:28	18:35	20:19	21:39	23:55

(1) Not TGV. No reservation or supplement. Light refreshments. (2) Runs Monday–Friday, except holidays. (3) Early July to late August: runs daily, except Saturday. Late August to early July: runs daily. (4) Runs Friday and Sunday. (5) Runs Monday-Saturday except holidays.

Paris - Evreux - Paris   120

Dep. Paris (St. Laz.)	08:06 (1)	09:21 (2)	10:32	11:47 (3)	12:48 (4)
Arr. Evreux	09:10	10:36	11:37	12:44	13:44

Sights in **Evreux**: The Cathedral of Notre Dame, a jumble of architectural styles due to having been built over a period of 6 centuries: from the 11th to the 17th. Goldsmith work in the Church of Stain Taurin. The ancient Eveche. The tower of The Clock. For lunch, try the Norman cuisine.

Dep. Evreux	13:27	14:31 (5)	15:34 (6)	17:10 (7)	18:32 (5+8)
Arr. Paris (St. Laz.)	14:35	15:34	16:37	18:22	19:41

(1) Light refreshments. (2) Runs Saturday only. (3) Runs daily, except Sunday and holidays. (4) Runs daily, except Saturdays. (5) Runs Sunday only. (6) Light refreshments. Early July to early September: runs daily. Early September to early July: runs daily, except Sundays and holidays. (7) Operates late June to early September. Runs daily. (8) Runs daily except Sundays & holidaysto July 1 and to September 2. (9) Plus other departures from Evreux at 18:48 (8), 19:10 (5) and 23:04 (7), arriving Paris 19:57, 20:27 and 00:12.

Paris - Fontainebleau - Paris   151a

Dep. Paris (Lyon)	Frequent times from 06:02 to 22:33
Arr. Fontainebleau-Avon	40 minutes later

Take the 10-minute bus ride from the railstation to the palace, open 08:00 to sunset, daily except Tuesdays.

Sights in **Fontainebleau:** It is advisable to plan on an entire day here for seeing the magnificent 16th century palace that many kings of France occupied, and the parks and gardens surrounding it. There are guided tours of the palace 10:00–12:30 and 14:00–18:00. Many visitors bring a picnic lunch.

Dep. Fontainebleau-Avon	Frequent times from 05:20 to 20:44 (1)
Arr. Paris (Lyon)	30–40 minutes later

(1) Plus another departure from Fontainebleau on Sundays at 21:20.

Paris - Granville - Paris   117

Dep. Paris (Montpar.)	07:13 (1)	08:15 (2)
Arr. Granville	10:47	12:12

Sights in **Granville:** This is a lively seaside town near Mont.-st.-Michel, with remarkably high tides and sandy beaches. The marina here can accommodate 1,000 yachts. The Regional Nautical Center offers instructions in sailing and wind surfing.

The Aquarium (with exhibits of sea life, shells and mineral stones) is along the walk to the lighthouse. The **Chausey Islands** can be seen from the shore, and there is daily boat service to them.

Visit the Church of Notre Dame. Try your luck in the Casino.

Dep. Granville	14:11 (1)	14:25 (3)	18:09 (4)	19:14
Arr. Paris (Montpar.)	17:44	18:29	21:52	22:46(4)

(1) Runs Monday–Friday, except holidays. (2) Runs Saturdays, Sundays and holidays. Light refreshments. (3) Runs Saturday and Sunday. (4) Runs Sundays only. Light refreshments.

Paris - Limoges - Paris   138

Dep. Paris (Aust.)	07:02 (1)	07:18 (8)	09:33 (3)	10:09 (4)	10:24 (5)
Arr. Limoges	10:47	10:20	12:58	13:10	13:28
Dep. Limoges	14:41 (2)	17:01 (2)	18:27 (6)	19:46 (7)	20:54
Arr. Paris (Aust.)	18:33	20:22	21:23	23:08	23:56(9)

(1) Runs Sunday only to July 1 and from Sept. 2. (2) Light refreshments. (3) Operates late June to early September. (4) Operates early September to late June. Light refreshments. (5) Operates late June to early September. Light refreshments. (6) Runs daily except Saturday. Supplement charged. Light refreshments. (7) Runs Sunday only. Light refreshments. (8) Supplement charged. Runs daily except Sundays & holidays. Restaurant car. (9) Runs Friday, Saturday and Sunday.

Paris - Lyon - Paris   150

All of these trains are TGV, require reservation, charge a supplement and have a restaurant car or light refreshments.

Dep. Paris (Lyon)	06:15 (1)	06:45 (2)	07:00(7)	07:30	08:15 (3)
Arr. Lyon (P.D.)	08:23	08:45	09:00	09:30	10:15
Dep. Lyon (P.D.)	14:00 (4)	15:00	16:00	17:00	17:25 (1)
Arr. Paris (Lyon)	16:02	17:04	18:00	19:10	19:30
Dep. Lyon (P.D.)	18:00	18:47	20:00	21:10(8)	21:49 (6)
Arr. Paris (Lyon)	20:04	20:49	22:04	23:20	23:59

(1) Operates late August to late June. Runs Monday–Friday, except holidays. (2) Runs Monday-Friday, except holidays. (3) Operates late August to late June. Runs daily, except Sundays and holidays. (4) Operates late August to late June. Runs daily. (5) Operates late June to late August. Runs daily. (6) Runs Sunday only. (7) Runs daily except holidays. (8) Runs daily except Saturdays.

Paris - Nancy - Paris   173

Dep. Paris (Est)	06:53 (1)	07:47 (2)	07:59 (3)	09:02 (4)
Arr. Nancy	09:37	10:31	11:35	11:50

Sights in **Nancy:** The Ducal Palace, with its museum of this city's 2,000-year history at 64 Grande Rue, open daily except Tuesdays and holidays 10:00–12:00 and 14:00–18:00. Its exhibits include a room on the history of Jews in this region.

The Church of the Cordeliers. The 14th century Porte de la Craffe, oldest monument in Nancy. The wrought-iron grillwork and fountains in Place Stanislas. Lovely 18th century houses on Place de la Carriere.

Visit the model rooms of early 20th century interior decor at the Musee de l'Ecole, 36–38 Rue Sergent Blandan, open daily, except Tuesdays and holidays. April–September: 10:00–12:00 and 14:00–18:00. October–March: 10:00–12:00 and 14:00–17:00. Much work by Emile Galle, Jacques Gruber, Eugene Vallin and other Art Nouveau artisans is exhibited there: glass bowls, tables, fireplaces, tooled leather wall coverings, inlaid bed headboards and footboards, inlaid chests, Galle's fantastic glass mushroom lamp, and the extraordinary Louis Majorelle grand piano, inlaid with irises and waterlillies.

Majorelle's house, a few blocks away at 1 Rue Majorelle (open Monday-Friday except holidays 8:30–12:00 and 13:00–18:00), is well worth visiting to see the exterior and interior ceramic work and the Gruber stained glass windows there.

Visitors can also see examples of Galle and Daum vases, lamps and other glass objects at the Musee Beaux-Arts, Place Stanislas, open daily except Tuesdays and holidays 10:00–12:00 and 14:00–18:00.

Pepiniere is a 57-acre park with gardens, a small zoo, and a restaurant.

Dep. Nancy	13:34 (2)	14:33 (5)	14:55	17:21 (7)	18:33 (8+9)
Arr. Paris (Est)	16:20	18:00	18:32 (10)	20:05	21:14

(1) Supplement charged. Operates early September to mid-July. Runs Mon-Fir, except holidays. Restaurant car. (2) Supplement charged. Restaurant car. (3) Light refreshments. (4) Runs daily, except Sundays and holidays. Light refreshments. (5) Runs Sundays (daily from June 21), Light Refreshments. (6) Runs Monday–Friday, except holidays. Light refreshments. (7) Runs daily, except Saturday. (8) Operates late August to mid-July. Runs daily, except Saturday. (9) Plus another Nancy departure at 19:34 (2), arriving Paris 22:18. (10) Runs daily except Sundays and holidays to June 21.

Paris - Nantes - Paris   123

All of these trains are TGV, require reservation, charge a supplement and have light refreshments.

Dep. Paris (Mont.)	06:45 (1)	07:15 (2)	08:50	09:50	10:55 (3)
Arr. Nantes	08:45	09:26	10:58	12:02	12:57

Sight in **Nantes**: See notes under "Bordeaux–Nantes"

Dep. Nantes	13:36	14:40	16:31 (4)	17:31 (5)	18:20 (6)	19:05 (7+10)
Arr. Paris (Mont.)	15:50	16:50	18:45	19:45	20:25	21:10

(1) Operates late August to early July. Runs Monday–Friday, except holidays. (2) Early July to late August: runs daily, except Sundays and holidays. Late August to early July: runs Monday–Friday, except holidays. (3) Operates late June to late August. (4) Early July to early September: runs daily. Early September to early July: runs daily, except Saturday. (5) Early July to late August: runs daily, except Sundays and holidays. Late August to early July: runs daily. (6) Runs daily, except Saturday. (7) Runs Sunday only. (8) Runs daily, except Sundays and holidays. (9) Runs Monday–Friday, except holidays. (10) Plus other departures from Nantes at 19:11 (8), 20:18 (9), 20:55 (7) and 21:48.

Paris - Neuilly - Paris

Take the Metro from Paris' Champs-Elysees station. **Neuilly** is the fourth stop.

The attraction here is The Museum of Women at 12 Rue de Centre, open daily except Sunday 14:30–18:00. The one guided tour starts at 15:00. Among the exhibits is the lavishly decorated bed used by France's most famous prostitute during the reign of Napoleon III, the Marchioness de La Paiva. While the bed cost her 10,000 gold francs, she recovered this expense quickly. She charged her clients 10,000 gold francs a night.

There is also the corset that Marie Antoinette wore in prison while waiting to be guillotined, a bronze cast of ballet dancer-choreographer Katherine Dunham's feet, a silk jacket that belonged to the last empress of China, a letter written by Nobel prize-winner Marie Curie, and many other curiosities.

Paris - Rheims - Paris 177

Dep. Paris (Est)	07:13 (1)	08:04	11:00	13:01 (1)
Arr. Rheims	08:46	09:55	12:36	14:40

Sights in **Rheims**: See the 13th century Cathedral of Notre Dame (open daily 07:30–19:30), longer and higher than Notre Dame in Paris. Most of this city was destroyed in World War I, and restoration of the Cathedral was not completed until 1938.

See church treasures in the Palais du Tau (2 Place du Cardinal-Lucon), open 10:00–12:00 and 14:00–18:00. The Porte Mars 13th century Arch. Saint Remi Basilica (open daily 08:00–18:30). Nearby, the great collection of 16th–19th century weapons in the St. Remi Museum (53 Rue Simon), open daily 14:00–18:30.

The Church of St. Jacquet. The museum at the Church of St. Denis.

See champagne processed. The public is invited to visit the Taitinger and Pommery caves.

Dep. Rheims	12:24 (6)	16:06 (3)	17:11 (3)	17:47 (4)	18:03 (5)	20:27
Arr. Paris (Est)	13:59	17:38	18:50	19:32	19:38	21:56

(1) Runs daily, except Sundays and holidays. (2) Runs daily, except holidays. (3) Runs Monday–Friday, except holidays. (4) Runs Saturdays, Sunday and holidays. (5) Runs Monday–Friday, except holidays. (6) Departs 12:35 Mon-Friday except holidays from August 8.

Paris - Rouen - Paris 115

Dep. Paris (St. Laz.)	06:45 (1)	07:39 (2)	08:15 (3)	09:15 (8)
Arr. Vernon	07:27	08:23	09:04	-0-
Arr. Rouen (Rive Dr.)	08:00	09:03	09:47	10:24

Sights in **Rouen**: Walk out of the railstation and then down Rue de Jeanne D'Arc about 1½ miles. Turn right onto Rue de la Grosse Horloge and continue a short distance to the remodeled ancient, large central market, Vieux Marche, the place where Joan of Arc was tied to a stake and burned. This is now the Church of St. Joan, built in 1977. It is in the shape of an upside-down boat and has magnificent stained-glass windows that were saved from the Church of Saint-Vincent, bombed during World War II. Try the regional specialty (terrine of duck) in one of the nearby restaurants.

Then, go back along Rue de la Gross Horloge (crossing Rue de Jeanne D'Arc). Straight ahead is the gigantic, ornate clock for which the street was named. The clock presents a spectacle of moving figures when each hour strikes.

Past the famous clock is the Cathedral, with its renowned Carillon of 56 bells. Nearby, see the sculptures on the doors of the Church of Saint-Maclou.

See the stained-glass windows in the Church of St. Godard and the Church of St. Patrice.

Visit the remains of a building located below the Palace of Justice. It was either an 11th century Jewish school or a synagogue. See the Hebrew graffiti written on the walls there more than 900 years ago, the elaborate carved columns and the 2 inverted Lions of Judah. It is open only on Saturdays.

The rose window of the Gothic Church of St. Ouen. The collection of fine faience ware for which Rouen was once famous, in the Museum of Fine Arts. The Gallo-Roman artifacts in the Museum of Antiquities. The late Gothic and Renaissance Bourgtheroulde mansion. The collection of old street signs and other ironwork pieces in the Musee Le Secq.

From Rouen, it is an easy bus trip to the colorful harbor at **Honfleur**.

Take a bus ($1.00) or taxi ($7.50) from Vernon about 4 miles to Giverny, to visit the home and spectacular garden of painter Claude Monet, both of them open daily except Monday, 10:00-18:00 April 1 through October 31. Admission is $6.00.

Dep. Rouen (Rive Dr.)	12:05 (3)	12:46 (4)	14:10 (3)	14:51 (3)
Dep. Vernon	12:55	-0-	14:51	-0-
Arr. Paris (St. Laz.)	13:44	14:01	15:40	16:08

Dep. Rouen (Rive Dr.)	16:47	17:27 (1)	18:30 (2)	19:37 (7+9)
Dep. Vernon	-0-	18:12	19:12	20:24
Arr. Paris (St. Laz.)	18:16	18:58	20:00	21:19

(1) Runs Monday–Friday, except holidays. (2) Runs Sunday only. (3) Runs daily, except Sundays and holidays. (4) Runs daily. except Sundays and holidays. Light refreshments. (6) Runs Saturday and Sunday. (7) Runs Sunday only. (8) Plus other departures from Paris at 10:42 (7) and 12:00 (3), arriving Rouen 12:11 and 13:35. (9) Plus other departures from Rouen at 20:19 (7), 20:28 (7) and 21:21 (7), arriving Paris 21:37, 21:43 and 22:55.

Paris - Strasbourg - Paris   173

This ride is along the Marne, with clear views of the area near famous World War I battlefields.

Dep. Paris (Est)	06:53 (1)	07:47 (2)	08:06 (3)
Arr. Strasbourg	10:59	11:42	12:51

Dep. Strasbourg	16:00 (4)	17:07 (5)	18:19 (2)	19:06 (6)
Arr. Paris (Est)	20:05	21:14	22:18	23:20

(1) Supplement charged. Operates early September to early July. Runs daily, except Sundays and holidays. Restaurant car. (2) Supplement charged. Restaurant car. (3) Runs Sundays only. Light refreshments. (4) Runs daily except Saturday. Light refreshments. (5) Operates early September to early July. Runs daily, except Saturday. Light refreshments. (6) Runs Friday and Sunday. Light refreshments.

Paris - Tours - Paris

This one-day excursion appears immediately following "Paris–Blois–Tours–Paris"

Paris - Trouville and Deauville - Paris   120

Dep. Paris (St. Laz.)	07:44 (1)	08:29 (2)	10:25 (3)	12:18 (4)
Arr. Trou Deau	09:53	10:53	12:20	14:20

Sights in **Trouville**: There is no chance of obtaining hotel rooms here in Summer without advance reservation. One of France's most beautiful swimming beaches. A gambling casino. Marvelous seafood.

Sights in **Deauville**: One of France's most beautiful swimming beaches. Two racetracks. Lovely gardens. To explore the Norman countryside, you can rent a car at the Deauville railstation.

Take a bus 6 miles to **Honfleur**, the beautiful fishing village that inspired many Impressionist paintings. Very crowded in July and August. Stroll along the bank of its old harbor on the English Channel. Visit the Eugene Bodin Museum (paintings of the Saint Simeon school) and the Marine Museum in the 14th century Church of St. Etiene.

Dep. Trou Deau	13:20 (11)	15:54 (6)	17:16 (7)	18:39 (8+10)
Arr. Paris (St. Laz.)	15:34	17:55	19:41	20:35

(1) Operates late June to early September. Runs Monday-Friday, except holidays. (2) Runs Saturdays, Sundays and holidays. (3) Operates early July to late August. (4) Operates late June to late August. Runs daily, except Sundays and holidays. (5) Change trains in Lisieux (arr. 14:39-dep. 14:47). Early July to early September: runs daily. Early September to early July: runs daily, except Fridays, Sundays and holidays. (6) Operates early July to early September. (7) Runs Sunday only. Light refreshments. (8) Runs Sunday only. (9) Operates early July to late August. Runs Monday–Friday, except holidays. (10) Plus other departures from Trou Deau at 19:18 (9) and 19:59 (8), arriving Paris 21:26 and 22:43. (11) Runs Sunday only July 3-Aug 28.

Paris - Troyes - Paris   171

Dep. Paris (Est)	07:08 (1)	07:52 (2)	08:37 (3)	12:40	13:30 (4)
Arr. Troyes	08:36	09:34	10:12	14:11	14:53

Sights in **Troyes**: This is the Champagne area. The most interesting places here are located along the 30-minute walk from the railstation to St. Pierre Cathedral, which has marvelous 13th, 14th and 16th century stained glass.

See the museum of tools used in French crafts at the 16th century Hotel de Mauroy, on

Rue de la Trinite. The 16th century religious art and the hosiery museum, both at the Musee de l'Hotel de Vauluisant. The mansions of Autry, des Ursins and Marisy. The Museum of Fine Arts, with its solid collection of 17th–18th century paintings and 13th–14th century sculptures.

The 12th century manuscripts in the Library. The Pharmacy Museum. The Archaeology Museum. The Natural History Museum

Dep. Troyes	12:09 (5)	12:41 (6)	16:36 (3)	17:53 (7)	19:19 (6+9)
Arr. Paris (Est)	13:40	14:10	18:05	19:36	21:06

(1) Runs daily, except Sundays and holidays. (2) Runs Sunday only. (3) Light refreshments. (4) Runs Saturday, Sunday and holidays. (5) Runs Monday–Friday, except holidays. Light refreshments. (6) Runs Saturday only. (7) Runs Sunday only. (8) Supplement charged. Runs Sunday only. Light refreshments. (9) Plus other departures from Troyes at 20:34 (2), 20:55 (8) and 22:15 (3), arr. Paris 22:17, 22:22 and 23:41.

Paris - Versailles - Paris 125 a

To reduce the often long wait for a guided tour, phone 30-84-76-18 to get the schedule and arrive 90 minutes before the desired tour. Some of the tours (taking either one or 2 hours) are given in English.

Dep. Paris (Austerlitz)	Frequent times from 05:30 to 00:30.
Arr. Versailles	37 minutes later

Versailles is also reached by suburban trains that stop in Paris at the Pont St. Michel, Invalides and Pont d'Alma stations.

Sights in **Versailles**: The fabulous palace where Louis XV lived like a king, and the elegant 250 acres of gardens here. Open daily except Mondays and public holidays. Bring a picnic lunch and eat in the gardens, by the mile-long Grand Canal.

During the time of Louis XV, about 5,000 members of the nobility lived in the palace's private apartments. Versailles became a museum in 1837.

Among its highlights are: the 237-foot-long by 33-foot-wide Hall of Mirrors (in which 17 mirror-lined arcades reflect 17 corresponding arched windows), throne room, queen's chambers, chapel, theater, the apartments of Madame de Pompadour and Madame du Barry, and the rooms named for Venus, Mercury, Diana and Mars.

The private apartment of the king can be seen only as a part of the guided tours of the palace, which start at various times from 9:45 to 15:30. However, most of the great rooms, such as the Hall of Mirrors and the king's bedroom, can be visited without a guide from 9:45 until the palace closes at 17:00. Visitors can purchase a book here which makes it possible to see and appreciate the palace without a guide.

Dep. Versaille	Frequent times from 06:30 to 01:30
Arr. Paris (Austerlitz)	37 minutes later

If you visit Versaille in the morning, it is possible to also see Chartres in early afternoon. There are frequent trains for the 30-minute ride from Versaille to Chartres.

TRIPS TO THE RIVIERA

Unless designated otherwise, all of these trains are TGV, require reservation, charge a supplement and have light refreshments or restaurant car.

Paris - Marseille - Paris 151

Dep. Paris (Lyon)	07:00 (1)	07:40	10:23	11:40	13:29 (6)
Arr. Marseille (St. Ch.)	11:46	12:38	15:03	16:23	18:10

• • •

Dep. Marseille (St. Ch.)	06:42 (2)	08:06	08:44	12:13	14:58 (7+8)
Arr. Paris (Lyon)	11:33	12:49	13:34	16:59	19:46

(1) Runs Monday–Friday, except holidays. (2) Operates late August to early July. Runs daily, except Saturday. (3) A non-TGV train that has couchettes and a second-class coach. (4) A non-TGV train that carries a sleeping car and also has couchettes. No coaches. (5) Runs daily, except Saturday. (6) Plus other departures from Paris at 15:40, 16:49, 17:47, 20:29 (3) and 22:36 (4), arriving Marseille 20:25, 21:44, 22:36, 23:24, 04:44 and 07:10. (7) Plus other departures from Marseille at 17:31, 18:17 (5), 21:45 (3) and 22:36 (4), arriving Paris 22:22, 23:20, 06:24 and 07:42. (8) Runs daily except Saturday and daily July 3-Sept 2.

Paris - Nice - Paris 151

All of these trains are TGV, require reservation and charge a supplement, unless designated otherwise.

Dep. Paris (Lyon)	07:30 (1)	10:41 (2)	15:05 (3)	20:29 (4)	22:36 (5)
Arr. Nice	14:26	17:38	22:02	08:20	09:55

• • •

Dep. Nice	10:02	15:18 (1)	18:18 (4)	19:38 (5)	
Arr. Paris (Lyon)	17:09	22:18	06:24	07:42	

(1) Light refreshments. (2) Restaurant car. (3) Operates mid-June to late August. Light refreshments. (4) A non-TGV train that has couchettes and a second-class coach. (5) A non-TGV train that carries a sleeping car and also has couchettes. No coaches.

SCENIC RAIL TRIPS

Chamonix - Vallorcine - Chamonix   268

Good mountain scenery on this short ride. It is easy to combine this with the one-day roundtrip from Geneva to Chamonix.

Dep. Chamonix	07:54	09:04 (1)	09:59 (1)	11:34	13:44	14:50(2)	16:18(1)
Arr. Vallorcine	08:28	09:44	10:38	12:07	14:12	15:21	16:46

Dep. Vallorcine	09:18	10:01 (1)	11:19	12:54	14:32 (2)	15:38	17:10
Arr. Chamonix	10:03	10:39	12:08	13:33	14:58	16:28	17:39

(1) Operates late June to early September. (2) Operates early July to late September.

Limoges - Toulouse - Limoges   138

Recommended for mountain scenery. This can be seen either as an easy one-day roundtrip between Limoges and Toulouse or as a portion of the route from Paris to Toulouse (and v.v.) via Limoges.

Dep. Limoges	10:22(1)	13:01 (2)	13:13(3)		
Arr. Toulouse (Mat.)	13:48	16:42	16:55		

Dep. Toulouse (Mat.)	13:41 (4)	14:02 (5)	17:31 (6)	18:02 (7)	19:26 (8)
Arr. Limoges	17:00	17:36	21:06	21:39	22:57

(1) Runs Sunday only. (2) Operates early July to early September. (3) Operates early September to early July. Light refreshments. (4) Light refreshments. (5) Runs Friday & Sunday. (6) Runs Monday–Thursday. (7) Runs Friday only. (8) Runs Saturday, Sunday and holidays.

Here is the schedule for the Paris-Toulouse route:
All of the TGV trains in this table depart/arrive at Paris Montparnasse railstation. All of the TGVs require a reservation and charge a supplement.

138

Dep. Paris (Aust.)	07:02 (1)	11:15 (3)	13:45 (4)	17:00 (5)	17:45 (6)
Dep. Limoges	10:01 (2)	-0-	16:55	-0-	20:59
Arr. Toulouse (Mat.)	13:25	16:31	20:35	22:09	00:20

Dep. Paris (Aust.)	18:00 (7)	21:31 (8)	22:18 (9)	22:53 (10)
Dep. Limoges	20:59	01:14	02:12	-0-
Arr. Toulouse (Mat.)	00:20	04:40	07:03	07:00

• • •

Dep. Toulouse (Mat.)	00:35 (11)	01:41 (12)	06:08 (13)	07:31 (1)	10:32 (15)
Dep. Limoges	04:01	05:05	-0-	10:50 (3)	14:04
Arr. Paris (Aust.)	07:45	08:36	11:25 (14)	13:55	17:15

Dep. Toulouse (Mat.)	13:41 (15)	13:47 (16)	17:19 (5)	23:00 (10)
Dep. Limoges	17:05	-0-	-0-	-0-
Arr. Paris (Aust.)	20:22	19:00 (14)	22:30 (14)	07:06

(1) Runs Sundays only to July 1 and from Sept. 2. Light refreshments. (2)Change trains in Brive (arr. 11:00, dep. 11:10). (3) Supplement charged. Runs daily except Sundays & holidays. Restaurant car. (4) Supplement charged. Light refreshments. (5) TGV. Runs daily, except Saturday. Restaurant car. (6) Runs Friday and Sunday. Light refreshments. (7) Supplement charged. Runs daily, except Saturday. Light refreshments. (8) Has couchettes. (9) Runs daily, except Friday and Sunday. (10) Carries a sleeping car. Also has couchettes. No coaches. (11) Operates early September to early July. Has couchettes. (12) Operates early July to early September. Has couchettes. Coach is second-class. (13) TGV. Runs daily, except Sundays and holidays. Light refreshments. (14) Arrives at Paris' Montparnasse railstation. (15) Light refreshments.

Lyon - Geneva   159

This trip is noted for scenic canyons. See details under "Lyon."

Marseille - Monaco (Monte Carlo) 164

Great views of the Mediterranean seashore.

Dep. Marseille	06:15 (1)	09:18	11:04	13:17	15:52 (2)
Arr. Nice	8:58 (1)	11:43	13:36	15:40	18:30
Change trains.					
Dep. Nice	09:10 (1)	11:55	14:12	16:16	19:15
Arr. Monaco	10:00	12:16	14:37	16:37	19:39

• • •

Dep. Monaco	11:07 (1)	12:59	15:50	18:05 (1)	21:07 (1)
Arr. Nice	11:20 (1)	13:21	16:12	18:24 (1)	21:20 (1)
Change trains.					
Dep. Nice	11:24	13:41	16:38 (2)	18:35	22:32
Arr. Marseille	13:43	16:09	19:09	21:13	01:05

(1) Direct train. No train change in Nice. (2) Light refreshments.

Narbonne - Carcassonne 139

Outstanding farm and vineyard scenery. Easy to make as a one-day roundtrip or can be covered in the route from Narbonne to Toulouse and Bordeaux.

Dep. Narbonne	06:51 (1)	08:41	09:50	12:04 (2)	15:20 (2)
Arr. Carcassonne	40–45 minutes later				

Sights in **Narbonne**: The Cloister adjacent to the Palace of the Archbishops. The choir of the incomplete Cathedral of Saint-Just.

Sights in **Carcassonne**: See notes under "Bordeaux–Carcassonne."

Dep. Carcassonne	09:52 (2)	12:19 (2)	12:49 (2)	15:01 (2)	18:11 (3+4)
Arr. Narbonne	40–45 minutes later				

(1) Runs Monday-Friday, except Holidays. (2) Light refreshments. (3) Operates all year. Light refreshments early September to early July. (4) Plus other departures from Carcassonne at 18:03 (2), 19:46 (2) and 21:54 (2).

Here is the daytime viewing schedule for the Narbonne-Bordeaux route:

Dep. Narbonne	08:24	09:45	11:58	15:20 (1)
Dep. Carcassonne	08:54	10:16	12:28	15:52
Arr. Toulouse (Matabiau)	09:44	11:14	13:26	16:48 (1)
Arr. Bordeaux (St. Jean)	11:57	13:27	-0-	19:04

• • •

Dep. Bordeaux (St. Jean)	06:39 (2)	08:23 (2)	11:47 (2)	14:48
Arr. Toulouse (Matabiau)	08:57	11:04 (3)	14:03	17:05
Dep. Carcassonne	09:52	11:13	15:01	18:03
Arr. Narbonne	10:20	12:26	15:29	18:31

(1) Light refreshments. Change trains in Toulouse at 16:36. (2) Light refreshments. (3) Change trains , departing Toulouse 11:13. Operates early July to early September. Light refreshments Toulouse–Narbonne.

Nice - Cuneo　356

There is spectacular scenery on the 74-mile long Nice–Cuneo rail route through the Alps and the **Roya Valley**, a service that first became operational in 1928. Severe damage during World War II caused it to be closed in 1940, and it was not re-opened until the Winter of 1979. An outstanding feat of engineering, this line is a succession of very high viaducts, bridges and 60 tunnels that span 27 miles of this route, interspersed with sections that look down into deep valleys. This route has attracted many tourists.

Dep. Nice	07:25	12:28(1)	Dep. Cuneo	10:32	16:16 (1)
Arr. Breil	08:29	-0-	Arr. Breil	12:14	-0-
Change trains.			*Change trains.*		
Dep Breil	10:08	-0-	Dep Breil	12:45	-0-
Arr. Cuneo	11:44	15:26	Arr. Nice	13:30	19:10

(1) Direct train. No train change in Breil.

Nice - Digne - Nice　151 d

This is a very scenic ride up the beautiful **Var Valley** on a self-propelled single car narrow-gauge train. The roundtrip ticket in 1993 cost $72 (U.S.) for first-class, $46 for second-class. Half-fare for holders of Eurailpass or any French pass. There is a great drop in temperature between sea-level Nice and 1,955-foot-high Digne. The scenery includes canyons, chateaus and forests. The train follows the route Napoleon took when he returned from exile in Elba in 1815. Plaques and monuments along the way mark that event.

Dep. Nice (Sud)	06:42	09:00	12:43
Arr. Digne	09:44	12:25	15:57

Sights in **Digne**: A popular mineral bath resort. See the 15th century Cathedral of Saint Jerome. Many fruit orchards. Digne is famed for the lavender cultivated here.

Dep. Digne	11:05	13:58	17:25
Arr. Nice (Sud)	14:17	17:15	20:35

Lyon - Torino (and Rome)   152 + 351

The Culoz-Modane portion of this trip offers outstanding lake and mountain scenery. The train goes through the 8.5-mile long Mont Cenis Tunnel, constructed in 1871.

Both of these trains have light refreshments.

Dep. Lyon (P-D)	06:59	Dep. Torino (P.N.)	12:22
Dep. Culoz	N/A	Dep. Modane	14:01
Arr. Modane	09:38	Dep. Culoz	N/A
Arr. Torino (P.N.)	11:16	Arr. Lyon (P-D)	16:40

Toulouse - La Tour-de-Carol - Toulouse   144

Excellent mountain and canyon scenery.

Dep. Toulouse (Mat.)	07:52	10:14	Dep. La Tour	10:40	13:35
Arr. La Tour	10:28	12:49	Arr. Toulouse (Mat.)	13:11	16:10

Toulouse - Limoges - Toulouse   138

Recommended for mountain scenery. This route can be seen either as an easy one-day roundtrip between Toulouse and Limoges or as a portion of the ride Toulouse–Paris and v.v. trip.

Dep. Toulouse (Mat.)	07:31 (1)	10:32 (2)	10:58 (3)	13:41 (2)	14:02 (4)
Arr. Limoges	10:48	14:04	14:21	17:00	17:36

• • •

Dep. Limoges	13:01 (5)	16:55 (6)	20:46 (6)
Arr. Toulouse (Mat.)	16:55	20:35	00:20

(1) Supplement charged. Runs daily, except Sundays and holidays. Light refreshments. (2)Runs daily. Light refreshments. (3) Operates mid-July to early September. Runs daily. (4) Runs Sunday and Friday only. (5) Runs daily. Light refreshments early September to early July. (6) Supplement charged. Runs Friday only. Light refreshments.

INTERNATIONAL ROUTES
FROM FRANCE

The French gateway for rail travel to Amsterdam, Bern (and on to Zurich and Vienna), Brussels, Cologne, Geneva, London and Madrid is Paris. Notes on the routes to London appear in Chapter 7.

From Marseille, there is rail service to Barcelona and Genoa (and on to Milan and Rome). From Paris, there are trains to Amsterdam, Barcelona, Bern, Brussels, Cologne, Geneva, Genoa, Lisbon, Madrid, Milan and Rome.

Nice - Marseille - Narbonne - Barcelona

163

Dep. Nice	06:00 (1)	-0-	-0-	11:56
Dep. Marseille	09:04	12:45 (1)	-0-	14:42
Arr. Narbonne	11:54	15:18	-0-	17:36

Change trains.
162

Dep. Narbonne	12:14	16:23	-0-	19:04
Arr. Port Bou	13:55	17:58	-0-	20:45

Change trains.
416

Dep. Port Bou	14:18 (2)	18:20 (2)	18:55 (4)	21:10 (2)
Arr. Barcelona (P. de G.)	16:50	21:32 (3)	20:50 (5)	23:22

(1) Light refreshments. (2) Second-class only. (3) Arrives at Barcelona's Sants railstation. (4) Restaurant car. (5) Arrives at Barcelona's Franca railstation.

Marseille - Nice - Genoa - Milan - Rome   90

There is marvelous Mediterranean coastal scenery on this route.

Dep. Marseille (St. Ch.)	-0-	05:00	06:15
Dep. Nice	07:15 (1)	08:08	09:10
Arr. Genoa (P.P.)	11:30	12:16	13:30
Arr. Milan (Cen.)	13:44	-0-	15:40
Arr. Rome	-0-	18:05	-0-
Dep. Marseille (St. Ch.)	16:39 (2)	17:28 (3)	20:35 (5)
Dep. Nice	19:10	20:29 (4)	23:12 (4)
Arr. Genoa (P.P.)	22:10	00:17	03:30
Arr. Milan (Cen.)	23:59	-0-	05:40
Arr. Rome	-0-	06:55	-0-

(1) Operates mid-July to late August. Second-class only. (2) Restaurant car. (3) Change trains in Nice at 20:19. (4) Carries a sleeping car. Also has couchettes. (5) Light refreshments. Change trains in Nice at 23:02.

Paris - Amsterdam 76

See "Amsterdam–Paris."

Paris - Basel 57

See "Paris–Basel."

Paris - Bordeaux - Lisbon 46

This train has couchettes Paris-Lisbon, plus a sleeping car, coaches and a restaurant car Irun-Lisbon.

Dep. Paris (Austerlitz)	13:54
Dep. Bordeaux (St. J.)	18:19
Set watch back one hour.	
Arr. Irun	20:51
Arr. Lisbon (S. Apol.)	13:05 Day 2

Paris - Bordeaux - Madrid 46

Dep. Paris (Aust.)	18:05 (1)	20:00 (2)
Dep. Bordeaux (St. J.)	22:35	00:26
Set your watch back one hour.		
Dep. Hendaye	01:57	02:37
Arr. Madrid (Cham.)	09:50	08:32

(1) Has only second-class couchettes. No coaches. Light refreshments Paris-Hendaye. (2) Has only first and second-class sleeping cars and a restaurant car. No couchettes or coaches.

Paris - Brussels - Amsterdam   18

Dep. Paris (Nord)	07:07 (1)	07:50 (3)	10:20 (3)	11:29 (4)	12:34 (5)	13:43 (6)
Arr. Brussels (Midi)	09:39	10:49 (3)	13:17 (3)	14:02	15:27	16:42
Change trains.						
Dep. Brussels (Midi)	10:10 (2)	11:04	13:29	14:10 (2)	16:10 (2)	17:10 (2)
Arr. Amsterdam	13:08	14:02	16:34	17:08	19:08	20:08

Dep. Paris (Nord)	14:33 (3)	16:36 (3)	17:25 (7)	18:38 (8)	23:22 (9)
Arr. Brussels (Midi)	17:42	19:49	20:01	21:10 (8)	04:32 (9)
Change trains.					
Dep. Brussels (Midi)	15:54	19:56	20:10	21:20	04:49
Arr. Amsterdam	21:01	22:47	23:08	23:59	08:05

(1) Supplement charged. Runs Monday–Friday. Restaurant car. (2) Light refreshments. (3) Direct train. No train change in Brussels. Light refreshments. (4) Supplement charged. Runs daily. Restaurant car. (5) Operates Monday-Friday late August to late June. Restaurant car. (6) Supplement charged. Restaurant car. (7) Restaurant car. Early September to early July: runs daily. Early July to early September: runs Monday-Friday. (8) Direct train. No train change in Brussels. Reservation required. Supplement charged. Runs daily, except Saturday. Restaurant car Paris–Brussels. (9) Direct train. No train change in Brussels. Has couchettes. (5) Runs Monday-Friday.

Paris - Cologne - Hamburg - Copenhagen   25

Dep. Paris (Nord)	07:31 (1)	13:43 (1)	16:32 (1)	21:30 (3)	23:14 (5)
Arr. Cologne	12:48	19:42	21:57	-0- (3)	05:52
Change trains.					
Dep. Cologne	13:10 (1)	20:10 (1)	-0-	-0- (3)	06:10 (1)
Arr. Hamburg (Hbf.)	17:11	00:11	-0-	07:11 (4)	-0-
Arr. Copenhagen	-0-	-0-	-0-	12:20	07:48

(1) Supplement charged. Restaurant car. (2) Direct train to Copenhagen. No train change in Cologne. Operates late May to late Ssptember. Carries a sleeping car. Also has couchettes. Coach is second-class. (3) Direct train to Hamburg. Does not call on Cologne. (4) Change trains in Hamburg, departing at 07:19 (1). (5) Carries a sleeping car. Also has couchettes and coaches. Light refreshments.

Paris - Geneva   159

All of these trains are TGV, require reservation and charge a supplement.

Dep. Paris (Lyon)	07:24 (1)	10:28 (1)	14:42 (2)	17:40 (1)	19:09 (1)
Arr. Geneva (Corn.)	10:51	-0-	18:14	21:11	22:45

(1) Restaurant car. (2) Light refreshments.

Paris - Dijon - Lausanne - Milan - Genoa - Rome or Venice 44

Dep. Paris (Lyon)	07:14 (1)	12:21 (1)	15:53 (1)	18:47 (3)	20:06 (3+8)
Arr. Lausanne	11:06	16:07	19:45	-0- (4)	-0- (4)
Change trains.					
Dep. Lausanne	11:13 (2)	16:13 (2)	19:53 (2)	-0-	-0-
Arr. Milan (Cen.)	14:40	19:45	23:40	-0-	04:43 (5)
Arr. Genoa (P.P.)	-0-	-0-	-0-	02:51	-0-
Arr. Rome (Ter.)	-0-	-0-	-0-	09:45	-0-
Arr. Venice (S.L.)	-0-	-0-	-0-	-0-	08:45

(1) TGV. Reservation required. Supplement charged. Restaurant car. (2) Restaurant car. (3) Light refreshments. This train has only sleeping cars and couchettes. No coaches. (4) Does not call on Lausanne. Direct train. (5) Arrives at Milan's Porta Garibaldi railstation. (6) Light refreshments. Carries a sleeping car. Also has couchettes. (7) Carries a sleeping car. Also has couchettes. Coach is second-class. (8) Plus another Paris departure at 20:56 (6), not calling on Lausanne, Genoa or Venice...arriving Rome's Ostiense railstaion at 14:19. There is also another Paris departure at 22:22 (4+7), terminating in Milan at 08:48.

THE FERRY-CROSSING TO IRELAND

Paris - Le Havre - Rosslare and Paris - Cherbourg - Rosslare

Operated by Irish Ferries Company. Passage *only* (without a seat or a berth) is free all year with a Eurailpass. The 1995 cost for "passage only" was $209 (U.S.) from July 10 to August 31, and was at lower prices in other times of the year.

Passage *plus a seat* was $217 (but only $10 with a Eurailpass) in mid-Summer when there are many more passengers than seats on the vessel and some passengers must sit on the deck for this 21-hour trip. Reserving and paying extra for a cabin is essential in Summer. A 6-berth cabin that was $221 per person in mid-Summer was onl y $13 with a Eurailpass. A 4-berth cabin with shower and private toilet (at $257 per person) was only $48 with a Eurailpass.

There are also sailings to and from Cork, Ireland during June, July and August.

Days of operation and departures times vary during 5 different periods of the year. For 1995 schedules, prices and reservations, contact the North American agent: Lynott Tours Inc., 350 Fifth Avenue, New York, NY 10118. Telephone: (212) 760-0101 or (800) 221-2474.

GERMANY

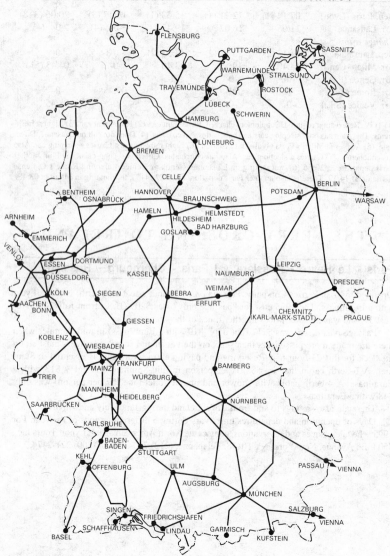

GERMANY

Overview

Train travel in Germany has changed radically since the Berlin wall came down and the Bundesrepublik reunified with the former East Germany. Although tremendous building projects have begun to help the eastern part of the country catch up materially with the west, there is still a vast gully between the two. Trains equipped to go twice as fast must slow down in parts of the east due to old and ill-maintained tracks. Cities like Berlin, Leipzig, Weimar, and Dresden are now easily connected to the major western German cities of Munich, Frankfurt, Hannover, Hamburg, etc. The German national train company, (Deutsche Bundesbahn, DB) is highly efficient and well equipped. The new fast trains, not unlike the French TGVs, run regularly between the major cities in record time and are teched-out with business conference rooms and on-board telephones. In Germany the train station functions as the hub of most downtown areas and after 6:30 PM when stores close in German cities, the train station (hauptbahnhof) is pretty much the only place to buy groceries, wine, etc.

General Information

• Children under four travel free. Half-fare for children 4-11. Children 12 and over pay full fare.

• Fast InterCity and EuroCity trains, connecting 50 important cities along five major rail routes, have easy cross-platform connections in such cities as Cologne, Wurzburg, Mannheim and Dortmund. The 6 DM supplement charged for IC and EC trains includes the cost of a seat reservation. Where timetable footnotes indicate that a supplement is charged by a particular train, a passenger using a Eurailpass or German Flexipass does not have to pay the extra charge. (All of those passes are also valid on all commuter rail services in major German cities.) The IC supplement must be paid when using the Inter-Rail Card, available only to residents of Europe. Some of the InterCity trains have top speeds of 125 mph. A conference compartment in them can be rented for the cost of four first-class tickets. Worldwide telephone calls can be made from all IC trains.

• When entering or leaving Germany on an international train, the customs, passport and currency control are usually performed in the train. Because of this, passengers traveling across Germany (such as from Amsterdam to Copenhagen) are required to travel in a special car or compartment.

• Porter service may be reserved in advance at many rail stations, including those at the Dusseldorf and Frankfurt airports. A program began in 1987 to install conveyor belts at stairways in 130 rail stations as well as escalators which can accommodate baggage carts in all major stations.

• The signs you will see at rail stations in Germany are the same as those listed earlier in this chapter under Austria.

GERMANY'S TRAIN PASSES

EuroCity and InterCity supplements are included in the prices listed below for all German train passes. Travelers arriving in Germany by airplane can validate all of them and also Eurailpass at the airport rail ticket office after exiting the customs area and use them for the rail trip from the airport to the city.

Wunder Flexipass Sold worldwide outside Germany by travel agencies and Rail Europe (U.S.A. and Canadian offices listed under "France").

Unlimited 4 days of first-class train travel plus one day of car rental (any 5 days) within 21 days. Prices vary (a) whether for one person or for 2 persons, and (b) the category of car. A third and fourth passenger needs to pay only for a 5-day German Railpass (see below).

The 1996 prices were not set at the end of 1995. The 1995 price *per person* for 2 persons (using the smallest size car) was: $225. A third and fourth passenger had to pay only $215 per person. Up to 5 more rail days could be added at $42 per day. Unlimited additional car days could be added also at $42 per day.

All of the following passes are sold worldwide outside Germany by travel agencies and by GermanRail. All of them are 'flexible,' valid for one month (example: July 3 to August 2). These 1996 prices are shown in U.S. dollars.

German Railpass For first-class: $260 for any 5 days, $410 for any 10 days, and $530 for any 15 days. For second-class: $178, $286 and $386.

A second-class Youthpass (under age 26 on first day of travel) costs $138, $188 and $238.

German Rail Twinpass The first-class price per person when 2 persons travel together is $234 for any 5 days, $369 for any 10 days, $477 for any 15 days. For second-class: $160, $257 and $331.

German Rail & Car Pass Provides 5 days of unlimited rail travel within Germany plus 3 days of rental car with unlimited mileage. All supplements for travel on high speed trains and the Value Added Tax on car rental are included. Cars may be picked up at one Hertz location in Germany and dropped off at another Hertz location in Germany.

Not included: train reservation fees, auto insurance, and gas. GermanRail will make train reservations up to 10 days prior to departure at a charge of $10 per person, per train, plus $10 per order for mailing and handling. Car reservations must be made either up to 7 days prior to departure or in Germany up to 2 business days before rental is to begin.

Prices vary (a) whether for one person or for 2 persons, (b) whether the rail portion is for first-class or second-class, and (c) the category of car. A third and fourth adult passenger needs to pay only the rail portion $240 for first-class, $160 for second-class. Children under age 12 need to pay only the rail portion: $120 for first-class, $80 for second-class.

The prices for all travel completed by March 31, 1996 per person for 2 persons (using second-class train seats and the smallest size car) is $209 plus $3.75 handling charge. More car days can be added at $35 per day.

BAHNCARDS

They allow 50% discount. The 1996 *first*-class prices are shown below. *Second*-class is 50% less.

BahnCard 440DM.

BahnCard fur Ehepartner (for married couples)   220DM for first person, 110 DM for the partner.

BahnCard fur Familien (for families — parents and all children) 220DM.

BahnCard fur Kinder (for chidren age 4–11)   100DM

BahnCard fur Jugendliche/Teens (for youths age 12–17)   100DM.

BahnCard fur Junioren (for youths age 18-22)   220DM.

BahnCard fur Senioren (for persons age 60 and older)   220DM.

ONE-DAY EXCURSIONS AND CULTURAL SIGHTSEEING

Here are 94 one-day rail trips that can be made comfortably from cities in Germany, returning to them in most cases before dinnertime. Notes are provided on a few possible recommended sights to see and do at each destination. The number after the name of each route corresponds to the Cook's Timetable. Details on 11 other rail trips recommended for exceptional scenery and schedules for international connections conclude this section. Sightseeing tours to Chemnitz (formerly Karl Marx Stadt), Dresden and Potsdam start in Berlin at Parkplatz Rankestrasse, near the Kurfurstendamm. For reservations, contact Deutsches Reiseburo, Kurfurstendamm 17, Berlin W.30, Germany.

The eight base cities for one-day excursions include Berlin, Cologne, Dresden, Frankfurt/Main, Hamburg, Hannover, Leipzig and Munich.

Berlin

Two-hour and 4-hour tours of West Berlin begin at 10:00 and occur at frequent intervals during the day, from 220 Kurfurstendamm, 216 Kurfurstendamm, and opposite from the bombed-out Gedachtniskirche (Memorial Church).

The stroll down tree-lined Kurfurstendamm is almost mandatory, to observe the city's fine stores, theaters, cafes, movie houses and bars. See the Zoo (started in 1843) and Aquarium, one of Europe's oldest and best animal exhibits, open daily until dusk. The New National Gallery, at Potsdamerstrasse 50, open daily except Monday 09:00–17:00.

The bust of Nefertiti and other important items in the Egyptian Museum at 70 Schloss Strasse, closed Friday. The rooms and gardens of Charlottenburg Castle, closed Monday, opposite the Egyptian Museum. The 1936 Olympic Stadium. The German History Museum, in the reconstructed Reichstag Building, on Paul-Lobe Strasse, open daily except Monday 10:00–17:00. The tent-shaped Philharmonic Hall. Take a boat ride on the Havel River.

See modern paintings at Brucke Museum, Bussardsteig 9, open Monday–Friday 11:00–17:00. Masterpieces by Durer, Cranach the Elder and Holbein the Younger, at the Dahlem Museum, Arnimallee 23–27, open Tuesday-Sunday 09:00–17:00. Models of everything that floats, flies or rolls, at the Transport Museum, Trebbinerstrasse 9, open Tuesday–Friday 09:00–18:00 and on Saturday and Sunday 10:00–18:00.

Exhibits about many modern architects in the Bauhaus Museum, Klingelhoferstrasse 13, open daily except Tuesday 11:00–17:00. The best collection of Durer drawings in Germany is at the Kupferstichkabinett.

Visit the sixth floor (called Feinschmecker Etage —"the gourmet's floor") of Kaufhaus des Westens (called KaDeWe "Kah-day-vay" by local people), a large department store on Tauentzienstrasse. It is the largest food store in Europe: 500 sales clerks dispensing 30,000 different products. Fruits and vegetables sold there include limes from Brazil, rare wild mushrooms from France and Poland, avocados from Israel, tiny beans from Kenya, tomatoes from Spain, apples from Hungary.

They sell 1,500 kinds of meats (250 varieties of salami). Then there are also eels, crawfish, catfish and carp. Live lobsters are delivered to the store in tank trucks. You will also find 400 types of bread. Three separate counters for 1,800 varieties of cheese from France, Italy and other countries. Eighteen kinds of herring salad. It also has 28 restaurants, counter services and stand-up bars.

Store hours are: 9:00–18:30 on Monday, Tuesday, Wednesday and Friday; 9:00–20:30 on Thursday; 9:00–14:00 on most Saturdays. KaDeWe has 30,000 customers on an ordinary day. Before holidays, there are 100,000 customers in a single day.

The Weissbierstube Restaurant in the Berlin Museum is acclaimed for its bounteous buffet tables. Both the Restaurant and the Museum are open daily except Mondays 11:00–18:00.

To see East Berlin, take the elevated railway from West Berlin's Zoo railstation to its Friedrichstrasse station. On leaving Friedrichstrasse station, turn right and walk 3 blocks to reach Berlin's famous boulevard, Unter den Linden, and the enormous Soviet embassy. A few blocks further, at the end of the boulevard, is the classical Brandenburg Gate and the ruins of the Berlin Wall.

Also see the reconstructed St. Hedwig's Cathedral. The National Gallery. The 18th century State Opera. The tremendous collection of Oriental, Greek and Roman antiquities, the Market Gate of Milet and the impressive Pergamon Altar, all at the Pergamon Museum on Bodestrasse, open Wednesday and Thursday 09:00–18:00 and Friday 10:00–18:00.

The Palace of the Republic. Bode Museum. The Altes Museum. The tiny 14th century church, Marienkirche. The Museum of German History.

Cologne (Koln)

All museums are closed on Monday.

It is a 10-minute bus ride from the Cologne/Bonn Airport to the center of Cologne.

Your city-sightseeing in Cologne should include, above all, the Cathedral, very near the railstation. Started in 1248 and not completed until 1880, it houses the world's largest reliquary, containing relics of the 3 kings, the Magi, as well as a splendid collection of illuminated books, vestments, ivories and liturgical articles. These can be seen Monday– Saturday 09:00–17:00, Sundays and holidays 12:30–17:00.

The best time to be inside the Cathedral is at the Sunday 10:00 mass, when the ceremony starts with a procession of church elders dressed in robes of burgundy, crimson and rose, and wearing white, embroidered, starched linen. If you climb the 502 steps to the top of the spire, past the 9 giant bells, you will see a magnificent view of Cologne, The Rhine River and the Rhine Valley.

Near the Cathedral, explore ancient Cologne. The Praetorium, a palace for Roman governors several centuries before Christ, located in the basement of the Town Hall, open daily 10:00–17:00. Its entrance, difficult to find, is across from the Restaurant-Bar-Cafe Oldtimer at 110 Kleine Budengasse. See the 3rd century Dionysus mosaic (once the dining hall floor of a Roman house) in the Roman Museum, open Tuesday–Sunday 10:00–20:00.

Also on view there is an outstanding collection of Roman glass, cooking utensils and 4th century jewelry. Visit the 3rd century Roman tower.

See the collection of paintings by Cologne masters of the 13th–17th and 19th centuries in the Wallraf Richartz Museum (1 Bischofsgartenstrasse, between the Cathedral and the Hauptbahnhoff), open Tuesday, Wednesday and Thursday 10:00–20:00. On Friday, Saturday and Sunday 10:00–18:00. Modern art is exhibited in the Ludwig Museum (same address and hours). Visit the Zoo. The 15th century Gurzenich. The Metropolitan Historical Museum. The Town Hall. St. Pantaleon Church. St. Andreas Church. Relics and treasures in the Golden Room at the Church of St. Ursula. The luxury shops on Hohestrasse and Schildergasse.

Dresden

Major works of Raphael, Rembrandt, Rubens, Tintoretto, Van Eyck, Vermeer and other great 16th and 17th century painters at the Picture Gallery in the Semper Building of Zwinger Palace. Another excellent collection of paintings in the National Gallery.

Hear the Silberman organ (235 years old in 1990) at the cathedral, Hofkirche. Visit the baroque Opera House. The Zoo in Stadtpark (also called Volkspark). The Block House.

Dresden Palace. The Japanese Castle. The treasures at the Albertinium Museum. The Palace of Culture. Take the cable car to Weisser Hirsch for the view of Dresden from the top of that hill.

It is a 17-mile ride by suburban railway from Dresdent to **Meissen**. See the 15th century castle (Albrechtsburg) and the Cathedral there. Shop in Meissen for Dresdent china and Albrecht porcelain.

Frankfurt

There is frequent rail service from Frankfurt's Hauptbahnhof railstation to the city's airport and vice versa (11-minute travel time) every 20 minutes from 04:14 to 23:54. From the airport to Frankfurt: every 30 minutes from 04:33 to 23:53 plus 00:33. Frequent trains per hour continue beyond the airport station to Mainz and Wiesbaden. Trains also depart the airport at frequent times for Bonn, Cologne, Dortmund, Dusseldorf, Koblenz, Ludwigshafen, Luxembourg, Mannheim, Nurnberg, Trier and Wurzburg.

Bus tours that cover in 2½ hours the city's most interesting places depart daily from the south side of the main railstation at 10:00 and 14:00. Most museums in Frankfurt are closed on Monday.

See the house where Goethe was born in 1749 (23 Grosser Hirschgraben), open daily, except Sunday: April–September, 09:00–18:00, October–March, 09:00–16:00. Next to it, the Goethe Museum (books, pictures, furniture and manuscripts associated with the writer) in the Grosser Hirschgraben, open Monday–Saturday 09:00–18:00, Sunday 10:00–15:00. The new (1991) Jewish Museum at 14–15 Untermainkal, in the former Rothschild Palace, is open daily except Monday.

The Zoo, one of the world's greatest, at Am Tiergarten, open 08:00–19:00 in Summer, 08:00–18:00 in October, 08:00–17:00 in Winter. Its Exoticarium (aquarium and reptile house) is open until 22:00. Buses #10, #13 and #15 go to the Zoo.

The emperor's coronation hall in the Romer complex at medieval Romerberg Square. The wonderful doors in the 13th century Leonhardskirche. The 13th century chapel of Saalhof in the remains of the palace of Frederick Barbarossa. Cloth Hall. The Botanical Garden. The pews and murals in the Cathedral of St. Bartholomew. The Church of St. Nicholas. The Church of St. Paul. Senckenberg Museum, the largest natural history museum in West Germany, open 09:00–16:00. The collection of Dutch primitives and 16th century German masters at the Stadel Art Institute and Municipal Gallery, open daily except Monday 10:00–17:00. The Liebighaus Exhibition of Sculpture.

The Museum of Plastic Art. The changing exhibits of European silver, porcelain, furniture and glass from the Middle Ages to the present time and also an Asian collection (3rd to 19th century) at the Museum of Arts and Crafts. The Henninger Tower in Sachsenhausen, the old quarter of the city (across the Main River, near the commercial district). The Postal Museum. The major shopping streets: Zeil and Kaiserstrasse.

The palm trees, other tropical plants, and Alpine gardens in the city's central park, Palmengarten. Nine miles away in **Offenbach,** center of West Germany's leather industry, is the German Leather Museum, open daily 10:00–17:00.

Hamburg

Most museums in Hamburg are closed Monday. See the port, one of the busiest in the world. There are splendid views of the enormous port from Stintfang Hill. Visit Hagenbeck Zoo, the first cageless zoo in the world, at Stellingen Gardens. St. James Church, with its famous organ, built in 1693. Rathausmarkt Square. The models of Old Hamburg, the port and the city's railway system, in the Museum of the History of Hamburg.

The Counting Houses in the business quarter, around Burchardplatz. The notorious Reperbahn. The view of the city from the Michel Tower of St, Michaelis Church. The Museum of Decorative Arts. The Art Gallery. The Botanical Garden. The "Sight and Sound" performances during Summer in the Planten un Blomen park. Take a flight over the city from Fuhlsbuttel Airport.

Hannover

The bus ride between Langenhagen Airport and Hannover's railstation takes 30 minutes. The bus terminal is located next to Track #14.

See the collection of art (from the Middle Ages to the beginning of the 20th century) in the Niedersachsische Landesgalerie. Modern painting and sculpture in the Sprengel Museum (Max Beckmann, Paul Klee, Pablo Picasso).

For an interesting 2-hour walking tour of Hannover, obtain the detailed brochure available at both of the railstation's 2 tourist information offices. Walk out of the station to the statue in front of it and start to follow the painted red line which leads to Passerelle (a pedestrian mall), the 19th century Opera House, the old city wall, Town Hall, and Hannover's oldest (16th century) half-timbered structure.

See the bronze doors by Marcks at Market Church. The outstanding collection of Egyptian antiquities in the Kestner Museum. The prehistoric objects in the Museum of Lower Saxony.

Take a short walk from the Central railstation to the station under Kropke Cafe and, from there, Tram #1 or #2 to the absolutely fantastic baroque Royal Gardens of Herrenhausen. Its ornamental fountains perform in Summer Monday–Friday, 11:00–12:00 and 15:30–16:30. On Saturdays and Sundays, they can be seen 10:00–12:00 and 15:30–17:30.

Next to Herrenhausen is the natural park, Georgengarten. Nearby, see the exotic plants in the greenhouses at Berggarten.

Take streetcar #6 from the Central railstation to Hannover's outstanding Zoo.

Leipzig

Concentrate on the area around Market Place. Visit the Museum of the History of Leipzig in the Renaissance Old Town Hall. The 17th century stock exchange (Alte Bourse), rebuilt in 1963. The weighinghouse (Alte Waage), where taxes were levied on imported goods. Auerbachs Keller, the old tavern on which Goethe based the locale of his Faust drama. Bach's tomb, at St. Thomas Church. The Museum of Fine Arts.

West of Market Place is the church where Johann Sebastian Bach is buried. Bach composed in that church the last 27 years of his life. Also see Gohliser Schlosschen, a rococo palace. Gohlis, the home of the poet Schiller. The Opera House in Karl Marx Platz. It is impossible to find a room in Leipzig during the semi-annual (March and September) trade fairs that attract visitors from all over the world.

Munich (Munchen)

A metropolitan train connects Munich's Hauptbahnhof and Ostbanhof railstations. It is a 10-minute bus ride between Munich's Riem Airport and the Hauptbahnhof railstation, where the city's monthly program of events (theaters, museums, exhibits, concerts, plays, etc.) can be obtained. The program is also sold at newsstands.

Most museums in Munich are closed on Monday. There are more than 50 — on coins, ethnology, theater, applied arts, hunting and fishing, folk music, graphic arts, mineralogy, Egyptian art, toys, fire fighting, beer making, prehistory, porcelains, paleontology, puppets, photography, even chamber pots.

See the works of Durer, El Greco, Raphael, Holbein, Rembrandt and many other great 14th to 18th century painters at Alte (Old) Pinakothek, at 27 Barer Strasse, open Tuesday-Sunday 09:00–16:30, and on Tuesday and Thursday 07:00–21:00. The Neue (New) Pinakothek at 29 Barer Strasse (same days and hours as the "Old" museum) has a collection of 19th and 20th century artists. The paintings of Kandinsky, Marcs and Klees in the Lenbachhaus, at 33 Luisen Strasse, open daily except Monday 10:00–18:00.

The 15th century Frauenkirche Cathedral, and the view of Munich from its north tower…and then later the view of Frauenkirche from the top of Neue Rathaus (New City Hall), where at 11:00 every day the mechanical figures in its bell tower perform a tournament of knights, a medieval royal wedding, and a dance. There are other fine views of Munich from Olympia Tower.

The paintings of Cezanne, Gauguin, Renoir and other impressionists at the Haus der Kunst at 1 Princregenten Strasse, open daily except Monday 09:00–16:30. On Thursday, it is also open 19:00–21:00. See Wittelsbach Fountain.

The fine exhibits and planetarium at Deutsches Museum, considered the best scientific museum in the world, open daily 09:00–17:00. It is across the Ludwigsbrucke, on an island in the Isar River. Displays of 16,000 items.

The view of the Alps from the top of Peterskirche. The best collection of tapestries and wood carvings in Germany, at the Bavarian National Museum. Munich's most famous beer palace, Hofbrauhaus.

The Schatzkammer in the Residenz palace (which houses the enormous Festaal and many museums that are open Tuesday–Saturday 10:00–16:30, Sunday 10:00–13:00), and the flower gardens in the park north of it. Words cannot describe the fabulous beauty of the Festaal.

At Schloss (Castle) Nymphenburg: the porcelain in the showrooms of Nymphenburger Porzellan Manufaktur, open daily except Monday 10:00–12:00 and 13:30–16:00. Also visit the park outside the castle. Located on the outskirts of Munich, Nymphenburg can be reached by taking the U-1 subway to the end of that line (Rotkreutzplatz) and transfering to the #12 streetcar. Alternate lines from the center of Munich are streetcars #17 or #21, or buses #41 or #42.

See the history of Munich in the Isartorplatz Museum. The impressive Renaissance Michalskirche on the Neuhauserstrasse pedestrian mall. Ancient Greek and Roman sculpture in the Glyptothek (Konigsplatz 3), open Tuesday, Wednesday, Friday and Sunday 10:00–16:30, on Thursday 12:00–20:30. Nearby, the Staatliche Antikensammlungen (State Collection of Antiquities) at Konigsplatz 1, open Tuesday and Thursday–Sunday 10:00–16:30, on Wednesday 12:00–20:30.

The collection of Medieval art and sculpture, arts and crafts, applied arts, folk art and folklore at the Bayerisches Nationalmuseum (Bavarian National Museum), at Prinzregenstrasse 3, open daily except Monday 09:30–17:00. Nearby, an exhibit of late 19th century Herman painters in Schackgalerie at Prinzregenstrasse 9, open daily except Tuesday 09:00–16:30.

Visit Schwabing, the Latin quarter. The palaces on Ludwigstrasse. The history of Bavarian Motor Works (aircraft, motorcycles, automobiles) in the BMW Museum, open daily 09:00–16:00.

Infamous Dachau is a 40-minute ride by commuter train #S-2 or bus #11. Although there are no guides at Dachau, an exhibit there details the operation of the concentration camp, and an English-language film is shown at 11:30 and 15:30.

Since 1870, an Alois Dallmayr food store has offered gourmet delicacies in Munich. It added a restaurant in 1978. As Fauchon's in Paris does, Dallmayr (15 Dienerstrasse) has a vast section of imported foods. Its most notable feature, however, is the enormous array it offers of West Germany's finest lunch meats, 22 varieties of smoked fish, and 27 types of bread.

Nearly everything edible can be found at Dallmayr's: local and imported fruits, cooked meats and poultry, live fish swimming in marble tanks, wines, more than 50 different salads, 200 different chocolates, 120 different sausages, 18 types of ham, and they also sell special cigars.

If you eat none of the splendid food there, at least see the statues, marble pillars and mounted deer heads that decorate the interior of the store. Another famous food emporium is Kafer's, at 73 Prinzregenten, Germany's largest delicatessen and caterer. Both stores have an excellent restaurant.

The Viktualienmarkt, behind St. Peter's Church, is one of Europe's largest outdoor food markets. Two blocks long, it has operated since 18:07: fruits, vegetables, poultry, cheeses, herbs, breads, pastries, wines, plants and flowers. It is open Monday–Friday 07:00–18:30, Saturday 07:00–17:00. Friday and Saturday are its busiest days. It is closed on Sundays.

The Most practical way to visit Neuschwanstein and Linderhof Castles is by taking the train-and-bus excursion operated by EurAide on Wednesday and Saturday during June, July and early August. Passsengers depart Munich at 07:35, returning there 17:30. For information and advisable advance reservations, write to EurAide, Bahnhofplatz 2, Am Gleissll, 80335 Munchen 2, Germnany. Telephone: (089) 59-38-89

In the following timetables, where a city has more than one railstation we have designated the particular station after the name of the city (in parentheses). Where no station is designated for cities in Austria, Switzerland and Germany, the station is "Hauptbahnhoff."

Reservations are advisable on most German trains!

Berlin - Chemnitz (formerly Karl Marx Stadt) - Berlin 680

All of these trains have light refreshments. Reservation is advisable for them.

Dep. Berlin (Lichtenberg)	07:24	11:24
Dep. Berlin (Schonefeld)	07:43	11:43
Arr. Chemnitz	09:51	13:51

Sights in **Chemnitz:** This was an East German post-World War II showplace new city before the 1990 unification of West and East Germany.

Dep. Chemnitz	14:17	16:17	18:17
Arr. Berlin (Schonefeld)	16:24	18:24	20:24
Arr. Berlin (Lichtenberg)	23 minutes later		

Berlin - Dresden - Berlin 680

All of these trains charge a supplement that includes reservation fee and have a restaurant car, unless designated otherwise.

Dep. Berlin (Hbf.)	06:24	08:24	10:24	12:24
Arr. Dresden (Hbf.)	08:12	10:06	12:06	14:06
Dep. Dresden (Hbf.)	13:36	15:36	17:36	19:36	21:36
Arr. Berlin (Hbf.)	15:15	17:15	19:15	21:15	23:15

Berlin - Erfurt - Berlin 670

Reservation is advisable for all of these trains. All of them have light refreshments, unless designated otherwise.

Dep. Berlin (Lichtenberg)	06:18	08:18	10:18
Dep. Berlin (Schonefeld)	20 minutes after departing Lichtenberg railstation		
Arr. Erfurt	10:01	12:03	14:01

Sights in **Erfurt:** The exquisite Gothic and German Renaissance houses. The Cathedral, where Martin Luther was ordained in 1507. The bridge, on which 33 houses stand. St. Severin Church.

Dep. Erfurt	13:48	15:48	17:48	19:48
Arr. Berlin (Schonefeld)	17:06	19:06	21:06	23:06
Arr. Berlin (Lichtenberg)	20 minutes later			

Berlin - Frankfurt   750

All of these trains charge a supplement that includes reservation fee and have a restaurant car.

Dep. Berlin (Zoo)	05:48	07:48	09:48	11:48	13:48	15:48 (1)
Arr. Frankfurt (Hbf.)	10:39	12:39	14:39	16:39	18:39	20:39

Dep. Frankfurt (Hbf.)	07:18	09:18	11:18	13:18	15:18	17:18 (2)
Arr. Berlin (Zoo)	12:15	14:15	16:15	18:15	20:15	22:15

(1) Plus another Berlin departure at 17:48, arriving Frankfurt 22:41. (2) Plus another Frankfurt departure at 19:18, arriving Berlin 00:15.

Berlin - Hamburg   680

All of these trains charge a supplement that includes reservation fee and have a restaurant car.

Dep. Berlin (Hbf.)	05:40	07:40	09:40	11:40	13:40	15:40 (1)
Dep. Berlin (Zoo)	06:00	08:00	10:00	12:00	14:00	16:00
Arr. Hamburg (Hbf.)	08:59	10:59	12:59	14:59	16:59	18:59

Dep. Hamburg (Hbf.)	06:51	08:51	10:51	12:51	14:51	16:51 (2)
Arr. Berlin (Zoo)	09:45	11:45	13:45	15:45	17:45	19:45
Arr. Berlin (Hbf.)	10:04	12:04	14:04	16:04	18:04	20:04

(1) Plus other Berlin (Hbf.) departures at 17:40 and 19:40, arriving Hamburg 20:59 and 22:59. (2) Plus other Hamburg departures at 18:51 and 20:51, arriving Berlin (Hbf.) 22:08 and 00:04.

Berlin - Hannover   700

All of these trains charge a supplement that includes reservation fee and have a restaurant car, unless designated otherwise.

Dep. Berlin (Hbf.)	-0-	-0-	-0-	
Dep. Berlin (Zoo)	07:23	09:07	11:07	
Arr. Hannover	10:54	11:54	13:54	
Dep. Hannover	16:04	18:04	19:04	20:04
Arr. Berlin (Zoo)	19:11	21:11	22:33	23:11
Arr. Berlin (Hbf.)	-0-	-0-	-0-	-0-

Berlin - Leipzig - Berlin   670

Dep. Berlin (Licht.)	06:12 (1)	09:36
Dep. Berlin (Hbf.)	-0-	-0-
Arr. Leipzig	08:25	11:45
Dep. Leipzig	14:40 (2)	16:40 (2)
Arr. Berlin (Hbf.)	16:49	18:49
Arr. Berlin (Licht.)	-0-	-0-

(1) Reservation advisable. Light refreshments. (2) Supplement charged includes reservation fee. Restaurant car.

Berlin - Munich and Munich - Berlin   670

All of the day trains charge a supplement that includes reservation fee and have a restaurant car.

Dep. Berlin (Hbf.)	07:06	09:06	11:06	13:06	15:06
Arr. Munich	15:03	17:06	19:03	21:03	23:03
Dep. Munich	06:56	08:56	10:56	12:56	14:56
Arr. Berlin (Hbf.)	14:49	16:49	18:49	20:49	22:49

Berlin - Potsdam - Berlin   700

There are frequent trains from Berlin's Hauptbahnhoff and Zoo stations 05:57 to 23:12 for this 50-minute ride. From Potsdam: 06:13 to 22:09. Reservations are advisable.

Sights in **Potsdam:** The Concert Room and the great paintings in the Picture Gallery at the 18th century Sans Souci Palace. The 17th century Palace, Cecillienhof, where Truman, Attlee and Stalin signed the Potsdam Agreement in 1945.

Berlin - Rostock - Berlin   669

Reservation is advisable for all of these trains.

Dep. Berlin (Lichtenberg)	06:51 (1)	08:51 (2)	10:51	12:51 (1)
Arr. Rostock	09:25	11:25	13:25	15:25

Sights in **Rostock:** East Germany's largest seaport. See St. Mary's Church. The ancient Town Hall.

Dep. Rostock	12:32 (1)	14:32 (1)	16:32	18:32	20:32 (1)
Arr. Berlin (Lichtenberg)	15:07	17:07	19:07	21:07	23:07

(1) Light refreshments.

Berlin - Stralsund - Berlin   669

Dep. Berlin (Licht.)	06:51 (1)	08:51 (2)	09:20 (5)
Arr. Stralsund (Hbf.)	10:18	12:22	12:122

Sights in **Stralsund:** Many old red-brick buildings and churches along the city's quaint Hanseatic streets.

Dep. Stralsund (Hbf.)	14:27 (3)	16:16 (3)	17:08	18:14 (3)
Arr. Berlin (Licht.)	17:07	19:07	20:11	21:07

(1) Reservation is advisable. Light refreshments. Change trains in Neustrelitz. (2) Change trains in Neubrandenburg. (3) Change trains in Neustrelitz. (4) Plus another Stralsund departure at 19:01 (5), arriving Berlin 21:40 (5). (5) Direct train. No train change.

Berlin - Warnemunde - Berlin   669

Reservation is advisable for all of these trains.

Dep. Berlin (Licht.)	00:09 (1)	06:51 (2)	08:51 (3)	12:51 (4)
Arr. Warnemunde	03:10	09:56	11:45	15:56

Sights in **Warnemunde:** A famous beach resort. A ferry connection to Denmark.

Dep. Warnemunde	04:08 (1)	12:01	15:50 (3)	18:01 (2)
Arr. Berlin (Licht.)	07:04	15:07	19:07	21:07

(1) Carries a sleeping car. Also has couchettes. Coach is second-class. Light refreshments. (2) Light refreshments. (3) Operates late June to mid-August.

Cologne - Aachen - Cologne   700

Dep. Cologne	07:14 (1)	08:14 (2)	09:14 (2)	10:50	11:14 (1)
Arr. Aachen	08:02	08:58	09:58	11:45	12:02
Dep. Aachen	12:53 (1)	14:04 (2)	14:12	15:53 (1)	17:12	17:51 (1+3)
Arr. Cologne	13:42	14:42	15:09	16:42	18:09	18:42

(1) Light refreshments. (2) Supplement charged includes reservation fee. Restaurant car. (3) Plus other Aachen departures at 18:12, 18:56 (2), 19:12, 19:58 (2), 21:12 (2), 21:35 (1), 21:55 (2) and 22:04.

Cologne - Amsterdam - Cologne   28

All of these trains charge a supplement that includes reservation fee and have light refreshments.

Dep. Cologne	07:17	09:17	11:17		
Arr. Amsterdam	09:54	11:51	13:51		
Dep. Amsterdam	15:06	17:00	19:06	20:05	20:56 (1)
Arr. Cologne	17:42	19:42	21:42	23:47	00:22

(1) Coach is second-class.

Cologne - Bonn - Cologne 650 + 710

| Dep. Cologne | Frequent times from 05:54 to 00:49 |
| Arr. Bonn | 22 minutes later |

Sights in **Bonn:** Beethoven-Halle and the museum at Bonngasse 20, where Beethoven was born in 1770. Drachenfels Mountain and the castle ruins that Byron immortalized. The 13th century Remigius Church. Jesu Church. The view of the Rhine and Siebengebirge from Alte Zoll. The university in the Electors' Castle. Poppelsdorf Castle. The Rhineland Museum. The Collegiate Church and Cloister. Take a cruise boat on the Rhine River to see the Siebengebirge Mountains.

| Dep. Bonn | Frequent times from 04:25 to 23:47 |
| Arr. Cologne | 22 minutes later |

Cologne - Brussels - Cologne 200

Dep. Cologne	05:08 (1)	06:30 (2)	07:14	09:14 (2)	
Arr. Brussels (Nord)	07:55	08:47	09:44	11:32	
Arr. Brussels (Cen.)	-0-	-0-	09:49	11:36	
Arr. Brussels (Midi)	08:06	09:01	09:59	11:42	
Dep. Brussels (Midi)	12:03 (2)	13:47	15:47	16:55 (2)	18:08 (2+3)
Dep. Brussels (Cen.)	-0-	13:52	15:52	-0-	18:12
Dep. Brussels (Nord)	12:12	13:57	15:57	17:03	18:18
Arr. Cologne	14:42	16:42	18:42	19:42	20:42

(1) Coaches are second-class. (2) Supplement charged includes reservation fee. Restaurant car or light refreshments. (3) Plus other departures from Brussels Midi/Zuid at 18:47,20:03 (2), arriving Cologne 21:39.

Cologne - Dortmund - Cologne 650 + 700

| Dep. Cologne | Frequent times from 05:03 to 23:16 |
| Arr. Dortmund | 70 minutes later |

Sights in **Dortmund:** The view of the city from the top of the Television Tower. Westphalia Park. The Ostwall Museum.

| Dep. Dortmund | Frequent times from 04:32 to 22:42 |
| Arr. Cologne | 70 minutes later |

Cologne - Dusseldorf - Cologne   650 + 700

There is frequent rail service between Dusseldorf's railstation and its airport. Travel time is 12 minutes (Table 699).

Dep. Cologne	Frequent times from 05:03 to 26:16
Arr. Dusseldorf	24–28 minutes later

Sights in **Dusseldorf:** Many sensational modern buildings, replacing the 85 of the city that was destroyed in World War II. See the Paul Klee collection at Kunsttammlung Nordhein-Westfallen. The Aquarium at the Museumbunker am Zoo.

The collection of 18th century Meissenware and 20th century art (Kadinsky, Chagall, Braque, etc., with 90 works by Paul Klee) at the 18th century Jagerhof Castle in the 30-acre Hofgarten (park), open daily except Monday 10:00–17:00 (until 20:00 on Wednesday).

The large collection of Goethe memorabilia (30,000 items: first editions, paintings, manuscripts) at the Goethe Museum, also in Hofgarten, open daily except Monday 10:00–17:00. An enormous collection of paintings in the Kunstmuseum.

The more than 4,000 manuscripts in the Heinrich Heine Institute, Bilkerstrasse 14, open daily except Monday 10:00–17:00. Near Altstadt ("Old Town"), stroll the half-mile long shopping street, Konigsallee (called "the Ko").

Take the 75-minute boat trip on the Rhine to Zons. Boats leave every 60 minutes 13:30–17:30 from the Rathausufer, at the edge of Old Town.

Take the 30-minute tram ride (#1 and #18, from Jan-Welem-Platz) to the 18th century Benrath Castle, surrounded by spectacular English-style and French- style gardens.

Sample the 8 local beers in Old Town and try the local food specialties: reibekuchen, a potato pancake; halve hahn, a caraway cheese eaten with mustard on roggelchen, small loaves of rye bread; spanferkel brotchen, slices of roast suckling pig served on a roll; bratwurst with hot mustard; and blutwurst, a black pudding served with raw onions.

Dep. Dusseldorf	Frequent times from 05:17 to 23:56
Arr. Cologne	24–28 minutes later

Cologne - Frankfurt - Cologne   650

All of these trains have a restaurant car or light refreshments.

Dep. Cologne	Frequent times from 05:54 to 21:25
Arr. Frankfurt	2–2½ hours later

Dep. Frankfurt	Frequent times from 06:50 to 21:49
Arr. Cologne	2–2½ hours later

Cologne - Hamburg - Cologne   650

All of these trains charge a supplement that includes reservation fee and have a restaurant car, unless designated otherwise.

Dep. Cologne	06:26	07:09	08:09	09:09	10:10	11:10 (1)
Arr. Hamburg (Hbf.)	10:11	11:11	12:11	13:11	14:24	15:11

Dep. Cologne	12:33	13:10	14:09	15:10	16:10	17:09 (4)
Arr. Hamburg (Hbf.)	16:11	17:24	18:11	19:11	20:11	21:24

Dep. Hamburg (Hbf.)	03:12 (2)	04:47	05:47	06:47 (1)	07:47	08:47
Arr. Cologne	07:57	08:50	09:50	10:50	11:50	12:50

Dep. Hamburg (Hbf.)	09:47	10:47	11:47	12:47	13:47 (1)	14:47 (1+5)
Arr. Cologne	13:50	14:50	15:50	16:50	17:50	18:50

(1) Light refreshments. (2) Reservation advisable. Light refreshments. (3) Runs daily, except Saturday. (4) Plus other Cologne departures at 18:09, 19:09, 20:10 and 22:00 (1). (5) Plus other Hamburg departures at 15:47, 16:47, 17:57 (3), 18:47 and 19:47.

Cologne - Heidelberg - Cologne   730

Reservation is advisable for all of these trains, and they have light refreshments.

Dep. Cologne	07:11	09:11
Arr. Heidelberg	09:59	11:57

Sights in **Heidelberg:** Take a short cable-car ride from the town center to see the gardens, Library, Great Terrace, Fat Tower, Elizabeth Gate, Freidrich's Wing, the Otto-Heinrich Wing, the Mirror Room Wing, the 10-room German Pharmaceutical Museum and the Great Vat (said to be the world's largest wine barrel, holding 55,000 gallons), all at Heidelberg Castle.

Visit Germany's oldest (13th century) university, immortalized in "The Student Prince" opera. The astounding 16th century carved wood Altar of the Twelve Apostles in the Kurpfalzisches Museum. The Jesuit Church. The Church of the Holy Ghost, where visitors often hear impromptu organ concerts.The 16th century wood-carved Windsheim Altar (Christ and the Twelve Apostles) plus many rooms furnished with period pieces and paintings in the Palatine Museum at the Palais Morass. Knight's Mansion. Student's Jail.

From Easter into October, there are boat trips on the **Neckar River** that begin each morning and afternoon, with views of many medieval villages and fortresses. It is only a 20-minute bus ride to **Neckargemund**, where you can wander ancient cobbled streets and see the view of the river and the countryside from Zum Ritter, a restaurant operating since 1579.

Dep. Heidelberg	13:58	17:58
Arr. Cologne	16:45	20:45

Cologne - Koblenz - Cologne   650

Most of these trains charge a supplement that includes reservation fee and have a restaurant car.

Dep. Cologne	Frequent times from 05:54 to 00:49
Arr. Koblenz	60 minutes later

Sights in **Koblenz:** Where the Rhine and Moselle rivers meet. See Old Town. St. Castor's Church. The Middle Rhine Museum. Stolzenfels Castle. The 18th century Prince Electors' Palace. The regional and Rhenish museums in the 19th century Ehrenbreitstein Fortress. The wine village.

The 13th century Old Castle. The 18th century Mint Master's House. The 18th century Baroque Franconian Royal Palace. The 13th century Romanesque Church of Our Lady. The 15th century Altes Kaufhaus. The 16th century Schoffenhaus.

The very scenic 4½-hour Koblenz–Cochem boat trip on the Mosel Rivel is covered by Eurailpass. Views include hillside vineyards and quaint "wine villages." There is a magnificent castle in Cochem.

A popular detour is to get off the boat before it arrives in Cochem—at Moselkern—and walk 45 minutes through the forest to Burg Eltz, one of Europe's loveliest castles. Then take a train from Moselkern to Cochem, and return to Koblenz from Cochem either by boat or by a 45 minute train ride.

Dep. Koblenz	Frequent times from 03:50 to 23:15
Arr. Cologne	60 minutes later

Cologne - Luxembourg - Cologne   720

Reservation is advisable for these trains, unless designated otherwise.

Dep. Cologne	06:11	08:11 (1)	10:11
Arr. Luxembourg	09:23	11:27	13:23

Dep.Luxembourg	12:30 (1)	14:33	18:26 (1)
Arr. Cologne	15:45	17:45	21:45

(1) Change trains in Trier.

Cologne - Mainz - Cologne   Boat   714

Here is a way to combine a cruise on the Rhine with a scenic rail trip.

Have lunch and Rhine wine on board the 09:00 boat just before arriving Mainz. Early in the trip, you can see Drachenfels Castle, near Bonn. During the Koblenz–Bingen portion of this cruise, you will see the best scenery on the Rhine, many hilltop castles, and the Lorelei.

Dep. Cologne (Rheingarten)	09:00 (1)	14:15
Dep. Bonn	09:40	14:55
Dep. Koblenz	11:05	11:00 (2)
Dep. Bingen	12:28	16:20
Arr. Mainz	13:10	18:45

(1) Hydrofoil boat express service. *Not* covered by Eurailpass. Supplement charged. Operates mid-April to late October. Runs daily, except Monday. (2) Operates May 1 to June 30 and September 1 to early October. Runs daily.

Sights in **Mainz:** The art collection in the 1,000-year-old Cathedral. Adjacent to it is the Gutenberg Museum, with the first printed bible and where a movie on the inventor's life can be viewed. Also visit the Museum of the Central Rhineland. Rare books in the World Museum of Printing in the Romischer Kaiser. Restored Baroque mansions on the Schillerplatz and Schillerstrasse, in the Kirschgarten. Old Town. Sculptures in the Diocesan Museum.

Then for the train ride back to Cologne:
All of these trains charge a supplement that includes reservation fee and have a restaurant car.

650

Dep. Mainz	14:18	19:48(1)	21:24	22:24
Arr. Koblenz	15:05	20:35	22:05	23:13
Arr. Bonn	15:37	21:07	22:37	23:45
Arr. Cologne	15:59	21:29	22:59	00:07

(1) Daily except Saturday.

Here is the schedule for visiting Mainz by taking the train both ways:

650

Dep. Cologne	Frequent times from 05:54 to 21:00
Arr. Mainz	2 hours later

• • •

Dep, Mainz	Frequent times from 06:36 to 20:37
Arr. Cologne	2 hours later

Cologne - Mannheim - Cologne   650

All of these trains charge a supplement that includes reservation fee and have a restaurant car, unless designated otherwise.

Dep. Cologne	06:30	07:00	07:30	08:00	08:30 (1)
Arr. Mannheim	08:53	09:22	09:52	10:22	10:53

(1) Plus other frequent departures from Cologne at 09:00 to 21:00.

Sights in **Mannheim:** The Squared Town. The first thing that strikes you about Mannheim is its "Squareness." Built to be a fortified town, it was designed as a chessboard of 144 residential blocks, each known by a letter and number that identifies its position on the grid.

See the Fine Arts Museum. The Reiss Municipal Museum. The Cathedral, Europe's largest Romanesque Church. The Water Tower. The old Town Hall and parish church in the Marketplatz. The Castle.

Dep. Mannheim	Frequent departures from 06:36 to 20:37.
Arr. Cologne	2½ hours later

Cologne - Siegen - Cologne   709

Dep. Cologne	Every hour 07:10-22:19
Arr. Siegen	1½ hours later

Sights in **Siegen:** The Upper Castle, with its Reubens paintings (he was born here) in the Siegerland Museum, which also offers the history of this region and a tour of the old iron mine under the Castle's cellar. See the crypts of the Princes of Nassau-Orange in the Castle.

Dep. Siegen	Every hour 08:10-21:10
Arr. Cologne	1½ hours later

Cologne - Trier - Cologne   720

Dep. Cologne	06:11	08:11	10:11	Dep. Trier	15:17	17:17
Arr. Trier	08:38	10:38	12:38	Arr. Cologne	17:45	19:45

Dresden - Berlin - Dresden   680

All of these trains charge a supplement that includes reservation fee and have a restaurant car, unless designated otherwise.

Dep. Dresden (Hbf.)	07:36	09:36	11:36		
Arr. Berlin (Hbf)	09:15	11:15	13:15		

Dep. Berlin (Hbf.)	12:24	14:24	16:24	18:24	20:24
Arr. Dresden (Hbf.)	14:06	16:06	18:06	20:06	22:06

(1) Reservation advisable. Light refreshments.

Dresden - Chemnitz (formerly Karl Marx Stadt) - Dresden   780

Reservation is advisable for all of these trains, unless designated otherwise.

Dep. Dresden (Hbf.)	07:52 (1)	09:52 (1)	10:40 (2)	11:52 (1)	12:40 (4)
Arr. Chemnitz	09:03	11:03	12:03	13:05	14:03

Sights in **Chemnitz**: An East German post-World War II showplace *new* city.

Dep. Chemnitz	11:53 (2)	12:58 (1)	13:53 (2)	14:58 (1)	15:53 (2+3)
Arr. Dresden (Hbf.)	13:07	14:06	15:07	16:06	17:29

(1) Light refreshments. (2) Reservation not available. (3) Plus other Chemnitz departures at 16:59 (1), 18:58 (1), 19:53 (2), 20:26 (1) and 21:53 (2), arriving Dresden 18:07, 20:06, 21:07, 21:34 and 23:07. (4) Runs daily except Sundays & holidays.

Dresden - Leipzig - Dresden   674

Dep. Dresden (Hbf.)	07:11 (1) 10:11 (2)
Dep. Dresden (Neu.)	8 minutes after departing Hauptbahnhof.
Arr. Leipzig	08:45 11:45

Dep. Leipzig	13:07 (2)	14:01 (2)	17:07 (2)	18:01 (2)	21:07 (1)
Arr. Dresden (Neu.)	14:40	15:30	18:34	19:33	22:34
Arr. Dresden (Hbf.)	8 minutes later				

(1) Reservation advisable. Restaurant car. (2) Reservation advisable. Light refreshments.

Frankfurt - Basel - Frankfurt   730

All of these trains charge a supplement that includes a reservation fee and have a restaurant car, unless designated otherwise.

Dep. Frankfurt (Hbf.)	05:40 (1)	07:43	08:43	09:43	10:09 (1)
Arr. Mannheim	-0- (1)	08:24	09:24	10:24	-0- (1)
Change trains.					
Dep. Manheim	-0-	08:31	09:31	10:31 (1)	-0-
Arr. Basel (Badisch.)	08:34	10:36	11:35	12:35	13:01
Arr. Basel (S.B.B.)	7 minutes later				

Dep. Basel (S.B.B.)	14:17	15:17	16:17	17:17	18:17 (2)
Dep. Basel (Badisch.)	7 minutes later				
Arr. Mannheim	16:27	17:27	18:27	19:27	20:27
Change trains.					
Dep. Mannheim	16:35	17:35	18:35	19:35	20:35
Arr. Frankfurt	17:14	18:14	19:14	20:14	21:14

(1) Direct train. No train change in Mannheim. (2) Plus other departures from Basel at 19:17 and 20:20, arriving Frankfurt 22:15 and 23:15.

Frankfurt - Bremen - Frankfurt

All of these trains charge a supplement that includes a reservtion fee, unless designated otherwise. Unless designated otherwise, the Frankfurt–Hannover (and v.v.) trains have a restaurant car — and the Hannover–Bremen and (v.v.) trains have light refreshments.

750

Dep. Frankfurt	06:17	08:18	08:51	10:18
Arr. Hannover	08:38	10:38	11:06	12:38
Change trains. 652				
Dep. Hannover	09:43	11:43 (1)	12:17 (1)	13:43
Arr. Bremen	10:48	12:48	13:37	14:48

Sights in **Bremen:** It is an easy walk, down Bahnhofstrasse, from the railstation to the fine buildings in Market Square. Starting there at the 18-foot-high statue of Roland (Sculpted in 1404), following the white dots on the sidewalk will lead you to most of the city's important places. The statue faces the 11th century St. Peter's Cathedral, open daily to tourists, except Saturday afternoon and Sunday morning.

Close by the Cathedral, the 17th century City Hall offers free guided morning tours daily, except Sunday. The interesting features in its upstairs hall are the oak-beamed ceiling, portraits of Holy Roman emperors from Charlemagne to Sigismund, and ship models. Also see the exceptional woodcarving in its Golden Chamber.

The largest rathskeller in Europe, serving only German wine (500,000 bottles a year), located under the City Hall, has been a tavern, restaurant and wine cellar for over 500 years. More than 800 people can be seated there. Very crowded at noon, it offers a choice of more than 500 wine varieties and vintages from Germany's 11 main wine areas. Its bottles and casks include vintages from as far back as 16:53.

Behind the City Hall is the 13th century Liebfrauenkirche (Church of Our Lady), whose 7 new stained glass windows were installed in 1966. It is open daily, but closed 12:30–14:00.

Walk from Market Square down Bottcherstrasse to see the Porcelain Carillon and Atlantic House, decorated with Zodiac signs.

The Ubersee (Overseas) Museum, across from the railstation at 13 Bahnofplatz, has exhibits of ethnology, world trade and natural history, gathered in the Middle Ages by Bremen ships. It is open daily, except Monday 10:00–18:00.

Visit the Focke Museum of Folklore and the Municipal Weights and Measures Office. See the old workshops, inns and houses in the Schnoor residential area.

Near Martini Church, 90-minute boat tours of Europe's third largest port depart 5 times a day in summer, at the river end of Bottcherstrasse.

In Bremerhaven, 36 miles away where the Weser River meets the North Sea, there is a maritime museum called Schiffahrts on Van Ronzelenstrasse. It is open daily, except Monday.

Dep. Bremen	13:10 (1)	14:21 (1)	15:10	16:21	17:10 (2)
Arr. Hannover	14:16	15:41	16:16	17:41	18:16
Change trains. 750					
Dep. Hannover	14:51	15:51	16:51	17:51	19:20
Arr. Frankfurt	17:06	18:06	19:06	20:06	21:39

(1) No supplement. (2) Plus another Bremen departure at 19:10, arriving Frankfurt 23:41.

Frankfurt - Brussels - Frankfurt   33

Dep. Frankfurt	06:50 (1)	08:50 (2)	Dep. Brussels (Midi)	15:47	16:55 (1+4)
Arr. Cologne	09:05	11:05	Arr. Cologne	18:42	19:42
Change trains.			*Change trains.*		
Dep. Cologne	09:14 (1)	11:14	Dep. Cologne	18:54 (3)	19:54 (1)
Arr. Brussels (Midi)	11:42	13:55	Arr. Frankfurt	21:08	22:08

(1) Supplement includes a reservation fee. Restaurant car. (2) Supplement includes reservation fee. (3) Supplement includes reservation fee. (4) Plus another Brussels departure at 18:08 (1), arriving Frankfurt 23:08.

Frankfurt - Cologne - Frankfurt   650

From Mainz to Bonn, the cliffs on both sides of the Rhine are topped by ruins of ancient castles. This portion of the river is crowded with barges, sailboats, recreational motorboats, ferries and cruise ships.

All of these trains charge a supplement that includes a reservation fee and have a restaurant car, unless designated otherwise.

Dep. Frankfurt	06:50	07:49	08:50	09:49	10:49		
Dep. Mainz	07:24	08:24	09:24	10:24	11:24		
Dep. Bonn	08:45	09:45	10:45	11:45	12:45		
Arr. Cologne	09:05	10:05	11:05	12:05	13:05		
Dep. Cologne	12:54	13:54	14:54	15:54	16:54	17:54	18:54 (2)
Dep. Bonn	13:14	14:14	15:14	16:14	17:14	18:14	19:14
Dep. Mainz	14:38	15:38	16:38	17:38	18:38	19:38	20:38
Arr. Frankfurt	15:08	16:08	17:08	18:08	19:08	20:08	21:08

(1) No supplement. Light refreshments. (2) Plus other departures from Cologne at 19:54, 20:37 (1), 20:54 and 21:33, arriving Frankfurt 22:08, 23:07, 23:08 and 23:30.

Frankfurt - Dusseldorf - Frankfurt   650

All of these trains charge a supplement that includes a reservation fee and have a restaurant car, unless designated otherwise.

Dep. Frankfurt	06:50	09:49 (1)			
Arr. Dusseldorf	09:31	12:31			
Dep. Dusseldorf	13:28	15:28	18:28 (1)	19:21 (2)	20:05 (3+5)
Arr. Frankfurt	16:08	18:08	21:08	22:08	23:07

(1) Light refreshments. (2) Light refreshments. Change trains in Cologne. (3) No supplement charged. Light refreshments. (4) Runs daily except Saturdays. Change trains in Cologne. No supplement charged. Light refreshments. (5) Plus another Dusseldorf departure at 20:56 (4), arriving Frankfurt 23:54.

Frankfurt - Essen - Frankfurt 650

All of these trains charge a supplement that includes a reservation fee and have a restaurant car, unless designated otherwise.

Dep. Frankfurt	06:50	07:49 (1)	10:04 (2)
Arr. Essen	09:57	11:22	12:59

Sights in **Essen**: One of the leading German collections of 18th, 19th and 20th century art (Menzel, Delacroix, Renoir, Gaugin, Vlaminck, Kandinsky, Klee, Rothko, Rodin) at the Folkwang Museum. The 10th century Cathedral and its collection of priceless 10th and 11th century processional crosses, the 9th century Golden Madonna (oldest Western statue of the Virgin Mary), and the sword of Cosmas and Damian, the martyr saints.

The chronicle of the Krupp family and business in the Annex at Villa Hugel, former residence of the Krupp family. The 12th century castle, Burg Altendorf. The Four Horsemen bronze door on the 11th century Marktkirche, Protestant since 1563.

Dep. Essen	15:01	15:35 (1)	16:35 (1)	18:01	19:31 (2)
Arr. Frankfurt	18:08	19:08	20:08	21:08	23:07

(1) Change trains in Cologne. (2) No supplement. Light refreshments.

Frankfurt - Hamburg - Frankfurt 750

All of these trains charge a supplement that includes a reservation fee and have a restaurant car, unless designated otherwise.

Dep. Frankfurt (Hbf.)	06:17	07:51	08:18	09:50	
Arr. Hamburg (Hbf.)	09:56	11:21	11:56	13:21	
Dep. Hamburg (Hbf.)	14:37	15:37	16:02	18:02	20:02 (2)
Arr. Frankfurt (Hbf.)	18:06	19:06	19:39	21:39	23:41

(1) Runs daily, except Sunday. (2) Runs daily, except Saturday.

Frankfurt - Hannover - Frankfurt   750

All of these trains charge a supplement that includes a reservation fee and have a restaurant car, unless designated otherwise.

Dep. Frankfurt	06:17	07:51	08:18	08:51	09:50	10:18
Dep. Hannover	08:38	10:06	10:38	11:06	12:06	12:38

Dep. Hannover	14:51	15:20	15:51	16:51	17:20	17:51 (2)
Arr. Frankfurt	17:06	17:39	18:06	19:06	19:39	20:06

(1) Runs daily, except Saturday. (2) Plus other Hannover departures at 18:51 (1), 19:20 and 21:23 (1), arriving Frankfurt 21:02, 21:39 and 23:41.

Frankfurt - Heidelberg - Frankfurt   730

Reservation is advisable for all of these trains, and they have light refreshments.

Dep. Frankfurt	Every 2 hours from 07:47 to 21:47
Arr. Heidelberg	One hour later

Dep. Heidelberg	Every 2 hours from 07:16 to 21:16 + 23:10
Arr. Frankfurt	One hour later

Frankfurt - Kassel - Frankfurt   750

All of these trains charge a supplement that includes a reservation fee and have a restaurant car.

Dep. Frankfurt (Hbf.)	Every hour from 06:18 to 21:18
Arr. Kassel (Wil.)	1½ hours later

Sights in **Kassel**: Take the bus #13 to see the enormous 233-foot high copper statue of Hercules, the 19th century Wilhelmshohe Castle, and the art museums (Rembrandt, Durer, Rubens) inside the Castle. Open daily except Monday, March–October, 10:00–17:00. Also see the collection of Brothers Grimm memorabilia in the City Museum. They wrote their fairy tales here. Other interesting sights are the 18th century Orangery Palace in Karlsaue Park. The paintings in the Landesmuseum. The Tapestry Museum. The Fredericianum Museum. The world's only Wallpaper Museum.

Dep. Kassel (Wil.)	Every hour from 06:15 to 22:15
Arr. Frankfurt (Hbf.)	1½ hours later

(1) Runs daily, except Saturday. (2) Plus other departures from Kassel at 19:16 (1), 20:16, 21:16 and 22:36, arriving Frankfurt 20:42, 21:42, 22:42 and 00:08.

Frankfurt - Luxembourg - Frankfurt

All of the Frankfurt–Koblenz (and v.v.) trains charge a supplement that includes reservation fee. Reservation is advisable for the Koblenz-Luxemburg (and v.v.) trains, unless designated otherwise.

650			720		
Dep. Frankfurt	07:49 (1)	09:51 (2)	Dep. Luxembourg	14:33	17:19 (4+5)
Arr. Koblenz	09:11	11:11	Arr. Koblenz	16:38	19:42
Change trains. 720			*Change trains. 650*		
Dep. Koblenz	09:19 (3)	11:19	Dep. Koblenz	16:46 (1)	19:46 (1)
Arr. Luxembourg	11:27	13:23	Arr. Frankfurt	18:08	21:08

(1) Restaurant car. (2) Light refreshments. (3) Change trains in Trier (arr. 10:38—dep. 10:44). (4) Reservations not available. Runs daily, except Sundays and holidays. Change trains in Trier (arr. 18:06—dep. 18:21). (5) Plus another departure from Luxembourg at 18:26. Change trains in Trier at 19:10 and in Koblenz at 20:38, departing Kolbenz 20:47, arriving Frankfurt 22:08.

Frankfurt - Mainz - Frankfurt   650

All of these trains charge a supplement that includes a reservation fee and have a restaurant car or light refreshments.

Dep. Frankfurt	49 minutes past each hour from 06:49 to 23:47
Arr. Mainz	30 minutes later
Dep. Mainz	38 minutes past each hour from 06:38 to 22:38
Arr. Frankfurt	30 minutes later

Frankfurt - Mannheim - Frankfurt   730

All of these trains charge a supplement that includes reservation fee and have a restaurant car or light refreshments.

Dep. Frankfurt	Frequent times from 05:42 to 22:58.
Arr. Mannheim	40 minutes later
Dep. Mannheim	Frequent times from 05:08 to 22:35.
Arr. Frankfurt	40 minutes later

Frankfurt - Munich - Frankfurt   760

All of these trains charge a supplement that includes reservation fee and have a restaurant car.

Dep. Frankfurt	06:31 (1)	07:43	08:43	09:43			
Arr. Munich	09:42	11:17	12:17	13:17			

Dep. Munich	12:46	13:46	14:46	15:46	16:46	17:46 (2)	18:46 (3)
Arr. Frankfurt	16:14	17:14	18:14	19:14	20:14	21:14	22:15

(1) Runs Monday–Friday. (2) Runs daily, except Saturday. (3) Plus another Munich departure at 19:46 (2), arriving Frankfurt 23:15.

Frankfurt - Nurnberg (and Bayreuth) - Frankfurt   740

All of these trains charge a supplement that includes reservation fee and have a restaurant car or light refreshments.

Dep. Frankfurt	Every hour form 06:22 to 21:22
Arr. Nurnberg	2 hours and 20 minutes later

Sights in **Nurnberg**: The bronze and silver Sebaldusgrab, excellent stained glass and the carved tomb of the Saint for whom it is named in the 13th century St. Sebaldus Church. Take a guided tour of the Kaiserburg (Imperial Castle), Burggrafenburg and Imperial Stables in the fort. See the Albrecht Durer Haus, with copies of his paintings. The kitchen is as it was, when the artist lived there from 1509 to 1528. It is open daily except Monday 10:00–13:00 and 14:00–17:00. The Rosette window, wood carving and statues in St. Lorenz Kirche.

Visit the 14th century Frauenkirche in the marketplace, where the moving figures in the clock perform every day at 12:00. Then lunch at a bratwurst restaurant. One is located next to St. Sebaldus Church; another is behind the rebuilt 17th century Rathaus (City Hall). There are guided tours of 14th century catacombs (torture chamber and dungeons) in the Rathaus.

The Alstadt Museum. The collection of toys, doll houses and other works in the German National Museum. The 40 gold figures of artists, emperors, philosophers, prophets and popes around the 14th century Schoner Brunnen (Beautiful Fountain) at Hauptmarkt, where farmers sell their produce from stalls.

On the little island in the Pegnitz River is the Holy Ghost Hospital, locale of the legendary Till Eulenspiegel. Disguised as a doctor, this is where the 14th century peasant clown told the man in charge of the hospital that he could cure all the patients in one day. The hospital authorities believed Till was a miracle worker when the patients rose from their beds and left the hospital after he whispered in each one's ear. He told the patients: "Those of you who are the most sick are going to be burned into a powder the hospital will use to heal the others."

Visit the collection of porcelains and the model of Old Nurnberg at Fembo House (The City Historical Museum), 15 Burgstrasse, open daily except Monday 10:00–17:00. The best collection of old trains in West Germany (including Germany's first locomotive) is in Nurnberg's Transport Museum, open Monday-Saturday 10:00–17:00 (closes at 16:00 in Winter) and Sunday 10:00–13:00. Toys from all over the world are exhibited at Spielzeug Museum, open daily except Monday 10:00–17:00.

From Nurnberg, it's a short trip to Bayreuth, site of a 5-week annual (over 100 years) Wagner opera festival at Festspielhaus, every year from late July to late August at 16:00.

Marvelous sights in nearby **Bayreuth**: Haus Wahnfried, Wagner's home. The breathtaking opera house. The Orangerie castle, open daily 10:00–11:30 and 13:30–15:00. Eremitage Park.

Dep. Nurnberg	Every hour form 05:17 to 21:17
Arr. Frankfurt	2 hours and 20 minutes later

Here are the connections between Nurnberg and Bayreuth:
There is great river and canyon scenery on the Nurnberg-Pegnitz portion of this trip.

778

Dep. Nurnberg	49 minutes after each hour from 05:49 to 23:49	Dep. Bayreuth	10 minutes after each hour from 05:10 to 22:10
Dep. Pegnitz	40 minutes later	Arr. Pegnitz	18 minutes later
Arr. Bayreuth	16 minutes after Pegnitz	Arr. Nurnberg	1 hour after Bayreuth

Frankfurt - Siegen - Frankfurt 709

Dep. Frankfurt	08:55	09:55 (1+2)	Dep. Siegen	13:54	15:54 (3)
Arr. Giessen	08:35	10:35	Arr. Giessen	14:48	16:48
Change trains.			*Change trains.*		
Dep. Giessen	09:08	11:08	Dep. Giessen	15:21 (1)	17:21 (1)
Arr. Siegen	10:05	12:05	Arr. Frankfurt	16:01	18:01

(1) Light refreshments. (2) Plus another departures from Frankfurt at 11:55 (1), arriving Siegen 14:05. (3) Plus other departures from Siegen at 17:54 and 19:54, departing Giessen 19:21 (1) and 21:21 (1), arriving Frankfurt 20:01 and 22:01.

Frankfurt - Strasbourg - Frankfurt

730			*727*		
Dep. Frankfurt	07:47 (1)	11:47 (1)	Dep. Strasbourg	09:21	17:57 (3)
Arr. Offenburg	09:51	13:51	Arr. Offenburg	09:47	18:31
Change trains. 727			*Change trains. 730*		
Dep. Offenburg	11:31	17:31	Dep. Offenburg	16:06 (1)	18:06 (1)
Arr. Strasbourg	12:04	18:05	Arr. Frankfurt	18:09	20:09

(1) Reservation advisable. Light refreshments. (2) Plus other departures from Strasbourg at 21:44 (3), departing Offenburg 22:17 (1), arriving Frankfurt 24:15. (3) Change trains in Kehl.

Frankfurt - Stuttgart - Frankfurt   760

All of these trains charge a supplement that includes reservation fee and have a restaurant car.

Dep. Frankfurt	Every hour from 07:43 to 21:43
Arr. Stuttgart	One hour and 20 minutes later

Sights in **Stuttgart:** Outstanding contemporary architecture, built since World War II. The Schillerplatz flower and vegetable market (Tuesday, Thursday and Saturday). Also on Schillerplatz, Swabian art and culture from the Middle Ages to Art Nouveau, at the Wuerttemberg Provincial Museum in the Altes Schloss. Europe's most modern planetarium, opened in 1977.

The largest Picasso collection in Germany (among the 4,000 paintings from the 14th to 20th century), at the State Gallery, Konrad Adenauer Strasse 32. The Daimler-Benz Automobile Museum, admission only by advance appointment. The Museum of Natural History, in Rosenstein Palace.

Dep. Stuttgart	Every hour from 05:53 to 21:53
Arr. Frankfurt	One hour and 20 minutes later

Frankfurt - Wiesbaden   717

Dep. Frankfurt	Frequent times from 05:18 to 00:18
Arr. Wiesbaden	33-40 minutes later

Sights in **Wiesbaden:** One of Europe's top mineral bath resorts. See Brunnenkolonnade, the longest colonnade in Europe.

Dep. Wiesbaden	Frequent times from 07:07 to 00:07
Arr. Frankfurt	33-40 minutes later

Hamburg - Berlin - Hamburg   665

See "Berlin-Hamburg."

Hamburg - Bremen - Hamburg 650

All of these trains charge a supplement that includes reservation fee and have a restaurant car or light refreshments.

Dep. Hamburg (Alt.)	Every hour from 05:33 to 20:33
Dep. Hamburg (Hbf.)	14 minutes later
Arr. Bremen	70 minutes after departing Altona railstation.

Dep. Bremen	Every hour from 07:16 to 20:16
Arr. Hamburg (Hbf.)	55 minutes later
Arr. Hamburg (Alt.)	13 minutes after arriving Hauptbahnhof railstation.

Hamburg - Munich and Munich - Hamburg 750

Germany inroduced its 165-miles-per-hour air-conditioned luxury trains on this route in 1991. All of its coaches have phone service, and the seats are fitted with earphones that carry a choice of music. These trains charge a supplement that includes the reservation fee and have a restaurant car.

Dep. Hamburg (Hbf.)	07:05	10:02	11:07	12:02	13:07 (3)
Dep. Hannover	08:28	11:28	12:21	13:15	14:21
Dep. Kassel	09:23	12:23	13:23	14:23	15:23
Dep. Augsburg	12:17	15:33	16:33	17:33	18:33
Arr. Munich	12:49	16:05	17:05	18:05	19:05
Dep. Munich	07:21 (1)	09:21	09:54	10:54	11:21 (4)
Dep. Augsburg	07:44	09:26	10:26	11:26	12:26
Dep. Kasse	10:37	12:37	13:37	14:37	15:37
Dep. Hannover	11:37	13:37	14:43	15:37	16:43
Arr. Hamburg (Hbf.)	12:51	15:05	15:56	16:51	16:51

(1) Runs daily, except Saturday. (2) Runs daily, except Sunday. (3) Plus other Hamburg departures at 14:02, 15:07 and 17:07 (1). (4) Plus other Munich departures at 13:21, 13:54, 15:21, 17:12 and 17:54.

Hamburg - Lubeck - Hamburg 665

Dep. Hamburg (Hbf.)	Frequent times from 06:02 to 00:34
Arr. Lubeck	40 minutes later

Sights in **Lubeck**: All museums here are closed Monday. April–September, they are open other days 10:00–17:00, October–March 10:00–16:00. It is an easy walk from the railstation down Konrad Adenauer Strasse, over the Puppenbrucke bridge, and straight ahead to the museum of the city's history in Holstentor, the immense 15th century fort. Particularly interesting there is the model of the town as it was in 1650.

Nearby, just off Holstenstrasse, is the 15th century St. Peter's Church. There is a marvelous view of the city and its harbors from the top of the church's 165-foot-high tower. Also see the elegant chapel in the 14th century St. Mary's Church. Across the square from it is Buddenbrookshaus, at 4 Mengstrasse, where Thomas Mann was born. Although it is now a bank, some of the upstairs rooms can be visited during the hours the bank is open.

There are dozens of interesting alleys and little passageways here with lovely cottages, shops and restaurants. See the mansions on Grosse Petersgrube, Engelsgrube, Fischergrube and Mengstrasse. See the 19th and 20th century paintings, handicrafts and sculptures in the Bennhaus, a magnificent 18th century merchant's house. The city's main museum is in St. Anne's Convent.

Cruise boats that go around the city and harbor leave from the front of Hotel Jensen (Trave Landing) daily in Spring, Summer and Fall every half hour from 10:00 to 18:00.

Dep. Lubeck	Frequent times from 05:24 to 24:00
Arr. Hamburg (Hbf.)	40 minutes later

Hannover - Berlin - Hannover   700

All of these trains charge a supplement that includes reservation fee and have a restaurant car, unless designated otherwise.

Dep. Hannover	06:00 (1)	07:46 (2)	09:04	
Arr. Berlin (Zoo)	08:58	10:40	12:53	
Dep. Berlin (Zoo)	14:34	16:32	17:07	18:47 (2)	20:38 (1)
Arr. Hannover	17:54	19:54	20:54	21:54	23:54

(1) No supplement. No restaurant car. Light refreshments. (2) Runs daily, except Sunday.

Hannover - Bremen - Hannover   652

Dep. Hannover	07:43 (1)	08:17	09:43 (1)	10:17	11:43 (1)	12:17
Arr. Bremen	08:48	09:37	10:48	11:37	12:48	13:37
Dep. Bremen	13:10 (1)	14:21	15:10 (1)	16:21	17:10 (1)	18:21 (2)
Arr. Hannover	14:16	15:41	16:16	17:41	18:16	19:41

(1) Supplement charged which includes a reservation fee. Light refreshments. (2) Plus other departures from Bremen at 19:10 (1), 20:21, 21:10 (1), 22:21 and 23:17.

Hannover - Celle - Hannover   750

Reservation is advisable for most of these trains.

Dep. Hannover	Frequent times from 05:21 to 22:49
Arr. Celle	25 minutes later

Sights in **Celle:** The beautifully decorated chapel and wonderful French Garden at the 13th century Duke's Palace. The 14th century Marienkirche. The exhibit of the local life and farm culture in the Bomann Museum. The heavy wood-beamed ceilings and quality wood panelling in the 14th century Rathaus (Town Hall), oldest tavern in Northern Germany. The Lower Saxony stud farm, home of the famous Hannoverian horses.

The 480 half-timbered houses, some dating back to the 15th century, many with carved beams. The Apiary Museum at the Institute for Bee Research. The nearby Wienhausen Monastery. Regional food specialties are *heidschnuckenbraten* (roasted lamb), *meissendorfer spiegelkarpfen* (carp) and *burgdorfer spargel* (asparagus). There are steamer cruises on the **Aller River.**

Dep. Celle	Frequent times from 05:45 to 22:57
Arr. Hannover	25 minutes later

Hannover - Dortmund - Hannover   700

All of these trains charge a supplement that includes reservation fee and have a restaurant car.

Dep. Hannover	06:57	07:57	08:57	09:57	10:57	11:57	
Arr. Dortmund	08:33	09:33	10:33	11:33	12:33	13:33	
Dep. Dortmund	13:27	14:27	15:27	16:27	17:27	18:27	19:27 (1)
Arr. Hannover	15:03	16:03	17:03	18:03	19:03	20:03	21:03

(1) Plus other departures from Dortmund at 20:27 and 21:27.

Hannover - Dusseldorf - Hannover   700

Dep. Hannover	09:57 (2)	11:57	13:57	
Arr. Dusseldorf	12:23	14:28	16:28	
Dep. Dusseldorf	15:33 (2)	16:33 (1)	19:45 (1)	20:33 (2)
Arr. Hannover	18:03	19:03	22:25	23:06

(1) Reservation advisable. Light refreshments. (2) Supplement includes reservation fee. Restaurant car.

Hannover - Frankfurt - Hannover　750

All of these trains charge a supplement that includes reservation fee and have a restaurant car.

Dep. Hannover	07:20	08:51	09:20	09:51	10:51	11:20
Arr. Frankfurt	09:39	11:06	11:39	12:06	13:06	13:39

Dep. Frankfurt	13:51	14:18	14:51	15:51	16:18	16:51	17:51 (3)
Arr. Hannover	16:06	16:38	17:06	17:52	18:38	19:06	20:06

(1) Runs daily, except Sunday. (2) Runs daily, except Saturday. (3) Plus other departures from Frankfurt at 18:18, 18:51 (2), 20:18 and 21:18 (2), arriving Hanover 20:38, 21:06, 22:38 and 23:38.

Hannover - Goslar - Hannover　697

Dep. Hannover	06:33	07:33	08:33	09:33	10:18 (1)	11:33
Arr. Goslar	07:57	08:57	09:57	10:57	11:45	12:57

Sights in **Goslar**: The many 13th–16th century half-timbered buildings and 19th century houses. The Eagle Fountain. The five 13th century churches. The chandeliers of reindeer horns in the 15th century Town Hall. The 16th century towers and old city walls. The 11th century Imperial Palace. The museums of natural science and antiquities.

　　Goslar is a popular base for touring the Harz Mountains.

Dep. Goslar	12:00	13:00	14:00	14:24 (1)	16:00	17:00 (2)	18:24 (3+4)
Arr. Hannover	13:25	14:25	15:25	15:40	17:25	18:25	19:40

(1) Light refreshments. (2) Runs Monday–Friday, except holidays. (3) Reservation advisable. Light refreshments. (4) Plus other departures from Goslar at 19:00 and 21:00.

Hannover - Hamburg - Hannover　750

All of these trains charge a supplement that includes reservation fee and have a restaurant car, unless designated otherwise.

Dep. Hannover	06:49 (1)	07:37	08:03 (1)	08:43	09:37	10:07
Arr. Hamburg (Hbf.)	08:16	08:51	10:01	09:56	10:51	11:21

Dep. Hamburg (Hbf.)	14:23	15:23	16:23	17:23	18:02 (5)
Arr. Hannover	15:49	16:49	17:49	18:49	19:15

(1) No supplement. Reservation advisable. Light refreshments. (2) Runs daily, except Sunday. (3) Runs daily, except Saturday. (4) No Supplement. No restaurant car. Reservation advisable. (5) Plus other departures from Hamburg at 19:02, 19:42 (1), 20:02 (3) and 21:42 (4), arriving Hannover 20:21, 21:09, 21:51 and 23:19.

Hannover - Hameln - Hannover   702

Dep. Hannover   Every hour from 06:48 to 22:48
Arr. Hameln   47 minutes later

Sights in **Hameln:** Every Sunday at Noon (mid-May through mid-September), see the reenactment of the Pied Piper leading children through the Town Square. Approximately 80 actors in historical costumes participate in the 30-minute performance.

Take the 90-minute guided walking tour (10:00–11:30) from the tourist information office. A stroll through the surrounding woods is pleasant. Or, try a steamboat trip on the **Weser River**.

Dep. Hameln   Every hour from 08:23 to 22:23
Arr. Hannover   47 minutes later

Hannover - Hildesheim - Hannover   697

Dep. Hannover   Every hour from 05:34 to 21:34
Arr. Hildesheim   30 minutes later

Sights in **Hildesheim**: The supposedly 1,100-year old rose tree (probably 300–500 years old) which survived World War II bombings that literally destroyed the city, on the grounds of the 11th century Cathedral.

The Cathedral houses marvelous 11th century art, particularly the 2 wings of the bronze door cast in 1015, showing 8 scenes from the Old and New Testaments.

Also see the Egyptian and Greco-Roman objects, as well as the collection of episcopal silverware and Chinese porcelain, in the Roemer und Pelizaeus Museum. The 12th century painted ceiling in the 11th century St. Michael's Church. The 15th century Tempelhaus.

The Gothic Town Hall. The collection of 15th century books and official records dating back to the 12th century at the Stadtarchiv.

Take a local train for the short ride to **Nordstemmen** and then it is a 20-minute walk from that railstation to see the medieval castle, Schloss Marianburg.

Dep. Hildesheim   Every hour from 05:54 to 21:54
Arr. Hannover   30 minutes later

Hannover - Kassel - Hannover   750

There is beautiful **Fulda River Valley** scenery 20 minutes before arriving in Kassel.

All of these trains charge a supplement that includes reservation fee. Most of them have a restaurant car.

Dep. Hannover	Frequent times from 06:28 to 21:20
Arr. Kassel (Wil.)	60 minutes later
Dep. Kassel (Wil.)	Frequent times from 06:34 to 22:44
Arr. Hannover	60 minutes later

Hannover - Luneburg - Hannover   750

Dep. Hannover	07:42	08:03 (1)	08:49 (2)	09:42	10:49 (1)	11:42
Arr. Luneburg	09:13	09:19	09:44	11:07	11:44	13:07

Sights in **Luneburg**: The 18th century crane at the waterfront. Guided tours of Town Hall, constructed over 5 centuries (1300-1800). The 17th century Ducal Palace. The view of the town from Kalkberg (Chalk Mountain).

The 15th–16th century wood carvings and paintings and the 16th–18th century organs in the 3 churches that have survived out of the city's 14 original churches: St. Johannis, St. Michaelis and St. Nicolai. There are magnificent tombs of the town's most important citizens inside St. Johannia, the oldest church here. The sound of its organ is unique.

Don't miss seeing the 12th century Monastery, slightly more than one mile northeast of the town.

Dep. Luneburg	14:12 (2)	14:45	16:12 (2)	16:45	18:12 (2+3)
Arr. Hannover	15:09	16:16	17:09	18:16	19:09

(1) Reservation advisable. Light refreshments. (2) Supplement charged which includes a reservation fee. Light refreshments. (3) Plus other departures from Luneburg at 18:45, 20:12 (1) and 20:33 (1), arriving Hannover 20:16, 21:09 and 21:57.

Leipzig - Berlin - Leipzig   670

Dep. Leipzig	06:22 (1)	06:48 (2)	08:48	10:40 (6)
Arr. Berlin (Hbf.)	08:39	09:09	11:07	12:49
Dep. Berlin (Licht.)	13:36 (6)	14:45 (6)	17:36 (6)	20:29 (1)
Arr. Leipzig	15:45	17:04	19:45	22:43

(1) Reservation advisable. Light refreshments. (2) Supplement charged which includes reservation fee. Light refreshments. (3) Runs daily, except Sunday. Supplement charged which includes reservation fee. Restaurant car. (4) Reservation advisable. (5) Depart/Arrive Berlin's Lichtenberg railstation. (6) Supplement charged which includes reservation fee. Restaurant car.

Leipzig - Chemnitz (formerly Karl Marx Stadt) - Leipzig   777

Dep. Leipzig	08:28	10:28	12:28	Dep. Chemnitz	12:41	14:41	16:41 (1)
Arr. Chemnitz	10:00	12:00	14:00	Arr. Leipzig		14:10	16:10	18:10

(1) Plus other departures from Chemnitz at 18:41, 19:39 and 20:41, arriving Leipzig 20:10, 22:10 and 24:10.

Sights in **Chemnitz**: An East German post-World War II showplace new city.

Leipzig - Dresden - Leipzig   660 + 775

Dep. Leipzig	06:52	08:07 (1)	09:18 (2)	09:52 (3)	10:07 (2)	12:07 (3)
Arr. Dresden (Neu.)	08:40	09:32	10:48	11:17	11:38	13:32
Arr. Dresden (Hbf.)	9 minutes later					

Dep. Dresden (Hbf.)	12:22 (2)	14:22 (2)	14:45 (3)	15:25 (2)	16:22 (3)	18:22 (2+7)
Dep. Dresden (Neu.)	8 minutes later					
Arr. Leipzig	13:51	15:51	16:09	16:52	17:51	19:51

(1) Reservation advisable. Restaurant car. (2) Reservation advisable. Light refreshments. (3) Supplement charged includes reservation fee. Restaurant car. (4) Supplement charged includes reservation fee. Light refreshments. (5) Runs daily, except Saturday. (6) Reservation advisable. (7) Plus other departures from Dresden (Hbf.) at 20:22 arriving 21:51.

Leipzig - Erfurt - Leipzig   775

Dep. Leipzig	08:12 (1)	10:12 (1)	12:12 (1)	
Arr. Erfurt	09:32	11:32	13:32	

Dep. Erfurt	14:20 (1)	16:20 (1)	18:20 (1)	20:20 (1+3)
Arr. Leipzig	15:43	17:43	19:43	21:43

(1) Supplement charged includes reservation fee. Restaurant car. (2) Reservation advisable. Restaurant car. (3) Plus another departure from Erfurt at 22:37 (1), arriving Leipzig 23:55.

Leipzig - Naumburg - Leipzig   770

All of these trains charge a supplement that includes reservation fee and have a restaurant car, unless designated otherwise.

Dep. Leipzig	07:13	09:13	11:13	13:13
Arr. Naumburg	40 minutes later			

Sights in **Naumburg**: A gem of a Medieval village.

Dep. Naumburg	12:02	14:02	16:02	18:02	20:02	22:02	23:16
Arr. Leipzig	40 minutes later						

Leipzig - Rostock - Leipzig   674

Reservation is advisable for all of these trains. All of them have light refreshments.

Dep. Leipzig	06:53	10:53 (1)	Dep. Rostock	15:38 (2)	17:50
Arr. Rostock	11:37	16:03	Arr. Leipzig	21:09 (1)	22:49

(1) Change trains in Magdeburg (arr. 09:39-dep. 09:50). (2) Change trains in Ludwigslust (arr. 17:48-dep. 17:54).

Sights in **Rostock**: Eastern Germany's largest seaport. St. Mary's Church. The ancient Town Hall.

Leipzig - Schwerin - Leipzig   674

Reservation is advisable for all of these trains, and all of them have light refreshments, unless designated otherwirs.

Dep. Leipzig	06:53	08:53 (1)	Dep. Schwerin	14:54	18:54 (2)
Arr. Schwerin	10:28	12:54	Arr. Leipzig	18:49	22:49

(1) Change trains in Magdeburg (arr. 09:39-dep. 09:54). (2) Reservations not available. No light refreshments. Change trains in Ludwigslust (arr. 17:48-dep. 17:54 restaurant car).

Sights in **Schwerin**: The Opera House. The fine castle.

Munich - Augsburg - Munich   750 + 760

Most of these trains charge a supplement that includes reservation fee and have a rest- aurant car or light refreshments.

Dep. Munich (Hbf.)	Frequent times from 04:54 to 23:10
Arr. Augsburg	30–40 minutes later

Sights in **Augsburg**: An ancient castled city, complete with splendid Gothic gate, moat, tower and ramparts. The Tourist Information Office, 7 Bahnhofstrasse, is open Monday-Friday 09:00–18:00, Saturday 09:00–13:00.

See the palatial, 8-story, 17th century City Hall. Next to it is the 11th century Perlachturm, a belltower. The oldest (12th century) Romanesque stained-glass in the world, great 11th century bronze doors, 4 altarpieces by Holbein and a huge 11th century bronze portal with scenes from the Old Testament in the 10th century Cathedral.

Just north of the Cathedral, on Frauentorstrasse, is the Mozart Museum (closed on Tuesday) in the house where the composer's father lived.

Schaezlerpalais, at 46 Maximilianstrasse, is an 18th century 60-room mansion that houses the Municipal Art Collections (Rubens, Rembrandt, Veronese, Tiepolo) and has a richly ornamented rococo ballroom on the second floor. The ballroom leads to an adjacent building that has a dazzling collection: Lucas Cranach, Holbein the Elder, Albrecht Durer. Both museums are open daily except Monday 10:00–16:00.

Also see the 15th century Basilica of St. Ulrich and St. Afra, the largest and most impressive church in Augsburg. The collection of manuscripts and drawings in the Municipal Library. The city's three 16th century fountains. Maximilianstrasse is considered by many to be the best Renaissance street in Germany.

Dep. Augsburg	Frequent times from 05:43 to 23:38
Arr. Munich (Hbf.)	30–40 minutes later

Munich - Bamberg - Munich   770

All of these trains charge a supplement that includes reservation fee and have a restaurant car.

Dep. Munich (H.)	06:56	08:56	10:56	Dep. Bamberg	16:44	18:44	20:44
Arr. Bamberg	09:12	11:12	13:12	Arr. Munich (H.)	19:15	21:15	23:15

Sights in **Bamberg**: A major port on the Rhine-Main-Danube Canal that connects the North Sea with the Black Sea. One of the few towns not damaged in World War II.

Visit the Town Hall, located in the center of the bridge that crosses the Regnitz River. The 16th century Geyerworth Castle. A History Museum is located in the 16th century Ratsstube. Nearby is the Old Imperial Court. The 17th cnetury Concordia House.

Walk 10 minutes up the hill to Domplatz (Cathedral Square), location of the 13th century Imperial Cathedral, to see many masterpieces of German medieval and early Renaissance sculpture (especially the 13th century life-size Knight of Bamberg astride his horse)... the 16th century tomb of Henry II with sculpted bas-relief panels showing scenes from his and his wife's life...the dazzling carved wood Marienaltar...the tile floors, frescoes and 18th century French tapestries in the Neue Residenz, the 15th and 16th century German paintings in the Museum there, and its 18th century rose garden.

The Cathedral is open dawn to sunset, daily except holidays. The Neue Residenz is open 09:00–12:00 and 13:30–17:00 (16:00 October through March). See the paintings of more than 600 different medicinal herbs in the ceiling of St. Michael, an 11th century church.

Munich - Bayreuth - Munich

All of the Munich–Nurnberg (and v.v.) trains charge a supplement that includes reservation fee and have a restaurant car.

770			778		
Dep. Munich (Hbf.)	06:56	08:56 (1)	Dep. Bayreuth	14:10	16:10 (2)
Arr. Nurnberg	08:40	10:40	Arr. Nurnberg	15:09	17:09
Change trains. 778			*Change trains. 770*		
Dep. Nurnberg	08:49	10:49	Dep. Nurnberg	15:18	17:18
Arr. Bayreuth	09:46	11:46	Arr. Munich (Hbf.)	17:15	19:15

(1) Plus another departure from Munich at 10:46, arriving Nurnberg 12:49, arriving Bayreuth 13:46. (2) Plus other departures from Bayreuth at 18:10 and 20:10, arriving Nurnberg 19:09 and 21:09, arriving Munich 21:15 and 23:15.

Sights in **Bayreuth**: Sight of a 5-week annual (over 100 years) Wagner opera festival at Festpielhaus, every year from late July to late August, at 16:00. See Haus Wahnfried, Wagner's home. The breathtaking opera house. Eremitage Park. The Orangerie castle, open daily 10:00–11:30 and 13:30–15:00.

Munich - Frankfurt - Munich   760

All of these trains charge a supplement that includes reservation fee and have a restaurant car.

Dep. Munich (Hbf.)	06:44	07:44	08:44	09:44	
Arr. Frankfurt	10:14	11:14	12:14	13:14	
Dep. Frankfurt	15:43	16:43	17:43	18:43	19:43
Arr. Munich (Hbf.)	19:17	20:17	21:17	22:17	23:19

Munich - Heidelberg - Munich   760

All of these trains charge a supplement that includes reservation fee and have a restaurant car.

Dep. Munich (Hbf.)	06:48	08:46	09:46
Arr. Heidelberg	09:52	11:52	12:52

Sights in **Heidelberg**: See notes under "Cologne–Heidelberg"

Dep. Heidelberg	14:07	15:07	16:07	17:07	18:07
Arr. Munich (Hbf.)	17:11	18:11	19:11	20:11	21:11

Munich - Innsbruck - Munich   70 + 795

Dep. Munich (Hbf.)	07:00 (1)	08:30 (2)	09:30 (1)	11:30 (1)	
Arr. Innsbruck	08:36	10:11	11:18	13:20	

Dep. Innsbruck	12:41 (1)	14:41 (1)	15:39 (1)	16:41 (1)	18:37 (2)	21:03 (1)
Arr. Munich (Hbf.)	14:30	16:30	17:30	18:30	20:30	22:40

(1) Supplement charged that includes reservation fee. Restaurant car. (2) Reservation advisable. Light refreshments.

Munich - Lindau - Munich   765

There are good views of the Allgau region and fine mountain scenery on this easy one-day roundtrip.

Dep. Munich (Hbf.)	06:19	06:52	08:10 (1)	08:19
Arr. Lindau	09:14	09:50	10:22	11:14

Sights in **Lindau**: An island resort town in the Bodensee (Lake Constance), third largest lake in central Europe and actually a part of the Rhine River. Departure times for the sightseeing boat can be obtained at the tourist information office across from the railstation.

See the 13th century lighthouse, Mangturm. The beautiful 15th century Old Town Hall on the Reichplatz. The Fountain of Linavia. The casino. The collection of furniture, arms, paintings and folk art in the 18th century mansion that now houses an art museum called Stadtische Kunstsammlungen, open Tuesday–Saturday 09:00–12:00 and 14:00–17:00, also Sunday 10:00–12:00.

The 15th century homes on Hauptstrasse, a pedestrian-only road. Enjoy a mid-day repast at one of the many sidewalk cafes along that street. The only existing wall mural by Hans Holbein The Elder, done between 1485 and 1490, depicting the Passion of Jesus, can be seen in the 11th century St. Peter's Church. Visit the wine tavern in the 16th century Pulverturm (Gun Powder Tower). Walk on the breakwater to the New Lighthouse and climb its 108-foot-high tower for a breathtaking view of the Alps.

Dep. Lindau	12:45	15:37 (2)	18:46 (6)
Arr. Munich (Hbf.)	15:29	17:51	21:29

(1) Supplement charged includes reservation fee. Restaurant car. (2) Change trains in Buchloe. (3) Runs Monday-Friday, except holidays. (4) Plus other departures from Lindau at 19:37 (2), 19:46 and 20:44 (3), arriving Munich 21:45, 22:29 and 23:31.

Munich - Mainz - Munich 650

All of these trains charge a supplement that includes reservation fee and have a restaurant car.

Dep. Munich (Hbf.)	06:48	08:48	09:48		
Arr. Mainz	10:46	12:46	13:46		
Dep. Mainz	14:12	15:12	16:12	17:12	19:12
Arr. Munich (Hbf.)	18:11	19:11	20:11	21:11	23:11

Munich - Mannheim - Munich 760

All of these trains charge a supplement that includes reservation and have a restaurant car.

Dep. Munich (Hbf.)	Frequent times from 05:40 to 19:05
Arr. Mannheim	3 hours later
Dep. Mannheim	Frequent times from 06:27 to 20:58
Arr. Munich (Hbf.)	3 hours later

Munich - Nurnberg - Munich 750

All of these trains charge a supplement that includes reservation and have a restaurant car, unless designated otherwise.

Dep. Munich (Hbf.)	07:54	08:54	09:54	10:54	11:54		
Arr. Nurnberg	09:32	10:32	11:32	12:32	13:32		
Dep. Nurnberg	13:24	14:24	15:24	16:24	17:24	18:24	19:24 (1+3)
Arr. Munich (Hbf.)	15:05	16:05	17:05	18:05	19:05	20:05	21:15

(1) Light refreshments. (2) Plus other departures from Nurnberg at 20:24, 21:23 and 22:24, arriving Munich 22:05, 23:05 and 00:05.

Munich - Oberammergau - Munich

There is very good mountain and lake scenery on the Murnau–Oberammergau portion of this trip.

785

Dep. Munich (Hbf.)	08:00	09:00	10:00	11:00	12:00
Arr. Murnau	08:52	09:56	10:52	11:56	12:52

Change trains. 786

Dep. Murnau	08:57	10:06	10:57	12:07	13:09
Arr. Oberammergau	40 minutes later				

Sights in **Oberammergau**: Every year ending in zero (1990, 2000, etc.), the famous Passion Play. Three hundred years ago the villagers here promised to produce this play every 10 years if the Black Plague ended. In the interval between decades, you can still see the unique theater and enjoy this interesting woodcarving capital of Bavaria. There is time to take a bus trip and see the lapis lazuli, gilt and crystal in King Ludwig II's glorious palace, Schloss Linderhof.

786

Dep. Oberammergau	10:57	12:07	13:09	14:07	15:07	16:10	17:07 (1)
Arr. Murnau	11:36	12:50	13:50	14:45	15:47	16:49	17:47

Change trains. 785

Dep. Murnau	11:58	12:54	13:58	14:54	15:58	16:54	18:00
Arr. Munich (Hbf.)	12:51	13:51	14:51	15:51	16:51	17:53	18:53

(1) Plus other departures by bus from Oberammergau at 18:07 and 20:07 that connect with trains departing Murnau 18:58 and 20:54, arriving Munich 19:56 and 21:51.

Munich - Regensburg - Munich   779

Dep. Munich (Hbf.)	07:48	09:48	11:48
Arr. Regensburg	09:13	11:13	13:13

* * *

Dep. Regensburg	13:37	14:44	16:44	19:37	21:37
Arr. Munich (Hbf.)	15:01	16:11	18:11	21:01	23:01

Sights in **Regensburg**: Founded by the Celts in about 500 B.C. It was made into an impregnable fort by the Romans in 179 A.D. How amazing that it still exists, intact! Its locat-ion on the Danube River made this city Germany's gateway to the Balkans and the Orient for several centuries.

Undamaged during World War II, this is the largest (130,000 population) and most perfectly preserved medieval city in Germany.

Because most of the streets here are too narrow for modern vehicles and also because its size is only one mile by a half-mile, Regensburg is ideal for strolling. A half-day guided walking tour is offered by the municipal tourist office, located in the 14th century Rathaus (City Hall). Many guided tours of the City Hall's ornate rooms are offered daily.

The ancient Roman 23-foot-high wall surrounding the city is built of enormous limestone blocks without mortar, and it runs more than a mile long. Christian tombstones here date back to the 4th century. The city's forum, temples, mint, and pottery and tile factories served a population of 12,000 in Roman times. This was also one of the most important cities in the German Holy Roman Empire from the 10th through the 18th centuries.

You will not even scratch the surface in a one-day visit. In order to see all of the 26 Romanesque and Gothic churches and the wonderful artwork displayed in them would require several weeks…and there is much more than those churches to see here.

Walk over the 12th century Steiner Brucke (Stone Bridge), one of the greatest engineering marvels of the Middle Ages. Riverboat rides on the Danube start near the Stone Bridge.

Visit St. Peter's Cathedral to see its lacework spires and its collection of sacral art dating back to the Middle Ages and the Renaissance, especially the 13th century gem-and-pearl-encrusted crucifix.

Hear the boys' choir (called "cathedral sparrows," they sing both secular and liturgical songs) in the adjacent Niedermunster. Famous since the year 975, the choir can be heard Sundays and holidays at the 9:00 a.m. mass.

See the 20 medieval tower houses (some are 12 stories high), especially the 13th century Goldener Turm on Wahlenstrasse and the Bamberger Turm on Watmarkt, near the City Hall. The Golden Cross, a magnificent hotel since the 16th century.

The Municipal Museum at Dachauplatz has several paintings by Albrecht Altdorfer, considered to be the world's first landscape painter and founder of the Danubian School in the 16th century. The collection there also includes Celtic, Roman, early German and medieval artifacts.

The 9th and 10th century sculptures and tombs in the 5th century St. Emmeramskirche are notable. There are many illuminated manuscripts and more than 200,000 ancient books in the adjacent abbey.

The enormous monastery at St. Emmerams's (named for a martyred 7th century missionary monk) is presently the palace of the princes of Thurn-und-Taxis. After Napoleon secularized the abbey in 1808, that family bought it and converted it into their palace. It is worth visiting to see the priceless art in its many lavishly decorated rooms.

The Thurn-und-Taxis family invented postal service in the 15th century and used a network of stage coaches. There is a very interesting stable museum across from St. Emmeram's, with exhibits of silver and gold harnesses, equestrian paintings and 19th century coaches.

Also near this church is the Diozesan Museum, which houses 1,000 years of ecclesiastical art.

The Shipping Museum is located on the other side of the Danube River. Weinstube zur

Stritzelback at No. 6 Watmarkt has been an inn since the 13th century. (Stritzel is a salty roll.)

There is an exhibit of 17th century mathematical instruments, astronomical tools and manuscripts that were used by the mathematician and astronomer Johann Kepler at No. 5 Keplerstrasse, the house in which he died in 1630.

Sample the chocolate pralines called "Barbara's kisses" at Cafe Prinzess (No. 2 Rathausplatz), Germany's oldest pastry shop and coffeehouse. It opened in 1686.

Try the fist-sized, white radishes that the locals eat as beer snacks.

Munich - Salzburg - Munich   790

These trains charge a supplement that includes reservation fee and have a restaurant car, unless designated otherwise.

Dep. Munich (Hbf.)	07:51	08:25	09:51 (1)	10:50 (2)
Arr. Salzburg	08:55	09:55	11:40	12:45

Dep. Salzburg	13:05	13:18 (2)	14:18 (1)	15:05	16:18 (1)	17:18 (2+4)
Arr. Munich (Hbf.)	14:35	15:10	16:07	16:34	18:07	19:10

(1) No supplement charged. Reservation advisable. Light refreshments. (2) Reservation not available. No supplement. No restaurant car. (3) No supplement charged. Reservation advisable. No restaurant car. (4) Plus other departures from Salzburg at 18:05, 18:18 (1), 19:05, 19:18 (2), 20:18 (1) and 22:15 (3), arriving Munich 20:07, 20:36, 21:10, 22:00 and 24:00.

Munich - Stuttgart - Munich   760

Many of these trains charge a supplement that includes reservation fee and have a restaurant car.

Dep. Munich (Hbf.)	Frequent times from 05:40 to 20:18
Arr. Stuttgart	2–3 hours later

Dep. Stuttgart	Frequent times from 05:02 to 22:01
Arr. Munich (Hbf.)	2–3 hours later

Munich - Tegernsee and Schliersee - Munich   759

Take a local train from Starnberger Bahnhof (the northern annex of Munich's Hauptbahnhof station) for this 37-mile ride that takes 66 minutes.

At the northern end of Tegernsee (an exceptionally beautiful lake) is **Gmund**, not to be confused with the 2 Austrian villages also named Gmund. A mile away from this Gmund is a smaller lake, **Schliersee**. It is only a 4-mile walk around Schliersee.

There is a lovely view of the lake from the ruins of Hohenwaldeck Castle and also from one of the many benches along the lake's shore. Sports (tennis, sailing, swimming)are very popular in this area.

The Taubenstein mountain railway goes to an area that provides extensive mountain hiking. Wandering through the Weissachau wildlife preserve, with its rare flowers, is worthwhile. Local food specialties in this region are white sausage, liver loaf, big white radishes and spicy Miesbacher cheese.

Sights in **Tegernsee**: The concerts (May–September) in the enormous Baroque dining hall of the Castle. The large collection of rustic furniture, weapons, craft utensils, traditional costumes and ancient books in the Tegernsee Museum. Try the beer in the Hofbrauhaus, located in the Museum building. Ludwig Schieffer of Cologne tells us the beer there is better than which is sold at Munich's famous Hofbrauhaus.

See the drawings, illustrations, sketches and caricatures by Olaf Gulbransson at the Kur-park Museum. Visit the lakeside gambling casino at **Wiessee**, across the lake.

Take the 10-minute boat trip (every half hour) across the lake to Wiessee. Both Tegernsee and Wiessee have been popular for centuries for their curative mineral waters, laden with iodine and sulphur. Swimming in the pristine lake is marvelous.

Take the cable car from nearby **Rottach-Egern** to the top of **Wallberg** for a view of the Tegernsee Valley and Austria's highest peak, the **Grossglockner**.

Munich - Ulm - Munich   760

All of these trains charge a supplement that includes reservation fee and have a restaurant car or light refreshments.

Dep. Munich   Frequent times from 05:40 to 22:18
Arr. Ulm   70–80 minutes later

Sights in **Ulm**: The Bakery Museum (tools, library, artwork pertaining to bread) on Fuersten-eckerstrasse. The display there includes breads made in ancient Egypt and in the Middle Ages. Open Monday-Friday 10:00–12:00 and 15:00–17:30.

The 14th century Gothic Cathedral has one of the highest towers in the world (528 feet) and a ceiling that is 100 feet above the central nave. When you hear an organ recital here (8,000 pipes !), you will experience an incredible affect from the exceptional acoustics. Don't miss seeing the magnificent 15th century carving on the choir stalls.

The views of the Alps while climbing the 528-feet-high tower are breathtaking. (You don't have to make the entire ascent.)

The 17th century Schworhaus, where Town Council members once took their oaths to perform their duties (where they were "sworn in").

Arts and crafts from this region are displayed in the Ulmer Museum, open Tuesday–Saturday 10:00–12:00 and 14:00–17:00, Sunday 10:00–13:00 and 14:00–17:00. See the 15th century fountain, Fischkasten, at the Marktplatz. Also on that square is the 14th century Town

Hall with an exceptional astronomical clock on its east wall.

Visit Metzgerturm, Ulm's 14th century leaning tower. Cross the bridge to New Ulm and walk along the Jahnufer promenade to see good views of the old city.

Dep. Ulm	Frequent times from 06:05 to 22:56
Arr. Munich	70–80 minutes later

Munich - Wurzburg - Munich   750

All of these trains charge a supplement that includes reservation fee and have a restaurant car.

Dep. Munich (Hbf.)	07:21	07:54	09:54	10:38 (1)
Arr. Wurzburg	09:32	10:32	12:32	13:13

Sights in **Wurzburg**: Vineyards and wineries galore. The tourist information center is located in Falcon House, on the square where bratwurst, vegetables, fruits and flowers are sold. See the Main-Franconia Museum (sculptures, wine presses, etc.) in the 13th century Miarienberg Fortress.

The view of the city from the restaurant at the Fortress. The rococo garden in the nearby Schloss Veitshochheim. The 12 statues of saints on the Old Main Bridge. Pilgrimage Church. The Tiepolo ceiling and the Emperor's Hall, in the Residenz. Neumunster Church. The Cathedral. The fine sculptures in the Mainfrankisches Museum at the Festung. Take a boat trip on the River Main to see **Randersacker** and **Sommerhausen**, both of them located in one of Germany's most important wine regions. Pfuelben, Sonnenstuhl and Tuefelskeller are among the leading wineries here.

Sights in **Randersacker**: There are many scenic walking tours near the **Main River** and through vineyards. Stroll the narrow Medieval streets lined with baroque houses. Many sculptures here (madonnas and pietas). See the Balthasar garden-pavilion. Try the delicious franconian meat and sausages. Fishing and many other watersports here.

Sights in **Sommerhausen:** Famous since the Middle Ages for winemaking. Its coat- of-arms features a radiant sun above a cluster of grapes. Its old town walls, gates and towers make it one of the most beautiful towns in the region. Sailing and motorboating are popular here. Visit the Rechteren-Limpurgsche Castle. The ancient City Hall.

Dep. Wurzburg	12:23	13:23	14:23	15:23	16:23	17:23 (4)
Arr. Munich (Hbf.)	15:05	16:05	17:05	18:05	19:05	20:05

(1) Runs daily, except Sunday. (2) No supplement. Reservation advisable. No restaurant car. (3) Runs daily, except, Saturday. (4) Plus other Wurzburg departures at 18:23, 19:23, 20:23 (3),and 21:23 (3), arriving Munich 20:49, 22:05, 23:05 and 00:05.

Munich - Zurich - Munich   768

Both of these trains charge a supplement that includes reservation fee and have a restaurant car.

Dep. Munich (H.)	08:11	Dep. Zurich	17:40
Arr. Zurich	12:21	Arr. Munich (H.)	21:45

SCENIC RAIL TRIPS

Cologne - Koblenz - Bullay - Cologne   720

There is beautiful farm, mountain and vineyard scenery on this easy one-day trip through the Moselle Valley. Very good river scenery on the Koblenz–Bullay portion.

Reservation is advisable for all of these trains.

Dep. Cologne	08:11	10:11	12:11	14:00
Dep. Koblenz	09:19	11:19	13:19	15:19
Arr. Bullay	50 minutes later			

* * *

Dep. Bullay	09:54	11:54	13:54	15:54
Arr. Koblenz	10:38	12:38	14:38	16:38
Arr. Cologne	57 minutes later			

Cologne - Mainz

See the fine mountain, vineyard and Rhine river scenery. Complete schedules appear under the "Cologne–Mainz–Cologne" one-day excursion.

Cologne - Giessen - Frankfurt - Koblenz - Cologne

View excellent mountain scenery on this ride, which can be made as a circle trip from either

709

Dep. Cologne	08:19	10:19	12:19			
Arr. Giessen	10:48	12:48	14:48			
Change trains.						
Dep. Giessen	11:21 (1)	13:21 (1)	15:21 (1)			
Arr. Frankfurt	12:01	14:01	16:01			
Change trains.	*650*					
Dep. Frankfurt	11:51 (2)	13:51 (2)	15:51 (2)	16:51 (2)	17:51 (2)	18:51 (2+3+4)
Dep. Koblenz	13:13	15:13	17:13	18:13	19:13	20:13
Arr. Cologne	14:05	16:05	18:05	19:05	20:05	21:05

(1) Light refreshments. (2) Supplement charged includes reservation fee. Restaurant car. (3) Plus other departures from Frankfurt at 19:51 (2), 20:51 (2) and 21:51 (2), arriving Cologne 22:05, 23:05 and 00:07. (4) runs daily except Saturday.

Dresden - Bad Schandau - Dresden

For best views of the **Elbe River** en route to **Bad Schandau**, sit on the left side of the 50-minute suburban train as it goes down the **Elbe Canyon**. Then, take a local tramway from the center of Bad Schandau into the mountains of the Sachsischer Schweiz to the **Lichtenhainer Waterfall**.

Frankfurt - Koblenz - Cologne - Giessen - Frankfurt

Here is the Frankfurt version of the circle trip shown on the previous trip:

650

Dep. Frankfurt	07:51 (1)	09:51 (1)	11:51 (1)	14:51 (1)
Dep. Koblenz	09:13	11:13	13:13	15:13
Arr. Cologne	10:05	12:05	14:05	16:05
Change trains. *709*				
Dep. Cologne	10:19	12:19	14:19	16:19
Arr. Giessen	12:48	14:48	16:48	18:48
Change trains.				
Dep. Giessen	13:21 (2)	15:21 (2)	17:21 (2)	19:21 (2)
Arr. Frankfurt	14:01	16:01	18:01	20:01

(1) Supplement charged includes reservation fee. Restaurant car. (2) Supplement charged includes reservation fee. Light refreshments.

Freiburg - Donaueschingen

The train runs through the heart of the Black Forest. Very good mountain scenery on this spur of the Frankfurt–Basel route.

730			*732*		
Dep. Frankfurt	10:09 (1)	11:43 (1+2)	Dep. Donau.	14:49	16:49
Arr. Freiburg	12:27	14:01	Arr. Neu. Schwarz.	15:25	17:25
Change trains. 731			*Change trains. 731*		
Dep. Freiburg	12:41	14:41	Dep. Neu. Schwarz.	15:31	17:31
Arr. Neu. Schwarz.	13:24	15:24	Arr. Freiburg	16:17	18:17
Change trains. 732			*Change trains. 730*		
Dep. Neu. Schwarz.	13:30	15:30	Dep. Freiburg	16:29 (1)	18:29 (1)
Arr. Donau.	14:10	16:08	Arr. Basel (SBB)	17:11	19:11

(1) Supplement charged includes reservation fee. Restaurant car. (2) Change trains in Mannheim (arr. 12:24-dep. 12:31).

Koblenz - Giessen   713

There is fine river scenery on this easy one-day roundtrip. This area can also be seen by taking an *indirect route* from Koblenz to Frankfurt. For the first way:

Dep. Koblenz	08:43 (1)	09:53 (2)	10:43 (1)	12:43	14:43
Arr. Giessen	10:39	12:14	12:39	14:39	16:39
		•	•	•	
Dep. Giessen	11:15	12:15 (3)	13:15	15:15	17:15
Arr. Koblenz	13:08	14:35	15:08	17:08	19:08

Here is the long route to Frankfurt which offers the same scenery:

713					
Dep. Koblenz	08:43 (1)	10:43 (1)	12:43	14:43 (4)	16:43 (4)
Arr. Giessen	10:39	12:39	14:39	16:39	18:39
Change trains. 709					
Dep. Giessen	11:21 (5)	13:21 (5)	15:21 (5)	17:21 (5)	19:21 (5)
Arr. Frankfurt	12:01	14:01	16:01	18:01	20:01

(1) Runs daily, except Sundays and holidays. (2) Runs Sunday only. (3) Runs Saturdays, Sundays and holidays. (4) Runs daily, except Saturday. (5) Reservation advisable. Light refreshments.

Here is the schedule for the reverse of the Koblenz–Frankfurt trip on previous page:

709

Dep. Frankfurt	07:55 (1)	09:55	-0-	-0-	11:55	13:55 (5)
Arr. Giessen	08:35	10:35	-0-	-0-	12:35	14:35

Change trains. 713

Dep. Giessen	09:15 (2)	11:15	11:55 (3)	12:15 (4)	12:35 (3)	13:15
Arr. Koblenz	11:08	13:08	14:15	14:35	15:02	15:08

(1) Light refreshments. (2) Runs daily, except Sundays and holidays. (3) Runs Monday-Friday, except holidays. (4) Runs Saturdays, Sundays and holidays. (5) Plus other Frankfurt departures at 14:22, 15:22 and 16:22, arriving Koblenz 17:08, 18:35 and 19:08.

Munich - Garmisch - Innsbruck - Munich

There is fine mountain scenery on this easy one-day circle trip.

785

Dep. Munich (Hbf.)	09:00	11:00	12:00	14:00
Arr. Garmisch	10:23	12:23	13:16	15:16
Arr. Mittenwald	10:46 (1)	12:47	13:43	15:39
Arr. Innsbruck	11:57	14:02	14:49	16:39

Change trains.   795

Dep. Innsbruck				
(via Kufstein)	12:41 (3)	14:41 (3)	15:39 (3)	16:41 (3+7)
Arr. Munich (Hbf.)	14:30	16:30	17:30	18:30

(1) Change trains in Mittenwald. (2) Change trains in Garmisch. (3) Supplement charged includes reservation fee. Restaurant car. (4) Reservation advisable. (5) Rervation advisable. Light refreshments. (6) Arrives at Munich's Ost railstation. (7) Plus other departures from Innsbruck at 17:05 (4), 18:37 (4), 21:03 (3) and 22:48 (5), arriving Munich 19:03, 20:30, 22:40 and 01:55 (6).

Garmisch - Zugspitzplatt - Zugspitzgipfel (summit) - Garmisch 783

The following schedule allows one to take one route to the summit of Zugspitze and a different route back to Garmisch.

Cook did not carry Schneefernerhaus schedules in 1994. Shown below are 1993 times.

Cog train.

Dep. Garmisch	07:35	08:35	09:35	10:35	11:35	12:35	13:35	14:35	15:35
Arr. Eibsee	08:15	09:15	10:15	11:15	12:15	13:15	14:15	15:15	16:15
Arr. Zugspitzplatt	08:40	09:40	10:40	11:40	12:40	13:40	14:40	15:40	16:40

Change to cable car.

Dep. Zugspitzplatt	08:45	09:45	10:45	11:45	12:45	13:45	14:45	15:45	16:45
Arr. Zugspitzgipfel	09:05	10:05	11:05	12:05	13:05	14:05	15:05	16:05	17:05

• • •

Dep. Zugspitzgipfel	09:15	10:15	11:15	12:15	13:15	14:15	15:15	16:15	17:05
Arr. Zugspitzplatt	09:35	10:35	11:35	12:35	13:35	14:35	15:35	16:35	17:35

Change cable cars.

Dep. Zugspitzplatt	09:45	10:45	11:45	12:45	13:45	14:45	15:45	16:45	17:45
Arr. Schneefernerhaus	09:49	10:49	11:49	12:49	13:49	14:49	15:49	16:49	17:49

Change to cog train.

Dep. Schneefernerhaus	10:00	11:00	12:00	13:00	14:00	15:00	16:00	17:00	18:00
Arr. Garmisch	11:20	12:20	13:20	14:20	15:20	16:20	17:20	18:20	19:20

Munich - Nurnberg - Heilbronn - Heidelberg

This schedule follows the route of the "Castle Road" and "Romantic Road"bus trips.

The 09:54 and 11:54 Munich departures must be made only Monday–Friday except holidays because of connection in Crailsheim.

750

Dep. Munich	07:56 (1)	09:56 (1)	11:56 (1)
Arr. Nurnberg	09:32	11:32	13:32

Change trains. 745

Dep. Nurnberg	09:45 (2)	11:45 (2)	13:45 (2)
Arr. Crailsheim	10:35	12:35	14:35

Change trains. 744

Dep. Crailsheim	10:48	12:48 (3)	14:48 (3)
Arr. Heilbronn	12:00	14:00	16:00

Sights in **Heilbronn**: More than 80% of the pre-World War II buildings in this city of 110,000 in the heart of Germany's wine country was obliterated by Allied bombing planes in 1944. The Wine Festival (one week in September) attracts 300,000 people every year.

742

Dep. Heilbronn	12:40	14:40	16:40
Arr. Heidelberg	13:59	16:13	17:59

(1) Supplement charged includes reservation fee. Restaurant car. (2) Reservation advisable. Light refreshements. (3) Runs Monday–Friday, except holidays.

Munich - Salzburg

This route offers good mountain scenery and is an easy one-day roundtrip. See schedules earlier in this section, under "One-Day Excursions."

Offenburg - Konstanz - Offenburg   730

This trip is recommended for exceptional mountain scenery.

Dep. Offenburg	07:02 (1)	07:56 (1)	08:37	09:53 (1)	10:37	11:53 (1)
Arr. Konstanz	09:17	10:11	11:18	12:11	13:18	14:11
Dep. Offenburg	12:37	13:53 (1)	14:37	15:53 (1)		
Arr. Konstanz	15:18	16:11	17:18	18:11		

* * *

Dep. Konstanz	09:49 (1)	10:50	11:49 (1)	12:50	13:49 (1)	14:50
Arr. Offenburg	12:04	13:18	14:04	15:18	16:04	17:18
Dep. Konstanz	15:49 (1)	16:45	17:49 (1)	18:50	19:49 (1)	20:55 (1)
Arr. Offenburg	18:04	19:18	20:04	21:15	21:44	23:09

(1) Reservation advisable. Light refreshments.

Offenburg - Singen - Schaffhausen - Offenburg

Excellent Black Forest scenery on this route. This trip can also be made as a detour en route from Frankfurt to Basel.

Reservation is advisable for all of the Offenburg-Singen (and v.v.) trains, and all of them have light refreshments.

730
Dep. Offenburg	07:56	09:53	11:53	13:53	15:53
Arr. Singen	09:48	11:47	13:47	15:47	17:47

Change trains.
734
Dep. Singen	12:14	14:14	16:14	18:14
Arr. Schaffhausen	12:32	14:32	16:32	18:32

Dep. Schaffhausen	11:29	13:29	15:29	17:29	19:29
Arr. Singen	11:45	13:45	15:45	17:45	19:45

Change trains.
730
Dep. Singen	12:13	14:12	16:13	18:13	20:13
Arr. Offenburg	14:04	16:04	18:04	20:04	21:44

Here is the detour from the Frankfurt-Basel ride:

730			734		
Dep. Frankfurt	07:47 (1)	09:47 (1)	Dep. Singen	12:14	14:14
Arr. Offenburg	09:51	11:51	Dep. Schaffhausen	12:34	14:34
Arr. Singen	11:47	13:47	Arr. Basel (Bad.)	13:48	15:48
Change trains.					

(1) Reservation advisable. Light refreshments.

Wurzburg - Zurich

There is exceptional Black Forest scenery on this ride.

741
Dep. Wurzburg	06:52 (1)	08:01 (2)	10:40	12:40
Arr. Stuttgart	09:15	10:21	12:58	14:58

Change trains. 74
Dep. Stuttgart	09:42 (3)	11:42 (3)	13:42	15:42	16:52 (4)	17:42
Arr. Zurich	12:47	14:47	16:47	18:47	19:50	20:47

(1) Runs daily, except Sunday. (2) Runs Sunday only. (3) Light refreshments. (4) Runs Monday-Friday. Supplement charged includes reservation fee. Restaurant car.

RHINE RIVER CRUISES

A variety of cruising on the Rhine is offered. The complete 5-day *down*stream route (from Basel to Amsterdam or Rotterdam) and the complete 6-day *up*stream route (Amsterdam or Rotterdam to Basel) are offered April to October.

A shorter portion (Rotterdam-Strasbourg and vice versa) is also available April to October. It is 4 days downstream and 5 upstream.

Still another service (3 days downstream and 4 upstream), between Amsterdam or Rotterdam and Mainz, is offered April to September.

On any of these, passengers may stop-over at points en route and resume the journey later (Cologne, Koblenz, etc.).

The most popular stretch of the Rhine (Koblenz to Mainz and Frankfurt) is covered by the Eurailpass. This is the portion famed for scenic vineyards and hilltop castles. The *entire* Rhine trip is *not* covered by Eurailpass. However, with a Eurailpass there is *no* charge for either the boat trip or train ride Mainz–Cologne or Cologne–Mainz.

The scenery between Mainz and Koblenz can be seen as well from a train as from a boat because the track on this run goes along the river bank.

Here are the schedules for taking the boat *Mainz–Cologne* and returning to Mainz by train the same day:

714 *(Boat)*		*650* *(Train)*	
Dep. Mainz	08:45 (1)	Dep. Cologne (Hbf.)	19:54 (2)
Arr. Koblenz	13:50	Dep. Koblenz	20:47
Arr. Cologne (Rheing'n)	18:50	Arr. Mainz	21:33

(1) Operates May 1 to October 3. (2) Supplement charged includes reservation fee. Restaurant car.

Here are the schedules for taking the hydrofoil *Cologne-Mainz* and returning to Cologne by train the same day:

714 *(Hydrofoil)*		*650* *(Train)*	
Dep. Cologne (Rheing'n)	09:00 (1)	Dep. Mainz	14:18 (2)
Arr. Koblenz	11:00	Dep. Koblenz	15:07
Arr. Mainz	13:10	Arr. Cologne (Hbf.)	15:59

(1) Operates April 1 to October 23. Runs daily, except Monday. Supplement charged. (2) Supplement charged includes reservation fee. Restaurant car. Plus other departures from Mainz at frequent times from 14:24 to 22:24.

THE ONE-DAY RHINE HYDROFOIL CRUISE ROUNDTRIP

Cologne - Mainz - Cologne   714

Operates April 1 to October 23. Runs daily, except Monday. Supplement charged.

Dep. Cologne (Rheing'n)	09:00	Dep. Mainz	14:25
Arr.. Koblenz	11:00	Dep. Koblenz	16:20
Arr. Mainz	13:10	Arr. Cologne (Rheing'n)	18:05

SCENIC BUS TRIPS COVERED BY EURAILPASS

Both of these extremely popular bus trips are covered by Eurailpass: "Roman tische Strasse" (**Romantic Road**) and "Burgenstrasse" (**Castle Road**). Advance seat reservations should be made at least 3 days before travel date. They can be obtained at no cost by writing to: Deutsche Touring GmbH, Am Roemerhof 17, D-6000 Frankfurt/M. 90, Germany, or by phoning: (069) 790-32-56. Be sure to indicate the dates you want to journey, which of the 2 different lines you want to travel, where you will start and end your trip, and the number of seats you want.

Passengers are allowed to break the journey at as many stops as they desire on both bus lines, and we recommend some specific places to do so in the text that follows. If that is your plan, be sure to provide all the specific dates this will involve when requesting a reservation.

The 2 lines connect in **Rothenburg**, making it easy to ride on all or part of both trips. Lodging in Rothenburg is good quality, but the supply is small and the demand very great. The Encyclopedia Britannica calls Rothenburg "probably the finest surviving example of a medieval town." It has been there for 1,000 years. Its 30 watchtowers and many dungeons, churches, patrician homes, ornamental fountains and market squares are perfectly preserved.

The town's most important buildings are on the old Market Square: Town Hall, Virgin's Pharmacy (Marienapotheque), the lovely stone fountain (Herterichbrunnen), the ancient city council drinking hall, and the mechanical clock that performs at 11:00, 13:00 and 14:00.

The Meistertrunk Legend When the town was under siege in the 17th century, the commander of the victorious Imperial Army was given his first taste of wine by the inhabitants. He offered to spare the lives of the city officials if any of them could empty in one drink the content of a tankard holding almost one gallon. One burgermeister rose to the challenge, accomplished the feat, and even quaffed more. The 3.24 liter Meistertrunk tankard is on display in the town's Reichstadt Museum. The legend is recreated every year in a pageant held on Whitsunday, 7 weeks after Easter.

Statues of the 7 deadly sins and 7 virtues adorn the Baumeisterhaus, on Schmiedgasse, near Market Square. This chiseled house is well worth seeing. The torture museum at the Dominican Nunnery is another attraction in the town.

Rothenburg has 15 hotels with 11 to 145 rooms each. It is an ideal stopover either for breaking the Romantische Strasse ride into 2 days or for transferring from or to the Burgenstrasse ride.

Also a recommended stopover on the Romantische Strasse ride is **Dinkelsbuhl,** another finely preserved medieval town with a surfeit of gates, bastions, towers, a moat equipped with floating swans and a sharp sense of ancient history. Its major pageant is every July, complete with sword dances and historic tableaux.

Augsburg is an ancient castled city. See notes under "Munich–Augsburg."

Castle Road   748

This bus trip operates from mid-May to late September.

Dep. Mannheim	08:37		Dep. Rothenburg	17:00
Dep. Heidelberg	08:56		Arr. Heidelberg	20:45
Arr. Rothenburg	13:27		Arr. Mannheim	21:10

Romantic Road   748

The portion of this bus trip which has the principal sights is Wurzburg–Augsburg (and v.v.). A stewardess-guide is provided for that part of the 2 schedules shown below.

These buses operate April 1 to October 31.

Dep. Frankfurt	08:15	-0-		Dep. Munich	09:00	-0-
Dep. Wurzburg	09:45	-0-		Dep. Fussen	-0-	08:00
Arr. Rothenburg	12:15 (1)	-0-		Dep. Augsburg	10:30	10:45
Dep. Rothenburg	13:00	14:45		Arr. Dinkelsbuhl	11:55 (1)	12:15
Arr. Dinkelsbuhl	13:40 (1)	15:25 (1)		Dep. Dinkelsbuhl	12:05	12:25
Dep. Dinkelsbuhl	16:20	16:15		Arr. Rothenburg	12:45 (1)	13:00 (2)
Arr. Augsburg	18:00	18:00		Dep. Rothenburg	17:00	17:00
Arr. Fussen	-0-	20:00		Arr. Wurzburg	18:25	18:25
Arr. Munich	19:15	-0-		Arr. Frankfurt	20:00	20:00

(1) Meal stop. Time to stroll. (2) Change buses.

SPECIAL RAIL TRIP FROM FUSSEN

For a marvelous extension from Fussen, here is a train trip that offers superb scenery: alpine meadows, deep river gorges, mountains. One of the most spectacular one-day rail routes in Europe.

Bus. German table.

Dep. Fussen	09:30	12:50
Arr. Reutte	10:03	13:43
Change to train.		
785		
Dep. Reutte	12:00 (1)	14:08
Arr. Garmisch	12:57 (1)	15:06
Change trains		
Dep. Garmisch	13:26	15:26
Arr. Innsbruck	14:41	16:43
Change trains.		
800		
Dep. Innsbruck	15:02 (2)	17:02 (2)
Arr. Salzburg	17:00	19:00

(1) Direct train Reutte–Innsbruck. No train change in Garmisch. (2) Supplement charged includes reservation fee. Restaurant car.

INTERNATIONAL ROUTES
FROM GERMANY

The German gateway for travel to Amsterdam and Brussels (and on to London) is Cologne. Frankfurt and Cologne are the access points to Paris (and on to Barcelona and Madrid). Frankfurt is also the starting point for travel to Basel and Zurich (and on to Milan and Genoa)…as well as to Warsaw.

Munich and Nurnberg are gateways for trips to Vienna (and on to Belgrade and Budapest), and Bologna (and on to Rome or Venice). Nurnberg and Berlin are departure points for getting to Prague. Berlin and Hamburg are the gateways to Copenhagen (and on to Oslo and Stockholm).

Berlin - Copenhagen   51

Dep. Berlin (Lichtenberg)	08:51 (1)	14:51 (2)	23:52 (3)
Arr. Copenhagen	16:55	22:55	08:31

(1) Carries first and second-class sleeping car. Also has second-class couchettes. Coach is second-class only. Runs June 23-August 20. (2) Operates late June to mid-August. (3) Restaurant car 16:00-20:55.

Berlin - Prague 680

Reservation is advisabe for all of these trains and they have a restaurant car, unless designated otherwise.

Dep. Berlin (Licht.)	02:14	09:24	17:23	18:48
Dep. Berlin (Sch'fld)	-0-	09:43	17:42	19:07
Arr. Prague (Hole.)	07:14	14:59	21:41	22:47
Arr. Prague (Hlavni)	-0-	-0-	-0-	-0-

Dep. Berlin (Licht.)	22:24	23:48
Dep. Berlin (Sch'fld)	22:43	00:07
Arr. Prague (Hole.)	01:59	05:14
Arr. Prague (Hlavni)	-0-	-0-

Berlin - Warsaw 56

Dep. Berlin (Hbf.)	08:10 (1)	-0-	-0-	16:32 (1)	-0-
Dep. Berlin (Licht.)	-0-	10:39 (2)	11:40 (3)	-0-	22:07 (4)
Arr. Warsaw (Centralna)	14:25	19:25	20:07	22:40	06:15
Arr. Warsaw (Wschodnia)	14:44	19:39	20:21	22:54	06:29

(1) Supplement charged includes reservation fee. Restaurant car. (2) Train has only first and second-class sleeping cars. *No* coaches. (3) Train has only second-class sleeping cars. *No* coaches. (4) Carries a sleeping car. Also has couchettes.

Cologne - Amsterdam 28

Sit on the right-hand side for best views of the marvelous Rhine River scenery.

All of these trains charge a supplement that includes reservation fee and have light refreshments, unless designated otherwise.

Dep. Cologne	07:17	09:17	11:17	13:17	15:17	17:17	18:02 (1+2)
Arr. Amsterdam	09:54	11:51	13:51	15:51	17:51	19:51	20:51

(1) Restaurant car. (2) Plus other departures from Cologne at 19:02 (1), and 21:17, arriving Amsterdam 21:51 and 23:51.

Cologne - Basel - Zurich   77

Dep. Cologne	07:00 (1)	08:00 (1)	09:00 (1)	11:00 (1)	12:00 (1+4)
Arr. Basel (S.B.B.)	11:43 (2)	12:43 (2)	13:43	15:43 (2)	16:43
Arr. Zurich	13:00	14:00	15:00	17:00	18:03

(1) Supplement charged includes reservation fee. Restaurant car. (2) Change trains in Basel. (3) Carries a sleeping car. Also has couchettes. (4) Plus other Cologne departures at frequent times from 13:00 to 17:00 plus 23:59 (3).

Cologne - Brussels   20

Dep. Cologne	05:08	06:30 (1)	07:14	11:14	12:14 (2)
Arr. Brussels (Nord)	07:55	08:50	09:44	13:44	14:14
Arr. Brussels (Midi)	08:04	09:01	09:55	13:55	14:55

(1) Supplement charged includes reservation fee. Restaurant car. (2) Plus other departures from Cologne at 13:14 (1), 14:14, 15:14 (1), 16:14, 18:14 and 20:14, arriving Brussels Nord 15:48, 16:44, 17:49, 18:44, 20:44 and 22:44.

Cologne - Paris   25

Dep. Cologne	00:07 (1)	05:46 (2)	08:14 (3)	13:14 (3)	17:08 (3)
Arr. Paris (Nord)	06:25	11:20	13:31	19:01	22:10

(1) Carries a sleeping car. Also has couchettes. Light refreshments. (2) Operates late May to late September. Coach is Second-class. (3) Supplement charged includes reservation fee. Restaurant car.

Munich - Bologna - Florence - Rome   76

Dep. Munich (Hbf.)	08:30	09:30 (1)	20:30 (2)	21:43 (3)	23:30 (2)
Arr. Bologna	16:14	17:16	04:08	05:32	07:47
Arr. Florence (S.M.N.)	-0-	18:23	-0-	-0-	09:06
Arr. Rome (Ter.)	-0-	20:30	08:15	-0-	-0-

(1) Supplement charged includes reservation fee. Restaurant car. (2) Carries a sleeping car. Also has couchettes. Coach is second-class. (3) Has couchettes. Coach is second-class.

Munich - Salzburg - Vienna   67

Dep. Munich (Hbf.)	06:50 (1)	08:25 (2)	09:51 (1)	10:50 (5)
Arr. Salzburg	08:45	09:55	11:40 (3)	12:45 (3)
Arr. Vienna (Westbf.)	-0-	13:25	15:25	16:25

(1) Reservation advisable. Light refreshments. (2) Supplement charged includes reservation fee. Restaurant car. (3) Change trains in Salzburg. (4) Has couchettes. (5) Plus other Munich departures at 12:25 (2+3), 13:25 (2+3), 13:51 (1+3), 15:25 (2+3), 16:25 (2), 16:50, 18:25 (2) and 23:19(4).

GREECE

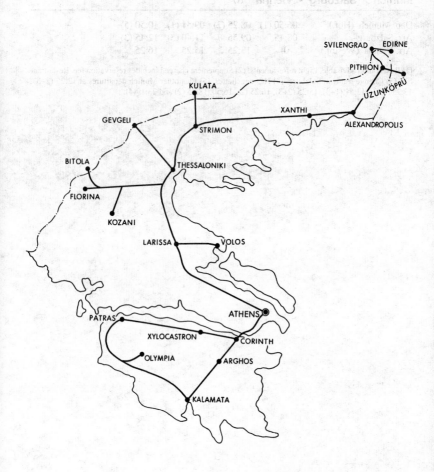

GREECE

Overview

In the days before the conflicts in Yugoslavia, many Eurailpass travelers took the train to Athens via Belgrade and Thessaloniki. Today most train to the Italian port of Brindisi and ferry across to Corfu and then continue by rail to the Greek capital via Patras. This is a long but not unpleasant ride.

General Information

• Children under four travel free if they do not occupy a separate seat.
• Greece changes to summer time on the last Sunday of March and converts back to standard time on the last Sunday of September.

Greek Holidays

January 1	New Year's Day		May 1	Labor Day
January 6	Epiphany		August 15	Virgin Mary's Day
	Ash Monday		October 28	National Day
March 25	Independence Day		December 25	Christmas
	Greek Good Friday		December 26	Boxing Day
	Greek Good Saturday			
	Greek Easter			
	Greek Easter Monday			

GREECE'S TRAIN PASSES

Sold worldwide outside Greece by travel agencies and Rail Europe (U.S.A. and Canadian offices listed under "France").

Greek Railpass Unlimited *first-class* train travel. The 1996 adult prices are: $80 for any 3 days within 15 days, $130 for any 5 days within 15 days, $223 for any 10 days within one month. Half-fare for children age 4-11.

Greek Rail'N Drive Unlimited 5 days of first-class train travel plus 3 days of car rental (any 8 days) within 15 days. Prices vary (a) whether for one person or for 2 persons, (b) the category of car, and (c) the season. High Season is July, August and September. The 1996 price *per person* for 2 persons (using the smallest size car) in High Season was: $132. A third and fourth passenger had to pay only for the Greek Railpass. And, more days of car rental could be added in increments of two or more consecutive days at $65 per day.

Greek Flexipasses Unlimited *first-class* train travel. The 1996 adult prices are: $86 for any 3 days in one month, $120 for any 5 days in one month. Children: $58 and $85.

The passes described below can be purchased only in Greece, at travel agencies and main railstations. Prices shown are for 1996 and are in drachmas.

Greek Tourist Card   Unlimited *second*-class travel on trains and CH buses.

Persons	10 days	20 days	30 days
1	6,000	9,000	10,000
2	10,000	15,000	22,000
3	13,000	21,000	20,000
4	15,000	25,000	34,000
5	17,000	27,000	37,000

Greek Senior Card   Valid for one year from date issued (except 10 days before and after Easter, 10 days before and after Christmas, and July 1 to September 30. For persons age 60 or older on the day that identity card or passport is presented. Allows 5 free journeys plus 50% discount for unlimited number of journeys after the first 5. The 1996 prices are: 6,000 drachmas for first-class; 4,000 drachmas for second-class.

Group Discount   A 30% discount is granted to groups of 10 or more persons.

EURAILPASS BONUSES IN GREECE

• The ferry crossing from Patras to Brindisi (see note under "Italy").
• There is also a 30% reduction on Adriatica di Navagazione Line for ships between Piraeus–Venice (and v.v.) and Piraeus–Alexandria (and v.v.).

ONE-DAY EXCURSIONS AND CITY-SIGHTSEEING

Here are 8 one-day rail trips that can be made comfortably from Athens and Thessaloniki, returning to them in most cases before dinnertime. Notes are provided on what to see and do at each destination. The number after the name of each route is the Cook's timetable.

Details on 2 longer rail trips in Greece follow the one-day excursions. Schedules for international connections conclude this section.

Athens (Athinai)

From 07:30 to sunset, and from 21:00 to 24:00 on nights of a full moon, visit the Parthenon, the elegant temple of the Wingless Victory and the Erechtheion at the ancient Acropolis. The monuments there can be seen 07:30–16:45 daily. The adjacent museum is closed Tuesday. Then walk northwest to the partly restored ancient Agora to see the best preserved Doric temple in Athens, the Hephaistos, also known as the Thesseion.

Also near the Acropolis are: The old theater of Dionyssos. The gravestones and sculptures in Kerameikos, the city's ancient cemetery. The Corinthia-style columns of the Temple of Olympian Zeus. Hadrian's Arch. The all-marble Athenian Stadium, where the Olympic Games were revived in 1896. The Clock of Kyrrestos, showing the prevailing wind on each of its 8 sides, standing in Aerides Square, named for the function of the clock. The Roman Forum.

Walk downhill to the Monastiraki area, where the daily "Flea Market" is held. See the view of Athens from the white chapel of Agios Georgios on the Hill of Lycabettus, climbed either by foot or by cable car.

Athens' best-known museums are the National Archaeological Museum at 1 Tositza Street; the collection of ancient coins at the Numismatic Museum, next to the Archaeological Museum; the Acropolis Museum (noted above), the Byzantine Museum at 22 Vassilis Sophias Avenue (closed Monday), for its collection of icons; the Museum of Greek Popular Art (closed Monday); the Museum of the Ancient Agora excavations in the Stoa, an ancient commercial community at Attalus (closed Tuesday). The work of contemporary Greek painters and sculptors in the National Gallery at 60 Vas Constantinou (closed Monday). The more than 2,000 items relating to the social and religious customs of Romanlot and Sephardic Jews in the Jewish Museum (third floor at 36 Amalias Avenue), open daily except Saturday 09:00–13:00. Displays include the reconstructed interior of a provincial synagogue, religious articles, costumes and objects of everyday life.

The 28 exhibit rooms at the fantastic Benaki Museum in central Athens (Vasilisis Sophias Avenue at Koumbari Street), arranged chronologically, cover the entire spectrum of Greek culture from the early Bronze Age to the start of the 20th century: gold, ornaments, jewelry, portraits, statues, embroidery, icons, rare 17th and 18th century bibles, and 8 centuries (10th to 18th) of Islamic art that includes ceramics, textiles and wood carvings. The Benaki is open daily except Tuesday 08:00 to 14:00.

Figurines of white marble from the Cycladic islands (in the Aegean Sea), created 5,000 years ago, in the Goulandris Museum of Cycladic Art (4 Neophytou Douka Street), open Monday–Friday 10:00-16:00, Saturday 10:00–15:00.

A collection of weapons since the Neolithic Age in the War Museum (Vasilisis Sophia Avenue at Rizari Street), open Tuesday-Saturday 09:00–14:00, Sunday 9:30–14:00. Nineteenth century arts and crafts (woodcarving, needlework, naive painting) at the Museum of Greek Folk Art (17 Kydathineon Street), open daily except Monday 10:00–14:00.

The collection (from the Archaic period through the Middle Ages) of stone sculptures, ceramics, bronzes and exceptionally beautiful icons in the Canellopoulos Museum (below the Acropolis, at Theorias and Panos streets), closed Tuesday, open other weekdays 08:45–15:00, Sundays 09:30–14:30.

There are sound-and-light performances in English at Pnyx Hill every night at 21:00. When it ends, cross the road and see native dances of Greece, performed nightly at 22:15 on the Hill of Philopappus.

For Greek arts and handicrafts (ceramics, hand-woven fabrics, alabaster articles, embroideries, hand-carved wood furniture), shop on the streets around Syntagma Square, the center of the city.

Athens - Arghos - Athens 980

| Dep. Athens | 06:30 | 08:30 | 09:28 | 14:59 | 16:09 |
| Arr. Arghos | 09:18 | 11:10 | 12:18 | 17:50 | 19:03 |

Sights in **Arghos:** The Museum, with its archaeological exhibits. From there, it is a 15-minute walk to the ancient theater, carved into the hillside, and to some Roman ruins. A 5-mile taxi ride to the 800 B.C. ruins of Tiryns is well worth the small fare. At the birthplace of Hercules you will see the ruins of Greece's oldest recognizable temple: underground galleries polished for many centuries by the woolly backs of innumerable sheep who sought shelter there during storms. Massive Cyclopean walls.

| Dep. Arghos | 10:18 | 13:53 | 17:51 | 19:25 |
| Arr. Athens | 13:02 | 16:38 | 20:46 | 22:13 |

Athens - Corinth (Korinthos) - Athens 980

Watch 80 minutes after departing Athens for the same view described above, under "Athens–Arghos." The arrival in Corinth is in the "modern" Corinth, built after the 1858 earthquake.

| Dep. Athens | 06:30 (1) | 07:56 | 08:30 (1) | 08:54 | 09:28 (3) |
| Arr. Corinth | 08:06 | 09:27 | 10:14 | 10:24 | 11:19 |

Sights in **Corinth:** The 2500-year old Temple of Apollo. The Kato Pirini Fountain. The rostrum from which St. Paul preached Christianity to the Corinthians.

| Dep. Corinth | 11:20 (2) | 11:56 | 12:36 (1) | 14:31 | 14:53 (1) | 15:57 (1) | 17:46 (2+4) |
| Arr. Athens | 13:08 | 13:50 | 14:27 | 15:58 | 16:38 | 17:42 | 19:12 |

(1) Light refreshments. (2) Restaurant car. (3) Plus other departures from Athens at 09:50 (1) and 12:02.
(4) Plus other departures from Corinth at 18:47, 19:55, 20:31 and 21:31.

Athens - Kalamata - Athens 980

| Dep. Athens | 06:30 (1) | 08:50 (2) | 09:20 (2) | 14:32 |
| Arr. Kalamata | 13:00 | 15:55 | 20:03 | 21:30 |

Sights in **Kalamata:** The exhibits at the Museum in the Kyriakos mansion, ranging from Stone Age weapons to Venetian mirrors and coins as well as relics from the 1821 War of Independence. The Byzantine-style Church of Aghii Apostoli. The splendid view from the Frankish castle and, descending from there, see the handmade silk articles at the Convent. Aghios Haralambos, one of the finest Byzantine churches in the area, is a short distance east of the

Convent. Stroll along the seafront.

Dep. Kalamata	06:30 (2)	10:00	15:40
Arr. Athens	14:25	16:38	22:13

(1) Via Xylocastron. (2) Via Arghos. (3) Light refreshments. Change trains in Patras (arr. 15:28-dep. 15:55). (4) Via Xylocastron. Change trains in Patras (arr. 15:10-dep. 15:50 light ref.).

Athens - Pirghos - Olympia - Athens

Most of this trip is alongside the sea, through green fields of citrus and olive trees. Between Athens and Corinth, the train goes across a bridge that spans the Korinthos Canal, which separates northern Greece from Peloponesia.

All of the trains Pirghos–Olympia (and v.v.) are second-class.

980

Dep. Athens	08:54 (1)	13:43
Arr. Pirghos	13:50	18:38
Change trains. 977		
Dep. Pirghos	14:40	20:00
Arr. Olympia	15:16	20:36

Sights in **Olympia:** The first Olympic Games (776 B.C.) were held here and continued here every 4 years for the next 12 centuries. See the Stadium. The fine Olympic Museum, with its marvelous Hermes of Praxiteles sculpture. The temples of Hera and Zeus.

Dep. Olympia	07:30	11:00	16:00
Arr. Pirghos	08:06	11:36	16:36
Change trains. 980			
Dep. Pirghos	09:10 (1)	11:08 (2)	16:29 (1)
Arr. Athens	14:02	17:53	21:22

(1) Light refreshments. Supplement charged. (2) Change trains in Patras (arr. 15:10-dep. 15:50 light refreshments).

Athens - Patras - Athens   980

Dep. Athens	06:30 (1)	08:54	09:50	12:02 (1)	13:43 (3+5)	
Arr. Patras	10:39	12:15	14:38	15:28 (5)	17:05	

Dep. Patras	06:00 (1)	09:35 (2)	10:42 (1)	13:25 (1)	15:57 (2)	18:03 (1+4)
Arr. Athens	09:20 (5)	13:42	14:02 (5)	17:53	19:12	21:20 (5)

(1) Light refreshments. (2) Restaurant car. (3) Plus other departures from Athens at 14:59 (2), 17:09 (1) and 19:19 (1+5), arriving Patras 19:05, 20:19 and 22:53. (4) Plus other departures from Patras at 19:16, arriving Athens 23:22. (5) Supplement payable.

Sights in **Patras:** Cross the street in front of the railstation to the park. Then walk from the Trion Fountain along Ayiou Nijulauo to the steps that ascend to the Patras Acropolis for a fine view of Patras, the surrounding mountains and the port, third largest of Greece.

After descending the steps, go to the left along Georgiou Street to the old Roman Theater, the Odeon. Another walk from the Trion Fountain is to the Archaeological Museum to see its collection of exhibits from the Mycenean, Geometric, Archaic and Roman periods. Also worth seeing are the Venetian castle and Greece's largest church, St. Andrews's. See the Clock of Patras, made entirely of flowers. Visit the century-old Achaia Clauss Winery, the leading producer of Greek wines.

Athens - Piraeus - Athens

Subway trains depart every few minutes from the southbound section of a combined north-and-south platform at Athens' Omonia Square railstation for the 20-minute ride to Piraeus. Be certain, at the same platform, you are not boarding the northbound train for Kifissia. There is also ordinary train service from Athens to Piraeus.

Sights in **Piraeus:** One of the largest ports on the Mediterranean. Ships sail daily from here to almost all the Aegean islands and to many other Greek ports. The 2 small adjoining ports of Zea and Mikrolimano are for pleasure craft. Bus #20 goes to those ports. The bus terminal is to the left of the railstation. See the neo-classical style Municipal Theater and the exhibits in the Archaeological Museum. The Maritime Museum, closed Monday, exhibits 13,000 items reflecting 5,000 years of Greek seafaring. Plays are performed at the open-air Theater of Kastella in the Summer.

Thessaloniki - Kavala - Thessaloniki

All of the Thessaloniki-Drama (and v.v.) trains have light refreshments.

974

Dep. Thessaloniki	07:50 (1)	09:31	13:30 (1+2)
Arr. Drama	11:32	13:00	16:11
Change to bus. (G.T.O. advice)			
Dep. Drama	10:00	16:00	18:00
Arr. Kavala	10:30	16:30	18:30

Sights in **Kavala:** The view from the Byzantine Fort. The colossal 16th century aqueduct, Kamares. Imaret, the group of Moslem buildings constructed a short time prior to the 1821 War of Independence. The ancient relics in the Archaeological Museum. Beautiful beaches.

Dep. Kavala	08:00	12:00	16:00	18:00
Arr. Drama	08:30	12:30	16:30	18:30
Change to train. 974				
Dep. Drama	10:03 (1)	13:01	17:08 (1)	01:56
Arr. Thessaloniki	12:43 (2)	16:39	20:42	05:20

(1) Reservations recommended. (2) Supplement payable.

SCENIC RAIL TRIPS

Athens - Thessaloniki and Thessaloniki - Athens

970 + Greek Timetable

From **Tithorea** to **Domokos,** the train winds along **Mt. Iti** and **Mt. Orthrys,** providing a panoramic view of many valleys and high mountains and, at one point, of the sea in the distance. Then the train goes along **Pinios River** and passes through **Tembi Valley.** About one hour before arriving **Katerini** (Athens–Thessaloniki), you can see on the left side of the train 9,000-foot-high **Mt. Olympus.**

Dep. Athens (Larissa)	07:00 (1)	08:10	10:00 (2)	13:00 (2)	15:00	17:00 (2+4)
Dep. Tithorea	N/A	N/A	N/A	N/A	N/A	N/A
Dep. Domokos	N/A	N/A	N/A	N/A	N/A	N/A
Dep. Katerini	11:55	14:27	14:50	18:08	20:45	22:02
Arr. Thessaloniki	12:55	15:32	15:51	19:15	21:58	23:13

Sights in **Thessaloniki:** Second largest city in Greece. See the ruins of the Roman Baths, north of the Church of Agios Demetrios. The Roman Market and Theater. Nym- phaion, the ancient circular building. The Arch of Galerius. The unique mosaics in the 4th century Rotunda, at the intersection of Agiou Georgiou and Filippou streets.

The 2 surviving early Christian churches: the 4th century Ahiropiitos and the 5th century Osios David. The 15th century White Tower. The collection of pre-historic to Byzantine items in the Archaeological Museum on YMCA Square. Articles from the past 3 centuries at the Folklore and Ethnological Museum, 68 Vasilisais Olgas.

Dep. Thessaloniki	08:00	13:07	17:07 (2)
Dep. Katerini	N/A	14:40	-0-
Dep. Domokos	N/A	N/A	N/A
Dep. Tithorea	N/A	N/A	N/A
Arr. Athens (Larissa)	15:19	18:58	23:16

Dep. Thessaloniki	18:00	22:04 (2)	23:30 (1)
Dep. Katerini	19:08	23:14	00:46
Dep. Domokos	N/A	N/A	N/A
Dep. Tithorea	N/A	N/A	N/A
Arr. Athens (Larissa)	00:58	05:45	07:26

(1) Carries a sleeping car. Also has couchettes. (2) Reservation required. Supplement charged. Light refreshments. (3) Reservation required. Supplement charged. (4) Plus other departures from Athens at 22:00 (1) arriving Thessaloniki 05:17.

INTERNATIONAL ROUTES FROM GREECE

Thessaloniki is Greece's gateway to Central Europe (and on to Western Europe), as well as to Turkey (and on to the Middle East).

Athens - Belgrade - Budapest

...Plus Salzburg, Vienna, Munich or Venice

	97 b +970	97 b +61	
Dep. Athens	10:00 (1)	23:30 (2)	
Arr. Thessaloniki	15:51	07:50 (3)	
Dep. Thessaloniki	-0-	08:26	
Set your watch back one hour from late September to early April, 2 hours from early April to late September.			
Arr. Belgrade	-0- (3)	21:23	
Change trains.			
Dep. Belgrade	-0-	21:45	
Arr. Budapest (Keleti)	-0-	05:55 (4)	
Change trains.		61	61
Dep. Budapset (Keleti)	-0-	05:55	12:25 (7)
Arr. Vienna (Westbf.)	-0-	09:20	15:50
Arr. Salzburg	-0-	-0-	19:00
Arr. Munich	-0-	-0-	20:36
Arr. Venice (S.L.)	-0-	-0-	-0-

(1) Carries a sleeping car. Also has couchettes. (2) Day 2. (3) Direct train Athens–Vienna. No train change in Belgrade or Budapest. Carries a sleeping car. Also has couchettes. Arrives Budapest and Vienna on day 2. (4) Day 3. (5) Restaurant car. (6) Arrives at Vienna's Sud railstation. (7) Supplement charged. Restaurant car.

Athens - Patras - Brindisi   980

The Patras-Brindisi boat trip is covered by Eurailpass and Eurail Youthpass but only if you go on Adriatica di Navagazione.

WARNING: The employees of other lines intimate that their ships honor the 2 passes and then charge fees after the boat leaves the pier.

With or without a Eurailpass or Eurail Youthpass, a reservation theoretically can be made on day of departure or day before departure but it is very unlikely that space will be available (particularly during July and August) unless a reservation is made many weeks in advance of departure date.

Those gambling on making a reservation after arriving in Patras can make application January 1 to June 9 and October 1 to December 31 only at the Adriatica di Navagazione embarkation office, located at Othonos Amalias Street 8.

From June 10 to September 30, those without advance reservations can apply also to any Patras travel agency that displays in its window the green badge "Eurail Information—Eurailpass."

Holders of advance reservations must go at all times directly to the Adriatica di Navagazione embarkation office to have their tickets checked, settle port taxes due and obtain the required Embarkation Ticket. That office is open 09:00–13:30 and 16:00–22:00.

Advance reservations before you start your trip can be made by contacting Extra Value Travel, 683 So. Collier Blvd., Marco Island, Florida 33937, U.S.A. Telephone: (813) 394-3384.

Another fee is charged for such special accommodations as aircraft type seats, pullman berths and cabins. There is also a port tax of 180 Drachmas that is not covered by Eurailpass and must be paid in Drachmas.

Passengers without advance reservations must obtain the Embarkation Ticket at least 2 hours prior to the ship's departure time. The ships reserve the right to cancel a reservation when that is not done and to give the space to a standby passenger.

Readers reported to us in 1990 that conditions on the boat were unsatisfactory.

For a view first of the Corinthian Canal and then the Corinthian Gulf, sit on the right side of the train Athens–Patras.

Dep. Athens	06:30	08:54 (1)	09:50	12:02 (1)	13:43 (3+4)
Arr. Patras	09:55	12:15	14:38	15:28 (4)	17:30

It is a 20-minute walk from the railstation to the harbor. A taxi costs about $5.00 (U.S.).

Change to boat. Check Cook's table 1490 for sailing dates.

Dep. Patras Harbor	19:00	22:00	
Arr. Brindisi	10:00	17:00	Both arrivals are on day 2

(1) Light refreshments. (2) Restaurant car. (3) Plus other departures from Athens at 14:59, 17:09 (4) and 19:19 (4), arriving Patras 19:05, 20:27 and 22:37. (4) Supplement payable.

Athens - Thessaloniki - Istanbul

Both of these trains have light refreshments.

970

Dep. Athens	07:00
Arr. Thessaloniki	12:55

Change trains.
974

Dep. Thessaloniki	15:04
Arr. Istanbul	07:20 Day 2. (Reservation recommended.)

IBERIAN PENINSULA
(SPAIN AND PORTUGAL)

Overview

It has become increasingly difficult to speak of Spain and Portugal as a single entity, as each country's tourist industry and infrastructure has progressed independently. Spain, of course, had a big year in 1992 when it hosted the Olympics in Barcelona, the World Expo in Seville, and the seat of the European Cultural Capital in Madrid, as so modernized considerably for the festivities. Lisbon has been the Cultural Capital of Europe in 1994 and some development and expansion has occurred.

Train travel in Spain is highly varied in that you can zoom across central and south Spain from Madrid to Seville in rocket time or take what seems like days to creek 50 kilometers across the Basque country or Galicia. Spain and Portugal have the broadest gauge railroad tracks in Western Europe It is therefore necessary in most crossings from Spain into France (at Irun/Hendaye, Port Bou/Cerbere, or La Tour-de-Carol) to change trains. A few trains running between Spain and France are adaptable to either gauge.

General Information

• Children under four travel free in Portugal and Spain if they do not occupy a separate seat. Half-fare for children 4-11 includes use of a separate seat. Children 12 and over must pay full fare.

• First-class sleeping cars in Spain have single-berth and two-berth compartments. Second-class sleeping cars have three-berth tourist compartments, except the Paris-Madrid and Barcelona Talgos, which have tourist compartments with four berths. There is a supplemental charge for air-conditioned sleeping cars. Neither berths nor this supplement are covered by Eurailpass. Some Spanish trains have second-class couchette cars, with six-berth compartments, as are also available in other Western European countries.

• First-class sleeping cars in Portugal have single and double-berth compartments. Second-class Portuguese sleeping cars have 3-berth compartments.

• Many Spanish train tickets include the price of a lunch or dinner, a fact that is wise to determine this in advance of a trip.

• For most Spanish trains, it is necessary to reserve a seat and have ones ticket stamped with the train number and departure date. Even when traveling with a Eurailpass or a Spanish pass, an endorsed ticket should be obtained for trains requiring them.

• Do not discard a ticket during the journey. Frequently, the ticket is collected at the termination of a ride. If it is not presented at the destination rail station, the passenger must purchase a second ticket.

• Every year, some tourists using Eurailpass or a Spanish pass report being ejected from a Spanish train either just before its departure or at a station en route to their destination for failing to obtain the required endorsed tickets. A person using a pass has been indoctrinated

266

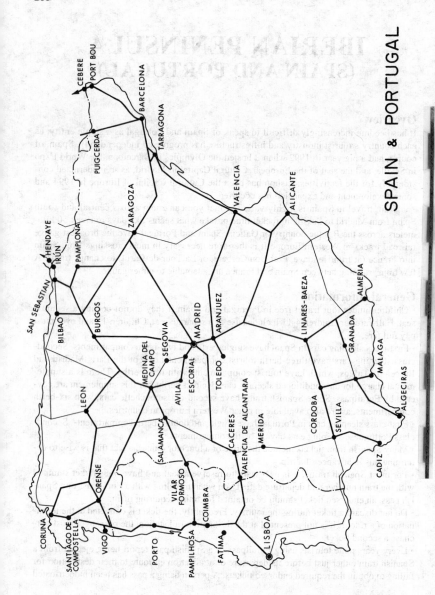

SPAIN & PORTUGAL

with the idea that he or she need not have either a ticket or (when riding an ordinary train) a seat reservation. This is confirmed everywhere in Europe outside Spain. Unaware of the Spanish Railway regulation, the passenger blithely steps aboard a train in Spain without having the ticket and seat reservation required there and a ticket can be obtained without charge upon presenting a Eurailpass or a Spanish pass. If the train is not exceptionally crowded that day and the conductor appears before the train departs, the passenger is told to get off the train, go back into the rail station, and obtain the required endorsed ticket. Frequently, the notice to do this is given so close to the departure time that the train leaves before the passenger is able to return to it. If the train departs before the conductor has discovered the omission of an endorsed ticket, often the passenger is forced to leave the train at the next stop to obtain a ticket. If that stop is typically brief, the train leaves that station before the passenger is able to return to the train.

• The justification for the Spanish ticket-and-reservation requirement is that Spain's first-class fares are substantially lower than those about 60% of what French National Railroads charges for the 7-hour trip from Paris to Avignon or what Norwegian State Railways charges for the 8-hour Bergen-Oslo trip. The demand for Spain's limited number of express train seats far exceeds the supply. Only by issuing endorsed tickets can they control the situation. The Spanish name for its national company is Red Nacional de los Ferrocar- riles Espanoles. Abbreviation: RENFE. Reservations can be made at RENFE offices both in the major rail stations and at numerous locations outside the station, as well as at various travel agencies in Spanish cities. Making train reservations in Spain is very easy. More than 90% of the stations in Spain are hooked-up with a computer in Madrid, making it usually possible to arrange at one time all of your reservations for train trips in Spain. Reservations can be made as much as two months in advance. Timetable information can be obtained at offices of RENFE and at Spanish travel agencies. Tell the clerk at the train information window your departure date, train number (which you can find in the rail station on the list of departures) and/or departure time, destination and number of seats required. You will be handed a form which you then take to a ticket window, where you will be handed a seat reservation computer card. It will show either an exact seat number or the symbol SR (Seat Reserved) under the column Asiento. If it is marked SR, the conductor will tell you which seat to occupy after you board the car designated on the reservation computer card.

Do not board a Spanish non-local train without a seat reservation!

• To ride without a Eurailpass or a Spanish pass on Spanish trains classified Rap, one must pay a supplement. An even higher supplement must be paid when riding a train classified Talgo, E.L.T. or T.E.R., all of which are air-conditioned. A Eurailpass or a Spanish pass entitles the bearer to ride these special trains without having to pay their supplemental charges, the same as when riding EuroCity or InterCity trains.

• In Spain, Rail Club Lounges are special rail station waiting rooms that have television sets, a bar, telephones, magazines and daily newspapers. These lounges are located at Madrid's Chamartin and Atocha stations, Barcelona's Sants, Valencias Termino, and at the rail station in Bilbao, Cordova, Malaga, Vigo and Zaragoza. These lounges are available to passengers who are ticketed for international trains: Madrid-Paris, Barcelona-Geneva, Barcelona-Paris, Barcelona-Bern…and also for domestic travelers holding first-class tickets for sleeping compartments as well as for coach seats on any Talgo or InterCity train.

In order to avoid waiting in the wrong line for Spanish tickets and seat reservations, take note of these signs you will find in large Spanish railstations:

TRENES DE SALIDA INMEDIATE   trains ready to depart
VENTA PARA HOY   trains leaving later in the day
VENTA ANTICIPADA   for trains leaving on a future day

Other **Spanish** railstation signs:

ANDEN   PLATFORM
ASIENTO   SEAT
BILLETTE   TICKET
CABALLEROS   MEN
COCHE-CAMA   SLEEPING CAR
COCHE-LITERA   COUCHETTES
COCHE-COMEDOR   RESTAURANT CAR
ENTRADA   ENTRANCE
ESTACION   STATION
HOMBRES   MEN
HORARIOS DE TRENES   TIMETABLES
LARGO RECORRIDO   LONG DISTANCE
LLEGADA   ARRIVAL
OFICINA DE INFORMACION   INFORMATION OFFICE
RESERVA   SEAT RESERVATION
SALA DE CONSIGNA   BAGGAGE CHECKROOM
SALIDA   DEPARTURE (EXIT)
SENORAS   WOMEN
TREN CON SUPLEMENTO   TRAIN WITH SURCHARGE
VIA   TRACK

Signs you will find in **Portuguese** railstations:

CARRUAGEM-CAMA   SLEEPING CAR
CARRUAGEM-RESTAURANTE   RESTAURANT CAR
CHEGADA   ARRIVAL
ESTACAO   STATION
HOMENS   MEN
HORARIO DOS CAMINHOS   TIMETABLES
PARTIDA   DEPARTURE
PLATAFORMA   PLATFORM (TRACK)
SAIDA   EXIT
SENHORAS   WOMEN

Spanish Holidays

A list of holidays is helpful because some trains will be noted later in this section as *not* running on holidays. Also, these trains which operate on holidays are filled, and it is necessary to make reservations for them long in advance.

January 1	New Year's Day		Ascension Day
January 6	Epiphany		Corpus Christi Day
March 19	Saint Joseph's Day	June 29	St. Peter and St. Paul
	Maundy Thursday	July 18	National Holiday
	Good Friday	July 25	Saint James' Day
	Easter	August 15	Assumption Day
	Easter Monday (Barcelona)	October 12	Columbus Day
April 1	Victory Day	November 1	All Saints Day
May 1	St. Joseph Artisan Day	December 8	Immaculate Conception
		December 25	Christmas Day

Portuguese Holidays

January 1	New Year's Day	August 15	Assumption of Our Lady
	Shrove Tuesday	October 5	Anniversary of the
	Good Friday		Proclamation of the
	Easter		Portuguese Republic
May 1	Labor Day	November 1	All Saints Day
	Corpus Christi Day	December 1	Restoration of Independence
June 10	Day of The Race	December 8	Immaculate Conception
	(Portuguese National Day)	December 25	Christmas
	Saint Anthony's Day (Lisbon)		

Summer Time

Portugal is one hour earlier than Spain all year. Portugal is on the same time as England nearly all year, except for a few weeks in the Spring and Fall. Both Portugal and Spain change to Summer Time on the last Sunday of March and convert back to Standard Time on the last Sunday of September. During Summer Time, when it is 12:00 in England, it is 12:00 in Portugal and 13:00 in Spain.

SPAIN'S TRAIN PASSES

Spain Flexipass and Spainrail'N Drive are sold both in Spain (at travel agencies and the offices of RENFE — the Spanish Railway) and also outside Spain worldwide by travel agencies and Rail Europe (U.S.A. and Canadian offices listed under "France"). Purchasers must prove by passport that they are *not* residents of Spain.

Spain Flexipass Unlimited train travel. The 1996 *first*-class prices are: $180 for any 3 days within one month. *Second*-class: $144. Additional days: $40 for *first*-class, $32 for *second*-class.

Spain Rail'N Drive   Unlimited 3 days of train travel plus 3 days of car rental (any 6 days) within one month. Prices vary (a) whether for one person or for 2 persons, and (b) the category of car. A third and fourth passenger needs to pay only for a 3-day Flexipass.

The 1995 prices *per person* for 2 persons (using the smallest size car) are: $249 for *first*-class train, $219 for *second*-class. More days of car rental could be added ($49 per day for smallest size).

All of the following are sold only in Spain, at main railstations and travel agencies.

Family Card   For at least 3 persons from the same family or living at the same address, a discount is given on train tickets for "Blue " periods of the day or all-day to certain destinations on certain trains. Not valid for high speed or inter-regional trains. The passholder pays full fare. All adults except the passholder receive 50% discount on tickets. For children 4–11 the discount is 75%. Valid for one year from date of purchase. Proof by marriage certificate or any other certifying documents is required. The 1996 price is 300 pesetas.

Golden Pass   (Senior Citizen and Disabled Person Discount)   For persons 60 and older and disabled persons of any age *—and who are residents of Spain*. One must first purchase a "Tarjeta Dorada" (Gold Card) for 300 pesetas at any railstation or Renfe ticket office. Proof of age (passport, etc.) required. Valid for one year. With the Gold Card, there is a 40% discount in "Blue " periods of the day or 25% discount all-day.

Under 26   For travelers under age 26. Valid for 2 months. Cannot be used for high speed trains. Allows discounts up to 15%. The 1996 price is 3,000 pesetas.

Roundtrip Discount   A 30% discount on both first-class and second-class roundtrips on high speed trains if both trips are on the same day, 20% discount if both trips are on different days within 2 months. There is a 10% discount for inter-regional trains. The discounts for other trains depends on destination and period of the day.

PORTUGAL'S TRAIN PASSES

Portuguese Railpass   Unlimited *first*-class train travel. The 1996 prices are: $99 for any 4 days within 15 days, $155 for any 7 days within 21 days.

Portuguese Rail'N Drive   Unlimited 3 days of *first*-class train travel plus 3 days of car rental (any 6 days) within one month. Prices vary (a) whether for one person or for 2 persons, and (b) the category of car. The 1996 prices were not set at the end of 1995. The 1995 price *per person* for 2 persons (using the smallest size car) was $135 and $45 per day for each additional day of car rental. Up to 5 more days of car rental could be added at $20 per day for each person. A third passenger had to pay only $65 for a 3-day *first*-class train pass.

All of the following are sold only in Portugal, at main railstations and travel agencies:

Tourist Ticket Unlimited train travel for any class. The 1995 price was: 15,200 escudos for 7 days, Esc-24,200 for 14 days, and Esc-34,600 for 21 days.

Senior Citizen Discount Persons 60 or older receive 30% reduction.

Family Ticket For 3 or more persons. Valid only for trips of more than 149 km. (92 miles). Passports and documents proving family relationship must be presented. One person must pay full fare. Half-fare for others who are age 13 or older. One-quarter fare for children 4–12. Children under 4 travel free.

EURAILPASS BONUSES

There are no Eurailpass bonuses in Portugal or Spain.

ONE-DAY EXCURSIONS AND CITY SIGHTSEEING

Here are 67 one-day rail trips that can be made comfortably from 13 major Spanish and Portuguese cities, returning to them in most cases before dinner-time. Notes are provided on what to see and do at each destination. The number after the name of each route is the Cook's timetable.

The 13 base cities are: Barcelona, Cordoba, Granada, Leon, Lisbon, Madrid, Porto, Regua, San Sebastian, Seville, Tarragona, Valencia and Vigo.

This section concludes with details on 12 rail trips recommended for exceptional scenery plus 6 trips to/from Madrid, the schedules for 2 other major routes (Barcelona-Valencia and Lisbon-Seville), and the international rail connections from Portugal and Spain.

Barcelona

There is rail service (Table 414) between the center of Barcelona (Sants railstation) and the city's airport every 30 minutes from 05:44 to 22:14. The rail service from the airport to the city is every 30 minutes from 06:12 to 22:42.

Local trains, not requiring seat reservations, depart from Barcelona's underground Pas de Gracia and Sants railstations. Faster express trains, requiring seat reservations, also depart from Pas de Gracia and from Sants, as well as from Barcelona's Termino station.

A guided walking-tour audiocassette (and Walkman adaptable to one or 2 headphones) can be rented from Libreria de la Virreina, at Rambla 99. It is closed Sunday of one week and Saturday of the alternate week. Open 10:00-14:00 and 16:30-20:30.

Your sightseeing here can be divided into covering 4 separate areas of Barcelona. In the Gothic Quarter: The cloisters in the 14th century Cathedral (La Seu), the Episcopal Palace, Palacio de la Generalidad, many elegant 14th and 15th century palaces, the Federico Mares Museum. The Picasso Museum.

In the Montjuich area: the Museum of Catalan Art in the National Palace, the collection of El Greco, Velasquez and Rembrandt paintings at the Archaeological Museum in Palacio Real, handicrafts and architecture representing every region of Spain in the Spanish Village.

In the Tibidado area: Pedralbes Palace, Pedralbes Monastery, and the view all the way to Montserrat and the Pyrenees.

In the modern city center: Stroll the mile-long Ramblas, from Plaza de Cataluna to Plaza Puerta de la Paz at the waterfront, with its Columbus monument. You will enjoy seeing the numerous stalls selling hundreds of varieties of birds, the many stands with flowers and plants, the very large central food market, cafes offering tapas (the local and varied between-meal snacks), and at least half the population of Barcelona. Visit the Picasso Museum, for exhibits of his early Impressionist works.

Another rewarding walk, in the opposite direction, is along beautiful Paseo de Gracia, from Plaza de Cataluna to Avenida del Generalismo Franco (also called "Diagonal," its original name), to see luxury shops, decorative sidewalks designed by Dali, and several buildings created by Barcelona's most radical and inventive architect, Antonio Gaudi.

In Plaza Gaudi, you must see the uncompleted and absolutely unique church, La Sagrada Familia, the architect's most important work. It was started in 1884. Because of lack of funds, Barcelonians believe construction will not be finished until 100 years from now.

What has been constructed in the last 100 years is well worth seeing: the 4 lofty towers (nearly 300 feet tall), the Nativity and Passion facades with the Tree of Life supported by the central arch, and the wrought-iron plants in the side chapels of the completed crypt.

Although public transportation is not available to the Gaudi-designed park, Parque Guell, we suggest you take a taxi there to see it and to see the view of Barcelona from its elevated plaza. The paths in this park are decorated with concrete pillars that imitate trees and vines. Also see the colorful undulating bench surfaced with broken ceramic pieces, on the plaza. And the gigantic tiled frog fountain on the steps leading down from the park's plaza.

Regular city tours include only the church and one apartment building designed by Gaudi. A guided tour of most of his projects is offered by the Municipal Tourist Office (Avenida Paralelo 202) for both individuals and groups.

Lisbon

Santa Apolonia is Lisbon's railstation for departure to Madrid and beyond (to France and the rest of Europe). It has currency exchange and hotel reservation services.

See the beautiful Avenida de Liberdade. The Tower of Belem (monument to Portugal's sailors). The view from the bi-cultural St. George's Castle, built by the Visigoths in the 5th century and by the Moors in the 9th century. Largo das Portas do Sol (Sun Gateway), one of the 7 gates into the ancient Arab City. Santa Cruz quarter. Alfama Quarter. Salazar Bridge.

The lovely Praco de Rossio. The marvelous collection of priceless Middle Eastern and European tapestries, jewelry, ceramics, and Dutch, Spanish, Italian and 15th to 18th century Portuguese paintings in the Ancient Art Museum (9 Rua das Janelas Verdes). The more than 3,000 art treasures (Rembrandt, Fragonard, Corot, many Impressionists, Egyptian sculpture, Persian art) in the Gulbenkian Museum (45 Avenida de Berna). Across the park from it is the Gulbenkian Center of Modern Art (Rua Dr. Nicolau Bettencourt).

Edward VII Park. The Zoological Garden. The Botanical Garden. The Museum of Modern Art. The Municipal Museum. The greatest collection in the world of royal coaches in the Belem Palace at Praca Afonso de Albuquerque. The Flea Market. The Military Museum. The collection of 17th and 18th century Portuguese and Indo-Portuguese furnishings in the Museum of Decorative Arts (2 Largo das Portas do Sol).

The Maritime Museum, in the West wing of Jeronimos Monastery. Jeronimo's Church. The Cathedral. House of Facets, its front entirely faced with dark stones that have been cut into diamond-like facets.

Madrid

There is train service connecting Madrid's Chamartin and Atocha stations. A Eurailpass *can* be used on it. At Chamartin station, look for the track marked "Linea de Atocha y Guadalajara." At Atocha, go to the separate small station, a short walk from the main station. "Atocha-Apeadero" is a lower level at Atocha railstation.

See the Prado Museum, with its breathtaking collection of great paintings (open Tuesday–Saturday 09:00–19:00, Sunday 09:00–13:45). Puerta del Sol. The Goya Pantheon. Plaza Mayor. San Miguel Basilica. San Isidor Cathedral.

Two-hour, guided tours of the Royal Palace take you nearly a mile through 52 sumptuously furnished rooms on the main floor. Open Monday-Saturday 09:30–17:15, Sundays and holidays only 09:30–12:45.

CAUTION: the Palace is closed to the public about 60 days a year for official functions. Check in advance about the day you plan to tour it.

At the Palace, you will see more than 400 antique clocks (keeping perfect time), paintings (Velasquez and Goya), and 15th and 18th century Flemish tapestries. Then, spend more hours seeing the magnificent Armory. Also, visit the Carriage Museum, near the west gate.

The Music Museum has 5 instruments made by Stradivari. Other fascinating rooms in the Palace are the State Apartments and Chapel, Apartments of Queen Maria Cristina of Hapsburg, the Private Apartments, Royal Pharmacy, Library, Numismatic Museum and Music Museum.

Additional interesting sights in Madrid are the Botanical Garden. The Bullfighting Museum. Descalzas Reales Convent. The Archaeological Museum. The Folk Museum. The Americas Museum. Retiro Park. University City. Plaza de Espana, with its stone monument to Cervantes. The Royal Tapestry Factory, closed Sunday during August.

For the best food in Spain, and it is moderately priced, dine at Restaurante Botin, at Calle de Cuchilleros 17. Every dish is marvelous. Their specialties are roast suckling pig and roast baby goat. These and many other foods are cooked there with oak wood in the original 16th century tiled oven. Botin is run by a very handsome gentleman, Antonio Gonzalez Jr. His family has operated Botin for more than 90 years.

San Sebastian

Excellent beaches. The Goya and El Greco collection at San Sebastian Picture Gallery. Santa Maria Church. San Telmo Museum. The Aquarium and Oceanographic Museum in Sea Palace, open daily 10:00–3:30 and 15:00–20:00. The picturesque fishing village nearby. Climb up Mount Urgull for a view of the bay from the Castle of Santa Cruz de la Mota.

Seville

The city of Don Juan and Carmen. You must not miss seeing Corpus Christi Cathedral, largest Gothic cathedral in the world and the site of Columbus' tomb.

The 14th century Alcazar Palace with its magnificent chambers, particularly the room where foreign ambassadors were received. Its colorful mosaics and tiles, delicate wrought-iron and carved wood ceilings are spellbinding. You can see nearby Segovia from the tower of Isabella's castle. Allow time to stroll through the elaborate gardens there: bronze and marble statues, lovely fountains and the extraordinary Pavillion of Carlos V.

On one side of the Alcazar is a university, formerly Antigua Fabrica de Tobacos, the tobacco factory Bizet immortalized in his opera, Carmen. On the other side of the Alcazar is Barrio de Santa Cruz, with its ancient buildings and narrow streets. Once a refuge for Jews fleeing the Inquisition, now it is a fashionable residential section of Seville.

You can enjoy spending many hours in Maria Luisa Park, seeing the beautiful buildings, gardens, pools and fountains there. Particularly noteworthy is the magnificent Plaza de Espana.

Other notable sights in Seville: The 12th century La Giralda Tower, a minaret when the Moors ruled here (open only on Sundays and holidays 11:00–14:00). The 12-sided Tower of Gold. Meander along the city's cobbled streets to see many picturesque homes.

RESERVATIONS ARE STRONGLY ADVISED
ON ALL SPANISH TRAINS!!

In the following timetables, where a city has more than one railstation we have designated the particular station (in parentheses).

Barcelona - Blanes - Barcelona   417 Costa Brava Resorts

Go to the "Estacion de Cercanias" (suburban section of Barcelona's Termino railstation) to board the train for Blanes. Seat reservations are *not* required for this ride. Board well before departure time to avoid standing for 70 minutes.

All of these trains are second-class only.

Take a bus or taxi from Blanes' railstation to the center of the village. It is a half-mile walk there from the station.

Dep. Barcelona (Sants)	Every 30 minutes from 06:12 to 22:12
Arr. Blanes	90 minutes later

Sights in **Blanes**: Stroll the waterfront. See the Aquarium and Botanical Garden, near the location of the daily fish auction, at 17:00. The Gothic fountain. The Church of Santa Maria. The view of the Bay of Blanes from the ruins of the castle on San Juan Mountain. it is a short drive to many popular beaches: Santa Catalina, Fanals, Lloret and Tossa.

Sights in **Lloret de Mar**: See the remains of the Tower of the Moors. The colored tiles that decorate the Church of San Roman. The 11th century castle at the beach. There is an active nightlife here (discotheques, nightclubs and casinos).

Sights in **Tossa de Mar**: Exhibits of Roman archaeology, modern paintings and sculptures (Catalan and foreign), and a 1933 painting of the town by Marc Chagall in the Town Museum, open 10:00–13:00 and 17:00–20:00. See the view from the lighthouse.

Dep. Blanes	Every 30 minutes from 06:00 to 21:30
Arr. Barcelona (Sants)	90 minutes later

Barcelona - Girona - Barcelona   416

All of these trains are second-class, unless designated otherwise.

Dep. Barcelona (Sants)	07:00 (1)	08:10	09:10	10:10 (2)	10:15
Dep. Barcelona (P. de G.)	-0-	08:15	09:15	-0-	10:20
Arr. Girona	08:32	09:32	10:19	11:12	11:27

Sights in **Girona**: The collection of paintings, sculptures, ceramics, glass objects, coins and silverware at the Art Museum in the former Episcopal Palace, open 10:00–13:00 and 16:30–19:00. Exhibits of local history and art in the Museum of the History of the city, open Monday–Saturday 10:00–14:00 and 17:00–19:00, Sundays and holidays 9:30–14:30.

The Museum in the magnificent 14th century Cathedral has such outstanding exhibits as the 11th century Tapestry of Creation. the 10th century Book of the Apocalypse, and the 10th century Arab chest of Hisham II, the oldest Hispanic-Arab work of silver. It is open daily 10:00–13:00 and 15:30–18:00.

The Provincial Archaeological Museum is open daily 10:30–13:00 and 16:30–19:00.

Visit the 12th century Arab Baths. See Sobreportes, the ancient gate. Stroll on the narrow 17th century streets.

Dep. Girona	11:36	12:30	13:29	14:34 (3)	15:26 (5)
Arr. Barcelona (P. de G.)	12:52	13:40	14:50	15:50	16:50
Arr. Barcelona (Sants)	12:57	13:45	14:55	14:55	16:55

(1) Reservation advisable. Has a first-class coach. Restaurant car. (2) Departs/arrives Barcelona's Estacio de Franca railstation. Reservation advisable. Supplement charged. Has a first-class coach. Restaurant car. (3) Has a first-class coach. (4) Light refreshments. Has a first-class coach. (5) Plus other departures from Girona at 16:24 (3), 17:28, 18:27, 19:23, 19:41 (2), 20:35 (4), 20:42 and 22:05, arriving Barcelona (Sants) 17:45, 18:55, 19:59, 21:32, 20:50 (2), 21:45, 22:16 and 23:28.

Barcelona - Lerida - Barcelona   410

It is advisable to make a reservation for this ride well in advance of departure date. Although departures are from other stations, go to Barcelona's Triunfo railstation to make this reservation. On boarding, find a seat on the left side so as to have a good view of the restored 13th century hilltop Seo Antiqua Cathedral before the arrival in Lerida.

Reservation advisable for all of these trains, unless designated otherwise.

Dep. Barcelona (Paseo de Gracia)	-0-	08:15 (2)
Dep. Barcelona (Sants)	07:30 (1)	08:30
Arr. Lerida	09:19	10:12

Sights in **Lerida**: The Archaeological Museum, in the Antiguo Hospital de Santa Maria, where the tourist office is located. A walking tour is easy with the city map available there. See the old Byzantine-Gothic-Moorish 13th century Cathedral. The Palacio de la Paheria. Stroll the maze of narrow streets in the interesting old section on the right bank of the Segre River, and visit the 12th century Alcazaba (castle).

Dep. Lerida	15:43 (3)	18:40 (2)	20:34 (2)	21:04 (1)
Arr. Barcelona (Sants)	18:00	20:35	22:35	23:04
Arr. Barcelona (Paseo de Gracia)	18:10	20:46	22:46	-0-

(1) Light refreshments. (2) Reservation advisable. Supplement charged. Restaurant car. (3) Restaurant car.

Barcelona - Montserrat - Barcelona   Barcelona T.O.

This trip is not covered by Eurailpass.

Dep. Barcelona (P. Espanya)	Every 2 hours from 09:11 to 15:11
	(Summer: until 17:11)
Arr. Martorell-Enllac	50–60 minutes later
Change to cable car.	
Dep. Martorell-Enllac	Every 15 minutes from 10:00 to 17:45
Arr. Monistrol (Monastery)	5 minutes after departing Martorell-Enllac

Sights in **Montserrat**: The 9th century Monastery, still occupied by hundreds of Benedictine monks, is 3700 feet above a valley. It ranks with Zaragoza and Santiago de Compostela as one of the most important pilgrimage sites in Spain. See the Grotto of the Virgin, the Mirador, the Chapel of San Miguel and the Chapel of Santa Cecilia. Then take a funicular to the Grotto of San Juan Garin and an aerial tram to the 4,000-foot-high Hermitage of San Jeronimo, from where you will have a view of the Eastern Pyrenees.

Dep. Monistrol (Monastery)	Every 15 minutes from 10:00 to 17:45
Arr. Martorell-Enllac	5 minutes after daparting Monistrol
Change to train.	
Dep. Martorell-Enllac	Every 2 hours from 11:26 to 19:26
	(Summer: from 09:26)
Arr. Barcelona (P. Espanya)	50–60 minutes later

Barcelona - Sitges - Barcelona

Frequent local trains run from Barcelona's Paseo de Gracia and Sants stations to Sitges, a 30-minute trip.

Sights in **Sitges:** The 18th century furnishings at Casa Llopis. Antique dolls collected from every part of Europe, in the Lola Anglada Museum. El Greco paintings at the Cap Ferrat Museum.

Barcelona - Tarragona - Barcelona

Frequent local trains run from Barcelona's Paseo de Gracia and Sants stations to Tarragona, a 90-minute trip.

Sights in **Tarragona:** Relics of pre-Roman, Roman, Visigothic and Moorish cultures.

It is a short, but severely uphill, walk from the railstation to the long promenade, Balcon del Mediterraneo, from which there is a marvelous view of the sea. Two strolling streets start at each end of the "balcony." The first is Rambla del Generalismo. The other is Rambla de San Carlos.

We suggest you rest a while at one of the many sidewalk cafes on either Rambla. Then, start your walking tour of Tarragona by going 2 blocks from the "balcony," down Rambla de San Carlos to where it intersects with San Augustin. Turn right (the street name changes to "Mayor") and walk one-quarter mile to the 12th century Cathedral, worth seeing for its large and architecturally unique Cloisters, influenced by Roman, Gothic and Moorish styles.

Next, return to Rambla de San Carlos and turn right. Walk down it 2 blocks until it intersects with Abalto. Turn right and walk uphill, alongside the Roman wall.

You will then be on the semi-circular Paseo Arqueologico walk, from which there are excellent views of the countryside surrounding Tarragona.

At the end of this walk, bear to the right and come downhill on Avenida de la Victoria for 5 minutes until you reach Plaza del Rey. There, you can visit both the museum in the 1st century B.C. Pretoria and also the marvelous mosaics and ancient coins in the Archaeological Museum.

Across from Plaza del Rey is the Roman Amphitheater. Having completed a circle, you will again be at Balcon del Mediterraneo, and it is all downhill to return to the railstation.

Granada - Malaga - Granada   426

Between Bobadilla and Malaga, the train travels through the spectacular **El Chorro Gorge**.

All of these trains are second-class.

Dep. Granada	08:20	Dep. Malaga	13:55	17:35
Arr. Bobadilla	10:05	Arr. Bobadilla	14:58	18:34
Change trains.		*Change trains.*		
Dep. Bobadilla	10:25	Dep. Bobadilla	15:20	18:40
Arr. Malaga	12:10	Arr. Granada	17:47	20:29

Sights in **Malaga**: Winter sun. The 9th century Alcazaba Moslem palace and the ruins of Gibralfaro Castle, 2 fortresses which made Malaga a major stronghold in the Middle Ages. The Fine Arts Museum. Sagrario, an unusual rectangular church that was originally a mosque. The Cathedral.

Lisbon - Algarve Resorts

The 100-mile Algarve (Lisbon-Vila Real de Santo Antonio) coastline, famous for its many popular resorts, consists of several centuries-old fishing villages and offers championship golf courses, tennis, horseback riding and all the watersports (windsurfing, fishing, water skiing, yachting).

Lisbon - Vila Real or Lagos 449

There is a bridge from **Vila Real** to **Ayamonte** (Spain) every 30 minutes. Summer: 08:30-23:30. Winter: 09:00-18:00.

Boat			*Train*		
Dep. Lisbon			Dep. Vila Real	-0-	06:03 (5)
(Ferry Ter.)	07:25 (1)	07:55 (2)	Dep. Faro	-0-	07:15
Arr. Barreiro	07:55 (9)	08:25	Dep. Albufeira	-0-	07:43
Change to train.			Dep. Lagos	06:10 (4)	-0-
Dep. Barreiro	08:05	08:35	Arr. Tunes	07:27 (3)	07:48
Arr. Tunes	11:0	12:17 (3)	Dep. Tunes	-0-	08:03
Dep. Tunes	11:05	12:29	Arr. Barreiro	-0-	11:11
Arr. Lagos	-0-	13:23	*Change to boat.*		
Arr. Albufeira	11:13	-0-	Dep. Barreiro	-0-	11:25
Dep. Faro	11:40	-0-	Arr. Lisbon		
Arr. Vila Real	-0-	-0-	(Ferry Ter.)	-0-	11:55

(1) Plus other Lisbon departures for Tunes, Albufeira, Faro and Vila Real at 13:25 (6), 17:30 (6), 18:50 (7) and 23:10. (2) Plus other departures for Tunes and Lagos at 17:30, 18:50 and 23:10, all requiring train change in Tunes. (3) Change trains in Tunes. (4) Plus other Lagos departures at 13:30 (8), 17:00 (8) and 22:30. (5) Plus other Via Real departures at 06:35 (8) and 21:35. (6) Reservation required. (7) Reservation advisable. (8) Light refreshments. (9) Runs daily July 1-August 31.

Sights in **Lagos**: This historic town was the center for the Portugal–Africa trade. See the marvelous tiles in the Baroque Chapel of San Antonio.

Sights in **Albufeira**: The Moorish ambiance here is striking. This is a very "arty" place. Has a colorful market.

Sights in **Faro**: The ancient church. The old quarter.

Lisbon - Setubal and Lisbon - Evora 448

Boat					
Dep. Lisbon (Ferry Ter.)	05:45	07:25	15:15	19:20	23:10 (5)
Arr. Barreiro	06:15	08:15	15:45	19:50	23:40
Change to train.					
Dep. Barreiro	06:20	08:20 (2)	16:00	20:05 (3)	23:50
Arr. Setubal	-0-	-0-	-0-	-0-0	-0-
Arr. Evora	-0-	10:30	18:10	-0-	-0-

Sights in **Setubal**: The paintings in the Town Museum. Next to it, the lovely Church of Jesus. The view from the 16th century Saint Philip's Castle, while having lunch there.

Many sardine canneries, some of them open to the public. The Maritime Museum. Take an inexpensive taxi ride to the nearby (5½ miles) Palmela Castle.

Sights in **Evora**: Portugal's "Museum City." The Tourist Information Office faces the main square, Praca Do Giraldo. See the beautiful Temple of Diana, oldest Roman remains on the Iberian Peninsula. Visit the excellent regional museum in what was once the Bishop's Palace. The 17th century monastery, now an inn called Pousada dos Loios. The Church of St. Francis, where the walls are decorated with the skulls and bones of nearly 5,000 monks.

Dep. Evora	-0-	-0-	19:25 (2)	23:03
Dep. Setubal	12:57 (3)	-0- (3)	-0-	-0-
Arr. Barreiro	15:10	15:10	21:41	00:12
Change to boat.				
Dep. Barreiro	15:20	15:12	21:50	00:40
Arr. Lisbon (Ferry Ter.)	30 minutes later			

(1) Runs Monday–Friday, except holidays. (2) Reservation advisable. Light refreshments. (3) Second-class.

Lisbon - Coimbra - Lisbon   445

Reservation is advisable for all of these trains and all of them have light refreshments, unless designated otherwise.

Dep. Lisbon						
(S. Apol.)	07:22 (1)	08:05	08:10	09:00	11:00	11:35 (2)
Arr. Coimbra	09:46	10:13	10:45	11:21	13:14	14:08

Sights in **Coimbra**: Walk uphill to the 13th century Old Cathedral, one of the finest Romanesque buildings in Portugal. Continue to the treasures at the Machado do Castro Museum. At the top of the hill is the 13th century University, where you must see the gilded carved stone and wood and the Baroque library. Also see the silver shrine in the magnificent interior of the New Convent of St. Clara. The Almedina Gate. Nearby, the Roman ruins at Conimbriga. Try the local food specialty, roasted suckling pig (leitao).

Dep. Coimbra	12:19	15:49 (3)	17:02 (1)	17:22	18:19 (3)	19:14 (5)
Arr. Lisbon						
(S. Apol.)	14:25	17:50	19:15	19:50	20:20	21:35

(1) Reservation *required*. (2) Runs Friday and Saturday. Reservation *required*. Supplement charged. (3) Reservation *required*. Supplement charged. (4) Reservation not available. No refreshments. (5) Plus other departures from Coimbra at 19:26 (4), 20:19 (6) and 21:29, arriving Lisbon 22:38, 22:23 23:35. (6) Runs Sunday.

Lisbon - Estoril and Cascais - Lisbon   P142

A scenic seashore ride that costs about one U.S. dollar.

All of these trains run daily, except Sundays and holidays.

Dep. Lisbon (Cais do Sordre)	Frequent times from 05:30 to 02:30
Arr. Estoril	35 minutes later
Arr. Cascais	4 minutes after departing Estoril

Sights in **Estoril:** Portugal's major beach resort. Try your luck in the gambling Casino.

Sights in **Cascais:** Bloodless bullfights on Summer Sundays. Surf fishing. Wednesday is market day, on the street that veers right from the railstation. There are taxis that will take you to Sintra (see "Lisbon–Sintra").

Dep. Cascais	Frequent times from 05:30 to 02:30.
Dep. Estoril	3 minutes later
Arr. Lisbon (Cais do Sordre)	35 minutes after departing Estoril

Lisbon - Fatima - Lisbon   P100-A

Dep. Lisbon (S. Apol.)	07:29	10:33	Dep. Fatima	14:33	20:38	(1)
Arr. Entroncamento	09:06	12:25	Arr. Entroncamento	14:52	-0-	(1)
Change trains.			*Change Trains.*			
Dep. Entroncamento	09:43	12:56	Dep. Entroncamento	15:13	-0-	
Arr. Fatima	10:05	13:16	Arr. Lisbon (S. Apol.)	17:00	22:38	

(1) Direct train. No train change in Entroncamento.

Sights in **Fatima:** Millions of pilgrims have come here from all over the world to worship at one of the world's most famous Marian Shrines.

Lisbon - Porto (Oporto) - Lisbon   445

Reservation is required for all these trains and they have light refreshments, unless designated otherwise.

Dep. Lisbon (S. Apol.)	07:00 (1)	08:05	09:00 (2)	11:00 (3)
Arr. Porto (Campanha)	10:00	11:30	13:15	14:25

Sights in **Porto**: The more than 80 wine stores occupying all of the Vila Nova de Gaia quarter. The 12th century Cathedral. The 3 great bridges: Dom Louis, Dona Maria and Ponte da Arrabida. Portugal's oldest chapel, Sao Martinho de Cedofeita. The gilded wood-carvings in the Church of San Francisco.

The Church of the Clerigos, with its 10-story tower. The city's many beautiful gardens. The 15th century Church of Santa Clara. The Moorish Hall of the Stock Exchange. The 14th century convent-fortress, Leca do Bailio Abbey. The fine paintings, sculpture, porcelain and jewelry at the Soares dos Reis Museum. The folklore objects of this region in the Ethnological Museum.

| Dep. Porto (Campanha) | 14:30 (4) | 15:30 (3) | 17:00 (4) | 19:00 (3) | 20:10 |
| Arr. Lisbon (S. Apol.) | 17:50 | 19:50 | 20:20 | 22:20 (7) | 23:20 |

(1) Runs Monday-Friday except holidays. Supplement charged. Restaurant car. (2) Runs daily, except Sundays and holidays. Supplement charged. (3) Reservation advisable. (4) Supplement charged. (5) Restaurant car. (6) Runs Monday-Friday and Sunday, except holidays.

Porto - Braga - Porto   446

| Dep. Porto (Cam.) | 06:27 (4) | 09:34 |
| Arr. Braga | 08:16 | 11:14 |

Sights in **Braga**: The most interesting buildings are on the narrow street that runs from Arco da Porta Nova to the Praca da Republica. (It changes its name along the way.)

See the beautiful Santa Barbara Gardens. The treasury at the Cathedral (gold and ivory crosiers, also damask and velvet vestments embroidered with heavy gold thread). The museum in the Casa dos Biscainhos. The terraced gardens that ascend uphill to the church of Bom Jesus.

| Dep. Braga | 12:16 | 14:29 (3) | 17:25 (2) | 21:02 (3) |
| Arr. Porto (Cam.) | 13:23 | 15:53 | 18:30 | 22:40 |

(1) Change trains in Nines. (2) Reservation *required*. Light refreshments. (3) Runs daily, except Saturday. (4) Runs daily except Sundays and holidays.

Lisbon - Sintra - Queluz - Lisbon   P 141

All of these trains run daily, except Sundays and holidays.

| Dep. Lisbon (Rossio) | Frequent times from 05:56 to 02:00 |
| Arr. Sintra | 45 minutes later |

Sights in **Sintra**: An outstanding old town, nestled on a mountaintop. There are many antique and craft shops on this village's winding, narrow streets. Take the "Sintra–Vila" bus from the railstation to the city's tourist office, where guide books and maps are available.

Use inexpensive taxis to see the view from the 19th century Palacio de Pena, the Moorish Castle, the Palacio Real, and the marvelous gardens at the Palacio de Monserrate. The palaces are closed on Tuesday.

Dep. Sintra	Frequent times from 05:15 to 01:15
Arr. Queluz	12 minutes later

Sights in **Queluz**: The beautiful gardens, the monument to Maria I and the exquisite restaurant at the 18th century Palacio de Queluz, a miniature Versailles.

Dep. Queluz	Frequent times from 05:39 to 01:38
Arr. Lisbon (Rossio)	37 minutes later

Madrid - Aranjuez - Madrid

	420	420	425	419
Dep. Madrid (Cham.)	08:00 (1)	09:00 (1)	09:05 (2)	-0-
Dep. Madrid (Atocha-Cer.)	08:15	09:15	09:20	-0-
Dep. Madrid (P. de Atocha)	-0-	-0-	-0-	09:35
Arr. Aranjuez	08:42	09:44	09:53	10:09

Sights in **Aranjuez**: The Museum of Royal Robes, the luxurious interiors of the Porcelain Room (walls and cielings covered with red and green figures depicting Chinese and Japanese themes), the intricately chiseled Moorish interior of the Arab Chamber, the more than 200 drawings from the Ching Dynasty in the Chinese Print Room, and the Throne Room all in the Royal Palace, which has guided tours that are usually in Spanish. See the bed of Queen Isabella II, inlaid with carvings, floral decorations and bronze ornaments.

There are guided tours of the magnificent furnishings in the 18 rooms at the 18th century Casa del Labrador, where a 19th century clock in the form of Hadrian's Column is exhibited in the sculpture gallery. (A ruby and pearl-studded star strikes the hour by spiraling up and down the column.) Platinum, gold and bronze decorations are displayed in the Platinum Chamber. There are many silk wall tapestries in this palace.

The Pastere and Island gardens. The collection of royal ships in the Casa de Marinos. The 300-acre forest, called Jardin del Principe (Prince's Garden). The Fountain of Hercules and the Fountain of Bacchus in the park called Jardin de la Isla.

	419	425	419	433	419
Dep. Aranjuez	14:08	15:00	15:57 (4)	16:11 (2)	17:18 (6)
Arr. Madrid (P. de Atocha)	14:48	-0-	16:34	-0-	17:55
Arr. Madrid (Atocha-Cer.)	-0-	15:52	-0-	16:46	-0-
Arr. Madrid (Ch.)	-0-	16:07	-0-	16:59	-0-

(1) Suppplement charged. Light refreshments. (2) Second-class. (3) Restaurant car. (4) Runs Monday-Friday, except holidays. (5) Light refreshments. (6) Plus other Aranjuez departures at [420] 19:26 (2), [419] 20:02, [433] 20:15 and [420] 20:25 (1).

Madrid - Avila - Madrid   431

| Dep. Madrid (Cham.) | 08:00 (1) | 09:00 (1) | 10:00 | 11:30 | 13:30 |
| Arr. Avila | 09:23 | 10:19 | 11:24 | 12:54 | 14:52 |

Sights in **Avila**: There are bus and inexpensive taxi services from Avila's railstation to the city center, about one mile from the station. Take a stroll on the 1½-mile long 11th century walls that circle Avila to see best the 88 semi-circular towers and more than 2,300 battlements (11:00–13:00 and 16:15–18:00, closed weekday afternoons from October through April).

Also see the El Greco painting and the enormous (nearly 200 pounds) silver monstrance in the fortress Cathedral. The baroque 17th century Convent of St. Teresa. The Basilica of St. Vincent.

| Dep. Avila | 13:25 (2) | 16:15 (2) | 17:50 (3) | 18:34 | 19:52 (4+5) |
| Arr. Madrid (Cham.) | 14:53 | 17:42 | 19:21 | 20:13 | 21:20 |

(1) Supplement charged. Light refreshments. (2) Light refreshments. (3) Second-class. (4) Supplement charged. (5) Plus other Avila departures at 20:57 (2) and 21:46, arriving Madrid 22:34 and 23:20.

Madrid - Burgos - Madrid   431

| Dep. Madrid (Ch.) | 09:20 (1) | 10:00 | Dep. Burgos | | 17:18 (1) | 19:03 (2) | 19:15 |
| Arr. Burgos | 12:25 | 13:32 | Arr. Madrid (Ch.) | | 21:05 | 22:09 | 23:20 |

(1) Second-class. (2) Supplement charged. Light refreshments.

Sights in **Burgos**: The many interesting chapels in the magnificent 13th century Cathedral of Santa Maria, where the remains are of Spain's greatest hero, El Cid, and those of his wife. The Archaeological Museum. Stroll 15 minutes on Paseo del Espolon, from the 14th century Arch of Santa Maria to the statue of El Cid.

To see the Royal Monastery of Las Huelgas, only a few minutes outside Burgos, take a bus from Plaza de Jose Antonio.

Madrid - Cuenca - Madrid   419

| Dep. Madrid (Ato.) | 09:35 | 11:30 | Dep. Cuenca | 15:29 | 18:07 (2) |
| Arr. Cuenca | 12:03 | 14:10 | Arr. Madrid (Ato.) | 17:55 | 20:49 |

(1) Runs Friday and Sunday. (2) Plus another Cuenca departure at 20:05 (1), arriving Madrid 22:46.

Sights in **Cuenca**: The Tourist Information Office (Calderon de la Barca 28) is only a 5-minute walk from the railstation.

Strolling down the winding lanes and narrow footpaths is marvelous. See the old houses hanging from sheer cliffs in this 15th century setting. The best modern art museum in Spain, Museo de Arte Abstrato. Wonderful El Greco paintings and 15th and 16th century altarpieces in the cathedral. A few steps away from the Cathedral, the collection of coins, statues and Roman mosaics at the Archaeological Museum in a restored 14th century granary.

Paleolithic red paintings of bison, wild boars, horses and archers at La Pena del Escrito National Monument.

Madrid - Escorial - Madrid

Timetables for this trip were were deleted from Cook's in 1992. The travel time is one hour. Below are 1991 schedules.

Dep. Madrid (Ato.)	09:15 (1)	12:05 (1)	Dep. Escorial	16:30	19:30 (1)
Dep. Madrid (Ch.)	09:30	12:20	Arr. Madrid (Ch.)	17:13	20:10
Arr. Escorial	10:14	13:07	Arr. Madrid (Ato.)	17:29	20:25

(1) Second-class only.

Sights in **Escorial**: Burial place of Spanish kings and queens. The Royal Monastery of San Lorenzo del Escorial, an enormous granite fortress (300 rooms), has more than 1,600 paintings (many of the finest Velasquez and El Greco) and murals, and it houses the Charter Hall Royal Library, containing 60,000 volumes.

See the Phillip II Apartments, the Throne Room, Apartments of the Bourbon kings, Whispering Hall, Casita del Principe, and the Basilica.

The Basilica was intended to copy St. Peter's in Rome, filled with gilt and marble carvings. Its 4 enormous pillars are 100 feet in circumference and support a cupola more than 300 feet high. Life-size bronze figures (royal families) surround the 100-foot-high altar.

The 18th century Prince's Cottage has 9 elaborately furnished rooms. Don't miss seeing the famous cross by Benvenuto Cellini and paintings by El Greco, Ribera and Velasquez in the church.

The circular, domed Royal Pantheon, crypt for most of the Spanish kings since the 17th century. Thirty feet underground, it contains 26 charcoal-gray marble coffins, in 5 tiers, and is illuminated by Italian baroque candelabra. Lesser royalty rest in white marble coffins in other rooms.

In planning a visit here, keep in mind that this enormous 16th century building covers 8 acres. It is open 10:00–13:00 and 15:30–18:30 (18:00 in Winter).

Also visit the nearby monumental Valley of the Fallen, memorializing those who died in Spain's civil war. A 492-foot-high cross of concrete faced with stone marks this crypt containing more than 100,000 bodies. Its 900-foot-long Basilica is a tunnel into the mountain. You can ride to the top of the cross in an elevator.

Madrid - Salamanca - Madrid   432

All of these trains are second-class only.

Dep. Madrid (Ch.)	09:35	Dep. Salamanca	17:35	20:10 (1)
Arr. Salamanca	12:55	Arr. Madrid (Ch.)	20:55	23:30

(1) Runs Sunday only.

Sights in **Salamanca:** The Convent of San Sebastian. The church and cloister at St. Stephens Monastery. The 15th and 16th century houses around the beautiful Plaza Mayor.

The oldest part of the city is the area between Plaza Mayor and the Tormes River. En route to the river, the 12th century Church of St. Martin is on Plaza del Corrillo. Opposite it is the 15th century Casa de las Conchas, named so because its facade is covered with 400 stone conch shells.

A few minutes walk from it is the third oldest university in Europe (after Oxford and Bologna), founded in 1218. A stone staircase leads to the university's magnificent Old Library which has 60,000 books from the 16th to 18th centuries and ancient manuscripts going as far back as 1059.

The city's Old and New cathedrals stand side by side behind the university. A magnificent altar and an elaborate ceiling are the highlights of the New Cathedral, begun in 1513. Its 16th century organ still works.

Madrid - Segovia - Madrid   432

All of these trains are second-class only. The arrivals are estimated.

Dep. Madrid (Chamartin)	06:25 (1)	09:16	10:16	12:16 (1)
Arr. Segovia	08:05	10:56	11:56	13:56

•   •   •

Dep. Segovia	12:55	14:55	16:55	18:55	19:36 (2)
Arr. Madrid (Chamartin)	14:35	16:35	18:35	20:35	21:16

(1) Runs daily, except Sundays and holidays. (2) Plus another Segovia departure at 20:55, arriving Madrid 22:35.

Madrid - Toledo - Madrid   432

Seat reservations are not required or obtainable for this ride. Board well before departure time to avoid standing for entire ride. The walk from Toledo's railstation to the center of that city is long. It is best to take a bus or taxi.

Most of these trains are second-class. The arrivals are estimated.

Dep. Madrid (Atocha-Cercarias)	07:20	09:09	10:50	12:20
Arr. Toledo	09:30	10:19	12:00	13:30

Sights in **Toledo**: The most spectacular Cathedral in Spain (750 stained-glass windows, priceless church clothing, jeweled ornaments, hundreds of tapestries, and paintings by Goya, El Greco, Velasquez, Tintoretto, Murillo and Titian). The house of El Greco, with a superb collection of his paintings. The 15th century Palace of the Duchess of Lerma. The Church of Santo Tome, containing El Greco's "Burial of the Count of Orgaz."

The Sefardi Museum in the 14th century El Transito Synagogue. The Provincial Museum of Archaeology and Fine Arts in the 16th century Hospital de Santa Cruz. The Army Museum in the Alcazar (fortress).

The Museum of Santa Cruz. Cristo de la Luz, the church first built in the 11th century as a Mosque (on the site of the ruins of a Visigothic church). It was then converted into a Catholic church in the 12th century. The works of Spain's leading modern sculptor, in the Vitorio Macho Museum.

Dep. Toledo	12:15	14:20	16:30	17:50	19:25 (1)
Arr. Madrid (Atocha-Cercarias)	13:25	15:30	17:40	19:00	20:35

(1) Plus another Toledo departure at 21:30, arriving Madrid 22:40.

Madrid - Valladolid - Madrid   431

Dep. Madrid (Cham.)	08:00 (1)	09:00 (1)	10:00
Arr. Valladolid	10:27	11:25	12:30

Sights in **Valladolid**: The National Museum of (Wood) Sculpture in San Gregorio College, founded in the 15th century by the confessor to Isabella, one of the finest museums in Spain, open Tuesday–Saturday 10:00–14:00 and 16:00–19:00. Its life-size 15th–16th century carvings are famous for their emotive and natural expressions, swirling draperies, and their realistic, vivid colors.

These sculptures were carved for religious processions and also to fill many of the magnificent and very complex altars that still remain in churches and museums throughout Spain. Visit the adjacent Church of San Pablo.

Sculptures, carvings and massive gold and silver objects are exhibited at the Cathedral in a museum that is open Tuesday–Friday 10:00–13:30 and 16:30–19:00; on Saturdays, Sundays and holidays 10:00–14:00.

See Vivero Palace, where Ferdinand and Isabella were married in 1474. The magnificent ceilings and wood sculptures at the National Museum of Sculpture, in the 15th century Colegio de San Gregorio. The wood sculptures in the 15th century Convent of Santa Clara. The 15th century Palace of Santa Cruz.

Cervantes' House, where he spent the last years of his life. Simancas Castle, 7 miles from Valladolid. Charles V converted the castle into a storehouse for state records. It holds 8,000,000 documents that provide a history of Spanish administration from the 16th through the 20th century.

Dep. Valladolid	15:00 (1)	16:35 (2)	17:30	18:45 (3)	19:55 (4+5)
Arr. Madrid (Cham.)	17:42	19:21	20:13	21:20	22:34

(1) Supplement charged. Light refreshments. (2) Second-class. (3) Supplement charged. (4) Light refreshments. (5) Plus another Valladolid departure at 20:40, arriving Madrid 23:20.

Madrid - Zaragoza - Madrid   410

All of these trains charge a supplement.

Dep. Madrid (Chamartin)	07:00 (1)	09:00 (1)	11:00 (2)
Arr. Zaragoza (Portillo)	10:00	12:10	14:13

Sights in **Zaragoza**: The Tapestry Museum in the Cathedral. The Exchange. Aljaferia, an 11th century Moorish palace. The Basilica de Pilar. The Goya and El Greco paintings at the Museo de Pintura.

Dep. Zaragoza (Portillo)	14:13 (3)	16:00 (2)	17:00 (1)	18:00 (1)	20:00 (1)
Arr. Madrid (Chamartin)	18:41	19:30	20:35	21:10	23:05

(1) Light refreshments. (2) Restaurant car. (3) Second-class.

San Sebastian - Biarritz - Bayonne - San Sebastian

46

Dep. San Sebastian (Donastia)	08:32			
Arr. Hendaye	09:10			

Change trains.

137

Dep. Hendaye	09:39 (1)			
Arr. Biarritz	10:00			
Arr. Bayonne	10:10			
Dep. Bayonne	14:15	14:40 (1)	15:53 (2)	20:40 (1)
Dep. Biarritz	14:24	14:53	16:05	20:53
Arr. Hendaye	14:49	15:16	16:29	21:17

Change trains.

46

Dep. Hendaye	-0-	15:20 (1)	21:25 (1)	
Arr. Irun	-0-	15:25	21:26	

Change trains.

Dep. Irun	-0-	15:35	22:15 (4)	
Arr. San Sebastian (Donastia)	-0-	15:50	22:30	

(1) TGV. Reservation required. Supplement charged. Light refreshments. (2) Light refreshments. (3) Direct train to San Sebastian. No train change in Irun. (4) Second-class.

San Sebastian - Bilbao - San Sebastian   436

*This second-class narrow-gauge rail trip is **not** covered by Eurailpass. Other (slower) trains, which depart/arrive Bilbao's Concordia railstation, run on this route at frequent times not listed in Cook.*

Dep. San Sebastian (Amara)	08:35	Dep. Bilbao (Axturi)	13:30	19:30
Arr. Bilbao (Axturi)	10:25	Arr. San Sebastian (Amara)	14:40	20:40

Sights in **Bilbao**: The Fine Arts Museum. The Biscay Historical Museum. The Begona Sanctuary.

San Sebastian - Burgos - San Sebastian   430

All of these trains have light refreshments.

Dep. San Sebastian	08:32	09:04
Arr. Burgos	11:11	12:20

Dep. Burgos	17:46	18:24 (1)
Arr. San Sebastian	21:05	21:17

(1) Supplement charged.

San Sebastian - Pamplona - San Sebastian   412

All of these trains have light refreshments.

Dep. San Sebastian (Dona.)	10:30 (1)	Dep. Pamplona	19:38
Arr. Pamplona	12:15	Arr. San Sebastian (Dona.)	21:28

(1) Operates June 25-September 25. Runs Monday, Wednesday, Friday and Sunday. (2) Runs Monday, Wednesday, Friday and Sunday.

Sights in **Pamplona**: The 14th century Gothic Cathedral, with its cloisters and Diocesan Museum. The Navarre Museum. The running of the bulls through the city's streets, every year between July 6 and July 15.

Seville - Cadiz - Seville   425

All of these trains are second-class, unless designated otherwise.

Dep. Seville (S.Justa)	07:30	08:20 (1)	08:45	10:00
Arr. Cadiz	09:57	10:28	10:47	12:02

Sights in **Cadiz**: The African environment. The Fine Arts Museum. The Museum of Archaeology and Art. The Cathedral, with its monumental Silver Tabernacle, decorated with almost 1,000,000 jewels. The Historical Museum.

Dep. Cadiz	13:05	15:05	16:30	18:20 (3)
Arr. Seville (S.Justa)	15:02	17:02	17:55	20:15 (4)

(1) Runs June 24-September 5 only.(2) Supplement charged. Restaurant car. (3) Plus other departures from Cadiz at 18:55 and 20:30 arriving Seville 20:49 and 22:35. (4) Runs Tuesday, Thursday and Sunday June 2- September 25.

Seville - Cordoba - Seville   425

Dep. Seville (S. Justa)	07:00 (1)	08:00 (2)	08:45 (1)	09:45 (1)	11:00 (1+5)
Arr. Cordoba	07:42	08:42	10:14	10:43	11:42

Sights in **Cordoba**: One thousand years ago, this was the most important city west of Constantinople (today's Istanbul). Its 200,000 houses *then* were double those of today. See the array of marble, jasper, onyx and granite on the 80 marble columns in the 8th century Mosque, built on top of what was first a Roman temple and later a Catholic church, before the Moors seized Cordoba.

Following the recapture of the city by the Spaniards and in the conversion of the building to a church again, most of the original 1,000 marble columns were removed to provide space for a nave and a high altar. Called "Mezquita," its interior is illuminated by 4,000 bronze and copper lamps. Its ceiling is carved cedar. Its mosaics are made from 35 tons of glass bits. The Mosque is closed 12:00–16:00, and the Alcazar palace fortress is closed 12:00–17:00.

Also see the 14th century Synagogue. The Fine Arts Museum. The Museum of Julio Romero de Torres. The Museum of Cordoban art, with its Bullfight Museum. The Provincial Archaeological Museum, one of the most important archaeological collections in Spain. The Roman Bridge, built in the time of Emperor Augustus. The home of the Marques de Viana, with its 14 flower-filled patios.

Dep. Cordoba	12:47 (1)	13:50 (3)	15:20 (3)	15:38 (1)	16:50 (3+6)
Arr. Seville (S. Justa)	13:40	15:43	17:13	16:25	18:43

(1) Supplement charged. Restaurant car. (2) Runs daily except Sundays and holidays. Supplement charged. Restaurant car. (3) Second-class. (4) Light refreshments. (5) Plus another Seville departure at 11:40 (3), arriving Cordoba 13:20. (6) Plus other departures from Cordoba at 18:00 (3), 18:49 (1), 20:20 (3), 20:40 (1) and 22:49 (1), arriving Seville 19:40, 19:45, 22:13, 21:35 and 23:40. (7) Does not run May 29-September 24 and December 16-January 9.

Seville - Granada - Seville   426

Both of these trains are second-class only.

Dep. Seville (S.Justa)	08:15	Dep. Granada	16:45
Arr. Granada	12:10	Arr. Seville (S. Justa)	20:46

Sights in **Granada**: The indescribable Alhambra complex, consisting of the Royal Palace, adjacent Partal Gardens, the 9th century Alcazaba watchtower fortress and, a quarter of a mile away, the Generalife (summer palace of Moorish caliphs), one of Europe's greatest gardens.

At the Royal Palace, be sure to see the Court of the Mexuar, the Hall of the Ambassadors, the Court of the Myrtle Trees, the Hall of the Two Sisters, the Court of the Lions, the

Royal Baths and the Daraxa courtyard. The Mocarabes Gallery and Abencerrrajes Gallery are near the Court of the Lions.

The Partal Gardens are a series of terraces featuring roses, poinsettias, orange and lime trees, lilies, bouganvillea and carnations.

Also see the crypts of Ferdinand and Isabella in the Cathedral's Royal Chapel. The Fine Arts Museum and Hispano-Moorish Museum in Charles V's Palace. The Royal Hospital. Casa Castril.

Seville - Jerez - Seville   425

All of these trains are second-class.

Dep. Seville (S. Justa)	07:50	08:20 (4)	08:45	10:00 (5)
Arr. Jerez	09:07	09:30	10:05	11:17

Sights in **Jerez**: A 3,000-year old city, famous for its horses, beautiful women and sherry wine. Its renowned Andalusian horses, bred from Spanish mares and stallions which the Moorish invaders brought here more than 1,500 year ago, do not date as far back as the wine does. Phoenicians started the vineyards here in 1100 B.C. Later Romans began the vinting of sherry. Many of the best wineries offer tours that conclude with tasting.

See the annual September Wine Festival. Its opening ceremony takes place on the steps that lead into the 17th century Collegiate Church of Santa Maria. Next to it is the 11th century Moorish fort, the Alcazar.

Also visit the 15th century San Dionisio Church. See the exhibit of Punic, Roman and Arabic pottery, tombstones, household implements and statues in the Archaeological Museum that occupies 2 small rooms inside Chapter House on tiny Plaza de la Asuncion, across from San Dionisio Church.

Look for the 7th century BC Corinthian helmet, believed to be the oldest Greek artifact ever found in Spain.

Dep. Jerez	13:43	15:48	17:17	18:55 (3+6)
Arr. Seville (S. Justa)	15:02	17:02	18:35	20:08

(1) Supplement charged. Light refreshments. (2) Restaurant car. (3) Plus other Jerez departures at 19:33, 21:15, and 22:58 (2), arriving Seville 20:49, 22:35 and 23:15. (4) Runs June 24-September 5 only. (5) Runs June 24-September 4, December 15-January 8. (6) Runs Tuesday, Thursday and Sunday June 2-September 25 and December 18-January 8. Also runs Sundays October 2-December 17 and January 15-May 25.

Seville - Malaga (via Bobadilla) - Seville   426

Both of these trains are second-class.

Dep. Seville (S. Justa)	08:15		Dep. Malaga	17:35
Arr. Malaga	11:20		Arr. Seville (S.Justa)	20:46

Sights in **Bobadilla:** An elegant modern resort, designed to resemble an Andalusian village. Recitals on a pipe orgen that has 1,595 pipes are presented in a copy of a 16th century church.

Seville - Torremolinos - Seville

426		*427 Electric train.*	
Dep. Seville (S.B.)	08:15	Dep. Torrenmolinos	17:04
Arr. Malaga	11:20	Arr. Malaga	17:22
Change to electric train.		*Change to ordinary train.*	
427		*426*	
Dep. Malaga	11:30	Dep. Malaga	17:35
Arr. Torremolinos	11:48	Arr. Seville (S.B.)	20:46

Sights in **Torremolinos:** Characters from all over the world, on and around this resort's 5-mile beach.

Tarragona - Tortosa - Tarragona   415

Dep. Tarragona	08:00 (1)	08:58	09:11	09:58 (1)	12:08 (3)
Arr. Tortosa	08:43	09:41	10:18	10:42 (2)	13:11

Sights in **Tortosa:** St. Louis College, founded in 1554 by Charles V for Moors converting to Christianity. The Cathedral. The Bishop's Palace.

Dep. Tortosa	13:15	15:06 (1)	15:45	17:00	18:40 (1+6)
Arr. Tarragona	14:19	15:53	16:53	17:57	20:12

(1) Supplement charged. Light refreshments. (2) Runs May 29-September 24 and December 15-January 8. (3) Second-class. (4) Runs daily, except Sundays and holidays. Supplement charged. Light refreshments. (5) Operates late June to early September. (6) Plus other Tortosa departures at 19:55 (2) and 21:10 (1), arriving Tarragona 20:55 and 22:00.

Valencia - Alicante - Valencia   415

Dep. Valencia (Ter.)	08:00	10:50 (2)	Dep. Alicante (Ter.)	17:05	18:34 (3+4)
Arr. Alicante (Ter.)	10:15	12:50	Arr. Valencia (Ter.)	19:05	21:19

(1) Operates late June to late September. Light refreshments. (2) Supplement charged. Light refreshments. (3) Second-class. (4) Plus other Alicante departures at 19:30 (1) and 20:25 (3), arriving Valencia 21:50 and 23:10.

Sights in **Alicante**: The avenue lined with date palms, part of the complete African atmosphere. The huge Moorish castle. Take the 26-mile bus trip to Elche to see the only palm forest in Europe.

Alicante - Benidorm - Denia - Alicante   418

There is marvelous scenery on a one-class narrow-gauge train that runs from Alicante (via **Benidorm**), to **Denia** and the time to take it (13:15–17:57) before returning to Valencia. *Not covered by Eurailpass.*

A special tourist train called "Limon Express" (*not covered by Eurailpass* and for which Cook's does not carry a timetable) runs between Benidorm and **Gata de Gorgos** on Wednesday and Friday. Taking "Limon Express" requires arriving Alicante the prior day and overnighting in Alicante.

Departing 08:15 from Alicante's FGV railstation, arriving Benidorm 09:21. Change to "Limon Express." Depart Benidorm 09:50 for this roundtrip, arriving back in Benidorm 13:50. Depart Benidorm 14:51, arriving Alicante (FGV) 15:57.

Tickets for "Limon Express" (sold by Alicante travel agencies) include visiting a guitar factory, and visiting Gata de Gogos, and a half-bottle of sparkling wine. The 1994 prices were: 1,250 pesetas for an adult, 650 pesetas for a child.

Valencia - Cuenca - Valencia   419

Dep. Valencia (Ter.)	08:40	11:50	Dep. Cuenca	14:15	18:30
Arr. Cuenca	11:58	15:27	Arr. Valencia (Ter.)	17:25	21:34

Sights in **Cuenca**: See notes under "Madrid–Cuenca"

Valencia - Murcia - Valencia   415

All of these trains are second-class.

Dep. Valencia (Ter.)	07:50	Dep. Murcia	17:14	22:15 (1)
Arr. Murcia	11:58	Arr. Valencia (Ter.)	21:19	02:00

(1) Light refreshments. Runs daily except Saturdays.

Sights in **Murcia**: The Moorish granary. The 14th century Gothic-Romanesque Cathedral. Glass, pottery and leather factories.

Valencia - Tarragona - Valencia   415

Dep. Valencia (Ter.)	06:30 (1)	08:15	09:45 (2)
Arr. Tarragona	09:50	10:59	12:22

Dep. Tarragona	15:28 (2)	18:28 (2)	19:35 (1)
Arr. Valencia (Ter.)	18:25	21:20	22:35

(1) Second-class coach. Restaurant car. (2) Supplement charged. Light refreshments.

SCENIC RAIL TRIPS

Here are 16 exceptionally scenic rail trips in Spain and Portugal.

Barcelona - La Tour-de-Carol - Villefranche - Perpignan - Barcelona

Passengers on the famous La Tour-de-Carol to Villefranche narrow-gauge service (called "The Yellow Train") may ride either in modern cars, an antique car or a completely open car, which John Zucker of New York City recommends for best glimpses of beautiful Pyrenees mountain scenery.

This very scenic route can be traveled either as a one-day circle trip from Barcelona (see schedules below) or when going from Spain to France. (A direct train Perpignan–Marseille [Table 162] departs Perpignan 20:01.)

You pass the popular **Mont-Louis** and **Font-Romeu** ski resorts and then ride alternately along very narrow ledges and also on very high bridges as the line criss-crosses canyons before arriving in the ancient walled-city of **Villefranche-de-Conflans**, a few miles from the **Vernet les Bains** sulfur-bath spa. The train-change in Villefranche is an easy cross-platform transfer.

The One-Day Circle Trip
All of these trains are second-class.

413				*143*		
Dep. Barcelona (Sants)	06:15	09:18		Dep. Villefranche	13:16	17:16 (2)
Arr. La Tour	09:59	12:48		Arr. Perpignan	14:03	18:04
Change to narrow-gauge				*Change trains.*		
"Yellow Train"				*163*		
143				Dep. Perpignan	17:11	18:25
Dep. La Tour	10:36	14:04		Arr. Port Bou	17:58	19:10
Dep. Font-Romeu	11:38	15:15		*Change trains.*		
Arr. Villefranche	12:53	16:42		*416*		
Change trains.				Dep. Port Bou	17:25	19:35 (1)
				Arr. Barcelona (P. de G.)	19:54	-0-
				Arr. Barccelona (Sants)	19:59	22:00

(1) Light Refreshments. (2) Plus another Villefranche departure at 18:24, arriving Barcelona (Sants) 23:28.

Barcelona - Massanes - Blanes - Barcelona   416

Fine coastline and mountain scenery on this easy one-day circle excursion. There are no tourist restaurants in Massanes or Blanes.

(Via Granollers)

Dep. Barcelona (Sants)	06:53 (1)	08:10 (2)	09:10	10:15	11:12 (2)	12:10
Arr. Massanes	08:00	09:08	10:00	11:08	12:59	13:03

•   •   •

Second-class only.

Dep. Massanes	08:00	09:52	11:58	12:50	13:53	15:52
Dep. Blanes	-0-	-0-	-0-	-0-	-0-	-0-
Arr. Barcelona (Sants)	09:02	10:54	12:57	13:45	14:55	16:55

(1) Runs daily, except Sundays and holidays. Second-class. (2) Second-class.

Barcelona - Zaragoza - Madrid 410

There are many ancient towns, castles, mountains and gorges to see on this route.

Dep. Barcelona (Sants)	08:30 (1)	10:00 (2)	12:00 (1)	15:30 (1)	23:10 (4)
Arr. Zaragoza	11:51	13:56	15:58	18:55	03:50
Arr. Madrid (Cham.)	15:05	17:45	19:30	22:10	08:00

(1) Supplement charged. Restaurant car. (2) Light refreshments. (3) Carries a sleeping car. Also has second-class couchettes. Restaurant car. (4) Carries a sleeping car. Coach is first-class. Restaurant car.

Barcelona - Puigcerda

There is beautiful Pyrenees mountain scenery on this portion of the Barcelona–Toulouse route. As shown below, this trip also can be made as a one-day excursion from Barcelona.

All of these trains are second-class, unless designated otherwise.

413

Dep. Barcelona (Sants)	06:15	09:18	15:06
Arr. Puigcerda	09:53	12:42	18:21
Arr. La Tour-de-Carol	09:59	12:48	18:26
Change trains. 144			
Dep. La Tour-de-Carol	10:40 (1)	13:35 (1)	19:17 (1)
Arr. Toulouse (Mat.)	13:11	16:10	22:17

(1) Has first class.

Here is the easy one-day excursion 413

All of these trains are second-class only.

Dep. Barcelona (Sants)	06:15	09:18	15:06
Arr. Puigcerda	09:53	12:42	18:21
Arr. La Tour-de-Carol	09:59	12:48	18:26
	•	•	•
Dep. La Tour-de-Carol	10:52	13:19	18:50
Dep. Puigcerda	10:58	13:25	18:56
Arr. Barcelona (Sants)	14:29	16:38	22:08

Barcelona - Tarragona

This trip is noted for excellent scenery along the Mediterranean coastline. Complete schedules can be found with "Barcelona" schedules.

Barcelona - Valencia

There are good views of the Mediterranean shoreline on this ride.
  Schedules appears with "Barcelona" schedules.

Cordoba - Malaga - Cordoba   426

Scenic canyons can be seen on this trip, an easy one-day excursion from Cordoba.

All of these trains are second-class, unless designated otherwise.

Dep. Cordoba	06:50	12:13 (1)
Arr. Malaga	09:35	14:45

Sights in **Malaga**: See notes under "Granada–Malaga"

Dep. Malaga	13:55	16:10 (2)	19:40 (3)	20:10	22:35 (4)
Arr. Cordoba	16:46	18:28	22:28	23:10	01:28

(1) Light refreshments. Subject to confirmation. Has both first and second-class coaches. (2) Restaurant car. Subject to confirmation. Has both first and second-class coaches. (3) Restaurant car. (4) Light refreshments.

Leon - Oviedo - Leon   435

Very good mountain scenery on this one-day roundtrip.

Sights in **Leon**: The stained-glass windows in the Cathedral and the 11th century Church of San Isidoro.

Dep. Leon	05:45 (1)	Dep. Oviedo	11:12 (1)	11:38 (2)
Arr. Oviedo	08:25	Arr. Leon	13:05	13:28

(1) Second-class. (2) Supplement charged. Light refreshments.

Leon - Monforte 440

The Leon–Monforte portion of the Leon–Vigo route is recommended for mountain scenery.

Both of these trains are second-class only.

Dep. Leon	08:05		Dep. Monforte	16:31
Arr. Monforte	12:03		Arr. Leon	20:55

Lisbon - Porto - Vigo - Santiago de Compostela...Lisbon

This table shows both extending the Leon-Vigo trip (above) from Vigo to Santiago de Compostela and also the route from Lisbon to Santiago. Notes on this marvelous attraction appear under "Madrid–Santiago."

445			*439*	
Dep. Lisbon (S. Apol.)	11:00		Dep. Santiago	08:40 (3)
Arr. Porto (Campanha)	14:25		Arr. Vigo	10:15
Change trains. 446			*Change trains. 446*	
Dep. Porto (Campanha)	15:09 (2)		Dep. Vigo	12:55
Set watch forward one hour			*Set watch back one hour*	
Arr. Vigo	18:42		Arr. Porto (Campanha)	16:05
Change trains. 439			*Change trains. 445*	
Dep. Vigo	20:12 (3)		Dep. Porto (Campanha)	17:00 (4)
Arr. Santiago	22:13		Arr. Lisbon (S. Apol.)	20:20

(1) Runs daily, except Sundays and holidays. Reservation required. Light refreshments. (2) Reservation advisable. Light refreshments. (3) Second-class. (4) Reservation required. Supplement charged. Light refreshments.

Porto - Viana do Castelo - Vigo 446

Schedules allow stopping over in Viana on the Porto–Vigo route.

Reservation is advisable for all of these trains. All of these trains have light refreshments.

Dep. Porto (Camphanha)	07:39	15:09	18:57
Arr. Viana do Castelo	-0-	16:39	20:15
Arr. Vigo	11:05	19:10	22:57

Sights in **Viana do Castelo**: A pretty, little fishing resort. Walk along the twisting road lined with pine and eucalyptus trees, up to the Basilica of Santa Luzia for marvelous views (or take the funicular).

See a collection of ceramics for which Portugal is famous, at the Municipal Museum. The Renaissance buildings in the Praca da Republica. The church of Sao Domingos.

Dep. Vigo	07:20
Arr. Viana do Castelo	09:18
Arr. Porto (Camphanha)	10:42

Porto - Regua - Porto   447

There is good river scenery on this easy one-day roundtrip.

Dep. Porto (S. Bento)	08:45	10:48 (1)	12:15 (2)	13:18	14:35 (1+4)
Dep. Porto (Campanha)	08:52	10:56	12:23	13:26	14:42
Arr. Regua	11:21	12:54	14:47	16:02	16:44

• • •

Dep. Regua	11:22 (1)	13:16	14:50 (3)	16:02 (1)	17:54 (5)
Arr. Porto (Campanha)	13:27	15:12	16:38	18:21	19:55
Arr. Porto (S. Bento)	13:35	15:18	16:45	18:30	20:02

(1) Reservation advisable. Light refreshments. (2) Runs daily, except Sundays and holidays. (3) Reservation advisable. (4) Plus another daytime Porto (S. Bento) departure at 16:15, arriving Regua 18:37. (5) Plus other Regua departures at 19:07 and 21:10 (1), arriving Porto (S. Bento) 21:41 and 23:30.

Madrid - Barcelona   Barcelona - Madrid   410

Many ancient towns, castles, mountains and canyons to see on this route.

Dep. Madrid (Cham.)	01:00 (1)	11:00 (2)	12:00 (4)	14:00 (2)	16:00 (2+8)
Arr. Barcelona (Franca)	08:50	18:00 (3)	20:20	20:55	22:55

• • •

Dep. Barcelona (Franca)	08:05 (2)	09:35 (5)	15:10 (2)	21:50 (1)
Arr. Madrid (Cham.)	15:05	17:4	22:10	05:40 (1)

(1) Departs/Arrives Madrid's Puerto de Atocha railstation. Carries only sleeping cars. (2) Supplement charged. Restaurant car. (3) Departs/Arrives Barcelona's Sants railstation. (4) Second-class. Light refreshments. (5) Light refreshments. (6) Carries a sleeping car. Also has couchettes. Light refreshments. (7) Carries a sleeping car. Also has couchettes. Coaches are first-class only. Light refreshments. (8) Plus other Madrid departures at 22:00 (6) and 23:10 (7), arriving Barcleona 07:00 (Sants) and 08:00 (Sants).

THE MAJORCA ONE-DAY RAIL TRIP

If you are planning on visiting the island of Majorca, you will enjoy this trip.

This narrow-gauge, easy one-day trip goes through olive groves before tunneling through a mountain and emerging high above **Soller**. At the tunnel exit, the train stops for 10 minutes to allow passengers to enjoy the view before the train spirals downhill to Soller. A quaint tram makes the short ride from Soller to the seaside **Puerto de Soller**.

Palma - Soller 422

*This ride is **not** covered by Eurailpass.*

Dep. Palma	08:00	10:40	13:00	15:15	19:45 (1)
Arr. Soller	55 minutes later				

• • •

Dep. Soller	06:45	09:15	11:50	14:10	18:30 (1)
Arr. Palma	55 minutes later				

(1)January 1-April 30 and November 1-December 31.

THE TRIP TO ANDORRA

Barcelona - La Tour-de-Carol - Andorra la Vella

All of these trains are second-class only.

413 Train			
Dep. Barcelona (Sants)	06:15	-0-	15:06
Arr. La Tour-de-Carol	09:59	-0-	18:26
Change to a bus (weather permitting). 144 a			
Dep. La Tour-de-Carol	11:10 (1)	12:00 (2)	18:35 (3)
Arr. Andorra la Vella	13:15	14:00	20:35

Sight in **Andorra la Vella**: Capital of the quaint, tiny (50,000 population) co-principality, governed jointly by the French government and the Spanish Bishop of Urgel. Both the Spanish peseta and the French franc are legal currency here.

The country's main export is postage stamps, created for philatelists. Small ski resorts and duty-free shops are the main attraction for the 6,000,000 tourists who come here every year. Located in the eastern Pyrenees, the country's mountain peaks reach heights of 9,800 feet.

Lying in one of Andorra's 6 valleys, this is the market town for the entire country (179 square miles). Catalan (the language of the Barcelona area), Spanish and French are spoken here.

Dep. Andorra la Vella	07:45	08:15 (5)	14:30 (3)
Arr. La Tour-de-Carol	10:00	10:30	17:00
Change to train. 413			
Dep. La Tour-de-Carol	-0-	10:52	18:50
Arr. Barcelona (Sants)	-0-	14:29	22:08

(1) Operates June 1 to September 30. (2) Operates October 1 to May 31. (3) Operates July 1 to September 30. (4) Operates May 1 to October 31. (5) Operates May 1-October 31.

THE MADRID ROUTES

Madrid is the hub of the Iberian Peninsula, with spokes going from it to the major cities of Spain and Portugal: Barcelona, Bilbao, Cordoba, Lisbon, San Sebastian, Santiago de Compostela, Seville and Valencia. Here are the schedules for reaching those cities from Madrid:

Madrid - Barcelona   Barcelona - Madrid

Covered under the description of scenic trips.

Madrid - Bilbao   430

Dep. Madrid (Chamartin)	15:30 (1)	23:00 (2)
Arr. Bilbao (Abando)	21:15	07:55

Sights in **Bilbao**: This is the largest Basque city. A major port and industrial city.

Dep. Bilbao (Abando)	16:25	23:00 (2)
Arr. Madrid (Chamartin)	22:09	07:45

(1) Supplement charged. Light refreshments. (2) Carries a sleeping car. Also has couchettes. Coaches are second-class.

Madrid - Lisbon 80 + 433

Both of these trains charge a supplement and have light refreshments.

Dep. Madrid (Chamartin)	-0- (2)	22:30 (1)
Dep. Madrid (Atocha)	14:00	-0-
Set your watch back one hour.		
Arr. Lisbon (S. Apolonia)	21:45	08:33

*   *   *

Dep. Lisbon (S. Apolonia)	11:55 (2)	22:05 (1)
Set your watch forward one hour.		
Arr. Madrid (Atocha)	19:56	-0-
Arr. Madrid (Chamartin)	-0-	08:40

(1) Carries a sleeping car. Also has couchettes. (2) Runs daily except Saturday.

Madrid - San Sebastian 430

Dep. Madrid (Cham.)	10:00 (1)	15:30 (1)	18:15 (2)	23:00 (3)
Arr. San Sebastian	16:16	21:27	01:35	07:55

Dep. San Sebastian	08:32 (4)	13:33 (5)	16:01 (1)	22:45 (3)
Arr. Madrid (Cham.)	14:53	20:25	22:09	07:45

(1) Light refreshments. (2) Coach is second-class. (3) No supplement charge. Carries a sleeping car. Also has couchettes. Coaches are second-class. (4) No supplement charged. (5) Operates late September to late May. Coaches are second-class.

Madrid - Santiago de Compostela 441

Dep. Madrid (Cham.)	14:00 (1)	21:45 (2)	
Arr. Santiago	21:15	07:40	

*   *   *

Dep. Santiago	09:49 (3)	13:40 (4)	22:18 (2)
Arr. Madrid (Cham.)	17:35	21:30	08:45

(1) Supplement charged. Light refreshments. (2) Carries a sleeping car. Also has couchettes. Coaches are second-class. Restaurant car. (3) Runs Saturday only. Supplement charged. Light refreshments. (4) Runs daily, except Saturday. Supplement charged. Light refreshments.

Sights in **Santiago de Compostela**: One of the 3 most sacred places in Christendom, ranking equally with Jerusalem and Rome since 812. It is believed that this is the repository of St. James (Santiago), a cousin of Jesus, son of Mary's sister, and the first follower of Jesus to attain martyrdom.

After witnessing the crucifixion, James came to Spain in A.D. 44, converted 9 Iberians to Christianity, was visited at Zaragoza by the Virgin Mary, returned to the Holy Land, and was beheaded there by King Herod Agrippa.

The legend which has generated the pilgrimage to Santiago de Compostela for the past 1,100 years is that, after the decapitation in Jerusalem, his body was disinterred and found to have the head intact. The body was brought to Spain's West Coast in A.D. 44.

Eight centuries later, a hermit saw a bright star (stela) over a vacant field (compo). Excavations were conducted, and the remains of James were found. Since that event, pilgrims have come to this shrine by horse and in vehicles, as well as on foot (from as far as Scandinavia) to pray and meditate here.

You would stop here to see the majestic Cathedral built in the 12th century.

See its beautiful Baroque sculptured Obradoire facade. The carved Romanesque 12th century Door of Glory. Touch the grooves left in the central pillar by the fingers of millions of pilgrims over the centuries.

Visit the Archaeological Museum in its basement, the art pieces in its Treasury, the collection of tapestries with designs by Goya and Rubens in the many halls of the Cathedral's Tapestry Museum.

Also see the gigantic 6-foot tall, 118-pound brass censer in the Library of the Cathedral.

In the early pilgrimage years, it was difficult for priests to tolerate the odor of worshippers from afar who had gone unbathed for weeks and months. The censer here, called Botafumeiro (smoke-thrower), masked the noxious odors.

A custom that originated in the early days of pilgrimages here is perpetuated today. On feast days, this censer is brought into the Cathedral, filled with incense, hung by ropes from the dome 104 feet above the floor, and swung in an arc, barely passing over the heads of people standing in the Cathedral. It is easy to explore Santiago de Compostela on foot. See the marvelous view of the town from Alameda Park. Santa Maria del Sar, one of the more than 40 churches here, is a splendid example of 12th century Romanesque architecture.

Madrid - Seville   425 + Government timetable

The introduction of high-speed trains (in excess of 156 mph) on this route in 1992 reduced this trip from 6 hours to 2½ hours. Called AVE (Tren de Alta Velocidad Espanola), they go between Madrid's Atocha railstation and Seville's Santa Justa station, on the grounds of the 1992 World Expo.

The 3 classes on an air-conditioned AVE train are: "Club" (the most luxurious, with boutiques and fax, video and secretarial services), "Preference" (equivalent to first-class on a French TGV), and "Tourist" (similar to TGV second-class, but with larger and lower windows. Each AVE has a cafeteria and a bar.

Each of these 3 classes is available on all of 3 types of trains (making 9 prices for the same journey!) — "Valle" stops in Cordoba and also in 2 other towns. Some "Llano" make the same 3 stops, while other "Llano" stop only in Cordoba. All of the "Punta" trains stop only in Cordoba.

As an example of the range of cost for 9 possible AVE services, the 1994 price of a one-way Tourist ticket on a "Valle" train was 6,000 pesetas. For a Club ticket on a "Punta" train it was 16,500 pesetas!

There was a 40% discount for children age 4-11. Holders of Eurailpass, Eurodomino and Tarjeta Turistica (Tourist Card) were given 60% discount for a Club ticket, 65% discount for Preference, and 85% discount for Tourist.

In North America, tickets and reservations can be obtained from Rail Europe.

Reservation is required for all of these AVE trains. All of them charge a higher supplement than other Spanish express trains. The AVE supplement includes a reservation fee and mandatory travel insurance. All have a restaurant car.

Dep. Madrid (Atocha AVE)	10:00 (3)	11:00	14:00	16:00 (4)	
Arr. Seville (S. Justa)	13:25	13:40	16:25	18:35	

Dep. Madrid (Atocha AVE)	17:00	18:00 (2)	19:00	20:00	21:00
Arr. Seville (S. Justa)	19:45	20:35	21:35	22:35 (4)	23:40

Dep Seville (S. Justa)	07:00	08:00	09:00	11:00	14:00	16:00
Arr. Madrid (Atocha AVE)	09:45	10:25(5)	11:45	13:35	16:25	18:35

Dep. Seville (S.Justa)	17:00	18:00 (2)	19:00	20:00 (1)	21:00
Arr. Madrid (Atocha AVE)	19:45	20:35	21:35	22:35 (4)	23:40

(1) Does not operate in August. (2) Runs Friday and Sunday. Does not operate in August. (3) Subject to confirmation. (4) Runs daily except Saturdays. (5) Runs daily except Sundays and holidays.

Madrid - Valencia - Madrid   420

All of these trains charge supplement and have light refreshments, unless designated otherwise.

Dep. Madrid					
(Atocha-Cer.)	07:15(2+6)	09:15 (6)	13:15 (1+6)	15:15 (1+6)	16:45 (5+6)
Arr. Valencia (Ter.)	11:10	13:10	17:10	19:10	20:40 (4)

Sights in **Valencia**: See the Holy Grail, the chalice used at the Last Supper, exhibited in the 13th century Cathedral. The great art collection in the Convent of Pio V. The Orange Court at the 15th century Lonja del Mercado. The popular beaches: Arenas, Nazaret and Pinedo y Saler. The scent of the vast surrounding orange groves, perfuming the night.

Dep. Valencia (Ter.)	07:00 (2)	09:00	13:00 (1)	15:00 (1)	16:30 (5)
Arr. Madrid (Atocha-Cer.)	10:55	12:55	16:55	18:55	20:25

(1) Runs daily, except Saturday. (2) Runs daily, except Sundays and holidays. (3) No supplement charged. Has couchettes. Coach is second-class. (4) Plus other departures from Madrid (Chamartin) at 18:45 (6) and 20:15 (2), arriving Valencia 22:40 and 00:50. (5) Plus other departures from Valencia at 18:30 and 20:00 (1), arriving Madrid 22:25 and 23:55(Chamartin). (6) Arrives/departs Madrid Puerta de Atocha.

Barcelona - Valencia - Barcelona   415

Dep. Barcelona (Franca)	06:40 (1)	-0-	-0-
Dep. Barcelona (P. de G.)	06:50	-0-	-0-
Dep. Barcelona (Sants)	07:00	08:00 (2)	09:00 (3)
Arr. Valencia (Termino)	10:55	11:45	12:50

Dep. Barcelona (Franca)	14:10 (1)	17:10 (1)
Dep. Barcelona (P. de G.)	14:20	17:21
Dep. Barcelona (Sants)	14:30	17:30
Arr. Valencia (Termino)	18:25	21:20

Dep. Valencia (Termino)	02:20 (7)	06:30 (6)	09:45 (1)
Arr. Barcelona (Sants)	07:30	11:00	13:30
Arr. Barcelona (P. de G.)	-0-	-0-	13:41
Arr. Barcelona (Franca)	-0-	-0-	13:50

Dep. Valencia (Termino)	13:15 (1)	15:10 (1)	16:30 (3+10)
Arr. Barcelona (Sants)	17:03	19:03	20:40
Arr. Barcelona (P. de G.)	17:11	19:11	-0-
Arr. Barcelona (Franca)	-0-	-0-	-0-

(1) Reservation *required*. Supplement charged. Light refreshments. (2) Restaurant car. (3) Operates late May to late September. Reservation *required*. Supplement charged. Light refreshments. (4) Second-class. (5) Reservation *required*. Supplement charged. Runs Monday-Friday, except holidays. Light refreshments. (6) Second-class. Restaurant car. (7) Runs daily, except Saturday. Carries a sleeping car. Also has couchettes. Coach is second-class. Light refreshments. (8) Operates late June to early September. Second-class. (9) Plus other departures from Barcelona (Sants) at 18:30 (1), 19:45 (8) and 22:45 (7), arriving Valencia 22:30, 00:45 and 03:25. (10) Plus other departures from Valencia at 18:00 (2) and 19:15 (1), arriving Barcelona (Sants) 22:05 and 23:07.

INTERNATIONAL ROUTES
FROM PORTUGAL

The 2 routes to France and beyond are Lisbon-Madrid and Lisbon-San Sebastian (see below).

The only practical way from Lisbon to southwestern Spain has been very indirect since 1991 — via Madrid. Lisbon-Madrid schedules appear under "Madrid-Lisbon."

Lisbon - San Sebastian - Bordeaux - Paris   46

The 2-hour stop in Hendaye is for changing the train's wheels to conform with the narrower track in France.

"Sud Express." Carries a sleeping car and restaurant car Lisbon-Irun. Hascouchettes Lisbon-Paris.

Arrival in Paris can be 4 hours earlier by changing in Hendaye to a TGV.

Dep. Lisbon (S. Apol.)	17:03 (1)	
Set your watch forward one hour.		
Dep. Salamanca	02:05	-0-
Dep. San Sebastian	08:32	-0-
Arr. Irun	09:00	-0-
Arr. Hendaye	09:10	-0-
Dep. Hendaye	09:34 (3)	09:49 (2)
Arr. Bordeaux	11:52	12:10
Arr. Paris (Austerlitz)	-0-	17:15
Arr. Paris (Montparnasse)	15:00	14:55

(1) "Sud Express." See headnote. (2) TGV. Supplement charged. Light refreshments. (3) Change trains in Hendaye.

INTERNATIONAL ROUTES
FROM SPAIN

Spanish National Railways (RENFE) makes reservations for only 4 trips to other countries: Madrid–Lisbon, Madrid–Paris, Barcelona–Geneva–Zurich and Barcelona–Milan.

When traveling by train from another country to Spain, if you want to travel later from Spain back into France and/or beyond France, it is necessary to book the trip from Spain to another country *before you enter Spain.*

The Spanish gateway for rail travel to London, Paris, Brussels and Amsterdam is Madrid.

From Barcelona, there is rail service to southwestern France (via Toulouse) and to southeastern France (Avignon, Marseille and Nice), from where there are connections to Italy, Austria and Switzerland (and on to Germany and Denmark)...plus Barcelona–Zurich and Barcelona–Milan on the fabulous "Pablo Casals" (see "Barcelona–Milan").

Seville - Lisbon

The only practical way to make this trip has been very indirect since 1991: Seville–Madrid–Lisbon.

Madrid - Bordeaux - Paris   46

All arrivals in Paris are on Day 2.

Dep. Madrid (Chamartin)	10:00 (5)	18:15 (6)	19:30 (7)	23:00 (8)
Arr. Hedaye	16:50	02:08 (6)	-0- (7)	08:30
Change trains.				
Dep. Hendaye	18:32 (2+4)	-0-	-0-	09:34
Arr. Bordeaux	20:39	05:51	03:55	11:50
Arr. Paris (Austerlitz)	-0-	10:55	08:30	-0-
Arr. Paris (Montparnasse)	23:45	-0-	-0-	14:55

(1) Second-class. (2) TGV. Reservation required. Supplement charged. (3) Runs daily, except Sundays and holidays. (4) Runs Sundays and holidays only. (5) Supplement charged. Light refreshments. (6) Direct train. No train change in Hendaye. Has only couchettes. No coaches. Light refreshments Hendaye-Paris. (7) Direct train. No train change in Hendaye. Has only sleeping cars and a restaurant car. (8) Carries a sleeping car. Also has couchettes. Coaches are second-class.

Barcelona - Avignon - Geneva - Bern - Zurich   81

The "Pablo Casals" began in 1990 to carry one "Gran Clase" sleeping car, the most luxurious cleeping car in Europe. Each of its large single and double 'staterooms' has a private, adjoining bathroom (circular shower stall, toilet and washbasin). Two armchairs are converted into beds by the compartment attendant.

Compartments in the first-class cars also have seating that converts to beds at night and a washbasin with towels. Second-class cars contain 4 berths and a washbasin. The 1994 second-class price (Barcelona-Geveva, Barcelona-Zurich or Barcelona-Milan) was 15,350 Pesetas Thursday-Saturday and 12,300 Pesetas Sunday-Wednesday.

Talk about secrecy! Spanish Railways flatly refused to divulge to the National Tourist Office of Spain what the 1995 price was for a full-course dinner, wine and dessert. It was $25-$40 in 1992, when the 2 government offices spoke to each other. Dinner is served in the restaurant car. Beverages and snacks are served in the bar car.

Substantial discounts are given to holders of Eurailpass and Eurodomino.

Dep. Barcelona (Franca)	-0-	10:10 (1)	20:15 (2)
Dep Barcelona (Sants)	08:02	-0-	-0-
Arr. Cerbere	10:45	12:30	-0-
Arr. Avignon	-0-	15:14	-0-
Arr. Geneva (Cornavin)	-0-	19:28	05:52
Arr. Bern	-0-	-0-	07:51
Arr. Zurich	-0-	-0-	09:15

(1) Supplement charged. Restaurant car. (2) "Pablo Casals." See description in headnote.

Barcelona - Torino - Milan   90

This is the second route of "Pablo Casals." A $10 continental breakfast can be purchased in one's compartment or the restaurant car.

Reservations for "Pablo Casals" can only be made in Spain. Substantial discounts are given to holders of Eurailpasses and Eurodomino passes.

Dep. Barcelona (Franca)	20:15
Arr. Torino (Porta Susa)	07:30
Arr. Milan (Centrale)	09:03

Barcelona - Paris   47

Dep. Barcelona (Sants)	07:10 (1)	17:16 (3)	17:35 (4)	18:40	21:00 (7)
Arr. Cerbere	09:50	20:25	19:35	20:50	- 0 - (7)
Change Trains					
Dep. Cerbere	10:27	- 0 -	20:40 (5)	22:13	- 0 -
Arr. Paris (Aus.)	20:22 (2)	- 0 -	07:33	08:36	08:15

(1) Second-class. (2) Arrives 20:45 on Saturday. (3) Departs from Barcelona's Franca railstation. Second-class. (4) Supplement charged. Light refreshments. (5) Carries only sleeping and couchette cars. (6) Operates early July to early September. Has couchettes. (7) Direct train. No change in Cerbere. Reservation can only be made in Spain. Carries only sleeping cars and a restaurant car. No coach cars.

Barcelona - Rome   90

This car has second-class couchettes.

Dep. Barcelona (Sants)	19:45
Arr. Rome (Termini)	18:05 Day 2

IRELAND

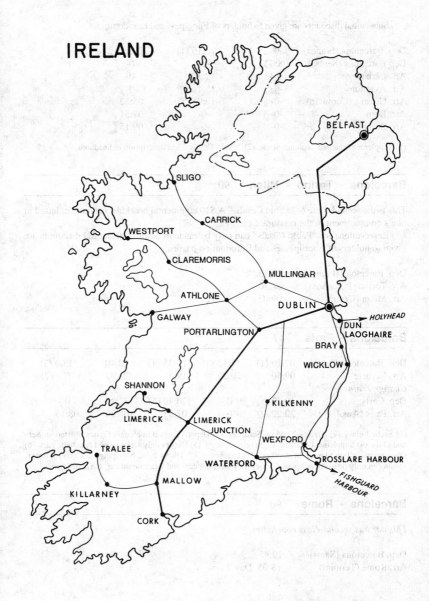

BELFAST

SLIGO

CARRICK

WESTPORT

CLAREMORRIS

MULLINGAR

ATHLONE

DUBLIN

GALWAY

DUN
LAOGHAIRE

→ *HOLYHEAD*

PORTARLINGTON

BRAY

WICKLOW

SHANNON

KILKENNY

LIMERICK

LIMERICK
JUNCTION

WEXFORD

TRALEE

WATERFORD

ROSSLARE HARBOUR

KILLARNEY

MALLOW

→ *FISHGUARD
HARBOUR*

CORK

REPUBLIC OF IRELAND

Overview

Ireland is not really known for its train system, but nonetheless a network sprawls from Cork in the south to Belfast in Northern Ireland with Dublin acting as the country's hub with some highly scenic lines stretching to Westport, Killarney, and Silgo.

General Information

• Children under five travel free. Half-fare for children 5-15. Children 16 and ocer must pay full fare.

• Ireland changes to summer on the last Sunday of March and coverts back to standard time on the last Sunday of October.

• Eurailpass Bonuses in Ireland: See introductory chapter on Eurail pass bonuses.

IRISH TRAIN PASSES

All of these passes are sold at rail and bus stations throughout the Irish Republic and in North America at CIE Tours, 108 Ridgedale Ave., P.O. box 2355, Morristown, NJ 07962. All of them provide unlimited second-class travel. Children age 5-15 pay half-fare.

Irish Explorer Rail (Republic of Ireland) Valid for any 5 days of train travel witin 15 days. The 1996 adult price is $102.

Irish Explorer Rail/Bus (Republic of Ireland) Valid for any 8 days within 15 days. The 1996 adult price is $153.

Irish Rover Rail (Republic of Ireland and Northern Ireland) Valid any 5 days within 15 days. The 1996 adult price is $128.

Emerald Card Rail/Bus (Republic of Ireland and Northern Ireland) The 1996 adult prices are: $179 for any 8 days within 15 days, and $306 for any 15 days within 30 days.

Dublin

Capital of the Irish Republic. See the outstanding Bronze Age gold ornaments, the 9th century Derrynaflan Chalice and the 12th century Cross of Cong, in the National Museum, open Tuesday-Saturday 10:00–17:00 and Sunday 14:00–17:00. The collection of paintings (Rubens, Rembrandt, Goya. Reynolds, Gainsborough) at the National Gallery of Art, open Monday–Saturday 10:00–18:00 and Sunday 14:00–17:00.

The 8th century Book of Kells, a richly illuminated bible regarded as one of the most beautiful books ever made, on view in the Old Library of Trinity College. The Hugh Lane Municipal Gallery of Modern Art.

The pulpit from which Jonathan Swift preached, at the 12th century St. Patrick's Cathedral, and a performance of the young boys' choir there. The collection of oriental manuscripts at Chester Beatty Library. The Zoo, in the 1,760-acre Phoenix Park. The 13th century Dublin Castle. Leinster House. The restored 12th century Christ Church Cathedral.

The 18th century mansions on St. Stephen's Green. Window-shop on Grafton Street. Stroll on O'Connell Street. See the historic General Post Office, site of the 1916 uprising. The Georgian houses on Parnell Square. The house where George Bernard Shaw was born. Take a tour of the facilities of the Irish Sweepstakes. A tour of Guinness's Brewery.

Belfast

This is the capital of Northern Ireland. A major port. See the elegant Queen's University. The collection of antique locomotives and train cars in the Transport Museum. The richly marbled interiorof the 19th century City Hall. The beautiful Grand Opera House. Across the street, the decorative interior of the Crown Bar. Palm House and the collection of modern Irish paintings, silver and glass and exhibits of the history, geology and botany in Ulster Museum, both at the BotanicGardens. Tour the Harland and Wolff Shipyard, location of the world's largest drydock and where many of the world's great ocean liners were built.

See the display of everything produced in Ulster factories (old farm implements, stage-coaches, a schooner, antique locomotives and train cars, modern aircraft) at the 180-acre open-air Ulster Folk and Transport Museum, a complex of 18 exhibit buildings. It also has cottages in styles spanning several centuries (some with original furniture), water-powered mills, and demonstrations of such traditional crafts as spinning and thatching.

Genealogical research can be done at the Public Record Office, 66 Balmoral Avenue as well as by mail with the Irish Genealogical Association, 164 Kingsway, Dunmurry, Belfast BT17 9AD.

Birth and death records since 1864 and copies of marriage registrations since 1922 can be obtained at General Register Office, Oxford House, 49-55 Chichester Street, Belfast BT1 4HL.

ONE-DAY EXCURSIONS AND CITY SIGHTSEEING

Here are 8 one-day rail trips that can be made comfortably from Belfast, Cork, Dublin, Galway and Limerick, returning to them in most cases before dinnertime. Notes are provided on what to see and do at each destination. The number after the name of each route is the Cook's timetable.

Dublin - Belfast - Dublin   630

| Dep. Dublin (Con.) | 07:55 (1) | 10:30 (2) | 11:00 (1) | 13:00 (3) | 15:00 (1+7) |
| Arr. Belfast (Cen.) | 10:10 | 13:05 | 13:32 | 15:20 | 17:16 |

•   •   •

| Dep. Belfast (Cen.) | 08:00 (1) | 09:00 (3) | 10:15 (2) | 11:00 (1) | 15:00 (5+8) |
| Arr. Dublin Con.) | 09:58 | 11:32 | 12:40 | 13:22 | 17:15 |

(1) Runs daily, except Sundays and holidays. Restaurant car. (2) Runs Sunday only. Light refreshments. (3) Runs daily, except Sundays and holidays. Light refreshments. (4) Runs daily. Restaurant car Monday–Saturday. Second-class and light refreshments on Sunday. (5) Runs daily, except holidays. Restaurant car. (6) Runs daily, except Sundays and holidays. Second-class. (7) Plus other Dublin departures at 18:20 (2), 18:34 (6) and 20:15 (3), arriving Belfast 20:18, 21:45 and 22:38. (8) Plus other Belfast departures at 17:00 (3) and 18:00 (4), arriving Dublin 19:20 and 20:00 (20:25 on Sunday).

Dublin - Cork - Dublin   640

This is a train ride through Ireland's lush southern area.

| Dep. Dublin (Heu.) | 07:30 (1) | 08:15 (2) | 10:15 (3) | 10:45 (4) | 13:20 (4+10) |
| Arr. Cork (Kent) | 10:05 | 10:50 | 13:30 | 13:45 | 16:20 |

Sights in **Cork:** Parnell Bridge. The Customs House, the finest building in Cork. The collection of 19th and 20th century works by leading Irish and English painters, in the Crawford Gallery on Emmet Place. Visit the shops on Paul Street and Patrick Street. The perpetual flea market and vegetable stands on Corn Market Street.

| Dep. Cork (Kent) | 05:20 (5) | 07:35 (4) | 09:00 (6) | 11:20 (4) | 14:45 (7+11) |
| Arr. Dublin (Heu.) | 08:40 | 10:05 | 12:10 | 14:25 | 17:35 |

(1) Runs Monday–Friday, except holidays. Restaurant car. (2) Runs Saturday only. Restaurant car. (3) Runs Sunday only. Second-class. Restaurant car. (4) Runs daily, except Sundays and holidays. Restaurant car. (5) Runs daily, except Sundays and holidays. Second-class. (6) Runs daily, except holidays. Restaurant car. Second-class on Sunday. (7) Runs daily, except holidays. Monday–Saturday: restaurant car. Sunday: light refreshments. Departs and arrives 15 minutes earlier on Sunday. (8) Runs Sunday only. Second-class. (9) Runs Sunday only. Second-class. Light refreshments. (10) Plus other departures from Dublin at 14:55 (4), 17:30 (4), 18:30 (3), 18:55 (4) and 21:15 (8). (11) Plus other departures from Cork at 17:30 (7) and18:30 (9).

Cork - Killarney - Tralee - Cork   647

There is much beautiful scenery throughout this fertile area.

These trains run daily, except Sundays and holidays, unless designated otherwise.

Dep. Cork	09:15	11:25	12:15 (1)	14:45 (1)	19:15 (2)
Dep. Killarney	11:10	13:20	14:16	16:40	21:05
Arr. Tralee	11:45	13:55	14:45	17:15	22:40

• • •

Dep. Tralee	08:50 (2)	12:00	14:00 (2)	16:05	18:00 (2)
Dep. Killarney	09:25	12:35	14:35	16:40	18:35
Arr. Cork	11:20	14:30	16:30	18:30	20:30

(1) Runs Sunday only. (2) Runs daily. Second-class.

Sights in **Killarney**: It is 85 miles from Shannon Airport. See the sculpture by Seamus Murphy, called The Shy Woman of Kerry. The marvelous garden and the exhibit of early crafts and housing at Muckross House, a 19th century mansion on the outskirts of Killarney. Shop here for linens, glassware and crocheted women's clothing.

Take the 112-mile, all-day "Ring of Kerry" bus sightseeing trip, a popular excursion. You will see many lakes and mountains.

Dublin - Galway - Dublin   645

The are many beautiful lakes in this area.

All of these trains run daily except Sundays and holidays, are second-class and have light refreshments, unless designated otherwise.

Dep. Dublin (Heu.)	08:00 (1)	09:20 (2)	11:00	14:10 (3)	18:45 (4)	20:20 (6)
Arr. Galway	10:55	12:20	13:50	16:55	21:15 (5)	23:05

Sights in **Galway:** The 14th century St. Nicholas' Church. The ruins of a 13th century Franciscan friary. The 13th century town walls.

Dep. Galway	08:00 (1)	08:50 (2)	11:35 (1)	14:50 (2)	15:15	18:05 (7)
Arr. Dublin (Heu.)	10:30	11:40	14:20	17:45	18:10	21:10

(1) Restaurant car. (2) Runs Sunday only. (3) Runs daily, except holidays. No light refreshments on Sunday. (4) Runs daily, except holidays. Also has first-class coach and restaurant car Monday–Saturday. (5) Arrives 25 minutes later on Sunday. (6) Runs Sunday only. No light refreshments. (7) Runs daily, except holidays. Departs 5 minutes later on Sunday.

Dublin - Kilkenny - Dublin   642

Dep. Dublin						
(Heuston)	07:35 (1)	09:50 (2)	11:35 (3)	14:50 (2)	15:00 (1)	18:10 (4+6)
Arr. Kilkenny	09:30	11:43	13:20	16:35	16:48	20:00

• • •

Dep. Kilkenny	08:17 (4)	10:32 (5)	11:39		15:26 (2)	16:02	18:50 (2+7)
Arr. Dublin							
(Heuston)	09:50	12:15	13:25	17:20	17:50		20:35

(1) Runs daily, except Sundays and holidays. Second-class. Light refreshments. (2) Runs Sunday only. Second-class. (3) Runs daily, except Sundays and holidays. Light refreshments. (4) Runs daily. Restaurant car. (5) Runs Sunday only. Second-class. Light refreshments. (6) Plus another Dublin departure at 18:15 (5), arriving Kilkenny 20:04. (7) Plus another Kilkenny departure at 19:13, arriving Dublin 21:00.

Sights in **Kilkenny:** The formal gardens and the 150-foot-long hall at Kilkenny Castle. The 13th century Saint Canice Cathedral, one of the loveliest in Ireland from that era. The 13th century Kytler's Inn, now a restaurant. The 19th century Saint Mary's Cathedral.

Dublin - Limerick - Dublin   638

There is bus service between Limerick and Shannon Airport.

Dep. Dublin (Heuston)	09:00 (1)	17:40	18:30 (4+5)
Arr. Ballybrophy	10:15	18:50	-0- (4)
Change trains.			
Dep. Ballybrophy	10:20 (2)	18:55 (2)	-0-
Arr. Limerick	11:54	20:20	20:55

• • •

Dep. Limerick	07:00 (2+4)	08:20 (1+4)	15:45 (2)	19:00 (3+4)
Arr. Ballybrophy	-0- (4)	-0- (4)	17:05	-0- (4)
Change trains.				
Dep. Ballybrophy	-0-	-0-	17:10 (2)	-0-
Arr. Dublin (Heuston)	09:25	10:25	18:20	22:30

(1) Runs daily, except Sundays and holidays. Restaurant car. (2) Runs daily, except Sundays and holidays. Second-class. (3) Runs Friday only. Second-class. (4) Direct train. No train change in Ballybrophy. (5) Runs Sunday only. Second-class.

THE FERRY-CROSSINGS
TO FRANCE

Rosslare - LeHavre - Paris and Rosslare - Cherbourg - Paris

Operated by Irish Ferries Company. Passage only (without a seat or a berth) is free all year with a Eurailpass. The 1993 cost for "passage only" was $209 (U.S.) from July 10 to August 31 and was lower prices in other times of the year. Passage *plus* a seat was $217 (but only $10 with Eurailpass) in mid-Summer when there are many more passengers than seats on the vessel and some passengers must sit on the deck for this 21-hour trip.

Reserving and paying extra for a cabin is essential in Summer. A 6-berth cabin that was $221 per person in mid-Summer was only $13 with a Eurailpass. A 4-berth cabin with shower and private toilet at $257 per personwas only $48 with a Eurailpass.

There are also sailings to and from Cork, Ireland during June, July and August.

Days of operation and departure times vary during 5 different periods of the year. For 1994 schedules, prices and reservations, contact the North American agent: Lynott Tours Inc., 350 Fifth Avenue, New York, NY 10118. Telephone: (212) 760-0101 or (800) 221-2474.

RAIL CONNECTIONS WITH ENGLAND
See Chapter 7.

ITALY

Overview

Italian train travel belongs to several centuries at once, depending where you are and how you are traveling. Trains south of Rome can be snail-like whereas Rapidos live up to their name and the pendolinos have been the most chic trains in Europe since 1990. To accommodate curves at very high speeds, Pendolinos tilt—using the motion of a pendulum.

General Information

• Except for EuroCity trains: children under four travel free. Half-fare for children 4-11. Children 12 and over must pay full fare.

• Italy has four types of fast trains: Pendolino (first-class only), EuroCity, InterCity, and Rapido. Passengers using individual tickets (not traveling with first-class Italian passes or one of the first-class Eurailpasses) must pay a supplemental charge when riding on all Pendolinos and most of the other three. The supplement includes a seat reservation and a meal. Reservations are required on all EuroCity and most InterCity trains.

• Sleeping-car service is offered by Wagon-Lits Company in first- and second-class compartments, first- and second-class couchette. All should be reserved in advance.

• Few Italian trains offer full meal services.

• The signs you will see at railstations in Italy are:

ARRIVI	ARRIVAL
BINARIO	TRACK
CARROZZA LETTI	SLEEPING CAR
CARROZZA RISTORANTE	RESTAURANT CAR
DONNE	WOMEN
ENTRATA	ENTRANCE
ORARIO FERROVIARIO	TIMETABLE
PARTENZE	DEPARTURE
PIATTAFORMA	PLATFORM
PRENOTAZIONE POSTI	SEAT RESERVATION
SCOMPARTIMENTO PER FUMATORI	SMOKING COMPARTMENT
STAZIONE FERROVIARIO	RAILSTATION
UFFICIO BAGAGLI	BAGGAGE CHECKROOM
UFFICIO BIGLIETTO	TICKET OFFICE
UOMINI	MEN
USCITA	EXIT

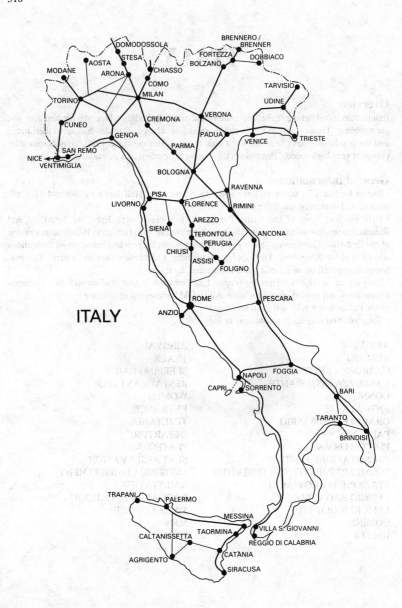

ITALY

Italian Holidays

A list of holidays is helpful because some trains will be noted later in this section as *not* running on holidays. Also, those trains which operate on holidays are filled, and it is necessary to make reservations for them long in advance.

January 1	New Year's Day		Proclamation of the Republic
January 6	Epiphany		(First Monday in June)
	Easter	August 15	Assumption Day
	Easter Monday		Victory Day (World War I)
April 25	Liberation Day		(First Monday in November)
May 1	Labor Day	December 8	Immaculate Conception
		December 25	Christmas Day
		December 26	St. Stephen's Day

Summer Time

Italy changes to Summer Time on the last Sunday of March and converts back to Standard Time on the last Sunday of September. Many Italian trains and international trains originating or terminating in Italy have different schedules during Summer Time than they do the balance of the year.

EURAILPASS BONUSES IN ITALY

A 30% reduction from the fare for the Venice–Piraeus (and v.v.) and Venice–Alexandria (and v.v.) boat trips.

The Brindisi-Patras boat trip (see schedules next page) is covered by the Eurailpasses — but only if you go on Adriatica di Navagazione Line or Hellenic Mediterranean Line. A bench seat or sitting on the deck is covered by Eurailpasses for this trip (the 1994 cost *without* Eurailpass was $108). However, pass holders are charged $14 for travel June 10 to September 30.

Other fees are charged for such special accommodations as aircraft type seats, pullman berths and cabins. There is also a port tax (10,000 Lira in 1993) that is *not* covered by Eurailpass and must be paid in Lira.

WARNING: The employees of other lines intimate that their ships honor the 2 passes and then charge fees after the boat leaves the pier.

With or without a Eurailpass, a reservation theoretically can be made on day of departure or day before departure — but it is very unlikely that space will be available (particularly during July and August) unless a reservation is made many weeks in advance of departure dates.

Those gambling on making a reservation after arriving in Brindisi can make application January 1–June 9 and October 1–December 31 only at the Adriatica di Navagazione embarkation office, located at Maritime Station, a 15-minute walk from Brindisi's Central railstation, along Corso Umberto and Corso Garibaldi. Taxis are available at the railstation.

From June 10 to September 30, those without advance reservations can apply also to any Brindisi travel agency that displays in its window the green badge "Eurail Information Euraipass."

Holders of advance reservations must go at all times directly to the Adriatica di Navagazione embarkation office to have their tickets checked, settle port taxes due and obtain the required Embarkation Ticket. That office is open 08:30–13:00 and 15:30–22:30.

Advance reservations before you start your trip can be made by contacting Extra Value Travel, 683 South Collier Boulevard, Marco Island, Florida 33937, U.S.A. Telephone: (813) 394-3384.

Passengers with advance reservation must obtain the Embarkation Ticket at least 2 hours prior to the ship's departure time. The ships reserve the right to cancel a reservation when that is not done and to give the space to a standby passenger.

The trains from northern Italy to Brindisi, timed to connect with the ferry departures, are frequently late. For that reason, it is *advisable* to arrive Brindisi the day before a ferry departure to Patras.

Brindisi - Patras - Athens   For sailing dates, see Cook's Table 1490.

Dep. Brindisi Harbor	20:00	22:30
Arr. Patras	13:00	18:00

It is a 20-minute walk from Patras' dock to its railstation. A taxi costs about $7 (U.S.)
Change to train. 980
For a view of the Corinthian Gulf and then the Corinthian Canal, sit on the left side of the train.

Dep. Patras	15:57 (1)	18:03 (1+2)	19:16
Arr. Athens	19:12	21:22	23:22

(1) Light refreshments. (2) Supplement payable.

ITALIAN TRAIN PASSES

When ordering any number of train tickets or any train pass *except Eurailpass* from the Italian State Railways, there is a $20 processing fee per order for ordinary tickets and a $10 fee per pass on all Italian train passes.

Anyone who purchases an Italian train pass may obtain a 10% discount on city sightseing and excursion tours by presenting the pass at any Compagnia Italiana Turismo (CIT) office in Florence, Milan, Naples, Rome and Venice.

Both the Italian Train Pass and Italy Flexi Railcard offer unlimited travel on all Italian trains (including InterCity and EuroCity trains), including free seat reservations (*which can be made only in Italy*) *on trains for which reservations are compulsory. If you choose to make a reservation on a train for which reservations are not compulsory, you must pay an additional reservation fee.* Sleeper and couchette services are *not* included. Both passes are available at travel agencies worldwide *outside* Italy and at all offices worldwide of CIT, including those in Italy.

Italian Railpass The 1995 prices were not available at the first printing of this book. The 1995 *first*-class prices were: $226 for 8 days, $284 for 15 days, $330 for 21 days, and $396 for 30 days. For *second*-class: $152, $190, $220, and $264. The 15, 21 and 30-day tickets can be extended to double their initial period. Half-fare for children 4–12 years old. Children under 4 travel free.

Italy Flexi Railcard The 1995 prices were not available at the first printing of this book. The 1995 *first*-class prices were: $176 for any 4 days within 9 days, $258 for any 8 days within 21 days, and $324 for any 12 days within 30 days. For *second*-class: $120, $168 and $216.

Kilometric Ticket Permits travel up to a maximum of 20 single trips totaling 3,000kms (1,875 miles) within 60 days. When used on a train that charges a supplement, the passengers using the Ticket must pay the supplement. Can be used by more than one person at a time, to a maximum of 5 persons. When a child 4–12 years old travels on this ticket, only half the mileage used is counted. Children under 4 travel free. Available before you leave home at both Italian State Railways and from travel agents worldwide. Also available in Italy at all railstations and from Italian travel agencies.

The 1996 prices were not available at the first printing of this book. The 1995 prices were: $264 for *first*-class, $156 for *second*-class.

ONE-DAY EXCURSIONS AND CITY SIGHTSEEING

Comprehensive maps which make it easy to find the worthwhile sights there can be obtained in most Italian cities in offices marked "Azienda Autonoma di Turismo" or "Ente Provinciale di Turismo," located on a principal street.

Here are 70 one-day rail trips that can be made comfortably from Agrigento, Bologna, Catania, Florence (Firenze), Genoa, Messina, Milan, Naples (Napoli), Palermo, Rome and Torino (Turin), returning to those cities in most cases before dinnertime. Notes are provided on what to see and do at each destination. The number after the name of each route is the Cook's timetable.

Bologna

See the dissection theater in the ancient medical school. The fantastic inlaid wood panels in the Chorus at San Domenico Church. (Be sure to turn on the electric lights there in order to get a good look at the marvelous woodwork.) The Church of San Petronio. The Art Gallery. Neptune's Fountain, wherePiazza Maggiore and Piazza Nettuno connect.

The 2 leaning towers in Piazza di Port Ravegnana: 165-foot tall Garisenda and the 330-foot high Asinelli. Climb the 486 steps of the Asinelli for the splendid view from the top of the tower. Visit the churches on Santo Stefano. The Municipal Archeological Museum. The Communale, Podesta, Mercanzia, Re Anzio and Bevilacqua palaces. Try the marvelous Bolognese food.

Florence (Firenze)

The 14th century Cathedral of Santa Maria del Fiore (open daily 07:00–12:00 and 14:30–18:00) is where most visitors begin sightseeing in Florence. Ascend its 292-foot high bell-tower for a great view of the city. Across from the Cathedral, see the magnificent sculptured bronze Ghiberti doors ("Gates of Paradise" was Michelangelo's description) on the octagonal Baptistry of San Giovanni (open 09:30–12:30 and 14:30–17:30).

See the 14th–19th century furniture and utensils representing domestic life in those eras, in the Davanzati Palace.

There is much more to see, in 2 different directions from the Cathedral-Baptistry complex. Facing the Baptistry, you proceed North on Via Ricasoli to visit Area #1. You go South, toward the Arno River, for the sightseeing in Area #2.

Area #1: See the Michelangelo sculptures and breathtaking marble floors, walls and crypts at the Medici Chapel. The street behind the Chapel is lined with vendors. On the other side of the street is an enormous food market where game with colorful furs and feathers make an unusual display.

An easy walk from the Chapel is the Academia (closed Monday), housing the stupendous statue of David. Nearby is the Fra Angelico Museum in the Church of San Marco, with its interesting frescoes and monk's cells.

Across the street from the Academia, you can board a city bus for the 20-minute ride uphill to the village of Fiesole, where there are Etruscan ruins, a Roman amphitheater, a 13th century Cathedral, the Convent of St. Francis, and a splendid view of Florence.

Area #2: The Piazza della Signoria and, next to it, the thousands of great art treasures in the 29 exhibit rooms of the Palazzo degli Uffizi (open Tuesday–Saturday 09:00–19:00, Sunday 09:00–13:00). Nearby is the Franciscan Church of Santa Croce, where Michelangelo, Machiavelli, Rossini and Galileo are buried. Also see the sculptures (Donatello's bronze David and the della Robbia glazed terra cottas) at the Bargello Palace and Museum, in a 13th century palace. Next, cross to the other side of the Arno River, over the Ponte Vecchio (lined with tiny jewelry shops) to visit the outstanding paintings, statues, tapestries and furniture in the 28 exhibit rooms and galleries of the Palazzo Pitti (closed Monday).

The Pitti is a complex of 5 different museums. The Palace itself contains the Palatine Gallery (noted for its Raphaels), the Modern Art Gallery, and the Silver Museum. Two other museums are located in the Boboli Gardens behind the Palace: the Costume Museum and the Porcelain Museum, both of which are open only on Tuesday, Thursday and Saturday (hours during May and June are 09:00–19:00).

The Medici Chapel, Academia, Bargello, Uffizi and Pitti are open Tuesdays–Saturdays 09:00–14:00 and Sundays and feast days from 09:00–13:00.

Genoa

Italy's largest port. See the house where Columbus is said to have been born, at Piazza Dante.

St. Lawrence Cathedral. *Do not fail* to walk down the 15th century streets near the waterfront, too narrow for a tour bus and unfortunately not seen by many visitors to Genoa. The incredible Monumental Cemetery, with its vast number of dramatic statues of many of the people buried there. The landscaped hillside with colorful plants painting a flowering tapestry of Columbus' fleet: the Nina, the Pinta and the Santa Maria.

The 16th century palaces on Via Garibaldi. The 17th century palaces on Via Balbi. The Cathedral of San Lorenzo, constructed from 1099 to 1250.

Milan

The Duomo Cathedral, holding more than 20,000 people, begun in 1386 and taking 5 centuries to complete. There are more than 3,000 statues on its exterior. Then go through the incredibly beautiful shopping arcade, the Galleria Vittorio Emanuele, to La Scala Opera House—one of the world's greatest theaters, accommodating 3,600 people, it was first constructed in 1776. Its opera museum is open Tuesdays–Saturdays 09:00–12:00 and 14:00–18:00.

Exhibited in the museum are old paintings and engravings of the opera house before its destruction by bombs in 1943 and its reconstruction in 1946, portraits of many famous singers, several of Verdi's pianos and such other Verdi memorabilia as his manuscripts and death mask.

Opposite La Scala, behind a statue of da Vinci, is the 16th century Palazzo Marino, now the City Hall. Just past the gate (Porta Nuova) at the end of Via Manzoni are the Museum of Natural History, the Zoo and the Planetarium.

See da Vinci's "Last Supper" at Santa Maria delle Grazie. It can be viewed daily 09:00–13:15 and 14:00–18:15. *Do not fail to see* the enormous and elaborate crypts at the Monumental Cemetery. Visit the Palazzo Dugnani, on Via Manin, to see the Tiepolo ceiling fresco there.

It is a short taxi ride from the Dugnani to the enormous Castello Sforzesco, which has a vast collection of paintings (including Michelangelo's last work, the Rondanini Pieta) and exhibits of harpsichords, wrought iron, tapestries and ceramics. The Castle is open daily except Monday 09:30–12:00 and 14:30–17:00.

See the collection of sculpture, Flemish and Persian tapestries, paintings, scientific instruments, glass and armor at Museo Poldi-Pezzoli, at 12 Via Manzoni, open Tuesday-Sunday 09:30–12:30 and 14:30–17:30. Many great paintings (Raphael, Tiepolo, Canaletto) are exhibited in the Accademia di Brera on Via Brera, open Tuesday–Saturday 09:00–14:00, and on Sunday 09:00–13:00.

Both the Modern Art Gallery (16 Via Palestra) and the Archaeological Museum (15 Corso Magenta) are open Wednesday–Saturday 09:30–12:30 and 14:30–17:30; on Sunday 09:30–13:00. There are marvelous paintings by Raphael, Caravaggi and Botticelli in the Ambrosian Library, open Mondays–Fridays except holidays 10:00–12:00 and 15:00–17:00 and Saturdays, Sundays and holidays 15:00–17:00.

Gourmets will want to visit the fantastic food store called Peck's, at No. 9 Via Spadari, opened in 1892 by a Czechoslovak named Frank Peck. It is the Italian equivalent of Hediard, described under "Paris" in the section of this chapter on France. What you will see at Peck's are: large wedges of parmigiano and reggiano cheese, Italian wines, roasts, loins, saddles and breasts of white veal, caviar, numerous cold seafood salads, mussels, langouste, squid, lobster, celery remoulade, pates, head cheese, scampi, sturgeon, hot vegetable dishes (baked fennel, baby zucchini, asparagus milanese), roasted quail skewered with sausages and wrapped in bacon, tripe in tomato sauce, a wide range of pasta (green ravioli al forno, tortellini, ravioli alla contadina), paella with saffron rice, white mushrooms in oil, many sausages and many fish (herring, smoked salmon, smoked eels, smoked trout).

If that is not enough, across the street from Peck's is a famous pork store, La Bottega del Maiale, with an enormous display of whole baby pigs, pork parts (loins, ears, fillets, tongue, liver) and such sausages as sopresa Calabra, salame Toscana, coppa, cacciatorini, stagionata, capocolla and finocchiona.

Next door to the pork store is Peschere Spadari, a great fish store, selling nearly everything that swims: scampi, Channel sole, mackerel, scampi, squid, mussels. A short distance down the street, at No. 1 Via Speroni, is a large cheese store.

Naples

Most museums in Naples are closed on Monday. See the view from Certosa de San Martino monastery and, inside, its National Museum. The 13th century Castel Nuovo. The National Library. The Archaeological Museum, with its great Grecian and Roman sculptures. The Capodimonte Park, Palace and Art Gallery. The Teatro San Carlo, home of Neapolitan opera. The Royal Palace and scores of other palaces. The Botanical Garden. There are good views of Naples Bay from the gardens of the Duca di Martina Museum of Ceramics at the Villa Floridiana. Splendid views of Mount Vesuvius from the quay at Santa Lucia. Nearby **Herculaneum** (now called **Ercolano**) is as interesting as Pompeii.

Rome

There is nonstop train service between Rome's da Vinci airport and the cities of Naples and Florence. Eurailpasses and Italian passes cover the train service from the airport to both the city's Ostiense and Termini railstations.

Visit St. Peter's, the most wonderful work by man in all the world. Take an elevator to the dome for views of Vatican City and Rome. Tour the Vatican to see the Sistine Chapel, Raphael Rooms, Pio-Clementino Museum, Picture Gallery, Tapestry Gallery, Map Gallery and Candelabra Gallery (all of them closed on Sunday, except the last Sunday of each month).

See Capitoline Hill. The Roman Forum. Palatine Hill. The Imperial Fora.

Marcellus Theatre. The Jewish Synagogue. The Temple of Avesta. Aventine Hill. St. Paul's Gate. The view of Rome from the Villa Borghese Park. The Protestant cemetery, with the graves of Keats and Shelley. The Colosseum. The Arch of Constantine. The Basilica of St. Paul Outside the Walls. Michelangelo's statue of Moses in the Church of St. Peter in Chains. The Pantheon. The mosaics at the Baths of Caracalla.

Castel Sant'Angelo (closed Monday). Trevi Fountain. The Zoo. The Etruscan Museum (closed Monday). The Napoleon Museum (closed Monday). The Spanish Square, Steps and Fountain. The National Modern Art Gallery (closed Monday). Diocletian's Baths.

The House of the Vestal Virgins. Marvelous views of Rome from Janiculum Hill. The Monument to Vittorio Emanuele. The Bernini sculptures in the Borghese Gallery (Villa

Borghese), open daily 09:00–13:30. The magnificent Velazquez portrait of Pope Innocent X in the Doria Gallery (Piazza del Collegio Romano), open Tuesday, Friday, Saturday and Sunday 10:00–13:00.

Displays of Etruscan art at the National Museum of Villa Giulia (Piazza di Villa Giulia), open daily except Monday 09:00–19:00, holidays 09:00–13:00. Exhibits of ancient Rome at the National Museum of Rome (in the Baths of Diocletian), open Tuesday–Saturday 09:00–14:00, Sunday 09:00–13:00. The Museum of Folklore (Piazza Sant' Egidio, in Trastevere), open Tuesday–Sunday 09:00–13:00, also Thursday evenings 17:00–19:30.

In the following timetables, where a city has more than one railstation we have designated the particular station after the name of the city (in parentheses).

Bologna - Florence - Bologna 375

Exceptional mountain scenery on this easy one-day roundtrip.

The train goes through the 11.5-mile long Apennine Tunnel, Italy's longest tunnel. Some trains stop almost midpoint in the tunnel at an underground station called **Precendenze**. Residents of a small village at the crest of the mountain, in order to return home, must climb 1,863 steps inside a diagonal shaft that was used for constructing the tunnel.

All of these trains require reservation and charge a supplement, unless designated otherwise.

| Dep. Bologna | 07:38 (1) | 08:44 (2) | 10:35 | 12:30 (4) | 16:30 (4) |
| Arr. Florence (S.M.N.) | 08:36 | 09:53 (3) | 11:44 | 13:56 | 17:27 (3) |

| Dep. Florence (S.M.N.) | 14:17 | 16:21 (4) | 18:17 | 20:17 (1) | 20:52 (3+4) |
| Arr. Bologna | 15:27 | 17:36 | 19:27 | 21:27 | 21:51 |

(1) Light refreshments. (2) "Pendolino." Supplement includes reservation fee and meal. First-class only. (3) Arrives/departs Florence's Rifredi railstation. (4) Restaurant car.

Bologna - Milan - Bologna 370

| Dep. Bologna | 07:46 | 08:16 | 08:38 | 09:16 (2) | 09:48 (1) | 10:00 |
| Arr. Milan (Cen.) | 09:50 | 09:55 (3) | 10:30 | 10:50 | 11:50 | 12:05 |

| Dep. Milan (Cen.) | 15:00 | 16:00 | 16:05 (3) | 16:35 | 17:05 | 17:50 (1+5) |
| Arr. Bologna | 16:52 | 17:42 (3) | 18:22 | 18:55 | 19:08 | 20:10 |

(1) Reservation *required*. Supplement charged. Light refreshments. (2) "Pendolino" Reservation *required*. Supplement includes reservation fee and meal. First-class only. (3) Light refreshments. (4) Reservation *required*. Supplement charged. Restaurant car. (5) Plus other departures from Milan at 17:55, 18:45, 19:40 (2), 20:00 and 22:05, arriving Bologna 20:20, 21:34, 21:16, 22:21 and 00:47.

Bologna - Parma - Bologna   374

Dep. Bologna	Frequent times from 02:04 to 22:41
Arr. Parma	50-65 minutes later

• • •

Dep. Parma	Frequent times from 06:45 to 02:55
Arr. Bologna	50-65 minutes later

Sights in **Parma:** The 19th century Teatro Reggio opera house. Nearby, the Lombardi Museum in the Palazzo di Riserva. The restored Palazzo della Pilotta, which houses the Farnese Theater, National Gallery, Palatina Library and the National Museum of Antiquities. The latter, Italy's most modern museum, has an outstanding collection of Etruscan, Roman, medieval and Renaissance works of art, including larger-than-life-size statues of members of the Julian-Claudian family (Britannicus, the 2 Drussii, Livia and Claudius) that are familiar to viewers of the "I Claudius" television program.

More than 40,000 rare books are displayed in the Library (Biblioteca). Particularly interesting are the De Rossi collection of Oriental manuscripts and the Bodoni Museum, a complete collection of all the volumes of the great 19th century typographer for whom it is named.

Visit the Cathedral to view the marvelous Assumption of the Virgin fresco by Corregio in the dome. Also the Camera di Corregio, a room near the Cathedral he frescoed in 1518. The 12th century sculptures by Benedetto Antelami, in the 5-story red marble Baptistry, one of Italy's finest buildings. See the early 19th century sculpture by Lorenzo Bartolini in the Madonna della Steccata church. Toscani's room at the Conservatory.

Bologna - Pisa - Bologna

All of the Florence–Pisa (and v.v.) trains shown here are second-class only.

375

Dep. Bologna	07:38 (1)	09:42 (2)	10:35 (2)	12:30 (2)	16:30 (2)
Arr. Florence (S.M.N.)	08:36 (3)	10:46	11:44	13:56	17:27 (3)
Change trains. 369					
Dep. Florence (S.M.N.)	09:40	11:40	12:40	13:40	14:06
Arr. Pisa	10:32	12:32	13:32	14:32	15:11

The #1 Bus takes you from the Pisa railstation to the Piazza del Duomo in 10 minutes.

• • •

Dep. Pisa	13:22	14:22	15:22	16:22	17:22
Arr. Florence (S.M.N.)	14:15	15:15	16:15	17:15	18:315
Change trains. 375					
Dep. Florence (S.M.N.)	14:17	16:21 (2)	17:15 (1)	18:17	20:17 (2)
Arr. Bologna	15:27	17:27	18:09	19:27	21:27

(1) Reservation *required*. Supplement charged. Light refreshments. (2) Reservation *required*. Supplement charged. Restaurant car. (3) Departs/arrives Firenze Rifredi.

Sights in **Pisa**: The Piazza del Duomo, with 4 major attractions. Walk up the spiral stairs of the Leaning Tower to its roof and see the view from there. A few feet from the base of the Tower is the majestic 11th century striped marble Cathedral. Key features of it are the magnificent bronze entrance doors and, inside, paintings, statues, mosaics, a fantastic pulpit, and Galileo's lamp. While watching the lamp swing, Galileo timed each arc by his pulse and observed that every swing, long or short, took the same time span. By that, he postulated "the isochronism of the pendular movement."

Next, walk the short distance from the Cathedral to the beautiful, enormous 11th century circular marble Baptistry to see its font and its 6 columns of porphyry, marble and oriental granite. Three of the columns rest on carved lions. Biblical scenes are carved on each panel.

A very short walk from the Baptistry is a large building with a cemetery in its central court. Each section of the building exhibits many frescoes. See the 50-foot by 19-foot "Triumph of Death" in the North Gallery.

Before the train from Florence reaches Pisa, it stops 2 minutes in **Campiglia Marittima**, which has a large statue of a mongrel dog at its railstation.The dog (named Lampo) appears to watch the procession of arriving and departing trains.

Lampo ("flash of lightning") liked train travel as much as we do. He learned the train schedules and took a trip every day—more than 3,000 train trips in his lifetime.

Owned by the assistant stationmaster, Lampo escorted his master's daughter to school every morning. For that reason, he made short rail trips on schooldays, longer journeys on weekends. Always, he would go only such distances and make the necessary connections so as to return home every day before dawn.

Prior to Lampo's death in 1961 (under a freight train), he had become known not only by every trainman in Italy but by the Italian public as well, through reports of his love of train travel that appeared on Italian television and in Italy's newspapers.

Local railway workers say only a person with a printed timetable could have equaled the dog's feat, when he once went past his stop on a certain trip and then managed to return home by taking a complex series of connecting trains to get back to Campiglia Marittima.

Bologna - Ravenna - Bologna   388

All of these trains are second-class.

| Dep. Bologna | 06:13 | 08:21 | 10:48 |
| Arr. Ravenna | 07:33 | 09:33 | 11:43 |

Sights in **Ravenna**: The marvelous 5th century monuments, the Mausoleum of Galla Placidia and the Orthodox Baptistry. Just behind the Mausoleum, see the mosaics at the Church of San Vitale. Great mosaics also in Sant'Appollinare Nuovo Church, where it is helpful to use binoculars or even an opera glass in order to see those mosaics that are at the top of the walls. There are more dazzling mosaics in the Archiepiscopal Chapel.

See the ivory pulpit in the Archbishop's Palace. Dante's Tomb. The Museum of Antiquities. The exhibits at the Academy of Fine Arts.

Dep. Ravenna	13:00	14:31	17:30	20:06 (1)
Arr. Bologna	14:35	15:44	18:52	21:18

(1) Runs daily, except Sundays and holidays.

Bologna - Rome   375

Dep. Bologna	05:40	07:38 (3)	08:44 (3)	10:35 (4)
Arr. Rome (Ter.)	09:30	10:15	11:55	13:45

Dep. Rome (Ter.)	14:15 (5)	16:15 (2)	18:15	19:15 (5)	19:20 (4)
Arr. Bologna	17:36	19:27	21:27	21:51	23:00

(1) Reservation *required*. Supplement charged. Light refreshments. (2) Light refreshments. (3) "Pendolino" Reservation *required*. Supplement includes reservation fee and meal. First-class only. (4) Second-class. (5) Reservation *required*. Supplement charged. Restaurant car.

Bologna - Siena - Bologna

375				373		
Dep. Bologna	06:27 (1)	08:44		Dep. Siena	15:45 (1)	15:45 (1+3)
Arr. Florence (S.M.N.)	07:53	09:53		Arr. Florence (S.M.N.)	17:13	17:30
Change trains. 373				*Change trains. 375*		
Dep. Florence (S.M.N.)	08:10 (1)	09:15 (1)		Dep. Florence (S.M.N.)	18:17 (2)	20:17 (2)
Arr. Siena	09:48	10:42		Arr. Bologna	19:08	21:27

(1) Second-class. (2) Reservation *required*. Supplement charged. Restaurant car. (3) Plus other departures from Siena at 17:40 (1), 18:38 (1) and 19:55 (1), departing Florence 20:28 (1) and 21:48, arriving Bologna 21:31 and 22:47.

Sights in Siena: The pervasive color, named for Siena, that dominates this hill town. The view of Italy's most unique square, Piazza del Campo, from the top of the Mangia Tower of the Palazzo Publico (with its marvelous 14th century murals) or from a window of the Palazzo Publico (open daily except Sunday 9:00–13:00), where records in unbelievably beautiful calligraphy going back to the 12th century are exhibited with 15th century costumes and fine frescoes. The Pisano sculpture and mosaic floors at the Cathedral, on Piazza del Duomo. The paneled Duccio Crucifixion in the Museum of the Cathedral. Climb from there to the top of Facciatone, the skeleton for a new cathedral whose construction ceased when the Black Death of 1348 ravished Siena.

Pinacoteca, the art museum, on a street that is down from the Cathedral. Fontebranda, the old fountain with 3 arches. The ancient houses along Via degli Archi, Vicolo della Fortuna, and Vicolo delle Scotto, all of these streets radiating out from the Piazza del Campo.

Bologna - Venice - Bologna   375

Dep. Bologna	06:02	07:40	08:40 (1)	11:29 (3)	11:40 (1)	
Arr. Venice (S.L.)	08:10	09:45	10:44	13:09	13:42	
			•	•	•	
Dep. Venice (S.L.)	13:20(1)	14:20 (1)	14:42 (3)	16:20	17:20	18:20 (5)
Arr. Bologna	15:23	16:33	16:23	18:27	19:23	20:22

(1) Light refreshments. (2) Reservation *required*. Supplement charged. Restaurant car. Change trains at Venice's Mestre railstation. (3) "Pendolino" Reservation *required*. Supplement includes reservation fee and meal. First-class only. (4) Reservation *required*. Supplementt charged. Restaurant car. (5) Plus other departures from Venice at 19:20, 20:20 and 20:54, arriving Bologna 21:28, 22:25 and 23:10.

Sights in **Venice**: After the obligatory gondola ride, stand at either end of Piazza San Marco and try to cope with the enormity and beauty of the most impressive square in the world. Next visit St. Mark's Cathedral, the most wonderful Byzantine structure in Europe. Next door, see the Doge's Palace. Then relax at one of the outdoor cafes on St. Mark's Square and take in the wonder of it all while waiting for the figures on the enormous 15th century clock to emerge and strike the bell.

For another view of St. Mark's Square and the entire Lagoon, go to the top of the Bell Tower. Walk through the colorful, narrow streets of shops to the 16th century Rialto Bridge and, standing there, watch the canal traffic. The Rialto is lined with stores selling jewelry, linens, hand-blown glass, clothing, gloves and fabrics. After crossing over the Bridge, walk a short distance to the extraordinary fish market, which is the most lively 07:00–11:00 and particularly on Friday.

Among the score of churches to see in Venice are: San Giuliano, Santa Maria Formosa, Santa Maria dei Miracoli, San Giovanni e Paolo, San Francesco della Vigna, San Zaccaria, Santo Stefano, Santa Maria Gloriosa dei Frari, Santa Maria del Carmine, San Sebastiano, Madonna dell'Orto and Santi Apostoli. There are also 5 synagogues here: the German (oldest), Spanish (most beautiful), Levantine, Italian and Canton.

See the Archaeological Museum (closed Monday) in the Old Library. The many beautiful palaces on the Grand Canal. The exquisite 18th century decor of the most beautiful small opera house in the world, the Gran Teatro La Fenice.

A 15-minute boat ride takes you to the **Lido**, Venice's beach resort and site of its largest gambling casino and a 14th century Jewish cemetery. It is only a 3-minute boat ride to the beautiful, white Church of Santa Maria della Salute, built on more than one million wood pilings.

It is a 15-minute boat ride to the island of **Murano** to watch glass-blowing and visit the Glassworks Museum (closed Tuesday) in Palazzo Giustiniani. Boats for Murano leave from the Fondamenta Nuove vaporetto dock. We recommend you get off the boat at the second stop, tour the Glassworks Museum, and then walk past many interesting shops to the first landing for the return ride to Venice. The Glassworks Museum displays ancient Roman work and many excellent glass pieces from the Middle Ages

To see lacemaking (tablecloths, handkerchiefs, bedspreads, dresses) and buy fine lace, take a 30-minute boat ride to **Burano**. It is only a few minutes by boat from Burano to **Torcelo**, a small island of orchards, vineyards and artichoke farms. The 11th century basilica there has splendid mosaics. Another sight on Torcello that interests some tourists is the display of the small skeleton of the martyr Santa Fosca in a glass coffin at the church there that is named for her.

Bologna - Verona - Bologna 380

Dep. Bologna	06:43	08:45	10:38 (3)	11:45	12:44
Arr. Verona	08:18	10:33	12:41	13:40	14:40

Sights in **Verona:** The large and excellently preserved first century Arena. Then take Via Mazzini (Verona's main shopping street) to Piazza della Herbe (Herb Square), where you will find a marvelous display of fruits, vegetables, live pet birds, and dead game birds. Only a few minutes walk from there, the Veronese marble lobby of the Hotel Due Torri is worth seeing.

At Piazza dei Signori are the tombs of the Della Scala Family, once rulers of Verona. La Scala Opera House in Milan is named after them. See the paintings in the Church of Sant'Anastasia. Visit the Cathedral and the Museum of Art in Castelvecchio, on Corso Cavour.

The main attraction in Verona, since Shakespeare, has always been Juliet's balcony, at Via Cappelo 17–25 (Shakespeare's "Capulet.")

Dep. Verona	12:23	13:30	15:01 (5)	15:18	15:30	17:29 (6)
Arr. Bologna	14:00	15:14	16:50	17:16	17:24	19:22

(1) Operates late May to late July and most of September. Runs Monday-Friday, except holidays. (2) Early September to late July: runs Saturday and Sunday. Late July to early September: runs daily. (3) Reservation *required*. Supplement charged. Restaurant car. (4) Reservation *required*. Supplement charged. Frist-class only. (5) Light refreshments. (6) Plus other departures from Verona at 19:30 and 21:56, arriving Bologna 21:14 and 23:42.

Florence - Arezzo - Florence 385

Dep. Florence (S.M.N.)	06:30		06:50	08:15	10:15 (2)	11:15	14:15 (2)
Arr. Arezzo		07:07	08:00	08:56	10:56	12:15	14:56

Sights in **Arezzo:** The 15th century Piero frescoes of the Legend of the True Cross that can be seen 12:00–14:30 and 19:00–21:30 in the Church of San Francesco. The carvings on the facade of the 11th century Church of Santa Maria della Pieve. Behind Pieve, the marvelous Piazza Grande, with its medieval palaces. There are many other fine palaces on Corso Italia.

The musical scale and staff of 4 lines was invented in the 10th century by Guido Monaco of Arezzo. The Piazza Guido Monaco is named for him.

See the 16th century stained glass and the great Renaissance organ in the Cathedral. Walk across the park to the enormous fortress, Medicea, built in the 16th century by the Medici family. See the collection of Etruscan and Roman artwork in the Archaeological Museum at the Convent, including the ancient Corallini vases. The remains of a Roman amphitheater can be seen in the park next to the Museum. A library and museum is maintained in the home where Petrarch was born.

The collection of ivories, goldsmith work, coins, furniture, weapons, ceramics and 13th–20th century sculptures and paintings (including Vasari's huge fresco "Feast in the House of Ahasuerus") in the Galleria e Museo Medievale e Moderno at the Bruni-Ciocchi Palace.

Other frescoes by Vasari are exhibited in the Casa del Vasari, on Via 20 Settembre.

See the 17th century frescoed dome of the Badia Church.

| Dep. Arezzo | 13:46 | 15:03 | 15:53 | 17:05 | 19:05 | 20:00 (5) | 21:05 (4) |
| Arr. Florence (S.M.N.) | 14:47 | 16:11 | 16:48 | 17:45 | 19:45 | 21:25 | 21:50 |

(1) Reservation *required*. Supplement charged. Light refreshments. (2) Reservation *required*. Supplement charged. Restaurant car. (3) Light refreshments. (4) Plus another departure from Arezzo at 22:08, arriving Florence 22:48. (5) Runs Monday-Friday except holidays.

Florence - Assisi - Florence

385			385		
Dep. Florence (S.M.N.)	06:50	10:15	Dep. Assisi	14:22	17:00
Arr. Terontola	08:27	11:20	Arr. Terontola	15:26	18:07
Change trains. 385			*Change trains.* 385		
Dep. Terontola	08:50	12:48	Dep. Terontola	16:41	18:41
Arr. Assisi	09:50	13:48	Arr. Florence (S.M.N.)	17:45	19:57

Sights in **Assisi**: St. Francis' tomb in the 13th century Basilica on the Hill of Paradise, and the many outstanding paintings there, considered to be the greatest museum of Italian Renaissance mural painting. St. Claire's Church. The medieval Castle. Piazza del Commune. The upper and lower churches at the Convent of St. Francis, with their many frescos. Prison Hermitage. The 16th century Church of Santa Maria degli Angeli. The 12th century Cathedral of St. Ruffino. The 14th century La Rocca Maggiore fortress. The Temple of Minerva.

Florence - Bologna - Florence   375

See Bologna schedules.

Florence - Livorno - Florence 369

On the departures from Livorno, there is time to taxi 10 minutes from Pisa's station to the Leaning Tower and return to the station for a later departure to Florence.

All of these trains are second-class, unless designated otherwise.

Dep. Florence (S.M.N.)	07:15	11:40	Dep. Livorno	13:05	15:05 (3)
Arr. Pisa	08:10	12:32	Arr. Pisa	13:15	15:17
Dep. Pisa	08:12	12:35	Dep. Pisa	13:17	15:19
Arr. Livorno	08:27	13:50	Arr. Florence (S.M.N.)	14:15	16:57

(1) Has a first-class coach. (2) Runs Saturdays, Sundays and holidays. (3) Plus other Livorno departures at 16:05, 18:05, 20:05, 21:05 and 21:45, departing Pisa 16:22, 18:22, 20:22, 21:22 and 22:12, arriving Florence 17:15, 19:15, 21:15, 22:20 and 23:35.

Sights in **Livorno**: The old and new forts, both from the 16th century. The marble statue of Ferdinand. Tacca's 17th century bronze statues of "The Four Moors." Villas once occupied by Shelley and Byron. Italy's Naval Academy. The paintings and the Communal Library, both in the Civic Museum.

Florence - Milan - Florence 370

Dep. Florence (S.M.N.)	06:58 (1)	07:23	08:35 (2)	09:04	10:07 (3)
Arr. Milan (Centrale)	09:55	10:30	11:50	12:15	13:10

Dep. Milan (Centrale)	15:00 (1)	16:00 (1)	17:00 (3)	17:55 (1)	20:00 (2)
Arr. Florence (S.M.N.)	17:46	18:46	19:46	21:19	22:58

(1) Reservation *required*. Supplement charged. Light refreshments. (2) "Pendolino." Reservation *required*. Supplement includes reservation fee and meal. First-class only. Departs/arrives Florence's Rifredi railstation. (3) Reservation *required*. Supplement charged. Restaurant car.

Florence - Padua - Florence 390

Dep. Florence (S.M.N.)	07:15 (1)	10:32 (2+4)	Dep. Padua	15:12 (3)	18:27 (5)
Arr. Padua	09:46	12:37	Arr. Florence (S.M.N.)	17:27 (6)	20:53

(1) Reservation *required*. Supplement charged. (2) "Pendolino." Reservation *required*. Supplement includes reservation fee and meal. First-class only. Departs from Florence's Rifredi railstation. (3) Reservation *required*. Supplement charged. Restaurant car. (4) Plus another departure from Florence at 14:17, arriving Padua at 16:46. (5) Plus another departure from Padua at 20:16, arriving Florence 22:54. (6) Arrives Florence's Rifredi station.

Sights in **Padua:** The 13th century university where Petrarch lectured and Galileo taught (on the Via 8 Febraio) has guided tours on each hour, 09:00-12:00 and 15:00-17:00. It is open daily, except Saturday afternoon and all day Sunday.

Scrovegni Chapel, noted for its Giotto frescoes, is open April-September 09:00-12:30 and 14:30-17:30. From October through March, it is open 09:00-12:30 and 13:30-16:30 daily, except Sunday afternoon, Christmas, New Year's Day and Easter.

The Church of Eremitani.

The Basilica of Sant'Antonio, a major Roman Catholic shrine with several statues by Donatello, is open daily 06:30-19:45. The Cathedral is open daily 08:00-12:00 and 16:00-19:00. The Art Gallery (Pinacoteca) is open daily except Sunday, 09:00-13:30;.

The Oratorio di San Giorgio and the Scuola di San Antonio are open daily except Monda y, Easter and Christmas. April-September: 09:00-12:00 and 14:30-18:30. October-March: closes at 18:00.

Santa Giu stina is open daily 07:30-12:00 and 15:30-19:30.

Florence - Parma - Florence 370

Dep. Florence (S.M.N.)	07:15	08:35	09:04
Arr. Bologna	08:23	09:11 (3)	10:18
Change trains.			
Dep. Bologna	08:38	09:38	10:30
Arr. Parma	09:30	10:31	11:24

Sights in **Parma:** See notes about Parma under "Bologna–Parma"

Dep. Parma	15:26 (2)	16:26	17:26 (2)	19:07 (3)
Arr. Bologna	16:18	17:27	18:22	-0- (3)
Change trains.				
Dep. Bologna	16:44 (4)	17:40 (4)	18:34	-0-
Arr. Florence (S.M.N.)	17:46	18:46	19:56	21:19

(1) "Pendolino" Reservation *required.* Supplement includes reservation fee and meal. First-class only. Departs/arrives Florence's Rifredi railstation. (2) Light refreshments. (3) Direct train. No train change in Bologna. Reservation *required.* Supplement charged. Light refreshments. (4) Reservation *required.* Supplement charged. Light refreshments.

Florence - Perugia - Florence   374

Dep. Florence (S.M.N.)	11:15	13:10 (2)	Dep. Perugia	16:34 (2)	17:30 (1+3)
Arr. Terontola *Change trains.*	-0-	-0- (2)	Arr. Terontola *Change trains.*	-0- (2)	18:11
Dep. Terontola	-0- (2)	-0-	Dep. Terontola	-0-	18:41
Arr. Perugia	13:26	15:20	Arr. Florence (S.M.N.)	18:46	19:45

(1) Second-class. (2) Direct train. No train change in Terontola. (3) Plus another Perugia departure at 19:28 (1), arriving Florence 21:50 (change trains in Terontola).

Sights in **Perugia:** Take a bus from the railstation rather than walk the steep climb uphill to the town. Visit the Municipal Palace, to see the magnificent carved and inlaid wood panels in the Library, the chapel of the Stock Exchange, and the great paintings in the National Gallery (Pinacoteca). On display to the left of the main door of the Stock Exchange chapel is the white onyx ring with which the Virgin Mary was married.

Also visit the 13th century Church of San Ercolano. Galleng Palace, with its Foreign University. The Pisano sculptures at the Fontana Maggiore in beautiful Piazza 4 Novembre. The fine collection of Tuscan paintings in the museum of the 13th century Palazzo dei Priori. Stroll along Maesta della Volte, Via dei Priori (to the Oratory of San Bernardino), Via Bagliona and Corso Vannucci, the main street.

Florence - Pisa - Florence   370

Dep Florence (S.M.N.)	Frequent times from 05:55 to 22:30
Arr. Pisa	50–60 minutes later

Sights in **Pisa**: See notes about Pisa under "Bologna–Pisa"

Dep. Pisa	Frequent times from 05:49 to 23:57
Arr. Florence (S.M.N.)	50–60 minutes later

Florence - Ravenna - Florence

375			*388*		
Dep. Flor. (S.M.N.)	07:15	09:47 (3)	Dep.Ravenna	13:00 (2)	14:31 (2+4)
Arr. Bologna	08:27	10:58	Arr. Bologna	14:35	15:44
Change trains. 388			*Change trains. 375*		
Dep. Bologna	08:21 (2)	10:48	Dep. Bologna	16:30 (3)	17:06 (3)
Arr. Ravenna	09:33	11:43	Arr. Flor. (S.M.N.)	17:27 (5)	18:16

(1) Reservation *required*. Supplement charged. Light refreshments. (2) Second-class. (3) Reservation *required*. Supplement charged. Restaurant car. (4) Plus another departure from Revenna at 17:30…departing Bologna 20:20…arriving Florence 21:19. (5) Arrives Florence's Rifredi station.

Florence - Rome - Florence   375

Dep. Florence (S.M.N.)	06:56 (1)	08:36 (3)	09:53 (3)	11:44	13:56 (4)
Arr. Rome (Ter.)	09:30	10:15	11:55	13:45	16:05

Dep. Rome (Ter.)	16:15 (2)	18:15	19:15 (3)	19:20 (4)
Arr. Florence (S.M.N.)	18:17	20:17	20:52 (3)	21:48

Dep. Rome (Ter.)	19:00 (3)	19:10 (3)	19:15	19:45 (3)	20:00 (1)
Arr. Florence (S.M.N.)	20:34 (3)	20:47 (3)	21:39	21:22 (3)	22:16

(1) Reservation *required*. Supplement charged. Light refreshments. (2) Light refreshments. (3) "Pendolino" Departs/arrives Florence's Rifredi railstaion. Reservation *required*. Supplement includes reservation fee and meal. (4) Reservation *required*. Supplement charged. Restaurant car.

Florence - Siena - Florence   373

All of these trains are second-class only.

Dep. Florence (S.M.N.)	06:35	08:10	09:15	11:45	13:25	14:13 (1)
Arr. Siena	08:02	09:48	10:42	13:25	15:05	15:33

Dep. Siena	13:35	15:45	16:33 (2)	17:37 (2)	18:38	19:55	21:15
Arr. Florence (S.M.N.)	15:05	17:30	18:20	19:22	20:00	21:24	22:33

(1) Runs daily, except Sundays and holidays. Change trains in Empoli. (2) Change trains in Empoli.

Florence - Verona - Florence

375

Dep. Florence (S.M.N.)	07:15	09:47	10:32	14:17 (2)
Arr. Bologna	08:27	10:58	11:30	15:27
Change trains. 380				
Dep. Bologna	08:45	-0-	11:45	12:44
Arr. Verona (P.N.)	10:33	12:41	13:40	14:40
Dep. Verona (P.N.)	15:18 (1)	15:30	17:29	
Arr. Bologna	-0- (1)	17:24	19:22	
Change trains. 375				
Dep. Bologna	-0-	17:46 (2)	19:44 (4)	
Arr. Florence (S.M.N.)	18:23	18:46	20:58	

(1) Reservation *required*. Supplement charged. Direct train. No train change in Bologna. Restaurant car. (2) Reservation *required*. Supplement charged. Light refreshments. (3) Late July to early September: runs daily. Early September to late July: runs Saturday and Sunday. (4) Second-class. (5) Arrives/departs Florence's Rifredi station.

Genoa - Bologna - Genoa   354

Dep. Genoa (Piazza Principe)	07:04	16:21	18:23
Arr. Bologna	10:08	19:20	21:36
Dep Bologna	07:38	13:38	17:38
Arr. Genoa (Piazza Principe)	10:35	16:48	20:35

Genoa - Cremona - Genoa

355

Dep. Genoa (P.P.)	05:48	09:13	11:54
Arr. Milan (Centrale)	07:40	10:50	13:44
Change trains. 363			
Dep. Milan (Centrale)	08:20	12:20	14:20
Arr. Cremona	09:32	13:33	15:27

Sights in **Cremona**: One of Italy's most impressive squares, the Piazza del Commune, with its octagonal Baptistry, 12th century Duomo Cathedral, Loggia de Militi, and the Gothic Torrazzo (tallest bell tower in Italy).

Cremona is where the art of violin-making reached its apex, with the works of Amati, Stradivari and Guarneri. It is possible to watch young violin makers following that great tradition by visiting La Scuola Internazionale de Liuteria, in a renovated 16th century palace.

At the City Museum every day at 11:00, an outstanding violin made by Stradivari is played by the museum curator. Located near the Liuteria are many shops which will make a special violin to order. On view at the City Hall are 2 original Stradivari, 2 Amatis and a Sacconi.

Dep. Cremona	12:37	15:42	17:58 (1)	-0-
Arr. Milan (Centrale)	13:50	16:45	19:22	-0-
Change trains. 356				
Dep. Milan (Centrale)	14:05	18:05	21:35	22:15
Arr. Genoa (P.P.)	15:49	19:55	22:47	00:04

(1) Arrived Milano Porta Garibaldi.

Genoa - Milan - Genoa   355

Genoa (P.P.)	07:13 (1)	07:54	09:13	11:13	11:54
Arr. Milan (Centrale)	08:47	09:40	10:50	13:05	13:45
Dep. Milan (Centrale.)	14:15	15:10	16:15	17:05	18:05
Arr. Genoa (P.P.)	16:10	16:45	18:00	18:44	19:55

(1) Reservation *required.* Supplement charged. Light refreshments. (2) Reservation *required.* Supplement charged. (3) Plus other departures from Milan at 19:05, 20:10 and 22:15, arriving Genoa 20:44, 21:54 and 00:05.

Genoa - Nice   90

Dep. Genoa (P.P.)	05:55	08:22 (1)	Dep. Nice (Ville)	19:10 (2)	20:29
Arr. Nice (Ville)	10:15	11:20	Arr. Genoa (P.P.)	22:10	00:17

(1) Reservation *required.* Supplement charged. Restaurant car. (2) Restaurant car.

Sights in **Nice**: See notes about Nice under France.

Genoa - Pisa - Genoa   355

There is exceptional mountain and Mediterranean coastline scenerey on this ride.

Dep. Genoa (P.P.)	06:17 (1)	12:16 (2)	13:05 (2)
Arr. Pisa (Cen.)	08:11	14:30	15:31

Sights in **Pisa:** See notes about Pisa under "Bologna–Pisa"

Dep. Pisa (Cen.)	15:00 (3)	16:02 (1)	21:27 (1)
Arr. Genoa (P.P.)	17:25	18:11	23:23

(1) Reservation *required.* Supplement charged. Light refreshments. (2) Light refreshments. (3) Operates late May to late September. Light refreshments. (4) "Pendolino" Reservation *required.* Supplement includes reservation fee and meal. First-class only.

Genoa - Rome   355

Dep. Genoa (P.Prin.)	00:40 (1)	06:17 (3)	12:16 (6)	13:05 (5)
Arr. Rome (Ter.)	06:55	10:35	18:05	19:20

(1) Carries a sleeping car. Also has couchettes. (2) "Pendolino" Reservation *required.* Supplement includes reservation fee and meal. First-class only. (3) Reservation *required.* Supplement charged. Light refreshments. (4) Change trains in Pisa. (5) Light refreshments.

Genoa - Torino - Genoa   360

Dep. Genoa (P.P.)	06:39	09:00	11:00 (1)	11:41 (2)
Arr. Torino (P.N.)	08:40	10:35	12:38	13:33

Sights in **Torino**: The marvelous facade of the Porta Nuova railstation, built in the 1860's. The beautiful Piazza Carlo Felice park, near the railstation.

Piazza San Carlo (considered second only to St. Mark's in Venice), dominated by a large statue (called "the bronze horse") of Emanuele Filiberto, hero king of the mid-16th century. In Piazza dello Statuto, the large monument dedicated to the completion of the Frejus rail tunnel between Italy and France in the late 19th century.

The imposing Palazzo Madama, with its enormous marble staircase and Royal Armory, in Piazza Castello, which is the heart of the city. (It is a museum.) The Museo Egizio in Palazzo Carignano, the third most important (after London and Cairo) Egyptian collection in the world. he university in Piazzo Carlo, where Erasmus of Rotterdam earned his doctorate in 1506. The view from the top of Mole Antonelliani, on Via Montebello. Parco del Valentino, with its splendid gardens and buildings.

The frescos in the Castello del Valentino. It is an easy walk from the Castle to Borgo

Medievale, a village built in 1884 to depict the lifestyle of this area in the year 1400. The Church of the Great Mother of God, patterned after Rome's Pantheon.

The 17th century Royal Palace. Near it, the black and white marble Chapel of the Holy Shroud in the Church of San Lorenzo. An urn holding what is believed to be the shroud placed on Jesus when he was taken from the cross is the major attraction there. The Auto Museum on Corso Unita d'Italia, with models going back to 1893.

Dep. Torino (P.N.)	12:28 (1)	13:28 (1)	14:28 (1)	16:28 (1)	17:28 (1)	18:28 (3)
Arr. Genoa (P.P.)	14:18	14:58	16:18	18:18	18:58	20:18

(1) Reservation *required*. Supplement charged. Light refreshments. (2) Operates mid-June to mid-September. (3) Plus other departures from Torino at 19:28 (2), 20:28, 22:00 and 23:05, arriving Genoa 20:58, 22:18, 23:53 and 00:56.

Milan - Bologna - Milan   370

Most of these trains charge a supplement and have either a restaurant car or buffet.

Dep. Milan (Cen.)	06:55 (1)	07:05 (2)	07:50 (2)	08:00 (4)	09:05 (2)	10:00 (2+6)
Arr. Bologna	08:31	08:57	09:28	09:44	10:52	11:42

Dep. Bologna	12:58 (2)	14:04 (2)	14:15 (2)	15:16 (2)	15:46 (2)	16:04 (4+7)
Arr. Milan (Cen.)	15:05	15:55	16:05	17:00	17:35	18:00

(1) "Pendolino" Reservation *required*. Supplement includes reservation fee and meal. First-class only. (2) Reservation *required*. Supplement charged. Restaurant car. (3) Light refreshments. (4) Reservation *required*. Supplement charged. Light refreshments. (5) Runs daily, except Sundays and holidays. Light refreshments. (6) Plus other departures from Milan at 11:05 (2) and 12:05 (2), arriving Bologna 12:56 and 13:42. (7) Plus other departures from Bologna at 17:16 (2), 18:16 (2), 19:16 (2) and 21:20 (2) arriving Milan 19:15, 20:07, 21:00 and 23:45.

Milan - Como - Milan   290

Reservation is required or advisable on most of these trains. All of them charge a supplement.

Milan (Cen.)	Frequent times from 07:25 to 21:25
Arr. Como (S.G.)	35–45 minutes later

Sights in **Como**: Take Bus #4, marked "Piazza Cavour," from the railstation to reach both the lakeshore and the cable car which ascends the 2300-foot high **Mount Brunate** in 7 minutes. At the peak, there is a wonderful view of **Lake Como** and the Alps.

Dep. Como (S.G.)	Frequent times from 06:12 to 22:56
Arr. Milan (Cen.)	35–45 minutes later

Milan - Faenza - Milan 390

Dep. Milan (Cen.)	08:05	10:05 (2)
Arr. Faenza	11:12	13:09

Sights in **Faenza**: This has been Italy's city of ceramics since 1100. See the collection in the Ceramics Museum.

Many of the factories have showrooms: Mazzotti (Via Firenze 240), Gatti (Pompignoli 4), Navarra (Via XX Septembre 42A) and Morigi (Via Barbavara 7). A wide selection of ceramics is sold at the Coopertiva Artigiana Ceramisti Faentini.

Dep. Faenza	13:43	15:53 (1)	17:43 (1)	19:43
Arr. Milan (Cen.)	16:53	19:08	20:50	23:05

(1) Light refreshments. (2) Runs Monday-Saturday only.

Milan - Cremona - Milan 363

Dep. Milan (Cen.)	08:20	12:20		Dep. Cremona	12:37	15:42	19:34
Arr. Cremona	09:29	13:02		Arr. Milan (Cen.)	13:50	16:45	20:45

Sights in **Cremona**: See "Genoa–Cremona."

Milan - Florence - Milan 375

Dep. Milan (Cen.)	06:55 (1)	07:55 (2)	08:55 (3)	09:55 (2)	10:35 (2)
Arr. Florence (S.M.N.)	09:24 (1)	10:46	11:46	12:46	13:51

Dep. Florence (S.M.N.)	14:11 (2)	15:10 (3)	16:15 (2)	17:05 (3)	18:10 (2+4)
Arr. Milan (Cen.)	17:00	18:00	19:15	20:07	21:00

(1) "Pendolino" Supplement includes reservation fee and meal. First-class only. Departs/arrives Florence's Rifredi railstation. (2) Reservation *required.* Supplement charged. Restaurant car. (3) Reservation *required.* Supplement charged. Light refreshments. (4) Plus other departures from Florence at 19:23 (2) and 21:27 (1), arriving Milan 22:40 and 23:59.

Milan - Genoa - Milan 355

See schedule under "Genoa-Milan."

Milan - Locarno - Milan

The Camedo–Locarno portion of this trip is one of the 5 most scenic rail trips in Europe, with outstanding mountain, canyon and river scenery.

365

Dep. Milan (Cen.)	07:23 (1)	08:25 (1)	09:05 (2)	10:25 (2)	12:25 (2)	14:00 (2)
Arr. Domodossola	09:00	09:58	10:33	11:58	13:58	15:31

Change trains.
Walk outside the Domodossola railstation and go to the underground track
in order to board the Centovalli narrow-gauge local railway.
272

Dep. Domodossola	09:02	10:18	11:12	12:16	15:16	16:00
Dep. Camedo	10:05	11:22	12:14	13:20	16:22	17:02
Arr. Locarno	10:40	11:55	12:48	13:55	16:55	17:37

Sights in **Locarno**: Stroll the gardens along the shore of **Lake Maggiore** and take the funicular ride to **Orselin** to see the art treasures in the Madonna del Sasso (Madonna of the Rock) church high above the village and, from there, the fine view of Locarno and Lake Maggiore. From Orselin, ride the cable-car to 4,400-foot-high **Cardada**. Then take the chair lift from **Cardada** to **Cimetta**, more than a mile high.

In nearby **Ascona,** see the frescoes depicting scenes of the Old and New Testament in the 14th century church of Santa Maria Misericordia and the adjoining cloisters of Collegio Papio.

Dep. Locarno	12:22	13:50	15:28	16:28	17:28	19:05
Dep. Camedo	12:57	14:23	16:01	17:01	18:01	19:40
Arr. Domodossola	14:00	15:30	17:00	18:00	19:00	20:46

Change trains. Walk from the underground Centovailli track, up to the main Domodossola railstation.
365

Dep. Domodossola	15:15 (2)	16:02 (4)	17:45 (3)	18:20 (2)	19:45	22:02 (2)
Arr. Milan (Cen.)	16:50	17:45	19:15	19:45	21:10	23:40

(1) Reservation *required*. Supplement charged. (2) Reservation *required*. Supplement charged. Light refreshments. (3) Reservation *required*. Supplement charged. Restaurant car. (4) Light refreshments.

CRUISING THE BORROMEAN ISLANDS ON LAKE MAGGIORE

An overnight stay in Locarno is worthwhile, in order to have a complete day for touring the **Borromean Islands** on Lake Maggiore.

Isola Madre is a fantastic garden island. See the 18th century palace and stroll through the lush gardens there (palm trees, orange and grapefruit trees, magnolias, roses, camelias, azaleas, and many gold and silver Chinese pheasants).

On **Isola Bella**, the fascinating and very unique 17th century palace where European leaders met in 1925 to sign the Locarno Pact is the attraction. You will be enchanted by the palace's 6-room Neptune Grotto, decorated with enormous plaster seashells, walls that simulate white coral, and floors that are mosaics of small pebbles. Stroll through the lavish 10-terrace garden.

The only schedule which allows visiting both islands in one day is to take the 10:30 hydrofoil (reservation required) from Locarno Pier. Arrive Isola Madre 11:45. Depart Isola Madre 13:00, arriving Isola Bella 13:20. Lunch there. Depart Isola Bella 16:35. Arrive back in Locarno at 18:30.

Milan - Lugano - Milan 290

Dep. Milan (Cen.)	07:25 (1)	08:25 (2)	09:20 (2)	10:25 (2)	11:25 (2)	12:25 (1)
Arr. Lugano	08:52	09:55	10:55	11:55	12:55	13:55

Sights in **Lugano**: Take the cable car from the railstation to Piazza Cioccaro. Walk downhill from there to the city center, Piazza Riforma. See the view of the city from the Cathedral of San Lorenzo. The collection of over 700 masterpieces (Rubens, Goya, Durer, Raphael, Tiepolo, Tintoretto, and some Americans) in the Thyssen Art Gallery of La Villa Favorita, open only from Easter to October.

Stroll the shore of lovely **Lake Lugano**.

It is 15 minutes by boat, bus, taxi or private car to **Campione** on the eastern shore of Lake Lugano, where a small gambling casino has operated since 1933. People under 18 years old are not admitted. Men must wear neckties and jackets. The Casino is open daily from 15:15 until dawn the next day.

Although Campione is located in Italian territory, no passport or any other identity document is required, and there is no customs checking.

Other sights in Campione are the frescoes in the church called Sanctuary of the Madonna dei Ghirli (Our Lady of the Swallows), first built in the Middle Ages and then rebuilt in the 18th century.

Another of the many boat trips on the lake is to the ceramic, clothing and craft shops in **Gandria**.

Dep. Lugano	14:06 (2)	15:06 (2)	16:32 (2)	17:06 (2)	18:06 (1+4)
Arr. Milan (Cen.)	15:35	16:35	17:35	18:35	19:35

(1) Reservation *required*. Supplement charged. Light refreshments. (2) Reservation *required*. Supplement charged. Restaurant car. (3) Light refreshments. (4) Plus other departures from Lugano at 19:06 (2), 20:06 (1), 21:19 (3) and 22:06 (2), arriving Milan 20:35, 21:30, 22:40 and 23:35.

Milan - Rome and Rome - Milan 370

Dep. Milan (Cen.)	06:55 (1)	07:50 (1)	09:00 (2)	10:00 (2)	10:55 (2)
Arr. Rome (Ter.)	11:05	12:48	14:00	15:05	16:15 (10)

Dep. Milan (Cen.)	12:55 (2)	14:00 (4)	15:00 (4)	16:00 (4)	17:00 (2+8)
Arr. Rome (Ter.)	17:50	18:50	19:52 (3)	20:50	21:50

●   ●   ●

Dep. Rome (Ter.)	06:55 (1)	08:05 (2)	09:05 (4)	11:05 (2)	12:05 (2)
Arr. Milan (Cen.)	10:50	13:10	14:32	16:05	17:00

Dep. Rome (Ter.)	13:05 (4)	14:05 (2)	15:05 (4)	16:05 (2)	17:05 (2+9)
Arr Milan (Cen.)	18:00	19:15	20:07	21:00	22:40

(1) "Pendolino." Reservation *required*. Supplement includes reservation fee and meal. First-class only. (2) Reservation *required*. Supplement charged. Restaurant car. (3) Depart/Arrive Rome's Tiburtina railstation. (4) Reservation *required*. Supplement charged. Light refreshments. (5) Has couchettes. (6) Carries a sleeping car. Also has couchettes. Coach is second-class. (7) Operates early September to late July. Carries only sleeping cars. (8) Plus other Milan departures at 17:50 (4), 19:30 (1), 19:40 (1), 22:15 (5), 22:55 (6) and 00:15. (9) Plus other Rome departures at 19:45 (1), 22:30 (5) and 22:50 (5). (10) Runs Sunday only.

Milan - Torino - Milan 350

Dep. Milan (Cen.)	07:10 (1)	08:20 (2)	09:10 (1)	11:20 (1)	12:20 (2)
Arr. Torino (P.N.)	08:45	09:58	10:55	13:13	13:58

Sights in **Torino**: See notes under "Genoa–Torino"

Dep. Torino (P.N.)	13:08 (1)	13:50 (2)	15:08 (1)	15:50	16:53 (2+5)
Arr. Milan (Cen.)	14:45	15:40	16:40	17:40	18:40

(1) Reservation *required*. Supplement charged. Light refreshments. (2) Light refreshments. (3) Depart/arrive Milan's Porta Garibaldi railstation. (4) Reservation *required*. Supplement charged. (5) Plus other Torino departures at 17:50, 19:08 (4), 19:50 (2), 21:32 (1), 21:50 and 22:50, arriving Milan 19:40, 20:50, 21:40, 23:05, 23:45 and 00:40.

Milan - Venice - Milan 350

Dep. Milan (Cen.)	06:10	07:05 (1)	08:10	11:05 (1)	11:10 (3)	12:10
Arr. Venice (S.L.)	09:16	09:52	11:18	13:59	14:25	15:25

Sights in **Venice**: See notes under "Bologna–Venice"

Dep. Venice (S.L.)	Frequent times from 05:10 to 00:05
Arr. Milan (Cen.)	3 hours later

(1) Reservation *required*. Supplement charged. Light refreshments. (2) Departs from Milan's Porta Garibaldi station. (3) Light refreshments.

Milan - Verona - Milan 350

Dep. Milan (Cen.)	06:10	07:00 (1)	08:10	09:05 (2)	11:05 (2)	12:10 (3)
Arr. Verona (P.N.)	07:44	08:26	09:44	10:27	12:27	13:53

Sights in **Verona**: See notes about Verona under "Bologna–Verona"

Dep. Verona (P.M.)	Frequent times from 05:35 to 22:14
Arr. Milan (Cen.)	1½ hours later

(1) Reservation *required*. Supplement charged. Restaurant car. (2) Light refreshments. (3) Restaurant car.

Naples - Bari - Naples 400

Dep. Naples (P. Garibaldi)	07:33	Dep. Bari	17:06
Arr. Bari	12:00	Arr. Naples (P. Garibaldi)	21:20

Naples - Pompeii - Naples 392

The standard-gauge trains that depart from Naples' Centrale railstation, (shown below) *are* covered by Eurailpass.

The narrow-gauge trains that leave from Naples' F.S. railstation are operated by Circumvesuviana Railway (Table 401) and are *not* covered by Eurailpass.

Salerno is as convenient a base for visiting Pompeii as Naples is.

Dep. Naples (Cen.)	07:10	08:05	11:41	13:10	14:10	15:10
Arr. Pompeii	25 minutes later					

Sights in **Pompeii:** See where 20,000 people were living and how they lived 1900 years ago when this city was buried within a few minutes under a volcanic rain of ashes from nearby (still active) Vesuvius, when it was young and strong.

Dep. Pompeii	11:19	14:39	15:42	17:22	20:19	22:00
Arr. Naples (Cen.)	25 minutes later					

Naples - Rome - Naples 405

Dep. Naples (Cen.)	06:47	07:05	07:47 (1)	08:35	08:57
Dep. Naples (P.G.)	-0-	-0-	-0-	-0-	-0-
Dep. Naples (Mer.)	-0-	-0-	07:50 (1)	-0-	-0-
Dep. Naples (C. Fl.)	-0-	-0-	07:54	-0-	-0-
Arr. Rome (Ter.)	09:10	09:20	09:50	10:45	10:50

Dep. Rome (Ter.)	13:20 (2)	14:00 (3)	15:15	16:10 (4)	17:10 (1+5)
Arr. Naples (C. Fl.)	15:18	-0-	-0-	-0-	-0-
Arr. Naples (Mer.)	15:24	-0-	-0-	-0-	17:42
Arr. Naples (P.G.)	-0-	-0-	-0-	-0-	17:53
Arr. Naples (Cen.)	15:53	16:18 (6)	17:26	18:08 (6)	19:00

(1) Reservation *required.* Supplement charged. Light refreshments. (2) Reservation *required.* Supplement charged. Light refreshments. First-class only. (3) Light refreshments. (4) Runs daily, except Sundays and holidays. (5) Plus other departures from Rome Termini at frequent times from 16:20 to 21:20. (6) Arrives Napoli Piazza Garibaldi.

Rome - Anzio - Rome 393

All of these trains are second-class only.

Dep. Rome (Ter.)	07:55	09:55	11:35	12:55	13:50	14:45	15:35 (1+2)
Arr. Anzio	66 minutes later						

Sights in **Anzio:** Has been a beach resort since ancient times. Many Americans visit the nearby military cemeteries, holding those killed in the January 22, 1944 Allied invasion.

Dep. Anzio	13:14	14:12 (1)	15:16	16:08	18:14	19:18	21:59
Arr. Rome (Ter.)	66 minutes later						

(1) Runs daily, except Sundays and holidays. (2) Plus other departures from Rome at 16:45, 17:45, 18:55, 20:15 and 22:00.

Rome - Assisi - Rome   385

Dep. Rome (Ter.)	07:00 (1)	07:30 (3)	10:15 (1)
Arr. Foligno	08:42	09:21	11:57
Change trains			
Dep. Foligno	08:45 (2)	09:35 (2)	12:02
Arr. Assisi	08:55	09:52	12:11

Sights in **Assisi**: See notes under "Florence-Assisi"

Dep. Assisi	11:51 (2)	14:44 (2)	17:41	18:51 (2)	20:38
Arr. Foligno	12:10	15:02	-0-	19:05	20:50
Change trains					
Dep. Foligno	12:32 (3)	15:58 (1)	17:56 (4)	19:38	21:17 (1)
Arr. Rome (Ter.)	14:30	17:45	19:40	21:40	23:10

(1) Reservation *required*. Supplement charged. Light refreshments. (2) Second-class. (3) Light refreshments. (4) Reservation *required*. Supplement charged. (5) Reservation *required*. Direct train.

Rome - Florence - Rome   375

Dep. Rome (Termini)	07:45 (1)	08:55 (1)	12:15 (3)	14:15 (3)
Arr. Florence (S.M.N.)	09:47 (2)	10:32 (2)	14:17	16:21 (2)
Dep. Florence (S.M.N.)	11:44 (3)	13:56 (3)	17:27 (1)	18:16 (3)
Arr. Rome (Termini)	13:45	16:05	19:05 (2)	20:20

(1) "Pendolino" Reservation *required*. Supplement includes reservation fee and meal. First-class only. (2) Arrives/Departs Florence's Rifredi railstation. (3) Reservation *required*. Supplement charged. Restaurant car. (4) Reservation *required*. Supplement charged. Light refreshments. (5) Operates late August to late July. Runs daily, except Saturday.

Rome - Genoa   355

Dep. Rome (Ter.)	-0-	-0-	-0-	-0-	07:20 (4)
Dep. Rome (Ost.)	00:20 (1)	01:04	03:23 (2)	05:05 (3)	07:30
Arr. Genoa (Brig.)	05:44	06:13	08:46	10:50	12:37
Arr. Genoa (P.Prin.)	05:52	06:23	08:56	10:58	12:45

Dep. Rome (Ter.)	-0-	12:25 (4)	12:40 (5)	14:50 (4)	-0- (7)
Dep. Rome (Ost.)	08:50 (4)	12:35	-0-	15:00	16:13 (5)
Arr. Genoa (Brig.)	14:02	17:37	18:18	20:00	21:36
Arr. Genoa (P.Prin.)	14:10	17:45	18:26	20:08	21:46

(1) Carries a sleeping car. Also has couchettes. (2) Has couchettes. (3) Operates mid-June to mid-September. Has couchettes. (4) Reservation *required*. Supplement charged. Light refreshments. (5) Light refreshments. (6) "Pendolino" Reservation *required*. Supplement includes reservation fee and meal. (7) Plus other departures from Rome (Termini) at 16:30 (4), 19:00 (6), 23:15 (1) and 23:30 (1), arriving Genoa (P. Principe) 21:54, 23:16, 04:50 and 05:35.

Rome - Naples - Rome   394

Dep. Rome (Ter.)	07:00 (1)	07:20 (2)	08:00 (3)	09:10 (2)	10:30 (4)
Arr. Naples (Mer.)	08:55	-0-	09:53	-0-	-0-
Arr. Naples (P.G.)	09:07	-0-	10:06	-0-	-0-
Arr. Naples (Cen.)	-0-	10:00	-0-	11:29	12:25

Dep. Naples (Cen.)	13:00 (3)	13:52 (2)	14:15 (2)	15:15 (7)	16:00(8+9)
Arr. Rome (Ter.)	15:05 (5)	16:03 (6)	16:55	18:00	17:40

(1) Runs daily, except Sundays and holidays. Reservation *required*. Supplement charged. (2) Light refreshments. (3) Reservation *required*. Supplement charged. Light refreshments. (4) Runs daily, except Sundays and holidays. Reservation *required*. Supplement charged. Light refreshments. (5) Arrives at Rome's Tiburtina railstation. (6) Arrives at Rome's Ostiense railstation. (7) Departs from Naples' Piazza Garibaldi railstation. (8) Departs from Naples' Mergelina railstation. First-class only. Light refreshments. (9) Plus other departures from Naples' Centrale at 16:37 (3+7), 17:15, 17:58 (2), 18:42 (3+7), 19:10, 19:20, 19:50, 20:04 (3), 20:23 and 21:28, arriving Rome's Termini 18:40, 19:55, 20:15, 20:50, 21:41 (5), 22:10, 22:25, 22:00, 23:00 and 00:04 (6).

Rome - Pisa - Rome   360

Dep. Rome (Ter.)	06:30	07:40 (2)	10:00 (3)	10:30
Arr. Pisa	10:25 (1)	10:37 (1)	12:53 (1)	14:26 (1)

Sights in **Pisa:** See notes about Pisa under "Bologna–Pisa"

Dep. Pisa	13:04 (2)	13:45	14:35 (5)	15:04	15:31	17:45 (2+7)
Arr. Rome (Ter.)	16:20	17:40	18:05	18:20 (3)	19:20 (5)	21:10 (8)

(1) The Leaning Tower is only 10 minutes by bus or taxi from the railstation. (2) Reservation *required*. Supplement charged. Light refreshments. (3) Reservation *required*. Supplement charged. Light refreshments. (4) Operates late May to late September. Light refreshments. (5) Light refreshments. (6) Arrives at Rome's Tiburtina railstation. (7) Plus another departure from Pisa at 19:45 (2), arriving Rome 23:40. (8) Arrives Rome's Ostiense station.

Rome - Pompeii - Rome   394 + 392

Trains departing Rome's Termini railstation at 07:00, 08:00, 08:55 and 09:10 arrive 2 hours later at Naples' Centrale or Piazza Garibaldi stations. Garibaldi is next to Centrale. A travel-ator provides transportation from Centrale to the F.S. station, from which it is a short walk to the Circumvesuviana station.

The ride from Circumvesuviana station to Pompeii is only 30 minutes, arriving there about 4 hours after having departed Rome.

Departures from Pompeii are at frequent times from noon to aproximately 20:00, arriving Rome 4–5 hours later.

Sights in **Pompeii**: See notes under "Naples–Pompeii"

Rome - Spoleto - Rome   385

Dep. Rome (Ter.)	07:00 (1)	07:30 (2)	10:15 (1)
Arr. Spoleto	08:19	08:58	11:24

Sights in **Spoleto:** The tourist office in the Piazza della Liberta has many brochures, including a town map and offers 3 half-day walking tours.

Dep. Spoleto	12:52 (2)	15:01 (2)	16:20 (1)	18:14 (1)	20:01	21:40 (1)
Arr. Rome ("Ter.)	14:30	16:40	17:45	19:38	21:40	23:10

(1) Reservation *required.* Supplement charged. Light refreshments. (2) Light refreshments.

Rome - Florence - Venice   390

Dep. Rome (Ter.)	07:45	08:55 (1)	-0-	12:15 (3)
Dep. Florence (S.M.N.)	09:47	10:32 (2)	11:30	14:17
Arr. Venice (S. Lucia)	-0-	13:09	14:40	17:15

Dep. Rome (Ter.)	14:15 (4)	16:15 (3)	18:15 (3)	19:15 (1)	19:20 (9)
Dep. Florence (S.M.N.)	16:21	18:20 (6)	20:17	20:52 (8)	21:48
Arr. Venice (S. Lucia)	19:45	21:40	23:15	23:38	-0-

(1) "Pendolino" Reservation *required.* Supplement includes reservation fee and meal. First-class only. (2) Departs from Florence's Rifredi railstation. (3) Reservation *required.* Supplement charged. (4) Reservation *required.* Supplement charged. First-class only. Change trains in Venice's Mestre railstation. (5) Departs from Rome's Ostiense railstation. Reservation *required.* Supplement charged. (6) Change trains in Venice's Mestre railstation (arr. 21:04-dep. 21:31). (7) Reservation *required.* Supplement charged. Restaurant car. (8) Arrives at Florence's Rifredi railstation. (9) Carries a sleeping car. Also has couchettes.

ROUTES TO THE TOE OF ITALY

Here is the rail route to southern Italy: along the Adriatic Sea from Pescara to Bari and the Ionian Sea from Taranto to Reggio di Calabria…and also north from Reggio di Calabria to Pescara.

See following page for the route to southern Italy along the Tyrrhenian seacoast from Rome to Naples and on to Reggio di Calabria…and north from Reggio to Rome.

Milan - Bologna - Pescara - Foggia - Barletta - Bari - Brindisi - Taranto - Catanzaro - Reggio di Calabria

This trip offers beautiful coastal scenery along both the Adriatic Sea (Pescara–Bari) and the Mediterranean (Taranto–Reggio di Calabria).

390

Dep. Milan (Cen.)	07:05 (1)	11:05 (1)	13:05 (1)		19:50 (10)	22:00 (3+9)
Dep. Bologna	09:01	13:00	14:59		22:11	00:15
Dep. Pescara	12:26	16:35	16:28		02:28	03:55
Dep. Foggia	14:28	18:32	20:27		04:30	06:13
Dep. Barletta	15:04	-0-	21:00		05:09	06:53
Arr. Bari	15:39	19:40	22:34		06:04	07:33
Dep. Bari	15:59	20:02	-0-		06:25	07:53
Arr. Brindisi	17:10	21:13	-0-		08:08	09:48

Change trains. 403

Dep. Brindisi	17:27(4)	21:29 (4)	-0-	-0-	08:28 (4)	10:29 (5)
Arr. Taranto	19:08	23:14	22:45	-0-	10:13	12:10

Change trains. 398

Dep. Taranto	-0-	-0-	23:05 (6)	09:59	-0-	14:08
Arr. Catanzaro	-0-	-0-	03:30	13:29	-0-	18:04
Arr. Reggio	-0-	-0-	06:14	15:41	-0-	20:13

(1) Reservation *required*. Supplement charged. Restaurant car. (2) Reservation *required*. Supplement charged. Light refreshments. (3) Train has only sleeping cars and couchettes. No coach cars. (4) Second-class. (5) Runs daily, except Sundays and holidays. Second-class. (6) Carries a sleeping car. (7) Carries a sleeping car. Also has couchettes. (8) Has couchettes. (9) Plus other departures from Milan at 00:05 (8), terminating in Brindisi at 11:42. (10) Only takes passengers for Rimini or beyond.

Sights in **Bari**: Much wine, olive oil and almonds in this area. Bari is actually a complex of 3 different cities. The "old town" is a peninsula which was the ancient port, rivaling Venice 900 years ago. Both the 11th century St. Nicola Basilica and the 12th century Romanesque Cathedral are located there.

"New Bari," built in the 19th century, is where the Archaeological Museum, the Picture Gallery, concert halls and fine restaurants are located. Industrial Bari encircles the other 2 areas (factories, oil refineries, low-income apartments).

Don't fail to visit the rebuilt Norman Castle.

Sights in **Barletta**: The 13th century S. Sepolcro Church. The Norman castle. The 12th century Gothic Cathedral.

Sights in **Brindisi:** Many Crusaders set out from here for Jerusalem. See the Roman column that marks the end of the Appian Way. The Civic Museum in the 11th century circular S. Giovanni al Sepolcro Church. Frederick II's 13th century castle. The rebuilt 11th century Cathedral.

Sights in **Catanzaro**: The Baroque S. Domenico Church. The paintings in the Museum.

Sights in **Foggia**: Much wool has been marketed here for centuries. See the ancient records of sheep tax at the Library. The city has an Art Gallery, a Museum and a Cathedral.

Sights in **Pescara**: A nice beach resort on the Adriatic coast.

Sights in **Reggio di Calabria**: A very popular tourist resort. Founded by the Greeks in 720 B.C. See the fine archaeological collection in the Museo Nazionale della Magna Grecia. The 15th century Aragonese Castle. The reconstructed Romanesque-Byzantine Cathedral. There are many Greek and Roman ruins in this area.

Sights in **Taranto**: A swing bridge connects the "old" city (on an island) with the new Taranto on the mainland. See the 15th century Aragonese castle. The 14th century S. Domenico Maggiore Church. The exhibit of Greek vases and statues in the Museo Nazionale. The early 19th century Arsenal. The 11th century Cathedral.

The Northbound Trip
398

Dep. Reggio	07:00 (1)	-0-	-0-	-0-	15:24 (1)	23:15
Dep. Catanzaro	09:13	-0-	-0-	-0-	17:33	01:55
Arr. Taranto	12:53 (1)	-0-	-0-	-0-	21:05	06:39
Change trains. 403						
Dep. Taranto	13:29	06:13 (4)	06:53 (4)	11:44 (4)		
Arr. Brindisi	15:00	08:00	08:42	13:30		
Change trains. 390						
Dep. Brindisi	13:13 (3)	16:57	20:02 (5)	21:52		
Arr. Bari	14:29	19:00	21:41	23:01		
Dep. Bari	14:48 (3)	19:49	21:57	23:20 (6)		
Dep. Barletta	15:19	20:23	22:30	-0-		
Arr. Foggia	15:57	21:06	23:13	00:31		
Arr. Pescara	17:44	23:24	01:26	02:38		
Arr. Bologna	21:16	03:30	05:23	06:38		
Arr. Milan (Cen.)	23:15	06:05	08:40	09:50		

(1) Reservation *required*. Supplement charged. Direct train to Bari. No train change in Taranto. Does not call at Brandisi. (2) Change trains in Bari. (3) Reservation *required*. Supplement charged. (4) Runs daily, except Sundays and holdays. Second-class. (5) Train has only sleeping cars and couchettes. No coach cars. (6) Carries a sleeping car. Also has couchettes. (7) Has couchettes. Light refreshments.

Rome - Naples - Villa San Giovanni - Reggio di Calabria and v.v. 400

There is great Tyrrhenian coastal scenery between Rome and Reggio.

Dep. Rome (Ter.)	-0-	-0-	08:10 (4)	12:10 (4)
Dep. Rome (Tib.)	03:30	04:24 (2+3)	-0-	-0-
Dep. Naples (Cen.)	05:36 (1)	06:46 (1)	10:10	13:42
Dep. Salerno	06:35	07:42	10:53	14:20
Arr. V.S. Giovanni	10:25	12:12	14:30	17:51
Arr. Reggio di Cal.	10:55	12:30	14:58	18:35
Dep. Rome (Ter.)	14:00 (4)	16:10 (4)	22:00	-0- (12)
Dep. Rome (Tib.)	-0-	-0-	-0-	22:30
Dep. Naples (Cen.)	16:05 (5)	17:57 (5)	00:57	00:46 (11)
Dep. Salerno	16:49	18:08	-0-	01:45
Arr. V.S. Giovanni	20:23	22:15	05:56	05:51
Arr. Reggio di Cal.	20:38	22:50	06:15	06:20
Dep. Rome (Ter.)	22:20 (3)	23:20 (7)		
Dep. Rome (Tib.)	-0-	-0-		
Dep. Naples (Cen.)	00:57	-0-		
Dep. Salerno	01:35	02:33		
Arr. V.S. Giovanni	05:20 (8)	08:31		
Arr. Reggio di Cal.	06:28	02:45		

The Northbound Return Trip

Dep. Reggio di Cal.	07:15 (4)	12:05	
Dep. V.S. Giovanni	07:49	12:27 (4)	
Dep. Salerno	11:20	15:55	
Arr. Naples (Cen.)	11:49 (5)	16:33	
Arr. Rome (Tib.)	-0-	-0-	
Arr. Rome (Ter.)	13:50	18:40	

Dep. Reggio di Cal.	14:15 (4)	15:05 (4)	17:20
Dep. V.S. Giovanni	14:24	15:40	17:40
Dep. Salerno	18:02	19:14	21:32
Arr. Naples (Cen.)	18:38 (5)	19:52	22:56 (11)
Arr. Rome (Tib.)	-0-	-0-	01:04
Arr. Rome (Ter.)	20:50	22:00	-0- (2)

Dep. Reggio di Cal.	19:30 (7)	20:27 (7)	20:42 (10)
Dep. V.S. Giovanni	19:58	21:04	21:30
Dep. Salerno	01:06	03:00	01:18
Arr. Naples (Cen.)	-0-	03:42	01:58
Arr. Rome (Tib.)	03:34	-0-	05:40
Arr. Rome (Ter.)	-0-	06:20	-0-

(1) Departs/Arrives Naples' Campi Flegrei railstation. (3) Has couchettes. (4) Reservation *required*. Supplement charged. Light refreshments. (5) Departs/Arrives Naple's Piazza Garibaldi railstation. (6) "Pendolino" Reservation *required*. Supplement includes reservation fee and meal. (7) Carries first and second-class sleeping cars. Also has first and second-class couchettes. (8) Change trains in Villa San Giovanni. (9) Second-class. (10) Carries only coach cars. (11) Departs Napoli Campi Flegrei. (12) Runs Friday, Saturday only.

THE RAIL TRIP TO SICILY

Milan, Florence, Rome and Naples to Messina and Palermo or Messina - Taormina - Catania - Siracusa   400

This trip includes a 35-minute ride on the ferry boat that runs between Villa S. Giovanni and Messina (Maritima).

There is beautiful seacoast scenery on this journey's Messina–Siracusa portion.

Dep. Milan (Cen.)	19:55 (1)	21:00 (2)	-0-	-0-	-0-
Dep. Florence (Campo)	23:34	00:34	-0-	-0-	-0-
Dep. Rome (Ter.)	-0-	-0-	04:29(3)	04:29 (3)	08:10 (4)
Dep. Rome (Tibur.)	-0-	03:30	-0-	-0-	-0-
Dep. Naples (Cen.)	-0-	05:46	06:56	06:56	-0-
Dep. Naples (C. Fleg.)	04:30	-0-	-0-	-0-	10:10 (5)
Arr. Messina (Cen.)	11:15	12:20	13:15	13:15	16:25
Arr. Palermo	-0-	16:55	-0-	17:38	-0-
Arr. Taormina	12:16	-0-	14:09	-0-	17:25
Arr. Catania	13:16	-0-	15:03	-0-	18:15
Arr. Siracusa	15:13	-0-	16:45	-0-	18:50
Dep. Milan (Cen.)	-0-	-0-	-0-	-0-	-0-
Dep. Florence (Campo)	-0-	-0-	-0-	-0-	-0-
Dep. Rome (Ter.)	08:10 (4)	12:10 (4)	12:10 (4)	19:35 (6)	20:40 (6)
Dep. Rome (Tibur.)	-0-	-0-	-0-	-0-	-0-
Dep. Naples (Cen.)	10:10 (5)	13:42	13:42	21:54	22:52
Dep. Naples (C. Fleg.)	-0-	-0-	-0-	-0-	-0-
Arr. Messina (Cen.)	16:25	19:50	19:50	03:55	05:20
Arr. Palermo	19:55	-0-	23:30	07:50	-0-
Arr. Taormina	-0-	20:31	-0-	-0-	06:27
Arr. Catania	-0-	21:30	-0-	-0-	07:25
Arr. Siracusa	-0-	22:50	-0-	-0-	09:05
Dep. Milan (Cen.)	15:59 (7)	16:35 (6)	-0-	-0-	22:46
Dep. Florence (Campo)	19:28	20:05	-0-	-0-	22:51 (6)
Dep. Rome (Ter.)	-0-	-0-	22:20 (8)	22:20 (9)	-0-
Dep. Rome (Tibur.)	21:53	23:23	-0-	-0-	-0-
Dep. Naples (Cen.)	-0-	-0-	00:57	00:57	-0-
Dep. Naples (C. Fleg.)	00:05	-0-	-0-	-0-	-0-
Arr. Messina (Cen.)	06:40	08:00	08:30	07:05	-0-
Arr. Palermo	10:30	-0-	-0-	-0-	-0-
Arr. Taormina	-0-	07:37	-0-	08:13	-0-
Arr. Catania	-0-	08:28	-0-	09:04	-0-
Arr. Siracusa	-0-	11:45	-0-	10:35	14:410

The Northbound Trip

Dep. Siracusa	08:15 (4)	-0-	-0-	10:50	12:30 (2)
Dep. Catania	09:25	-0-	-0-	12:00	14:05
Dep. Taormina	10:02	-0-	-0-	12:46	14:49
Dep. Palermo	-0-	08:00 (4)	10:35 (4)	-0-	-0-
Dep. Messina (Cen.)	11:05	10:40	13:40	13:50	15:55
Arr. Naples (C. Fleg.)	-0-	-0-	-0-	-0-	-0-
Arr. Naples (Cen.)	16:45	16:33	19:52	19:52	-0-
Arr. Rome (Tibur.)	-0-	-0-	-0-	-0-	01:04
Arr. Rome (Ter.)	18:50	18:40	22:00	22:00	-0-
Arr. Florence (Campo)	-0-	-0-	-0-	-0-	-0-
Arr. Milan (Cen.)	-0-	-0-	-0-	-0-	-0-

Dep. Siracusa	-0-	-0-	15:15 (6)	-0-
Dep. Catania	-0-	-0-	16:50	-0-
Dep. Taormina	-0-	-0-	17:31	-0-
Dep. Palermo	12:00 (2)	13:30 (6)	-0-	15:40 (6)
Dep. Messina (Mari.)	15:55	16:45	18:30	19:05
Arr. Naples (C. Fleg.)	-0-	-0-	-0-	-0-
Arr. Naples (Cen.)	-0-	-0-	-0-	-0-
Arr. Rome (Tibur.)	01:04	-0-	03:31	03:53
Arr. Rome (Ter.)	-0-	-0-	-0-	-0-
Arr. Florence (Campo)	-0-	-0-	05:42	05:59
Arr. Milan (Cen.)	-0-	-0-	09:05	09:45

Dep. Siracusa	-0-	18:10 (9)
Dep. Catania	-0-	19:40
Dep. Taormina	-0-	20:37
Dep. Palermo	16:30 (10)	-0-
Dep. Messina (Mari.)	20:20	21:45
Arr. Naples (C. Fleg.)	-0-	-0-
Arr. Naples (Cen.)	02:28	-0-
Arr. Rome (Tibur.)	04:42	-0-
Arr. Rome (Ter.)	-0-	-0-
Arr. Florence (Campo)	07:22	08:55 (12)
Arr. Milan (Cen.)	11:20	12:15

(1) Operates late July to early September. (2) Carries only coach cars. (3) Departs/Arrives Rome's Ostiense railstation. Carries only coach cars. (4) Reservation *required*. Supplement charged. Light refreshments. (5) Departs/Arrives Naples' Piazza Garibaldi railstation. (6) Train has only sleeping cars and couchettes. (7) Carries first and second-class sleeping cars. Also has first and second-class couchettes. Coach cars are second-class. (8) Carries a sleeping car. (9) Has couchettes. (10) Carries a sleeping car. Also has couchettes. (11) Arrives at Rome's Ostiense railstation. (12) Arrives at Florence's S.M.N. railstation.

Sights in **Messina**: The Cathedral and the Annunciata dei Catalani Church, both rebuilt in the 12th century by Norman occupiers. The beautiful astronomical clock in the modern Bell Tower, next to the Cathedral. The art in the Museo Nazionale. The Botanical Gardens.

Sights in **Catania**: Founded 729 B.C. by Greek settlers. Now a very busy seaport and a popular Winter beach resort. Whatever could happen to a city happened here in the 16th and 17th centuries: famines, civil wars, epidemics, pirate raids, earthquakes, and the eruption of Mt. Etna in 1693, after which Catania was almost completely rebuilt. The dark gray color of the city results from the use of volcanic matter in constructing buildings.

See the Greek and Roman theaters, aqueducts and baths. The excellent collection of art and archaeological relics in the Civic Museum of the 13th century Castello Ursino. The tomb of the composer Vincenzo Bellini in the rebuilt 11th century Cathedral, also containing relics of St. Agatha. Sicily's largest church, San Nicolo. Next to it, the Benedictine San Nicolo Monastery, started in the 14th century.

The medieval manuscripts in the library of the University. The royal chapel, Collegiata. The 18th century palaces circling the Piazza del Duomo, with its Elephan Fountain. The museum at the birthplace of Bellini. The Astronomical Observatory.

Sights in **Siracusa**: Settled by Greeks in 734 B.C., 5 years after the founding of nearby Catania. An earthquake that destroyed much of Catania leveled Siracusa in 1693, after which Siracusa was rebuilt.

A comprehensive tour of Siracusa starts by visiting on the hill of Neapolis the Roman Amphitheater (which held 15,000 people attending gladiator fights), constructed during the reign of Augustus, before the birth of Christ. This structure was severely stripped in 1526 for the building of the city's defensive walls.

Above the Amphitheater is the 600-foot-long altar of Hieron II, where 450 oxen were simultaneously sacrificed on pagan religious days. Nearby is the ancient Paradise Quarry in which the cave called "the ear of Dionysius" is located. Next to it is the 5th century B.C. Greek Theater, where Plato and Aeschylus performed.

Behind the Theater is the "Grotto of the Nymphs." The views are wonderful from the walkway to the Paradise Grotto and from the Viale Rizzo, looking down into the Greek Theater and out toward the harbor. The archaeological area is open daily except Monday 09:00–17:00 (later in Summer).

Five miles further, on the hill of Epipoli overlooking Siracusa, is the Castle of Euryalus, the mightiest and most complete fortress of Greek times.

Returning downhill, along Corso Gelone, you come to the ruins of the Roman Forum, at Piazzale Marconi. Go along Corso Umberto I and cross the Ponte Nuovo to reach the island of **Ortygia**. There, in Piazza Pancali, are the remains of the Temple of Apollo, which the conquering Arabs turned into a mosque.

Other sights in Ortygia are the 16th century Santa Maria dei Miracoli church, the 15th century arch (Porta Marina), the Maniace Castle, and the 13th century Bellomo Palace, which houses a museum of medieval and modern art. The 17th century Palazzo del Municipo (Town Hall), the 18th century Palazzo of Benevantano del Bosco.

The National Archaelogical Museum, which has one of the most important collections

(Greek, Roman and Byzantine) of sarcophagi, pottery, coins and bronzes in Italy. Its most famous treasure is the 2nd century B.C. Venus Landolina sculpture.

The ancient Cathedral is dominated by the Doric columns of the original Temple of Minerva, where many works of art are exhibited.

Sights in **Palermo**: This city was entirely Arabic in ancient times. It is the modern capital of Sicily. Severely damaged by bombs in July of 1943. Most museums and galleries here are closed on Monday. Their hours are 09:00 to 12:30 or 13:30. Most of them re-open from 15:00 to 18:00 on certain days. All are open Sunday 09:00 to 12:00 or 13:00.

See the exhibits of carretti (Sicilian horsecarts) and many other phases of traditional Sicilian life (bridal dresses, fishing boats, whips used for self-flagellation during Holy Week processions) at the Pitre Ethnological Museum. The fine archaeological collection in the Museo Nazionale on Via Roma. The Risorgimento Museum at Piazza San Domenico. The International Museum of Marionettes (located at Via Butera 1), open daily 10:00–13:00 and 17:00–19:00.

Watch tin, copper and iron being shaped into utensils in the stalls along Via dei Calderai, near Piazza Bellini. See tombs of important Sicilians, in the San Domenico Church.

The 800-year old Cathedral and, next to it, The Archepiscopal Palace, both on Vittorio Emanuele. Nearby, the marvelous Oriental garden at the Church of San Giovanni degli Eremiti, a converted mosque.

See statues of former Spanish rulers in the Quattro Canti (Four Corners), a small octagonal piazza. Near it are 2 very interesting street markets, Vucciria and Il Capo. Located on a small, twisting street, Vucciria offers Sicilian pastries, cheeses and many foods that are exotic to non-Mediterranean tastebuds: fried lungs and spleen, sea urchins, pork sausage encased in the skin of a pig's foot.

The great array of food at Il Capo (which starts at the intersection of Via Volturno and Via Carini) includes squash, cheese, mounds of tomato paste, grapes, melons, swordfish, eggplant as well as shirts, blouses, sweaters, leather handbags, etc.

See the antiques sold at Il Papireto, the flea market. Decorative tiles, Italian Victorian furniture, filigree jewelry, coins, religious art.

One of the most splendid opera houses in Europe, the Teatro Massimo, built in 1897. The 12th century Royal Palace. The Cuba and Zisa palaces. The catacombs under the Convent of the Capuchin Friars.

There are dazzling mosaics at the 12th century Sala di re Roggero, open to the public on Monday, Friday and Saturday mornings if no official meetings of the Regional Assembly are taking place. This is only one of the many local churches and palaces built when Norman knights returned to Europe from the Crusades, ending Saracen rule of Sicily. Additional ancient mosaics can be seen in the Martorana Church in Piazza Bellini.

Don't fail to see other Norman mosaics in the Palace of the Norman Kings and at the 12th century Arabic-Norman Palatine Chapel in nearby **Monreale**, a 5-mile bus ride (#9) from Palermo. It is one of the most outstanding architectural achievements in Italy, open in the morning on Wednesday and Sunday, all other days 09:00–13:00 and 15:00–17:30 (hours vary in Winter). Also the excellent mosaics in the 12th century Cathedral there.

Take the #14 or #77 bus to the bathing beach, Mondello. There are half-day bus excursions and local train service to **Segesta** and **Selinunte**, sites of substantial Greek ruins.

A local train leaves almost hourly for the 15-minute ride to **Bagheria**, where the eccentric 18th century Villa Palagonia and the beautiful Villa Valguarnera are located.

There is hydrofoil service in the Spring and Summer to 2 interesting islands. The Blue Grotto on **Ustica** attracts many visitors. The Archaeological Museum on **Lipari** is worthwhile. From Lipari, there is boat service to other nearby islands: **Alicudi, Filicudi, Salina, Stromboli** (immortalized by Ingrid and Roberto with more passion off the silver screen than they invested in the motion picture) and **Vulcano**.

Passenger ships run from Palermo to Tunisia.

TRAIN ROUTES IN SICILY
(INCLUDING ONE-DAY EXCURSIONS)

Messina - Milazzo - Palermo 400

Dep. Messina	05:30	06:10 (1)	07:07	08:10	10:05	
Dep. Milazzo	06:00	06:52	08:05	09:32	10:42	
Arr. Palermo	09:10	09:40	10:30	11:35	13:35	
Dep. Messina	11:00	13:40	16:10 (2)	18:15	20:05 (2)	
Dep. Milazzo	11:32	14:12	16:40	18:50	20:37	
Arr. Palermo	14:25	17:38	19:10	21:50	23:30	

Sights in **Milazzo**: Founded 7 centuries before Christ. An important naval victory over the Carthaginians was won by the Romans in Milazzo's bay more than 2,200 years ago. See the 13th century Norman castle and the 16th century Spanish walls at the old town, on a hill above the modern city.

Dep. Palermo	04:20 (3)	06:20	08:00 (2)	10:10 (2)	10:40	11:30 (3)
Dep. Milazzo	07:18	09:01	10:15	12:52	13:45	14:41
Arr. Messina	09:35	09:35	10:50	13:30	14:30	15:23
Dep. Palermo	12:00	13:30	13:50 (3)	15:40	18:10	20:40
Dep. Milazzo	15:00	16:05	16:35	18:14	20:55	23:25
Arr. Messina	15:40	16:42	17:20	18:50	21:35	23:59

(1) Second-class. (2) Reservation *required*. Supplement charged. Light refreshments. (3) Runs daily, except Sundays and holidays.

Messina - Taormina - Catania - Siracusa   400

There is beautiful seacoast scenery on this route.

Dep. Messina (Cen.)	07:07	08:20 (1)	11:05	13:35	15:32 (4)
Arr. Taormina	-0-	08:50	11:40	14:10	16:10
Arr. Catania	-0-	09:45	12:38	15:03	17:02
Arr. Siracusa	-0-	11:45	14:30	16:45	18:30

Sights in **Taormina**: A year-around resort, with very mild Winter weather, consisting mainly of 3 streets, each on a different level, connected to each other by many stairways, all on one side of Mont Venere. One funicular provides access to the beaches below the little town (4,000 population).

Stroll and shop for pottery, embroidery and carved wood figures along Corso Umberto, the main street. See the 3rd century Roman theater, facing Mt. Etna. The medieval great halls in the 15th century Palazzo Corvaja. The 14th century Palace of the Duke of St. Stephen. The 13th century Cathedral.

Dep. Siracusa	05:10 (4)	07:00 (7)	08:15 (3)	10:50 (3)	12:30	15:15 (6)
Arr. Catania	06:24	07:55	09:25	11:56	13:46	16:30
Arr. Taormina	07:08	08:49	10:02	12:42	14:45	17:27
Arr. Messina (Cen.)	07:55	10:00	10:48	13:30	15:38	18:15

(1) Operates late July to early September. (2) Change trains in Catania. From Siracusa: runs daily. From Catania: runs daily, except Sundays and holidays. (3) Reservation *required*. Supplement charged. Light refreshments. (4) Runs daily, except Sundays and holidays. (5) Plus other departure from Messina at 20:10 (3), arriving Siracusa 22:50. (6) Plus other departures from Siracusa at 18:14 (1) arriving Messina 18:50. (7) Runs Sunday only.

Palermo - Agrigento - Palermo   407

Dep. Palermo	07:35	10:05	11:05	13:02	14:20	16:20 (2)
Arr. Agrigento	09:32	12:10	13:10	15:05	16:20	18:35

Sights in **Agrigento**: Founded by Greeks in 581 B.C. See the extremely fine Greek ruins: 7 Doric temples in the Valley of the Temples, many ancient aqueducts and cemeteries. The 14th century Cathedral. The 13th century churches: S. Nicola, Santa Maria dei Greci and S. Spirito. Baroque palaces. There is an especially good Archaeological Museum here.

Dep. Agrigento	06:45	08:22 (1)	10:12	11:35	13:30	16:35 (3)
Arr. Palermo	08:50	10:18	12:15	13:40	15:30	18:35

(1) Runs daily, except Sundays and holidays. (2) Plus other departures from Palermo at 17:20, 18:55 (1) and 20:10, arriving Agrigento 19:15, 20:55 and 22:05. (3) Plus other Agrigento departures at 17:50 and 20:00, arriving Palermo 19:50 and 22:00.

Palermo - Caltanissetta - Palermo   407

Dep. Palermo	05:55 (1)	08:10	12:05 (1)	14:00	16:10 (1)	18:20
Arr. Caltan. (Xirbi)	07:36	10:00	14:06	15:46	18:00	20:02

Sights in **Caltanissetta**: The Greek, Arabic and Norman ruins at the Pietrarossa Castle. The excellent archaeological collection in the Civic Museum. The Baroque Cathedral and Palazzo Moncada.

Dep. Caltan. (Xirbi)	07:41 (1)	10:04	13:00 (1)	16:02 (1)	18:17	21:05
Arr. Palermo	09:20	11:40	14:50	17:40	20:05	22:50

(1) Runs daily, except Sundays and holidays.

Palermo - Catania - Siracusa

407						
Dep. Palermo	05:55 (1)	08:10	09:20 (2)	12:05 (1)	14:00	16:01 (1)
Arr. Catania	09:30 (1)	11:50	13:25	16:05	17:35	20:00
Change trains. 400						
Dep Catania	10:00	12:50	15:14	17:05 (1)	18:40	21:32 (4)
Arr. Siracusa	11:45	14:00	16:45	18:30	20:05 (1)	22:50

Dep. Siracusa	-0-	06:40	12:27	14:10	15:15 (7)
Arr. Catania	-0-	07:55	13:46	15:30	16:30
Change trains. 407					
Dep Catania	05:50 (1)	08:07	14:06 (1)	16:05	18:05 (7)
Arr. Palermo	09:20	11:40	17:33	20:00	21:55

(1) Runs daily, except Sundays and holidays. Direct train (no train change) late July to early September. (2) Change train in Agrigento. (3) Operates late July to early September. (4) Reservation *required*. supplement charged. Light refreshments.

Palermo - Trapani - Palermo   392

Dep. Palermo	05:20	07:10 (1)	09:00	10:40	13:00 (1)	13:50 (3)
Arr. Trapani	07:26	08:56	11:06	12:46	15:06	15:56

Sights in **Trapani**: A major Carthaginian and Roman naval base in the 3rd century B.C. See the outstanding 14th century Santuario dell'Annunziata, rebuilt in the 18th century. The 14th century Santa Agostino Church. The excellent sculpture and paintings in the Museo Nazionale Pepoli. The 17th century Cathedral. The Baroque Palazzo della Giudecca. The 15th century Santa Maria di Gesu Church.

| Dep. Trapani | 04:25 | 04:55 (1) | 08:00 | 09:25 | 11:00 | 12:35 | 16:08 (4) |
| Arr. Palermo | 06:31 | 07:01 | 10:06 | 11:31 | 13:06 | 14:41 | 18:14 |

(1) Runs daily, except Sundays and holidays. (2) Runs Sunday only. (3) Plus other departures from Palermo at 14:55 (1), 16:05, 17:20, 18:50 and 20:35, arriving Trapani 17:01, 18:11, 19:26, 20:56 and 22:41. (4) Plus other departures from Trapani at 17:10 and 19:10, arriving Palermo 19:21 and 21:16.

Agrigento - Caltanissetta - Agrigento   407

Dep. Agrigento	06:55 (1)	10:00	15:20	17:20
Arr. Caltanissetta (Cen.)	08:22	11:14	16:45	18:45
Arr. Caltanissetta (Xirbi)	10 minutes after arriving Centrale station

Sights in **Caltanissetta:** See "Palermo–Caltanissetta"

Dep. Caltanissetta (Xirbi)	07:41 (1)	10:04	10:40	12:40	17:20 (1)	20:10 (3)
Dep. Caltanissetta (Cen.)	-0-	10:16	11:00	12:43	17:35	20:20
Arr. Agrigento	-0-	11:35	12:45	14:40	19:00	21:45

(1) Runs daily, except Sundays and holidays. (2) Runs daily, except Sundays and holidays. Second-class. (3) Second-class.

Catania - Caltanissetta - Catania   407

| Dep. Catania | 05:50 (1) | 08:05 | 08:27 | 10:35 | 13:10 | 14:13 (1+3) |
| Arr. Caltanissetta (Xirbi) | 07:35 | 10:04 | 10:40 | 12:40 | 15:05 | 15:55 |

Sights in **Caltanissetta:** See "Palermo–Caltanissetta"

| Dep. Caltanissetta (Xirbi) | 07:38 (1) | 08:35 | 10:01 | 11:35 | 14:12 (1) | 15:46 (4) |
| Arr. Catania | 09:30 | 10:45 | 11:50 | 13:25 | 16:05 | 17:25 |

(1) Runs daily, except Sundays and holidays. (2) Second-class. (3) Plus other departures from Catania at 16:14, 18:15, 18:10 and 21:40, arriving Caltanissetta 18:14, 20:05, 20:58 and 23:45. (4) Plus other departures from Caltanissetta at 16:10, (1), 19:10 and 20:08, arriving Catania 19:15, 21:20 and 21:50.

The Malta Cruise

Reggio di Calabria, Catania and Siracusa are gateways for the boat trip to Malta.

1476

Dep. Reggio	08:30 (1)	Dep. Malta	05:30 (2)
Dep. Catania	11:00 (1)	Arr. Siracusa	14:00
Dep. Siracusa	16:30	Dep. Catania	17:45
Arr. Malta	21:30	Arr. Reggio	22:00

(1) Runs Tuesday + Saturday July 19-September 4. (2) Runs Tuesday + Saturday April 1-May 31; Tuesday, Friday + Saturday June 1- October 10.

SCENIC RAIL TRIPS

Arona - Brig   82

There is beautiful lake and mountain scenery on this portion of the Milan–Lausanne route.

Dep. Milan (Cen.)	07:23	09:10 (1)	14:00 (1)	15:25 (1)	17:25 (5)
Dep. Arona	08:16	09:53	14:43	17:16 (3)	18:15 (4)
Dep. Brig	09:48	11:16	16:15	18:48	19:48
Arr. Lausanne	11:27	12:40	17:40	20:27	21:11

(1) Reservation *required*. Supplement charged. Light refreshments. (2) Reservation *required*. Supplement charged. Restaurant car. (3) Change trains in Brig. (4) Reservation *required*. Supplement charged. (5) Plus another Milan departure at 19:05 (4), arriving Lausanne 22:55.

Bologna - Florence   374

Excellent mountain scenery on this ride.

The train goes through the 11.5-mile long Apennine Tunnel, Italy's longest tunnel.

Complete schedules appear under the "Bologna–Florence" and "Florence–Bologna"one-day excursions.

Bolzano - Brennero

Beautiful views of medieval castles and wild alpine mountain scenery on this portion of the route from Verona to Innsbruck, and on to Munich.

Sights in **Bolzano**: Has been Italian since only 1919. The language spoken here (called "Bozen" during the nearly 6 centuries it was ruled by the Hapsburgs, from 1363 until World War I) is German.

Take at least one of the 3 funiculars that climb up the Alps. See the 16th to 18th century house on both Bindnergasse and Silbergasse. The vegetable and fruit market on Piazza delle Erbe. The 18th century Neptune fountain.

The exceptional carved altar depicting the Nativity, in the Holy Virgin Chapel of the Franciscan church. The frescoes at both the Cathedral and the Dominican church.

Stroll along the Talvera River first to the 13th century Maretsch Castle and then to Runkelstein Castle, whose lovely frescoes can be seen on guided tours Tuesday–Saturday, 10:00–12:00 and 15:00–18:00.

Buses are available to make short trips of less than an hour to many vineyard villages. Traminer and Gewurztraminer are produced in this area.

Verona - Innsbruck - Munich   76

Dep. Verona (P.N.)	08:32 (1)	10:54 (1)	12:55 (1)	14:06
Dep. Bolzano	10:20	12:30	14:28	16:00
Arr. Fortezza	11:06 (3)	13:06 (3)	15:03 (3)	16:45 (3)
Dep. Brennero	12:04	14:04	16:04	17:50
Arr. Innsbruck	12:37	14:37	16:37	18:28
Arr. Munich	14:30	16:30	18:30	20:30

(1) Reservation *required*. Supplement charged. Restaurant car. (2) Light refreshments. 3) Estimated. Cook deleted Fortezza from this timetable in 1993.

Fortezza - Dobbiaco

Very good mountain scenery on this spur off the Bolzano–Brennero route, appearing above. The following schedule shows how the Verona–Innsbruck–Munich trip can accommodate this en route detour.

380		381	
Dep. Verona (P.N.)	08:32 (1)	Dep. Dobbiaco	12:55 (3)
Arr. Fortezza	11:04	Arr. Fortezza	14:02
Change trains. 381		Arr. Bolzano	14:54
Dep. Fortezza	11:24	*Change trains. 76*	
Arr. Dobbiaco	12:32	Dep. Bolzano	16:00
		Arr. Innsbruck	18:28
		Arr. Munich	20:30

(1) Reservation *required*. Supplement charged. Restaurant car. (2) Restaurant car. (3) Runs daily except Sundays & holidays.

Torino - Cuneo - Breil - Nice 356

There is spectacular scenery on the 74-mile-long Cuneo–Nice rail route through the Roya Valley and the Alps, a service that first became operational in 1928. Severe damage during World War II caused it to be closed in 1940, and it was not re-opened until the Winter of 1979.

An outstanding feat of engineering, this line is a succession of very high viaducts, bridges and 60 tunnels that span 27 miles of this route, interspersed with sections that look down into deep valleys. This route has attracted many tourists.

Dep. Torino (P.N.)	08:59 (2)	10:10 (3)
Arr. Cuneo	10:24	11:00
Change trains.		
Dep. Cuneo	10:39	14:00 (2)
Arr. Breil	11:38	15:32 (2)
Change trains.		
Dep. Breil	12:45	18:05
Arr. Nice	13:43	19:10

(1) Departs from Torino's Porta Susa railstation. (2) Direct train to Breil. (3) This schedule includes a Breil-Nice train that runs only on Sunday.

Sights in **Cuneo:** The 10th century Cathedral. The 13th century Church of San Francesco. The marvelous viaduct over the Stura di Demonte. The Civic Museum in the 18th century Palazzo Audiffredi. The 18th century Town Hall.

The magnificent Cuneo–Breil scenery can also be seen on the following easy one-day roundtrip from Torino.

Torino - Cuneo - Torino 356

All of these trips require changing trains in Cuneo.

Dep. Torino(P.N.)	08:59	07:45 (1)	Dep. Breil	17:44 (1)	16:29
Arr. Cuneo	10:24		Arr. Cuneo	19:12	18:00
Dep. Cuneo	10:39	08:44	Dep. Cuneo	15:58	18:12
Arr. Breil	12:08	10:07	Arr. Torino (P.N.)	20:16	19:18

(1) Direct train, no change in Cuneo.

Genoa - Torino - Cuneo - Ventimiglia - Genoa and v.v.

The right-hand column allows a layover in Torino (see footnote #4) for sightseeing and for dinner.

360		*355*	
Dep. Genoa (P.P.)	06:39 (1)	Dep. Genoa (P.P.)	12:05 (1)
Arr. Torino (P.N.)	08:50	Arr. Ventimiglia	15:10
Change trains. 356		*Change trains. 356*	
Dep. Torino (P.N.)	08:59	Dep. Ventimiglia	15:29
Arr. Cuneo	13:35	Arr. Breil	16:24
Dep. Breil	10:13	Arr. Cuneo	18:00 (2)
Arr. Ventimiglia	12:01	Arr. Torino (P.N.)	19:18 (5)
Change trains. 3555		*Change trains. 360*	
Dep. Ventimiglia	13:15	Dep. Torino (P.N.)	19:33 (1+4)
Arr. Genoa (P.P.)	15:40	Arr. Genoa (P.P.)	21:27

(1) Reservation *required*. Supplement charged. Light refreshments. (2) Change trains in Cuneo. (3) Operates mid-June to mid-September. (4) Plus other departures from Torino at 17:28, 18:26 (1), 19:28 (3), 20:28 and 22:20, arriving Genoa 19:10, 20:31, 20:04, 21:00, 22:27 and 00:25. (5) Arrives on Sunday only.

Brindisi - Reggio and Reggio - Brindisi

There is splendid coastline scenery on this trip.

404		*398*		
Dep. Brindisi	06:14	Dep. Reggio (Cen.)	07:00 (1)	-0-
Arr. Taranto	07:50	Arr. Taranto	12:53	-0-
Change trains. 398		*Change trains. 403*		
Dep. Taranto	09:59 (1)	Dep. Taranto	13:29	14:35
Arr. Reggio (Cen.)	15:52	Arr. Brindisi	15:15	16:20

(1) Reservation *required*. Supplement charged. (2) Runs daily, except Sundays and holidays.

Genoa - Pisa

There is exceptional mountain and Mediterranean coastline scenery on this ride. Complete schedules appear under the "Genoa–Pisa" one-day excursion.

Genoa - Nice - Cannes - Marseille   90

A close look at more than 100 miles of outstanding seashore resorts along the Mediterranean's Ligure coastline: the Savona and San Remo beaches (on the Italian Riviera) and the Monaco, Nice, Antibes, Cannes and St. Raphael beaches (on the French Riviera).

Dep. Genoa (P.P.)	05:55	08:22 (3)	16:20	18:16
Arr. Nice	10:15 (1)	11:20	19:46	22:00
Dep. Nice	10:38 (2)	11:25	19:51	22:05
Arr. Cannes	11:01	11:47	20:30	22:45
Arr. Marseille (St. Ch.)	12:53	13:43	22:41	01:00

(1) Change trains in Nice. (2) Light refreshments. (3) Reservation *required*. Supplement charged. Restaurant car.

Milan - Barcelona   90

The "Pablo Casals" (20:00 departure) began in 1990 to carry one "Gran Clase" sleeping car, the most luxurious sleeping car in Europe. Each of its large single and double compartments has a shower and toilet. The train also has ordinary sleeping compartments and 4-berth tourist compartments. There are *no* coach seats. The train has a restaurant car. Substantial discounts are given to holders of Eurailpass and Eurodomino. Reservation is required but can be made only in Spain!

Dep. Milan (Cen.)	18:15 (1)	20:00 (2)
Arr. Barcelona (Sants)	09:35 (3)	09:10

(1) Operates mid-July to late August. Has couchettes. (2) "Pablo Casals" (see description above the timetable). Arrives Barcelona Franca. (3) Change trains in Porto Bou.

Milan - Bern   82

The Brig–Bern portion of this ride is one of the 5 most outstanding scenic rail trips in Europe, with a fabulous array of lakes, mountains and rivers.

Dep. Milan (Cen.)	07:25	08:25 (2)	10:25 (2)	12:25 (3)	14:00 (4+7)
Dep. Brig	10:01 (1)	10:43	12:46	14:43	16:22 (5)
Arr. Bern	11:38	12:12	14:38	16:12	18:04

(1) Change trains in Brig. Light refreshments Brig-Bern. (2) Reservation *required*. Supplement charged. Restaurant car. (3) Reservation *required*. Supplement charged. Light refreshments. (4) Reservation *required*. Supplement charged. (5) Light refreshments. (6) Restaurant car. (7) Plus other Milan departures at 15:25 (3), 16:25 (1) and 17:25 (2), arriving Bern 19:38, 20:38 and 21:38.

Milan - Genoa   356

Great views of marble quarries, mountains, farms and the Mediterranean coast, all in 2 hours. An easy one-day roundtrip.

Milan - Locarno

Great canyon, mountain and river scenery is seen from a narrow-gauge local train over the Domodossola-Locarno portion of this route. This Centovalli (one hundred valley) ride is one of the 5 most outstanding scenic rail trips in Europe. Complete schedules appear under the "Milan–Locarno" one-day excursion.

Milan - Zurich   84

This is one of the 5 most outstanding scenic rail trips in Europe.

A feast of beautiful farms, lakes, mountains, rivers and vineyards. You go through the 9.3-mile long Gotthard Tunnel. Before it was opened to traffic in 1882, there was no direct rail route from Italy to eastern Switzerland through the Alps.

Prior to entering the Gotthard, the train goes through the beautiful Ticino Valley.

Immediately upon exiting the first of a series of 9 tunnels, you first see the small, white Wassen Church on your right, 170 feet below the track. The next time the church comes into view, after exiting tunnel #4, the church is to your left and nearly level with the track.

Later, after exiting tunnel #6, you have a third view of the church, again to your left, this time nearly 230 feet above the track, but you will see it there only if you look far ahead and before being alongside the church. (The train is in the Kirchberg Tunnel when it is directly alongside the church.)

The turns inside 3 semi-circular tunnels in this area (Leggistein, Wattinger and Pfaffensprung) are engineered so well that there is no sensation of the curves that the train is making inside those tunnels.

Try this interesting experiment: make a pendulum of any object, holding the top of a weighted string, chain or handkerchief against the inner face of a train window (a left-hand window when inside Leggistein, and a right-hand window when inside Wattinger and Pfaffensprung). As the train goes around a curve, the weighted bottom will move away from the window.

The Mediterranean climate on the Italian end of the tunnel is usually much warmer than the Alpine temperature on the Swiss end. The train makes 3 gradients at 45–50 miles per hour.

Dep. Milan (Cen.)	08:25 (1)	10:25	12:25	14:25	15:00 (2+5)
Arr. Zurich	12:57	14:57	16:57	18:57	19:28

Dep. Zurich	13:33 (3)	15:03 (4)	17:03 (2)	19:03 (2)	-0-
Arr. Milan (Cen.)	17:35	19:30	21:30	23:35	-0-

(1) Restaurant car. (2) Reservation *required*. Supplement charged. Restaurant car. (3) Reservtion *required*. Supplement charged. Light refreshments. (4) Reservation *required*. Supplement charged. (5) Plus other Milan departures at 16:25, 17:20 (2) and 19:25 (3), arriving Zurich 20:57, 21:48 and 23:36.

Milan - Tirano - St. Moritz - Chur - Zurich

This is an alternate route from Milan to Zurich. Many rivers and lakes are seen between Milan and Tirano. There is great mountain scenery on the Tirano-St. Moritz narrow-gauge portion of this easy one-day excursion. The track reaches 7,405-foot altitude going through the Bernina Pass, Europe's highest main rail line. The descent from St. Moritz to Chur is spectacular.

362

Dep. Milan (Cen.)	05:04 (1)	06:15 (2)	08:15	-0-	09:15
Arr. Tirano	08:23	08:23	10:20	-0-	12:06
Change trains. 328					
Dep. Tirano	-0-	08:40	10:30	11:30	12:24
Arr. St. Moritz	-0-	10:58	13:02	13:56	14:56
Change trains. 330					
Dep. St. Moritz	-0-	11:00 (8)	13:00 (4)	14:00	15:00 (4)
Arr. Chur	-0-	13:07	15:07	16:07	17:07
Change trains. 310					
Dep. Chur	-0-	13:15	-0-	16:23 (6)	17:15 (7)
Arr. Zurich	-0-	14:50	-0-	17:50	18:50

(1) Runs daily, except Sundays and holidays. (2) Runs only on Sunday. (3) Runs daily, except Sundays and holidays. (4) Runs Saturday, Sunday and holidays. (5) Late May to late October: runs daily. Late October to mid-May: runs daily, except Sundays and holidays. (6) Reservation *required*. Supplement charged. Restaurant car. (7) Light refreshments. (8) Runs Saturdays, Sundays & holidays except Saturdays June 18-September 24.

Milan - St. Moritz - Milan

Very good river and lake scenery Milan-Tirano. Great mountain scenery on the Tirano-St. Moritz narrow-gauge portion of this one-day roundtrip. The track reaches 7,405-foot altitude going through the Bernina Pass, Europe's highest main rail line.

362
Dep.Milan	05:04 (1)	06:15 (2)	08:15	09:15	12:05	14:05
Arr. Tirano	08:23	08:23	10:20	12:06	14:42	16:36

Change trains. 328
Dep. Tirano	-0-	08:40	13:30	12:24	15:30	17:30
Arr. St. Moritz	-0-	10:58	13:02	14:56	17:56	19:56

• • •

Dep. St. Moritz	11:05	16:00	17:00
Arr. Tirano	13:30	18:28	19:28

Change trains. 362
Dep. Tirano	15:02	19:02 (1)	20:02 (2)
Arr. Milan	17:30	21:40	22:30

(1) Runs daily except Sundays and holidays. (2) Runs only Sunday. (3) Runs daily, except Sundays and holidays. Change trains in Sondrio at 11:12.

Naples - Siracusa

There is wonderful Mediterranean coastline scenery on this trip. See details earlier in this section, under "The Rail Trip To Sicily."

Naples - Sorrento   401

There is excellent Mediterranean coastline scenery on this ride.

Dep. Naples (Circumvesuviana) and Naples (F.S.) at one or 2 times per hour from 05:31 until 22:48 for the 55–65 minute ride to Sorrento.

• • •

Dep. Sorrento at one or 2 times every hour from 04:13 to 22:41 for the ride back to Naples. (There are stops in both directions at Pompeii.) A travolator provides transportation between Naples' F.S. station and Naples' Centrale station.

Naples - Taranto

There is very good mountain scenery on this route.

390		*398*	
Dep. Naples (P. Gari.)	07:33	Dep. Taranto	20:24
Arr. Bari	12:00	Arr. Bari	23:04
Change trains. 398		*Change trains. 390*	
Dep. Bari	12:35 (1)	Dep. Bari	22:31
Arr. Taranto	14:08	Arr. Naples (P. Gari.)	05:00

(1) Reservation *required.* Supplement charged.

Reggio Calabria - Taranto - Brindisi

There is excellent coastline scenery on this ride, which allows a sightseeing stopover in Taranto.

Brindisi is the gateway for the cruise to Greece.

398		
Dep. Reggio Calabria (Cen.)	07:00 (1)	15:24 (1)
Arr. Taranto	13:09	21:08
Change trains. 403		

Dep. Taranto	13:29	14:35	16:43	17:45	19:00	21:38
Arr. Brindisi	15:15	17:20	18:17	19:21	20:25	23:25

(1) Reservation *required.* Supplement charged. (2) Runs daily, except Sundays and holidays.

Rimini - Pescara - Brindisi   390

The excellent scenery on this route includes olive groves, vineyards and superb beaches on the Adriatic coastline. This can be broken into a 2-day trip by *stopping in Pescara one night and then continuing on to Brindisi the next day.*

Also, this trip can be extended by continuing on from Brindisi to Reggio di Calabria, a ride that offers fine coastline scenery.

Dep. Rimini	09:00 (1)	10:07 (2)	14:09 (2)
Arr. Pescara (Cen.)	11:46	12:22	16:30
Dep. Pescara (Cen.)	11:49	12:26	16:35
Arr. Brindisi (Cen.)	16:30	17:15	21:18

(1) Operates late June to early September. (2) Reservation *required.* Supplement charged. Restaurant car.

Rome - Foligno - Terontola - Foligno - Rome   385

Between Foligno and Terontola, there are magnificent views of vineyards, olive groves, the hillside towns of **Spello** and **Assisi, Lake Trasimente**, and the city of **Perugia**.

These Schedules allow a sightseeing stopover in Foligno or Perugia.

Dep. Rome (Ter.)	10:15 (1)	13:25	14:20 (1)
Arr. Foligno	11:46	15:16 (1)	16:30
Change trains			
Dep. Foligno	12:00	16:00	16:44
Dep. Perugia	12:36	16:34	17:21
Arr. Terontola	13:17	17:22	18:07

Sights in **Foligno**: An ancient Roman city that was badly damaged by earthquake in 1832 and then by heavy bombing during World War II. See the restored 12th century Cathedral. The archaeological museum and picture gallery, in the 14th century Palazzo Trinci.

You can go by bus from Foligno 8 miles to the mountain-top 14th century village called **Montefalco**. Its main attraction is the vista from the top of its Communal Tower (Torre Comunale). Also see the interiors of St. Augustine's Church and St. Francis's Church.

Sights in **Perugia**: see notes under "Florence–Perugia"

Dep. Terontola	13:33 (3)	17:44	18:46 (3)
Dep. Perugia	14:27	18:25	19:36
Arr. Foligno	15:02	19:05	20:18
Change trains.			
Dep. Foligno	15:58 (1)	19:40	21:20 (1)
Arr. Rome (Ter.)	17:45	21:30	23:03

(1) Reservation *required*. Supplement charged. Light refreshments. (2) Light refreshments. (3) Second-class.

Udine - Trieste

This portion of the Venice-Trieste ride has excellent scenery of the Adriatic coastline. Sit on the right side for best viewing. The schedules allow a sightseeing stopover in Udine.

377					
Dep. Venice (S. L.)	06:34	09:10 (2)	11:10	11:47 (2)	14:10
Arr. Udine	08:48	10:50	13:03	13:50	16:00
Change trains. 378					
Dep. Udine	09:50 (3)	12:35	13:30 (2)	17:01 (3)	17:40 (2+4)
Arr. Trieste (Cen.)	10:48	13:45	15:06 (3)	18:21	19:07

(1) Restaurant car. (2) Second-class. (3) Runs daily, except Sundays and holidays. Second-class. (4) Plus other departures from Udine at 18:50 (2), 19:45 (3) and 20:45, arriving Trieste 19:58, 20:54 and 21:53.

Sights in **Udine**: see notes under "Trieste–Udine"

INTERNATIONAL ROUTES
FROM ITALY

The primary Italian gateway for rail travel to Switzerland, western Germany, Luxembourg, Belgium, Holland and northeastern France (Paris) is Milan. A secondary gateway for rail travel from Italy to Switzerland is from Torino, via Aosta, to either Brig or Geneva.

There is rail service to southern France (Nice, Marseille and Avignon), Paris, and to Spain from Milan and Genoa.

The gateways for travel to Austria, Germany and Denmark are Verona and Venice.

Venice is also the starting point for trips to Yugoslavia, Czechoslovakia, eastern Germany and the rest of Eastern Europe (Bulgaria, Greece, Romania, Hungary, Poland and Russia).

Milan - Genoa - Nice - Marseille - Barcelona 90

"Pablo Casals" (departing Milan 20:00) began in 1990 carrying one "Gran Clase" sleeping car, called by Cook "probably the most luxurious sleeping car in Europe." Each of its large single and double compartments has both a shower and a toilet. Substantial discounts are given to holders of Eurailpass and Eurodomino. Reservation is required but can be made only in Spain!

Dep. Milan (Cen.)	06:40 (1)	07:10 (2)	14:15	-0-	20:00 (5)
Dep. Genoa (P. Principe)	08:22	-0-	16:10	18:16 (3)	-0-
Arr. Nice	11:20	-0-	19:46	22:00	-0-
Arr. Marseille	13:43	-0-	22:41	01:00	-0-
Arr. Port Bou	-0-	-0-	-0-	05:52 (4)	-0-
Arr. Barcelona	-0-	20:50	-0-	09:35	09:10

(1) Reservation *required*. Supplement charged. Restaurant car. (2) Reservation *required*. Supplement charged. Light refreshments. Change trains in Chambery at 11:38. Depart Chambery 12:48 (1). (3) Has couchettes Genoa–Port Bou. (4) Change trains. Depart Port Bou 07:15. (5) "Pablo Casals" (see note above the timetable.). Reservation *required*. Supplement charged. Train has only sleeping cars. (No coaches.) Offers 4 different classes of accommodation: Gran Clase, single, double and 4-berth tourist compartments. Restaurant car.

Milan - Luzern - Basel   290

Dep. Milan (Cen.)	07:25 (1)	09:20 (2)	11:25 (2)	13:25 (2)
Arr. Luzern	11:46	13:39	15:39	17:39
Arr. Basel (S.B.B)	13:09	14:53	16:53	18:53

Dep. Milan (Cen.)	15:25 (2)	17:25 (1)	18:25	19:03
Arr. Luzern	19:39	21:39	22:39	-0-
Arr. Basel (S.B.B.)	20:53	22:53	23:59	00:08

(1) Reservation *required*. Supplement charged. Light refreshments. (2) Reservation *required*. Supplement charged. Restaurant car.

TORINO - AOSTA
GATEWAYS TO SWITZERLAND

(1) Via Le Grand St. Bernard

Torino - Aosta - Martigny - Brig or Lausanne

All of the Torino-Aosta trains are second-class.

353

Dep. Torino (Porto Nvova)	06:30 (1)	11:20	13:20	
Arr. Aosta	08:55	13:32	15:20	
Change to a bus.				

269

Dep. Aosta (Place Narbonne)	10:00 (3)	14:15 (3)	16:25 (5)	
Arr. Orsieres	-0-	17:19	17:58	
Change to a train.				
Dep. Orsieres	-0- (3)	17:24 (8)	18:03	
Arr. Martigny	11:10	17:58	18:44	
Change trains.				

270

Dep. Martigny	11:25	14:21 (6)	18:25 (6)	
Arr. Brig	12:23	15:12	19:23	

OR

Dep. Martigny	11:34	15:34	19:38 (7)	20:37 (9)
Arr. Lausanne	12:27	16:27	20:27	21:27

(1) Runs daily, except Sundays and holidays. (2) Runs only Sunday. (3) Runs June 10-September 18. (4) Operates mid-June to mid-September. (5) Via the St. Bernard Tunnel. (6) Light refreshments. (7) Restaurant car. (8) Runs daily June 10- October 9. (9) Runs Saturdays, Sundays and holidays June 5-September 24.

(2) Via Mt. Blanc Tunnel

Torino - Aosta - Chamonix - Geneva

A layover in Chamonix (11:30–16:31) allows for sightseeing there.

353

Dep. Torino (Place Nvova)	06:30 (1)	09:01	13:20
Arr. Aosta	08:55	11:00	15:20
Change to bus.			

192

Dep. Aosta	09:40 (2)	11:30 (2)	12:15 (2)
Arr. Courmayeur	10:40	12:20	14:05
Change buses.			
Dep. Courmayeur	10:50	12:30	14:15
Arr. Chamonix	11:30	13:10	14:55

All of the Chamonix–Geneva train changes are "cross-platform," each taking less than one minute.

268

Dep. Chamonix	12:12 (5)	13:27	16:16
Arr. St. Gervais	12:52	14:06	16:55
Change trains. 167			
Dep. St. Gervais	13:07 (6)	14:32 (6)	17:23 (6)
Arr. La-Roche-sur-Foron	13:58	15:20	18:08
Change trains. 167			
Dep. La-Roche-sur-Foron	14:00 (7)	15:30	18:15 (4)
Arr. Geneva (Eaux-Vives)	14:32	16:03	19:06

(1) Runs daily, except Sundays and holidays. (2) Operates early July to mid-September. (3) Runs Monday-Friday, except holidays. (4) Change trains in Annemasse at 18:36. (5) Runs daily. July 4-28 runs 16 minutes earlier. (6) Does not run July 4-28. (7) Runs 5 minutes earlier July 4-28.

ROUTES TO OTHER COUNTRIES

Rome - Milan - Genoa - Lausanne - Dijon - Avignon - Lyon - Paris

44

Dep. Rome (Ter.)	-0-	-0-	08:05 (1)	-0-
Dep. Florence (SMN)	-0-	-0-	10:16	-0-
Arr. Bologna	-0-	-0-	11:10	-0-
Dep. Bologna	-0-	-0-	11:20	-0-
Dep. Genoa (P.P.)	-0-	07:05 (3)	-0-	11:50
Arr. Milan (Cen.)	-0-	08:47 (4)	13:10 (4)	13:44 (4)
Dep. Milan (Cen.)	07:10 (1)	09:10 (1)	→	14:00 (1)
Arr. Lausanne	-0-	12:40 (4)		17:40 (4)
Dep. Lausanne	-0-	12:46		17:54 (2)
Arr. Dijon	-0-	14:44		19:57
Arr. Paris (Lyon)	16:02	16:28		21:39

Dep. Rome (Ter.)	-0-	16:22 (6)	-0-	19:10 (7)
Dep. Florence (SMN)	-0-	-0-	19:43 (7)	-0-
Arr. Bologna	-0-	-0-	-0-	-0-
Dep. Bologna	-0-	-0-	21:00	-0-
Dep. Genoa (P.P.)	-0-	22:04	-0-	00:18
Arr. Milan (Cen.)	21:10 (5)	-0-	-0-	-0-
Dep. Milan (Cen.)	-0-	-0-	-0-	-0-
Arr. Lausanne	-0-	-0-	04:02	-0-
Dep. Lausanne	-0-	-0-	04:07	-0-
Arr. Dijon	04:32	05:58	06:39	07:37
Arr. Paris (L yon)	07:22	08:52	09:21	10:07

(1) Reservation *required*. Supplement charged. Restaurant car. Change trains in Lyon (2) TGV. Reservation *required*. Supplement charged. Light refreshments. (3) Reservation *required*. Supplement charged. (4) Change trains. (5) Carries a sleeping car. Also has couchettes. Coach is second-class. (6) Departs from Rome's Ostiense railstation. Carries a sleeping car. Also has couchettes Light refreshments Rome-Genoa. (7) Train carries only sleeping cars and couchettes. No coach cars. Light refreshments.

Rome - Venice - Budapest - Kiev to St. Petersburg or Moscow 88

This train carries only sleeping cars. It does not have coach cars. Runs Monday, Wednesday and Friday.

Dep. Rome (Termini)	19:20	Day 1
Dep. Venice (Santa Lucia)	-0-	Day 2
Arr. Budapest (Keleti)	-0-	
Train divides		
Dep. Budapest (Keleti)	16:15	
Arr. St. Petersburg	-0-	Day 3
Arr. Kiev	17:38	Day 3
Arr. Moscow (Kievski)	11:21	Day 4

Milan - Venice - Innsbruck - Munich 76

Dep. Milan (Cen.)	-0- (4)	07:00 (2)	-0-	15:30 (2)
Dep. Venice (S.L.)	06:25 (3)	-0-	08:55 (2+7)	-0-
Arr. Innsbruck	-0-	12:37	14:37	20:58
Arr. Munich (Hbf.)	14:30	14:30	16:30	22:40

(1) Carries a sleeping car. Also has couchettes. Coach is second-class. (2) Reservation *required*. Supplement charged. Restaurant car. (3) Change trains in Verona. (4) Reservation *required*. Supplement charged. Light refreshments. (5) Light refreshments. (6) Has couchettes. Coach is second-class. (7) Plus other Venice departures at 10:25 (3), 12:05 (3+4), 15:25 (2) and 22:05 (6), arriving Munich 18:30, 20:30, 22:40 and 06:35.

Venice - Milan - Geneva 83

Dep. Venice (Santa Lucia)	10:25	12:25 (2)	14:05 (3+4)	22:05 (3+5)
Arr. Milan (Cen.)	13:54	15:50	17:20 (3)	-0- (3)
Change trains.				
Dep. Milan (Cen.)	14:00 (1)	16:25 (2)	17:25	-0-
Arr. Geneva	18:17	21:12 (1)	21:48	06:39

(1) Reservation *required*. supplement charged. (2) Restaurant car. (3) Direct train to Geneva. No train change in Milan. (4) Reservation *required*. Supplement charged. Restaurant car. (5) Carries a sleeping car. Also has couchettes. Coaches are second-class.

Bologna - Venice - Milan - Lausanne - Paris 44

Dep. Bologna	11:16 (1+2)	-0-	-0	-0-
Dep. Venice (S.L.)	-0-	10:25	-0-	20:10 (6)
Arr. Padua	-0- (1)	10:54	-0-	-0- (6)
Change trains.				
Dep. Padua	-0-	11:00 (3)	-0-	-0-
Arr. Milan (Cen.)	13:10	13:40	-0-	23:08 (7)
Change trains.				
Dep. Milan (Cen.)	-0-	14:00 (2)	21:10 (5)	23:13 (7)
Arr. Lausanne	-0-	17:40	-0-	-0- (6)
Change trains.				
Dep. Lausanne	-0-	17:54 (4)	-0-	-0-
Arr. Paris (Lyon)	-0-	21:39	07:22	08:25

(1) Direct train to Milan. No train change in Padua. (2) Reservation *required*. Supplement charged. Restaurant car. (3) Lignt refreshments. (4) TGV. Reservation *required*. Supplement charged. Restaurant car. (5) Direct train to Paris. No train change in Lausanne. Carries a sleeping car. Also has couchettes. Coach is second-class. (6) Direct train to Paris. No train changes en toute from Venice. Train has only sleeping cars and couchettes. No coach cars. Has light refreshments. (7) Arrives/departs Milan's Porta Garibaldi railstation. (8) Direct train to Paris. No train changes en route from Venice. Operates late June to early September. Carries a sleeping car. Also has couchettes. Coach is second-class.

Venice - Salzburg 88

Dep. Venice (S. Lucia)	07:30
Arr. Villach (Hbf.)	11:33
Change trains.	
Dep. Villach (Hbf.)	16:00 (2)
Arr. Salzburg	18:53

(1) Restaurant car. (2) Reservation *required*. Supplement charged. Restaurant car. (3) Departs from Venice's Mestre railstation. Direct train to Salzburg. No train change in Villach.

Venice - Vienna 88

Dep. Venice (S. Lucia)	07:30	-0-	20:50 (3)	23:55 (4)
Dep. Venice (Mestre)	07:42	12:41 (2)	21:01	00:06
Arr. Vienna (Sud.)	16:40	20:40	06:23	08:49

(1) Restaurant car. (2) Reservation *required*. Supplement charged. Restaurant car. (3) Carries a sleeping car. Also has couchettes. Coach is second-class. (4) Runs daily.

SCANDINAVIA
(DENMARK, FINLAND, NORWAY, AND SWEDEN)

Children under 4 travel free on trains in Denmark and Norway, under 6 in Finland, and under 12 in Sweden.

SCANRAILPASS

Unlimited travel on all trains and several ferries throughout Denmark, Finland, Norway and Sweden — such as Stockholm–Turku, Rodby–Puttgarden and Trelleborg–Sassnitz. Also allows 50% discount on such ferries as Copenhagen–Malmo, Stockholm–Helsinki and Bergen–Flam.

Both "Scanrailpass" and "Scanrail'N Drive" (below) are sold worldwide (except Scandinavia) by travel agencies, tour operators, and Rail Europe (U.S.A. and Canadian offices listed under "France").

The 1996 *first*-class prices are $222 for any 5 days within 15 days, $346 for any 10 days within one month. For *second*-class: $176 and $278. First-class youth:$167 and $260. Second-class youth: $132 and $209. Children under 4 travel free.

For passengers aged 55 and over, the following prices apply: $193 for *first*-class for any 5 days within 15, *second*-class $153. For any 10 days within one month: $301, $242 respectively.

SCANRAIL'N DRIVE

Unlimited 5 days of train travel plus 3 days of car rental (any 8 days) within 15 day. Prices vary (a) whether for one person or for 2 persons, and (b) the category of car. A third and fourth passenger needs to pay only for a Scanrailpass. The 1996 prices *per person* for 2 persons (using the smallest size car) with the 8-day pass are: $289 for *first*-class train, $249 for *second*-class. Unlimited additional car rental days can be added to either pass at $55 per day.

NORDTURIST RAIL TICKET

Sold only in Denmark, Finland, Norway and Sweden — at all railstations. Unlimited travel for 21 consecutive days on all government railways and on the Oslo–Copenhagen (and v.v.) and the Stockholm–Helsinki (and v.v.) ferries, plus 50% discount on the Bodo/Fauske–Kirkenes (and v.v.) bus in Norway. Depending on the currency exchange rate, the approximate 1996 first-class prices are: $430 for adults, $332 for youths age 12–25, and $215 for children age 4–11. For second-class: $332, $250 and $166.

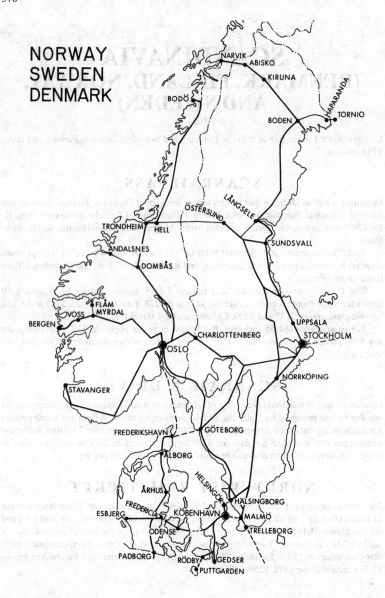

NORWAY
SWEDEN
DENMARK

MIDNIGHT SUN CALENDAR

An average June day has over 17 hours of daylight in Copenhagen and almost 19 in Helsinki, Oslo and Stockholm. Above the Arctic Circle, the whole disc of the sun remains visible throughout the night for periods of 30 to 120 days, depending how far north a city is. Some of the best vantage points are:

NORWAY					SWEDEN				
Green Harbor	April	21	– Aug	23	Bjorkliden	May	26	– July	19
North Cape	May	14	– July	30	Abisko	May	31	– July	14
Hammerfest	May	17	– July	28	Kiruna	May	31	– July	14
Tromso	May	21	– July	23	Gallivare	June	2	– July	12
Harstad	May	26	– July	19	Boden	June	4	– July	10
Narvik	May	26	– July	19					
Svolvaer	May	26	– July	19	FINLAND				
Bodo	June	5	– July	9	Utsjoki	May	22	– July	24
Trondheim	June	8	– July	6	Kilpisjarvi	May	27	– July	18
Andalsnes	June	5	– July	3	Pallastunturi	May	30	– July	15

Gallivare, Kiruna and Abisko are on the rail route from Boden to Narvik. Andalsnes, Trondheim and Bodo can be reached by train service from Oslo. Trondheim also can be reached by rail from Stockholm.

DENMARK

General Information

• Children under four travel free. Half-fare for children 4-11. Children 12 and over must pay full fare. Denmark's two categories of fast trains are IC (Intercity Trains) and EC (EuroCity Trains).

• Seats are reserved on IC and EC trains, and reservations are required between Copenhagen-Frediricia-Aalburg, Copenhagen-Fredericia-Herning and Copenhagen-Fredericia-Esbjerg. Ferry service to England operates from Esbjerg.

The signs you will see at rail stations in Denmark:

AFGANG	DEPARTURE
ANKOMST	ARRIVAL
BANEGARDEN	RAILSTATION
BILLETKONTORET	TICKET OFFICE
DAMER	WOMEN
GARDEROBEN	CHECKROOM
HERRER	MEN
INDGANG	ENTRANCE
KOREPLAN	TIMETABLE
LYNTOG	FAST INTERCITY TRAIN
OPLYSNING	INFORMATION
PLADSBESTILLINGEN	RESERVATIONS
PERRON	TRACK
RYGEKUPES	MOKING COMPARTMENT
SOVEVOGN	SLEEPING CAR
SPISEVOGN	RESTAURANT CAR
TIL PERRONERNE TO	THE PLATFORMS
TOG AFGAR	DEPARTURE TIMETABLE
TOG ANKOMMER	ARRIVAL TIMETABLE
UDGANG	EXIT

Danish Holidays

A list of holidays is helpful because some trains will be noted later in this section as *not* running on holidays. Also, those trains which operate on holidays are filled, and it is necessary to make reservations for them long in advance.

January 1	New Year's Day	June 5	Constitution Day
	Maundy Thursday		(from Noon)
	Good Friday		Whit Sunday
	Easter		Whit Monday
	Easter Monday	December 24	(From Noon)
	Prayer Day	December 25	Christmas Day
	(4th Fri. after Easter)	December 26	Boxing Day
	Ascension Day		

Summer Time

Denmark, Finland, Norway and Sweden change to Summer Time on the last Sunday of March and convert back to Standard Time on the last Sunday of September. Finland is one hour ahead of Denmark, Norway and Sweden all year.

DENMARK'S TRAIN PASSES

All of Denmark's passes must be purchased in Denmark.

Cheap Day Discount Allows discount of about 20% on *first-class* tickets only, on distances of over 100kms (62 miles). Valid all year on Tuesday, Wednesday, Thursday and Saturday.

Child's Discount One child plus one adult traveling a minimum of 100kms in *second-class* only pay the price of 2 children's tickets. On a "cheap day" (see above), the price is even lower. Children under 4 travel free. Half-fare for children 4–11.

65-Ticket Persons 65 and older receive discounts of 25–40% on both first and second-class tickets, depending on the day of the week. Valid most days except Fridays, Sundays, the Wednesday before Easter, Maundy Thursday, Easter Monday, Common Prayer Eve, Ascension Eve, and Dec. 22 to Jan. 2. Can be used in combination with the Cheap Day Discount (which includes Mondays when using 65 Ticket).

Group Ticket Discounts of 20% and more on tickets. The group must be a minimum of 3 adults traveling together in second-class.

ONE-DAY EXCURSIONS AND
CITY-SIGHTSEEING

Here are 12 one-day rail trips that can be made comfortably from Copenhagen and Odense, returning to them in most cases before dinnertime. Notes are provided on what to see and do at each destination.

Copenhagen

Travel on commuter trains is covered by train passes. Trains depart every 20 minutes to most commuter stations.

City tours start from Town Hall Square, in front of the Palace Hotel. To get to the Mermaid or Amalienborg Castle (changing of the guard daily at 12:00) on your own, take bus #1 or #6. For brewery visits, take bus #6 to Carlsberg, or take bus #1 to Tuborg.

Tivoli Gardens, one of the world's most famous amusement parks, is open eaarly April to mid-September. Fireworks are presented several nights each week.

Also see Thorvaldsen Museum, with his sculptures and tomb. Christiansborg Palace, where the Danish Parliament meets. The Danish Resistance Museum. The Zoo. Windowshop in the walking area, Stroget.

The vast collection in the National Museum (12 Frederiksholms Kanal) reflecting Danish life from the Ice Age to the late 17th century plus Danish sculptures and paintings by European artists, open daily except Monday. From mid-June to mid-September: 10:00–16:00. From mid-September to mid-June: 11:00–15:00 Tuesday–Friday and 12:00–16:00 on Saturday and Sunday.

Danish and European paintings (an excellent Matisse collection) at the Royal Museum of Fine Arts, on Solvgade, open daily 10:00–17:00. An exhibit of superb French Impressionists and also Egyptian, Greek, Roman and French sculptures at Carlsberg Glypotek (behind Tivoli Gardens), open daily except Monday. From May through September: 10:00–16:00. From October through April: 12:00–15:00 (10:00–16:00 on Sunday).

The Toy Museum is open all year Wednesday-Sunday 10:00–16:00. There is a good collection of weapons and uniforms in the Royal Arsenal. From May through September: 13:00–16:00 on weekdays, 10:00–16:00 on Sunday. From October through April: 13:00–15:00 on weekdays, 11:00–16:00 on Sunday.

The City Museum, at 59 Vesterbrogade. The view from the top of Town Hall's 350-foot-high tower. Borsen, the oldest stock exchange in the world, still functioning.

The gilded spiral staircase of the Old Saviour's Church (Vor Frelsers Kirke), and the view at the top, from its tower. Regensen, a residential university since 1623. Thorvaldsen's marble statues of Christ and the Apostles in Our Lady's Church (Vor Frue Kirke).

The picturesque buildings along Nyhavn Canal. The line of foreign naval ships along Langelinie Promenade.

The crown jewels and other possessions of Danish monarchs in the museum at Rosenborg Palace (open daily in Summer, only on Tuesday, Friday and Sunday the rest of the year), particularly the pearl-encrusted saddle of Christian IV. Nearby, the 25-acre Botanical Garden and the National Art Gallery.

The Frilandsmuseet open-air museum of Danish houses and farms in suburban **Sorgenfri**, open daily except Monday 10:00–17:00. mid-March to the end of September and 10:00–15:00 the first half of October. the excellent English-language guidebook sold at the ticket counter is essential for understanding the exhibits. Allow at least 2 hours here to stroll the 2 miles of paths.

The farms here are complete with livestock. You will see sheep being sheared, the carding of wool and the spinning of cloth. There are folk dances on Saturday and Sunday.

Commuter trains run 3 times every hour during the day for the 30-minute ride.

In the following timetables, where a city has more than one railstation we have designated the particular station after the name of the city (in parentheses).

Copenhagen - Alborg - Copenhagen   450

All of these trains require reservation and have light refreshments.

Dep. Copenhagen	06:55	07:55	08:55
Arr. Alborg	12:46	13:46	14:46

Sights in **Alborg**: This thousand-year old town is the most important in the north Jutland area. You will find many medieval houses, down the lanes that wind off the modern boulevards. The early 15th century Monastery of the Holy Ghost. The early 16th century Aalborghus Castle.

The basement Duus Wine Cellar in the outstanding ornate, 5-story, 17th century Jens Bang House. The 16th century paintings, depicting the Ten Commandments, in the 12th century Budolphi Cathedral.

The oak-paneled room from 1602 in the Historical Museum, open daily June through August 10:00–19:00 (48 Algade). Works by Scandinavian modern artists in the North Jutland Museum of Modern and Contemporary Art, open daily except Monday 10:00–17:00 (50 Kong Christians Alle).

The more than 300 restaurants (Greek, Italian, Lebanese, Danish) on Jomfru Ane Gade. The Shipping and naval Museum, open daily 10:00–19:00 (75 Vestre Fjordvej). Lindholm Hoje, a museum devoted to Viking archaeology, open daily 10:00–19:00 (11 Vendilavej).

Dep. Alborg	15:51	16:51	17:51	18:51
Arr. Copenhagen	21:48	22:48	23:48	01:05

Copenhagen - Aarhus - Copenhagen

There are 2 ways to make this trip. The first is by train between Copenhagen and Kalundborg, then by boat between Kalundborg and Aarhus. The boat has a smorgasbord cafeteria, and the scenery on the cruise is good.

The second way to Aarhus, entirely by train, is via Fredericia.

It makes an interesting day to go to Aarhus by the combination of train and boat via Kalundborg and return to Copenhagen by train via Fredericia.

Boat - via Kalundborg 451

The tickets for the ferry must be purchased before boarding the train.

Train			Boat		
Dep. Copenhagen (H.)	06:58 (1)	08:50 (8)	Dep. Aarhus (Pier)	12:40 (1)	14:40 (4+7)
Arr. Kalundborg	08:34	10:11	Arr. Kalundborg	14:10	16:10
Change to boat.			*Change to train.*		
Dep. Kalundborg	09:10 (1)	10:25 (8)	Dep. Kalundborg	14:23 (1)	16:23 (5)
Arr. Aarhus (Pier)	12:20	11:55	Arr. Copenhagen (H.)	15:42	17:42

(1) Runs daily, except Sundays and holidays. (2) Reservation *required*. Runs Monday-Friday, except holidays. (3) Runs Monday-Friday, except holidays. (4) Runs Sunday only. (5) Reservation *required*. Runs Sunday only. (6) Runs daily except Saturdays. (7) Plus other Aarhus departures at 16:05 (6) and 18:40 (5), arriving Copenhagen 21:17 and 21:42. (8) Runs Saturday only. Reservation required.

Sights in **Aarhus**: Board the train at the Aarhus pier and take it to Aarhus' railstation. Don't fail to visit the 17th century Clausholm Castle and its Italian garden. The owners have been restoring their home since 1965 in order to make its extraordinary interior accessible to the public.

The magnificent decor, paintings, tapestries and furnishings of the Castle are worth going to Aarhus.

It is a one-hour drive from the city to the Castle, which is open only Easter to October 15. In Spring and Autumn, it is open only on Saturday and Sunday. From June 1 to August 15, Clausholm is open daily 11:00–17:00.

See the 60 completely furnished medieval houses and the 400-year-old mayor's residence at the Old Town open-air museum (Den Gamle By) in the Botanical Gardens. The 15th century Cathedral, noted for the magnificent tones of its twin organs and for the altar's woodcarvings. The ancient University. The Tivoli Friheden amusement park in Marselisborg Woods.

Take bus #6 from the railstation for the 5-mile drive to see the great collection of primitive relics (Stone Age to Viking Era) in the Prehistoric Museum at **Moesgaard**, open daily in Summer 10:00–17:00. It is closed Mondays the rest of the year.

Train - via Fredericia 450

All of these trains require reservation and have light refreshments.

Dep. Copenhagen (H.)	05:55 (1)	06:55	07:55	08:55	09:55
Arr. Aarhus	10:15	11:15	12:15	13:15	14:15
		•	•	•	
Dep. Aarhus	13:26	14:26	15:26	16:26	17:26 (3)
Arr. Copenhagen (H.)	17:48	18:48	19:48	20:48	21:48

(1) Runs daily, except Sundays and holidays. (2) The Friday departure from Aarthus arrives Copenhagen 00:48 on Saturday morning. (3) Plus other departures from Aarhus at 18:26, 19:26 and 20:26 (2), arriving Copenhagen 22:48, 23:48 and 01:05 (2)

THE TRIP TO LEGOLAND

Copenhagen - Billund - Copenhagen

All of these trains require reservation and have light refreshments.

Train 450

Dep. Copenhagen	05:55	06:55	07:55	08:55	09:55 (2)
Arr. Vejle	09:25	10:25	11:25	12:25	13:25

Change to bus.

Dep. Vejle	Frequent times from 10:00 to 24:00
Arr. Billund	55 minutes later

Sights in **Billund**: Although the visit to Legoland can be made as a one-day excursion, an overnight stay in or near Billund is recommended so as to have adequate time to see everything at this 21-acre park that features the world's most popular toy.

The outdoor exhibit of buildings, monuments, cities and villages modeled after sites from all over the world (including the Statue of Liberty and Mount Rushmore sculptures in the U.S.A., the Rhine River and an African wildlife scene) is constructed from more than 33 million plastic interlocking pieces. It is open May 1 to mid-September, 10:00–20:00.

Both a monorail and a small train provide overviews of the park to see details one might miss while walking. Children can make projects at several large playrooms on tables equipped with Legos kits.

Dep. Billund	Frequent times from 05:00 to 24:00
Arr. Vejle	55 minutes later

Change to train.

Dep. Vejle	18:13	19:13	20:13	21:13 (3)
Arr. Copenhagen	21:48	22:48	23:48	01:05

(1) Runs daily, except Sundays and holidays. (2) Plus other departures from Copenhagen every hour 10:55 to 19:55. (3) Friday departure arrives Copenhagen 00:48 Saturday morning.

Copenhagen - Frederickshavn and Frederickshavn - Copenhagen　450

Most of these trains require reservation and have light refreshments.

Dep. Copenhagen (H.)	05:55 (1)	06:55	07:55	08:55	09:55 (6)
Dep. Odense	08:35	09:35	10:35	11:35	12:35
Dep. Fredericia	09:13	10:13	11:13	12:13	13:13
Arr. Arhus	10:15	11:15	12:15	13:15	14:15
Arr. Alborg	11:46 (2)	12:46	13:46 (2)	14:46	15:46 (2)
Arr. Frederickshavn	13:00	13:53	15:00	15:53	17:00

Sights in **Frederickshavn**: The military museum at the 17th century fort. The museum in the 18th century manor house called Bangsbo.

Dep. Frederickshavn	04:40 (3)	05:39 (1)	06:38(2)	07:16 (1)	08:47 (7)
Dep. Alborg	05:51 (1)	06:51	07:51	08:51 (2)	09:51
Dep. Arhus	07:27	08:27	09:27	10:27	11:27
Dep. Fredericia	08:33	09:33	10:33	11:33	12:33
Dep. Odense	09:08	10:08	11:08	12:08	13:08
Arr. Copenhagen (H.)	11:48	12:48	13:48	14:48	15:48

(1) Runs daily, except Sundays and holidays. (2) Change trains. (3) Runs Monday-Friday, except holidays. (4) *No* reservation required. Train has only sleeping cars and couchettes. *No* refreshments. Coach cars are second-class. (5) Runs daily, except Saturday. (6) Plus other departures from Copenhagen every hour from 10:55 to 18:55 (4). (7) Plus other Frederickshavn departures at 09:36, 10:47, 11:36, 12:47, 14:47, 15:36 (5), 16:47, 17:36 (5) and 22:07 (4).

Copenhagen - Helsingborg - Copenhagen   463

Train

Dep. Copenhagen (H.)	07:25 (3)	07:55	08:25	08:55	09:25	09:55 (1)
Arr. Helsingor	08:20	08:50	09:20	09:50	10:20	10:50
Change to ferry						
Dep. Helsingor	08:30	09:10	09:30	10:10	10:30	11:10
Arr. Helsingborg	25 minutes later					

Sights in **Helsingborg**: Stained-glass windows, depicting the city's 900 years of history, in the Radhuset (Town Hall). Karnan, the 14th century fort with walls up to 15 feet thick, one of the best preserved Medieval buildings in Scandinavia. To reach it, take the elevator at the left of The Terrace, from the Main Square.

See the view of the Sound from Rosengarden, and the beautiful roses there. The Municipal Museum. The magnificent pulpit in the 15th century Mariakyrkan (Church of St. Mary). The handsome Concert Hall in Stadsbiblioteket (Town Library). The bronze statue in Hamntoget (Harbor Square).

Ferry

Dep. Helsingborg	13:10	13:30	14:10	14:30	15:10	15:30 (2)
Arr. Helsingor	13:35	13:55	14:35	14:55	15:35	15:55
Change to train						
Dep. Helsingor	13:44	14:14	14:44	15:14	15:44	16:14
Arr. Copenhagen (H.)	14:39	15:09	15:39	16:09	16:39	17:09

(1) Plus other departures from Copenhagen at 10:25, 10:55 and 11:25, arriving Helsingborg 1½ hours later. (2) Plus other departures from Helsingborg at 10 and 30 minutes after each hour until 23:30 (less frequent after 23:30), arriving Copenhagen 1½ hours later. (3) Runs Monday-Friday except holidays.

Copenhagen - Helsingor - Copenhagen   463

Dep. Copenhagen (H.)   07:25 (1)   07:55   08:25   08:55 (2)
Arr. Helsingor   55 minutes later

Sights in **Helsingor**: Kronborg Castle (of Shakespeare's Hamlet). The stained-glass, depicting the town's history, in the Council Chamber of the Radhus (Town Hall). If time allows you to visit only Helsingor or Hillerod (described in the next listing), do *not* choose Helsingor. Fredericksborg Castle at Hillerod is by far the more interesting of the two.

Dep. Helsingor   12:14   12:44   13:14   13:44 (3)
Arr. Copenhagen (H.)   55 minutes later

(1) Runs Monday to Friday, except holidays. (2) Plus other Copenhagen departures at the same frequencies until 18:25, then every 30 minutes until 22:55, plus 23:55 and 00:55. (3) Plus other Helsingor departures at the same frequencies until 18:14, then every 30 minutes until 21:44, plus 22:44 and 23:44.

Copenhagen - Hillerod - Copenhagen   STB

This is an excellent one-day trip by local commuter train on which Eurailpass is valid. We recommend leaving Copenhagen (Central) between 08:00 or 09:00 for the 50-minute ride. (There is service 3 times every hour during the day.) It is a 25-minute walk from the **Hillerod** rail-staion, through the village, past the lake and market square, to the 17th century Fredericksborg Castle and its National Historic Museum of both worldwide art and Danish history. One of the most beautiful castles in Europe, it is located on an island in a small lake, reached by walking over a short bridge. You could spend many days enjoying its contents. A full morning will fly by.

The Castle is open 10:00–17:00 May through September, 10:00–16:00 April and October, and 10:00–15:00 November through March.

Market days in Hillerod are Monday, Thursday and Saturday (09:00–13:00).

You can eat lunch at the Castle's restaurant or in the village on your walk back to the railstation, for departures to Copenhagen every hour at 8 minutes past the hour (05:08–00:08).

By leaving Copenhagen early in the day, it is easy to combine a visit to both Hillerod and **Gilleleje**, a colorful fishing port that is 40 minutes beyond Hillerod. The attractions in Gilleleje are the daily fish auction and the famous Adamsens Fiske-Udsalgr take-out stand which sells fish salads and sandwiches made of fresh-caught crab, shrimp, cod and tuna. It is only a 5-minute walk from Gilleleje's railstation to its port.

The train for Gilleleje leaves Hillerod's track #14 hourly Monday–Friday, every 90 minutes on Saturday and Sunday.

Copenhagen - Humlebaek - Copenhagen STB

Dep. Copenhagen   Frequent times from 05:25 to 00:55
Arr. Humlebaek   30 minutes later

Sights in **Humlebaek**: Exhibits of Giacometti sculptures, painters of the "Cobra" group, and post-1950 art (Warhol, Picasso, Lichtenstein, Calder) in the Louisiana Museum of Modern Art, open daily except Wednesday 10:00–17:00, on Wednesday 10:00–22:00. It is a 15-minute walk from the railstation to the Museum.

Dep. Humlebaek   Frequent times from 05:05 to 00:05
Arr. Copenhagen   30 minutes later

Copenhagen - Malmo - Copenhagen 1215

This popular roundtrip ferry-boat ride to Sweden's West Coast is inexpensive (1994: $44-U.S. for first-class, $28 for second-class), and a 50% discount from first-class is given to holders of a Eurailpass, 25% discount from second-class for Eurail Youthpass.

There are 16–22 saillings daily from Copenhagen (Havnegade) and Malmo for this 45-minute cruise.

Sights in **Malmo**: The Art, Archaeology, Military, Technical and Carriage Museums, all in the Castle. Town Hall. St. Peter's Church. The Sailor's House (3 Fiskehamnsgatan). The 17th and 18th century houses on Lilla Torg (Small Square). Malmo is the gateway to Skane, the beautiful chateau country of Sweden.

Copenhagen - Odense - Copenhagen 450

En route, the train drives onto a ferry for the 65-minute boat ride between Korsor and Nyborg. Passengers can leave the train and stroll on the boat for fine views of the shoreline.

All of these trains require reservation and have light refreshments.

Dep. Copenhagen (H.)   Every hour from 06:55 to 19:55
Arr. Odense   2½ hours later

Sights in **Odense**: The home of Hans Christian Andersen, now a museum, on Hans Jensenstraede. You can visit another Andersen Museum at Munkemollestraede 3. Also see the National Railway Museum in the Dannebrogsgade. The 13th century Cathedral of St. Knud.

Dep. Odense   Every hour from 06:08 to 22:08
Arr. Copenhagen (H.) 2½ hours later

Copenhagen - Roskilde - Copenhagen   450

All of these trains require reservation and have light refreshments.

Dep. Copenhagen (H.)   Frequent times from 06:55 to 19:55
Arr. Roskilde   18 minutes later

Sights in **Roskilde:** The 40 tombs of Denmark's kings and queens, a 500-year old clock, and the post on which such royalty as Peter the Great and the 20th century Duke of Windsor marked their heights (some of them with humorous exaggeration), all in the red brick Cathedral. Open for tours weekdays April–September 09:00–17:45 and October–March 10:00–15:45. Also on Sundays and holidays 12:30–17:45 June–August and 12:30–15:45 September–May.

Also see the exhibits of 5 ancient boats (39 to 59-feet long) in the Viking Ship Museum. Open daily 09:00–17:00 April-October, 10:00–16:00 November-March. It is a 20-minute walk from the town center.

The town center and the Cathedral are a short walk from the railstation. The tourist office (near the Cathedral) supplies an excellent English-language brochure, a city map, and a printed description of a walking tour that includes the town's most important sights.

Dep. Roskilde   Frequent times from 08:29 to 00:41
Arr. Copenh   (H)   18 minutes later

SCENIC RAIL TRIPS

Jaegersborg–Naerum

Called "Denmark's most scenic train ride" by Danish State Railways, this trip begins at Copenhagen's Central railstation. Change trains 30 minutes after departing Copenhagen, at Jaegersborg.

The 30-minute rail trip Jaersborg–Naerum (frequent departures) is along meadows, forests and small lakes. It is covered by train passes.

Naerum is a modern town.

Odense - Fredericia - Odense 450

There is fine coastline scenery on this easy one-day roundtrip. This can also be seen as a portion of the Copenhagen–Frederickshavn route.

All of these trains require reservation and have light refeshments..

Dep. Odense	35 minutes after each hour, from 07:35 to 22:35
Arr. Fredericia	35 minutes later

• • •

Dep. Fredericia	33 minutes after each hour, from 06:33 to 22:33 (1)
Arr. Odense	39 minutes later

(1) Plus another departure from Fredericia at 23:33 daily except Saturday.

INTERNATIONAL ROUTES
FROM DENMARK

Copenhagen is the gateway for travel from Denmark, Norway and Sweden to Western Europe, starting with its connections to Berlin and Hamburg, and then on from those cities to the rest of Western Europe.

Copenhagen - Berlin - Prague 51

The trains are carried Gedser–Warnemunde (a 2-hour trip) by ferries that have a restaurant.

Dep. Copenhagen (Hovedbanegard)	07:20	12:41 (2)	22:30 (3)
Dep. Gedser	09:25	15:25	01:00
Arr. Warnemunde	11:20 (1)	17:20	03:05
Arr. Berlin (Lichtenberg)	15:07 (4)	21:07	07:04
Arr. Prague (Holesovice)	20:59	-0-	-0-

(1) Restaurant car Warnemunde-Prague. (2) Operates late June to mid-August. (3) Carries a sleeping car. Also has couchettes. Coach is second-class. (4) Change trains.

Copenhagen - Hamburg 460

The trains are carried Rodby–Puttgarden (a 65-minute trip) by ferries that have a restaurant.

Dep. Copenhagen (H.)	07:30 (1)	09:20 (1)	12:30	15:20
Dep. Rodby Ferry	09:30	11:30	14:30	17:30
Arr. Hamburg (Hbf.)	12:29	14:29	17:22	20:27

Dep. Copenhagen	17:30 (1)	19:05 (4)	20:05 (5)	21:05 (6+9)
Dep. Rodby Ferry	19:30	21:30	22:30	23:30
Arr. Hamburg (Hbf.)	22:29	00:40	01:35	02:40

(1) Reservation advisable. Supplement charged. Light refreshments. (2) Operates early June to late September. (3) Operates late June to mid-August. (4) Second-class. (5) Operates June 17-September 11. Coach is second-class. (6) Has couchettes. Light refreshments. Coach is second-class. (7) Operates late June to late August. Has couchettes. Coach is second-class. (8) Opearates late May to late September. Has couchettes. (9) Plus other Copenhagen departures at 22:05 (7), arriving Hamburg 04:10.

Copenhagen - Oslo 466

Dep. Copenhagen (H.)	09:45 (1)	21:45 (2)
Arr. Oslo (Sen.)	19:43	07:10

(1) Restaurant car. (2) Runs May 29-August 28. Carries a sleeping car. Also has couchettes. Coach is second-class.

Copenhagen - Stockholm 465

All of these trains require reservation.

Dep. Copenhagen (H.)	11:15 (1)	15:15 (1)	22:15 (2)
Arr. Stockholm (Cen.)	19:35	23:26	07:47

(1) Restaurant car. (2) Carries a sleeping car. Also has couchettes. Coach is second-class.

FINLAND

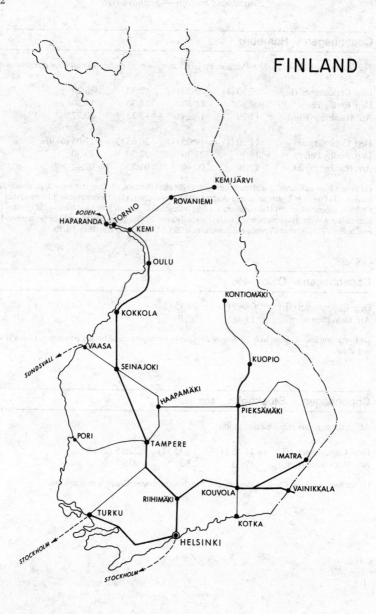

KEMIJÄRVI

ROVANIEMI

BODEN ← TORNIO

HAPARANDA KEMI

OULU

KONTIOMÄKI

KOKKOLA

VAASA

SUNDSVALL ←

SEINÄJOKI

KUOPIO

HAAPAMÄKI

PIEKSÄMÄKI

PORI

TAMPERE

IMATRA

KOUVOLA VAINIKKALA

RIIHIMÄKI

TURKU

KOTKA

STOCKHOLM ←

HELSINKI

STOCKHOLM ←

FINLAND

Overview

Many Eurailpass holders arrive in Finland via the country's ancient capital of Turku and connect with the train immediately to the contemporary capital of Helsinki. Finland's national timetable is called Suomen Kulkuneuvot.

The northern line is dependable and mostly tree-lined.

General Information

• Travel on Finnish trains titled EP or IC requires payment of a supplement.

• The tracks in Finland are constructed with the wide Russian gauge of 50". This makes for spacious cars. The rail service extends as far north as Lapland. Service is maintained during severe Winter weather. All major Finnish Express trains are equipped with radiotelephones for passenger use.

• The signs you will see at railstations in Finland are:

AIKATAULUT	TIMETABLE
LAHTO	DEPARTURE
LAITURILTA	TRACK
LIPPULUUKKU	TICKET OFFICE
MAKUUVAUNU	SLEEPING CAR
MATKALIPPUJEN MYYNTI	RESERVATIONS
MIEHILLE	MEN
NAISILLE	WOMEN
NEUVONTA (TOIMISTO)	INFORMATION
ODOTUSSALI	CHECKROOM
RAUTATIEASEMALLE	RAILSTATION
RAVINTOLAVAUNU	RESTAURANT CAR
SAAPUMINEN	ARRIVAL
SISAAN	ENTRANCE
TUPAKOITSEVILLE	SMOKING COMPARTMENT
ULOS	EXIT

FINLAND'S TRAIN PASSES

Finnrailpass Unlimited rail travel. Can be purchased worldwide and at railstations and ports of arrival in Finland. Sales agents in North America are Holiday Tours of America (425 Madison Ave., New York, N.Y. 10017) Rahim Tours (12 S. Dixie Highway, Suite #203, Lake Worth, FL 33460), Scantours Inc. (1535 Sixth St., Suite #205, Santa Monica,

CA 90401), and Rail Europe (U.S.A. and Canadian offices listed under "France"). Valid for one month, the 1996 *first*-class prices are: $179 for any 3 days, $249 for any 5 days, and $339 for any 10 days. For *second*-class: $119, $169 and $229. Half-fare for children age 6–16. Children under 6 travel free.

Senior Citizens Rail Card Available at railstations. Buyer must pay 50 Finnish marks and provide photo. Allows persons over 65 a 50% discount on each trip that is at least 48 miles.

Group Reduction Groups of 3 or more persons traveling together on a trip of at least 48 miles are allowed discounts of 20% on ticket prices, 25–50% discount for groups of 11 or more.

Child Reduction Tickets are half-price for children 6–16. Children under 6 travel free.

FINNISH HOLIDAYS

A list of holidays is helpful because some trains will be noted later in this section as *not* running on holidays. Also, those trains which operate on holidays are filled, and it is necessary to make reservations for them long in advance.

January 1	New Year's Day		Whit Saturday
	Epiphany		Whit Sunday
	Good Friday	June	Midsummer Eve
	Easter		Midsummer's Day
	Easter Monday		All Saint's Day
May 1	May Day	December 6	Independence Day
	Ascension Day	December 25	Christmas Day
		December 26	Boxing Day

ONE-DAY EXCURSIONS AND CITY-SIGHTSEEING

Here are 7 one-day rail trips that can be made comfortably from Helsinki, returning there in most cases before dinnertime. Notes are provided on what to see and do at each destination. The number after the name of each route is the Cook's timetable.

Helsinki

Helsinki's single most inspiring sight is Temppeliaukio Church, known since its 1969 dedication as the "Rock Church." This fantastic structure was quarried on its site, out of the bedrock in the middle of one of the oldest residential districts of Helsinki. Because the area occupied by worshipers is below the street level, all that can be seen as you walk toward the church is a low rock wall and the massive (70-foot diameter) copper dome.

Also see the large tubular steel sculpture, symbolizing music, in Sibelius Park. Tapiola, the model "new town." Finlandia Hall. The National Museum (closed Mondays September through May). The floral cemetery. The onion towers on the Greek Orthodox Uspenski Cathedral.

It is best to visit Market Square before Noon, to see the flowers, fish and mountains of berries. Also see the Town Hall. The Empress Stone obelisk. (Ferries from a pier near the obelisk go every hour to the island Suomenlinna Fortress.) See the impressive columns of Parliament House. The University Library and the Cathedral, in Senate Square.

The paintings and sculptures in the National Art Gallery. The National Theater. The Elaintarhantie shopping complex, opposite the railstation. The Botanical Gardens, in Elaintarha Park. The Linnanmaki amusement center, closed Mondays. The collection of Finnish wood houses at the open-air Museum of Seurasaari.

The Ateneum Art Gallery. The Gallen-Kallela Museum. The art and furniture at the Helsinki Municipal Museum. Old-fashioned and modern farm tools and implements in the Agricultural Museum. The Military Museum (Maurinkatu 1.) There are good views of the South Harbor and the waterfront from Observatory Hill (Tahtitornin Vuori). See the displays in the Architectural Museum of Finland (Puistokatu 4).

Take the #6 tram to Arabia and see the original site of Helsinki, Old Town. Take the ferry from North Harbor to the Korkeasaari Island Zoo. See the displays in the Architectural Museum of Finland (Puistokatu 4).

Helsinki - Hameenlinna - Helsinki   495

All of these trains have light refreshments, unless designated otherwise.

Dep. Helsinki	06:58	07:58 (1)	08:58	09:58	10:58	11:58 (5)
Arr. Hameenlinna	65 minutes later					

Sights in **Hameenlinna**: The medieval castle. Ahvenisto Tower. The Art Museum. The City Museum.

Dep. Hameenlinna	11:46	12:42 (2)	13:46	14:46	15:46 (3)	17:08 (6)
Arr. Helsinki	74 minutes later					

(1) Reservation *required*. (2) Reservation *required*. Restaurant car. (3) Restaurant car. (4) Runs daily, except Sundays and holidays. (5) Plus another departure from Helsinki at 12:58 (3). (6) Plus other departures from Hameenlinna at 18:48 (3), 19:46 (4), 20:41, 21:46 and 22:58 (2).

Helsinki - Hanko - Helsinki   490 + Finnish timetable

A beautiful ride through woods and along lakes,

All of the trains Helsinki–Karjaa and v.v. have light refresments.

Dep. Helsinki	06:50	09:02	12:02
Arr. Karjaa	07:50	10:00	13:00
Change to local train.			
Dep. Karjaa	07:52	10:02	13:02
Arr. Hanko	08:42	10:52	13:57

Sights in **Hanko**: The southernmost town in Finland. The tourist office is open all year Monday–Friday, 09:00–16:00 and in Summer also on Saturday 09:00–16:00, Sunday 11:00–15:00. Take a 2-hour cruise, leaving from the eastern harbor, operating June through mid-August. There is good fishing here. See the statue dedicated to the many Finns who disembarked from here to migrate to the United States between 1880 and 1930. Dance or try your luck at the Casino.

Dep. Hanko	14:10	16:10	21:18
Arr. Karjaa	14:52	16:52	22:02
Change to a standard train.			
Dep. Karjaa	15:02	17:02	22:09
Arr. Helsinki	16:02	18:02	23:10

Helsinki - Lahti - Helsinki   496

All of these trains have light refreshments, unless designated otherwise.

Dep. Helsinki	07:04	08:04	09:10 (1)	10:26	11:26	12:26 (2)
Arr. Lahti	08:23	09:23	10:52	11:45	12:45	13:45

Sights in **Lahti**: A Winter sports center. The tourist office (closed Sunday) is in the rear of the Town Hall (intersection of Vesijarvenkatu and Aleksanterinkatu). See the view from the top of the 90-meter high ski jump, its elevators operating June through September, 10:00–19:30. It is only a 10-minute walk from the Town Hall.

Visit the Art Gallery. The Ethnographic Museum. The Radio Museum, open Sundays 13:00–15:00. In Summer, there are open-air concerts at the Mukkula Tourist Center. Shop here for marvelous Finnish glassware.

Dep. Lahti	12:07	14:03 (1)	14:58	16:30 (2)	17:55	18:30 (5)
Arr. Helsinki	13:32	15:50	16:34	17:54	19:56	19:54

(1) Second-class. No light refreshments. (2) Runs daily, except Saturday. No light refreshments. (3) Runs Sunday only. Second-class. No light refreshments. (4) Runs Sunday only. Reservation *required*. (5) Plus other Lahti departures at 19:36 (3), 19:53 (4), 20:30 and 21:41.

Helsinki - Riihimaki - Helsinki   495 + 496

Dep. Helsinki   Frequent times from 06:26 to 23:04
Arr. Riihimaki   50 minutes later

Sights in **Riihimaki**: The wood-working mills of H. G. Paloheimo. The glass factories of Riihimaen Lasi Oy. The Museum Peltosaari. The Municipal Museum.

Dep. Riihimaki   Frequent times from 05:58 to 23:20
Arr. Helsinki   50 minutes later

Helsinki - Rovaniemi   495

A trip to Lapland.

Dep. Helsinki	07:00 (1)	09:58 (1)	19:26 (2)	22:00 (2)
Arr. Rovaniemi	16:40	20:05	07:42	11:09
Dep. Rovaniemi	07:00 (3)	13:00 (1)	18:05 (2)	20:10 (5+6)
Arr. Helsinki	16:58	22:58	07:10	08:15

(1) Light refreshments. (2) Carries a sleeping car. Coaches are second-class. Light refreshments. (3) Restaurant car. (4) Runs Sunday only. Carries a sleeping car. Coaches are second-class. (5) Runs Friday and Sunday. Carries a sleeping car. Coaches are second-class. Light refreshments. (6) Plus another Rovaniemi departure at 21:05, arriving Helsinki 08:27.

Helsinki - Savonlinna   499

Dep. Helsinki	07:02 (1)	10:26 (1)	17:02 (2)
Arr. Parikkala	10:47	14:19	20:44
Change trains.			
Dep. Parikkala	10:52	14:24 (4)	20:49
Arr. Savonlinna	11:45	15:41	21:45

Sights in **Savonlinna**: A charming town in the Lake Region, near the Russian border. The Tourist Office (Olavinkatu 35) is open in Summer daily 07:15–22:00. There is an English-language guided tour at Olavinlinna, a medieval castle. Shop for food at the open-air market.

Dep. Savonlinna	06:20 (2)	16:25 (3)	16:47
Arr. Parikkala	07:16	16:23	16:48
Change trains.			
Dep. Parikkala	07:20 (2)	16:25 (3)	16:50 (1+5)
Arr. Helsinki	11:02	20:56	21:58

(1) Light refreshments. (2) Reservation *required*. Restaurant car. (3) Runs Sunday only. Reservation required. Light refreshments.(4) Runs May 29-August 14 only. (5) Runs daily except Sundays and holidays.

Helsinki - Tampere - Helsinki   495

All of these trains have light refreshments, unless designated otherwise.

Dep. Helsinki	06:58	07:58 (1)	08:58	09:58	10:58	11:58
Arr. Tampere	2 hours later					

Sights in **Tampere**: The aquarium, planetarium, children's zoo, amusement park, observation tower and planetarium at the Sarkanniemi Recreation Center. The more than 30,000 objects exhibited in the Hame Museum, particularly the handwoven rugs and tapestries. Many excellent artworks, frescoes and the altarpiece in the Cathedral, completed in 1907. The fine modern architecture of Kaleva Church. The National history Museum. The Haihara Doll Museum. The largest church bells in Finland, at the Orthodox Church.

See a performance at Tampere's Summer Theater in Pyynikki Park, from a seat in the unique bowl-shaped auditorium that rotates 360 degrees. Everyone sitting in the last row at the beginning of a performance also has a front-row seat during the show.

Dep. Tampere	12:00 (2)	12:58	13:58	15:00 (3)	16:00 (1)	16:20 (5)
Arr. Helsinki	2 hours later					

(1) Reservation *required.* (2) Reservation *required.* Restaurant car. (3) Restaurant car. (4) Reservation *required.* Runs daily, except Saturday. Restaurant car. (5) Runs, daily, except Sundays and holidays. (6) Runs Friday and Sunday. Reservation *required.* (7) Plus other departures from Tampere at 18:04 (3), 18:58 (5), 19:56, 20:10 (6), 20:58 and 22:10 (2).

Helsinki - Turku - Helsinki   490

All of these trains have light refreshments.

Dep. Helsinki	06:50	09:02	12:02
Arr. Turku (Stn.)	09:12	11:16	14:16

Sights in **Turku**: A "Turku Card," good for city buses, museum admissions and discounts in restaurants and shops is sold at the City Tourist Office, near Market Square, at Kasityolaiskatu 4.

See the Provincial Museum and the marvelous Banquet Hall in the 13th century Castle, a short walk from the Silja Lane railstation, only a few minutes ride past the Main railstation. The Castle is open 10:00–18:00 May–September, 11:00–15:00 the rest of the year. The great organ (6,057 pipes) in the 13th century Cathedral.

The composer's instruments and personal possessions in the Sibelius Museum. The cobbled marketplace (fruits, flowers, fish and produce), Monday Saturday 08:00–14:00

Dep. Turku (Stn.)	13:43	15:43	17:00	19:35	20:55
Helsinki	16:02	18:02	19:18	22:00	23:10

INTERNATIONAL ROUTES
FROM FINLAND

Helsinki is the gateway both to Russia (Leningrad, and on to Moscow) and Western Scandinavia (Stockholm, and on to Oslo and Copenhagen). Oulu is the starting point for trips to northern Sweden (Boden) and northern Norway (Narvik).

Helsinki - St. Petersburg 902

These trains require reservation and have a restaurant car.

Dep. Helsinki	06:26	15:32
Arr. St. Petersburg (Fin.)	13:55	23:20

Helsinki - Moscow 902

This train carries a sleeping car and a restaurant car.

Dep. Helsinki	17:08	Arr. Moscow	09:10

Helsinki - Stockholm 490

The price for the cruise across the Gulf of Bothnia (Turku-Stockholm) on the comfortable and pleasant Silja Line ships is $46 for first-class and $37 for second-class in 1994. This passage *is* covered by Eurailpass. The fare for a sleeping cabin is *not* covered by Eurailpass — but only for those who reserve and pay for a bed. Food on the ship is varied and delicious.

We recommend the daytime sailing in order to see the thousands of tiny islands on the ride through this extremely interesting archipelago. During the daytime cruise, there is a good smorgasbord for both lunch and dinner. On the night cruise, a live band plays music in the ship's nightclub. On both day and night cruises, the major activity is duty-free shopping.

490 Train			*1250 Ship*		
Dep. Helsinki	06:50 (1)	17:06 (1)	Dep. Turku (Abo)	10:00 (2)	20:00 (3)
Arr. Turku (Harbor)	09:27	19:26	*Set watch back one hour.*		
Walk to Abo Pier.			Arr. Stockholm (Var.)	19:00	07:00

(1) Light refreshments. (2) Runs daily except January 1,3,10,17,24, April 17-21, September 12,13 and December 24, 25. (3) Runs daily except May 29, 30, September 4-8, December 24, 25, 31.

Helsinki - Oulu - Haparanda - Boden - Narvik

495

Dep. Helsinki	06:58 (1)	-0-	12:58 (2)	19:26 (3)	22:00 (3)
Arr. Oulu	13:52	-0-	20:05	04:20	07:33

Sights in **Oulu:** The Art Museum. The Zoological Museum. The Cathedral. The Water Tower, on top of Puolivalinkangas, open May-October. Picturesque, ancient waterfront warehouses. The Church and Open Air Museum. Kastelli Church.

Dep. Oulu	13:57	-0-	04:25	07:38
Arr. Kemi	15:09	-0-	05:55	09:18
Change to bus. 474				
Dep. Kemi	15:15	-0-	06:42 (4)	09:23 (4)
Arr. Torino	15:43	-0-	06:58	09:55
Change buses. 474				
Dep Torino	-0-	-0-	-0-	-0-
Set your watch back one hour.				
Arr. Haparanda	-0-	-0-	-0-	-0-
Change buses. 474				
Dep. Haparanda	14:25	-0-	-0-	10:10 (5)
Arr. Boden	16:45	-0-	-0-	12:35
Change to train. 475				

We recommend stopping-over in Boden for the night so as to travel Boden–Narvik during the daylight hours in order to be able to see the fine mountain scenery on that route. You cross the Arctic Circle going from Boden to Narvik.

Dep. Boden	07:35 (6)	10:43 (7)	-0-	-0-	-0-
Arr. Kiruna	11:03	14:12	-0-	-0-	-0-
Dep Kiruna	11:18 (6)	14:23 (7)	-0-	-0-	-0-
Arr. Narvik	14:23	17:34	-0-	-0-	-0-

(1) Light refreshments. (2) Restaurant car. (3) Carries a sleeping car. Coach is second-class. Light refreshments. (4) Runs daily, except Sundays and holidays. (5) Runs Monday-Friday, except holidays. (6) Reservation *required*. Coach is second-class. (7) Reservation *required*. Coach is second-class. Light refreshments.

NORWAY

Overview

Norway's train service extends to the very top of the country in the Land of the Midnight Sun and to the western port of Bergen. A delightful way of touring the country, train travel in Norway can boast of the most number of scenic rail trips of any Scandinavian country.

General Information

• Children under four travel free. Half-fare for children 4-15. Children 16 and over must pay full fare.

• Norway is the most glorious places in which to experience the wonder of the Midnight Sun.

• Norwegian State Railways have one coach on the Oslo-Bergen and Bergen-Oslo runs (and similar service on other long-distance routes) designed for conveying handicapped persons and other passengers requiring special care, such as mothers traveling with young children. These special cars have a compartment accommodating two wheel chairs that are lifted aboard. An 8-seat compartment in these cars, equipped for mothers and their infants, is provided with a baby-chair, bottle heater, and other equipment helpful when caring for small children. This compartment is adjacent to a space with fitted toilets and a diaper-changing table. The car also has oxygen tanks, a stretcher and a small wheel chair for handicapped persons to use in moving about inside the train.

• From Dombas and on north, you are in the land of the Midnight Sun. (See Midnight Sun Calendar.)

The signs you will see at railstations in Norway are:

ANKOMIST	ARRIVAL
AVGANG	DEPARTURE
BANESTASJONEN	RAILSTATION
BILLETLUKEN	TICKET OFFICE
DAMER	WOMEN
GARDEROBEN	CHECKROOM
HERRER	MEN
INFORMASJON	INFORMATION
INGANG	ENTRANCE
RESERVASJONSLUKEN	RESERVATIONS
ROKERE	SMOKING COMPARTMENT
SOVEVOGN	SLEEPING CAR
SPISEVOGN	RESTAURANT CAR
SPOR	TRACK
TIL PLATTFORMENTE	TO THE PLATFORMS
TOGTABELL	TIMETABLE
UTGANG	EXIT
VEKSLIGSKONTOR	CURRENCY EXCHANGE
VINDUSPLASS	WINDOW SEAT

Norwegian Holidays

A list of holidays is helpful because some trains will be noted later in this section as *not* running on holidays. Also, those trains which operate on holidays are filled, and it is necessary to make reservations for them long in advance.

January 1	New Year's Day		Ascension Day
	Maundy Thursday	May 17	Constitution Day
	Good Friday		Whit Monday
	Easter	December 25	Christmas Day
	Easter Monday	December 26	Boxing Day
May 1	Labor Day		

EURAILPASS BONUSES

A 30% reduction on the fares of the Color Line Steamship Company for the cruise between Kristiansand and Hirtshals (Denmark).

NORWAY'S TRAIN PASSES

Norway Rail Pass Unlimited train travel. The *second-class* prices during May-September are: $190 for 7 days, $255 for 14 days. During October-April, 1996: $150 and $205. Half-fare for children age 4-15. *First-class* 1996 prices: May-September $250 for 7 days, $330 for 14 days. October-April $200 for 7 days, $265 for 14 days. Sold in North America by travel agencies and Scanam World tours, 933 Highway 23, Pompton Plains, NJ 07444. Telephone: (800) 545-2204. **Flexipasses** also available: *First-class* for any 3 days in one month! May-September $190; October-April $170. *Second-class:* $135 and $120.

All of the following train passes can be purchased only at Norwegian railstations.

"Green Departures" are at times when traffic volume is low. All of the following discounts are restricted to "Green Departures," marked with a green dot in Norwegian timetables.

Senior Citizen Discount Persons over 67 years old are allowed a 50% discount on both first-class and second-class tickets. Must obtain an ID card, available at railstations.

Mini-Price Tickets A one-way, *second*-class train ticket available either (a) at discount for a *specific* trip, such as $51 Oslo–Bergen versus $66 normal fare for an ordinary second-class ticket, or (b) at $67 for an *unlimited* distance. Must be purchased at least one day in advance.

The Oslo–Bodo–Tronheim 1,282 km trip (797 miles) costs about $246 for an ordinary second-class ticket. This $492 roundtrip can be covered with 2 "Mini-Price Tickets" for only $164.

ONE-DAY EXCURSIONS AND CITY-SIGHTSEEING

Here are 11 one-day rail trips that can be made comfortably from Bergen, Oslo and Stavanger, returning to them at or shortly after dinnertime. Notes are provided on what to see and do at each destination. The number after the name of each route is the Cook's timetable.

In the following timetables, where a city has more than one railstation, we have designated the particular station after the name of the city (in parentheses).

Oslo

Free admission to most Oslo museums and the Tusen Fryd amusement park; 50% discount on sightseeing by bus and boat; free travel on public city boats, buses, trams and trains; and discounts at cinemas, theaters and opera with "Oslo Card." Sold at most Oslo hotels, the Tourist Offices, Norway Information Center, and Oslo's Central railstation.

The 1995 prices are: Adult one-day: $16; two-day:$27; three-day: $34. Children one day: $8; two-day:$12; three-day:$16.

Walk from the railstation, up Karl Johansgate, to the Royal Palace. En route, you will pass the National Theater. Behind it is the underground suburban train station. See the massive mural, in the post World War II City Hall, commemorating the Nazi occupation of Norway.

From the pier behind City Hall, take the 4-minute boat ride to Bygdoy (or take Bus #30 from the center of town) to see the 4 interesting museums there: Viking ships (daily 09:00–18:00); the balsa Kon Tiki and reed Ra II rafts used by Thor Heyerdahl to recreate ancient voyages (daily 09:00–18:00); Roald Amunden's polar exploration ship Fram in the National Maritime Museum (daily 09:00–17:45); and the outdoor collection of 170 historical buildings brought to Oslo from all over Norway along with more than 80,000 items exhibited in the Norwegian Folk Museum (daily 10:00-18:00).

The walk from the Maritime Museum to the Viking ships and the Folk Museum takes only 20 minutes.

Later, see the bronze and granite sculptures of Gustav Vigeland in Frogner Park. Its highlight is a 55-foot-high monolith that has 121 intertwined figures. The Vigeland Museum at Nobelsgate 32. The collection of 1,100 Munch paintings and 18,000 Munch prints in the Edvard Munch Museum (53 Toyengata). The Historical Museum. Norway's largest art collection, at the National Gallery (13 Univesitetsgaten), open Monday and Wednesday-Saturday 10:00-16:00, Sunday 11:00-14:00. Oslo Cathedral.

Visit Aker Brygge (pier), a huge entertainment, shopping and residential project. The Museum of Applied Art. The 12th century, stone Gamle Aker Church (open Tuesday and Thursday in Summer).

The Resistance Museum and Defense Museum (commemorating the German occupation of Norway during World War II) in the Hjemmefront, at the 14th century Akershus Castle and Fortress, only a 5-minute walk from City Hall.

The Sonja Henie-Nils Onstad collection of modern paintings at Henie-Onstad Art Center (Monday-Saturday 09:00–22:00, Sunday 11:00–22:00). The Museum of Contemporary Art, opened in 1991. Marvelous views of Oslo and the Fjord from the Ski Jump and Ski Museum at

Holmenkollen. Take the trolley to the Merchant Marine Academy at Sjomannsskolen.

Take Bus #36 from Town Hall Square for a one-hour ride to **Sundvollen**. Beautiful Tyri Fjord scenery.

Oslo - Goteborg - Oslo   480

All of these trains require reservation and have a restaurant car.

Dep. Oslo (Sen.)	08:10 (1)		Dep. Goteborg	14:48 (2)	18:00(1)
Arr. Goteborg	12:10		Arr. Oslo (Sen.)	19:43	22:10

(1) Second class only. (2) Runs Friday, Saturday and Sunday (daily May 29-Sept. 24)

Oslo - Hamar - Oslo   483

Be sure to sit on the left side for the best view of the fantastic scenery along the western shore of **Lake Mjosa**. Norway's largest lake (75 miles long).

All of these trains have light refreshments and are second-class, unless designated otherwise.

Dep. Oslo (Sen.)	08:00 (1)	09:05	10:05	11:00 (2)	13:05
Arr. Hamar	09:26	10:40	11:43	12:36	14:47

Sights in **Hamar**: The enormous outdoor Hedmark Museum complex of more than 40 buildings, most of them from the 18th and 19th century, brought here from other places. One of the buildings is a house built in 1871 in North Dakota, U.S.A., by a Norwegian emigrant.

Also visit the 7½-acre Railway Museum, open May–September, to see many early coaches and locomotives as well as Norway's first railstation.

Dep. Hamar	13:56 (4)	15:09 (2)	16:26 (8)	17:15 (2)	19:17 (2)	20:23 (6+7)
Arr. Oslo (Sen.)	14:27	16:55	18:25	18:55	20:55	22:07

(1) Reservation *required*. Has first-class coach seats. Restaurant car. (2) Reservation *required*. (3) Runs daily, except Saturday. (4) Reservation *required*. Has first-class seats. (5) Restaurant car. (6) Runs Sunday only. (7) Plus another Hamar departure at 20:58 (4), arriving Oslo 22:28. (8) Runs Friday and Sunday.

Oslo - Lillehammer - Oslo   483

All of these trains have light refreshments and are second-class, unless designated otherwise.

Dep. Oslo (Sen.)	08:05 (1)	09:05	11:05 (2)
Arr. Lillehammer	10:09	11:36	13:23

Sights in **Lillehammer**: Site of the 1994 Winter Olympic Games. Visit the Sandvig collection of more than 100 old buildings and craftwork demonstration at the 100-acre open-air Maihaugen Museum, open daily 11:00–19:00 from late June to early August and 11:00–14:00 the rest of the year. See the "White Swan" paddle-wheel steamboat, Skibladner, at the city's dock.

Dep. Lillehammer	12:12 (3)	14:13 (1)	16:30 (2)	18:29 (2)	20:15 (3)
Arr. Oslo (Sen.)	14:27	16:46	18:55	20:55	22:28

(1) Reservation *required*. Has first-class coach. Restaurant car. (2) Reservation *required*. (3) Reservation *required*. Has first-class coach. (4) Restaurant car.

Oslo - Vinstra - Oslo   483

All of these trains have light refreshments and are second-class, unless designated otherwise

Dep. Oslo (Sen.)	08:05 (1)	09:05	11:05 (2)
Arr. Vinstra	11:05	12:47	14:27

Sights in **Vinstra:** A mountain resort. Home of the legendary Peer Gynt. See the memorial over his grave in the village church. Cross-country skiing is popular here.

Dep. Vinstra	11:07 (3)	13:06 (1)	17:13 (2)	18:08 (5)	19:15 (2)
Arr. Oslo (Sen.)	14:27	16:46	20:46	22:07	22:28

(1) Reservation *required*. Has first-class coach seats. Restaurant car. (2) Reservation *required*. (3) Reservation *required*. Has first-class coach. (4) Restaurant car. (5) Runs Sunday only.

THE FJORD TRAIN ROUTE

Oslo - Drammen - Tonsberg - Sandefjord - Larvik - Skien - Nordagutu - Oslo 488

This one-day excursion offers great views of several fjords (starting with the Oslofjord), wooded countryside, and lovely lakes. As the schedules indicate, stops can be made for sightseeing in several of the towns on this route.

All of these trains are second-class and have light refreshments Oslo-Skien (and v.v.), unless designated otherwise.

A train change in Skien is necessary in both directions.

Oslo (Sen.)	06:21 (9)	09:09 (9)	11:09 (9)	13:09 (9)	14:18 (3+7)
Arr. Drammen	07:04	09:37	11:37	13:38	14:37
Arr. Tonsberg	08:02	10:31	12:31	14:32	15:33
Arr. Sandefjord	08:25	10:58	12:55	14:56	15:57
Arr. Larvik	08:43	11:14	13:11	15:12	16:18
Arr. Skien	09:28	11:58	13:56	15:57	17:02
Dep. Skien	09:49	-0-	-0-	16:12	18:36 (2)
Arr. Nordagutu	10:21	-0-	-0-	17:11	19:10

Dep. Nordagutu	-0-	10:28	12:42 (1)	14:45 (1)	16:48 (8)
Arr. Skien	-0-	10:52	13:35	15:18	17:20
Dep. Skien	09:50 (9)	11:38 (4)	13:40	15:40 (4)	17:35
Dep. Larvik	10:23	12:23	14:23	16:23	18:23
Dep. Sandefjord	10:39	12:39	14:39	16:39	18:39
Dep. Tonsberg	11:02	13:02	15:02	17:02	19:02
Dep. Drammen	12:01	14:02	16:02	18:02	20:02
Arr. Oslo (Sen.)	12:43	14:43	16:43	18:43	20:43

(1) No light refreshments. (2) Skien–Nordagatu (and v.v.): runs daily, except Saturday. No light refreshments. (3) Runs Monday–Friday, except holidays. (4) Runs daily. (5) Runs daily, except holidays Nordagatu–Skien. No light refreshments. (6) Runs daily, except Saturday. No light refreshments. (7) Plus another departure from Oslo at 15:09, arriving Skien 17:56, Nordagatu 19:10 (2). (8) Plus another departure from Nordagatu at 18:50 (6+9), arriving Oslo 22:51. (9) Reservation required.

Sights in **Drammen**: The activity along the busy docks. Many attractive old buildings. Watching the Drommensfjorden meet the Drammen River.

Sights in **Tonsberg**: Norway's oldest town. See today's whaling ships and the ruins of an ancient Viking castle, Tonsberghus. Also, the Vestfold Museum, the 12th century St. Michael's Church, the 12th century Sem Church, and the 13th century Royal Castle.

Sights in **Sandefjord**: The main port for Norway's whaling ships. See the whaling monument in the square. The Whaling Museum. Nearby are the mouth of the Oslofjorden and the head of the Sandefjorden.

Sights in **Larvik**: The Museum. The fjord.

Sights in **Skien**: The large sawmill operations. The meeting of Skien River and Lake Hjelle.

"NORWAY IN A NUTSHELL"

The easiest way to take the Myrdal-Flam scenic train ride is to buy either one of the one-day "Norway In A Nutshell" packages. The Bergen roundtrip, which cost 390 Norwegian Kroner in 1994 (NOK-195 for children under 16), includes the train Bergen–Myrdal, the "Flam Line" cogwheel train Myrdal–Flam, the fjord boat trip Flam–Gudvangen, the bus Gudvangen–Voss, and the train from Voss back to Bergen = 7 to 9 hours.

The Oslo roundtrip, which cost 596 Norwegian Kroner in 1994 (NOK-298 for children under 16), includes the train Oslo–Myrdal, the "Flam Line" cogwheel train Myrdal–Flam, the fjord boat trip Flam–Gudvangen, the bus Gudvangen–Voss, and the train from Voss back to Oslo =15 hours.

Both the one-way Bergen-Oslo "Nutshell" (13-15 hours) and the one-way Oslo-Bergen "Nutshell" (11 hours) cost NOK-557 for an adult in 1994, and NOK-278 for a child age 4-15.

For North American booking of "Nutshell," phone Passage Tours of Scandinavia at (800) 548-5960 or Nordique Tours at (800) 995-7997.

When these packages are purchased in Norway, either a Eurailpass or a Scanrailpass can be used for all of the train rides, reducing the prices above substantially.

Sights in **Bergen**: Free admission to most Bergen museums, rides on the funicular to the top of Mt. Flojen, and discounts at cinemas, theaters, concerts, sightseeing, boat excurions, parking and car rental with "Bergen Card." Sold at Bergen hotels, Tourist Information and the bus station.

The 1995 adult prices are: 100 Norwegian Kroner for one day, NOK-150 for 2 days. For children age 4-15: NOK-50 and NOK-75.

Visit Torget, a fish market that has been operating for 9 centuries (weekdays: 08:30–15:00). See Bergenhus Fortress, with its 13th century Hakon Hall. The 12th century Maria-kirken (St. Mary's Church). Europe's most modern aquarium and the collection of 19th century houses in Gamle Bergen (Old Bergen). Edvard Grieg's home in **Troldhaugen**.

Take the 5-minute funicular ride to the top of 2,000-foot-high **Mt. Floien**. See the Hanseatic Museum. The Maritime Museum. The Arts and Crafts Museum. The Bryggen Museum. The Leprosy Museum. Take the cable car to the top of **Mt. Ulriken**.

It is only 22 minutes for the bus ride and short walk to see the 13th century Fana Church and Fantoft, the 12th century Stave Church.

SCENIC RAIL TRIPS

Bergen to Oslo...and The Stalheim-Flam Detour   481

Indisputably, the most scenic rail route in Europe. There are several ways to make the detour, either in a single day or by adding one or 2 days to the Bergen-Oslo trip.

The most carefree way to make the detour in a single day is to check baggage direct from Bergen to Oslo, rather than be bothered with it all day.

The complete Bergen–Oslo line was opened in 1909 as the only year-round land transportation between Norway's 2 larges cities. It was electrified in 1964. Terrain and climate both caused construction problems which prior to then had never been encountered in building a railway line. The 300-mile length of track must pass through 200 tunnels and 18 miles of snow sheds in addition to crossing more than 300 bridges.

The first 40 minutes after leaving Bergen is along the lovely Sorfjorden. Travelers are frustrated by the interruptions of viewing the scenery caused by the many snow sheds.

However, it would be impossible for the trains to operate daily year round on this route and stick to a strict timetable if it were not for these structures.

When taking the Voss-Stalheim–Flam–Myrdal detour we have been recommending since 1971, you omit the 63-minute Voss–Myrdal portion of the main Bergen–Oslo line.

Voss - Stalheim - Flam - Myrdal Detour

The Gudvangen-Flam cruise on the Sognefjord (called "King of the Fjords") is the most scenic fjord trip in Norway.

481		*481*	
Dep. Bergen	07:33 (1)	Dep. Oslo (Sen.)	07:42 (1)
Arr. Voss	08:39	Arr. Myrdal	12:17
Change to bus. (Nor.)		*Change to narrow-gauge train (481)*	
Dep. Voss	09:50	Dep. Myrdal	12:25
Arr. Stalheim	10:25	Arr. Flam	13:25
Dep. Stalheim	10:35	*Change to fjord boat.*	
Arr. Gudvangen	11:20	Dep. Flam	14:30 (2)
Change to fjord boat.		Arr. Gudvangen	16:35
Dep. Gudvangen	11:30 (2)	*Change to bus. (Nor.)*	
Arr. Flam	13:30	Dep. Gudvangen	16:55
Change to narrow-gauge train (481)		Arr. Stalheim	17:40
Dep. Flam	15:00	Dep. Stalheim	17:50
Arr. Myrdal	15:55	Arr. Voss	18:10
Change trains. 481		*Change to train. 481*	
Dep. Myrdal	16:58 (3+5)	Dep. Voss	18:46 (4)
Arr. Oslo (Sen.)	21:55	Arr. Bergen	20:01

(1) Reservation *required*. Light refreshments. (2) Operates mid-April to mid-October. (3) Reservation *required*. Light refreshments. Plus another Myrdal departure (reservation *required*, runs daily, restaurant car) at 17:21, arriving Oslo 22:12. (4) Second-class. (5) Runs daily except Sat. May 29-Sept. 28 and Fridays + Sundays Sept. 19-May 27.

Sights in **Voss**: The 13th century church. The restored farmhouses and other buildings in the outdoor folk museum.

NOTE: On the Oslo-Bergen route (right-hand column above), there are only 8 minutes to change trains in Myrdal. *In mid-Summer, hundreds of people compete for the few seats on the Flam Line train.* Bus tour groups which board the Flam Line in Vatnahalsen (3 minutes after Myrdal) have to stand, which is very difficult on this route.

En route Bergen-Oslo, the one-hour bus ride from Voss to **Stalheim** passes (on your left) the spectacular Tvinde waterfall. At Stalheim there is only a Norwegian village museum and a hotel—which we recommended with high praise for 23 years.

Reports we received from readers in 1993, sadly, told us that the hotel is concentrating its services on tour groups. Its management is discouraging individual travelers.

Those traveling independently were told there were no porters to help with luggage and that they could not be seated in the dining room until groups were finished with lunch, by which time the fabled smorgasbord had been decimated.

The jouney via Stalheim is still recommended. The change is withdrawing our recommendation about staying or dining at the hotel. We also no longer recommend staying at the Fretheim Hotel in Flam.

There is a view here of such magnificence that Kaiser Wilhelm II came to Stalheim annually for 25 years to look at it.

The land here has been farmed since 400 A.D. Some facility for food and lodging has existed here since 1647 when mail was carried by Norway's "pony express" from Bergen to Oslo, and Stalheim was one of the stations for changing horses and riders, right up until 1900.

An inn was operated at Stalheim before 1700. The first hotel here, constructed in 1885, burned in 1900. A second hotel, built in 1901, met the same fate in 1902. Another hotel, constructed and used first in Voss, was moved to Stalheim in 1906, enlarged in 1912, and burned down in 1959.

The present Stalheim Hotel was built in the Winter of 1959–60 and enlarged in 1967 to its present capacity of 130 units, ranging from single rooms to doubles and then suites consisting of a double room plus sitting-room with fireplace. Stalheim can accommodate 219 guests, and it is filled nearly every day in its April-September operation with tour groups.

The terrace of the hotel provides a view over the Naro, Brekke and Jordal valleys, the Sivle and Stalheim waterfalls, and the conical peak of Mt. Jordal.

Two mounds on the right-hand side of the hotel's terrace date from 800 A.D. These were opened in 1890, revealing the remains of a woman who had been buried with her frying-pan, loom, bronze brooches and bracelets and the remains of a man, with his sword, axes and other utensils. These relics were given to the museum in Bergen. The mounds have been reconstructed, and photos of the relics are displayed in the hotel's entrance hall.

The hotel will arrange (for guests) a tour of its open air Ancient Village Museum. A commentary is on the old log buildings, the lives that were led in them, the white mansion of the landowner who built it in 1726, and the contents of all the structures. These objects dramatize the contrasting life-style between the rich and the poor of that era. Among the contents are antique Norwegian furniture, arms, glass, silver, pewter and brass, some of which are also displayed in the hotel lobby.

If your schedule does not allow staying overnight at Stalheim, from mid-June to mid-August a boat leaves Gudvangen (only a 30-minute bus ride from Stalheim) at 16:50 and 19:50 for a cruise along the Sognefjord, all in Midnight Sun daylight, arriving Aurland at 18:15 and 21:20.

You can leave Stalheim by bus on Day 2 at 10:35 to connect with the Gudvangen–Flam boat ride on the **Sognefjord**, starting at 11:35 for arrival in Flam at 13:30. Snacks and beverages are available on the boat, or you can have lunch after you reach **Flam**.

On the morning of the following day, start the 12½-mile "Flam Line" railway ride to Myrdal (Table 481) late May to mid-September at 10:00 or mid-September to late May at 10:40, arriving Myrdal 10:55 or 11:35, changing to the 12:25 departure for Oslo, and arrive Oslo 18:10.

The 41-minute Flam-Myrdal trip is one of the 5 most beautiful train rides in Europe.

"Flam Line" goes along the **Aurlandsfjord**, a branch of the Sognefjord. Watch for sturdy, wild mountain goats that often cluster on huge granite boulders only a few feet from the track. There is an ascent of 2,845 feet from sea level in the first 12 miles. This railway has the greatest incline of any Norwegian track, 5.5 percent at one stretch.

The descent is so steep that the train takes a longer time to go downhill than it does to go up. It has 5 different braking systems, any one of which is sufficient to stop the train.

The mountainside is so steep along one stretch that the train has to go through reverse tunnels. In one particular short distance, the track must go on 3 different levels on one side of Kjosfossen Gorge and on 2 levels on the other side of the Gorge. There are 20 tunnels with a combined length of 3.7 miles in the 12½-mile route.

The train proceeds slowly or stops completely at the finest scenic sections in order for passengers to have the best possible views of magnificent scenery and of a road that was built in 1895 to supply materials for building the railway. This road has 21 hairpin bends. Along another stretch, the train crosses a 110-yard-long embankment and stops there for several minutes so that passengers can get off and walk closer to the enormous raging Kjos waterfall that cascades close to the train. Its force is marvellous to see and hear.

The first stop en route from Myrdal to Oslo is at **Finse**, highest elevation (4,267 feet) of the entire Bergen–Oslo line. Workers are stationed permanently at Finse to fight snow on the tracks 9 months out of the year and repair the snow sheds during the 3-month Spring-Summer-Autumn there.

Between Finse and Oslo, the scenery changes from glacier to ski resorts, waterfalls, and then beautiful valley farms and fast-moving rivers.

If time does not permit going to Stalheim, you can leave Bergen (late May to mid-September) at 08:45, terminating in Myrdal at 11:00. Depart Myrdal 11:45 on "Flam Line," arriving Flam 12:45. Depart Flam 15:00 for the ride back to Myrdal, arriving Myrdal 15:55 and connecting with the train that departed Bergan at 15:30. Depart Myrdal on that train at 17:21 (reservation required). Arrive Oslo at 22:12. Despite the late arrival, you will see all of the interesting scenery between Myrdal and Oslo in daylight if you are taking this trip in Summer.

Oslo to Bergen with Myrdal-Flam Detour 481

Depart Oslo (Sentral) 07:42, 10:48, 14:55 (daily except Saturday) or 16:09 for the direct trip to Bergen, arriving there 14:07, 18:26, 20:45 and 22:14. The 07:30 has light refreshments. the other 3 trains have a restaurant car. All 4 trains require reservation.

To take the Myrdal–Flam–Myrdal roundtrip detour, leave Oslo 07:30 or 10:30, arriving Bergen 18:26 or 20:45. The 14:30 and 15:42 Olso departures reach Myrdal too late for making the detour.

For a 2-day Oslo-Bergen trip, overnight in Flam. Then, on the morning of Day 2, leave Flam Pier 08:45 for the boat trip on Sognefjord to Gudvangen, take the bus Gudvangen-Stalheim-Voss, and then by train Voss to Bergen.

All of these trains are second-class, unless designated otherwise.

Dep. Voss	06:33 (1)	08:42 (1)	10:30	12:30 (2)	13:16 (3+5)
Arr. Bergen	07:51	09:56	12:07	13:44	14:07

(1) Runs daily, except Sundays and holidays. (2) Runs Monday–Friday, except holidays. (3) Reservation *required*. Light refreshments or restaurant car. Has a first-class coach. (4) Operates late June to mid-September. Runs daily. (5) Plus other departures from Voss at 14:55, 16:00, 17:20 (3), 18:46, and 21:37 (3), arriving Bergen 16:03, 17:30, 18:26, 19:47 and 22:42.

Hotel Grand Terminus is a 2-minute walk from the Bergen railstation.

If time does not permit going to Stalheim on Day 2, you can depart Flam by fjord boat [table 481a] at 14:35 (early June to mid-September), arriving Bergen at 20:35 the same day.

Oslo - Dombas - Andalsnes 483

This 71-mile "Rauma Line" detour off the "Dovre Line" (Oslo to Trondheim) is, mile for mile, one of the 5 greatest scenic rides in Europe.

Even for one who is not going further north than Dombas, the 2-day roundtrip is well worth the time involved. There is no question that the route is worth seeing twice, and from 2 perspectives.

Be sure to obtain a free brochure at Oslo's Central railstation before beginning the trip. We would enjoy riding "Rauma Line" every day of our lives. Depart Oslo (Sentral) at 08:55 or 14:27. Arrive Andalsnes 15:30 or 20:50. In the Summer, you can read a newspaper there by sunlight at Midnight.

Soon after the train leaves Dombas it crosses the granite Jora Bridge, which spans a 120-foot deep gorge. At **Bjorli,** the Romsdal Valley comes into view, and you will see (at least in late Spring and early Summer) unmatched foaming torrents of thawed- glacier water, rushing at 80 miles an hour down vertical mountain slopes and through the boulder-strewn Rauma River bed.

The descent from Bjorli involves a double spiral through 2 circular mountain tunnels, first the 1,550-yard-long Stavem Tunnel, then through the 500-yard-long Kylling Tunnel.

Between these 2 tunnels, at **Verma** railstation, there is a monument that commemorates the opening of the Rauma Line by King Haakon in 1924. Along the opposite side of the Rauma River are small, well-kept farms, lush from the benefit of the warmth of the Gulf Stream, which keeps temperatures moderate along most of the coast of Norway.

The train next crosses Kylling Bridge, 200 feet above a thundering run of the Rauma River through a steep, narrow gorge. You are now approaching the valley floor.

Near **Flatmark,** you cross Foss Bridge and see Bridal Veil, best known of the numerous waterfalls on this route. At **Marstein** railstation, the sun is visible only 7 months of the year due to the combination of the tall surrounding mountains and the arc of the sun at this latitude.

After passing along the glaciated foot of the majestic Romsdalshorn Montain, whose peak rivals the Matterhorn as a climber's challenge, one can see on the left the highest vertical rock face in northern Europe, the "Troll's Wall" (Trollveggen), which is 3,000 feet high.

The "Rauma Line" reaches sea level in the Romsdall Valley before ending at **Andalsnes** (population 2,500) on the shore of Isfjord, at the head of the Romsdallfjord.

There is a bus connection between Andalsnes and **Alesund.** At Alesund, one can make flights to Oslo, Bergen or Trondheim, or make coastal express boat trips to Bergen or Trondheim.

The Rauma River is fished by sportsmen for salmon and trout.

To return to Oslo, depart Andalsnes 10:05. Depart Dombas 11:53. Arrive Oslo 16:46… or, depart Andalsnes 16:25, change trains in Dombas at 18:00, depart Dombas 18:06, arrive Oslo 22:16. Both trains require reservation and have light refreshments.

The Oslo-Andalsnes-Oslo roundtrip can be made without stopping overnight in Andalsnes. There is a night departure from Andalsnes at 23:10 [table 483], arriving Oslo the next morning at 07:16. What a shame, to take this ride at night!

The only overnight lodging we know of in **Andalsnes** is at the 65-room Grand Hotel Bellevue. Advance room reservations are recommended.

There is a 2-hour bus/ferry connection [483] from Andalsnes to **Molde**, Norway's "town of roses" located on a fjord and surrounded by 87 beautiful snowcapped peaks. In Molde, see the many ancient wood buildings from the 11th century. The Romsdal Museum, largest Norwegian provincial museum. The floral decorations in the modern concrete and glass Town Hall. The view of the Norwegian Sea and the countryside from the Varden Restaurant, 1300 feet above the town. An International Jazz Festival (music, art, poetry and theatrical events) has been held in Molde the first week of August every year since 1960.

Take the Eide bus 18 miles to visit the grottos and caves at the Troll's Church and the waterfall that tumbles against a marble mountain.

Oslo - Andalsnes - Trondheim - Bodo - Narvik

This is a marvelous 5-day rail trip up Norway's Gulfstream-warmed coastline. There is very good mountain and lake scenery Oslo–Trondheim, and excellent mountain, lake and seacoast scenery Trondheim-Bodo.

Keep in mind when reading the timetables that there is constant daylight on this route during June and July.

A transplanted herd of gigantic musk oxen live along the Dombas–Trondheim route, Day 2 of this journey. On one of our trips, we saw a mother and baby grazing late at night on a grassy slope near the train track.

The scenery of forests, rich valleys, waterfalls, rivers and farms is lovely almost all the way to the crossing of the Arctic Circle, on the ride from Trondheim to **Bodo**.

Passengers are given a brochure with details about the Arctic Circle trip. Announcements during the ride over a public address system alert passengers to approaching points of interest. A steward or hostess is on board to provide information.

Upon reaching the stone monument that marks the Arctic Circle, the train stops there for 5 minutes, allowing passengers adequate time to take photographs.

We were fortunate that it was snowing on our first crossing of the Arctic Circle one June, giving the trip the feeling of a polar environment. A few hours later, as the train's route came close to the coastline, and when we were considerably north of the Arctic Circle, the weather was sunny and warm.

Because of the sunny, balmy weather that day, there was no sensation of being so far north, nor was there in Narvik the next day, by which time we were 700 miles above the Arctic Circle.

The northernmost rail service from Oslo is to Bodo. Passage from Bodo to Narvik is via an all-day bus trip through beautiful countryside interspersed by 3 ferry-boat crossings.

There are schedules on this page for a recommended rail trip from Oslo to Narvik, and then from Narvik across northern Norway to northern Sweden and then south to Stockholm. On the trip from Narvik to Sweden (Boden), you cross the Arctic Circle north-to-south, although without the interesting ceremony that is presented on the south-to-north Trondheim–Bodo ride.

Day 1 (*table 483*)			*Day 3* in *Trondheim*	
Dep. Oslo (Sen.)	09:05 (1)			
Arr. Andalsnes	15:30		*Day 4* (*table 484*)	
			Dep. Trondheim	08:55 (4)
Day 2 (*table 483*)			*Cross the Arctic Circle.*	16:10
Dep. Andalsnes	16:35 (2)		Arr. Bodo	18:40
Arr. Dombas	18:00			
Change trains.			*Day 5* Bus.	
Dep. Dombas	18:52 (3)		Dep. Bodo	07:30 (5)
Arr. Trondheim	21:50		Arr. Narvik	14:35

(1) Second-class. Light refreshments. (2) Second-class. (3) Second-class. Restaurant car. (4) Reservation *required*. Restaurant car. (5) Food is available at occasional stops.

Keep in mind that during late June, all of July and most of August, the Midnight Sun allows you to see the scenery all the way to Trondheim, despite the 21:50 arrival time there. The light is not blinding, but you can read a newspaper by it straight through the night.

Deleting Overnight in Andalsnes and Trondheim

Here are schedules for those wishing to continue on from Andalsnes to Narvik without spending 21 hours in Andalsnes or a night in either Trondheim or Bodo and who don't mind missing a daytime view of the Andalsnes–Dombas "Rauma Line." The bus Fauske–Narvik is *not* covered by Eurailpass. Its cost in 1994 was 245 Norwegian kroner.

483				*483*		
Dep. Oslo (Sen.)	09:05 (1)	14:205 (5)		Dep. Dombas	18:41 (4)	04:26 (4)
Arr. Dombas	13:51	19:08		Arr. Trondheim	21:20	07:20
Arr. Andalsnes	15:30	20:15		*Change trains. 484*		
Return to Dombas.				Dep. Trondheim	23:00 (4)	08:55 (5)
Dep. Andalsnes	16:35 (2)	23:15 (4)		*Cross the Arctic Circle.*		
Arr. Dombas	18:00	01:00		Arr. Fauske	09:05	17:55
Change trains.				*Change to a bus.*		
				Dep. Fauske	09:10	18:15
				Arr. Narvik	13:55	22:55

(1) Second-class only. Light refreshments. (2) Second-class only. (3) Second-class only. Restaurant car. (4) Reservation *required*. Carries a sleeping car. Coach is second-class only. (5) Reservation *required*. Has a first-class coach. Restaurant car.

Sights in **Trondheim**: This is the gateway for northern cruises. See the old Nidaros Cathedral, the largest medieval structure in Scandinavia. The 18th century rococo Strift-sgarden royal residence. The Bishop's Palace. The open-air Folk Museum, open daily 10:00–18:00. The dazzling array of unusual musical instruments in the Ringve Museum of Musical History (including an Eskimo drum made from a walrus stomach, a Tibetan trumpet, a violin made of matches).

Sights in **Narvik**: The second (after Murmansk) most northern rail passenger terminus in the world.

Founded in 1901 at the western tip of **Ofot Fjord** to provide an ice-free port for the mid-Winter export of iron ore from Swedish mines which cannot ship via the frozen Bay of Bothnia during Winter.

For the most breathtaking view of Midnight Sun sky, fjords, mountains and the town of Narvik, take the 10-minute walk from Grand Hotel Royal to the base of the cable that lifts you 2,000 feet in 13 minutes to the top of **Mt. Fagernesfjell**.

Food and beverages are sold in the Fjellsheimen restaurant on the peak, an ideal site for taking spectacular photos and watching the sun revolve clockwise around the horizon.

A crucial British-German naval battle (commemorated at a small museum in the center of town) was fought in Narvik's fjords during World War II. Destroyed in 1940, Narvik was completely rebuilt after the war.

The Direct Trip

Oslo - Trondheim and Trondheim - Oslo 483

Dep. Oslo (Sen.)	08:00 (1)	10:05 (2)	14:05 (1)	16:05 (1)	22:30 (4+7)
Arr. Trondheim	14:45	18:20	21:20	22:35	07:05

• • •

Dep. Trondheim	07:45 (1)	09:20 (1)	09:25 (6)	15:50 (1)	22:45 (1+8)
Arr. Oslo (Sen.)	14:46	16:46	17:46	22:28	06:55

(1) Reservation *required*. Restaurant car or light refreshments. (2) Second-class. Light refreshments. (3) Second-class. Restaurant car. (4) Runs daily, except Saturday. Reservation *required*. Carries a sleeping car. Coach is second-class. (5) Runs daily. Reservation *required*. Coach is second-class. (6) Restaurant car. (7) Plus another Oslo departure at 23:00 (5), arriving Trondheim 07:20. (8) Plus another Trondheim departure at 22:25 (4) (5), arriving Olso 07:16.

Narvik - Boden - Stockholm 476

There is fine mountain scenery Narvik–Kiruna.

Day 6

Dep. Narvik	13:45	Day 6 of the Oslo–Narvik–Stockholm trip.
Arr. Kiruna	16:25	
Dep. Kiruna	17:05 (1)	
Arr. Boden	20:20	
Arr. Stockholm (Cen.)	10:45	Day 7 of the Oslo–Narvik–Stockholm trip.

(1) Reservation *required*. Carries a sleeping car. Also has couchettes. Restaurant car.

Oslo - Kritiansand - Stavanger 482

There is excellent mountain scenery between Kristiansand and Stavanger.

Dep. Oslo (Sen.)	07:18 (2)	15:39 (2)	22:39 (3)	22:48 (4)
Dep. Kristiansand	12:02	20:26	04:10	04:30
Arr. Stavanger	14:48	23:15	07:32	07:56

Sights in **Stavanger**: Many old streets and houses in this 1100-year old town. See the market of fruits, vegetables, flowers and fish. The 11th century Cathedral. Outside the city, see the prehistoric Viste Cave. Try a deep-sea fishing trip.

Dep. Stavanger	07:00(2)	12:06 (1)	22:00 (4)
Arr. Kristiansand	09:40	15:17	01:25
Arr. Oslo (Sen.)	14:21	20:42	07:18

(1) Reservation *required*. Second-class. Light refreshments. (2) Reservation *required*. Restaurant car. (3) Operates all year except most of July. Runs Sunday only. Carries a sleeping car. Coach is second-class. (4) Carries a sleeping car. Coach is second-class. Runs daily, except Saturday.

Stavanger - Kristiansand - Stavanger   482

From Stavanger, it is an easy one-day roundtrip to see the fine mountain scenery en route to Kristiansand.

All of these trains require reservation and have light refreshments, unless designated otherwise.

Dep. Stavanger	07:00 (1)	12:06		Dep. Kristiansand	12:02 (2)	20:26 (1)
Arr. Kristiansand	09:140	15:17		Arr. Stavanger	14:48	23:15

(1) Restaurant car. (2) Second-class.

Voss - Ulvik

This spur off the Bergen–Oslo route affords great farm, mountain and river scenery. It is an easy one-day roundtrip.

481 Train			
Dep. Bergen	10:20 (1)	13:30 (2)	15:45 (1)
Arr. Voss	11:25	14:42	16:47
Change to bus. 489			
Dep. Voss	11:40 (3)	15:40 (3)	17:20 (4)
Arr. Ulvik	12:45	16:45	18:25

* * *

Dep. Ulvik	13:55 (4)	16:50 (4)	18:45 (3)
Ar. Voss	15:00	17:55	19:50
Change to train. 481			
Dep. Voss	16:00 (2)	18:46 (2)	21:37 (1)
Arr. Bergen	17:15	20:01	22:42

(1) Reservation *required*. Restaurant car. (2) Second-class. (3) Runs daily, except Sundays and holidays. (4) Runs daily, except Saturday. (5) Runs daily, except Sundays and holidays. Second-class.

INTERNATIONAL ROUTES
FROM NORWAY

Bergen is Norway's starting point for *cruises* to England. Oslo is the gateway for *rail* trips to Sweden (Stockholm, and on to Finland) and Denmark (Copenhagen, and on to Germany and the rest of Western Europe).

Bergen - Newcastle 1050

The arrivals in Newcastle are on Day 2 after departing Bergen.

Dep. Bergen	11:00 (1)	11:00 (2)	14:30 (3)	17:00 (4)	17:00 (5)
Dep. Stavanger	17:45	18:00	21:15	23:30	23:59
Arr. Newcastle (Tyne)	12:00	12:00	14:30	16:45	19:00

(1) Operates late Monday only Jan 1 - June 3 and Sept 3 - December 31. Runs Friday only. (2) Runs Friday only June 4-Sept 2. (3) Operates June 4-Sept 2. Runs Sunday only. (4) Operates June 4 - Sept 2. Runs Tuesday only. (5) Runs Thursday only.

Narvik - Boden - Haparanda - Kemi - Oulu - Helsinki

The schedule below indicates that it is necessary to layover one night in Boden when going from Narvik to Helsinki. In order to see the entire Boden–Oulu portion during daylight, take the 08:00 departure from Boden. To see the entire Oulu–Helsinki portion during daylight, layover one or more nights in Oulu and on Day 3 or later depart Oulu 09:56.

475 Train

Dep. Narvik	010:05 (1)	13:45 (2)			
Arr. Boden	16:56	20:11			
Change to bus. 474					
Dep. Boden	08:05	10:55 (4)	13:35 (3)		
Arr. Haparanda	10:20	13:30	15:55		
Change buses. 474					
Dep. Haparanda	11:05 (3)	13:50 (4)	16:05		
Set your watch forward one hour.					
Arr. Kemi	12:50	15:35	17:52		
Change to a train. 495					
Dep. Kemi	14:22 (5)	-0-	20:10 (6)	22:43 (6)	08:30 (7)
Dep. Oulu	16:03	-0-	22:10	00:12	09:56
Arr. Helsinki	22:58	-0-	07:10	08:27	16:58

(1) Reservation *required*. Second-class. Light refreshments. (2) Reservation *required*. Second-class. (3) Runs daily, except Sundays and holidays. (4) Runs Monday-Friday, except holidays. (5) Light refreshments. (6) Carries a sleeping car. Coach is second-class. Light refreshments. (7) Restaurant car.

Oslo - Stockholm   470

| Dep. Oslo (Sen.) | 08:20 (1) | 16:20 (1) | 22:50 (3) |
| Arr. Stockholm | 14:41 | 22:41 | 06:47 |

(1) Reservation *required*. Restaurant car. (2) Restaurant car. Mid-June to mid-August: runs daily. Mid-August to mid-June: runs daily, except Saturday. (3) Carries a sleeping car. Also has couchettes. Coach is second-class.

Oslo - Copenhagen   466

All of these trains require reservation.

Dep. Oslo (Sen.)	10:15 (1)	22:43 (2)
Arr. Helsingborg	18:20	05:58
Arr. Copenhagen (H.)	20:15	08:20

(1) Restaurant car. (2) Carries a sleeping car. Also has couchettes. Coach is second-class. Runs May 29-August 28.

SWEDEN

Overview

Most train travelers coming into Sweden cross over on one of the quick ferries from Denmark (Helsingborg-Helsingor) which connects to the Stockholm line.

General Information

• Children under 12 travel free when accompanied by an adult (to a maximum of two children for each adult). Half-fare for children 12-15. Children 16 and over must pay full fare.

• The signs you will see at railstations in Sweden are:

ANKOMST	ARRIVAL
AVGANG	DEPARTURE
BILJETTLUCKAN	TICKET OFFICE
DAMER	WOMEN
GARDEROBEN	CHECKROOM
HERRAR	MEN
JARNVAGSTATION	RAILWAY STATION
INGANG	ENTRANCE
INFORMATIONSDISKEN	INFORMATION
LIGGPLATSVAGN	COUCHETTE CAR
PLATSBILJETTER	RESERVATIONS
RESTAURANGVAGN	RESTAURANT CAR
SOVVAGN	SLEEPING CAR
SPAR	TRACK
TILL SPAREN	TO THE PLATFORMS
UTGANG	EXIT
VAXELKONTORET	CURRENCY EXCHANGE

Swedish Holidays

A list of holidays is helpful because some trains will be noted later in this section as *not* running on holidays. Also, those trains which operate on holidays are filled, and it is necessary to make reservations for them long in advance.

January 1	New Year's Day		Ascension Day
	Epiphany		Whit Monday
	Good Friday		Midsummer Day
	Easter		All Saint's Day
	Easter Monday	December 25	Christmas Day
May 1	Labor Day	December 26	Boxing Day

EURAILPASS BONUSES IN SWEDEN

These boat trips: Goteborg–Fredrickshavn, Helsingborg–Helsingor, Stockholm–-Helsinki, Stockholm–Turku and Stockholm–Aland Islands–Turku. There is also a 50% reduction of the fares of the ferries between Malmo and Lubeck-Travemunde (Germany) and between Trelleborg and Sassnitz (Germany). From Stockholm or Oslo, Sassnitz is the most direct gateway to Berlin, with both day and night trains operating Sassnitz–Berlin.

SWEDEN'S TRAIN PASSES

All of Sweden's passes are sold *only* in Sweden, at main railstations and travel agencies.

Reslust Card Entitles the holder to 25% discount on *all* trains on Tuesday, Wednesday, Thursday and Saturday — plus other advantages such as restaurant car discounts and special Summer rates. The 1996 price is $18 (only $6 for persons over 67).

Red Departure Discount Ticket The holder is allowed 50% discount for trains marked in red on Finnish timetables on *second*-class tickets that are valid for 36 hours. No stopovers. The minimum ticket must be $14, or $10 for persons holding the "Reslust Card" (see above). If the station's ticket office is closed when the train departs, "Red Departure" can be purchased on the train. Seat reservation, at $3 each, is required for InterCity trains and for many long distance trains.

ONE-DAY EXCURSIONS AND
CITY SIGHTSEEING

Here are 9 one-day rail trips that can be made comfortably from Stockholm and Goteborg, returning to them in most cases before dinnertime. Notes are provided on what to see and do at each destination. The number after the name of each route is the Cook's timetable.

Goteborg

A great seaport. The one-hour sightseeing bus tour leaves from Stora Teatern. There are one-hour boat trips covering the 7-mile harbor and its canals, leaving from Kungsportsbron. See the view of the harbor and city from the Sailor's Tower near the Maritime Museum at Gamla Varvsparken. The Liseberg amusement park. The magnificent City Theater, Concert House and Art Museum, all in the large square, Gotaplatsen. Antikhallarna, Scandinavia's largest permanent antiques and collectors market.

The view from Ramberget, highest point on the Hisingen side of Goteborg. The Botanical Garden. The 07:00 fish auction, weekdays, at Scandinavia's largest fish market. The 17th century Elfsborg Fortress. The historical and archaeological collections at the Goteborg Museum, located in the city's oldest (1643) building. Art from all over the world, at the Rohss Museum. Slottsskogen Zoo. The view of the harbor and city from the top of Sjomanjtornet, a 193-foot-high tower. Stroll down the broad Kungsportsavenyn, hub of the city.

Stockholm

Maps, literature and advice can be obtained at the Stockholm Tourist Association in Sweden House (Hamngatan 27), in the central business-shopping district (open Monday–Friday 08:30–18:00, Saturday and Sunday 08:00–17:00).

Bus connections to the city's airport are available at a terminal across the street from the Central railstation. Stockholm's subways depart from the same level as the Tourist Information Office in Central railstation. A Tourist Ticket, good for rides on both buses and subways, is sold for 2 periods: one day and 3 days. These can be purchased at the Tourist Information Office in Central railstation.

Bus #47 can be taken from across the street from Central railstation to the 75-acre Skansen amusement park, open 08:00–23:30 June through August. Its prime attraction is the Vasa Museum (open daily 09:30–19:00 June through mid-August, 10:00–17:00 the rest of the year), where a 17th century battleship is on exhibit. This ancient ship sank in Stockholm harbor at the moment she set forth on her first voyage as flagship of the Swedish Navy and rested in 100 feet of water from 1628 until it was raised in 1956, restored and turned into a museum.

Located near the Nordic Museum in the Galarvarv area of Djurgarden Island, the Vasa Museum can be reached by bus or by ferries that leave continuously from Nybroplan and from the end of Gamla Stan. It is an easy 5-minute walk from where the ferries dock at the island to the Vasa Museum.

Also popular are Skansen's Zoo and its outdoor museum of life in early Stockholm (more than 150 buildings from the 18th and 19th centuries).

At the Royal Palace, the treasury and Armory are open in Summer 10:00–16:00. The king's silver throne in the Hall of State can be seen 12:00–15:00. Also see the Bernadotte and Festival suites. The historic and art treasures in the Royal Chapel. The Changing of the Guard in the courtyard takes place daily at 12:10.

Other sights: the 15th century Storkyrkan Cathedral, with its sculpture of St. George and the Dragon, is a short walk from the Palace. The tall old houses and Stock Exchange on Stortorget, the city's oldest square. The modern architecture in Skarholmen, a suburb

The collection of Carl Milles statues at Millesgarden sculpture park. Fine views of the city and the archipelago from the 504-foot-high Kaknas television tower, open May through August 09:00–24:00. The exhibit of 16th through 19th century paintings by European masters at the National Museum of Fine Arts, open daily 10:00–16:00 (see the 9 Rembrandts on the second floor). Rosendal Palace, closed Monday. The Chinese Pavilion, Court Theater and Museum, all at Drottingholm Palace, open April through October.

Do not miss seeing the Golden Hall, Blue Hall, Prince's Gallery, Terrace and the view from the Tower, all at Town Hall (1 Hantverkgatan), one of Europe's most famous buildings, where guided tours are offered daily at 10:00 (plus 12:00 on Sundays and holidays). The Nobel festivities take place there.

Goteborg - Kalmar - Goteborg   467

| Dep. Goteborg | 08:00 (1) | | Dep. Kalmar | 17:26 (2) |
| Arr. Kalmar | 12:37 | | Arr. Goteborg | 22:00 |

(1) Runs Saturdays only. (2) Runs daily, except Saturday. Light refreshments.

Sights in **Kalmar**: The moat, courts and towers of the Castle. A bus trip to the nearby glass-works.

Stockholm - Eskilstuna - Stockholm   471 Bus

Dep. Stockholm	08:10	10:10	12:10	14:10
Arr. Eskilstuna	10:25	12:15	14:15	16:25
		•		
Dep. Eskilstuna	13:30	15:30	17:30 (1)	19:30
Arr. Stockholm	15:35	17:50	19:35	21:40

(1) Runs Saturdays, Sundays and holidays.

Sights in **Eskilstuna**: The 6 Rademacher Forges that are more than 300 years old, on display in the center of town. Eskilstuna is the capital of Sweden's steel industry. Also see the wooden Fors Church and the statue of the 10th century English missionary, Saint Eskil, for whom the town was named in 1659, one year after Reinhold Rademacher built the forges which launched the local industry.

The Zoo and Amusement Park. The 12th century church. The wonderful collection of Scandinavian art in the Art Museum. Take a local bus 8 miles to Sundbyholm Castle. Shop for gold, iron and copper souvenirs.

Stockholm - Gavle - Stockholm   476

All of these trains require reservation.

| Dep. Stockholm (Cen.) | 05:40 (1) | 07:13 (2) | 08:13 (4) | 10:13 (12) | 12:13 (13) |
| Arr. Gavle | 07:47 | 09:11 | 10:19 | 12:06 | 14:15 |

Sights in **Gavle**: The Swedish Railway Museum.

| Dep. Gavle | 11:49 (4) | 13:49 (9) | 15:49 (4) | 16:47 (2) | 19:11 (4+11) |
| Arr. Stockholm (Cen.) | 13:44 | 15:44 (9) | 17:44 | 18:44 | 21:30 |

(1) Runs Monday–Friday, except holidays. Light refreshments. (2) Restaurant car. (3) Runs Saturday only. Light refreshments. (4) Light refreshments. (5) Runs Monday-Thursday. Restaurant car. (6) Runs daily, except Saturdays and Sundays. (7) July: runs daily. August-June: runs Friday, Saturday and Sunday. Resaurant car. (8) Operates August-June. Runs Monday-Thursday. Restaurant car. (9) Runs daily, except Saturday. Light refreshments. (10) Plus another Stockholm departure at 12:13 (7), arriving Gavle 14:08. (11) Plus other departures from Gavle at 20:34 (2) and 21:106 (14), arriving Stockholm 22:27 and 22:57. (12) Runs Friday, Saturday only. (13) Runs Friday, Saturday and Sunday only. (14) Runs Sunday only.

Stockholm - Goteborg - Stockholm   469

All of these trains require reservation and have a restaurant car, unless designated otherwise.

Dep. Stockholm (Cen.)	07:00 (1+3)	08:00 (1+2)	08:12	
Arr. Goteborg (Cen.)	10:10	11:04	12:55	
Dep. Goteborg (Cen.)	15:10	16:05 (4)	17:05 (1+3)	17:10 (9)
Arr. Stockholm (Cen.)	19:47	19:17 (5)	20:11	21:35

(1) X2000 high speed train. Supplement charged includes reservation fee and meal. Operates mid-August to early June. (2) Runs daily except holidays. (3) Runs Monday–Thursday. (4) X2000 high speed train. Supplement charged includes reservation fee and meal. Operates all year. (5) Runs daily , except Saturday. (6) Runs Friday and Sunday. (7) Runs Monday-Thursday and Sunday. (8) Train carries only sleeping car and couchettes. Reservation *not* required. *No* restaurant car. (9) Plus other Goteburg departures at 19:10 (6), and 23:55 (5), arriving Stockholm 23:33, and 06:17.

Stockholm - Malmo - Stockholm   465

This trip is impratical as a one-day Stockholm excursion.

All of these trains require reservation and have a restaurant car., unless designated otherwise.

Dep. Stockholm (Cen.)	06:12	08:06	10:06	12:06	14:06	16:12 (6)
Arr. Malmo (Cen.)	12:48	14:50	10:58	18:53	20:45	22:37
Dep. Malmo (Cen.)	05:15 (2)	07:14	09:17	11:17	13:17	15:00 (7)
Arr. Stockholm (Cen.)	11:53	13:53	15:53	17:53	19:35	21:53

(1) Runs Saturday only. (2) Runs Monday–Friday, except holidays. (3) Runs daily, except Saturday. (4) Runs Saturday only. Train carries only sleeping cars and couchettes. No coaches. Reservation *not* required. *No* restaurant car. (5) Early June to mid-August: runs daily. Mid-August to early June: runs daily, except Saturday. Train carries only sleeping cars and couchettes. No coaches. Reservation *not* required. *No* restaurant car. (6) Plus other departures from Stockholm at 23:12 (5), arriving Malmo 06:45. (7) Plus other departures from Malmo at 17:17 and 23:00 (5), arriving Stockholm 23:26 and 06:47.

Stockholm - Borlange - Mora - Stockholm   478

There is excellent lake and mountain scenery Borlange-Mora.

All of these trains require reservation and have light refreshments, unless designated otherwise.

Dep. Stockholm (Cen.)	06:10 (7)	09:32	Dep. Mora	11:38 (2)	14:29 (6+7)
Arr. Borlange	08:52 (2)	11:51 (4)	Arr. Borlange	13:23	15:53 (2)
Arr. Mora	10:33	13:35	Arr. Stockholm (Cen.)	16:02	18:57 (4)

(1) Runs Monday-Friday, except holidays. (2) Change trains in Borlange. (3) Mid-June to mid-August: runs daily. Mid-August to mid-June: runs Saturday and Sunday. (4) Runs Sunday only. (5) Mid-June to mid-August: runs daily, except Saturday. Change trains in Borlange on Friday and Sunday. Mid-August to early June: runs Monday and Thursday.(6) Plus other departures from Mora at 17:51 arriving Stockholm 22:44. The 17:51 train runs daily except Saturday. (7) Runs daily except Sundays and holidays. (8) Runs July 4-31 only.

Sights in **Mora**: The outdoor museum of 40 timber buildings, some 600 years old. The collection of Anders Zorn, Swden's most famous painter.

Stockholm - Norrkoping - Stockholm   465

All of these trains require reservation and have a restaurant car, unless designated otherwise.

Dep. Stockholm (Cen.)	06:12	08:06	10:30	12:06
Arr. Norrkoping	08:05	10:05	12:15	14:05

Sights in **Norrkoping**: The amazing collection of more than 25,000 cactus plants in beautiful Karl Johans Park. Take the short sightseeing trip by boat, from the pier at the end of this park.

See the 3,000-year old Bronze Age carvings and also the display of roses in Himmelstalund Park, to the right of the railstation. On the other (east) side of the railstation, visit the ruins of the star-shaped Johannisborg Fort. See the Lindo Canal.

Hear the bell-chiming at 13:00 in front of the Radhuset (Council House). See Hedvigs Kyrka, the German Church.

See the demonstration of antique textiles (from rugs to doilies) and textile machinery in the museum of old factory buildings and tour the restored residence of the factory owner, the Stadsmuseet, a short walk from the railstation. Also exhibited there are interesting scale models of the city as it was in various past centuries.

Dep. Norrkoping	11:55	13:55	15:55	17:05 (1)	17:55 (4)
Arr. Stockholm (Cen.)	13:53	15:53	17:53	19:11	19:35

(1) Runs Monday-Friday except holidays. Reservation not required. No restaurant car.(2) Runs Friday only. *No* restaurant car. (3) Runs Sunday only. *No* restaurant car. (4) Plus other departures from Norrkoping at 18:55 (3), 19:55, 21:40 arriving Stockholm 20:53, 21:53, 23:26.

Stockholm - Uppsala - Stockholm

All of these trains require reservation, unless designated otherwise.

	476	478	476	476
Dep. Stockholm (Cen.)	08:13 (1)	09:32 (2)	10:13 (11)	12:13 (5)
Arr. Uppsala	40–50 minutes later			

Sights in **Uppsala:** The Cathedral, a short walk from the railstation, is the largest church in Scandinavia.

England's Princess Louise (after whom Lake Louise in Canada is named) visited it in 1929. An anecdote about that occasion has been passed on to generations of Britains:

The Swedish bishop whose command of the English language was imperfect, led the Princess on a tour of the church. After having shown her many priceless religious objects in several areas of the Cathedral, he led her into the sacristry where he conducted her to a large cabinet of severals drawers and began to open one of them. In halting English, he announced to her: "I will now open these trousers and show your Royal Highness even more precious treasures."

Also visit Sweden's largest library, Carolina Rediviva, with more than 20,000 hand-illuminated medieval manuscripts, including the only book in existence that is written in pure Gothic, the famous Codex Argentus, the 5th century Silver Bible. The Great Hall of State in the old red Castle, open 11:00–18:00 from mid-May to mid-September.

The 18th century Linnaeus Garden at 27 Svartsbacksgatan (open May–December 09:00–21:00) was created for the study of plant species by Karl von Linne, Sweden's "Prince of Botanists." The present collection numbers 1,300 plants. It was Linne who originated the system of sexual plant classification and the dual nomenclature for natural science.

Take a bus marked "Gamla Uppsala" for a 2-mile ride to see relics of heathen worship going back to the 5th century.

	476	476	478	476
Dep. Uppsala	12:57 (6)	14:57 (9)	15:28	17:57 (10)
Arr. Stockholm (Cen.)	40–50 minutes later			

(1) Runs Saturday only. Light refreshments. (2) Runs daily except Sundays and holidays. (3) Runs Monday–Friday, except holidays. (4) Operates August through June. Runs Monday-Thursday. Restaurant car. (5) Runs Friday, Saturday and Sunday. (6) Light refreshments. (7) Runs Sunday only. Light refreshments. (8) Restaurant car. (9) Runs daily, except Saturday. Light refreshments. (10) Plus other Uppsala departures (all table 476) at 21:40 (8) and 22:10 (7). (11) Runs Monday-Saturday.

INTERNATIONAL ROUTES
FROM SWEDEN

Stockholm is the gateway for rail trips to northern Norway (Trondheim and Narvik) and to northern Finland (Oulu), as well as by boat to Helsinki, and on to Leningrad. It is also the gateway for travel to southern Norway (Oslo, and on to Bergen or Stavanger). Malmo is the starting point for rail travel to Denmark, (Copenhagen, and on to Germany and the rest of Western Europe).

There is fine lake scenery on the Ostersund–Storlien portion of this route.

Stockholm - Trondheim

476

Dep. Stockholm (Cen.)	07:13 (1)	11:45 (2)	12:13 (3)	22:10 (4)
Dep. Ostersund	13:26	18:15	18:42	06:35
Arr. Storlien	15:51	21:22	21:28	09:34
Change to a bus. 484				
Dep. Storlien	16:10	21:35	21:35	10:05
Arr. Trondheim	18:25	23:25	23:25	12:00

(1) Reservation *required*. Restaurant car. (2) Runs Monday-Thursday. Restaurant car. (3) Runs Friday, Saturday and Sunday. (4) Carries a sleeping car. Also has couchettes. Coach is second-class only.

Stockholm - Copenhagen 465

All of these trains require reservation and have a restaurant car, unless designated otherwise.

Dep. Stockholm (Cen.)	06:12	10:30	22:12
Arr. Copenhagen (Hoved.)	14:51	18:51	07:05

Stockholm - Helsinki   Boat and Train

This is the short route to Helsinki, *across* the Gulf of Bothnia.

The price for the cruise across the Gulf of Bothnia on the comfortable and pleasant Silja Line ships in 1995 is $46 for first-class and $37 for second-class. Passage is free on day sailings of the Silja Line ferry for Eurailpass holders. On night sailings a bed in at least a 4-bed cabin must be used, at $12. It can be upgraded to higher cabin class at extra charge. The fare for a sleeping cabin is *not* covered by Eurailpass. Food on the ship is varied and delicious.

We recommended the 08:00 sailing in order to see the thousands of tiny islands on the ride through this extremely interesting archipelago. During the daytime cruise, there is a good smorgasbord for both lunch and dinner.

A small band plays music in a delightful bar area. Movies are shown in a small theater. There is a duty-free shop on board. The ships ferry autos.

All of the Turku–Helsinki trains have light refreshments.

1250 Boat

Dep. Stockholm (Var.)	08:00 (1)	20:00 (2)
Arr. Turku (Harbor)	19:00	08:00

Walk to either railstation.

493

Dep. Turku (Harbor)	-0-	08:30
Dep. Turku (Stn.)	19:35	08:43
Arr. Helsinki	22:00	11:02

(1) Runs daily except January 1,3,10,17,24; May 30,31;September 5-9; December 24,25. (2) Runs daily except April 17-21, September 11,12 and December 24,25.

Stockholm - Narvik

There is good mountain scenery on the Kiruna–Narvik portion of this trip.

Both of these trains require reservation. Coach cars on both trains are second-class.

476			*475*	
Dep. Stockholm (Central)	17:30 (1)		Dep. Lulea	10:00 (2)
Arr. Lulea	07:53		Arr. Boden	10:23
Change trains.			Arr. Kiruna	14:12
			Arr. Narvik	17:34

(1) Carries a sleeping car. Also has couchettes. Restaurant car. (2) Light refreshments.

Stockholm - Oslo   470

Dep. Stockholm (Cen.)	07:36 (1)	15:35 (1)	23:00 (3)
Arr. Oslo (Sen.)	14:00	21:50	07:35

(1) Reservation *required.*Restaurant car. (2) Early June to mid-August: runs daily. Mid-August to early June: runs daily, except Saturday. (3) Carries a sleeping car. Also has couchettes. Coach is second-class.

Stockholm - Oulu - Helsinki

By stopping-over one night in Oulu, the Oulu-Helsinki trip can be made the next day in daylight by departing Oulu 07:15, 09:56 or 12:52.

476

Dep. Stockholm (Cen.)	17:30 (1)	20:10 (1)	-0-	
Arr. Boden	07:14	10:30	-0-	
Change to bus. 474				
Dep. Boden	08:05	10:55 (3)	13:35 (3)	
Arr. Haparanda	10:20	13:30	15:55	
Change buses.				
Dep. Haparanda	11:05 (2)	13:50 (3)	16:05 (2)	
Set your watch forward one hour.				
Arr. Kemi	12:50	15:35	17:52	
Change to a train. 495				
Dep. Kemi	14:22 (4)	17:23 (5)	20:10 (6)	-0-
Arr. Oulu	15:58	18:45	22:05	-0-
Dep. Oulu	16:03	-0-	22:10	07:15 (7+8)
Arr. Helsinki	22:58	-0-	07:10	13:54

(1) Reservation *required*. Carries a sleeping car. Also has couchettes and a cinema/bistro car. Coach is second-class. (2) Runs daily, except Sun. and holidays. (3) Runs Mon.-Fri., except holidays. (4) Runs daily. Light refreshments. (5) Second-class. (6) Carries a sleeping car. Coach is second-class. Light refreshments. (7) Restaurant car. (8) Plus other Oulu departures at 9:56 (7), 12:52 (7) and 16:03 (4), arriving Helsinki 16.58, 19:58 and 22:58.

SWITZERLAND

Overview

Switzerland is the scenic treasure that it is made out to be, although its people and their traditions are relatively little known outside of the country. Train travel here is easy and predictably efficient, with a range of modern and rather traditional train services available to Eurailpass holders. Switzerland is one country where the train can get you places that the automobile could not.

General Information

• See "Swiss Family Card" for children's free fares.
• The signs you will see at rail stations in Switzerland are those you would see in France, Germany or Italy depending on the section of the country you are in.
• French is the language south and southwest of Bern. Italian is dominant in the southeast corner of Switzerland. Elsewhere, the prevailing language is German.
• There are free timetables distributed at most rail stations.
• Seat reservations are advised for most EuroCity and Intercity trains.
• A traveler with a confirmed flight reservation for a departure from Zurich or Geneva airport can check bags at a special counter in the rail station at nearly 100 Swiss cities.
• Unencumbered with luggage, the passenger using "Fly Luggage Service" rides a train from places such as Bern, Locarno, and Luzern directly to the airport, checks-in at the airport's "Express" counter, boards the airplane and claims the luggage at the end of the flight. The time required for baggage deposit in advance of train departure varies from one Swiss rail station to another. Be sure to obtain that information before departure day. Because of USA security procedures, "Fly Luggage Service" is not available to passengers who are departing on a US airline.

SWITZERLAND'S TRAIN PASSES

These passes are good for unlimited travel on all trains covered by Eurailpass, *plus* many expensive trains that do *not* honor Eurailpass, and on lake steamers and postal buses *not* covered by Eurailpass…plus local subways, buses and trams in 25 major Swiss cities.

Swiss Pass Sold worldwide, including in Switzerland. In addition to the services described above, also provides either free travel or discounts up to 50% on many extremely scenic and very expensive privately-owned mountain railroad and aerial cable car routes that are *not* covered by a Eurailpass. Valid for consecutive days.

The 1996 *first*-class prices for one adult are: $316 for 8 days, $368 for 15 days, and

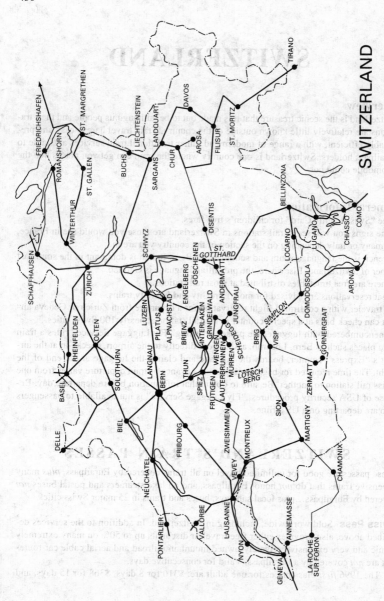

SWITZERLAND

$508 for one month. *Second*-class: $220, $256 and $350. Children under age 16 with an adult travel free. For two adults traveling together (**"Swiss Pass Companion"**) 1996 *first*-class for 8 days, 15 days, and one month respectively: $237, $276, $381 for each adult.

Swiss Flexipass Allows unlimited travel any 3 days within a 15-day period. Includes everything covered by Swiss Pass. The 1996 prices for one adult are: $264 for *first*-class, $176 for *second*-class. For two adults traveling together, (**"Swiss Couples Flexi Pass"**), 1996 prices are as follows: *first*-class $198, *second*-class $132 each.

Swiss Card A free one-day trip from any entry point (airport or border station) to any single destination in Switzerland and a free one-day trip from any place in Switzerland to any departure point. In addition, the holder can purchase an unlimited number of both roundtrip and one-way tickets for Swiss trains postal buses and lake steamers at 50% discount (25% discount on some mountain railroads). Valid for one month, the 1996 prices are: *first*-class $142, *second*-class $116.

Swiss Rail'N Drive 3 days of unlimited train travel plus 3 days of car rental (any 6 days) within 15 days. Prices vary (a) whether for one person or for 2 persons, (b) time of year, and (c) the category of car. A third and fouth passenger needs to pay only for a 3-day Swiss Flexipass.

The 1996 prices *per person* for 2 persons (using the smallest size car trav eling between May 1-October 31) were: $275 for *first*-class, $205 for *second*-class. More days of car rental could be added at $55 per day. All prices include all of the Swiss government railways, most of the private mountain railroads and aerial cable cars (except some short routes), lake steamers and distance buses, plus ocal buses and trains in 25 major Swiss cities. All prices for Hertz auto rental include Value-added Tax, unlimited mileage, basic liability insurance, and free drop-off in Switzerland.

Swiss Family Card Children under 16 travel free if accompanied by at least one parent and holder of a Swiss Pass, Swiss Flexi Pass or Swiss Card. If the Swiss Family Card is purchased in Switzerland (sold at rail stations), it costs 20 Swiss francs. There is no charge for this card when it is obtained from Rail Europe in conjunction with the purchase of a Swiss train ticket or a Swiss train pass.

Regional Passes Sold only in Switzerland. For details on 8 separate passes, obtain a brochure from Swiss National Tourist Office (U.S.A. and Canadian listed in introductory material).

SWISS HOLIDAYS

A list of holidays is helpful because some trains will be noted later in this section as not running on holidays. Also, those trains which operate on holidays are filled, and it is necessary to make reservations for some Inter-City, Euro City and TGV trains.

January 1	New Year's Day		Ascension Day
January 2			Whit Monday
	Good Friday	December 25	Christmas Day
	Easter Monday	December 26	

ONE-DAY EXCURSIONS AND CITY-SIGHTSEEING

Here are 129 one-day rail trips that can be made comfortably from cities in Switzerland, returning to them in most cases before dinnertime. Notes are provided on what to see at each destination. The number after the name of each route is the Cook's timetable. The 13 base cities are: Basel, Bern, Brig, Chur, Geneva, Interlaken, Lausanne, Locarno, Luzern, St. Moritz, Spiez, Zermatt and Zurich. When no station is designated for cities in Austria, Switzerland and West Germany, the station is "Hauptbahnhof."

Basel (Appears as *Bale* in French timetables)

The superb Picasso, Holbein, Delacroix, Gauguin, Matisse, Ingres, Courbet and Van Gogh paintings in the Kunstmuseum. The Historical Museum in the Franciscan Church in Barfusserplatz. The Municipal Casino. The collection of 18th century clothing, ceramics and watches in the Kirschgarten mansion. Shop on Freiestrasse. See the 16th century Town Hall. The fishmarket. The 15th century New University.

The beautiful Munsterplatz. Fifteenth century tapestries in the 14th century Barfuserkirche. The tombs of Queen Anne and Erasmus of Rotterdam at Munster, the 13th century Cathedral. Nearby, the Folk Art Museum.

The more than 100,000 rarities from every continent (particularly those from New Guinea and the South Seas) in the Ethnological Museum at Augustinerstrasse 2. In the same complex, the extraordinary geological section at the Museum of Natural History.

The Jewish Museum of Switzerland, at Kornhausgasse 18, where Theodore Herzl presided over the first Zionist Congress, in 1897. One of the world's greatest collection of animals, at the Zoo (Binningerstrasse 40), open 08:00–18:30 in Summer, 08:00–17:30 in Winter. Switzerland's largest, it is a short stroll from the SNCF and SBB railstations. Or, take Trolleys #4 and #7 from the stations.

Take a boat excursion from the pier in the back of the Hotel Three Kings. See the view of the city from the Wettstein Bridge.

Bern

The capital of Switzerland. See the comic antics of the denizens of the Bear Pit. How they love figs! The Rose Gardens, north of the Bear Pit. The performance of the 16th century clock tower, the Zytglockenturm, at 11:57. The nearby old arcaded streets. Lunch on the terrace of the Casino restaurant and enjoy the view from there of the River Aare. The Art Museum, with the largest Klee collection in the world.

Climb the 254 steps to the top of one of the towers of the Cathedral for a marvelous view. Play chess with people-size chessmen on the huge slate chessboard near the Cathedral. The elaborate statue honoring the world postal system, without which it would be impossible to have one country handle and deliver to an addressee a mailing for which another country had been paid the postage by the addressor.

One of the world's largest stamp collections, at the Swiss PTT Museum. The view of the Alps from the terrace of the Federal Palace, and the nearby open-air flower and produce market (Tuesday and Saturday mornings). The Swiss Alpine Museum. The Natural History Museum. Prison Tower. Holy Ghost Church. The Botanical Gardens. The many window-boxes with flowering geraniums throughout the streets in the city center.

Geneva

The 6-minute train ride [table 250] *from* the airport to the center of Geneva runs 05:39 to 23:46. From the center of Geneva *to* the airport, it runs 06:14 to 23:12.

Walk from the railstation, down Rue du Mont Blanc, to the shore of Lake Leman. See the enormous Jet d'Eau (water fountain). Walk on the bridge across the lake to the Jardin Anglais. It has a fabulous clock of living flowers and plants and a monument to international Protestantism. It is on that side of the lake you will find the city's old narrow streets and, in St. Peter's Cathedral, the pulpit from which Calvin preached. See the view of Geneva and Lake Leman from the top of the Cathedral's North Tower, a climb of 153 steps.

In modern Geneva: Palais des Nations, today the European headquarters of the United Nations Organization. The chinaware collection in the Ariana Museum, open daily except Monday during Summer. The Far East art (Japanese jade, Chinese porcelain, many pieces from Sri Lanka) at the Baur Collection. The Botanical Garden. The Museum of Historic Musical Instruments, open Tuesday, Thursday and Friday. The Ethnographic Museum, closed Monday.

The Art and History Museum, 2 Rue Charles-Galland (Bus #1 from the railstation) has an archaeological collection, paintings, decorative art and sculptures, open daily except Monday 10:00–17:00. The National History Museum, 11 route de Malagnou (Bus #5 from the railstation), one of the most modern museums in Europe, open Tuesday–Sunday 10:00–12:00 and 14:00–18:00, on Monday 14:00–18:00. Nearby, at 15 route de Malagnou, is the Watch and

The Voltaire Museum, 25 rue des Delices (Bus #6 from the railstation), open Monday-Friday 14:00–17:00. The world-famous Davidoff's Cigar Store at Rue de Rive 2, open Monday-Friday 08:30–18:45 and Saturday 08:00–17:00, where the No. 2 coronas sold for $8.00 (U.S.) each in 1993. Also in stock there: the world's biggest choice of cigars and enormous ebony and mahogany humidors.

Luzern

Walk across the 14th and 15th century bridges spanning the Reuss River and see the 120 paintings on the ceiling of Kappelbrucke depicting Luzern's history and the 45 "Dance of Death" paintings inside the Spreuerbrucke.

See the immense 30-foot high, 42-foot long Lion of Luzern, carved in 1821 into a sandstone cliff which became in 1872 the entrance to the Glacier Gardens outdoor museum. The lion commemorates the bravery of those Swiss soldiers who defended Marie Antoinette during the French Revolution.

You will see at the Glacier Museum, open 08:00–18:00, the absolute proof that palm trees grew here 20,000,000 years ago when this area was tropical. A bank manager, planning to augment his income by turning a meadow into a vineyard, blasted this area so as to make a wine cellar in the rock. A geologist friend spotted a bowl-like recess in the sandstone and convinced the banker to cease the blasting. The 32 round holes found there were made by the erosion from ice-age waterfalls.

The old railway cars, locomotives, trolley cars, buses, autos, many scale models, and the simulated ride in an engine cab at the Swiss National Transport Museum at Lidostrasse 5, largest museum of its kind in Europe. There is also a very interesting model of the Gotthard Tunnel (see "Zurich–Lugano"). The museum is open 09:00–18:00 March-October, 10:00–16:00 November–February. Next door is a Planetarium. Visit the Art Museum, near the railstation. The August Music Festival.

The giant (12,000 square foot) canvas Grand Panorama, depicting the Winter campaign of the 1870–71 Franco-Prussian War.

Zurich

There is 12-minute rail service [Table 310] *from* the airport to Zurich's Hauptbahnhof (Main Railstation) from 06:05 to 23:40. From Zurich's Hauptbahnhof *to* the airport, it runs 07:00 to 23:00. A cruise on Lake Zurich is covered by Eurailpass. Board the boat at the lake end of Bahnhofstrasse.

Here is a great 2-hour walk: Upon arriving at the main Zurich railstation, take the escalator down one level and enjoy a snack or meal in Shopville, the enormous underground shopping center beneath Bahnhof Platz, the square in front of the station. Come up from Shopville on the other side of Bahnhof Platz. Walk one mile down one side of Bahnhofstrasse, lined with smart stores. When this city's Fifth Avenue ends at the shore of Lake Zurich, take in the lakeside promenade before returning to the railstation by walking along the opposite side of Bahnhofstrasse that you walked earlier.

Upon returning to the station, go all the way through it, cross Museumstrasse, and visit the National Museum to see its collection of medieval and Renaissance art, prehistoric artifacts, elaborately carved ancient peasant furniture and much more. Open Tuesday- Friday and Sunday 10:00–12:00 and 14:00–17:00, on Saturday 14:00–16:00.

Other sights: The Bellevue Platz amusement center. The paintings and sculptures at the Kunsthaus. African and Asian art at the Rietberg Museum. Kunstgewerbemuseum (The Museum of Applied Arts): handicrafts, architecture and industrial design. The Zoo. The Botanical Garden. The 5 Chagall stained-glass windows (red, blue and green) in the 13th century Fraumunsterkirche, open Monday–Saturday 10:00–16:00, Sunday 14:00–16:00.

Basel - Baden Baden - Basel   730

Reservation is advisable for all of these trains and all of them have a restaurant car, unless designated otherwise.

Dep. Basel (S.B.B.)	-0-	07:17 (1)	08:17 (1)	08:51 (1)	09:17
Dep. Basel (Bad. Bf.)	06:20	07:58	08:24	08:58	09:24
Arr. Baden-Baden	07:40	09:06	10:02	10:21	10:40

Sights in **Baden-Baden:** Praised for its hot salt springs since the Romans discovered the curative water in this area nearly 2,000 years ago. The illnesses treated here include rheumatism, abnormal blood pressure, metabolic disturbances, respiratory ailments, and problems caused by lack of physical exercise.

Nearly 300 prominent European families once had their permanent homes here. Fantastic landscape. The Oos Valley has been called the most beautiful valley in the world. Exotic trees include the Japanese maple, American tulip, East Asian ginkgo, Chinese trumpet, magnolia and fig. The colors of many deciduous trees make Autumn glorious here.

See the Louis XIII and Louis XIV decor of the halls in the casino. The fancy boutique shops. Exhibitions of international art in the Staatliche Kunsthalle (City Art Gallery).

Motorized vehicles are not permitted in the central area of Baden-Baden. There is a constant schedule of balls, fashion shows and concerts. Food specialties here are Grunkernsuppe (a vegetable soup), game pate, pike dumplings, Blaufelchen (a kind of whitefish, from Lake Constance), raspberry schnapps and kirsch with smoked bacon, bread baked by charcoal, and pate of truffled goose-liver from nearby Strasbourg.

Dep. Baden-Baden	11:11	11:30 (2)	13:11	13:47 (1)	15:11 (3)
Arr. Basel (Bad Bf.)	12:35	13:01	14:35	15:36	16:35
Arr. Basel (S.B.B.)	8 minutes later				

(1) Change trains in Offenburg. (2) Change trains in Offenburg. Light refeshments Offenburg-Basel. (3) Plus other Baden Baden departures at 15:47 (1), 17:30 (1), 19:11, 19:47 (1), 21:11.

Basel - Bern - Basel   280

Reservation is advisable for most of these trains.

Dep. Basel (S.B.B.)	07:01 (1)	07:23 (2)	08:01 (1)	08:11	09:01 (2+3)
Arr. Bern	08:12	08:36	09:12	09:36	10:12

Dep. Bern	11:48 (2)	12:48 (1)	13:48 (2)	14:48 (1)	15:48 (2+4)
Arr. Basel (S.B.B.)	12:59	13:59	14:59	15:59	16:59

(1) Restaurant car. (2) Light refreshments. (3) Plus other departures from Basel at 10:01 (2), 11:01 (1) and 12:01, arriving Bern 11:12, 12:12 and 13:12. (4) Plus other departures from Bern at 16:48 (1), 17:48 (2), 18:48 (1), 19:48, 20:48 (1), 21:48 (2) and 22:45, arriving Basel at 17:59, 18:59, 19:59, 20:59, 21:59, 22:59 and 23:59.

Basel - Interlaken - Basel   280

Reservation is advisable for most of these trains, and most of them have light refreshments, unless designated otherwise.

Dep. Basel (S.B.B.)	07:01 (1)	08:01 (2)	09:01 (3)	10:01	11:01 (1+5)
Arr. Interlaken (West)	09:12	10:12	11:12	12:12	13:12
Arr. Inerlaken (Ost)	5 minutes later				

Sights in **Interlaken**: A fine Summer resort and health spa. Take the funicular to **Heimwehfluh** for a marvelous view of the mountains.

Dep. Interlaken (Ost)	12:39	13:39 (3)	14:39 (3)	15:39 (3)	16:39 (6)
Dep. Interlaken (West)	5 minutes later				
Arr. Basel (S.B.B.)	14:59	15:59	16:59	17:59	18:59

(1) Restaurant car. Change trains in Speiz. (2) Restaurant car. (3) Change trains in Speiz. (4) No light refreshments. (5) Plus another departure from Basel at 12:01 (4), arriving Interlaken (West) 14:12. (6) Plus other departures from Interlaken (Ost) at 17:39 (3), 18:39 (3), 19:39 (2) and 20:40 (3+4), arriving Basel 19:59, 20:59, 21:59 and 22:59.

Basel - Luxembourg - Basel   176

Dep. Basel (SNCF)	08:32 (1)		Dep. Luxembourg	14:59 (2)	18:02	20:43 (3)
Arr. Luxembourg	12:00		Arr. Basel (SNCF)	18:25	21:30	00:35

(1) Restaurant car. (2) Reservation advisable. Supplement charged. Restaurant car. (3) Runs Friday only.

Basel - Luzern - Basel   290

Dep. Basel (S.B.B.)	06:00 (1)	07:07 (2)	07:51 (1)	09:07 (3)	09:51 (1+4)
Arr. Luzern	70 minutes later				

Dep. Luzern	09:56	10:56 (1)	11:56 (2)	12:56 (1)	13:46 (3+5)
Arr. Basel (S.B.B.)	70 minutes later (6)				

(1) Light refreshments. (2) Reservation advisable. Light refreshments. (3) Reservation advisable. Restaurant car. (4) Plus other departures from Basel at 11:07 (3), 11:51 (1) and 13:07 (3). (5) Plus other departures from Luzern at 14:56 (1), 15:46 (3), 15:56, 16:56 (1), 17:46 (3), 17:56, 18:56 (1), 19:46 (3), 19:56, 20:56 (1), 21:46 (2) and 22:46. (6) Supplement charged.

Basel - Rheinfelden - Basel   300

Dep. Basel (S.B.B.)	Every hour from 07:49 to 22:49 + 23:32.
Arr. Rheinfelden	15 minutes later

Sights in **Rheinfelden**: This has been a world-famed health spa since 1844. There are tours of the Cardinal and Feldschlosschen breweries. Visit the island park on the Rhine River.

Dep. Rheinfelden	07:28 + every hour from 07:58 to 22:58 and 00:36.
Arr. Basel (S.B.B.)	15 minutes later

Basel - Strasbourg - Basel   176

Dep. Basel (SNCF)	07:04 (1)	08:32 (2)	09:33 (3)	11:12 (6)	12:30 (3)
Arr. Strasbourg	08:41	09:54	10:50	12:36	13:48

Dep. Strasbourg	14:01 (4)	16:28 (4)	17:07 (5)	17:14 (7)	19:22 (6)
Arr. Basel (SNCF)	15:50	18:02	18:25	18:44	20:39

(1) Runs Monday-Friday, except Sundays and holidays. (2) Restaurant car. (3) Runs daily, except Sundays and holidays. (4) Change trains in Mulhouse. Runs Monday-Friday, except holidays. (5) Reservation advisable. Supplement charged. Restaurant car. (6) Runs daily, except Saturday. (7) Runs daily except holidays.

Basel - Zurich - Basel   310

Dep. Basel (S.B.B.)	Frequent times from 05:49 to 21:17
Arr. Zurich	60 minutes later

Dep. Zurich	Frequent times from 06:51 to 23:50
Arr. Basel (S.B.B.)	60 minutes later

Bern - Basel - Bern   280

Dep. Bern	Frequent times from 06:48 to 22:51
Arr. Basel (S.B.B.)	70–80 minutes later

Dep. Basel (S.B.B.)	Frequent times from 05:50 to 21:52
Arr. Bern	70–80 minutes later

Bern - Geneva - Bern   260

Dep. Bern	06:10	06:38 (1)	07:18 (2)	08:18 (2)	08:38 (3+4)
Arr. Geneva (Corn.)	08:02	08:34	09:02	10:02	10:34
Dep. Geneva (Corn.)	11:48 (2)	12:48 (2)	13:15 (3)	13:48 (2)	14:48 (2+5)
Arr. Bern	13:42	14:42	15:22	15:42	16:42

(1) Runs daily, except Sundays and holidays. (2) Reservation advisable. Restaurant car. (3) Light refreshments. (4) Plus other Bern departures at frequent times from 09:18 to 23:26. (5) Plus other Geneva departures at frequent times from 15:25 to 21:57.

Bern - Interlaken - Bern   280

Dep. Bern	06:56 (1)	07:28	08:28 (2)	09:28 (3)	10:28 (2+4)
Arr. Interlaken (West)	07:41	08:13	09:13	10:13	11:16
Arr. Interlaken (Ost)	8 minutes later				

Dep. Interlaken (Ost)	Frequent times from 05:31 to 22:32
Dep. Interlaken (West)	4 minutes after departing Ost railstation
Arr. Bern	55 minutes after departing Interlaken (Ost)

(1) Reservation advisable. Light refreshments. (2) Light refreshments. (3) Reservation advisable. Restaurant car. (4) Plus other departures from Bern at frequent times from 11:28 to 22:28.

Bern - Lausanne - Bern 260

| Dep. Bern | Frequent departures from 06:10 to 23:26 |
| Arr. Lausanne | 70 minutes later |

Sights in **Lausanne:** The Cathedral. The Castle of St. Maire. City Hall. The Federal Palace of Justice. There are 13 museums here, including the collection of photographs at Musee Cantonal de l'Elysee (18 Avenue de l'Elysee), and the Pipe Museum (7 Rue de l'Academie).

| Dep. Lausanne | Frequent departures from 05:31 to 22:33 |
| Arr. Bern | 70 minutes later |

Bern - Fribourg - Lausanne - Bern 260

It is possible to stop and sightsee in both Fribourg and Lausanne on the same one-day excursion.

Dep. Bern	08:18	08:38	09:18	10:18	10:38	11:18	12:18
Arr. Fribourg	08:39	08:59	09:39	10:39	11:59	11:39	12:39

Sights in **Fribourg:** The 17th century altar in the Church of the Augustines. Farmers and their wives in traditional local dress, at the Wednesday and Saturday markets. The many stone fountains in the winding streets that lead to the 16th century Town Hall.

Dep. Fribourg	10:41	11:01	11:41	12:41	13:01	13:41	14:41
Arr. Lausanne	12:26	11:50	12:26	13:26	13:50	14:26	15:26

| Dep. Lausanne | Frequent times from 05:31 to 22:33 |
| Arr. Bern | 70 minutes later |

Bern - Fribourg - Bern 260

Here are the schedules for a one-day excursion involving only Fribourg.

| Dep. Bern | Frequent times from 06:10 to 23:26 |
| Arr. Fribourg | 20 minutes later |

Sights in **Fribourg:** See notes in preceding listing.

| Dep. Fribourg | Frequent times from 06:18 to 23:20 |
| Arr. Bern | 20 minutes later |

Bern - Luzern - Bern   265

Outstanding farm and forest scenery as you travel through Switzerland's beautiful Emmental (valley of the Emme River).

All of these trains have light refreshments.

Dep. Bern	06:48	07:31	08:48	09:31	10:48	11:31	12:48 (1)
Arr. Luzern	08:12	08:46	10:12	10:46	12:12	12:46	14:12

Dep. Luzern	11:13	11:56	13:13	13:46	15:13	15:46	17:13 (2)
Arr. Bern	12:24	13:36	14:29	15:12	16:24	17:12	18:24

(1) Plus frequent other Bern departures from 13:31 to 22:45. (2) Plus frequent other Luzern departures from 17:46 to 23:20.

Bern - Langnau - Luzern - Bern   265

It is possible to stop and sightsee in both Langnau and Luzern on the same one-day excursion.

All of these trains have light refreshments, unless designated otherwise.

Dep. Bern	07:31	09:31	11:31	13:31
Arr. Langnau	25 minutes later			

Sights in **Langnau:** The antique household utensils and local industry products (linen-weaving, tanning embroidery) in the museum housed in a 16th century wood building.

Dep. Langnau	10:00	12:00	14:00	16:00	17:00		
Arr. Luzern	10:46	12:46	14:46	16:46	17:46		

Dep. Luzern	13:13	15:13	15:46	17:13	17:46	18:13	19:13 (2)
Arr. Bern	14:24	16:24	17:12	18:24	19:12	19:29	20:24

(1) No light refreshments. (2) Plus other departures from Luzern at 19:46, 21:01, 22:01 (1), 22:46 arriving Bern 21:12, 22:15, 23:15, 00:25.

Bern - Langnau - Bern   265

Here are the schedules for a one-day excursion involving only Langnau.

All of these trains have light refreshments, unless designated otherwise.

Dep. Bern	07:31	09:31	11:31	13:31			
Arr. Langnau	30 minutes later						

Dep. Langnau	10:01	12:01	14:01	16:01	18:01	19:01	20:01
Arr. Bern	30 minutes later						

(1) No light refreshments.

Bern - Neuchatel - Bern   255

Dep. Bern	Frequent time from 06:05 to 23:46
Arr. Neuchatel	40–60 minutes later

Sights in **Neuchatel:** The 16th and 17th century houses, fountains and towers. Painted, carved 16th century statues. The exhibit of androids, a seated draftsman, scribe and musician, that have been performing since 1774 and attracting tourists from all over the world since then.

After many years of recommending a visit to the Suchard chocolate factory, we received a letter from the Suchard people telling us it *does not offer tours during July and August* when its employees take vacations and it slows down production during those months. At any time of year, Suchard requires advance notice "of at least a couple of days" before it can provide a factory tour. For chocolate maniacs such as we are, if a tour of Suchard is imperative try phoning them at (038) 21-11-55.

Failing the Suchard tour, see the city's museum of mechanical dolls and music boxes. Take a stroll up winding streets, past elegant Renaissance and 17th century houses, to the hilltop Castle. Visit the Fine Art Museum. Take the funicular to the top (3,839 feet) of Chaumont for a view of the Alps.

Boat rides on the 2 nearby lakes (Biel and Neuchatel) *are* covered by Eurailpass.

Try the great Fondue Neuchatelois, made from white wine and kirsch schnapps. On the first Sunday of October, the local grape harvest is celebrated with a colorful Parade and Battle of Flowers. On this day, wine flows from the city's outdoor fountains instead of water.

Dep. Neuchatel	Frequent times from 07:02 to 23:10
Arr. Bern	40–60 minutes later

Bern - Zurich - Bern   260

Most of these trains have a restaurant car or light refreshments.

Dep. Bern	Frequent times from 04:51 to 23:50
Arr. Zurich	60–90 minutes later
Dep. Zurich	Frequent times from 04:45 to 0:03
Arr. Bern	60–90 minutes later

Chur - Andermatt - Chur   320

Not covered by Eurailpass. The 1995 prices for a roundtrip ticket *without* a Swiss Pass: 109.20 Swiss francs for first-class, Sfr-64.80 for second-class. *With* a Swiss Pass: Free.

Dep. Chur	05:45 (1)	06:48	08:11	09:03 (2)	09:45	10:55 (2)
Arr. Disentis	07:17	08:15	09:32	-0- (2)	11:08	-0- (2)
Change trains.						
Dep. Disentis	07:22	08:22	09:36	-0- (2)	11:35	-0- (2)
Arr. Andermatt	08:29	09:37	10:58	11:34	12:46	13:25

Sights in **Andermatt:** A great ski resort. See the rock crystal altar crucifix and other treasures in the baroque St. Peter and St. Paul Church.

Dep. Andermatt	08:29	10:30	12:00 (2)	12:18	13:34 (2)	14:18 (3)
Arr. Disentis	09:36	11:34	-0- (2)	13:33	-0- (2)	15:26
Change trains.						
Dep. Disentis	09:40	11:40	-0- (2)	13:40	-0- (2)	15:40
Arr. Chur	11:03	13:03	14:18	15:03	16:10	17:03

(1) Runs daily except Sundays and holidays. (2) "Glacier Express." Runs May 29-October 16 only. Reservation required (tel. 081-22-1425). Supplement charged. Direct train to and from Anermatt. No train change in Disentis. Light refreshments. (3) Plus other departures from Andermatt at 16:18(4), and 18:18(4), arriving Chur 19:03, and 21:03. (4) Runs May 14-October 16 only.

Chur - Arosa - Chur   324

These are cogwheel trains that leave from the front of the Chur railstation. A very scenic ride.

Dep. Chur	06:31	08:13	09:00	09:55	10:55	11:55	12:55 (1)
Arr. Arosa	61 minutes later						

Sights in **Arosa**: Great Summer and Winter sports. Fantastic mountain scenery.

Dep. Arosa	07:45	09:05	10:05	11:05	12:05	13:05	14:05 (2)
Arr. Chur	61 minutes later						

(1) Plus other departures from Chur every hour 13:55–17:55, plus 19:07, 19:55, 21:05 and 23:00. (2) Plus other departures from Arosa every hour 15:05–21:05.

Chur - Filisur - St. Moritz - Chur 330

Dep. Chur	06:40	08:08 (1)	09:00 (1)	09:52 (1)	10:52	11:52 (2+3)
Arr. Filisur	08:00	09:15	10:14	11:00 (5)	12:00	13:00 (5)
Arr. St. Moritz	09:00	10:18	11:18	11:58	12:58	13:58

• • •

Dep. St. Moritz	10:00 (2)	11:00 (1)	12:00 (1)	13:00 (5)	14:00	15:00 (1+4)
Arr. Filisur	11:02	12:02 (5)	13:02	14:02	15:02	16:02 (5)
Arr. Chur	12:07	13:07	14:07	15:07	16:07	17:07

(1) Light refreshments. (2) Restaurant car. (3) Plus other departures from Chur at 12:52 (1), 13:52, 14:52 (2), 15:52, 16:52, 17:52, 18:52, 19:52 and 20:57. (4) Plus other departures from St. Moritz at 05:45, 07:05, 08:05, 09:00, 16:00 (1), 17:00 (1), 18:00 (2), 19:00 and 20:00 (5) Runs Fridays, Saturdays and Sundays.

Sights in **Filisur:** Near a very high railway bridge, Filisur is located in a narrow valley. The Hotel Grischuna, close to the railstation, has some rooms with a view of the village and the valley. Train fans might prefer other rooms that face the rail line.

It is only a 30-minute walk to the edge of the roaring **Landwasser River**, where you can look up at the trains going over the bridge.

Chur - Zurich - Chur 310

Dep. Chur	06:13 (1)	07:15 (1)	08:23 (2)	09:15 (3)	10:23 (2)	11:15 (3)
Arr. Zurich	07:51	08:50	09:50	10:50	11:50	12:50

Dep. Zurich	11:10 (1)	12:10 (4)	13:10 (3)	14:10 (2)	15:09 (2)	16:10 (4+5)
Arr. Chur	12:45	13:37	14:45	15:37	16:37	17:37

(1) Restaurant car. (2) Reservation advisable. Restaurant car. (3) Light refreshments. (4) Reservation advisable. Light refreshments. (5) Plus other departures from Zurich at 17:10 (3), 18:10 (2), 19:10 (1), 20:10 (3), 21:10 (1) and 22:10.

Geneva - Annecy - Geneva   167

The train changes in La Roche-sur-Foron are easy cross-platform transfers.

Dep. Geneva (Eaux-Vives)	08:27 (6)	11:10 (1)	13:20 (6)
Arr. La Roche-sur-Foron	08:57	11:46 (6)	13:56
Change trains.			
Dep. La Roche-sur-Foron	09:04 (2)	11:57 (2)	14:06 (7)
Arr. Annecy	09:48 (6)	12:30 (6)	14:41

Sights in **Annecy**: Pronounced "Ahn–see." This is a beautiful lake resort. See the 12th century Island Palace. The shops in the old quarter.

Dep. Annecy	11:14 (6)	12:42 (3)	14:48 (6)	16:41 (6)	17:31 (4)
Arr. La Roche-sur-Foron	11:46	13:17 (6)	15:21	17:13	18:13 (6)
Change trains.					
Dep. La Roche-sur-Foron	11:56 (6)	13:21 (3)	15:30	-0-	18:15 (4+5)
Arr. Geneva (Eaux-Vives)	12:36	13:52 (6)	16:03	-0-	19:06

(1) Runs Saturdays, Sundays and holidays. (2) Light refreshments. (3) Runs daily, except Sundays and holidays. (4) Runs Monday-Friday, except holidays. (5) Change trains in Annemasse (arr. 18:36-dep. 18:56). (6) Does not run July 5-29. (7) Does not July 4-28.

Geneva - Basel - Geneva   260

Dep. Geneva (Corn.)	07:38 (1)	08:15 (2)	09:44	10:15 (2)	11:44 (2)
Arr Basel (S.B.B.)	10:37	11:37	12:37	13:37	14:37
Dep. Basel	13:23 (1)	14:23	15:23 (1)	16:23	17:23 (4+6)
Arr. Geneva (Corn.)	16:06	17:34	18:06	19:34	20:06

(1) Reservation advisable. Light refreshments. (2) Light Refreshments. (3) Reservation advisable. (4) Reservation advisable. Restaurant car. (5) Change trains in Biel. (6) Plus other departures from Basel at 18:23, 19:23 (5), 20:23 and 21:23 (5), arriving Geneva 21:34, 22:37, 23:37 and 00:34.

Geneva - Bern - Geneva   260

All of these trains have a restaurant car, unless designated otherwise.

Dep. Geneva (Corn.)	06:25 (1)	06:57 (2)	07:57 (3)	08:57 (3)	09:25 (3+5)
Arr. Bern	08:22	08:42	09:42	10:42	11:22
Dep. Bern	13:18 (3)	14:18 (3)	14:38 (4)	15:18 (3)	16:18 (3+6)
Arr. Geneva (Corn.)	15:02	16:02	16:34	17:02	18:02

(1) No restaurant car or light refreshments. (2) Reservation advisable. (3) Reservation advisable. Restaurant car. (4) Light refreshments. (5) Plus other departures from Geneva at 09:57 (3) and 10:57 (3). (6) Plus other departures from Bern 16:38, 17:18 (3), 18:18 (3), 18:38 (4), 19:18 (3), 20:18 (3), 20:38, 21:18 (3), 22:21 (3) and 23:26.

Geneva - Dijon - Geneva

250

Dep. Geneva (Corn.)	06:38	08:48 (1)	11:48 (1)
Arr. Lausanne	07:27	09:31	12:31
Change trains. 157			
Dep. Lausanne	07:31 (2)	10:15 (3)	12:46 (2)
Arr. Dijon	09:42	12:16	14:45
Dep. Dijon	14:00 (2)	17:31 (3)	19:46 (2)
Arr. Lausanne	16:07	19:45	21:57
Change trains. 250			
Dep. Lausanne	16:28 (1)	19:55	22:28 (1)
Arr. Geneva	35-50 minutes later		

(1) Reservation advisable. Restaurant car. (2) TGV. Reservation advisable. Restaurant car. (3) TGV. Reservation advisable. Light refreshments. (4) Restaurant car.

Geneva - Grenoble - Geneva 165

Dep. Geneva (Corn.)	09:44	10:34 (2)	11:32 (1)
Arr. Grenoble	11:39	12:47	13:29
Dep. Grenoble	15:07	17:29 (1)	18:25 (2)
Arr. Geneva (Corn.)	17:18	19:28	20:44

(1) Supplement charged. Restaurant car. (2) Operates early July to early September. Light refreshments.

Geneva - Lausanne - Montreux - Geneva 270

As these schedules indicate, a stopover in Lausanne en route to Montreux is possible.

Dep. Geneva (Corn.)	07:38 (1)	08:38 (1)	09:38 (1)	10:38	11:38 (1)	12:38 (1+2)
Arr. Lausanne	08:30	09:30	10:30	11:30	12:30	13:30
Arr. Montreux	23 minutes later					

Sights in **Montreux:** The casino offers gambling, a cabaret and a disco. The 13th century Chillon Castle, about 1½ miles from Montreux, was immortalized by Byron. Its dungeon, used as a model for many movies, is the attraction. Board the bus to Chillon across from the Montreux railstation.

Dep. Montreux	11:07	12:07	13:07 (1)	14:07	15:07 (1)	16:07 (3)
Dep. Lausanne	11:30	12:30	13:30	14:30	15:30	16:30
Arr. Geneva (Corn.)	50 minutes later

(1) Light refreshments. (2) Plus another departure from Geneva at 13:38. (3) Plus other departures from Montreux at frequent times from 17:07 to 22:07.

Montreux - Gstaad - Zweisimmen - Montreux   275

This is the scenic route of both the "Panoramic Express" and "Crystal Panoramic Express." See details about these special Observation Trains as well as the scenery and interesting places on this line under "Geneva–Montreux–Zweisimmen – Geneva"

Reservations for "Crystal Panoramic Express" are accepted only for groups, but individuals may ride if there are any vacant seats.

Dep. Montreux	09:00 (1)	08:54	10:00 (2)	11:00	12:21 (3)
Dep. Gstaad	10:11	10:30	11:18	12:30	13:42
Arr. Zweisimmen	10:36	11:00	11:45	13:00	14:10

Sight in **Gstaad:** A *very* expensive ski village.

Dep. Zweisimmen	10:43 (1)	10:50	12:00	12:50	14:00 (4)
Dep. Gstaad	11:14	11:20	12:32	13:20	14:32
Arr. Montreux	12:30	12:38	14:00	14:38	16:00

(1) Reservation required. Supplement charged. "Crystal Panoramic Express." First-class only. Runs Saturdays, Sundays and holidays. (2) Reservation required for first-class, advisable for second-class. Supplement charged. "Panoramic Express." Runs daily. (3) Plus other Montreux departures at 14:00 (1), 14:21 (2) and 15:00. (4) Plus other Zweisimmen departures at 14:50 (2), 16:00, 16:50, 17:15 (1), 18:00 and 20:00, arriving Montreux at 16:38, 18:00, 18:38, 19:00, 20:00 and 22:00.

Geneva - Lyon - Geneva   159

The first 90 minutes from Geneva is noted for scenic canyons. Occasionally, 2 trains depart from the same track at Lyon's Perrache railstation, heading in opposite directions. Be sure to stand at the correct end (North or South) of the track in order to board the train you want to ride. Check the departure signs at the underground passageway. Do not rely merely on a track number when departing from Perrache railstation!

Next to the North passageway of Track "A" is a take-out restaurant, handy for provisioning your trip.

Dep. Geneva (Corn.)	07:04	10:22	12:54
Arr. Lyon (Part-Dieu)	08:53	12:12	14:46
Arr. Lyon (Per.)	9 minutes later		

Dep. Lyon (Per.)	12:13 (1)	17:10	19:21
Dep. Lyon (Part-Dieu)	9 minutes later		
Arr. Geneva (Corn.)	14:16	19:08	21:29

(1) Light refreshments.

Geneva - Neuchatel - Geneva   260

Dep. Geneva (Corn.)	07:54 (1)	08:54 (1)	09:54	10:54 (1)	11:54 (1+6)
Arr. Neuchatel	09:04	10:04	11:04	12:04	13:04

Sights in **Neuchatel**: See notes under "Bern–Neuchatel"

Dep. Neuchatel	12:55 (1)	13:01 (3)	13:55 (4)	14:55 (1)	15:55 (4+7)
Arr. Geneva (Corn.)	14:06	14:34	15:06	16:06	17:06

(1) Reservtion advisable. Light refreshments. (2) Reservtion advisable. (3) Change trains in Lausanne. (4) Reservtion advisable. Restaurant car. (5) Restaurant car. (6) Plus another departure from Geneva at 12:54(4). (7) Plus other departures from Neuchatel at 16:01,16:55 (1), 17:55 (1), 18:55 (4), 19:01 (3), 19:55 (1), 20:01, 21:01 (5), 22:01 and 23:01 (1).

Geneva - Zurich - Geneva   260

Reservation is advisable for all of these trains and all of them have a restaurant car or light refreshments.

Dep. Geneva (Cor.)	Frequent times from 04:49 to 21:57
Arr. Zurich	3 hours later

Dep. Zurich (Hbf.)	Every hour from 06:00 to 21:06
Arr. Geneva (Cor.)	3 hours later

Interlaken - Bern - Interlaken   280

Dep. Interlaken (Ost)	Every hour from 05:31 to 22:32
Dep. Interlaken (West)	5 minutes after departing Ost railstation
Arr. Bern	53 minutes after departing Interlaken (Ost)
Dep. Bern	Every hour from 06:56 to 23:28
Arr. Interlaken (West)	48 minutes after departing Bern
Arr. Interlaken (Ost)	5 minutes later

Interlaken - Lausanne - Interlaken

280

Dep. Interlaken (Ost)	07:11 (1)	07:39 (2)	08:11 (3)	08:39 (3)	09:39 (1)
Dep. Interlaken (West)	5 minutes later				
Arr. Bern	08:04	08:32	09:04	09:32	10:32
Change trains. 260					
Dep. Bern	08:18 (1)	08:38 (2)	09:18 (1)	10:18 (1)	10:38 (2)
Arr. Lausanne	09:26	09:50	10:26	11:26	11:50
Dep. Lausanne	12:33 (1)	13:33 (1)	14:10 (2)	14:33 (1)	15:33 (1+5)
Arr. Bern	13:42	14:42	15:22	15:42	16:42
Change trains. 280					
Dep. Bern	13:56 (4)	15:28 (2)	-0-	16:28 (2)	17:28 (1)
Arr. Interlaken (West)	14:44	16:16	-0-	17:16	18:16
Arr. Interlaken (Ost)	5 minutes later				

(1) Reservation advisable. Restaurant car. (2) Light refreshments. (3) Reservation advisable. Light refreshments. (4) Reservation advisable. (5) Plus other Lausanne departures at 16:10 (2), 16:33 (1), 17:10 (2), 17:33 (1), 19:10 and 21:10, arriving Interlaken (West) 18:16, 19:00, 19:16, 20:21, 21:23 and 23:23.

Interlaken - Murren - Jungfraujoch - Interlaken

This one-day trip covers the heart of the Bernese Oberland area. *It is not covered by Eurailpass.* The 1995 total price of tickets *without* a Swiss Pass: 170.80 Swiss francs for first-class, and Sfr-161.40 for second-class. *With* a Swiss Pass: Sfr-95.10.

All of the train changes shown here take less than one minute.

Hiking and trout fishing are Summer activities in **Murren**. Both it and **Wengen** are postcard Alpine villages. There have been top ski resorts in this area since 1906. **Jungfraujoch** is the highest (11,333 feet) railstation in Europe. From there, you can see the Jungfrau, Eiger and Monch peaks. The highest waterfall in Europe (2,000-foot drop) is spectacular there in late Spring and early Summer.

287

Dep. Interlaken (Ost)	08:32 (1)	Dep. Scheidegg	11:30 (3)
Arr. Lauterbrunnen	08:54	Arr. Jungfraujoch	12:22
Change to funicular. 289		*Change trains*	
Dep. Lauterbrunnen	09:02	Dep. Jungfraujoch	12:30 (2)
Arr. Murren	09:32	Arr. Scheidegg	13:21
Return to Lauterbrunnen.		*Change trains. 288*	
Dep. Murren	09:45	Dep. Scheidegg	14:00
Arr. Lauterbrunnen	10:15	Arr. Grindelwald	14:45
Change to a train. 287		*Change trains. 288*	
Dep. Lauterbrunnen	10:35	Dep Grindelwald	14:50
Dep. Wengen	10:55	Arr. Interlaken (Ost)	15:27
Arr. Scheidegg	11:20 (3)		
Change trains.			

(1) Plus other circle trips departing Interlaken at 09:02(3), 10:02(3), 10:32(3), 11:02, 11:32 and 12:32, arriving back in Interlaken at 15:57, 16:27, 17:57, 18:27 and 19:27. (2) Plus other departures from Jungfraujoch (via Grindelwald) at 13:00, 14:00, 14:30, 15:30, 16:00, 17:00 and 18:00, arriving Interlaken (Ost) at 15:57, 16:27, 16:57, 17:57, 18:27, 19:27 and 20:27. (3) Does not run May 29-June 23.

Interlaken - Luzern - Interlaken   285

There is a very scenic 48-mile panorama of the Alps on this trip along the shore of Lake Brienz.

Dep. Interlaken (Ost)	06:32	07:37	08:44	09:37	10:44 (1)
Arr. Luzern	08:36	09:36	10:36	11:36	12:36
Dep. Luzern	11:24	12:24 (2)	13:24 (1)	14:24 (2)	15:24 (2+3)
Arr. Interlaken (Ost)	13:16	14:23	15:16	16:23	17:16

(1) Restaurant car. (2) Light refreshments. (3) Plus other departures from Luzern at 16:24, 17:24, 18:24, 19:09 and 20:09, arriving Interlaken 18:23, 19:20, 20:23, 21:25 and 22:25.

Lausanne - Sion - Lausanne   270

Dep. Lausanne	08:09(1)	08:32 (2)	09:00 (2)	09:32 (2)	09:56 (2)	10:32 (4)
Arr. Sion	09:02	09:40	10:08	10:41	11:04	11:41

Sights in **Sion**: Ruins of the 13th century Valere Castle and the 4th–11th century religious art in the museum there. The world's oldest operable pipe organ (built in 1390), carved and painted wood chests and 15th century frescoes in the Church of Our Lady of Valere, open daily except Monday, 9:00–12:00 and 14:00–18:00.

The collection of Roman antiquities in the Cantonal Archaeological Museum on rue des Chateaux. Paintings by artists of this area in the Majorie Fine Arts Museum. Both museums are open daily except Monday 9:00–12:00 and 14:00–18:00.

The astronomical clock and carved doors of the 17th century City Hall. The ancient Tour de Sorciers (Tower of the Wizards). The 9th century Romanesque bell-tower of the Cathedral. Supersaxo, the 16th century mansion of a Renaissance nobleman.

Dep. Sion	13:23	14:17	15:17	15:52	16:17 (2+5)
Arr. Lausanne	14:27	15:27	16:27	17:03	17:27

(1) Reservation advisable. Light refreshments. (2) Light refreshments. (3) Reservation advisable. Restaurant car. (4) Plus other departures from Lausanne at 11:13 (3), 11:32, 11:56 (2) and 12:32 (2). (5) Plus other departures from Sion at frequent times from 16:45 to 22:03.

Luzern - Andermatt - Luzern

The Goschenen-Andermatt-Goschenen portion of this one-day excursion (a thrilling ride in the Schollenen Canyon) is by rack railway and is *not* covered by Eurailpass. The 1994 price of a roundtrip ticket *without* a Swiss Pass: 20.80 Swiss francs for first-class, Sfr-12.40 for second class. *With* a Swiss Pass: free.

290

Dep. Luzern	08:14 (1)	10:19 (1)	12:19 (2)	13:14 (3)
Arr. Goschenen	09:45	11:45	13:45	14:45
Change trains. 320				
Dep. Goschenen	09:55	11:55	13:55	15:55
Arr. Andermatt	10:06	12:06	14:06	16:06

Sights in **Andermatt**: A great ski resort.

Dep. Andermatt	12:50	16:50 (4)	18:50
Arr. Goschenen	13:05	17:05	19:05
Change trains. 290			
Dep. Goschenen	13:13 (3)	17:13 (5)	19:13
Arr. Luzern	14:46	18:46	20:46

(1) Reservation advisable. Light refreshments. Change trains in Arth-Goldau. (2) Reservation advisable. Restaurant car. Change trains in Arth Goldau. Supplement charged. (3) Light refreshments. (4) Operates late May to late October. (5) Light refreshments. Change trains in Arth Goldau.

Luzern - Basel - Luzern   290

Dep. Luzern	06:35 (1)	07:56 (1)	08:56	09:56	10:56 (1)
Arr. Basel (S.B.B.)	07:49	09:09	10:09	11:09	12:09
Dep. Basel (S.B.B.)	11:07 (2)	11:51 (1)	13:07 (2)	13:51 (1)	15:07 (2+3)
Arr. Luzern	12:12	13:04	14:12	15:04	16:12

(1) Light refreshments. (2) Reservation advisable. Supplement charged. Restaurant car. (3) Plus other departures from Basel at frequent times from 15:51 to 23:02.

Luzern - Bern - Luzern   265

Most of these trains have light refreshments.

Dep. Luzern	06:35	07:13 (1)	07:56	08:13 (2)	08:46	09:13 (1)	09:56
Arr. Olten	07:15	-0- (1)	08:37	-0- (2)	09:25	-0- (1)	10:37
Change trains.							
Dep. Olten	07:29	-0-	08:48	-0-	09:29	-0-	10:48
Arr. Bern	08:12	08:27	09:36	09:29	10:12	10:27	11:36
Dep. Bern	13:31 (1)	14:48	15:31 (1)	16:31 (1)	16:51	18:31 (1+3)	
Arr. Olten	-0- (1)	15:30	-0- (1)	-0- (1)	17:39	-0- (1)	
Change trains.							
Dep. Olten	-0-	15:35	-0-	-0-	17:49	-0-	
Arr. Luzern	14:46	16:12	16:46	17:46	18:27	19:46	

(1) Direct train. No train change in Olten. (2) Direct train. No train change in Olten. Runs Saturdays, Sundays and holidays. (3) Plus other departures from Bern at 18:51, 19:31 (1), 19:51 (1), 20:51, 21:48 (1), 22:21 (1) and 22:45, arriving Luzern 20:27, 20:46, 21:41, 22:52, 22:59, 23:57 and 00:16.

Luzern - Interlaken - Luzern   285

Dep. Luzern	06:03 (1)	07:24 (2)	08:24 (3)	09:24 (2)	10:24 (4)
Arr. Interlaken (Ost)	08:23	09:16 (6)	10:23	11:16	12:23
Dep. Interlaken (Ost)	10:44 (3)	11:37	12:44 (2)	13:37	14:44 (5)
Arr. Luzern	12:36	13:36	14:36	15:36	16:36

(1) Runs daily, except holidays. (2) Light refreshments. (3) Restaurant car. (4) Plus other departures from Luzern at frequent times from 11:24 to 20:09. (5) Plus other departures from Interlaken at frequent times from 15:37 to 20:37. (6) Reservation recommended.

Luzern - Neuchatel - Luzern

265

Dep. Luzern	06:35 (1)	07:13 (2)	08:46 (1)	09:13 (2)	09:56 (1)	11:56 (1)
Arr. Bern	08:12	08:27	10:12	10:27	11:36	13:36

Change trains. 255

Dep. Bern	08:22	09:22	10:22	11:22	12:22	14:22
Arr. Neuchatel	08:57	09:57	10:57	11:57	12:57	14:57
Dep. Neuchatel	14:02	15:02	16:02	17:02	18:02	19:02 (3)
Arr. Bern	14:38	15:38	16:38	17:38	18:38	19:38

Change trains. 265

Dep. Bern	14:48 (1)	16:31 (2)	16:51	18:31 (1)	18:51 (2)	19:51 (1)
Arr. Luzern	16:12	17:46	18:27	19:46	20:27	21:41

(1) Change trains in Olten. Light refreshments. (2) Light refreshments. (3) Plus other departures from Neuchatel at 21:08 and 22:06, arriving Luzern 23:57 and 00:16.

Luzern - Schwyz - Luzern   290

Dep. Luzern	08:14 (1)	09:14 (2)	10:19 (3)	11:14 (2)	12:19 (3)	13:14 (2)
Arr. Schwyz	50 minutes later					

Sights in **Schwyz:** Visit the Staatsarcivmuseum (National Archive Museum), to see the 13th century Oath of Eternal Alliance, the document which marks the founding of Switzerland. This village's name became the name of the country (Schweiz). The Museum is one mile (uphill) from the railstation. A bus meets every train. There are also nicely restored 17th and 18th century patrician homes here.

Dep. Schwyz	12:01 (2)	13:01 (4)	14:01 (1)	15:01 (4)	16:01 (2)	17:01 (4+5)
Arr. Luzern	50 minutes later					

(1) Change trains in Arth Goldau. (2) Light refreshments. (3) Reservation advisable. Restaurant car. Change trains in Arth Goldau. (4) Light refreshments. Change trains in Arth Goldau. (5) Plus other departures from Schwyz at 18:01 (2), 19:01 (4), 20:01 (4), 22:01 and 22:55.

Luzern - Zurich - Luzern 295

Most of these trains have light refreshments.

Dep. Luzern   Frequent times from 06:04 to 23:08
Arr. Zurich   50 minutes later

Dep. Zurich   Frequent times from 07:07 to 00:13
Arr. Luzern   50 minutes later

Zurich - Andermatt - Zurich

The Goschenen–Andermatt–Goschenen portion of this one-day excursion (a thrilling ride down the **Schollenen Canyon**) is by rack railway and is not covered by Eurailpass. The 1995 prices of a roundtrip ticket without a Swiss Pass were: 20.80 Swiss francs for first-class, Sfr-12.40 for second-class. *With* a Swiss Pass: free.

*All of the trains **Zurich–Gochenen** and vice-versa, have light refreshments, unless designated otherwise.*

290

Dep. Zurich	08:03 (1)	10:03 (2)	12:03 (3)
Arr. Goschenen	09:45	11:45	13:47
Change trains. 320			
Dep. Goschenen	09:55	11:55	13:55
Arrr. Andermatt	10 minutes later		

Sights in **Andermatt**: A great ski resort.

Dep. Andermatt	11:27	12:50	16:50 (4)	18:50
Arr. Goschenen	11:42	13:05	17:05	19:05
Change trains. 290				
Dep. Goschenen	12:13	13:13 (2)	17:13 (2)	19:13 (2)
Arr. Zurich	13:57	14:57	18:57	20:57

(1) Reservation advisable. Restaurant car. Change trains in Arth Goldau. (2) Light refreshments. Change trains in Arth Goldau. (3) Light refreshments. (4) Runs May 14-October 16 only.

Zurich - Arosa - Zurich

310

Dep. Zurich	06:33 (1)	07:33 (2)	08:10 (3)	09:10 (1)	10:10 (3)	11:10 (4)
Arr. Chur	08:03	08:51	09:37	10:45	11:37	12:45

Change trains. 324

The Chur–Arosa cogwheel train leaves from the front of the Chur railstation. This is a very scenic ride.

Dep. Chur	08:13	09:00	09:55	10:55	11:55	12:55
Arr. Arosa	one hour later					

Sights in **Arosa**: Great Summer and Winter sports. Fantastic mountain scenery.

Dep. Arosa	10:05	11:05	12:05	13:05	14:05	15:05 (5)
Arr. Chur	11:07	12:07	13:07	14:07	15:07	16:07

Change trains. 310

Dep. Chur	11:15 (1)	12:23 (3)	13:15 (4)	14:23 (3)	15:15 (1)	16:23 (2)
Arr. Zurich	12:50	13:50	14:50	15:50	16:50	17:50

(1) Light refreshments. (2) Reservation advisable. Restaurant car. (3) Reservation advisable. Light refreshments. (4) Restaurant car. (5) Plus other departures from Arosa (parenthesis designate Chur–Arosa service) at 16:05 (1), 17:05 (3), 18:05 (1), 19:05 (4) and 20:05, arriving Zurich 18:50, 19:50, 20:50, 21:50 and 22:50.

Zurich - Basel - Zurich   300

Many of these trains have a restaurant car or light refreshments.

Dep. Zurich	Frequent times from 06:30 to 23:37
Arr. Basel (S.B.B.)	60–70 minutes later

Dep. Basel (S.B.B.)	Frequent times from 05:23 to 23:32
Arr. Zurich	60–70 minutes later

Zurich - Bern - Zurich   260

Many of these trains have a restaurant car or light refreshments.

Dep. Zurich	Frequent times from 06:00 to 00:03
Arr. Bern	90 minutes later

Dep. Bern	Frequent times from 04:51 to 23:50
Arr. Zurich	90 minutes later

Zurich - Chur - Zurich   310

Many of these trains have a restaurant car or light refreshments.

Dep. Zurich	Frequent times from 06:33 to 22:10
Arr. Chur	90 minutes later

Sights in **Chur:** This 2100-year old village is located at what has been a strategic pass in the Alps since Roman times. Walk from the station up through the small business area to a hilltop church and see the unusual cemetery there. The modern portion of it has rows of graves that are solidly decorated with living, blossoming plants.

Also see the fine stained-glass and the 12th century carved altar in the 15th century Cathedral. The Bishop's Palace. A one-hour walking tour of Chur is made easy by following red and green footprints painted on the sidewalks. The footprints are matched to a map available at the city's tourist office.

Dep. Chur	Frequent times from 06:13 to 21:13
Arr. Zurich	90 minutes later

Zurich - Landquart - Davos - Zurich

310

Dep. Zurich	07:33 (1)	08:10 (2)	09:10 (3)	10:10 (2)	11:10 (4)
Arr. Landquart	08:36	09:23	10:31	11:23	12:31
Change trains. 327					
Dep. Landquart	08:56	09:40	10:40	11:40	12:40
Arr. Klosters	09:34	10:18	11:18	12:18	13:18
Arr. Davos (Platz)	28 minutes after arriving Klosters.				

Sights in **Davos**: One of the world's most popular ski resorts. Also popular for its skating rinks, hiking trails, a sled run, horse-drawn sleigh rides, indoor swimming, hang-gliding, horseback riding and ice hockey.

Take the 22-minute ride on the Parsenn cable railway, once described by Vogue Magazine as "the Rolls Royce of mountain railways," to the ridge of **Weissfluh**. A cable car ascends from there to the summit, the start of the different ski runs to **Serneus**, **Sass** and **Klosters**.

A general-fare ticket (Sfr-280 for adults, Sfr-173 for children in 1994) allows unlimited use of the entire network of funicular railways, ski lifts and cable cars for 6 days. It also covers the buses that run every 15 minutes from one end of Davos to the other.

Dep. Davos (Platz)	12:05	13:05	14:05	15:05	16:05 (5)
Dep. Klosters	29 minutes after departing Davos				
Arr. Landquart	13:17	14:17	15:17	16:17	17:17
Change trains. 310					
Dep. Landquart	13:26 (4)	14:34 (2)	15:26 (3)	16:34 (1)	17:26 (3)
Arr. Zurich	14:50	15:50	16:50	17:50	18:50

(1) Reservation advisable. Restaurant car. (2) Reservation advisable. Light refreshments. (3) Light refreshments. (4) Restaurant car. (5) Plus other departures from Davos (parenthesis designate Landquart–Zurich service) at 17:05, 18:05, 19:05, 20:00 and 21:00, arriving Zurich 19:50, 20:50, 21:50, 22:50 and 23:50.

Zurich - Frankfurt - Zurich 77

Both of these trains charge a supplement that includes reservation fee and have a restaurant car.

Dep. Zurich	06:45	08:00 (1)		Dep. Frankfurt	16:09	16:43 (2)	17:43 (2+3)
Arr. Frankfurt	10:47	12:14		Arr. Zurich	20:15	21:00	22:00

(1) Change trains in Basel and Mannheim. (2) Change trains in Mannheim and Basel. (3) Plus another Zurich departure at 18:43 (2).

Zurich - Geneva - Zurich 260

Most of these trains have a restaurant car or light refreshments. Reservation is advisable

Dep. Zurich	Frequent times from 06:00 to 21:06
Arr. Geneva (Corn.)	3 hours later
Dep. Geneva (Corn.)	Frequent times from 04:49 to 21:57
Arr Zurich	3 hours later

Zurich - Interlaken - Zurich   280

All of these trains have light refreshments, unless designated otherwise.

Dep. Zurich	06:25	07:30 (1)	08:30	09:30 (1)	10:30	11:30 (1)
Arr. Interlaken (Ost)	09:21	10:21	11:21	12:21	13:21	14:21

Sights in **Interlaken**: See notes about sightseeing in Interlaken under "Basel–Interlaken"

Dep. Interlaken (Ost)	13:39	14:39	15:39	16:39 (2)	17:39	18:39 (4)
Arr. Zurich	16:30	17:30	18:30	19:30	20:30	21:30

(1) Change trains in Spiez. (2) Reservation advisable. Change trains in Olten. (3) Reservation advisable. Restaurant car. Change trains in Olten. (4) Plus another departure from Interlaken at 19:39 (3). Restaurant car to Olten, arriving Olten 21:30, depart Olten 21:42, arriving Zurich 22:31.

Zurich - Lugano - Zurich   290

Dep. Zurich	06:30 (1)	07:03 (2)	08:03 (2)	09:03 (2)	10:03 (3)	11:03 (2)
Arr. Lugano	09:45	10:04	11:04	12:04	13:04	14:04

Dep. Lugano	12:41 (1)	13:57 (4)	14:41 (1)	15:57 (2)	16:33 (2)	17:57 (2+6)
Arr. Zurich	15:57	16:57	17:57	18:57	19:28	20:57

(1) Light refreshments. (2) Reservation advisable. Supplement charged. Restaurant car. (3) Change trains in Arth Goldau at 10:45 (2). (4) Reservation advisable. Light refreshments. (5) Runs daily, except holidays. Light refreshments. (6) Plus other Lugano departures at 18:47 (2), 19:41 (5) arriving Zurich, 21:48 and 23:15.

Zurich - Luzern - Zurich   295

Most of these trains have light refreshments.

Dep. Zurich	Frequent times from 07:07 to 00:13
Arr. Luzern	50 minutes later

Dep. Luzern	Frequent times from 06:04 to 23:08
Arr. Zurich	50 minutes later

Zurich - Milan - Zurich 290

See the description of this very scenic trip under either "Zurich–Bellinzona–Lugano"

Reservation is advisable for all of these trains, and all of them have a restaurant car.

Dep. Zurich	07:03	08:03 (1)	Dep. Milan (Cen.)	16:25	17:20(1)
Arr. Milan (Cen.)	11:35	12:35	Arr. Zurich	20:57	21:50

(1) Supplement charged.

Zurich - Munich - Zurich 75

Reservation is advisable for all of these trains, and all of them have a restaurant car.

Dep. Zurich	07:40 (1)	09:40 (1)	Dep. Munich	14:02 (1)	18:37 (1)
Arr. Munich	11:51	13:56	Arr. Zurich	18:23	22:56

(1) Supplement payable.

Zurich - Neuchatel - Zurich 260

Dep. Zurich	07:06 (1)	08:06 (2)	09:06 (1)	10:06 (2)	11:06 (4)
Arr. Neuchatel	08:59	09:53	10:59	11:53	12:59
Dep. Neuchatel	12:06 (3)	13:01 (1)	14:06 (2)	15:01 (1)	16:06 (3+5)
Arr. Zurich	13:53	14:53	15:53	16:53	17:53

(1) Light refreshments. (2) Reservation advisable. Restaurant car. (3) Reservation advisable. Light refreshments. (4) Plus another Zurich departure at 12:06 (2), arriving Neuchatel 13:55. (5) Plus other Neuchatel departures at 17:01 (1), 18:06 (2), 19:01 (1), 20:06 (2) and 21:01 (1), arriving Zurich 18:53, 19:53, 20:53, 21:53 and 22:53.

Zurich - Rheinfelden - Zurich 300

Dep. Zurich	06:30 (1)	07:00	08:00 (2)	09:00 (2)	10:00 (3+7)
Dep. Brugg	06:57	07:25	08:25	09:25	10:31
Arr. Rheinfelden	07:26	07:56	08:56	09:58	11:08

Sights in **Rheinfelden**: A world-famed health spa since 1844. There are tours of the Cardinal and Feldschlosschen breweries. Visit the island park on the Rhine River.

Dep. Rheinfelden   13:01 (4)   13:50 (5)   15:01 (6)   16:01 (1)   17:01 (1+8)
Arr. Zurich   65 minutes later

(1) Light refreshments. (2) Restaurant car. (3) Reservation advisable. Restaurant car. Change trains in Brugg. (4) Reservation advisable. Restaurant car. (5) Change tains in Brugg. (6) Reservation advisable. Light refreshments. (7) Plus other departures from Zurich at 11:00 (1), 13:00 (1) and 14:00 (6). (8) Plus other departures from Rheinfelden at 18:00 (2), 19:01 (1), 20:01 (2), 21:01 (1), 22:02 (1), 23:05 and 23:45.

Zurich - St. Moritz - Zurich

310			*330*		
Dep. Zurich	07:33 (1)	08:10 (1)	Dep. St. Moritz	12:00 (2)	13:00 (5)
Arr. Chur	08:51	09:37	Arr. Chur	14:07	15:07 (6)
Change trains. 330			*Change trains. 310*		
Dep. Chur	09:00 (2)	09:52 (2+6)	Dep. Chur	14:23 (3)	15:15 (2)
Arr. St. Moritz	11:18	11:58	Arr. Zurich	15:50	16:50

(1) Reservation advisble. Restaurant car. (2) Light refreshments. (3) Reservation advisable. Light refreshments. (4) Restaurant car. (5) Plus other departures from St. Moritz at 14:00, 15:00 (2+6), 16:00 (2), 17:00 (2), 18:00 (4), 19:00 and 20:00...departing Chur 16:23 (1), 17:15 (2), 18:23 (3), 19:15 (2), 20:13 (4), 21:13 and 22:13...arriving Zurich 17:50, 18:50, 19:50, 20:50, 21:50, 22:50 and 23:50. (6) Runs Saturdays, Sundays and holidays.

Sights in **St. Moritz:** The lovely scenery of the Alps, reflected on the Lake of St. Moritz. The curative waters. Great Summer sports (swimming, sailing, fishing, golf, mountain climbing) as well as Winter sports. The creme de la creme of the international jet set is here December to April.

See the collection of porcelain stoves, furniture and carved woodwork in the Engadine Museum, open Monday–Saturday 09:30–12:00 and 14:00–17:00, also on Sunday 10:00–12:00. Many paintings of this beautiful area by Giovanni Segantini in the Segantini Museum, open Monday–Saturday 09:30–12:00 and 14:00–16:00, on Sunday 14:30–16:00.

Zurich - Schwyz - Zurich   290

Dep. Zurich	07:30	08:03(3)	09:03(3)	10:03(4)	11:03(3)	12:03(6)	
Arr. Schwyz	one hour later						

Dep. Schwyz	11:01	12:01(5)	13:01	14:01(5)	15:01(6)	16:01(5)	17:01(6+7)
Arr. Zurich	one hour later						

(1) Operates early April to late October. Light refreshments. (2) Change trains in Arth Goldau. (3) Reservation advisable. Restaurant car. Change trains in Arth Goldau. Supplement charged. (4) Light refreshments. Change trains in Arth Goldau. (5) Change in Arth Goldau to a train for which reservation is advisable. (6) Light refreshments. (7) Plus other departures from Schwyz at 17:36 (6), 18:01 (5) and 19:01 (6) .

Zurich - Solothurn - Zurich 260

All of these trains have a restaurant car or light refreshments.

Dep. Zurich	Frequent times from 06:06 to 23:03
Arr. Solothurn	60 minutes later

Sights in **Solothurn**: Switzerland's oldest town. (It and Trier, in Germany, are the 2 oldest towns north of the Alps.) This is the best preserved Baroque town in Switzerland, located in the **Aare Valley**, at the foot of the **Jura Mountains**. Everything worth seeing here can be reached by walking the town's narrow streets: the town's many fine statues, 11 churches and chapels, 11 ornamental fountains…and the 11 steps leading to the entrance of the Cathedral of St. Ours which has 11 bells, 11 towers and 11 altars.

Solothurn became in 1481 the *eleventh* canton to join the Swiss Federation!

See the outstanding ancient art here. Holbein's Madonna in the Museum. Traces of the 4th century Roman wall. Farmers selling flowers, fruits and vegetables in the town center every Wednesday and Saturday. The marvelous Assumption over the high altar in the Jesuit church.

The bulb domes on the twin towers of the Town Hall. The comprehensive collection of arms and armor in the Old Arsenal Museum, said to be the second largest collection of weapons in Europe. It has 400 suits of armor among its exhibits. The Italian belltower of the Cathedral.

Dep. Solothurn	Frequent times from 05:41 to 22:56
Arr. Zurich	60 minutes later

Zurich - Stuttgart - Zurich 74

Dep. Zurich	06:30 (1)	07:13	09:13	
Arr. Stuttgart	09:13 (2)	10:22	12:22	
Dep. Stuttgart	13:42	15:42	16:52 (1+2)	17:42	19:42 (3)
Arr. Zurich	16:47	18:47	19:50	20:49	22:47

(1) Reservation advisable. Supplement charged. Restaurant car. (2) Runs Monday-Friday. (3) Runs Friday only July 1-August 26.

Zurich - Winterthur - Zurich 308

Dep. Zurich	Frequent times from 06:39 to 23:15
Arr. Winterthur	22 minutes later

Sights in **Winterthur**: More art treasures than any other place in Switzerland, at the country's National Gallery in the Am Roemerholz mansion. Great Austrian, German and Swiss paintings.

Dep. Winterthur	Frequent times from 06:27 to 23:27
Arr. Zurich	22 minutes later

Zurich - Zug - Zurich 295

Dep. Zurich	Frequent times from 07:07 to 00:13
Arr. Zug	26 minutes later

Sights in **Zug**: This village is located on the northeast shore of the 14-mile long Lake Zug. See the spires and massive towers of the 15th century Church of St. Oswald. The stained-glass for which this area is noted and also gold and silver work, embroidery and wood carvings in the Museum at the 16th century Town Hall.

See the narrow, ancient houses (most of them with overlapping second and upper floors) on Ober-Alstadt and Unter-Alstadt. The elaborately-carved choir stalls in the 15th century St. Oswald's Church.

To reach the top floor of the 3,255-foot-high **Zugerberg**, either take the 20-minute bus ride from the railstation to the **Schoenegg** suburb and then a cable railway from there, or make the 2-hour climb by foot. The splendid view at the top is of **Lake Zug** and parts of **Lake Luzern**, framed by the Alpine giants Mount Pilatus, Mount Rigi, Jungfrau, Eiger and Finsterahorn.

Visit the 7-story Glass House, facing the railstation. Its shopping center has stores that offer fine shoes, gourmet food, wine, jewelry and flowers.

There are short boat trips, to **Walchwil** and to **Arth**.

Try the local specialties: *rotel* (a tasty salmon-like fish from the lake), the local cherries that are used for producing the liqueur kirsch, and the local cake, kirsch-torte, laced with the cherry liqueur.

Dep. Zug	Frequent times from 06:28 to 23:32
Arr. Zurich	26 minutes later

SCENIC RAIL TRIPS IN SWITZERLAND

Basel - Schaffhausen - Basel   734

An easy one-day roundtrip, to see the marvelous Rhine Falls.

Dep. Basel (Bad Bf.)	08:16	10:16	12:16	14:16	16:15
Arr. Schaffhausen	09:28	11:28	13:28	15:28	17:28

Dep. Schaffhausen	10:34	12:34	14:34	16:34	18:34
Arr. Basel (Bad Bf.)	11:48	13:48	15:48	17:48	19:48

Bern - Brig - Bern   280

An easy one-day roundtrip that affords a view of **Rhone Valley** and **Lonza Valley** canyons, lakes and mountains plus the Lake Thun scenery at Spiez about which we enthuse in the "Geneva–Spiez" trip .and going through the 9-mile Lotschberg Tunnel and over the Bietschtal Bridge. This structure takes the train 255 feet above the ravine it crosses.

Dep. Bern	06:22 (1)	06:50 (3)	07:22 (1)	08:22 (3)	08:51 (4)	09:22 (1+6)
Arr. Spiez	06:52	07:20	07:52	08:52	09:21	09:52
Dep. Spiez	06:54	07:22	07:54	08:54	09:23	09:54 (7)
Arr. Brig	07:59	08:18	08:59	09:59	10:19	10:59

Sights in **Brig**: Switzerland's largest private residence, the 17th century Stockalper Castle, built by a very successful businessman.

Dep. Brig	08:01 (1)	09:01 (1)	10:01 (4)	10:42 (2)	11:01 (3)	12:01 (5+8)
Arr. Spiez	09:05	10:05	11:05	11:40	12:05	13:05
Dep. Spiez	09:07	10:07	11:07	11:42	12:07	13:07 (9)
Arr. Bern	31 minutes after departing Spiez.					

(1) Light refreshments. (2) Reservation advisable. (3) Reservation advisable. Restaurant car. (4) Reservation advisable. Light refreshments. (5) Restaurant car. (6) Plus other departures from Bern at frequent times from 10:22 to 23:28. (7) Plus other departures from Spiez at frequent times from 10:54 to 00:06. (8) Plus other departures from Brig at frequent times from 13:01 to 21:35. (9) Plus other departures from Spiez at frequent times from 13:33 to 22:01.

Bern - Brig - Domodossola - Bern

To see all of the scenery and Lotschberg Tunnel noted above under "Bern–Brig" plus having the experience of going through the 11.9-mile Simplon (Europe's longest rail tunnel), make the Bern–Domodossola portion of the Bern–Milan trip.

The Simplon is actually 2 tunnels, one southbound and a 65-foot longer bore for the separate northbound tunnel.

280

Dep. Bern	06:50 (1)	07:22 (2)	08:51 (3)	10:22 (4)	12:56 (4)
Arr. Brig	- 0 - (1)	08:59	10:21 (9)	11:59	14:27

Change trains.
365

Dep. Brig	- 0 -	09:34 (3)	10:31	12:38 (5)	14:31 (3)
Arr. Domodossola	08:50	10:02	11:00	13:07	15:00

• • •

Dep. Domodossola	09:15	10:11 (4)	10:46 (4)	12:13 (5)	14:11 (4+8)
Arr. Brig	09:45	10:40	11:14	12:43	14:40

Change trains.
280

Dep. Brig	10:01 (3)	11:01 (5)	12:01 (6)	13:01 (5)	15:01 (5)
Arr. Bern	11:38	12:38	13:38	14:38	16:38

(1) Reservation advisable. Direct train. No train change in Brig. Restaurant car or light refreshments. (2) Light refreshments. (3) Reservation advisable. Light refreshments. (4) Reservation advisable. (5) Reservation advisable. Restaurant car. (6) Restaurant car. (7) Operates late May to mid-October. Runs Saturdays, Sundays . (8) Plus other Domodossola departures at 17:13 (1), 18:13 (6) and 18:50 (7), arriving Bern 19:38, 20:38 and 21:38. (9) Runs Fridays and Saturdays July 2-August 27.

Bern - Interlaken - Brienz - Interlaken - Bern

There is fine canyon, lake and mountain scenery on this easy one-day roundtrip.

Most of the trains Bern–Interlaken and v.v. have light refreshments.

280

Dep. Bern	07:28	08:28	09:28 (1)	10:28	11:28 (2+3)
Arr. Interlaken (Ost)	08:21	09:21	10:21	11:21	12:21
Change trains. 285					
Dep. Interlaken (Ost)	08:44	09:37	10:44	11:37	12:44
Arr. Brienz	09:00	09:58	11:00	11:58	13:00

• • •

Dep. Brienz	09:01 (2)	10:02	11:00	12:02	13:00
Arr. Interlaken (Ost)	09:16	10:23	11:16	12:23	13:16
Change trains. 280					
Dep. Interlaken (Ost)	09:39 (1)	10:39	11:39 (1)	12:39 (2)	13:39
Arr. Bern	10:32	11:32	12:32	13:32	14:32

(1) Reservation advisable. Restaurant car. (2) Reservation advisable. (3) Plus other departures from Bern (that allow the same roundtrip) at 12:28, 13:28 (2), 14:28, 15:28, 16:28 and 17:28 (1), arriving back in Bern 15:32, 16:32, 17:32, 18:32, 19:32 and 20:32.

Bern - Interlaken - Wengen - Jungfrau - Grindelwald - Interlaken - Bern

This easy one-day trip covers the heart of the Bernese Oberland area and offers very good gorge, lake and mountain scenery. There have been popular ski resorts in this area since 1906.

The Interlaken-Jungfraujoch-Interlaken portion of this excursion is *not* covered by Eurailpass. The 1994 prices *without* a Swiss Pass were: 155.20 Swiss francs for first-class, Sfr-145.80 for second-class. *With* a Swiss Pass: Sfr-95.10.

At **Jungfraujoch**, passengers alight to look down on the great Jungfrau glacier and stroll in the "Ice Palace" carved inside the glacier. Jungfraujoch is the highest (11,333 feet) railstation in Europe. Fabulous views of the Jungfrau, Eiger and Monch peaks can be seen from the revolving restaurant, which rotates completely every 50 minutes. The highest waterfall in Europe (2,000-foot drop) is spectacular in late Spring and early Summer.

We suggest, for variety, you go from Interlaken to Jungfraujoch *via Wengen* and then return to Interlaken *via Grindelwald*.

280

Dep. Bern	07:28	08:28 (1)
Arr. Interlaken (Ost)	08:21	09:21
Change trains.		

287

Dep. Interlaken (Ost)	08:32	09:32
Arr. Wengen	09:14	10:24
Arr. Scheidegg	09:45	10:55
Change trains.		
Dep. Scheidegg	10:02	11:02
Arr. Jungfraujoch	10:53	11:53
Sightsee in Jungfraujoch		

287

Dep. Jungfraujoch	12:00	13:00
Arr. Scheidegg	12:49	13:49
Change trains. (table 288)		
Dep. Scheidegg	13:02	14:02
Arr. Grindelwald	13:45	14:45
Change trains.		
Dep. Grindelwald	13:50	14:50
Arr. Interlaken (Ost)	14:27	15:27
Change trains.		

280

Dep. Interlaken (Ost)	14:39	15:39 (1)
Arr. Bern	15:32	16:32

(1) Light refreshments.

Bern - Lausanne - Brig - Spiez - Bern

Excellent canyon, lake and mountain scenery on this easy one-day circle trip. There is time for a stopover in Lausanne and/or Spiez. You go through the 9-mile Lotschberg Tunnel after leaving Brig.

260

Dep. Bern	06:38 (1)	07:18 (2)	08:38 (3)	09:18 (2)	10:18 (2+7)
Arr. Lausanne	07:50	08:26	09:50	10:26	11:26
Change trains.	*(table 270)*				
Dep. Lausanne	07:56	08:32 (3)	09:56 (3)	10:32	11:32
Arr. Brig	09:53	10:18	11:52	12:23	13:23
Change trains.	*(table 280)*				
Dep. Brig	10:01 (4)	10:42	12:01 (3)	12:26 (3)	14:01 (2)
Arr. Spiez	11:05	11:40	13:05	13:30	15:05
Dep. Spiez	11:07	11:42	13:07	13:33	15:07
Arr. Bern	11:38	12:12	13:38	14:04	15:38

(1) Runs daily except Sundays and holidays. (2) Reservation advisable. Restaurant car. (3) Light refreshments. (4) Reservation advisable. Light refreshments. (5) Restaurant car. (6) Reservation advisable. (7) The same circle trip can be made in daylight by leaving Bern at 10:38 (3), 11:18 (2), 12:38 (3), 13:18 (2) and 14:38 (3)...depart Lausanne 11:56 (3), 12:32 (3), 13:56 (3), 14:32 (3) and 15:56 (3).depart Brig 14:01 (4), 14:42 (4), 16:01 (3), 17:01 (2) and 18:01 (6)...arriving back in Bern 15:38, 16:12, 17:38, 18:38 and 19:38.

Bern - Locarno - Bern

Complete notes on the Domodossola–Locarno portion of this easy one-day roundtrip, one of the 5 most scenic rail journeys in Europe, appear under "Brig–Domodossola—Locarno" on page 392.

280

Dep. Bern	06:50 (4)	07:56	08:51 (2)	10:22 (2)	12:56 (1)	13:22 (3)
Arr. Brig	08:18	09:29	10:19 (7)	11:59	14:27	14:59

Change trains   (table 365)

Dep. Brig	08:22 (1)	09:34 (2)	10:31 (4)	12:38 (4)	14:31 (1)	15:17 (3)
Arr. Domodossola	08:50	10:02	11:00	13:07	15:00	15:47

Change trains.

Walk from the Domodossola station and go to the underground Centovalli track. Hurry!

272

Dep. Domodossola	09:02	10:18	11:12	13:18	15:16	16:00
Arr. Locarno	10:40	11:56	12:48	14:55	16:55	17:37

Dep. Locarno	12:22	13:50	15:28	16:28	17:28	19:05
Arr. Domodossola	14:00	15:30	17:00	18:00	19:00	20:46

Change trains.

Walk from the underground Centovalli track, up to the main Domodossola station. Hurry!

365

Dep. Domodossola	14:11 (1)	15:44 (1)	17:13 (1)	18:13 (6)	19:13 (4)	21:00 (1)
Arr. Brig	14:40	16:13	17:43	18:43	19:43	21:30

Change trains   (table 280)

Dep. Brig	14:42 (2)	17:01 (4)	18:01 (1)	19:01 (3)	20:01 (2)	21:35
Arr. Bern	16:12	18:38	19:38	20:38	21:38	23:10

(1) Reservation advisable. (2) Reservation advisable. Light refreshments. (3) Light refreshments. (4) Reservation advisable. Restaurant car. (5) Operates late March to late October. (6) Restaurant car. (7) Runs Friday-Saturday July 2-August 27.

Bern - Luzern - Alpnachstad - Pilatus

Very nice canyon, lake and mountain scenery on this easy one-day roundtrip that can include a stopover in Luzern. There are good views and several restaurants at the peak of **Pilatus.**

Note in the footnotes that the Pilatus Rack Railway trip (Alpnachstad–Pilatus–Alpnachstad) operates *only* May through November. The 1994 price *without* a Swiss Pass for the one-class roundtrip was: 53 Swiss francs. *With* a Swiss Pass: Sfr-39.75.

265			286		
Dep. Bern	07:31 (1)	09:31 (1+2)	Dep. Pilatus Kulm	10:45	13:45 (3)
Arr. Luzern	08:46	10:46	Arr. Alpachstad	11:25	14:25
Change trains. 285			*Change to ordinary train.* 285		
Dep. Luzern	09:09	11:09	Dep. Alpachstad	11:30	14:30
Arr. Alpnachstad	09:26	11:26	Arr. Luzern	11:50	14:50
Change to rack railway. 286			*Change trains.* 265		
Dep. Alpnachstad	09:30	11:30	Dep. Luzern	11:56 (1)	15:13 (1)
Arr. Pilatus Kulm	10:00	12:00	Arr. Bern	13:36	16:29

(1) Light refreshments. (2) Plus other departures from Bern at 11:31 (1) and 12:48, arriving Pilatus Kulm 14:20 and 15:00. (3) Plus other departures from Pilatus Kulm at 15:45 and 16:25, arriving Bern 18:26 and 19:29.

Bern - Spiez - Bern   280

Great canyon, lake and mountain scenery on this easy one-day roundtrip. This is a portion of the "Geneva–Spiez–Geneva" trip listed earlier. Plenty of time to stroll in Spiez and enjoy the beauty of Lake Thun and the mountains above it.

Dep. Bern	Frequent times from 06:22 to 23:28
Arr. Spiez	30 minutes later
Dep. Spiez	Frequent times from 05:58 to 22:56
Arr. Bern	30 minutes later

Bern - Spiez - Brig - Lausanne - Bern

Marvelous canyon, lake, mountain and river scenery on this easy one-day circle trip. This is the reverse of the "Bern–Lausanne–Spiez–Bern" ride listed earlier. A stroll in Spiez is a nice way to break the journey. You go through the 10-mile Lotschberg Tunnel after leaving Spiez.

All of these trains have light refreshments, unless designated otherwise.

280

Dep. Bern	07:22	08:22 (1)	08:51 (2)	09:22 (3)	10:22 (3)	11:22 (3+5)
Arr. Spiez	07:52	08:52	09:21	09:52	10:52	11:52
Dep. Spiez	07:54	08:54	09:23	09:54	10:54	11:54
Arr. Brig	08:59	09:59	10:19	10:59	11:59	12:59

Change trains. 270

Dep. Brig	09:07	10:07 (3)	10:36 (3)	11:16 (2)	12:07	13:36
Arr. Lausanne	11:03	12:03	12:27	12:40	14:03	15:27

Change trains. 260

Dep. Lausanne	11:33 (1)	12:10 (3)	12:33 (1)	13:33 (1)	14:10 (3)	15:33 (1+6)
Arr. Bern	12:42	13:22	13:42	14:42	15:22	16:42

(1) Reservation advisable. Restaurant car. (2) Reservation advisable. Light refreshments. (3) Light refreshments. (4) Reservation advisable. (5) Plus others Bern departure at 12:22 (1) and 13:22 (3), arriving back in Bern 17:22 and 18:22. (6) Plus other departures from Lausanne at frequent times from 16:10 to 22:33. (7) Runs Fridays and Saturdays July 2-August 27.

Brienz - Rothorn - Brienz   283

This is a cogwheel line. It goes through forests, mountains and meadows to the magnificent view from the 7,714-foot-high peak of **Rothorn**, from which there is an excellent 4-hour walk on a good mountain path to **Brunig**. There ia a superb network of well-maintained hiking trails in this area. Extra trains run at busy times. No trains operate from late October to early June.

Not covered by Eurailpass. The 1994 price for a one-class roundtrip ticket *without* a Swiss Pass was 58 Swiss francs. *With* a SwissPass: Sfr-43.50.

Dep. Brienz	08:05 (1)	09:05 (1)	09:35 (2)	10:15 (1)	11:15 (1)
Arr. Rothorn	50-60 minutes later				

Dep. Brienz	13:05 (1)	14:15 (1)	15:15 (1)	16:15 (3)
Arr. Rothorn	50-60 minutes later			

• • •

Dep. Rothorn	09:05 (1)	10:10 (1)	11:20 (1)	13:00 (1)	13:40 (1)
Arr. Brienz	50-60 minutes later				

Dep. Rothorn	14:45 (1)	15:45 (1)	16:45 (1)	17:20 (3)
Arr. Brienz	50-60 minutes later			

(1) Operates early June 4—October 23. (2) Operates July 1 to August 31. (3) Operates early June 4-September 25.

Brig - Andermatt - Disentis - Brig 320

Fine canyon and mountain scenery on this easy one-day roundtrip. A stopover can be made (08:25 to 17:48 or 19:07) in Andermatt, a great ski resort.

This trip is a portion of the "Glacier Express" route. See details about reservations and prices under "St. Moritz–Zermatt and Zermatt–St. Moritz"

Sit on the right side for best views from Brig, on the left side from Disentis.

This trip is *not* covered by Eurailpass. The 1994 roundtrip ticket price for an ordinary train (not "Glacier Express," which charges a supplement) *without* a Swiss Pass was 115 Swiss francs for first-class, Sfr-66 for second-class. *With* a Swiss Pass: Free.

Dep. Brig	06:27 (3)	08:49	09:44 (1)	10:30 (1)	11:44 (1)
Arr. Andermatt	08:25	10:22	11:22 (2)	11:58 (2)	13:22 (2)
Arr. Disentis	09:36	11:34	12:40	13:00	14:37

Sights in **Disentis**: The stained glass in the Cathedral

Dep. Disentis	10:28 (1)	12:20 (1)	13:40 (2)	16:35	17:35 (3)
Dep. Andermatt	11:36 (2)	13:37 (2)	15:12 (1)	17:48	19:08 (3)
Arr. Brig	13:14	15:14	17:17	19:35	20:58

(1) "Glacier Express." See details about reservations and prices under "St. Moritz–Zermatt" Plus another "Glacier Express" at 13:44, arriving Disentis 16:25. (2) Operates late May to late October. (3) Change trains in Andermatt.

Brig - Arona - Brig 365

Beautiful lake and mountain scenery on this easy one-day roundtrip, which can also be seen as a portion of the Lausanne–Milan route. This ride takes you through Europe's longest (19.8km or 11.9 miles) tunnel, the Simplon.

It is the third longest tunnel in the world, after Japan's Seikan Tunnel (33.4 miles, between Tappi and Yoshioka) and Japan's Daishimizu Tunnel (13.4 miles, between Tokyo and Niigata).

Dep. Brig	08:22	09:34 (2)	10:31 (3)	14:31	15:17 (2)
Arr. Arona	09:46 (2)	10:55	11:52	15:57 (2)	16:45

* * *

Dep. Arona	09:53 (4)	11:16	13:16	14:43	16:16	17:16 (6)
Arr. Brig	11:14	12:43 (2)	14:40 (2)	16:13 (2)	17:43 (2)	18:43

(1) Reservation advisable. (2) Reservation advisable. Light refreshments. (3) Reservation advisable. Supplement charged. Restaurant car or light refreshments. (4) Reservation advisable. Supplement charged. (5) Light refreshments. (6) Restaurant car. (7) Plus other departures from Arona at 17:41 (8) and 18:15 (3) arriving Brig 19:20 and 19:43. (8) Runs Saturdays and Sundays June 5-September 24.

Here is the daytime schedule for the Lausanne–Milan route.

82

Dep. Lausanne	06:37 (1)	08:09 (3)	08:57 (4)	11:13 (4+5)	12:32 (6)	13:32 (3)
Arr. Brig	08:17 (1)	09:32	10:22	12:36	14:23 (1)	15:12
Dep. Brig	08:22 (2)	09:34	10:31	12:38	14:31	15:17
Dep. Arona	09:48	10:57	11:54	-0- (5)	15:43	16:47
Arr. Milan (Cen.)	10:45	11:45	12:40	14:40	16:50	17:45

(1) Change trains in Brig. (2) Reservation advisable. (3) Reservation advisable. Light refreshments. (4) Res-ervation advisable. Supplement charged. Restaurant car. (5) Train does not stop in Arona. (6) Light refreshments. Change trains in Brig.

Brig - Bern - Brig 280

An easy one-day roundtrip that affords a view of Rhone Valley and Lonza Valley farms, canyons, lakes and mountains plus the Lake Thun scenery at Spiez about which we enthuse in the "Geneva–Spiez" trip and going through the 10-mile-long Lotschberg Tunnel and over the Bietschtal Bridge. This structure takes the train 255 feet above the ravine it crosses.

We recommend a stop in Spiez and a stroll there on either the outbound or homebound leg of this trip.

For best views, sit on the right side Brig to Spiez, on the left side Spiez to Brig.

Dep. Brig	07:01 (3)	08:01 (2)	09:01 (2)	10:01 (1)	11:01 (2+4)
Arr. Spiez	08:05	09:05	10:05	11:05	12:05
Dep. Spiez	08:07	09:07	10:07	11:07	12:07
Arr. Bern	30 minutes after departing Spiez.				

* * *

Dep. Bern	09:22 (2)	10:22 (1)	11:22 (2)	12:22 (3)	13:22 (2+5)
Arr. Spiez	09:52	10:52	11:52	12:52	13:52
Dep. Spiez	09:54	10:54	11:54	12:54	13:54
Arr. Brig	66 minutes after departing Spiez.				

(1) Reservation advisable. Light refreshments. (2) Light refreshments. (3) Reservation advisable. Res-taurant car. (4) Plus other departures from Brig that allow daylight viewing in Summer months at fre-quent times from 12:01 to 21:35. (5) Plus other departures from Bern at frequent times from 14:22 to 19:09.

Brig - Domodossola - Locarno - Domodossola - Brig

We call the Domodossola–Locarno portion of this one-day roundtrip one of the 5 most scenic rail trips in Europe. It is a spectacular narrow-gauge local train ride offering great gorge, mountain and river scenery on the Centovalli (one hundred valleys) route.

Be sure to have your passport with you. On this trip, you go from Switzerland to Italy, then Switzerland, back to Italy, and then again to Switzerland.

This ride takes you through Europe's longest (19.8km or 11.9 miles) tunnel, the Simplon (between Brig and Domodossola). It is the third longest tunnel in the world, after Japan's Seikan (33.4 miles, between Tappi and Yoshioka) and Japan's Daishimizu Tunnel (13.4 miles, between Tokyo and Niigata).

When departing Locarno, look for the "Ferrovia Centovalli" sign that directs you to stairs descending to an underground track. Stops en route from Locarno include **Intragna**, with its many churches; **Verdasio,** which has a train connection to the mountain town of **Rasa; Palagnedra,** which has a lake; **Camedo**; and **Druogno,** the highest point on this scenic route.

See detailed notes about Locarno under "Milan–Locarno–Milan."

When changing trains in Domodossola, keep in mind that trains to and from Brig are located at street level. Trains to and from Locarno are on an underground track, connected by a walkway to the street level.

365
Dep. Brig	08:22 (1)	09:34 (2)	10:31 (3)	12:38 (3)	14:31 (4)
Arr. Domodossola	08:50	10:02	11:00	13:07	15:00
Change trains. 272					
Dep. Domodossola	09:02	10:18	11:12	13:18	15:16
Arr. Locarno	10:40	11:55	12:48	14:55	16:55

•   •   •

Dep. Locarno	12:22	13:50	16:28	17:28	19:05
Arr. Domodossola	14:00	15:30	18:00	19:00	20:46
Change trains. 365					
Dep. Domodossola	14:11 (4)	15:44 (3)	18:13 (6)	19:13 (3)	21:00 (2)
Arr. Brig	30 minutes later				

(1) Reservation advisable. (2) Reservation advisable. Light refreshments. (3) Reservation advisable. Supplement charged. Restaurant car or light refreshments. (4) Reservation advisable. Supplement charged. (5) Operates late March to late October. (6) Restsaurant car.

Brig - Spiez - Interlaken - Brienz - Interlaken - Brig

Very good canyon, lake and mountain scenery on this easy one-day roundtrip.

For best views, sit on the right side Brig to Spiez, on the left side Spiez to Brig. Between Brig and Spiez, the train goes through the 10-mile-long Lotschberg Tunnel and over the Bietschtal Bridge. This structure takes the train 255 feet above the ravine it crosses.

Most of the trains Brig–Spiez (and v.v.) and Spiez-Interlaken (and v.v.) below have light refreshments.

280			285		
Dep. Brig	09:01	10:01	Dep. Brienz	12:02	13:00
Arr.Spiez	10:05	11:05	Arr. Interlaken (Ost)	12:23	13:16
Change trains.			*Change trains. 280*		
Dep. Spiez	11:01	12:01	Dep. Interlaken (Ost)	12:39	13:39
Arr. Interlaken (Ost)	11:21	12:21	Arr. Spiez	12:59	13:59
Change trains. 285			*Change trains.*		
Dep. Interlaken (Ost)	11:37	12:44	Dep. Spiez	13:28	14:54
Arr. Brienz	11:58	13:00	Arr. Brig	14:29	15:59

Brig - Interlaken - Wengen - Jungfrau - Grindelwald - Brig

There is excellent canyon, lake and mountain scenery on this easy one-day roundtrip. See "Bern–Interlaken–Wengen–Jungfrau"

The Interlaken-Jungfraujoch-Interlaken portion of this trip is not covered by Eurailpass. The 1994 prices of tickets without a Swiss Pass were 155.20 Swiss francs for first-class, Sfr-145.80 for second-class. With a Swiss Pass, both the Interlaken-Wengen and Grindelwald–Interlaken portions were free, and the one-class Wengen–Scheidegg, Scheidegg–Jungfraujoch–Scheidegg and Scheidegg–Grindelwald portions were at 25% discount, making the entire trip cost Sfr-95.10.

It is for variety that we suggest you go from Interlaken to Jungfraujoch via Wengen and then return to Interlaken via Grindelwald.

Most of the trains Brig–Spiez (and v.v.) below have light refreshments or a restaurant car.

280				287		
Dep. Brig	08:01	09:01		Dep. Jungfraujoch	14:00	15:00
Arr. Spiez	09:05	10:05		Arr. Scheidegg	14:49	15:45
Change trains.				*Change trains.*		
280				Dep. Scheidegg	15:02	16:02
Dep. Spiez	10:01	11:01		Arr. Grindelwald	15:45	16:45
Arr. Interlaken (Ost)	10:21	11:21		*Change trains.*		
Change trains.				Dep. Grindelwald	15:50	16:50
287				Arr. Interlaken(Ost)	16:27	17:27
Dep. Interlaken (Ost)	10:32	11:32		*Change trains.*		
Arr. Wengen	11:14	12:24		280		
Arr. Scheidegg	11:45	12:55		Dep. Interlaken (Ost)	16:39	17:39
Change trains.				Arr. Spiez	16:59	18:59
Dep. Scheidegg	12:02	13:02		*Change trains.*		
Arr. Jungfraujoch	12:53	13:53		280		
Sightsee in Jungfraujoch.				Dep. Spiez	17:54	18:54
				Arr. Brig	18:59	19:59

Brig - Zermatt - Gornergrat - Zermatt - Brig

Great canyon and mountain scenery on this easy one-day roundtrip that includes an outstanding 5½–mile narrow-gauge cogwheel train ride to Gornergrat (10,200 feet) for a close view of the **Gorner Glacier**, the **Matterhorn** (14,692 feet) and more than 50 other peaks.

This trip is *not* covered by Eurailpass. The 1994 prices of roundtrip tickets *without* a Swiss Pass were 141 Swiss francs for first-class, Sfr-106 for second-class. *With* a Swiss Pass, the Brig-Zermatt–Brig trip is free and the Zermatt–Gornergrat–Zermatt trip is at 25% discount, making the entire trip Sfr-39.75.

320

| Dep. Brig | Frequent times from 05:10 to 20:23 |
| Arr. Zermatt | 90 minutes later |

Change trains. 321

| Dep. Zermatt | Frequent times from 07:05 to 18:00 |
| Arr. Gornergrat | 45 minutes later |

• • •

| Dep. Gornergrat | Frequent times from 07:55 to 19:07 |
| Arr. Zermatt | 45 minutes later |

Change trains. 320

| Dep. Zermatt | Frequent times from 06:00 to 21:10 |
| Arr. Brig | 90 minutes later |

Lausanne - Zermatt - Gornergrat - Lausanne

Nice canyon, lake, mountain and river scenery on this easy one-day roundtrip. The Visp–Zermatt–Gornergrat roundtrip is *not* covered by Eurailpass.

The 1994 prices of roundtrip tickets for an *ordinary* train (not "Glacier Express," which charge a supplement) *without* a Swiss Pass were 138 Swiss francs for first-class, Sfr-105 second-class. *With* a Swiss Pass, the Visp–Zermatt–Visp trip is free and the Zermatt–Gornergrat–Zermatt trip is at 25% discount, making the entire trip cost Sfr-39:75.

270

| Dep. Lausanne | 06:56 | 07:32 (1) | 08:32 (1) | 09:32 (1) | 10:32 (1) | 11:32 |
| Arr. Visp | 08:33 | 09:14 | 10:09 | 11:14 | 12:14 | 13:14 |

Change trains. 320

| Dep. Visp | 08:36 | 09:36 | 10:36 | 11:36 | 12:36 | 13:36 (6) |
| Arr. Zermatt | 09:45 | 10:47 | 11:45 | 12:47 | 13:47 | 14:45 |

Change trains. 321

| Dep. Zermatt | 10:00 | 11:12 (3) | 12:00 | 13:12 | 14:00 | 14:48 (7) |
| Arr. Gornergrat | 10:43 | 11:55 | 12:43 | 13:55 | 14:43 | 15:31 |

• • •

| Dep. Gornergrat | 11:07 | 12:19 (7) | 13:07 | 14:19 (7) | 15:07 | 16:19 (7) |
| Arr. Zermatt | 11:50 | 13:02 | 13:50 | 15:02 | 15:50 | 17:02 |

Change trains. 320

| Dep. Zermatt | 12:10 (2) | 13:10 | 14:10 | 15:10 | 16:10 | 17:10 |
| Arr. Visp | 13:22 | 14:22 | 15:22 | 16:22 | 17:22 | 18:22 |

Change trains. 270

| Dep. Visp | 13:42 (1) | 14:42 | 15:42 (1) | 16:38 (1) | 17:42 | 19:39 |
| Arr. Lausanne | 15:27 | 16:27 | 17:27 | 18:27 | 19:27 | 21:27 |

(1) Light refreshments. (2) "Glacier Express." See details about reservations and prices under "St. Moritz–Zermatt" (3) Operates late November to late October. (4) Operates mid-December to late April and mid-June to mid-October. (5) Operates May 29-October 16. (6) Runs October 17-December 16 only. (7) Runs daily except May 29-June 10.

Chur - Brig - Zermatt - Gornergrat - Zermatt

There is fabulous Rhone Valley scenery on this ride plus crossing Oberalp Pass (6,700 feet) and going through the 8-mile long Furka Tunnel on the Chur–Brig portion. This trip crosses the highest bridges in Europe and includes the outstanding cogwheel train ride to Gornergrat (10,200 feet) for a close view of the Matterhorn (14,692 feet) and more than 50 other Alpine peaks.

This trip is *not* covered by Eurailpass. The 1994 prices for this trip on an ordinary train (not "Glacier Express," which charges a supplement) *without* a Swiss Pass were: 203 Swiss francs for first-class, Sfr-143 for second-class. *With* a Swiss Pass, the Chur–Zermatt portion was free, and the Zermatt–Gornergrat–Zermatt roundtrip was at 25% discount, making the entire trip Sfr-39.75.

320

Dep. Chur	09:03 (1+4)					
Arr. Zermatt	14:45					

Change to a narrow-gauge train. 321

Dep. Zermatt	15:12	15:36 (3)	16:00	17:12	18:00	-0-
Arr. Gornergrat	15:55	16:19	16:43	17:55	18:43	-0-

• • •

Dep. Gornergrat	16:19 (3)	16:43 (3)	17:07	17:55	19:07	-0-
Arr. Zermatt	45 minutes later					

(1) "Glacier Express." Restaurant car or light refreshments. See details about reservations and prices under "St. Moritz–Zermatt" (2) Operates late November to late October. (3) Runs daily except May 29-June 10. (4) Runs May 29-October 16.

Chur - St. Moritz - Chur   330

Marvelous canyon, lake and mountain scenery on this easy one-day roundtrip. It is a very scenic ride involving going through double spiral tunnels and across the amazing Landwasser Viaduct. Ask at the Chur railstation which trains have open-air cars. The views from them are even more thrilling than from the closed cars.

All of these trains have light refreshments, unless designated otherwise.

Dep. Chur	06:40	08:08	09:00	09:52 (4)	10:52	11:52 (1+2)
Arr. St. Moritz	09:00	10:18	11:18	11:58	12:58	13:58 (4)

• •

Dep. St. Moritz	10:00 (1)	11:00 (5)	12:00	13:00 (4)	14:00	15:00 (3)
Arr. Chur	12:07	13:07	14:07	15:07	16:07	17:07 (4)

(1) Restaurant car. (2) Plus frequent other departures from Chur 12:52 to 20:57. (3) Plus other departures from St. Moritz 16:00, 17:00, 18:00 (1), 19:00 and 20:00. (4) Runs Saturdays, Sundays and holidays. (5) Runs Sundays and holidays June 18-September 24.

Geneva - Lausanne - Brig - Spiez - Bern - Lausanne - Geneva

One of the 5 most scenic rail trips in Europe.

The succession of beautiful scenes defy verbal description: 15 miles of terraced vineyards and Lake Geneva shoreline between Geneva and Lausanne. Great river scenery en route from Martigny to Brig. Upon leaving Brig, take a seat on the side of the train that faces the Brig railstation. In the 52 miles between Brig and Thun, the train goes through 37 tunnels (including the 10-mile Lotschberg) and crosses the top of 25 bridges and viaducts. The 866-foot-long **Kander Viaduct** is 92-feet high.

Upon emerging from the Lotschberg Tunnel, there is such beautiful farm and mountain scenery around tiny **Kandersteg** and **Fruitigen** that you want to get off the train and spend the rest of your life there. It is only a 15-minute downhill walk from the Spiez railstation to the castle overlooking Lake Thun, the most beautiful lake scene on this planet. If the view of Lake Thun and the mountains reflected on its surface does not thrill you, pack up and go home because you will not find any landscape more beautiful in this world. From here, you can see the peaks of Jungfrau, Eiger, Monch and Finsteraarhorn.

You can return to Geneva (via Bern) either by boarding a train in Spiez or by first taking the 45-minute boat ride (covered by Eurailpass) from Spiez to **Thun** village and then boarding the train in Thun. It is a 10-minute downhill walk from the Spiez railstation to the Spiez pier. The lake steamer ties up 100 feet from Thun's railstation.

On the way back to Geneva from Bern, you pass through the same lake and vineyard scenery you saw between Lausanne and Geneva that morning, at the start of this fabulous one-day trip.

The schedules shown below allow a stopover in Bern (see footnotes #6 and #7).

270

Dep. Geneva (Corn.)	07:48 (1)	08:20 (2)	08:48 (1)	09:48 (1)	10:34 (2+7)
Dep. Lausanne	08:32	08:57	09:32	10:32	11:13
Dep. Martigny	09:25	-0-	10:25	11:25	-0-
Arr. Brig	10:18	10:22	11:23	12:23	12:36
Change trains. 280					
Dep. Brig	10:42 (3)	11:01 (1)	12:01 (1)	-0-	13:01 (2)
Arr. Spiez	11:40	12:05	13:05	-0-	14:05
Dep. Spiez	11:42	12:07	13:07	-0-	14:07
Dep. Thun	11:53	12:18	13:18	-0-	14:18
Arr. Bern	12:12	12:38	13:38	-0-	14:38
Change trains. 260					
Dep. Bern	12:38 (1)	13:18 (5)	14:18 (5)	-0-	15:18 (5+8)
Arr. Lausanne	13:50	14:26	15:26	-0-	16:26
Arr. Geneva (Corn.)	14:34	15:02	16:02	-0-	17:02

(1) Light refreshments. (2) Reservation advisable. Supplement charged. Restaurant car. (3) Reservation advisable. (4) Restaurant car. (5) Reservation advisable. Restaurant car. (6) Reservation advisable. Supplement charged. Light refreshments. (7) Plus other Geneva departures at 10:48, 11:48 (1), 12:48

(1) and 13:48 (1)....Departing Brig at 14:01(2), 15:01 (2), 16:01 (1) and 17:01 (2)...Departing Bern at 16:18 (2), 17:18 (2), 18:18 (2) and 19:18 (2)...Arriving back in Geneva at 18:02, 19:02, 20:02 and 21:02. (8) Plus other Bern depatures at 16:18 (2), 16:38, 17:18 (2), 18:18 (2), 18:38 (1), 19:18 (2), 20:18 (2), 20:38, 21:18 (2), 22:21 (2) and 23:26.

Here are the Lake Thun (Spiez–Thun) boat schedules (covered by Eurailpass) to combine with departures from Thun village for Bern.

281 Boat

Dep. Spiez	13:17 (1)	13:49 (2)	14:58 (1)	15:14 (3)	16:03 (1)	16:43 (4+5)
Arr. Thun (Pier)	14:02	14:53	15:46	16:00	16:48	17:38

It is a 2-minute walk from the boat pier to the train.

280 Train

Dep. Thun (Stn.)	14:12	15:12	15:53	16:44 (6)	17:12 (4)	17:44 (4)
Arr. Bern	20 minutes later					

(1) Has restaurant. (2) Late May to mid-June: light refreshments. Mid-June to late September: restaurant car. (3) Paddlesteamer. Runs daily, except Monday. Supplement charged. (4) Light refreshments. (5) Plus other boat departures from Spiez at 17:04 (4), 18:03 (1), 18:59 (1) and 20:11 (2), connecting in Thun with trains that arrive Bern 18:32, 19:32, 20:32 and 21:38. (6) Runs Sunday only.

Geneva - Chamonix (Mt. Blanc) - Geneva   167

Be sure to have your passport with you on this trip filled with fantastic mountain scenery, as you will be going from Switzerland to France. From Chamonix, take the 2-mile-high cable-car ride that goes nearly to the top of the tallest mountain in Europe, the 15,771-foot Mt. Blanc, towering almost 10,000 feet above Chamonix, for a view of Alpine peaks extending 80 miles.

After descending, there is just time to also take the narrow-gauge train to see the "Sea of Ice" glacier bed (which does not operate in Winter). The tombstones in the small cemetery, a 5-minute walk from the railstation, are fascinating. Nearly one-fourth of the headstones read "died on the mountain" (climbers and their rescuers).

All of these connections are easy cross-platform train changes, each taking less than one minute.

Dep. Geneva			Dep. Chamonix	13:27	17:48
(Eaux Vives)	07:10 (1)	08:27 (4)	Arr. St. Gervais	14:18	18:27
Arr. La Roche	07:42 (4)	08:57	*Change trains.*		
Change trains.			Dep. St. Gervais	14:32 (6)	17:23 (6)
Dep. La Roche	07:50 (5)	10:00 (4)	Arr. La Roche	15:15	18:08
Arr. St. Gervais	08:52	10:43	*Change trains.*		
Change trains. 268			Dep. La Roche	15:30	-0-
Dep. St. Gervais	09:16	10:53	Arr. Geneva		
Arr. Chamonix	09:43	11:30	(Eaux Vives)	16:03	-0-

(1) Runs daily, except Sundays and holidays. (2) Runs 18 minutes later early July to early September. (3) Runs Monday-Friday, except holidays. (4) Not July 5-29. (5) July 5-29. (6) not July 4-28.

Geneva - Martigny - Chamonix - Geneva

This one-day circle trip avoids the repetition involved in the Geneva–Annemasse–Chamonix–Geneva roundtrip described in the previous listing and also allows time for the activities in Chamonix described above. The scenery Martigny–Vallorcine–Chamonix is fantastic!

All of the Chamonix–Geneva connections are easy cross-platform train changes, each taking less than one minute.

270			268		
Dep. Geneva (Corn.)	06:48 (1)	07:48 (1)	Dep. Chamonix	13:27	16:16
Arr. Martigny	08:20	09:20	Arr. St. Gervais	14:06	16:55
Change trains. 268			*Change trains. 167*		
Dep. Martigny	08:59	10:09	Dep. St. Gervais	14:32 (5)	17:23 (5)
Arr. Le Chatelard	09:48 (2)	10:45 (2)	Arr. La Roche	15:15	18:08
Dep. Le Chatelard	09:55	11:11	*Change trains.*		
Arr. Vallorcine	09:18	10:56	Dep. La Roche	15:30	-0-
Arr. Chamonix	10:03	11:50	Arr. Geneva (Eaux-Vives)	16:03	-0-

(1) Light refreshments. (2) Change trains in Le Chatelard-Frontiere. (3) Runs Chamonix-Geneva on Monday-Friday, except holidays. Must change trains in Annemasse en route La Roche to Geneva. (4) July 4-Sept. 4. (5) Not July 4-28.

Geneva - Lausanne - Geneva

Here is a short trip packed with fine scenery of 15 miles of terraced vineyards, nearly the entire route following the lovely shoreline of Lake Geneva. Complete schedules are listed under the "Geneva–Lausanne" one-day excursion on.

Geneva - Lyon - Geneva 159

The first 1½ hours from Geneva is noted for scenic canyons.

Geneva - Martigny - Geneva 270

This is a scenic trip of intermediate length, longer than the Geneva–Lausanne ride and shorter than the Geneva–Brig–Bern–Geneva circle trip. Very good canyon, lake, mountain and vineyard scenery.

Dep. Geneva (Corn.)	06:48 (1)	07:48 (1)	08:48 (1)	09:48 (1)	10:48 (2)
Arr. Martigny	08:20	09:20	10:20	11:20	12:20

* * *

Dep. Martigny	08:34	09:38 (1)	10:40 (1)	11:34	12:34 (1+3)
Arr. Geneva (Corn.)	10:12	11:12	12:12	13:12	14:12

(1) Light refreshments. (2) Plus other departures from Geneva at frequent times from 11:48 to 22:52. (3) Plus other departures from Martigny at frequent times from 13:38 to 21:34.

Geneva - Montreux - Zweisimmen - Spiez - Bern - Geneva

This narrow-gauge variation on the scenic trip described earlier (Geneva–Brig–Bern–Geneva) runs parallel and north of the Martigny–Brig route. You miss going through the Lotschberg Tunnel, but you are able to see all of the Geneva–Lausanne vineyard and Lake Geneva scenery plus Lake Thun (Spiez) and a possible stopover in Bern, en route back to Geneva.

Before traveling the normal-guage Zweisimmen–Spiez leg, there is time to take the very scenic narrow-guage 13km (9 miles) detour from Zweisimmen to Lenk (and back to Zweisimmen). Upon first arriving Zweisimmen 13:00, 15:45 or 17:00, passengers can arrive back in Zweisimmen from Lenk at 14:11, 16:55 or 18:11 before continuing on to Speiz.

There is time to leave the train in Spiez, take the lake boat from Spiez to Thun, and then take the train from Thun to Bern. See notes under the "Geneva–Brig–Bern–Geneva" scenic trip.

The narrow-guage ascent from Montreux to Zweisimmen is very scenic as the train climbs from the shore of Lac Leman to Les Avants in a series of hairpin bends. The funicular ride from **Les Avants** to **Sonloup** is worth stopping over in Les Avants and rejoining the Montreux–Zweisimmen route later in the day. **Gstaad** is a very expensive ski resort.

We recommend departing Montreux on "Panoramic Express" or "Crystal Panoramic Express." The comfortable coaches of these special narrow-gauge Observation Trains have glass domes and large side windows for viewing the marvelous scenery. Refreshments are available from vending machines in their bar car.

For "Crystal Panoramic," reservations are accepted only for groups. Individuals may ride it if there are any vacant seats.

There are seats in the front car, which has an elevated cab for the engineer. The next car is a bar car which seats 45 passengers. The third and last car is the locomotive.

Regardless which train you ride, sit on the right side Montreux-Zweisimmen for best views.

270

Dep. Geneva (Corn.)	08:48 (1)	09:48 (1)	10:48	11:48 (1)	12:48 (1)
Arr. Montreux	09:51	10:51	11:51	12:51	13:51
Change trains. 275					
Dep. Montreux	10:00 (2)	11:00	12:21	13:00	14:00 (3)
Arr. Les Avants	10:22	11:22	12:42	13:22	– 0 – (8)
Dep. Gstaad	11:18	12:30	13:42	14:30	15:18
Arr. Zweisimmen	11:45	13:00	14:10	15:00	15:45
Change trains. 276					
Dep. Zweisimmen	12:21	13:05	14:21	15:05	16:05
Arr. Spiez	12:57	13:51	14:57	15:51	16:51

Spiez: See notes under "Geneva-Brig-Bern-Geneva." For marvelous views of mountains and lakes, walk to the Burg Woods and Burg Hill. Spiez is an ideal base for one-day rail trips to Bern, Interlaken, Luzern, Gstaad, Montreux, Zermatt, Grindelwald, Stresa, Yungfraujoch and Solothurn.

Change trains. 280					
Dep. Spiez	13:07 (4)	14:01 (1)	15:07 (6)	16:01 (1)	17:01 (5)
Dep. Thun	13:18	14:12	15:18	16:12	17:12
Arr. Bern	13:38	14:32	15:38	16:32	17:32
Change trains. 260					
Dep. Bern	14:18 (6)	15:18 (6)	16:18 (6)	17:18 (6)	18:18 (6+7)
Arr. Geneva (Corn.)	16:02	17:02	18:02	19:02	20:02

(1) Light refreshments. (2) "Panoramic Express." See details in text on previous page. (3) "Crystal Panoramic." See details in text on previous page. (4) Restaurant car. (5) Reservation advisable. Light refreshments. (6) Reservation advisable. Restaurant car. (7) Plus other departures from Bern at 18:38 (1), 19:18 (6), 20:18 (6), 20:38, 21:18 (6) and 22:21 (6), arriving Geneva 20:34, 21:02, 22:02, 22:37, 23:02 and 00:09. (8) Reservation required.

Geneva - Nyon - Geneva   250

See the magnificent views of **Lac Leman** (the Lake of Geneva) and the Alps, particularly of Mont Blanc, from **Nyon**, a medieval hilltop village on the shore of Lac Leman.

Dep. Geneva (Corn.)	Frequent times from 04:49 to 00:01
Arr. Nyon	14 minutes later

Sights in **Nyon**: Sailing is popular here.

Dep. Nyon	Frequent times from 06:00 to 01:06
Arr. Geneva (Corn.)	14 minutes later

Interlaken - Mt. Pilatus - Interlaken

Great canyon and mountain scenery on this easy one-day narrow-gauge roundtrip. There are good views and several restaurants at the peak of Pilatus.

A roundtrip ticket is available in Luzern covering train or boat Luzern-Alpnachstad, rack railway Alpnachstad-Pilatus Kulm, cablecar and gondolas Pilatus-Kriens, and trolley-bus Kriens-Luzern.

The Alpnachstad–Pilatus–Alpnachstad rack railway portion operates only May through November. The 1994 price of a one-class roundtrip ticket without a Swiss Pass was 53 Swiss francs. With a Swiss Pass: Sfr-39.75.

285

Dep. Interlaken (Ost)	08:44	09:37 (2)	10:44 (1)	11:37 (2)	12:44 (2)	13:37
Arr. Giswil	09:56	10:56	11:56	12:56	13:56	14:56

Change trains.

Dep. Giswil	10:06	11:06	12:06	13:06	14:06	15:06
Arr. Alpnachstad	10:28	11:28	12:28	13:28	14:28	15:28

Change to rack railway for the ride to the top of Mt. Pilatus. table 286

Dep. Alpnachstad	10:50	11:30	13:10	13:50	14:30	15:50
Arr. Pilatus Kulm	11:20	12:00	13:40	14:20	15:00	16:20

•   •   •

Dep. Pilatus Kulm	12:05	13:05	14:25	15:45	16:25
Arr. Alpnachstad	12:45	13:45	15:05	16:25	17:05

Change to a standard train. 285

Dep. Alpnachstad	13:29	14:29	15:29	16:29	17:29
Arr. Giswil	13:51	14:51	15:51	16:51	17:51

Change trains

Dep. Giswil		14:00(1)	15:00 (2)	16:00(2)	17:00	18:00
Arr. Interlaken (Ost)	15:16	16:23	17:16	18:23	19:20

(1) Restaurant car. (2) Light refreshments.

Interlaken - Luzern - Interlaken

A very scenic 48-mile panorama of the Alps on this trip along Lake Brienz, an easy one-day excursion. Schedules appear under "Interlaken–Luzern."

Interlaken - Spiez - Bern - Spiez - Interlaken 280

Excellent canyon, lake and mountain scenery on this easy one-day roundtrip that includes visiting Lake Thun and a possible stopover in Bern. See earlier notes about Spiez and taking a boat on Lake Thun from Spiez to Thun village, under "Geneva–Brig–Bern–Geneva."

Dep. Interlaken (Ost)	07:39	08:11 (3)	08:39 (2)	09:39 (4)	10:39 (4)	11:39 (1)
Dep. Interlaken (West)	5 minutes later					
Dep. Spiez	08:01	08:33	09:01	10:01	11:01	12:01
Dep. Thun	08:12	08:44	09:12	10:12	11:12	12:12
Arr. Bern	20 minutes later					
Dep. Bern	Frequent times from 06:56 to 23:28					
Arr. Interlaken (West)	45–60 minutes later					
Arr. Interlaken (Ost)	5 minutes after arriving West station					

(1) Light refreshments. (2) Reservation advisable. Light refreshments. (3) Reservation advisable. (4) Reservation advisable. Restaurant car.

Interlaken - Spiez - Brig - Spiez - Interlaken 280

Nice canyon, lake and mountain scenery on this easy one-day roundtrip which includes visiting Lake Thun and going through the 10-mile Lotschberg Tunnel.

The schedules below allow time to stopover in Spiez.

Most of the trains Spiez–Brig and v.v. have light refreshments.

Dep. Interlaken (Ost)	06:39 (1)	07:11 (2)	07:39	08:11 (4)	08:39 (1)	09:39 (2+5)
Dep. Interlaken (West)	5 minutes later					
Arr. Spiez	07:04	07:31	07:59	08:31	08:59	09:59
Change trains.						
Dep. Spiez	07:22 (1)	07:54	08:28	08:54	09:23	10:54
Arr. Brig	08:20	08:59	09:29	09:59	10:21	11:59

Dep. Brig	Frequent times from 05:38 to 21:35
Arr. Spiez	70 minutes later
Change trains.	
Dep. Spiez	Frequent times from 07:29 to 23:01
Arr. Interlaken (West)	15 minutes later
Arr. Interlaken (Ost)	5 minutes after arriving West station

(1) Reservation advisable. (2) Reservation advisable. Restaurant car. (3) Light refreshments. (4) Reservation advisable. Light refreshments. (5) Plus other Interlaken departures at 10:39 (2), 11:39 (3), 12:39(3), 13:39(3), 14:39(3) and 15:39(3), arriving Brig 2½ hours later.

Interlaken - Jungfraujoch - Interlaken 287

Great canyon and mountain scenery on this easy one-day roundtrip. This spectacular route ends at Europe's highest (11,333 feet) railstation. It includes 2 stops in the tunnel through Mount Eiger, for viewing through "windows" which the railroad's builders cut in the face of the cliff.

At Jungfraujoch, passengers alight to look down on the great Jungfrau glacier and stroll in the "Ice Palace" carved inside the glacier. Fabulous views can be seen from the revolving restaurant, which rotates completely every 50 minutes. For variety, we show how to go from Interlaken to Jungfraujoch via Wengen, and then return to Interlaken via Grindelwald.

Grindelwald sits at 3400-feet altitude. The majestic peaks that rise around this village are: **Jungfrau** (13,642 feet), **Eiger** (13,026), **Wetterhorn** (12,142), **Breithorn** (12,409), **Monch** (13,449), **Schreckhorn** (13,380), **Gspaltenhorn** (11,277) and **Tschingelhorn** (11,736).

This trip is not covered by Eurailpass. The 1994 prices of a ticket without a Swiss Pass were: 170.80 Swiss francs for first-class, Sfr-161.40 for second-class.

With a Swiss Pass, both the Interlaken–Wengen and Grindelwald–Interlaken portions were free, and the one-class Wengen–Scheidegg–Jungfraujoch–Scheidegg and Scheidegg–Grindelwald portions were at 25% discount making the entire trip cost Sfr-95.10.

(Via Wengen)						
Dep. Interlaken (Ost)	07:38	08:05 (1)	08:32	09:02 (1)	09:32	10:02 (1)	10:32 (2)
Arr. Scheidegg	08:55	09:20	09:45	10:10	10:55	11:20	11:45
Change trains.						
Dep. Scheidegg	09:02	09:30 (1)	10:02	10:30 (1)	11:02	11:30 (1)	12:02
Arr. Jungfraujoch	09:53	10:22	10:53	11:22	11:53	12:22	12:53
Dep. Jungfraujoch	11:00 (1)	12:00	13:00	14:00	14:30 (1)	15:00	
Arr. Scheidegg	11:49	12:49	13:49	14:49	15:19	15:45	
Change trains. (via Grindelwald) 288						
Dep. Scheidegg	12:00	13:00	14:00	15:00	15:32 (1)	16:00	
Arr. Grindelwald	12:45	13:45	14:45	15:45	16:15	16:45	
Change trains.						
Dep. Grindelwald	12:50	13:50	14:50	15:50	16:20 (1)	16:50	
Arr. Interlaken (Ost)	13:27	14:27	15:27	16:27	16:57	17:27	

(1) Does not operate May 29-June 3. (2) Plus other departures from Interlaken at 11:32, 12:32, 13:32 and 14:32, arriving back in Interlaken 16:27, 17:27, 18:27 and 19:27. (3) Plus other departures from Jungfraujoch at 14:00, 15:00, 16:00, 17:00 and 18:00 (1), arriving Interlaken 16:27, 17:27, 18:27, 19:27 and 20:27.

Lausanne - Brig - Lausanne   270

Enjoy the fine canyon, lake, mountain and river scenery on this easy one-day roundtrip.

Dep. Lausanne	Frequent times from 06:56 to 23:45
Arr. Brig	1½–2 hours later

Sight in **Brig**: Switzerland's largest private residence, the 17th century Stockalper Castle, built by a very successful businessman.

Dep. Brig	Frequent times from 05:25 to 21:36
Arr. Lausanne	1½–2 hours later

Lausanne - Brig - Spiez - Bern - Lausanne

Marvelous canyon, lake, mountain and river scenery on this easy one-day roundtrip, a portion of the "Geneva–Lausanne–Spiez–Bern–Geneva" scenic trip.

Locarno - Camedo - Locarno   272

One of the 5 most scenic rail trips in Europe. Fantastic canyon, river and mountain scenery. Hillside farms that are nearly vertical. The ride is called "Centovalli," and you will see a hundred valleys. This trip can be made either as an easy one-day roundtrip or as a portion of these routes: Milan–Locarno, Bern–Locarno, Brig–Locarno, Luzern–Locarno, and Locarno–Brig.

Please note that this trip does not start from the Locarno railstation. You catch what looks like a trolley car at the central bus stop, across from the train station.

At Camedo, a small hotel (Osteria Grutly) is only a 5-minute walk from the railstation. The granite slab roofs on the houses in this area are unique.

Dep. Locarno	08:54	10:28	12:22	13:50	15:28	16:28	17:28
Arr. Camedo	09:25	10:59	12:55	14:21	15:59	16:59	17:59

• • •

Dep. Camedo	10:05	11:22	13:20	14:23	16:22	17:02	19:24
Arr. Locarno	35 minutes later						

Locarno - Domodossola - Brig - Domodossola - Locarno

Very good canyon, mountain and river scenery on this one-day roundtrip that includes the wonderful **Centovalli** ride described in the previous trip plus going through the 12-mile

Simplon, longest main line rail tunnel in the world. Be sure to take your passport on this trip from Switzerland to Italy, Switzerland, back to Italy and then again to Switzerland.

Follow the "Ferrovia Centovalli" sign down a flight of stairs to the underground portion of Locarno's railstation. Stops en route include **Intragna**, with its many churches; **Verdasio**, which has a train connection to the mountain town of **Rasa**; **Palagnedra**, which has a lake; **Camedo** ; and **Druogno**, highest point on this scenic route.

The Domodossola–Brig (and v.v.) portion of this route takes you through Europe's longest (19.8km - 11.9 miles) tunnel, the Simplon. It is the world's second-longest tunnel, after Japan's Daishimizu Tunnel between Tokyo and Niigata (22.3km - 13.4 miles).

272		
Dep. Locarno	08:54	10:28
Arr. Domo.	10:34	12:00

Change trains. Walk from the underground Centovalli track, up to the main Domodossola station. Hurry!

365		
Dep. Domo.	10:46 (1)	12:13 (1)
Arr. Brig	11:14	12:43

365		
Dep. Brig	12:38 (2)	14:31 (1)
Arr. Domo.	13:07	15:00

Change trains. Walk outside the Domodossola station and go to the underground Centovalli track. Hurry!

272		
Dep. Domo.	13:18	15:16
Arr. Locarno	14:55	16:55

(1) Reservation advisable. Light refreshments. (2) Restaurant car. Reservation required.

Luzern - Brunnen - Fluelen - Luzern   294

Here is an excellent one-day roundtrip boat ride on Lake Luzern, that is covered by Eurailpass.

All of these boats have a restaurant, unless designated otherwise.

Dep. Luzern (Stn. Quay)	09:05 (1)	09:30 (2)	10:25	11:15 (3)	11:25 (1+7)
Arr. Brunnen	10:59	11:50	12:35	12:55	13:52
Arr. Fluelen	11:50	12:40	13:40	13:45	14:52

• • •

Dep. Fluelen	11:55 (1)	12:51 (2)	13:51	14:20 (4)	15:00 (1+8)
Dep. Brunnen	12:46	13:42	14:45	15:30	16:00
Arr. Luzern (Stn. Quay)	14:54	16:10	16:46	17:36	18:36

(1) Paddlesteamer. Runs daily. (2) Paddlesteamer in July and August, daily except Sundays and holidays. (3) Paddlesteamer. Runs Sunday only. No restaurant. (4) Runs Sunday only. (5) Runs daily all year. July and August: paddlesteamer daily. September to June: paddlesteamer only on Sunday. (6) Light refreshments. (7) Plus other departures from Luzern at 13:15, 14:20 (6) and 15:15 (6). (8) Plus other departures from Fluelen at 16:20 (5) and 17:45 (6).

Luzern - Interlaken - Luzern

Great canyon and mountain scenery on this easy one-day roundtrip. Complete schedules are listed under "Luzern–Interlaken–Luzern."

Luzern - Interlaken - Brig - Domodossola - Locarno - Luzern

This circle route includes going through the 9-mile Lotschberg Tunnel, the 12-mile Simplon and the 9-mile St. Gotthard, as well as seeing the beautiful Centovalli scenery between Domodossola and Locarno.

285		272	
Dep. Luzern	07:24 (1)	Dep. Domodossola	13:18
Arr. Interlaken (Ost)	09:16 (5)	Arr. Locarno	14:55
Change trains. 280		*Change trains*	
Dep. Interlaken (Ost)	09:39 (3)	*291*	
Arr. Spiez	09:59	Dep. Locarno	15:03 (4)
Change trains. 280		Arr. Bellinzona	15:21
Dep. Spiez	10:54 (2)	*Change trains. 290*	
Arr. Brig	11:59	Dep. Bellinzona	15:27 (3)
Change trains. 270		Arr. Luzern	17:39 (6)
Dep. Brig	12:38 (3)		
Arr. Domodossola	13:07		

(1) Light refreshments. (2) Reservation advisable. Light refreshments. (3) Reservation advisable. Restaurant car. (4) Plus other departures from Locarno at 17:03 and 18:03, arriving Luzern 19:39 and 21:39. (5) reservation advisable. (6) Supplement charged.

Luzern - Interlaken - Jungfraujoch - Interlaken - Luzern

There is marvelous canyon, lake and mountain scenery on this easy one-day roundtrip. See details about Jungfraujoch under "Interlaken–Jungfraujoch."

For variety, we suggest you go from Interlaken to Jungfraujoch via Wengen, and then return to Interlaken via Grindelwald. The Interlaken–Jungfraujoch–Interlaken portion is not covered by Eurailpass. The 1994 prices of tickets *without* a Swiss Pass were 170.80 Swiss francs for first-class, Sfr-161.40 for second-class. *With* a Swiss Pass, both the Interlaken–Wengen and Grindelwald–Interlaken portions were free, and the one-class Wengen–Scheidegg, Scheidegg–Jungfraujoch–Scheidegg and Scheidegg–Grindelwald portions were at 25% discount making the entire trip cost Sfr-95.10.

For the best views, sit on the right-hand side Luzern–Meiringen, on the left side Meringen–Interlaken. For the return ride, sit on the right Interlaken–Meiringen and on the left Meiringen–Luzern.

285	
Dep. Luzern	08:24 (1)
Arr. Meiringen	09:41
Arr. Interlaken (Ost)	10:23
Change trains. 287	
Dep. Interlaken (Ost)	
(*via Wengen*)	10:32
Arr. Scheidegg	11:45
Change trains. 287	
Dep. Scheidegg	12:02
Arr. Jungfraujoch	12:53

(1) Restaurant car.

287		
Dep. Jungfraujoch	13:00	14:00
Arr. Scheidegg	13:49	14:49
Change trains. 288		
Dep. Scheidegg		
(*via Grindelwald*)	14:00	15:00
Arr. Interlaken (Ost)	15:27	16:27
Change trains. 285		
Dep. Interlaken (Ost)	15:37	16:44 (1)
Arr. Meiringen	16:12	17:12
Arr. Luzern	17:36	18:36

Luzern - Interlaken - Spiez - Brig - Andermatt - Goschenen - Luzern

Here is a marvelous one-day circle trip, crammed with outstanding scenery. Although this schedule allows only 50 minutes in Spiez, if you take a packed lunch from Luzern there are benches outside the Spiez railstation where you can sit while eating and have a fabulous view of the village, Lake Thun and the mountains reflected on its surface.

From Spiez to Brig, there is a good view of the Matterhorn from the right side of the train. Walk to the front of the Brig railstation to board the train to Andermatt.

En route from Brig to Andermatt, you see the beautiful Rhone Valley and go through the 8-mile long Furka Tunnel. The Brig–Andermatt–Goschenen portion of this trip is *not* covered by Eurailpass. The 1994 ticket prices for an ordinary train (not for "Glacier Express," which charges a supplement) *without* a Swiss Pass were 58 Swiss francs for first-class, Sfr-35 for second-class. *With* a Swiss Pass: Free.

285		
Dep. Luzern	08:24 (1)	09:24 (2)
Arr. Interlaken (Ost)	10:23	11:16
Change trains. 280		
Dep. Interlaken (Ost)	10:39	11:39
Arr. Spiez	10:59	11:59
Change trains. 280		
Dep. Spiez	11:54 (3)	12:54 (3)
Arr. Brig	12:59	13:59
Change trains.		

320	
Dep. Brig	14:17 (4+5)
Arr. Andermatt	16:25
Dep. Andermatt	16:27 (5)
Arr. Goschenen	16:42
Change trains. 290	
Dep. Goschenen	17:13 (2)
Arr. Luzern	18:46

(1) Restaurant car. (2) Light refreshments. (3) Restaurant car. (4) Plus another Brig departure at 16:17, arriving Luzern 20:46. (5) Runs May 14-October 16 only.

Luzern - Mt. Pilatus - Luzern   285   286

See the fine canyon and mountain scenery on this easy one-day roundtrip. The Alpnachstad–Pilatus–Alpnachstad rack railway portion operates only from May to the end of November. The 1994 price for a one-class roundtrip ticket *without* a Swiss Pass was 53 Swiss francs. *With* a Swiss Pass: Sfr-39.75. There are good views and several restaurants at the peak of Pilatus.

Dep. Luzern	08:09	09:09	10:09	11:09	12:09	13:09	14:09 (1)
Arr. Alpnachstad	08:26	09:26	10:26	11:26	12:26	13:26	14:26

Change to rack railway for the ride to the top of Mt. Pilatus.

Dep. Alpnachstad	08:50	09:30	10:50	11:30	13:10	13:50	14:30
Arr. Pilatus Kulm	09:20	10:00	11:20	12:00	13:40	14:20	15:00

• • •

Dep. Pilatus Kulm	09:25	10:45	11:25	12:05	13:45	14:25	15:05 (2)
Arr. Alpnachstad	10:05	10:25	12:05	12:45	14:25	15:05	15:45

Change to standard trains.

Dep. Alpnachstad	10:30	11:30	12:30	13:30	14:30	15:30	16:30
Arr. Luzern	18 minutes later						

(1) Plus another departure from Luzern at 15:09, arriving Pilatus Kulm 16:20. (2) Plus another departure from Pilatus Kulm at 16:25.

Luzern - Engelberg - Mt. Titlis - Luzern   293

There is very good canyon and mountain scenery on this easy one-day roundtrip. The Engelberg–Titlis–Engelberg rack railway is *not* covered by Eurailpass and does not operate late October to early December. The 1994 price of a one-class roundtrip ticket *without* a Swiss Pass was 66 Swiss francs. *With* a Swiss Pass: Sfr-49.50.

Engelberg is a popular ski resort. It also has more than 20 miles of level walking and hiking paths, toboggan runs, a gambling casino and indoor swimming pools.

There are great views from the restaurant on the top of **Mt. Titlis**. See the 11th century illuminated manuscripts in the Benedictine monastery.

Dep. Luzern	07:24 (3)	08:14	09:14	10:14	11:14	12:14	13:14 (1)
Arr. Engelberg	08:20	09:12	10:12	11:12	12:12	13:12	14:12

Change to the funicular.

Dep. Engelberg	Frequent times
Arr. Mt. Titlis	60 minutes later

• • •

Dep. Mt. Titlis	Frequent times
Arr. Engelberg	60 minutes later

Change to the train.

Dep. Engelberg	10:45	11:45	12:45	13:45	14:45	15:45	16:45 (2)
Arr. Luzern	60–65 minutes later						

(1) Plus other departures from Luzern at frequent times from 14:14 to 19:14 for Luzern roundtrip. (2) Plus other departures from Engelberg at 17:45, 18:45, 19:45 and 20:50. (3) Change trains at Hergiswil.

Luzern - Engelberg - Mt. Titlis - Luzern - Mt. Pilatus - Luzern

From May through October, *all 3* mountains can be ascended in one day by following this schedule.

Neither the Engelberg-Titlis nor Alpnachstad-Pilatus one-class roundtrips are covered by Eurailpass. The 1994 ticket prices for them without a Swiss Pass totaled 119 Swiss francs. With a Swiss Pass: Sfr-89.25.

293		*285*	
Dep. Luzern	07:24 (5)	Dep. Luzern	13:09 (3)
Arr. Engelberg	08:20	Arr. Alpnachstad	13:27
Change to the funicular.		*Change to the rack railway. 286*	
Dep. Engelberg	08:30 (1)	Dep. Alpnachstad	13:50
Arr. Mt. Titlis	09:30 (1)	Arr. Pilatus Kulm	14:20
• • •		• • •	
Dep. Mt. Titlis	10:00 (1)	Dep. Pilatus Kulm	14:25 (4)
Arr. Engelberg	11:00 (1)	Arr. Alpnachstad	15:05
Change to the train. 293		*Change to the train. 285*	
Dep. Engelberg	11:45 (2)	Dep. Alpnachstad	15:30
Arr. Luzern	12:45	Arr. Luzern	15:50

(1) Estimated. Thomas Cook Timetables does not publish Engleberg-Titlis schedules. (2) Plus other Engleberg departures. See above table. (3) Plus other Luzern departures at 14:09, arriving Pilatus 15:00. (4) Plus other Pilatus Kulm departures at 15:45 and 16:25, arriving Luzern 16:50 and 17:50. (5) Change trains at Hergiswill.

Luzern - Mt. Rigi (via Arth-Goldau) - Luzern

The excellent canyon and mountain scenery on this route (unlike the route via Vitznau that follows) is entirely by train. This is an easy one-day roundtrip. The rides between Arth-Goldau and Rigi are *not* covered by Eurailpass. The 1994 price for a one-class roundtrip ticket *without* a Swiss Pass was 48 Swiss francs. *With* a Swiss Pass: Sfr-36.

The Arth-Goldau to Regi Kulm (and v.v.) trains operate late May to mid-October. Times shown below are for the period early July to mid-October.

290

Dep. Luzern	09:14	10:19 (3)	12:19	14:19	15:14 (1)
Arr. Arth Goldau	09:40	10:44	12:44	14:44	15:40
Change to rack railway. 296					
Dep. Arth Goldau	10:03	11:03	13:03	15:03	16:03
Arr. Rigi Kulm	10:33	11:33	13:33	15:33	16:33

•   •   •

Dep Rigi Kulm	11:10	12:10	14:10	16:10	17:10 (2)
Arr Arth Goldau	11:50	12:50	14:50	16:50	17:50
Change to standard train. 290					
Dep. Arth Goldau	12:20	13:14 (4)	15:14 (4)	17:14 (4)	18:20
Arr. Luzern	25 minutes later				

(1) Plus another Luzern departure at 16:19 (4), arriving Rigi Kulm 17:30. (2) Plus another Rigi Kulm departure at 19:10, arriving Luzern 20:46. (3) Reservation recommended. (4) Reservation required. Supplement charged.

Luzern - Mt. Rigi (via Vitznau) - Luzern

There is very nice canyon, lake and mountain scenery on this easy one-day roundtrip that includes a boat ride (*covered by Eurailpass*) on Lake Luzern. From Vitznau to Mt. Rigi, the train climbs 4,000 feet in 4¼ miles. Over 450,000 passengers take this ride every year. There is good skiing at **Rigi** in the Winter. This line was constructed in 1871.

The Vitznau–Rigi ride is *not* covered by Eurailpass. The 1994 price of the (one-class) roundtrip ticket for the Vitznau–Rigi portion *without* a Swiss Pass was 48 Swiss francs. *With* a Swiss Pass: Sfr-36. *All of the boats have a restaurant or light refreshments.*

294 Boat

Dep. Luzern (Bahnhof.)	09:05 (1)	09:30 (2)	10:25 (3)	11:25 (1)	12:00 (3)	13:15 (4+7)
Arr. Vitznau (Pier)	09:52	10:17	11:30	12:26	12:41	14:05
Change to rack railway adjacent to the quay. 296						
Dep. Vitznau	10:10	10:45	11:45	12:40	13:30	16:10
Arr. Rigi Kulm	10:40	11:15	12:15	13:10	14:00	17:00

•   •   •

Dep. Rigi Kulm	10:45	11:40	12:40	14:15	15:00	16:00
Arr. Vitznau	11:25	12:20	13:20	14:55	15:45	17:00

Change to boat adjacent to the railstation. 294

Dep. Vitznau (Pier)	11:33 (5)	12:52 (6)	13:47 (1)	15:10 (2)	15:50 (6)	17:30 (1)
Arr. Luzern						
(Bahnhof.)	55–70 minutes later					

(1) Paddlesteamer. Has a restaurant. (2) Runs daily except Sundays and holidays July 1-August 31. (3) Boat has a restaurant. (4) Runs daily. July and August: this is a paddlesteamer daily. May, June and September: this is a paddlesteamer only on Sunday. (5) Light refreshments. (6) Restaurant car. (7) Plus another departure from Luzern at 14:20 (1), arriving Rigi Kulm 15:45.

St. Moritz - Tirano - St. Moritz   328

Great mountain scenery on this easy one-day narrow-gauge roundtrip into Italy. (Take your passport!) It is absolutely breathtaking. The track goes through the Bernina Pass, making this Europe's highest main rail line, reaching 7,400 feet at Bernina Hospiz. Buy a lunch in St. Moritz to eat on the train.

Dep. St. Moritz	07:45	09:05	09:30	10:00	11:05
Arr. Tirano	10:22	11:28	11:46	12:24	13:30

•   •   •

Dep. Tirano	10:30 (4)	11:30 (5)	12:24	13:05 (5+6)	14:05 (1+2++8)
Arr. St. Moritz	13:02	13:56	14:56	15:56	16:22

(1) Special tourist train. Reservation required. Supplement charged. (2) "Summer Bernina Express." Operates mid-May to late October. (3) "Winter Bernina Express." Operates late October to late May. (4) Mid-December to mid-April: runs daily. Late May to late October: runs Saturdays, Sundays and holidays. (5) Late October to mid-May: runsdaily, except Sundays and holidays. Mid-May to late October: runs daily. (6) Change trains in Poschiavo. (7) Runs Monday–Friday, except holidays. (8) Plus other Tirano departures at 14:40 (1+2),15:05 (1+2), 15:30, 16:10 (7) and 17:30, arriving St. Moritz 16:56, 16:50, 17:39, 17:56, 18:53 and 19:56.

St. Moritz - Zermatt   and   Zermat - St. Moritz   320 + SNTO

Many ordinary trains which do not require reservation, are *not* packed, and have seats that are as comfortable as those of "Glacier Express" run every day. Their only disadvantage is that they require changing trains 4 times: in Chur, Disentis, Andermatt and Brig.

All of the schedules below are for the direct-ride, luxury, "Glacier Express," for which a reservation is required. During the summer, seats in its elegant 34-seat restaurant car are usually reserved several months in advance. Reservations both for assigned seats and also for lunch in the elegant 34-seat paneled restaurant car can be made as much as 2 months in advance of travel date through a travel agency — and must be made 14 or more days prior to departure from the U.S.A. Passengers may also have food served at their seats from a minibar that is rolled down the aisle.

St. Moritz–Zermatt, sit on the left for the best views, on the right Zermatt– St. Moritz. There is marvelous canyon, mountain and Rhone Valley scenery on this ride, which crosses 291 bridges (including Europe's highest ones) and goes through 91 tunnels, including the 9-mile-long Furka, as the train traverses the 6,700-foot Oberalp Pass. This "Albula Line" is one of the world's greatest feats of railroad engineering. Its **Landwasser Viaduct** towers over a rampaging Alpine stream. Some of its tunnels are spirals inside the mountains, tunnels that you exit traveling in the same direction as you entered them, but at either a higher or lower level.

On "Glacier Express," the entire route is free with Swiss Pass and Swiss Flexipass. There is no discount for Eurailpass. The 1994 charges for the Disentis–Brig or v.v. portion was $61 (U.S.) for first-class, $37 for second-class. The Brig–Zermatt–Brig portion was $90 and $54.

Dep. St. Moritz	07:05 (1)	09:00 (2)	10:00 (2)
Dep. Chur	09:03 (2)	10:55	12:16
Dep. Disentis	10:29	12:22	13:35
Dep. Andermatt	11:36	13:37	14:36
Dep. Brig	13:23	15:23	16:08
Arr. Zermatt	14:45	16:45	17:22
	• • •		
Dep. Zermatt	08:54 (2)	10:10	12:10 (2)
Dep. Brig	10:30	11:44 (2)	13:44
Dep. Andermatt	12:00	13:53	15:23
Dep. Disentis	13:10	15:00	16:52
Arr.Chur	14:18	16:10	18:13 (3)
Arr. St. Moritz	16:58	17:58	19:58

(1) Change trains to "Glacier Express" in Chur. (2) Operates May 29-October 16. (3) Change to ordinary train in Chur.

Sights in **Zermatt**: Access to the Matterhorn. Great skiing in woods, pastures and hills. Displays of the challenges that mountaineers face are exhibited at the Alpine Museum. There are many hiking trails here, so easy that neither special shoes nor gear is necessary. Although each trail climbs about 2,000 feet, they are effortless because the incline is spread over many miles. Because autos have to park several miles away, the air here is pristine.

Sights in **Disentis**: The stained glass in the Cathedral.

Zermatt - Gornergrat - Zermatt 321

This is a great cogwheel train ride to the 10,200-foot high Gornergrat for a close view of the Matterhorn (14,692 feet) and more than 50 other Alpine peaks.

This ride is not covered by Eurailpass. The 1994 price of a one-class rountrip ticket without a Swiss Pass was 53 Swiss francs. With a Swiss Pass: Sfr-39.75.

Dep. Zermatt	07:05, 08:00, 08:24 (1), 08:48 (1), 09:12, 09:36 (1), 10:00, 10:24 (1), 10:48, 11:12, 11:36 (1), 12:00, 12:24 (1), 12:48 (1), 13:12, 13:36 (1), 14:00, 14:24 (1), 14:48 (1), 15:12, 15:36 (1), 16:00, 16:24 (1), 17:12, 18:00.
Arr. Gornergrat	43 minutes later

• • •

Dep. Gornergrat	07:55, 08:43 (1), 09:07, 09:31 (1), 09:55, 10:19 (1), 10:43 (1), 11:07, 11:31, 11:55, 12:19 (1), 12:43 (1), 13:07, 13:31 (1), 13:55, 14:19 (1), 14:43 (1), 15:07, 15:31 (1), 15:55, 16:19 (1), 16:43 (1), 17:07, 17:55, 19:07.
Arr. Zermatt	43 minutes later

(1) Runs daily except May 29-June 10.

Zurich - Sargans - Vaduz - Zurich   (The Trip To Liechtenstein)

There is fine scenery along the shores of **Lake Zurich** and **Lake Walen** on this easy one-day roundtrip.

It is only a 30-minute *bus ride* from Sargans to **Vaduz**, in the tiny country of Liechtenstein. Buses leave Sargans' railstation every 20 minutes for the 27-minute ride to Vaduz.

310

Dep. Zurich	07:35 (2)	08:10 (1)	09:10 (3)	09:33 (1)	10:10 (2)	11:10 (4+6)
Arr. Sargans	08:31	09:11	10:18	10:31	11:11	12:19
Change to bus.	*Table 311*					
Dep. Sargans	08:33	09:33	10:33	10:53 (5)	11:28	12:33
Arr. Vaduz	09:02	10:02	11:02	11:32 (8)	11:57	13:02

• • •

Dep. Vaduz	13:05	14:05	15:05	16:05	17:05	18:05 (7)
Arr. Sargans	13:34	14:34	15:34	16:34	17:34	18:34
Change to train.	*Table 310*					
Dep. Sargans	13:39 (4)	14:45 (2)	15:39 (3)	16:45 (1)	17:39 (3)	18:45 (2)
Arr. Zurich	14:50	15:50	16:50	17:50	18:50	19:50

(1) Reservation advisable. Restaurant car. (2) Reservation advisable. Light refreshments. (3) Light refreshments. (4) Restaurant car. (5) Runs daily, except Sundays and holidays. (6) Plus other departures from Zurich at 11:20 (1) and 12:10 (3), arriving Vaduz 13:02 and 13:42. (7) Plus other departures from Vaduz at 19:00, 20:00, 21:00 and 22:00, arriving Zurich 20:50, 21:50, 22:50 and 23:50. (8) Also August 1, not June 2, August 15, September 18.

Sights in **Vaduz**: Capital of the principality of Liechtenstein, a country that is 16 miles long by 4 miles wide, nestled between Switzerland and Austria. The extensive network of walking paths is very popular. Many excellent restaurants here.

See the collection of paintings by Rubens and other old masters at the National Art Gallery, open daily (April–October: 10:00–12:00 and 13:30–17:30. November–March: 10:00–12:00 and 14:00–17:30.) The exhibits of prehistoric and Roman articles: ancient weapons, coins, wood carvings, folk art and handicrafts, items from the area's medieval castles and other historical artifacts in the National Museum, open May–September daily 10:00–12:00 and 13:30–17:30. October–April: daily except Monday, 14:00–17:30.

The Postage Stamp Museum is open daily all year 10:00–12:00 and 14:00–18:00.

Zurich - Chur - Arosa - Chur - Zurich

See the good canyon, lake and mountain scenery on this easy one-day roundtrip. There is time for a stopover in Chur, as shown by the schedules below.

Most of the Zurich–Chur and Chur–Zurich trains have a restaurant car or light refreshments.

310

Dep. Zurich	07:33 (1)	08:10 (1)	09:10	10:10 (1)	11:10	12:10 (1+2)
Arr. Chur	08:51	09:37	10:45	11:37	12:45	13:37
Change trains.	324					
Dep. Chur	09:00	09:55	10:55	11:55	12:55	13:55
Arr. Arosa	60 minutes later					

Sights in **Arosa**: Great Summer and Winter Sports. Fantastic mountain scenery.

Dep. Arosa	10:05	11:05	12:05	13:05	14:05	15:05
Arr. Chur	11:07	12:07	13:07	14:07	15:07	16:07
Change trains.	310					
Dep. Chur	11:15	12:23 (1)	13:15	14:23 (1)	15:15	16:23 (1+3)
Arr. Zurich	12:50	13:50	14:50	15:50	16:50	17:50

(1) Reservation advisable. (2) Plus another Zurich departure at 13:10, arriving back in Zurich 18:50. (3) Plus other departures from Chur at 17:15, 18:23 (1), 19:15, 20:13, 21:13 and 22:13, arriving Zurich 18:50, 19:50, 20:50, 21:50, 22:50 and 23:50.

Zurich - Chur - Zermatt - Gornergrat - Zermatt

There is fabulous Rhone Valley scenery on this ride plus crossing Oberalp Pass (6,700 feet) and going through the 8-mile long Furka Tunnel on the Chur–Brig portion.

This trip includes going over the highest bridges in Europe and, by departing Zurich at 07:10 or 09:10, you can include the outstanding cogwheel train ride to Gornergrat (10,200 feet) for a close view of the Matterhorn (14,692 feet) and more than 50 other Alpine peaks.

The Chur–Zermatt, Zermatt–Gornergrat and Gornergrat–Zermatt portions of this trip are not covered by Eurailpass.

The 1994 prices of tickets for those rides without a Swiss Pass were: 203 Swiss francs for first-class, Sfr-143 for second-class. With a Swiss Pass, the Chur–Zermatt portion was free, and the Zermatt–Gornergrat–Zermatt roundtrip was at 25% discount, making the entire trip Sfr-39.75.

All of the Chur–Zermatt trains in this timetable are "Glacier Express," for which reservation is required. For services, prices and reservations, see "St. Moritz–Zermatt."

Do not let this timetable discourage you. This trip is easier to make than it was to prepare the table!

310				321		
Dep. Zurich	07:10 (1)	09:10 (1)		Dep. Zermatt	14:48 (7)	17:12
Arr. Chur	08:45	10:45		Arr. Gornergrat	15:29	17:55
Change trains. 320					• • •	
Dep. Chur	09:03 (2)	10:55 (2)		Dep. Gornergrat	15:31 (6)	17:55 (4+5)
Arr. Zermatt	14:45 (6)	16:45 (6)		Arr. Zermatt	16:15	18:37
Change trains.						

(1) Light refreshments. (2) "Glacier Express." See details about reservations and prices under "St. Moritz–Zermatt" (3) Operates mid-June to mid-October. Plus another Zermatt departure all year at 16:00. (4) Does not operates late October to late November. (5) Plus other departures from Gornergrat at 15:55, 16:19 (7), 16:43 (7), 17:07 (all year), 17:55 and 19:07, arriving Zermatt 16:39, 17:03, 17:27, 17:51, 18:38 and 19:49. (6) Runs May 29-October 16. (7) Runs daily except May 29-June 10.

Zurich - Davos - Filisur - Thusis - Zurich

In order to make a scenic *circle-trip* that avoids repeating the Landquart–Filisur route in the Zurich–Davos roundtrip, return to Zurich from Filisur via Thusis.

The Davos–Filisur portion of this trip is *not* covered by Eurailpass. The 1994 prices *without* a Swiss pass were: 14 Swiss francs for first-class, Sfr-8.40 for second-class. *With* a Swiss Pass: Free.

310

Dep. Zurich	07:10 (1)	08:10 (5)	09:10 (1)	10:10 (1)	11:10 (3+6)
Arr. Landquart	08:31	09:23	10:31	11:23	12:31

Change trains. 327

Dep. Landquart	08:56	09:40	10:47	11:40	12:47
Dep. Klosters	09:52	10:20	11:43	12:20	13:43
Arr. Davos Platz	10:24 (4)	10:46 (4)	12:13 (4)	12:46 (4)	14:13 (4)
Arr. Filisur	10:52	11:52	12:52	13:52	14:52

Change trains. 330

Dep. Filisur	11:04 (3)	12:04 (1)	13:04 (1)	14:04 (8)	15:04
Dep Thusis	11:37	12:37 (7)	13:37	14:37	15:37
Arr. Chur	12:07	13:07	14:07	15:07	16:07

Change trains. 310

Dep. Chur	12:23 (2)	13:15 (3)	14:23 (2)	15:15 (1)	16:23 (5)
Arr. Zurich	13:50	14:50	15:50	16:50	17:50

(1) Light refreshments. (2) Reservation advisable. Light refreshments. (3) Restaurant car. (4) Change trains. (5) Reservation advisable. Restaurant car. (6) Plus other departures from Zurich at 12:10 (2) and 13:10 (1), arriving back in Zurich 18:50 and 19:50. (7) Runs Sundays + holidays June 18-September 24. (8) Runs Saturdays, Sundays and holidays.

Zurich - Landquart - Davos - Landquart - Zurich

Excellent canyon, lake and mountain scenery may be viewed on this easy one-day round-trip.

Zurich - Bellinzona - Lugano   290

The Zurich – Lugano portion of the Zurich-Milan route (one of the 5 most scenic rail trips in Europe) can be seen on a one-day roundtrip from Zurich. A feast of beautiful farms, lakes, mountains, rivers and vineyards. You go through the 9.3-mile long Gotthard Tunnel.

Before the Gotthard was opened to traffic in 1882, there was no direct rail route from eastern Switzerland through the Alps to Italy. For 7 years and 5 months, 2500 men worked in 3% shifts day and night to build this engineering marvel. Immediately after exiting the third of a series of 9 tunnels, the train passes the small, white Wassen Church to your right, and about 230 feet above the track. The next time the church comes into view, after leaving Wassen Station, it is also to your right, and nearly level with the track. Later, after exiting tunnel #7, you have a third view of the church, this time to your left and 170 feet above the track.

The turns inside 3 semi-circular tunnels in this area (Pfaffensprung, Wattinger and Leggistein) are engineered so well that there is no sensation of the curves that the train is making inside those tunnels.

Try this interesting experiment: make a pendulum of any object, holding the top of a weighted string, chain or handkerchief against the inner face of a train window (a left-hand window when inside Pfaffensprung and Wattinger, a right-hand window when inside Leggistein). As the train goes around a curve, the weighted bottom will move away from the window.

Climate on the Swiss side of the tunnel is usually much cooler than the Mediterranean temperature on the Italian end. There is a beautiful descent from the Italian end of the tunnel down the Ticino Valley. The train makes 3% gradients at 45–50 miles per hour.

At Bellinzona, the line forks. One branch goes to Locarno, the other to Lugano and Milan.

Dep. Zurich	07:03 (1)	08:03 (1)	09:03 (1)	10:03 (2)	11:03 (1)
Arr. Bellinzona	09:33	10:33 (7)	11:33 (7)	12:33	13:33
Arr. Lugano	10:03	11:03	12:03	13:03	14:03

Sights in **Bellinzona**: The Museum of Costumes and Prints, located in Castello di Sasso Corbaro, 320 feet above the town. Open daily except Monday 09:00–12:00 and 14:00–17:00, there are great views from it of the Alps, the Ticino River Valley and Lago (Lake) Maggiore.

The outdoor Saturday market: peasant sausages, breads, mountain cheeses, kitchenware, clothing. The 4th century Castello Grande, sitting on a 150-foot-hight hill in the center of the town.

The Post Office on Viale della Stazione is the newest (1990) tourist attraction because of its post-modernism architecture.

One can take a passageway under the railraod tracks (starting at a point between the railstation and the Post Office) to begin walking up a hillside to the 15th century Castel Piccolo (small castle) for good views of the area.

See the views of the Ticino River Valley and the collection of medieval art, ancient coins and old weapons at the Civic Museum in the former dungeons of Castle Piccolo, open daily except Monday June–September 09:30–12:00 and 14:00–17:30: October–May 09:30–12:00 and 14:00–17:00.

The frescoed and arcaded old houses with wrought-iron balconies and marble portals, particularly Ca Rossa, called "Red House" because of the terra cotta ornaments on its facade.

The elegant clock tower on the ancient Town Hall, at Piazza Nosetto. Nearby the large rose window on the Collegiate Church and the beautiful sculptured 15th century font there. A 10-minute walk from it is the interesting frescoed wall at Santa Maria delle Grazie Church.

Dep. Lugano	10:41	11:57 (1)	12:41 (3)	13:57 (4)	14:41 (3+6)
Dep. Bellinzona	11:09	12:27	13:09	14:27	15:09
Arr. Zurich	13:57	14:57	15:57	16:57	17:57

(1) Reservation advisable. Restaurant car. (2) Light refreshments to 10:45 arrival and train change in Arth Goldau. Depart Arth Goldau 10:49 (1). (3) Light refreshments. (4) Reservation advisable. Light refreshments. (5) Reservation *required*. Restaurant car. (6) Plus other departures from Lugano at 15:57 (1), 16:33 (1), 17:57 (1), 18:47 (7), 19:41 and 20:31 (5), arriving Zurich 18:57, 19:28, 20:57, 21:48, 23:03 and 23:36. (7) Supplement payable.

Zurich - Mt. Rigi - Zurich

The Arth Goldau–Mt. Rigi-Arth Goldau roundtrip portion of this trip is not covered by Eurailpass. The 1994 price of a one-class roundtrip ticket without a Swiss Pass was 48 Swiss francs. With a Swiss Pass: Sfr-36.

The Arth Goldau–Rigi Kulm (and v.v.) schedules shown here are for the period early April to mid-October. Arth Goldau-Rigi (and v.v.) trains additional to those shown below operate early July to mid-October.

290
Dep. Zurich	09:03 (1)	10:03 (2)	12:03 (2)	14:03 (2)	15:03 (3)
Arr. Arth Goldau	09:45 (4)	10:45	12:45	14:45	15:44 (4)

Change to rack railway.
296
Dep. Arth Goldau	10:03	11:03	13:03	15:03	16:03
Arr. Rigi Kulm	10:33	11:33	13:33	15:33	16:33

• • •

296
Dep. Rigi Kulm	11:10	12:10	14:10	16:10	17:10	19:10
Arr. Arth Goldau	11:50	12:50	14:50	16:50	17:50	19:50

Change from rack railway to a standard train
290
Dep. Arth Goldau	12:15 (1)	13:15	15:15 (2)	17:15 (2)	18:15 (1)	20:15 (1)
Arr. Zurich	12:57 (4)	13:57	15:57	17:57	18:57	20:57

(1) Reservation advisable. Restaurant car. (2) Light refreshments. (3) Reservation advisable. Light refreshments. (4) Supplement payable.

Zurich - Luzern - Mt. Pilatus - Luzern - Zurich

There is fine canyon and mountain scenery on this easy one-day roundtrip.

The Alpnachstad–Pilatus–Alpnachstad rack railway portion operates only from May to the end of November. The 1994 price of a one-class roundtrip ticket without a Swiss Pass was: 53 Swiss francs. With a Swiss Pass: Sfr-39.75.

There are good views and several restaurants at the top of Pilatus.

Most of the trains Zurich-Luzern (and v.v.) have light refreshments.

295

Dep. Zurich	07:07	08:07 (3)	09:07 (3)	10:07	11:07	12:07	13:07 (1)
Arr. Luzern	07:56	08:56	09:56	10:56	11:56	12:56	13:56

Change trains. Table 285

Dep. Luzern	08:09	09:09	10:09	11:09	12:09	13:09	14:09
Arr. Alpnachstad	08:27	09:27	10:27	11:27	12:27	13:27	14:27

Change to rack railway. Table 286

Dep. Alpnachstad	08:50	09:30	10:50	11:30	13:10	13:50	14:30
Arr. Pilatus Kulm	09:20	10:00	11:20	12:00	13:40	14:20	15:00

* * *

Dep. Pilatus Kulm	09:25	10:45	11:25	12:05	13:45	14:25	15:05 (2)
Arr. Alpnachstad	10:05	11:25	12:05	12:45	14:25	15:05	15:45

Change to standard train. Table 285

Dep. Alpnachstad	10:30	11:30	12:30	13:30	14:30	15:30	16:30
Arr. Luzern	10:50	11:50	12:50	13:50	14:50	15:50	16:50

Change trains. Table 295

Dep. Luzern	Frequent times from 06:04 to 23:08
Arr. Zurich	50 minutes later

(1) Plus another departure from Zurich at 14:07, arriving Pilatus Kulm 16:20. (2) Plus other Pilatus departures at 15:45 and 16:25, arriving Zurich 17:53 and 18:53. (3) Runs Monday-Friday except holidays.

Zurich - Romanshorn - St. Gallen (St. Gall) - Zurich

There is excellent lake and mountain scenery on this easy one-day circle roundtrip that visits **Lake Constance** (**Konstanz** in German). One hundred miles of the lake's shore are in Germany, 16 in Austria, 43 in Switzerland. The microclimate here is so balmy taht even palm trees grow in this area.

Sights in **St. Gallen:** The history of lacemaking and embroidery from the 16th century to the present, and lacework worn by European nobility, at the Gewerbemuseum (Embroidery Museum). The paintings in the Historisches Museum. The 100,000 volumes (including illuminated manuscripts), more than 1,000 years old, in the rebuilt rococo library of the ancient abbey. The twin-towered baroque 18th century Cathedral. Near it, many old houses decorated with frescoes and oriel windows, in the city's old quarter.

305

Dep. Zurich	08:10 (1)	09:10 (2)	10:10 (2)	11:10	12:10 (4+5)
Arr. Romanshorn	09:21	10:21	11:21 (3)	12:21	13:21

Take time for a boat ride on Lake Konstanz. Table 312
(09:36–11:24, 10:36–12:24 or 11:36–13:24 — 50% discount with Eurailpass.)

Dep. Romanshorn	10:08 (1)	10:32	12:08 (1)	12:32	14:32
Arr. St. Gallen	10:40	10:55	12:40	13:00	15:00

Change trains. Table 308

Dep. St. Gallen	Frequent times from 06:03 to 23:15
Arr. Zurich	70 minutes later

(1) Light refreshments. (2) Restaurant car. (3) Reservation advisable. (4) Reservation advisable. Light refreshments. (5) Plus other departures from Zurich at 13:10, 14:10 (4) and 15:10…with departures from Romanshorn, at 15:08, 16:08 (1) and 16:32…arriving back in Zurich 16:53, 17:53 and 18:21.

Romanshorn - Friedrichshafen 314

This is the ferry service between Romanshorn and Friedrichshafen (50% discount with Eurailpass).

All of these boats have a restaurant.

Dep. Romanshorn	09:36	10:36 (1)	11:36	12:36 (1)	13:36	14:36 (1+2)
Arr. Friedrichshafen	40–45 minutes later

Sights in **Friedrichschafen**: The first rigid airship, the Zeppelin, was built here in 1900, and this town became the principal European terminal for regularly scheduled trans-Atlantic airship service to New York and Rio de Janeiro. See the models, documents, photographs and collection of engines and other parts at the Zeppelin Museum.

Many of the towns on the German shore of Lake Constance (or Konstanz) have attractions. The local wine, pleasant inns and cozy taverns along their steep, winding cobblestoned streets bring crowds of visitors to them.

At **Unteruhldingen,** the open air museum of Stone Age and Bronze Age villages features reconstructed thatch-roofed, adobe houses built on wood piles between 4,000 and 1,000 B.C.

For devotees of Baroque and roccoco decor, there are the 18th century church at **Birnau** and the banquet hall, reception rooms, library and private chambers of the palace and the interior of the 12th century abbey at **Salem.**

See **Ueberlingen,** a living page from the Middle Ages and the Renaissance: massive walls, 15th and 16th century house, a lavish Town Hall.

Konstanz is the largest city on the lake (70,000). Because it is surrounded by Switzerland, it was spared from air raids in World War II. Founded about 300 A.D., it is the best base for visiting the lake's most popular islands: **Mainau** and **Reichenau**. The sights on Mainau are its tropical orchards (bananas, lemon, orange and mandarin trees) and profusion of flowers. It also has a Baroque castle.

The Benedictine abbeys and 3 churches on Reichenau provide a view of monastic life in the Middle Ages. See the Byzantine, Baroque and Gothic art at the treasury in St. Mary's Church.

The 18th century Montfort Palace in **Tettnang** is one of the most richly decorated and lavishly furnished chateaus in southern Germany.

Dep. Friedrichshafen   10:43   11:43 (1)   12:43   13:43 (1)   14:43   15:43 (1+3)
Arr. Romanshorn   40–45 minutes later

(1) Operates March 18-May 27, 1995. (2) Plus other departures from Romanshorn at 15:36, 16:36 (1), 17:36, 18:36 (1) and 19:36 (2). (3) Plus other departures from Friedrichshafen at 16:43, 17:43 (1), 18:43(2) and 19:43 (1).

Zurich - Schaffhausen - Zurich   302

A trip to see the marvelous **Rhine Falls**.

Dep. Zurich   Frequent times from 07:13 to 23:13
Arr. Schaffhausen   38 minutes later

Sights in **Schaffhausen**: A bus takes you in 10 minutes from the railstation to the cataracts below the tumultous 7-story-high Rhine Falls (less than an hour walk from the town's waterfront). The most impressive sight is usually in early July, when the snow in the Swiss and Austrian Alps is melting. For a great view of the Rhine River, climb to the 16th century Munot Fortress.

Visit the gold and silver room in the Allerheiligen Museum. The Thursday market.

Take the uphill path, through vineyards, a 15-minute walk to the hilltop castle, for the view from there. Ride the cable car to the summit of 8,215-foot-high **Mt. Santis** for a spectacular view of many Alpine peaks, including Germany's Zugspitze.

Take the 90 minute river boat to **Stein am Rhein** to see the 11th century Hohenklingen Castle. See the depiction of 11th century life in the museum at the 11th century St. George Monastery, the ruins of Tasgetium (a Roman fort), and the stained glass, wood walls and medieval firearms on the top floor of the 16th century Town Hall.

Dep. Schaffhausen   Frequent times from 06:06 to 22:08
Arr. Zurich   38 minutes later

A GLORIOUS WEEK IN SWITZERLAND

Here is a great 7-day circle itinerary of Switzerland that gives you, in the span of one week, a visit to most of the country's major cities plus a view of much of Switzerland's great scenery. (The rides to Jungfraujoch and Mt. Rigi are *not* covered by Eurailpass.)

Day 1   Geneva, Montreux, Zweisimmen, Spiez (Lunch). Lake Thun boat to Interlaken.
Day 2   Interlaken, Jungfraujoch, Grindelwald (lunch), Interlaken.
Day 3   Interlaken, Luzern.
Day 4   Luzern, Vitznau, Mt. Rigi (lunch), Arth-Goldau, Lugano.
Day 5   Lugano, Bellinzona, Locarno.
Day 6   Locarno, Domodossola, Bern.
Day 7   Bern to Geneva or Zurich.

A MAGNIFICENT ONE-DAY TRIP

Here are several of the most scenic rail trips in Europe, combined in a single day.

All of these rides are covered by Eurailpass.

Table	280	Dep. Spiez	07:54 (1)	....	Arr. Brig	08:59
	365	Dep. Brig	09:34 (2)	....	Arr. Domodossola	10:02
	272	Dep. Domodossola	10:18	....	Arr. Locarno	11:55
	291	Dep. Locarno	12:03	....	Arr. Bellinzona	12:21
	290	Dep. Bellinzona	13:27 (3)	....	Arr. Luzern	15:39
	285	Dep. Luzern	16:24	....	Arr. Interlaken (Ost)	18:23
	280	Dep. Interlaken (Ost)(1)	18:39	....	Arr. Spiez	18:59

(1) Light refreshments. (2) Reservation advisable. Light refreshments. (3) Reservation advisable. Restaurant car. Supplement charged.

THE "GOLDEN PASS" ROUTE

Luzern - Interlaken - Spiez - Zweisimmen - Montreux - Lausanne

There are snowcapped Alpine peaks, flowering meadows, and sparkling mountain streams on this marvelous one-day trip. As the timetables show, a layover in Spiez is possible.

285	
Dep. Luzern	08:24 (1)
Arr. Interlaken (Ost)	10:23
Change trains.	
280	
Dep. Interlaken (Ost)	10:39 (1)
Arr. Spiez	10:59
Change trains.	

276		
Dep. Spiez	11:08	12:03 (2)
Arr. Zweisimmen	11:55	12:39
Change trains. 275		
Dep. Zweisimmen	12:00	12:50
Arr. Montreux	14:00	14:38
Change trains. 270		
Dep. Montreux	14:07	15:07
Arr. Lausanne	14:27	15:27

(1) Restaurant car. (2) Plus other departures from Spiez at 13:08, 14:03 (transferring to "Panoramic Express" for the Zweisimmen-Montreux portion — Reservation required...see pages 398-399) and 15:08...changing trains in Zweisimmen 13:55, 14:39 and 15:55...changing trains in Montreux 16:00, 16:38 and 18:00...arriving Lausanne 16:27, 17:03 and 18:27.

INTERNATIONAL ROUTES
FROM SWITZERLAND

The Swiss gateways for travel to West Germany are Basel (to Cologne), Geneva (to Frankfurt), and Zurich (to Munich). Zurich is also the starting point for the train trip to Austria (Innsbruck, and on to Vienna and East Europe) and for train travel to Italy (Milan and beyond).

Basel is also a starting point for trips to Belgium, Holland and France (Paris, and on to London or Madrid).

Geneva (via Aosta, and on to Torino) as well as Bern and Brig (via Domodossola) are also departure cities for rail rides to Italy (Milan, and beyond).

There is also rail service from Geneva to Paris, and from Geneva to southern France (Avignon) and on to Spain (Barcelona).

Basel - Amsterdam 38

Dep. Basel (S.B.B.)	13:17 (2)	14:17 (2)	23:25 (3)
Arr. Amsterdam	20:51	21:51	09:40

(1) Change trains in Maastricht at 15:22. (2) Reservation advisable. Supplement charged. Restaurant car. (3) Has couchettes.

Basel - Cologne   650 + 730

Sit on the right side of the train for best views of the marvelous Rhine River scenery.

Reservation is advisable for all of the Basel–Cologne day trains. All of them have a restaurant car.

Dep. Basel (SBB)	Every hour 07:17 to 18:17
Dep. Basel (Bad.)	7 minutes after departing S.B.B. railstation
Arr. Cologne	11:59 to 22:59

Basel - Hamburg - Copenhagen - Oslo - Stockholm   50

Dep. Basel (SBB)	07:51 (1)	11:51 (1)	-0-	17:49 (4+5)	-0-
Arr. Hamburg (Hbf.)	14:21	18:21	-0-	03:54 (5)	-0-
Change trains.					
Dep. Hamburg	15:19(2)	19:34 (4)	19:34 (4)	04:04	-0-
Arr. Copenhagen	20:20	-0-	-0-	09:25	-0-
Change trains.					
Dep. Copengagen	21:45 (3)	-0-	-0-	09:45 (6)	11:15 (6)
Arr. Oslo (Sen.)	07:37	11:46	-0-	19:42	-0- (7)
Arr. Stockholm (Cen.)	-0-	-0-	10:05	-0-	19:53

(1) Reservation advisable. Supplement charged. Restaurnt car. (2) Reservation advisable. Supplement charged. Light refreshments. (3) Reservation *required*. Carries a sleeping car. Also has couchettes. Coach is second-class. (4) Train has only sleeping cars and couchettes. No coaches. (5) Direct train to Copenhagen. No train change in Hamburg. (6) Reservation *required*. Restaurant car. (7) Runs daily to August 14.

Zurich - Munich   75

Reservation is advisable for all of these trains. All of them charge a supplement and have restaurant car.

Dep. Zurich	07:40	09:40	13:40	17:40
Arr. Munich	11:51	13:56	17:48	21:45

Zurich - Innsbruck - Salzburg - Vienna   86

About 2½ hours out of Zurich, the train passes through one of Europe's largest tunnels, the 6.3-mile long Arlberg. There is a very beautiful view of Alpine scenery as the train comes out of the tunnel.

Dep. Zurich	09:33 (1)	13:35 (1)	22:33 (3)
Arr. Innsbruck	13:16	17:16	02:46
Arr. Salzburg	15:22	19:22	04:45
Arr. Vienna (West.)	18:30	22:30	08:05

(1) Reservation advisable. Supplement charged. Restaurant car. (2) Change trains in Feldkirch [arr. 17:11/dep. 17:44 (1)]. (3) Reservaion advisable. (4) Change trains in Innsbruck, departing Innsbruck 23:29 (has couchettes). (5) Carries a sleeping car. Also has couchettes.

Bern - Brig - Milan   280

This trip takes you on the marvelous scenic route via Spiez (see "Geneva–Spiez") and through both the 10-mile long Lotschberg Tunnel Bern–Brig) and the 11.9-mile long Simplon (Brig–Milan), longest tunnel in Europe and world's third longest, after Japan's Seikan Tunnel (33.4 miles, between Tappi and Yoshioka) and Japan's Daishimizu Tunnel (13.4 miles, between Tokyo and Niigata).

Reservation is advisable for all of these trains.

Dep. Bern	06:50 (2)	08:51 (1)	12:56 (1)	15:22 (2)	17:22 (1)
Arr. Brig	08:15	10:16 (3)	14:24	16:54	18:54
Arr. Milan (Cen.)	10:45	12:40	16:50	19:15	21:10

(1) Light refreshments. (2) Restaurant car. (3)Runs Friday and Saturdays July 2-August 27.

Zurich - Milan   84

See detailed notes about the wonderful scenery on this route (one of the 5 most scenic rail trips in Europe) under "Zurich–Lugano"

Reservation is advisable for all of these trains.

Dep. Zurich	07:03 (1)	08:03 (1)	09:03 (1)	11:03	13:33 (2+3)
Arr. Milan (Cen.)	11:35	12:35 (4)	13:30 (4)	15:35	17:35

(1) Restaurant car. (2) Light refreshments. (3) Plus other Zurich departures at 15:03,17:03 (1) and 19:03, arriving Milan 19:30, 21:30 and 23:35. (4) Supplement charged.

Basel - Luxembourg - Brussels 40

Dep. Basel (S.B.B.)	08:32	13:30 (3)	16:26 (3)
Arr. Luxembourg	12:06	16:59	20:06
Arr. Brussels (Q.L.)	14:17	19:10	22:18
Arr. Brussels (Nord)	14:27	19:20	22:28
Arr. Brussels (Midi)	8 minutes after arriving Nord railstation.		

(1) Carries a sleeping car. Also has couchettes. (2) Restaurant car. (3) Reservation advisable. Supplement charged. Restaurant car.

Geneva - Milan - Venice 83

Dep. Geneva (Corn.)	08:20 (1)	10:34 (1)	11:48 (4)	23:02 (5)
Arr. Milan (Cen.)	12:40	14:40 (2)	16:50 (7+8)	-0- (6)
Dep. Milan (Cen.)	12:50	15:05 (3)	17:05 (3)	-0- (6)
Arr. Venice (S.L.)	15:52	17:57	20:02	07:00

(1) Reservation advisable. Restaurant car. (2) Change trains. (3) Reservation advisable. Supplement charged. Light refreshments. (4) Light refrehments. Change trains in Brig [arr. 14:23—dep. 14:31 (1)]. (5) Carries a sleeping car. Also has couchettes. (6) Does not call on Milan. (7) Arrives Venice Mestre. (8) Also change in Milan.

Bern - Paris 42

Dep. Bern	07:00 (1)	09:22	17:05
Arr. Frasne	08:28	10:59 (2)	18:38 (2)
Dep. Frasne	08:30	11:06 (1)	18:45 (1)
Arr. Paris (Lyon)	11:24	13:59	21:39

(1) TGV. Reservation advisable. Supplement charged. Restaurant car. (2) Change trains in Frasne.

Geneva - Paris 159

Reservtion is advisable for these trains. All are TGV, run daily and have a restaurant car, unless designated otherwise.

Dep. Geneva (Corn.)	05:40 (1)	07:45	10:00	12:37	16:50	19:10
Arr. Paris (Lyon)	09:15 (2)	11:12	13:29	16:11	20:30	22:42

(1) Runs Monday-Friday, except holidays. (2) Not July 15.

Zurich - Bern (or Basel) - Geneva - Avignon - Barcelona 81

The "Pablo Casals" (19:33 departure from Zurich) began in 1990 to carry one "Gran Clase" sleeping car, the most luxurious sleeping car in Europe. Each of its large single and double compartments has a shower and toilet. The train also has ordinary sleeping compartments and 4-berth tourist compartments. There are no coach seats. The train has a restaurant car. Travel is not covered by any rail passes. A supplement is charged. This is a direct train. No train change in Port Bou.

Dep. Zurich	-0-	-0-	-0-	19:33 (4)
Dep. Bern	-0-	-0-	-0-	20:47
Dep. Basel (S.B.B.)	-0-	-0-	18:23 (3)	-0-
Dep. Geneva (Cor.)	10:34 (1)	11:32 (2)	21:54	22:46
Dep. Avignon	15:10	15:47	01:45	-0-
Arr. Port Bou	18:23	18:51	05:25 (3)	-0-
Arr. Barcelona (Sants)	19:53	-0-	09:35	-0-
Arr. Barcelona (Franca)	-0-	20:50	-0-	09:10

(1) Operates early July to early September. Light refreshments. Geneva-Port Bou. (2) Restaurant car. (3) Has couchettes. Change trains in Port Bou at 05:25. (4) "Pablo Casals." See description above.

AOSTA-TORINO GATEWAYS TO ITALY

(1) Via San Bernardo Tunnel

Lausanne or Brig to Martigny and Martigny - Aosta - Torino

270 (Train)			270 (Train)		
Dep. Lausanne	06:56	15:32 (1)	Dep. Brig	06:48	15:36 (1)
Arr. Martigny	07:45	16:21	Arr. Martigny	07:36	16:32

• • •

269 (Bus)				
Dep. Martigny (Stn.)	07:55	10:55 (2)	16:30	-0-
Arr. Aosta (P. Narbonne)	10:00	17:25	18:35	-0-
Change to a train. 353				
Dep. Aosta	14:42	18:26	19:32	20:42
Arr. Torino (Porta Nuova)	16:34	20:35	21:37	22:29

(1) Light refreshments. (2) Train Martigny-Orsieres, bus Orsieres-Le Grand St. Bernard, then change buses and depart Le Grand 16:15 (operates early June to mid-September).

(2) Via Mt. Blanc Tunnel

Geneva - Chamonix - Aosta - Torino

All of the train changes Geneva–Chamonix are cross-platform, taking less than one minute.

167
Dep. Geneva (Eaux-Vives)	07:10 (1)	08:27 (3)	11:10	14:30
Arr. La Roche-sur-Foron	07:42 (3)	08:57	11:46	15:11

Change trains.
Dep. La Roche-sur-Foron	07:50	09:56	11:53	15:35
Arr. St. Gervais	08:52	10:43	12:38	16:21

Change trains. 268
Dep. St. Gervais	09:16	10:53	13:04	16:45
Arr. Chamonix	09:52	11:30	13:42	17:21

Change to a bus. 192
Dep. Chamonix	10:05 (3)	15:00 (3)	16:15 (3)	17:30
Arr. Aosta	11:40	17:00	18:00	19:30

(1) Runs daily, except Sundays and holidays. (2) Runs Saturdays, Sundays and holidays. (3) Operates late June to mid-September.

Change to a train. 353
Dep. Aosta (P. Narbonne)	14:42	18:26	-0-	19:32	20:42
Arr. Torino (P. S.)	16:34	20:35	-0-	21:24	22:29

A good break in this journey is to spend the night in Aosta and continue on to Torino the next day. Here are the schedules for the other departures from Aosta:

Dep. Aosta (P. Narbonne)	07:42	09:42 (1)
Arr. Torino (P. S.)	09:32	10:35

(1) Runs daily, except Sundays and holidays.

CHAPTER 7

BRITAIN
ENGLAND, WALES AND SCOTLAND

Children under 5 travel free. Half-fare for children 5–15. Children 16 and over must pay full fare.

On British trains, first-class sleeping cars have single compartments; standard-class sleeping cars have 2-berth compartments. Sleeping-car passengers are served morning tea and biscuits free of charge. Generally, overnight passengers may remain in sleeping cars at destinations the next morning until 07:30. Pullman trains, for which reservation is advisable, offer full meals to first-class passengers at their seats.

Britain's 750 "InterCity" trains, linking more than 200 towns each weekday, average 98 to 100 miles per hour on some routes.

Reservations are required on the fast day trains. If there are vacant spaces, the conductor at the departure platform can allocate available places.

British Rail usually makes repairs to train lines on Sundays, as late as 16:00. If you plan to travel by train here on a Sunday, it is advisable to telephone the railstation and confirm the time for routes you intend to use.

BRITAIN'S TRAIN PASSES

BritRail Pass The BritRail Pass, similar to Eurailpass (which does *not* cover Britain), provides unlimited rail travel in England, Scotland and Wales. Youth-Pass (limited to ages 16 to under 25) is for standard-class space. The 1996 prices are:

	8 Days	15 Days	22 Days	One Month
First-class	$ 325.00	$ 525.00	$ 665.00	$ 765.00
Standard-class	235.00	365.00	465.00	545.00
Child 5-15				
First-class	157.50	257.50	322.50	375.00
Standard-class	115.00	177.50	222.50	260.00
Youth 16-under 25				
Standard-class	189.00	289.00	369.00	435.00
Senior Citizen 60 +				
First-class	275.00	445.00	565.00	650.00

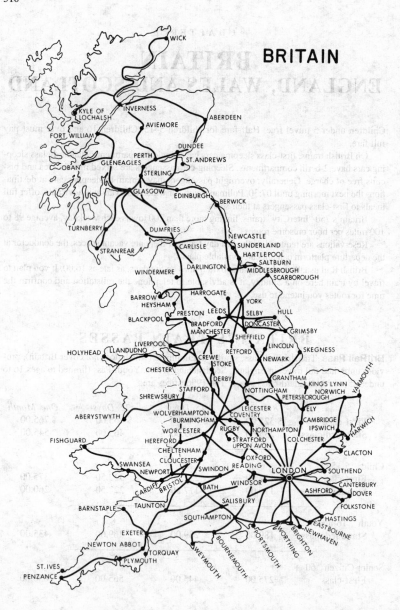

BRITAIN

WICK
KYLE OF LOCHALSH
INVERNESS
FORT WILLIAM
AVIEMORE
ABERDEEN
PERTH
DUNDEE
OBAN
GLENEAGLES
ST. ANDREWS
STERLING
GLASGOW
EDINBURGH
BERWICK
TURNBERRY
DUMFRIES
NEWCASTLE
STRANREAR
CARLISLE
SUNDERLAND
HARTLEPOOL
SALTBURN
DARLINGTON
MIDDLESBROUGH
WINDERMERE
SCARBOROUGH
HARROGATE
BARROW
HEYSHAM
YORK
LEEDS
SELBY
HULL
PRESTON
BLACKPOOL
BRADFORD
DONCASTER
MANCHESTER
SHEFFIELD
GRIMSBY
LIVERPOOL
RETFORD
LINCOLN
SKEGNESS
HOLYHEAD
LLANDUDNO
CREWE
STOKE
NEWARK
CHESTER
DERBY
GRANTHAM
STAFFORD
NOTTINGHAM
KING'S LYNN
SHREWSBURY
LEICESTER
PETERSBOROUGH
NORWICH
YARMOUTH
WOLVERHAMPTON
COVENTRY
ELY
ABERYSTWYTH
BURMINGHAM
CAMBRIDGE
IPSWICH
WORCESTER
RUGBY
NORTHAMPTON
HARWICH
HEREFORD
STRATFORD
UPON AVON
COLCHESTER
FISHGUARD
CHELTENHAM
CLACTON
GLOUCESTER
OXFORD
SWANSEA
SWINDON
READING
LONDON
SOUTHEND
NEWPORT
CARDIFF
BRISTOL
BATH
WINDSOR
CANTERBURY
ASHFORD
DOVER
BARNSTAPLE
TAUNTON
SALISBURY
FOLKSTONE
SOUTHAMPTON
HASTINGS
EASTBOURNE
EXETER
BRIGHTON
NEWHAVEN
NEWTON ABBOT
TORQUAY
WEYMOUTH
BOURNEMOUTH
PORTSMOUTH
WORTHING
ST. IVES
PLYMOUTH
PENZANCE

These passes do not cover travel in the Republic of Ireland or in Northern Ireland (which is covered by BritIreland Railpass - see next page) and *they cannot be purchased in Britain.* They can be purchased worldwide through the offices of BritRail Travel International, its representatives, and travel agencies outside Britain. Validate these passes at the rail-station's "Travel Centre" before starting your first trip with them. The rail official will mark your pass with that day's date and also the appropriate expiration date.

It is a good idea to protect yourself from having your pass rendered partly or wholly invalid because the validity dates were entered incorrectly.

Before the rail official writes on the pass the first and last day it can be used, you should write a note with what you believe are the correct validity dates, show it to the seller, and ask if he or she agrees with those dates. Only when the official says your dates are correct, or explains why they are not, should you have the dates entered on your pass.

(Be sure to follow the European custom of showing the day of the month first, followed by the number of the month. In Europe, July 8 is 8/7. If you wanted to take a train to Edinburgh, leaving London at 2:00 PM on July 8, your note for a reservation would read: "Edinburgh 14:00 8/7.")

BritRail Flexipass Valid for one month. (For "Youth," the 15-day pass can be used within two months.) Same conditions and purchase locations as BritRail Pass. The 1996 prices are:

	4 Days	8 Days	15 Days
First-class	$ 289.00	$ 399.00	$ 615.00
Standard-class	199.00	280.00	425.00
Child 5–15			
First-class	144.50	199.50	307.50
Standard-class	99.50	140.00	212.50
Youth 16–25			
Standard-class	160.00	225.00	340.00
Senior Citizen 60 +			
First-class	245.00	339.00	490.00

BritRail/Drive Provides 2 options, both within one month. Either 3 days of BritRail Flexipass plus 3 days of car rental, or 6 days of BritRail Flexipass plus 7 days of car rental.

Prices vary (a) how many people travel together, (b) whether the rail portion is for first-class or standard-class, (c) whether the car is manual or automatic transmission, and (d) the size of the car. There is a very small Senior discount for those over age 60. Half-fare for children age 5-15.

UK-France Sampler See France

BritIreland Pass Unlimited train travel in England, Scotland, Wales, Northern Ireland and the Republic of Ireland (plus roundtrip ferry between the 2 Irelands). Sold in North America by both BritRail Travel International and C.I.E. Tours International. The 1996 adult *first*-class prices are: $405 for any 5 days within one month, and $599 for any 10 days within one month. Standard-class: $299 and $429. Half-fare for children age 5–15. Children under 5 travel free.

England/Wales Pass Unlimited train travel any 4 days within one month throughout Wales and as far north in England as Berwick and Carlisle (including trips to Bath, Cambridge, Chester, Exeter, Oxford, York, the Lake District and Cotswold villages).

   The 1996 prices were not available in late 1995. The 1995 adult prices were $205 for *first*-class, $155 for *standard*-class. For children age 5–15: $102.50 and $77.50.

Southeast Railpass This is a new pass for 1996. Unlimited train travel in southeast England. The 1996 *first*-class prices are: For any 3 days in 8: $90. For any 4 days in 8: $120. For any 7 days in 15: $169. *Second*-class prices: $69, $89, $119 respectively.

London Extra Flexipass *Cannot be purchased in England*. Unlimited travel on trains in Southeast England plus a London Visitor Card (see below) for same duration. Does *not* include airport transfers. The 2 passes need not be used together. The 1996 adult *first*-class prices are: $105 for any 3 of 8 days, $145 for any 4 of 8 days, and $219 for any 7 of 15 days. For children age 5–15: $35, $39 and $45. The 1995 adult *standard*-class prices are: $85, $115 and $175. For children age 5–15: $29, $30 and $35.

London Visitor Travelcard Can be purchased worldwide. Valid for unlimited travel on London's buses and subways, plus discounts on the admission prices at such attractions as London Transport Museum, London Zoo, Madame Tussaud's, Kensington Palace, Tower Bridge and the Cabinet War Rooms. (A version sold in Britain does not include discounts at historical sites.) The 1996 adult prices prices are: $25 for 3 days, $32 for 4 days, $49 for 7 days. Children age 5–15: $11, $13 and $25.

SCOTLAND'S TRAIN PASSES

Scottish Area Rover passes are sold at main railstations and Travel Centres in the area of the "ticket." All of these allow 33% discount for children 5–15. Children under 5 travel free.

   The 2 passes described below are sold at main British railstations and in the U.S.A. by BritRail Travel International, 1500 Broadway, New York, NY 10036-4015...and by Scots-American Travel Advisors, 26 Rugen Drive, Harrington Park, NJ 07640. telephone: (201) 768-5505. They do not have discounts for children.

Freedom of Scotland Travelpass Unlimited *standard*-class train travel on British Rail lines north of Berwick and Carlisle (see "England/Wales Pass" for train travel between southeast England and those cities)...also on ferries to many scenic islands, plus discounts on ferries to Orkney and Shetland islands, and travel on some local bus services.

   The 1996 prices are $159 for 8 days and $220 for 15 days.

Freedom of Scotland Flexipass Unlimited *standard*-class travel on the same train, ferry and bus services as the pass above for consecutive days. The 1996 price for any 8 days within 15 days is $185 .

NORTHERN IRELAND'S TRAIN PASSES

Both of these passes are sold in Belfast at: Tourist Information Centre, 59 North Street; NIR Travel Ltd., 28-30 Wellington Place; and Central Station.

Irish Rover Covers unlimited travel on all sceduled rail services of Northern Ireland Railways and Irish Rail. The 1996 adult prices are: £55 for any 8 days within 15 days, and £80 for any 15 days within 30 days. Children age 5-15: £27.50 and £42.50. Operates all year.

Rail Runabout Provides 7 consecutive days of unlimited train travel in Northern Ireland. The 1996 price are: £25 for adults, £12.50 for children age 5-15. Operates April-October.

COMBINING BRITAIN AND
THE CONTINENT

When planning to travel both in Britain and on the European Continent, keep in mind that the maximum value of combining a British train pass with a Eurailpass is achieved by scheduling Britain for either the start or end of a tour (see also "Eurostar" for Channel Tunnel connections). For example, to start a tour in Amsterdam and have one's itinerary then go to Paris, London, and then return to the continent for additional Eurailpass traveling would require a longer (and more expensive) Eurailpass because of consuming Eurailpass days while in Britain.

Conversely, to start a tour in London, followed by travel on the Continent, and then concluding with more travel in Britain will require a longer and more expensive British pass since the days spent on the Continent will consume British pass days.

We present in this chapter descriptions of 4 categories of rail service. First, the train connection services between London and the Continent (Paris, Brussels and Amsterdam). Next, 41 one-day rail trips that can be made comfortably out of London, with departure and arrival times, on-board-services, and what to see and do at each destination before returning to London, in most cases at dinnertime.

Third, readers will find itineraries for 4 long trips from and to London: Cork, Shannon Airport, Dublin and Edinburgh. This chapter concludes with details on 12 rail trips in Scotland from Aberdeen, Edinburgh, Glasgow and Inverness. Several of those routes are very scenic.

The extensive notes in this book about train times are intended to both help you *plan* your itinerary and are also useful after your trip begins (if you bring *Eurail Guide* along!) for making impromptu last-minute travel plans.

Before commencing any journey, always — without exception — doublecheck the

times in this book or in any published timetable, as they are subject to change without prior notice. Eurail Guide has made every effort possible to publish correct departure and arrival times, but schedules are subject to constant change.

WARNING: Many cities have 2 or more railstations. London has 8 railstations. We take pains to tell you for every trip in this book the name of the railstation from which your train departs, by noting the station in parenthesis immediately after the name of the city, such as: London (King's Cross).

All of London's railstations are interconnected by subway service, providing far easier and quicker transfers than by surface streets. For example, when entering England by rail from France, at Dover, you will come into Victoria station. To continue on to Edinburgh, it is necessary to first transfer by subway (Circle line) from Victoria (along to Thames River) to King's Cross station, on the opposite side of London from Victoria station.

A brief description of the areas served by London's 8 major railstations:

CHARING CROSS STATION This station services suburban commuters between London and Folkestone, and between London and Hastings. It connects at Dover (Priory station) with Hovercraft service to and from France.

EUSTON STATION A part of Central England and the northwestern area of Britain are reached from Euston station, starting with Coventry and Birmingham, and then running through Stafford, Chester, Liverpool, Manchester and Blackpool, on into Glasgow. Also, Holyhead, gateway to Dublin.

KING'S CROSS STATION Northeastern England (Leeds, York, Hull, Newcastle) and Edinburgh are reached by trains from King's Cross station. Newcastle is the gateway to Norway. Hull is a gateway to Denmark, Germany and Holland.

LIVERPOOL STREET STATION This station services the area immediately northeast of London: Colchester, Cambridge, Ipswich, Harwich (gateway to Holland, Germany, Austria, Yugoslavia and Norway), Norwich and King's Lynn.

PADDINGTON STATION The area in southern England, west from Weymouth (Exeter, Plymouth and Penzance), is reached out of Paddington station as is also that portion of southwestern England running north to Bristol, Swansea, Fishguard (gateway to Rosslare, at the southeastern tip of the Republic of Ireland), Gloucester, Worcester, Hereford and Oxford.

ST. PANCRAS STATION Trains going due north from London to Leicester, Derby, Nottingham and Sheffield leave from St. Pancras station.

VICTORIA STATION The London airport for charter flights is Gatwick, which is serviced from 05:30 to 23:00 by a train every 15 minutes (and hourly from 01:00 to 05:00) for the 40-minute ride to and from London's Victoria station. The transfer from airplane to train, or vice versa, is entirely indoor as the railstation at Gatwick is a part of the airport.

Victoria station services the small area of Southern England just East of but not including Portsmouth: Worthing, Brighton, Newhaven, Eastbourne, Hastings and Dover (gateway to France, Spain, Belgium, Switzerland, Italy, Austria and Yugoslavia).

WATERLOO STATION   Services South Central England: Southampton, Bournemouth and Weymouth.

HEATHROW – LONDON
UNDERGROUND CONNECTION

The train service is between Heathrow airport and every subway station on Piccadilly Line between Heathrow and Kings Cross railstation. Trains depart both terminals every 4-10 minutes 05:30-23:00 daily except Sundays and holidays, and 07:30-23:30 on Sundays. Journey time is 50–58 minutes.

GATWICK – LONDON
TRAIN CONNECTION

This service takes 30 minutes daytime, 45 minutes at night. Trains depart Gatwick Airport 00:10, 01:05, 02:05, 03:05, 04:05, 05:05, plus every 15 minutes 05:20-21:50, plus 22:20, 22:50, 23:20 and 23:50. Departures from Victoria railstation are 00:15, 01:00, 02:00, 03:00, 04:00, plus every 15 minutes 04:30-21:00, plus 21:30, 22:00, 22:30 and 23:00.

   The transfer from airplane to train, or vice versa, is entirely indoor as the railstation at Gatwick is a part of the airport.

Gatwick Express Tickets   1996 prices: *First*-class $23, *Second*-class $17.

SUMMER TIME

Britain changes to Summer Time on the last Sunday of March and converts back to Standard Time on the last Sunday of October.

DAYS OF THE WEEK VARIANCES

For the time schedules given in this book, "daily" means Monday through Sunday. Where Sunday departure and arrival times are specified in conjunction with a list of daily schedules, this refers to *additional* service on Sunday, not to substitute service.

   In other words, if a daily schedule lists departures at 10:00 and 11:12, and the Sunday schedule indicates a departure at 13:05, there are 3 departures on Sunday: at 10:00, 11:12 and 13:05.

   Conversely, if Monday-Friday or Monday-Saturday schedules show departures at 10:00 and 11:12, and there is a listing of a Sunday departure at 13:05, then the only departure on Sunday for that trip is 13:05.

The same treatment applies to "Saturday only" schedules in connection with times given as "Monday–Friday" or as "daily."

SUMMER AND WINTER SCHEDULES

In most European countries, Winter schedules usually start on the Sunday following the last Saturday of September and runs through the Saturday preceding the last Sunday in May of the following year.

British timetables differ from the Continental pattern. Summer timetables for British rail service begin on the second Monday in May. There are two changes in Winter schedules, occuring on the first Monday in October and on the first Monday in January.

Unless designated otherwise, the departure and arrival times given in this chapter are for the Summer season and apply to trips that are made from early May to early October.

HOLIDAY TRAVEL

Nearly all train, bus and subway services cease on holidays. The main holidays on which to avoid travel are all "Bank" holidays (whose dates vary) and the period from December 25 through January 1. If you cannot avoid intra-city travel on a holiday, it is advisable to reserve a taxi by telephone the day prior.

London

The capital of England. See the changing of the guard at Buckingham Palace. Downing Street, official residence of the Prime Minister. The Tower of London. London Bridge. The Houses of Parliament. The Wellington Museum (Aiseley House) and Wellington Arch. Hyde Park. Tate Gallery. The London Transport Museum at 39 Wellington Street, Covent Garden, is open daily 10:00–18:00. The Kensington Gardens complex of Royal Albert Hall, the Science Museum, Geological Museum, Natural History Museum, and the Victoria and Albert Museum (closed on Fridays). Piccadilly Circus. The National Gallery and National Portrait Gallery.

The British Museum. Dickens' House (closed Sunday). St. Paul's Cathedral. Gray's Inn. The Imperial War Museum. The Royal Botanic Gardens (Kew). Regent's Park. Westminster Abbey. Nelson's Monument in Trafalgar Square. St. James's Palace. St. James's Park. The 53-acre Green Park.

Admiralty Arch.The Museum of London. The Royal Academy. The Museum of Mankind. The Sunday orators at Speaker's Corner. Marble Arch. Lambeth Palace, the residence of the Archbishop of Canterbury.

The dragon at Temple Bar Memorial. Mansion House, the residence of the Lord Mayor of London. Tower Bridge. The South Bank Arts Centre complex of National Theatre, Queen Elizabeth Hall, Royal Festival Hall, and Hayward Gallery. The Victoria Tower. Whitehall, the compound of government offices.

One of the world's greatest food stores, in Harrods Department Store, presents a spectacle of more than 500 cheeses, 120 different breads, 21 kinds of butter, produce from California, and a meat hall 90 feet long by 60 feet wide containing hams, pork, sausages, beef and lamb. There is also venison, shellfish, poultry, salmon (smoked and fresh), tinned foods from all over the world, eggs, teas from everywhere, caviars, wine, and the list goes on forever.

Don't miss London's other great food store, in Fortnum and Mason (also a complete department store), operating since 1707 on Picadilly Circus. Open 09:30–18:00, daily except Sunday. 'Fortnums', as Londoners call it, has 3 restaurants. "The Fountain," in the basement, has an American-style soda fountain. It is open 09:30–24:00, very popular for after-theater snacks. "The Patio," on a mezzanine, offers the same light menu as "The Fountain" but also has grilled meats. It is open 09:30–16:30. The elegant fourth-floor "St. James" offers more extensive and more expensive food, open 11:30–18:00.

For a different view of food, visit Smithfield Meat Market, England's largest meat and poultry market, covering over 10 acres and employing almost 3,000 people. On a busy day, it sells in 19 hours more than 4,000 tons of meat, poultry and game: grouse, ducks, partridges, rabbits, pheasant, hams, green bacon, Danish bacon, smoked bacon, Irish bacon, lamb, beef and many exotic imported meats. Open Monday-Friday 05:00–12:00.

Near Smithfield is the very interesting 12th century St. Bartholomew the Great Church. Stroll the entire area: St. John's Lane, Charterhouse Street and many narrow alleys for a look at the London of 300 years ago.

For a different view of London, explore the city on a Sunday, by foot. Walk along Whitechapel Road to see the (still working) foundry where the Liberty Bell was cast. From Whitechapel, it's an easy walk to the Tower of London and the St. Katherine marina.

CONNECTIONS WITH THE CONTINENT

Aside from the new Channel Tunnel route (see "Eurostar" for prices, conditions, schedules), the shortest route from England to the Continent is Dover to Calais or Boulogne.

The validity of one's BritRail Pass stops or starts, as the case may be, at the British shore. Similarly, the validity of one's Eurailpass stops or starts at the Continental port where your boat ride begins or ends. In all cases, the channel boat fare is *not covered* by either pass. However, the Brit France Pass *does* include a Hovercraft roundtrip Dover–Boulogne-Dover and Dover–Calais–Dover, as well as Boulogne–Dover–Boulogne and Calais–Dover–Calais.

Regular ferries run the following routes: Dover–Calais, Dover–Oostende, Folkestone–Boulogne, Harwich–Hoek van Holland and Newhaven–Dieppe.

Hovercraft service, faster and more expensive, is provided Dover–Boulogne, Dover–Calais, Dover–Oostende, Newhaven–Dieppe, Portsmouth–Cherbourg, and Ramsgate–Dunkerque.

Both regular ferries and hovercraft carry autos. *All of the regular ferries have a restaurant.*

London - Paris via Newhaven and Dieppe   and v.v. 10

Dep. London (Vic.)	08:32 (1)	20:40	Dep. Paris (St. Laz.)	10:42 (1)	22:09
Arr. Newhaven Harbour	09:55 (1)	21:55	Dep. Rouen (Rive Dr.)	12:13	23:49
Change to a ferry.			Arr. Dieppe	13:09	00:42
Dep. Newhaven Harbour	10:30	22:30	*Change to a ferry.*		
Set your watch forward one hour,			Dep. Dieppe	14:00	02:00
except late Sept. to late Oct.			*Set your watch back one hour,*		
Arr. Dieppe	15:30	03:30	*except late Sept. to late Oct.*		
Change to a train.			Arr. Newhaven Harbour	17:00	05:00
Dep. Dieppe	15:49	04:44	*Change to a train.*		
Arr. Rouen (Rive Dr.)	16:45	05:34	Dep. Newhaven Harbour	17:35	05:40
Arr. Paris (St. Laz.)	18:16	07:01	Arr. London (Vic.)	19:05	06:45

(1) Departs 7–10 minutes earlier on Sunday.

London - Paris via Portsmouth and Le Havre (regular ferry) and v.v.

Frequent trains make the 83–108 minute ride London (Waterloo) to Portsmouth and v.v.

1030 Ferry

Dep. Portsmouth	08:30 (1)	14:45 (2)	23:00 (3)
Set your watch forward one hour, except late September to late October.			
Arr. Le Havre	15:15 (8)	21:30	07:00
Change to train. 115			
Dep. Le Havre	16:44 (10)	06:43 (4)	07:57
Arr. Paris (St. Laz.)	18:52	08:57	10:01

• • •

Dep. Paris (St. Laz.)	12:34 (5)	17:48
Arr. Le Havre	14:40	19:57
Change to a ferry. 1030		
Dep. Le Havre	16:45 (6)	23:00 (7)
Set your watch back one hour, except late September to late October.		
Arr. Portsmouth	22:30	07:00

(1) July 1-August 31: runs daily. September 1-June 30: runs daily, except Monday. (2) Runs daily January 1- December 23. (3) Early May to mid-September: runs Friday and Saturday. (4) Runs Monday-Friday, except holidays to July 8 and from August 22. (5) Runs daily, except Sundays and holidays. (6) Runs one hour earlier September 25-October 22. Runs daily except December 24, 25, 26. (7) Runs daily except December 24, 25,26. (8) Arives one hour earlier September 25-October 22. (9) Departs one hour later September 25-October 22. (10) Runs Sunday to June 26 and from September 4.

OTHER CHANNEL-CROSSING SCHEDULES

London - Paris via Calais or Boulogne   and v.v. 10

Schedules shown here are for early June to late September.

All of the trains from French ports to Paris and v.v. have light refreshments, unless designated otherwise.

Train			
Dep. London (Vic.)	08:55	09:25	12:25 (3)
Arr. Folkestone		10:51	13:59
Arr. Dover (West.)	10:26		
Change to ferry.			
Dep. Folkestone		11:15 (1)	14:30 (1)
Dep. Dover (West.)	11:00		
Set your watch forward one hour.			
Arr. Boulogne		13:15	16:30
Arr. Calais	13:30		
Change to train.			
Dep. Boulogne		13:45	16:57
Dep. Calais	14:09		
Arr. Paris (Nord)	18:19	16:12	19:35

Train			
Dep. Paris (Nord)	07:47 (4)	10:58	14:18 (3)
Arr. Calais	10:44		
Arr. Boulogne		13:20	16:50
Change to ferry.			
Dep. Calais	11:15		
Dep. Boulogne		14:00 (1)	17:15 (1)
Set your watch back one hour.			
Arr. Dover (West.)	11:45 (2)		
Arr. Folkestone		14:05	17:20
Change to train.			
Dep. Dover (West.)	12:40		
Dep. Folkestone		14:45	18:00
Arr. London (Vic.)	14:07	16:23	19:37

(1) Hoverspeed catamaran. Reservation required. Supplement charged. (2) Arrives at Dover's Eastern Docks. A free bus transfers passengers to the railstation. (3) May 29-Sept. 4. (4) July 10-Sept. 4.

London - Brussels via Oostende (Jetfoil)   12

Reservation is required on all of the London–Dover trains. Reservation is required and supplement charged for the one-class jetfoil, which has light refreshements.

Passengers from London *must* check-in at the Jetfoil Lounge in Victoria railstation and obtain the Jetfoil boarding card at least 60 minutes before train departs.

Change to jetfoil in Dover.

Dep. London (Vict.)	08:05	11:05	13:05	16:05
Dep. Dover Docks	09:35	13:20	15:30	18:25
Set your watch forward one hour.				
Arr. Oostende	12:15	16:00	18:10	20:55
Change to train.				
Dep. Oostende	12:34	16:34	18:34	21:34
Arr. Brussels (Midi)	14:43	17:43	19:43	22:43
Arr. Brussels (Nord)	12 minutes later			

London - Brussels via Oostende (regular ferry)   12

Reservation is required for all the London–Dover trains and these ferries.
   Times shown below are for Summer service (early June to late September). Change to a ferry in Dover. All of the ferries have a restaurant.

Dep. London (Vict.)	08:05	11:05	22:05
Arr. Dover Docks	09:07	12:24	23:58
Set your watch forward one hour.			
Arr. Oostende	15:30	18:45	06:00
Change to train.			
Dep. Oostende	16:34	19:34	06:34
Arr. Brussels (Midi)	17:43	20:43	07:43
Arr. Brussels (Nord)	12 minutes later		

London - Amsterdam via Hoek van Holland (regular ferry) and v.v. 5

Change to ferry in Harwich Parkeston Quay (en route to Amsterdam) and in Hoek van Holland (en route to London).

Dep. London (Liverpool Street)	09:25	19:00
Dep. Harwich	11:30 (2)	21:30 (1)
Set your watch forward one hour, except from late Sept. to late Oct.		
Arr. Hoek van Holland	19:00 (3)	07:00
Arr. Amsterdam (Cen.)	21:32	09:49

• • •

Dep. Amsterdam (Cen.)	09:32	19:48
Arr. Hoek van Holland	10:57	21:13
Dep. Hoek van Holland	12:00 (2)	22:00 (1)
Set your watch back one hour, except from late Sept. to late Oct.		
Arr. Harwich	18:00	07:00
Arr. London (Liverpool Street)	20:00	09:00

(1) Ferry reservation required. (2) Change trains. (3) Runs daily except Friday

ONE-DAY EXCURSIONS FROM LONDON

Here are 39 one-day rail trips that can be made comfortably, returning to London in most cases at dinnertime. Notes are provided on what to see and do at each destination.

The notation "frequent times" in these schedules means at least one departure (and usually more) every hour.

London - Bath - London   530

Dep. London (Pad.)	07:15 (1)	08:15 (1)	08:30 (3)	09:15 (1)	09:30 (3+4)
Arr. Bath	08:37	09:36	10:04	10:32	11:04

Sights in **Bath**: For interesting walking tours here, go to the Tourist Information Centre and purchase "Official Guidebook" and "Walks Around Bath." During Summer, guide 1½-hour tours on foot (at no charge) start at the churchyard of the abbey.

See the Roman baths. Buy a glass of curative mineral water in the 18th century Pump Room, above the baths. Visit antique shops around Abbey Green. The Circus, a group of 3-story, classical 18th century houses constructed of honey-colored Bath Stone, located on Gay Street. Nearby, the Museum of Costume in the Assembly Rooms. The Royal Crescent row of town houses. Queen Square. The shops on Pulteney Bridge.

The American Museum at Claverton Manor, open daily except Monday 14:00–17:00. The collection of Eltonware and Nailsea glass in the 14th century Clevedon Court manor house, open Wednesday, Thursday and Sunday 14:30–17:30. There is much elegant 18th century architecture here.

Bath is a great base for seeing many of the best sights in England. Several good, inexpensive motorcoach tours go to Gloucester, Salisbury, Stonehenge and Cheddar Gorge. These buses stop for photo-taking along the way.

Dep. Bath	12:12 (3)	12:27 (2)	13:12 (3)	13:27 (2)	14:12 (3+5)
Arr. London (Pad.)	14:05	14:00	15:05	15:00	16:05

(1) Runs Monday-Friday except holidays. (2) Runs Monday-Saturday except holidays. (3) Runs Sunday only. (4) Plus other departures from London at frequent times from 09:45 to 23:10. (5) Plus other departures from Bath at frequent times from 14:27 to 21:25.

London - Birmingham -London   540

Dep. London (Eus.)	07:15 (1)	07:45	08:05 (2)	08:35 (2)	09:05 (7)
Arr. Birmingham (New St.)	08:55	09:19 (9)	09:50 (10)	10:19 (10)	10:54 (2+10)

Sights in **Birmingham**: The Tourist Information Centre has brochures on walking tours. The Cadbury Company's "World Chocolate Experience" museum at its factory here features an exhibit on the history of chocolate. Visitors can sample a chocolate drink made from an ancient Aztec recipe, see chocolate being made, and sample chocolate at the factory's restaurant, ice cream parlor and souvenir shop.

See the restored 18th century water mill, Sarehole Mill. The 17th century house furnished as it was in its era, Blakesley Hall. The first (1734) English locomotive can be seen at the Science Museum.

Dep. Birmingham (New St.)	12:15 (2)	12:45 (2)	13:15 (6)	13:45 (6)	14:15 (6+8)
Arr. London (Eus.)	13:56	14:49	15:04	15:29	15:56

(1) Runs Monday-Friday except holidays. Restaurant car. (2) Runs daily except Sundays and holidays. Restaurant car. (3) Runs daily except holidays. Restaurant car. (4) Arrives 34 minutes later on Sunday. (5) Runs Monday-Friday, except holidays. (6) Runs daily, except Sundays and holidays. (7) Plus other departures from London at frequent times from 09:40 to 23:40. (8) Plus other Birmingham departures at frequent times from 14:48 to 22:48. (9) Runs Sunday only. (10) Departs 10 min. earlier Mon-Friday only, except holidays.

London - Bournemouth - London   502 + ABC 60

Most of these trains have buffet.

Dep. London (Wat.)	Frequent times Monday–Saturday: 05:40–23:45.
	Sunday: 07:45–22:45
Arr. Bournemouth	Monday–Saturday: 2 hours later
	Sunday: 2½ hours later

Sights in **Bournemouth**: A large seaside resort. Stroll through Pavillion Rock Garden. There are 3 gambling casinos. Many lovely parks and gardens.

Dep. Bournemouth	Frequent times Monday–Saturday: 05:15–23:02.
	Sunday: 06:14–21:45
Arr. London (Wat.)	Monday–Saturday: 2 hours later
	Sunday: 2½ hours later

London - Brighton - London   ABC 31

Dep. London (Vic.)	Frequent times Monday–Saturday: 05:17–01:00.
	Sunday: 07:47–23:10
Arr. Brighton	55–70 minutes later

Sights in **Brighton**: Walk from the railstation down Queen Street to the seashore and the Aquarium at Palace Pier. See the antique shops in the many alleys, called "The Lanes." The Regency architecture prevalent here. The Royal Pavillion. The ornate chandelier in Banquet Hall.

This is one of Britain's leading antique centers. An outdoor antique market is held on Saturdays starting at 07:00, on Upper Gerdner Street, near the railstation. See the collection of Art Nouveau and Art Deco furniture and furnishings in the City Museum.

Dep. Brighton	Frequent times Monday–Saturday: 06:23–23:35.
	Sunday: 07:15–22:15
Arr. London (Vict.)	55–70 minutes later

London - Bristol - London   530

Dep. London (Paddington)	Frequent times 07:15 to 23:59 (from 08:20 on Sunday)
Arr. Bristol (Temple Meads)	90 minutes later

•   •   •

Dep. Bristol (Temple Meads)	Frequent times 05:45 to 21:25 (from 07:30 on Sunday)
Arr. London (Paddington)	90 minutes later

Sights in **Bristol**: A famous seaport. Everything here is either a short walk or can be reached by bus. The city operates 1½-hour guided walking tours June, July and August from the Exchange on Corn Street at 11:00 on Monday and Tuesday, at 14:30 on other days. Some of Bristol can be seen from a tour boat at the harbor. That tour operates daily at 12:00, 14:00, 15:00 and 16:00.

See the many excellent Georgian buildings on Royal York Crescent, Cornwallis Crescent, Windsor Terrace, West Mall, Caledonia Place, Queen Square and Berkeley Square. The Christmas Steps, built in 1669. The 12th century St. James' Church.

The John Wesley Chapel, world's first Methodist preaching house, with a bronze statue of Wesley in the courtyard. The 11th century St. Mary-le-Port Church. St. John's Church. The 13th century St. Mary Redcliffe, one of England's largest churches. The 12th century Cathedral.

The exhibit of period furniture in the 18th century Georgian House. The view from the top of Cabot Tower, on Brandon Hill. The collection of porcelain, models of early sailing ships and paintings of the waterfront in the Bristol Museum and Art Gallery, open every day 10:00–17:00. See the beautiful gardens and the rare animals (including the Okapi and the white tigers) at the Zoo. Brunel's Clifton Suspension Bridge, built in 1864, straddling Avon Gorge, 245 feet above the water. Tour Brunel's iron steampship, The Great Britain (the first ocean screw steamship, launched in 1843), returned to Bristol in 1970 from the Falkland Islands. It is open 10:00–18:00.

London - Cardiff - London   530

Dep. London (Paddington)	Frequent times from 07:00 to 22:00 (from 09:00 on Sunday)
Arr. Cardiff (Central)	2 hours later

Sights in **Cardiff**: Llandaff Cathedral. Cardiff Castle. The National Museum of Wales, featuring Welsh handicraft and art. It is a short train ride from Cardiff's Queen Street railstation to **Caerphilly**, whose castle is nearly as large as Windsor Castle and has many interesting exhibits.

Dep. Cardiff (Central)	Frequent times from 06:25 to 19:25 (from 08:00 on Sunday)
Arr. London (Paddington)	2 hours later

London - Bristol - Cardiff - London

As these schedules indicate, it is easy to visit both Cardiff and Bristol in one day.

These schedules are for travel daily, except Sundays and holidays.

530		530	
Dep. London (Pad.)	08:15	Dep. Cardiff (Cen.)	16:25 (1)
Arr. Bristol (T.M.)	09:51	Arr. London (Pad.)	18:35
Sightsee in Bristol			
532			
Dep. Bristol (T.M.)	12:25		
Arr. Cardiff (Cen.)	13:11		

(1) Plus other departures from Cardiff at 17:25, 18:25, 19:25 and 21:25.

Sights in **Bristol:** The Temple Meads railstation, completed in 1841, is one of the most beautiful in England.

In Summer, open-top buses make a circle tour that includes Temple Meads, Clifton Bridge, the Zoo, downtown, the harbor and the 13th century Church of St. Mary Redcliffe (one of England's largest churches). Queen Elizabeth I described it as "the fairest, goodliest and most famous parish church in England."

London - Cambridge - London 581

Dep. London (King's X)	06:52(1)	07:42 (2)	08:45 (5)	09:45 (2)	10:45 (2+4)
Arr. Cambridge	70–80 minutes later				

• • •

Dep. Cambridge	Monday–Saturday: frequent times from 06:54 to 23:10
	Sundays: frequent times from 14:36 to 22:41
Arr. London (King's X)	70–80 minutes later

(1) Runs Monday–Friday, except holidays. (2) Runs daily, except Sundays and holidays. (3) Runs Sunday only. (4) Plus other departures from London Monday–Saturday at frequent times from 10:45 (2) to 21:45 (3) (5) Runs Monday-Saturday except holidays.

Sights in **Cambridge:** To see buildings that have housed great colleges for more than 700 years, take bus #101 to Market Street. See King's College Chapel and Queen's College. Visit the Wren Library at Trinity College. The medieval and renaissance armor, weapons, tapestries and manuscripts in the Fitzwilliam Museum on Trumpington Street.

The Botanical Gardens. On Castle Street, see the Folk Museum and the modern paintings and sculpture at Kettles Yard Art Gallery. Hire a boat at Mill Bridge or Anchor Inn, and paddle along the idyllic Cam River. Four miles away is the American Cemetery

London - Canterbury - London   ABC 10 + 17

For this 2-hour ride, there are frequent departures both from London's Waterloo and Charing Cross railstations to Canterbury's West railstation. There are also frequent departures from London's Victoria station to Canterbury's East station. The walk from Canterbury's *West* station to the famous Cathedral allows you to view interesting buildings.

Canterbury's *East* railstation is nearer the Cathedral and therefore more convenient to use for returning to London after visiting the Cathedral than the West station. A departure from Canterbury's East station will take you to London's Victoria station. Or, you can depart from Canterbury's West station, arriving London's Waterloo or Charing Cross stations.

Sights in **Canterbury**: Guided tours (Monday–Friday) start at 14:15 at a kiosk in Longmarket, a pedestrian area next to Christ Church Gate.

See the great Cathedral, housing the tomb of Thomas a Becket. Medieval inns (Falstaff, Beverlie, Olive Branch). The cemetery, where Christopher Marlowe and Joseph Conrad are buried. The Old Weaver's House, built in 1500. Excavated Roman ruins. Plays, ballet, cricket.

London - Sevenoaks - Chartwell - London   ABC 15

There are many departures daily from London's Charing Cross railstation for the 45-minute ride to Sevenoaks. Take a taxi for the 7-mile trip from Sevenoaks to Chartwell.

Sights in **Chartwell:** The country house that Winston Churchill bought in 1922, where he painted and wrote his books during the years he was out of power. You will see here the best collection of Churchilliana in the world: his collection of eccentric hats, his World War II "jump suit," Knight of the Garter uniform, many of his paintings, and a model of the Invasion Day harbor at Arromanches. Also the brick wall and cottage he built with his own hands on a small part of the 79 acres there. The main house is open Wednesday, Thursday, Saturday and Sunday from April to mid-October.

London - Chester - London   555

| Dep. London (Euston) | 10:20 (1) | | Dep. Chester | 15:14 (3) | 17:20 (3) |
| Arr. Chester | 12:35 | | Arr. London (Euston) | 18:02 | 20:08 |

(1) Runs Monday-Friday, except holidays. Restaurant car. (2) Runs daily, except Sundays and holidays. Restaurant car Monday-Friday. (3) Runs Sunday only.

Sights in **Chester**: The 2-mile-long Roman Wall. The excellent collection of Roman artifacts (glass, tools, coins, weapons, tombstones) at Grosvenor Museum. The "Rows," long covered balconies (to protect shoppers from rain) that are full-length streets above the streets of Chester. These are lined with shops. Also see St. Werburgh's Cathedral. The castle overlooking the **River Dee**. The marvelous carving of animals and historic scenes on the front of the 17th century Bishop Lloyd's House on Watergate Street. The antique shops on Lower Bridge Street and Watergate Street. The 16th century mansion, Stanley Palace. The 30-minute slide show of Chester's history, in the British Heritage Centre.

Sightseeing bus tours start in Market Square, opposite the Tourist Office at the Victorian Gothic Town Hall. Guided *walking* tours of 1 to 3 hours cost £1.95 for adults in 1992 (£1.25 for children and senior citizens). Leave from the Tourist Information Office at the Town Hall at 10:45 (May-October: daily. November–April: daily, except Sunday)...and at 14:30 (April–October: daily. November–March: daily, except Sunday).

The 130-acre open-space Zoo, just north of the city, attracts nearly 1,000,000 people a year.

London - Chichester - London   ABC 35

This service is daily. Most of these trains have light refreshments Monday–Saturday.

Dep. London (Vic.)	Frequent times 07:50 – 22:21
Arr. Chichester	About 100 minutes later

Sights in **Chichester**: The Marc Chagall stained glass window and the John Piper Holy Trinity tapestry in the 12th century Norman Cathedral. The 2nd century Roman wall. The 16th century arcaded Market Cross. The 200-year-old "stately homes" on streets called East, West, North and South Pallant.

Go two miles westto see the museum and mosaic floors in the 3rd century Palace at Fishbourne, the largest Roman residence in Britain, open daily, March through October. See the attractive mosaic floors in the 1st century Roman villa at **Bignor**, 2 miles east, open daily except Monday, March through October.

There is extraordinary fillegree woodcarving in the 17th century Petworth House, 13 miles northeast. It is open April through October on Wednesday, Thursday, Saturday and Sunday 14:00–18:00.

A few miles west of Chichester is an 11th century Saxon church and a marvelous yacht harbor at **Bosham**, a beautiful seashore village.

Dep. Chichester	Frequent times 07:30 to 21:16
Arr. London (Vic.)	About 100 minutes later

London - Coventry - London   540

Dep. London (Eus.)	07:15 (2)	07:35 (1)	08:05 (1)	08:35 (1)	09:05 (1)	09:35 (1+9)
Arr. Coventry	08:20	08:48 (11)	09:18 (11)	09:48 (11)	10:23 (11)	10:48

Sights in **Coventry**: Completely rebuilt since the Nazi air attacks, Coventry was the site of

Lady Godiva's notorious horseback ride. See the Graham Sutherland tapestry, the abstract stained-glass windows and the enormous engraved glass wall at the new (1962) Cathedral.

Dep. Coventry	12:07 (4)	12:37 (6)	13:07 (4)	13:37 (6)	14:07 (6)	14:37 (6+10)
Arr. London (Eus.)	13:26	13:56	14:29	15:04	15:29	15:56

(1) Runs daily, except Sundays and holidays. Restaurant car. (2) Runs Monday–Friday, except holidays. Restaurant car. (3) Runs daily, except holidays. (4) Runs daily, except holidays. Restaurant car Monday–Friday. (5) Runs Monday–Friday, except holidays. (6) Runs daily, except Sundays and holidays. (7) Runs daily, except holidays. Restaurant car Monday–Saturday. (8) Runs daily, except Saturdays and holidays. (9) Plus other departures from London at 10:05 (1+11), 11:05 (1+11), 11:35 (1+11), 12:05 (1+11), 12:35 (2 +11), 13:05 (2+11) and 13:35 (1+11). (10) Plus other departures from Coventry at 15:07 (4), 15:37 (1), 16:07 (6), 16:37 (1), 17:07 (4), 17:37 (6), 18:07 (4), 18:37 (6), 19:37 (5), 20:37 (6) and 21:37 (6). (11) Departs 10 minutes earlier on Monday-Friday, except holidays.

London - Dover - London   ABC 10 + 506

Dep. London (Char. Cr)	08:30 (1)	09:30 (1)	10:00 (1)
Arr. Dover (Priory)	10:17	11:17	11:41

Sights in **Dover**: It is a short walk downhill from the Priory railstation to the village. Or, you can ride a bus. See the legendary white cliffs. The mighty castle. The busy harbor. The museum in the 4th century Roman painted house.

Dep. Dover (Priory)	15:05 (1)	15:50 (1)	16:05 (3)	16:51 (1+9)
Arr. London (Char. Cr)	16:46	18:15 (1)	17:56 (1)	18:47

(1) Runs daily, except Sundays and holidays. Light refreshments. (2) Runs Sunday only. (3) Runs daily, except Sundays and holidays. (4) Runs daily, except Saturday. Light refreshments Monday–Friday. (5) Arrives 19:15 on Sunday. (6) Runs Saturday only. Light refreshments. (7) Runs daily. (8) Runs Saturday only. (9) Plus other Dover departures at 17:05 (1), 17:49 (1), 18:49 (1), 19:49 (1) and 20:49 (1).

London - Exeter - London   (main line via Reading)

(Paddington station)   510

Dep. London (Pad.)	07:40 (1)	09:03 (2)	09:15 (4)	09:45 (1)	10:15 (4)
Arr. Exeter (St. David's)	10:16	11:12	11:57	12:40	12:47

Dep. London (Pad.)	10:35 (1)	11:35 (2)	11:45 (2)	12:35 (2)
Arr. Exeter (St. David's)	12:36	13:52	14:30	14:41 (12)

Sights in **Exeter**: The 11th century Cathedral, with its 300-foot nave and row of statutes. Rougemont Castle. The Mint. The underground water channel at Princesshay. The paintings and oak paneling in Exeter Guildhall.

The exhibit of boats from all parts of the world at the very interesting Maritime Museum.

Dep. Exeter (St. David's)	14:37 (1)	15:02 (2)	15:29 (1)	15:42	16:37 (1)
Arr. London (Pad.)	17:05	17:25 (1)	17:45	18:25 (4)	18:40

Dep. Exeter (St. David's)	16:57 (4)	17:29 (1)	17:38 (2)	18:13 (2)	18:57 (4+11)
Arr. London (Pad.)	19:50	19:45	20:50	21:05	21:50

(1) Runs Monday-Friday, except holidays. (2) Runs Saturday only. (3) Runs daily, except holidays. (4) Runs Sunday only. (5) Runs daily, except Sundays and holidays. Restaurant car Monday-Friday. (6) Runs daily, except Sundays and holidays. (7) Runs daily, except Saturdays and holidays. (8) Arrives 17:25 on Sunday. (9) Runs Saturday and Sunday. (10) Runs daily, except Sundays and holidays. Restaurant car. (11) Plus other departures from Exeter at 19:37 (1) and 20:07 (4), arriving London 22:10 and 23:05. (12) Runs until September 17.

OR

London - Exeter - London   (via Salisbury)

Most of these trains have light refreshments.

(Waterloo Station) 511					
Dep. London (Waterloo)	07:09 (1)	07:35 (2)	08:35 (3)	08:55 (4)	10:12 (2)
Arr. Exeter (Central)	10:23	10:54	11:36	12:20	12:58
Arr. Exeter (St. David's)	5 minutes later				

• • •

Dep. Exeter (St. David's)	15:35 (2)	16:18 (4)	17:41 (1)	18:22 (2)	19:15 (4)
Dep. Exeter (Central)	5 minutes later				
Arr. London (Waterloo)	18:43	19:44	21:17	22:22	22:35

(1) Runs Monday–Friday, except holidays. (2) Runs Saturday only. (3) Runs daily, except Sundays and holidays. (4) Runs Sunday only. (5) Runs daily, except holidays. (6) Arrives 21:44 on Saturday.

London - Greenwich - London   suburban train

Sights in **Greenwich**: Take the Docklands Light Railway, opposite the Tower of London, for the 20-minute ride to the "Island Gardens" terminus. Walk from it through the pedestrian tunnel that goes under the Thames River, ending next to the famous 1870 clipper ship Cutty Sark. Near the Cutty Sark, see the 53-foot Gypsy Moth sailboat which Chichester sailed solo around the world in 1966–67. Both Cutty Sark and Gypsy Moth are open May–September 14:30–18:00 daily…October–April 11:00–17:00 Monday–Saturday and 14:30–17:00 Sunday.

Visit the Royal Observatory's museum of navigation, astronomy and chronometry (astrolabes, hourglasses, clockwork planetariums, quadrants, chronometers). See the Meridian Building's brass strip which marks the division of the eastern and western hemispheres. All distances and time worldwide are measured from this, the prime meridian.

See the marvelous exhibits (ship models, scientific instruments, marine paintings, chronometers, naval uniforms) in the National Maritime Museum.

Both the Royal Observatory and the Maritime Museum are open Monday–Saturday 10:00–17:00, Sunday 14:00–17:00 (October–April) and 14:00–18:00 (May–September).

See the enormous Painted Hall in the Royal Naval College, open daily except Thursday 14:30–17:00. Lunch in one of the good "pubs" at the riverside.

For the return to London, a boat ride on the Thames is an enjoyable alternative to the train.

London - Hampton Court - London   ABC 50

Dep. London (Waterloo)	Monday–Saturday: Frequent times from 06:22 to 23:24
	Sunday: Frequent times from 07:37 to 23:07
Arr. Hampton Court	35 minutes later

Sights in **Hampton Court**: This is the riverside Palace built by Cardinal Wolsey and then given to Henry VIII, after he expressed his desire to have it. Walk through the ancient maze.

Dep. Hampton Court	Monday–Saturday: Frequent times from 06:08 to 22:39
	Sunday: Frequent times from 08:06 to 23:06
Arr. London (Waterloo)	35 minutes later

London - Hastings - London   ABC 501

All of these trains have light refreshments.

Dep. London (Char. X)	08:15 (1)	09:10	10:10 (2)	11:10 (2)	12:10 (2)
Arr. Hastings	09:43	10:44	11:39	12:38	13:38

Sights in **Hastings**: This is where William became the Conqueror, of the Saxons. Take buses #5, #252, #485 or #486 to see the ancient battlefield. Visit the old fishing harbor and stroll the 3-mile promenade along the beach. Obtain a printed description of the Castle at the Tourist Information Center, 4 Robertson Terrace.

See the 243-foot-long tapestry in Town Hall, illustrating the 81 greatest events of British history since 1066: the battle of Hastings, the Boston Tea Party, the first television broadcast, etc.

Dep. Hastings	13:52 (3)	14:11 (2)	15:11 (2)	15:52 (3)	16:10 (3+6)
Arr. London (Char. X)	15:19	15:53	17:04	17:19	17:55

(1) Runs Monday-Friday, except holidays. (2) Runs daily, except holidays. (3) Runs daily, except Sundays and holidays. (4) Runs Saturday only. (5) Runs daily, except Saturdays and holidays. (6) Plus other departures from Hastings at frequent times from 17:11 to 21:11.

London - Isle of Wight (Yarmouth) - London   (via Lymington)

There are 148 miles of well-posted footpaths on Wight, including a 60-mile path along the entire coastline of this island that measures 13 miles at its widest by 23 miles at its longest. Also several bus lines. Many quiet beaches. Good fishing.

Twenty-two orchid species grow here. See the dinosaur bones in the Museum of Wight Geology over the Public Library. Carisbrooke Castle. Quarr Abbey, near Ryde. Take the boat trip that starts at Alum Bar.

ABC 60 (*Train*)			*ABC 61* (*Ferry*)		
Dep. London (Wat.)	08:32 (1)	09:32 (1)	Dep. Yarmouth	14:00 (1)	14:30 (1+2)
Arr. Brockenhurst	09:55	10:53	Arr. Lym. Pier	14:30	15:00
Change trains. ABC 61			*Change to train*		
Dep. Brockenhurst	09:58	10:57	Dep. Lym. Pier	14:40	15:10
Arr. Lym. Pier	10:07	11:06	Arr. Brockenhurst	14:49	15:19
Change to ferry.			*Change trains. ABC 60*		
Dep. Lym. Pier	10:15	11:15	Dep. Brockenhurst	14:58	15:38
Arr. Yarmouth	10:45	11:45	Arr. London (Wat.)	16:36	17:06

(1) Runs Monday–Saturday. (2) Plus other Yarmouth departures every 30 minutes from 15:00 to 18:30, plus 19:30, 20:30 and 21:00.

London - Kings Lynn - London   581

Dep. London (Kings X)	08:45 (1)	09:45 (1)	10:45 (1)	11:45 (1)
Arr. Kings Lynn	10:25	11:29	12:25	13:29

Sights in **Kings Lynn**: The "Town Trail" brochure, available at the City Information Center, is very helpful for touring the winding, twisting streets here in one of England's most historic towns.

See the attractive merchants' houses on Queen Street. The King John Cup and one of the oldest paper books in the world (the Red Register), at the Treasury in the 15th century Town Hall. The country market, every Tuesday near Duke's Head Hotel and every Saturday opposite Town Hall.

Dep. Kings Lynn	14:03 (1)	15:10 (5)	16:02 (1)	16:18 (3+6)
Arr. London (Kings X)	15:49	16:49	17:49	18:17

(1) Runs Monday–Saturday, except holidays. (2) Runs daily, except holidays. (3) Runs Sunday only. (4) Runs Saturday and Sunday. (5) Runs Monday-Friday, except holidays. (6) Plus other departures from Kings Lynn at 17:05 (1), 17:18 (3), 18:09 (5), 18:18 (3), 19:09 (5), 19:18 (3), 20:18 (3), 20:42 (1), 21:14 (3), 21:42 (7) and 22:14 (5). (7) Runs Saturdays only.

London - Leicester - London 560

Dep. London (St. Pan.)	07:00 (1)	07:30 (2)	08:00 (3)	08:30 (4+13)
Arr. Leicester	08:20	08:45	09:13	09:48

Sights in **Leicester**: The Jewry Wall, to see outstanding Roman ruins. The Church of St. Mary de Castro.

Dep. Leicester	12:30 (1)	13:00 (4)	13:30 (1)	14:00 (9+14)
Arr. London (St. Pan.)	13:47	14:15	14:50	15:17

(1) Runs Monday-Friday, except holidays. (2) Runs Saturday only. (3) Runs Monday–Friday, except holidays. Restaurant car. (4) Runs Monday-Saturday, except holidays. (5) Runs Sunday only. (6) Arrives 30 minutes later on Sunday. (7) Runs daily, except Saturday. Restaurant car Monday-Friday. (8) Runs Monday-Saturday, except holidays. Restaurant car Monday-Friday. (9) Runs daily, except holidays. (10) Runs daily, except Saturdays and holidays. (11) Runs daily, except holidays. (12) Runs Monday-Thursday. (13) Plus other London departures at 09:00 (3), 09:30 (3), 10:00 (3), 10:30 (3), 11:00 (1), 11:30 (4), 12:00 (1) and 12:30 (1). (14) Plus other Leicester departures at 14:30 (1), 14:45 (14), 15:00 (1), 15:30 (9), 15:57 (5), 16:30 (1),17:30 (10), 18:00 (10), 18:30 (11), 19:30 (11), 20:00 (5), 20:30 (4). (14) Runs Saturdays and Sundays only.

London - Lincoln - London

570

Dep. London (Kings X)	07:00 (3)	08:20 (3)	09:10 (3)	11:10 (3)
Arr. Newark (Northgate)	08:23	09:31	10:26	12:26
Change trains. 574				
Dep Newark	08:54 (6)	10:45 (1)	12:10 (7)	12:45 (1)
Arr. Lincoln (Cen.)	09:19	11:10	12:38	13:10

Sights in **Lincoln**: The wonderful Cathedral. Newport Arch. Roman relics in the City and County Museums. The houses on High Bridge.

Dep. Lincoln (Cen.)	13:13 (7)	15:24 (1)	16:57 (8)	17:17 (6)	19:15 (7)
Arr. Newark	13:40	15:54	17:27	17:47	19:39
Change trains. 570					
Dep Newark	14:21	16:03 (6)	17:14	18:10 (6)	20:31 (3)
Arr. London (Kings X)	15:45	17:33	18:47	19:37	21:57

(1) Runs daily, except Sundays and holidays. (2) Runs daily, except Sundays and holidays. Restaurant car Monday-Friday. (3) Runs Monday–Friday, except holidays. Restaurant car. (4) Runs daily, except Sundays and holidays. Restaurant car. (5) Runs daily, except Saturdays and holidays. (6) Runs Monday-Friday, except holidays.

London - Norwich - London   580

Dep. London (L'pool)	07:30 (1)	08:00 (2)	08:30 (4)	09:30 (4)	10:30 (5+8)
Arr. Norwich	09:26	09:42	10:23	11:23	12:23

Sights in **Norwich**: Norwich Grammar School. (Its alumni include Lord Nelson.) The Cathedral. The collection of lace, pottery, teapots, paintings and coins at the Museum in the Castle, built in 1068 by William the Conqueror.

Walk down the Elm Hill alley. See the view of Norwich from the Castle. Assembly House. The Strangers Hall. The 16th century house on the 12th century High Bridge.

Dep. Norwich	13:05 (5)	14:05 (6)	15:05 (6)	16:05 (5)	17:05 (5+9)
Arr. London (L'pool)	14:53	15:52	16:52	17:58	18:53

(1) Runs Saturday only. (2) Runs Monday–Friday, except holidays. Restaurant car. (3) Runs daily, except holidays. (4) Runs daily, except Sundays and holidays. Restaurant car. (5) Runs daily, except holidays. Restaurant car Monday-Saturday. (6) Runs daily, except holidays. (7) Runs daily, except Sundays and holidays. (8) Plus another London departure at 11:30 (7). (9) Plus other Norwich departures at 18:05 (5), 19:05 (6) and 20:40 (6).

London - Nottingham - London   560

Dep. London (St. Pan.)	07:30 (7)	08:30 (2)	09:15 (7)	10:30 (8)	12:00 (2+10)
Arr. Nottingham	09:11	10:14	11:12	12:11 (5)	13:07

Sights in **Nottingham**: The Duke of Newcastle's castle. which was a new Newcastle castle in 1679...with its art collection. The great council house. The Natural History Museum in Wollaton Hall.

Dep. Nottingham	12:33 (2)	13:39	14:24 (7)	14:38 (2)	15:33 (2+11)
Arr. London (St. Pan.)	14:15	15:17 (2)	16:02	16:29	17:17

(1) Runs daily, except Sundays and holidays. (2) Runs Monday-Friday, except holidays. (3) Runs daily, except Sundays and holidays. Restaurant car Monday–Friday. (4) Runs daily, except holidays. (5) Arrives 30–50 minutes later on Sunday. (6) Runs daily, except Saturday and holidays. (7) Runs Saturday only. (8) Runs Sunday only. (9) Runs Saturday and Sunday. (10) Plus other departures from London at 12:15 (7) and 13:30 (5), arriving Nottingham 14:14 and 15:11. (11) Plus other departures from Nottingham at 16:33 (2), 17:33 (2), 18:02 (8), 19:03 (1) and 19:30 (8), arriving London 17:50, 18:23, 19:07, 19:34, 20:01, 21:03 and 21:36.

London - Oxford - London   525

| Dep. London (Pad.) | 08:20 (6) | 08:48 (2) | 09:03 (3) | 09:18 (2) | 09:48 (2+5) |
| Arr. Oxford | 60–70 minutes later | | | | |

Sights in **Oxford**: Daily guided tours by open-top, double-decker bus depart the railstation every 15 minutes 09:30–17:30 (until 18:30 in July and August). The 1994 prices were £6 for adults, £1.50 for children 5-11 years old.

This is the home of one of the greatest universities in the world, comprising 23 different colleges. Start your stroll at the center of Oxford (Carfax Tower), where the Information Center is located. There is bus service from the railstation to Carfax Tower.

Begin by walking south from Carfax Tower, down St. Aldates Street to Folly Bridge, the Cathedral and the numerous portraits (John Wesley, William Penn, Lewis Carroll, William Gladstone) at Christ Church College. Founded by Cardinal Wolsey and Henry VIII, it is the largest and most splendid of all the colleges here.

Later, see Merton College and Corpus Christi before continuing on to Oriel and then into High Street. See Bodleian Library, which has a copy of every book published in England. See the decorative bookcases in the library of Queen's College. Most popular among visitors is Magdalen College, with its beautiful main quadrangle.

At 20:55, hear "Great Tom's" 101 strokes every night as the heavy bell calls the original number of Osney Abbey's students to return to their rooms before the nightly closing of its gates.

Stroll the lane behind Holywell Street to see attractive Tudor and Elizabethan houses. There are many late 18th century houses on Beaumont Street.

| Dep. Oxford | Frequent times from 07:09 to 22:38 |
| Arr. London (Pad.) | 60–70 minutes later |

(1) Runs daily, except Saturdays and holidays. (2) Runs daily, except Sundays and holidays. (3) Runs Sunday only. (4) Runs daily, except holidays. (5) Plus other departures from London at 10:07 (2), 11:07 (2), 11:48 (2), 12:07 (2), 12:40, 13:07 (2), 13:40 (3) and frequent other times until 23:48. (6) Runs Monday-Friday except holidays.

Nearby: Blenheim Palace (Churchill's Birthplace)

To see lovely Blenheim Palace, take a bus in Oxford from Gloucester Green bus station for the 8-mile trip to **Woodstock**. This magnificent 18th century structure was the birthplace of Winston Churchill in 1874.

A gift from Britain to the Duke of Marlborough after this ancestor of Churchill defeated the French in 1704 at Blenheim in Bavaria, the beautiful 300-room mansion is open daily March–October, with guided tours 11:30–17:00.

Letters, documents, photos, even a lock of Churchill's hair (at the age of 5) are exhibited in the tiny room where he was born prematurely and unexpectedly on November 30, 1874, in his mother's seventh month of pregnancy.

Other rooms throughout the palace have more memorabilia: some of Churchill's paintings (see "London–Chartwell"), recordings of his speeches, his letters, etc. A visit here is worthwhile if only to see the 180-foot-long library, with its marvelous Willis pipe organ.

There is time in the same day to visit nearby Bladon Churchyard. A simple tombstone there that reads merely "Winston Leonard Spencer Churchill 1874/1965" marks the burial place (alongside his American mother Jenny Spencer) of the greatest Englishman of the last 1,000 years.

London - Penzance - London   515

Reservation is advisable for all of these trains, especially for sleeping cars and pullman service

Dep. Lon. (Pad.)	07:35 (1)	07:40 (2)	09:03 (1)	10:15 (3)	12:15 (3)
Arr. Penzance	12:50	13:20	14:15	15:55	18:00

Dep. Lon. (Pad.)	13:35 (2)	14:15 (3)	15:35 (2)	17:35 (9)	17:55 (1+17)
Arr. Penzance	19:00	19:50	21:00	22:30	23:20

• • •

Dep. Penzance	05:15 (9)	06:45 (1)	08:36 (3)	09:38 (1)	10:39 (3)	11:29 (3)
Arr. Lon. (Pad.)	10:00	11:50	13:45	14:55	16:30	17:25

Dep. Penzance	12:40 (3)	14:45 (2)	15:40 (3)	16:41 (1)	17:16 (3)	22:15 (15)
Arr. Lon. (Pad.)	18:45	19:45	21:05	22:10	23:05	06:10

(1) Runs Saturday only. (2) Runs Monday–Friday except holidays. (3) Runs Sunday only. (4) Runs daily, except Sundays and holidays. Restaurant car. (5) Runs Monday–Thursday (restaurant car) and Saturday. (6) Runs Friday (restaurant car) and Saturday. (7) Arrives 18:50 on Saturday. (8) Runs Friday and Saturday. (9) Runs Monday–Friday, except holidays. Pullman service (for which reservation is advisable) availabe in first-class. (10) Runs daily, except Sundays and holidays. (11) Runs Saturday and Sunday. (12) Arrives 30–50 minutes later on Sun. (13) Runs daily, except holidays. (14) Runs Monday-Friday, except holidays. Restaurant car. (15) Runs daily, except Saturday. Carries a sleeping car. Coach is second-class. Light refreshments. (16) Runs Monday-Friday. (17) Plus other London departures at 18:35 (18) and 23:55 (15), arriving Penzanee 00:10 and 08:19. (18) Runs Friday + Sunday.

Penzance and the rest of Cornwall deserve a stay of several days, although Penzance can be visited on a one-day train excursion from London. Sights in **Penzance**: Take the walk described in the free brochure called "A day in Chapel Street, Abbey Street and Quay Street" and visit Egyptian Shop, the Admiral Benbow Inn, the Nautical Museum and Morrab Gardens. See the view of Mount's Bay from Bolitho Gardens.

It is only a 10-mile bus trip to **Land's End**, the westernmost edge of England and a beautiful seascape of waves crashing against the granite cliffs. In another direction, it is also only a 10-mile bus ride to **St. Ives**, a quaint fishing village and the location of The Hepworth Gallery, containing the work of Britain's best-known sculptress. (Both buses leave from the terminal next to the railstation.)

Go a mere 3 miles by city bus to **Marazion** and then by small motorboat to visit **St. Michael's Mount,** a tiny island only a half-mile offshore. There has been a church at the summit since 1135. The castle has been occupied by the St. Aubyn family from 1659 to the present day. Visitors are allowed to enter most of the rooms of the castle and are provided a brochure describing its history and the many interesting contents: furniture, costumes, guns, maps, portraits, banners.

Penzance is also the gateway to the more than 100 **Isles of Scilly**. The largest island is the 3-miles-by-2-miles St. Mary's. For information, about the 2½-hour ferry-boat ride to it (600 passengers), contact Isles of Scilly Steamship Company, Quay St., Penzance, Cornwall TR18 4BD, United Kingdom.

There is 20-minute helicopter service from Penzance to both St. Mary's Island and Tresco Island. For current schedules, write to: British International Helicopters, Heliport, Eastern Green, Cornwall, England.

The northern half of **Tresco**, dominated by the ruins of the 16th century King Charles Castle and the 17th century Cromwell's Castle, is windswept and treeless. Its southern half, lush and semitropical, has wide beaches, a roofless 16th century stone fort from which there are beautiful views, and the marvelous Abbey Gardens with its collection of restored figureheads salvaged from ships that were wrecked in this area.

There is boat service from Tresco to **St. Mary's**, the commercial center of the archipelago, where the main attractions are a 16th century Star Castle and a museum open every day except rainless Sundays 09:30–12:30, 13:30–16:30 and 19:30–21:00 (old rowboats, Roman pottery, stone tools).

St. Mary's also offers sandy beaches (washed by frigid water), many beautiful gardens of sub-tropical plants, coastal walks, nature trails, and a 9-hole golf course along the seacoast. Small launches can be taken to the other inhabited islands: **Bryher**, **St. Agnes** and **St. Martin's**.

London - Portsmouth - London   ABC 56 + 504

See Cook's table 509 for service to Portsmouth from London's Victoria railstation and Gatwick Airport.

Dep. London (Waterloo)	07:15 (1)	07:23 (12)	08:15 (5)	08:45 (12)	09:15 (5+10)
Arr. Portsmouth (Hbr.)	08:40	08:53	09:42	10:33	10:40

Sights in **Portsmouth**: England's great naval base. See Lord Nelson's flagship H.M.S. Victory, which won the battle of Trafalgar over the combined Spanish and French fleets. The nearby Victory Museum (Nelson relics, good marine paintings, ship models) at the Naval Yard. Nearby is Henry VIII's man-of-war, "Mary Rose," raised in 1982 from the seabed where it had lain since it sank in 1545.

The Dickens Museum at the house where the author was born, 393 Commercial Road. Many fine 17th and 18th century houses on Lombard Street and High Street.

Dep. Portsmouth (Hbr.)	14:17 (6)	15:02 (5)	15:17 (7)	16:02 (8)	16:20 (4)	16:36 (12+11)
Arr. London (Waterloo)	15:59	16:30	16:59	17:33	17:59	18:29

(1) Runs Saturday only. (2) Runs daily, except Sundays and holidays. Light refreshments. Monday-Friday. (3) Arrives 40 minutes later on Saturday. (4) Runs Sunday only. (5) Runs daily, except Sundays and holidays. Light refreshments. (6) Runs daily, except Sundays and holidays. (7) Runs Saturday and Sunday. (8) Runs daily, except holidays. Light refreshments. (9) Runs daily, except holidays. (10) Plus other London departures at 10:15 (8), 10:48 (6), 11:15 (8) and 11:48 to 22:50. (11) Plus other departures from Portsmouth at frequent times 17:02 to 22:17. (12) Runs Monday-Friday only, except holidays.

London - Isle of Wight (Shanklin) - London   (via Portsmouth)

As these schedules indicate, it is easy to visit both Portsmouth and the Isle of Wight in one day by stopping-over in Portsmouth at 08:53 or 09:42…until 11:30, 12:00 or 12:30.

504

Dep. London (Wat.)	07:23 (1)	08:15 (2)	08:25 (3)	08:45 (2)	09:15 (4+11)
Arr. Portsmoth (Hbr.)	08:53	09:42	10:00	10:33	10:40
Change to ferry. ABC 57					
Dep. Portsmouth (Hbr.)	09:30	10:00	10:30	11:00	11:30
Arr. Ryde Pier Head	09:48	10:18	10:48	11:18	11:48
Change to train.					
Dp. Ryde Pier Head	10:00	10:22	11:00	11:22	12:00
Arr. Shanklin	10:25	10:45	11:25	11:45	12:25

There are full-day and half-day bus tours of the island, starting from Ryde Esplanade.

Sights in **Ryde**: Six miles of pretty beaches. many nice gardens. Take the 9-mile island train from Ryde Pier to Shanklin. En route is Ryde Esplanade, a working-class resort. A 3-mile steam railway roundtrip from there offers pretty views.

Sights in **Shanklin**: One of Britain's loveliest towns. Ten minutes' walk from the railstation there are views of the sea and farms from East Cliff Promenade. On the way back to Shanklin, walk through the Chine (deep ravine) to the mile-long beach and see lovely Old Village. Buses (on Carter Avenue, 2 blocks from the railstation) go to Cowes on the north coast. Near Cowes is Osborne House, queen Victoria's summer mansion, which can be toured from the day after Easter through early October.

Dep. Shanklin	13:52	14:52	15:52	16:32	16:52 (12)
Arr. Ryde Pier Head	14:17	15:17	16:17	16:56	17:17
Change to ferry.					
Dep. Ryde Pier Head	14:30	15:30	16:30	17:00	17:30
Arr. Portsmouth (Hbr.)	14:48	15:48	16:48	17:18	17:48
Change to train. 504					
Dep. Portsmouth (Hbr.)	15:20 (4)	15:02 (5)	17:01 (2)	17:20 (3)	18:01 (2)
Arr. London (Wat.)	16:30	17:33	18:34	19:32	19:32

(1) Runs daily, except Sundays and holidays. Light refreshments Monday-Friday. (2) Runs daily, except Sundays and holidays. Light refreshments. (3) Runs Sunday only. (4) Runs daily, except holidays. Light refreshments Monday-Saturday. (5) Runs daily, except holidays. Light refreshments. (6) Runs daily. Light refreshments. (7) Runs Monday–Friday, except holidays. Light refreshments. (8) Runs daily, except holidays. Light refreshments on Saturday. (9) Runs daily, except holidays. Light refreshments. (10) Runs Sunday only. Light refreshments. (11) Plus another London departure at 10:15 (4), arriving Shanklin 13:25. (12) Plus other departures from Shanklin (Portsmouth service shown in parentheses) at 17:32 (3), 17:52 (2), 18:32 (3), 19:50 (7), 20:50 (8), 22:17 (9) and 22:32 (10).

London - Rochester - London   ABC 9

Dep. London   Frequent times from 05:22 to 00:14 (08:02 to 23:17 on Sunday)
    (Charing X)
Arr. Rochester   60 minutes later

Sights in **Rochester**: The 17th century Bull Hotel, where Charles Dickens' characters, Pickwick and his friends, spent the first night of their long and memorable trip

See the little house at 11 Ordinance Terrace, where Dickens lived from the time he was 4 until he was 9 years old, Visit the red brick mansion where he lived his last 10 years and died. The cemetery here has many markers from which Dickens took the names for the people he cast in his stories.

Visit the City Museum in Eastgate House, open daily except Friday 14:00-17:30.

Dep. Rochester   Frequent times from 05:31 to 22:29 (06:52 to 21:20 on Sunday)
Arr. London (Charing X)   60 minutes later

London - Rye - London   ABC 20

Dep. London (Charing Cross)   Frequent times from 05:35 to 21:00
                               (08:57 to 19:57 on Sunday)
Change from suburban train 90 minutes later, in Ashford.
Arr. Rye   2 hours after departing London.

Sights in **Rye**: This delightful little hilltop town was once an important seaport, but it is now 2 miles from the sea. See the 14th century city walls. The 14th century wood Monastery, now housing one of the town's 6 potteries.

It is a 10-minute walk up Conduit Hill to the 12th century Norman church and then to the oldest structure in Rye, the 13th century Ypres Tower, now the city Museum, open from Easter to the end of September, Monday-Saturday 10:30–12:30 and 14:15–17:30, Sunday 11:15–12:30.

Dep. Rye   Frequent times from 05:50 to 21:42
                           (10:21 to 20:21 on Sunday)
Change to Suburban train 30 minutes later, in Ashford.
Arr. London (Charing Cross)   2 hours after departing Rye.

London - Salisbury - Stonehenge - London   511

Most of these trains have light refreshments.

Dep. London (Wat.)	07:35 (1)	07:54 (2)	08:35 (3)	08:55 (4)	09:35 (2)	10:12 (1+8)
Arr. Salisbury	09:04	09:21	09:51	10:37	11:00	11:31

Sights in **Salisbury**: The Cathedral, with its tombs of Crusaders and one of the 4 existing copies of the Magna Carta.

Buses operate between the Salisbury railstation and Stonehenge to view the mysterious oval of 50-ton stones there, about 4,000 years old. This is the most important prehistoric relic in Britain. How were these stupendous weights moved 20 miles from their quarry…and why?

The nearly 2-hour roundtrip departs Salisbury Monday–Friday at 10:15, 11:15, 12:15, 13:15, 14:15 and 16:15 (different but similar times on Saturday and Sunday). The 1994 prices were £3.90 for adults, £2.90 for children and senior citizens.

Dep. Salisbury	13:20 (2)	13:50 (1)	14:15 (2)	14:29 (4)	15:21 (3)	16:15 (6+9)
Arr. London (Wat.)	14:44	15:17	15:44	16:25	16:44 (5)	17:45

(1) Runs Saturday only. (2) Runs Monday-Friday, except holidays. (3) Runs daily, except Sundays and holidays. (4) Runs Sunday only. (5) Arrives 30 minutes later on Saturday. (6) Runs daily, except holidays. (7) Runs daily, except Saturdays and holidays. (8) Plus other departures from London at 10:35 (2), 10:55 (4), 11:35 (2) and 12:35 (3). (9) Plus other departures from Salisbury at 16:52 (2), 17:17 (1), 17:50 (2), 18:15 (3), 18:18 (4), 19:53 (2), 20:18 (1), 20:45 (2) and 21:06 (4).

London - Stratford on Avon - London

Although there is service between London's *Paddington* railstation and Coventry, it requires changing trains en route.

The escorted "Shakespeare Connection" service between London's *Euston* railstation, Coventry and (by bus) Stratford is preferable. Details are available from British Travel Centre, 12 Regent Street, London. The special bus that transfers passengers between Coventry and Stratford has a guide and stops near the Stratford office that books various local tours.

Dep. London (Euston)	08:55 (3)	09:45 (2)	10:25 (3)
Arr. Coventry	10:26	12:02	11:51
Change to bus.			
Dep. Coventry	10:35	12:10	12:00
Arr. Strarford	11:10	12:45	12:35

• • •

Dep. Stratford	17:15 (1)	17:55 (2)	23:15 (1)
Arr. Coventry	17:50	18:25	23:45
Change to train.			
Dep. Coventry	18:07 (4)	18:37 (3)	00:37
Arr. London (Euston)	19:29	20:17	02:37

(1) Runs Monday–Saturday. (2) Runs Sunday only (3) Runs daily except Sundays + holidays. (4) Runs daily except holidays.

Those wishing to attend a performance at the Royal Shakespeare Theater *cannot* purchase tickets for that night's performance until arriving at the theater and chance the possibility that all tickets have been sold.

The "Shakespeare Connection" combination train-and-bus ticket can be purchased only in England — at either of British Rail's central London offices (Regent Street or Oxford Street), or at London's Euston railstation.

There are many restaurants and pubs in Stratford, and visitors may picnic either by the theater or in the garden along the river.

See the house of Mary Arden, his mother. The cottage of Anne Hathaway, his wife. Shakespeare's tomb in Trinity Church. The home of John Harvard, founder of America's great university.

There are afternoon performances at the Royal Shakespeare Theater on some Thursdays and Saturdays.

London - Torquay - Paignton - London   510

Dep. London (Pad.)	07:15	08:35 (3)	09:35 (3)	10:45 (4)	11:45 (3)
Dep. Exeter (St. Davids)	10:25 (3)	-0-	12:01	12:59	14:03
Arr. Torquay	11:07	11:41	12:41	13:29	14:43
Arr. Paignton	6–10 minutes later				

Sights in **Torquay:** An 11-mile coastline that resembles a Mediterranean resort, palm trees and all. The British "Riviera." Pronounced "tor-kee." Stroll the walk along the formal gardens at the waterfront to the park, where concerts and dances are held in the Summer. Visit the Model Railroad and House Miniatures in the Victoria Arcade at the harbor.

See the collection of 17th century silver and 18th century glass at the Municipal Art Gallery and Museum in the 18th century building next to the ruins of the 12th century Torre Abbey. Nearby is the Model Village, open in Summer 09:00-22:00, in Winter 09:00 to dusk. The exhibits of archaeology, natural history and Devon folk life in the Museum of Natural History, open daily except Sunday from March through October 10:00–16:45, and Monday-Friday from November through February.

Paignton has many bed-and-breakfast inns. Sights there include the restored 14th century Great Hall of Compton Castle, open May through October on Monday, Wednesday and Thursday 10:00–17:00. The ballroom filled with silver mirrors at Oldway House, called "a miniature Versailles," open Monday-Saturday 09:00–13:00 and 14:15–17:00, Sundays 14:00–17:00.

Dep. Paignton	15:21 (3)	16:09 (6)	17:20 (3+11)
Dep. Torquay	6 minutes after departing Paignton		
Dep. Exeter (St. Davids)	15:58	16:53	18:16
Arr. London (Pad.)	19:06	19:50	20:45

(1) Runs Monday–Friday, except holidays. Restaurant car. (2) Operates early July to late August. Runs Saturday only. (3) Runs Saturday only. (4) Runs daily, except Sundays and holidays. (5) Runs Saturday and Sunday. (6) Runs Sunday only. (7) Runs Saturday only. Change trains in Exeter. (8) Runs Monday-Friday, except holidays. Light refreshments. Change trains in Exeter. (9) Runs daily, except Saturdays and holidays. Change trains in Exeter. (10) Arrives 55 minutes later on Sunday. (11) Plus another Paignton departure at 18:25 (9), arriving London 22:10 (10).

London - Winchester - London   ABC 59 + 502

All of these trains run daily.

Dep. London (Wat.)	Frequent times from 05:40 to 23:45 (07:45 to 22:45 on Sunday)
Arr. Winchester	60 minutes later (80 minutes later on Sunday)

Sights in **Winchester**: King Arthur's roundtable in the Great Hall at the Castle. The 11th century Cathedral, with the tombs of King Alfred, Jane Austen and Izaak Walton.

Dep. Winchester	Frequent times from 06:21 to 23:14 (08:02 to 23:02 on Sunday)
Arr. London (Wat.)	60 minutes later (80 minutes later on Sunday)

London - Windsor - London   ABC 67

Dep. London (Waterloo)	Monday–Saturday: Frequent times from 06:13 to 23:17
	Sunday: Frequent times from 07:50 to 22:50
Arr. Windsor (Riverside)	40–60 minutes later

Sights in **Windsor**: Windsor Castle with its collection of Da Vinci drawings and, occasionally, members of the Royal Family. See the Changing of the Guard there, at 10:25. Queen Mary's Doll House. St. George's Chapel.

In the town, stroll down the 3-mile "Long Walk." See Eton College, where once it did not matter if you won or lost, in the days when observing niceties was more important than the final score.

Dep. Windsor (Riverside)	Monday–Saturday: Frequent times from 06:08 to 22:40
	Sunday: Frequent times from 07:05 to 23:05
Arr. London (Waterloo)	40–60 minutes later

London - York - London   570

Dep. London (Kings X)	06:00 (7)	07:00 (2)	07:30 (3)	08:00 (8)	09:00 (3)
Arr. York	08:29	09:09	09:28	09:53	10:54

Dep. London (Kings X)	09:30 (3)	10:00 (3)	10:30 (3)	11:00 (3)	11:30 (3)
Arr. York	11:35	11:54	12:26	13:00	13:36 (10)

Dep. York	14:35 (7)	14:52 (3)	15:32 (3)	16:00 (2)	16:32 (7)
Arr. London (Kings X)	16:49	16:57	17:39	18:13	18:35

Dep. York	16:55 (7)	17:00 (2)	17:20 (8)	17:51 (7)	18:27 (3+9)
Arr. London (Kings X)	18:55	19:23	19:10	20:07	20:38

(1) Runs daily, except Sundays and holidays. (2) Runs Saturday only. (3) Runs Monday–Friday, except holidays. Restaurant car. (4) Runs daily, except Sundays and holidays. Pullman service available in first-class Monday–Friday. (5) Runs daily, except Sundays and holidays. Restaurant car Monday–Friday. (6) Runs daily, except Sundays and holidays. Restaurant car. (7) Runs Monday-Friday, except holidays. (8) Runs Monday-Friday, except holidays. Pullman service available in first-class. (9) Plus other York departures at 19:41 (3), 20:03 (3) and 21:39 (7). (10) Runs to June 24+ from September 5.

Sights in **York**: Free walking tours in Summer leave from the fountain across from the Information Center (Exhibition Square) daily at 10:15, 14:15 and 19:15.

Founded by Romans in A.D. 71. Very crowded with tourists in July and August. Most of the interesting places are located within the one square mile that is encircled by 3 miles of ancient walls.

York Minister, the largest Gothic cathedral in Britain (open daily 07:30 to dusk) has fantastic stained glass. Its Great East Window is the size of a tennis court. It is advisable to use binoculars to study the detail on both the windows and the plaster work on the ceilings.

See the 14th and 15th century stained glass in All Saints Church, on North Street. The brass rubbings center at St. Williams College (outside the cathedral's Great East Window). Stroll along the top of the city walls for a great view of the ancient buildings that surround the cathedral.

Walk down "The Shambles." Visit the restored Guildhall on St. Helen's Square to see its modern stained glass and timbered roof. Castle Museum, Britain's largest folk museum, off

Tower Street (open daily 09:30–18:30). The shrine commemorating the 12th century massacre of Jews at Clifford Tower, in the center of York.

Exhibits of Bronze Age, Iron Age and Roman-era remains, in the Yorkshire Museum on Museum Street (open Monday–Saturday 10:00–17:00, Sunday 13:00–17:00). The 25 old locomotives and many train cars (including Queen Victoria's ornate coach) at the National Railway Museum on Leeman Road.

There are special excursion trains from London, to the Railway Museum, for a few days in August, September, October and November each year. The all-day excursions include round-trip train service from London and 4 hours touring the Museum.

SCENIC TRAIN TRIPS

There is much fine scenery on nearly every rail route in England. The next 4 train rides offer exceptional scenic views, as do several rail trips in Scotland.

London - Pwllheli - London   ABC page 126

There is excellent coastal scenery on this ride plus a splendid view of Harlech Castle.

This trip is too long as a one-day London roundtrip.

All of these departures require changing trains at one or 2 railstations among 5 different stations—in Birmingham for most trips. The ticket office at London (Euston) will advise where to make a train change.

A layover in Birmingham should be considered.

Dep. London (Euston)	07:00 (1)	09:30	11:30 (1)	13:30	15:30 (1)
Arr. Pwllheli	14:54	16:26 (2)	18:37	20:50 (3)	22:49

Sights in **Pwllheli**: This summer seaside resort is located on the southern side of the Lleyn Peninsula. The major attraction here is boating in **Tremadog Bay**.

Dep. Pwllheli	07:11 (1)	09:27 (1)	10:25 (4)	12:39 (1)	13:16 (4+7)
Arr. London (Euston)	14:29	16:29	18:10	21:03 (5)	20:16

(1) Runs Monday–Saturday. (2) Arrives 17:35 on Sunday. (3) Arrives 21:36 on Sunday. (4) Runs Sunday only.(5) Arrives 21:48 on Saturday. (6) Arrives 23:59 on Saturday. (7) Plus other Pwllheli departures at 14:59 (1), 15:25 (4) and 17:49 (1), arriving London 23:19 (6), 22:10 and 00:48.

Leeds - Settle - Carlisle   562

The 62-mile Settle–Carlisle portion of this route is considered by many to be the most scenic train route in England. It goes through the **Pennine Hills** and the **Yorkshire Dales Na-**

tional Park, close to the Lake district. This line has 14 tunnels and 21 viaducts, including the 104-foot-high Ribblehead Viaduct.

All of these trains have light refreshments, unless designated otherwise.

Dep. Leeds	08:45 (2)	09:49 (6)	10:49 (2)	12:49 (2)	13:32 (3)	14:49 (4)
Dep. Settle	09:47	10:53	11:46	13:45	14:27	15:45
Arr. Carlisle	11:28	12:36	13:29	15:28	16:10	17:30

Sights in **Settle**: A pretty town. Since 1429, a market has been held here every Tuesday.

Dep. Carlisle	14:16 (2)	15:20 (7)	16:26 (2)	16:49 (3)	17:45 (4)	18:21 (5)
Dep. Settle	15:59	16:59	18:09	18:29	19:24	19:57
Arr. Leeds	17:01	18:07	19:09	19:30	20:22	20:59

(1) Runs daily, except holidays. (2) Runs daily, except Sundays and holidays. (3) Runs Sunday only. (4) Runs Monday–Friday, except holidays. (5) Runs Saturday only. (6) Runs daily except Sundays & holidays July 18-September 2, also July 2,9,16, September 3, 10, 17, 24. (7) Runs Saturday only.

London - Windermere - London

The breathtaking scenery of England's "Lake country."

The Oxenholme–Windermere (and v.v.) trains are second-class only.

550

Dep. London (Euston)	08:40 (1)	12:40 (2+3)
Arr. Oxenholme	12:01	16:00

Change trains.
547

Dep. Oxenholme	13:38	16:08
Arr. Windermere	13:58	16:34

Dep. Windermere	15:00	15:47	16:39	18:33
Arr. Oxenholme	15:19	16:06	17:02	18:50

Change trains.
550

Dep. Oxenholme	15:39 (1)	16:20 (2+3)	17:12	18:42 (3)
Arr. London (Euston)	19:02	20:22 (4)	21:07 (3)	22:28

(1) Runs daily, except Sundays and holidays. Restaurant car. (2) Change trains in Preston. (3) Runs Sunday only. (4) Train from Preston runs daily, except Sundays & holidays.

A DAY THROUGH WALES

There is a marvelous one-day circle train trip from London that takes you through the incredibly beautiful rural scenery in the heart of Wales, between Swansea and Shrewsbury. As shown below, this trip can be made either clockwise or counter-clockwise.

London - Swansea - Shrewsbury - London

530			*540*	
Dep. London (Pad.)	09:00 (1)		Dep. London (Euston)	07:05 (10)
Arr. Swansea	11:55 (2)		Arr Birmingham (New St.)	08:55
Change trains.			*Change trains*	
535			Dep.Birmingham (New St.)	09:25 (6)
Dep. Swansea	12:29 (9)		Arr. Shrewsbury	10:50 (11)
Arr. Shrewsbury	16:28 (8)		*Change trains.*	
Change trains.			*535*	
540			Dep. Shrewsbury	11:10 (7)
Dep. Shrewsbury	16:38 (7)		Arr. Swansea	15:22
Arr Birmingham (New St.)	17:54		*Change trains*	
Change trains			*530*	
Dep.Birmingham	18:15		Dep. Swansea	15:32 (6)
Arr. London (Euston)	20:13 (7)		Arr. London (Pad.)	18:30

(1) Runs daily, except holidays. Restaurant car Monday–Saturday. (2) Arrives 30–40 minutes later on Sunday. (3) Runs daily, except holidays. Light refreshments. (4) Runs daily, except holidays. (5) Runs daily, except Sundays and holidays. Restaurant car. (6) Runs daily, except Sundays and holidays. (7) Runs daily, except Sundays and holidays. Light refreshments. (8) Runs from July 17. (9) Runs Sunday only. (10) Runs Saturday only. (11) Change trains in Wolverhampton.

Sights in **Shrewsbury**: The 1,000-year-old castle. In **Wroxeter**, a short bus ride from here, are the reconstructed ruins of Roman baths built there 2,000 years ago.

RAIL CONNECTION WITH IRELAND
VIA WALES

There is bus service between Swansea's railstation and its ferryport.

London - Swansea - Cork		Cork - Swansea - London		
530 Train		*621 Ferry*		
Dep. London (Pad.)	17:00 (1)	Dep. Cork	09:00 (2)	21:00 (2)
Arr. Swansea	19:50	Arr. Swansea	19:00	07:00
Change to ferry. 621		*Change to train. 530*		
Dep. Swansea	21:00 (2)	Dep. Swansea	20:22 (3)	08:00 (4)
Arr. Cork	07:00	Arr. London (Pad.)	23:53	11:40

(1) Runs Monday-Friday, except holidays. (2) Runs Monday, Wednesday, Thursday, Friday and Sunday June 23-September 18; Runs Tuesday, Thursday, Friday and Sunday September 20-December 23. (3) Runs Monday-Thursday only. (3) Runs Sunday only.

RAIL CONNECTIONS WITH SCOTLAND

These are the schedules for rail travel between London (*Kings Cross* railstation) and the capital of Scotland.

London - Edinburgh and Edinburgh - London   570

Seat reservation is advisable for all of these trains, particularly for Pullman service—which is more comfortable and provides meals and refreshment service at seats.

Dep. London	06:00 (1)	07:00 (2)	08:00 (3)	09:00 (6)	10:00 (4)
Arr. Edinburgh	11:09	11:45	12:15	13:30	14:15
Dep. London	10:30 (5)	11:00 (6)	11:30 (4)	12:00 (6)	13:00 (6)
Arr. Edinburgh	14:51	15:30	16:10 (13)	16:30	17:25
Dep. London	13:30 (1)	14:00 (6)	15:00 (3)	16:00 (6)	17:00 (3)
Arr. Edinburgh	18:11	18:29	19:06	20:29	21:15
Dep. London	18:00 (6)				
Arr. Edinburgh	22:25 (8)				

•   •   •

| Dep. Edinburgh | 06:00 (1) | 07:00 (6) | 08:00 (6) | 08:30 (2) | 09:00 (6) |
| Arr. London | 11:07 | 11:45 | 12:44 | 13:07 | 13:39 |

| Dep. Edinburgh | 09:30 (1) | 10:00 (1) | 10:30 (6) | 11:00 (6) | 11:30 (6) |
| Arr. London | 14:08 | 14:40 (14) | 14:57 | 15:45 | 15:57 |

| Dep. Edinburgh | 12:00 (6) | 12:30 (6) | 13:00 (6) | 13:30 (2) | 14:100 (1) |
| Arr. London | 16:49 (14) | 16:57 | 17:39 | 18:13 | 18:55 |

| Dep. Edinburgh | 15:00 (11) | 15:30 (2) | 16:00 (6) | 16:30 (2) | 17:00 (6) |
| Arr. London | 19:10 | 20:21 | 20:40 | 21:25 | 21:57 |

| Dep. Edinburgh | 18:00 (11) |
| Arr. London | 23:30 |

(1) Runs Monday–Friday except holidays. (2) Runs Saturday only. (3) Runs Monday–Saturday, except holidays. Pullman service available Monday-Friday in first-class. (4) Runs Monday–Saturday, except holidays. Restaurant car Monday–Friday. (5) Runs Monday-Saturday, except holidays. Restaurant car. (6) Runs Monday-Friday, except holidays. Restaurant car. (7) Runs Monday–Saturday, except holidays. (8) Arrives 20–60 minutes later on Sunday. (9) Runs Monday-Saturday, except holidays. (10) Late June to late August: runs daily, except Sundays and holidays and has a restaurant car. Late August to late June: runs Saturday only. (11) Runs Monday-Friday, except holidays. Pullman service available in first-class. (12) Runs Sunday only. (13) RUns to June 24 & from Sept. 5. (14) Runs June 27-Sept. 2.

SCOTLAND

The 2 rail trips north from Edinburgh (to Dundee–Aberdeen and to Perth–Inverness) are very scenic. There is also train service between Aberdeen and Inverness.

From Inverness, there is a rail route to Wick in northernmost Scotland, and to Kyle of Lochalsh on the west coast of Scotland. Other train routes to the same coastal area are from Glasgow to both Oban and to Mallaig. The other principal rail service in Scotland is between Edinburgh and Glasgow.

We list 36 one-day rail excursions in Scotland.

(See "Freedom of Scotland Travelpass and Flexipass.")

Edinburgh

The capital of Scotland. Most of the 25-acre railstation is under glass. Visit Edinburgh Castle, sitting on a cliff 270 feet above the city, on a site where there have been forts since the 6th century. A cannon has been fired from there every day since 1858. The Castle is open every day in the Summer: 09:30–18:00 Monday-Saturday, 11:00–18:00 on Sundays.

The panoramic view of Edinburgh from the Castle is breathtaking.

At the Castle, see the hammer-beamed timbered ceiling in the Great Hall of James IV, the Scottish Crown Jewels, the small St. Margaret's Chapel, and the State Apartments, including the rooms once occupied by Mary Queen of Scots.

Below the Castle is the 37-acre Princess Street Gardens, with the city's main rail tracks running through it, at a lower level than the surface of the park.

Also visit the 17th century Palace of Holyrood House to see the Throne Room and also the portraits of 110 Scottish kings (painted by the same artist) in the gallery. You will notice that all 110 noses are the same ! Stroll through 648-acre Holyrood Park, which has 3 lakes.

Other interesting sights in Edinburgh: the paintings at both the National Gallery of Scotland and in the National Portrait Gallery. The National Museum of Antiquities. The collection of technology, art, archaeology, geology and natural history in the Royal Scottish Museum. The Museum of Childhood (historic books, toys and materials about child rearing), closed on Sundays. The adaptation of Athens' Temple of Theseus. The month-long International Festival of Music and Drama.

The pottery, handcrafted glass, textiles and woodwork at the Scottish Craft Center, in Acheson House, open daily except Sunday 10:00–17:00. The collection of Robert Burns, Sir Walter Scott and Robert Louis Stevenson manuscripts and memorabilia in the 17th century Lady Stair's House.

The exhibit (Picasso, Hockney, etc.) at the Scottish National Gallery of Modern Art on Belford Road, open Monday–Saturday 10:00–17:00, Sunday 14:00–17:00. Henry Moore sculptures decorate the grounds. A sign behind this museum directs you to a path that goes to Dean Village, once a grain-milling center. Nearby is St. Bernard's Well, a Doric temple built at a mineral spring in 1789.

Then stroll to Stockbridge (once an industrial village) on St. Stephen Street, where many interesting antique shops are located. Stockbridge is next to New Town, notable for its Georgian houses and elegant crescents.

Edinburgh - Dundee - Aberdeen 600

This is a very scenic rail trip.

Dep. Edinburgh	07:05 (1)	08:10 (1)	09:10 (2)	10:20 (4)	11:10 (2)
Arr. Dundee	08:27	09:26	10:26 (3)	11:35	12:26 (3)
Arr. Aberdeen	09:42	10:45	11:40	12:50	13:40

* * *

Dep. Aberdeen	13:10 (1)	13:10 (5)	13:35 (6)	14:20 (1)	14:55 (7+10)
Arr. Dundee	14:27	-0- (5)	15:01	15:30	16:06
Arr. Edinburgh	15:48	16:15	16:18	16:48	17:20

(1) Runs daily, except Sun. and holidays. Light refreshments. (2) Runs daily, except holidays. Departs 15 minutes earlier on Sunday. Light refreshments Monday–Saturday. (3) Arrives 15 minutes earlier on Sunday. (4) Runs daily, except Sundays and holidays. (5) Runs Sunday only. Light refreshments. Change

trains in Perth. (6) Runs Saturday and Sunday. (7) Runs daily, except Sundays & holidays. Restaurant car Monday–Friday. Light refreshments on Sunday. (8) Runs Sunday only. Light refreshments. (9) Runs Sunday only. (10) Plus other departures from Aberdeen at 15:23 (1), 16:15 (1), 17:12 (1), 18:15 (4), 19:00 (8), 20:00 (1), 20:50 (9) and 21:14 (1).

Sights in **Dundee**: A very ancient city, predating Roman occupation. Mountains of jam and preserves are processed here. Visit the Spalding Golf Museum in nearby Camperdown Park. The frigate "Unicorn," launched in 1824, now tied at Victoria Dock. The 4 castles: Dudhope, Claypotts, Broughty and Mains.

Sights in **Aberdeen:** A very popular tourist center and busy seaport. The center of Scotland's fishing industry (see the 07:00 fish market). Straddles 2 rivers. See the 15th century Cathedral of St. Machar. Streets that were laid out in the 13th and 14th centuries. The local history museum in the 17th century Provost Skene's House.

The 16th century Provost Ross's House. The 18th century St. Nicholas Church. Two very old bridges: the 14th century Brig o'Balgownie and the 16th century Old Bridge of Dee. The 19th century Music Hall. The 19th century Marischal College, considered the world's largest and finest granite building.

Edinburgh - Perth - Inverness 600

A very scenic train ride through the heart of the **Grampian Mountains**. Winter sports, including skiing, are the attraction at the **Aviemore** vacation resort.

Dep. Edinburgh	06:48 (1)	09:35 (6)	13:40	15:40 (3)
Dep. Perth	08:08 (1)	10:51	14:53 (6)	17:02
Dep. Aviemore	09:51	12:40	16:41	18:54
Arr. Inverness	10:32	13:23	17:18	19:45

• • •

Dep. Inverness	12:20 (1)	14:32 (6)	18:30 (5)
Dep. Aviemore	12:58	15:21	19:16
Dep. Perth	15:00 (1)	16:55	20:50
Arr. Edinburgh	16:15	18:12	22:10

(1) Runs daily, except Sundays and holidays. Change trains in Perth. Light refreshments Perth–Inverness (and v.v.). (2) Runs daily except holidays. Change trains in Perth. Sunday: light refreshments entire trip. Monday-Saturday: light refreshments Perth-Inverness. (3) Runs daily, except Sundays and holidays. Light refreshments. (4) Runs daily, except holidays. Change trains in Perth. Light refreshments Perth–Inverness (and v.v.). (5) Runs daily, except holidays. Light refreshments. (6) Runs Sunday only.

Sights in **Perth**: A popular tourist center. There is much whiskey distilling and weaving of tartans here. Good Winter sports. Sailing and water skiing in the Summer. See the 360-degree panoramic color slide-show and hear the stereophonic presentation at the Round House waterworks. St. John's Kirk. The Perth Art Gallery and Museum, on George Street.

A short distance from there, at North Post, visit the Fair Maid's House, an important locale in Sir Walter Scott's novel, "The Fair Maid of Perth."

Sights in **Inverness**: Located in the mountainous Highlands. Very cold Winters and cool Summers here. A popular tourist resort for hunting of grouse and deer, hiking, fishing, sailing, camping and Winter sports. Many whiskey distillers in this area. Visit the Castle. Stroll the garden paths along the River Ness. Nearby is Great Britain's highest mountain, Ben Nevis (4,406 feet).

Take a cruise on **Loch Ness,** and see if you can spot the "monster." Boats go from the lake through the **Caledonian Canal** and return to Inverness on cruises that take 2½ hours in the morning, 3½ hours in the afternoon, and 2½ hours in the evening.

Aberdeen - Inverness   595

Dep. Aberdeen	06:27 (1)	07:27 (2)	09:20 (2)	10:00 (3)	11:36 (2+6)	
Arr. Inverness	08:48	09:49	11:52	12:16	13:52	
Dep. Inverness	04:52 (2)	06:00 (2)	08:07 (2)	09:55 (3)	10:45 (2)	12:20 (4+7)
Arr. Aberdeen	07:14	08:20	10:32	12:13	12:58	14:45

(1) Runs daily, except Sundays and holidays. (2) Runs daily, except Sundays and holidays. Light refreshments. (3) Runs Sunday only. Light refreshments. (4) Runs daily, except holidays. Light refreshments. (5) Runs daily, except holidays. Light refreshments. (6) Plus other Aberdeen departures at 13:00 (2), 15:16 (2), 17:14 (2), 18:12 (2), 20:10 (4) and 21:48 (3), arriving Inverness 15:20, 17:50, 19:40, 20:35, 22:37, 23:50 and 23:58. (7) Plus other Inverness departures at 13:52 (2), 15:23 (4), 17:06 (4), 18:06 (2) and 20:45 (4), arriving Aberdeen 16:05, 17:38, 19:33, 20:33 and 23:00.

Inverness - Kyle of Lochalsh - Inverness   597

This is one of the most scenic train trips in Britain. The track climbs and descends, turns and twists through the **Wester Ross Mountains** as it often goes along the shoreline of lovely lakes through the heart of the Highlands. In the Spring, there are fields of red and orange rhododendrons. The fields of purple heather can be seen all year.

In the high **Luib Summit** area there are forests and snowcapped mountains. It is only an 8-minute ferry-boat ride from Kyle to the **Isle of Skye**.

| Dep. Inverness | 06:55 (1) | 08:00 (1) | 10:40 (2) | 12:40 (3) | 18:38 (4) |
| Arr. Kyle | 09:27 | 10:30 | 14:00 | 15:08 | 21:15 |

• • •

| Dep. Kyle | 07:10 (1) | 10:00 (6) | 11:48 (1) | 15:10 (7) | 17:05 (1) |
| Arr. Inverness | 09:29 | 12:30 | 14:20 | 17:52 | 19:48 |

(1) Runs daily, except Sundays and holidays. Light refreshments. (2) Operates late June to early Septem-

ber. Runs Sunday only. (3) Operates early June to early September. Runs daily, except Sundays and holidays. Light refreshments. (4) Late June to early September: runs daily except holidays. Light refreshments all year. (5) Runs daily, except Sunday and holidays. (6) Runs Sunday only July 3-August 28. (7) Runs daily except Sundays & holidays July 4-Sept. 3; Sunday only July 3-Sept. 18.

Edinburgh - Dunbar - Edinburgh   570

Dep. Edinburgh	09:30 (1)	14:00 (1)	17:00 (1)
Arr. Dunbar	20-25 minutes later		

Sights in **Dunbar**: A small fishing port, the birthplace of naturalist John Muir (128 High Street). See the Castle ruins at the harbor.

Take a 45-minute walk and visit the Old Harbor with its Lifeboat Museum, the roost for domesticated pigeons in Friar's Croft, and the Georgian houses (Castellau and Lauderdale). This walk is detailed in a guidebook available at the town's tourist information center in the 17th century Town House on High Street, open during Summer Monday-Saturday 09:00–19:00, Sunday 11:00–13:00.

Also visit the 1,667-acre John Muir Country Park, containing a wide variety of birds and plants. Near it are the restored 17th century Preston watermill and many old towns and villages: **Gifford**, **Haddington**, **Dirleton** and **North Berwick**. A list of hotels, guest houses and bed-and-breakfast places can be obtained by writing to the Dunbar Tourist Information Centre, if sufficient international reply coupons are enclosed.

Dep. Dunbar	07:47 (1)	09:46 (1)	13:09 (1)	16:56 (1)
Arr. Edinburgh	20-25 minutes later			

(1) Runs Monday–Friday, except holidays.

Edinburgh - Glasgow - Edinburgh   590

Dep. Edinburgh	Monday–Saturday: Frequent times from 05:50 to 23:30
	Sunday: Frequent times from 08:30 to 23:30
Arr. Glasgow (Queen St.)	50–70 minutes later

• • •

Dep. Glasgow (Queen St.)	Monday–Saturday: Frequent times from 06:22 to 23:30
	Sunday: Frequent times from 08:00 to 18:48
Arr. Edinburgh	50–70 minutes later

Sights in **Glasgow**: A major seaport. Largest city in Scotland. See the great shipyards on the River Clyde.

The dozens of antique streetcars, motorcycles and trains (including King George VI's 72-foot-long railway coach, built in 1941 with wartime armor-plated shutters) in the Museum of Transport at Kelvin Hall on Albert Drive, open Monday-Saturday 10:00–17:00, Sunday

14:00–17:00. Nearby, the fine collection of weapons, paintings (Rembrandt, Monet), Mackintosh furniture and natural history exhibits in Kelvingrove Art Galleries and Museum.

The vast collection of paintings by James Abbott McNeil Whistler—the world's best collection—in the Hunterian Art Gallery at Glasgow University, open Monday-Friday 10:30–12:30 and 13:30–17:30, Saturday 09:30–13:00. The Gallery also features a reconstruction of 3 floors of the home of the great architect Charles Mackintosh.

Many fine paintings in the Glasgow Art Gallery. The Botanic Gardens. Scottish genealogy at the Mitchell Library on North Street, Europe's largest municipal reference library. It holds over 1,250,000 books and subscribes to 40 newspapers and more than 200 periodicals. It has a helpful, knowledgeable staff and modern studying facilities.

The more than 8,000 treasures of The Burrell Collection, in Pollok House: over 700 stained glass items (one of the world's best collections). Paintings by Rembrandt, Bellini, Memling, Degas, Manet. Excellent Chou Dynasty pieces. Neolithic burial urns. The more than 8-ton marble Warwick Vase, discovered in Rome in 1771. Also on view: jade, carpets, porcelain, silver, furniture, glass and gold. Open Monday-Saturday 10:00–17:00, Sunday 14:00–17:00.

Glasgow - Oban - Glasgow   593

There is marvelous Highland scenery on this route.

Dep. Glasgow (Queen St.)	08:40 (6)	12:42 (5)	18:12 (5)
Arr. Oban	11:40	15:40	21:24

Sights in **Oban**: This has been a holiday resort for nearly a century, and a fishing port for even longer.

Dep. Oban	08:05 (6)	12:35 (7)	18:08 (5)
Arr. Glasgow (Queen St.)	11:14	15:44	21:28

(1) Operates early September to mid-June. Runs daily, except Sundays and holidays. (2) Operates mid-June to early September. Runs daily, except Sundays and holidays. (3) Late June to early September: runs Sunday only. Early September to late June: runs daily, except Sundays and holidays. (4) Operates early July to early September. Runs daily, except Sundays and holidays. (5) Runs daily, except holidays. (6) Runs daily, except Sundays & holidays. (7) Runs Sunday only.

Glasgow - Fort William - Mallaig - Glasgow   593

The Fort William–Mallaig portion, the train ride with the most beautiful scenery in Britain, offers better views than an alternative auto route does of many lochs (lakes), glens (valleys) and bens (mountains).

These trains provide a guide who tells about the sights on this route: the 4,406-foot-high Ben Nevis (highest peak in Britain), the Caledonian Canal built in 1822, Loch Long, fabled

Loch Lomond, the heather-encrusted wild Rannoch Moor, the man-made Loch Trieg, the forested Loch Eil, Bonnie Prince Charlie's monument, and the 1,000-foot-long Glenfinnan Viaduct. The highest altitude on British rail is 347 feet, at Corrour Summit, between Glasgow and Fort William.

Dep. Glasgow (Queen St.)	08:12 (11)	12:42 (11)	18:12 (11)
Arr. Crianlarich	09:53	14:25	20:11
Dep. Crianlarich	10:10	14:37	20:17
Arr. Fort William	11:55	16:22	22:08
Dep. Fort William	12:02	16:30	22:15
Arr. Mallaig	13:24	17:54	23:37

Sights in **Mallaig:** There is a 2-hour ferryboat ride from this little fishing village to Kyle of Lochalsh.

Dep. Mallaig	06:00 (11)	10:30 (11)	10:25 (7+9)
Arr. Fort William	07:22	11:47	11:47
Dep. Fort William	07:30	11:57	12:37
Arr. Crianlarich	09:15	13:46	14:21
Dep. Crianlarich	09:22	13:52	14:28
Arr. Glasgow (Queen St.)	11:14	15:44	16:28

(1) Operates early September to mid-June. Runs daily, except Sundays and holidays. (2) Operates late June to early September. Runs Sunday only. (3) Operates early September to late June. Runs daily, except holidays. (4) Operates late June to early September. Runs daily, except Sundays and holidays. (5) Train has only sleepling cars (London-Fort William and v.v.). Runs daily, except Saturdays and holidays. Departs 45-70 minutes earlier on Sunday. (6) Change trains in Crianlarich. (7) Operates late June to early September. Runs daily, except holidays. (8) Runs Sunday only. (9) Plus another Mallaig departure at 16:10 (8), arriving Glasgow 21:30. (10) Plus another Fort William departure at 17:42 (8), arriving Glasgow 21:30. (11) Runs daily except Sundays & holidays.

CHAPTER 8

CENTRAL AND EASTERN EUROPE

Overview

Everyone will tell you the same thing: travel conditions have been changing in central and eastern Europe at such a turbulent pace that guidebooks cannot possibly keep up. Travel in general has grown phenomenally in eastern Europe, and so more people need more and better information in order to experience the region in an interesting and rewarding way. With that in mind, we have investigated numerous new sources of up-to-date information and surfed through the region's offerings on the Internet. We also interviewed seasoned train travelers with recent eastern European experience and local residents in the countries represented here.

A few areas of concensus emerged. Because eastern Europe is in a state of social, economic, and political flux, it is absolutely necessary that travelers confirm and reconfirm travel information. So, remember to check information and then reconfirm newly acquired information with still other people. Then check again. A train connection time printed on a schedule at the time you purchased your ticket may very well change the morning of your trip. The 3-hour layover in Warsaw you were informed of may be reduced to an hour and half at the last minute. Track 8 may not even exist. And on and on. Jim Haynes, Paris's most famous American expatriate and author of the *People to People* guides to eastern Europe, maintains that local people "know the current situation better than any up-to-date guidebook." People who live in the countries you are about to visit are your greatest source of "real info, friendship, and security," Jim acknowledges.

Although train travel in the region is quickly coming into greater homogeny with train travel in Western Europe, train travel east of Poland remains highly exotic, often disorienting, and at times less than reassuring for western travelers. Many experienced travelers love those exciting trips through the Ukraine, Russia, and the Baltic States and are the first to advise neophyte travelers to proceed with great caution and informed intelligence. Urban train stations in the Commonwealth of Independent States and the former Yugoslavia can range from confusing and seedy to outright dangerous. Try to sort out the myth from the truth. Horror stories of theft on night trains, rowdy gangs, sleeping gas, sordid violence, and roaming pirates in the East abound, but much is lore. As the economies of the region evolve, the public relationship to money responds. In that western travelers bring cash, care must be taken in how one travels and how one handles ambiguous situations. Bring one-dollar bills and take them out sparingly and one at a time—they buy a lot and they don't require change. Jody Jenkins, an American writer who lives on a barge in Burgundy and has recently completed *The Low Lights of Winter*, a collection of stories about life in contemporary eastern Europe, contends that travelers in the East must be able to "flow with the tide." Ghengis Khan–type characters were habitually harassing Jody and his girlfriend Gwen as they trained from Moscow to Tashkent in Uzbekistan. First-class tickets cost them $5 each, but it was the on-board bribes of $10 each and a pack of chewing gum that allowed them to win over the conductor and to feel secure in an otherwise alienating environment.

Jim Haynes strongly advises western travelers to be met and dropped off at train stations in the East. And don't hang out at stations; you will invite unwelcome experiences. It's always better to hail a taxi or private car a few hundred meters from the station than to subject yourself to being ripped off by a taxi waiting at the station.

Another shared point. In the more exotic places and for the overnight and long hauls, always bring your own food. Bring an extra supply for your neighbors, conductors, and compartment mates, for whom a small act of generosity and openness will buy solidarity. Cigarettes, gum, and trinkets work wonders in gaining instant companions and bodyguards. Also think ahead in terms of your travel needs. Toilet paper, for one, is a must, as Catrinel Plescu from Bucharest reported on her recent trip from the Romanian capital to Vienna, Austria. Bottles of water, flashlights, and matches are all good ideas.

Lastly, there are now scores of general travel guides to eastern Europe. Pick up at least one or two to accompany your Eurail guide. Select editions that are as recent as possible. The travel information included here will serve as a good start, but for more detailed descriptions and commentary you'll need a more general source of data. Pick up brochures along the way and share them with other travelers. Of course, we're open to receiving your comments, suggestions, and experiences in order to better report on the region in each successive update.

TRAIN PRICES AND INFORMATION

There is one rail pass that will let you see Eastern Europe. The Central European Rail Pass was discontinued in 1995.

Eastern European Pass Unlimited first-class train travel in Austria, Czechoslovakia, Hungary and Poland. The 1996 prices are: $195 for any 5 days within 15 days, $299 for any 10 days within one month.

ALBANIA

Currently there is only one international rail connection in and out of Albania—it consists of the passenger link with Mali izi, Montenegro to the north via Lezhe and Shkoder. The longest train journey in the country runs a total of 96 miles between the capital, Tirana, and the southern port of Vlorë, and it takes approximately five hours. Otherwise, boat connections from Vlorë to Brindisi, Italy, which is only 80 miles away, and from Sarande to Corfu, just 16 miles south, exist, although travel details are difficult to confirm in advance. The train system runs east-west also between Durrës on the Adriatic Coast and Pogradec on the eastern lake frontier with Greek Macedonia. Some of the most interesting mountain villages are off the train route and must be visited by bus or car.

Train travel within the country requires tolerance and time. One seasoned traveler, John Hodgson, recently back from Albania, writes: "I have traveled by train in all the countries of Eastern Europe, and the best train journey is in Albania, from Tirana to Pogradec. The line is 147 kilometers, the journey takes seven hours, and it costs $1.50 U.S. All the railways in Albania were built by 'volunteer' young people under communism, and their technical standards are very low. Poor maintenance has also meant that speed limits are down to a crawl. Albanian railways have Czech-built diesels, and used to have Chinese carriages, but most of these were reduced to bits in the 1991 revolution and have been replaced by cast-off carriages donated by Italian railways. In 1992 I traveled from Tirana to Shkoder in an unlit train with no glass in the windows, holding an umbrella inside the compartment and 'protected' by a sinister-looking character carrying pistols under both armpits.

The Tirana-Pogradec train leaves at 5:40 A.M. and passes through most of central Albania, via Durrës, Rrogozhine, Elbasan, and Librazhd. The later part of the journey, up the Shkumbin valley, is exceptionally beautiful, with many tunnels and bridges. After a final tunnel the line emerges on lovely Lake Ohrid, which forms the border with Macedonia.

The trains are very dirty, but are companionable. Take your own food, and indeed take some to share around. Reservations are not possible. The train is normally very crowded and smoky.

Anyone who visits Albania and proposes going by train will have to fight with his Albanian host for the right to do so, because the trains are thought to be too horrible for foreigners to support. It is worth fighting for—and worth going to Albania, which is a wonderful country."

PLACES TO VISIT AND EXCURSIONS

Tirana

The predominance of indestructible and ubiquitous concrete bunkers, or "pillboxes," sprinkled throughout the countryside perpetually remind visitors of the past and this country's century-long trail of invasions. Tirana's inroads into Western Europe were best heard via its notorious attacks on capitalism on Radio Tirana broadcasts in English. Although intrigue still lurks in contemporary Tirana and tourism remains greatly undeveloped, a new atmosphere of possibility pervades daily life. There is little traffic, and at times an unsettling calm cloaks the city. Air connections to and from Rinas Airport exist with Istanbul, Athens, Sophia, Rome, Budapest, Vienna, Lubliana, and Zurich.

The Albanian capital with its 400,000 inhabitants hosts some 170 museums. The Museum of Natural History houses a worthwhile yet limited collection of prehistoric and Illyrian objects and folk art from the region as well as an imposing mosaic mural depicting examples of warriors through the ages struggling for "freedom." A large room dedicated to the communist period has been roped off but not yet removed or reorganized, a detail that indicates the conflict of the national debate on the treatment of history.

Crowning the highest hill in the city is a mammoth statue commemorating "The Heroes," which guards the cemetery below. The major buildings around the main square capture the nation's history. There is the old Byzantine church, which long ago was converted into a mosque with the addition of a tall and narrow minaret. The government buildings date from World War II, when Mussolini's troops occupied the city (1939–1944).

As the Albanian-born New York writer Fron Nazi states, contemporary Albanian life transpires in the coffee shops, where right- and left-wing politicians, corrupt intellectuals, charming criminals, ideologue artists, spies and double agents, and sleazy businesspeople all congregate and swap stories, rumors, dreams, plots, and plans for deals, articles, government reforms, and revolutionary projects.

Durrës

Albania's Adriatic port, Durrës, built on the ruins of Greek and Roman towns, offers excellent sand beaches. This city has served as the nation's resort area, offering functional hotels built for "the people." The city also has a Roman amphitheater, several interesting bazaars, and a variety of Moslem mosques, the largest located in the main square. A curiosity: a beached boat now serves as a popular coffee shop. Durrës is a good starting point for exploration to nearby villages. All train trips in Albania pass through Durrës. Each day seven trains make the 36-kilometer haul in 90 minutes between Durrës and Tirana.

Kruje

Kruje is a mountainside city north of Tirane. An interesting citadel/museum is dedicated to Skanderbeg, the national hero who led a revolt against the Turks in the middle 1400s, resulting in a brief period of independence. There is a quaint marketplace street that offers folkloric items.

Berat

Crowning the isolated steep hill is a walled citadel overlooking the broad valley below. Inside is an ancient Byzantine church which had been converted into an icon museum during the decades when religious practices were prohibited. The old part of Berat, along the riverbanks, has been preserved and restored as a museum town. The hilltop 16th-century Ardenitza Monastery has been converted into an inn.

Vlorë

This ancient seaport is surrounded by hills of olive trees which serve the local olive oil refinery. Popular lore has it that the city takes its name from the "Turk" who declared Albania's independence in 1912, Ismail Kemal Bey Vlorë. This is not so—the name dates to Roman times. The Tirana-Vlorë train makes the 155-kilometer trek in under six hours.

Sarande

Sarande is the southernmost city on the Adriatic coast, almost on the border with Greece and across a narrow body of water from the island of Corfu. The town is on a curved shoreline, making it most attractive. The walls and houses are ablaze with bougainvillea and the streets are shaded with palms. A few miles farther south are the ruins of Butrint, a city founded in pre-Greek times by Illyrians and perhaps exiled Trojans, followed by the civilizations of Greece, Rome, and Byzantium. The layers of stone ruins are clearly visible. Foundations, walls, heroic gates, colorful mosaics, fallen columns, and the citadel atop the hill all combine to make this a most interesting site.

Gjirokaster

The small mountainside city of Gjirokaster, crowned by a citadel that was used by the Italians, Nazis, and communists as a prison, is now a war museum. The monumental statue of the deceased dictator recently had been removed from this prominent spot.

Other villages worth visiting include Apollonia, Fiera, Shkodra, and Butrinti. Other train travel in Albania includes the Shkodra to Podgorica, Yugoslavia, run initiated in 1986, but this is primarily used for freight.

For information about Albanian tours, contact the Kutrubes Travel Agency, 328 Tremont Street, Boston, MA 02116; (800) 878-8566.

Tirane - Durres - Vlore   and v.v. 949

Dep. Tirane	15:25		Dep. Vlore	05:20
Dep. Durres	16:45		Dep. Durres	09:20
Arr. Vlore	20:25		Arr. Tirane	10:30

BULGARIA

BULGARIAN HOLIDAYS

January 1	New Year's Day	June 2	Memorial Day
May 1 and 2	Labor Day	Sept. 9 and 10	Liberation Day
May 24	Education Day	November 7	Revolution Day

BULGARIAN RAIL PASS

Unlimited first-class train travel in Bulgaria for 3 days in one month: $70

Bulgarians will often advise you not to take their trains—they'll tell you that they are dirty and unreliable. However, there still is no better way to see the "Jewel of the Balkans" than by rail, and the highly useful Bulgarian Flexipass is a great asset.

The most significant travel destinations in Bulgaria are the capital city of Sofia, the ancient trading center of Plovdiv, and the Black Sea resort towns of Varna and Burgas.

Train travel into Bulgaria is dominated by its routes from Bucharest, Romania; Nis, Yugoslavia; Thessaloniki, Greece; and Edirne, Turkey; with major connections to Athens, Berlin, Budapest, Warsaw, Kiev, Moscow, Vilnius, and St. Petersburg. As elsewhere in Eastern Europe, buses are often cheaper and more reliable than trains, and this is especially true when traveling between Bulgaria and Romania. The Romanian train into Bulgaria originates in Russia, and travelers often report being told they were not allowed on these trains despite their purchased tickets. A $10 "tip" in almost all cases will resolve any potential conflict. Don't get too righteous about these things—have small bills, cigarettes, and chewing gum conveniently ready. The 11-hour Bucharest-Sofia jaunt can only be taken on an overnight and unreserved basis. Be ready for horrible crowding and arrive at the station well in advance of the departure time.

The famous Orient Express from the late 1800s ran through Sofia on its way from Paris to Istanbul, and the legacy is carried forward in the form of the Istanbul Express coming from Munich and the Balkan Express coming from Warsaw. Some cost-sensitive travelers recommend buying westbound tickets up to the Turkish frontier town of Kapikule and then paying for the additional fare into Bulgaria on the train.

Traveling to Bulgaria from Greece has been reported as difficult and painful, especially at the border. The bus is preferable. However, train travel in the other direction seems less problematic. The overnight Transbalkan Express links Sofia and Athens in 18 hours. Other Greek-Bulgarian connections include the Plovdiv and Alexandroupolis run.

The Meridian Express is a daily linking Berlin and Sofia by way of Prague, Budapest, and Belgrade. The Istanbul Express runs four days a week from Munich to Istanbul via Salzburg, Belgrade, and Sofia. Since the war in former Yugoslavia, these train routes to Belgrade and beyond host all sorts of unsavory characters. Caution should be used in making this journey. No one will understand why you are heading to Belgrade and it is not certain that you'll be allowed to carry on.

The BDZ Bulgarian State Railway has an extensive system of more than 4,000 kilometers of track, and the trains come in three speeds: express, fast, or slow (putnichki). The popular Sofia-Burgas route passes by either Karlovo or Plovdiv, and travelers often opt to break up this stint with a stopover. Similarly, the Sofia-Ruse route passes by Pleven or Gorna Oryahovitsa. Book a seat and/or sleeper reservations in a Rila tourist office well in advance for the express trains to the Black Sea.

As elsewhere in Eastern Europe, train stations in Bulgaria are not always clearly marked and it is easy to miss your stop, especially when the name is written in cyrillic script! Pay attention and ask locals on the train to announce when you've arrived.

Many seasoned travelers agree that Bulgaria's most spectacular train trip is the Sofia-Mezdra climb up the Iskar Gorge on the line to Vidin and Pleven. This can be accomplished as a day trip, but two days are preferable. The Central Railway Station in Sofia is located at Maria Luiza Blvd. Call for train information or have a Bulgarian person call for you. The telephone number is 3-11-11 to 3-11-20. For international train ticket information, call 87-59-35 or stop in at 5 Gurko Street. The official train ticket offices are called Rila and are located in all Bulgarian towns served by rail.

PLACES TO VISIT AND EXCURSIONS

Sofia

Sofia's central train station has little charm and can be a bit disorienting. Platforms are called *peron* and are numbered in Roman type while the tracks or *kolovoz* are marked with Arabic numbers. Don't panic, just keep asking. There is a waiting room that is slightly more comfortable than elsewhere in the station but there is a small fee to gain access.

Ticket windows are separated by floors depending on national or international destinations. Same-day, Bulgarian train tickets are sold on the lower level. But these things change so keep asking.

Although daily life in Sofia has been transformed since the end of communist rule, the Bulgarian capital remains oppressively sedate, well behaved, and rather uneventful. The former Communist Party, under a new name, still holds the most seats in the national government, and change comes begrudgingly. The cyrillic alphabet and the Turkish mosques are clear reminders of this nation's eastern roots. Sophia hosts some of the most memorable icons in Europe, notably those found at Alexander Nevsky Memorial Church and the Byzantine 6th-century Sancta Sophia church. The Archaelogical Museum in Bouyouk, the largest mosque in Sophia, requires a visit, as do the early renaissance frescos in the brick Rotunda of the St. Georgi Church, the city's oldest standing building. Art enthusiasts should also plan to visit the medieval Boyanna Church just outside the city and the Rila Monastery, an hour and a half from the capital.

Sofia is noted for its remarkable churches. The official religion in Bulgaria is Christian Orthodox, and most of the churches in Sofia perform Orthodox services. A few key sites not to

miss include the following:
• Alexander Nevsky Cathedral. This central landmark shines from every part of the city.
• The Rotunda of St. George. This red brick rotunda church dating from the 4th century is considered the oldest structure in Sofia.
• St. Sophia Church. St. George is the oldest church, but St. Sofia is the oldest Eastern Orthodox church in Sofia.
• Banya Bashi Mosque. This Islamic shrine was built in 1576.
• Church of St. Cyril and St. Methodius and Their Five Disciples. Bearing the name Sveti Sedmochislenitsi, this church dates to 1528.

The art scene is focused on the National Art Gallery, located at 1 Alexander Batenberg Square. It's open Tuesday through Sunday 10:00 to 17:30 and is closed on Mondays. Standing exhibitions feature Bulgarian and foreign art from the Middle Ages to the present day. Extention in a crypt of the Alexander Nevsky Cathedral displays one of the largest original icon collections in Bulgaria. In addition, a surprising number of private art galleries have been appearing in downtown Sofia.

Sofia also hosts a number of restaurants, where traditional national dishes can be sampled. Try *gyuvech,* a meat and mixed vegetables dish, or *sarmi,* vine leaves filled with spicy mince meat. *Palneni chushki* (dolmas) are peppers stuffed with spicy minced meat. *Tarator* is a cold yogurt soup with chopped cucumbers and garlic, ideal in the summer. The traditional drink is what the Bulgarians consider their world famous and cheap Bulgarian wine, both red and white, and *rakiya,* a strong brandy distilled from grapes and plums. In both cases, be prepared for a headache the next morning.

The Rila Mountains

The Rila Mountains are an absolute must for travelers to Bulgaria, offering exquisite hiking possibilities. A trip across these mountainous wonders, a visit to the Complex Malyovitsa and the Rila Monastery, 74 miles from Sofia, are unforgettable. The monastery, founded in 927 as a colony of hermetic monks by Ivan Rilski, is best visited by bus. Other important sites include the 14th-century Cherepish Monastery, found in the Iskar Gorge on the way from Sofia to Vidin close to the Lakatnik rocks, approximately 35 kilometers from the capital city. Legend links the monastery with the battles of the last Bulgarian medieval tsar, Ivan Shishman, who clashed with the Turks.

Plovdiv

An ancient strategic trading hub on the Maritsa River serving early caravans that moved between Europe, Asia Minor, and Africa, Plovdiv today is Bulgaria's second largest city. The train station is an easy 10-minute walk from the Central Square and the historic old town. A visit to the Roman Forum and amphiteatre is recommended, as are visits to the Djoumaya and Imaret Mosques. The Archeological Museum houses excellent exhibits of Tracian gold utensils, although some of the most famous pieces have been moved to Sofia.

Varna

Bulgaria's largest Black Sea port dominates summer life in the country. Dating back to the days of ancient Rome and Greece, this lively seaside resort city enjoys a colorful past. When the train connecting Varna to Ruse was completed in the 1860s, a direct trade route from the Danube to the Black Sea was created. Today the city offers excellent beaches, parks, street life, and restaurants. The center of the city can be reached on foot from the train station, and a convenient luggage storage office is located across the street. The celebrated summer hydrofoil service from Varna to Nesebar, Burgas, and Sozopol was shut down in 1993 for economic reasons, although a hydrobus still runs from Varna to Balchik.

Train travel to the coast is recommended, but bus travel up and down the coast between Varna and Burgas is the most convenient form of transportation. Nesebar, which can be reached by bus or taxi, hosts the ruins of thirteen churches dating back as early as the 9th century.

Burgas

Burgas, a beach resort on the Black Sea, is less crowded than Varna. The city's connection to the national train system via Plovdiv at the turn of the century accounts greatly for its growth. A bit too industrial for many vacationers' taste, Burgas still serves as a good seaside base for Black Sea exploration. The art gallery in the former synagogue is worth a visit. The old opera house, however, has been rented out as a car showroom, an indication of the realities of post-communist Bulgaria. Thirty-six kilometers north of Burgas is Bulgaria's largest tourist resort, Sunny Beach, which offers beaches, sailing, family restaurants, and babysitting services—perhaps a relaxing destination for families.

Ruse

Ruse is Bulgaria's leading port on the Danube River and a prime stopover for Russian river traffic, despite the air pollution. A daily train from Bucharest also arrives in Ruse, bringing with it hoards of Romanians and other visitors. Ruse is only a few kilometers from the longest steel bridge in Europe, ironically named the Friendship Bridge, which carries both car and train traffic and links Bulgaria and Romania. Train-lovers should plan on a visit to the Transportation Museum near the Danube—it was here that Bulgaria inaugurated its first train station, which was built in 1866.

Gorna Oryathovitsa

This town is important as a train junction and transit point that travelers often pass through on their Bulgarian journeys. Connection times often require long waits here despite your impression that you had a through ticket. Some smart travelers opt for a bus from Gorna to save time. The Sofia-Varna and Ruse–Veliko Tarnovo routes meet at Gorna.

Pleven

Famous for its battles between Turkish pashas and Russo-Romanian armies, Pleven is located between Ruse and Sofia and offers an authentic Bulgarian experience. Osman Pasha surrendered his sword to Tsar Alexandrer II of Russia here, and you can see the sword at the National Revival Park. The greatest advantages to Pleven are that it is less visited by travelers than other towns are and that its location is on the train route that follows the stunning Iskar Gorge. From Pleven, many spirited train travelers with an open ticket jump on the unreserved 8-hour Bucharest train in the middle of the night.

ONE-DAY EXCURSIONS

Sofia - Burgas - Sofia   962

Dep. Sofia	06:30 (1)	07:00 (2)	10:15 (5)	13:35 (2)	14:15 (2)	16:00 (1)	22:45 (4)
Arr. Burgas	12:40 (1)	13:55	17:15	19:50	21:05	21:45	06:10

Sights in **Burgas**: A good beach resort.

Dep. Burgas	05:15 (3)	06:00 (1)	10:30 (2)	11:00 (5)	15:10 (2)	16:00 (1)	23:10 (4)
Arr. Sofia	11:24	11:44	16:48	18:13	21:36	22:05	06:23

(1) Reservation required. Light refreshments. (2) Light refreshments. (3) Reservation *required*. Restaurant car. (4) Carries a sleeping car. Light refreshments. (5) Restaurant car.

Sofia - Plovdiv - Sofia   962

Dep. Sofia	06:30 (1)	08:15 (4)	10:15 (7)	12:15 (4)	14:15 (4)	17:15 (1)
Arr. Plovdiv	08:26	10:40	12:39	14:42	16:34	19:20

Sights in **Plovdiv**: This city has been a commercial center for more than 2,000 years, serving the early caravans that moved between Europe, Asia and Africa. There are excellent exhibits of Thracian gold utensils in the Archaeological Museum. See the Bachkovo Monastery and, near it, the ruins of Tsar Ivan Asen II's fort. The Roman ruins. The Church of Constantine and Helena. The Turkish Imaret Djamiya.

Dep. Plovdiv	04:00 (6)	09:00 (1)	10:00 (4)	11:00 (4)	14:00 (4)
Arr. Sofia	06:30	11:10	12:25	13:35	16:23

(1) Reservation required. Light refreshments. (2) Second-class. (3) Reservation *required*. Restaurant car. (4) Light refreshments. (5) Reservation *required*. First-class only. (6) Carries a sleeping car. Light refreshments. (7) Restaurant car. (8) Plus other Sofia departures at 18:50 and 23:00 (4).

Sofia - Varna - Sofia   962

Dep. Sofia	06:30 (1)	10:30 (2)	12:15 (3)	14:15 (1)	22:00 (5+6)
Arr. Varna	14:35	18:35	20:45	21:35	06:30

Sights in **Varna:** An ancient, lively and important seaport and a very popular beach resort.

See the relics of Greek, Roman, Byzantine, Turkish and Bulgarian eras in the Museum of Art and History (41 Boulevard Dimitar Blagoev), open daily except Monday 09:00–17:00 in Summer, 10:00–17:00 in Winter. Many museums and art galleries. The oldest gold ever found (from 3,500 years B.C.) is displayed there: jewelry and decorations from a burial site.

The Roman Bath. The cells and the chapel carved into the side of a chalk cliff at the 13th century Aladzha Monastery in **Druzhba**, a few miles to the north. It is open daily except Monday 10:00–17:00.

During the Summer, a hydrofoil service goes from Varna to Nesebar, Burgas and Sozopol. In **Nesebar** (a $7-U.S. taxi ride from Burgas), there are ruins of 13 churches dating back as early as the 9th century on this small islet at the end of a causeway. See the Church of John Aliturgetus and the 16th century St. Stephen's Church.

Dep. Varna	07:10 (1)	08:10 (3)	10:30 (1)	14:00 (1)	22:15 (5)	22:40 (5)
Arr. Sofia	14:40	16:23	18:30	21:40	06:39	07:31

(1) Reservation *required*. Restaurant car. (2) Restaurant car. (3) Light refreshments. (4) Change trains in Plovdiv at 21:18. Sleeping car and light refreshments Plovdiv-Varna. (5) Carries a sleeping car. Light refreshments. (6) Plus another Sofia departure at 23:00 (5), arriving Varna 07:05.

INTERNATIONAL ROUTES
FROM BULGARIA

Sofia is the gateway for train travel to Yugoslavia (and on to Western Europe), Romania and Greece (and on to Turkey).

Sofia - Belgrade   945

There is great mountain scenery on the Dragomagoman-Crveni Krst portion of this route.

Dep. Sofia	08:20	23:10 (1)
Set your watch back one hour.		
Arr. Belgrade (Belgrade)	15:32	06:29

(1) Carries a sleeping car. Also has couchettes. Coach is second-class.

Sofia - Bucharest - Kiev or **St Petersburg** or **Moscow**   94d

All of these trains have only sleeping cars. No coaches.

Dep. Sofia	13:00 (4)	11:15 (6)	21:40 (8)
Arr. Bucharest (Nord)	23:40 (5)	23:16 (7)	09:04 (2)
Arr. Kiev	01:28 (3)	03:06 (3)	11:26 (3)
Arr. St. Petersburg	18:24	-0-	-0-
Arr. Moscow (Kievski)	-0-	21:14	-0-

(1) Runs Monday, Wednesday, Friday and Sunday. (2) Day 2. (3) Day 3. (4) Day 2. The section of this train that originated in Athens departs from Bucharest's Baneasa railstation. The section from Istanbul departs from Bucharest's Chitila railstation. Then, the 2 sections are combined. (6) Runs Tuesday and Friday. Restaurant car on Day 2. (7) Day 2. Departs from Bucharest's Chitila railststation. (8) Runs Tuesday, Thursday and Saturday. Restaurant car.

Sofia - **Athens** or **Istanbul**   57 + 84 + 965 + 975

	975	965
Dep. Sofia	07:40	08:05 (3)
Arr. Athens	00:58	-0-
Arr. Istanbul	-0-	19:59

(1) Carries only sleeping cars. (2) Carries only sleeping cars and couchettes. (3) Reservation *required*. Has couchettes. Carries a sleeping car on Thursday. Coach is second-class.

COMMONWEALTH OF INDEPENDENT STATES

The CIS, the catch phrase replacing the former Soviet Union (FSU), has come to suggest many unclear notions in the minds of travelers. Few westerners can name more than a few of the fifteen states, and travel beyond Moscow and St. Petersburg is still complicated and at times even surrealist. Train travel in Russia and the Ukraine as well as the Baltic States of Estonia, Latvia, and Lituania, however, has generally become far more accessible to western travelers since 1990. For political and cultural reasons, each country in this section of this guide has been listed separately, although in many cases the rail infrastructure of one small country is connected to that of another.

Most seasoned travelers agree that Russia and its related states present some of the most exciting train trips available today. Most also agree that the sensibilities of travelers never cease to be shocked when traveling in that region, and that mental preparation for the journey is required. One highly experienced world traveler reports that he could not remember even one moment of relaxation during his month-long trek from Paris to Tashkent via Moscow. Be ready for some wonderful experiences mixed with some trying and tiring moments of international survival.

As soon as you reach the eastern border of Poland, you are confronted with a major shift in aesthetics and functionality. When the train pulls into the station at Brest in Belarussia, it is lifted into the air and its wheels are changed to adapt to the wider Russian tracks. Walking underneath the train is a strange experience. At one border crossing, passengers are intructed to disembark while the train pulls onto a siding for a wheel change. Stay close by: it is often difficult to find the train again or to find the access to that siding. A garbled announcement shouts that the train will be leaving shortly, and hoards of panicked travelers push and scramble, jump onto the tracks to get to another platform, pass battered suitcases over their heads, and so on. Then, after surviving this pandemonium on the quai, you may find yourself in an Old World dining car drinking Bulgarian champagne and downing spoonfuls of red caviar for a whopping $2! Such is the charm of Russian train travel.

Lastly, one cannot generalize about trains in the CIS. They are all different, and they depend on everything from time of year, available equipment, mood of the conductor, exchange rates, weather, destination, application of laws, and luck.

SUMMER TIME

The Commonwealth changes to Summer Time the last Sunday of March and converts back to Standard Time on the last Sunday of September.

TRAIN PRICES AND INFORMATION

Children under five travel free. Half-fare for children between the ages five and nine. Reservations are usually required for all trains. In the case you do not have reservations but need to get on a train, it's up to you to negotiate with the conductor. Don't be too passive or quick to pay a lot, but definitely be sensitive to the fact that an extra $5 or $10 may represent a month's salary to the conductor.

There are two classes of train cars in the CIS. Soft Class is the upholstered seats which convert to bunks in four-berth compartments and Hard Class are plastic or fake leather seats which sometimes convert into bunks and sometimes do not. Bedding is available at an extra charge.

Sleeping cars are also available in two-berth compartments equipped with folding tables, a closet, and a speaker over which music and announcements come. Conductors on these trains serve tea from large samovars, one of the few features you can always count on.

Because the tracks in the CIS are five feet wide, passenger cars are roomy. Of course the change of wheels at the Polish border represents a delay, but you can't have everything. One border crossing through the north of Poland on the way to the Baltic States is organized differently and instead of changing the wheels, passengers walk across the border and board an awaiting Lituanian train.

Athough the CIS has nine different time zones, all timetables indicate Moscow time only.

The topography of Uzbekistan is highly diverse. The southeast portion contains the foothills and valleys of the Tian Shan (Tien Shan) mountain range. The north central lowland portion is occupied by desert.

ARMENIA

The good news is that Armenia is a fantastically interesting country with a rich and diverse cultural heritage. The bad news is that Armenia is enduring a transportation and natural gas embargo that is causing severe food and medical shortages, frequent interruptions in electrical power, and shortages of transportation fuel. Internal travel, especially by air, may be disrupted by fuel shortages and other problems. Tourist facilities are not highly developed, and many of the goods and services taken for granted in other countries are not yet available, according to the United States State Department.

If you do go, remember that a visa is required. Without a visa, travelers cannot register at hotels and may be required to leave the country immediately via the route by which they entered.

Yerevan is the capital of Armenia. Since 1988, armed conflict has taken place in and around the enclave of Nagorno-Karabakh (located within Azerbaijan), and there is frequent shelling along many areas of the Armenian-Azerbaijani border. A ceasefire has been in effect since May 1994, though there have been some reports of minor violations.

Train transportation may be unreliable and uncomfortable. Train service to neighboring Georgia is subject to frequent disruptions and delays, and crime on board is an increasing problem.

AZERBAIJAN

Azerbaijan is located in southwestern Asia, between Armenia and Turkmenistan, bordering the Caspian Sea. With its capital in Baku, it is slightly larger than the state of Maine including the Nakhichevan Autonomous Republic and Nagorno-Karabakh, whose autonomy was abolished by the Azerbaijani Supreme Soviet in 1991. Azerbaijan borders with Armenia to the west, Georgia and Iran to the south, and Russia, Turkey, and the Caspian Sea to the east.

The country is ethnically dominated by Azeris and is predominantly Muslim. Its violent and longstanding disputes with ethnic Armenians of Nagorno-Karabakh and with the ethnic Azeri portion of Iran have not been resolved. Additionally, severe pollution problems have not helped encourage visitors to the region.

Azerbaijan is less developed industrially than either Armenia or Georgia, the other Transcaucasian states. It resembles the other Central Asian states in its majority Muslim population, high unemployment, and low standard of living. The country has more than 2,000 kilometers of railroad track, but connections with Europe are long and tiring.

BELARUS

Located east of Poland, Belarus with its 10 million people is slightly smaller than the state of Kansas. It borders with Latvia, Lithuania, Poland, Russia, and the Ukraine, with Minsk as its capital. Its people speak primarily Byelorussian and belong to the Eastern Orthodox church.

Known for its cold winters, Belarus is flat and marshy. On April 26, 1986, Belarus was severely hit by the fallout of radioactive dust from the Chernobyl nuclear power plant. In December of 1991, with Russia and the Ukraine, Belarus formed the core of the CIS.

More modernized than other CIS states, Belarus has always served as a transport link for Russian oil exports to the Baltic states and eastern and western Europe. Train travelers to Moscow undoubtedly pass through Belarus and thus get a good glimpse of the state.

GEORGIA

Located in southwestern Asia between Turkey and Russia, bordering the Black Sea, Georgia is slightly larger than the state of South Carolina. It borders Armenia, Azerbaijan, Russia, and Turkey. Georgia is a nation undergoing profound political and economic change. A newly independent nation, it is in the process of stabilizing its relations with neighboring countries.

Tourist facilities outside of the capital are not highly developed, and many of the goods and services taken for granted in other countries are not yet available. Travel, especially by air, may be disrupted by fuel shortages and other problems. The recent assasination attempt of Georgian speaker of parliament Eduard Shevardnadze hasn't helped to reassure tourists, who are eager to experience the otherwise calm Mediterranean-like Crimea.

Visitors who enter at the Tbilisi airport receive a temporary passport stamp and are instructed to obtain a visa from the Consular Division of the Ministry of Foreign Affairs.

Travelers who have a valid multiple-entry visa from Armenia or Azerbaijan are not required to obtain a Georgian visa. Those arriving from or departing to other countries, including other former Soviet states, must obtain a Georgian visa in order to leave the country. On an exceptional basis, the Georgian Ministry of Foreign Affairs can assist travelers in obtaining visas at the checkpoint at Sarpi (on the border with Turkey) and at the port of Batumi on the Black Sea. Arrangements must be made *in advance* to issue a visa at one of these entry points.

Travel in the separatist-controlled Georgian autonomous Republic of Abkhazia remains hazardous. Since March 1995, there has been increased Abkhaz terrorist activity in southern Abkhazia and attacks on United Nations personnel in the Sukhumi and Gali districts of Abkhazia. In addition, land mines pose a threat to all travelers in Abkhazia. This should tell you enough about the prospects of enjoyable travel in the region. Also, the U.S. government does not recognize an independent republic of Abkhazia separate from the Republic of Georgia. For the time being, it is recommended that you choose other countries in which to rail around.

Another warning: high crime rates in south Ossetia make unofficial and unescorted travel there risky. All train and vehicular traffic is vulnerable to robbery. Please note that terrorist incidents have occurred in the country in connection with regional conflicts. Passenger trains traveling between Georgia and Armenia have been the targets of bombings.

Georgia currently has a cash-only economy, with the use of Russian ruble being banned in July 1993.

KAZAKHSTAN

Located in Central Asia, northwest of China, Kazakhstan is immense, nearly four times the size of Texas. It borders China, Kyrgyzstan, Russia, Turkmenistan, and Uzbekistan, as well as the Aral Sea and the Caspian Sea, whose international borders are not yet determined. The country has a population of more than 17 million, of which most are ethnically Kazakh and Russian, and equally split between Muslim and Russian Orthodox religions.

The capital is Almaty. Kazakhstan is so far from Moscow by train that, other than foreign travelers on their way to Beijing, the country is seldom a selected destination.

KYRGYZSTAN

Kyrgyzstan is a newly independent nation in a state of dramatic change. Do not take anything for granted if traveling to or through this region. The capital is Bishkek (formerly Frunze). Visas from Russia and neighboring Commonwealth of Independent States, except Georgia and Tajikistan, allow for temporary stays in Kyrgyzstan for up to three days.

With the breakup of Aeroflot into many small airlines, air travel in the former Soviet Union is often unreliable. Travelers must often cope with unpredictable schedules and difficult conditions, including poor quality of service and overloading. At present, no airline provides dependable, regularly scheduled international air service into Bishkek. Most international air travelers fly to Almaty and then travel overland (approximately 3 hours) to Bishkek.

Train travel in Central Asia is irregular and arduous. About four-fifths of Kyrgyzstan is mountainous. The mountains include the Tian Shan (Tien Shan) range, extending into the Xinjiang (Sinkiang) region of northwestern China, the Kirghiz Mountains of north Kyrgyzstan, and the Alai range in the southwest. The highest elevation is Pobeda (Victory) Peak on the Chinese border (7,437 meters/24,400 feet).

Kyrgyzstan, like the other Central Asian countries, is a cash-only economy.

MOLDOVA

Moldova, according to the U.S. State Department Travelers Warning, is "a nation undergoing profound political and economic change. It is a newly independent nation still in the process of stabilizing its relations with neighboring countries. Tourist facilities are not highly developed, and many of the goods and services taken for granted in other countries are not yet available. Internal travel, especially by air, may be disrupted by fuel shortages and other problems."

Visas for travel to other former Soviet states are necessary and difficult to obtain in Moldova. The U.S. embassy in Chisinau advises that only essential travel should be undertaken into or through the Transnistria region. There are frequent checkpoints in Transnistria that are manned by armed, young, inexperienced paramilitary units who are not under the control of the Moldovan government and whose members rarely understand English. Tourists and truckers may be subject to extortion or robbery at checkpoints.

Only Air Moldova and Tarom (Romania's national airline) regularly fly to Moldova. Air Moldova service is well below Western standards. Aircraft appear to be old and cabin areas are in poor condition. Train service is also below Western standards, and an increasing number of Americans have been victimized while traveling on international trains to and from Moldova.

Mumansk

The largest city in the world north of the Arctic Circle, Mumansk was founded in 1915 as a supply post in World War I. Used in World War II as Russia's principal port for receiving supplies from Britain and the United States, the city exudes historic exoticism beneath its current commercial fishing and ship repair industries.

RUSSIA

Russia has for many years been a land of mystery and intrigue to the people of the West. For hundreds of years it has been an enigma, friend, or enemy, as the political climate has shifted time and again. Since the dissolution of the Soviet Union, Russia has bounded in diverse and often contradictory directions socially, politically, culturally, and economically, making travel hard to predict yet extremely interesting.

Traveling to Russia by train has been an experience that more and more westerners have indulged in, and most come back with fantastic stories and a will to return or venture deeper into this vast land. Most also come back with words of caution. Jody Jenkins and Gwen

Strauss tell of a horrific journey by train from Moscow to Tashkent: a band of drunken nuclear submarine captains took over one compartment while Ghengis Khan look-alikes proceeded to shake down the most vulnerable travelers. American expatriate Jim Haynes, who has traveled throughout eastern Europe and has written five books, admits that the train south through the Ukraine to Odessa and the Black Sea is the route that has peaked his imagination the most.

For first-time visitors to Russia, the train to Moscow and the Moscow–St. Petersburg route are wonderful initiations.

Due to the extraordinary political changes in Russia and changing attitudes in the United States, most sources of local information confirm loudly that it is now possible for individuals and companies to do business in Russia. Runaway inflation, however, is causing contact with local travelers to be tainted by an air of mercantilism. While there is relatively little inflation in dollar terms, inflation in ruble terms is terrifying. This situation has caused local hardship and is affecting the security of travel.

Russia is technically located in northern Asia between Europe and the North Pacific Ocean, although the area west of the Urals is sometimes considered to be Europe. Russia is the world's largest country and borders Azerbaijan, Belarus, China, Estonia, Finland, Georgia, Kazakhstan, North Korea, Latvia, Lithuania, Mongolia, Norway, Poland, and the Ukraine.

As of July 1994, the Russian population alone totaled nearly 150 million people.

Pricilla Sharp is an experienced travel writer whose comments on trains appear regularly on-line in the Train Forum on CompuServe. She has traveled extensively on trains in Russia, Belarus, and a bit of Ukraine, specifically from Moscow to St. Petersburg, St. Petersburg to Minsk, Minsk to Gomel, Gomel to Kiev, Kiev to Moscow, and St. Petersburg to Archangel. She swears that the overnight trips are the best: "You must travel first-class, and it is preferable to buy all four tickets in the compartment to ensure privacy, especially on the 'overnighters.' The trains are well-worn, creaky monstrosities. For example, on the Kiev–Moscow train, our compartment was directly over the wheels, which groaned, clanked, crunched, and made various other loud noises all night long! There is no air conditioning in summer, but the only time I was uncomfortable was on the 'local' three-hour Minsk to Gomel. There were forest fires all the way (thus, unfortunately, stirring up the radioactivity which had settled in the area from Chernobyl) and the heat was unbearable. The windows in the compartments rarely open, but the windows in the hallways do."

Pricilla also states that the bathrooms are uniformly filthy. There is nothing you can do about it except do *not* sit down. Russians will very often stand on the toilet seat and squat, thus, in her words, adding boot mud to the mixture. "Whenever I travel in Russia I always bring my own toilet paper—at least one and a half rolls per week! And, don't laugh, but I always wear long skirts when riding on trains. It's much cleaner and easier to pull something *up* around my neck than *down* toward that filthy floor!" Successful train travel in difficult places relies on the sharing of practical information like Pricilla's.

"Edible food is almost nonexistent. I always pack my own: sausages, bread, cheese, hard-boiled eggs, peanut butter, etc. We always bring our own single-pack coffee bags and just ask for hot water, which is provided by the train attendant from a huge samovar that's constantly kept boiling hot in each car. Actually, the tea is always very good, if you prefer tea. Whenever the train stops, there are usually vendors at the stations who come and offer vegetables, pirogis (little popovers of meat and bread), cookies, and the like. On the overnight trains, such as one from Moscow to St. Petersburg, you won't need any food because the train arrives at about 7:00 A.M. in St. Petersburg."

When in Moscow and in need of reliable train or other travel information, try contacting the Travelers Guest House at 50 Bolshaya Pereyaslavskaya, 10th Floor, Moscow, Russia 129401; Tel. (7095) 971-4059, 280-8562; Fax (7095) 280-7686. The Travelers Guest House is very close to the downtown area, including Red Square and the Kremlin. It would take approximately 20 minutes to get there from the closest metro station and only a few stops on the metro.

IRO Travel, an American owned and managed agency, can help in issuing train tickets, visas, and invitation letters when needed.

The Europe Library of The Travel Forum on CompuServe stores a healthy supply of relevant rail information. Here is more on the various Trans-Siberian options.

Moscow

Start at the Kremlin, the Grand Kremlin Palace, or Red Square, and satisfy the great mythic draw of this international landmark. Closed on Thursdays. Red Square, with Lenin's Mausoleum, is open daily except Monday and Friday.

The Cathedral of Saint Basil the Blessed has become a symbol of Russia to those in the West. This colorful 16th-century church sits on the north side of the Kremlin. Interestingly, Red Square is not named for the red bricks which pave it, but for the Russian word meaning beautiful, literally "Beautiful Square."

On a sunny fall afternoon Red Square is crowded with families, tourists, and vendors selling stacking dolls, shish kebab, and other small goods. The prices here, as in any area in the world frequented by tourists, will be higher than elsewhere. If you have the time, the best place to do your souvenir shopping is at Izmailovsky Park. Here there is a large flea market with hundreds of vendors selling everything under the sun. It is open on weekends only.

The south side of Red Square is bounded by Lenin's tomb (now closed to the public) and the wall of the Kremlin. The church above has beautiful bells which are rung on weekends and other times. It is well worth the time to soak in the sites and sounds of Red Square on a sunny day. Weekends are best as there are few official events. Remember that the Kremlin is the seat of government, so during the week Red Square may be closed when officials or visiting dignitaries are arriving and leaving. Try to visit at night. The buildings are caught in strong spotlights and the scene is filled with magic.

The south side of Red Square is the north side of the Kremlin, a 13th-century fortress that's surrounded by a high brick wall and many towers. Most of the towers are still crowned with illuminated red stars. It is not impossible to visit the inside of the Kremlin during some days and hours, but you should ask your Russian hosts to help set this up.

Americans and others who visit Russia for the first time will be amazed at how expensive it is. A quality hotel room will cost from $100 to $300 per night. Restaurant meals are on par with those in New York in cost, but not necessarily in quality. A taxi ride is similar in cost to those in any major city. While there are dispatched taxis, most any private car headed in your direction will give you a ride for a small fee. Hailing a taxi in Moscow rarely takes more than 30 seconds on a busy street, which is far from the reality of St. Petersburg! Agree on the fee ahead of time, and if at all possible have a Russian do the talking and negotiate the price.

Moscow has the world's busiest METRO (subway) system. It carries nearly 4 billion people each year. There are many English newspapers and maps available—most of them are free and will have a METRO map in them.

Russian cultural performances and exhibitions are truly world class. Pick up a copy of the *Moscow Times* for listings. Tickets for most events are very reasonable.

In Moscow, don't miss the Tretyakov Gallery, which just reopened after several years of renovations. Another important cultural insight is the Orthodox church. Try to stop by a functioning church. If a service is going on, don't be intimidated—services are long and most Russians don't stay for the whole thing. Orthodox church music is unbelievably beautiful.

Also see the Uspensky, Blagoveshchensky, and Archangelsky cathedrals, which date to the 15th century. The priceless jewelry, costumes, gold and and silver objects, Fabergé eggs, and weapons located in the Armory Museum will impress you. Don't miss the 16th-century 38-ton canon, Czar Pushka. The weekend bird market on Kalitnikovskaya Street is highly original. The Bolshoi Theater should be attended if possible, as well as the Lenin State Library and Lenin Museum. For public art deco, make sure you pass through the Komsololskaya, Ploshchad, Revutsi, Kropotkinskay, and Mayakovskaya metro stations.

In Moscow, there are culinary alternatives to the bland hotel food, the incredibly expensive western hotel food, and McDonald's and Pizza Hut. Georgian food comes highly recommended. Watch out the beautiful bowl of fruit on your table trick. If you want a reasonably priced meal, *don't eat the fruit*—your pocketbook will regret it.

Fun weekend things to do in Moscow include the Ismailovsky Park flea market. Russian handicrafts, souvenirs, etc., for cheap prices. Haggle. Good stuff, much cheaper than in shops. If you buy lacquered boxes, make sure they're painted, not decoupaged—a common trick.

Note that Moscow has *nine* major railroad stations:

      Byelorussia—trips to Warsaw and on to western Europe
      Kazanski—trips to Tashkent and Samarkand
      Kievski—trips to Kiev and Eastern Europe
      Kurski—trips to Sochi and the Caspian Sea
      Leningradski—trips to St. Petersburg and on to Helsinki
      Paveletski—check Thomas Cook timetables
      Riga—trips to Riga and the Baltic States
      Savelovski—check Thomas Cook timetables
      Yaroslavski—trips to Siberia, Central Asia, and Beijing

LONG-DISTANCE TRIPS
FROM MOSCOW

Here are schedules for rail trips from Moscow to 9 interesting cities, with notes on what to see at each destination.

Moscow - Kiev   and v.v. 924

The following trains are ones we recommend.

Dep. Moscow (Kiev.)	09:56 (1)	11:47 (1)	11:54 (1)	13:07 (2)	14:20 (2)	14:44 (1)
Arr. Kiev	00:01	01:57	03:16	03:30	06:00	05:53

Sights in **Kiev:** See notes about sightseeing in Kiev under "St. Petersburg–Kiev"

Dep. Kiev	04:50 (1)	10:00 (1)	11:22 (1)	12:28 (1)	16:45	17:15 (2)
Arr. Moscow (Kiev.)	21:41	04:00	05:09	06:17	09:09	10:24

(1) Restaurant car. (2) Light refreshments.

Moscow - St. Petersburg   and v.v. 901

Dep. Moscow (St. P.)	01:05	01:56	12:26	13:28	17:18	20:35
Arr. St. Petersburg (Mos.)	09:16	10:30	20:15	22:36	23:19	05:15

Moscow - Riga   and v.v. 915

Dep. Moscow (Riga)	16:55	19:53	21:08
Arr. Riga	09:20	10:55	12:25

Sights in **Riga:** An important Baltic seaport. See the great pipe organ at the 13th–15th century Cathedral. The 14th century Riga Castle.

Dep. Riga	17:40	18:30
Arr. Moscow (Riga)	10:46	12:06

Moscow - Sochi - Sukhumi   and v.v. 5025 + 5080

Dep. Moscow (Kurski)	13:40 (1)	16:50 (1)	22:30 (1)	23:17 (2)	23:50 (1)
Arr. Sochi	01:12 (4)	03:14 (4)	08:24 (4)	11:16 (4)	11:51 (4)
Arr. Sukhumi	05:33	06:50	12:30	15:08	16:12

•   •   •

Dep. Sukhumi	00:57 (1)	02:16 (1)	04:10 (3)	22:45 (1)	23:00 (2+5)
Dep Sochi	04:38	06:19	08:53	02:42 (4)	05:23 (4)
Arr. Moscow (Kurski)	14:54 (4)	16:02 (4)	21:43 (4)	12:09	16:12

(1) Carries a first-class sleeping car. Coach is second-class. Restaurant car. (2) Coach is second-class. Restaurant car. (3) Coach is second-class. (4) Day 2. (5) Plus another Sukhumi departure at 23:44 (1), arriving Moscow 15:22 (4).

Sights in **Sochi:** A popular Black Sea resort. Over 800 species of trees at the Dendrarium. Scenic Lake Ritsa is a 5-hour bus trip away.

   Sights in **Sukhumi:** This is the heart of Russia's subtropical area: citrus fruits, tobacco, etc. See the monkey farm used by Russian scientists in their program of studying human behavior.

Moscow - Tashkent - Samarkand   and v.v.

5031

Dep. Moscow (Kaz.)	11:46 (1)	13:55 (3)	22:03 (3)
Arr. Tashkent	04:00 (2)	04:16 (2)	08:00 (2)

Change trains. 5133

Dep. Tashkent	-0-	07:34 (4)	09:15 (4)	15:30 (5)	17:05 (5+7)
Arr. Samarkand	-0-	17:48	19:33	21:38	22:46

•   •   •

Dep. Samarkand	00:20 (5)	04:23 (5)	22:10	23:20 (5)	
Arr. Tashkent	06:10	09:50	03:45	05:05	

Change trains. 5031

Dep. Tashkent	11:45	14:29	04:40 (3)	-0-	
Arr. Moscow (Kaz)	05:08 (6)	05:41 (6)	14:30 (6)	-0-	

(1) Coach is second-class. Restaurant car. (2) Day 4 from Moscow. (3) Carries a first-class sleeping car. Also has second-class couchettes. Restaurant car. (4) Second-class. (5) Has first and second-class coaches. Restaurant car. (6) Day 4 from Tashkent. (7) Plus additional Tashkent departures at 17:35 (5) and 21:25.

Sights in **Tashkent**: This has been an important center of trade and handcraft on the major caravan route (the "silk road") between Europe and China and India for nearly 2,000 years. There are many 15th and 16th century churches. Heavy Muslim cultural influence here. See:

The Academy of Sciences. The Navoi Public Library. The Navoi Theater of Opera and Ballet.

Sights in **Samarkand:** One of the oldest cities in Central Asia. Alexander the Great captured Samarkand 2300 years ago. Heavy Turkish cultural influence here since the 6th century. Uninhabited from 1720 to 1770 due to an economic decline at that time caused by constant attacks by nomad tribes. The inception of train service in 1896 revived the city. See: The enormous colored domes of the 14th century mausoleums, decorated in marble and gold. The 14th century mosque. The ruins of a 16th century aqueduct.

Moscow - Volgograd - Rostov — Rostov - Moscow

Here is a great combination train and boat trip: a circle, from Moscow to Volgograd by train, and from Volgograd to Rostov by ship on the Volga–Don Canal. Then, return to Moscow by train.

5030

Dep. Moscow (Pav.)	01:40 (1)	14:15 (2)	15:05 (2)
Arr. Volgograd	09:00	11:10	13:09

(1) Second-class couchettes. Restaurant car. (2) Carries a first-class sleeping car. Also has second-class couchettes. Restaurant car.

Change to a ship for the Volgograd–Rostov cruise. Check Intourist for current Volga–Don Canal cruise timetables. The complete 2,000-mile ship trip runs from Moscow to Rostov. Change to a train in Rostov.

5085

Dep. Rostov	Frequent times from 00:11 to 23:27
Arr. Moscow (Kur.)	22 hours later

(1) Operates late May to late September. (2) Carries a first-class sleeping car. Also has second-class couchettes. Restaurant car.

Sights in **Volgograd:** Renamed (from Stalingrad) after being destroyed during a 7-month battle in 1942–43. See: The enormous 63-mile canal. The huge industrial complex, particularly the Tractor Factory. But, most of all, the Soviet Union's Eternal Flame, memorial to their millions of World War II dead, in the Hall of Valor. All of those names are carved in its walls.

Sights in **Rostov:** Another post-World War II metropolis based on heavy industrial manufacturing. See the enormous theater on Teatralnaya Square. Window-shop Engels St.

Here is the reverse route for this circle trip:

5085

Dep. Moscow (Kur.)	Frequent times from 00:05 to 23:59
Arr. Rostov	22 hours later

(1) Carries a first-class sleeping car. Also has second-class couchettes. Restaurant car. (2) Operates late May to late September. (3) Plus another Moscow departure at 23:59 (1), arriving Rostov 20:25.

Change to a ship for the Rostov-Volgograd cruise. Check Intourist for current Don Canal-Volga cruise timetables. Change to a train in Volgograd.

5030

Dep. Volgograd	05:49 (1)	12:45 (1)	13:10 (1)	16:00 (3)
Arr. Moscow (Pav.)	05:15 (2)	10:10	11:00	22:42

(1) Carries a first-class sleeping car. Also has second-class couchettes. Restaurant car. (2) Arrives at Moscow's Kazanski railstation. (3) Has only second-class couchettes. Restaurant car.

Trans-Siberian Express

1. The *Trans-Mongolian* (Chinese train #4) leaves Moscow every Tuesday at 7:45 P.M. This train takes you via Ulan Bator, Mongolia, and after five and a half days and 7,885 kilometres you arrive in Beijing on Monday at 15:33 P.M.

2. The *Trans-Manchurian* (Russian train #20) leaves Moscow every Friday at 8:25 P.M. This train takes you thru Manzhouli and Harbin, and after 9,001 kilometres and six and a half days you arrive in Beijing on Friday at 6:32 A.M.

3. *To Beijing with stop in Irkutsk for 4 days and Mongolia for 4 Days (3/3 days in winter).* This highly popular trip allows you to see and enjoy both Irkutsk and Mongolia to their fullest. You will stop in Irkutsk and Lake Baikal for a total of four days and three nights.

4. *To Beijing with 1 day/1 night stop in Irkutsk and Ulan Bator.* This quick stopover option lets you get a feel for Irkutsk with maximum freedom to do it on your own. Departure from Moscow every Wednesday at 9:15 P.M.

5. *To Beijing with stop in Irkutsk for 4 days/4 nights.* You will stay in both Irkutsk and in the village of Listvyanka, right on the shores of Lake Baikal. At least one full day is spent sightseeing in Irkutsk and visiting two or three museums and churches throughout the city. Part of the tour is spent at Lake Baikal, where you will be shown the Lymnological Institute and Museum of Wooden Architecture. You'll have plenty of free time to enjoy an exciting view of Baikal Lake and its shores. This stopover includes all meals, guides, and transfers. You will stay in either a hotel or with a family (one to two people in a room) in Irkutsk. Accommodation in Listvyanka is a typical Siberian wooden house for at least one night. Departure from Moscow every Tuesday at 9:15 P.M.

6. *Stop in Mongolia for 3 days/3 nights or 5 days/5 nights.* Minimum 2 nights will be spent in a traditional Mongolian Ger (*yurt*) in a camp at Terelj (70 kilometres outside of Ulan Bator) in the beautiful Mongolian countryside, which features vast grasslands, rugged hills, and horses running free. On the remaining nights you will stay at a hotel in Ulan Bator (either

the Negdelchin or Zul).

7. *The Trans-Siberian to Vladivostok (train #2: The Russia Express)* leaves Moscow every odd day at 2:00 P.M. This train travels straight through Siberia, and after 9296 kilometres and six and half days, you arrive at Vladivostok at 9:45 A.M. local time.

Safety Tips on Traveling in Russia

One travel writer, Kathryn Coombs, offers these practical tips that all train travelers should take to heart.

If you take the train from St. Petersburg to Moscow, take a bicycle lock and one of those flexible wire "chain" things that you wind through the spokes of your bike. There have been a lot of robberies/attacks on the trains. If you loop this through the door handle of your compartment, then attach it to the luggage rack, the bad guys can't get in. When you leave the compartment for any reason during the day, chain your luggage to the luggage rack with this. And lock the luggage. Bring train munchies (all the Russians do), it's a long trip and all they offer you is endless tea. There is a big samovar (hot water boiler) on the train, so pot noodles are a good idea.

Do not drink the water in St. Petersburg. It is contaminated with an intestinal parasite that you'll have trouble getting rid of. Drink bottled water and brush your teeth in bottled water. If you take baths instead of showers, bring water purification tablets with you and drop a few in the bath and wait about 10 minutes (follow directions on package) before you get in. These parasites can enter you through either end (yuck!). This happened to a friend of mine.

Moscow water is generally safe to drink if boiled first, unlike St. Pete's, but do use water purification tablets there as well. It's all right to shower. The way to avoid getting mugged is to avoid looking obviously foreign or rich. Leave your fancy jewelry at home.

Don't wear clothes that scream out "I am an American tourist" (if you're not American, sorry for presuming). This means no plaid trousers or bright preppy greens. Do not sling your camera around your neck. Most Russians carry some kind of shoulder bag with them—as they tend to do shopping on the way home from work. Find a camera bag that doesn't look like a camera bag, and you'll blend in.

Hang around with a Russian guide whenever you can. There are good people you can hire for the whole day, or your whole stay in a city, who are cheap. They will add to your enjoyment and understanding and increase your safety, helping you blend in.

Regarding arrival at Sheremetyevo Airport, make sure your travel agent arranges your airport transport in advance. The taxi drivers that congregate in the international terminal are real sharks (will charge you as much as $100 to get to town, whereas you can book a cab in advance for about $40). Most of these sharks are safe at least, but some are not, and you never know.

Watch out for "gypsy" kids—there have been some recent problems. An elderly Canadian gentleman was mugged in front of the Moskva Hotel and beaten by 8-year-old kids. They tend to hang around the less expensive tourist hotels. Often they will pretend to be begging, or trying to sell you something (postcards, usually) with the idea that when you open your wallet, ZAP! Sadly, the best policy is to avoid giving to begging children, many of whom have been put up to it by their parents. However, the metros are full of begging grannies and disabled veterans. *Always* give to them if you can—consider it reparations for winning the cold war. These pensioners are trying to live on $9 a month and are some of the nicest people you'll meet. Grannies (babuski) are the victims of crimes, not the perpetrators, so you're safe here.

Try to keep your spending money (for ice cream, beggars, small purchases, etc.) separate from your main stash of cash, to avoid flashing large wads of bills around. Sensible advice in any big city.

You will be less conspicious if you are not in a huge group of foreigners. If you stray off the beaten track, keep to small groups of, say, four people, and have your Russian guide with you.

Watch your property when you're in restaurants—a new trick is "kidnapping" property. If they think you're a foreign businessperson, they might take your papers—worthless to anyone but you—and then send a representative to negotiate your payment to get them back. This happened when I had escorted a group to dinner at the Minsk Restaurant on Tverskaya Street, where an Azeri gang hangs out. When I had checked out the restaurant the night before, everything was OK, but I was with a group of Russians and they thought I was Russian.

Get cholera and diptheria shots before you go, just to make sure. Outbreaks in Moscow/St. Petersburg have been only a few cases, and the risk is minimal, but its best to make sure, just in case, particularly if you are older. If you have any medical problems while you are there, the place to go is the American Medical Center (takes credit cards)—all hotels know how to find number. Also, State Department travel advisory bulletins are worth getting for any country you're visiting. You can access these via CompuServe.

Trans-Siberian Express: Moscow to Vladivostok

Nothing excites the imagination more than a train ride for six days across the former Soviet Union. Six days on a train. Thoughts of Pasternak's *Doctor Zhivago* rush to mind. Heading west, the train leaves Vladivostock station at midnight. Vladivostock, rich in natural resources and labeled the Seattle of Russia, has emerged in the mid-1990s as a wild town of gangsters and street warfare. Most people get on in Moscow, but the few who manage to take the train in the other direction have a particularly pure experience, especially for the first half of the trip, when very few foreigner are on board. The problem many have with the Moscow-Vladivostock run is getting back. It's easier to continue east to Japan and fly from there. One American couple recently shared their westbound journey on CompuServe's Train Forum and some of their impressions have been incorporated here.

The Trans-Siberian Express across the nation is the longest single train ride in the world. Curiously, the entire journey is quoted in Moscow time—stops, meals, everything —even though the capital can be as much as six days away.

As is true on all long voyages in the CIS, it is advised that you bring your own food, and plenty of it. Food in varying degrees of quantity and quality is always attainable, but the negotiations and "backshish" needed to come by it is too unreliable and tiring to make the effort worth it.

The route traveled covers just under 6,000 miles: from the Pacific coast along the Amur River, across the Siberian taiga, by Lake Baikal (the biggest freshwater lake in the world), through industrial towns such as Sverdlovsk (now renamed Ekaterinberg), past enormous coal fields, over the Urals (the great Europe/Asia divide) and between huge wheat fields.

"Over the six days of the journey, we must have spent more than forty hours propped in the corridor staring out of the window. And the views? Well, interesting, but not spectacular. Or rather, we expected more. But the memories will be of the people, not the views. We had come prepared with a library of books to stave off boredom. We read Eric Newby's *Big Red Train Ride*—his account of the Trans-Siberian Railway from Moscow to the east—which was excellent read backwards. Apart from that we hardly dipped into any of the books. Time—perhaps not the train itself—certainly flew by.

Surprisingly, some of the most attractive scenery on the whole journey was on the outskirts of Moscow. As we came into the area called the Golden Triangle, we could see in the distance golden spires glowing in the sunset; we were passing through green fields and forests and then suddenly we were in Moscow. After six days, across seven time zones, in a country that seemed to be falling apart at the seams, the train pulled into Yaroslavl Station ten minutes late."

The Moscow-Khabarovsk-Yokohama route of the Trans-Siberian Express is much like the above the journey, except it is advisable to stop over in Novosibirsk and Irkutsk on the 5300 mile trip.

Czar Nicholas officiated at the ceremony in Vladivostock when construction of the line began in 1891. Six separate sections were developed independently. Prisoners sent to Siberia were offered reduced sentences for working on the construction 8 months of work reduced a sentence by one year. By 1900 two unconnected sections had been completed: Moscow–Sretensk (east of Lake Baykal) and Khabarovsk–Vladivostock. Passengers traveled from Sretensk to Khabarovsk by river boat.

A line from Lake Baykal to Khabarovsk (the Chinese Eastern Railway, via Manchuria) was completed in 1903 and was much shorter than the present line. Russia lost it one year later, after the 1904 Russo-Japanese War, and had to begin building the present line from Baykal to Khabarovsk. Twelve years later the present Moscow–Vladivostock line, entirely on Russian territory, was completed and Russia began to develop Siberia.

It is necessary to check 1996 sailing dates of the Nakhodka–Yokohama (and v.v.) ships before determining dates on which to reserve Moscow or Nakhodka train departures.

929 + 5020 (Train)		
Dep. Moscow		
(Yar.)	14:00 (1)	
Arr. Novosibirsk	N/A (2)	Day 3
Arr. Irkutsk	01:38	Day 5
Arr. Khabarovsk	03:10 (3)	Day 7
Change trains.		
Dep. Khabarovsk	13:20 (4)	
Arr. Nakhodka	N/A (2)	Day 8
Change to boat.		
5050		
Dep. Nakhodka	12:00 (5)	Day 8
Arr. Yokohama	15:00	Day 10

5050 (Boat)		
Dep. Yokohama	12:00 (5)	
Arr. Nakhodka	17:00	Day 3
Change to train.		
929 + 5020		
Dep. Nakhodka	N/A (2+6)	Day 3
Arr. Khabarovsk	07:35 (3)	Day 4
Change trains.		
Dep. Khabarovsk	18:05 (1+3)	Day 4
Arr. Irkutsk	16:10	Day 6
Arr. Novosibirsk	N/A (2)	Day 7
Arr. Moscow		
(Yar.)	06:45	Day 10

(1) Carries a first-class sleeping car. Also has second-class coaches with seats that convert to berths. Restaurant car. (2) Time not available in 1993 for first time in more than 23 years. (3) Local time (7 hours later than Moscow). (4) Local time (7 hours later than Moscow). Runs only on days prior to sailings from Nakhodka to Yokohama. Carries a sleeping car. Also has second-class coaches that convert to berths. Restaurant car. (5) For specific sailing dates, check Far Eastern Shipping Co. (6) Local time (7 hours later than Moscow). Runs only on days that sailings from Yokohama arrive in Nakhodka. Carries a sleeping car. Also has second-class coaches that convert to berths. Restaurant car.

Sights in **Novosibirsk**: The Theater of Opera and Ballet, which is larger than Moscow's Bolshoi Theater. Take the 18-mile bus ride to **Akademgorodok**, the "Science Town," located along the Ob Sea, a man-made reservoir. There, top Soviet scientists and technicians live, work and shop in the USSR's most modern apartments, office buildings and stores.

Sights in **Irkutsk**: A large industrial city with no major tourist attraction. However, Irkutsk is the gateway for visiting the most unique place in the Soviet Union: **Lake Baykal**. Buses take tourists through a virgin forest to the shore of the world's deepest (6,365 feet) lake, 380 miles long and 12 to 50 miles wide, containing one-fifth of the fresh water on the earth's surface (four-fifths of the fresh water in the U.S.S.R.). Its waves sometimes measure over 15 feet.

Formed nearly 30,000,000 years ago by a rupture in the earth's crust, it is fed by 336 rivers and streams. There are 1,800 species of animals and plants in the lake. About three-quarters of them are found nowhere else in the world.

The day-trip includes a stop at the Limnological Museum, where hundreds of local flora and fauna are exhibited. The excursion to Baykal ends with a 90-minute hydrofoil ride from the Museum, up the **Angara River**, to Irkutsk.

Sights in **Khabarovsk**: Named after Yerofei Khabarov, a Slavak Daniel Boone who led a Cossack expedition to explore this area in the 17th century. Khabarovsk was first settled in 1858 by a handful of people living in tents along the banks of the **Amur River.**

When the Bolsheviks came into power in 1917, Khabarovsk was too far from Moscow for the embryonic Soviet regime to defend it, and the city was grabbed by Manchuria. Soviet rule here was re-established in 1922. By then, the old Khabarovsk had been reduced to ruins by the Manchurians. The city that exists today was started from scratch in 1922.

Its commercial air connections with Japan make Khabarovsk the Eastern gateway to the Soviet Union. Japanese tourism to Moscow and Leningrad begins and ends in Khabarovsk. The city is so geared to Japanese tourism and has so little tourism from elsewhere that several of its tourist brochures are printed only in the Japanese language.

There is a good museum here, with exhibits on the natural and political history of this area. The many 19th century wood and brick buildings are interesting. River boat excursions depart hourly from a dock that is across the park from the Intourist Hotel (one of the best hotels in Russia). **Vladivostok**, a major naval and long-range missile base, was opened to tourists in 1991 for the first time since the 1917 revolution.

Moscow - Khabarovsk - Yokohama   and v.v.

This is the eastward route of the Trans-Siberian Express.

It is advisable to stopover in Novosibirsk (population 1,500,000) and Irkutsk on the 7½-day 5,301-mile-long Moscow–Khabarovsk trip. The Hotel Novosibirsk used to have better accommodations than were available in either Irkutsk or Khabarovsk. It is always recommended to bring toilet paper and soap when traveling on Soviet trains, including the Trans-Siberian Express.

The times shown here are Moscow Time, considerably different than actual arrival and departure times as this 5,777-mile route covers 8 time zones.

For example, the real arrival time in Khabarovsk and Vladivostock is 7 hours *later* than the Moscow Time listed. Also the real departure time from Vladivostock and Khabarovsk (for the westward trip to Moscow) is 7 hours *earlier* than indicated.

The number of travel days is represented by capital letters: B = Day 2, C = Day 3 etc.

Moscow - Khabarovsk - Vladivostock   and v.v. 5020

Dep. Moscow (Yar.)	09:35 (1)	17:25 (2)	14:00 (3)	21:50 (4)
Dep. Kirov	01:22 B	07:31 B	03:56 B	20:01 B
Dep. Ekaterinberg	17:00	21:04	19:00	11:20 C
Dep. Omsk	05:10 C	08:29 C	07:03 C	02:35 D
Dep. Novosibirsk	14:51	16:42	N/A (5)	12:33
Dep. Krasnoyarsk	04:21 D	05:02 D	N/A (5) D	02:02 E
Dep. Irkutsk	23:59	23:10	01:38 E	22:13
Dep. Ulan Ude	08:14 E	07:02 E	N/A (5)	06:18 F
Dep. Chita	18:20	16:34	N/A (5)	17:03
Dep. Skovorodino	16:23 F	13:10 F	N/A (5) F	15:10
Arr. Khabarovsk	14:53	08:57 G	13:10	13:40
Arr. Vladivostock	05:35 H	22:05	02:45 H	-0-

• • •

Dep. Vladivostock	-0-	01:20 (4)	12:30 (6)	18:05 (3)
Dep. Khabarovsk	02:30 (1)	15:56	01:50 B	07:35 B
Dep. Belogorsk	14:35	04:25 B	12:46	18:44
Dep. Skovorodino	00:33 B	14:06	21:45	03:35 C
Dep. Chita	22:23	11:20 D	18:30 C	00:58 D
Dep. Ulan Ude	08:22 D	22:40	04:06 D	N/A (5)
Dep. Irkutsk	16:23	07:22 E	11:51	19:01 E
Dep. Krasnoyarsk	12:18 D	03:04 F	06:08 E	N/A (5)
Dep. Novosibirsk	01:50 E	17:02	18:25	N/A (5)
Dep. Omsk	11:39	03:10 G	02:28 F	13:15 F
Dep. Ekaterinberg	03:17 F	17:04	14:34	02:15 G
Dep. Kirov	20:00	08:28 H	04:33 G	N/A (5)
Arr. Moscow (Yar.)	17:12 G	23:00	18:55	06:45 H
Dep. Belogorsk	02:02 G	22:13	N/A (5) G	01:00 G

(1) Has second-class coaches with seats that convert to berths. Restaurant car. (2) Runs Wednesday and Sunday. Restaurant car. Has first and second-class coaches with seats that convert to berths. (3) "Rossia." Carries a first-class sleeping car. Also has second-class coaches with seats that convert to berths. Restaurant car. (4) Has second-class coaches with seats that convert to berths. Restaurant car. (5) Time not available for the first time in more than 23 years. (6) Runs Tuesday and Thursday. Restaurant car. Has second-class coaches with seats that convert to berths.

St. Petersburg

Many travelers consider St. Petersburg, formerly Leningrad, the most beautiful and stimulating city in the CIS. The Hermitage Museum with its 2.5 million works of art could keep you hostage for days alone. Don't miss the Summer Palace, and of course the 112 columns and gold cupolas at St. Isaac's Cathedral. The 600-ton Alexandrovskaya Column marking Russia's victory over Napoleon, the Summer Gardens of Peter the Great, and the Monument to the Heroes of the Revolution should not be overlooked. Nor should the excursion to the magnificent Yekaterinsky Palace in Pushkin be forgotten. In the summer, take a hydrofoil cruise on the River Neva.

Do not miss Tsarskoye Selo, just outside of town. A former Royal Palace turned into a school, there are entire rooms of malachite walls and columns. It is breathtaking.

The St. Petersburg metro operates from 5:30 A.M. to 12:30 A.M. Unless you really want massive intimate contact with the Russian people, try to avoid traveling during the peak commuter hours. Note that the doors in the stations weigh a ton and swing back and forth with the force of a wrecking ball.

Tickets for the two trains from Helsinki to St. Petersburg can be bought right in Helsinki. The Sibelius, whose departure is at 6:30 and arrives at 1:55, and the Repin, whose departure is at 3:32 and arrives at 11:20. The price is around $60 one way.

LONG-DISTANCE TRIPS FROM ST. PETERSBURG

Here are schedules for rail trips from St. Petersburg to 5 other interesting cities, with notes on what to see at each destination.

St. Petersburg (Leningrad)

The Commonwealth's most interesting city. The Hermitage Museum (closed Monday) has the world's largest exhibition of fine arts, over 2,500,000 articles. Visit the Summer Palace (open daily except Tuesday, May through November). See the 112 columns, gold cupola and priceless paintings and mosaics at St. Isaac's Cathedral (closed Tuesday, Wednesday and the last Monday of each month).

The park and palace at Petrodvorets. The Winter Palace. The 600-ton, 154-foot high Alexandrovskaya Column, marking Russia's victory over Napoleon. The Peter-Paul Fortress and Cathedral. The Summer Gardens of Peter the Great. The Museum of the History of Religion and Atheism, in Kazansky Cathedral (closed Wednesday).

The Monument to the Heroes of the Revolution, in the Field of Mars. The Central Museum, at the Marble Palace. The State Museum of the History of St. Petersburg (closed Wednesday). The State Museum of Russian Art, in Mikhailovsky Palace (closed Tuesday). The Arctic and Antarctic Museum (closed Monday and Tuesday).

In the Kunstkammer, the Peter the Great Museum of Anthropology and Ethnography and the Lomonosov Museum (closed Friday and Saturday). The Botanical Garden and Museum (the museum open only Wed., Sat. and Sun.). The Railway Museum.

Take an excursion to **Pushkin** to see the magnificent Yekaterinsky Palace (closed Tuesday and the last Monday of each month). In the Summer, hydrofoils cruise the **River Neva.**

St. Petersburg - Kiev   and v.v. 907

| Dep. St. P. (Viteb.) | 12:52 (1) | 21:53 (1) | Dep. Kiev | 09:08 (1) | 22:37 (1) |
| Arr. Kiev | 19:57 (2) | 23:32 (2) | Arr. St. P. (Viteb.) | 15:56 (2) | 09:29 (3) |

(1) Restaurant car. (2) Day 2. (3) Day 3.

Sights in **Kiev:** The 11th century catacombs at the Pecherskaya Lavra Monastery. The frescos and mosaics at the 11th century St. Sophia Cathedral. The Golden Gate (Zolotiya Vorota) at the intersection of Sverlovskaya and Vladimirskaya. The Museum of Russian Art. The Museum of Western and Oriental Art.

Below are schedules for continuing on from Kiev to Odessa:

Kiev - Odessa   and v.v. 925

The coaches on all of these trains are second-class only.

| Dep. Kiev | 03:35 (1) | 11:33 (1+3) | Dep. Odessa | 11:26 | 21:40 (4) |
| Arr. Odessa | 15:05 | 22:45 | Arr.Kiev | 22:50 | 09:02 |

(1) Restaurant car. (2) Light refreshments. (3) Plus another Kiev departure at 20:41, arriving Odessa 08:09. (4) Plus another Odessa departure at 23:30 (1), arriving Kiev 11:06.

Sights in **Odessa**: A sea resort and Russia'a largest port. See the beautiful Opera and Ballet Theater. The Potemkin Stairway, descending 455 feet from Primorsky Boulevard to the waterfront.

St. Petersburg - Moscow 901

Dep. St. Petersburg (Mos.)	00:35	12:56	15:50	20:20	21:55
Arr. Moscow (Len.)	10:57	22:09	21:50	04:56	06:22

Dep. St. Petersburg (Mos.)	22:30	22:45	23:10	23:55	23:59
Arr. Moscow (Len.)	06:35	07:10	07:19	08:25	08:29

St. Petersburg - Murmansk and v.v. 903

Murmansk is the world's northernmost passenger rail terminus.

All of these trains have a restaurant car and arrive on Day 2, unless designated otherwise.

Dep. St. Petersburg (Moskovski)	13:54	23:20
Arr. Murmansk	21:00	06:47

Sights in **Murmansk**: The largest city in the world north of the Arctic Circle. Founded in 1915 as a supply post in the First World War. Valuable in World War II as Russia's principal port for receiving war supplies from Britain and the U.S. Its ice-free harbor has made Murmansk a major ship repair center and commercial fishing base.

Dep. Murmansk	08:35	01:00
Arr. St. Petersburg (Moskovski)	14:14	08:41

St. Petersburg - Tallinn and v.v. 910

Dep. St. Petersburg (Varshavski)	21:28 (1)	23:25 (2)
Arr. Tallinn	05:35	08:45

Sights in **Tallinn**: A fortified town for more than 2,000 years. The capital of Estonia from 1918 until that country was annexed in 1940 by the former Soviet Union, Tallinn became the capital again when Estonia left the U.S.S.R. in 1991. In the walled Lower Town, see the 13th century Toom Church. The 13th century Great Guildhall. The 14th century Town Hall. Ruins of the 13th century fort built by invading Danes on Toompea Hill. The Gothic churches, Niguliste and Oleviste. The old castle.

Dep. Tallinn	20:10 (2)	23:00 (1)
Arr. St. Petersburg (Varshavski)	07:25	09:35

(1) Reservation *required*. Carries a first-class and second-class sleeping car. Coach is second-class. Light refreshments. (2) Reservation *required*. Carries a second-class sleeping car. Coach is second-class.

INTERNATIONAL ROUTES
FROM RUSSIA

Here are the schedules for rail trips from St. Petersburg to Helsinki (and on to the rest of Scandinavia) and to Warsaw (and on to Western Europe).

Also, from Moscow to Bucharest (and on to the rest of Eastern Europe as well as to Athens and Istanbul), Khabarovsk (and on to Nakhodka, and from there to Yokohama and Hong Kong), Beijing, Tehran and Warsaw (and on to Western Europe).

St. Petersburg - Helsinki and Moscow-Helsinki   902

All of these trains have a restaurant car.

Dep. St. Petersburg (Finlandski)	-0-	08:05 (2)	15:55 (2)
Dep. Moscow (St. Petersburg)	18:17 (1)	-0-	-0-
Set your watch back one hour.			
Arr. Helsinki	09:02	14:03	21:26

(1) Carries only first and second-class sleeping cars and a restaurant car. No coaches. (2) Reservation required. Has first-class and second-class coach cars.

St. Petersburg - Warsaw   857

Dep. St. Petersburg (Varshavski)	12:10 (1)	20:25 (1)
Arr. Grodno	08:15 (2)	13:57 (2)
Set your watch back one hour.		
Arr. Warsaw (Gdanska)	15:13	21:14

(1) Carries only first and second-class sleeping cars. No coaches. (2) Day 2.

Moscow - Warsaw - Berlin   56

A 2½-hour layover in Brest is for changing train wheels to conform with Western Europe's narrower tracks.

Dep. Moscow (Smol.)	13:10 (1)	20:15 (3)
Dep. Brest	08:00 (2)	14:36 (2)
Set your watch back one hour.		
Arr. Warsaw (Cen.)	10:53	19:25
Arr. Berlin (Licht.)	17:23	-0-

(1) Carries only first-class and second-class sleeping cars. No coaches. (2) Day 2 from Moscow. (3) Carries first and second-class sleeping cars. Also has second-class couchettes. Coach is second-class.

Moscow - Beijing 5000

Both of these trains carry a first-class sleeping car. They also have first and second-class coaches that convert at night to berths and bunks, and a restaurant car.

Dep. Moscow (Yar.)	19:50 (1)	21:25 (4)
Dep. Irkutsk	03:49 (2)	05:36 (2)
Arr. Beijing	15:33 (3)	06:32 (5)

(1) Runs Tuesday only. Route is via Ulan Bator. (2) Day 5. (3) Day 7. (4) Runs Monday, Friday and Saturday. Route is via Shenyang. (5) Day 8.

Moscow - Bucharest 955

All of these trains carry only sleeping cars.

Dep. Moscow (Kievski)	14:44	16:45 (5)
Arr. Bucharest (Nord)	07:41 (2+3)	11:15 (2+4)

(1) Light refreshments. (2) Day 3. (3) Arrives at Bucharest's Baneasa Railstation. (4) Arrives at Bucharest's Chitila railstation. (5) Reservation required.

Moscow - Warsaw - Frankfurt - Berlin - Cologne - Geneva - Paris - Madrid

	94a	55	56	24	56
Dep. Moscow (Smol.)	09:01 (1)	13:10 (3)	13:10 (7)	20:15 (8)	20:15 (7)
Dep. Brest	-0-	-0-	08:00 (4)	14:36 (4)	14:36 (4)
Set your watch back one hour.					
Arr. Warsaw (Wsch.)	05:32 (2)	11:50 (4)	10:15	19:10	18:15
Arr. Warsaw (Cen.)	-0-	12:20	10:40	19:25	18:30
Arr. Frankfurt/Main	-0-	06:00 (5)	-0-	-0-	-0-
Arr. Berlin (Licht.)	-0-	-0-	18:49	-0-	-0-
Arr. Cologne	-0-	-0-	-0-	-0-	09:58 (5)
Arr. Geneva	-0-	-0-	-0-	-0-	-0-
Arr. Paris (Nord)	-0-	-0-	-0-	17:08 (5)	-0-
Arr. Madrid (Cham.)	-0-	-0-	-0-	-0- (9)	-0-

(1) Carries only second-class sleeping cars. (2) Day 2. Arrives at Warsaw's Gdanska railstation. (3) Carries only sleeping cars. Moscow-Geneva: operates all year; runs Tuesday, Thursday and Sunday. Moscow-Madrid: operates late June to late August; runs Sunday only. (4) Day 2. (5) Day 3. (6) Day 4. (7) Carries only sleeping cars. (8) Carries sleeping cars. Also has couchettes. Coach is second-class. (9) Change trains in Brussels.

Moscow - Pyongyang   5000

Dep. Moscow (Yar.)	14:00 (1)	21:25 (5)
Dep. Irutsk	01:38 (2)	05:36 (2)
Dep. Khabarovsk	13:10 (3)	-0-
Dep. Shenyang	-0-	03:46 (6)
Arr. Pyongyang	10:40 (4)	15:55 (6)

(1) Carries a first-class sleeping car. Coach is second-class. (2) Day 5. (3) Day 7. (4) Day 9. (5) Runs Saturday only. Carries a first-class sleeping car. Has first and second-class coaches. Restaurant car. (6) Day 8.

TAJIKISTAN

Tajikistan is a Central Asian country bounded on the south by Afghanistan, on the west by Uzbekistan, on the north by Uzbekistan and Kyrgyzstan, and on the east by the Xinjiang (Sinkiang) region of northwestern China. Its capital city is Dushanbe. The Russian military continues to play a major role in the region.

More than 90 percent of Tajikistan is mountainous; all of its eastern territory is in the high Pamirs, known as "the roof of the world." The highest elevation was named Communism Peak (7,495 meters).

The Tajik people, who form over half of the population, are Sunni Muslims. Unlike their Turkic neighbors, they are of Iranian origin, descended from the Persian-speaking peoples that occupied the Trans-Oxus region long before the coming of the Uzbeks and other conquerors.

Tajikistan is a poor country. Its per capita income in 1989 was the lowest of all the Soviet republics. Sheep breeding remain the leading activity, and the reality is that most westerner travelers don't spend much time in Tajikistan.

TURKMENISTAN

Turkmenistan, with its capital in Ashkabad, is a country in Central Asia bounded on the west by the Caspian Sea, on the north by Kazakhstan and Uzbekistan, on the east by Uzbekistan, and on the south by Afghanistan and Iran.

More than 80 percent of Turkmenistan consists of the Kara Kum Desert. Along the border with Iran is the Kopet Dagh, a dramatic mountain range that rises to nearly 3,000 meters.

The population is concentrated in oases in the east, along the foot of the Kopet Dagh, and along the Murgab and Tedzhen rivers. The Turkmen population, Sunnite Muslims, speak a Turkic language.

Passenger train travel is limited, although since independence, travel has increased, mostly American and European businesses negotiating agreements to develop the country's natural gas reserves, and a rail line has been started to connect Ashkhabad with the Persian Gulf via Iran. Still too exotic for the casual backpacker!

UKRAINE

Kiev

Kiev, the capital of Ukraine and the country's largest city with more than 2.5 million people, is located on the banks of the Dnepr River, at the halfway point of its 2,255 kilometers (1,400 miles) route from northwest Russia to the Black Sea. Originally founded on the river's right bank, on terrain marked by steep hills, Kiev sprawls onto both sides of the Dnepr

As the country's capital, Kiev is Ukraine's political, industrial, and cultural center and a major transportation hub and river port. Kiev is also the Ukraine's most important educational and research center. It is the seat of the Ukrainian Academy of Sciences and a number of other research institutions. The city boasts of excellent and numerous theaters and concert halls, including the Ivan Franko Ukrainian Drama Theater, the Taras Shevchenko Opera, the Ballet Theater, and the Philharmonic Concert Hall.

Most of the city's historic monuments are in Old Kiev, on the right bank of the Dnepr. The city's oldest surviving church, St. Sophia's (Holy Wisdom) Cathedral, dates from 1037 and contains the tomb of Yaroslav the Wise, the 11th-century ruler of Kiev. Other architectural monuments include the 11th-century Golden Gate, one of the city's original gates, and St. Andrew's Church (1747–53), a fine example of the Russian baroque style. Kiev's most celebrated historic site is the Pechersky Lavra, or Monastery of the Caves. Dating from 1051, the monastery covers a sprawling campus and comprises many churches, cathedrals, bell towers, and monastic cells. Two separate networks of underground caves beneath the monastery contain the mummified bodies of more than 100 monks and six subterranean churches. Of utmost importance is the Babi Yar monument (1976) marking the site where thousands of Jews and Soviet prisoners of war were massacred by the Germans during World War II, an event that the Russian poet Yevgeny Yevtuskenko immortalized in his 1961 poem "Babi Yar."

See the 11th-centruy catacombs at the Pecherskaya Lavra Monastery in Kiev. The frescos and mosaics at the 11th-century St Sophia Cathedral is definietly worth a visit. The Golden Gate at the intersection of Sverlovskaya and Vladimirskaya and the Museum of Russian Art should be included in Kiev town visits.

L'viv

L'viv, located exactly 600 kilometers from both the Baltic and the Black Sea, was founded as a fort in the mid-13th century by Prince Danylo Halitski of Galicia, a former principality of Kyivan Rus. The first mention of Lviv in early chronicles is from 1256, although archeological excavation in 1993 revealed that the first settlements appeared in the 6th century.

The city's favorable location on the crossroads of trade routes led to its rapid economic development. Galicia was taken over by Poland in the 14th century. Its nobility eventually adopted the Polish language and Roman Catholicism but the vast majority of people remained Ukrainian Orthodox and later joined the Greek Catholic Church which acknowledged the Pope's spiritual supremacy but adhered to the area's Orthodox forms of worship. Thus, you begin to understand the cultural complexity of the city.

L'viv was occupied by the Nazis from 1941 to 1944. Almost the entire Jewish population was murdered in concentration camps in and around L'viv. Under Soviet rule, L'viv became an important center of activities of Ukrainian dissidents. Since the late 1980s the city has emerged as a leading force in Ukraine's movement toward sovereignty.

On the square next to the town hall the buildings captivate visitors with their beauty. Nearby is L'viv's world reknown Great Theatre, the I. Franko Theatre. This is not to be missed.

Odessa

This major seaport of the Black Sea has inspired tourists, world travelers, and immigrants for centuries. Russia's leading sea port, maritime traffic is impressive heading through the Bosporus at Istanbul. The Opera House and Ballet Theater are particularly worth seeing, as is the famous Potemkin Stairway, which descends 455 feet from Primorsky Boulevard to the waterfront. This is where you want to send your postcards from.

UZBEKISTAN

Uzbekistan is a country in Central Asia, bordered by Kazakhstan on the north and west, Turkmenistan on the southwest, Afghanistan on the south, and Tajikistan and Kyrgyzstan on the east with its capital in Tashkent. It has the largest population of the Central Asian states; among the former Soviet republics it is exceeded in population only by Russia and Ukraine. Uzbekistan is also the main heir to the rich Islamic civilization of Central Asia, containing within its borders the historic Muslim cities of Samarkand, Bukhara, and Khiva.

Tashkent

Tashkent, the capital, with a population of more than 2 million, is the largest single city in Central Asia and has been a center of Islamic civilization in that area since medieval times. Situated in the foothills of the Tian Shan mountains in an oasis irrigated by the Chirchik River, Tashkent today is a major manufacturing and transport center and cotton-textile mill, based on its cotton-fiber production. To its credit, the urban area is served by a subway system.

An opera and ballet theater and both Uzbek and Russian drama theaters are based in Tashkent six museums including a Uzbekistan history museum and an Uzbek arts museum grace the capital.

Annexed by Russia only in 1865, Tashkent now consists of an old Asian section, with winding narrow streets, and a modern city, dating from the mid–19th century. Rail connections with Russia were completed in 1898, and industrial development followed. The city's growth was spurred in World War II, when many industries were evacuated there from the European part of the USSR. A devastating earthquake in 1966 was followed by large-scale reconstruction.

Samarkand

Samarkand, the ancient city of southern Uzbekistan, situated in the valley of the Zeravshan River about 275 kilometers southwest of Tashkent, is one of the oldest cities of central Asia. Samarkand has many noted architectural remains from the 14th to the 17th century, when it flourished as the fabled capital of the Mongol empire of Timur. The ruins of the mosque of Bibi Khanom (1399–1404), with its distinctive turquoise cupola, and the great open Registan Square, lined with the remains of three Muslim religious colleges, can be seen.

Known in antiquity as Maracanda, Samarkand is believed to date back to the 6th century B.C., when it was the capital of ancient Sogdiana. It was destroyed in 329 B.C. by Alexander the Great. After the 8th-century Arab conquest it flourished under the Samanid dynasty of the 9th and 10th centuries before it fell to Genghis Khan in 1219.

Following completion of a railroad in 1888, the city's economy developed. Samarkand served as the capital of the Uzbekistan from 1924 until 1930, when the capital was moved to Tashkent. Access is possible by train, but adventurous travelers often opt for the small plane. Recently returning Americans explained that they paid $64 to get to Samarkand from Tashkent by plane and $1 for the return portion to Tashkent! Don't try to understand.

BALTIC STATES

Estonia

Bordering the Baltic Sea, between Sweden and Russia, Estonia, with Tellinn as its capital, is slightly larger than New Hampshire and Vermont combined including its 1,500 islands in the

Baltic Sea. It borders with Latvia and Russia. Only slightly more than a million and a half people occupy this small but proud Lutheran nation, which occupies a strategic geographic position in Eastern Europe.

Bolstered by a widespread national desire to reintegrate into Western Europe, the Estonian government has pursued a program of market reforms and rough stabilization measures, which is rapidly transforming the economy. Two years after independence—and one year after the introduction of the kroon—Estonians are beginning to reap tangible benefits; inflation is low; production declines appear to have bottomed out; and living standards are rising.

The Estonian World Festival is scheduled for early August, and folk culture is at the heart of Estonian spirit.

The oldest Estonian religious beliefs probably reach back to the Stone Age. These included the belief that the spirit of a witch could leave the body and gain wisdom from the place of the dead (shamanism) and belief in the image of an animal as the emblem of tribal ancestor (totemism). The cosmogonic myths about the creation of the world from the egg of a miraculous bird, and the creation of the Milky Way from a giant tree have been preserved in folklore, and are just as old. Everything in nature (trees, stones, arable land, bodies of water, fire, wind, and so on) was believed to have a spirit (animism). The most important holiday in Estonian tradition was Christmas, which was endowed with fertility magic. The most original part of Estonian folklore, the runic folksong, originated in the 1st millennium BC, as a result of interaction between primitive Balto-Finnic singing (warbling, keening) and the songs of the Baltic tribes. Heroic legends have blended with legends about hills. Estonian proverbs have been researched in detail, and 82,000 have been published.

Major train routes include the "Balti Ekspress from Warsaw and Sestokai, the Brest-Minsk connection, the "Tallinna Ekspress" between Moscow, St. Petersburg and Tallinn, the "Admiraltejets" to and from Riga. Jim Haynes's *People to People* guide on Estonia, Lativa, and Lithuania provides valuable contacts in these towns. For train information to and from Tallinn call (+372 2) 446 756, 456 851.

Estonia, located on the Baltic Sea, is considered to be one of the most progressive of the former Soviet Republics. U.S. citizens do not need an entry visa at this time. This small country is strategically located as a transportation hub. Many of you may remember the tragic loss of life from the loss of a passenger ferry in the fall of 1994. The port of Tallinn has regular links to Helsinki Finland, it was on the way to Helsinki that the ferry was lost.

Tallinn

In Tallinn, definitely plan to walk around the Lower Walled Town. Check out the 13th-century Toom Church and the fort built by the invading Danes on Toompea Hill. Visitors to Tallinn truly feel like they have rediscovered a long lost medieval Europe.

Latvia

The Republic of Latvia, with its capital in Riga, one of the "Baltic States" of northern Europe, is bordered by the Baltic Sea on the west, Russia on the east, Lithuania and Belarus on the south, and Estonia on the north. It was independent from 1918 to 1940, when it was forcibly annexed by the USSR, an event that indelibly marked the Latvians. Independence was restored in 1991. Russian intellectuals will confirm that Riga, after Moscow, is the cultural hub of the CIS. Many small publishing houses and literary journals have emerged there since independence.

Latvia's landscape with many lakes and rivers and its seaside location have strongly effected the commercial and cultural life of the country. The river estuaries provide ice-free commercial and fishing harbors, and Latvia enjoys a moderate climate, with cool summers and mild winters.

The Latvians speak a Baltic language related to Lithuanian, use Latin script, and have a mostly Lutheran background. Ethnic Russians constitute 33 percent of the population, reduced from nearly 50 since independence when many Russians were more or less forced to leave.

Riga

Riga, the capital of Latvia with nearly a million people, is situated on the Western Dvina (Daugava) River, near the river's mouth on the Gulf of Riga, an arm of the Baltic Sea. Riga consists of an old medieval city center, with narrow, winding streets and distinctive Gothic architecture, and a newer section with a grid street plan and modern buildings. The city has a cool, maritime climate. An attractive seacoast of sand dunes to the west of the city is the site of a popular beach resort, Jurmala.

The port of Riga carries on an active commercial cargo trade with Western Europe and serves as the base for an Atlantic deep-sea fishing fleet. As the cultural center of Latvia, the city is the seat of Latvian University (1919) and of the Latvian Academy of Sciences. Founded in 1201 by the Teutonic Knights, Riga developed as a trading center between Russia and the Baltic Sea. It was a member of the Hanseatic League. It passed to Russia in 1721 and became one of that country's major seaports; manufacturing followed during the second half of the 19th century.

Lithuania

Lithuania borders the Baltic Sea between Latvia and Russia and also borders with Belarus and Poland. Interestingly, it has a dispute with Russia in that the Nemen River border is presently located on the Lithuanian bank and not in midriver as by international standards. Its nearly 4 million inhabitants have adjusted well to a system set on distancing itself from the old Soviet ways, and many travelers will remember the tension in Vilnius, the capital, reported in the international news in 1990.

Significant outbreaks of diphtheria have occurred during the winter of 1993-94. Street crime, including purse snatchings and muggings, occur, especially at night near major tourist hotels and restaurants. Robberies have occurred on trains, in train stations, and in hotel rooms. Be careful.

Vilnius

Vilnius, the capital of Lithuania, is located on the Neris River. With a population of over a half a million, the city is an important cultural and industrial center, accounting for about one-fourth of the manufacturing output of Lithuania.

Vilnius has the ruins of a 14th-century castle and buildings in a variety of architectural styles, ranging from Gothic to baroque. It is the seat of the Lithuanian Academy of Sciences and has a university, founded in 1579.

Settled during the 10th century, Vilnius became the capital of the Grand Duchy of Lithuania in 1323 and, despite destruction by the Teutonic Knights in 1377, developed into a major trading center. It declined after Lithuania was formally united with Poland in 1569. Vilnius passed to Russia in 1795. After World War I the city was disputed between the new governments of Lithuania and Poland; the Poles won control of it in 1920. The USSR took Vilnius from Poland in 1939 and ceded it to Lithuania, only to annex all of Lithuania the following year.

Vilnius was also an important Jewish center of Eastern Europe until the Nazi extermination of the Jews in World War II.

THE CZECH REPUBLIC

As most travelers know, the country Czechoslovakia is now two countries, the Czech Republic and the Slovak Republic. And although the two republics are intimately connected—they both take the same telephone country code—the languages are different, the currency is different, and ultimately the experience of traveling in the two countries is distinct. The Czech Republic is made up of two distinct regions, Bohemia and Moravia, both of which offer travelers a wealth of attractions.

After the fall of communism in Czechoslovakia, the success of the Velvet Revolution, and the election of dissident playwright Vaclav Havel, Prague opened up spiritually and materially not only to the Czechs but to the West—and at a pace that has rarely been seen before. In two years, nearly 40,000 Americans moved to Prague is search of new horizons, a Bohemian existence, and economic success. Then the prices of apartments and consumer goods shot up.

Today, among the wonders of this equisite city, it is difficult to mill around without hearing an English twang. For Czechs, the brunt of their new ethnic jokes are Americans, their new immigrants. Upon arriving at the Prague airport or train station you are greeted by the neon sign MASTERCARD WELCOMES YOU TO THE CZECH REPUBLIC, and quickly you begin to understand who really won the cold war! Prague is particularly overrun in the summer, but don't let that dissuade you—it is still one of the most enchanting cities in Europe, where the old and the new mix and the spirit of Franz Kafka still lurks.

Travel conditions in the Czech Republic, especially in Prague, are now up to snuff with conditions in other European countries. You can buy telephone debit cards in tobacco shops for international use in telephone booths. You can reach your AT&T operator at 00-420-00101, MCI operator at 00-420-0011, and Sprint operator at 00-420-87187. There are beeper services and Internet service providers galore if you want to be accessible as you get lost in the Bohemian landscape.

Train travel within the Czech Republic is relatively easy and well developed. There is even a Prague Excursion Pass, an enhancement to holders of the Eurailpass, Germanrail pass, or Austrian Railpass. This allows you to travel from any Czech border crossing to Prague and return for as little as $49.00 for adults within a 7-day period. The Czech railways distinguish themselves between the following types of trains:

• Personal train (*osobní vlak*). Local trains that stop at all stations and have only second-class seats.

• Speed train (*spesn vlak*). Usually provide longer routes over more than one track. They stop at important stations only. The importance of a station, however, depends on the particular route. For instance, a speed train from Prague to a mountain region will stop at every village in the mountains but will skip small stations on the remainder of the route. Speed trains have first- and second-class cars. In the timetables, speed train schedules are printed in bold.

• Fast train (*rychlék*). Long-distance trains that stop at certain stations only. Some of them have dining cars, some are overnight trains and have couchettes and sleepers. You can reserve your seat in a fast train, and reservations are required for some connections. In the timetables, fast train schudules are printed bold on a gray background.

• Express train (express). Only about two connections are called express today. The difference between express trains and fast trains is too insignificant to discern.

The actual speed of the Czech trains depends on the quality of the track. For example, a personal train on the main track from Prague to Ceske Trebove may be faster than a fast train from Prague to Chomutov.

Several trains have cars or sections for smokers. In general, smoking is forbidden in all trains and stations (including platforms), but be prepared for violators. Remember, this country's president smokes three packs a day.

A word on train tickets. In addition to ticket windows, there are machines at some stations that sell tickets for rides of up to 100 kilometers. You can pay with coins or with debit cards. If you arrive late, you can buy your ticket from the conductor. If you do not have a valid ticket, report to the conductor before he approaches you and pay a surcharge of only Kc 10. Otherwise, the surcharge will be Kc 100. If there is no ticket office at your departure station (or it is not open), the conductor will sell the tickets without any surcharge. Local fares in Czech krowns are reasonable. The fares for first class are 50 percent higher than second class. There are special fares for children and dogs. No special surcharge is required for fast trains if you buy a full-fare ticket. A passenger can book a seat on a fast train for which he has got a valid ticket as long as 30 days and as little as 15 minutes before the departure. It is always advisable to reserve, and a reservation costs only Kc 10.

A note: you probably will not be traveling with a canoe, but if you are, you'll be pleased to know that in the summer months it is permissible to lug such fluvial items on the train as checked luggage.

Rail travel to and from Prague mainly revolves around two international stations: Praha Hlavni nádraze and Praha Holesovice, both accessible by subway line C. Hlavni, Prague's largest station, serves the Cheb, Karlovy Vary, Kosice, and Tabor connections. Holesovice serves the Berlin and Budapest connections. Trains to Bratislava and Brno stop in both stations, usually. To be sure, recheck connections, times, and stations before heading to catch a train.

For domestic train travel there are several other important stations: Praha Masarykovo nádraze for trains to Chomutov, Zsté nad Labem and Kolén. Train and other travel reservations and services are obtainable from the Czech national tourist agency Satur, which until 1994 was the ubiquitous CEDOK.

A visa is required to enter the Czech Republic. As of October 1995, foreigners must prove that they have a minimum of $20 U.S. cash available per day for the first ten days or a fixed amount of $270 U.S. for longer visits. (The Czech Republic has just opened a second consulate in Los Angeles to serve the demand for visas.) This measure is designed to limit the flow of drifters making Prague their beat. A fascinating update on the conditions in Prague was posted recently in the Travel Forum on CompuServe: it reported that of the thousands of Americans who are now long-term residents of the Czech Republic, many wrote for their college newspaper and hoped that the experience would land them a job at the *Prague Post* or *Prognosis,* the now defunct arts weekly. They have since learned otherwise. Be prepared to bus tables, pour beer at a sports bar, or to be a night manager of a laundromat in between English tutoring gigs. Also be aware that apartment rental rates in central parts of Prague are now comparable to those in San Francisco. Unless you have a good source of income, you'll either be living on the outskirts or sharing a one-bedroom with three or four people.

HOLIDAYS

January 1	New Year's Day	May 9	Liberation Day
	Easter	October 28	Nationalization Day
	Easter Monday	December 25	Christmas Day
May 1	Labor Day	December 26	Additional Holiday

SUMMER TIME

Czechoslovakia changes to Summer Time on the last Sunday of March and converts back to Standard Time on the last Sunday of September.

TRAIN PASSES

Czech Flexipass Unlimited *first*-class train travel any 5 days within 15 days. the 1996 price is $69. Half-fare for children age 4–12. Children under 4 travel free.

CITY-SIGHTSEEING NOTES

Prague

Despite the rapid influx of foreigners, Prague is a delight. When those who have read Kafka's *The Castle* see Prague's Hradcany Castle complex (where the government is situated), they know it is worth the visit alone. Visit the awesome medieval Jewish cemetery and nearby synagogue, the oldest in Europe, and the majestic 14th-century Charles Bridge (Karlov Most) with its thirty statues of saints and hordes of street people. The charming back streets of Mala Strana district echo Mozart and Milos Forman's film *Amadeus*.Visit the little streets beyond the Hradcany Castle and stop in at Kafka's house, number 22, on the Golden Lane (Zlata Ulicka), now a bookshop. If you have a prerevolution guidebook, references to Kafka will be glaringly absent.

There is no lack of freshly updated travel guides to Prague, though, and you'll need one. Kakfa's grave is a few tram rides from the city center; it takes a bit of an effort to find, but it's worth it. Starímestskí namesti Square is the heartbeat of the old Prague with its ancient clock tower, its 1410 Gothic horologe, the Baroque St. Nicholas Church and Tyn Church, and the medieval Carolinum, the oldest remnant of the original Prague University.

One of the great pleasures of being in Prague is simply sitting in the café of the Hotel Europa and watching people. Waiters in polyester tuxedos rush around brusquely serving sparkling water, shots of slivovitz, and portions of strudel. You will find yourself in a quirky time warp that is indicative of today's Prague.

Getting around Prague is quick and easy: aside from walking, the public transportation system is excellent. There is an underground tram system with three lines connecting all areas of the city, a dense network of trams with Lazarská as the central change point, buses serving the outskirts, and a funicular that runs from Malá Strana to the hill of Petrín.

Prague taxi drivers don't enjoy the best of reputations due to their habit of overcharging and taking circular routes. Be vigilant and never give the impression that you don't know where you are. Insist that the driver uses the meter, watch that he doesn't change the rate on the taximeter, and always ask for a receipt.

To get to the Praha Ruzyne International Airport, in the northwestern suburbs, take the 119 bus from the subway station Dejvická on the A line.

Brno

Located in the Moravian part of the Czech Republic, often overshadowed by Bohemia, Brno is noted for its craftsmanship—fine woodcarvings, lace, pottery, and costumes, as well as its excellent art galleries.

Culturally speaking, Brno is rich, and theater buffs and art enthusiasts will love it here, especially because the over-the-top commercialism that has invaded Prague has yet to reach user-friendly Brno. A visit to the Macocha and Sloup grottoes via an underground cruise is a highlight. Don't miss the Brno Castle, Moravian Museum, and the open-air market Brno makes for a perfect stop between Prague and Budapest. Highly recommended.

Ceske Budejovice

Home of the original Budweiser (Budvar) Brewery, this virtually unchanged medieval city and capital of southern Bohemia is filled with Old World wonder: it has a fascinating history. Halfway between Vienna and Plzen, Ceske Budejovice is where the Vltava meets the Malse River. Railroad buffs will want to know that it was here that the first horse-drawn railway arrived in 1832, coming from Linz, Austria. The brewery here does not have the same charm as the Urquell Brewery in Plzen, and is probably not worth the time. The best thing to do in Ceske Budejovice is to simply walk through the old streets off the large square and around Samson's Fountain and down by the river.

Cheb

Cheb is a medieval town on the Ohre River in the western part of the country. An easy day trip from either Karlovy Vary or Marianske Lazne, it is a Germanic town with scenic burgher houses in its old section. The area around the train station is reported to be particularly ugly, so don't judge Cheb by your first impressions.

Karlovy Vary

Formerly Carlsbad, Karlovy Vary is a scenic city that is world renown since the 1300s for its curative waters. Peter the Great, Bismarck, Goethe, Tolstoy, Beethoven, Mozart, Edward VII, and Karl Marx are among the people who have visited this spa for its water. The city is also famous worldwide for its Bohemian crystal.

There are express trains from Prague and Cheb to and from the Karlovy Vary station on the north side of the town. Trains to and from Marianske Lazne use the Karlovy Vary station near the bus depot.

Liberec

Noted for its 17th-centruy Reichenberg architecture, Liberec lends itself to lovely walks in the old town and in the scenic Jested Hills area on the outskirts.

Marianske Lazne

You would most likely recognize this famous spa town by its old name, Marienbad, which has been frequented by an impressive list of international celebrities. Local life revolves around the spas, walks, and the Maxim Gorky Colonnade.

Plzen

Plzen, or Pilsen, a traditional trading center halfway between Prague and Nuremberg, is the capital of West Bohemia. The 19th-century ironworks factory founded by Emile Skoda gave its name to the famous Czech car the Skoda. Beer brewing in this town is so historic that it has left its name on the process: pils. The Pilsner trademark known as Urquell internationally comes from Plzen. Go on a brewery tour and do visit the Museum of Beer Brewing, located in an original medieval malt house (but don't count on ambitious sightseeing afterwards!). Also visit the underground corridors.

Tabor

Founded in 1420 on a religious principle of communal life, contributing to the modern sense of the word *Bohemian,* Tabor is a perfect day trip from Prague. Visit the Museum of the Hussite Movement—it is all one needs to understand the history and significance of Tabor and its 14th-century reformation.

ONE-DAY EXCURSIONS

Prague - Bratislava - Prague   880

Dep. Prague (Hole.)	00:28 (1)	05:58 (2)	07:39 (3)	15:10 (2)	-0-
Dep. Prague (Hlav.)	-0- (10)	-0- (10)	-0- (10)	-0- (10)	14:41 (10)
Arr. Bratislava	05:39	11:30	12:40	19:52	20:34

Sights in **Bratislava**: An important Danube port in ancient Roman times. See the 14th–15th century castle. The Hussite House. The Old City Hall. The Cathedral. The palaces on Mirove Square, Michalska Street and Gottwald Square. Few of the museums here offer information in English language.

Dep. Bratislava	00:43 (2+10)	03:55 (2)	09:43 (3)	11:52 (10)	14:51 (10)
Arri. Prague (Hlav.)	06:29	-0-	-0- (10)	18:07	20:40
Arr. Prague (Hole.)	-0-	09:24	14:20	-0-	-0-

(1) Carries a sleeping car. Also has couchettes. (2) Carries a sleeping car. Also has couchettes. (3) Restaurant car. (6) Arrives at Prague's Holesovice railstation. (7) Operates late March to early November. (8) Plus other departures from Prague (Hlavni) at 17:36 (10) and 22:10 (10) arriving Bratslava 22:3 and 04:20. (10) Supplement charged.

Prague - Brno - Prague   880

Dep. Prague (Hole.)	05:58	07:39 (1)	09:16 (2)
Arr. Brno	09:24	10:58	12:50

Sights in **Brno**: The folk-art exhibit of woodcarving, laces, pottery and costumes in the Moravian Museum. Brno Castle. Take a cruise on one of the underground rivers to see the Macocha and Sloup grottos. The outstanding 13th century Pernstejn Castle, near Brno.

Dep. Brno	13:28 (1)	15:21 (1)	16:54 (5)	19:14 (4)	20:17
Arr. Prague (Hole.)	16:37 (5)	18:40 (3)	20:42 (3)	22:28 (5)	23:37 (5)

(1) Restaurant car. (2) Departs/Arrives Prague's Masarykovo railstation. (3) Arrives at Prague's Hlavni railstation.(4) Departs from Brno's Kralovo Pole railstation. Operates late March to early November. Restaurant car. (5) Supplement charged.

Prague - Ceske Budejovice - Prague   875

Dep. Prague (Hlavni)	06:23	07:49 (1)	Dep. Ceske Bude.	13:18	16:17 (4)
Arr. Ceske Bude.	09:05	11:10	Arr. Prague (Hlavni)	16:07	18:46

(1) Second-class. (2) Runs Sunday only. (3) Runs daily, except Saturday. (4) Plus other Ceske departures at 18:02 (2), 18:55 and 20:14 (3), arriving Prague 20:45, 21:48 and 23:01. (5) Will not run July 5-October 28, December 24,25, April 16, 30 and May 7.

Sights in **Ceske Budejovice**: This city appears the same now as it did in the Middle Ages. Visit the Budvar brewery.

Prague - Karlovy Vary - Prague   874

Dep. Prague (Hole.)	04:29	06:23 (1)	09:43	12:04
Arr. Karlovy Vary	08:50	09:47	13:40	16:20

Sights in **Karlovy Vary:** Once called Carlsbad, famous for its curative waters since 1347. Peter the Great, Beethoven, Mozart and England's Edward VII are among the celebrities that have come here to drink the elixir and use the monumental baths in their search for improved health. An international film festival is held here every July. Visit the Moser crystal glass factory. There is an interesting porcelain factory in nearby **Slakov**.

Dep. Karlovy Vary	05:01 (4)	09:52	14:10	17:44	18:37
Arr. Prague (Hole.)	08:47 (2)	14:00	18:07	21:35 (3)	22:32

(1) Departs from Prague's Hlavni railstation. (2) Departs/arrives Prague's Masarykovo railstation. (3) Arrives at Prague's Hlavni railstation. (4) Second-class. (5) Plus another departure from Prague (Masarykovo) at 23:46 (4), arriving Karlovy Vary 03:39.

Prague - Liberec - Prague   876

Both of these trains are second-class.

Dep. Prague (Hlavni)	06:51		Dep. Liberec	17:23
Arr. Liberec	10:03		Arr. Prague (Hlavni)	20:10

Sights in **Liberec:** This town is noted for its 17th century Reichenberg architecture. Walks in the encircling Jested Hills are recommended.

Prague - Marianske Lazne - Prague   870

Dep. Prague (Hlav.)	04:06	08:55	11:22	13:08 (1)	14:32	17:012 (1)	19:16 (4)
Arr. Marianske	07:34 (3)	12:03	14:23	15:49 (6)	17:52	20:13	22:23

Sights in **Marianske Lazne**: Once called Marienbad, still a famous health spa.

Dep. Marianske	05:03	05:47	06:38 (1)	12:40 (1)	14:02 (1)	15:24	17:21 (5)
Arr. Prague (Hlav.)	08:16	08:46	10:03	15:56	16:45 (6)	18:25	20:26

(1) Restaurant car. (2) Light refreshments. (3) Carries a sleeping car. Also has couchettes. (4) Plus other Prague departures at 20:47 and 23:52, arriving Marianske Lazne 23:49 and 03:00. (5) Plus another Marianske Lazne departure at 19:57, arriving Prague 23:04. (6) Supplement charged.

Prague - Plzen - Prague   870

| Dep. Prague (Hlavni) | 07:23 (1) | 08:55 | 11:22 |
| Arr. Plzen | 09:00 (3) | 10:30 | 13:07 |

Sights in **Plzen:** Visit the enormous Urquell brewery, where more than 200 million pints of beer are bottled annually. They have been producing beer here (hence "Pilsener") for over 800 years.

| Dep. Plzen | 14:10 (1) | 15:06 (1) | 16:40 | 18:41 | 19:03 (1+2) |
| Arr. Prague (Hlavni) | 15:56 | 16:45 (3) | 18:25 | 20:30 | 20:37 (3) |

(1) Restaurant car. (2) Plus another Plzen departure at 21:18 (1), arriving Prague 22:57. (3) Supplement charged.

Prague - Tabor - Prague   875

| Dep. Prague (Hlv.) | 07:49 (1) | 09:00 (1) | Dep. Tabor | 14:26 | 18:01 (2+5) |
| Arr. Tabor | 09:53 | 11:48 | Arr. Prague (Hlv.) | 16:07 | 19:34 |

(1) Second-class. (2) Restaurant car. (3) Runs Sunday only. (4) Runs daily, except Saturday. (5) Plus other Tabor departures at 19:05 (3), 20:02 and 21:28 (4), arriving Prague 20:45, 21:48 and 23:01.

Sights in **Tabor:** A museum town, preserved to immortalize the unusual Hussite 14th century reform movement which held that all people are brothers and equal.

SCENIC RAIL TRIPS

Bratislava - Kosice - Bratislava   885

Very good mountain scenery, through the Low and High Tatras Mountains.

All of these trains have a restaurant car.

| Dep. Bratislava | 05:45 (1) | 07:50 (1) | Dep. Kosice | 12:15 | 16:00(1+2) |
| Arr. Kosice | 10:50 | 14:11 (2) | Arr. Bratislava | 18:28 | 21:20 |

(1) Reservation required. (2) Supplement charged.

Poprad-Tatry to Stary Smokovec and Tatranska Lomnica

This spur off the Bratislava-Kosice route is the most scenic rail trip in Czechoslovakia. Forty minutes of the spectacular Tatras Mountains. Then, you can continue on to the **Tatranska Lomnica** ski resort and take a funicular to the top of 8,645-foot **Lomnicky Stit**.

"Pleso" means "lake." It is a popular one-hour stroll to Poprodske Pleso, another of the more than 100 glacial lakes in this area. Strbske Pleso is the main ski resort in the 16-mile-long Tatra mountain range.

885		887	
Dep. Bratislava	07:50 (1)	Dep. Tatranska Lomnica	15:07 (2)
Arr. Poprad-Tatry	12:50 (4)	*Change trains.*	
Change trains.			
887			
Dep. Poprad-Tatry	14:00 (2)	Arr. Poprad-Tatry	15:45 (2)
Arr. Tatranska Lomnica	14:25 (3)	*Change trains.*	
		885	
		Dep. Poprad-Tatry	17:10 (1)
		Arr. Bratislava	21:20 (4+5)

(1) Restaurant car. (2) Change at Studeny Park. There are 25 departures each day. (3) Estimated. There are 20 departures each day. (4) Supplement charged. (5) Reservation required.

Strba - Strbske Pleso

This other spur off the Bratislava–Kosice line is a second great Tatras Mountain scenic rail trip. There are much Winter sports in the area around Strbske Pleso.

All of the Bratislava–Strba (and v.v.) trains have a restaurant car.

885			887		
Dep. Bratislava	05:50 (2)	07:50 (2)	Dep. Strbske Pleso	Frequent times	
Arr. Strba	09:42	12:34	Arr. Strba	13 minutes later	
Change trains.			*Change trains*		
887			885		
Dep. Strba	Frequent times		Dep. Strba	14:02 (2)	16:02
Arr. Strbske Pleso	13 minutes later		Arr. Bratislava	18:28	20:30 (2)

(1) Carries a sleeping car. Also has couchettes. (2) Supplement charged.

INTERNATIONAL ROUTES
FROM THE CZECH REPUBLIC

Prague is the Czech Republic's gateway to Berlin (and on to Copenhagen and all of Scandinavia), Belgrade, Budapest, Bucharest (and on to Athens), Nurnberg (and on to the rest of Western Europe), Vienna, and Warsaw (and on to Moscow).

Because the Czech Republic is not a Eurailpass country, passengers traveling from Prague to Austria, Germany (and on, to Switzerland or France) and Hungary must pay for a ticket from Prague to the border of those Eurailpass countries. None of the travel from Prague into Poland is covered by Eurailpass. Travel to Austria, Hungary and Poland is covered by European East Pass.

Prague - Berlin   680

All of these trains require reservation, unless designated otherwise. All night trains carry a sleeping car and have couchettes. All day trains have a restaurant car.

Dep. Prague (Hlavni)	-0-	-0- (1)	-0-	-0-
Dep. Prague (Holesovice)	00:35	02:05	08:47 (1)	12:47
Arr. Berlin (Licht.)	05:51	07:14	13:06 (3)	17:26 (2)

Dep. Prague (Hlavni)	-0-	-0-	-0-	-0-
Dep. Prague (Holesovice)	14:37	16:47	18:47 (4)	22:49 (1)
Arr. Berlin (Licht.)	19:26 (2)	21:26 (2)	23:15 (2)	02:51

(1) Restaurant car. (2) Arrives at Berlin's Hauptbahnhof railstation. (3) Arrives Berlins' Schonefeld. (4) Not December 24, 31.

Prague - Budapest - Belgrade or Bucharest   96b

Dep. Prague (Holesovice)	05:58 (1)	07:39 (1)	15:11 (3)	14:41 (4+5)
Arr. Budapest (Keleti)	14:42	16:28	22:42	23:50
Arr. Belgrade	-0-	-0-	-0-	07:11 (2)
Arr. Bucharest (Nord)	06:20 (2)	-0-	-0-	-0-

Dep. Prague (Holesovice)	15:10 (3)	22:22 (4+6)	23:08 (7)
Arr. Budapest (Keleti)	22:37	07:47 (2)	08:28 (2)
Arr. Belgrade	-0-	-0-	-0-
Arr. Bucharest (Nord)	-0-	23:25	-0-

(1) Carries a sleeping car. Also has couchettes. (2) Day 2. (3) Restaurant car. (4) Departs from Prague's Hlavni railstation. (5) Carries only sleeping cars. Runs Wednesday, Thursday and Friday. (6) Carries a sleeping car. Also has couchettes. (7) Carries a sleeping car. Also has couchettes. Restaurant car.

Prague - Frankfurt - Paris

	57	30	30+57
Dep. Prague (Hlavni)	13:08 (1)	16:55 (2)	20:47 (3)
Arr. Frankfurt/Main	20:43	-0-	05:35
Dep. Frankfurt/Main	-0-	-0-	-0-
Arr. Paris (Est)	-0-	09:37	-0-

(1) Reservation advisable. Supplement charged. Restaurant car. (2) Operates late May to late September. Carries a first-class sleeping car. Also has second-class couchettes and coaches. Restaurant car 17:54 to 23:40. (3) Carries a first-class sleeping car. Also has second-class couchettes. Coaches are first and second-class.

Prague - Nurnberg or Munich and Zurich   57

	07:23 (1)	13:08 (1+2)	16:23 (1+3)	20:50 (4+5)
Dep. Prague (Hlavni)	07:23 (1)	13:08 (1+2)	16:23 (1+3)	20:50 (4+5)
Arr. Nurnberg	-0-	17:56	22:03	02:50
Arr. Munich	13:51	21:12	23:12	06:07
Arr. Zurich	18:23	-0-	-0-	-0-

(1) Supplement charged. Restaurant car. (2) For Munich, change trains in Marktredwitz at 16:36. (3) For Munich, change trains in Schwandorf at 20:54. (4)Carries a sleeping car. Also has couchettes. Light refreshments. (4) Carries a sleeping car. Also has couchettes. (5) Plus another Prague departure at 23:52 (4), terminating in Nurnberg 05:47.

Prague - Vienna   96a

	-0-	03:24 (2)	13:11 (3)	17:11 (4)
Dep. Prague (Hole.)	-0-	03:24 (2)	13:11 (3)	17:11 (4)
Dep. Prague (Hlavni)	00:11 (1)	-0-	-0-	-0-
Arr. Vienna (F. J. Bf.)	06:06	-0-	-0-	-0-
Arr. Vienna (Sud.)	-0-	08:52	18:02	21:58

(1) Runs daily, except Sundays and holidays. (2) Second-class. (3) Restaurant car. (4) "Antonin Dvorak."

Prague - Warsaw   95a

	13:40 (1)	18:13 (2)	21:16 (2)
Dep. Prague (Hlavni)	13:40 (1)	18:13 (2)	21:16 (2)
Arr. Warsaw (Centralna)	22:50	06:43	07:20
Arr. Warsaw (Gdanska)	23:04	06:57	07:34

(1) Reservation required. Restaurant car. (2) Carries a sleeping car. Also has couchettes.

SLOVAK REPUBLIC

The eastern half of the former Czechoslavakia, the Slovak Republic today is tucked in below Poland to the north, Hungary to the south, the Ukraine to the east, and Austria and the Czech Republic to the west.

Europe's newest country, Slovakia managed to break away from the Czechs in 1993. The country has a tremendous amount to offer nature-lovers and sport-oriented visitors. Its Tatra mountain region is ideal for hikers and skiers; its unspoiled medieval villages are priceless for their beauty and authenticity. Visitors are received in an open and friendly manner. Travelers will experience the discovery of a long-lost part of Eastern European history and tradition at reasonable prices by including Slavakia, beyond Bratislava, in their itineraries. Bratislava, of course, the country's cultural and intellectual center, necessitates a visit on its own terms.

The easiest access to Slovakia is via the Vienna-Bratislava connection. Only 64 kilometers away, 4 direct trains make this 2-hour jaunt daily. For trains from Germany and other western European countries that pass through the Czech Republic, a transit visa may be required. Other trains to Slovakia from eastern European countries that pass through the Czech Republic may also present visa problems for travelers: if travelers do not hold Czech transit visas and the train enters the Czech Republic in the middle of the night, on-board visas will not be issued and voyagers risk being put off the train. This is not like the CIS, where a huffy conductor may be tamed at the sight of Abraham Lincoln or Queen Elizabeth. Inquire. Bratislava enjoys four direct trains from Budapest (Hungaria, Balt-Orient, and Pannonia leaving from Keleti station, and the Metropol train leaving from Nyugati station), which is only three hours away. All travel via Sturovo. Many guides recommend the morning Hungaria and afternoon Metropol for getting to Bratislava; they originate in Budapest and run on time. The others connect to Budapest from Romania and are often late. Several express night trains pass through Slovakia at Trencin, but reservations are mandatory in order to board, and, again, if you don't have the Czech transit visa you may find yourself sitting in the chill of the night on the tracks at the border wondering how this happened.

The eastern Slovak city of Kosice enjoys train connections twice a day with the Hungarian towns of Miskolc and Satoraljaujhely, if that helps you. The Rakoczi express train makes the Budapest-Kosice run in under 5 hours, leaving Budapest-Keleti in the morning and Kosice in the afternoon with a partial service continuing to Poprad-Tatry. And, the Polish Cracovia express train passes through Kosice between Budapest and Kracow in the middle of the night, as does the Karpaty Express between Krakow and Warsaw.

Reservations are required and precision planning is needed to coordinate these travel options. Jumping on an express train at whistle stop in the middle of the night excites the imagination, but also requires willpower. Crawling into a sleepy compartment of strangers is not the easiest way to make friends, but at times a late-night connection may be the most practical way of joining up segments of your trip.

Kosice also serves as a stop between Prague and Moscow (the Dukla Express) and Bratislava and Moscow (the Slovakia Express). Both trains pass through Kiev in the Ukraine.

Visitors to Slovakia are required to have at least $15 U.S. or equivalent per day of their stay in Slovakia when entering the Slovak Republic.

Bratislava

Slovakia's largest city, Bratislava, aside from being the cultural and administrative capital of this young country, sits at a strategic geographic location on the Austrian border, minutes from Hungary, on the Danube River, at the foot of the Carpathians. The geography contributes to the city's historic diversity with Hungarian influence felt in the architecture and names.

The main train station is actually located slightly north of the city and is easily reached by tram. But note that there is another train station that is on the eastern side of the city, called stanica Bratislava-Nove. It is not as often used for major train connections, but things are always changing.

With its 450, 000 inhabitants, Bratislava offers a rich cultural program and ambitious economic aspirations. Start your visit with the Bratislava Castle; built on a hill it dominates the center of Bratislava, and its four towers have become a symbol of this Danube port city. Inhabited from Neolithic Hallstadt and Roman eras, the castle was first mentioned in 907. Today, after reconstruction, it shelters the historical part of the Slovak National Museum. Bratislava Castle is also the residence of the president of the Slovak Republic, with the Slovak parliament residing in the new building nearby.

The Slovak National Museum, a key point of interest, is located opposite the hydrofoil terminal on the river. Contrasting the traditional aesthetics of this museum is the very contemporary Slavak National Gallery, which holds Bratislava's most important art collection. Add to your cultural itinerary the art nouveau Reduta Palace concert hall and the turn-of-the-century National Theater, which recently celebrated its 75th anniversary.

Walking around the city is a pleasant experience. In the evening, Bratislava excels in its choice of wine cellars. Tourists are advised not to chance money on the streets—black marketeers have been known to stick gullible visitors with wads of worthless banknotes from defunct despotic republics.

Regular train connections between Bratislava and Kosice are frequent and efficient. The night train with its couchette service is a particularly good idea, and some savvy travelers who've found it difficult to land an affordable hotel room in Bratislava have even booked a couchette to Kosice as a lodging and transportation solution.

Trencin

This town of 50,000 hosts a noted castle at one of the gateways to Slovakia. Once the most northern Roman military camp, Trencin today is a textile center. The city serves aa a stopover between Bratislava and Kosice via Zilina.

Poprad-Tatry

Industrial and of little interest to travelers, Poprad requires a mention nonetheless in that it is a train hub, north and south, and the pivot point for the electric train that climbs 13 kilometers to the Tatry mountain resort of Stary Smokovec.

Kosice

The second largest city in Slovakia with nearly 250,000 inhabitants, this formerly Hungarian town is now an industrial hub specializing in metalurgy. The old town nonetheless presents much of interest to visitors, and many have used Kosice as a base for regional travel. Trains run every day to Krakow, Poland, and Budapest, Hungary. Visit the remarkable Gothic Cathedral of St. Elizabeth.

HUNGARY

Overview

Hungary has always held a special place for travels in the East. Even in the days of the communist bloc, Budapest remained the most popular holiday destination for eastern visitors. Thus, it wasn't surprising that Hungary became the first of the former communist countries to join the Eurail pass system countries, becoming the seventeenth. Just behind Prague in its massive tourist attraction to western travelers, Budapest offers cultural splendor and aesthetic pleasure, full-bodied red wine, peppery food, lively folk music, and an atmosphere of openness. Budapest represents all the positive aspects of Prague without the excess of grotesque commercialism. The prices have increased, but are still manageable. Just a jump away from Vienna, Hungary was always the first step into the East. Aside from the train, many travelers opt for the pleasant Danube river trip between the two cities via Bratislava by hydrofoil, which can be convenient (but sometimes less so). One British historian recently reported that the 5-hour river trip is almost always delayed due to insufficient water level on the Danube. The boat slows to a standstill waiting for the water level to rise. You might just prefer the train.

Ethnically unique, Hungarians are of Finno-Ugrian descent and speak Magyar, linguistically related only to Finnish and Estonian. There are slightly more than 10 million people in Hungary, of which two-thirds are Catholic. The once vibrant Jewish population of nearly 800,000 today stands at just 10 percent of that, representing nonetheless the largest Jewish community today in Eastern Europe. Hungary has one of the highest rates of suicide in the world, and also performs the highest per capita amount of abortions.

Literary and cultural life is intense with more writers in Hungary per capita than in any other European country. The president of Hungary himself is a leading contemporary writer.

Train travel to and from Hungary, aside from the Eurail passes, has gone up substantially in price over the last five years. There are direct rail links between Budapest and 25 capital cities of Europe, and 54 scheduled international trains arrive every day in Budapest. All international trains have dining and sleeping cars. Most international express trains arrive and depart from the Eastern (Keleti) Railway Station with the exception of the following trains, which use Budapest-Dáli: Adriatica, Agram, Lehár, Eurocity, Maestral, Graz.

The following trains use Budapest-Nyugati: Amicus, Aquincum, Budapest Express, Claudiopolis, Corona, Gerecse, Metropol, Partium, Varadium, Visegrád, Baia Mare, Saxonia, Miskolc, Karpaty, Pécs, Sopianae, Zagreb.

The following are railroad station information numbers:

Budapest Southern (Dáli): 175-6293
Budapest Eastern (Keleti): 113-6835
Budapest Western (Nyugati): 149-0115
For information on international fares: 122-8035

trains that run to Vienna in three hours. These trains include the Liszt Ferenc from Dortmund and Nuremberg, the Orient Express from Paris and Munich, and the Wiener Waltzer from Basel and Innsbruck. There are special Eurocity return trip fares between Vienna and Budapest as well. There are also many local trains that run between smaller cities in Austria and Hungary; reservations are not needed. The Prague-Budapest voyage is made in nine hours, a popular route among Eurailers. One traveler sharing his Prague-Budapest overnight train experience reported that he woke in the night "to find the porter had chained the car doors shut. We were on a siding somewhere around Brataslavia. He was able to make me understand he had wanted to sleep and to insure the safety of his charges had chained and padlocked the doors."

Some travelers recommend first class for its comfort; others prefer second class where it's easier to encounter local people. The Balt-Orient and Meridian express trains serve Budapest from Berlin, Prague, and Bratislava, and then continue east to Romania and Bulgaria. There are daily Budapest-Warsaw connections on the Bathory and Polonia express trains depending on which route you choose. The Bem express train from Szczecin, Poznan, and Wroclaw serves Budapest via Trencin. The Varsovia arrives from Gdansk. For Czech and Slovak connections, see those chapters in this guide. Train connections with points further east include the Ovidius Express, which runs from the Black Sea at Constanta, and the Claudiopolis train via Cluj to Budapest. The Corona from Brasov arrives in Budapest 14 hours later. For points south, Budapest is a hub. The Budapest-Belgrade express train currently is a strange shuttle for all sorts of traffic. To Croatia there is the Budapest-Zagreb express train (Adriatica, Agram, Drava, and Maestral). If you plan on departing from Budapest for a journey by train through Russia and China, see David Stanley's comments on and recommendation of Star Tours in Budapest, which is published in his excellent Lonely Planet edition on Eastern Europe. In any case, train travelers experience a rush of excitement just thinking about such journeys.

In general, connections and access in Hungary are excellent. There are eight daily

"Once you have your train ticket and reservations you can apply for a Chinese tourist visa (allow three days for processing), then a Russian transit visa ($60 U.S.), which you may be able to get in one day. If time is short, ask for the Russian train via Manchuria, which eliminates the need for a Mongolian transit visa (another three days' processing). Three-day Ukraininan transit visas are usually available at the border for $50."

There is also a car–train service operating on the Vienna-Budapest Eastern Station-Thessaloniki route during the main tourist season, July 1 to September 25. Car loading time at Budapest Keleti Station: 11:45 to 12:00 A.M. At Thessaloniki: 6:30 to 7:30 P.M. for the return voyage.

Subway service between the Keleti and Dáli railway stations exists on the M2 metro line (seven stops).

Other Intercity and express trains from Budapest to the major tourist regions in Hungary include Northern Transdanubia, Lake Balaton (north shore), Southern Transdanubia, Northern Hungary, and Great Plain.

One Budapest company called Nostalgia Trains Ltd. organizes specialized train trips in the summer months. Contact: Nostalgia Ltd., H-1055 Budapest, Teréz krt. 55. Telephone/fax: (36) 1/269-5242.

Of special interest are fifteen narrow-gauge specialized railways operating in Hungary, generally from May to September. For information contact TOURINFORM, telephone 117-9800.

Specialized information on Hungary called The Hungary Report can be obtained on-line from hungary-report-request@hungary.yak.net. For other up-to-date sources of information on Hungary consult the *Budapest Business Journal* at 100263.213@compuserve.com. You can reach the *Budapest Sun* at 100275.456@compuserve.com. You can reach *Budapest Week* at 100324.141@compuserve.com and/or Central Europe Today (free online) cet-info@eunet.cz.

The Hungary Report writes about a local train service that operates from Budapest to Csepel Island to the south of the city and to the nearby towns of Szentendre and Ráckeve. Here you can experience the majestic Danube River Bend.

Transportation buffs will be pleased to note that the first underground railway or public subway on the continent, Millenary Underground Railway (the second in the world after London's) was built in Budapest in the late 1800s and has been restored to its original state for its 100th anniversary.

Additionally, the Funicular from the Buda side of the Chain Bridge to the Buda Castle Palace has been operating since the turn of the century.

Hungarian Holidays

January 1	New Year's Day	August 20	Constitution Day
	Easter	November 7	Revolution
	Easter Monday		Remembrance Day
April 4	Liberation Day	December 25	Christmas Day
May 1	Labor Day	December 26	Additional Holiday

HUNGARY'S TRAIN PASSES

Hungarian Flexipass First-class only, unlimited train travel. The 1996 adult prices are: $55 for any 5 in 15 days, and $69 for any 10 days in a month (example June 3–July 2). Half-fare for children age 5–14. Children under 5 travel free. Sold worldwide by travel agencies and Rail Europe (U.S.A. and Canadian offices listed under "France").

CITY-SIGHTSEEING NOTES

Budapest

The city is divided into two cities, Buda and Pest, by the Danube, and locals and tourists alike will playfully disagree about which they like better and for what reasons. The great width of the river in Budapest contributes to the split personality of the city. Buda in general is the historically endowed side while Pest is the commercially vibrant side. The city's public transportation system is highly expansive and efficient, reaching far on both sides of the river with key lines converging at Deak tár.

The theater district is focused on Andrassy ut, and the offering of theatrical performances on any given night is impressive. Go see a play in Hungarian! You'll never have been more concentrated on the acting and set design than during those two hours of pure Magyar bliss.

In Buda, a visit up Castle Hill is a must. This is where the vestiges of medieval Budapest lurk. There are several possibilities for exploring the Buda Hills around the city: the Cogwheel Railway from Városmajor (2 stops from Moszkva tár on the No. 56 tram) to Széchenyi Hill and the Chairlift (Libegé) from Zugliget (at the terminus of No. 28 bus from Moszkva tár) to the look-out on János Hill (Budapest's highest point: 526 meters) are two good approaches. Plan on visiting both the National Gallery and the Historical Museum, both of which are located in the Palace of Buda Castle. From the castle you can catch the funicular down to the tunnel under Castle Hill at the foot of the famous Chain Bridge.

On Gellert Hill, above the Hotel Gellert, which, aside from being known for its unusual swimming pool that made artificial waves, was a hotbed for high-end espionage in the 1960s and 70s, you'll find the Citadella, a fort built by the Austrians, now a hotel and commemoration to the Soviet soldiers who gave their lives to liberate Hungary in 1945. In 1956, the statute on this spot was knocked down, but was later restored. From here you are afforded the finest view Budapest has to offer. On the Pest side of the world you'll want to visit the City Park, the Grand Circus, the Budapest Zoo, the Museum of Fine Arts, and St. Stephen's Basilica. For a picturesque visit of the city, try riding the newly restored Number 2 Tram on the Pest side of the river.

A fun activity for the family is a ride on the Children's Railway. This narrow-gauge railway runs a distance of 12 kilometres through the Buda forests. Don't overlook the very lovely Margaret Island and its spacious 112-acre park. Special pedal-operated vehicles for 2 to 6 persons can be hired to ride in this park.

Gyor

Well connected by express train, halfway between Budapest and Vienna, Gyor is Hungary's third-largest city. With an interesting old town, historic churches, and the striking new Kisfaludy Theater, Gyor is worth a stop.

Fertod

The Esterhazy Palace with its more than 100 rooms and grand Versailles-style baroque details merits a visit to Fertod.

Szeged

This gateway town to and from Romania and the former Yugoslavia is best known for its paprika salami and the Votive Church, which was built in the 1920s in remembrance of the devastating flood of 1879 that changed the face and history of Szeged.

Lake Balaton

This long and lively lake, the largest freshwater lake in Europe, is a popular summer swimming resort and family vacation spot. The south shore is sandier and more developed while the north shore is more scenic and historically rich. For ecological reasons motorboats are prohibited, making the lake ideal for sailing. There is constant train traffic between Balaton and Budapest and a train route around the lake as well. Kezthely, at the western end of the lake, is a large town with lots of lakefront and boating services. Siofok and Balatonszentgyorgy are also accessible by train and offer lakeside pleasures.

Heviz

This famous spa town, with its 1,500 thermal baths, is a natural wonder. Located on a thermal lake, Gyogy, the water temperature averages 30 degrees Celsius at the surface. In the winter the haze off the water renders the experience particularly strange and appealing. In addition, there are lake baths and thermal baths in Heviz.

Kecskemet

A perfect day trip from Budapest, this town in central Hungary is best known for its fruit production, more specifically its production of apricot brandy.

Pecs

In the Southern Transdanubian part of Hungary near Croatia, Pecs is Mediterranean in feel. Pecs is on the direct line to Zagreb and thus has become a departure point for Croatian travel. The first King of Hungary, Stephane I, proclaimed Pecs a bishopric in the year 1009.

ONE-DAY EXCURSIONS

Budapest - Kecskemet - Szeged - Budapest   895

As these schedules show, it is possible to visit both Kecskemet and Szeged in the same day.

Dep. Budapest (Nyugati)	07:00 (1)	10:30 (1)	11:00 (2)	14:00 (1,2 +6)
Arr. Kecskemet	08:13 (2)	11:40 (2)	12:27	15:13
Arr. Szeged	09:10	12:48	13:35	16:10
Dep. Szeged	05:20 (2)	06:20 (1)	09:50 (1)	13:20 (7)
Dep. Kecskemet	06:25	07:23 (2)	10:48	14:25 (1)
Arr. Budapest (Nyugati)	07:48	08:42	12:00	15:48 (2)

(1) Reservation required. (2) Light refreshments. (3) Second-class. (4) Runs Monday-Friday, except holidays. (5) Runs Saturdays, Sundays and holidays. (6) Plus other Budapest departures at 16:25, 18:25 (2) and 19:25 (2), arriving Szeged 18:46, 20:50 and 22:20. (7) Plus other Szeged departures at 15:30 (2), 18:10 (1), 19:35 (4) and 20:20 (5), arriving Budapest 17:48, 20:45, 22:45 and 23:07.

Budapest - Lake Balaton (Siofok and Balantonszentgyorgy)
and v.v.

It is a short train and bus ride to reach Hungary's most popular resort area, the 46-mile long **Lake Balaton**, circled with spas, motels and campgrounds along its 118 miles of shoreline. Great sailboating and fishing here. Frequent ferries link the many towns on both sides of the lake.

893

Dep. Budapest (Deli)	07:00	07:15	13:15	14:25 (3)	15:45 (4)
Arr. Siofok	08:41 (2)	08:48	15:06	16:09	18:03 (5)
Arr. Balatonszentgyorgy	09:48	10:40	16:35	17:20	19:27

* * *

Dep. Balatonszentgyorgy	06:23 (2)	07:02	10:41	12:40 (2)	14:58 (2+6)
Dep. Siofok	07:26	08:39	12:08	13:52	16:08 (7)
Arr. Budapest (Deli)	09:08	10:28	14:03	15:28	17:48

(1) Restaurant car. (2) Light refreshments. (3) Departs/Arrives Budapest's Keleti railstation. (4) Plus other Budapest departures at 18:05, (2), 19:35, and 20:30 (3). (5) Plus other Siofok departures at 20:10, 21:22, and 22:42. (6) Plus other Balatonszentgyorgy departures at 16:49 (3), 18:43 and 20:18 (3). (7) Plus other Siofok departures at 18:04 (3), 20:12, 21:20 (3).

INTERNATIONAL CONNECTIONS
FROM HUNGARY

Budapest is Hungary's gateway for rail travel to Belgrade (and on to Athens and Istanbul), to Moscow, to Prague (and on to Berlin and Scandinavia), to Vienna (and on to the rest of Western Europe), and to Zagreb (and on to Italy).

Budapest - Belgrade 940

Dep. Budapest (Keleti)	06:25 (3)	11:25 (3)	15:10	17:15 (3)
Arr. Belgrade	12:18	17:12	21:38	23:30

(1) Carries a sleeping car. Also has couchettes. (2) Reservation required. Second-class. (3) Reservation required. Restaurant car. (4) Restaurant car.

Budapest - Moscow 94c

This train carries only sleeping cars.

Dep. Budapest (Keleti)	16:15
Arr. Moscow (Kievski)	11:21 Day 3

Budapest - Prague 880

Dep. Budapest (K.)	06:55 (1)	13:20 (1)	15:00 (5)	18:25 (2)	21:20 (3)
Arr. Prague (Hlav.)	-0- (4)	-0- (5)	-0-	-0-	06:29
Arr. Prague (Hole.)	14:20	22:28	23:21	02:53	-0-

(1) Restaurant car. (2) Departs from Budapest's Nyugati railstation. Carries a sleeping car. Also has couchettes. Restaurant car. (3) Carries a sleeping car. Also has couchettes. (4) Supplement payable. (5) Supplement payable in Slovakia.

Budapest - Vienna 61.

Dep. Budapest (Keleti)	05:55	08:20 (1)	09:55	12:25 (1)	13:30
Arr. Vienna (Westbf.)	09:20	11:50	12:57 (2)	15:50	19:00

Dep. Budapest (Keleti)	15:30	17:20 (3)	18:30	19:10 (4)	21:00 (3)
Arr. Vienna (Westbf.)	19:00	20:50	21:45 (2)	21:58 (2)	00:27

(1) Reservation required. Supplement charged. (2) Arrives Vienna's Subbahnhof station. (3) No restaurant car. (4) Departs from Budapest's Deli station.

POLAND

Children under 4 travel free. Half-fare for children 4–10. Children 11 and over must pay full fare.

As the *CIA World Factbook* reminds readers, Poland is slightly smaller than New Mexico and borders with Belarus, the Czech Republic, Slovakia, Germany, Lithuania, Russia, and the Ukraine. For train travelers, that comparative scale doesn't really help orient travel nor plan itineraries. The size of Poland and the placement of its national borders, however, has always been a sensitive issue in history. Poland's boundaries have responded with the elasticity of political events, and anyone with access to a chronological atlas of Europe will note that Poland, with its vulnerable flatness and lack of natural boundaries has both sprawled with expansion and retracted out of existence only to return a century later as a geographic double of its former self. In 1943, at the Teheran Conference, Churchill, Stalin, and Roosevelt decided that land east of the Oder River and Neisse River was to be returned to Poland after centuries of German control, while the eastern provinces would become part of the Soviet Union and thus postwar Poland became 20 percent of its prewar self, and yet closer to the nation it once was back in the 1200s! And this border agreement was ratified in the famous Warsaw Pact of 1955. More than a country, its cities that have maintained a consistent cultural phenomenon, with Krakow being one of the historic intellectual capitals of Europe. An hour away by car or train, one visits Auschwitz and Birkenau, perhaps the quintessential living symbol of humanity's ability to inflict horror and cruelty. Poland is many things indeed.

Poland's Solidarnosc trade union, led by Lech Walesa, played a pioneering role in the transformation of Eastern Europe. Walesa went on to become Poland's elected president. The fact that there is a Polish Pope has not been an inconsequential factor as well in the transformation of the region. Poland, if anything, must be viewed as a vital stage on which many of the world's major issues appear and reappear. Today, despite the growing pains of converting to a market economy, Poland has a vibrant people with a fertive urge to create both art and commerce. And at this writing, Poland is by far the largest country in eastern Europe.

Poland is highly accessible by trains, and trains have played a deeply felt role in 20th-century Polish history. It is quite easy to move around the country by rail, and in general the atmosphere and openness of the Poles and their new system has removed the heaviness and oppression previously experienced when traveling in Poland.

If you have not opted for a train pass that includes Poland (the Inter-Rail pass includes Poland), you should note that train tickets purchased for Poland in the eastern countries are much cheaper than those prebought in the West. And domestic train tickets are rather reasonable. So, when planning your Polish itinerary, you can stop at the first Polish city of interest to you after crossing the border and buying the continuing tickets there.

To get to Poland from Western Europe, note that the celebrated Ost-West express train leaves Paris-Nord station everyday and arrives in Warsaw 22 hours later. This train functions like a puzzle, and cars from around northern Europe, the United Kingdom, Holland, Belgium, and so on, get coupled on along the way. Some travelers have reported that the morning train from London is a better connection than the afternoon one, which requires a change in Germany.

There are many trains between Germany and Poland, with Berlin being only an hour from the Polish border. If you're not familiar with German geography, note that Frankfurt/Oder and Frankfurt/Main are not the same place! The former is the border crossing with Poland in eastern Germany; the latter is the large city. The Eurocity Berolina makes the Berlin-Warsaw journey in under 7 hours. The Gedania Express between Berlin and Dynia by way of Szczecin takes 10 hours and has sleeping cars. There is also an overnight train between Cologne and Warsaw and Cologne and Krakow via Leipzig, Dresden, and Wroclaw.

From the other eastern countries, Poland is accessible via numerous routes. The Prague-Warsaw train, the overnight Bohemia, takes 12 hours. The Silesia Express goes between Prague and Warsaw by way of Katowice, while the Baltic Express from Prague to Gdansk via Wroclaw and Poznan takes 16 hours. From Vienna the Sobieski and Chopin express trains run both at night in the days and pass by Breclav and Katowice. Other connections may be noted in the chapters on Hungary, the Czech Republic, and Slovakia. Good deals on the Trans-Siberian Railraod can be found in Warsaw.

If you are inexperienced in international train travel in the East, the following story of an innocent traveler attempting to make two sets of reservations between Poland and Romania may be instructive: "We went to the ticket office to book our train. The woman did not speak English and there were loads of people behind us waiting (despite there being being about 15 empty windows). Using a pen and paper as our only common language we were told we didn't need a reservation on that day from Warsaw to Krakow, so we just asked for one from Krakow to Bucharest for the following day. Instead of just reservations, she issued us tickets, which we didn't want, so we had a row about that until someone helped out, and we ended up with some reservations. After we'd paid, a Polish kid came up and asked if he could help us, as he spoke English. It turned out we'd been given reservations from Warsaw to Krakow for the following day. Totally useless."

The Polish national railroad takes the ubiquitous initials PKP. Express trains with reservations assure you the fastest and most comfortable way of traveling, whereas the direct trains and local trains are slower and more crowded but afford you a greater taste of local life.

The national tourist agency Orbis serves as reservation center for all train travel, and the ease and inexpensive fees are strong reasons to use this service. The express trains heading to or coming from the capital all have dining cars and comfortable seats. And the new Intercity trains between Warsaw and Krakow in under 3 hours are state of the art. As in France or Germany, second class is perfectly comfortable. One experienced rail user adds, "First-class accommodations are inexpensive and should be used where possible. The language problem is the largest difficulty, and missing a train in a larger station a reality." Another Polish rail aficionado, Jeff Dobek, enjoys answering questions and chatting with others about Poland's railways. Contact Jeff Dobek at 76645.3660@compuserve.com. Jeff adds that travelers shouldn't leave luggage unattended in the train, even when you go to the dining car.

Others have added that travelers should be careful not to take currency that is marked in any way; only perfectly clean notes will be accepted by change bureaus or banks. Still others openly write of fearful and sleepless nights on Polish trains—one is not certain if thieves are really plotting to steal your luggage, money, passport, and travelers checks or if the ambiance of total insecurity prods the imagination into zones of paranoia.

POLISH HOLIDAYS

January 1	New Year's Day		Assumption
	Easter	November 1	All Saints' Day
	Easter Monday	November 11	Day of Independence
May 1	Labor Day	December 25	Christmas Day
	Corpus Christi	December 26	Additional Holiday

SUMMER TIME

Poland changes to Summer Time on the last Sunday of March and converts back to Standard Time on the last Sunday in September.

CITY-SIGHTSEEING NOTES

Warsaw

Warsaw has been the capital of Poland since the beginning of the 17th century. At present it has about 2 million inhabitants, which ranks it seventh in Europe both in population and area. The Main Town and Old Town are on the higher, left bank of the Vistula River, with parks and squares sloping gently down to the river. Within an easy day's travel from Berlin, Prague, Vienna, and Budapest, Warsaw is relatively accessible by train. The population of Warsaw suffered brutally under the Third Reich and the city was ultimately leveled. Some 35 percent of the Warsaw population was Jewish before the war, with the Warsaw Ghetto representing the last holdout of surviving Jews. Miraculously, the old city was reconstructed in a highly convincing way.

Most travelers arrive at the lower level of the Central Station, which has four levels. The station is well equipped with services—and pickpockets. So be warned: the thieves here are organized and efficient, working in small groups. And be wary when getting on and off trains: pairs of thieves arrange to climb on in front of and behind you, one serving to distract your attention while the other grabs the goodies.

Note that when you check your luggage at the train station, you'll be asked to assign a value to your belongings and pay a fee according to that value. This is normal. Plac Zamkowy is at the mouth of the old city (Stare Miastro) and is a good place to start your walking tour. Visit the Barbicon Wall, Blacha Palace, the Royal Way, and the ancient market here. A visit to the reconstructed Chopin Family Drawing Room in the side wing of the former Raczynski Palace should be on your list. For a bright view of the city, climb to the top of the 37th floor of the

Palace of Culture and Science. Also visit the Monument to the Heroes of the Ghetto and the Lenin Museum. For Warsaw information you can now consult the *Warsaw Voice,* Poland's only general-interest English-language weekly newspaper, now on-line on the World Wide Web.

Warsaw is also noted for its music, its art scene, and it cultural festivals.

Krakow

Undoubtedly one of Europe's most beautiful cities, Krakow was spared by the Nazis during World War II at the negotiated request of the Vatican. Krakow is the former capital of Poland, the royal residence, and a symbol of Polish culture that constantly shines with the reflection of its one-time splendor.

Krakovians see their city as the place which is said to be a mystical city: once a center of magic and astrology where Faustus began his studies; one of the seven places in the world protected by magical stones…

Start in the middle of the city at the medieval Wawel Castle. Krakow gets its name from Prince Krak, who founded a settlement on Wawel Hill. Krakow emerged as a student town in the Middle Ages, and Jagiellonian University was founded here in 1364. Spend some time walking though the Market Square or rynek Glowny and its quaint archways, and the Renaissance Cloth Hall, where crafted goods are sold. The live trumpet sounds that call out every hour from the top of the Church of Our Lady and end abruptly is a tradition dating from the 13th century, when the trumpeter was pierced in the neck by a Tatar arrow. The Kazimierz district is now silent with echos and ghosts; it was here that the Jewish community, and later, the ghetto, was situated. Spielberg filmed much of the movie *Schindler's List* on location. Nearly all the Jews of Krakow were sent to the death camps, and Oswiecim (Auschwitz in German) is only an hour from the city. The site of the Plaszow work camp can be visited outside the city.

Krakovians will suggest that a visitor buy grain for Kracow's pigeons (this is a tradition), or give a flower from the Krakow flower sellers to a passing beauty (another tradition). Rest in the "Planty" in the shade of a 100-year-old chestnut and the 600-year-old university. Walk through Kazimierz through Wolnica between Sw. Wawrzynca, Dajwor, Miodowa and Krakowska Streets. Spend some time on a street which is a really a small, elongated square, called Szeroka Street. Here you will find the Remu'h Synagogue and cemetery. In the renaissance Old Synagogue you will see a beautiful collection of Jewish art and objects.

Check the schedule for cultural events in Krakow; the city hosts a rich selection of festivals, including the Short Film Festival and Music in Old Krakow.

Auschwitz

After this day trip from Krakow, a 60-kilometer trip, you will never be the same. Be prepared to do nothing else all day. After a tour of the concentration camp, make sure you also witness the extermination camp of Birkenau, 2 kilometers away. One and a half million people, mostly Eastern European Jews from nearly 30 countries, were murdered here. One traveler reminds others not to be tempted to pay 50 zloty for an organized trip to Auschwitz from Krakow. A coach from the central bus station to Oswiecim costs just 4 zloty each way and leaves from

Stand 3. The Oswiecim rail station is 2 kilometers north of the Auschwitz camp, a 20-minute walk. There are 6 daily trains from Krakow Glowny station, 12 per day from Krakow Plaszow station, and 15 per day from Katowice.

Zakopane

Zakopane, an Alp-like mountain resort in the Tatras, has attracted visitors, hikers, skiers, and vacationers for centuries. The Tatra National Park costs 1 zloty to enter, and is highly regulated to protect the natural setting. For example, it is forbidden to pick berries, herbs, mushrooms, and so on. The guidebook *Zakopane and Its Vicinity*, by Maciej Pinkwart, available in many languages including English, is highly recommended. Should you decide to take the raft trip down the Dunajec Gorge in the Pieniny National Park, book in advance via Orbis Tourist. The queues are quite horrendous on fine days.

The train to Zakopane from Krakow took nearly 5 hours via Nowy Targ in the prewar days. Today, the Kasprowy makes the run in half that time twice a day leaving from Krakow, and the Giewont leaving from Zakopane. There is also a funicular railway up Mt. Gubalowska that offers a memorable view of the mountain valley.

The Zakopane bus trip to Morskie Oko, the largest lake in the Tatras, is available via the village of Plana Palenica; the lake is a 9-kilometer walk from there.

The seasonal Tatry Express takes 6 hours from Warsaw to Zakopane. To cover the entire north-south expanse of Poland you can ride the overnight Zakopane-Gdansk train, which stops in Wroclaw, Poznan, and Warsaw.

Wroclaw

In the heart of Lower Silesia, this tongue-twister dates back to the 13th century. On the Odra, this city boasts of more than 120 canals. Cultural life and student activity are vibrant here. The pubs fill with young people nightly. St. Dorothy's Church demands a visit.

Lublin

An ancient city with the oldest private university in the country, Lublin is worth visiting because it is authentic and deeply historic. From the castlelike architecture of the main train station slightly out of town, Lublin's old town affords visitors a taste of the decadence of times gone by. Visit the castle and the Krakoski Gate as well as the many impressive old churches.

Poznan

Between Berlin and Warsaw, Poznan is famous for its Przemyslaw Castle and sculptures at the Dzialynski Castle. Walk through the old town and then visit the unique Musical Instrument Museum. The stained glass at the Church of the Holy Virgin is of particular beauty, as is the brick Gothic cathedral at Ostorw Tumski. For train travelers, Poznan is actually easy to visit— many trains pass through the city.

Torun

This Teutonic medieval city is located on the Vistula River between Gdansk and Poznan. Visit the Gothic churches. Birthplace of Copernicus (1473), travelers can visit his house and inspect the instruments he used to determine that the earth revolves around the sun. The Church of St. John contains one of the largest bells in Poland. The honey gingerbread is a local specialty.

The Kujawiak express train serves Torun from Warsaw every day, but requires reservations.

Czestochowa

This sacred place of pilgrimage attracts Catholic worshipers from all over the country. They come to the Luminous Mountain Monastery (Jasna Gora) to worship the image of the Black Madonna, the holiest icon in Poland. There are direct train connections from Warsaw, Krakow, and Zakopane.

Gdansk, Gdynia, and Sopot

Gdansk, Gdynia, and Sopot, known as the tri-cities, are sprawled for 30 kilometers along the Gulf of Gdansk on the Baltic Sea, with Gdansk serving as Poland's leading port and shipbuilding center. Its shipyard is the birthplace of Lech Walesa's Solidarnosc labor party. Also known as Danzig, it was declared a free city in the Treaty of Versailles after World War II. There is international ferry service to and from Finland and Sweden.

Gdynia, a leading port and fishing center, is the most northern of the three cities and the only one technically on the Baltic.

Sopot is the chic seaside resort that has attracted international bathers for centuries. Connected by electric train, Sopot offers wide white beaches, but the local pollution is so intense that swimming is no longer thinkable.

Major trains stop in all three cities, while southbound trains usually originate in Gdynia. The Warsaw-Gdansk trains Neptun, Slupia, and Kaszub take 3½ hours, while the Lajkonik Express between Krakow and Gdansk takes 7 hours.

ONE-DAY EXCURSIONS

Warsaw - Czestochowa - Warsaw 864

It is only a 2½-hour drive from Warsaw by taxi on Poland's best highway.

Dep. Warsaw (Wsch.)	06:05	09:05 (2)	Dep. Czestochowa	05:37	17:47
Dep. Warsaw (Cen.)	06:25	08:15	Arr. Warsaw (Cen.)	09:25	21:40
Arr. Czestochowa	09:47	12:55	Arr. Warsaw (Wsch.)	09:39	21:54

(1) Restaurant car. (2)Change trains in Koluszki.

Warsaw - Gdansk - Gdynia - Warsaw 855

Dep. Warsaw (Cen.)	-0-	02:22 (2)	-0-	08:57 (3+6)
Dep. Warsaw (Wsch.)	01:29 (1)	02:32	07:02 (3)	09:07
Arr. Gdansk	05:36	06:35	10:31 (9)	12:30
Arr Gdynia	06:08	07:03	10:57	12:55

* * *

Dep. Gdynia	04:44 (3)	05:40 (3)	06:48 (3)	08:42 (5+7)
Dep. Gdansk	05:10	06:10 (9)	07:10	09:10 (8)
Arr. Warsaw (Wsch.)	08:33	09:22	10:33	13:12
Arr. Warsaw (Cen.)	10 minutes after arriving Wschodnia railstation			

(1) Carries a sleeping car. Also has couchettes. Light refreshments. (2) Carries a sleeping car. Also has couchettes. (3) Reservation required. Light refreshments. (4) Operates late June to late August. Reservations required. Light refreshments. (5) Light refreshments. (6) Plus other Warsaw (Cen.) departures 10:57 (3), 15:02 (3), 16:02 (3), 18:57 (5) and 21:02 (2),...arriving Gdansk 15:31, 18:56, 19:28, 20:17, 21:30, 23:01 and 01:30...arriving Gdynia 16:05, 19:30, 19:51, 20:48, 21:57, 23:30 and 02:07. (7) Plus other frequent Gdynia departures from 10:44 to 22:25. (8) Plus frequent other Gdansk departures from 11:10 to 22:55. (9) Runs daily except Sundays & holidays.

Warsaw - Krakow - Warsaw 865

Dep. Warsaw (Cen.)	07:00 (1)	09:00 (1)	11:00 (1)	13:00 (1)	15:00 (5)
Arr. Krakow (Glowny)	09:35	11:40	13:35	15:40	17:37 (1)
Dep. Krakow (Glowny)	01:10 (2)	02:15 (2)	06:15 (1)	07:15 (3)	08:15 (1+6)
Arr. Warsaw (Cen.)	06:00	05:25	08:45	09:45	10:45

(1) Reservation required. Restaurant car. (2) Carries a sleeping car. Also has couchettes. (3) Runs daily, except Sundays and holidays. Reservation required. Restaurant car. (4) Runs daily, except Saturday. Reservation required. Restaurant car. (5) Plus other Warsaw departures at 15:45 (4), 16:45 (4), 17:45 (4), 18:45 (1), 21:25 and 22:48, arriving Krakow 18:41, 19:35, 20:35, 22:35, 01:50 and 03:58. (6) Plus other Krakow frequent times from 10:10 to 23:00.

Warsaw - Lublin - Warsaw   869

Dep. Warsaw (Centralna)	-0-	06:47	10:47	14:47 (3)
Dep. Warsaw (Wschodnia)	02:45	06:57	10:57	14:57
Arr. Lublin	05:08	09:15	13:15	17:15

Dep. Lublin	07:00 (1)	10:30	12:30	15:00 (4)
Arr. Warsaw (Wschodnia)	09:00	12:44	14:47	17:05
Arr. Warsaw (Centralna)	10 minutes after arriving Wschodnia railstation			

(1) Reservation required. Light refreshments. (2) Light refreshments. (3) Plus other Warsaw (Cen.) departures at 16:47 (2), 18:47 (1) and 20:47 (2), arriving Lublin 19:11, 21:02 and 23:14. (4) Plus another Lublin departure at 16:30, arriving Warsaw (Cen.) 18:57.

Warsaw - Poznan - Warsaw   850

Dep. Warsaw (Wsch.)	06:15 (1)	06:30 (5)	09:10 (1)	13:25 (2)	15:15 (3)
Dep. Warsaw (Cen.)	15 minutes after departing Wschodnia station				
Arr. Poznan (Gl.)	09:37	11:00	12:45	17:00	18:38 (10)

Dep. Warsaw (Wsch.)	16:35 (11)	17:15 (1)	19:10 (3)	21:35	23:15 (5)
Dep. Warsaw (Cen.)	15 minutes after departing Wschodnia station				
Arr. Poznan (Gl.)	19:50	20:35	22:45	01:40	03:15

Dep. Poznan (Gl.)	02:05 (5)	06:30 (4)	07:08 (1)
Arr. Warsaw (Cen.)	05:55	10:15	10:20
Arr. Warsaw (Wsch.)	14 minutes after arriving Centralna station		

Dep. Poznan (Gl.)	10:07 91)	11:12 (1)	15:03 (1+9)
Arr. Warsaw (Cen.)	13:25	14:25 (12)	18:30
Arr. Warsaw (Wsch.)	14 minutes after arriving Centralna station		

(1) Reservation required. Restaurant car. (2) Light refreshments. (3) Reservation required. Second-class. (4) Reservation required. Light refreshments. (5) Carries a sleeping car. Also has couchettes. (6) Reservation required. Carries a sleeping car. Also has couchettes. (7) Runs daily, except Sundays and holidays. Reservation required. Restaurant car. (8) Runs Monday-Friday, except holidays. (9) Plus other Poznan departures at 17:17 (1), 18:18 and 19:31 (1), arriving Warsaw (Cen.) 20:20, 21:20 and 22:40. (10) Runs daily except Saturday. (11) Will not run December 24, 31. (12) Will not run December 25, Jan. 1.

Warsaw - Sopot - Warsaw   852

Dep. Warsaw (Cen.)	16:02 (2)	21:02 (1)
Dep. Warsaw (Wsch.)	10 minutes after departing Centralna station	
Arr. Sopot	19:48	01:39

Dep. Sopot	06:57 (2)	01:07
Arr. Warsaw (Wsch.)	10:42	05:47
Arr. Warsaw (Cen.)	15 minutes after arriving Wschodnia station	

(1) Carries a sleeping car. Also has couchettes. (2) Reservation required. Light refreshments. (3) Light refreshments. (4) Operates late June to late August. (5) Plus other Warsaw (Cen.) departures at 14:57 (3), 15:57 (2), 16:57 (2), 17:57 (2), 18:57 (3) and 21:07 (1), arriving Sopot 19:16, 19:41, 20:36, 21:47, 23:20 and 01:53. (6) Plus other Sopot departures at 10:54 (3), 12:50 (3), 15:55 (2), 17:55 (2), 18:36 (4) and 21:50 (1), arriving Warsaw (Wsch.) 15:12, 17:12, 19:33, 21:36, 22:22 and 02:32.

Warsaw - Torun - Warsaw   859

Dep. Warsaw (Wsch.)	06:25 (1)	16:40 (3)	22:45 (2)
Dep. Warsaw (Cen.)	06:40	17:00	23:10
Arr. Torun	09:36	19:48 (1)	02:18

Dep. Torun	06:56 (1+3)	18:24 (1)	03:55 (2)
Arr. Warsaw (Cen.)	09:45	21:15	07:10
Arr. Warsaw (Wsch.)	09:59	21:29	07:29

(1) Light refreshments. (2) Carries a sleeping car. (3) Reservation required.

INTERNATIONAL CONNECTIONS
FROM POLAND

Warsaw is Poland's gateway for rail travel to Berlin (and on to both Scandinavia and north-western Europe), Moscow, and Vienna (and on to Italy, southeastern Europe and south-western Europe).

Warsaw - Berlin 850

Dep. Warsaw (Wsch.)	06:00 (1)	16:35 (1)	22:05 (2)	23:40 (3)
Dep. Warsaw (Cen.)	06:15 (4)	16:50 (5)	-0-	23:50 (6)
Arr. Berlin (Licht.)	-0-	-0-	06:25	08:00
Arr. Berlin (Hbf.)	12:40	23:25	-0-	-0-
Arr. Berlin (Zoo)	12:25	23:01	-0-	-0-

(1) Reservation required. Restaurant car. (2) Departs from Warsaw's Gdanska railstation. Carries only sleeping cars. (3) Carries a sleeping car. Also has couchettes. (4) Will not run December 25, January 1. (5) Will not run December 24, 31. (6) Reservation required.

Warsaw - Moscow 900

Dep. Warsaw (Gdan.)	-0-	-0-	-0-	14:55 (4)
Dep. Warsaw (Cen.)	09:02 (2)	10:22 (1)	14:54 (2)	-0-
Set your watch forward one hour.				
Arr. Brest	14:26	16:00	20:53	-0-

A short distance from the Brest railstation, the train is held for about 2 hours while the train's wheels are changed so as to conform to the wider Soviet track.

Dep. Brest	16:30	18:08	20:58	-0-
Arr. Moscow (Smol.)	10:00	11:49	12:15	21:54

(1) Carries only sleeping cars. (2) Carries only sleeping cars. Has restaurant car Brest–Moscow. (3) Carries a sleeping car. Also has couchettes. Coaches are second-class. (4) Light refreshments.

Warsaw - Vienna 95a

Dep. Warsaw (Wschodnia)	08:55 (1)	20:20 (2)
Dep. Warsaw (Centralna)	09:10	20:35
Arr. Vienna (Sudbf.)	17:04	06:52

(1) Reservations required. Restaurant car. (2) Carries a sleeping car. Also has couchettes.

ROMANIA

Passengers who board a train that requires reservation whithout obtaining a reservation are charged a penalty fee.

To buy a Romanian timetable, ask for "Mersul Trenurillor." The **1996 Romanian Rail are**: $60 for 3 days rail travel in any 15 days. Children 4-11: half adult fare.

ROMANIAN HOLIDAYS

January 1	New Year's Day	August 23	Liberation Day
January 2	Additional Holiday	August 24	Additional Holiday
May 1	Labor Day	December 30	Republic Day
May 2	Additional Holiday		

SUMMER TIME

Romania changes to Summer Time on the last Sunday of March and converts back to Standard Time on the last Sunday in September.

It has taken time, but the dark and perverse images of Romania that used to correspond to the reality of Ceausescu's Romania are fading quickly as the country, its people, and its institutions respond to a new world of possibilities. Romania today offers travelers more than they might have previously anticipated. Romania's history, language, and geographic beauty position it as a country worth the time one is willing spend to discover its treasures. Aside from its time-warped capital, Bucharest, Romania offers visitors the lush and romantic medieval mountain villages of Transylvania, the iconoclastic monasteries of proud Moldavia and intellectual Bukovina, and the Roman- and Turkish-influenced resort towns on the Black Sea. The infrastructure of material life in this least developed of the new Eastern European countries is still unpredictable and seemingly illogical, and many Romanians have a strangely ironic take on reality, having emerged from the horrors of one of the century's most twisted dictators. But give them a chance and show some sensitivity toward their history and you'll be touched by the local readiness to open up and share the best of the indigenous culture. If you are seeking an experience that is real, inexpensive, and filled with emotional challenge, a trip through Romania by train is highly recommended.

Romania is farther east and south than most westerners imagine, with the Ukraine and Moldova to the north and east, the Black Sea to the east, Bulgaria to the south, Yugoslavia to the southwest, and Hungary to the west. Making the journey by train from western Europe requires some time and a few long stints on the tracks. Due to the very low salaries that they receive, Romanian intellectuals and artists eager to visit other cities in Europe are almost always obliged to take the train, and thus you'll often meet fascinating folks on the Bucharest-Vienna run, for example.

Catrinel Plescu, program director at the Romanian Cultural Foundation in Bucharest, shared her recent experience on the Dacia express train to Vienna: "We left Bucharest at 4:30 and I was a bit nervous about the journey, fearing the old, worn-out carriages. Having to cross three frontiers, a nightmare in itself for an Eastern European, I am worried about the rumors we hear about train attacks in the night. Surprisingly, the carriage is brand-new and cheerfully colorful, navy blue and red, not that terrible military green that reminds one of war convoys and typified Romanians trains. The sheets and the blankets are clean; the towels are threadbare but clean too. The loo is impeccable. I am almost moved. It's the Romanian human touch of gentle corruption—I notice that the toilet paper, paper towels, and liquid soap has already been stolen. The stern schoolmarm in me wants to tell the conductor that this is not civilized, that it spoils our image, that it only confirms that Romanians have no 'klo-kultur,' as the Germans would say. But he helps us with the luggage, he has a nice face with a drooping mustache, two children, a small salary...so I let it be, the tired Romanian in me says...at least he is friendly and human. I've got my own toilet paper (ancestral wisdom) anyway."

Catrinel goes on to report of an incident at the first border crossing. "I refuse to pay the compulsory tourist tax that the custom officer tells me has just been passed in parliament. I want him to show me the law, and secondly, I tell him I'm not a tourist. My fear of people in uniforms turns to anger. This has helped me many times to be brave before 1989. I control my anger and try to sound rational, feminine, and sweet. The man in uniform threatens to put me off the train. This is Hegeshalom; I don't want to spend the night in Hegeshalom. I remember my father's advice: 'Never show them you are frightened; if they feel your fear you are finished'. At the same time I wonder if this is worth the fight. I state that I am expected at a journalists' conference and if he wants an uproar, that's OK with me. He goes off to talk to a superior, and I hear him say that that woman threatened him.They glare at me and I glare back and smile sweetly. My tummy aches. The other Romanians are staring at me because I have dared to be different. This is painfully familiar. I reaffirm what I already know; they want to make the others hate you for defending your rights. I wonder what will happen. I wait. Nothing happens. What a relief; what happiness.

"I've shown them for once, for the first time, that we are stronger than they. The conductor comes back and we drink a glass to each other's health and he tells me, 'Madame, I was so frightened for you! Why did you do that? You know people in uniforms are always right!' Well, this time they weren't. The Hungarian customs officer then asked a Japanese couple to get off the train because there was something wrong with their visas. They got off in tears, not understanding what it was all about. If I could only have explained it to them! Cultural misunderstanding!"

As for domestic travel in Romania, stories vary from western tourists, but in almost all cases a deep sense of contentment seems to pervade those who have decided to commit a part of their itineraries to this still crude land of surprises. Contact with Romanians seems to outstrip the geography or landmarks as the most rewarding aspect of Romanian travels.

One of the most moving travelogues written on Romania was penned on-line on CompuServe's Travel Forum by Melissa Harris, an assistant professor of architecture on exchange in Vienna who spent two weeks exploring the Romanian landscape and mindset by train. "When we arrived in Arad, Romania, at 5:00 A.M., we couldn't decide if it was necessary to get off the train to buy our tickets onto Bucharest. When purchased in the country of travel, tickets are significantly less expensive. We decided to get off, but failed to reboard in time and the train left without us. It would be five hours before the next train departed. It was still dark in Arad as we fumbled our way about the station, looking first for a place to purchase tickets and then for baggage storage which would free us to roam the city during our layover. At the end of the waiting room, we were instructed, there was luggage storage. When I first pushed open the swinging doors, a terrible odor confronted us. Sudden darkness blinded us temporarily. The air was thick and heavy—dank, stagnant air that stank of alcohol and caused us to choke. Perhaps it, like the people who emerged from it, had not stirred for hours. If one can conceive of space as a solid, this waiting room seemed impenetrable.

"As our eyes adjusted, we saw motionless people packed densely on the floors and benches. We moved through the room like a small wave causing ripples in a tangle of arms and legs. Coughing and moaning jostled the unconscious, though daybreak was still an hour away. Time froze as the faint light signaling the end of the room never seem to get any closer. We were moving in slow motion through invisible mud, fighting the paralysis of this violent act of contrast—the 'haves' slicing through the 'have nots.' But if one believes in fate, our ignorance of the train system blessed us with the opportunity to meet our first guardian, Imre, a 23-year-old budding businessman from Brasov. For me, Romania is best summarized by the characters of three people we met, who in each individual situation framed my perceptions and actions."

Imre went on to escort her to his colorful, rural Transylvanian village of Sacele, where, aside from slaughtering a lamb, our heroine learned the routine of daily Romanian life in the countryside.

When it came to looking for more classical means of lodging, like a hotel, Melissa writes that "this is where the myth of cheap travel in Eastern Europe is exposed. Our running joke throughout the trip was the parrotlike response we got when we asked 'How much does this cost?' The answer was always another question: 'Where are you from?' 'America' insured the highest possible rate. If you are a tourist, it is almost impossible to find a hotel room for less than $80 to $100 per night. In other Eastern European countries, accommodations in private homes cost much less, but this doesn't exist yet in Romania. If you are Romanian with proper identification, the same room costs $6."

Bucharest's Gara du Nord train station is reknown for its confusion, so take your time and keep your head. "No visitor leaves without a brush against the sticky fibers of an invisible web of complications almost too bizarre to handle," Melissa recounts. "Many innocent visitors, in fact, become stunned and temporarily paralyzed. We still have no idea if some of the people we encountered were intertwined, but as the night progressed into morning, it seemed more and more likely that we were tangled in a broader net than we could imagine." Again, just be careful, be discreet, be less than trusting, and, when possible, have local Romanians meet you and send you off. It's better to start off overprotected than find your holiday ruined by a black market scam or an unfriendly shakedown.

Melissa's description of the approach to Gara du Nord is realistic, and it should help you imagine what you may head into: "The dingy yellow light of a large bonfire in front of the station cast a spooky glow over hovering bodies and lighted our path to the entrance. A man without legs, almost indistinguishable from the color of the ground. dragged himself past as we dodged the spit of a crippled Gypsy boy retaliating against another throwing sand. My desire to flee was mounting. We were about to discover the underbelly of the infamous Gara du Nord."

If there weren't so many consistent stories about conspiring groups of thieves it would be hard to believe these horrific tales as true. Undoubtedly, things have improved since 1993 but to what degree is unclear. Melissa completed her Romanian experience in style. Her train was delayed for hours; she waited huddled on the platform with her travel companions in the station, only to discover that the track number had been changed at the last minute, and then it was a mad rush to catch it at all.

"Panic swept through our small crowd. Dave ran off to reinspect the information board and the rest of us scurried, looking for anyone in a uniform. I found the closest guy and managed to communicate that we were looking for the train to Sofia. Sympathizing with our desire, our need to get out, this man knew immediately that we were in trouble. He began to run and motioned us to follow. He wanted us to make it. We ran. Rounding the corner, passing track after track, I prayed he knew where he was going. We had pinned all of our hopes on this guy. There was maybe a minute left, maybe seconds, before departure. No more room for errors. As we raced with our packs bouncing, I was running as fast as I possibly could not for the train to Sofia but from the idea of a night in the Gara du Nord."

Of course the train was packed—other people were in their reserved seats and refused obstinately to budge—and Melissa and friends tried to obtain justice. "We remained patient as the conductor pushed his way to the controversial cabin. But when he, too, returned empty handed, irritation began to rise. We paid for these seats and we wanted them. The conductor told us to wait while he conferred with his buddies in their compartment. When he emerged, he escorted us into the business compartment as the other conductors gathered their belongings. They were giving up their seats. If things weren't complicated enough already, we then had to purchase our tickets to Sofia. We only had tickets to the border, where you must get off to buy the rest. Or you can buy them from the conductor for a slightly higher price. So before we all moved in to occupy our places for the night, this guy pulls out a price book and begins to write out the prices. Dave and I were watching closely. 'Don't trust anyone,' the man at the Romania Travel Bureau in Vienna had told us. 'No one.'

"And considering the hassle we had encountered previously with the Arad conductor who was so drunk he couldn't focus and refused to give us our return tickets back, requiring that we essentially push him aside and grab them, we were on high alert. Everything looked feasible until he slapped down a 3,200-lei figure. None of our tickets had been more than 800 lei. Now he was telling us our total would be 5,200 lei each. Though it is only ten dollars, we knew it was severely escalated. Despite our questioning, the guy remained firm. He had us and he knew it. We all forked over the money. It was worth knowing that we had our places for the rest of the night and morning. We got him to write down all the seat numbers again. Who cared about a sleeper at this point? I couldn't wait to have this seat, the protection that such a bribe would provide.

"Just as we had all settled back, leaning wearily into the vinyl seats, Ted's face dropped. He pointed to the aisle window. Briefly speechless, he then gasped, 'It's him. Oh, no. It's that fat—' It was the round man who had pushed over my shoulder while I was buying the tickets. He was now pushing his way toward our compartment. When he attempted to open the door, Ted said no, and held it closed. The guy pressed his face and hands against the glass like some horror movie. Dave quickly pulled the curtains. The man said his wife was pregnant and his family needed a place to sit. Certainly it was his crew who had already occupied our original seats. It seemed as though the entire mass of people standing outside the door wanted into our compartment. They began to pull on the door, pressing their faces to the window. Ted and Dave moved swiftly. With collected belts and luggage straps and harnessed the door and secured it. Ted sat right by the door. There would be no sleeping tonight. The frustrations, the discomfort of the weary travelers outside our door could easily turn on us. They had the numbers. Each time this nightmare seemed to end, another face appeared. We rode like this for three hours. Strangely, when we got to Ruse, just over the Romanian border, the entire train emptied."

CITY-SIGHTSEEING NOTES

Bucharest

This city needs to be walked. Have local friends or a well-recommended guide take you around. Much of prewar Bucharest remains untouched and some of the most elegant properties are now returning to their pre-Ceausescu owners. You can even visit the streets and residences that belonged to the dictator and his wife, entire portions of the city that was off-limits to citizens. One mansion is noted as having solid gold scales in the kitchen which were used to weigh the meat fed to Ceausescu's pack of doberman and German shepherds.

The gargantuan Casa Poporului, the administrative office bloc that was to be Ceausescu's legacy, rose from the ruins of churches, monasteries, and other historic buildings, now looms over the city center in front of a boulevard that dwarfs Paris's Champs-Elysées. Fountains burst in obscene spurts for kilometers in the center of this avenue while the residents of Bucharest weere deprived of drinking water in a harsh rationing scheme. The People's House was never finished and there is talk today among intellectuals of converting the monster into a Museum of Human Folly!

Near the Atheneum concert hall is Revolution Square, the site of the dramatic events of December 1989, flanked by the former royal palace, now housing the national art collection, and the former Communist Party headquarters, now housing the Romanian Senate. Visit all of these.

Brasov

Excellent Transylvania mountain scenery. Visit the 14th-century Black Church.

Bukovina

Northeast of Bucharest in the northern Moldavian region of Bukovina, priceless monasteries beckon your attention: Voronet, Humor, Sucevita, Moldovita, and Arbore. What makes these monasteries unique are the extraordinary frescoes.

Sighisoara

Sighisoara, with its lovely old citadel square, includes the birthplace of Vlad Tepes, the historical Count Dracula. Visit the museum of the walled town.

Sinaia

This lovely winter resort town, filled with mystique and lore, is noted for its late-19th-century extravaganza, Peles Castle, which Prince Carol of Hohenzollern built. Peles was designed as a residence with large halls, elaborate carving, and sumptuous decorations. Access to this and other gems of the Romanian patrimony were restricted during the long and harsh reign of Ceausescu.

ONE-DAY EXCURSIONS

Bucharest - Brasov - Bucharest 950

All of these trains require reservation, unless designated otherwise.

Dep. Bucharest (Nord)	00:50 (1)	07:45 (2)	09:08 (2)	13:25 (2+4)
Arr. Brasov	03:42	10:33	11:35	15:59

Sights in **Brasov:** Excellent Transylvania Mountain scenery in this area. See the 14th century Black Church. The Museum of History. The Art Museum. The Museum of the Romanian School. A popular Winter resort, **Poiana Brasov**, is 9 miles from here.

Dep. Brasov	02:35	03:31 (1)	04:51 (1)	05:42 (1)	06:30 (5)
Arr. Bucharest (Nord)	05:19	06:20	07:24	08:16	09:27

(1) Carries a sleeping car. Also has couchettes. (2) Restaurant car. (3) Runs Monday-Friday, except holidays. Restaurant car. (4) Plus other Bucharest departures at frequent times from 15:00 to 23:35. (5) Plus other Brasov departures at 09:33, 11:10, 12:26 (3), 15:40 (2), 17:15 (2), 17:59 (2), 19:47 (2) and 20:50 (2).

Bucharest - Constantza - Eforie - Mangalia and v.v. 958

Dep. Bucharest (Nord)	06:05 (1)	07:05 (2)	09:15 (1)	10:05 (3)	10:30 (1+6)
Arr. Constantza	09:13	10:16 (1)	11:46 (2)	12:40	13:24
Dep. Constantza	09:41	-0-	-0-	12:52	-0-
Arr. Eforie (Nord)	10:02	-0-	-0-	13:10	-0-
Arr. Mangalia	10:55	-0-	-0-	14:05	-0-

•   •   •

Dep. Mangalia	05:05 (1)	-0-	-0-	13:45 (3+7)	-0-
Dep. Eforie (Nord)	05:55	-0-	-0-	14:43	-0-
Arr. Constantza	06:25	-0-	-0-	15:02	-0-
Dep. Constantza	06:44	08:50 (1)	13:15 (1)	15:15	16:10 (1)
Arr. Bucharest (Nord)	10:00	12:00	16:30	18:40 (4)	18:50

(1) Reservations required. (2) Restaurant car. (3) Operates mid-June to late September. Reservations required. (4) Arrives at Bucharest's Baneasa railstation. (5) Operates late May to late September. Reservation required. (6) Plus other Bucharest departures at 16:05 (1) and 19:00 (5), arriving Mangalia 21:08 and 23:25. (7) Plus other Mangalia departures at 15:00 (3), 15:40 (3), 17:10 (1), 18:05 (3) and 23:30 (5), arriving Bucharest 19:25, 20:48 (4), 21:55, 22:35 and 04:30.

Sights: **Constantza** is a very large resort. See the Museum of Archaeology Parvan. The Open Air Museum of Archaeology. The Roman Mosaic. The Museum of the Black Sea. **Eforie** and **Mangalia** are popular Black Sea beach resorts.

Bucharest - Galati - Bucharest   953

Dep. Bucharest (Nord)	06:10 (2)	13:35 (2)	15:10 (1)	18:10 (2)
Arr. Galati	10:05	17:07	18:50 (2)	21:55

Sights in **Galati**: The most splendid array of birdlife in all of Europe.

Dep. Galati	06:10 (2)	11:05 (1)	13:40 (2)	19:50 (2)
Arr. Bucharest (Nord)	09:45	14:50 (2)	17:29	23:21

(1) Runs daily, except Saturday. (2) Reservations required. Restaurant car.

Bucharest - Sighisoara - Bucharest   950

All of these trains require reservation.

Dep. Bucharest (Nord)	07:45	13:25 (1)
Arr. Sighisoara	11:33	17:57

Sights in **Sighisoara**: The birthplace of Count Dracula. This is an interesting medieval fortress city. See the Museum of the Walled Town. Stroll through the old section.

Dep. Sighisoara	17:49 (1)	18:55 (1)
Arr. Bucharest (Nord)	22:22	23:25

(1) Restaurant car.

Bucharest - Sinaia - Bucharest 950

All of these trains require reservation.

Dep. Bucharest (Nord)	00:55	06:38 (1)	07:45 (1)	09:08 (1)	13:25 (1)
Arr. Sinaia	02:35	08:13	09:32	10:37	15:01

Dep. Bucharest (Nord)	15:00	15:55 (2)	17:31	19:42	20:00 (3)
Arr. Sinaia	16:43	17:26	19:13	21:21	21:47

Sights in **Sinaia**: This is a major Winter resort.

Dep. Sinaia	03:36	04:34 (1)	05:55	06:10	07:32
Arr. Bucharest (Nord)	05:19	06:20	07:44	08:00	09:27

Dep. Sinaia	10:27	12:55	13:23 (2)	16:35 (1)	18:08 (1+4)
Arr. Bucharest (Nord)	11:58	14:40	15:05	18:19	19:45

(1) Restaurant car. (2) Runs Monday-Friday, except holidays. Restaurant car. (3) Plus other Bucharest departures at 21:40 and 23:15. (4) Plus other Sinaia departures at19:02 (1), 20:43 (1) and 21:45.

INTERNATIONAL ROUTES
FROM ROMANIA

Bucharest is Romania's gateway for rail travel to Belgrade (and on to Yugoslavia's Adriatic cities), Budapest (and on to Western Europe), Kiev (and on to Moscow and Leningrad), and Sofia (and on to Athens and Istanbul).

Bucharest - Belgrade 954

This train requires reservation and carries a sleeping car.

Dep. Bucharest (Nord)	23:00
Set your watch back one hour.	
Arr. Belgrade (Dunav)	10:40

Bucharest - Budapest   950

All of these trains require reservation.

Dep. Bucharest (Nord)   00:55 (1)   20:54 (1)
Set your watch back one hour.
Arr. Budapest (Nyugati)   -0-   -0-
Arr. Budapest (Keleti)   14:22   09:32

(1) Carries a sleeping car. Also has couchettes. (2) Restaurant car. (3) runs Monday-Friday except holidays. Restaurant car. Change trains in Brasov at 18:25.

Bucharest - Kiev - Moscow

All of these trains carry only sleeping cars, unless designated otherwise.

	925	94d	94d
Dep. Bucharest (Nord)	09:06	23:16	23:55 (5)
Arr. Ungeni	-0-	06:10 (3)	-0-
Arr. Vadu Siret	19:37 (2)	-0-	08:15 (3)

Ungeni and **Vadu Siret** are the Russian border stations where the wheels of the trains are changed to fit the wider Soviet rail gauge.

Dep. Ungeni	-0-	08:30 (2)	-0-
Dep. Vadu Siret	17:28	-0-	10:30 (2)
Arr. Kiev	11:26 (3)	-0-	01:13 (6)
Set your watch forward one hour.			
Arr. Moscow (Kievski)	-0-	21:14	19:33

(1) Departs from Budapest's Chitila railstation. Runs Tuesday and Friday. Restaurant car Ungeni to Moscow. (2) Estimated. (3) Day 2. (4) Runs Wednesday, Friday and Sunday. Light refreshments. (5) Restaurant car. (6) Day 3.

Bucharest - Sofia - Istanbul   98

This train runs Thursday only and carries only sleeping cars.

Dep. Bucharest (Baneasa)   08:15
Dep. Sofia   22:30
Arr. Istanbul   10:50

YUGOSLAVIA
(Serbia, Montenegro, and Kosova)

Technically, present-day Yugoslavia is the combined states of Serbia and Montenegro. Croatia, Macedonia, Slovenia, and Bosnia-Herzegovina are all independent countries and are treated separately.

Former Yugoslavia is the term referring to the whole nation prior to 1991. The war in the region has rendered daily life, let alone train travel, unpredictable. International train access to Belgrade is exclusively routed via Budapest, Subotica, and Novi Sad. The Meridian originates in Berlin and Sofia, the Skopje-Istanbul in Munich, and the Avala and Beograd in Vienna. Travel from Zagreb in Croatia to Belgrade in Serbia requires the circuitous route through Budapest, Hungary. Via Timisoara, the Bucuresti connects Bucharest and Belgrade. Other local trains connect western Romania and Yugoslavia. The Istanbul Express from Munich passes through Belgrade, as does the Meridian from Berlin to Sofia. Athens and Belgrade are linked via Skopje and Thessaloniki twice a day.

Internally, there is a very scenic route between Belgrade and the coastal town of Bar on which overnight sleeper cars are available. Interail passes are honored in Yugoslavia, but Eurail passes are not. Belgrade is gray and uninspiring, was once a popular transit city in the summer months when northern European students would migrate to the beaches of the Greek islands. Today, Belgrade, aside from being grim, is prohibitively expensive. Some travelers courageous enough to make this leg of the trip spend the day in Belgrade and book a sleeper bunk on the night train out. Most have decided not to include Yugoslavia this year.

Montenegro is seated north of Albania in the southwest corner of the country. Aside from the Adriatic city of Bar, Montenegro hosts a bucolic rail line between Podorica and Kolasin. The 100-mile Tara Canyon is located beyond Kolasin. Montenegro is highly isolated now in times of war and only the port of Bar seems like a unique contact with the outside world. Budva is the best beach in the region.

Montenegro hosts a surprising variety of natural beauty. It is difficult not to be amazed by the stunning changes that occur at frequent intervals in the landscape. Hence the fantastic and inspired descriptions of Montenegro. Nature is harsh and gentle. The region hosts some of the deepest canyons in the world.

YUGOSLAVIAN HOLIDAYS

January 1	New Year's Day	May 9	Victory Day (WWr II)
January 2	Additional Holiday	July 4	Veterans Day
May 1	Labor Day	November 29	Republic Day
May 2	Additional Holiday	November 30	Additional Holiday

SUMMER TIME

Yugoslavia changes to Summer Time on the last Sunday of March and converts back to Standard Time on the last Sunday of September.

KOSOVA

Kosova, also known as Kosovo, is the region disputed over by its Albanian majority and Serbia. The Serbian government has imposed a police state in Kosova by stripping away its autonomy, closing Albanian-language schools, dismissing Albanians from their jobs, suspending Kosova's legal parliament and government—the systematic oppression and flagrant violations of basic rights of Albanians in Kosova. The 90 percent Albanian majority of Kosova have held free elections in which they have chosen their leadership, expressed their determiniation for the independence of Kosova in the 1992 referendum, and declared the independence of Kosova, first from Serbia, then from the Yugoslav federation. The Albanian leadership has declared that it will seek a peaceful resolution of the problem of Kosova. Prishtina is the capital of Kosova.

BOSNIA-HERZEGOVINA

The Department of State warns U.S. citizens not to travel to the Republic of Bosnia-Herzegovina because of ongoing tensions. Instability around Sarajevo severely restricts the American embassy's ability to assist U.S. citizens, even in emergencies.

The Republic of Bosnia and Herzegovina, formerly one of the Yugoslav republics, continues to be in a tortured state of war. The resulting deaths, destruction, food shortages, and travel disruptions affecting roads, airports and railways, make travel to all parts of Bosnia and Herzegovina extremely hazardous. The popular religious shrine at Medjugorje is located within Bosnia and Herzegovina's borders, but tourism in the region is virtually nonexistent and the idea of travel here at this time in history is unthinkable.

Permission to enter Bosnia and Herzegovina is currently granted at the border on a case-by-case basis. Over 70 percent of Bosnia is under the control of Bosnian Serb military forces. General lawlessness and deteriorating economic conditions have brought an increase in crime, and adequate police response in the event of an emergency is doubtful. Anti-American sentiments run high in many parts of the country, particularly in Serb-dominated areas. Roadblocks manned by local militias are numerous. These militia groups frequently confiscate relief goods and trucks, and may otherwise behave unprofessionally. Sarajevo, the beautiful city of Oriental mosques which hosted the 1984 Winter Olympics, is now characterized by its main avenue, popularly called Sniper Alley.

SLOVENIA

This small country tucked in between northeastern Italy and southern Austria enjoys the geography of the Julian Alps and the north Adriatic. In 1990 Slovenia was the first to break away from communist Yugoslavia. That sense of freedom and independence is strongly felt in Slovenian cultural production—the nation offers excellent original music and a dynamic avant art scene called Neue Slowenische Kunst which not only runs an excellent Web site on the Internet but has issued its own passports to a virtual country that is wholly peaceful.

Slovenia, even today, makes for a pleasurable and surprisingly peaceful journey. Don't think of Slovenia as former Yugoslavia. Llubljana, the capital, is filled with interesting sites and activities. The most popular train routes into Slovenia are via Vienna and Salzburg to Jesenice and Llubljana. Routes from Munich and other German cities are functioning, and five trains a day run from Trieste to Llubljana. Slovenian-Croatian connections require a change of train mid-route, and via Croatia one can connect from Llubljana to Budapest.

Aside from Llubljana with its old town, Presernov Square, and triple bridge, side trips to the chic resort lake town of Bled is a must. Marshal Tito kept his summer house on a hill above this sparkling lake.

CROATIA

Before the war, the Croatian coast on the Adriatic attracted millions of tourists with its resort towns of Split and Dubrovnik. All that has changed. The islands off the coast, curiously, have not been disrupted by the war and are lovely and safe although desolate.

Zagreb, the capital and center of cultural life, remains bright and vibrant. There are overnight intercity trains from Munich to Zagreb via Salzburg and Ljubljana. Reservations southbound are required but only recommended northbound. From Vienna to Zagreb, there is the Eurocity Croatia daily. Three express trains run between Venice and Zagreb via Trieste and Ljublijana. The Simplon Express offers a connecting service from Geneva and Rome; Budapest-Zagreb connections are plentiful. Note though that there are no Serbian-Croatian train connections.

Zagreb - Ljubljana - Zargreb   935

Dep. Zagreb	05:40 (1)	06:50	08:10 (2)	10:35	
Arr. Ljubljana	08:00	09:13	10:17	12:54	
			• • •		
Dep. Ljubljana	12:35	15:05	19:40 (2)	20:45 (1)	21:45 (3)
Arr. Zagreb	14:50	17:30	21:50	22:55	23:59

(1) Restaurant car. (2) Reservation required. Restaurant car. (3) Second class.

Sights in **Ljubljana**: Several walking tours are described in "Ljubljana City Guide," a book with maps that is sold at the bookstore at Titov Cesta, near the corner of Subiceva Ulica in the new city. All of the walks begin at the square called Presernov Trg, where the17th century Franciscan Church of the Anunciation is located.

See the triple bridge that crosses Ljubljana River (2 for pedestrians, one for vehicles). Ascend a hill to reach the castle for a view of the city from it.

There is free sampling of hundreds of different Yugoslav wines at the Autumn Wine Fair.

SCENIC RAIL TRIPS

Belgrade - Priboj - Bar   and v.v.   942

This is the most scenic rail route in Yugoslavia. Steep canyons, turbulent rivers and mountains. The world's highest railway span, completed in 1976, is the 495-foot-high Mala Rijeka Bridge on this route.

The 325-mile line has 254 tunnels and 234 concrete and steel bridges. The trip climbs from the Danube to heights of 4,000 feet before descending to sea level on the Adriatic coast. The line from Priboj to Bar is narrow-gauge as the train descends to the valley of the **Rzav River**.

Dep. Belgrade	05:10 (1+2)	10:30 (3)	14:20 (4)	21:30 (5)	22:40 (5+6)
Dep. Priboj	08:47	14:40	18:03	01:45	-0- (7)
Arr. Bar	12:34	18:22	21:30	05:44	06:04

Dep. Bar	09:55 (3)	14:10 (4)	15:35 (1+8)	22:00 (6)	22:20 (5)
Dep. Priboj	13:33	17:41	19:15	01:42	02:18
Arr. Belgrade	17:39	21:14	23:04	05:28	06:38

(1) Operates mid-June to mid-September. (2) Reservation required. Light refreshments. (3) Light refreshments. (4) Reservation required. First-class only. Light refreshments. (5) Carries a sleeping car. Also has couchettes. (6) Operates early June to late September. Carries a sleeping car. Also has couchettes. (7) Does not stop in Priboj. (8) Reservation required.

Ljubljana - Postojna - Ljubljana   930

The longest and most beautiful river cave of Europe is near **Postojna**, where the **Pivka River** flows through an underground passage.

Tourists, traveling through the cave on a small train, are able to see wonderful rows of stalactites and stalagmites, gigantic underground rooms, chasms and little lakes. A 16th century castle is at the entrance to the cave. Conducted tours are offered daily, every half-hour. June 1–September 1, from 08:30–16:00, plus 17:00 and 18:00. September 2 to May 31, from 09:30–13:30.

Because the cave is not deep, visitors can go a long distance through it. It extends 19 miles! A narrow-gauge railway takes passengers more than one mile into the cave. Its terminal (Postojna Station) is larger than New York's Grand Central. English-speaking guides conduct tourists from it on a 1½-mile figure-eight walk. Great Mountain Room is more than 900-feet high.

Dep. Ljubljana	Frequent times from 03:40 to 20:20
Arr. Postojna	55-65 minutes later

• • •

Dep. Postojna	Frequent times from 02:20 to 22:21
Arr. Ljubljana	55–65 minutes later

Ljubljana - Jesenice - Sezana - Ljublana

We show the long scenic route for a daylight ride to Sezana and then the shorter route for returning to Ljubljana from Sezana at the end of the day.

935

Dep. Ljubljana	10:20 (1)	15:45 (4)
Dep. Kranj	-0-	16:12
Dep. Lesce-Bled	11:00	16:34
Arr. Jesenice	11:14	16:49
Change trains. 931		
Dep. Jesenice	11:20 (2)	16:55 (4)
Arr. Nova Gorica	-0- (2)	18:40
Change trains.		
Dep. Nova Gorica	-0-	18:43 (4)
Arr. Sezana	14:15	19:35
Change trains. 930		
Dep. Sezana	19:03 (3)	21:35
Arr. Ljubljana	20:42	23:20

(1) Reservation required. Has first-class and second-class coaches. Restaurant car. (2) Direct train. No train change in Nova Gorica. (3) Restaurant car. (4) Second-class.

INTERNATIONAL ROUTES
FROM YUGOSLAVIA

There are rail connections from Belgrade to Athens (and on to Istanbul), Bucharest (and on to Kiev and Moscow), Budapest (and on to Moscow, Prague, Vienna and Warsaw), Salzburg (and on to the rest of Western Europe and to Scandinavia), Sofia (and on to Athens and Istanbul), and to Venice (and on to the rest of Italy and Southern Europe).

Belgrade - Athens   970

Dep. Belgrade	07:45 (1)	11:00 (2)	21:40 (1)
Set your watch forward one hour.			
Arr. Athens (Larissa)	06:33	08:10	20:00

(1) Carries a sleeping car. Also has couchettes. (2) Carries only sleeping cars and couchettes.

Belgrade - Bucharest   954

Dep. Belgrade (Dunav)   18:00 (1)
Set your watch forward one hour.
Arr. Timisoara (Nord)   23:39
Arr. Bucharest (Nord)   07:35

(1) Reservation required. Carries a sleeping car.

A stopover in **Timisoara** is worthwhile, to see the opulence of the Hapsburg rulers at the Dicasterial Palace. Also the Catholic and Serbian cathedrals and the Museum of Fine Arts on Piata Unirii, a picturesque square. See a show at Puppet Theater, on Piata Furtuna.

Belgrade - Budapest - Vienna   61

Dep. Belgrade	12:35 (1)	19:30 (3)	22:05 (4)
Arr. Budapest (Keleti)	18:30 (1)	-0-	06:00
Arr. Vienna (West)	21:45 (2)	05:30	09:20

(1) Restaurant car. (2) Arrives at Vienna Sud railstation. (3) Carries a sleeping car. Also has couchettes. (4) Second class.

Belgrade - Sofia   945

Dep. Belgrade	10:15 (1)	12:50	22:00 (2)
Set your watch forward one hour.			
Arr. Sofia	19:30	22:05	07:22

(1) Light Refreshments. (2) Has couchettes.

CHAPTER 9

THE MIDDLE EAST

IRAN

Children under 7 travel free. Half-fare for children 7–13. Children 14 and over must pay full fare.

Five rail routes radiate from Tehran: (west to Tabriz (and on to both Russia and Turkey), south to Khorramshahr on the Persian Gulf (and on to Iraq), southeast to Zarand (with a spur to Isfahan, a popular tourist resort), and west to both Mashhad and Gorgan. A short line runs from Zahedan into Pakistan.

The country's oldest rail line has been operating only 60 some years. The rail service to Turkey was completed in 1971. Engineering and equipment are both highly modern.

Third-class has only wood or plastic seats. Sleeping cars and couchettes are available on trains to Turkey and to the USSR.

Tehran

See the museums in the fantastic Shahyad Monument, built to commemmorate Iran's 2500th anniversary, only a few years ago. The 6-mile labyrinth of the city's Bazaar. The House of Strength. Gulistan Palace. The 19th century Sepahsalar Mosque. Shah Mosque. The Crown Jewels Museum in Markazi Bank.

The gardens and museums of Golestan Palace. The Ethnological Museum. The Archaeological Museum. The Mausoleum of Reza Shah The Great. The Marble Palace. The Decorative Art Museum. The National Art Museum.

Take a one-day excursion to the Shemshak ski resort or to see carpet-washing in the Cheshmeh Ali Stream.

Tehran - Esfahan   4510 Bus

Buses depart Tehran hourly	05:00–20:00, plus 12:45 and 14:00.
Buses depart Esfahan hourly	05:00–20:00.
	Journey time is 7 hours.

Sights in **Esfahan**: (This is the spelling used by Cook. Iranians spell it Isfahan.) A popular tourist resort.

See the blue enameled domes of the mosques. Visit the Ali Qapu Palace. View the breathtaking frescoes at the Palace of Four Columns. Visit ancient Friday Mosque and the Theological School. Browse through the Bazaar. Walk across the tiered bridges. Wonderful textiles, rugs and tiles can be purchased here. Esfahan carpets are magnificent.

Tehran - Gorgan   4503

Dep. Tehran	07:25	Dep. Gorgan	07:10
Arr. Gorgan	19:25	Arr. Tehran	18:50

Sights in **Gorgan:** This city was rebuilt after being destroyed in an earthquake during the 1930's.

Tehran - Kerman   4505

Both trains are air-conditioned and have a restaurant car.

Dep. Tehran	13:30	Dep. Kerman	13:35
Arr. Kerman	07:55 (1)	Arr. Tehran	0755 (1)

(1) Day 2.

Sights in **Kerman**: Founded in the 3rd century and situated 5,738 feet above sea level. The largest carpet-exporting center of Iran. See the 11th century mosque, Masjed-e-Malek. Visit the 18th century Qajar citadel, the many very old mosques and the ruins of a 3rd century castle. Browse through the large bazaar.

Tehran - Neyshabur - Meshhad   4504

There is excellent mountain scenery on this trip.

Dep. Tehran	06:20	15:20	16:00 (1)	16:50 (1)	18:10
Dep. Neyshabur	N/A (2)	N/A (2)	N/A (2)	05:35	06:53
Arr. Meshhad	17:40	05:50	06:45	07:15	08:15

Sights in **Neyshabur:** This is the birthplace and burial site of Omar Khayyam, Persia's famous astronomer, mathematician and poet.

Sights in **Meshhad**: The holiest city in Iran, Shiite Muslims make pilgrimages to this city because Imam Ali Reza, their religious leader, was buried here in 817 in the great gold-domed shrine. Also see: Gowhar Shad Mosque. The Tomb of Nader Shah. The Meshhad Museum.

Dep. Meshhad	06:00	12:35	15:10 (1)	16:00 (1)	18:25
Dep. Neyshabur	N/A (2)	N/A (2)	17:10	17:50	N/A
Arr. Tehran	21:20	04:45	05:20	06:15	09:00

(1) Air-conditioned. Carries a first-class sleeping car. (2) Departure times from Neyshabur not available at first printing of this guide.

Tehran - Tabriz 4500

There is interesting mountain scenery on this ride. Tabriz is the gateway for rail travel to Turkey (see "International Routes From Iran").

All of these trains are air-conditioned in first-class, unless designated otherwise.

Dep. Tehran	17:00	18:00	20:25(1)
Arr. Tabriz	06:00	06:55	10:05

Sights in **Tabriz**: This is one of the major carpet producing areas in Iran. A popular Summer resort. Do not fail to see the fantastic 15th century Blue Mosque.

Dep. Tabriz	16:10 (2)	17:00(3)	17:55
Arr. Tehran	05:40	06:00	07:30

(1) Runs Tuesday only. *Not air-conditioned*. (2) Runs Thursday only. *Not air-conditioned*. (3) Runs daily, except Tuesday. (4) Runs Tuesday and Saturday.

INTERNATIONAL ROUTES
FROM IRAN

The gateway for train travel from Iran to Russia is Tehran. Timetables for this route were not available at the time of first printing of this guide. A line starting in Zahedan leads into Pakistan.

Zahedan - Quetta 5942 + 4510

This is the rail route from Iran into Pakistan. The Zahedan railstation is 2 miles east of the city.

Mirjawa is on the Iran-Pakistan border. Rail service Mirjawa-Kuhi Taftan was suspended 1984-1992, and the Zahedan-Mirjawa rail service was suspended 1985-1992, replaced by buses. Both services resumed operation in 1993.

This train runs Monday only. It has a first-class coach and a restaurant car.

Dep. Zahedan	08:00
Dep. Mirjawa	11:10
Dep. Kuhi Taftan	13:45
Arr. Quetta	11:20 Tuesday

IRAQ

Children under 4 travel free. Half-fare for children 4–9. Children 10 and over must pay full fare.

Iraqi trains have 3 classes of space: first, second and tourist. First-class and second-class seats convert into berths for overnight travel.

Baghdad

More than 100 mosques and minarets here, including the spectacular gold-domed Kazimayn Mosque. The 13th century Abbasid Palace and its museum. The 13th century Mustansiriyah law college. The selection of copper, cloth and silver in the many bazaars. The collection of Arabic history and literature at the Library of Waqfs.

The Central Library of Baghdad University. The Costumes and Ethnographic Museum. The Iraq Museum. The Iraq Natural History Museum. The Museum of Arab Antiquities. The National Museum of Modern Art. Nearby, the tombs of 2 imams.

Baghdad - Basra   4152

This scenic route follows the Tigris River to the Persian Gulf.

| Dep. Baghdad (West) | 9:00 | 20:45 | 22:45 |
| Arr. Basra (Ma'qil) | 19:15 | 8:35 | 13:30 |

Sights in **Basra**: This is a prominent river harbor. Many date palm groves in this area.

| Dep. Basra (Ma'qil) | N/A (1) |
| Arr. Baghdad (West) | N/A (1) |

(1) Return times were not available at first printing of this book.

Baghdad - Al Mawsil (also "Mosul")   4151

These trains are air-conditioned in all three classes. Overnight trains have first and second-class coach seats that convert to berths. These services are subject to confirmation.

Dep. Baghdad (West)	12:00	20:50	22:10
Arr. Al Mawsil	19:00	05:06	05:49
Dep. Al Mawsil	11:30	20:40	22:10
Arr. Bagdad (West)	18:50	05:30	05:40

Sights in **Mosul**: The ruins of ancient Nineveh are near here. The word "muslin" came from the production here once of fine cotton goods. See: The Great Mosque and its leaning minaret. The 13th century Red Mosque.

There are NO INTERNATIONAL ROUTES from Iraq.

ISRAEL

Children under 4 travel free. Half-fare for children 4–9. Children 10 and over must pay full fare.

Plan rail trips in Israel carefully to avoid the crowded conditions on public holidays and Friday afternoons and the suspension of nearly all transportation service from Friday sunset to Saturday sunset in conformance with the Jewish sabbath, which causes heavy traffic on Friday afternoon. Most museums and historical facilities are closed from 14:00 Friday until Sunday morning.

The country's principal train route is south from Nahariyya to Haifa, Tel Aviv and Ashdod. Its west–east line goes from Tel Aviv to Lod and Jerusalem.

There are *no* rail connections between Israel and countries adjacent to it.

The heaviest passenger train traffic in Israel is during August. Lightest is in February. Israel Railways urges tourists to make advance seat reservations at all times. Direct requests to: Traffic and Commercial Manager, Israel Railways, P.O. Box 44, Haifa, Israel.

MAIN ISRAELI RAILSTATIONS

Haifa (Bat Galim)	Telephone (04) 564182
Jerusalem	Telephone (02) 733764
Netanya	Telephone (09) 823470
Tel Aviv	Telephone (03) 5421515

Haifa

This is Israel's main port. See the Bahai Shrine and Persian Gardens, open 09:00–12:00 (open in the afternoon for strolling). The Museum of Prehistory, a Nature Museum and Zoo complex, open Sunday-Thursday 08:00–14:00; Fridays 08:00–12:00; Saturdays 09:00–14:00.

The collection of Islamic folk art and costumes at the Museum of Ethnology, open 10:00–13:00 every day, plus 17:00–19:00 on Monday and Wednesday. The Clandestine Immigration Museum. The Carmelite Monastery. The Dagon Grain Museum. The Statue Garden.

Objects from 5,000 years of this area's maritime history, exhibited at the National Maritime Museum (198 Allenby Road), open Sunday-Thursday 10:00–16:00; Saturday 10:00–13:00. See the 4,000-year-old Egyptian funerary boat; a painting from 700 B.C. of a ship; ancient clay jars in which oil, wine and wheat were shipped to and from Israel; coins with maritime motifs from all over the world; rare 15th century maps; ship models; a 10th century Chinese jade astronomical device.

The Museum of Japanese Art on the summit of **Mt. Carmel** (89 Hanassi Avenue), open Sunday–Thursday 10:00–17:00; Saturday 10:00–14:00. (Israel's only subway is the one-mile "Carmelit" that goes to the top of Mt. Carmel.) Its exhibits include textiles, ceramics, metal objects, lacquers, scrolls and screens as well as 2,500 books and catalogs on Japanese art and culture. See the 18th and 19th century woodblock prints. The sliding, paper doors there create a perfect Japanese ambiance.

Israel's advancements in hi-tech and communications can be seen at the Institute of

Technology (on Balfour Street), open Monday–Thursday 08:00–16:00; Friday 08:00–14:00. The program there includes an electronic newspaper and a 3-dimensional hologram exhibit. Nearby, see the exhibit of trains from the 19th century Turkish period, at the Railway Museum in the East Railway Station.

The paintings and drawings at the Museum of Ancient and Modern Art, open Sunday-Thursday 10:00–13:00 and 16:00–19:00; Friday and Saturday 10:00–13:00.

Tel Aviv

One of the oldest cities in the world, called Yafo 4,000 years ago.

See the photography and paintings (Van Gogh, Chagall, Vlaminck, Renoir, Utrillo, Degas) at the Tel Aviv Museum (27 Shaul Hamelech Boulevard), open Sunday–Thursday 10:00–22:00; Saturday 10:00–14:00 and 19:00–22:00. Its annex is the Helena Rubinstein Pavillion (7 Tarsat Boulevard), open Sunday–Thursday 09:00–13:00 and 17:00–19:00; Friday 09:00–11:00.

The animals at the 250-acre drive-through Safari Park, open Saturday–Thursday 09:00–15:00; Friday 09:00–13:00. The view from the observation terrace of the Shalom Building. The fascinating museum of the Jewish underground movement of the 1930's and 1940's, in the Bet Jabotinsky Building on King George Street.

The Museum of the Diaspora, recounting the cultural, social and religious events of those Jews who settled in different countries all over the world between 70 A.D. and the 20th century. Open Sunday, Monday, Tuesday and Thursday 10:00–17:00, Wednes- day 10:00–21:00, closed Friday and Saturday. There are guided tours in English, Hebrew and many other languages. The exhibits are in the categories of Family, Community, Faith, Culture, Among The Nations, Return and Martyrdom. Located on the campus of Tel Aviv University, this museum is reached by Bus #25 from the beachfront hotels, or by taxi.

Models of 20 famous synagogues (including the 18th century one in Newport, Rhode Island and the one in Kai Feng Fu, the only known Jewish community in China) are part of the "Faith" exhibit. One of the dioramas in the "Community" section is an array of more than 100 figures re-enacting life in a 13th century German village.

The nearby Haaretz Museum complex consists of a planetarium, an archaeological dig, and exhibits of coins, folklore, science and technology. It is open Sunday–Thursday 09:00–16:00; Friday 09:00–13:00; Saturday 10:00–14:00.

Take a 20-minute bus ride to **Jaffa**, the ancient port, and browse in the artists' colony there. Nearly 100 commercial galleries there stay open until late night. The "Israel Experience," located in Old Jaffa, has 4 floors of craft shops, restaurants, a duty-free shop, and a tourist information center. A 40-minute slide show is presented there.

One-day bus tours from Tel Aviv go to the occupied **Golan Heights** (Thursday); the northwestern frontier at **Rosh Hanikra**, the Roman, Byzantine and Crusader ruins at Caesarea, and remains of the Crusaders at Acre (Tuesday, Friday and Sunday); Christian holy sites (Monday, Wednesday and Saturday); and to the **Dead Sea** plus a 1,000-foot ascent by cable car to the **Masada** fortress, daily except Fridays (see more about Masada under "Jerusalem").

The Tel Aviv Marina offers boating, surfing and windsurfing. Nearby **Herzliya**, **Netanya** and **Caesarea** are popular beach resorts along Israel's Riviera. Take a guided tour of the Diamond Center in Netanya and shop for gems there.

Jerusalem

Bus #99 travels between 32 major tourist sites. A roundtrip ticket ($2 U.S.), sold at both the Central Bus Station and aboard the bus, allows getting on and off the bus all day.

The best way to see the Armenian, Christian, Jewish and Muslim quarters of the Old City is by walking. Brochures describing several walks, are available at the Ministry of Tourism (24 King George Street or at the Jaffa Gate).

Three-hour tours with an English speaking guide leave from the Tower of David courtyard at 09:00 and 14:00 Sunday–Friday and at 14:00 on Saturday.

There are other walking tours that include the ruins of the Second Jewish Temple (beneath the Dome of the Rock), the ramparts of the walls of the Old City, and a tunnel that reveals more of the Western Wall. Schedules for this walk can be obtained at the tour office at 34 Habad Street.

Visit the History of Jerusalem Museum in the restored ruins of the 2,000-year-old King David Citadel, the Tower of David. This is just inside the Jaffa Gate in the Old City. Entry begins by crossing a 12th century moat, built by the crusaders. This museum's exhibits trace the city's history from its Canaanite origins to the present day and offers a sound-and-light show every evening April–October at 21:30 in English, at 22:30 in French and German (on alternate nights). The museum is open Sunday–Thursday 10:00–17:00, Friday and Saturday 10:00–14:00.

The Dead Sea Scrolls are the highlight of the exhibits in the Israel Museum. This museum also has archaeological finds from the prehistoric era to the Middle Ages, a large collection of Jewish ceremonial art and artifacts, ancient coins, and a fine art collection. Four tours are offered: a 2-hour look at exhibits in the galleries, a 90-minute inspection of the ruins of the fort, a 40-minute look at the Old City, and rooftop views from the Citadel's towers.

Don't fail to see the enormous diorama of the Jewish Second Temple, from the First Century. Also notable is the miniature of the 7th century Muslim Dome of the Rock. Statues of Crusader knights guard the entrance to a hall that is devoted to their reign over Jerusalem.

The Bezalel National Art Museum, Samuel Bronfman Biblical and Archaeological Museum, and Billy Rose Art Garden, all in the Israel Museum complex.
The Knesset (Israel's Parliament) and the President's Garden are opposite the Israel Museum.

A prominent satellite of the Israel Museum is the Rockefeller Museum, containing objects from prehistory to the Ottoman Empire: the skull of Galilee Man (100,000 B.C.), a carved wood beam from the 8th century al Aqsa Mo que, plaster pieces from the 8th century Islamic Hisham Palace, ivories from 12th century B.C. Armageddon, superlative Roman and Byzantine gold jewelry. The Rockefeller Museum is open Sunday–Thursday 10:00–17:00; Friday and Saturday 10:00–14:00.

Visit the Western (Wailing) Wall of the Temple Mount. The Dome of the Rock (Mosque of Omar). The al-Aqsa Mosque. The Church of the Holy Sepulchre. The 14 stations of the cross, along Via Dolorosa.

Shop at the nonprofit Benevolent Arts Workshop on Via Dolorosa for hand-embroidered dresses and tablecloths made by Christian Arab women. Next door to it, the Jerusalem Pottery sells what are said to be the best ceramics to be found in the Old City section: jars, plates and bowls decorated with Arabesque designs reproduced from 6th century mosaics and manuscripts.

Visit Hadrian's Arch and Roman Square, at Damascus Gate. The 6th century Nea Church. The archaeological park next to the City Museum at Jaffa Gate's Citadel. The 1,500-year-old artifacts in the Greek Orthodox Patriarchate Museum. Colorful oriental markets. The exhibits from the 1948–67 occupation at Tourjeman Post Museum in the Mandelbaum Gate area. The displays from the same period at the Cable Car Museum on Hebron Road.

Mount Zion, with the Tomb of the House of David, Cenacle (the room of the Last Supper), and the Abbey of the Dormition. The Tombs of the Sanhedrin. En Karem, birthplace of John the Baptist. The Chagall stained-glass windows, depicting the Tribes of Israel, at the Synagogue of the Hadassah Medical Center.

Don't fail to see the 24-foot-long Book of Isaiah, most ancient of the Dead Sea Scrolls. It is the centerpiece at the Shrine of the Book, where a beautiful copper scepter from 3,500 B.C. and the illuminated Italian Rothschild manuscript from 1470 are also exhibited.

See the 11th century mosaics and 17th century frescoes at the Monastery of the Holy Cross, open Monday–Thursday and Saturday 09:00–17:00, Friday 09:00–13:30, closed Sunday. The 30 dioramas telling the history of the Jewish people from 4,000 years ago to the re-establishment of Israel in 1948, Jewish ceremonial objects of all eras, and an 18th century carved ivory kiddush cup in the Wolfson Museum, open Sunday–Thursday 09:00-13:00, Friday 09:00–12:00.

Visit the Biblical Zoo. The Kennedy Memorial. The completely furnished, reconstructed mid-19th century Palestinian home (costumes, utensils, tools, and furniture used by Jews of that era) in the Old Yishuv Court Museum on Or Hahayim Street.

Yad Vashem Holocaust Memorial, open Sunday–Thursday 09:00–17:00 and Friday 09:00–13:00, commemorates the 6,000,000 Jews killed by the Nazis 1935–1944. Near its entrance is a grove of trees called "Garden of the Rightegous," memorializing individuals and groups who saved Jews during that period. More than 3,000 Christian families in France, Germany, Holland and Poland have been honored here. Inside, the names of the 22 largest death camps are stamped on a floor and there is a vault containing ashes recovered from camp gas chambers. There are also exhibits tracing the rise of Adolph Hitler, concluding with the Nuremberg war-criminal trials.

The L.A. Mayer Memorial Institute of Islamic Art, at 2 Hapalmach Street is open Sunday–Thursday 10:00–13:00 and 15:00–18:00, Saturday 10:00–13:00, closed Friday. It was founded by the Jewish granddaughter of a Lord Mayor of London, in honor of a Jewish professor of Islamic art. Its purpose is to acquaint non-Moslems with the heritage of Islam. The displays here of rugs, glassware, pottery, jewelry and calligraphy trace the history of Islamic art since the 7th century.

Two Islamic traditions are represented: the Eastern one that originated in Iraq and Iran, and the Western tradition that originated in Syria and Egypt. Among the exhibits are 12th and 14th century miniature paintings that illustrated manuscripts, an elegant Koran with beautiful calligraphy, bronze pieces inlaid with gold and silver thread, brilliantly-colored ceramic tiles that once ornamented mosques, and a collection of cameo glass, enameled glass and cut glass with geometric designs (7th to 19th centuries).

Southwest of the city are the ancient Jewish cemetery at the Mount of Olives and the Christian shrines at the Garden of Gethsemane. Below the Mount of Olives: Absalom's Pillar, the Tomb of Zechariah, and the toms of Bnei Hezir.

Northeast of the city are the Tombs of the Kings of Judah, the Garden Tomb, the Tomb of Simon the Just, the Cave of King Zedekiah (also known as Solomon's Quarries).

Masada

Masada is a 90-minute drive south. Buses leave daily, except Saturday and Jewish holy days, from the central Egged Bus Station (224 Yafo Road). The 4-minute cable-car ride to King Herod's palaces and fort on the top of the mountain runs every half-hour from 08:00 to 15:30.

After the fall of Jerusalem in 70 A.D., a group of Jewish zealots making the last attempt to revolt against the Romans barricaded themselves and held the mountain-top for 3 years against Roman siege. Masada has remained a symbol of heroism, and it is the modern scene of annual pilgrimages by young Israelis.

Tourists can inspect 2 large palaces, villas, bathhouses, storerooms, a fortified wall, the Herodian Synagogue (oldest synagogue in the world), cisterns and a 5th century Byzantine chapel.

All times shown for Isreal are Summer schedules.

Haifa - Tel Aviv   4000

Dep. Haifa (Merkaz)	05:54 (1)	06:14 (1)	06:36 (2)	07:09 (3)	07:28 (1+8)
Dep. Haifa (Bat Galim)	6 minutes after departing Merkaz station				
Arr. Tel Aviv (Merkaz)	07:30	07:50	08:02	08:20	08:59

• • •

Dep. Tel Aviv (Merkaz)	06:00 (1)	06:25 (2)	07:18 (3)	08:03 (1)	08:42 (3+9)
Arr. Haifa (Bat Galim)	07:31	08:00	08:23	09:26	09:47
Arr. Haifa (Merkaz)	6 minutes after departing Bat Galim station				

(1) Runs daily except Sat. (2) Runs daily, except Fri. and Sat. (3) Runs daily, except Fri. and Sat. Air conditioned train. Light refreshments. (4) Runs Fri. only. (5) Runs Fri. only. Air-conditioned train. Light refreshments. (6) Runs Sat. only. (7) Runs one hour later mid-March to mid- September. (8) Plus other departures from Haifa (Merkaz) at 08:17 (1), 08:54(3), 09:24 (4), 09:54 (5), 10:24 (1), 11:24 (3), 12:24 (2), 12:54 (4), 13:24 (3), 13:54 (4), 14:24 (2), 15:22 (3), 16:24 (2), 17:24 (2), 18:24 (2), 18:54 (4) and 19:25 (4). (9) Plus other departures from Tel Aviv at 09:00 (1), 10:00 (4), 10:30 (3), 11:00 (4), 11:40 (5), 12:00 (1), 13:00 (3), 14:00 (1), 15:00 (2), 16:00 (2), 16:40 (3), 17:00 (2), 18:00 (3), 19:00 (2), 20:00 (2), and 21:00 (7).

Haifa - Tel Aviv - Lod - Jerusalem

This ride through the Judean wilderness, in operation since 1892, is the most scenic train trip and most exciting travel experience in Israel.

The train winds from the Mediterranean coast through orange groves before climbing into the Judean mountains, covered with pine and cypress trees. Then it passes **Zor'a** and **Eshtaol** and the **Valley of Sorek**, where Samson lived and met Delilah, according to the Bible.

Next, this route goes through a breach in the wall the Romans built around **Bittir** (called Beitar in biblical days), where Simeon Bar Kochba in 135 A.D. led the unsuccesful second Jewish revolt against the Romans, marking the beginning of the long Jewish diaspora.

4000

Dep. Haifa (Merkaz)	07:09 (1)	07:24 (2)	10:24 (2)	14:24 (3)
Dep. Haifa (Bat Galim)	07:15	07:30	10:30	14:30
Arr. Tel Aviv (Merkaz)	08:20	08:35	11:50	15:55
Change trains.				

4005

Dep. Tel Aviv (Merkaz)	08:25 (3)	08:40 (2)	11:55 (2)	16:00 (3)
Dep. Lod	08:46	09:01	12:16	16:21
Arr. Jerusalem	10:10	10:25	13:40	17:45

* * *

Dep. Jerusalem	08:35 (3)	08:50 (2)	12:05 (2)	16:10 (3)
Dep. Lod	09:59	10:13	13:28	17:33
Arr. Tel Aviv (Merkaz)	10:21	10:35	13:50	17:55
Change trains.				

4000

Dep. Tel Aviv (Merkaz)	10:30 (1)	11:00 (2)	14:00 (2)	18:00 (1)
Arr. Haifa (Bat Galim)	11:30	12:18	15:30	19:10
Arr. Haifa (Merkaz)	6 minutes after arriving Bat Galim station			

(1) Runs daily, except Friday and Saturday. Air-conditioned train. Light refreshments. (2) Runs Friday only. (3) Runs daily, except Friday and Saturday.

SAUDI ARABIA

Children under 4 travel free. Half-fare for children 4–11. Children 12 and over must pay full fare. Disabled passengers and those accompanying them travel at half-fare.

The only passenger rail route in Saudi Arabia is from the port of Dammam on the Persian Gulf to Riyadh, the inland capital. There are no train connections between Saudi Arabia and countries adjacent to it. The trains are modern air-conditioned diesels.

Dammam - Riyadh   4200

All of these trains run daily except Thursday. These trains are air-conditioned and have a restaurant car.

| Dep. Dammam | 07:30 | 16:00 | Dep. Riyadh | 07:51 | 16:21 |
| Arr. Riyadh | 11:30 | 20:00 | Arr. Dammam | 11:51 | 20:21 |

Sights in **Riyadh**: The Museum of Antiquities. The Zoo.

SYRIA

Children under 4 travel free. Half-fare for children 4–9. Children 10 and over must pay full fare.

When they were functioning, all of Syria's train routes became international connections. The rail lines in Syria which ceased operating after 1983 were the north-south standard-gauge from Kamechlie to Baghdad, the north-south standard-gauge from Halab (Aleppo) to Akkari (and on to Lebanon), the north-south special 3'5G" gauge Hedjaz (also spelled "Hijaz") Railway from Dimashq (Damascus) to Deraa (and on to Jordan), a narrow-gauge from Dimashq (Damascus) to Beirut, and 2 short lines running north from Halab, one of which went to Karkamis (and on into eastern Turkey).

The only remaining passenger train services in recent years are: (1) Halab-Fevzipasa (and on into central and western Turkey, en route to Ankara and Istanbul [table 4020], (2) the route from Halab to Kamechlie [table 4075], and (3) Halab to Dimashq (Damascus) [table 4075].

Passenger train service was once possible from Europe, through Istanbul, via Turkey, Syria and Jordan all the way to Aqaba on the Red Sea. The interruption of service in Jordan from Amman to Ma'an, has made that intercontinental train travel impossible since 1917.

Halab (Aleppo)

Founded before 2,000 B.C. See the remains of the ancient Cathedral of St. Helena, converted into a mosque in the 12th century A.D. The 11th century minaret on the 8th century Great Umayyad Mosque. The ancient Citadel, built before the 13th century. Fantastic 16th and 17th century bazaars. The archaeological exhibits in the National Museum.

Dimashq (Damascus)

"The pearl of the east." Oldest inhabited city in the world, founded about 3,000 B.C. See the Great Umayyad Mosque. Al-Marjah Square, in the center of the city. The National Museum.

The Qasr al-'Azm Museum. The Arab Academy, containing the national library. The fabulous orchards of the Ghutah.

Deraa

The ancient Greco-Roman ruins. The 13th century mosque.

Halab (Aleppo) - Haydarpasa (Istanbul)   4020 + 4022

Dep. Halab	12:20 (1)
Arr. Fevzipasa	18:00
Dep. Fevzipasa	19:50 (2)
Arr. Haydarpasa	21:25 (3)

(1) June–September: runs Tuesday and Saturday. October–May: runs Saturday only. (2) Runs Tuesday, Thursday and Saturday all year. Carries a sleeping car. (3) Day 2 from Fevzipasa.

When making connections for trains in Istanbul, allow 8 hours from arrival in Haydarpasa even though the boat trip from Haydarpasa to Istanbul is only a 20-minute ride. Haydarpasa is the eastern section of Istanbul.

Halab - Qamishli (Kamechlie)   4075

Dep. Halab	01:40 (1)	05:50	15:28 (2)	22:15 (2)
Arr. Qamishli	08:52	12:36	23:07	06:14
		• • •		
Dep. Qamishli	07:00 (2)	14:45	18:18 (1)	22:06 (2)
Arr. Halab	14:27	21:45	01:24	05:47

(1) Carries a sleeping car and a restaurant car. (2) Second-class only. Air-conditioned.

Halab - Dimashq (Damascus)   4075

Dep. Halab	00:35(1)	01:55 (2)	15:18 (3)
Arr. Dimashq (Kadem)	07:02	08:21	21:51
		• • •	
Dep. Dimashq (Kadem)	00:01 (1)	16:18 (3)	19:20 (2)
Arr. Halab	06:07	22:12	01:12

(1) Carries a sleeping car. Light refreshments. (2) Carries a sleeping car and a restaurant car. (3) Restaurant car.

TURKEY

Children under 7 travel free. Half-fare for children 7–11. Children 12 and over must pay full fare.

The first-class sleeping cars here have single compartments. Second-class sleeping cars have 2-berth and 3-berth compartments. Some trains also have first-class 6-berth couchette cars or reclining-seat cars (designated "Pullman"). Express and Mail trains charge higher fares than local trains. There is no air-conditioned space on Turkish trains.

Turkish trains in Asia are liable to cancellation or change.

Most of the train trips in Turkey for which we provide schedules are also the international rail routes to countries adjacent to Turkey. For that reason, we do not show a separate International Route list in this section.

Shoppers come to Turkey for alabaster (vases, lamps, chess sets), copper (trays, pitchers, bowls), inlaid wood (boxes, backgammon boards), leather and suede (coats, skirts, bags, brief-cases), carpets, jewelry, ceramics and meerschaum (pipes, necklaces, bracelets).

TURKEY'S TRAIN DISCOUNTS

Students .... 10% discount.
Groups .... 30% discount for groups of 24 or more.
Roundtrips .... 20% discount for roundtrip tickets.
Sport Teams of 5 or more .... 50% discount.

Ankara

Capital of the Turkish Republic. See: The Anitkabir, tomb of Mustafa Kemal Ataturk, father of modern Turkey. The collection of relics from prehistoric times until the present in the magnificent Ataturk Mausoleum, and the view of Ankara from there. The Museum of the National Assembly. The third century Roman Baths. The Columns of Julian. The Temple of Augustus.

The Byzantine Citadel. The finest collection of Hittite and pre-Hittite artifacts in Turkey can be seen in the Museum of Anatolian Civilizations. Visit the exhibits of an- cient clothing, jewelry, manuscripts, tapestries, wood carving, musical instruments and weapons in the Ethnographic Museum.

Next to it is the Museum of Modern Art and Sculpture. Nearby, the Zoo at Ataturk's Farm. Ankara has several fine mosques: Haci Bayram, Alaettin, Ahielvan, Arslanhane and Yeni.

Istanbul

Colonized 2,600 years ago. First called Byzantium, then Constantinople. The city that links Europe and Asia. Haydarpasa is the eastern section of Istanbul.

See several exceptional mosques: The 17th century Blue Mosque (Sultanahmet), the rich tiles and stained-glass in the 16th century Suleymaniye (the greatest building here), the enormous Fatih, the 15th century Eyup, the extraordinary jasper columns in the 15th century

Beyazit, lovely tile decorations in the 17th century Yeni and in the 16th century Rustempasa.

Mosques are open to non-Muslims 09:00–12:00 and 13:00–17:00. Most mosques are closed to non-Muslims at prayer times (dawn, noon and dusk).

One of the world's richest museums, Topkapi Sarayi, palace of sultans from the 15th to mid 19th century (open daily except Tuesday 09:00–17:00). The turbans, swords and tea cups encrusted with emeralds, rubies and diamonds as well as the satins embroidered with pearls will dazzle you. The kitchens there contain what is said to be the world's finest collection of Chinese porcelain.

The 19th century white marble Palace of Dolmabahce. Two other splendid palaces: Yildiz and Beylerbeyi. The blue and green tiled interior of the 15th century Cinili kiosk.

Istanbul's churches are outstanding: Ayasofia (St. Sophia), first built in 325, reconstructed in 532, later converted to a mosque, now a museum with fine Byzantine mosaics (closed Monday). The 4th century Church of St. Irene. The Byzantine frescoes and mosaics depicting the life of Christ and Old Testament scenes in the ancient Church of St. Saviour, now called Kaariye Mosque. The 14th century beautiful gilded mosaics in the old Church of St. Mary. The exquisite mosaics in the 12th century church, Pammakaristos (now called Fethiye Mosque).

The Summer open-air folklore performances at Rumeli Castle. The 4th century fortification. The Ramparts. Tour the great underground cistern, Yerebatan Sarayi. This storage facility, connected to the 4th century Aqueduct of Valens, supplied water to the Imperial Palace. It is built with 336 columns that have corinthian capitals.

Visit the Grand Bazaar. See the ancient Hippodrome of Constantinople, where chariot races took place. One of the 3 tall columns there was taken from the Egyptian Temple of Karnak. Another was removed from the Greek Temple of Apollo at Delphi.

The views of the Bosphorus from the luxury restaurant on Galata Tower and from the top of the Tower of Leander, and the view of Istanbul from the top of the white marble Beyazit Tower.

There are 2 incredibly beautiful fountains: Ahmet II (behind St. Sophia Cathedral) and the marble Tophane.

Istanbul has many excellent museums: The immense Greco-Roman collection at the Archaeological Museum (closed Monday). Next to it, the Assyrian, Babylonian, Sumerian and Hittite treasures in the Museum of Oriental Antiquities (closed Monday). The Museum of Mosaics (closed Tuesday).

The Museum of Turkish and Islamic Art (closed Monday). The Municipal Museum. The Naval Museum and the Military Museum (both closed Monday and Tuesday). During Summer, folk dances are performed at Gulhane Park every night except Sunday.

The spectacular view from the ancient fort at the first of the 96 gates along the 5th century 4-mile-long wall (15 feet thick by 35 feet high) that stretches from the Golden Horn to the Sea of Marmara.

Other interesting sights along the ancient wall are: the ancient spring of Zoodochos Pege near the Belgrade Gate, the Ottoman tombs outside the Edirne Gate, the 13th century Palace of Porphyrogenitus (tenanted in succession by Ottoman royalty, a Jewish poorhouse, a brothel, a pottery and a bottle works).

Istanbul - Haydarpasa (Boat Trip) 4042

Haydarpasa is the eastern section of Istanbul.

The boat departs both piers frequent times from 06:00 to 24:00 for the 20-minute journey.
Allow at least 12 hours for making connections with trains.

Istanbul - Athens

974		*970*	
Dep. Istanbul	23:40 (1)	Dep. Thessaloniki	18:17
Dep. Pithion	08:00 Day 2	Arr. Athens	01:42
Arr. Thessaloniki	18:02		
Change trains.			

(1) Light refreshments. Pithion-Thessaloniki.

Istanbul - Edirne - Svilengrad - Sofia - Belgrade - Munich

	945 + 965	*61+ 965*
Dep. Istanbul (Sirkeci)	18:30 (1)	22:15 (2+3)
Dep. Svilengrad	02:48 Day 2	05:35 Day 2
Arr. Sofia	07:45	09:52
Dep. Sofia	08:20	10:20
Set your watch back one hour.		
Arr. Belgrade	15:32	17:29 (3)
Change trains. 61		
Dep. Belgrade	18:30 (2)	18:30 (3)
Arr. Munich	10:56 Day 3	10:56 Day 3

(1) Reservation required. Carries a sleeping car Tuesday and Saturday. Has couchettes daily. (2) Carries
a sleeping car. Also has couchettes. (3) Direct train to Munich. No train change in Belgrade. Carries a
sleeping car. Also has couchettes. No coach cars.

Istanbul - Bandirma - Manisa - Izmir

Travel between Istanbul and Bandirma is by boat.

4041			*4035*		
Dep. Istanbul	09:00	21:00	Dep. Izmir (Bas.)	08:00 (1)	19:10 (2)
Arr. Bandirma (Quay)	13:15	01:15	Dep. Manisa	09:20	20:21
Change to train. 4035			Arr. Bandirma (Quay)	14:05	01:00
Dep. Bandirma (Quay)	15:00 (1)	02:00 (2)	*Change to boat. 4041*		
Dep. Manisa	-0-	-0-	Dep. Bandirma(Quay)	14:15	02:30
Arr. Izmir (Bas.)	21:10	08:05	Arr. Istanbul	18:30	07:00

(1) Light refreshments. (2) Restaurant car.

Sights in **Manisa:** The 14th century Ulu Cami (Great Mosque) and the 16th century Muradiye Mosque.

Sights in **Izmir:** Third largest city in Turkey and its largest Aegean port. Once known as Smyrna. Walk along Ataturk Caddesi on the seafront.

See the elegant Moorish-style clock tower at Konak Meydani. The Bazaar. Three very attractive mosques: Kemeralti, Hisar and Sadirvan. Remains of the second-century Roman Agora. The Archaeological Museum in Culture Park. The magnificent view of the city from Velvet Castle, on Mount Pagos. The fortress of Kadifekale, built by one of Alexander the Great's generals.

Izmir - Ankara   4023

All of these trains have a restaurant car.

Dep. Izmir (Basmane)	18:00 (1)	20:30 (2)
Arr. Ankara	08:46	10:35

• • •

Dep. Ankara	18:00 (1)	21:50 (2)
Arr. Izmir (Basmane)	09:00	11:25

(1) Carries a sleeping car. (2) Reservation required. Supplement charged. First-class only. Has couchettes. The coach seats recline.

Fevzipasa - Halab (Aleppo)   4020 + 4022

Dep. Fevzipasa	10:40 (1)	Dep. Halab	12:20 (2)
Arr. Halab	17:01	Arr. Fevzipasa	19:50

(1) October–May: runs Friday only. June–September: runs Monday and Friday. (2) October–May: runs Saturday only. June–September: runs Tuesday and Saturday.

Izmir - Selcuk - Ephesus

In contrast to the train schedule shown below, there is also a more frequent guided bus service direct from Izmir to Ephesus and v.v. and it is only a 2-hour trip each way.

4026				
Dep. Izmir (Bas.)	08:15		Dep. Ephesus	Frequent times
Arr. Selcuk	09:50		Arr. Selcuk	15 minutes later
Change to mini-bus.			*Change to train.*	
Dep. Selcuk	Frequent times		*4026*	
Arr. Ephesus	15 minutes later		Dep. Selcuk	17:52	18:37
			Arr. Izmir (Bas.)	19:35 (1)	20:15

(1) Arrives at Izmir's Alsancak railstation

Sights in **Ephesus:** St. Paul preached here. The Virgin Mary spent her last days nearby. The Turkish Culture and Information office claims: "This vast ruined city has more to see than any other classical city anywhere. It is the grandest of ancient cities. Ephesus was famous as a center for worship of Artemis. The goddess' temple here was among the Seven Wonders of the World. The city is one of the Churches of the Revelation."

Ankara - Kars - Tbilisi - Leninakan - Rostov - Kharkov - Moscow

Service within Armenia on part of the Tbilisi-Moscow route may be suspended frequently due to military action in that area.

4030					
Dep. Ankara	18:15 (1)		*Change trains.*		
Dep. Kayseri	02:40 (2)		*Set your watch to Moscow time.*		
Dep. Erzurum	18:35		*5090*		
Arr. Kars	22:58		Dep. Leninakan	15:33 (4)	10:18 (8)
Change trains.			Arr. Tbilisi	22:20	16:50 (8)
Dep. Kars	10:45 (3)		*Change trains.*		
Arr. Leninakan	14:50		*5025 + 5080*		
			Dep. Tbilisi	14:00 (5)	17:15 (8)
			Dep. Rostov	14:59 (6)	18:01 (9)
			Dep. Kharkov	23:18 (6)	02:32 (6)
			Arr. Moscow (Kurski)	12:09 (7)	16:02 (6)

(1) Carries a sleeping car and restaurant car. Also has couchettes. (2) Day 2 from Ankara. (3) Day 3 from Ankara. Winter: runs Tuesday only. Rest of the year: runs Tuesday and Friday. Has only second-class coaches. (4) Second-class only. Compartments convert to bunks. (5) Day 2 from Leninakan. Carries a sleeping car and a restaurant car Tbilisi-Moscow. (6) Day 3 from Leninakan. (7) Day 4 from Leninakan. (8) Direct train. No train change in Tbilisi. Carries a first-class sleeping car, second-class coaches and a restaurant car Leninakan-Moscow. (9) Day 2 from Leninakan.

Sights in **Kayseri:** Called Caesarea when it was the capital of a Roman province. See the Byzantine Citadel and, in it, the Faith Mosque. East of the Citadel, the 13th century Huand Mosque and College, and the geometric designs in the Baths of Princess Mahperi. Nearby, the beautifully decorated 13th century Doner Kumbet (Mausoleum). West of the Citadel is the interesting covered market. Also see the Archaeological Museum. The 13th century Koluk Mosque.

Sights in **Erzurum:** The Seljuk fort. The collonaded courtyard at the 12th century Ulu Cami Mosque. The Cifte Minareli Madrese Museum. The Hatuniye Medrese Mausoleum.

Sights in **Kars:** The 10th century Church of the Holy Apostles, now a museum. The ancient Georgian fort. The Kumbet Mosque. The 11th century Cathedral. The murals in the Church of St. Gregory. The Evliya Mosque.

Sights in **Rostov:** A post-World War II Russian metropolis, designed for heavy industrial manufacturing. See the enormous theater on Teatralnaya Square.

Sights in **Tbilisi:** This is one of the oldest and most important cities in the former Soviet Union. But, it was almost entirely rebuilt since it became part of the Russian empire in 1801.

At the State Museum of Art, see the exhibits of outstanding 6th to 11th century Byzantine enamels, splendid gold and bronze crosses decorated with pearls and colored stones, the great 12-pound gold altarpiece, an 18th century solid gold bishop's miter, and Scythian-style gold jewelry from the fifth century B.C.

Sights in **Kharkov:** Almost totally reconstructed after World War II with wide streets. Sixth largest city in the USSR. Among the few old treasures that survived Nazi destruction are the 17th century Pokrovsky Cathedral, a belltower commemorating the 1812 victory over Napoleon, the 19th century Patriarchal Cathedral, and an 18th century theater.

Ankara - Haydarpasa (Istanbul) 4027

All of these trains require reservation and have a restaurant car, unless designated otherwise.

Dep. Ankara	08:10 (1)	09:50 (2)	17:30	22:20 (4)	23:30 (3)
Arr. Haydarpasa	16:25	17:05	04:00	07:17	07:45

Dep. Haydarpasa	10:30 (1)	13:15 (2)	20:00 (3)	22:00 (4)	23:50 (2)
Arr. Ankara	17:50	20:40	05:54	07:18	08:02

(1) Supplement charged. First-class only. (2) Supplement charged. Has only reclining-seat coaches. (3) Coaches have both couchettes and reclining seats. No restaurant car. (4) Carries only sleeping cars.

Haydarpasa (Istanbul) - Ankara - Kayseri - Tatvan - Van

4027

Dep Haydarpasa	22:00 (1)
Arr Ankara	07:50
Change trains. 4030	
Dep Ankara	10:40 (2)
Dep Kayseri	18:55
Arr Tatvan Pier	17:10 (2+3)
Change to a boat. 4045	
Dep Tatvan Pier — Every 4 hours	
around the clock from 02:00	
Arr Van Pier 4 hours later	

4045 (Boat)

Dep Van Pier — Every 4 hours	
around the clock from 23:59.	
Arr Tatvan Pier 4 hours later	
Change to a train. 4030	
Dep Tatvan Pier	09:10 (4)
Dep Kayseri	07:45 (5)
Arr Ankara	16:10 (5)
Change trains. 4027	
Dep Ankara	21:30 (6+8)
Arr Haydarpasa	07:00 (3)

(1) Reservation required. Carries only first and second-class sleeping cars and a restaurant car. (2) Runs Tuesday, Thursday and Sunday. Carries first-class sleeping cars. Also has couchettes. The Tuesday and Thursday departures terminate in Tatvan City at 16:40. (3) Day 2 from Ankara. (4) Runs Tuesday, Thursday and Saturday. The Tuesday and Saturday departures originate in Tatvan City at 09:50. (5) Day 2 from Tatvan. (6) Coaches have couchettes and reclining seats. Restaurant car. (7) Reservation required. Supplement charged. Has reclining seats and a restaurant car. (8) Plus other departures from Ankara at 22:20 (1) and 23:00 (7), arriving Haydarpasa 07:43 and 08:05.

Sights in **Van:** This city is on a vast, salt lake. A famous trading place for carpets and rugs. See: The old fort. The 2 small Seljuk mosques. The 10th century Church of the Holy Cross, on an island in Lake Van, reached by frequent boats operated for tourists.

Samsun - Sivas   4025

Dep. Samsun	07:30 (1)	18:00 (2)	Dep. Sivas	08:30 (2)	19:15 (1)
Arr. Sivas	19:10	05:40	Arr. Samsun	19:36	06:20

(1) Runs Monday, Wednesday, Friday and Sunday. (2) Runs Tuesday, Thursday and Saturday.

Sights in **Samsun:** Birthplace of the Turkish Republic, in 1919. This is the largest Turkish port on the Black Sea.

Sights in **Sivas:** Excelent remains of 13th century Seljuq Turkish architecture. See the 11th century Great Mosque. The museum in the 13th century Blue Medrese (theological college). The mausoleum of Sultan Kay-Kaus I in the 13th century Medresesi. The intricately-carved facade and minarets of the Cifte Minare Medrese. The royal throne and other relics in the nearby Armenian Monastery of the Holy Cross.

Haydarpasa (Istanbul) - Mersin   4022

4032			4033	
Dep. Haydarpasa	09:00 (1)		Dep. Mersin	17:26
Arr. Yenice	05:25 (2)		Arr. Yenice	18:06
Change trains.			*Change trains.*	
4033			4032	
Dep. Yenice	06:43		Dep. Yenice	23:59 (3)
Arr. Mersin	07:26		Arr. Haydarpasa	21:25 (4)

(1) Runs Tuesday, Thursday and Sunday. Restaurant Car. (2) Day 2 from Haydarpasa. (3) Runs Tuesday, Thursday and Saturday. Restaurant Car. (4) Day 2 from Yenice.

Sights in **Mersin:** This is Turkey's principal port on the Mediterranean, surrounded by citrus groves. See Eski Cami (the Old Mosque) and Yeni Cami (the New Mosque). Crusaders' castles. Roman ruins.

Haydarpasa (Istanbul) - Ankara - Adana

All of these trains are first-class only, require reservation, charge a supplement, and have a restaurant car.

4027			4021	
Dep. Haydarpasa	10:00		Dep. Adana	19:30 (1)
Arr. Ankara	17:10		Arr. Ankara	08:05 (2)
Change trains.			*Change trains.*	
4021			4027	
Dep. Ankara	20:10 (1)		Dep. Ankara	09:50
Arr. Adana	07:55 (2)		Arr. Haydarpasa	17:05

(1) Train has only sleeping cars and couchettes. (2) Day 2.

Sights in **Adana:** This city was founded about 1,000 B.C. See: The second-century stone bridge, Tas Kopru. The 16th century Ulu (Great) Mosque. The 15th century Akca and Ramazanoglu mosques. The Archaelogical Museum.

Haydarpasa (Istanbul) - Izmit   4027

All of these trains have a restaurant car, unless designated otherwise.

Dep. Haydarpasa	08:55 (1+2)	13:15 (3)	17:30	18:30 (8)	21:50 (1+7)
Arr. Izmit	10:24	14:44	18:59	20:15	22:35

Dep. Izmit	04:56	05:22 (4)	06:21 (3)	07:34 (3)	15:38 (9)
Arr. Haydarpasa	06:30	07:00	08:05	09:05	17:27

(1) Departs/Arrives Haydarpasa's Sogutlucesme railstation. (2) Runs Tuesday, Thursday and Sunday. (3) Reservation required. Supplement charged. First class only. (4) First class only. (5) Supplement charged. First-class only. (6) Supplement charged. First-class only. Light refreshments. (7) Runs Wednesday, Friday and Sunday. (8) Plus other departures from Haydarpasa at 21:00(4), 23:00(3) and 23:15(6). (9) Plus other departures from Izmit at 16:48 (3) and 19:45(1+7).

Haydarpasa (Istanbul) - Konya   4020 + 4032

Dep. Haydarpasa	09:00 (1)	18:40 (2)	23:15 (3)
Arr. Konya	22:50	08:10	13:00

Sights in **Konya:** Inhabited since 3,000 B.C. This has been a holy Islamic city since the death there of the 13th century Mevlana Jalludin Rumi, founder of the Mevlevi order.

The legend is that when Mevlana walked by a goldsmith's shop one day, he heard "Allah" every time a worker hit the metal with a hammer. Mevlana whirled in ecstasy in the middle of the street. This started the tradition of the Whirling Dervishes. The 13th century Mevlana Mausoleum, ancient monastery of the Whirling Dervishes, decorated with greenish-blue tiles, is now a museum. See the ebony pulpit, 42 Roman columns and sarcophagi of many sultans in the 13th century Alaeddin Mosque. Nearby, the 13th century Karaty College and the interesting ceramics in the ruins of the Seljuk Palace. The Museum of Wood and Stone Carving in the Minare Medrese (Koranic school). The collection of Roman sarcophagi and statues in the Archaeological Museum, next to the Seljuk Sahip Ata Mosque. The 13th century Iplikci Mosque and Sircali College. The 16th century Selimiye Mosque. The collection of Islamic Art in the Koyunoglu Museum.

Dep. Konya	07:50 (4)	16:35 (2)	20:10 (3)
Arr. Haydarpasa	21:25	06:30	09:05

(1) Sleeper and couchette. Runs Tuesday, Thursday and Sunday. Restaurant car. (2) Carries a sleeping car and restaurant car. (3) Reservation required. Supplement charged. First-class only. Has couchettes and a car with reclining seats. Light refreshments. (4) Runs Tuesday, Thursday and Saturday. Restaurant car.

Haydarpasa (Istanbul) - Adana - Fevzipasa - Halab (Aleppo)   4020

En route to Halab, this train divides in Fevzipasa. Be sure to board the "Halab" coaches.

Both trains carry a sleeping car and have couchettes and a restaurant car.

Dep. Haydarpasa	09:00 (1)		Dep. Haleb	12:20 (4)
Arr. Adana	06:00 (2)		Arr. Fevzipasa	18:00 (4)
Dep. Adana	06:50 (3)		Arr. Adana	22:40 (4)
Arr. Fevzipasa	10:07		Dep. Adana	23:30 (4)
Arr. Halab	17:01		Arr. Haydarpasa	21.25 (5)

(1) June—September: runs Tuesday, Thursday and Sunday. October–May: runs Thursday only. (2) Day 2 from Haydarpasa. (3) June—September: runs Friday and Monday. October—May: runs Friday only. (4) June-September: runs Tuesday and Saturday. October-May: runs Saturday only. (5) Day 2 from Halab.

CHAPTER 10

AFRICA

The longest rail trip in this continent is from Johannesburg, South Africa to Dar es Salem, Tanzania. This journey takes you through Botswana, Zimbabwe and Zambia. It can take up to 7 days, depending on the intervals between connections.

Here are the various segments:

> Johannesburg—Harare
> Harare—Bulawayo—Victoroa Falls
> Taxi   Victoria Falls—Livingstone
> Livingstone—Lusaka—Dar es Salaam

ALGERIA

Children under 4 travel free. Half-fare for children 4–9. Children 10 and over must pay full fare.

The train lines here are standard-gauge. Algeria's rail system consists of one east-west route (connecting Tunisia with Morocco) from which there are 4 spurs heading north to Mediterranean ports (Annaba, Skikda, Bejaia and Tizi Ouzou) and 3 southern routes (Annaba–Tebessa, Constantine–Touggourt, and Mohammadia–Bechar, the last 2 going through the Atlas Mountains to the Sahara Desert).

Algiers

See the shops, cafes and unique narrow streets of the Kasbah. The Marechal Franchet d'Esperey Museum. The fabulous palaces (Summer and Winter) of the Governor-General. Many fine mosques. The view of little islands, harbor and city from Notre-Dame d'Afrique Church.

The splendid Jardin d'Essai du Hamma botanical gardens. The view from Saint-Raphael Park. Nearby, several good seashore resorts: **Moretti, Zeralda**, etc.

Constantine

Located on the eastern edge of the Kabylia mountain area. Rebuilt by the Roman emperor Constantine in AD 312, after the city was destroyed in the previous year. The ancient section of the city is on top of a steep rock. See: The spectacular gorges of the **Rhummel River**, which surround 3 sides of the city.

The elaborate Ahmed Bey Palace. Medina, the Moslem Quarter. The Gustav Mercier Museum. Nearby: restored ruins of ancient Roman towns: Tebessa, Timgad, Djemila. Several Berber villages.

There is much good Berber handicraft in this area: pottery, carved furniture, enamel-inlaid jewelry. Shoes and saddles made here are famous for exceptional leatherwork.

TRANSCONTINENTAL ALGERIAN RAIL ROUTES

The following 3 services are Algeria's only train connections with the countries adjacent to it, Tunisia and Morocco.

Algiers - Constantine - Annaba - Tunis

All of these trains require a reservation, unless designated otherwise.

2545

Dep. Algiers	08:05 (1)	16:10 (3)	20:30 (5)
Arr. Constantine	14:50	01:55	03:20
Dep. Constantine	14:55	02:00	03:29
Arr. Annaba	17:42	07:34	06:13

Change trains.
2550

Dep. Annaba	08:20 (6)
Arr. Ghardimaou	12:42

2601

Dep. Ghardimaou	13:45 (6)
Arr. Tunis	16:53

(1) Light refreshments. (2) Supplement charged. First-class is air-conditioned. Restaurant car. (3) Supplement charged. First-class is air-conditioned. Has couchettes. Buffet car. (4) Reservation is *not* required. (5) Has couchettes. Light refreshments. (6) First-class is air-conditioned. Light refreshments until 10:28, then buffet 13:40–16:47.

Sights in **Annaba:** This old city was settled by Phoenicians in the 12th century B.C. See: The narrow streets of the old town. The 11th century Sidi Bou Merouan Mosque. (Its columns were taken from Roman ruins.) The 18th century Salah Bey Mosque. The Place d'Armes. **Hippo Regius**, one mile south, was a rich city of Roman Africa until AD 300. Many of the archaeological finds from it are exhibited at the Hippo Museum.

Algiers - Oran 2542

Dep. Algiers (Agha)	07:30 (1)	11:30	17:15	21:30	22:30
Arr. Oran	12:30	17:40	23:07	05:25	06:06

Sights in **Oran:** This city has 3 sections: La Blanca (the 16th century Spanish city on the hill), La Marine (near the Mediterranean) and La Ville Nouvelle (on the right bank of the Raz el-Ain River). The Turkish Citadel, Santa Cruz. The early 19th century Cathedral of Saint-Louis. The fountain in the 18th century Place Emerat. The 18th century Porte de Canastel. The Great Mosque. The Sidi al-Hawwari Mosque. Nearby, the Kasbah. Chateau Neuf, once the residence of the rulers and later the headquarters of the French colonial army. The harem of the rulers. The 18th century Jewish cemetery. The Roman and Punic exhibits at the Municipal Museum. The collection of Islamic art in the Tlemcen Museum. The Aubert Library.

Dep. Oran	06:35 (2)	15:20 (1)	22:50 (5)
Arr. Algiers (Agha)	12:29	20:15	05:45

(1) Reservation required. Supplement charged. First-class coach is air-conditioned. Light refreshments.

Algiers - Oran - Fez - Meknes - Rabat - Casablanca - Marrakech

2542
Dep. Algiers	07:30 (1)		
Arr. Oran	12:30		

Change trains.
2540
Dep. Oran	13:10 (2)		
Arr. Oujda	17:55		

Change trains.
2510
Dep. Oujda	21:25 (3)		
Dep. Fez	03:15		
Dep. Meknes	04:09		
Dep. Rabat (Ville)	07:13		
Arr. Casablanca (Port)	08:18		

*Change trains **and stations** !*
2512
Dep. Casablanca (Voy.)	09:14 (4)	11:56 (4)	16:52 (4)
Arr. Marrakech	12:23	15:20	20:20

(1) Reservation required. Supplement charged. Has an air-conditioned coach. Buffet or light refreshments. (2) Reservation required. No supplement charged. (3)Reservation required. Supplement charged. Carries an air-conditioned sleeping car. Also has air-conditioned couchettes and air-conditioned coach cars. Buffet car. (4) Supplement charged. Air-conditioned train. Light refreshments or buffet.

NORTHERN ALGERIAN RAIL ROUTES

Here are the schedules for the 3 short spurs heading north from the transcontinental train route.

Constantine - Skikda   2547

All of these trains are second-class only.

Dep. Constantine	06:05	18:10	Dep. Skikda	05:50	17:20
Arr. Skikda	07:37	19:44	Arr. Constantine	07:29	19:03

Sights in **Skikda:** Ruins of the largest Roman theater in the Algeria. Roman antiquities in the City Museum.

Skikda - Annaba

All of these trains are second-class only.

2547

Dep. Skikda	05:30 (1)	05:50 (2)
Arr. Ramdane Djamal	-0- (1)	06:03
Change trains. 2545		
Dep. Ramdane Djamal	05:54 (1)	06:50
Arr. Annaba	07:34	08:42

• • •

Dep. Annaba	17:26 (1)	-0-
Arr. Ramdane Djamal	19:02 (1)	-0-
Change trains. 2547		
Dep. Ramdane Djamal	19:04 (1)	-0-
Arr. Skikda	19:27	-0-

(1) Second-class only. Direct train. No train change in Ramdane Djamal. (2) Second-class only.

Algiers - Bejaia   2545

Dep. Algiers	06:00 (1)	07:35 (2)	13:00 (4)	14:55 (1)
Arr. Beni Mansour	-0- (1)	10:12 (3)	15:36 (3)	-0- (1)
Change trains				
Dep. Beni Mansour	-0- (1)	10:22 (3)	15:46 (3)	-0- (1)
Arr. Bejaia	11:22	12:24	17:54	20:17

• • •

Dep. Bejaia	06:00 (1)	12:35	14:25 (1)	16:10
Arr. Beni Mansour	-0- (1)	15:09 (3)	-0- (1)	18:10 (3)
Change trains.				
Dep. Beni Mansour	-0- (1)	15:19 (4)	-0- (1)	18:20 (2)
Arr. Algiers	11:32	18:12	19:57	21:10

(1) Direct train. No train change in Beni Mansour. (2) Reservation required. Light refreshments. (3) Estimated. (4) Reservation required. Supplement charged. Restaurant car.

Sights in **Bejaia:** There are many Roman ruins in this area.

SOUTHERN ALGERIAN RAIL ROUTES

The following schedules are for the 2 Algerian train lines going south from the transcontinental route.

Annaba - Souk Ahras - Tebessa   2550

Both of these trains are second-class only.

Dep. Annaba	16:35	Dep. Tebessa	04:20
Arr. Tebessa	21:51	Arr. Annaba	09:17

Sights in **Tebessa:** Founded by Romans in AD 71. Some of the finest Roman remains in Africa are in this area, including the 2nd century Arch of Caracalla. Only one mile to the north are the Roman ruins of the Temple of Minerva, thermal baths, and an amphitheater at the same site as a beautiful Christian basilica.

See the 6th century walled Byzantine Citadel, with 4 gates and 12 towers.

Carpets made here are among the best manufactured in Algeria.

Constantine - Biskra - Touggourt   2551

All of these trains are second-class only.

Dep. Constantine	06:25	16:32	Dep. Touggourt	00:45 (1)	10:30 (2)
Arr. Biskra	10:13	20:25	Arr. Biskra	05:06	15:09
Change trains.			*Change trains.*		
Dep. Biskra	10:45 (1)	18:10 (2)	Dep. Biskra	05:20	15:50
Arr. Touggourt	15:10	22:39	Arr. Constantine	08:55	19:45

(1) Operates mid-October to mid-April. (2) Operates mid-April to mid-October.

Sights in **Biskra:** An ancient Roman outpost, now a popular Winter resort. Five miles to the west is the hot sulphur spring famous for medicinal value, Hamman Salahin ("Bath of the Saints"). Many oases here.

Sights in **Touggourt:** A typical Saharan town. There are many dried mud buildings here. See the tremendous fortress minaret. The clock tower in the Kasbah. The tombs of the kings. Many date palms in this oasis. Nearby, the tomb of Sidi el-Hadj Ali.

ANGOLA

Children under 3 travel free. Half-fare for children 3–11. Children 12 and over must pay full fare.

The 3 parallel west–east rail lines in Angola start at seaports on the South Atlantic coastline and run inland. Trains in Angola run "when circumstances permit." In the last year, four out of the five routes we suggested were discontinued.

Luanda - Malanje   3420

This line has 2 short spurs, one to Dondo and another to a hill station, Golungo Alta.

Both of these trains run Monday, Wednesday and Friday, are second and third-class, and have light refreshments.

Dep. Luanda   00:55
Arr. N'Dalatando   10:06
Arr. Malanje   16:03

Sights in **Luanda**: The capital of Angola. A major harbor. See the Angola Museum. The Bunda Museum. The old Sao Miguel Fort. The 17th century Chapel of Nazareth. The Zoological Museum.

Sights in **Malanje**: The 350-foot high Duque de Braganca Falls. The Pungo Andongo stones, enormous black monoliths that figure in tribal legends. To the south, the Game Reserve.

Dep. Malanje   19:10
Dep. N'Dalatando   01:11
Arr. Luanda   09:22

BENIN

Previously called Dahomey.

Children under 4 travel free. Half-fare for children 4–9. Children 10 and over must pay full fare.

Only first-class has fully upholstered seats.

Cotonou - Parakou   3020

All of these trains have light refreshments.

Dep. Cotonou	08:22 (1)	19:15 (2)
Arr. Parakou	16:22	06:34
	• • •	
Dep. Parakou	08:18 (1)	18:00
Arr Cotonou	16:19	06:30

(1) Runs daily. (2) Has couchettes.

Sights in **Cotonou**: Many interesting markets. The Supreme Court. The National Assembly. Nearby are Abomey and Ouidah (see notes above).

Cotonou - Pobe   3021

Both of these trains are second-class only.

Dep. Cotonou	17:02	Dep. Pobe	06:00
Arr. Pobe	20:55	Arr. Cotonou	09:54

BOTSWANA

Children under 7 travel free. Half-fare for children 7–11. Children 12 and over must pay full fare.

First-class coaches have very confortable airline-style reclining seats. Second-class has comfortable, *non*-reclining seats. Sleeper-class consists of 2 and 4-berth "cabins" with separate shower compartments.

The one rail trip in landlocked Botswana (operated by Rhodesian Railways) leads north from Ramatlhabama near South Africa's border to Plumtree and into Rhodesia.

The major tourist attraction here is wilderness preserves, comprising one-eighth of the country's area. They are: Chobe National Park, Moremi Game Reserve, Central Kalahari Game Reserve, Khutse Game Reserve, Gemsbok National Park and Makuasehube Game Reserve.

Gaborone - Plumtree - Harrare (Salisbury)

3475			
Dep. Gaborone	21:00 (1)	21:00 (3)	
Arr. Plumtree	08:30	08:30 (4)	
Arr. Bulawayo	14:05	14:05 (5)	
Change trains.			
3451			
Dep. Bulawayo	08:00 (2)	20:00 (6)	21:00 (8)
Arr. Harrare	16:00	05:55 (7)	06:40 (7)

(1) Runs Wednesday only (3) Runs daily. Has second and third-class seats. Buffet car. (4) Runs daily. Has air-conditioned sleeper-class and a second-class coach. Buffet car service until 06:45 on day 2. (5) Day 2 from Gaborone. (6) Time was not available in 1993. Estimated from 1992 travel time. (7) Runs Friday and Sunday. Second-Class only. (8) Day 2 from Bulawayo. (9) Runs daily. Has first-class seats except Friday and Saturday. Light refreshments every day.

BURKINA FASO (UPPER VOLTA)

Landlocked Burkina Faso has one train route, from Ouagadougou to Bobo Dioulasso, and on to Abidjan (Ivory Coast). For schedules, see "Treichville–Abidjan–Bouake–Bobo Dioulasso–Ouagadougou" under Ivory Coast.

CAMEROON

Children under 5 travel free. Half-fare for children 5–9. Children 10 and over must pay full fare.

Only first-class has upholstered seats.

Douala - Nkongsamba   3131

Both of these trains are second-class only.

Dep. Douala	06:00		Dep. Nkongsamba	13:05
Arr. Nkongsamba	12:20		Arr. Douala	19:20

Sights in **Douala**: The 13,000-foot high Mount Cameroun, tallest mountain in West Africa. The beautiful view of the enormous bridge over the Wouri River.

Sights in **Nkongsamba**: Pleasant climate. A popular tourist resort. Many banana, coffee and palm-oil plantations.

Douala - Yaounde   3131

All of these trains require a reservation, have air-conditioning in first-class and a restaurant car, unless designated otherwise.

Dep. Douala	07:15	13:00 (1)	19:00
Arr. Yaounde	10:31	16:45	22:22

Sights in **Yaounde**: Capital of Cameroun. Many streams and shaded avenues. Nearby: The cocoa plantations in a very large forest. The Ekom Waterfalls and the Dschang health resort at the 4,000-foot high Bamileke Plateau. Nachtigal Falls. The Grottos of the Pygmies.

Dep. Yaounde	07:15	07:30 (2)	12:50 (1)	19:00
Arr. Douala	10:37	16:05	16:43	22:31

(1) Does *not* have air-conditioning or restaurant car. (2) Reservation *not* required. *No* air-conditioning *or* restaurant car. Second-class only.

Yaounde - N'gaoundere   3130

Both of these trains require reservation and have second-class couch seats and first-class couchettes.

Dep. Yaounde	19:35
Arr. N'gaoundere	07:24

* * *

Dep. N'gaoundere	19:00
Arr. Yaounde	05:55

Sights in **N'gaoundere**: Big-game hunting and photography are the attractions here. There are large game reserves nearby.

CONGO

Children under 5 travel free. Half-fare for children 5–9. Children 10 and over must pay full fare.

The rail system in Congo starts at the South Atlantic seaport of Pointe Noire and runs inland to Loubomo, where it forms the two top arms of a "Y," one fork heading north to M'Binda, the other going east to **Brazzaville**, the nation's capital. Kinshasa, across the border in Zaire, has a rail line running to Matadi.

Pointe Noire

The country's main seaport is located on the coast of the Atlantic Ocean, at the end of the Congo–Ocean Railway. The railway was completed in 1934. The city grew rapidly after the port was opened five years later. This city of 200,000 has an international airport.

Brazzaville

This is the capital of the Congo. It is a major port, located in a luxuriant tropical forest on a broad section of the **Zaire River**. This city of 500,000, has an international airport. Visit the nearby scenic rapids.

Pointe Noire - Brazzaville   3170

This is the principal Congo–Ocean Railway.

Dep. Pointe Noire	06:15	10:30 (1)	18:20 (2)
Arr. Brazzaville	19:36	20:34	06:08 (3)

• • •

Dep. Brazzaville	06:15	10:30 (1)	18:15 (2)
Arr. Pointe Noire	19:47	20:48	05:34 (3)

(1) Reservation required. Supplement charged. Buffet car. (2) Has first-class couchettes. Buffet car. (3) Day 2.

Pointe Noire - M'Binda   3170

Dep. Pointe Noire	06:15	Dep. M'Binda	04:45
Arr. Loubomo	10:50	Arr. Loubomo	12:23
Change trains.		*Change trains.*	
Dep. Loubomo	14:15	Dep. Loubomo	15:01
Arr. M'Binda	21:45	Arr. Pointe Noire	19:43

DJIBOUTI

This was formerly the northwestern corner of Somalia. Its only passenger rail service is the 63-mile portion of the line running from its Gulf of Aden seaport, Djibouti, to Ethiopia's Addis Abeba.

Djibouti - Dire Daoua - Addis Abeba 3251

Information about this journey will be found in the Ethopia train schedules.

Sights in **Djibouti City:** A major seaport on the Gulf of Aden. See the Palace, on Menelik Square. The Great Mosque, on Place Rimbaud, where a large camel market is conducted.

EGYPT

Children under 4 travel free. Half-fare for children 4–9. Children 10 and over must pay full fare.

Most Westerners prefer to visit Egypt November-March. Summer months are extremely hot.

First-class sleeping cars have single or double berths in modern cars. Second-class sleeping cars are older and only have compartments with double berths. First-class coaches are luxurious, while second-class coaches are comfortable. There are only wood seats in third-class.

From Cairo, there is one rail line south, to Sadd-el-Ali, where a connection can be made for train travel across the desert in Sudan. This is the only international rail route between Egypt and countries adjacent to it.

The 3 other Egyptian rail routes from Cairo are northwest to Alexandria, northeast to Ismailia (and on to Port Said), and east to Suez.

There is also train service along the Suez Canal, from the city of Suez to Ismailia. Egypt's Mediterranean coastal train trip is between Alexandria and Mersa Matruh.

EGYPTIAN HOLIDAYS

mid-April	Shams en-Nassim	July 23	Revolution Day
June 18	Evacuation Day	September 1	Arab Republic Day
mid-July	Feast of the Nile	December 23	Victory Day

Cairo

See the world's greatest collection of pharaonic treasures, covering the 30 dynasties of ancient Egypt from the dawn of civilization to the coming of the Romans, in the Egyptian Antiquities Museum at Tahrir Square, near the Nile Hilton Hotel. It is open daily 09:00–16:00 (closed Friday 11:15–13:30). The more than 3,000 world-famous treasures of Tutankhamun are on the second floor.

Egyptian life, as it was in the days of the pharaos, can be seen at The Pharaonic Village, on a 33-acre island in the Nile River, open daily 09:00–17:00.

This 2-hour excursion on a barge moves through canals showing activities of ancient daily life: sowing of seed, plowing, papyrus boats, brick-making, carpentry, home building and the making of linen, perfume, pottery, statues and papyrus. There is also a tour of a temple and the house of a nobleman.

There are marvelous views of the city from the top of the 12th century Citadel. Located inside the Citadel are both the Military Museum and the Jewel Palace (open 09:00–17:00), in which 19th century items are exhibited, including King Farouk's wedding throne.

Near the Citadel is the 14th century Mosque of Sultan Hussein, which has the tallest minarets in Cairo and is a veritable fortress. Adjacent is Rifai Mosque, worth seeing for its ornate, marble-inlaid floors. It contains the tomb of the last Shah of Iran. See the silver domes and ornate ceilings of the 19th century Mohammed Ali Mosque (also called the Alabaster Mosque for its marble interior).

The 600 stucco filigree windows (each with a different design) at the 9th century Mosque of Ibn Tulun, oldest in Cairo and noted as the world's finest example of pure Islamic architecture. It is near Anderson House, a museum on how a prosperous Cairo family would have lived in the 17th century (open daily except Friday 11:00–13:00).

In Old Cairo, visit the Coptic Museum that is open daily 09:00–6:00 (closed Friday 11:15–13:30), to see its ancient textiles, manuscripts, wood carvings and ivories.

Nearby, the 4th century Church of Abu Sarga (St. Sergius) where, according to legend, the Holy Family stayed when fleeing from Herod. The ancient El Muallaga Church. The 10th century gate, Bab Zuweilla.

The Papyrus Museum, in houseboats near the Sheraton Hotel, has an exhibit on making the early writing material. Nearby, the work of one of Egypt's best sculptors, in the Mukhtar Museum.

The ornate 10th century Al-Azhar Mosque is the oldest university in the Moslem world. Nearby is Wekalet el Ghouri, where local craft from different parts of Egypt are exhibited.

Cairo has several hundred mosques that are open to visitors except during Friday prayers. Women are not allowed to enter mosques after sunset.

See King Farouk's tomb, at El Rifai Mosque. The view of the city and the Nile from the revolving restaurant on the top of Cairo Tower. The Khan al-Khalili Market's tinsmiths, tentmakers, hand-hammered copper and brass trays, cotton caftans, and local inexpensive perfumes. The Ben Ezra Synagogue.

There are exceptional carved wood panels, hand-painted glass, carpets, coins, mosaics, weapons, pottery, copper and silver inlay, jewelry, manuscripts, calligraphy and Persian daggers at the Islamic Museum on Ahmed Maher Square (open same hours as the Egyptian Antiquities Museum). Thousands of bazaars in Cairo.

Cheops (the largest pyramid) and the Sphinx are in Giza, a 25-minute taxi ride from the center of Cairo. A visit to the pyramids at sunset is recommended and also the Sound and Light Pageant in an outdoor theater at the Sphinx. October-March, the first show is 18:30 and the second show is 19:30. April-September, the shows are presented at 20:30 and 21:30. An English language commentary on the history of the pharaohs is performed on Monday, Wednesday, Friday and Saturday at the early show and on Thursday at the late show.

The state-owned MISR Travel has a full-day tour to the pyramids that cost $19 (U.S.) in 1993. MISR's U.S.A. office is 630 Fifth Ave., New York, NY 10111.

A one-hour sailboat ride in the evening on the Nile costs about $10. The boats leave from docks near the Shepheards and Meridien hotels.

Alexandria

Egypt's most important port and second-largest city. A very popular beach resort.

Cairo - Alexandria - Cairo 2651

These trains require reservation and have air-conditioned first and second-class coaches. Most of these trains have a restaurant car.

Dep. Cairo (Main)	Frequent times from 06:20 to 21:35
Arr. Alexandria	2½–3½ hours later

•   •   •

Dep. Alexandria	Frequent times from 06:10 to 21:35
Arr. Cairo	2½–3½ hours later

Alexandria - El Alamein 2656

These trains have only second-class and third-class space.

Dep. Alexandria	06:30	10:00
Arr. El Alamein	09:43	13:15

•   •   •

Dep. El Alamein	10:46	14:18
Arr. Alexandria	14:20	17:10

Sights in **El Alamein:** There is a small museum commemorating General Montgomery's defeat of Field Marshal Rommel in one of the most famous battles of World War II. More than 8,000 soldiers are buried in large cemeteries in this area.

Cairo - Ismailia - Bur Said   2652

These trains have only 2nd and 3rd-class space, unless designated otherwise.

Dep. Cairo (Main)	06:20 (1)	08:20 (2)	14:35 (1)	15:20 (1+3)
Dep. Ismailia	09:09	10:52	17:41	18:14
Arr. Bur Said	10:30	12:10	19:00	19:35

• • •

Dep. Bur Said	05:30 (1)	10:35 (2)	19:15 (1)	18:25 (2+4)
Dep. Ismailia	06:58	12:05	19:50	19:48
Arr. Cairo (Main)	09:45	14:35	22:30	-0-

(1) Air-conditioned in second-class. (2) Reservation required. Air-conditioned in first and second-class. Light refreshments. (3) Plus another departure from Cairo at 18:45 (1), arriving Ismailia 21:35...Bur Said 23:00. (4) Plus another departure from Bur Said at 19:40 (1), arriving Ismailia 21:05, arriving Cairo 23:45.

Sights in **Ismailia:** Many parks and gardens. The Suez Canal. The Sweet Water Canal, built in 1863 to provide thousands of canal workers with drinking water. There are several ancient ruins 10 miles west of here.

Sights in **Port Said:** This is Egypt's second most important seaport.

Cairo - El Suweis (Suez)   2654

Dep. Cairo (Ain Shams)	06:10 (1)	16:05 (1)	18:45 (2)
Arr. El Suweis	08:10	18:00	20:35

• • •

Dep. El Suweis	05:55 (1)	10:00 (1)	19:00 (1)
Arr. Cairo (Ain Shams)	07:55	12:05	21:05

(1) Second and third-class only. (2) Reservation required. Air-conditioned train. Has first and second-class coaches. Restaurant car.

Sights in **Suez:** The Canal and this city's 2 harbors. This is a departure point for pilgrimages to Mecca.

Cairo - Luxor - Aswan - El Sadd el Ali (the High Dam)   2655

Pyramids, ancient temples and camel trains can be seen on this route.

In 1995, the price for a reserved seat in an air-conditioned coach was only $21.90 for the 558-mile trip from Cairo to El Sadd el Ali. A sleeping compartment for one person

Cairo–Luxor or Cairo–Aswan roundtrip was $194 and $252 for 2 persons. This included the ticket, compartment, dinner and breakfast.

The train's $15 lunch was not appetizing. Better to bring food from one's hotel.

Dep. Cairo (Main)	07:30 (1)	12:00 (1)	14:00 (2)	21:35 (2)
Arr. Luxor	18:20	22:50	23:00	09:00
Arr. Aswan	23:00	-0-	-0-	14:40
Arr. El Sadd el Ali	-0-	-0-	-0-	15:50
Dep. El Sadd el Ali	-0-	-0-	-0-	-0-
Dep. Aswan	-0-	-0-	06:10 (1)	-0-
Dep. Luxor	04:10 (2)	05:15 (1)	11:45	15:25 (2)
Arr. Cairo (Main)	16:25	17:10	21:45	04:55

(1) Reservation required. Air-conditioned train. Restaurant car. (2) Reservation required. Air-conditioned train.

Sights in **Luxor:** In 2133 B.C. this was Thebes, capital of the Egyptian empire, and on the opposite side of the Nile it was Karnak, the "city of the dead," with the kings' mortuary temples. The obelisk now standing in Paris' Place de la Concorde was brought there by Napoleon from the Temple of Luxor. The ruins of the great temples of Karnak, Amon, Mont, Mut and Khons, and the complex of temples called Amon-Re are the interesting places to see here today. Also, the Colossi of Memnon, more than 60 tombs in the Valley of the Kings, burial grounds of the great pharaohs and their queens.

Sights in **Aswan**: A Winter resort. You can see the ancient quarries from which granite was taken for building the pharaohs' monuments. Four miles north is the Aswan High Dam, completed in 1970, one of the greatest engineering accomplishments in the world. It is 1½ miles long and has 180 sluices.

THE RAIL ROUTE TO SUDAN

Egypt's train connection with Sudan starts with a Nile boat trip from El Sadd el Ali to Wadi Halfa. These schedules are subject to serious delays.

El Sadd el Ali - Wadi Halfa   2680

Dep. El Sadd el Ali	09:00 (1)	Dep. Wadi Halfa	16:00 (3)
Arr. Wadi Halfa	08:00 (2)	Arr. El Sadd el Ali	08:00 (2)

(1) Runs Monday and Saturday only. (2) Day 3. (3) Days of operation were not available when this edition was printed.

Wadi Halfa - Khartoum   2700

This trip crosses the Nubian Desert.

The train runs Tuesday and Sunday. It carries a sleeping car and a restaurant car.

Dep. Wadi Halfa	16:40
Arr. Khartoum	16:45 Day 2

ETHIOPIA

Children under 4 travel free. Half-fare for children 4–9. Children 10 and over must pay full fare.

Addis Abeba - Dire Daoua - Djibouti   3251

This ride descending from 8,000-foot high Addis Abeba to Dire Daoua is very scenic, similar to Colorado mountain scenery in the United States.

All of these trains are subject to confirmation

Dep. Addis Abeba	06:00	07:30	19:30 (1)
Arr. Dire Daoua	20:50	17:24	08:45 (2)
Change trains.			
Dep. Dire Daoua		19:30	
Arr. Djibouti		07:40 (2)	

• • •

Dep. Djibouti		20:00	
Arr. Dire Daoua		06:55 (2)	
Change trains.			
Dep. Dire Daoua	06:00	07:30	19:30 (1)
Arr. Addis Abeba	16:27	17:27	08:50 (2)

(1) Carries a sleeping car. (2) Day 2.

Sights in **Addis Abeba**: The depiction of Africa's past struggles, present problems and future progress in the magnificent stained-glass window at All Africa Hall. The lavishly decorated National Palace. The mosaics, ceiling carvings and stained-glass at Holy Trinity Cathedral. The obelisk on Miazia 27 Square.

The Natural History Museum. The Imperial Lion House. The handicrafts for sale in the Empress Menen Handicraft School. The view of the city from Mount Entoto. Haile Selassie I Square. The National Museum's archaeology exhibits. The paintings in the Institute of Ethiopian Studies. The activities every Saturday at Mercato, the city's large marketplace. The heavy traffic of domestic animals on some of the downtown streets. The imperial lions in the small zoo at Jubilee Palace. Several other palaces. St. George's Cathedral.

Sights in **Dire Daoua**: The Mosque. The Muslim cemeteries. Prehistoric paintings in the nearby caves. The Palace.

GABON

Children under 4 travel free. Half-fare for children 4–11. Children 12 and over must pay full fare.

Under construction since 1980, the 293-mile track Ndjole–Franceville went into service at the end of 1986. Cost of the complete 403-mile Trans-Gabon route (Owendo-Ndjole–Franceville) was $3 billion.

Scenery on this trip includes grasslands, the rushing rapids of the **Ogooue River**, and dense rain forests.

All of the locomotives and passenger cars were new in 1987.

Owendo

A seaport and suburb of **Libreville**, the capital.

Owendo (Libreville) - Franceville   3160

All of these trains have air-conditioned first-class and buffet service.

Dep. Owendo	08:30 (1)	21:00 (2)	
Dep. Ndjole	11:25	23:50	
Arr. Franceville	18:00	06:30	

• • •

Dep. Franceville	09:30 (3)	20:10 (5)	21:10 (6)
Dep. Ndjole	16:15	03:20	04:00
Arr. Owendo	19:30	06:35	07:05

(1) Runs Tuesday and Saturday. (2) Runs Wednesday, Friday, Sunday and holidays. Has couchettes. (3) Runs Thursday only. (4) Runs Saturday. (5) Runs Friday only. Has couchettes. (6) Runs Sunday only. Has couchettes.

GHANA

Children under 3 travel free. Half-fare for children 3–11. Children 12 and over must pay full fare.

This country's rail system forms the letter "A," with the western arm running from the Atlantic seaport of Takoradi north to inland Kumasi, the eastern segment going from the port of Accra north to Kumasi, and the cross-arm extending from Tarkwa (on the western route) to the eastern route. The cross-arm is the Takoradi–Accra route.

First-class sleeping car compartments have one berth. Second-class has 4 berths per compartment.

Ghana's rail authorities advised travelers in 1985 that its engines "are old and not wholly reliable" and therefore "breakdowns may occur during the course of travel." They also stated: "The situation is being ameliorated but will definitely take some time."

Accra

See the port longshoremen carrying crates and bundles on their heads. The spirited nightlife here. The Arts Council of Ghana. The Ethnological Museum. The Science Museum. Nearby: The enormous Volta Dam and, behind it, the largest manmade lake in the world, **Lake Volta**.

Accra-Tarkwa-Takoradi   3060

Both of these trains carry a second-class coach and a second class-sleeping car. They have light refreshments.

Dep. Accra	19:25	Dep. Takoradi	19:15
Dep. Tarkwa	N/A (1)	Dep. Tarkwa	N/A (1)
Arr. Takoradi	07:15	Arr. Accra	07:10

(1) Time has not been available since 1990.

Takoradi - Tarkwa - Kumasi   3062

Dep. Takoradi	06:00 (1)	12:00 (1)	14:30 (3)	20:00 (4)
Dep. Tarkwa	N/A (2)	N/A (2)	N/A (2)	N/A (2)
Arr. Kumasi	13:45	20:15	21:57	05:15

Sights in **Tarkwa:** There is much mining here for gold, diamonds, manganese and bauxite. Because of the sand that is found in this area, there is a substantial glass industry here.

Sights in **Kumasi:** The "Garden City of West Africa." The Ashanti kings rule from here. The area is dense forest. See: The Ghana Regiment Museum in the old British fort. The museum, zoo and library at the Ashanti Cultural Center. Good textiles are available here.

Dep. Kumasi	06:00 (1)	11:40 (5)	14:30 (3)	20:00 (4)
Dep. Tarkwa	N/A (2)	N/A (2)	N/A (2)	N/A (2)
Arr. Takoradi	13:40	20:30	21:40	05:15

(1) Runs daily, except Sunday. (2) Times have not been available since 1984. (3) Runs Sunday only. (4) Reservation required. Runs daily. Carries first and second-class sleeping cars. Light refreshments. (5) Runs daily.

Accra - Kumasi   3061

Dep. Accra	20:30	Dep. Kumasi	20:30
Arr. Kumasi	06:38	Arr. Accra	06:21

GUINEA

No discounts are allowed for children.

Guinea's 2 rail lines are from Conakry and Kamsar on the Atlantic seacoast to inland **Kankan** and **Sangaredi**.

Conakry - Kankan

Rail service for this route is no longer offered. Bus service on Fridays is available from 13:50 on.

Sights in **Conakry:** Good beaches. The Corniche, a lovely promenade along the seashore. The African exhibits at the Museum. The Mosque. The monument to anti-colonial martyrs. The picturesque Boulbinet fishing harbor. Nearby, the Botanical Garden in Camayenne.

Sights in **Kankan:** This was an 18th century caravan center. The ambience is very Moslem. Many mosques. Much wood, gold and ivory craftsmanship here. A center for trading in reptile skins, sesame, cattle, rice.

Kamsar - Sangaredi   2851

Both of these trains are second-class only.

Dep. Kamsar	09:55(1)	Dep. Sangaredi	13:45(1)
Arr. Sangaredi	13:15	Arr. Kamsar	16:35

(1) Except Tuesday and Wednesday.

IVORY COAST

Children under 4 travel free. Half-fare for children 4–9. Children 10 and over must pay full fare.

This country's single passenger rail route is the 725-mile narrow-gauge Abidjan–Niger Line (constructed by France), running from Abidjan on the shore of the Gulf of Guinea to Bouake, Bobo Dioulasso and then on to Ouagadougou in the grasslands of landlocked Burkina Faso (Upper Volta).

Treichville - Abidjan - Bouake - Bobo Dioulasso - Ouagadougou

This is the route from the Republic of Ivory Coast to Burkina Faso. People from several different tribes make this trip. Many of the women passengers wear very high-heeled shoes, colorful long dresses, turban-style hats.

The ride was said in 1981 to be quite smooth due to the modern rails and good roadbed. En route to Ougadougou, the train goes through a heavily-foliaged rain forest before arriving at **Dimbokro**. After leaving Dimbokro, the train travels alongside a village of dirt streets and many thatched-roof huts. Women can be seen in that village walking with lumber, large packages and trays balanced on their heads.

Next seen on the route are large banana plantations and a jungle with bright flowers. Adjacent to the Bouake railstation is a 66-room hotel built in 1975, with swimming pool and a restaurant that at least once featured French cuisine in a pleasant dining-room.

3100

Dep. Treichville	06:00 (1)	N/A (2)	15:00 (1)
Dep. Abidjan	06:07	09:45 (3)	N/A (5)
Dep. Dimbokro	09:20	N/A (2)	19:08
Arr. Bouake	11:25	N/A (2)	21:40
Dep. Bouake	-0-	N/A (2)	-0-
Arr. Bobo Dioulasso	-0-	13:10 (3+4)	-0-

2740

Dep. Bobo Dioulasso	06:00 (6)	12:30 (6)	19:00 (6)
Arr. Ouagadougou	11:00	17:30	24:00

(1) Air-conditioned train. Light refreshments. (2) Time was not available in 1993. (3) Direct train Treichville–Ouagadougou. Has first-class coaches and couchettes. Carries a restaurant car and also has light refreshments. (4) Day 2. (5) Time has not been available since 1991. (6) Has air-conditioned first and second-class coaches. Buffet.

Sights in **Treichville:** This section of Abidjan is best known for one of the city's main shopping streets (Boulevard du 6 Fevrier) and for its many nightclubs.

Sights in **Abidjan**: Chief port and largest city in the Republic of Ivory Coast. See the exhibits of traditional Ivorian art in the National Museum. The handicrafts at Plateau Market in the enormous Square Bressoles. The 2-story bazaar in Treichville, a suburb. The Adme market. The extravagant President's Palace. The wonderful tropical rain forest, Parc National du Banco, north of the city.

Sights in **Bouake**: Many mosques here. Good textile products for sale. You cannot miss seeing the brilliant-colored clothing worn by the crowds at the open-air market.

Sights in **Bobo Dioulasso**: This is an Islamic center, with many clay mosques. There are good buys here in ivory and bronze products, also traditional jewelry.

Sights in **Ouagadougou**: This is the capital of Burkina Faso. The large street market is very interesting.

KENYA

Children under 3 travel free. Half-fare for children 3–15. Children 16 and over must pay full fare.

First-class compartments convert to 4 berths at night, second-class to 6 berths.

Kenya's one train line is from Mombasa on the Indian Ocean, inland to Nairobi. From there, the rail route forks, one tine running to Kisumu at Lake Victoria and a second tine going to Tororo on the Kenya–Uganda border, and to Kampala, in landlocked Uganda.

Passengers have a view of Tsavo National Park, teeming with African game. West of Nairobi, there are extraordinary views of flamingos and of tea and coffee plantations.

Mombasa - Nairobi - Kisumu   3270

Dep. Mombasa	19:00 (4)		Dep. Kisumu	18:00 (1)
Arr. Nairobi	08:30 (2)		Arr. Nairobi	06:20 (2)
Change trains.			*Change trains.*	
Dep. Nairobi	18:00 (1)		Dep. Nairobi	19:00 (4)
Arr. Kisumu	07:10 (3)		Arr. Mombasa	08:06 (5)

(1) Reservations required. Light refreshments. Except Wednesday. (2) Day 2. (3) Day 3 after departing Mombasa. (4) Reservations required. Restaurant car. (5) Day 3 after departing Kisumu.

Sights in **Mombasa:** More than 2,000 years old, Kenya's second-largest city (after Nairobi) sits on an offshore island, linked to the mainland by causeway, bridge and ferry. It has been an important seaport since Arab traders developed it in the 11th century.

See the Persian, Portuguese and medieval Chinese porcelain and other artifacts in the museum at the 2-acre, 16th century Fort Jesus, open daily. Behind the fort, on Treasury Street, there is an exhibit of elephant tusks, hippopotamus teeth and rhinocerous horns in the Game

Department Ivory Room, where those items (confiscated from poachers or taken from dead animals on the game reserves) can be purchased legally at semi-annual auctions. The silver door at Lord Shiva Temple. The Moorish-style Anglican Memorial Cathedral, with its silver roof.

The stalls of ivory carvers, perfume makers, goldsmiths, spice merchants, tailors, tinsmiths, moneylenders and silk dealers in the winding, narrow streets of Old Town. Colorful articles from the Middle East, Persia, Pakistan and India are sold there. Vendors in the middle of Salim Road offer a large variety of African carvings and other goods. See the National Museum in the 16th century Fort Jesus, built by Portuguese to fend off Turks. In the modern part of the city, visit the African market in Mwembe Tayari to buy Swahili costumes. See the 16th century Manadhara/Mandhry Mosque. Sheikh Jundani Mosque. Kilindini Mosque. The 4 enormous sheet-metal elephant tusks forming an arch over Kilindini Road, the main street. Take a cruise of Kilindini Harbor.

Board a dhow at the quayside of the old port to bargain for brass chests, Arab silverware, Persian carpets, furniture, spices and dates. Take a short ferry-boat ride to the white-sand beaches south of Mombasa. North of the city, see the 20 acres of flowers and lawns in landscaped coral gardens at Nyali Beach. Go on a glass-bottomed boat to look at the colorful sea life.

Try the excellent world-record deep-sea fishing (marlin, sailfish, baracuda) and scuba diving. There are several special marine parks.

A few miles to the north are the 15th century Arab ruins at **Jumba La Mtwana**. Other Arab ruins are 10 miles south of **Malindi**, a colorful resort area where the largest (220 species) aviary in East Africa is located. In Malindi, see the Cross of Vasco da Gama, erected by the Portuguese explorer in 1499. It is a short airplane ride and ferry trip to **Lamu Island**, where there are no automobiles and the scene is the same as it was 200 years ago: robed peddlers riding donkeys on the dusty streets, prayers chanted from the mosques, dhows anchored along the ancient harbor, wood-carvers working on the street corners.

Sights in **Nairobi:** The capital of Kenya, Nairobi is the largest (800,000 population) city in East Africa. It is almost on the equator. However, it is one mile high, making for temperate climate.

See the treasures of Kenya's past and the exhibits of a vast number of birds, insects, mammals, fish, musical instruments, ornaments and tribal weapons in the National Museum of Kenya, a 15-minute walk from the center of Nairobi, open daily 09:30–18:00. Its exhibits include world-famous fossils from the Olduvai Gorge in Tanzania, remnants of earliest toolmaking man, and remains of such remarkable prehistoric animals as a giant ostrich, an enormous rhinoceros, and a 2-million-year-old elephant which was brought into the museum by knocking down one of the walls.

Across the street from the museum is Snake Park. Its collection of 200 varieties of snakes, crocodiles and alligators is open daily 09:30–18:00. Visit the Sorsbie Art Gallery. Jeevanjee Gardens on Muindi Mbingu Street. The City Market is farther up that street.

See the trees and flowering plants in the 100-acre Arboretum. Tribal dances performed 14:30–16:00 Monday–Friday and 15:00–17:00 on Saturday and Sunday, as well as tribal jewelry, baskets and 16 replicas of tribal villages at the Bomas of Kenya cultural center. Near it, the lions, wildebeeste, ostriches, hartebeest, cheetahs, rhinos, buffalos, zebras and deer in the

44-square-mile Nairobi Game Park. Hunting in the area has been prohibited since 1977.

A fantastic collection of African railway relics at the Railway Museum, a 5-minute walk from the railstation. African and Western contemporary art at Paa-ya-Paa Gallery. The curios and exotic fruits, vegetables and fowers sold in Municipal Market. Jamia Mosque. The African exhibits at McMillan Memorial Library. The fascinating rust-red and white International House. At the Aquarium, a fine collection of marine life from the offshore coral reefs.

The tapestries, murals, tribal shields and the conference table made from 33 kinds of Kenya wood, in the National Assembly. The Tuesday morning coffee auction at Kahawa ("coffee") House. City Nurseries, with its enormous number of different species of bougainvillaea.

The old books and newspapers in the McMillan Memorial Library, open Monday–Friday 09:00–17:00; Saturday 09:00–13:00.

Sights in **Kisumu:** Kenya's third largest (300,000) city. There are many small fisheries here, on Lake Victoria.

Mombasa - Nairobi - Nakuru - Eldoret - Tororo - Kampala

3270

Dep. Mombasa	19:00 (6)	
Arr. Nairobi	08:40 (2)	
Change trains.		
Dep. Nairobi	15:00 (3)	18:00 (1)
Arr. Nakuru	20:35 (3)	23:35 (7)
Dep. Eldoret	03:40 (3)	-0-
Arr. Malaba	07:45 (5)	-0-
3285		
Change trains. (6)		
Dep. Tororo	03:05 (8)	
Arr. Kampala	08:55	

• • •

Dep. Kampala	16:00 (8)	
Arr. Tororo	21:45 (5)	
Change trains. (6)		
3270		
Dep. Malaba	17:00 (4)	-0-
Dep. Eldoret	21:35 (4)	-0-
Dep. Nakuru	03:30 (10)	01:30 (1)
Arr. Nairobi	08:25	06:20
Change trains.		
Dep. Nairobi	19:00 (6)	
Arr. Mombasa	08:05 (12)	

(1) Runs daily. Light refreshments. Reservation required. (2) Day 2. (3) Runs Tuesday, Friday and Saturday. Restaurant car. Reservation required. (4) Day 3. Runs Wednesday, Saturday and Sunday. Restaurant car. Reservation required. (5) There is frequent service by jitney-van Malaba–Tororo and v.v. (6) Runs daily. Restaurant car. Reservation required (7) Day 2 from Nairobi. (8) Runs Wednesday only. Restaurant car. (9) Runs Tuesday, Thursday and Sunday. (10) Day 2. Runs Thursday, Sunday and Monday. Restaurant car. (11) Day 3 from Malaba. (12) Day 2 from Nakuru.

Sights in **Nakuru:** The pelicans on the inland saline **Lake Nakuru**. Lake Nakuru National Park.

Sights in **Eldoret:** The temperate climate here is due to the 6,800-foot altitude, which attracted many European settlers in the period when this was an English colony.

Sights in **Kampala:** See notes about Kampala under "Tororo–Jinja–Kampala–Kasese."

MADAGASCAR (MALAGSAY REPUBLIC)

Children under 4 travel free. Half-fare for children 4–6. Children 7 and over must pay full fare.

Maximum health precautions are advisable, particularly against malaria. Tourists (mostly young Europeans) swarm to Madagascar at Christmas, Easter and in August. The most preferable tour season is September and October, when there is the least rain and while the lemurs are having babies.

Twenty nine species of lemurs thrive here (and only here) where there are no monkeys, the most virulent predator of lemurs wherever they are found in the rest of the world. The largest member of the lemur family, the Indri, can propel itself 30 feet backwards, turn in mid-air, and land facing the opposite direction it was facing before it leapt.

There are 3 short rail lines in north Madagascar: Antananarivo–Moramanga–Tamatave, Moramanga to Ambatosoratra, and Antananarivo to Antsirabe. (Antananarivo is also called Tananarive.)

The southern train route is Finanarantsoa to Manakara.

Antananarivo (Tana) - Moramanga - Toamasina (Tamatave) 3330

This is called "one of the world's great rail trips" by British travel writer Mark Ottaway, who also recommends Hilary Bradt's book "Guide to Madagascar."

In 1989, the train carried only one 54-seat first-class coach. Reservations are essential because the second-class cars are very crowded and require standing for tickets in a line at the railstation as early as 2 hours before departure. The 1988 first-class price for this 13-hour ride was $8.00.

Of the thousands of Chinese coolies who worked on constructing this line 1910–1913, hundreds of them lost their lives. The train goes along the edge of cliffs overlooking raging rivers. From Antananarivo (also called "Tana"), the scenery on the ascent to **Anjiro** (not shown in Cook) includes patty fields and a forest.

Just before Anjiro, the track makes a very large hairpin bend and then descends through a green, bamboo rainforest and goes along the **Mangoro River**. The train's lunch stop at **Perinet** (also called **Andasibe**) allows passengers to dine in the Hotel de Gare there. Staying over in Perinet is recommended for viewing 9 species of lemurs and many reptiles and insects, including leeches. Perinet is *not* shown in Cook.

Shortly before nightfall, the train goes through palm tree groves and along the seacoast (too late to be able to see the view!).

Antananarivo

Capital of Madagascar. Also called "Tana." At 4,000 feet, the air here is fresh and clear. See the 19th century towered palaces of the Imerina kings on the royal estate, above the city. The exhibits of Malagsay culture and archaeology in the Organisation pour la Recherche Scientifique et Technique. The collection of lemurs and other Malagsay animals in the Zoo.

The Queen's Palace, called "Rova," open Tuesday-Saturday 14:00–17:00, Sunday 09:00–12:00 and 14:00–17:00. The Art and Archaeology Museum (17 Rue Docteur Villette)

The stupendous Friday outdoor market (called Zoma), on Independence Avenue. Thousands of booths and "blanket shops" offering leather goods, semiprecious stones, woven baskets, etc. This is the place to flex your bargaining muscles. Most items in this market are intended to sell for half the asking price, and buyers are expected to start bidding below that figure.

Take a taxi or bus 2½ miles from the center of town to the Natural History and Ethnology Museum, garden and zoo complex, called Tsimbazaza. A prize exhibit at the Museum is the skeleton of the "elephant bird," considerably larger than an ostrich and extinct for 800 years.

Sights in **Toamasina:** (Also called Tamatave.) This is the country's chief seaport, on the Indian Ocean. Stroll down tree-lined Avenue Poincare.

There is a wonderful beach and good snorkeling at **Nosy Tanikely.** Drive or fly to **Fort Dauphin** to visit the Berenty Lemur Reserve.

Dep. Antananarivo	06:45
Dep. Moramanga	10:45
Arr. Toamasina	18:40

• • •

Dep. Toamasina	06:00
Dep. Moramanga	09:50
Arr. Antananarivo	13:10

Moramanga - Ambatosoratra   3330

Dep. Moramanga	10:45	Dep. Ambatosoratra	06:00
Arr. Ambatosoratra	14:10	Arr. Moramanga	09:40

Sights in **Ambatosorata:** Lake Alaotra.

Antananarivo - Antsirabe   3330

This is a very scenic 92-mile ride to 4,000-foot high Antsirabe.

Dep. Antananarivo	06:30	Dep. Antsirabe	06:30
Arr. Antsirabe	13:00	Arr. Antananarivo	11:50

Sights in **Antsirabe:** This is a thermal springs resort, situated under 8,674-foot high **Mt. Tsiafajavona**, the top of the Ankaratra volcanic mass. Attracted by the cool climate here, Norwegian missionaries founded this elegant city in 1872. It is actually cold here May-September. The former European area is to the right of the railstation. The Malagsay section with the town's market (Asabotsy) is to the left of the station.

Go a half-mile from the railstation, down the imposing grand avenue, to see the colonial-style (British) Hotel des Thermes.

Among the many short excursions from Antsirabe is the 3-mile one to the volcanic **Lake Andraikiba**. Another is 7 miles to **Lake Tritriva**, particularly interesting for ornithologists and botanists. Also, the 12-mile trip to **Betafo** to see **Lake Tatamarina** and the **Antafofo Waterfalls**.

Fianarantsoa (Fianar) - Manakara   3331

Even more scenic than the Antananarivo–Toamasina route.

Dep. Fianarantsoa	07:00	Dep. Manakara	06:45
Arr. Manakara	15:00	Arr. Fianarantsoa	15:00

Sights in **Manakara:** The Antaimoro tribe migrated to this area more than 600 years ago. Although they are now Christian, they brought with them and continue to follow many Moslem customs: Arab style clothing and Arabic script. They adapted the script to the Malagsay language. The Antaimoro are located near **Vohipeno**, a village about 24 miles from Manakara.

MALI

Children under 3 travel free. Half-fare for children 3–9. Children 10 and over must pay full fare.

The 2 rail lines in landlocked Mali are from its capital, Bamako, northeast only 33 miles to Koulikoro, and west to Kidira (and then on to Dakar in Senegal).

The hot season is March to May. The rainy season is June to September.

Cholera, yellow fever, hepatitis, polio, meningitis, malaria and AIDS are widespread in Mali.

Bamako

This city is on the Niger River. See: The fine display of prehistoric-to-modern exhibits in the National Museum. The handicraft (weaving, jewelry, ironwork, sculpture, leatherwork) in Maison des Artisans (Artisans' House). The interesting marketplaces. The excellent Zoo. The Botanical Gardens.

Nearby, the forests at Lake Mandingues, La Boule National Game Reserve, Lake Ouegna, the Korounkorokale Grottoes, Oyako Waterfalls.

Bamako - Koulikoro   2761

Dep. Bamako	18:00		Dep. Koulikoro	05:45
Arr. Koulikoro	20:10		Arr. Bamako	08:15

MAURITANIA

The only passenger rail service in Mauritania is a second-class, limited facility on an overnight iron-ore freight train that runs the 392 miles between **Nouadhibou**, a West African Atlantic fishing and freight port, and **Zouerate**, a mining town.

Nouadhibou-Zouerate   2800

Both of these trains are second-class only and have couchettes.
Both arrivals are on Day 2.

Dep. Nouadhibou	14:50		Dep. Zouerate	12:15
Arr. Zouerate	05:40		Arr. Nouadhibou	06:18

MOROCCO

Children under 4 travel free. Half-fare for children 4–10. Children 11 and over must pay full fare.

Moroccan trains are all standard gauge. A substantial supplement is charged for air-conditioned trains. The country's 3 classes of trains are: first-class, second-class and economy.

Morocco's rail system runs east from Marrakech to Casablanca and Rabat. It then forks at Sidi Kacem, one tine going to Tangier, the other to Oran (and on to Algeria).

Casablanca

Morocco's major seaport. See: The stained-glass at the white Cathedral of the Sacre Coeur. The gardens in the Park of the Arab League. Busy Muhammad V Square. The Municipal College of Fine Arts. Many good beaches.

Fes

Founded in the 9th century. See: The hundreds of columns and brilliant mosaics in the 9th century Qarawiyn Mosque (which can hold 20,000 people), oldest mosque in North Africa, housing the tomb of Idris II, but open only to Muslims.

However, the Attarine Medersa (prayer school), a former dormitory attached to the mosque, can be visited by non-Muslims and is worthwhile seeing for its Marinid decorative art.

The area around the mosque is interesting for its shops: silk, silver, incense, Moroccan leather with gold leaf, nougats, brass, books, copper objects, spices, beadwork, caftans and candles.

See how the rich Moroccans live, at the Museum of Moroccan Art in the 19th century Dar Batha Museum, which is also an ancient university (older than Oxford). The fascinating gate of the Andalusian Mosque. The charming 14th century Medersa Bou Inania (open to non-Muslims).

The Bon Jelud gardens. The multi-colored minaret on the Great Mosque, in the 13th century Fes Jalid complex. Nearby, the olive groves. The extremely high dam, Bin el Widane. The Royal Palace has not been open to the public since 1983.

Marrakech

A popular Winter resort. Good skiing at the nearby 8,000-foot Atlas Mountains. This area is a vast 30,000-acre date palm grove. See: Africa's most famous mosque: the 12th century Koutoubia, with its pale green 220-foot high minaret and the thrilling voice of its muezzin. The 16th century Sa'di Mausoleum. The 18th century Dar el-Beida Palace.

The Moorish gardens at the 19th century Bahia Palace. Marvelous fountains: El Mouasine and Eshrob ou Shouf. The fantastic scenes (dancers, acrobats, musicians, snake charmers, costumed water boys) in the tremendous square, Place Djemaa el-F'na.

The gardens of the Hotel Mamounia. The casino. The olive orchards of the walled 1,000-

acre Agdal gardens and the Menara gardens, at the edge of which the Sahara Desert begins.

The costumes of the mountain and desert people, on a shopping visit. The green and blue tiles on the walls of the central court of the 16th century Medrassa of ben Yussef. The monumental palace, El-Badi, with its small museum and nesting storks. Take a ride around the Old City in a horse-drawn carriage.

Meknes

Founded in the 10th century. Stroll on narrow, ancient streets that veer off from the enormous square, Place El Hedim.

See the 25 miles of 17th century walls that circle the city. The heavily decorated gate, Bab Mansour El Aleuj. The large Royal Palace. The immense and beautiful stables and granary (once housing 12,000 horses and their feed) at Moulay Ismail's tomb. Many big gardens, irrigated by a 10-acre artificial lake, and several other large artificial lakes here. The shops with outstanding rugs.

The exhibits of silver jewelry, filigreed boxes, textiles, carpets, luxurious furniture and guns that have nielloed barrels and stocks that are inlaid with mother-of-pearl at Dar Jamai, open daily except Thursday 09:00–12:00 and 14:00–18:00.

The lovely tiles of the Nejjarine Fountain. The bronze doors of the 14th century Bou Inania Medersa (school for studying the Koran) and its beautiful courtyard, paved in marble and onyx. The building is open daily 09:00–12:00 and 15:00–18:00. Nearby, the ruins of the Roman Volubilis.

Rabat

This has been a military post since the 12th century. There are many splendid gardens here: Belvedere, Essai, Udayia, Triangle de Vue. See: The Kasbah. The 12th century Tour Hassan, largest Arabian minaret, once part of a now ruined mosque. The collection of Moroccan art in the King Muhammed V Memorial, and the view from its roof.

The Old Town. G'Naoua, the old fort. The Royal Palace, built in the 1950's. The Friday procession of the king, from his palace to Djamaa Abel Fez Mosque. Fine work is done here in carpets, blankets and leather handicrafts.

Near the Bou Regreg River, the collection of jewelry, costumes, weapons, carpets and pottery in the Museum of Moroccan Arts, located in the Andalusian Gardens. This 17th century building was originally a palace. It is open 08:30–12:00 and 16:00–18:00.

Shops featuring carpets, leatherware, brass, mosaics, thula-wood boxes, spices, clothes and jewelry line Rue des Consuls and Rue Souika. Visit the Museum of Traditional Arts, open 08:30–12:00 and 15:00–18:30. The 12th century Bab ar-Rouah (Gate of the Wind) and the Archaeological Museum. Nearby, the Roman ruins at Sala Colonia (Chellah).

Tangier

Excellent beaches. Extensive night life. See: Grand Socco, the colorful square in the Old Town, and the market stalls by walking through the twisting alleys to the Petit Socco.

Marrakech - Casablanca - Rabat - Meknes - Fes - Oujda - Algiers

2512	
Dep. Marrakech (Gue.)	17:05 (1)
Arr. Casablanca (Voy.)	21:03
Change trains.	
2510	
Dep. Casablanca (Voy.)	12:55 (2)
Dep. Rabat (Ville)	13:30
Dep. Meknes	16:30
Arr. Fes	17:20
Change trains.	

2510	
Dep. Fes	20:20 (3)
Arr. Oujda	02:23 (4)
Change trains.	
2540	
Dep. Oujda	08:30 (5)
Arr. Algiers (Agha)	14:48

(1) Supplement charged. Air-conditioned. Light refreshments. (2) Air-conditioned. Buffet. (3) Light refreshments. (4) Day 2. (5) Reservation required. Has air-conditioned-class coach and non-air-conditioned first-class coach. Light refreshments.

Oran - Algiers   2542

All of these trains require a reservation.

Dep. Oran	06:35 (1)	15:20 (2)	22:50 (3)	
Arr. Algiers (Agha)	12:29	20:15	05:45	

• • •

Dep. Algiers (Agha)	07:30 (2)	11:30 (1)	17:15 (1)	21:30 (3)
Arr. Oran	12:30	17:40	23:07	05:25

(1) Supplement charged. Air-conditioned first-class. Buffet. (2) Supplement charged. Has air-conditioned-class coach. (3) Has first and second-class couchettes. Light Refreshments.

Marrakech - Casablanca - Rabat

See Cook's Table 2511 for frequent departures from Casablanca's Port railstation, to Rabat and v.v.

2512

Dep. Marrakech	07:00	09:00 (1)	14:00 (2)	19:00 (2)
Arr. Casablanca (Voy.)	10:45	12:24	17:12	21:29

2510

Dep. Casablanca (Voy.)	10:45	12:25 (1)	15:55 (2)	22:18 (2)
Arr. Rabat (Ville)	12:00	13:27	16:56	23:20

• • •

Dep. Rabat (Ville)	04:37 (3)	08:16 (1)	10:58 (2)	18:10 (2)
Arr. Casablanca (Voy.)	05:47	09:12	11:54	19:05

2512

Dep. Casablanca (Voy.)	06:00 (3)	09:14 (1)	11:56 (2)	19:12 (2)
Arr. Marrakech	09:33	12:23	15:20	22:35

(1) Supplement charged. Air-conditioned. (2) Supplement charged. Air-conditioned. Buffet or light refreshments. (3) First and second class couchettes.

Marrakech - Casablanca - Meknes - Fes

2512

Dep. Marrakech	01:30	07:00	09:00 (1)	14:00 (1)	17:00 (4)
Arr. Casablanca (Voy.)	05:08	10:41	12:21	17:21	21:03

Change trains.
2510

Dep. Casablanca (Voy.)	06:05 (4)	10:47 (4)	12:25 (3)	17:30 (4)	22:35 (6)
Dep. Meknes	10:47	15:05	16:37	21:41	02:40
Arr. Fes	11:37	15:50	17:26	22:29	04:00

• • •

Dep. Fes	01:45 (6)	07:00 (3)	09:00 (4)	10:40 (4)	14:35 (3+7)
Dep. Meknes	02:40	08:09	09:54	11:44	15:21
Arr. Casablanca (Voy.)	06:50	12:06 (2)	13:36	16:47	19:23

Change trains.
2512

Dep. Casablanca (Voy.)	09:14 (3)	11:56 (2)	14:45 (2)	-0-	19:12 (2)
Arr. Marrakech	12:23	15:20	18:08	-0-	22:35

(1) Supplement charged. Air-conditioned. (2) Direct train. No change in Casablanca. Supplement charged. Buffet. (3) Supplement charged. Air-conditioned. Light refreshments or buffet. (4) Light refreshments. (5) Has couchettes. Light Refreshments. (6) Plus another Fes departure at 19:43 (4), arriving Casablanca 00:46.

Casablanca - Rabat - Tangier   2510

Dep. Casablanca (Port)	06:45 (1)	10:47 (2+3)
Dep. Rabat (Ville)	07:48	11:59
Arr. Sidi Kacem	-0- (1)	-0- (3)
Change trains.		
Dep. Sidi Kacem	09:12 (1)	13:55 (3)
Arr. Tangier (Gare)	12:32	15:05

* * *

Dep. Tangier (Gare)	01:30 (4)	16:25 (1)
Arr. Sidi Kacem	04:16	-0- (1)
Change trains.		
Dep. Sidi Kacem	05:17 (5)	-0- (1)
Dep. Rabat (Ville)	07:13	21:35
Arr. Casablanca (Port)	08:18	22:25

(1) Direct train. No train change in Sidi Kacem. Supplement charged. Air-conditioned. Buffet. (2) Departs from Casablanca's *Voyageurs* railstation. Light refreshments. (3) Direct train. No train change in Sidi Kacem. Has couchettes. Light refreshments. (4) Reservation required. Supplement charged. Air-conditioned. Buffet. (5) Light refreshments. (6) Arrives at Casablanca's *Voyageurs* railstation.

MOZAMBIQUE

Children under 7 travel free. Half-fare for children 7–16. Children 17 and over must pay full fare. Third-class has only wood seats.

This country's 3 major rail terminals are its Indian Ocean seaports: **Nacala**, **Beira** and **Maputo**, the capital.

Nacala - Nkaya - Chipoka

The Nacala–Cuamba rail line (second and third sections of the left-hand column) has been undergoing reconstruction since 1991. The following schedules are subject to delays and alterations.

3345				*3371*	
Dep. Nacala	04:00 (1)			Dep. Entre Lagos	13:50 (40
Arr. Nampula	12:04			Arr. Nkaya	18:52
Change trains.				*Change trains.*	
Dep. Nampula	15:30 (2)	17:10 (3)		*3370*	
Arr. Cuamba	03:43	03:38		Dep. Nkaya	09:20 (5)
Change trains.				Arr. Chipoka	15:00
Dep. Cuamba		16:00 (4)			
Arr. Entre Lagos		18:18			
Change trains.					

(1) Runs daily. (2) Runs Monday, Wednesday and Saturday. Carries a sleeping car on Monday and Saturday. (3) Runs Thursday only. Carries a sleeping car. (4) Runs daily. Third-class only. (5) Runs daily. Has third-class seats every day and also has second-class seats on Tuesday and Friday.

Quelimane - Nicoadala - Mocuba   3340

Quelimane is a seaport on the Quelimane River. This town was established by Portuguese in 1761. A 78 square mile coconut plantation is located here.

All of these trains are second and third-class only, unless designated otherwise, and are subject to local confirmation.

Dep. Quelimane	03:00 (1)	03:30 (2)	07:00 (3)	13:00 (6)	18:30 (7)
Arr. Nicoadala	03:31	04:28	08:01 (4)	14:01	19:28
Arr. Mocuba	06:09	-0-	11:46 (5)	17:46	-0-
		•	• •		
Dep. Mocuba	-0-	04:00 (6)	06:00 (8)	13:00 (9)	14:00 (10)
Dep. Nicoadala	04:45 (2)	07:50	09:50	15:28	17:50 (11)
Arr. Quelimane	05:43	08:46	10:46	16:09	18:46

(1) Runs Monday only. (2) Runs daily, except Sunday and holidays. Third-class only. (3) Runs Monday, Wednesday, Friday and Saturday. (4) Arrives 07:31 on Saturday. (5) Arrives 10:09 on Saturday. (6) Runs Saturday only. (7) Runs Monday–Friday, except holidays. Third-class only. (8) Runs Tuesday and Thursday. (9) Runs Monday and Saturday. *All times are 15 minutes later on Saturday*. (10) Runs Sunday and holidays only. (11) Plus another departure from Nicoadala at 19:45 (7), arriving Quelimane 20:43.

NAMIBIA

These services were run by South African Railways until April, 1989, when the transitional Namibian government took over complete control.

Children under 2 travel free. Half-fare for children 2–11. Children 12 and over must pay the full fare.

For overnight travel, seats in first-class compartments convert to 4 couchettes and seats in second-class compartments to 6 couchettes.

This is a former German colony, now subject to the administrative control and protection of South Africa. The key tourist attractions are **Etosha National Park** and the **Namib Desert**, said to be the world's oldest desert. Its unusual vegetation is supported only by occasional mists. A specialized world of plants, insects and reptiles has adapted to this environment.

Among the interesting sights in the Desert are the strange "Finger of God" rock formation, one of the most celebrated prehistoric rock paintings (near the tin-mining town of **Uis**, in the wild **Isisab Gorge**), and the 97-mile-long by 16-mile-wide superscenic **Fish River Canyon** which has a modern hot springs resort at **Ai-Ais**.

When the 80-by-30-mile **Etosha Park** is flooded annually, vast numbers of birds and game are attracted there.

Otavi - Windhoek - Keetmanshoop - De Aar   3607 (Bus)

Dep. Otavi	10:00 (1)	13:45 (2)	19:30 (3)	
Arr. Windhoek	15:45	19:30	00:45	
Change to train.				
3600				
Dep. Windhoek	-0-	20:00 (4)	11:00 (6)	
Arr. De Aar	-0-	06:27 (5)	20:33 (7)	
		• • •		
Dep. De Aar	-0-	00:55 (14)	-0-	
Arr. Windhoek	-0-	10:10 (8)	-0-	
Change to bus.				
3607				
Dep. Windhoek	07:00 (10)	09:30 (11)	10:00 (12)	17:00 (13)
Arr. Otavi	12:45	15:15	15:45	22:45

(1) Runs Monday and Friday. (2) Runs Monday, Wednesday, Friday and Sunday. (3) Runs Monday and Sunday. (4) Runs Wednesday and Sunday. Light refreshments on Wednesday only. (5) Day 3 from Windhoek. (6) Runs Wednesday only. Buffet. (7) Day 2 from Windhoek. (8) Day 2 from De Aar. (9) Runs Monday and Thursday. Light refreshments on Monday only. (10) Runs Monday, Wednesday, Friday and Saturday. (11) Runs Thursday only. (12) Runs Sunday only. (13) Runs Thursday and Friday. (14) Runs Friday only.

Sights in **Windhoek:** The capital of South West Africa (Namibia). See notes about Windhoek under "Johannesburg-Windhoek."

Walvisbaai - Swakopmund - Windhoek - Tsumeb

3602
Dep. Walvisbaai	18:35 (1)	
Dep. Swakopmund	20:35	
Arr. Windhoek	06:21 Day 2	

Change to bus.
3607
Dep. Windhoek	07:00 (2)
Arr. Tsumeb	16:00

• • •

Dep. Tsumeb	07:00 (7)	13:00 (8)
Arr. Windhoek	16:00	22:00

Change to train.
3602
Dep. Windhoek	20:00 (1)
Dep. Swakopmund	05:45 (11)
Arr. Walvisbaai	07:05

(1) Runs every day except Sunday. (2) Runs Monday, Wednesday, Friday and Saturday. (3) Runs Thursday only. (4) Runs Sunday only. (5) Runs Thursday and Friday. (6) Day 2 from Windhoek. (7) Runs Monday and Friday. (8) Runs Monday, Wednesday, Friday and Sunday. (9) Runs Monday and Sunday. (10) Day 2 from Tsumeb. (11) Day 2 from Windhoek.

Sights in **Swakopmund:** The government moves here from Windhoek, the capital, during the Summer (December and January) because it is cooler here than in Windhoek. This is South West Africa's principal seaside resort. Good fishing. See the exhibits of natural history, marine life and mineralogy in the Swakopmund Museum.

Sights in **Tsumeb:** The chief copper-mining center of this area. Lead, silver and vanadium are also mined here.

Luderitz - Keetmanshoop   3607 (Bus)

Dep. Luderitz	06:00 (1)	19:00 (2)
Arr. Keetmanshoop	10:30	23:30

Sights in **Luderitz:** There is much diamond mining in this area. One cannot enter the prohibited area outside the town without a permit. Rock lobster fishing and processing is extensive here. See the small museum's collection of Bushman tools and other archaeological objects.

Dep. Keetmanshoop	14:00 (2)	18:00 (3)
Arr. Luderitz	18:30	22:30

(1) Runs Saturday only. (2) Runs Sunday only. (3) Runs Friday only.

SENEGAL

Children under 3 travel free. Half-fare for children 3–9. Children 10 and over must pay full fare. Senegal's 2 rail lines are the short ride from Dakar to St. Louis and the long route from Dakar to Kidira and on to Bamako in landlocked Mali.

The rainy season is June–September. The hot season is March–May. Nighttime temperatures are sometimes over 100 degrees Fahrenheit, overpowering hotel air-conditioners. Cholera, yellow fever, hepatitis, polio, meningitis, malaria and AIDS are widespread in Senegal.

Sights in **Dakar**: A major seaport. Capital of Senegal. About 1,000,000 population. There are good museums here on the sea, ethnography and archaeology. Also see: The Victorian railstation. The Zoo. The outstanding scarlet uniforms of the sentries at the President's Palace.

The green tile mosaics in the Moorish-style Great Mosque. The beautiful Church of Our Lady of Fatima in the Cathedral du Souvenir Africain. The making of leather-work, baskets, jewelry and woodwork at the Soumbedioune Artisnal Village. The collection of African art in the Museum of Dakar. The array of gold, silver, exotic musical instruments, produce, spices, jewelry and embroidered African garments sewn to order in a few minutes, all at the covered Sandaga central market. Nearby, the picturesque fishing village, Cayar.

Take the 20-minute ferry ride to Goree Island for a tour of the Slave House Museum. Goree was once the main port for the slave trade. You can see the cells where chained slaves were held before they were moved onto crowded ships.

Dakar - St. Louis   2811

Both of these trains have light refreshments.

Dep. Dakar	15:00		Dep. St. Louis	06:30
Arr. St. Louis	20:00		Arr. Dakar	12:00

Dakar - Kidira - Bamako, (Mali)   2760 + 2810

Passengers are subjected to hot wind, dust and diesel smoke on this ride. Prior to 1992 the *non* air-conditioned train carried a mail car, 4 very old second-class coaches with wood slat seats, first-class coaches with padded seats dating from the 1950's (similar to a car on a commuter train in the western U.S.A.), and a restaurant car that had a small counter, a refrigerator and an old gas stove. At the end of the train were sleeping cars with dirty compartments, dirty linen, an openable window and an overhead fan.

Because the restaurant car had no tables, diners balanced the plate on their lap. Neither towels nor wash water was available. By the end of the trip, the train was filthy, and the stench from the toilets was very strong.

That abysmal equipment was replaced in 1992 with cars from Europe's most magnificent train, the French "Mistral." It had elegant, air-conditioned first-class sleeping cars, air-conditioned coaches and a modern restaurant car. Both trains run Wednesday and Saturday

Dep. Dakar	10:00		Dep. Bamako	09:15	
Arr. Kidira	00:15 Day 2		Arr. Kidira	00:10 Day 2	
Arr. Bamako	14:30		Arr. Dakar	14:55	

SOUTH AFRICA

Travel is free for children under 2 years old accompanied by an adult who has paid the full advertised ticket price. Half-fare for children 2–11 who either are traveling alone or when they travel with an adult who has paid a reduced ticket price. Children 12 and over must pay the full price.

Summer climate here is November to mid-April. The peak Summer holiday period is December 12 to January 30.

All major rail lines in South Africa are narrow-gauge (3'6") because so much track is over mountain terrain. However, carriages are only slightly narrower than those used on British, European and North American railways.

Reservations can be made up to 2 months in advance, with one exception: up to 11½ months for "Blue Train" (Pretoria-Johannesburg-Cape Town).

First-class coupes carry 2 passengers. First-class compartments carry 4. Second-class coupes carry 3, and second-class compartments accommodate 6. By paying a higher fare, one person can reserve a first-class coupe, and first-class compartments can be reserved for the use of 2 or 3 people.

Reservation is recommended for all night travel. On night trains, first -class compartments convert to 4 couchette berths and second-class to 6 berths. Passengers are charged for sterilized bedding, packed in a sealed canvas bag. The seal is broken in the passenger's presence, when the attendant makes up the berth. However, bedding and meals are included in the fare charged for Blue Train.

Holders of first-class tickets are permitted up to 100 pounds of free luggage.

A pocket timetable is available free from Spoornet (called South African Railways prior to 1990).

The country's extensive rail system connects inland Johannesburg with 5 seaports: Durban, East London, Port Elizabeth, Mossel Bay and Cape Town. There is train service from South Africa to 3 of the 4 countries adjacent to it: Zimbabwe (formerly Rhodesia), Botswana and South West Africa (Namibia). There was also train service from Johannesburg into Mozambique until guerrilla attacks forced it to cease. In 1989, that service terminated at Komatipoort, near the Mozambique border (table 3346).

The U.S.A. source for reservations on South Africa's main-line trains is: SARtravel Ltd, 1100 E. Broadway, Glendale, CA 91205. Telephones: (800) 727-7207 and (818) 549-1921.

Johannesburg

There are many museums here on archaeology, costumes, transportation, Judaica, geology, medicine and South African history. The railstation, largest in the African continent, has a splendid railway museum. Among the exhibits there are models of locomotives and rolling stock from early days to modern times, and old restaurant car menus, tickets, signalling systems, uniforms and badges

See the collection of South African and European paintings (Manet, Monet, Pissaro, Van Gogh, Degas, Renoir, Rembrandt) at the Art Gallery. The Mosque. The Money Museum. Jan Smuts House. The Bensuan Museum of Photography. The Museum of History and Medicine. Replicas of the huts of many different South African tribes in the riverside African Village that is the central display of the Africana Museum.

Hermann Eckstein Park, a complex of a large zoo, the National Museum of Military History, and the Museum of Rock Art. The view of the city from the Carlton Panorama. Visit the Gold Museum at nearby Crown Mines, called "Gold Reef City."

Pretoria - Johannesburg - Pietermaritzburg - Durban

3521

Dep. Pretoria	Frequent times from 04:12 to 22:12
Arr. Johannesburg	90 minutes later

Change trains. 3510

Dep. Johannesburg	18:30 (1+4)
Dep. Pietermaritzburg	05:51 (2)
Arr. Durban	08:00

• • •

Dep. Durban	18:30 (1+4)
Dep. Pietermaritzburg	20:51
Arr. Johannesburg	07:44 (3)

Change trains. 3521

Dep. Johannesburg	Frequent times from 04:03 to 22:03
Arr. Pretoria	90 minutes later

(1) Reservation suggested. (2) Runs Wednesday only. Restaurant car. (3) Day 2. (4) Runs daily. Restaurant car. (5) Runs daily.

Sights in **Pretoria:** The streets lined with jacaranda trees. Some of the oldest and most beautiful buildings in town are located around Church Square, the center of the city and the site of the first settlement in the region.

See Paul Kruger's house. The National Cultural History and Open Air Museum. The sunken gardens at Venning Park. The National Zoological Gardens. The Museum of Science and Technology, the only one of this kind on the African continent.

The Voortrekker Monument, commemorating the journey of the pioneers who fought Zulus in 1838. Made of marble and granite, its 27 panels depict the leaders of the battle. There are also 64 life-size ox wagons, the number that were present at the battle.

The collection of coins and minerals from around the world, at the South African Mint. The natural history exhibit at the Transvaal Museum. Works by South African artics at the Art Museum. The National Botanic Gardens.

Sights in **Pietermaritzburg:** Called "City of Flowers" for its many fine botanical gardens and parks. See the Voortrekker Museum. The Natal Museum.

The model native village in nearby Mountain Rise. Many nearby mountain resorts and game preserves, including the Natal Lion and Game Park (lions, giraffes, zebras, ostriches, rhinos and antelope).

Sights in **Durban:** This is South Africa's largest port and the country's major seaside resort, popular for sailing, swimming and deep-sea fishing in the Indian Ocean. Shop for brassware, ivory, carved masks and figurines, spices, fruits, beads, jewelry, gold, silver and semi-precious stones at the Indian Market.

Visit the fabled Orchid House in the Botanic Garden, a wooded area in the center of the city's business district. Also in the city center is the Old Fort, occupied by British soldiers during the Anglo-Boer War. See Snake Park. Japanese Water Gardens. The rose gardens in Jameson Park. The Oceanarium. The motorized cars, trains, ships and airplanes that move around and through a scaled-down (1/24th) reproduction of the city, called Minitown.

There are many nearby game and nature reserves: **Umfolzi** (the rare white rhino), **Hluhluwe** (black rhino), **Mkuzi** (for photographing wildlife congregating at waterholes), **Ndumu** (birdwatching) and **St. Lucia Estuary** (for birdwatching and to see hippos and crocodiles).

Johannesburg - Bloemfontein - East London   3508

All of these trains have an air-conditioned restaurant car.

Dep. Johannesburg	12:45
Arr. Bloemfontein	19:40
Arr. East London	08:30 (1)

•   •   •

Dep. East London	12:00
Dep. Bloemfontein	00:55 (1)
Arr. Johannesburg	08:15

(1) Runs every day except Saturday. Reservation required.

Sights in **Bloemfontein:** The beautiful 300-acre King's Park. The Franklin Game Reserve. Two astronomical observatories: Lamont-Hussey and Boyden Station. The enormous dinosaur and other fossils at the National Museum.

Sights in **East London:** The 80-acre Queen's Park. This Indian Ocean seaport's Museum has a coelacanth, a primeval fish. Beautiful beaches here. See the Victorian artifacts exhibited at the Gately House Historical Museum. Paintings by South African and English artists at the Ann Bryant Art Gallery.

Johannesburg - Bloemfontein - Port Elizabeth   3520

Both of these trains have an air-conditioned restaurant car.

Dep. Johannesburg	14:30 (1)	Dep. Port Elizabeth	14:45 (3)
Dep. Bloemfontein	21:20	Arr. Bloemfontein	02:15 (2)
Arr. Port Elizabeth	09:45(2)	Arr. Johannesburg	09:00

(1) Runs Tuesday, Thursday and Sunday. Reservation required. (2) Day 2. (3) Runs Monday, Wednesday and Friday. Reservation required.

Sights in **Port Elizabeth:** Popular for swimming beaches and deep-sea fishing expeditions. Many fine parks, including St. George's Park. See Fort Frederick, built in 1799 to accommodate British troops. The milking of a puff adder's venom, at Snake Park. Dolphin performing in the oceanarium at Settler's Park Nature Preserve. Nearby is Addo Elephant National Park.

Climb the 204 steps to the top of the 52-meter-high Memorial Campanile for the View from the platform at the top, and hear the ring changes of its 23 bells, performed 3 times a day. Visit the King George VI Art Gallery. Enjoy the fine beaches with gigantic sand dunes at nearby coastal resorts: The Willows, Swartkops, Sea View, etc.

Take a one-day excursion on the narrow-gauge "Apple Express" hauled by a little steam locomotive. Used mainly to transport fruit from the Long Kloof orchards, it becomes a special sightseeing train only on the first Saturday of each month, except during the December holiday period when several additional days are added. Reservations are recommended for this popular $10 trip.

This very scenic 171-mile route is ablaze with wild flowers, fruit blossoms and the fragrance of ripe fruit. "Apple Express" departs Humewood Road Station (near Port Elizabeth's harbor) at 08:30, arriving Loerie at 12:05. The 12:50 departure from Loerie brings passengers back to Port Elizabeth at 16:30. At the railstation, the Humerail Museum has exhibits of the 2-foot gauge system.

Pretoria - Johannesburg - Kimberley - Cape Town

This is the route of the wonderful, all first-class Blue Train, which provides 5 categories: "A" (a suite consisting of a bedroom with twin beds, private lounge and a bathroom with tub and toilet), "B" (compartment with one or 3 berths, with its own bathroom having a tub and toilet), "C" (compartment with one or 3 berths, private shower and toilet), "D" (compartment with one or 2 berths that can be converted to 3 berths) and "E" (compartment with 2 berths and a private toilet). There is only one "A" compartment. Passengers traveling in "D" and "E" compartments have use of a shower in the carriage.

The food is cordon bleu quality.

Blue Train is so popular that advance seat reservations are nearly always necessary. Due to the heavy demand for travel on this train, space on it can be reserved as much as 11 months in advance of travel date.

Air-conditioning with individual controls. Electrically operated venetian blinds sealed between windows. Suites equipped with refrigerator, wine rack and FM radio reception. Double insulation and advanced construction techniques make this train vibrationless and noiseless. The seats are upholstered.

Valet service is available for coffee and tea in the morning as well as at 16:30 with tea and an after noon news paper.

The schedule provides daytime viewing in both directions of the scenic area through the Cape mountains and over the Hex River Pass between Touws River and Cape Town, during which the line descends or ascends 2,352 feet within one 36-mile section, into or out of De Doorns Valley.

The U.S.A. source for reservations is SAR Travel Ltd., 1100 E. Broadway, Glendale, CA 91205. Telephones: (800) 727-7207 and (818) 549-1921.

	3519
Dep. Pretoria	10:10
Dep. Johannesburg	12:30 (3)
Dep. Kimberley	21:00
Dep. De Aar	00:54 (2)
Arr. Cape Town	14:15

• • •

	3519	3500
Dep. Cape Town	09:20 (3)	10:50 (1)
Dep. De Aar	22:28	01:20 (2)
Dep. Kimberley	02:15 (2)	04:44
Arr. Johannesburg	10:00	11:50
Arr. Pretoria	11:40	12:55

(1) Blue train. January 1-April 16 and Sept. 15- December 31. Runs Monday, Wednesday & Friday. Runs on "limited days" the rest of the year. Has only sleeping cars. Suites and staterooms are available. Reservation required. Supplement charged. Air conditioned restaurant car. (2) Day 2 (3)"Trans-Karoo Express" - Air conditioned restaurant car. Reservation required. Car carrier.

Sights in **Kimberley:** Many diamond mines in this area. See the exhibit of diamonds at the Mine Museum. Visit the De Beers Mine Observation Platform to view the mine that produces most of South Africa's diamonds. The block square, 14-story Harry Oppenheimer House. The Ernest Oppenheimer Memorial Garden.

The William Humphrey's Art Museum. The collection of Bushman artifacts in both the Dugglin-Cronin Bantu Gallery and in McGregor Memorial Museum.

Durban - Bloemfontein - Cape Town   3501

Both of these trains have an air-conditioned restaurant car.

Dep. Durban	17:30 (1)	Dep. Cape Town	18:50 (4)
Dep. Bloemfontein	09:45 (2)	Dep. Bloemfontein	15:46 (2)
Arr. Cape Town	06:15 (3)	Arr. Durban	07:45 (3)

(1) Runs Thursday only. Reservation required. (2) Day 2. (3) Day 3. (4) Runs Monday only. Reservation required.

Cape Town - Bitterfontein

This is now a 7-hour bus trip.

Dep. Cape Town	14:00 (1)	
Arr. Bitterfontein	21:00	
Dep. Bitterfontein	06:45 (2)	10:00
Arr. Cape Town	13:45	17:00

(1) Runs Tuesday, Thursday, Friday and Saturday. (2) Runs Monday, Tuesday, Thursday and Saturday.

Johannesburg - De Aar - Keetmanshoop - Windhoek

This is one of the 2 train routes to Namibia.

"Trans-Karoo" is the only practical connection Johannesburg–De Aar and v.v. because of reservation restrictions imposed by "Blue Train" on passengers riding only this portion of its Johannesburg–Cape Town route. Seats convert to couchettes on all of the overnight trains shown here.

3519			*3600*		
Dep. J'burg	10:10 (1)	12:30 (2)	Dep. Windhoek	11:00 (3)	20:00 (7)
Arr. De Aar	22:11	00:30	Arr. De Aar	20:33 (6)	06:27 (6)
Change trains.			*Change trains*		
3600			*3519*		
Dep. De Aar	00:55 (3)	02:00 (5)	Dep. De Aar	22:28 (2)	00:17 (1)
Arr. Windhoek	10:10 (4)	13:12 (4)	Arr. J'burg	10:00 (8)	10:40

(1) "Blue Train." January 11-April 30 and October 1-December 31: runs Mon, Wed and Fri. Runs on "Limited Days" the rest of the year. Has only sleeping cars. No coaches. Suites and staterooms are available. Reservation required. Supplement charged. Air-conditioned train. Restaurant car. (2) "Trans-Karoo." Runs daily. Air-conditioned restaurant car. (3) Runs Sat only. Buffet. (4) Day 2 from De Aar. (5) Runs Mon and Thurs. Light refreshments only on Mon. (6) Day 2 from Windhoek. (7) Runs Wed and Sun. Light refreshments only on Wed. (8) Day 3 from Windhoek.

Sights in **De Aar:** A major rail junction. Train buffs come here to see old steam trains. A very hot desert climate .

Sights in **Windhoek:** The capital of Namibia. Many hot springs in this area. Karakul (Persian lamb) graze here, and the furs are processed in this area. See the collection of very large meteorites in the State Museum. The lovely gardens around Christ Church. The 3 hilltop castles. Tourists come here for the Carnival (late April, early May) and the big Oktoberfest.

Cape Town - De Aar - Windhoek

This isone of the 2 train routes to Namibia

3501+3519			3600		
Dep. Cape Town	09:20 (1)	18:50 (4)	Dep. Windhoek	11:00 (2)	20:00'(7)
Arr. De Aar	22:11	07:43	Arr. De Aar	20:33 (6)	06:27 (8)
Change trains.			*Change trains.*		
3600			3501 + 3519		
Dep. De Aar	00:55 (2)	02:00 (5)	Dep. De Aar	00:52 (1)	17:00 (9)
Arr. Windhoek	10:10 (3)	13:12 (3)	Arr. Cape Town	13:55 (8)	06:15 (10)

(1) "Trans Karoo." Runs daily. Air-conditioned restaurant car. Reservation required. (2) Runs Friday only. Buffet. (3) Day 2 from De Aar. (4) Runs Mon only. Restaurant car. (5) Runs Mon and Thurs. Has light refreshments only on Mon. (6) Day 2 from Windhoek. (7) Runs Wed and Sun. Light refreshments only on Wed. (8) Day 3 from Windhoek. (9) Runs Fri only. Restaurant car. (10) Day 4 from Windhoek.

SUDAN

Children under 3 travel free. Half-fare for children 3–11. Children 12 and over must pay full fare.

Routes in Sudan are very dusty. Little vegetation is seen in Sudan. Grass fires engulf more than half the country every year.

Sudan's rail system links Port Sudan on the Red Sea with the inland capital, Khartoum. At Haiya, there are 2 possible train routes to Khartoum. A northern one goes via Atbara, and a southern route runs via Kassala.

There is rail service north from Khartoum to Wadi Halfa and, from there, on to the Nile and to Cairo by a combination of boat and train. This is the only rail connection between Sudan and a country adjacent to it. A short spur from this route goes west to Karima.

Two lines run south from Khartoum, one to Ed Damazine and the other to Kosti (from which there is a slow, 11-day boat trip to Juba) and to Babanusa.

A short spur runs from Kosti northwest to El Obeid. Another spur continues from Babanusa, going northwest to Nyala.

Bur (Port) Sudan - Khartoum   2701   Via Atbara

In recent years, foreigners have not been allowed to travel on this line due to the civil war.
All of these trains carry a sleeping car and a restaurant car.

Dep. Bur Sudan	18:00 (1)	20:15 (3)	Dep. Khartoum	08:15 (1)	10:45 (5)
Arr. Khartoum	06:00 (2)	16:00 (4)	Arr. Bur Sudan	06:00 (4)	20:15 (4)

(1) Runs Saturday only. (2) Day 3. (3) Runs Monday only. (4) Day 2. (5) Runs Thursday only.

Sights in **Khartoum:** It is very hot here. The temperature reaches more than 100 degrees Fahrenheit every month and goes as high as 117 degrees. The city was founded by Egyptians as an army camp in 1824. See the Republican Palace, the Sudan Museum. The Ethnographical Museum. The Natural History Museum. The Zoo, along the river. The meeting of the White Nile and Blue Nile, viewed from the White Nile Bridge. Across the bridge is the sister town, **Om Durman**, with its fabulous Mosque Square that holds 100,000 people. The silver Khalifa's Mosque. The Mahdi-Khalifiana Museum.

Sights in **Bur Sudan:** African Moslems stop here en route on their pilgrimage to Mecca. This is Sudan's principal port.

Bur (Port) Sudan - Khartoum   2703   Via Kassala

| Dep. Bur Sudan | 18:00 (1) | | Dep. Khartoum | 13:00 (3) |
| Arr. Khartoum | 08:45 (2) | | Arr. Bur Sudan | 09:05 (2) |

(1) Runs Friday only. (2) Day 3. (3) Runs Thursday only.

Khartoum - Ed Damazine   2702

These services are subject to confirmation.

| Dep. Khartoum | 17:00 | Mon. | | Dep. Ed Damazine | 08:00 | Wed. |
| Arr. Ed Damazine | 11:20 | Tues. | | Arr. Khartoum | 03:05 | Thurs. |

Khartoum - Kosti - El Obeid   2702

Both of these trains carry a sleeping car and a restaurant car.

Dep. Khartoum	17:50	Tues.		Dep. El Obeid	07:00	Thurs.
Dep. Kosti	08:25	Wed.		Dep. Kosti	17:50	Thurs.
Arr. El Obeid	17:30	Wed.		Arr. Khartoum	07:00	Fri.

Sights in **El Obeid:** Also called al-Ubayyid. Founded by Egyptians in 1821. The city was once encircled by a forest preserve, designed to alleviate frequent dust storms. The main activity here is trading in gum arabic.

Khartoum - Nyala   2702

Both of these trains carry a sleeping car and a restaurant car.

Dep. Khartoum	10:30	Mon.	Dep. Nyala	10:00	Thurs.
Arr. Nyala	10:30	Wed.	Arr. Khartoum	10:30	Sat.

Sights in **Nyala:** This is a trade center for gum arabic.

Khartoum - Kosti - Juba

2702 *(Train)*			2706 *(Boat)*	
Dep. Khartoum	10:30 (1)	17:50 (2)	Dep. Juba	N/A (3)
Arr. Kosti	02:20	08:15	Dep. Malakal	N/A
Change to boat.			Arr. Kosti	N/A (5)
2706			*Change to train.*	
Dep. Kosti	N/A (3)		2702	
Dep. Malakal	N/A		Dep. Kosti	17:50 (6)	20:35 (6)
Arr. Juba	N/A (4)		Arr. Khartoum	07:00 (7)	10:30 (7)

(1) Runs Monday only. Carries sleeping car and restaurant car. (2) Runs Tuesday only. Carries sleeping car and restaurant car.(3) Service was "temporarily" suspended in 1987. When running, service operates "about every 4 weeks." Schedules vary according to depth of water in river. Has a restaurant. (4) Arrives 8–11 days after departing Khartoum, depending on full moon periods. (5) Arrives 5–9 days after departing Juba, depending on full moon periods. (6) Runs Thursday only. Carries a sleeping car and restaurant car. (7) Day 2 after departing Kosti. (8) Runs Friday only. Carries a sleeping car and restaurant car.

Kosti - Babanusa   2702

Both of these trains carry a sleeping car and a restaurant car.

Dep. Kosti	02:30	Mon.	Dep. Babanusa	23:10	Thurs.
Arr. Babanusa	02:50	Tues.	Arr. Kosti	20:25	Fri.

Babanusa - Nyala   2702

Both of these trains carry a sleeping car and a restaurant car.

Dep. Babanusa	03:00	Mon.	Dep. Nyala	10:00	Thurs.
Arr. Nyala	10:30		Arr. Babanusa	23:00	

Sights in **Nyala**: This is a trade center for gum arabic.

Wadi Halfa - Khartoum 2700

Both of these trains carry a sleeping car and a restaurant car.

Dep. Wadi Halfa	16:40 (1)		Dep. Khartoum	16:40 (2)	
Arr. Khartoum	16:45	Day 2	Arr. Wadi Halfa	15:40	Day 2

(1) Runs Tuesday and Sunday. (2) Runs Wednesday and Sunday.

Sights in **Wadi Halfa:** This area was the center of archaeological activities in the 1970's to save Egyptian monuments from being covered by the Aswan High Dam reservoir. Egyptian ruins from 2,000 B.C. (the ruins of Buchen) are across the river from Wadi Halfa. An Egyptian colony was here until the Roman invasion.

THE RAIL ROUTE TO EGYPT

Sudan's train connection with Egypt from Khartoum involves a Nile boat trip from Wadi Halfa to Sadd el Ali.

Khartoum - Wadi Halfa - El Sadd el Ali - Cairo

This trip crosses the vast Nubian Desert. It is subject to serious delays.

2700 (Train)			*2680 (Boat—Nile Valley River Transport)*		
Dep. Khartoum	16:40 (1)		Dep. Wadi Halfa	16:00 (3)	
Arr. Wadi Halfa	15:40 (2)		Arr. El Sadd el Ali	08:00 Day 3	
Change to boat.			*Change to train.*		
			2655		
			Dep. El Sadd el Ali	18:25 (4)	19:35 (4)
			Arr. Cairo (Main)	13:25 (5)	13:40 (5)

(1) Runs Wednesday and Sunday. Carries sleeping cars and a restaurant car. (2) Day 2 from Khartoum. (3) Days of operation are not currently available. (4) Runs daily. Reservation required. Air-conditioned train. (5) Day 2 from El Sadd el Ali.

Khartoum - Karima 2700

Dep. Khartoum	10:50 (1)		Dep. Karima	12:25 (1)
Arr. Karima	14:00 (2)		Arr. Khartoum	16:00 (2)

(1) Runs Wednesday and Sunday. (2) Day 2.

TANZANIA

Children under 3 travel free. Half-fare for children 3–13. Children 14 and over must pay full fare.

This country's rail system is the modern Tanzam Line that was completed in 1976, running from the seaport of Dar es Salaam to Tunduma (and on into Zambia, to Kapiri Mposhi), plus 2 routes going north from Dar es Salaam and 2 that head west from there. One of the northern lines connects Tanga, another of Tanzania's seaports, with Dar es Salaam.

The trains from Dar es Salaam to Kapiri Mposhi (see below) have first-class compartments that convert to 4 berths and second-class compartments that convert to 6 berths. On all other Tanzanian trains, first-class compartments convert to 2 berths.

There is also train-ferry service on Lake Victoria.

Tanzania has many excellent national parks, offering splendid viewing of monkeys, elephants, rhinos, antelopes, lions, zebras and giraffes: Arusha (45 minutes from Dar es-Salaam), Ngorongoro Crater, Lake Manyara, Tarangire, Mikumi, Gombe and the 5,000-square-mile Serengeti.

Dar es Salaam

Means "Haven of Peace" in Arabic. This is Tanzania's main Indian Ocean seaport. See the 1,700,000-year old skull at the National Museum, as well as abstract Makonde wood carving, Masai weapons, drums and Zanzibar chests and elaborately carved doors. The Botanical Gardens. The Askari Monument. The picturesque boats at Dhow Wharf. The Asian Bazaar, called "Uhindini." An extensive complex of seaside resorts is located 15 miles to the north.

Dar es Salaam Kapiri Mposhi   3301

This train runs Tuesday and Friday, charges a supplement and has a restaurant car. Reservation required.

During this ride, the train climbs as high as 6,000 feet altitude. If you do not like curry and local maize cuisine, it is advisable to bring your own food for this 37–43 hours of travel.

Dr. Norbert Brockman, returning to the U.S.A. in 1990, after 5 years in East Africa, advised us that conditions on the Tanzanian portion of this route (Dar es Salaam to Tunduma) are inferior to the Zambian portion (Tunduma to Kapiri Mposhi). Poor service, running out of food, or food available only by paying a bribe. Also unclean conditions.

Dep. Dar es Salaam	17:34
Dep. Tunduma	15:48
Arr. Kapiri Mposhi	08:38

Tanga - Korogwe - Moshi   3300

There are no hotels suitable for tourists in either Korogwe or Moshi.

Dep. Tanga	19:30 (1)	Dep. Moshi	16:00 (1)
Arr. Korogwe	22:20	Arr. Korogwe	23:00
Change trains.		*Change trains.*	
Dep. Korogwe	00:20 (2)	Dep. Korogwe	02:00 (3)
Arr. Moshi	07:05	Arr. Tanga	04:45

(1) Runs Tues,Thurs and Sun. (2) Runs Monday, Wednesday and Friday. Reservation required. (3) Runs Tuesday, Thursday and Saturday. Reservation required.

Dar es Salaam - Moshi

This trip goes to the southern foot of Mt. Kilimanjaro, highest mountain in Africa (over 19,000 feet).

	3300	3315	3315
Dep. Dar es Salaam	16:00 (1+2)	N/A (4)	N/A (4)
Arr. Moshi	07:05 (3)	N/A (4)	N/A (4)

• • •

	3315	3300	3315
Dep. Moshi	N/A (4)	16:00 (5)	N/A (4)
Arr. Dar es Salaam	N/A (4)	07:00 (1)	N/A (4)

(1) Departs/Arrives about 5 miles from Dar es Salaam's Tazara railstation. (2) Train. Runs Monday, Wednesday and Friday. Reservation required. (4) Bus. Time was not available in 1994. (5) Train. Runs Tuesday, Thursday and Sunday. Reservation required.

Dar es Salaam - Mwanza   3300

This rail trip goes to Lake Victoria.

Both of these trains carry a restaurant car and have first-class seats that convert to berths.

Dep. Dar es Salaam	17:00 (1)	Dep. Mwanza	18:00 (3)
Arr. Mwanza	07:35 (2)	Arr. Dar es Salaam	08:50 (4)

(1) Runs Tuesday, Wednesday, Friday and Sunday. Reservation required. (2) Day 3 from Dar es Salaam. (3) Runs Tuesday, Thursday, Friday and Sunday. Reservation required. (4) Day 3 from Mwanza.

Dar es Salaam - Morogoro - Dodoma - Tabora - Kigoma   3300

Here are the schedules for the train ride to **Lake Tanganyika**. There is boat service across the lake, from **Kigoma** to **Kalemie (Zaire)**.

On this 900-mile trip, **Dodoma** and **Tabora** are fine stopping places en route, which at least until 1979 had good and picturesque railway hotels near both stations.

There is taxi service for the 5-mile trip from Kigoma to **Ujiji**. This is the village where on October 28, 1871, after many months of ordeal, Henry Stanley found Dr. David Livingstone. A small monument marks the site.

The Dar es Salaam departure and arrival is a railstation that is about 5 miles from Dar es Salaam's Tazara railstation. All of these trains have first-class seats that convert to berths.

Dep. Dar es Salaam	17:00 (1)	Dep. Kigoma	17:00 (5)
Dep. Morogoro	00:15 (2)	Arr. Tabora	04:30 (6)
Dep. Dodoma	08:10	*Change trains.*	
Arr. Tabora	18:25	Dep. Tabora	07:25 (5)
Change trains.		Dep. Dodoma	18:40 (5)
Dep. Tabora	20:10 (3)	Dep. Morogoro	02:15 (8)
Arr. Kigoma	07:35 (4)	Arr. Dar es Salaam	08:50

(1) Runs Tuesday, Wednesday, Friday and Sunday. Restaurant car. Reservation required. (2) Day 2 from Dar es Salaam. (3) Runs Monday, Wednesday, Thursday and Saturday. (4) Day 3 frkom Dar es Salaam. Reservation required. (5) Day 2 from Kigoma.(6) Runs Monday, Wednesday, Friday and Saturday. (7) Day 3 from Kigoma.

From Dar es Salaam to **Morogoro** is only 7 hours by train. It took Stanley 29 days to walk this 121-mile distance. Here, as at many stations in Africa, one can buy hard-boiled eggs, peanuts, tea, oranges and samosas (spicy meat knishes) from vendors along the platform.

Sights in **Tabora:** Long avenues, shaded by mango trees that grew from seeds spitted by end-less lines of slaves who were herded down these streets.

There is a small Livingstone museum in nearby **Kwihara** (reached by taxi from Tabora), where Stanley rested many weeks during his search for Livingstone in 1871.

Mpanda - Tabora - Kigoma 3300

This is the train route from Mpanda to **Lake Tanganyika.**

Dep. Mpanda	13:00 (1)		Dep. Kigoma	17:00 (1)
Arr. Tabora	02:45 (2)		Arr. Tabora	04:30 (5)
Change trains.			*Change trains.*	
Dep. Tabora	20:10 (3)		Dep. Tabora	21:00 (6)
Arr. Kigoma	07:35 (4)		Arr. Mpanda	10:30 (7)

(1) Runs Tuesday, Thursday, Friday and Sunday. Reservation required. (2) Day 2 from Mpanda. (3) Runs Monday, Wednesday, Thursday and Saturday. Reservation required. (4) Day 2 from Tabora. (5) Day 2 from Kigoma. (6) Runs Monday, Wednesday, Thursday and Saturday. (7) Day 3 from Kigoma.

TOGO

Children under 5 travel free. Half-fare for children 5–9. Children 10 and over must pay full fare. Only one, spartan class is available, comparable to third-class in other African countries. The official language in Togo is French.

Lome - Kpalime 3051

Dep. Lome	06:30(1)		Dep. Kpalime	12:45 (1)
Arr. Kpalime	11:30		Arr. Lome	17:45

(1)Runs Tuesday, Thursday and Saturday. (2)Runs Monday, Wednesday, Friday and Sunday.

Sights in **Kpalime:** The ride from Lome is through many small villages and tropical forest. Experience the Friday night frivolities before each Saturday's market day, where thousands of people from the outlying area come here to do their weekly shopping. Do not fail to see the famous fantastic kente cloth that has irridescent silk and cotton threads woven into geometric patterns.

Lome - Blitta 3050

Dep. Lome	07:00 (1)
Arr. Blitta	16:30

• • •

Dep. Blitta	07:30 (1)
Arr. Lome	16:30

(1) Runs Tuesday, Thursday and Saturday.

TUNISIA

Children under 4 travel free. Children 4–9 pay 75%. Children 10 and over must pay full fare.

Because Tunisia is only 2 hours by air from Paris and one hour from Rome, it is a popular vacation place for Europeans.

Tunisia's rail system is 2 lines running west from Tunis (one to Bizerte and the other to Ghardimaou, and on to Algeria) and one heading south from Tunis, to Gabes. An 11-mile spur from Bir-bou-Rekba on this southern line goes to Hammamet and Nabeul.

The 3 classes of seats are grand-comfort, first-class and second-class.

Tunis

There are more than 700 exceptional monuments to see here. The finest and largest collection of Roman mosaics in the world are on exhibit at the National Museum of the Bardo, as well as Punic, Byzantine, Arab and other Roman objects (open daily except Monday 09:00–12:00 and 14:00–17:30). Shop the native quarter for famous Kairouan rugs.

See the fantastic 9th century Great Mosque Zitouna (Mosque of the Olive Tree). A marvelous collection of illuminated Korans and other Arabic manuscripts in the National Library. The beautiful interior of the Zaouia (temple) of Sidi Mahrez. The marble and sculptured wood in the lovely Dar Ben Abdullah, an example of Tunis' many 19th century "great houses."

The Lapidary Museum of Sidi Bou Krissan. The valuable objects from Egypt, Persia and Turkey at the Dar Hussein Museum of Islamic Art, in an 18th century mansion. The 17th century Mosque of Hamouda Pasha. The 16th century Mosque El Youssefi (Mosque of the Kasbah). The Belvedere Zoo. The many beach resorts south of Tunis. There are half-day tours to **Carthage** and **Sidi Bou Said**. A full-day tour goes to Dougga.

Dougga

It is a short drive from Tunis to Dougga. See the 2nd century B.C. Dougga Mausoleum, a prince's tomb. There are also many temples and an ancient Market Place, all very well preserved. The Comedie Francaise often performs in the large open-air theater. Dougga is Tunisia's largest archaeological site, one of the best-preserved Roman towns in Tunisia.

Kerkouane

This city is near Tunis. It is the only unmutilated Punic town, the only one that was not built upon by succeeding generations.

Thuburo Majus

Near both Tunis and Sousse, Thuburo Majus is home to many fabulous ruins: temples, a Forum, public buildings and an excellently preserved Roman town.

Utica

Also near both Tunis and Bizerte, Utica was a Phoenician port in the 11th century B.C. Some vaults from that period and many fine Roman ruins can be seen here. The Museum has a fine collection of ancient jewels and funeral furniture.

Tunis - Bizerte   2602

Dep. Tunis	04:55 (1)	11:20	14:05	19:10
Arr. Bizerte	06:40	12:55	15:51	20:49

* * *

Dep. Bizerte	04:45 (1)	07:20	13:55	18:30
Arr. Tunis	06:27	08:52	15:36	20:10

(1) Runs daily except Sundays and Holidays.

Sights in **Bizerte:** This city has been ruled by Punic, Roman, Byzantine, Arab and Turkish leaders. See: The Er-Rimel beach. The Old Port, with docks for fishing boats. Nearby there are many interesting villages: Tabarka, Utica, Raf-Raf, Ain Draham, Ghar El Melh (Porto Farina), Ras Djebel, Metline, Sounine, Aousdja, Zouaouine, El Alia, Kalaat El An-dalous, Sedjenane.

Tunis - Carthage   2603

It is a short ride from Tunis to **Carthage** on a 1908 wooden train which starts at Place d'Afrique in the center of Tunis and stops at several fashionable seaside resorts.

Get off at Carthage's Hannibal station to visit the birthplace of Hannibal. This city was founded in 814 B.C. and are many outstanding Punic and Roman ruins here. Plays, dances, musical performances and sound and light performances are presented every July and August in both the Roman Theater and in the Baths of Antonin. Other sights: the very large and beautifully decorated 2nd century Roman baths, nearly 700 feet long; The National Museum of Carthage; the ancient Theater, built in a marble quarry. The Basilica of St. Cyprian.Get off at Carthage's Salammbo station to see The Tophet, now an open-air museum, where humans once were sacrificed.

Dep. Tunis (Nord)	Frequent times *except* 01:00 to 03:49
Arr. Carthage	25 minutes later

* * *

Dep. Carthage	Frequent times *except* 01:15 to 03:49
Arr. Tunis (Nord)	25 minutes later

Tunis - Ghardimaou   2601

Dep. Tunis	05:45(1)	10:20 (2)	12:40 (3)	16:30 (3)	18:40 (3)
Arr. Ghardimaou	08:55	13:32	15:50	19:45	21:50

* * *

Dep. Ghardimaou	05:10 (3)	9:50 (3)	12:40 (3)	13:45 (2)	17:35 (3)
Arr. Tunis	08:25	12:58	15:53	16:53	20:47

(1) Reservation required. Has air-conditioned luxury-class. For lunch a supplement is charged. Light refreshments.(2) Reservation required. Has air-conditioned first-class, for which a supplement is charged. Buffet. (3) Has air-conditioned luxury-class, for which a supplement is charged. Light refreshments.

Tunis - Ghardimaou - Algiers

All of these trains require a reservation and are air-conditioned in first-class.

2550+2601		2545	
Dep. Tunis	10:20 (1)	Dep. Algiers	20:30 (2)
Dep. Ghardimaou	14:25	Dep. Constantine	03:29
Arr. Annaba	18:48	Arr. Annaba	06:13
Change trains.		*Change trains.*	
2545		2550+2601	
Dep. Annaba	18:36 (2)	Dep. Annaba	06:13 (1)
Dep. Constantine	23:04	Arr. Ghardimaou	12:32
Arr. Algiers	06:23	Arr. Tunis	16:53

(1) Light refreshments. (2) Supplement charged. Has couchettes. Buffet. Reservation required.

Tunis - Kairouan   2620   (Bus)

Dep. Tunis	09:30	12:00	14:30	17:00	20:00	21:15
Arr. Kairouan	3–4 hours later					

      •   •   •

Dep. Kairouan	02:00	03:30	06:30	07:30	11:30	13:00
Arr. Tunis	3–4 hours later					

Sights in **Kairouan:** The unbelievably beautiful carved wood panels of the Minibar (pulpit) and gilded 9th century tiles in the massive 9th century Great Mosque of Okba Ibn Nafaa, the founder of Kairouan. The fourth holiest city of Islam (after Mecca, Medina and Jerusalem). It is open to non-Muslims. Its roof is supported by 414 columns of marble, porphiry and granite. See the splendid collection of parchment manuscripts of the Koran, 9th century bookbindings, ceramics and glassware in the Museum of Islamic Art.The 17th century Zaouia of Abou Zamaa El Balaoui (Mosque of the Barber). The 9th century reservoirs, Bassins Aghlabides. Narrow streets that are 1,000 years old. The 9th century facade on the Mosque of Three Doors. The Museum of Rugs. The ruins of nearby Rakada.

Sights in **Rakada**: Taste the date cakes, dipped in honey. Famous piled rugs are made here. Also outstanding copperware: coffee and tea pots, jars, plates, cooking pots.

Tunis - Hammamet - Nabeul   2600

A one-day roundtrip from Tunis to Hammamet and/or Nabeul is possible, as these schedules indicate.

Dep. Tunis (East)	07:10 (1)	12:05 (1)	15:30 (4)
Arr. Bir-bou-Rekba	08:08	13:05	16:38
Change trains.			
Dep. Bir-bou-Rekba	08:12	13:10	16:42
Arr. Hammamet	08:17	13:17	16:47
Arr. Nabeul	08:36	13:35	17:07

Dep. Tunis (East)	17:30 (1)	18:05 (2+5)	18:40 (6)
Arr. Bir-bou-Rekba	18:27	-0- (2)	19:50
Change trains.			
Dep. Bir-bou-Rekba	18:30	-0-	19:55
Arr. Hammamet	18:35	19:31	20:00
Arr. Nabeul	18:53	19:51	20:20

Sights in **Hammamet:** This is a popular seashore resort. See: The medieval fortress with its fantastic gardens of flowers and fruit trees.

Sights in **Nabeul:** There are many fine mosaics here.

Dep. Nabeul	05:40 (2+7)	06:25 (7)	07:40	08:45
Dep. Hammamet	05:58	06:44	07:58	09:03
Arr. Bir-bou-Rekba	-0- (2)	06:50	08:04	09:09
Change trains.				
Dep. Bir-bou-Rekba	-0-	06:53 (8)	08:09 (9)	09:13 (1)
Arr. Tunis (East)	07:20	07:59	09:13	10:13

Dep. Nabeul	12:37	16:10	19:00
Dep. Hammamet	12:56	16:27	19:17
Arr. Bir-bou-Rekba	13:02	16:33	19:23
Change trains.			
Dep. Bir-bou-Rekba	14:38 (10)	16:38 (1)	19:53 (1)
Arr. Tunis (East)	15:38	17:38	20:53

(1) Reservation required. Has air-conditioned luxury-class. Light refreshments. (2) Direct train. No train change in Bir-bou-Rekba. (3) Runs Friday and Saturday. (4) Runs daily, except Sundays and holidays. Light refreshments. (5) Runs Monday–Thursday. (6) Light refreshments. (7) Runs daily, expect Sundays and holidays. (8) Reservation required. Runs daily, except Sundays and holidays. Light refreshments. (9) Reservation required. Has air-conditioned luxury-class. Light refreshments. (10) Runs Sundays & Holidays olny.

Tunis - Sousse - El Djem - Sfax - Gabes - Jerba

2600 Train				
Dep. Tunis (East)	07:10 (1)	12:05 (1)	13:05 (1)	14:10 (1+2)
Arr. Sousse	09:15	14:20	15:10	16:20
Dep. Sousse	09:25	-0-	15:20	16:30
Arr. El Djem	10:15	-0-	16:12	17:20
Arr. Sfax	11:18	-0-	17:10	18:18
Dep. Sfax	11:28	-0-	-0-	-0-
Arr. Gabes	13:53	-0-	-0-	-0-
Change to bus. Timetable 2620				
Dep. Gabes	02:15	-0-	-0-	-0-
Arr. Jerba	04:45	-0-	-0-	-0-

Dep. Tunis (East)	15:30 (3)	17:30 (1)	18:40 (4)	21:20 (1)
Arr. Sousse	18:07	19:33	21:21	23:28
Dep. Sousee	-0-	19:43	-0-	23:38
Arr. El Djem	-0-	20:37	-0-	00:25
Arr. Sfax	-0-	21:47	-0-	01:30
Dep. Sfax	-0-	-0-	-0-	02:19
Arr. Gabes	-0-	-0-	-0-	04:38

(1) Reservation required. Has air-conditioned luxury and first-class, for which a supplement is charged. Light refreshments. (2) Early June to mid-October: runs daily. Mid-October to early June: runs Saturday only. (3) Runs daily, except Sundays and holidays. (4) Light refreshments.

Jerba - Gabes - Sfax - El Djem - Sousse - Tunis

2600 Train

Dep. Gabes	-0-	-0-	-0-	-0-
Arr. Sfax	-0-	-0-	-0-	-0-
Dep. Sfax	-0-	-0-	06:00 (2)	12:30 (2+3)
Dep. El Djem	-0-	-0-	06:55	13:24
Dep. Sousse	05:25 (1+2)	06:50 (2)	07:55	14:22
Arr. Tunis (East)	07:59	09:13	10:13	16:44

2620 Bus

Dep. Jerba	-0-	-0-	-0-	20:00
Arr. Gabes	-0-	-0-	-0-	22:30
Change to train. Timetable 2600				
Dep. Gabes	-0-	-0-	15:35(2)	23:10 (2)
Arr. Sfax	-0-	-0-	18:20	01:37
Dep. Sfax	13:30 (2)	-0-	18:30	01:45
Dep. El Djem	14:24	-0-	19:24	02:40
Dep. Sousse	15:22	18:35 (4)	20:21	03:37
Arr. Tunis (East)	17:38	20:53	22:33	05:51

(1) Runs daily, except Sundays and holidays. (2) Reservation required. Has air-conditioned luxury-class and first-class (for which a supplement is charged). Light refreshents. (3) Early June to mid-October: runs daily. Mid-October to early June: runs Sundays and holidays only. (4) Reservation required. Has air-conditioned luxury-class and first-class (for which a supplement is charged).

UGANDA

Children under 3 travel free. Half-fare for children 3–13. Children 14 and over must pay full fare. The 3 classes are called "upper, first and second," which we show as first, second and third-class. First-class coach seats convert into couchette-type sleeping accommodations on overnight trips.

Landlocked Uganda's rail lines radiate from Tororo: northwest to Lira, west to Kasese, and southeast to Nairobi (and on to Mombasa).

Dr. Norbert Brockman, returning to the U.S.A. in 1990 after 5 years in East Africa, advised us that Ugandan trains "are filthy and overbooking is customary." On one ride he took, 12 people were issued a ticket for a 4-person compartment.

Tororo - Jinja - Kampala - Kasese   3285

This line touches the northern shore of Lake Victoria at Kampala.

Service between Kampala and Kasese is subject to local confirmation due to frequent flood damage on this route.

Dep. Tororo	03:05 (1)		Dep. Kasese	16:00 (5)
Dep. Jinja	06:15		Arr. Kampala	06:00 (3)
Arr. Kampala	08:50		*Change trains.*	
Change trains.			Dep. Kampala	16:00 (6)
Dep. Kampala	15:00 (2)		Dep. Jinja	18:52
Arr. Kasese	03:40 (3)		Arr. Tororo	21:45

(1) Runs Wednesday only. (2) Runs Monday, Wednesday and Friday. Has first-class seats that convert to couchettes. (3) Day 2. (4) Third-class only. (5) Runs Tuesday, Thursday and Saturday. Has first-class seats that convert to couchettes. (6) Runs Tuesday, Thursday and Sunday. (7) This arrival requires laying-over in Kampala in order to continue on to Jinja.

Sights in **Kampala:** The capital of Uganda. See the tombs of the kings of Baganda. The collection of African musical instruments in the Uganda Museum. Several Hindu temples. Rubaga Cathedral. The white Kibuli Mosque. The "apocalypse" ceiling of St. Francis' Chapel at Makerere University. The Botanical Garden in **Entebbe**, 20 miles away.

Tororo - Nairobi - Mombasa   3270

All of these trains have first-class coach seats that convert to berths.

Dep. Tororo	N/A (1)		Dep. Mombasa	19:00 (6)
Dep. Malaba	17:00 (2)		Arr. Nairobi	08:30 (7)
Arr. Nairobi	08:25 (3)		*Change trains.*	
Change trains.			Dep. Nairobi	15:00 (8)
Dep. Nairobi	19:00 (6)		Arr. Malaba	07:50 (1+5)
Arr. Mombasa	08:06 (5)		Arr. Tororo	N/A (1)

(1) Service to and from Uganda (Malaba - Tororo and v.v.) was suspended prior to 1981. There is said to be taxi service 18km (11 miles) on the road Tororo–Malaba and v.v. (2) Runs Wednesday, Saturday and Sunday. Restaurant car. Reservation required. (3) Day 2 from Malaba. (4) Runs daily. Light refreshments. (5) Day 2 from Nairobi. (6) Runs daily. Restaurant car. Reservation required. (7) Day 2 from Mombasa. (8) Runs Friday and Saturday. Restaurant car. Reservation required.

UPPER VOLTA (BURKINA FASO)

Landlocked Upper Volta has one train route, from Ouagadougou to Bobo Dioulasso, and on to Abidjan (Ivory Coast). For schedules, see "Treichville–Bobo Dioulasso- Ouagadougou" under Ivory Coast.

ZAIRE

Children under 3 travel free. Half-fare for children 3–9. Children 10 and over must pay full fare.

Zaire's trains have 4 classes: de luxe, first, second and third. Even de luxe and first-class are not comparable to European standards.

This country's rail system is Y-shaped, with Lubumbashi at the bottom of the vertical South-North line and Kamina at the point that one route goes northwest to Ilebo, where there is boat service to Kinshasa and train facility from there to the port of Pointe Noire on the coastline of Congo.

Another route goes northeast from Kamina to Kalemie (on the west shore of Lake Tanganyika), where there is boat service across the lake to Kigoma in Tanzania, and trains from Kigoma to Dar es-Salaam.

Lubumbashi - Tenke - Kamina 3201

Dep. Lubumbashi	09:00 (1)	12:00 (3)	22:00 (5)		
Dep. Tenke	17:15	21:40	23:20 (6)		
Arr. Kamina	06:00 (2)	12:30 (4)	04:20 (7)		

• • •

Dep. Kamina	04:30 (8)	05:20 (9)	08:50 (10)	14:20 (11)	16:00 (10+12)
Dep. Tenke	19:30	17:30	21:50	05:30 (4)	04:50 (4)
Arr. Lubumbashi	06:05 (4)	01:10 (4)	06:05 (4)	15:55	15:55

(1) Runs Monday, Thursday and Friday. Has deluxe, first and second-class seats. Also has couchettes. Restaurant car. (2) Day 2. Arrives 05:10 on Tuesday. (3) Runs Wednesday and Saturday. Restaurant car. (4) Day 2. (5) Runs Sunday only. (6) Day 2 from Lubumbashi. Runs Monday only. (7) Day 4 after departing Lubumbashi on Sunday. (8) Runs Thursday only. Restaurant car. (9) Runs Wednesday only. Has deluxe and first-class seats. Also has couchettes. Restaurant car. (10) Runs Monday only. Has deluxe and first-class seats. Also has couchettes. Restaurant car. (11) Runs Sunday only. Restaurant car. (12) Plus another departure from Kamina at 18:00 Wednesday, departing Tenke 04:00 Thursday, arriving Lubumbashi 23:30 Thursday.

Kamina - Kalemie - Kigoma - Tabora - Dar es Salaam

Kalemie, on the west shore of Lake Tanganyika, is a foreign trade transport center. This is the trip into Tanzania.

3200			*3300*	
Dep. Kamina	08:00 (1)		Dep. Kigoma	17:00 (5)
Arr. Kalemie	06:20 (2)		Arr. Tabora	04:30 (6)
Change to boat.			*Change trains.*	
3215			Dep. Tabora	07:25 (7)
Dep. Kalemie	16:30 (3)		Dep. Dodoma	18:40 (7)
Arr. Kigoma	07:00 (4)		Dep. Morogoro	02:15 (8)
Change to train.			Arr. Dar es Salaam	08:50 (9)

(1) Runs Saturday only. Has both de luxe and first-class seats. Also has couchettes. Restaurant car. (2) Arrives on Sunday. (3) Runs Monday only. Restaurant on ship. Reservation required. (4) Arrives on Tuesday. (5) Runs Tuesday, Thursday, Friday and Sunday. Reservation required. (6) Day 2 from Kigoma. (7) Runs Wednesday, Friday, Saturday and Monday. Restaurant car. Reservation required. (8) Runs Thursday, Saturday, Sunday and Tuesday. Restaurant car. (9) Day 3 from Kigoma. Day 2 from Tabora.

ZAMBIA

Children under 3 travel free. Half-fare for children 3–15. Children 16 and over must pay full fare. First-class seats are upholstered. Second-class seats have leather covering.

On a map of landlocked Zambia, the outline of its rail system is a sloppy "Y," with Livingstone in the south at the bottom of the "Y." The right-arm runs east from Kapiri Mposhi to Tunduma and on into Tanzania. This is Zambia's portion of the Tanzam Railway, which terminates at the port of Dar es Salaam.

The left-arm of the "Y" goes from Kapiri Mposhi to Ndola and on into Zaire. A small spur runs off this route, from Ndola to Kitwe.

South of Livingstone is the border with Zimbabwe and a connection (before 1989) to Victoria Falls, and on to Bulawayo, a junction for continuing southwest to South Africa. There is also service from Bulawayo northeast to Harare (Salisbury). The train service to Mozambique has been "temporarily" suspended since 1977.

Livingstone - Victoria Falls - Bulawayo - Harare (Salisbury)

3453		3451	
Dep. Livingstone	15:30 (1)	Dep. Harare	21:00 (4+8)
Arr. Victoria Falls	16:00	Arr. Bulawayo	06:40
Change trains.		*Change trains.*	
Dep. Victoria Falls	18:30 (2)	3453	
Arr. Bulawayo	07:05 (3)	Dep. Bulawayo	19:00 (2)
Change trains.		Arr. Victoria Falls	07:00 (3)
3451		*Change trains.*	
Dep. Bulawayo	21:00 (4+7)	Dep. Victoria Falls	10:00 (1)
Arr. Harare	06:55	Arr. Livingstone	10:30

(1)E-class: hard upholstered seating. (2) Runs daily. First and second-class seats convert to couchettes. Buffet. Reservation required. (3) Day 2. (4) Runs Friday and Sunday. Third-class only. Reservation required. (5) Runs daily. First and second class seats convert to couchettes. Light refreshments.

Sights in **Livingstone:** This is the most popular tourist center in Zambia. See the flowers and aviary in Barotse Gardens. The Livingstone Museum's archaeological, historical and ethnological exhibits. Traditional dances, performed at Maramba Cultural Center. Visit the Railway Museum.

Nearby, Lake Kariba, Livingstone Game Park, Kafue National Park and Wankie National Park. Take a cruise on the Zambesi River.

The most important sight here is seen by taking an excursion to the nearby majestic Victoria Falls, which are more than 5,500 feet wide and have a minimum drop of 355 feet. The falls are the border between Zambia and Zimbabwe (formerly Rhodesia). There is a great view from Knife Edge Bridge. However, the best view is from the Zimbabwe side, looking at the two-thirds of the falls owned by Zambia.

Sights in **Victoria Falls:** See notes about Victoria Falls.

Livingstone - Lusaka - Kapiri Mposhi - Dar es Salaam

Dr. Norbert Brockman, returning to the U.S.A. in 1990 after 5 years in East Africa, advised us that the Zambian portion on the Tanzam Railway (Livingstone–Kapiri Mposhi) is superior to the Tanzanian portion (Kapiri Mposhi to Dar es-Salaam). Better food and service. Also cleaner conditions.

Much wildlife can be seen as the train passes through **Mkumi National Park**.

The train climbs as high as 6,000 feet altitude during this ride. If you do not like curry and local maize cuisine, it is advisable to bring your own food for this 37–43 hours of travel.

3400

Dep. Livingstone	09:00 (1)	
Dep. Lusaka	21:05	
Arr. Kapiri Mposhi (ZR)	02:50 (2)	

*Change trains **and railstations** (**about 1 mile apart**).*
3301

Dep. Kapiri Mposhi (New)	-0-	13:45 (4)
Dep. Tunduma	-0-	08:24 (5)
Arr. Dar es Salaam (TAZ)	-0-	06:48 (6)

* * *

Dep. Dar es Salaam (TAZ)	17:34 (4)	-0-
Dep. Tunduma	15:48 (7)	-0-
Arr. Kapiri Mposhi (New)	08:38 (8)	-0-

*Change trains **and railstations** (**about 1 mile apart**).*
3400

Dep. Kapiri Mposhi (ZR)	02:16 (3)	
Dep. Lusaka	08:00	
Arr. Livingstone	19:40	

(1) Reservation required. Runs daily. Reservation required. Carries a sleeping car. Has first and second-class coaches. Light refreshments. (2) Day 2 from Livingstone. (3) Reservation required. Supplement charged. Runs daily. Carries a sleeping car. Has first and second-class coaches. Light refreshments. (4) Supplement charged. Runs Tuesday and Friday. Restaurant car. (5) Day 2 from Kapiri Mposhi. (6) Day 3 from Kapiri Mposhi. (7) Day 2 from Dar es Salaam. (8) Day 3 from Dar es Salaam.

Sights in **Lusaka:** The capital of Zambia. Although the population is almost one million, the hotels and restaurants here are very primitive. See the large copper cross over the altar in the Anglican Cathedral of the Holy Cross. Luburma Central Market. The Tobacco Auction Floor. The 8-acre Twickenham Road Archaeological Site in **Olympia Park,** a suburb.

Nearby, Munda Wanga Park and Botanical Gardens, Kafue Gorge. The Ayrshire Farm Rock Engravings national monument. Blue Lagoon National Park.

Kapiri Mopshi - Ndola - Lubumbashi

This is the route into Zaire.

All of these trains require reservation and have light refreshments.

3400
Dep. Kapiri Mposhi	05:13 (1)	13:24 (3)
Arr. Ndola	09:50	16:35

Change to bus.
3410
Dep. Ndola	N/A (2)	N/A (2)
Arr. Lubumbashi	N/A	N/A

• • •

Dep. Lubumbashi	N/A (2)	N/A (2)
Arr. Ndola	N/A	N/A

Change to train.
3400
Dep. Ndola	08:55 (4)	22:11 (1)
Arr. Kapiri Mposhi	11:49	02:06

(1) Runs daily. Reservation required. (2) Times have not been available since 1980.

Livingstone - Mulobezi 3401

This is a spur off the Victoria Falls-Kapiri Mposhi line.

Both of these trains are third-class only.

Dep. Livingstone	10:30 Sat.		Dep. Mulobezi	08:00 Sun.
Arr. Mulobezi	22:50		Arr. Livingstone	21:10

ZIMBABWE
(FORMERLY RHODESIA)

Children under 3 travel free. Half-fare for children 3–11. Children 12 and over must pay full fare. There are 3 classes of seats. First-class compartments convert to 4 berths at night and second-class to 6 berths. There is a charge for bedding.

There are rail connections between Harare (formerly Salisbury) in landlocked Zimbabwe and Zambia, Mozambique, Botswana and South Africa.

Sights in **Harare** (formerly Salisbury): The capital. See the Queen Victoria Memorial Library and Museum. The collection of talented African artisans in the National Gallery, open Monday-Friday 09:00–17:00. The more than 750 species of plants indigenous to Zimbabwe, in the National Botanic Gardens.

Sights in **Bulawayo:** The Railway Museum. The National Museum. Nearby, Cecil Rhodes' Tomb in the granite Matapo Hills, where cave paintings made 2,000 to 4,000 years ago can be viewed. The 75,000 specimens of mammals in the Natural History Museum. The 17th century Khami Ruins.

Sights in **Victoria Falls:** These spectacular falls are more than 5,500 feet wide and have a maximum drop of 355 feet, twice that of Niagara Falls. This is the border between Zimbabwe (formerly Rhodesia) and Zambia. The best view is from the Zimbabwe side, looking at the two-thirds of the falls that is in Zambia. Watch local artists carve soapstone at the African Craft Village.

Harare (Salisbury) - Bulawayo - Mafikeng - Johannesburg

The route to Botswana and South Africa.

3451
Dep. Harare	08:00 (1)	20:00 (2)	21:00 (4)
Arr. Bulawayo	16:10	05:35 (3)	06:40 (3)
Change trains. 3475			
Dep. Bulawayo	10:30 (5)	N/A (7)	
Arr. Gaborone	00:15 (6)	06:30 (3)	
Dep. Ramatlhabana	03:30	-0-	
Arr. Mafikeng	04:00 (5)	-0-	
Change trains. 3518			
Dep. Mafikeng	04:30 (6)	20:45 (8)	22:52 (8)
Arr. Johannesburg	10:35	04:55 (3)	05:22 (3)

(1) Runs daily. Second and third-class only. Buffet. (2) Runs Friday and Sunday. Third-class only. (3) Day 2. (4) Runs daily. Has first-class coaches. Light refreshments. (5) Reservation required. Runs Thursday only. Direct train to Johannesburg. No train change in Mafikeng. Has a first-class coach. Buffet. (6) Day 2 from Bulawayo. Runs Friday only. (7) Time was not available in 1993. Runs daily. Carries an air-conditioned first-class coach. Buffet from 21:00. (8) Runs Sunday only. Has a first-class coach.

CHAPTER 11

ASIA

BANGLADESH

Children under 3 travel free. Half-fare for children 3–9. Children 10 and over must pay full fare. Bangladesh offers 6 classes of train space: air-conditioned, executive, first-class, second-class, economy and third-class (which is tantamount to sixth-class). Air-conditioned class converts to 2 berths at night and first-class converts to 4 berths. "Express" and "Mail" trains provide better accommodation and charge higher fares.

The principal cities in Bangladesh having train service are Chittagong and Dhaka.

Chittagong

This is Bangladesh's largest port. See the slab believed to bear the imprint of Mohammed's foot, in the Qadam Mubarik Mosque. The Chandanpura Shahi Jame Mosque. The tortoises at the tomb of Hazrat Bayazid Bostami.

Dhaka (Dacca)

The nearly 400-year old capital of Bangladesh. See the 17th Century Lalbagh Fort and the tomb of Pari Bibi. The 4 bazaars in the Chowk (old market). The 17th century Chowk Mosque. Other notable mosques: The Star, Kar Talab, Baidul Mukarram, and Sat Gumbad. The collection of coins, paintings, and stone, wood and metal sculptures in the Museum of Antiquities. There are many interesting archaeological digs at **Mainamati** and **Lalmai**, 5 miles west of **Comilla**.

Dhaka (Dacca) - Comilla - Chittagong   6602

All of these trains charge a supplement.

Dep. Dhaka	06:30 (1)	08:00 (2+3)	09:00 (1)	12:20 (1+5)
Dep. Comilla	09:38	-0-	13:28	16:30
Arr. Chittagong	12:30	13:05	17:15	20:00

* * *

Dep. Chittagong	06:40 (2)	07:45 (1+3)	09:05 (1)	12:05 (4+6)
Dep. Comilla	-0-	10:31	12:35	14:59
Arr. Dhaka	11:45	13:55	17:35	19:10

(1) Has first-class. Buffet. (2) Reservation required. Has air-conditioned class and first-class. Restau-

rant car. (3) Runs daily, except Friday. (4) Has air-conditioned class and first-class with seats that convert to berths. (5) Plus other departures from Dhaka at 15:00 (1+3), 16:30 (2) and 22:30 (4), arriving Chittagong 20:10, 21:35 and 07:15. (6) Plus other departures from Chittagong at 13:30 (1), 15:10 (2+3) (4), arriving Dhaka 19:35, 20:15.

BURMA (MYANMAR)

Children under 3 travel free. Half-fare for children 3–9. Children 10 and over must pay full fare.

The 3 classes on Burmese trains are: upper-class (3 upholstered seats abreast), first-class (4 upholstered seats abreast), and ordinary-class (5 wood seats abreast), which we show as *first, second and third-class*.

Burma does not publish timetables. Those timetables that are posted at railstations are in Burmese script, including the numerals.

An English-speaking duty officer at the Information Office in Rangoon's railstation will assist foreigners with ticket purchases and will provide information about train connections.

Tickets may be purchased up to 3 days in advance of travel date, and it is usually necessary to make reservations 2 days in advance for first-class space on the Yangon (Rangoon)–Mandalay ride. Lower class space is very unsatisfactory.

Only tea and soft drinks are served on Burma's trains. Vendors at many stations sell food. This is Burmese food and does not appeal to all Westerners. It is advisable to bring your own food and a container of water. Both Burma Airways and Tourist Burma's office in Yangon (Rangoon) arrange tours of Burma and a 3-hour guided tour of Yangon (Rangoon).

Yangon (Rangoon)

The 320-foot high stupa of the enormous 2400-year old Shwe Dagon Pagoda is completely covered with gold leaf. Value of the 8,688 foot-square gold plates on the plantian bud at the top has been computed at over $2,500,000. There are 5,448 diamonds and more than 2,000 other precious stones at the top of the bud.

A 25-ton bell is located at one corner of the platform. The British took the bell, as a prize of war, and dropped it into the Yangon (Rangoon) River as they were attempting to load it onto a ship. Unable to raise the bell, the British abandoned it. Burmese workers raised it by tying enough bamboo poles to it until it floated.

The Shwe Dagon is said to be the most revered pagoda of the world's one billion Buddhists.

In central Yangon (Rangoon), see: The 2300-year old Sule Pagoda. The National Museum. Burmese students learning their dances at the State School of music and Drama in Jubilee Hall. Bogyoke Market on Park Road, only a few minutes' walk from the town center, has many shops and stalle selling handcrafts. Also visit the Zoo, which has an excellent collection of monkeys. North of the city's center is the contemporary Kaba Aye Pagoda, built in 1956. In nearby **Regu**, a 2-hour auto ride, there is a 180-foot long reclining Buddha.

Yangon - Mandalay   6700

The 06:00 departures are usually less crowded than the other departures.

All of these trains have first-class space.

Dep. Yangon	06:00	11:45	19:30 (1)	21:00 (1)
Arr. Mandalay	20:00	07:15	10:35	10:40

• • •

Dep. Mandalay	06:00	15:15	18:35 (2)	21:00 (1)
Arr. Yangon	20:00	05:20 (3)	08:20	10:40

(1) Carries a sleeping car. (2) Reservation required. (3) Couchettes.

Sights in **Mandalay:** This is one of Burma's youngest cities, existing since only 1857. Great Buddhist carvings here. Fine Burmese timber architecture. Many interesting monasteries, beautiful small pagodas.

Mandalay - Pagan   6720 Bus

Dep. Mandalay	04:00	Dep. Pagan	04:00
Arr. Pagan	13:00	Arr. Mandalay	13:00

Sights in **Pagan**: Once a fantastic city of many millions and called City of Four Million Pagodas, before Kublai Khan sacked it in the 13th century. Now, there are splendid ruins of more than 5,000 structures to see: great temples and pagodas.

Here are schedules for 3 other long train trips from Mandalay:

Mandalay - Lashio   6701

This route has fine scenery.

Dep. Manadalay	04:45	Dep. Lashio	05:30
Arr. Lashio	19:00	Arr. Mandalay	19:55

Mandalay - Myitkyina   6701

All of these trains have first-class space. All arrivals are day 2.

| Dep. Mandalay | 15:00 | 16:00 (1) | | Dep. Myitkyina | 07:00 | 08:00 (1) |
| Arr. Myitkyina | 13:10 | 16:00 | | Arr. Mandalay | 04:15 | 08:00 |

(1) Carries sleeping car.

Mandalay - Thazi - Shwenyaung - Taunggyi   6700

All of these trains have first-class space.

Dep. Mandalay	06:00		Dep. Shweyaung	10:00	
Arr. Thazi	08:28		Arr. Thazi	20:20	
Change trains.			*Change trains.*		
Dep. Thazi	09:00		Dep. Thazi	03:34	05:36 (1)
Arr. Shwenyaung	16:10		Arr. Mandalay	08:30	08:20

(1) Reservation required.

It is an 11-mile taxi ride from **Shwenyaung** to **Taunggyi**, a hill station located at 4,712 feet.

HONG KONG

Children under 3 travel free. Half-fare for children 3–9. Children 10 and over must pay full fare.

This country owns the Kowloon-Canton Railway, which operates 40 passenger trains daily between Kowloon and Lo Wu, the border station for non-direct rail trips into the People's Republic of China. Nearly 2,000,000 people make this ride every year. There is ferry service from Hong Kong to Kowloon.

Prior to 1979, it had always been necessary to go through customs formalities in Lo Wu and then walk across the bridge spanning the Shum Chun River to the Chinese railstation on the north side of the river before boarding a second train in Shenzhen and proceeding to Guangzhou (Canton).

Since 1979, several trains per day make a direct ride from Hong Kong to Guangzhou and v.v., without requiring passengers to change trains in Lo Wu. These direct trains are operated by the People's Republic of China and are first-class only.

Hong Kong

See the art objects in Fung Ping Shan Museum at the University of Hong Kong. Take the cruise to Yaumati Typhoon Shelter to see the "floating people" who live their entire lives on small boats. Go on the bus tour to Aberdeen and several interesting villages. The bus also stops at the unique Tiger Balm Gardens.

Visit the Sung Dynasty village at Laichikok in Kowloon to see the architecture, costumes and food of the 10th–12th centuries. There are 3-hour guided group tours there Monday-Friday 10:00–13:00 (lunch included), 12:30–15:30 (lunch included), 15:00–18:00 (light snacks), and 17:30–20:00 (dinner). The village is also open to individuals on Saturdays and Sundays 12:30–17:00.

Eat at some of the 27 restaurants in the one-square-block called Food Street, in the Causeway Bay section everything from Sichuan to Cantonese, Taiwanese, Peking, Vietnamese, Indian, Pakistani, Indonesian, Japanese, Malaysan, Singapore, Sri Lanka...and European food. Also visit the complex of food stalls located in Kowloon between the Star Ferry Terminal and the Peninsula Hotel. Shop for aphrodisiacs in the alleys behind Queen's Road Central.

See the 7-story-high Buddha (said to be the largest outdoor bronze Buddha in the world) on Lantau Island. The $2(U.S.) round trip ferry leaves from the pier in Central District.

Buses on Lantau take visitors from the Ferry Terminal there to the mountain-top Po Lin Monastery, near the Buddha. The mountain and coastal views from there are breathtaking.

Visitors can explore the island on their own or take a guided tour. There are many miles of marked mountain trails and stone paths, several 18th century stone forts and a tea plantation.

Kowloon (Hong Kong) - Guangzhou (Canton) 5400

These trains require reservation, are first-class only, are air-conditioned and have light refreshments unless designated otherwise.

Dep. Kowloon (H. Hom)	07:50	08:35	12:25	14:10	16:21	17:56
Arr. Guangzhou	10:30	11:15	15:05	16:50	18:51	20:26

•   •   •

Dep. Guangzhou	08:15	10:00	12:15	14:15	16:13	18:00
Arr. Kowloon (H. Hom)	10:55	12:45	14:45	16:45	18:53	20:40

INDIA

Children under 5 travel free. Half-fare for children 5–11. Children 12 and over must pay full fare. Every day, more than 10,000,000 people ride India's 11,000 trains, connecting 7,085 railstations. This is Asia's largest railway system.

The 5 classes of space on Indian Railways are: first-class air-conditioned, second-class air-conditioned, air-conditioned chair car, first-class, and second-class. First-class air-conditioned converts at night to 2 berths, second-class air-conditioned to 4 berths. First-class (not air-conditioned) compartments convert at night to 4, 5 or 6 berths. Second-class sleepercoaches convert into sleeping bunks between 21:00 and 06:00.

Reservations are recommended for all overnight and long-distance journeys. Foreign tourists can reserve air-conditioned classes and ordinary first-class space up to 180 days in advance of travel date. To determine which of the 7 rail offices in India you need contact for advance reservations, first communicate your itinerary to any Government of India Tourist Office. That office will advise you whether to direct your reservation order to the Central, Eastern, North Eastern, Northern, South Central, South Eastern or Western offices of Indian Railways.

Breaking of a journey at any station en route is permitted with single journey tickets when the entire trip is more than 200 miles, at the rate of one day for every 100 miles. However, the first break of journey cannot be made until the passenger has traveled at least 150 miles from his or her starting station.

There are restaurants at important railstations. The leading passenger trains have restaurant cars which offer both Indian and Western food. India Government Tourist Offices provide a "Tourist Timetable."

INDIA'S TRAIN PASS

Indrail Pass. Unlimited rail travel. Available to citizens of countries other than India and to those Indians residing outside India who hold valid passports. The bearer is not required to pay for reservations *but must make reservations. You'll need a xerox copy of your passport to get a train pass. There's also a $15 service charge per pass.*

Even when full use of the pass is not made, having it avoids having to stand in long lines to buy tickets. Furthermore, on many trains that are ostensibly "sold-out," authorities somehow find seats for pass-holders.

Don't even consider the second-class pass. That class is usually so crowded that it is extremely uncomfortable. On the other hand, the highest-priced pass (air-conditioned) is frequently a waste of money because many routes don't have air-conditioned coaches.

The great advantage to the first-class pass is that both reservations and sleeping compartments are easier to obtain with it than with the second-class pass. Also, passengers having it can use comfortable first-class waiting rooms in the railstations.

The 1996 prices in U.S. dollars (children shown in parenthesis) are:

	Air-conditioned		First-class		Second-class	
1 day	$ 78	(39)	$ 35	(18)	$ 15	(8)
7 days	270	(135)	135	(68)	70	(35)
15 days	330	(165)	165	(83)	80	(40)
21 days	400	(200)	200	(100)	90	(45)
30 days	500	(250)	250	(125)	110	(55)
60 days	720	(360)	360	(180)	165	(83)

Sold by Hari World Travel. In the U.S.A.: 30 Rockefeller Plaza, Room 21, New York, NY 10112. Telephone: (212) 957-3000. In Canada: Royal York Hotel, 100 Front St. W., Toronto, Ont. M5J 1E3. Telephone: (416) 366-2000.

India's 4 principal cities (Bombay, Calcutta, Delhi and Madras) are connected by rail routes.

Bombay

This is a seaport. See the Zoo and the Victoria and Albert Museum at Victoria Gardens. The Mahatma Phule Market. Jehangir Art Gallery. The collection of Chinese jade and porcelain and the Tata Collection of paintings at The Prince of Wales Museum. The Rajabai Tower. Elephant Caves. Gateway of India.

Calcutta

A major seaport, although it is 100 miles from the Bay of Bengal. See the many alleys with shops called Bara Bazaar. The stone carvings in the India Museum. The large Nakhoda Mosque. The Botanical Gardens. The Kali Temple. The Jain Temple. The white tigers at the Zoo. The assortment of both great art objects and junk in the Marble Palace. The Victoria Memorial. Howrah Bridge. Belur Math. The National Library. The Philatelic Museum.

Delhi

See the 16th century Lodi Tombs. The Great Mosque. Teen Murtis House, once the home of Nehru and his daughter, Indira Gandhi. The Pearl Mosque. The 2200-year old Ashoka Pillar. The 17th century Red Fort. Humayun's Tomb. The 13th century 238-foot high, red sandstone Qutub Minar Tower.

The Zoo. The National Museum. For shopping, stroll Connaught Place and see the marvelous jewelry assortment (emeralds, diamonds, rubies and sapphires) in both the leading stores and at the Sundar Nagar Market. Visit the Central Cottage Industries Emporium on Janpath and the silver and cloth stores on Chandni Chowk.

The 43 locomotives and 17 coaches in New Delhi's enormous Rail Transport Museum (closed Monday), including the world's oldest (1855) and still operational steam locomotive. This museum also has a model train for children and a floating restaurant.

Madras

Visit the archaeological exhibit at the Government Museum on Pantheon Road near the Egmore railstation, open 09:00–17:00 daily except Fridays and holidays. In the first of the Museum's 3 buildings, see the miniature paintings of the Moguls and court processions. Also, 18th and 19th century carved ivory miniatures.

The second building, the Bronze Gallery, has 9th century Chola sculpture masterpieces. The third building displays ivory temple models, weapons, musical instruments, votive toys and wood carvings. Its major exhibit is 3rd and 4th century granite sculptures.

See the collection of weapons, chinaware and costumes in the Fort Museum. The view of the harbor from the top of the lighthouse. The fine beach. The South Indian bronzes at the National Art Gallery. Fort St. George, the oldest Anglican church in the Orient. San Thome Basilica, where the remains of the apostle Thomas are said to lie.

Bombay - Ahmadabad   6067

Dep. Bombay (Cen.)	05:45	07:45	13:40 (1)	17:10 (2)	20:10 (2+3)
Arr. Ahmadabad	15:05	19:35	21:20	01:32	05:20

Sights in **Ahmadabad**: Free guides are provided by the city, at Lal Darwaja, a few blocks from the Manek Chowk Bazaar. Spices, incense, brass, copper, hand-painted cottons, silver, jewelry, fruits and vegetables are sold in the streets of that bazaar. See the collection of rare 11th-16th century miniature paintings in the Sanskar Kendra Cultural Center.

The terra-cotta sculptures at the National Institute of Design. The exhibits of musical instruments, ceremonial costumes and jewelry at the Shreyas Folk Museum. The students practicing traditional dance, music and puppetry at the Darpana Academy. The 250 beautifully carved pillars at the lovely 15th century Jumma Masjid Mosque. The exquisite filligree marble windows at Sidi Said's Mosque. The promenades, boating, gardens and museums at **Lake Kankaria**.

Visit the **Sabarmati Ashram**, a colony of small cottages Gandhi established in 1915 and where he worked to promote Indian independence for the next 15 years.

Dep. Ahmadabad	03:30 (2)	05:10 (1)	07:15	22:00 (1)	22:40 (2)
Arr. Bombay (Cen.)	12:15	12:45	16:25	06:40	08:05

(1) Runs daily except Wednesday. Has both first and second-class air-conditioned compartments that convert to berths. (2) Has second-class air-conditioned compartments that convert to berths. (3) Plus another departure from Bombay at 21:25 (1), arriving Ahmadabad 06:35.

Bombay - Allahabad   6080

All arrivals are on day 2.

Dep. Bombay (Vict.)	05:00 (1)	06:40 (2)	11:25 (3)	21:00 (3)	23:55 (4)
Arr. Allahabad	05:10	08:15	11:10	23:15	23:50

Sights in **Allahabad** (City of God): The confluence of the Ganges, Jamuna and mythical Sarawati rivers. See the Pillar of Asoka at the 16th century fort. The Jami Masjid (Great Mosque). The Museum. The beautiful Victorian Nehru House.

Dep. Allahabad	08:20 (3)	11:15 (4)	15:05 (4)	17:00	21:05 (5)
Arr. Bombay (Vict.)	11:50 (3)	11:25	15:15	20:00 (2)	23:35

(1) Supp. charged (exc. Sat) . Runs Monday, Wednesday, Thursday. (2) Depart/Arrive Bombay's Dadar station. (3) Depart/Arrive Bombay's Kurla railstation. Has second-class air-conditioned compartments that convert to berths. (4) Has second-class air-conditioned compartments that convert to berths. (5) Supplement charged. Runs Sunday only.

Bombay - Bangalore - Mysore

Bangalore - Mysore - Bangalore is an easy one-day excursion.

None of these trains are air-conditioned, unless designated otherwise.

6010
Dep. Bombay	-0-	17:50	20:45 (2)			
Arr. Miraj	-0-	05:00 (1)	06:10 (1)			
Change trains. Table 6155						
Dep. Miraj	-0-	-0-	13:10			
Arr. Bangalore	-0-	-0-	08:30 (3)			
Change trains. Table 6172						
Dep. Bangalore	06:00	07:00	14:05	16:45	18:20	23:45
Arr. Mysore	09:20	10:00	17:55	20:30	22:00	04:15

Sights in **Bangalore**: The palace of the Maharajah of Mysore. The 18th century Lal Bagh botanic garden. The Mysore Government Museum. The **Nandi Hill Station**, summer resort, 38 miles from here. The nearby **Hesaraghatta Lake**.

Sights in **Mysore**: Brindavn Gardens, at a dam, beautifully lighted at night.

Dep. Mysore	06:00	10:00	14:00	16:25	19:20	23:05
Arr. Bangalore	09:20	13:35	15:55	20:15	21:50	04:15
Change trains. Table 6155						
Dep. Bangalore	-0-	-0-	19:25	-0-		
Arr. Miraj	-0-	-0-	14:30 (4)	-0-		
Change trains. Table 6010						
Dep. Miraj	-0-	-0-	22:15 (2)	23:40		
Arr. Bombay	-0-	-0-	07:50 (5)	12:05 (5)		

(1) Day 2. from Bombay. (2) Has second-class air-conditioned compartments that converts to berths. (3) Day 3 from Bombay. (4) Day 2 from Mysore. (5) Day 3 from Mysore.

Bombay - Calcutta   6105

Dep. Bombay (Vic.)	06:05 (1)	20:15 (3)	21:30 (5)
Arr. Calcutta (How.)	15:15 (2)	08:10 (4)	15:00 (4)
Dep. Calcutta (How.)	11:20 (1+5)	12:30 (1)	20:15 (3)
Arr. Bombay (Vic.)	06:00 (2)	21:45 (2)	07:40 (4)

(1) Supplement charged. Has second-class air-conditioned compartments that convert to berths. (2) Day 2. (3) Has first-class and second-class air-conditioned compartments that convert to berths. Restaurant car. (4) Day 3. (5) Not air-conditioned.

Bombay - Madras   6095

All of these trains have second-class air-conditioned compartments that convert to berths.

Dep. Bombay (Victoria)	-0-	-0-	23:15
Dep. Bombay (Dadar)	14:25	19:50 (2)	23:30
Arr. Madras (Cen.)	16:35 (1)	20:00 (1)	05:45 (3)
Dep. Madras (Cen.)	07:00 (4)	09:15	22:20
Arr. Bombay (Dadar)	07:05 (1)	12:00 (1)	04:28 (3)
Arr. Bombay (Victoria)	-0-	-0-	04:50

(1) Day 2. (2) Supplement charged. Runs daily, except Monday and Saturday. (3) Day 3. (4) Supplement charged. Runs daily, except Wednesday and Friday.

Bombay - New Delhi   6070

All of these trains charge a supplement. All arrivals are "Day 2."

Dep. Bombay (Central)	08:25 (1)	11:20 (2)	16:55 (3)	21:10 (2)
Arr. New Delhi	04:45	10:35	09:55	19:00
Dep. New Delhi	08:10 (2)	16:05 (3)	16:55 (2)	21:45 (1)
Arr. Bombay (Central)	06:00	08:35	10:10	18:10

(1) From Bombay: Runs Monday, Thursday, Friday and Sunday. From New Delhi: Runs Tuesday, Wednesday, Friday and Saturday. Has second-class air-conditioned seats that convert to berths. (2) Has both first and second-class air-conditioned seats that convert to berths. Restaurant car. (3) Reservation required. Restaurant car. From Bombay: Runs daily except Monday. From New Delhi: Runs daily except Tuesday. Has both first and second-class air-conditioned seats that convert to berths and also has an air-conditioned chair car. (4) Runs Daily except Wednesday. Reservation required.

Bombay - Patna

6080

Dep. Bombay (Dadar)	05:18 (1)	06:40	11:25 (3+4)	21:25 (4)	23:55 (4+5)
Arr. Allahabad	05:10 (2)	08:15 (2)	11:10 (2)	20:45 (2)	23:35 (2)

Change trains. Table 6060

Dep. Allahabad	04:20 (6)	10:50	19:50	22:45	23:55 (7)
Arr. Patna	11:45	18:25	04:15	05:52	07:50 (8)

Sights in **Patna**: Many fine mosques. The collection of rare Arabic and Persian manuscripts in the Khudabuksh Oriental Library. An important Sikh temple.

Dep. Patna	05:00 (6)	07:25	13:30 (6)	23:45 (7)
Arr. Allahabad	10:55	15:45	20:05	07:45 (2)

Change trains. Table 6080

Dep. Allahabad	11:10 (7)	17:00	21:05 (9)	08:20 (7)
Arr. Bombay (Dadar)	10:53 (2)	20:00 (2)	23:03 (2)	11:50 (10)

(1) Supplement charged. Runs Monday, Wednesday, Thursday. (2) Day 2. (3) Departs from Bombay's Kurla railstation. (4) Has second-class air-conditioned seats that convert to berths. (5) Departs from Bombay's Victoria railstation. (6) Supplement charged. Has second-class air-conditioned seats. (7) Has second-class air-conditioned seats that convert to berths. (8) Day 3 from Bombay. (9) Supplement charged. Runs Sunday only. (10) Day 3 from Patna.

Bombay - Pune   6095

The first double-deck passenger train in India started operating in 1978 on the 115-mile long Bombay–Pune line. Its coaches seat 148 (versus 90 in ordinary second-class coaches).

From Bombay to Pune, the train climbs 2,000 feet through the Western Ghat. There are extraordinary views of the Sahyadri mountain range from the high viaducts on this route.

Only trains that have air-conditioned compartments are listed here.

Dep. Bombay (Vic.)	07:55	12:35	14:25 (1)	15:35 (3)
Arr. Pune	3½–4½ hours later			

Sights in **Pune**: Many ancient palaces and temples. This route involves 25 tunnels and many high bridges and viaducts. Can be made as a one-day roundtrip. The very picturesque narrow-gauge Matheran Hill Railway is near this route and can be visited during the day.

Dep. Pune	00:30	01:00	02:20 (2)	03:25 (1+2)	04:05 (1+4)
Arr. Bombay (Vic.)	3½–4½ hours later				

(1) Depart/Arrive Bombay's Dadar railstation. (2) Supplement charged (3) Plus other Bombay departures at 19:50 (1+2), 20:45 (1), 21:55 (2) and 23:15. (4) Plus other departures from Pune at 07:45 (1), 08:55, 16:15 and 16:20.

Calcutta - Allahabad   6060

Dep. Calcutta (How.)	09:45 (1)	19:20 (3)	20:00 (4)	
Arr. Allahabad	00:30 (2)	09:05 (2)	10:30 (2)	
Dep. Allahabad	00:24 (5)	02:25 (1)	16:30 (4+6)	21:15 (4)
Arr. Calcutta (How.)	11:30	17:30	07:30 (2)	13:15 (2)

(1) Supplement charged. Has first and second-class air-conditioned seats that convert to berths and also has an air-conditioned chair car. (2) Day 2. (3) Supplement charged. Has first and second-class air-conditioned seats that convert to berths. Restaurant car. (4) Has second-class air-conditioned compartments that convert to berths. (5) Reservation required. Supplement charged. Runs daily, except Monday and Friday. Has first and second-class air-conditioned seats that convert to berths. Restaurant car. (6) Runs Monday, Tuesday, Friday and Saturday only.

Calcutta - New Jalpaiguri - Darjeeling

The New Jalpaiguri–Darjeeling narrow-gauge rail line was completed in 1881. It has been known as "the toy train."

This tortuous 53-mile route (crossing 550 bridges and making 6 switchbacks and 4 complete loops) takes more than 8 hours. The train moves so slowly that there are constant opportunities to take photos and to observe villages.

The scenic beauty along this route includes giant bamboos, ferns, mosses, orchids, magnolias, rhododendrons and many trees fig, oak, chestnut, birch, walnut.

6108		*6123*	
Dep. Calcutta (Sealdah)	19:15 (1)	Dep. Darjeeling	08:25
Arr. New Jalpaiguri	08:30	Arr. New Jalpaiguri	16:20
Change trains.		*Change trains.*	
6123		*6108*	
Dep. New Jalpaiguri	09:00	Dep. New Jalpaiguri	18:45
Arr. Darjeeling	17:30	Arr. Calcutta (Sealdah)	08:45

(1) Has air-conditioned first and second-class seats that convert to berths or bunks, and also has an air-conditioned chair car.

Sights in **Darjeeling**: At 7,000 feet, this is a cool and beautiful area. Many famous tea plantations. The town's name comes from the word "dorjee," the mystic thunderbolt of Indra, and "ling," meaning place. There is a large population of Tibetans in Darjeeling. Many arts and crafts are sold at the Tibetan Refugee Center. The interesting items to purchase there are jewelry, carvings, colorful fabrics, carpets, prayer wheels. Nearby is the Zoo and the Museum of Himalayan Mountaineering. Visit the shrines in the Mahakala Temple complex. Tour a factory that processes tea. Ride the longest cable chairlift in Asia, 5 miles to the village of **Singla**. Take a land-rover ride through spectacular forests to the very interesting Saturday market in **Kalimpong**. Go to the **Jaldapara** game sanctuary (about 120 miles away) to see rhinos and elephants. Excursions by 4-wheel-drive vehicles are made from Darjeeling to Nepal, Sikkim and Bhutan. One can walk or take a jeep to Tiger Hill to see the sunrise. There is a hotel there. The preferred visit is to spend the night in Tiger Hill, see the sunrise the next morning (and a view of 4 countries: Nepal, Bhutan, Sikkim and India), and then catch the train from Darjeeling for the ride back to Calcutta.

Calcutta - Madras   6150

Midway between Madras and **Visakhapatnam**, the train goes over **Godavari River**. This is the second longest bridge in India.
All of these trains have second-class air-conditioned seats that convert to berths.

Dep. Calcutta (Howrah)	14:10 (1)	20:30	22:35 (4)
Arr. Madras (Central)	17:35 (2)	05:15 (3)	04:10 (3)
Dep. Madras (Central)	07:20 (4)	08:10 (1)	22:30
Arr. Calcutta (Howrah)	13:45 (2)	12:15 (2)	07:00 (3)

(1) Supplement charged. Restaurant car. (2) Day 2. (3) Day 3. (4) Supplement charged.

Calcutta - New Delhi   6060

The train passes through several different regions on this trip. Climate, language and clothing change every few hours.

All of these trains charge a supplement and have first and second-class air-conditioned seats that convert to berths.

Dep. Calcutta (Howrah)	09:45 (1)	19:55 (3)
Arr. New Delhi	09:50 (2)	-0-
Arr. Delhi	-0-	19:55 (2)
Dep. Delhi	-0- (1)	16:00
Dep. New Delhi	08:00	-0-
Arr. Calcutta (Howrah)	18:15 (2)	05:25 (2)

(1) Also has an air-conditioned chair car. (2) Day 2. (3) Restaurant car.

Delhi - Agra   6080

The 07:05 departure from New Delhi is "Taj Express." It is met on 09:50 arrival in Agra by an air-conditioned government-operated tourist bus and an official guide. Its tour includes the 17th century Taj Mahal and Fatehpur Sikri Fort. Avoid private guides. They *do not* provide as complete a tour as the government does. Another interesting sight in Agra is the tomb of Itmad-ud-Daullah. The bus brings you back to the Agra station for the 18:45 departure of "Taj Express," arriving back in New Delhi at 22:00.

Dep. New Delhi	06:15 (1)	07:15 (2)	08:00	10:50 (3)	11:30 (4)
Arr. Agra	08:05	10:13	12:10	13:48	14:12

Dep. New Delhi	14:55 (5)	17:50 (6)	19:15 (3+8)	21:15 (3+8)	-0-
Arr. Agra	18:35	20:25	22:10	23:47	-0-

• • •

Dep. Agra	01:35 (3)	05:43 (6)	07:28 (6)	08:03 (3+8)	12:00 (4)
Arr. New Delhi	07:10	08:40	11:45	12:10	15:15

Dep. Agra	15:30	16:45 (3)	17:28 (3)	18:45 (2)	20:18 (7)
Arr. New Delhi	21:25	20:15	21:05	22:00	22:25

(1) "Shatabdi Express." Its schedule is ideal for a day of sightseeing in Agra, but a reservation is essential because it carries only 201 passengers (3 coaches of 67) to Agra. This train has only air-conditioned chair cars. Seats recline and have a foot-rest. Each coach has 3 restrooms: 2 Indian style and one Western style. (2) "Taj Express." Reservation required. Supplement charged. Has air-conditioned chair car. Restaurant car. (3) Has second-class air-conditioned compartments. (4) Supplement charged. Has second-class air-conditioned compartments. Restaurant car. (5) Runs Monday, Wednesday, Friday and Sunday. (6) Supplement charged. Has second-class air-conditioned compartments and air-conditioned chair car. (7) Has air-conditioned chair car. (8) Supplement charged.

Delhi - Ahmadabad   6036

Dep. Delhi	09:20	15:55 (2)	18:10 (3)	21:55 (4)
Arr. Ahmadabad	10:00 (1)	16:15 (1)	11:55 (1)	21:15 (1)

Dep. Ahmadabad	05:45 (2)	08:25 (4)	17:00 (3)	18:00
Arr. Delhi	05:30 (1)	07:40 (1)	10:00 (1)	19:00 (1)

(1) Day 2. (2) **Warning!** First-class is carried only from Delhi to Palapur and v.v. First-class passengers must transfer to second-class Palapur to Ahmadabad and v.v. (for about 3½ hours). (3) Supplement charged. Has second-class air-conditioned seats that convert to berths. (4) Has first and second-class air-conditioned seats that convert to berths.

Delhi - Allahabad   6060

All of these trains charge a supplement and have second-class air-conditioned seats that convert to berths, unless designated otherwise.

Dep. Delhi	-0-	08:00 (1+2)	-0-	18:45	-0-
Dep. New Delhi	06:25 (1)	-0-	16:00 (2+3)	-0-	19:45 (7)
Arr. Allahabad	15:20	17:50	02:20 (4)	04:10 (4)	05:10 (4)

Dep. Allahabad	00:30 (2+3)	02:00	02:28 (5)	09:15 (1+2)	11:00 (8)
Arr. New Delhi	10:40	11:55	09:50	-0-	20:15
Arr. Delhi	-0-	-0-	-0-	19:55	-0-

(1) Restaurant car. (2) Has both first and second-class air-conditioned seats that convert to berths. (3) Also has air-conditioned chair car. (4) Day 2. (5) Reservation required. Runs daily, except Wednesday and Saturday. Has both first and second-class air-conditioned seats that convert to berths and an air-conditioned chair car. Restaurant car. (6) No supplement charged. (7) Plus other departures from New Delhi at 21:15 (6) and 22:00 (2), arriving Allahabad 11:35 and 08:00. (8) Plus other departures from Allahabad at 14:40 (6) and 21:00 (2), arriving New Delhi 06:25 and 06:50.

Delhi - Jaipur   6036

One of India's fastest trains, Pink City Express (colored pink), departs from a station that is a few miles away from the main Delhi station. Provide extra time to get there.

Dep. Delhi	06:00 (1)	09:20	13:00	18:10 (2)	21:55 (3)
Arr. Jaipur	11:50	18:20	21:40	23:35	06:25

Sights in **Jaipur**: This city is noted for the unusually colorful clothes worn by its people. See the pink Palace of the Winds.

Dep. Jaipur	00:15 (3)	04:30 (2)	06:25	10:20	16:45 (1)
Arr. Delhi	07:30	10:00	14:15	19:00	22:05

(1) "Pink City Express." Supplement charged. Buffet. (2) Supplement charged. Has second-class air-conditioned seats. (3) Has first and second-class air-conditioned seats that convert to berths.

Delhi - Madras

	6080	6080	6007
Dep. New Delhi	14:55 (1)	18:40 (3)	22:30 (3)
Arr. Madras (Central)	12:35 (2)	07:00 (2)	07:50 (2)

	6007	6080	6080
Dep. Madras (Central)	21:00 (3)	22:15 (3)	23:50 (5)
Arr. New Delhi	06:45 (4)	11:45 (4)	23:05 (4)

(1) Runs Wednesday, Saturday and Sunday.. Not air-conditioned. (2) Day 3 from New Delhi. (3) Supplement charged. Has second-class air-conditioned seats that convert to berths. Also has air-conditioned chair car. Restaurant car or buffet. (4) Day 3 from Madras. (5) Runs Wednesday, Thursday and Sunday. Not air-conditioned.

Madras - Ernakulam - Cochin 6175

En route to Cochin, it is possible to leave the train in Ernakulum, sightsee there, and then later the same day take the trip of a few minutes to Cochin either by ferry boat or by bus across the bridge that connects the 2 cities.

Both trains run Monday, Thursday Friday and Sunday and have second-class air-conditioned seats that convert to berths.

Dep. Madras (Cen.)	01:20	Dep. Cochin	08:40
Dep. Ernakulam (Junction)	15:35	Dep. Ernakulam (Junction)	09:15
Arr. Cochin	16:00	Arr. Madras (Cen.)	23:20

Sights in **Ernakulam**: The week-long festival at the Siva temple, every January. Performances of the unusual Kathakali dance.

Sights in **Cochin:** This is actually a conglomerate of several islands and 3 cities. See the 16th century Santa Cruz Cathedral. The 16th century synagogue. The blue willow-patterned tiles on the floor of a second synagogue. The 16th century tomb of the great Spanish explorer Vasco de Gama. The Dutch Palace. Picturesque palm-lined beaches.

INTERNATIONAL ROUTES
FROM INDIA

New Delhi is the gateway for train travel to Pakistan. The rail route to Sri Lanka (Ceylon) is via Madras and Rameswaram.

New Delhi - Amritsar - Lahore - Hyderabad - Karachi

Unless designated otherwise, all of the New Delhi–Amritsar trains have second-class air-conditioned seats that convert to berths, and all of the Lahore–Karachi trains have first-class air-conditioned-class seats that convert to berths.

6022

Dep. New Delhi	20:05 (1)	06:45 (2)	08:00 (1)	11:10 (3)	12:15 (9)
Arr. Amritsar	06:15	13:40	18:25	19:20	21:00

Sights in **Amistar**: This is the holiest city of the Sikh religion. Home of the wonderful Golden Temple.

Change trains
6013

Dep. Amritsar	09:30 (4)
Arr. Lahore	13:35

Change trains
5910

Dep. Lahore	07:00 (6)	09:15 (7)	14:30 (1)
Dep. Hyderabad	21:20	04:15 (5)	08:50 (5)
Arr. Karachi (Can.)	23:40	07:00	11:30

(1)Restaurant car. (2) *No* second-class air-conditioned seats. Has air-conditioned chair car. (3) Supplement charged. Also has first-class air-conditioned seats. Restaurant car. (4) *Not* air-conditioned. (5) Day 2 from Lahore. (6) Supplement charged. Restaurant car. (7) Reservation required. Restaurant car. (8) *Not* air-conditioned. Restaurant car. (9) Plus other departures from New Delhi at 20:05 and 23:10(3), arriving Amritsar 06:15 and 08:05. (10) Plus other departures from Lahore at 18:30 (7) and 22:50 (8), arriving Karachi 16:10 and 21:40.

INDONESIA

Children under 3 travel free. Half-fare for children 3–7. Children 8 and over must pay full fare. There are 4 classes of coaches. First and second-class are air-conditioned. Cook says the first 3 classes are "quite comfortable."

Nearly every train ride in Indonesia offers views of extinct volcanoes, mountains, water buffalo and rain forests.

Jakarta

The main railstation is Kota. See Bali dancing at Gedung Kesenian. The world's finest collection of Hindu-Javanese antiquities (coins, archaeological objects, Chinese ceramics) at the National Museum on Medan Merdeka. Its treasure room, containing Javanese gold ornaments from thousands of years ago, is open *only* on Sunday.

Do not miss seeing the morning activity at the Pasar Ikan, a large fish market. At the wharf, the unloading of spices, bananas, indigo and teak. The Maritime Museum, in what were once the warehouses of the old Dutch fort.

The National Mosque. The Museum Kota. Presidential Palace. The very tall National Monument. Spend an evening (plays, concerts, art exhibits, dances) at Taman Ismail Marzuki Cultural Complex, Jalan Cikini Raya 13. Go to the enormous park, Taman Mini, to see the exhibit (arts, crafts and building) from all the different islands of Indonesia. The interesting Dutch houses and the canals in Chinatown.

Ride out to **Bogoru** by bus or taxi to see the old Dutch palace (Merdeka Palace) and the fantastic 275-acre Botanical Garden: 10,000 species of trees and more than 500,000 other plants, including more than 100,000 orchid plants. Nothing in the world to compare with these gardens.

Before shopping for batik in the air-conditioned Aldiron Plaza, visit the Textile Museum on Jalan Satsuit Tubun and Keramik Museum on Fatahillah Square to learn how to differentiate between more than 300 types of Indonesian fabrics and many different styles of weaving. Across from the Keramik is the fantastic collection of puppets (Balinese, Javan, etc.) at Wayang Museum.

Browse in the flea markets along Jalan Surabaya: Chinese and European chinaware, Balinese wood sculptures, silver filigree from Jogjakarta, Javanese daggers. Shop for quality antiques at the stores on Jalan Kebon Sirih Timur Dalam, near the Hyatt Hotel. The specialty on Pasar Baru is fabrics. Check-out the art, curio and handicraft stalls in the 12-acre Indonesian Bazaar, next to the Hilton Hotel, open daily 10:00–18:00.

Visit the bird market (cockatoos and many other tropical birds) on Jalan Pramuka. The orchid markets, at Cipete and Cilandak. At Taman Fatahillah (a square in the center of Old Batavia) see: the Historical Museum in the 18th century Town Hall, the Wayang puppets in the Wayang Museum, and Balai Seni Rupa (the city art gallery).

Surabaja

There are 3 railstations. Trains for Jakarta depart from Gubeng. Trains for Bandung depart from Kota. Tasar Turi is the third railstation.

This is a major seaport. A 30-minute ferry-boat ride takes you to **Madura**, where the major attraction is the racing of bulls. Surabaja is a convenient point for visiting **Mount Bromo**.

Jakarta - Surabaja (via Bandung)   7406

Dep. Jakarta (Gambir)	05:42 (1)	09:33 (1)	11:33 (1)	13:33 (1)	15:33 (1)
Arr. Bandung	08:33	12:33	14:33	16:33	18:33
Change trains.					
Dep. Bandung				17:40 (2)	05:35 (3)
Arr. Surabaja (Gubeng)				06:54	20:39

Sights in **Bandung**: This is a much nicer and cooler city than Jakarta. Quinine is derived from cinchona bark. This is the center of Indonesia's quinine industry, with many cinchona tree plantations here. There are also numerous tea plantations in this area, See the collection of crocodiles, birds and snakes at the Zoological Garden.

Dep. Surabaja (Gubeng)	05:23 (3)	17:50 (2)			
Arr. Bandung	19:15	07:03			
Change trains.					
Dep. Bandung	05:00 (1)	06:00 (1)	09:00 (1)	11:00 (1)	13:00 (1+4)
Arr. Jakarta (Gambir)	07:51	08:59	11:51	13:51	15:51

(1) Has air-condtioned first and second-class. Restaurant car. (2) Has air-conditioned second-class. Restaurant car. (3) Has only third and fourth-class. Buffet. (4) Plus other Bandung departures at 15:00 (1), 17:00 (1), 1820 (1) and 1930 (1).

Jakarta - Jogjakarta   7406

Dep. Jakarta (Gambir)	06:15 (1)	16:00 (2)	17:50 (3)	19:30 (1)
Arr. Jogjakarta	14:24	00:30	03:05	04:43

• • •

Dep. Jogjakarta	07:00 (1)	18:00 (1)	19:20 (3)	21:10 (2)
Arr. Jakarta (Gambir)	15:27	03:03	04:11	05:31

(1) Has air-conditioned first and second-class. Restaurant car. (2) Supplement charged. Has air-conditioned first and second-class. Restaurant car. (3) Third-class only. Buffet.

Sights in **Jogjakarta**: The batik schools, 2 museums, the mosques and the Sultan's Palace, all inside the walled Kraton complex. Be sure to see the carved teak pillars in the Bengsal Kencono (Golden Pavillion) and the gold pillars, gems and sacred weapons displayed in Gadjah Mada University. It is a short rickshaw ride to the village of **Kota Gede**, to see fine silver filigree being made.

Visit the shops stocked with excellent batik, along Jalan Tirtodipuran. The seated Buddha at the Mendut Temple. Taman Siri, the Water Castle. Nearby is a bird market. Watch the complex dyeing of fabric at the Batik Research Center (Jalan Kusumanegara 2).

The dances at the 10th century Roro Djonggrang Temple, 10 miles from Jogjakarta.

There is an air-conditioned bus tour to the 9th century Borobudur, 35 miles from the city. The lower terraces of this low pyramid have 432 statues and 1,460 reliefs of the Buddha. It is a 15-mile trip to **Prambanam**, a temple complex dedicated to Shiva, Hindu deity.

Jogjakarta - Solo   7406

This is an easy one-day roundtrip.

Dep. Jogjakarta	00:40 (1)	01:35 (2)	03:15 (3)	14:12 (3)	18:49 (4)
Arr. Solo	70–80 minutes later				

Sights in **Solo**: A quite attractive village. Famous for its good batik cloth and its Sriwedai Amusement Park, which has a fine Zoological Garden.

Dep. Solo	09:35 (3)	12:50 (4)	18:00 (3)	19:45 (1)	22:00 (2)
Arr. Jogjakarta	70–80 minutes later				

(1) Supplement charged. Has air-conditioned first and second-class. Restaurant car. (2) Has air-conditioned second-class. Restaurant car. (3) Third-class only. Buffet. (4) Has only fourth-class. Light refreshments.

Medan - Rantau Prapaet - Tanjon Balai   7400

The one rail route on Sumatra is across the bay from Penang. A one-day roundtrip from Medan to Tanjong Balai is possible.

Dep. Medan	07:00 (1)	09:15 (2)	14:30 (3)	21:30 (1)
Arr. Rantau Prapaet	-0-	16:14	-0-	04:30
Arr. Tanjong Balai	11:12	-0-	18:48	-0-

Sights in **Medan**: An ugly city of almost one million people. There are large oil palm and rubber tree plantations here. See the tamed Sumatran orangutans being trained so they can be returned to the jungle. Their "school" is in nearby **Mount Leuser Nature Reserve**, open to the public every afternoon.

To view rhinoceroses, elephants and tigers, go on the boat trip up the **Alas River**, into the rain forest.

Sights in **Rantau Prapaet**: A small resort. Visit the Saturday market for souvenirs. See the exhibitions of Batak music and dance every night at Hotel Prapaet.

Rantau Prapaet is the gateway to **Samosir Island** on large nearby 400-square-mile **Lake Toba** (twice the size of Lake Geneva). Only a short distance from the Equator, Samosir is 3,000-feet high and has a remarkably cool climate for its location. Take the ferry from Rantau Prapaet to see the unique Batak houses there, built without nails and up to 60 feet long. These windowless houses are decorated with incredible carvings and mosaics of humanlike figures, mythical birds, monsters, lizards and snakes. See the tomb of King Sidabutar. Walk the many paths that connect the island's villages.

Dep. Tanjong Balai	06:30 (1)	-0-	14:15 (3)	-0-
Dep. Rantau Prapaet	-0-	08:00 (2)	-0-	22:15 (1)
Arr. Medan	10:44	15:05	18:27	05:20

(1) Fourth-class only. Light refreshments. (2) Third-class only. Buffet. (3) Third and fourth class only. Buffet.

JAPAN

Children under 6 travel free. Half-fare for children 6–11. Children 12 and over must pay full fare. The 2 elements that are necessary for top quality rail service both exist in Japan: high population density and short distances.

In major cities, railstations have "Green Windows" where travel advice in English can be obtained.

Personnel who speak English and can render advice and information are also on duty at these offices of Japan National Tourist Organization:

Tokyo: 6-6 Yurakucho 1-Chome

Kyoto: Kyoto Tower Building, Higashi-Shiokojicho, Shimogyo-ku

Narita: The Terminal Building

Tickets for all Japanese trains which require reservation go on sale one month before travel day and can be purchased at Japanese Railways railstations and at major travel agencies throughout Japan.

Passengers are permitted to take 2 suitcases weighing a total of 44 pounds into their car and may also check 3 additional suitcases at a small fee for transit in the baggage car. Also, for little cost, arrangements can be made either to have baggage delivered from the train to one's residence or to be stored at a railstation. Although porters are available at all main railstations, they are very scarce.

Principal trains have restaurant cars. There are refreshment vendors on almost all other long-distance trains. Both Japanese and "Western" food are provided.

There are 4 classes of trains in Japan: Super-Express (Hikari and Kodama), Limited Express, Ordinary Express and Local. A surcharge is required for all types of express trains. When any express train arrives 2 hours or more late, the express surcharge is refunded at the destination.

Each express train has one or more "Green Cars." Seat reservations, at an additional charge, are required for space in a Green Car.

Sleeping cars have roomettes (for one person) and double compartments in Class "A" cars. Class "B" cars provide 2-berth and 3-berth compartments.

Combination tickets (for both hotel rooms and seats on bullet trains) can be purchased from either Japanese Railways or from Japan Travel Bureau. All of Japan's many privately owned trains are single-class and require seat reservations. Many of these trains serve resort areas.

Japan enacted in 1970 its "Law for Construction of Nationwide High-Speed Railways" calling for speeds up to 150 miles per hour on many routes. Completed in 1985, the 33.4-mile-long undersea Seikan Tunnel (world's longest) connects Tappi and Yoshioka, linking Hokkaido by rail with the rest of Japan. Passenger service began in 1988.

The hazardous 4½-hour ferry ride between Aomori and Hakodate (suspended an average of 80 days every year because of rough seas) was eliminated, and the 16-hour trip from Tokyo to Sapporo was reduced to 11 hours on bullet trains. Construction of the tunnel began in 1964. Its cost ($2.8 Billion) was more than 3 times the original estimate. It is actually a complex of 3 separate tunnels: the main one, plus narrower pilot and service tunnels. A 14.5-mile segment of the Seikan runs beneath the Tsugaru Strait, from Cape Tappi on Honshu Island to Yoshioka on Hokkaido Island.

At some locations the tunnel is 787 feet beneath the surface of the water and 328 feet beneath the seabed. There was one 4-month period that construction advanced only 120 feet.

Japan Railways Group surpasses all other rail systems in the world as to service and size. It operates more than 26,000 trains a day. Express trains between Tokyo and Osaka (345 miles) usually run at 125mph, sometimes going as fast as 137mph. Passengers can follow the trains' speed on speedometers located throughout the trains. On the stretch from Tokyo to Kyushu Island, some trains reach a speed of 156mph.

The most famous Japanese trains are its Shinkansen "bullet trains." The great "Hikari," leaving Tokyo every 15 or 20 minutes, runs the 345 miles from Tokyo to Osaka in 2 hours 26 minutes. The 455-mile run from Tokyo to Okayama is made in 3 hours 50 minutes. From Tokyo to Hakata (735 miles), it is only 5 hours 57 minutes.

Bullet trains, while traveling, have telephone service to 26 cities.

When we rode a bullet train both from Tokyo to Kyoto, and then the next day back to Tokyo, the speed was so great that it was difficult to focus on scenery or objects within 1,000 feet from the train. The interior was immaculately clean. It is one of the world's best travel experiences.

And the bullet trains are very safe. To guard against natural disasters, the Japanese installed seismoscopes, anemometers and rain gauges along the entire line. In case of an earthquake exceeding a certain intensity, the electrical current that runs the trains in the area concerned will automatically cut off.

If there are excessive rains or winds, the running speed of the train is restricted or the train is stopped. Each train window is made of double-layer glass with a dry air space between so as to minimize noise, wind pressure and moisture condensation, as well as guard against flying stones.

In planning a tour of Japan, keep in mind that the country is 4 major islands: Honshu (Tokyo and Kyoto), Shikoku (Takamatsu), Kyushu to the south (Hakata and Nagasaki), and Hokkaido, the wild northern land of Japan (Sapporo).

JAPAN'S TRAIN PASSES

Japan Railpass. *Cannot* be purchased in Japan. Unlimited travel on the trains, buses and ferries of the 6 Japanese rail companies (all of which also sell separate passes, which can be purchased only in Japan). Vouchers for Japan Railpass are sold only outside Japan, at offices of Japan Air Lines (for passengers only), Nippon Travel Agency and Japan Travel Bureau. After arriving in Japan, the voucher is exchanged for the pass at the Travel Service Center at Tokyo International Airport (Narita) and at these Tokyo railstations: Ikebukuro, Shibuya, Shinjuku, Tokyo and Ueno. Also at the railstation in 19 other main cities.

Passengers must show the pass to board a train and also flash it again to get out of a station.

Travel must start within 3 months after the voucher is purchased. With a Japan Railpass there is no charge for seat reservations, which can be made only in Japan and at either any Travel Service Center or any railstation. Refundable at a 10% fee before the first day of use if presented at a Travel Service Center in a JR station that is designated to handle this pass.

The adult *first*-class prices in late 1995 were: Y-37,000 for 7 days, Y-60,000 for 14 days, and Y-78,000 for 21 days. Children 6-11: Y-18,500, Y-30,000 and Y-39,000.*Second* Y-27,800, Y-44,200 and Y-56,600. For children 6-11: Y-13,900, Y-22,100 and Y-28,300.

Combinations (for example two 7-day passes, or a 7-day plus a 14-day pass) allow remaining several days in one city without depleting a pass.

Japan Tour Tickets. These cover a variety of routes listed by Japan Railways Group. Offering reduced-rate excursions, they can be obtained at principal Japanese railstations, or at the Kobe, Kyoto and Tokyo offices of Japan Travel Bureau, and also at all offices of Kinki Nippon Tourist.

Hiroshima

Rebuilt since 1955. All major sites can be reached by bus from the railstation: Shuk-keien Garden, Hiroshima Castle, Asa Zoological Park, the Buddhist Fudoin Temple, the monuments at Peace Memorial Park and the interesting exhibits in the Peace Memorial Museum. It is a 25-minute train ride to Miyajimaguchi and then a 10-minute ferryboat ride from there to the magnificent landscape and 6th century Itsukushima Shrine of Miyajima (Shrine Island).

Kyoto

You will not see all worth seeing here in a few days. There are more than 200 Shinto shrines, over 1500 temples, plus 9 museums, 3 palaces and an imposing castle in Kyoto.

The 17th century Nijo Castle is first on everyone's list. Beautiful gold ceilings, wood sculptures, and murals to see at this complex.

Other sights in Kyoto: the 13th century 393-foot long Sanjusangendo (Hall of 33 Bays). The incredible halls at Nishi Hongan-ji. The 200-acre park in the center of Kyoto, with the Imperial Palace. The 3 large gardens of the 68-acre Shugaku-in. The 22 subtemples at Daitoku-ji, one of the city's many Zen temples. The Library, Zoo, Art Gallery and Heian Jingu Shrine, all in Okazaki Park. Hundreds of narrow streets, each with interesting shops, food stores and inns.

Kinkaku-ji (Temple of the Golden Pavilion). Ryoan-ji (Temple of the Peaceful Dragon). Kokedera (The Moss Temple), with many different types of moss in its lovely garden. The 17th century Kiyomizu (Clear Spring Temple). The view from the 8th century Kiyomizu Temple. The tallest (5-story) pagoda in Japan, at Toji Temple.

Osaka

The 16th century Osaka Castle, and its fine museum. Shitenno-ji Temple. Nishi Temple. Higashi Hongan-ji Temple. The Kabuki Theater. The view from the top of 338-foot high Tsutenkaku (Tower Leading to Heaven). The view from the top of the 340-foot high observation platform on Osaka Tower.

Sumiyoshi Taisha Shrine. Temmangu Shrine. The Bunraku puppet theater. The dozen different farmhouses with hundreds of utensils in the Museum of Japanese Farmhouses. The Japan Handicraft Museum. Ancient and modern art at the Municipal Art Museum in Tennoji Park, where the Zoo and Botanical Garden are also located.

The Electric Science Museum. The Transportation Museum. The Natural Science Museum. The Fujita Art Museum. A tourist specialty in Osaka is visiting factories: clothing, beverages, ice cream, chocolate, cameras, autos, bread, etc.

Tokyo

Schedules for the 60-minute train ride between Tokyo's "Tokyo" station and Narita Airport appear under "Tokyo–Narita."

There is monorail and bus service between Haneda Airport and the center of Tokyo.

Several English language daily newspapers list entertainment events.

Any tour of Tokyo must focus on visiting the massive park surrounding the Palace, in the center of the city. Then see: The gardens at the Meiji Shrine. The enormous Zoo (open 09:30–16:30, closed Monday), the National Museum of Western Art, and the Tokyo National Museum (greatest collection in the world of Japanese art and archaeology), and the Shitamachi Museum, all in the 210-acre Ueno Park, next to Ueno Railstation.

Shitamachi features the lifestyle of common people in the 19th and early 20th centuries: a merchant's house, a candy shop, the house of a clog-maker, women's teeth-blackening utensils, early firefighting equipment. Closed Monday, Shitamachi is open other days 09:30–16:30.

Stroll the Ginza, particularly after dark to view the extraordinary illuminations. See the tremendous assortment of sealife very early in the morning at the wholesale fish market at

Tsukiji (a 10-minute walk from the Ginza). See the elegant lobby of the Imperial Hotel. The Iris Garden (Shobu-en). The gardens at Shin-juku Gyoen. Kiyosumi Garden. The 60-acre Hama Rikyu Park. Buddhist art at Goto Museum. The collection of ancient Japanese and Chinese art in the Nezu Museum and at the Matsuoka Art Museum.

Koishikawa Botanical Garden. The Railway Museum. Ihinkan, a small museum of World War II memorabilia (human torpedos, warplanes, models of battleships) open daily 09:30–16:30. The gigantic paper lantern suspended from a gate made of 1700-year-old Japanese cypress, at the 7th century Asakusa Kannon Temple. Folkcrafts in Bingo-Ya. Kabuki-Za, the leading Kabuki theater.

The city's largest department stores have amusement parks and many restaurants on their roofs Several have undergrounds malls connected to Tokyo Railstation. The best in the Ginza are Matsuya, Mitsukoshi and Wako.

Hiroshima - Fukuoka (Hakata)   8000

All of these services are Bullet Trains which require reservation for first-class, have facilities for disabled passengers, and are air-conditioned. Most have a restaurant car or light refreshments.

Dep. Hiroshima	Frequent times from 06:40 to 22:30
Arr. Fukuoka (Hakata)	90 minutes later

Sights in **Hakata**: Hakata is the railstation for Fukuoka. This twin-city is famous for Hakata dolls. Much nightlife here. Only a few miles from away, there is cormorant fishing at **Harazuru**.

Dep. Fukuoka (Hakata)	Frequent times from 6:00 to 21:46
Arr. Hiroshima	90 minutes later

Hiroshima - Kagoshima

All of the services Hiroshima–Fukuoka and v.v. are Bullet Trains which require reservation for first-class, have facilities for disabled passengers, and are air-conditioned. Most have a restaurant car or light refreshments. All the Fukuoka–Kagoshima and v.v. trains require reservation for first-class and are air-conditioned. All have light refreshments.

8000

Dep. Hiroshima	Frequent times from 06:40 to 22:30		
Arr. Fukuoka (Hakata)	2 hours later		
Change trains. Table 8024			
Dep. Fukuoka (Hakata)	09:04	11:04	13:04
Arr. Kagoshima (Nishi)	17:10	19:13	21:02

Sights in **Kagoshima**: Rebuilt since 1945. An old castle town, often called "Naples of the Orient." A good base for visiting the beautiful crater lake, many live volcanoes and the thick forests of **Kirishima-Yaku National Park**. See the view of **Kagoshima Bay** and **Sakurajima** (a volcanic island) from the hilltop Shiroyama Park. **Ibusuki Spa**, only one hour by train from Nishi-Kagoshima station, is one of Japan's most popular hot springs resorts because of its lovely white seashore and the lush subtropical plants that surround it.

Dep. Kagoshima (Nishi)	07:10	09:15	12:15
Arr. Fukuoka (Hakata)	15:15	17:15	20:13

Change trains. 8000

Dep. Fukuoka (Hakata)	Frequent times from 06:00 to 21:46
Arr. Hiroshima	90 minutes later

Nishi-Kagoshima to Makurazaki   (Government Timetable)

The trip to the southern end of Japan's railway system

Dep. Nishi-Kagoshima	05:13	12:12	15:20	16:20	18:30
Arr. Makurazaki	15:15	14:16	17:53	19:12	21:00

Sights in **Makurazaki**: A popular beach resort.

Dep. Makurazaki	05:11	06:35	07:50	14:25	18:03	19:52
Arr. Nishi-Kagoshima	07:23	09:07	10:06	16:55	20:25	22:19

Hiroshima - Kumamoto

All of the services Hiroshima–Fukuoka and v.v. are Bullet Trains which require reservation for first-class, have facilities for disabled passengers, and are air-conditioned . Most have a restaurant car or light refreshments.

All the Fukuoka–Kumamoto and v.v. trains require reservation for first-class and have either buffet or light refreshments.

8000

Dep. Hiroshima	Frequent times from 06:40 to 22:30
Arr. Fukuoka (Hakata)	90 minutes later

Change trains. 8022

Dep. Fukuoka (Hakata)	Frequent times from 07:00 to 22:35
Arr. Kumamoto	90 minutes later

Sights in **Kumamoto**: It is a short drive from here to marvelous Suizenji Park.

Dep. Kumamoto	Frequent times from 06:20 to 22:04
Arr. Fukuoka (Hakata)	90 minutes later
Change trains. 8000	
Dep. Fukuoka (Hakata)	Frequent times from 06:00 to 21:46
Arr. Hiroshima	90 minutes later

Hiroshima - Nagasaki

All of the services Hiroshima–Fukuoka and v.v. are Bullet Trains which require reservation for first-class, have facilities for disabled passengers, and are air-conditioned . Most have a restaurant car or light refreshments.

All the Fukuoka–Nagasaki and v.v. trains require reservation for first-class and are air-conditioned. Most have buffet or light refreshments.

8000

Dep. Hiroshima	Frequent times from 06:40 to 22:51
Arr. Fukuoka (Hakata)	90 minutes later
Change trains.	

There is great scenery of **Omura Bay** on the ride from Fukuoka (Hakata) to Nagasaki. Sit on the right-hand side for the best view in this direction.

8023

Dep. Fukuoka (Hakata)	07:02	07:32	09:21	10:21	10:51	11:21 (1)
Arr. Nagasaki	09:05	09:51	11:26	12:31	12:55	13:36

Sights in **Nagasaki**: Japan's first contact with the Western world was here, as well as the country's early traffic with China. That explains both the Chinese and Catholic influence on this area. At Saints Martyrdom there is a chapel with twin towers reminiscent of Gaudi's Sagrada Familia church in Barcelona. This is the site of the crucifixion in 1597 of 6 foreign and 20 Japanese Christians for refusing to renounce their faith after Christianity was banned.

The local tradition is flying the huge kites that were first flown in China. Two other Chinese influences seen here even now are the annual June racing of large rowboats to the tempo of a drum that is beaten amidship and an annual October festival featuring Chinese-style costumes, floats and dragons.

See the Catholic Cathedral. (Nearly half of Japan's small Catholic population lives in this area.) The view of the city and harbor from Glover House, the place where Madame Butterfly (in Puccini's imagination) waited for Pinkerton to return. The exhibit at International Cultural Hall at Peace Park (daily 09:00–17:00), commemorating the August 9, 1945 atomic bomb blast. The 17th century Chinese Buddhist temple. The 33-foot high bronze torii at the Suwa Shrine. Much marvelous seacoast scenery in this area.

Dep. Nagasaki	06:30	07:09	07:57	08:31	09:00	09:24 (2)
Arr. Fukuoka (Hakata)	08:48	09:20	10:08	10:35	10:58	11:29

Change trains. 8000

Dep. Fukuoka (Hakata)	Frequent times from 06:00 to 21:46
Arr. Hiroshima	90 minutes later

(1) Plus other departures from Fukuoka (Hakata) at frequent times from 11:51 to 22:08. (2) Plus other departures from Nagasaki at frequent times from 10:04 to 21:31.

Kyoto - Gifu

All of the services Kyoto–Nagoya and v.v. are Bullet Trains which require reservation for first-class, have facilities for disabled passengers, and are air-conditioned . Most have a restaurant car or light refreshments.

All the Nagoya–Gifu and v.v. trains require reservation for first-class, are air-conditioned and have light refreshments.

8000					*8015*			
Dep. Kyoto	07:47	08:44	11:14		Dep. Gifu	15:28	16:30	18:26
Arr. Nagoya	08:29	09:26	12:12		Arr. Nagoya	15:49	16:49	18:47
Change trains.					*Change trains*			
8015					*8000*			
Dep. Nagoya	08:40	09:40	12:40		Dep. Nagoya	16:01	17:16	19:16
Arr. Gifu	09:00	09:59	13:00		Arr. Kyoto	16:45	17:58	19:58

Sights in **Gifu**: There is large production of lovely paper lanterns and paper umbrellas here. Numerous hot springs resorts in this area. See the cormorant fishing, almost every night from mid-May to mid-October.

Kyoto - Kobe   8000

All of these services are Bullet Trains which require reservation for first-class, have facilities for disabled passengers, and are air-conditioned . Most have a restaurant car or light refreshments.

Dep. Kyoto	Frequent times from 07:15 to 22:50
Arr. Kobe	32 minutes later

Sights in **Kobe**: This is Japan's largest seaport. See the Ikuta Shrine. Take a bus tour to Minatogawa Shrine and the ancient Temple in **Sumadera**. There are great cherry tree blossoms there every Spring. Equally beautiful maple tree foliage, every Autumn, at Zenshoji Temple. See the Hakutsuru Gallery of Oriental Art, near Mikage station. Visit the Zoo, Botanical Garden and all-girl opera at nearby **Takarazuka**.

Dep. Kobe	Frequent times from 06:24 to 21:33
Arr. Kyoto	32 minutes later

Kyoto - Okayama - Matsuyama -Uwajima

This ride to Shikoku Island includes traveling over the $8 Billion Seto-Ohashi bridge that is 213-feet wide and has 4 highway lanes and 2 rail tracks. It crosses 5½ miles of water (the Inland Sea). Passengers can stare down at huge cargo ships.

All of the services Kyoto–Okayama and v.v. are Bullet Trains which require a reservation for first-class, have facilities for disabled passengers, and are air-conditioned. Most have a restaurant car or light refreshments.

All of the Okayama–Uwajima and v.v. trains require reservation for first-class, are air-conditioned and have light refreshments.

8000

Dep. Kyoto	08:38	10:34	12:34	13:20	15:34	16:34	18:34 (1)
Arr. Okayama	09:52	11:51	13:51	14:48	16:52	17:51	19:51
Change trains. Table 8021							
Dep. Okayama	11:19	13:19	14:19	16:19	17:19	20:19	
Arr. Matsuyama	14:08 (2)	16:05	17:04	19:07	20:08	22:50	
Arr. Uwajima	15:43	-0-	18:29	20:39	21:36	00:08	

Sights in **Okayama**: See "Kyoto-Okayama"

Sights in **Matsuyama**: This is a popular hot springs resort. See the lovely maple trees in nearby Omogo Valley. There is a fine castle here. The local sport is bullfighting.

Sights in **Uwajima**: Near the railstation, the 17th century 3-story dungeon at the 17th century Uwajima Castle. Also see Uwatsuhiko Shrine at the foot of Atago Park, and the view from the park. Visit Tenshaen, a beautiful garden.

Dep. Uwajima	-0-	06:45	08:38	10:01	11:47	12:53	14:52
Dep. Matsuyama	05:27	08:12	10:07	11:31	13:23	14:20	16:11
Arr. Okayama	08:16	11:00	13:01	14:01	16:01	17:01	19:01
Change trains. Table 8000							
Dep. Okayama	08:31	11:09	12:09	14:09	15:09	17:09	18:09
Arr. Kyoto	09:55	12:10	13:05	15:05	16:05	18:05	19:05

(1) For complete schedules, see "Kyoto-Okayama" (2) Change trains in Matsuyama.

Kyoto - Nagoya   8000

All of these services are Bullet Trains which require reservation for first-class, have facilities for disabled passengers, and are air-conditioned. Most have a restaurant car or light refreshments.

Dep. Kyoto	Frequent times from 06:17 to 21:56
Arr. Nagoya	40–50 Minutes later

Sights in **Nagoya**: The art objects in the recently re-built 5-story 17th century castle. The view of Nagoya from the top of the 350-foot high television tower. The modern Nittaiji Temple, a gift from Thailand. The 1700-year old Atsuta Shrine. The Tokugawa Art Museum. Shop for fine Noritake chinaware and Ando cloisonne.

It is only a 45-minute train ride to **Inuyama** to see the 16th century castle and the Kiso rapids there.

There is bus service every 20 minutes at the Nagoya station for the 1H-hour ride to the marvelous preservation park at **Meiji**, a 172-acre mountain village that has reproduced the lifestyle that existed in Japan at the end of the 19th century. Among the many monuments from the 1868–1912 era are: the railroad coach of the Meiji Emperor, the lobby of the original Frank Lloyd Wright Imperial Hotel (a Tokyo landmark for almost 50 years until it was demolished in the 1960's), a public bath, a merchant's townhouse, a teahouse, a Kabuki theater, antique railway machines, a hand-printing press, and textile spinning, weaving and threading machines. The village is open 10:00–17:00 March–October and 10:00–16:00 November–February.

Dep. Nagoya	Frequent times from 06:21 to 22:55
Arr. Kyoto	40–50 minutes later

Kyoto - Nara   8073

Dep. Kyoto	Frequent times from 08:30 to 22:50
Arr. Nara	35 minutes later

Sights in **Nara**: This is a very crowded tourist town. Weekends should be avoided. See the 1250-acre Nara Park and its temples.

Dep. Nara	Frequent times from 06:18 to 21:00
Arr. Kyoto	35 minutes later

Kyoto - Okayama   8000

All of these services are Bullet Trains which require reservation for first-class, have facilities for disabled passengers, and are air-conditioned. Most have a restaurant car or light refreshments.

Dep. Kyoto   Frequent times from 07:15 to 22:28
Arr. Okayama   90 minutes later

Sights in **Okayama**: The bamboo groves, tea plantation, streams and ponds in the 28.5-acre Korakuen Park, one of Japan's finest gardens, established in 1700. Nearby, the lovely Kibitsu Shrine and the Saidaiji Temple. There is much extraordinary fruit in this area: white peaches, muscat grapes and unusual pears.

Dep. Okayama   Frequent times from 06:00 to 20:42
Arr. Kyoto   90 minutes later

Okayama - Matsuyama - Uwajima

See "Kyoto–Okayama–Matsuyama–Uwajima"

Kyoto - Takamatsu

All of the services Kyoto–Okayama and v.v. are Bullet Trains which require reservation for first-class, have facilities for disabled passengers, and are air-conditioneds. Most have a restaurant car or light refreshments.

All the Okayama–Uwajima and v.v. trains require reservation for first-class, are air-conditioned and have light refreshments.

8000
Dep. Kyoto   Frequent times from 07:15 to 22:12
Arr. Okayama   1½ hours later
Change trains. 8021
Dep. Okayama   Frequent times from 05:25 to 23:45.
Arr. Takamatsu   60 minutes later

Sights in **Takamatsu**: The museum of 12th century battle relics in **Yashima Temple**, 5 miles away. The outstanding Ritsurin Park and Zoo. The Kimpira Shrines, only a one-hour ride by electric train to **Kotohira**. Nearby **Kotobiki Park**.

Dep. Takamatsu	Frequent times from 04:38 to 22:52.
Arr. Okayama	60 minutes later
Change trains. 8000	
Dep. Okayama	Frequent times from 06:00 to 20:42
Arr. Kyoto	1½ hours later

Kyoto - Toba   8120

All of these trains require reservation for first-class and are air-conditioned . All have light refreshments, unless designated otherwise.

| Dep. Kyoto | 07:15 (1) | 08:15 | 09:15 | 10:15 | 11:15 | 12:15 | 13:15 (2) |
| Arr. Toba | 09:31 | 10:31 | 11:31 | 12:31 | 13:31 | 14:31 | 15:31 |

Sights in **Toba**: See women divers gathering oysters into which an irritant is inserted which starts the process of pearl formation. A program is presented at **Pearl Island**, near the waterfront. Then continue on to **Kashikojima**, where you will want to visit the Cultured Pearl Institute to see the exhibition there.

| Dep. Toba | 08:57 | 09:57 | 10:57 | 11:57 | 12:57 | 13:57 | 14:57 (3) |
| Arr. Kyoto | 11:18 | 12:18 | 13:18 | 14:18 | 15:18 | 16:18 | 17:18 |

(1) No light refreshments. (2) Plus other departures from Kyoto at 14:15, 15:15, 16:15 and 18:15. (3) Plus other departures from Toba at 15:57, 16:57, 17:57 and 18:57 (1).

Kyoto - Tokyo   8000

All of these services are Bullet Trains which require reservation for first-class, have facilities for disabled passengers, and are air-conditioned . Most have a restaurant car or light refreshments.

| Dep. Kyoto | Frequently 06:17 to 21:35 | Dep. Tokyo | Frequently 06:07-21:18 |
| Arr. Tokyo | 2 hours and 40 minutes later | Arr. Kyoto | 2 hours and 40 minutes later |

Osaka - Himeji   8000

All of these services are Bullet Trains which require reservation for first-class, have facilities for disabled passengers, and are air-conditioned . Most have a restaurant car or light refreshments.

Dep. Osaka (1)	Frequent times from 06:10 to 23:10
Arr. Himeji	40 minutes later

Sights in **Himeji**: The 5-story 17th century White Herron Castle.

Dep. Himeji	Frequent times from 06:00 to 22:44
Arr. Osaka (1)	40 minutes later

(1) Shin-Osaka, a commuter station.

Osaka - Kanazawa   8017

These trains have light refreshments.

Dep. Osaka (Umeda)	Frequent times from 07:05 to 20:10
Arr. Kanazawa	2 hours 35 minutes later

Sights in **Kanazawa**: A lovely castle city on Japan's seacoast. Mountain-climbing trips start from here. See Kenrokuen, the beautiful garden with ponds and waterfalls, next to the castle. Seisonkaku Villa (08:30–16:30, closed Wednesday), in the garden. Behind Seisonkaku is the Ishikawa Art Museum, which features Kutani ceramics. See artists painting intricate designs on silk at the Saihitsuan Yuzen Silk Center (09:00–12:00 and 13:00–16:30, closed Thursday).

Dep. Kanazawa	Frequent times from 06:05 to 19:55
Arr. Osaka (Umeda)	2 hours 35 minutes later

Osaka - Kobe   8000

All of these services are Bullet Trains which require reservation for first-class, have facilities for disabled passengers, and are air-conditioned . Most have a restaurant car or light refreshments.

Dep. Osaka (1)	Frequently 06:00 to 23:10	Dep. Kobe	Frequently 06:24-23:19
Arr. Kobe	14 minutes later	Arr. Osaka (1)	14 minures later

(1) Shin-Osaka, a commuter station.

Sights in **Kobe**: See notes under "Kyoto–Kobe"

Osaka - Nagoya   8000

All of these services are Bullet Trains which require reservation for first-class, have facilities for disabled passengers, and are air-conditioned . Most have a restaurant car or light refreshments.

Dep. Osaka (1)	Frequent times from 06:00 to 21:39
Arr. Nagoya	60–70 minutes later

Sights in **Nagoya**: See notes under "Kyoto–Nagoya"

Dep. Nagoya	Frequent times from 06:21 to 22:55
Arr. Osaka (1)	60–70 minutes later

(1) Shin-Osaka, a commuter station.

Osaka - Okayama   8000

All of these services are Bullet Trains which require reservation for first-class, have facilities for disabled passengers, and are air-conditioned . Most have a restaurant car or light refreshments.

Dep. Osaka (1)	Frequent times from 06:00 to 22:28
Arr. Okayama	60–70 minutes later

Sights in **Okayama**: See notes under "Kyoto–Okayama"

Dep. Okayama	Frequent times from 06:00 to 22:40
Arr. Osaka (1)	60–70 minutes later

(1) Shin-Osaka, a commuter station.

Osaka - Tottori   8018

All of these trains require reservation for first-class, have light refreshments, and are air-conditioned, unless designated otherwise.

Dep. Osaka (Shin)	-0-	09:27	-0-	17:51
Dep.Osaka (Umeda)	09:05 (1)	09:35	12:20	18:02
Arr. Tottori	13:10	13:50	16:31	22:19

Sights in **Tottori**: Many hotsprings here. See the sand dunes on the nearby shore.

Dep. Tottori	01:12 (2)	06:55	11:25	15:57	16:56 (1)
Arr. Osaka (Umeda)	07:09	10:55	15:35	20:10	21:03
Arr. Osaka (Shin)	-0-	-0-	15:48	20:19	-0-

(1) Second-class only. (2) *Not* air-conditioned. Carries a second-class sleeping car. Coaches are second-class only.

Osaka - Toyama 8017

All trains on this route have light refreshments and are air-conditioned.

Dep. Osaka (Umeda)	Frequent times from 07:05 to 20:10
Arr. Toyama	3¼–3½ hours later

Sights in **Toyama**: Famous since the 17th century for its medical powders, pills, drugs and other pharmaceutical items.

Dep. Toyama	Frequent times from 05:25 to 19:16
Arr. Osaka (Umeda)	3¼–3½ hours later

Tokyo - Hakone (Lake Ashi) 8049

Beautiful scenery on this easy one-day roundtrip.

Dep. Tokyo (Shinjuku)   07:00 then every 30 minutes from 10:00 to 18:30
    Saturdays & Sundays: as above + 07:30, 08:00, 08:30, 09:00, 09:30 and 19:00
Arr. Hakone-Yumoto   90 minutes later
Take a taxi or bus from Yumoto to the lake.

•   •   •

Dep. Hakone-Yumoto   09:13 then every 30 minutes to 20:13
    Saturdays & Sundays: as above + 20:43
Arr. Tokyo (Shinjuku)   90 minutes later

Sights in **Hakone**: A very popular resort, wedged between Mt. Fuji and Izu Peninsula. Volcanic topography, hot springs, historic relics and the beautiful scenery of deep glens, ravines and lovely **Lake Ashi**.

Odakyu Railways offers a "Hakone Pass" which includes the Tokyo (Shinjuku)-Hakone rail fare plus the Hakone Tozen Railway (30 minutes from Hakone–Yumoto to Gora), the Sounzan Cablecar (9 minutes from Gora to Sounzan), the Hakone Ropeway (33 minutes from Sounzan to Togendai), the Hakone Cruise Boat (30 minutes from Togendai to Moto–

Hakone), a 20-minute walk from Moto–Hakone to Hakone–Machi, then the Hakone Tozen Bus (80 minutes from Hakone–Machi to the Atami railstation), and the train from Atami to Tokyo.

The 1994 price was Y-4,850 (Y-2,430 for children).

The unique craft in Hakone is elaborate inlaid and mosaic work made with cherry and camphor wood. Called "Hakone-Zaiku," the technique is used for dolls, toys, boxes and various accessories.

Tokyo - Kofu - Matsumoto   8011

All of these trains require reservation for first-class, have light refreshments, and are air-conditioned.

Dep. Tokyo (Shinjuku)	07:00	07:30	08:00	09:00	10:00	10:30 (1)
Arr. Kofu	08:33	09:05	09:34	10:37	11:34	12:07
Arr. Matsumoto	09:51	10:23	10:51	11:54	12:46	13:24

Sights in **Kofu:** Good views of the Japanese Alps. Fine Summer and Winter sports facilities. There are connections from Kofu to Lake Suwa.

Sights in **Matsumoto**: Great mountain scenery. Gateway to the Japanese Alps. See the Castle (open daily 08:30–17:00) and its 5-story donjon, from which there are magnificent views of the mountain peaks and the Utsukushigahara Plateau. At the Folklore Museum (open daily 09:00–16:30) there are over 50,000 exhibits on the archaeology, history, folklore and mountains of this area.

It is only 30 minutes by train from Matsumoto to Hotaka, and then a 7-minute walk from there to the Rokuzan Art Museum, open daily except Monday 09:00–17:00 April–October, 09:00–16:00 November–March. It features the sculptures of Rokuzan Ogiwara. He is called "the Rodin of the Orient."

A 40-minute walk from Hotaka's railstation, down a hiking road, leads to the very picturesque view of the country's largest Japanese horseradish farm-fields of green leaves of the "wasabi," surrounded by acacia and poplar trees.

Dep. Matsumoto	06:05	06:32	07:42	08:47	09:12	09:54 (2)
Dep. Kofu	07:22	07:49	09:03	10:04	10:29	11:05
Arr. Tokyo (Shinjuku)	09:12	09:25	10:36	11:36	12:06	12:36

(1) Plus frequent other Tokyo departures every hour 11:00–21:00. (2) Plus frequent other Matsumoto departures 10:47–19:42.

Tokyo - Kyoto - Osaka 8000

All of these services are Bullet Trains which require reservation for first-class, have facilities for disabled passengers, and are air-conditioned . Most have a restaurant car or light refreshments.

Dep. Tokyo	Frequent times from 06:00 to 21:18
Arr. Kyoto	2¾ hours later
Arr. Osaka	15 minutes after departing Kyoto

Sights in **Kyoto:** See notes about Kyoto.

Sights in **Osaka**: See notes about Osaka.

Dep. Osaka	Frequent times from 06:00 to 21:18
Dep. Kyoto	Frequent times from 06:17 to 21:34
Arr. Tokyo	3 hours after departing Osaka

Tokyo - Mito 8008

All of these trains require reservation for first-class, have light refreshments and are air-conditioned.

Dep. Tokyo (Ueno)	Frequent times from 07:00 to 22:30
Arr. Mito	70 to 90 minutes later

Sights in **Mito**: Visit Kairaku-en Park, noted for its apricot blossoms, about one mile west of the railstation. The special flowering season is late February to mid-March.

The beaches here are popular for swimming in Summer. See the orchid and hydrangea flowers at the Howaen Garden.

Dep. Mito	Frequent times from 06:00 to 21:47
Arr. Tokyo (Ueno)	70 to 90 minutes later

Tokyo - Narita Government Timetable

The 90-minute taxi ride to and from the international jet airport that serves Tokyo cost Y-25,000 ($238 when the exchange rate was Y-102 to the U.S. dollar in mid-1994), while the 60-minute train ride was Y-4,890 for first-class and Y-2,890 for second-class ($46 and $27 at Y-105 to the U.S. dollar).

Because there are 2 terminals (one mile apart) at Narita Airport, be sure to get off the train at the terminal that is correct for the airline you are boarding.

Non-stop trains depart Tokyo's Ueno railstation at frequent times from 06:30 to 20:00 for this 60-minute trip.

Sights in **Narita**: Located 40 miles from Tokyo and only 15 minutes by taxi from the international airport. Many Buddhist temples here. Visit the Historical Museum (08:30–16:00, closed Monday and national holidays) to see art objects relating to the 10th century Shinshoji Temple, located in front of the Museum, as well as archaeological and folkloric articles found in the northern part of the Boso Peninsula. Be sure to see the daily Goma ceremony at the Shinshoji. The Issaikyodo Temple is also worthwhile.

Nearby is the 45-acre Naritasan Park with flowering trees and plants, waterfalls and reflecting ponds. There are many country-inn restaurants on Monzen-Dori, Narita's narrow main street.

Tokyo - Niigata   8001

High-speed trains began operating in 1982 on this route through the 22.3km-long Daishimizu Tunnel. It is the world's second-longest, after Japan's 33.4-mile undersea Seikan Tunnel. At 200km (120 miles) per hour, the "bullet train" runs through the Daishimizu in 7 minutes.

All of these services are Bullet Trains which require reservation for first-class, have facilities for disabled passengers, and are air-conditioned . Most have light refreshments.

Dep. Tokyo (Ueno)	Frequent times from 06:14 to 21:14
Arr. Niigata	2¼–2½ hours later

Sights in **Niigata**: The leading Sea of Japan seaport.

Dep. Niigata	Frequent times from 06:21 to 21:28
Arr. Tokyo (Ueno)	2¼–2½ hours later

Tokyo - Nikko   8046

These trains are first-class only and require reservation.

Dep. Tokyo (Asakusa)	Frequent times from 07:20 to 20:10
Arr. Nikko	2 hours later

Sights in **Nikko**: A cool retreat from hot Tokyo in Summer. Beautiful foliage in Autumn. Fine Winter sports. Many mountain lakes in this area. Lake Chuzenji and Kegon Falls (nearly twice as high as Niagara Falls) are 30 minutes by bus, taxi or rental car from the railstation.

Dep. Nikko	Frequent times from 07:30 to 19:38
Arr. Tokyo (Asakusa)	2 hours later

Tokyo - Sendai   8002

All of these services are Bullet Trains which require reservation for first-class, have facilities for disabled passengers, and are air-conditioned . Most have light refreshments.

Dep. Tokyo (Ueno)	Frequent times from 06:00 to 21:34
Arr. Sendai	2 hours later

Sights in **Sendai**: The black-lacquered main building of the Osaki Hachiman Shrine, reminiscent of Tokugawa's mausoleum at Nikko. Near it, see Sendai's finest Buddhist temple, Rinnoji. Sendai Castle, built in 1602 by a feudal lord and residence for the next 270 years of 13 generations of his family.

The Star Festival (early August) is the most splendid display of color in Japan. Each year at that time, Sendai's streets are decorated with brilliant paper streamers. The celebration goes 24 hours. Also see the nearby Matsushima National Park. Nearly every night in August, you can see the Summer Dance Festival, illuminated by lanterns painted by school children. See many artcrafts and the portraits and old records of the ancient lords at the Municipal Museum (09:00–16:00, closed Monday). Only a 30-minute bus ride from Sendai are several pinetree mountain hot springs resorts with inns. Much beautiful foliage there. Skiing at nearby **Mt. Zao**.

Dep. Sendai	Frequent times from 06:06 to 21:26
Arr. Tokyo (Ueno)	2 hours later

Tokyo - Karuizawa   8010

All of these trains require reservation for first-class, are air-conditioned, and have light refreshments.

Dep. Tokyo (Ueno)	Frequent times from 07:00 to 21:00 plus 23:58
Arr. Karuizawa	2 hours later

Sights in **Karuizawa**: Japanese alpine scenery. There are connections in Karuizawa for **Lake Nojiri** and **Akakura**, where there is good skiing.

Dep. Karuizawa	Frequent times from 07:27 to 20:54 plus 01:44
Arr. Tokyo (Ueno)	2 hours later

Tokyo - Toyama   8028

Both of these trains carry only air-conditioned first and second-class sleeping cars and have light refreshments.

Dep. Tokyo (Ueno)	23:03		Dep. Toyama	22:58
Arr. Toyama	05:40		Arr. Tokyo (Ueno)	06:19

Sights in **Toyama**: See notes under "Osaka–Toyama"

Tokyo - Yokohama   8000 + 8013 + 8027 + 8031

Both of these trains carry only air-conditioned first and second-class sleeping cars and have light refreshments.

Dep. Tokyo	Frequent times from 06:00 to 23:00
Arr. Yokohama	17 minutes later

Sights in **Yokohama**: The Chinatown area. The boutiques in the Motomachi section. The 19th century garden, Sankei-en. A stroll outside Myohoji Temple. The thousands of Buddhas in the Taya Caves. The history written on the tombstones in the Foreign Cemetery.

Dep. Yokohama	Frequent times from 06:18 to 23:26
Arr. Tokyo	17 minutes later

HOKKAIDO TRAIN TRIPS

What Hokkaido offers tourists is wild, primitive scenery: great lakes, fierce animals, aborigines, large herds of cattle, a severe northern climate, fine Winter sports, scenic mountains and forests. The 5 main train routes on Hokkaido are: Hakodate–Sapporo, Sapporo–Abashiri, Sapporo–Kushiro, Abashiri–Kushiro and Sapporo–Wakkanai.

Hakodate

This is the starting point for rail trips to Japan's northernmost frontier. See the only Western castle in Japan: Goryokaku fortress, constructed in the form of a 5-pointed star. Take a cable car to see the view from the top of **Mt. Hakodate**.

Sapporo

Known as "Little Tokyo," this 1.3 million metropolis has marvelous skiing and is also a hot springs resort. Its most famous event is the annual February Show Festival, featuring 10-foot high snow sculptures of subjects ranging from Colonel Sanders to Donald Duck. Visit the **Shikotsu-Toya National Park**, **Akan National Park** (a reservation for Ainu aborigines) and **Daisetsuzan National Park**.

See the azalea and rose gardens and 2 small museums in the Hokkaido University Botanical Garden. The collection of Ainu handicrafts in the Batchelor Museum, founded by an English minister. The 2 underground shopping arcades: Pole Town (running from the Minami–Odori to the Susukino subway stations) and Aurora Town (from Odori-Sanchome to the TV tower).

Tokyo - Hakodate (via Sendai) - Sapporo   8028

All of these are overnight trains, are air-conditioned and carry only first and second class sleeping cars and a restaurant car..

Dep. Tokyo (Ueno)	16:50	17:17	19:03
Arr. Hakodate	04:24	04:52	06:34
Arr. Sapporo	08:53	09:23	10:57
		• • •	
Dep. Sapporo	17:13	18:14	19:24
Dep. Hakodate	21:46	22:38	23:41
Arr. Tokyo (Ueno)	09:17	10:12	11:12

Tokyo - Fukushima - Sapporo   Government Timetable

None of the "Northern Star" trains have coach cars. All of them carry only first and second-class sleeping cars and a restaurant car. All "Northern Star" trains have a shower in their "lobby car." They charged $3.00 (U.S.) in 1994 for 6 minutes of hot water plus 24 minutes to lounge in a bathrobe after the shower.

Dep. Tokyo (Ueno)	16:50 (1)	17:17 (1)	19:03 (1)	19:23
Dep. Fukushima	20:10	20:42	22:31	23:00
Arr. Sapporo	08:53	09:20	10:50	12:30
		• • •		
Dep. Sapporo	17:13 (1)	18:14 (1)	19:24 (1)	19:39
Dep. Fukushima	05:50	06:47	07:49	09:07
Arr. Tokyo (Ueno)	09:20	10:12	11:12	12:45

(1) "Northern Star."

Hakodate - Sapporo and Sapporo - Hakodate 8003

All of these trains require reservation for first-class, are air-conditioned, and have light refreshments unless designated otherwise.

Dep. Hakodate	01:37 (1)	07:30	09:06	10:12	11:38	13:00	14:58 (2)
Arr. Sapporo	06:18	11:11	12:41	13:41	15:11	16:43	18:41

• • •

Dep. Sapporo	07:06	08:00	09:40	11:40	13:01	15:01	17:01 (3)
Arr. Hakodate	10:46	11:42	13:27	15:27	16:41	18:41	20:39

(1) Second-class only. No light refreshments. (2) Plus other departures from Hakodate at 17:05 and 19:01, arriving Sapporo 20:49 and 22:40. (3) Plus other departures from Sapporo at 19:16 and 22:00 (1), arriving Hakodate 23:02 and 02:42.

Sapporo - Asahikawa - Abashiri 8003

All of these trains require reservation for first-class, are air-conditioned, and have light refreshments unless designated otherwise.

Dep. Sapporo	07:05	07:30 (1)	09:40	15:15	17:15	23:00
Arr. Asahikawa	08:35	09:00	11:12	16:50	18:44	01:10
Arr. Abashiri	12:24	– 0 –	15:09	20:43	22:36	06:15

Sights in **Abashiri**: Take a sightseeing bus or taxi to view the magnificent seacoast. See the unique igloo sculptures during February Snow Festival, including blocks of ice containing frozen fish.

Sights in **Asahikawa**: The aborigine Ainu village at **Chikabumi**, a few minutes away. Instead of stopping in Asahigawa, many tourists drive by rental car to the hot spring resorts a few hours away (**Shirogane** and **Sounkyo**), where there are good inns, skiing and beautiful mountain scenery. This is in the excellent Daisetsuzan National Park. There is excellent fishing in this area.

Dep. Abashiri	– 0 –	06:43	09:30	13:53	17:19	22:15
Dep. Asahikawa	07:20 (2)	10:33	13:10	17:36	21:00	04:20
Arr. Sapporo	08:45	12:09	14:48	19:11	22:34	06:30

(1) Plus other Sapporo – Asahikawa services (most second-class only) at frequent times 08:00 – 23:00. (2) Plus other Ashikawa – Sapporo services (most second-class only) at frequent times 07:45 – 21:00.

Sapporo - Kushiro   8003

All of these trains require reservation for first-class, are air-conditioned, and have light re-freshments unless designated otherwise.

Dep. Sapporo	07:20	09:53	12:16	14:41	16:31	18:46 (2)
Arr. Kushiro	12:19	14:46	17:05	19:35	21:00	23:32

• • •

Dep. Kushiro	07:03	09:31	11:04	13:29	15:08	17:50 (3)
Arr. Sapporo	11:41	13:56	15:56	18:26	19:56	22:33

(1) Carries a second-class sleeping car and a second-class coach. *Not* air-conditioned. *No* light refreshments. (2) Plus another departure from Sapporo at 23:00 (1), arriving Kushiro 06:10. (3) Plus another departure from Kushiro at 22:30 (1), arriving Sapporo 06:26.

Abashiri - Shari - Kushiro   Government Timetable

Dep. Abashiri	06:44	10:00	10:56	12:48	13:56	15:40	18:02 (1)
Arr. Shari	07:23	10:38	11:44	13:40	14:35	16:23	18:47
Arr. Kushiro	10:00	13:00	-0-	-0-	-0-	19:23	21:36

Sights in **Shari**: Exhibits of this area's wildlife and geology, at the Shiretoko Museum, open April-September 08:30–17:00, October-March 09:00–16:00.

Sights in **Kushiro**: One of the bases for visiting **Akan National Park**.

Dep. Kushiro	06:13	-0-	08:55	-0-	-0-	-0-	14:58 (2)
Dep. Shari	08:42	09:43	11:09	13:03	14:46	16:27	17:18
Arr. Abashiri	09:23	10:58	11:48	13:48	15:34	17:12	17:58

(1) Plus other departures from Abashiri at 19:19 and 21:10, terminating in Shari 20:02 and 21:48. (2) Plus another departure from Kushiro at 17:40, departing Shari at 19:56, arriving Abashiri 20:42.

Sapporo - Asahikawa - Wakkanai   8003

The trip to Japan's northernmost rail terminal.

Dep. Sapporo	07:05 (1)	11:32 (2)	16:32 (2)	22:00 (3)
Dep. Asahikawa	08:49 (1)	13:18	18:19	00:32
Arr. Wakkanai	12:45	17:27	22:16	06:00

Sights in **Wakkanai**: Japan's northernmost city, situated on the west shore of Soya Bay. Because the Tsushima Current that touches it is warm, this port does not freeze in Winter.

The main activity here is the processing of marine products. It is a 70-minute bus ride to the ruins of Soya Gokokuji Temple in **Cape Soya**, a small port village.

Dep. Wakkanai	07:52 (2)	12:56 (2)	16:06 (4)	22:03 (3)
Dep. Asahikawa	12:04	17:04	20:00	03:39
Arr. Sapporo	13:46	18:46	21:20	06:00

(1) Reservations required for first-class coaches. Light refreshments. Change trains in Asahikawa at 08:41. The Asahikawa–Wakkanai train is only second-class and has light refreshments. (2) Only second-class. Light refreshments. (3) Carries a second-class sleeping car and second-class coach. (4) Only second-class. Change trains in Asahikawa at 19:57. The Asahikawa–Sapporo train has a first-class coach requiring reservation, is air-conditioned, and has light refreshments.

Sapporo - Oshamambe - Sapporo   8004

Called "an incredibly scenic route" in the Thomas Cook Overseas Timetable. An easy one-day roundtrip.
All of these trains are second-class.

Dep. Sapporo	07:12 (1)	11:11	14:11	15:33	18:53
Arr. Oshamambe	11:18	15:15	18:15	19:44	22:47

Sights in **Oshamambe**: The nearby **Lake Doya**.

Dep. Oshamambe	14:25	15:53(1)	17:23 (1)	19:56	06:00 (2)
Arr. Sapporo	18:29	20:28	21:44	23:53	09:48

(1) Change trains in Otaru. (2) Plus other Oshamambe departures at 06:24, 08:55 and 10:29, arriving Sapporo 10:37, 12:54 and 15:00.

THE TRANS-SIBERIAN RAIL TRIP

This is the westward ride on the Trans-Siberian Express.

Yokohama - Khabarovsk - Moscow

5050			*5000 + 5020*		
Dep. Yokohama	12:00 (1)	Day 1	Dep. Khabarovsk	07:35 (3)	Day 4
Arr. Nakhodka	17:00	Day 3	Dep. Ulan Ude	11:02	Day 6
Set your watch back 8 hours to			Arr. Irkutsk	18:41	Day 6
Moscow time.			Dep. Krasnoyarsk	124:34	Day 7
Change to train. 5020			Arr. Omsk	13:10	Day 8
Dep. Nakhodka	12:50 (2)	Day 3	Arr. Ekaterinberg	01:44	Day 8
Arr. Khabarovsk	05:52	Day 4	Arr. Moscow (Yar.)	06:45	Day 9
Change trains.					

(1) No Winter Sailings. For specific sailing dates, check a current Cooks "Overseas" Timetable. (2) Runs only on days that ships arrive from Yokohama. Carries first-class coaches that convert to couchettes at night and a restaurant car. (3) Runs daily. Carries a first-class sleeping car and a restaurant car. Coaches are second-class only.

The Khabarovsk arrival and departure times (as well as all the other Khabarovsk– Moscow times) are shown in "Moscow time." In Khabarovsk time, the actual arrival time in Khaba-rovsk from Nakhodka is 21:52 on Day 3, and the departure from Khabarovsk for Moscow is 22:09 on Day 3.

MALAYSIA

Children under 4 travel free. Half-fare for children 4–11. Children 12 and over must pay full fare.

The 3 classes of trains are: De Luxe (upholstered seats), Eksekutif (padded leather seats) and Ekonomi (cushioned plastic seats), shown in our footnotes as first, second and third-class.

There is passenger rail service from Kuala Lumpur to 2 Malayan seaports: Penang and Padang Besar on its westcoast. There is also train service from Kuala Lumpur south to Singapore.

The views through Malaysia include pepper-vine farms, rice paddies, colorfully clothed people at small railstations, water buffalo, and many different tree farms: rubber, banana, tapioca, coconut and palm oil nut (used in making soap and margarine).

MALAYSIA'S TRAIN PASS

Malayan Railway Pass Unlimited train travel on all classes of coach on all rail lines within Peninsular Malaysia, including travel to and from Singapore. The 1995 prices were: 85 Malaysian Ringgit for 10 days, MR-175 for 30 days. Half-fare for children 4–12. Space in first-class air-conditioned coaches (for which a supplement is charged) must be reserved. (The single air-conditioned coach operated between Kuala Lumpur and Singapore has seats for only 22 people.)

Reservations for first-class and second-class can be made up to 3 months in advance of travel date from: Director of Commerce, Malayan Railway, Jalan Sultan Hishamuddin, Kuala Lumpur.

This pass is sold at stations in Butterworth, Johore Bahru, Kuala Lumpur, Padang Besar, Port Kelang, Rantau Panjang, Wakaf Bhuru and Singapore.

Kuala Lumpur

The railstation, built in 1911, is an architectural jewel, built in the Indian Mogul style. Across the street from it is the exhibit of 1,700 works by Malaysian artists in the National

Art Gallery, open daily 10:00–18:00 (except Friday, when it closes at 15:00).

See the marvelous collection of dioramas portraying primitive Malay life, costumes, ancient vehicles, silver, brass and weapons in the National Museum (Muzium Negara), open daily 09:00–18:00 except Friday when it closes at 14:45.

The breathtaking modern Masjid Negara (National Mosque), measuring 5 acres and surrounded by 8 acres of gardens and reflecting pools. Its Grand Hall and encircling veranda accomodate 8,000 people.

Visit Parliament House. Rubber and pewter factories. Tin mines. The old Central Mosque.

The Chan See Shu Yuen Society Temple. The Sunday Market (to be visited Saturday night) on Jalan Raja Muda Musa, to sample Malay food. The antiques and art in Wisma Loke, formerly the residence of a wealthy Chinese merchant, on Jalan Medan Tuanku. Visit the zoo.

Embroidery, tapestry, beadwork, teak furniture, ceramics and knitwear representative of Malaysia's 13 states and the federal district can be purchased at the 14 huts in the Karyaneka Handicraft Village, open daily 09:00–18:00 (except Saturday, when it closes at 18:30).

The National Monument, featuring a group of bronze hero figures (sculpted by the American, Felix W. de Weldon, who made the Iwo Jima statue near Arlington National Cemetery). Open daily, 07:00–18:00, it is dedicated to those killed in World Wars I and II, as well as those who fell while fighting Communist insurgents in Malaysia during the 1950's.

The Batu Caves are 8 miles from Kuala Lumpu. The main sight there is a Hindu shrine more than a century old in a cavern at the top of 272 steps, alongside of which a rail car runs. Who walks the steps? Thousands of pilgrims — on their knees and with skewers in their faces and bodies — as an annual penance. The caverns have large stalactites and stalagmites, as well as religious decorations and souvenir vendors.

Penang

An island, just off **Butterworth**. See the Snake Temple. Ayer Hitami Temple. Khoo Kongsi Temple. The view of the island from the top (2500 feet) of Penang Hill, reached by a funicular. Siva Temple. Goddess of Mercy Temple. The sociable monkeys at the Botanical Gardens. The shops on Campbell Street. The pagoda at Kek Lok Si Temple. Kapitan Kling Mosque.

Kuala Lumpur - Gemas - Tumpat

7005		*7006*	
Dep. Kuala Lumpur	21:00 (1)	Dep. Tumpat	19:00 (4)
Arr. Gemas	00:43 (2)	Arr. Gemas	04:00
Change trains. Table 7006		*Change trains. Table 7005*	
Dep. Gemas	01:41 (4)	Dep. Gemas	10:56 (1)
Arr. Tumpat	10:30	Arr. Kuala Lumpur	13:45

(1) Has air-conditioned first and second-class coaches. Buffet. (2) Estimated. (3) Runs Tuesday, Thursday and Saturday. Non-airconditioned second and third-class coaches. (4) Runs Wednesday, Friday and Sunday. Non-airconditioned second and third-class coaches.

INTERNATIONAL ROUTES
FROM MALAYSIA

Butterworth is Malaysia's train gateway to Thailand. Kuala Lumpur is the starting point for rail trips to Singapore.

Kuala Lumpur - Butterworth - Bangkok

7005

Dep. Kuala Lumpur	07:30 (1)	13:50 (2)	21:15 (3)	22:30 (4)
Arr. Butterworth	14:10	21:00	06:00	06:25

Change trains.

7050

Dep. Butterworth	13:45 (5)
Arr. Bangkok	08:35

(1) Has air-conditioned first and second-class coaches. Buffet. (2) Reservation required. Has air-conditioned first and second-class. Buffet. (3) Second and third-class only. (4) Carries an air-conditioned first-class sleeping car. Also has non-airconditioned first and second-class coach cars. Buffet. (5) Carries an air-conditioned first-class sleeping car. Also has non-airconditioned second-class coach cars.

Kuala Lumpur - Singapore   7005

Dep. Kuala Lumpur	07:45 (1)	14:10 (1+3) 21:00 (2)	22:25 (4)
Arr. Singapore	16:00	22:35 06:35	07:25

(1) Has air-conditioned first and second-class coach cars. Buffet. (2) Has only *non*-air-conditioned second and third-class coach cars. Buffet. (3) Reservation required. (4) Carries an air-conditioned first-class sleeping car. Also has *non*-airconditioned first and second-class coach cars. Buffet.

NEPAL

Nepal's only passenger train service is the 31-mile Jaynagar–Bizalpura route. The main attraction for tourists in Nepal is guided treks into the Himalayas with Sherpa guides.

Jaynagar - Janakpurdham - Bizalpura   6200

Dep. Jaynagar	07:30	15:30	Dep. Bizalpura	08:30	-0-
Arr. Janakpurdham	09:30	17:30	Arr. Janakpurdham	10:05	-0-
Change trains.			*Change trains.*		
Dep. Janakpurdham	14:45	-0-	Dep. Janakpurdham	15:30	07:30
Arr. Bizalpura	16:20	-0-	Arr. Jaynagar	17:30	09:30

NORTH KOREA
(DEM. REP. OF KOREA)

Children under 3 travel free. Half-fare for children 3–9. Children 10 and over must pay full fare.

Pyongyang - Chongjin   5255

All of these trains have a restaurant car.

Dep. Pyongyang	06:43 (1)	17:30 (2)	Dep. Chongjin	01:07 (1)	08:14 (3)
Arr. Chongjin	03:44	09:37	Arr. Pyongyang	21:23 (1)	23:15

(1) Depart/Arrive Pyongyang's West railstation. Second-class only. (2) Plus another Pyongyang departure at 19:50, arriving Chongjin 11:36. (3) Plus another Chongjin departure at 17:40, arriving Pyongyang 09:35.

Pyongyang - Dandong - Shenyang - Beijing (Pekin)

The scenery on this route is mostly rice paddies. The 16-car train from Pyonyang to Beijing is pulled by an electric engine. About half of the cars have sleeping facilities. These are occupied mainly by non-Koreans. The other cars have 4-seat benches. Passage between the 2 classes of cars is prevented by locked doors. A restaurant car is accessible to the first-class sleeping cars. In it, passengers can buy food, beer and Pullosul, a yellow liqueur containing an alcohol-preserved pit viper snake.

Before reaching the Chinese border, the train crosses the Yalu River. On the other side of the Yalu, a steam engine replaces the electric Korean locomotive. Chinese immigration officers board the train when it stops in **Dandong**, where a Chinese restaurant car replaces the Korean one. After reaching Beijing, there are connections by train from there to both Moscow and to Hanoi (and on from there to Ho Chi Minh City, formerly called Saigon).

5250 + 5282		*5280*	
Dep. Pyongyang	11:50 (1)	Dep. Shenyang	23:23 (2)
Arr. Shenyang	23:08	Arr. Beijing	10:00
Change trains.			

(1) Runs Monday, Wednesday, Thursday and Saturday. Restaurant car. Change trains in Dandong at 16:23, departing Dandong [Table #5282] at16:53 (supplement charged, restaurant car). (2) Runs Monday, Wednesday, Thursday and Saturday. Supplement charged. Restaurant car.

Pyongyang -Moscow 5000

Dep. Pyongyang	10:10 (1)	11:50 (4)
Dep. Shenyang	-0-	07:20 (5)
Dep. Khabaruvsk	07:35 (2)	-0-
Arr. Moscow (Yaroslavski)	06:45 (3)	20:50 (6)

(1) Runs only when required. Carries a first-class sleeping car. Also has a second-class coach. (2) Day 3. (3) Day 8. (4) Runs Saturday only. Carries a first-class sleeping car. Also has a first-class coach and a restaurant car. (5) Day 2. (6) Day 7.

PAKISTAN

Children under 3 travel free. Half-fare for children 3–11. Children 12 and over must pay full fare. Most trains in Pakistan provide "special ladies' accommodation" which both male and female children under 12 may use if they are traveling with an adult female relative or companion.

There are 4 classes of train travel here: air-conditioned, first-class, second-class and third-class. Air-conditioned class converts into sleeping compartments with 2 berths for night travel. First-class converts to 4 berths. Second-class converts to couchettes.

Reservations are recommended for all overnight and long-distance journeys. Advance application is recommended to reserve bedding rolls in air-conditioned class. Passengers in air-conditioned coaches on certain trains can obtain (at extra charge) bedding, soap, toilet paper and a towel.

The 3 major train routes in Pakistan are from Karachi: northeast to Lahore, north to Peshawar, and northwest to Quetta.

Karachi

See Burns Gardens. The Ghanshyam Art Center. The Zoo in Ghandi Gardens. The 270-acre Botanical Garden. The National Museum, with its Greco-Buddhist art, near Cantonment Railstation. Adamji Mosque. The Memorial Museum. Mamon Mosque. The Hindu Temple. Jahangir Park. You will find every thing from mangos to silver anklets in these typical Eastern bazaars: Juna, Khajoor, Jodia, Sarafa and Bahri.

Visit Fire Temple. Islamia College. "Mazaar," the Mausoleum of Quaid-E-Azam Mohammad Ali Jinnah, who guided Pakistan to independence. The Aquarium and amusement park, at Clifton.

This is a natural harbor. Half-day and full-day excursions can be made to many secluded swimming and fishing beaches, archaeological sites and bird sanctuaries. Only 17 miles away are the exquisitely carved gravestones of medieval kings, princes and Baluchi tribesmen.

Engraved red sandstone mausoleums over 600 years old, where some of the great Moghul governors are buried, can be seen at Makli Hill. The main attraction there is the Shah Jehan Mosque, one of the finest surviving works of Muslim architecture. It was built in 1644 by Jehan, the same emperor who constructed the TajMahal in India and, in 1632, the fabulous Shish Mahal in Lahore. Its series of 93 domes enables a prayer leader to be heard in every corner of the massive brick building. The Mosque's brick enamel and glazed tiles are unsurpassed.

An airplane excursion can be made to **Moenjodaro** (Mound of the Dead), a 25-acre split-level town, site of one of the earliest Asian civilizations. It had a covered sewage system, a huge public bath, a large granary, a religious seminary, and many private homes.

Karachi - Hyderabad 5910

Dep. Karachi (Can.)	07:00 (1)	07:15	07:35	08:20 (2)	10:00 (3+7)
Arr. Hyderabad	09:00	09:45	11:13	11:00	12:15

Sights in **Hyderabad**: Much lacquerware, ornamented silks and items of gold and silver are made here. See the large 18th century fort. The 1½ mile-long Shahi Bazaar, running from the fort to the Market Tower. The old palaces. The tombs of ancient rulers.

Dep. Hyderabad	03:15 (4)	04:15 (2)	05:45 (5)	06:50 (5)	07:15 (6+8)
Arr. Karachi (Can.)	06:40	07:00	08:35	09:52	10:20

(1) Supplement charged. Has an airconditioned-class coach. Restaurant car. (2) Reservation required. Has an airconditioned-class coach. Restaurant car. (3) Has a first-class coach. Restaurant car. (4) Reservation required. Has an airconditioned-class coach. (5) Has an airconditioned-class coach. (6) Reservation required. Has a first-class coach. (7) Plus other departures from Karachi at 11:35 (2), 17:00 (3), 18:05 (2), 18:30 (5), 20:10 (2), 22:00 (2) and 22:25 (5). (8) Plus other departures from Hyderabad at 08:50 (5), 11:10 (2), 13:25 (2), 15:40 (2), 16:50, 18:00 and 21:20 (1).

Karachi - Lahore   5910

All of these trains have a restaurant car and a coach with seats that convert to berths.

Dep. Karachi (Can.)	07:00 (1)	08:20 (2)	10:00 (3)	17:00 (4)	18:05 (5+7)
Arr. Lahore	23:40	05:35	06:20	12:00	15:35

• • •

Dep. Lahore	07:00 (1)	09:15 (2)	16:30 (6)	17:15 (6)	18:30 (2+8)
Arr. Karachi (Can.)	23:40	07:00	11:30	13:20	16:10

(1) Supplement charged. Has an airconditioned-class coach. (2) Reservation required. Has an air-conditioned-class coach. (3) Has a first-class coach. (4) Reservation required. Carries a sleeping car. Also has an airconditioned-class coach. (5) Reservation required. Has an airconditioned-class coach. Change trains in Khanewal Junction at 08:05 on day 2. Depart Khanewal 10:45 (no restaurant car). (6) Carries a sleeping car. Also has an airconditioned-class coach. (7) Plus another Karachi departure at 22:00 (4). (8) Plus another Lahore departure at 22:50 (6), arriving Karachi 21:40.

Sights in **Lahore**: Pakistan's second-largest city. Often called "the city of gardens." This is a busy rail center, with 10,000,000 passengers handled here every year.

See the complex of 16th–18th century palaces and halls inside Lahore Fort. The Shish Mahal (Palace of Mirrors) with its fretted screens, colored mirrors and marble, often called the most ornately decorated royal salon in the world. It was built in 1632 by the same Shah Jehan who built the great Mosque outside Karachi in 1644 and the Taj Mahal in India.

Also in the Fort, the museum of 18th and early 19th century maps, drawings and weapons. The small Moti Masjid Mosque. The royal apartments and throne room. The marble hall, Diwan-i-Khas.

At one of the world's largest places of worship, across from the Fort (on the other side of Hazuri Bagh Square), see the marble ornamentation at the 17th century Badshahi (Imperial) Mosque. Its courtyard, nearly 600-feet long, can hold 70,000 people praying at the same time. The view of Lahore from its minarets is worth climbing the more than 200 stairs to them.

Take the 2-mile walk from the Fort through many colorful bazaars (jewelry, leather, copper, brass, cloth). Also see the mirrored ceilings and glass mosaics in the mausoleum of the 18th century playboy, Maharajah Ranjit Singh. The ashes of his 4 wives and 7 concubines, cremated at his death, are also stored there. See the marvelous collection of Gandhara and Greco-Buddhist art (particularly the "starving Buddha") at the Lahore Museum.

Without fail, go 6 miles east of Lahore to the incredibly magnificent 40-acre **Shalimar Gardens**, one of the greatest gardens in the world. It was designed in the 17th century to rival the one of the same name at Srinigar in **Kashmir**.

Near Shalimar is Jehangir's Mausoleum, located in a 55-acre garden. The emperor Jehangir is resting in a white marble sarcophagus ornamented with mosaics of flowers and with the Arabic and Persian inscriptions that list the 99 attributes of God.

Karachi - Peshawar   5910

This is a 1,100-mile journey.

All of these trains have airconditioned-class seats that convert to berths, and have a restaurant car.

| Dep. Karachi (Canton.) | 08:20 (1) | 17:00 (3) | 20:10 (1) | 22:00 (1) |
| Arr. Peshawar (Canton.) | 16:15 (2) | 22:00 (2) | 08:35 (4) | 06:20 (4) |

Sights in **Peshawar**: Stroll down the ancient Qissah Khawani Bazar (Street of Storytellers), with its stores selling dried fruits, rugs, sheepskin coats and lambskin (karacul) caps. In past centuries, travelers from Persia, Russia and Afghanistan sat in these narrow alleys and told stories of their journeys.

See the 17th century pure white Mahabat Khan Mosque. The 16th century Bala Hisar Fort. The shoes sold at Mochilara Bazaar. The central square, Chowk Yaad Gar. The former Buddhist Monastery, Gor Khatri. The famed **Khyber Pass**, 10 miles from Peshawar.

| Dep. Peshawar (Canton.) | 06:30 (3) | 08:05 (1) | 20:05 | 22:30 (1) |
| Arr. Karachi (Canton.) | 11:30 (2) | 16:10 (2) | 08:10 (4) | 07:00 (4) |

(1) Reservation required. (2) Day 2. (3) Carries a sleeping car. (4) Day 3.

Lahore - Peshawar   5910

All of these trains have an airconditioned-class coach that converts to berths and a restaurant car.

| Dep. Lahore | 06:05 (1) | 12:30 | 20:10 (2) | 22:45 (4) |
| Arr. Peshawar (Can.) | 16:15 | 22:00 | 06:20 (3) | 09:35 (3) |

• • •

| Dep. Peshawar (Can.) | 06:30 | 08:05 (1) | 18:35 | 22:30 (2) |
| Arr. Lahore | 16:00 | 18:00 | 05:30 (3) | 08:40 |

(1) Reservation required. (2) Reservation required. Carries a sleeping car. (3) Day 2. (4) No food service.

Karachi - Quetta   5940

Both of these trains require reservation, have an airconditioned coach with seats that convert to berths at night, and carry a restaurant car.

Dep. Karachi (Can.)	11:30		Dep. Quetta	15:35
Arr. Quetta	09:30		Arr. Karachi (Can.)	14:00

Sights in **Quetta**: A popular Summer resort. This town developed around a fort occupied by British troops in 1876. It is a market center for western Afghanistan, eastern Iran and part of Central Asia. See: The Sandeman Library. The Geological Survey of Pakistan (there was severe earthquake damage here in 1935.)

Lahore - Quetta

*Although Cook uses 2 tables for this trip, all of the trains shown below are direct and there is **no** train changing in Rohri.*

5910			*5940*	
Dep. Lahore	06:30 (1)		Dep. Quetta	10:50 (3)
Arr. Rohri	17:00		Arr. Rohri	21:40

5940			*5910*	
Dep. Rohri	17:50		Dep. Rohri	22:10 (3)
Arr. Quetta	08:05 (2)		Arr. Lahore	13:35 (2)

(1) Has air-conditioned class and first-class coaches that convert to berths. (2) Day 2 . (3) Reservation required. Carries a sleeping car. Also has airconditioned-class and first-class coaches that convert to berths. Restaurant car.

INTERNATIONAL ROUTES
FROM PAKISTAN

The Pakistani rail gateway to Iran is Quetta. Lahore is the departure point for train travel to India.

Quetta - Zahedan   5942 + 4510

Mirjawa is on the Pakistan-Iran border. Rail service Kuhi Taftan-Mirjawa was suspended 1984-1992, and the Mirjawa-Zahedan rail service was suspended 1985-1992, replaced by buses. Both services resumed operation in 1993.

This train runs from Quetta only on Saturdays and Wednesdays. It has a first-class coach and a restaurant car.

Dep. Quetta	12:30	
Arr. Kuhi Taftan	08:45	Sunday
Dep. Mirjawa	13:15	
Arr. Zahedan	16:45	

Lahore - Amristar - Delhi - New Delhi   6013

Dep. Lahore	11:30	
Arr. Amritsar	15:00	
Change trains. 6006 + 6022		
Dep. Amritsar	16:00 (1)	07:45 (2)
Arr. New Delhi	05:00	16:10

(1) Has air-conditioned second-class seats which convert to bunks. Restaurant car. (2) Supplement charged. Has air-conditioned first and second-class coaches. Restaurant car. (3) Has air-conditioned second-class coaches. Restaurant car. (4) Supplement charged. Has air-conditioned second-class. (5) Supplement charged. Has air-conditioned chair car class. (6) Has air-conditioned first-class and second-class coaches, also ordinary first-class, all of which convert to berths. (7) Plus other departures from Amritsar at 14:20 (5), 20:45 (1), arriving New Delhi 21:40, 07:05 and 11:45.

Sights in **Amritsar**: This is the holiest city of the Sikh Religion. Home of the wonderful Golden Temple.

PEOPLE'S REPUBLIC OF CHINA

Children under 1 meter tall travel free. Quarter-fare for children 1.00 to 1.29 meters. Children 1.30 meters and taller must pay full fare.

Short-distance trains have soft and hard (first and second-class) seat accommodations. Long-distance trains have first-class seats that convert to berths with complete bedding, and second-class seats that convert to hard bunks.

We learned on our rail trips (Shanghai-Changsha, Changsha-Guilin and Canton-Hong Kong) that Chinese trains do *not* provide drinking water, toilet paper, or soap, although each sleeping compartment is supplied with a thermos of hot water, tea and cups. There is enough storage space in each 4-person compartment for 6 large suitcases. Each berth has a reading lamp.

You can count on 2 things when touring China: the government will keep you on the go 10-14 hours every day, and you will be placed in a Friendship Store from one to 3 hours almost every day. These emporiums sell every possible souvenir you could want to bring home from China: jade, ivory, fabrics, furniture, porcelain, clothing, lacquerware, jewelry, books, etc.

Canton (Guangzhou, pronounced "Kwang-chow")

In the 64-acre Memorial Garden to the Martyrs (also called Red Uprising, the 1927 massacre of many Chinese Communist Party members by government soldiers), holding more than 5,000 bodies. Also: The Pavillion of Sino-Korean Friendship and the Memorial Pavillion. The Tomb of the 72 Martyrs, honoring leaders of the unsuccessful 1911 revolution, located at Huanghuagang (Yellow Flower Hill Park). The Sun Yat-sen Memorial Hall.

At the enormous Yuexiu Park, go to the top of the 600-year-old Zhen Hai Tower (also called Five-Storied Building) for a view of all of the city. Also located in this park are the Museum of Liberation and many other museums: prehistory, Ming Dynasty, the Manchu era, the Opium Wars, and one on the industrialization of Canton.

There is an excellent Chinese Orchid Garden at the west side of Yuexiu Park. The 82-acre Zoo, with more than 200 varieties of birds and animals, is considered one of the best in Asia and is famous for its Panda bears.

Other notable sights: the 6th century Lu Yung Temple (Temple of the Six Banyan Trees). The 7th century Huaisheng Mosque. The 4th century (B.C.) Kwang Shiao Temple. Many parks and lakes. The view from White Cloud Mountain. The Monument to the Struggle Against the British Invasion, at **Sanyuanli**, north of the city.

Beijing (Pekin)

It is said that everyone starts a tour of Beijing from the enormous Tiananmen Square (nearly 100 acres), where Chairman Mao Zedong first raised the flag of the People's Republic of China and initiated the contemporary era of China.

At the north side of the Square is Tian'anmen (Gate of Heavenly Peace), the entrance to the fabled Forbidden City, a 250-acre compound containing many palaces, museums, pavillions and gardens.

You walk first through the Upright Gate, then down Sightseer's Route to Meridian Gate and then through Gate of Supreme Harmony, next reaching the exhibits inside Hall of Supreme Harmony, followed by Hall of Complete Harmony, Hall of Preserving Harmony, Gate of Heavenly Purity, Palace of Heavenly Purity, Hall of Union, Hall of Earthly Peace, Gate of Earthly Peace, and finally reach hall of Imperial Peace, surrounded by the Imperial Garden.

East of Tiananmen Square are the Chinese History Museum and the Museum of the Chinese Revolution. West of the Square is the Great Hall of the People. Its banquet room seats 5,000 people. A theater near it holds 10,000. At the south side of the Square is the magnificent Chairman Mao Memorial Hall and the Monument to the People's Heroes.

Other important sights in Beijing are: The large Zoo, featuring Giant Pandas. The 770-

foot long white marble Marco Polo Bridge, spanning the Yungting River. The National Art Gallery. The fantastic 15th century Temple of Heaven, located in a complex measuring 16 square miles.

It is a 90-minute bus ride from Beijing to the Great Wall, the mightiest human construction in history. Although a special excursion train departs Beijing daily at 07:03 (arriving back in Beijing at 13:30), the train leaves passengers about ¼-mile from the Great Wall. Buses from Beijing take you directly to the section of the Great Wall at **Badaling** that was restored in 1957 for visitors.

Most of the 3,600-mile long wall was built 476–221 (B.C.), with more than another 100 years of work performed to restore and reinforce it in the 14th–15th century A.D.).

Seven miles from Beijing is the Summer Palace, set in a 700-acre park that includes the lovely Kunming Lake and many museums. The walk down the beautifully decorated "Long Corridor," along the lakeshore, is memorable.

Thirty miles from Beijing, the Ming Tombs cover an area of several square miles. The sculptured animals along the road leading to the exhibit tomb are very interesting.

Beijing - Tianjin - Harbin   5280 + 5284

All of these trains have a first-class coach and a restaurant car.

Dep. Beijing	00:18	01:13 (1)	08:14	15:50 (3)	20:32 (4)
Dep. Tianjin bei	02:28	03:21	10:29	-0-	22:19
Arr. Harbin	22:01	22:43	05:21 (2)	05:12 (2)	14:55 (2)

Sights in **Tianjin**: see notes under "Shanghai – Bejing"

Sights in **Harbin:** Called "Moscow of the East." It became a large Russian settlement when refugees surged here in 1917 to avoid capture by Soviet communists. The major annual event is the Ice Lantern Festival that runs all of January and February, when Harbin is filled with monumental ice sculptures.

Dep. Harbin	06:42	07:14	12:20 (4)	18:18	20:40 (3)
Dep. Tianjin bei	02:30	02:24 (2)	04:55 (2)	13:05 (2)	-0-
Arr. Beijing	04:12 (2)	04:10	06:32	15:13 (1)	13:10

(1) Depart/Arrive Beijing's Nan railstation. (2) Day 2. (3) Supplement charged. (4) Supplement charged. Carries a first-class sleeping car.

Canton (Guangzhou) - Changsha 5320

All of these trains have a restaurant car.

Dep. Canton	08:05	20:52 (1)	23:58 (1)
Arr. Changsha	21:26	08:28 (2)	11:55 (2)

• • •

Dep. Changsha	07:32	17:32 (1)	19:46 (1)
Arr. Canton	20:57	05:30 (2)	07:25

(1) Supplement charged. (2) Day 2.

Sights in **Changsha**: At the Hunan Provincial Museum, over 3,000 valuable artifacts from the Han Tomb excavations. Among the valuable relics from 2,100 years ago, you can view the well-preserved body of a woman. Also on exhibit, displayed in glass jars, are her vital organs.

Other exhibits include beautiful lacquerware, wind and stringed musical instruments, delicate silk fabrics, wood figurines in singing and dancing positions, silk paintings, huge colored wood coffins, bronzes over 3,000 years old, and porcelain pieces produced more than 1,000 years ago.

A tour of the Hunan Provincial Embroidery Factory is worthwhile not only to see the incredible work done there but also to experience the curiousity of the crowds of Chinese people who wait outside the factory to stare at tourists.

Canton (Guangzhou) - Kowloon - Hong Kong 5400

Prior to 1979, it had always been necessary to get off the train in Shenzhen, walk across the bridge spanning the Shum Chun River to the Lo Wu railstation on the south side of the river, and go through customs formalities there before boarding a second train and proceeding on to Kowloon and Hong Kong.

Since 1979, several trains per day make a direct ride from Hong Kong to Guangzhou and v.v. without requiring passengers to change trains inLo Wu. These direct trains are operated by the People's Republic of China and are first-class only.

There are frequent departures for the short ferry-boat ride from Kowloon to Hong Kong.

All of these trains are first-class only, require reservation, are air-conditioned and have light refreshments.

Dep. Canton	08:15	10:00	14:00	16:13	18:00
Arr. Kowloon (Hung Hom)	10:55	12:40	16:40	18:53	20:40

Canton - (Guangzhou) - Shanghai   5334

Both of these trains charge a supplement and have a restaurant car.

| Dep. Canton | 10:46 | Dep. Shanghai | 10:04 |
| Arr. Shanghai | 20:48 Day 2 | Arr. Canton | 19:10 Day 2 |

Sights in **Shanghai**: With more than 11,000,000 people, this is the second (after Mexico City) most populous city in the world. See Chung Shan Lu Street, on the waterfront, called "the Bund," with its European-style buildings, from the period when foreigners controlled the city. You will want to visit the Number One Department Store while strolling this famous street. Also see People's Park, once a race track.

The enormous People's Square. The goods displayed at the Industrial Exhibit, everything from jade to ship-building.

Next to the City God Temple are the Yueyuan Gardens and the Temple of the Town Gods and the Garden of the Purple Clouds of Autumn.

Do not miss the 3rd century pagoda, rebuilt in the 10th century, located in Lung Hua Park. The laughing Buddha in the temple there is a major attraction.

Visit the large natural exhibit Zoo in Si Jiao Park and the smaller Zoo in Fu Hsing Park. The vast collection of artwork in the Museum of Shanghai.

The white jade Buddha in the Jade Buddha Temple. The antiques for sale at the Antique and Curio Branch of Shanghai Friendship Store. The Children's Palace. Swan Lake in West Suburb Park.

Shanghai - Suzhou - Wuxi - Nanjing - Tianjin - Beijing   5330

At most stops on this route, passengers alight to buy local food items sold along the platforms. At Tianjin (Tientsin), the favorite is meat-filled dumplings that the Chinese regard as the best in their country.

The route actually originates in Fuzhou (Foochow). Located in a critical military area, Fuzhou is closed to most foreigners.

Compartments are fitted with loudspeakers from which pour a steady combination of propaganda and music, the same as we experienced on the "Trans Siberia Express."

However, where the Soviet off-switch is in plain sight, the Chinese have placed theirs more obscurely under a small reading table.

The compartments on the Shanghai-Peking Express have a *fin de siecle* elegance: potted plants, porcelain cups, and tea bags. An acupuncturist is available for anyone requiring that service. As on most Chinese express trains, women workers are constantly scrubbing and mopping the interior. Boiling water is provided free in large thermos containers.

Each compartment has 4 berths. However, foreigners traveling in pairs are usually given an entire compartment. Early in the trip the train goes along the Grand Canal that was being used before Marco Polo saw it 6 centuries ago. It still has heavy boat traffic.

All of these trains have first-class seats that convert to berths (a supplement charged for bedding) and a restaurant car.

Dep. Shanghai	10:10 (1+2)	13:01 (2)	16:49 (2)	21:56
Dep. Suzhou	-0-	14:16	18:15	23:19
Dep. Wuxi	11:40	14:55	18:54	23:59
Dep. Nanjing	14:32	17:45	21:49	03:41 (3)
Arr. Tianjin (xi)	04:07 (3)	09:52 (3)	14:10 (3)	22:32
Arr. Beijing	05:45	11:42	16:20	00:29 (4)

. . .

Dep. Beijing	10:40 (1)	17:14 (1)	15:23	20:58
Dep. Tianjin (xi)	12:29	19:31	17:36	23:15
Dep. Nanjing	03:01 (3)	12:27	10:22 (3)	15:53 (3)
Dep. Wuxi	05:33	15:11	13:09	18:42
Dep. Suzhou	-0-	15:50	13:57	19:22
Arr. Shanghai	07:14	16:50 (3)	15:01 (2)	20:39

(1) Supplement charged. (2) Depart/Arrive Shanghai's Xi railstation. (3) Day 2. (4) Day 3 arrives in Beijing Nan.

Sights in **Tianjin:** China's third largest city, only a 2-hour train ride from Beijing. See the attractive lakes (with rowboats) and pavilions in the large "Water Park" (Shui Shang Gong Yuan).

The most important factories of handwoven carpets in China can be toured every day. Visits run about 90 minutes. Carpets purchased there are shipped to the buyer's home.

This city is also popular for purchasing Chinese antiques (jade carvings and jewelry, porcelains, scroll paintings). Very good contemporary scroll paintings on silk can be purchased at the Yang Liu Qing Art Society.

See the collection of jade objects, stone rubbings, ceramics, bronzes and 1500 year-old calligraphy at the Museum of History, open daily 08:30–16:45. Hire a car to go to the nearby 17th century Qing Tombs, which the Chinese regard as more interesting and more beautiful than the Ming Tombs outside Beijing.

INTERNATIONAL ROUTES FROM THE PEOPLE'S REPUBLIC OF CHINA

Here are the routes from Beijing to Russia and North Korea.

Beijing - Moscow   5000

Both of these trains carry a sleeping car and a restaurant car.

Dep. Beijing	07:40 (1)	20:32 (3)
Arr. Moscow	17:25(2)	20:30 (4)

(1) Runs Wednesday only. (2) Day 6, Monday. (3) Runs Monday, Friday and Saturday. (4) Day 7, Friday.

Beijing - Dandong - Pyongyang - Chongjin

In Dandong, a Korean restaurant car replaces the Chinese one. It is accessble to the first-class sleeping cars. Passengers can buy food, beer and Pullosul, a yellow liqueur containing an alcohol preserved pit viper snake. An electric Korean locomotive replaces the Chinese steam engine, and the train crosses the **Yalu River**. About half of the cars have sleeping facilities. These are occupied mainly by non-Koreans. The other cars have 4-seat benches. Passage between the 2 classes of cars is prevented by locked doors.

5280		*5250*		
Dep. Beijing	16:48 (1)	Dep. Dandong	09:35 (3)	
Arr. Shenyang	03:31 (2)	Arr. Pyongyang	15:55	
5282		*Change trains and railstations.*		
Dep. Shenyang	03:46 (6)	*5255*		
Arr. Dandong	08:07	Dep. Pyonyang	17:30 (4)	19:50 (4)
		Arr. Chongin	09:37 (5)	11:36 (5)

(1) Direct train Beijing-Pyongyang. No train change in Shenyang or Dandong. Runs Monday, Wednesday, Thursday and Saturday. Supplement charged for travel and bedding. (2) Day 2. (3) Runs Tuesday, Thursday, Friday and Sunday. Restaurant car. Carries sleeping car on Friday. (4) Restaurant car. (5) Day 3 from Beijing. (6) Runs Monday, Wednesday, Thursday and Saturday.

PHILIPPINES

Children under 3 travel free. Half-fare for children 3–9. Children 10 and over must pay full fare.

The rail system on Luzon is 2 lines, north from Manila to San Fernando and south from Manila to Camalig.

Manila

See representations of the country's major regions (Visayas, Mindanao, Vigan and the Mountain Provinces) at the Philippine Village, next to the airport. Excellent souvenirs are sold there. Visit the complex of Cultural Center, Folks Art Theater and Convention Center.

The sidewalk cafes, Chinese and Japanese gardens, planetarium and the lagoon with "dancing" fountains, all in Rizal Park. The Rizal Monument in Luneta Park. Windowshop on Dasmarinas and Escolta streets.

Fort Santiago, San Augustine Church (which has artifacts from the era of Spanish rule) and Manila Cathedral, all in the 16th century walled city called Intramuros. Near it, Chinatown and the marble tombs in the Chinese cemetery. The Zoological and Botanical Garden.

The 18th century 12-foot wide Bamboo Organ of **Las Pinas** is only a few miles from Manila. Take a hydrofoil for the short trip to see the ruins of **Corregidor**, the famous World War II fort.

Manila - Camalig   7700

There are great views of **Mayon Volcano** between Naga and Camalig and of **Pagsanjan Falls and Rapids**.

All of these trains have a restaurant car.

Dep. Manila (Paco)	13:35 (1)	20:40 (3)
Arr. Naga	03:10 (2)	07:00 (2)
Arr. Camalig	N/A	N/A
	• • •	
Dep. Camalig	N/A (2)	N/A (2)
Dep. Naga	16:30 (1)	20:00 (3)
Arr. Manila (Paco)	03:12	06:13

(1) Has only second-class coaches and third-class couchettes. Restaurant car. (2) Service Naga–Camalig and v.v. was "temporarily" suspended in 1987. (3) Has air-conditioned first-class coaches and non-airconditioned first-class couchettes.

REPUBLIC OF CHINA (TAIWAN)

Children under 3 travel free. Half-fare for children 3–13. Children 14 and over must pay full fare.

Train tickets can be purchased at most major Taipei hotels as well as at the main railstation.

The 5 classes of trains are: First-class Air-conditioned, Air-conditioned, Air-conditioned Limited, Limited and Ordinary. Every train is entirely one of those classes. There is First-class Air-conditioned service from the northernmost part of Taiwan, at Keelung, extending south to Taipei and then along western Taiwain to Kaohsiung and Pingtung.

From Pingtung, local trains run to a fork at Chen-an. From Chen-an, one local spur goes to Tung-chiang and another to Fanh-liao. Another rail line runs from Keelung along the eastern side of the island, south to Hualien and Tai-tung Hai-an.

CHINESE HOLIDAYS

Jan. 1	Founding of the Republic of China	Oct. 10	Double Tenth National Day
Jan. 2	Additional holiday	Oct. 25	Retrocession Day
Mar. 29	Youth Day	Oct. 31	Veterans' Day and
April 5	Tomb Sweeping Day and		birth of Chiang Kai-shek
	death of Chaing Kai-shek	Nov. 12	Dr. Sun Yat-sen's birthday
June	Dragon Boat Festival	Dec. 25	Constitution Day
Sept. 28	Confucius' Birthday also		
	Teacher's day		

Taipei

Among the leading sights to see in Taipei are the fabulous art treasures from mainland China in the National Palace Museum (open daily 09:00–17:00), the world's greatest collection of Chinese art since it was founded here in 1965. About 12,000 of its 620,000 objects are displayed on a 3–6 month rotation. They represent the last 5,000 years.

Its treasures include bronzes (cooking pots, bells, wine containers) used 1700–1200 B.C., paintings on silk and paper, 11th century opaque Ju vases, a 19th century translucent jade cabbage, ancient lacquer (14th to 20th century), 15th century blue-and-white porcelains, cloisonne, and miniature carvings from ivory, different kinds of wood and fruit stones. A store at the Museum sells good reproductions of the objects.

Also see the Monument of the Martyrs. The Memorial to Dr. Sun Yat Sen. Luan Shen Temple, and the street of food stores across from the Temple. The lobby and halls of the world's most extravagant and most beautiful hotel, The Grand Hotel, atop a hill that overlooks all of Taipei.

Chiang Kai-Shek Memorial Hall, a classical Chinese structure, honoring the country's first president. Lungshan Temple. Art objects and Chinese currency exhibited at the National Museum of History. Aboriginal artifacts at the Taiwan Provincial Museum.

"Window on China," 33 miles southwest of Taipei, features Lilliputian (1:25 scale) beautiful reproductions of many of China's historical sites, including the Temple of Heaven in Beijing.

Taipei - Taichung - Chiayi - Tainan - Kaohsiung
Government Timetable

Taiwan's railstations and other of its public places have enormous mirrors. Personal appearance is very important to the Taiwanese, who like to inspect themselves when starting and ending a journey.

No one could become mussed on the air-conditioned, non-stop ride we made from Taipei to Taichung. A few minutes after leaving Taipei, Chinese-language and English-language newspapers were given to each passenger without charge. Next, an attendant brought hot, damp wash-cloths, and everyone washed face and hands. Meanwhile, recorded Western and Chinese music was played over the train's public address system.

Other train employees placed tea bags and hot water into large glasses that fit into holders along the wall, next to where one is sitting and within easy reach. More hot water was served frequently during the trip.

Vendors come through the train with sandwiches, candies and cigarettes. An hour before arriving in Taichung, a hot meal of pork, rice and a hardboiled egg flavored with tea could be purchased at one's seat for NT $60 in 1994 (about U.S. $2.30). This train has airplane style seating, all passengers facing forward. Each car has separate lavatories for men and women. The 1993 price for the all-first-class express train was NT $320 Taipei–Taichung, and NT $392 Taipei–Kaohsiung.

All of these trains run daily, are first-class, have light refreshments and are air-conditioned.

Dep. Taipei	08:00	09:00	10:00	11:00	13:09	14:00 (1)
Dep. Taichung	10:13	11:24	12:14	13:12	-0-	-0-
Dep. Chiayi	11:15	12:29	13:16	14:15	-0-	16:53
Dep. Tainan	11:53	13:09	13:54	14:53	16:27	17:31
Arr. Kaohsiung	12:22	13:38	14:23	15:22	16:56	18:00

• • •

Dep. Kaohsiung	08:00	09:30	13:00	14:15	14:45	15:25 (2)
Dep. Tainan	08:31	10:01	13:31	14:45	15:19	15:56
Dep. Chiayi	09:09	10:41	14:09	-0-	15:59	16:34
Dep. Taichung	10:13	11:51	15:16	-0-	17:07	17:38
Arr. Taipei	12:29	14:04	17:29	18:03	19:16	19:52

(1) Plus other departures from Taipei at 16:37 and 18:58. (2) Plus other departures from Kaohsiung at 16:35, 18:00 and 19:15.

Sights in **Taichung**: Classical Chinese landscaping in the city-center 50-acre Chungshan

Park. Primitive dwelling and artifacts representing each of the island's 9 major aborigine tribes are exhibited at the Aboriginal Culture Village.

In **Changhua**, 12 miles southwest of Taichung, see the Giant Buddha (72-feet tall, resting on a 14-foot-high lotus-shaped pedestal). An interior staircase leads to the head of the statue, from whose eyes (actually windows) there is a panoramic view of the area.

Sights in **Tainan**: Taiwan's oldest city. See the shrine to Koxinga (Cheng Chengkung), the Ming Dynasty loyalist who in 1661 restored Taiwan to Chinese rule after 37 years of Dutch occupation. The Confucian temple. Yitsai Castle.

Sights in **Kaohsiung**: Second-largest city in Taiwan (1,350,000). See the view of the city from Shou Shan, a hill topped by a martyr's shrine. This city is a gateway to several popular tourist attractions: Taiwan's newest Confucian Temple and the Dragon and Tiger Pagodas at **Lotus Lake**. The Chung Hsing Pagoda, one of Taiwan's best-known landmarks, at the nearby **Chen Ching Lake** resort area (aquariums, boating, fishing, hiking, golf, swimming).

Kaohsiung is also used as the base for trips to such other attractions as the picturesque bay at **Kenting National Park** and **Fo Kuang Shan** (Light of Buddha Mountain).

Taipei - Taichung - Sun Moon Lake

All of the Taipei–Taichung and v.v. trains are air-conditioned.

7800

Dep. Taipei	-0-	06:10	11:00 (1)	12:57 (2)
Arr. Taichung	-0-	08:59	13:02	15:35
Change to bus. (Government timetable)				
Dep. Taichung	08:30	09:50	13:30	15:50
Arr. Sun Moon Lake	10:30	11:50	15:30	17:50

One of Taiwan's 2 most famous tourist attractions is the incredibly beautiful Sun Moon Lake, a 50-mile trip from Taichung on the Golden Horse Bus. Motor launches offer cruises on the lake. Tourist sites include Wen Fu Temple and the Pagoda of Filial Piety.

The Handicraft Exhibition Hall is on this highway. Items of bamboo and rattan, lanterns, jewelry, lacquerware and toys can be purchased in this air-conditioned, 4-story building.

Dep. Sun Moon Lake	18:30	10:30	12:30	18:00
Arr. Taichung	20:30	12:30	02:30	20:00
Change to train. Table 7800				
Dep. Taichung	10:13 (1)	13:20	16:31	19:40 (3)
Arr. Taipei	12:29	15:58	19:27	22:25

(1) Light refreshments. (2) Plus other Taipei departures at frequent times from 05:15 to 23:30. (3) Plus other Taichung departures at frequent times from 06:12 to 02:55.

Here is an easy stopover in Taichung, en route from Taipei to Kaohsiung or vice versa, with a side-trip to Sun Moon Lake.

7800		7800	
Dep. Taipei	11:00 (1)	Dep. Kaohsiung	10:30 (2)
Arr. Taichung	13:02	Arr. Taichung	13:10
Take bus to Sun Moon Lake.		*Take bus to Sun Moon Lake.*	
Government timetable		*Government timetable*	
Dep. Taichung	13:30	Dep. Taichung	13:30
Arr. Sun Moon Lake	15:30	Arr. Sun Moon Lake	15:30
Dep. Sun Moon Lake	18:00	Dep. Sun Moon Lake	18:00
Arr. Taichung	20:00	Arr. Taichung	20:00
Change to train. 7800		*Change to train. 7800*	
Dep. Taichung	21:10 (1)	Dep. Taichung	19:53 (2)
Arr. Kaohsiung	23:29	Arr. Taipei	22:47

(1) Air-conditioned train. Light refreshments. (2) Air-conditioned train.

Chiayi - Alishan

This spur off the Kaohsiung–Taipei line has great Ali Shan Forest mountain scenery. The station at Alishan (7,461 feet) is the highest railstation in East Asia.

7800		7801	
Dep. Kaohsiung	12:00 (1)	Dep. Alishan	13:10
Arr. Chiayi	13:17	Arr. Chiayi	16:35
Change trains.		*Change trains.*	
7801		7800	
Dep. Chiayi	13:30	Dep. Chiayi	16:53 (1)
Arr. Alishan	16:55	Arr. Taipei	21:05

(1) Air-conditioned train.

Sights in **Alishan**: People come to this forest recreation area for its smog-free mountain air and the spectacular view of the "Sea of Clouds" that rings 13,110-foot-high **Yushan** (Jade Mountain), the highest peak in Northwest Asia.

Taipei - New Hualien - Taitung   7803

A very scenic train ride down Taiwan's east coast.

All of these trains are air-conditioned.

Dep. Taipei	06:50 (1)	07:20 (1)	08:00	09:00	10:00 (3)
Arr. New Hualien	09:35	10:00	11:44 (4)	-0-	-0-
Arr. Taitung	12:16	12:46	14:59	16:04	17:27

• • •

Dep. Taitung	00:01	06:25 (1)	06:57	08:12	09:50 (1+5)
Dep. New Hualien	03:18	08:56	09:54	11:32	12:48 (1+6)
Arr. Taipei	07:23	12:01	13:59	15:21	15:40

(1) Light refreshments. (2) Plus other departures from Taipei at 13:20 (1), 16:00, 17:00 (1), 19:28 (1), 20:41 and 23:05. (3) Plus other departures from New Hualien at 20:10 (1), 00:43 and 03:20. (4) Plus other departures from Taitung at 12:55 (1), 15:10 (1), 16:15 (1) and 21:38. (5) Plus other departures from New Hualien at 13:15 (1), 15:46 (1), 16:38, 18:00 (1), 19:00 (1) and 01:00.

Sights in **Hualien:** It is only a 20-minute auto (or bus) ride from Hualien to the eastern end of Taiwan's most fantastic scenic subject: **Taroko Gorge.**

Spectacular marble mountains and, in the river along which you drive, marble boulders of various colors and patterns, larger than a sightseeing bus.

Within an hour, the road comes to a long, carved marble bridge. Do not drive over it. Instead, be sure you get out of your car and walk across this bridge in order to get a good view of a raging waterfall under the bridge and the massive boulders that have been polished by the extremely heavy and fast-falling watercourse.

The 3,000-foot-high cliffs along this 12-mile ride contain millions of tons of marble.

There are many marble factories on the outskirts of Hualien. We went through the largest, RSEA Marble Plant. It is well worth visiting. You can watch blocks of unpolished raw marble the size of a large automobile being sawed into smaller pieces and then see the smaller pieces being carved and buffed into ornamental vases, urns, tables, chairs, ash trays, wine glasses, lamps, chessboards, dragons, etc. The other great attraction in Hualien is the marvelous show presented 2 times during the day and once at night that features dancing and singing by very attractive, beautifully-costumed aborigine Taiwanese.

Sights in **Taitung**: This city faces the Pacific Ocean and has a subtropical temperature. Many orchids grow here. Crops include pineapple, oranges and sugarcane. There are many caves, waterfalls and lakes in this area.

SABAH

Extraordinary scenery of dense jungles, wild animals and high mountains is seen on the short rail trips in Sabah, one north from **Beaufort** and the other south from Beaufort.

Tenom - Beaufort - Tanjong Aru (Koto Kinabalu) 7014

Dep. Tenom	06:40 (1)	07:20 (2)	07:30 (3)	07:55 (4)
Arr. Beaufort	08:11	08:54	09:45	10:10
Arr. Tanjong Aru	-0-	-0-	12:30	-0-

Sights in **Tanjong Aru**: A marvelous beach resort that is next to Kota Kinabulu.

Sights in **Kota Kinabalu:** A modern seaport. The capital of Sabah.
    See the museum complex on Old Palace Hill, a mile and a half from the center of the city. Its main building, in the style of a traditional longhouse, exhibits collections of ethnography, ceramics, history, archaeology and natural history with one display on headhunting (actively pursued here as late as 1915). Other exhibits include traditional uses of bamboo and a mounted Sumatra rhino, now almost extinct. There is also, in separate buildings, a Science Center, Conservation Center and an Art Gallery/Theater. Visit nearby Kinabalu National Park.

Dep. Tanjong Aru	-0-	-0-	-0-	08:00 (3)	11:00 (3+7)
Dep. Beaufort	06:45 (4)	08:25 (1)	10:50	12:00	13:55
Arr. Tenom	08:45	09:56	12:51(1)	14:44	15:55

(1) Runs daily, except Sunday and holidays. First-class only. (2) Runs Sunday and holidays only. First-class only. (3) Runs daily, except Sunday and holidays. Third-class only. (4) Runs Sunday and holidays only. Third-class only. (5) Runs daily. Third-class only. (6) Plus another departure from Tenom at 12:10 (4), arriving Beaufort 14:20, Tanjong Aru 17:10…and other departures from Tenom at 13:40 (3), 15:05 (4) and 16:00 (1), terminating in Beaufort 15:41, 17:10 and 17:30. (7) Plus another departure from Tanjong Aru at 11:20 (4), arriving Beaufort 14:20, Tenom 16:37.

SINGAPORE

The 3 classes of trains (operated by Malayan Railways) are De Luxe (upholstered seats), Eksekutif (padded leather seats), and Ekonomi (cushioned plastic seats), shown in our footnotes as first, second and third-class.

The long train ride from Singapore is to Kuala Lumpur, and on to Butterworth (Penang) and Bangkok. The short trip from Singapore is to Johore Bahru.

Singapore

A great seaport and the most modern city in Asia. See: the excellent exhibit of Malay culture at the National Museum. The view of the city and harbor from the top of Fort Canning Hill. The museum in the transformed 1854 courthouse, now called Empress Place. Songbirds in wood and wicker cages at various songbird cafes. Take a subway ride to the Eunos Station to see a market that tour buses don't reach.

The 50-foot tall, 300-ton statue of Buddha and other wonders in the Temple of 1,000 Lights in the Indian section, near Serangoon Road. The Thian Hock Keng Taoist temple. The ornately-carved Sri Mariammon Hindu Temple. The wood and marble carvings in Sian Lim Sian Si temple. The orchids (some of which we contributed in 1975 from our then 28-year-old nursery) and the monkeys at the excellent Botanical Garden. The Chettiar Hindu temple. The Sultan Mosque. Twin Grove temple. Sakya Muni Gaya temple.

Take a one-hour cruise to see the hundreds of ships anchored in the world's fourth busiest harbor, only 77 miles north of the Equator. The cable car or ferry trip to **Sentosa Island**, to see its beaches, the museum of corals and shells, and the 18-hole golf course. A 3-hour out-of-town tour, visiting the nearby Malay villages, rubber and coconut plantations, temples and a crocodile farm.

Participate in the open-air eating that starts at 17:00 at the dozens of food stalls and pushcarts which vend Chinese, Indonesian and Malaysian delicacies. The most prominent locations: Newton Circus, around the corner from Orchard Road (near many hotels); Teklok Ayer Food Center, at the intersection of Cross Street and Robinson Road; and the Seafood Center, on East Coast Parkway.

Sample prawn fritters, fried pork, satay, beef curry, fish-head fried rice, carrot cake, exotic fruits, a rice dish called Nasi Goreng, and on and on. In Singapore , the gourmet can find 9 styles of Chinese cuisine plus Thai, Indian, Malay, Italian, German, French and Japanese Food.

See the many Chinese and Indian shops on narrow, twisting Change Alley. The more than 7,000 birds of 350 species in aviaries (some so large that visitors can walk through them) in Jurong Bird Park, open daily 09:00–18:00. Near it, the elaborately landscaped Chinese and Japanese Gardens.

Also see the tremendous collection of jade from every important Chinese dynasty, in the House of Jade. The daily cultural show at Instant Asia. The exhibit of more than 3,000 fish and the many corals at Van Kleef Aquarium. Over 600 animals in the 70-acre Zoological Garden. Souvenirs and antiques in the stalls at Thieves' Market.

Singapore - Kuala Lumpur - Butterworth - Bangkok

Passengers must be at Singapore's railstation 30 minutes before departure time in order to complete customs formalities before boarding train.

7005

Dep. Singapore	07:30 (1)	08:30 (2)	14:45 (4)	23:00 (5)
Arr. Kuala Lumpur	13:45 (1)	19:05	20:55	07:10
Change trains.				
Dep. Kuala Lumpur	13:50 (1)	21:25 (3)	22:30 (5)	08:20 (4)
Arr. Butterworth	21:00	06:50	06:25	15:40
Change trains. 7050				
Dep. Butterworth			13:45 (6)	
Arr. Bangkok			09:50	

(1) Reservation required. Direct train to Butterworth. No train change in Kuala Lumpur. Has air-conditioned first and second-class coaches. Buffet. (2) Second and third-class coaches only. Buffet. (3) Second and third-class coaches only. (4) Has air-conditioned first and second-class coaches. Buffet. (5) Carries air-conditioned first-class sleeping cars and non-air-conditioned second-class sleeping cars. Also has non-air-conditioned first and second-class coaches. Buffet. (6) Carries air-conditioned first-class sleeping cars. Also has non-air-conditioned second-class sleeping cars and second-class coaches. Restaurant car 17:05–08:35.

Singapore - Johor Bahru   Bus 7019

Dep. Singapore	Frequent times from 06:30 to 23:30
Arr. Johor Bahru	40 minutes later

• • •

Dep. Johor Bahru	Frequent times from 06:00 to 23:30
Arr. Singapore	40 minutes later

Sights in **Johor Bahru**: Do not forget to bring your passport. This short trip takes you from the Republic of Singapore to Malaysia. See: The Hindu Mariamman Temple. The Sultan Suleiman Mosque. The Chinese Goddess of Mercy Temple. The National Museum collection of arts, crafts and Malaysian culture.

Singapore - Kota Bharu

Very beautiful jungle and high mountain scenery on this route.

A passport is required at the Singapore/Malaysia border.

7005 (Train)		*7018 (Bus)*	
Dep. Singapore	22:30 (1)	Dep. Kota Bharu	08:30
Arr. Kuala Lumpur	06:05 (2)	Arr. Kuala Lumpur	20:30
Change to bus. 7018		*Change to train. 7005*	
Dep. Kuala Lumpur	08:30	Dep. Kuala Lumpur	22:25 (1)
Arr. Kota Bharu	20:30	Arr. Singapore	07:10 (2)

(1) Carries air-conditioned first-class and non-air-conditioned second-class sleeping cars. Also has first and second-class coaches. Buffet. (2) Day 2.

SOUTH KOREA

Children under 6 travel free. Half-fare for children 6–12. Children 13 and over must pay full fare.

Seoul is the focal point for rail trips in South Korea, to 3 different seaports: Gangreung, Mokpo and Pusan.

Seoul

See the Kyonghweru Banquet Hall and the Throne Hall in the 14th century Kyongbok (Great Happiness) Palace, rebuilt in 1867 after a 16th century Japanese invasion destroyed it (open Spring to Fall 09:00–18:00, Winter 09:00–17:00).

Nearby, the beautiful Pagoda, the National Folklore Museum (19th century houses, tools, pottery and artwork plus 14th century ceramic vases, dishes, statuary, bowls, incense burners), and Kwanghwa Gate. The collection of metal craft, pottery, paintings and sculpture in the National Museum.

The fantastic 78-acre Secret Garden in the 17th century Changdok (Illustrious Virtue) Palace, with its museum. This is the only palace in Seoul that can be entered only on a guided tour. English-speaking guides usually lead tours of Changdok Palace at 11:30, 13:30 and 15:30. Its beautiful garden has streams and lotus ponds among its pine, maple and cherry-blossom trees as well as flowers that bloom in different seasons.

Nearby, the Yun Kyung Dang residence, Changgyongwon (Garden of Bright Happiness), the Zoo and the Chongmyo Royal Ancestors' Shrine. In the center of Seoul, the Tok-su (Virtuous Longevity) Palace. The view from the 763-foot high hill in Namsan Park. The exhibits of music, dance, architecture and art at Korea House. The colorful Chogye-sa Buddhist Temple.

The great silks, jewelry, antiques, fresh fish and lacquerware on sale at the 2-mile-long East Gate Market. The folk dances and reproduction of rural Yi-dynasty lifestyles at Korean Folk Village, a one-hour drive south of Seoul.

The Korean Tourist Office provides information about one-day excursions to **Panmunjom**, the village that was the site of 1953 cease-fire talks at the end of the Korean War. The Freedom House there has a pagoda-style tower from which American soldiers watch movements on the Communist side of the 38th parallel.

Seoul - Mokpo   5506

Dep. Seoul (Main)	07:20 (1)	10:05 (2)	11:20 (1)	13:05 (1)	16:05 (2+5)
Arr. Mokpo	12:40	14:38	17:05	18:26	20:38

• • •

Dep. Mokpo	08:35 (2)	09:35 (1)	11:35 (1)	12:25 (1)	14:10 (3+6)
Arr. Seoul (Main)	13:10	15:29	16:59	18:00	19:59

(1) Has air-conditioned first and second-class coaches. (2) Has air-conditioned first and second-class coaches. Restaurant car. (3) Has only air-conditioned second-class coaches. (4) Carries an air-conditioned first-class sleeping car and first and second-class coaches. (5) Plus other departures from Seoul at 20:50 (1),22:15 (4) and 23:05 (3), arriving Mokpo 03:05, 04:38 and 05:35. (6) Plus other departures from Mokpo at 15:20 (1), 17:40 (2), 21:05 (1), 22:00 (4) and 23:20 (3), arriving Seoul 20:50, 22:20, 03:05, 04:15 and 05:40.

Seoul - Chonju - Yosu   5502

All of these trains are air-conditioned.

Dep. Seoul (Main)	08:05 (1)	09:40 (1)	10:20 (2)	12:05 (2)	13:20 (2+5)
Dep. Chonju	11:27	12:39	13:53	15:39	16:48
Arr. Yosu	14:04	15:13	16:47	18:45	19:37

• • •

Dep. Yosu	07:40 (3)	08:45 (1)	10:20 (2)	11:40 (2)	14:20 (2+6)
Dep. Chonju	10:15	11:17	13:07	14:03	16:58
Arr. Seoul (Main)	13:36	14:19	16:54	18:39	20:27

(1) Has first and second-class coaches. Restaurant car. (2) Has first and second-class coaches. (3) Has only second-class coaches. (4) Carries a first-class sleeping car and first and second-class coaches. (5) Plus other departures from Seoul at 16:10 (2), 18:05 (1), 21:45 (2) and 22:45 (4), arriving Chonju 19:25, 20:57, 01:44 and 02:34, arriving Yosu 22:10, 23:35, 04:55 and 05:40. The 23:50 (4) Seoul departure terminates in Chonju 04:00. (6) Plus other departures from Yosu at 16:00 (2), 17:10 (2), 20:10 (3) and 22:10 (4), arriving Chonju 18:40, 19:34, 23:20 and 01:05, arriving Seoul 22:14, 22:39, 03:40 and 05:08.

Sights in **Chonju:** The Tourist Information Office is in front of the railstation. This city is also spelled "**Gyeongiu**," "**Jeonju**" and "**Kyonju**." It is South Korea's most popular tourist resort and has been called "a museum without walls" because of the number of historical attractions here. See the ceramics, bejeweled sword hilts, elaborate gold jewelry, and the gold Silla crown and helmets in the National Museum, open daily 09:00–17:00.

On leaving the museum, turn left and go about one mile to the more than 200-year-old Sungdok-jon Shrine. Then walk through the oldest part of Chonju, Choe Village. After that, take 2 succesive left turns to reach Chomsong-dae, a 7th century stone tower that was built as an observatory. Continuing on the same street takes you to Tumli Park, open daily 09:00–17:00. Its 20 ancient earth-mound tombs are interesting.

On the outskirts of Chonju are many interesting sculptures, temples and royal tombs. The hotels have rental cars for driving to many such nearby places of interest. See the 8th century Bulgugsa Temple, one of Korea's national treasures.

Seoul - Inch'on   5503

An extremely picturesque narrow-guage, 18-mile ride.

Dep. Seoul (Main)	Frequent times from 05:30 to 23:12
Arr. Inch'on	58 minutes later

• • •

Dep Inch'on	Frequent times from 05:05 to 23:32
Arr. Seoul (Main)	58 minutes later

Seoul - Pusan (via Taejeon)   5501

Most of these trains are air-conditioned and have a restaurant car. Some overnight trains carry sleeping cars.

Dep. Seoul (Main)	Frequent times from 06:10 to 23:55
Arr. Pusan	4–5 hours later

• • •

Dep. Pusan	Frequent times from 06:00 to 23:55
Arr. Seoul (Main)	4–5 hours later

Sights in **Pusan**: This is South Korea's principal seaport. Many beaches, monasteries and hot springs resorts a few miles from here.

See the museums and temple at the Chung-Yol Shrine (open during daylight hours), where brightly-costumed dancers, singers and musicians perform. This Shrine honors 16th century patriots who resisted Japanese invaders.

The view of the city and harbor from the Pusan Observation Tower in Youngdusan (Dragonhead) Park. The enormous range of fish sold at "Visit The Fisheries" in the downtown dock area, amounting to an outdoor aquarium. The busy shopping center, called Kuk-

Je to buy jewelry, silk items, masks and ginseng. The marvelous wood tile and the many carvings in Pomosa Temple.

The Zoo, Botanical Gardens and ancient fort in Kumgang Park. Pusan has the world's only United Nations Military Cemetery, where graves are decorated with the flags of the many nations that contributed soldiers to the battles in Korea in the 1950's. Visit **Boma-Sa** (15 miles north of Pusan), a temple complex with 30 buildings.

Seoul - Onyang   5502

These trains are second-class only and are air-conditioned, unless designated otherwise.

Dep. Seoul (Main)	07:35	08:35	09:30 (1)	10:40	11:35	12:35(1)	13:40 (3)
Arr. Onyang		08:55	09:57	10:39	11:57	12:57	13:54	14:56

Sights in **Onyang**: A major hot springs resort, surrounded by beautiful scenery.

Dep. Onyang	09:23	10:16	11:25	13:17	14:18	15:22	15:59 (4)
Arr. Seoul (Main)	10:45	11:38	12:47	14:43	15:39	16:43	17:26

(1) Has a first-class coach and a restaurant car. (2) Has a first-class coach. (3) Plus other departures from Seoul at 14:35, 16:35, 17:35, 18:35 and 19:35. (4) Plus other departures from Onyang at 17:00,17:21 (1), 18:17, 19:17 (2), 20:32 and 21:44.

SRI LANKA (CEYLON)

Children under 3 travel free. Half-fare for children 3–11. Children 12 and over must pay full fare.

Reservations can be made only up to 10 days before travel date. Contact the Government Railway Reservation Office, Fort Railway Station, Colombo.

Telephones: 434215 and 21281, extension 433 (extension 536 for information).

Among the sights to see in this tiny (270-mile by 140-mile) island off the southern tip of India are ancient palaces, shrines, temples, libraries and pleasure gardens.

The 3 train tour package that were offered in 1994 included bus transportation between hotel and railstation, all meals, hotel rooms, guides and city sightseeing.

They included the 4-day Nuwara Eliya Tour (Colombo-Kandy-Nuwara-Eliya) at $335 (U.S.) per person. **Nuwara Eliya** is a cool mountain resort (more than 6,000 feet altitude) from which a visit can be made to Hakgala Botanic Gardens and to a tea plantation to see the harvesting, blending and "proper" brewing of tea.

A 3-day Cultural Triangle Tour (Colombo-Anuradhapura-Polonnaruwa) was $162. A one-day Colombo-Kandy-Colombo roundtrip was $108.

Colombo

See the exhibit of stone and bronze sculptures at the Museum. Nearby, the performing elephants at the Zoo. Also a short distance away, the Buddhist murals in Kelaniya, at Raja Maha Vihara Temple.

Bentota, **Mount Lavinia** and **Negombo** are beach resorts a short distance from Colombo.

Colombo - Colombo Airport   6304

All of these trains are third-class only.

Dep. Colombo (Fort)	05:10	15:10
Arr. Colombo Airport	06:56	16:26
	• • •	
Dep. Colombo Airport	07:40	18:00
Arr. Colombo (Fort)	08:55	19:22 (1)

(1) Arrives at Colombo's Maradana railstation.

Colombo - Badulla   6306

Dep. Colombo (Fort)	05:55 (1)	09:45 (1)	20:15 (2)
Dep. Nanu Oya	13:31	15:40	03:56
Arr. Badulla	17:00	19:05	07:48

This extremely scenic rail trip is through mountains and tea plantations. The area at **Nanu Oya** (6,000 feet) is cool and green. **Badulla** is 5,000-foot altitude.

Dep. Badulla	05:55 (1)	08:50 (1)	17:45 (2)
Dep. Nanu Oya	09:36	12:44	22:06
Arr. Colombo (Fort)	15:23	20:00	05:40

(1) Carries a first-class observation car. Has second and third-class coaches. Buffet. (2) Carries first and second-class sleeping cars. Also has third-class couchettes (which Thomas Cook advises "should be avoided") and both second and third-class coaches. Buffet.

Colombo - Kandy   6306

For the best views on this ride, sit on the right-hand side en route to Kandy, on the left-hand side when going to Colombo.

These trains have only second and third-class coaches, unless designated otherwise.

Dep. Colombo (Fort)	05:55 (1)	06:55 (2)	10:15 (3)	13:25	15:35 (2+5)
Arr. Kandy	08:54	09:30	13:36	16:35	18:05

• • •

Dep. Kandy	06:30 (2)	06:50	10:00	15:00 (2)	15:30 (3+6)
Arr. Colombo (Fort)	09:00	10:05	13:00	17:30	18:50

(1) Has a first-class observation car. Buffet. (2) Reservation required. Second-class only. Buffet. (3) Buffet. (4) Carries first and second-class sleeping cars. Also has third-class couchettes (which should be avoided). Buffet. (5) Plus other departures from Colombo at 16:20 and 20:15(4), arriving Kandy 19:25 and 23:55. (6) Plus other departures from Kandy at 17:05 (1) and 01:30 (4), arriving Colombo 20:00 and 05:40.

Sights in **Kandy**: The praying and ceremonies at the pink-domed Dalada Maligawa (Temple of the Tooth), so-named because it claims to have an authentic tooth of Buddha. A ceremony, during which the sacred relic can be viewed in a golden casket, occurs daily at approximately 11:00 and 18:30. Many fine art treasures are exhibited adjacent to the Temple, in the Archaeological Museum and National Museum.

See the jewelry and gems in the shops along the narrow streets of the Bazaar. The spices and great variety of fruits at the Market. Local brassware, lacquerware, carvings and silver items are displayed and sold at the Kandyan Arts and Crafts Centre. The Tea Factory. Elephants taking baths, nearly all afternoon. See wonderful orchids displayed at the 147-acre Botanical Gardens in nearby **Peradeniya**.

Kandy - Matale   6303

All of these trains are third-class only.

Dep. Kandy	04:25 (1)	05:25 (2)	06:55 (1)	13:40 (2)	14:18 (1)	16:55 (1+3)
Arr. Matale	06:08	06:52	08:09	15:00	15:39	17:57

• • •

Dep. Matale	04:53 (1)	05:30 (2)	06:56 (1)	08:15 (1)	10:20 (1)	13:55 (1+4)
Arr. Kandy	06:03	06:50	08:07	09:27	11:31	14:57

(1) Runs daily, except Sunday and holidays. (2) Runs Monday–Friday, except holidays. (3) Plus another departure from Kandy at 18:45 (1), arriving Matale 19:57. (4) Plus other departures from Matale at 15:10 (2) and 16:45 (1), arriving Kandy 16:22 and 18:06.

Colombo - Bentota - Galle - Matara   6307

This very scenic train ride, along Sri Lanka's coastline, offers many miles of palm-fringed beaches washed by turquoise ocean.

These trains have only second and third-class coaches, unless designated otherwise.

Dep. Colombo (Fort)	07:30	08:45 (1)	13:35 (2)	13:35 (3)	15:45 (8)
Dep. Bentota	09:04	– 0 –	15:03	15:03	– 0 –
Arr. Galle	10:20	11:21	16:16	16:26	18:13
Arr. Matara	11:40	12:15	-0-	17:52	19:10

Dep. Matara	– 0 –	– 0 –	– 0 –	05:40	07:05 (3+9)
Dep. Galle	03:50 (4)	04:40 (5)	05:00 (6)	06:46	08:25 (10)
Dep. Bentota	05:11	06:13	06:33	– 0 –	09:31
Arr. Colombo (Fort)	07:10	08:25	08:06	09:07	10:46

(1) Runs Saturdays, Sundays and holidays. (2) Runs Saturday only. Third-class only. (3) Runs Monday–Friday, except holidays. (4) Runs daily, except Sundays and holidays. Third-class only. (5) Runs Sundays and holidays only. Third-class only. (6) Runs daily, except Sundays and holidays. Third-class only on Saturday. (7) Third-class only. (8) Plus other departures from Colombo at 16:50 (3), 17:20 (7) and 19:15, terminating in Galle at 20:00, 20:57 and 22:30. (9) Plus other departures from Matara at 13:25 and 15:57 (1), arriving Colombo (Fort) 17:35 and 19:31. (10) Plus other departures from Galle at 08:40, 14:56 and 17:00 (1), arriving Colombo (Fort) 12:20, 17:35 and 19:31.

Sights in **Bentota**: A seaside resort.

Sights in **Galle**: A Portuguese seaport before the Dutch seized it and then Sri Lanka's chief port until Colombo was developed in the 1880's.

Sights in **Matara**: An ancient fort town. See the old Dutch Reformed Church. Swim and snorkel at nearby **Polhena**.

Colombo - Negombo   6307

Dep. Colombo (Fort)	03:40 (1)	-0-
Dep. Colombo (Maradana)	03:45	10:40 (2)
Arr. Negombo	05:29	12:21

Sights in **Negombo**: A fishing port and beach resort. See the remarkable murals in Raja Maha Vihara, a famous temple. Visit the old Dutch fort.

Dep. Negombo	08:30 (2)	20:25 (1)
Arr. Colombo (Maradana)	10:20	23:10
Arr. Colombo (Fort)	-0-	-0-

(1) Runs Monday–Friday, except holidays. Third-class only. (2) Third-class only.

Colombo - Trincomalee 6301

Dep. Colombo (Fort)	06:05 (1)	Dep. Trincomalee	07:40
Arr. Galoya	11:20	Arr. Galoya	13:16
Change trains.		*Change trains.*	
Dep. Galoya	11:30	Dep. Galoya	13:20 (1)
Arr. Trincomalee	14:00	Arr. Colombo Fort	18:20

(1) Has only second and third-class coaches. Buffet.

Sights in **Trincomalee**: One of the world's finest natural harbors. The 17th century fort constructed by Portuguese invaders from the ancient Temple of a Thousand Columns.

Colombo - Anuradhapura - Jaffna 6300

The fantastic Elephant's Pass is on this route.

Dep. Colombo (Fort)	05:45 (1)	06:35 (3)	14:05 (3)
Arr. Anuradhapura	09:42 (2)	12:30 (2)	18:52 (2)
Arr. Jaffna	N/A	N/A	N/A

• • •

Dep. Jaffna	N/A (2)	N/A (2)	N/A (2)
Dep. Anuradhapura	05:05 (3)	14:28 (1)	15:40 (3)
Arr. Colombo (Fort)	09:40	18:45	20:43

(1) Air-conditioned train. Has a first-class coach. (2) Service Anuradhapura–Jaffna and v.v. was suspended "temporarily" in 1988. (3) Has only second-class and third-class coach seats.

Sights in **Anuradhapura**: Ruins of many ancient palaces and temples. The worl oldest documented tree, the sacred Sri Maha Bodhi. The 300-foot diameter dome of the Ruwanveliseya.

Sights in **Jaffna**: Many ancient ruins. An outstanding exhibit at the Archaeological Museum.

Colombo - Puttalam 6305

| Dep. Colombo (Maradana) | 03:45 (1) | 10:40 |
| Arr. Puttalam | 09:01 | 15:20 |

• • •

| Dep. Puttalam | 05:35 | 16:30 (1) |
| Arr. Colombo (Maradana) | 10:20 | 23:10 |

(1) Runs Monday–Friday, except holidays.

INTERNATIONAL ROUTE
FROM SRI LANKA

There is ferry service from Talaimannar to Rameswaram in southern India. (Rail service is provided from Rameswaram to Bombay and Calcutta, via Madras.)

Colombo - Talaimannar - Rameswaram - Madras 6300

Dep. Colombo (Fort)	05:45 (1)	Dep. Anuradhapura	N/A (2)
Arr. Anuradhapura	09:43	Arr. Talaimannar (Pier)	N/A
Change trains			

(1) Air-conditioned train. Has a first-class coach. (2) A connection in Anuradhapura for travel Colombo–Talaimannar has not been possible since 1989 due to the "temporary" suspension of the Anuradhapura–Tailamannar service .

6186 (Boat)		*6182 (Train)*		
Dep. Talaimannar Pier	09:00 (1)	Dep. Rameswaram	12:35 (2)	15:50 (2+4)
Arr. Rameswaram	12:00	Arr. Madras (Eg.)	06:05 (3)	06:20 (3)
Change to train.				

(1) Runs Tuesday, Thursday and Saturday. (2) Runs daily. (3) Day 2. (4) Plus another departure from Rameswaram at 20:45 (2), arriving Madras 19:15 (3).

THAILAND

Children under 4 who are less than 100cm tall travel free. Half-fare for children 4–11 who are not more than 150cm tall. Children 12 and over must pay full fare.

Reservations in Thailand can be made 80 days before travel date. A supplement is charged for fast trains, sleeping berths and air-conditioned coaches.

Thai Rail Pass Provides unlimited 20 days of both second and third-class travel. The 1993 prices for the pass that includes supplementary charges: 2,000 bahts for adults 1,000 bahts for children. For the pass that does *not* include supplementsary charges: 1,100 bahts and 550 bahts.

Bangkok

A boat ride on the klongs (canals) during peak activity in early morning to a floating market boats full of exotic tropical fruits and vegetables, plus cook-boats that prepare stir-fried dishes and a visit to the Royal Palace are the 2 major tourist attractions in Bangkok. The best place to hire a boat is at the pier in back of the Oriental Hotel.

Cruises on the Chao Phya River also start from there. The boats stop at Wat Arun (Temple of Dawn) and also to see the gilded royal barges (entry daily 08:30–15:30), of which the most spectacular one is about 130-feet-long, carved from a single teak log.

In the Royal Palace complex (open daily 08:00–17:00), see: Chakri Palace, the gold thrones in the Amarin, Dusit Hall, the Chapel of the Emerald Buddha. Nearby, the Temple of the 160-foot long Reclining Buddha (the most sacred object for Thai Buddhists). The exhibit of the history of this area since 4,000 B.C., at Southeast Asia's largest museum, the excellent Thai National Museum, open daily except Monday and Friday 09:00–16:00.

Also visit the Weekend Market at Pramane Ground. The Pasteur Institute Snake Farm. The collection of Thai paintings, pottery and Thai houses at Jim Thompson's House, open Monday–Saturday 08:00–17:00. Another collection of Thai art at Kamthiang House.

Suan Pakkad Palace. The Marble Temple, open daily 09:00–17:00.

Bangkok - Chiang Mai   7060 + Government timetable

Second-class "Sprinter" trains, introduced in 1991, have an air-conditioned locomotive car seating 72 passengers and an air-conditioned coach seating 80. Both feature adjustable seats, telephones and fax machines.

All of these trains have meals that are served to the passengers' seats.

Dep. Bangkok	06:40 (1)	08:10 (2)	15:00 (3)	18:00(5)	19:40 (6)	22:00 (7)
Arr. Chiang Mai	19:50	19:00	05:15 (4)	07:25 (4)	08:05 (4)	11:55 (4)

•   •   •

Dep. Chiang Mai	06:35 (8)	15:30 (7)	16:40 (5)	19:50 (6)	20:40 (2)	21:05 (7)
Arr. Bangkok	20:05	05:30 (4)	06:00 (4)	06:25	10:25 (4)	09:40 (4)

(1) Has second and thrid-class coaches. (2) Sprinter train (see description above). (3) Carries a second-class sleeping car. Has an air-conditioned second-class coach. (4) Day 2. (5) Carries a second-class sleeping car. Has air-conditioned first and second-class coaches. (6) Supplement charged. Carries first and second-class sleeping cars. Has a first-class coach. (7) Carries a second-class sleeping car. Coaches are second and third-class. (8) Has an air-conditioned second-class coach.

Sights in **Chiang Mai:** An abundance of Thai handicrafts are available here: lacquer-ware, woodcarving, pottery, weaving, batik cloth, silk and pottery. See: the 14th century temple, Wat Chian Man. The porcelain decorated 17th century Wat Koo Tao. The 14th century Wat Phra Singh. The beautiful bronze Buddha in Wat Kao Tue.

The view from the mountain-top Wat Doi Suthrep, 3500 feet above Chiang Mai. Climbing its 290 steep steps is an exertion on a hot, sultry day. See the display of fruits and vegetables at Varoros Market. The 7 spires at Wat Ched Yod Temple. Take a tour outside the city to see local aborigines. Also, another tour, a 30-minute ride, to watch elephants perform logging work.

Bangkok - Thon Buri - River Khwae Bridge - Nam Tok   7067

This trip is through one of the most scenic areas of Thailand, abounding with wild orchids. The legendary wood bridge (rebuilt after World War II with steel and concrete) and original rail line were built by 18,000 Dutch and 700 U.S. prisoners, often forced by their Japanese captors to work 19 hours a day in tropical heat.

These prisoners were fed less than one pound of food a day, which the captives supplemented with tree fungus, rats, cats and dogs. Also conscripted to work on the construction were 200,000 Asian laborers. The deaths of 18,000 prisoners of war and 100,000 Asian workers occurred by the time the entire Bangkok-Nam Tok line was completed on October 25, 1943 — 15 months after construction began.

This is a special tourist train that requires reservation and has light refreshments. It runs in both directions only on Saturdays, Sundays and holidays.

On the return to Bangkok, the train stops at the allied cemetery in **Kanchanaburi.**

Dep. Bangkok (Hual.)	06:30	Dep. Nam Tok	14:40
Dep. River Khwae Bridge	-0-	Arr. Kanchanaburi	N/A
Arr. Nam Tok	11:35	Arr. Bangkok (Hual.)	19:35

Bangkok - Ubon Ratchathani   7065

All of these trains have buffet service, unless designated otherwise..

Dep. Bangkok (Hual.)	06:50 (1)	15:25 (1)	18:45 (1)	21:00 (1)	22:45 (1+5)
Arr. Ubon Ratchathani	16:45	04:05	05:20	07:05	09:30

•   •   •

Dep. Ubon Ratchathani	06:40 (1)	07:10 (1)	08:20 (3)	13:45 (1)	16:50 (1+6)
Arr. Bangkok (Hual.)	17:25	19:40	20:50	03:00	03:30

(1) Has only second and third-class coaches. (2) Has only air-conditioned second-class coaches. (3) No buffet. Third-class only. (4) Carries first and second-class sleeping cars. Also has first, second and third-class coaches. (5) Plus other departures from Bangkok at 23:25 (1), arriving Ubon Ratchathani 12:20. (6) Plus other departures from Ubon Ratchathani at 17:45 (1), 19:00 (4) arriving Bangkok 04:35, 05:20

Bangkok - Butterworth (Penang) - Kuala Lumpur - Singapore

7050

Dep. Bangkok	15:15 (1)			
Arr Butterworth	12:25 (2)			

Change trains. 7005

Dep. Butterworth	13:30 (3)	20:40	22:30 (4)	07:30 (7)
Arr. Kuala Lumpur	21:20 (2)	06:10 (5)	07:00 (5)	14:40 (7)

Change trains.

Dep. Kuala Lumpur	22:45 (4)	08:05 (3)	08:50 (6)	14:45 (7)
Arr. Singapore	07:25 (5)	16:00	18:50	22:35

(1) Carries air-conditioned sleeping cars. Has restaurant car until 07:04 on Day 2. (2) Day 2 from Bangkok. (3) Air-conditioned train. Buffet. (4) Carries an air-conditioned first-class sleeping car. Has first and second-class coaches. Buffet. (5) Day 3 from Bangkok. (6) Has only second and third-class coaches. Buffet. (7) Reservation required. Direct train. No train change in Kuala Lumpur. Has air-conditioned first and second-class coaches. Buffet.

VIETNAM

Children under 5 travel free. Half-fare for children 5–9. Children 10 and over must pay full fare.

Hanoi - Hue - Da Nang - Ho Chi Minh City   7305

All of these trains have a restaurant car and the coach cars are second-class only, unless designated otherwise.

Dep. Hanoi	07:50 (1)	19:00 (4)	19:40 (4)
Dep. Hue	01:32 (2)	08:52 (2)	11:41 (2)
Dep. Da Nang	05:51	11:57	15:20
Arr. Ho Chi Minh City	05:00 (3)	06:45 (3)	12:10 (3)

Sights in **Ho Chi Minh City**: Chinese, Japanese, Vietnamese, Cham and Khmer art objects in the National Museum. The Zoo. The Cho Ben Thanh Market. The Botanical Garden. The Flower Market. The Chinese temples in Cholon, the city's Chinatown suburb.

Sights in **Danang**: The Buddhist monastery at Marble Mountain.

Sights in **Hue**: Thai Hoa (Palace of the Full Peace). Dien Tho (Everlasting Longevity) Palace. The-Mieu Temple. Ngu Phung (Five Phoenix Building). Tin Tam (Serenity of Heart) Lake. The 7-story Phuoc Duyen Tower. The imperial tombs of the Nguyen emperors.

Dep. Ho Chi Minh City	08:00 (1)	19:00 (4)	19:40 (4)
Dep. Da Nang	07:39 (2)	14:10 (2)	17:07 (2)
Dep. Hue	11:26	16:59	20:09
Arr. Hanoi	05:00 (3)	06:45 (3)	12:10 (3)

(1) Has first and second-class couchettes and a first-class coach. (2) Day 2. (3) Day 3. (4) Each train runs twice weekly: Monday and Friday. (5) From Hanoi: runs Monday, Wednesday, Friday and Sunday. From Ho Chi Minh: runs Monday, Tuesday, Thursday and Saturday.

Hanoi - Haiphong   7300

All of these trains are third-class only.

Dep. Hanoi	05:00	08:00	12:00	17:50
Arr. Haiphong	09:25	12:30	16:25	21:50

· · ·

Dep. Haiphong	05:10	11:00	14:20	18:10
Arr. Hanoi	09:45	15:25·	18:45	22:10

Hanoi - Yen Bai   and   Lang Son   7300

All of these trains are third-class only.

Dep. Hanoi	05:30	13:20	19:10	22:50	23:30
Arr. Yen Bai	15:20	22:40	04:30	-0-	09:10
Arr. Lang Son	-0-	-0-	-0-	07:55	-0-

· · ·

Dep. Lang Son	-0-	09:30	-0-	-0-	-0-
Dep. Yen Bai	07:00	-0-	11:00	17:10	18:30
Arr. Hanoi	16:30	18:55	20:45	02:50	04:50

INTERNATIONAL ROUTES FROM VIETNAM

There are no train connections to other countries.

CHAPTER 12

AUSTRALIA

Children under 4 travel free if space has not been reserved for them. Half-fare for children 4–15. Children 16 and over must pay full fare.

Summer here is December 1 to February 28. Winter is June 1 to August 31.

To make advance reservations, write to: Australian National Travel Centre, 132 No. Terrace, Adelaide, S.A. 5000, Australia. Telephone: (08) 231-7699.

The State Rail Authority of New South Wales offers 4 different special one-day train tours that leave Sydney between 07:40 and 09:20, arriving back in Sydney between 16:30 and 21:45.

Typical of a day's outing is the "Riverboat Postman Tour" which runs every Wednesday. An air-conditioned double-deck train takes you to **Hawkesbury River**, where you board the last Riverboat Mail Run operating in Australia. While enjoying the wonderful Hawkesbury River scenery, you are served a scrumptious smorgasbord lunch. After leaving the boat at **Patonga**, passengers enjoy a bus tour of the Central Coast before boarding the train in **Gosford Station** for the journey back to Sydney.

The 3 most outstanding train rides in Australia are luxurious and long.

1. "Indian Pacific" makes a 68-hour run between Sydney and Perth, a 2,461-mile journey from Australia's East Coast to its West Coast, and return. This trip involves 3 nights on board as the train crosses the rugged **Blue Mountains**, pastoral and grazing country, the wheat belt of South Australia, the arid **Nullarbor Plain**, the wheat belt between Kalgoorlie and the seacoast, and the **Darling Ranges**.

The portion of the trip on the Nullarbor Plain has the world's longest stretch of straight rail — 287 miles without a curve.

Fully air-conditioned and sound-proofed, this train carries first and second-class sleeping cars and coach cars.

Three types of sleeping accomodation are available.

First-class Twinette compartments have a shower, toilet, wash basin and a folding table. Holiday-class (economy) Twinette passengers have the use of showers and toilets located at the end of each car. Both Twinette versions have a lower and an upper berth with complete bedding.

Roomettes are for only one person, are soley First-class and are the same size as Holiday-class Twinette. Each of these has a toilet, wash basin and foldaway table. The one-seater lounge chair in it converts at night to a lower berth with complete bedding. Roomette passengers have use of showers at the end of each car.

This train has one deluxe compartment, a luxurious bed-sitting room with armchairs.

"Indian Pacific" carries a restaurant car, lounge car for first-class passengers (with piano, videotape programs, taped music and bar service), and a cafeteria club car that serves morning and afternoon teas, ice cream, sandwiches, snacks and liquor. All food served on this train is prepared on board. The "Indian Pacific" is famous for its lavish breakfast: fruit juice, cereal, bacon and eggs, steak or sausage, potatoes, toast and beverage.

On this route, temperatures outside the train average 109 degrees Fahrenheit in February. Overseas tourists are allowed up to 176 pounds of free luggage.

The best time to take this ride is August–November, during the spectacular wildflower season. Reservations can and should be made 6 months in advance. Stops may be made at station en route and journey resumed later at no extra cost, provided that the whole journey is completed within 2 months.

2. The second extraordinary Australian rail trip goes 1,043 miles from subtropical Brisbane across many coastal estuaries to Cairns, the gateway to several Barrier Reef resorts. The 2 trains, "Queenslander" and "Sunlander," are air-conditioned and have a Lounge Car for first-class passengers that has a bar, recorded music and a VCR. Both their roomette sleeping cars and their sitting cars have a shower room.

"Queenslander," renovated in 1992 and very beautiful, is one of the last narrow-gauge passenger trains in Australia.

The variety of landscapes is so interesting that the Queensland Government Travel Centre offers 5 and 6 day versions of this 37-hour trip (with 4 overnight stays en route to Brisbane, 5 nights en route to Cairns) so that all of the scenery can be observed during daylight.

3. The third exceptional Australian train service is "The Ghan" Adelaide to Alice Springs. It won the National Tourism Award in 1990 after it was refurbished. For details, see end of chapter.

AUSTRALIA'S TRAIN PASSES

All of the state railways offer separate train passes, valid for travel within their state borders.

Although sleeping berths and meals are included in the price of some Australian *tickets*, they are *not* covered by passes but can be obtained at additional cost.

Reservations are essential for travel on many days and should be made before arriving in Australia, for which a $25 (U.S.) deposit must accompany information that includes your name as it appears on your passport, your passport number and nationality, and a copy of your air ticket to Australia.

Use of the passes must start within 12 months from the date they are issued. The passes can be used from the first day of travel until midnight on the last day of validity.

"Australpass" and "Austrail Flexi-Pass" can*not* be purchased in Australia. Both are sold in most countries by travel agencies and in the U.S.A. also by ATS/Tours: 2381 Rosecrans, Suite #325, El Segundo, CA 90245. Telephone: (800) 423-2880.

To order, send: a cashier's check, your name as it appears on your passport, a copy of your airline ticket, and the number and nationality of your passport.

Australpass Unlimited travel on all Australian railways, including metropolitan trains. The 1996 *first*-class prices are: $780 (U.S.) for 14 days, $985 (21), $1,210 (30), $1,700

(60) and $1,950 (90). *Economy*-class: $460, $595, $720, $1,030 and $1,180.

Austrail Flexi-Pass The 8-day version is *not* valid for travel on "Ghan" or "Indian Pacific" Adelaide–Perth (and v.v.). The 1996 *first*-class prices are: $620 (U.S.) for any 8 days within 60 days, $870 for any 15 days within 90 days, $1,210 for any 22 days within 90 days, and $1,540 for any 29 days within 90 days. *Economy*-class: $360, $520, $735 and $945.

Sydney

Stop by Central Station and get a copy of the brochure which has details on 7 short, one-day rides by train, bus and/or ferry to such interesting destinations as Taronga Zoo, Manly Oceanarium and the Blue Mountains

See the view from the top of Centrepoint Tower, the highest point in the city. Take the guided tour of Sydney Opera House. Go on a walking tour around The Rocks, the oldest part of Sydney, after obtaining information from the Visitors' Centre at 104 George Street North. See the excellent collection of traditional and modern Australian and European art at Art Gallery of New South Wales, open Monday-Saturday 10:00–17:00, Sunday 12:00–17:00.

Visit the exhibit of Aboriginal artifacts and relics and the country's largest natural history collection in the Australian Museum, at College and William Streets, open everyday 10:00–17:00. The craft, gift and curio shops at Argyle Arts Center, open daily 10:00–18:00. Lush tropical plants and exotic trees at Royal Botanic Gardens, open daily 08:00 to sunset.

Australia's largest museum is the Powerhouse Museum, displaying collections in applied arts and sciences.

Ride the monorail that links Sydney with Darling Harbour. At Darling Harbour, see the Aquarium (one of the world's largest) and the National Maritime Museum.

The changing of the guard every Thursday at 13:30 at the ANZAC Memorial in beautiful Hyde Park.

See the sharks and other Australian fish at Oceanworld. Take the ferry or jetcat from Circular Quay, also the location of the Museum of Contemporary Arts and the departure point for visits to Taronga Zoo Park. There are many excellent beaches, easy to reach from the center of Sydney. Rail tours operate to Old Sydney Town, 44 miles to the north, where the settlement of 1810 has been re-created complete with convict dwellings, jail, church, shops and 2 old ships.

Take a day tour to visit nearby sheep and cattle stations. It is a comfortable 2-hour train ride to the scenic Blue Mountains.

Adelaide

The collection of prints, drawings, sculpture, graphic arts, coins and paintings at the Art Gallery of South Australia, open 10:00–17:00. The Australian birds and animals in the South Australian Museum. The spectacular water-lilies at the Botanical Gardens. The view of Adelaide from Light's Vision. Australian native animals in nearby Cleland Wildlife Reserve, where visitors are allowed to hold koalas and feed kangaroos.

Winery tours in the nearby McLaren Vale and Barossa Valley wine districts. Coach and 4-

wheel drive vehicle tours go from Adelaide to the **Andamooka** and **Coober Pedy** opal fields, often visiting Alice Springs and **Ayers Rock**. Day tours by ferry or short-flight air are available to see abundant plants and wildlife on **Kangaroo Island**: koalas, sealions and fairy penguins.

Take a tram trip 5 miles west, to the coastal suburb of **Glenelg**. The attractions there include a beautiful beach along a balmy sea, golf courses, fishing, scuba diving, horse racing and an amusement park. The tram operates daily.

Sydney - Adelaide - Kalgoorlie - Perth   9000 + Rail Australia

---

This is the air-conditioned "Indian Pacific." Reservation required. Restaurant car. Carries first and second-class sleeping cars and a lounge car. Coaches are second-class only.

Dep. Sydney (Ter.)	14:40 (1)		Dep. Perth (East)	13:35 (5)
Set watch back 30 minutes.			Dep. Kalgoorlie	22:35
Arr. Broken Hill	08:50 (2)		*Set watch forward 1½ hours.*	
Arr. Adelaide (Kes.)	16:00		Arr. Adelaide (Kes.)	07:00 (3)
Dep. Adelaide (Kes.)	18:00		Dep. Adelaide (Kes.)	07:45
Set watch back 1½ hours.			Arr. Broken Hill	14:50
Arr. Kalgoorlie	20:27 (3)		*Set watch forward 30 minutes.*	
Arr. Perth (East)	07:00 (4)		Arr. Sydney (Ter.)	09:15 (4)

(1) Runs Monday and Thursday. (2) Day 2. (3) Day 3. (4) Day 4. (5) Runs Monday and Friday.

Sights in **Broken Hill**: This is the area of the dry, sunburnt "outback." The city is built over huge silver, lead and zinc deposits. Visits to mines can be arranged. Take an underground tour of Delprat's Mine. Also see the collection of coins, minerals, shells and Aboriginal artifacts at Carlton Gardens and Art Gallery. The restored Afghan Mosque, once used by the camel drivers imported to carry supplies through the region.

The unique School Of The Air conducts lessons via 2-way radio for children living in remote areas. It is open to visitors during school hours.

Scenic air tours operate from here to various nearby points of interest such as the diggings of the world's only source of black opals at **White Cliffs**, plus trips to **Kinchega National Park, Menindee Lakes** and several outback stations. Only 82 miles northeast are ancient Aboriginal rock carvings, at **Mootwingee**. The restored **Silverton ghost town** is also nearby.

Sights in **Kalgoorlie**: This famous goldrush town is still Australia's largest producer of gold. Tours of a mine can be arranged. Take a camel ride!

Sights in **Perth**: Wide sandy beaches on the Indian Ocean, with good surfing. Tours to wildflower and forest areas nearby from August to November, when it is Spring here. See the marvelous display of wildflowers in the 1,000-acre King's Park. London Court, a shopping area recreated as a 16th century English street. The folk museum of early pioneering days, Old Mill.

The exhibit of the large Blue Whale skeletons, meteorites, Aborigine culture and paintings in the Art Gallery of Western Australia, which has a major collection of comtemporary Australian art (open daily 10:00–17:00). Take a river cruise. Visit wineries. The lovely Georgian-style Old Court House, in Stirling Gardens. The marvelous horses 37 miles away at El Caballo Blanco, where Andalusian dancing horses are bred. The 6,000-acre **Yanchep Park**, only 37 miles away, with its koalas, black swans, limestone caves and profusion of wildflowers.

The Maritime Museum and Art Center in nearby **Fremantle**, and the great views of the city and harbor from the Round House there. Trains depart Perth every 20 minutes for the 35-minute trip to this small, cosmopolitan seaport. Its uniqueness is that most of the buildings there (Federation architecture) were built shortly after it was settled in 1830. There is excellent access to outback tours from here.

Ferries make a 45-minute ride from Freemantle to the popular **Rottnest Island** resort, 12 miles offshore, at 7:00, 9:00 and 11:00. Ferries depart from the island at 15:00 and 17:00. There are one and 2-hour bus tours on Rottnest. Rental bicycles allow access to secluded coves and beaches. Skin-diving is popular there.

EASTERN AUSTRALIA RAIL ROUTES

An extensive rail system in eastern Australia radiates west and north from Melbourne.

Melbourne

Opened in 1985, the Victorian Arts Centre consists of the 2,600-seat Concert Hall, the 2,000-seat State Theatre (for opera and dance), the 400-seat Studio (experimental theater), and the 850-seat Playhouse (plays and musicals). Two-hour tours of the Victorian Arts Centre are offered daily 10:00–17:00, except when there are matinee performances. These guided tours start at the Smorgon Family Plaza.

See the largest plant collection in the Southern Hemisphere, at the Royal Botanical Gardens, open daily 08:30 to sunset. The butterfly house, kangaroos, koalas, and Gorilla Rainforest at the Royal Milbourne Zoological Gardens in Royal Park. Treasury Gardens, near Parliament House. The superb collection of Australian trees, shrubs and plants at Maranoa Gardens in Balwyn.

Australia's largest art collection, at National Gallery, St. Kilda Road, open daily except Wednesday 10:00–17:00, Wednesday 10:00–21:00. Old Melbourne Gaol and Penal Museum, Russell Street. Institute of Applied Science Museum, Swanston Street. Australian birds, animals and minerals, as well as Aborigine artifacts, at the National Museum, Russell Street, open Monday-Saturday 10:00–17:00, Sunday 14:00–17:00.

The exhibit of Australian ceramics, weaving and hand-made jewelry in the Galaxy of Handicrafts, 99 Cardigan Street. Captain Cook's Cottage, in Fitzroy Gardens, honoring the discoverer of eastern Australia. The Australian Gallery of sport, at the Melbourne Cricket Ground.

Take a ride on one of Melbourne's trams, particularly to enjoy gourmet dining on the Colonial Tramcar Restaurant. The only traveling tramcar restaurant in the world, it cruises

Melbourne's scenic streets. Because its maximum capacity is 36 passengers, advance reservation is advisable: 319 Clarendon St., South Melbourne, 3205 Victoria, Australia. Telephone: 696-4000.

Visit The Railway Museum at **North Williamstown**, open 13:00-17:00 on Saturdays, Sundays and holidays. Take a flight on the Melbourne Gooney Bird, a refurbished 3-propeller Dakota.

A day-tour every Wednesday to the Ned Kelly Museum in nearby **Glenrowan** is operated by V/Line Travel, 589 Collins Street, Melbourne. Kelly was the most famous bush-ranger.

See the Rhododendron garden at 100-acre Olinda. The demonstrations of sheep dogs working, sheep shearing, wool classing and freeze branding of cattle at **Grevisfield**, 24 miles from Melbourne. Take the bus to **Philip Island** to see the "Penguin Parade," a large number of Penguins coming onto the shore to feed their young.

Suburban electric trains run frequently from Melbourne's Flinders Street station for the 70-minute ride to Belgrave. Several different 2-hour roundtrip steam-train excursions on "Puffing Billy" offer fine mountain scenery on the 8-mile ride between **Belgrave** and beautiful **Emerald Lake Reserve.** A collection of early steam locomotives can be seen at the Steam Museum in **Menzies Creek**, one of the stops on that line.

See the collection of kangaroos, koalas, emus, wombats and platypuses at **Healesville Sanctuary**, 39 miles east of Melbourne.

Melbourne - Adelaide   9035

This route includes wheat-growing areas, the 1,891-foot-long railway bridge spanning the Murray River, and the beautiful Mount Lofty Ranges.

Both trains require reservations, are air-conditioned, carry sleeping cars and a club car, and have light refreshments.

Dep. Melbourne (Spencer St.)	20:00	Dep. Adelaide (Kes.)	19:30
Arr. Adelaide (Kes.)	08:00	Arr. Melbourne (Spencer St.)	08:00

Melbourne - Sydney   9026

All of these trains require reservation, are air-conditioned and have buffet service.

Dep. Melbourne (Spen.)	20:05 (1)	Dep. Sydney (Ter.)	20:42 (1)
Arr. Sydney (Ter.)	06:45	Arr. Melbourne (Spen.)	07:00

(1) Carries a sleeping car.

Sydney - Canberra   9021

All of these trains are air-conditioned and have light refreshments.

Dep. Sydney (Ter.)	07:43	11:43	Dep. Canberra	06:50	12:20
Arr. Canberra	11:50	15:50	Arr. Sydney (Ter.)	10:56	10:28

Sights in **Canberra**: This is the capital of Australia. Individual sightseeing here is easy with a day ticket on an Explorer Bus that allows getting on and off at all of the city's major attractions…or you can take the inexpensive city tour offered by the ACT Tourist Bureau, located in the Civic Center. See the modern art exhibit at National Library. The 6 tons of water jetting 450 feet into the air by the Captain Cook Memorial Water Jet on Lake Burley Griffin (10:00–12:00 and 14:00–16:00). The Sunday afternoon (14:45–15:30) concerts of the 53-bell carillon on **Aspen Island**.

The daily exhibits at the Indonesian Pavilion. The view of the marvelous surroundings of Canberra from Mt. Ainslie, Mt. Pleasant or Red Hill Lookout. All Saints' Anglican Church in a railway station that was built in 1868. Its bell is from an old locomotive.

The 98-acre Botanic Gardens, containing 6,000 native Australian plants representing 2,000 species. Parliament House, open to the public every day. The coin museum at the Royal Australian Mint and seeing production of money there. An art gallery and the Museum of War Relics, at the Australian War Memorial. The Academy of Science.

The miniature village, called Cockington Green. The view from the revolving restaurant at the top of Telecom Tower on Black Mountain. The National Science and Technology Centre. High Court. The Australian National Gallery.

The **Tidbinbilla Nature Reserve** collection of kangaroos, emus and koalas is 24 miles from Canberra.

Melbourne - Bendigo - Swan Hill   9032

All of these trains have air-conditioned first and second-class coaches and have buffet or light refreshments, unless designated otherwise.

Dep. Mel., (Spen.)	08:35 (1)	09:50 (2)	12:10 (3)	15:50 (4)	17:05 (2)
Arr. Bendigo	10:37	11:57	14:10	18:00	19:15
Arr. Swan Hill	-0-	-0-	-0-	20:20	21:30

Sights in **Bendigo**: Central Deborah Gold Mine. Pottery Centre. Joss House. The Historical Museum and Art Gallery at nearby **Castlemaine**.

Sights in **Swan Hill**: The re-creation of pioneer days at the Folk Museum.

Dep. Swan Hill	-0-	06:35	06:45 (1+12)	-0-	-0-
Dep. Bendigo	06:35 (5)	07:25 (6)	09:00	11:25 (3)	15:05 (7)
Arr. Mel. (Spen.)	08:55 (5)	09:22	11:00	13:24	17:10

(1) Reservation required. Runs daily, except Sundays and holidays. (2) Reservation required. Runs Sundays and holidays only. (3) Runs daily, except Sundays and holidays. (4) Runs Monday–Friday. Reservation required. Has neither buffet nor light refreshments. (5) Runs daily, except Sundays and holidays. Has neither buffet nor light refreshments. (6) Runs Sundays and holidays only. Has neither buffet nor light refreshments. (7) Reservation required. Runs Monday–Friday, except holidays. (8) Runs Monday-Friday, except holidays. (9) Runs Friday only. Has neither buffet nor light refreshments. (10) Reservation required. Runs Saturdays, Sundays and holidays.

Sydney - Brisbane   9017

Watch for the outstanding forest and river scenery between Sydney and Gosford en route to Brisbane. This area comes in view about 30 minutes after departing Sydney. The best way to see this area is by taking a ride on a suburban train from Sydney, returning to Sydney the same day.

All of these trains require reservation, are air-conditioned and have buffet.

| Dep. Sydney (Ter.) | 07:05 | 16:24 | Dep. Brisbane (Roma) | 07:30 | 19:00 |
| Arr. Brisbane (Roma) | 22:50 | 06:05 | Arr. Sydney (Ter.) | 21:35 | 10:30 |

Sights in **Brisbane**: The view from the observation platform of the clock tower at City Hall. Sub-tropical flowers and shrubs in the 50-acre Botanic Gardens, which provides moorings for visiting yachts. The simulated rainforest in Mount Coot-tha Botanic Gardens, open daily 08:00–17:00. (Australia's largest planetarium is also located there.)

The views from lookout points in Brisbane Forest Park. Brass-rubbing workshops Wednesday and Friday 10:00–15:00 at St. John's Cathedral, open daily 07:00–17:30. The collection of dolls and more than 700 different teddy bears at the Teddy Bear Land and Museum, 118 Edward St., open Monday–Friday 09:00–16:00, Saturday 08:30–12:00.

Queensland Art Gallery's fine collection of paintings, sculptures, photographs and prints, open daily 10:00–17:00 (until 20:00 on Wednesday). Many good ship models as well as an old frigate at Queensland Maritime Museum, open Wednesday 10:00–15:30, on Saturday and Sunday 10:00–16:30.

The exhibits at Queensland Museum (open daily 10:00–16:55) include dinosaurs, the only surviving World War I German tank and the airplane in which the first solo flight from England to Australia was made, in 1928. The lovely lake and the exotic animals, birds and plants at Alma Park Zoo and 32-acre Tropical Palm Gardens, open daily 09:00–17:00.

The 12,000 rose trees in bloom from September through November (and avenues of jacaranda and poinciana trees) in New Farm Park, along Brisbane River.

Brisbane's oldest home is Newstead House, built in 1846, open Monday-Thursday 11:00–15:00, Sunday 14:00–17:00. Several memorials, including the Australian-American Memorial, are located in its garden, now a public park. Nearby is the Miegunyah Folk Museum, another historic home, open Tuesday and Wednesday 10:30–15:00; Saturday and Sunday 10:30–16:00.

See the old buildings (hotel, store, slab hut, worker's cottage and a colonial mansion in 5 acres of natural forest) in Earlystreet Village, open Monday-Friday 09:30–16:30, Saturday and Sunday 10:30–16:30.

You can hold a koala and watch the kangaroos and wallabies at the Lone Pine Koala Sanctuary, open daily 09:30–17:00, reached by road or by taking a launch at Victoria Bridge. Another collection of Australian animals can be seen at Bunya Park Wildlife Sanctuary, open daily 09:30–17:00.

Brisbane's only Chinese temple, the Joss House, on Higgs Street (phone 262-5588 for an appointment). See the more than 5,000 toys, doll houses, model cars and planes, money boxes and teddy bears at Panaroo's Playthings, in nearby **Windsor**, open Wednesday, Thursday and Friday from 10:30–15:30, and on Saturdays, Sundays and holidays from 11:00–16:00.

Dozens of arts and crafts galleries. The collection of steam locomotives at the large Railway Museum, adjacent to the suburban Redbank station. The Australian Railway Historical Society runs several steam trains here.

"Southern Cross," the first airplane to cross the Pacific Ocean from California to Queensland (in 1928), displayed 24 hours at Brisbane Airport.

The Victorian opulence of the National Bank. The beauty of the Treasury Building and City Hall. Many tropical and sub-tropical parks and gardens. Shop in Queen Street Mall. Take the 2½-hour boat trip to **Moreton Island**, or a day cruise to **Stradbroke Island**.

Sydney - Lithgow - Sydney   (Interurban schedule)

Marvelous Blue Mountain scenery on this easy one-day roundtrip by frequent suburban service. Departing Sydney, the best views are seen from the left side of the train as it climbs into the Blue Mountains.

Interurban trains depart from Sydney's Terminal railstation frequently for the 3-hour trip to Lithgow.

Sydney - Newcastle - Sydney   9014 + 9015

It is an easy one-day roundtrip to take Australia's most scenic rail route. This line travels through the **Ku-ring-gai National Park**, the **Hawkesbury River** estuary (famous for its oyster farms), Australia's longest rail tunnel and the Lake Macquarie district. Departing Sydney, the best views of the Hawkesbury River estuary are from the *right side* of the train.

Dep. Sydney (Ter.)	Frequent departures from 04:55 to 23:17
Arr. Newcastle	3 hours later

•   •   •

Dep. Newcastle	Frequent departures from 04:02 to 23:24
Arr. Sydney (Ter.)	3 hours later

Brisbane - Rockhampton - Townsville - Cairns

All of these trains are air-conditioned. See descriptions of "Sunlander" (table 9002 below) and "Queenslander" (table 9004 below). "Spirit of Capricorn" (table 9013 below) features the service of meals, light refreshments and beverages to passengers' seats, airline style.

Dep. Brisbane (Roma St.)	08:25 (1)	10:00 (4)	10:00 (3)
Arr. Rockhampton	17:40 (1)	20:30	21:05
Dep. Rockhampton	20:55 (2)	20:55	21:30
Arr. Townsville	10:15	10"15	11" :05
Arr. Cairns	17:15	17:15	18:10

* * *

Dep. Cairns	07:45 (3)	08:00 (4)	08:00 (1)
Dep. Townsville	14:50	15:10	15:10
Arr. Rockhampton	04:20	04:15	04:15 (1)
Dep. Rockhampton	04:45	04:40	04:40 (2)
Arr. Brisbane (Roma St.)	16:00	15:25	15:25

(1) Change trains in Rockhampton. The Brisbane–Rockhampton and v. v. train requires a reservation, runs daily and has light refreshments. (2) Rockhampton-Cairns: runs Sunday only. Cairns-Rockhampton: runs Tuesday only. Light refreshments in both directions. (3) Brisbane-Cairns: runs Tuesday, Thursday and Saturday. Cairns-Brisbane: runs Monday, Thursday and Saturday. Restaurant car in both directions. (4) Operates early April to late January. Reservation required. Brisbane–Cairns: runs Sunday only. Cairns–Brisbane: runs Tuesday only. Reservation required. Carries first-class sleeping cars and second-class coaches. Restaurant car in both directions.

Sights in **Cairns**: Visitors can study coral gardens and colorful marine life from the Underwater Observatory or from a glass-bottomed boat at **Green Island**, only 17 miles from Cairns. The **Atherton Tableland Rainforest**, teeming with birdlife, is to the west of Cairns. Aerial tours of the **Great Barrier Reef** take tourists from Cairns along the jungle coastline and over many cattle stations. Twenty minutes by car north of Cairns' International Airport is the **Kewarra**, a resort on the Coral Sea beach.

Brisbane - Toowoomba   9009

The ascent through the Great Dividing Range offers outstanding scenery on this easy one-day roundtrip.

This service is by train from Brisbane–Ipswich and v.v. then by bus Ipswich–Toowoomba and v.v.

Dep. Bris. (Cen.)	06:35 (1)	06:37 (2)	07:05 (3)	07:31 (1)	07:35 (2)	08:31
	09:05 (5)	10:05 (1)	12:01 (5)	13:05 (1)	13:31 (2)	14:31
	16:10 (6)	17:05 (1)	18:05 (7)	18:31 (2)	20:05 (3)	21:31
Dep. Bris. (Roma)	2 minutes after departing Central station					
Arr. Toowoomba	2½ hours later					

Sights in **Toowoomba**: This is a garden city in the center of the very rich 8,500,000-acre Darling Downs agricultural area. A week-long Carnival of Flowers takes place here every September. The dense rainforest with many species of birds in **Ravensbourne National Park** is 28 miles from here.

Dep. Toowoomba	04:40 (4)	06:30 (6)	07:30 (5)	09:30 (5)	11:00 (4)
	12:30 (7)	13:00(2)	16:27 (7)	16:30 (3)	17:15 (6)

Arr. Bris. (Roma)   2¼–2½ hours later
Arr. Bris. (Cen.)   2 minutes after arriving Roma railstation.

(1) Sat. only. (2) Mon.–Fri. except holidays. (3) Sun. and holidays only. (4) Daily except Sun. and holidays. (5) Daily. (6) Daily, except Sat. (7) Sat., Sun. and holidays. (8) Fri. only.

Brisbane - Longreach   Rail Australia Timetable

This service ("The Spirit of the Outback") was initiated in late 1993. Travel between the coastal town of Rockhampton and Longreach is during daylight so that passengers can view the outback, including wild kangaroos.

Reservations can be made up to 6 months prior to travel date for first-class 2-berth and single-berth compartments, economy 3-berth compartments, or economy coach reclining seats.

These trains have a restaurant car, take-out meals and a bar for all sleeping-berth passengers. Both trains require reservations.

Dep. Brisbane (Roma)	19:00 (1)	Dep. Longreach	06:30 (3)
Dep. Rockhampton	06:25 (2)	Dep. Rockhampton	19:30
Arr. Longreach	19:00	Arr. Brisbane (Roma)	06:30 (2)

(1) Runs Wednesday and Saturday. (2) Day 2. (3) Runs Thursday and Sunday.

Sights in **Longreach:** The home of the "Stockman's Hall of Fame."

Townsville - Mount Isa   9008

Both of these trains require reservation, are air-conditioned, carry a first-class sleeping car and second-class coaches, and have buffet. Both arrivals are day 2.

Dep. Townsville	18:00 (1)	Dep. Mount Isa	17:00 (2)
Arr. Mount Isa	13:00	Arr. Townsville	11:00

(1) Runs Wednesday and Sunday. (2) Runs Monday and Friday.

Sights in **Mount Isa**: Visit the National Trust Tent House. See mining memorabilia at the Undergound Museum. The lifestyle of the Kalkadoon Aborigines. The Flying Doctor Base. The School of the Air, giving students in remote areas lessons by 2-way radio. Nearby, **Lake Moondarra**.

Visitors may inspect one of the world's richest copper, silver-lead and zinc mines.

Cairns - Kuranda - Cairns 9007

Kuranda is Australia's most northern rail terminal. This is one of the world's most scenic rail trips, through the most lush, tropical rain forests in Australia filled with tropical flowers. It is an easy one-day roundtrip through the massive **Stoney Creek Gorge**. Opened in 1891, this 34km (21-mile) line was an amazing engineering feat. Hundreds of men, equipped with only picks and shovels, had toiled 7 years to triumph over steep grades, dense jungle and hostile natives.

Sights in **Kuranda:** The railstation, built in 1915 is covered by such a beautiful array of tropical plants, ferns and shrubs that it is the major tourist attraction here.

All of these trains are second-class.

Dep. Cairns	09:00		Dep. Kuranda	12:30 (1)
Arr. Kuranda	10:30		Arr. Cairns	13:55

(1) Runs daily, except Saturday.

THE CENTRAL AUSTRALIAN
RAIL ROUTE

Adelaide - Alice Springs 9003 + 9034 + Rail Australia

A standard-gauge train, "The Ghan" is the 1980 successor to the original narrow-gauge operation of the same name that ran from Port Pirie to Alice Springs from 1930 to 1980. The name is in tribute to the Afghan traders who in the 19th century carried passengers and goods on camels between Port Pirie and Oodnadatta, the end of the original rail line.

"The Ghan" requires reservation, carries air-conditioned first-class, 2-berth and single-berth sleeping cars and also coach cars. Its restaurant car is available to sleeping car passengers. Buffet is available to all passengers. Both Sleeping cars and Sitting cars have a shower room.

Dep. Adelaide (Keswick)	14:00 (1)		Dep. Alice Springs	14:00 (3)
Arr. Alice Springs	09:30 (2)		Arr. Adelaide (Keswick)	11:30 (2)

(1) April to November: runs Monday and Thursday. December to March: runs Thursday only. (2) Day 2.
(3) April to November: runs Tuesday and Friday. December to March: runs Friday only.

Sights in **Alice Springs**: This is the ideal base for tours to the "Great Outback." It is a frontier town with modern homes and wide, tree-lined streets. Alice Springs is the headquarters for both the Royal Flying Doctor Service and the unique School of the Air, the sole means of education for those living in the deserted areas of Australia.

Visitors can listen to the children and the teachers, and visit the Flying Doctor facility.

See the museum in the Old Telegraph Station. Many art galleries and souvenir shops.

The Pitchi-Richi Bird Sanctuary, 2 miles from Alice Springs, has a collection of Aboriginal sculptures and implements, also Australian gemstones.

Take a tour to awe-inspiring **Ayers Rock** to see it change color at sunset and sunrise. Alice Springs is also the gateway to **Kings Canyon** and the Olgas.

Alice Springs - Darwin   9125 (Bus)

All arrivals are on Day 2.

Dep. Alice Springs	14:45	20:00
Arr. Darwin	08:00	16:00

Sights in **Darwin**: Tropical flowers, shrubs and trees in the jungle-like Botanical Gardens. The crocodiles and water buffaloes at Kakadu National Park. The excellent Mandorah Beach.

Dep. Darwin	10:00	12:45	12:45
Arr. Alice Springs	05:15	08:00	08:40

WESTERN AUSTRALIAN ROUTES

Perth - Albany   9139 (Bus)

All of these buses require reservations.

Dep. Perth (Ter.)	09:00 (1)	09:00 (2)	14:15 (4)	15:00 (5)	17:30 (6)
Arr. Albany	15:00	16:55 (3)	22:00	21:00	24:00

Sights in **Albany**: A magnificent harbor. This is the starting point for tours through the Porongurup and Stirling mountain ranges for scenic walks and viewing marvelous wildflowers August–November. Visit the Whaling Museum.

Dep. Albany	09:00 (7)	09:15 (8)	13:15 (4)	15:00 (5)	17:30 (6)
Arr. Perth (Ter.)	15:00	16:35	21:10	21:00'	24:00

(1) Via Kojonup. Runs Monday-Friday. (2) Via Katanning. Runs Monday, Friday and Saturday. (3) Monday arrival time. Arrives Albany Friday at 16:20, Saturday at 15:45. (4) Via Katanning. Runs Sunday only. (5) Via Kojonup. Runs Sunday only. (6) Via Kojonup. Runs Friday only. (7) Via Kojonup. Runs daily, except Sunday. (8) Via Katanning. Runs Monday and Thursday.

Perth - Bunbury   9036

All of these trains require reservation and have buffet unless designated otherwise.

Dep. Perth	10:00 (1)	19:00	Dep. Bunbury	06:30 (1)	15:40
Arr. Bunbury	12:20	21:20	Arr. Perth	08:52	18:00

(1) Runs daily, except Sunday.

Sights in **Bunbury**: An important port. Good fishing and surfing here.

Perth - Fremantle   9037

These trains are second-class only.

Dep. East Perth	Mon.-Fri.	Frequent times	05:28 — 23:28
	Saturday	Frequent times	05:28 — 23:28
	Sun. and holidays	Frequent times	07:30 — 20:28
Arr. Fremantle		30 minutes later	

Dep. Fremantle	Mon.-Fri	Frequent times	05:30 — 23:59
	Saturday	Frequent times	06:00 — 23:59
	Sun. and holidays	Frequent times	07:30 — 20:30
Arr. East Perth		30 minutes later	

Sights in **Fremantle**: This is Western Australia's principal port. See the Maritime Museum and Art Center. The great views of the city and harbor from The Round House.

Perth - Kalgoorlie   9000 + 9034 + Air Australia

The "Prospector" trains are among Australia's fastest, making their 407-mile (655km) trip in 6–7½ hours. Stewardesses bring hot meals to the passengers' seats: lunch at 12:30, dinner at 18:30.

Dep. East Perth	09:25 (1)	15:00 (7)	16:10 (4)	18:00 (5)
Arr. Kalgoorlie	16:55	22:25 (3)	23:45	24:00

Sights in **Kalgoorlie:** See notes about sightseeing in Kalgoorlie, under "Sydney–Port Pirie–Kalgoorlie–Perth."

Dep. Kalgoorlie	07:15 (5)	08:55 (8)	16:10 (2)	17:50 (6)
Arr. East Perth	13:20	16:25	23:35	00:15

(1) Runs Monday–Thursday. Does not run Monday on holiday weekends. (2) Runs Fridays, Sundays and holidays. (Plus Monday of holiday weekends). (3) Arrives 21:00 on Friday. (4)Runs Friday only. (5) Runs Saturday only. (6) Runs Thursday only. (7) Runs Fridays and Sundays. (8) Runs Tuesday, Wednesday and Thursday.

TASMANIA

Australia's island state, 150 miles south of mainland Victoria, measures 190 miles from east to west and 180 miles from north to south. Visitors can inspect historic homes and folk museums, stay at old inns, see the ruins of old penal colonies, enjoy fine beaches, swimming and excellent mountain and rural scenery.

Tasmania's one rail route ceased operating in 1978. It ran north from **Hobart** to **Launceston** and then west to **Devonport** and **Wynyard**.

CHAPTER 13

NEW ZEALAND

Children under 5 travel free. Lower fares for children 4–14. Children 15 and over must pay full fare. All trains are non-smoking. Advance reservations are advisable.

The country is 2 islands: North Island and South Island. There is ferry service between the 2 islands, connecting Wellington (at the southern tip of North Island) with Picton (the north tip of South Island).

NEW ZEALAND'S TRAIN PASS

New Zealand TravelPass. Available worldwide from travel agencies. Also available in New Zealand at train and bus depots, offices of Intercity Travel, and travel agencies. In the U.S.A.: from New Zealand Central Reservations Office, Suite 1270, 6033 West Century Blvd., Los Angeles, CA 90045. The toll free telephone is (800) 351-2323.

Unlimited travel on all trains, Intercity buses and Interisland Line ferries. Not transferable or refundable.

The single-class 1996 adult prices (after March 31, 1996) are: $296 for any 8 days within 21 days, $372 for any 15 days within 35 days, and $435 for any 22 days within 56 days. For children age 4-14: $283, $248 and $290.

NORTH ISLAND RAIL ROUTES

This system joins the main cities of Auckland and Wellington. Emanating from it are the Auckland–Tauranga, Auckland–Rotorura, Wellington–Masterson and Wellington–Napier rail lines.

Auckland

Walking tours are so popular here that the city publishes 2 brochures: "Go Strolling in Your Lunch Hour" and "Coast to Coast Walking." (It is only an 8-mile walk from the Pacific Ocean on the east side of Auckland to the Tasman Sea on the west side of the city.) All interesting sights are outlined in a free map, and the routes are marked clearly.

See the sculptures and fountains in Queen Elizabeth II Square. Parnell Rose Gardens. Westhaven Marina. The view of Waitemata Harbor from the War Memorial Museum (open daily 10:00–17:00), which has a good collection of Maori artifacts, native New Zealand animals and plants, and relics of both wars.

Heritage Park. The exhibits and Pioneer Village at the Museum of Transport and Technology, reached by double-decker buses from and to major downtown hotels. The outstanding collection of mammals, fish, reptiles and birds (including the local non-flying Kiwi) at the Zoo.

Marvelous views of Auckland, its beaches and harbors as well as many streams and waterfalls, at Centennial Memorial Park. See the Cathedral of the Holy Trinity. The Waitakere Scenic Reserve. The view of the city from Mt. Eden, a dormant volcano. The Emily Nixon Garden of Memories. The views of Hauraki Gulf from Musick Point. Take a bus tour to the Earth Satellite Tracking Station near **Warkworth**, 50 miles from Auckland. Travel in a clear tunnel through the huge Underwater World aquarium (open daily 09:00–21:00). Swim in the thermal pools at nearby **Waiwera**.

Take a 2-day motorcoach tour to **Waitomo** (to see its caves and Glowworm Grotto). Visit some of the 19 wineries in West Auckland's Henderson Valley.

Wellington

Many fine beaches here. See the view of the city, harbor and Hutt Valley from the 548-foot high Mount Victoria. Lady Norwood Rose Gardens. The Zoological Gardens. The crafts at the New Zealand Display Center. Conducted tours of the marble-faced House of Parliament. Freyberg Tepid Pool.

Government Building, one of the largest wood structures in the Southern Hemisphere. The South Pacific manuscripts and maps in Turnbull Library. The collection of Maori exhibits at Dominion Museum and National Art Gallery. Nearby, the Carillon and Hall of Memories. The Carter Observatory. Many fine beaches.

The information Center (corner of Wakefield and Victoria Streets) has brochures that outline independent walking tours.

Take the cable car from Lambton Quay 397 feet up to the 62-acre Botanical Gardens in Kelburn Park.

Wellington - Hamilton - Auckland   9750

This scenic trip includes the breathtaking Raurimu Spiral, rivers, forests, seascapes and 3 high volcanoes: Ngauruhoe (7,515 feet), Ruapehu (9,175) and Tongariro (6,517).

All of these trains require a reservation, are first-class only, have facilities for disabled persons and have light refreshments.

Dep. Wellington	08:20	20:10 (1)	Dep. Auckland	08:50	20:40 (1)
Dep. Hamilton	16:39	04:48	Dep. Hamilton	10:48	22:41
Arr. Auckland	18:45	06:35	Arr. Wellington	19:12	07:12

(1) Runs daily, except Saturday.

Auckland - Hamilton - Rotorua   9750

This journey offers the rolling pastures of the Waikato region and the forests of the Mamaku ranges.

All of these trains require reservation, are first-class only, run daily, are air-conditioned, and have buffet and bar.

Dep. Auckland	08:20	13:00	Dep. Rotorua	13:05	17:55
Dep. Hamilton (Frankton)	10:13	14:54	Dep. Hamilton (Frankton)	15:20	20:10
Arr. Rotorua	12:20	17:03	Arr. Auckland	17:15	22:05

Sights in **Hamilton**: Popular for boating and swimming on Lake Rotorua. See Garden Place, on Victoria Street. Stroll the parklands on both sides of the Waikato River and cruise on the River

Sights in **Rotorua**: An interesting place with thermal swimming pools, the beautiful Government Gardens, the Maori Arts and Crafts Institute (a school for young woodcarvers and weavers), trout fishing, the Whakarewarewa Maori Village, St. Faith's Maori Church, TeWairoa (an excavated Maori village), the exhibits of sheepshearing, wool spinning, working sheep dogs and performing rams at Agrodome, the hand-fed trout at Rainbow Springs, and the overall Polynesian ambiance.

Wellington - Palmerston North - Napier - Gisborne   9750

This route includes the scenic shoreline of Hawkes Bay (Wairoa–Gisborne). These trains stop for refreshments at Palmerston North and Napier.

These trains require reservation, are first-class only, have an observation car and have buffet.

Dep. Wellington	08:00	Dep. Gisborne	09:15 (1)
Dep. Palmerston North	10:08	Dep. Wairoa	11:00
Arr. Napier	13:15 (1)	Dep. Napier	14:15
Arr. Wairoa	15:45	Dep. Palmerston North	17:25
Arr. Gisborne	17:30	Arr. Wellington	19:30

(1) Napier–Gisborne and v.v. is by bus service.

Sights in **Napier**: The exhibit of dolphins, sea lions, sea leopards, penguins and other animals and sea birds at Marineland. The assortment of birds in the Botanic Gardens. The fine swimming and fishing beaches. The beautiful Sunken Garden and lovely Golden Mile Park, along the shore.

Wellington - Masterton   9751

All of these trains are second-class only.

Dep. Wellington	07:58 (1)	09:58 (2)	12:58 (1)	16:11 (1)	17:42 (1)	17:58 (2+4)
Arr. Masterton	09:28	11:28	14:28	17:41	19:12	19:28

• • •

Dep. Masterton	06:03 (1)	06:43 (1)	07:59 (2)	09:59 (1)	14:59 (1)	15:59 (2+5)
Arr. Wellington	07:33	08:23	09:29	11:29	16:29	17:29

(1) Runs Monday–Friday, except holidays. 2) Runs Saturdays, Sunday, and holidays. (3) Runs Friday only. (4) Plus another departure from Well. at 21:28 (3), arriving Masterson 22:58.(5) Plus another departure from Masterson at 19:29 (3), arriving Wellington 20:59.

Auckland - Hamilton - Tauranga   9750

Both of these trains require reservation, are first-class only, and have buffet and bar.

Dep. Auckland	17:50		Dep. Tauranga	08:35
Dep. Hamilton (Cen.)	19:44		Dep. Hamilton (Cen.)	10:01
Arr. Tauranga	21:10		Arr. Auckland	11:55

Sights in **Tauranga**: The historical village.

SOUTH ISLAND RAIL ROUTES

A ferry service connects North Island and South Island.

The rail system on South Island is one route along the South Pacific shoreline due south from Picton via Christchurch and terminating in Invercargill, plus a single cross-island line running from Christchurch to Greymouth.

Wellington - Picton - Christchurch

The notable scenery on this ride includes views of man-made lakes of Grassmere Saltworks, ocean surf, many attractive beaches, and the Kaikoura mountain range.

These ferries carry both automobiles and passengers. They have food and beverage service.

9780 *(Bus)*			
Dep. Wellington (Railst'n)	08:55	13:45 (1)	16:55 (1)
Arr. Wellington (Ferry Ter.)	09:20	14:10	17:20
Change to ferry.			
Dep. Wellington (Ferry Ter.)	09:30 (1)	14:20 (1)	17:30 (1)
Arr. Picton	12:30	17:40	20:30
Change to train. Table 9800			
Dep. Picton		21:21 (2)	
Dep. Kaikoura		16:51	
Arr. Christchurch		24:00	

• • •

Dep. Christchurh			07:30 (2)
Dep. Kaikoura			16:22
Arr. Picton			12:45
Change to ferry. Table 9780			
Dep. Picton	05:30 (4)	10:00 (1)	18:40
Arr. Wellington (Ferry Ter.)	09:00	13:20	22:40
Change to bus.			
Dep. Wellington (Ferry Ter.)	09:10	13:50	22:35
Arr. Wellington (Railst'n)	15 minutes after departing from Ferry Terminal		

(1) Runs daily, except Monday. (2) Reservation required. First-class only. Buffet. (3) Runs daily, except Sunday. (4) Runs daily, except Monday.

Sights in **Kaikoura:** Whale-watching and dolphin-watching cruises. The Aquarium. The early-whaling-era cottage. The seal colony. Take a half-day horse trek.

Sights in **Christchurch:** Takahe, the carved Maori meeting house. The beautiful Botanical Gardens in Hagley Park. The mementos from Captain Cook's 3 voyages, displays on Antarctica explorations, and the exhibit of Maori articles (including a 47-foot wood war canoe) in the Canterbury Museum on the side of Hagley Park. Cathedral Square. The view from Summit Road. Take a hydrofoil boat tour through **Waimakariri Gorge**.

Christchurch - Timaru - Dunedin - Invercargill 9800

Invercargill is the most southerly rail terminal in the world – latitude 46 degrees.

There is fine scenery of the South Pacific coastline and the Canterbury Plains on this ride. Looking to the west, one can see the New Zealand Alps. Other views: rivers, sheep runs and wheatfields.

The schedules below are for "Southerner," a first-class only, luxury train with buffet service. Reservations are required. These trains run Monday–Friday, except holidays. All cars are non-smoking.

Seats can be reserved up to 6 months prior to travel date. As you board, you are given a folder about the journey, with a map and notes on points of interest en route.

A hostess will serve morning and afternoon teas and light meals to anyone who is physically unable to eat in the buffet car and to mothers traveling with young children. Arrangements can be made to have a rental car or taxi waiting for one's arrival. In the smoking carriage, passengers are served wine, cocktails and liquor at their seat.

Dep. Christchurch	08:30		Dep. Invercargil	08:30
Dep. Timaru	10:45		Dep. Dunedin	11:43
Dep. Dunedin	14:10		Dep. Timaru	15:09
Arr. Invercargill	17:25		Arr. Christchurch	17:14

Sights in **Timaru**: A large port. A great beach. Good fishing in this area. Nearby, the **Mount Cook National Park** with its many 2-mile-high mountains.

Sights in **Dunedin**: Attractive old stone buildings such as the Railstation. The enjoyable miles of beaches. The Kauri wood, Italian marble and Venetian glass in Larnach Castle, perched on top of a 1,000-foot-high hill on Otago Peninsula, and the view from it. Originally the 19th century mansion of a wealthy banker, the castle is now a hotel.

The Jacobean-style Olveston House. Glenfalloch Woodland Gardens. A Maori village. Penguin Place. Nearby, Mount Aspiring National Park and several lovely lakes: **Manapouri**, **Te Anau**, **Ohau**, **Pukaki** and **Tekakpo**.

Sights in **Invercargill**: The view of the city from the seventh floor of the Kelvin Hotel. The collection of Maori exhibits and art gallery at the Southland Centennial Museum in the 200-acre Queen's Park, located in the center of Invercargill. The park features a display of native and exotic trees and plants, a group of statues for children, a large sunken rose garden surrounded by flowering prunus and cherry trees, and a special iris garden. At the eastern side of this park is a wide variety of tropical plants, a large pond containing aquatic plants and fish, a large lily pond, and a well-stocked aviary, all in the Steans Memorial

Winter Garden.

Also see the City Gardens, along the Otepuni stream that runs through the center of Invercargill. Rose Gardens. The display of provincial history in the Southland Centennial Museum and Art Gallery. The 85-acre Waihopai Scenic Reserve. The City Art Gallery in the 60-acre Anderson Park. The 25-mile long sandy Oreti Beach, fine for swimming.

Christchurch - Arthur's Pass - Greymouth   9800

This is the most scenic rail trip in New Zealand. After departing Christchurch, the train climbs to 2,500 feet at Arthur's Pass before going through the 5½-mile Otira Tunnel. Some grades are as great as 3% on this steep ride. On the approach to Greymouth, there are splendid views of the Tasman Coast.

Recommended reading about this line: "On the Transalpine Trail" and "The Midland Line," both published by IPL Books, P.O. Box 10215, The Terrace, Wellington, New Zealand

These trains require reservation and are first-class only.

Dep. Christchurch	09:15	Dep. Greymouth	14:35
Dep. Arthur's Pass	11:36	Dep. Arthur's Pass	16:34
Arr. Greymouth	13:25	Arr. Christchurch	18:40

Sights in **Arthur's Pass**: Take walking paths to waterfalls and alpine viewing sites.

Sights in **Greymouth**: Visit a coal mine. Take a jet-boat ride up the Taramakau River to the Kaniere gold dredge and see the little museum of the gold-rush days and greenstone factory at Hokitika, 25 miles to the south. Trout fishing at nearby **Lake Brunner** (train stop at Moana).

Kingston - Fairlight   9802

A special 6-mile steam train trip Kingston–Fairlight on "Kingston Flyer" to the south shore of **Lake Wakatipu** operates only on a charter basis. The operator, Kingston Flyer Company, gives only a 48-hour notice prior to days there is service.

CHAPTER 14

NORTH AMERICA

Winter in North America is from December 21 to March 20. Summer is from June 21 to September 20.

CANADA

Children under 2 not occupying a separate seat travel free with each passenger 18 or older. Half-fare for children 2–11. Children 12 and over must pay full fare,

The national Canadian passenger train network is called "VIA RailCanada." Since the Spring of 1992, all trains operating between Vancouver and Toronto were completely refurbished, including showers on all sleeping cars. "Silver & Blue Class" service, introduced in April of 1992, includes upgraded amenities such as enhanced restaurant car services.

For reservations and information, contact a travel agency.

Canada's other train systems are: Algoma Central Railway, British Columbia Railway, Great Canadian Railtour Company Ltd., Ontario Northland Railway, Quebec North Shore & Labrador Railways, and Toronto Hamilton & Buffalo Railway.

The Canrailpass described below is valid only on VIA routes.

CANADA'S TRAIN PASSES

Canrailpass Must be purchased before you arrive in Canada. Sold at travel agencies worldwide outside Canada.

Valid for unlimited train travel on the single-class VIA lines any 12 days within 30 days from first day of travel.

Coach seats can be upgraded at additional charge to a sleeping compartment with upper and/or lower berths, for which early reservation is advisable.

If a trip involves the use of a pass either completely on High-Season days or on a combination of High-Season *and* Low-Season days, then a High-Season pass must be used.

Low Seasons are January 6 through May 31 and October 1 to December 14. High Season is June 1 through September 30.

"Youths" are passengers under age 25. "Seniors" are passengers age 60 and over.

The 1995 adult Low Season price was $349 (Can.). For Youths and Seniors: $319. The 1995 adult High Season price was $510. For Youths and Seniors: $460.

The price structure for ordinary tickets allows 25% discount from Peak season prices for Off-Peak season and 40% discount for super Saver Season. Peak Season is June 1 through September 30. Off-Peak is May 1 through May 31, and October 1 through October 31, and December 15 through January 5. Super saver is January 6 through April 30 and November 1 through December 14.

Montreal

See the 23,400-pound bell ("Le Gros Bourdon") and marvelous stained-glass windows in the Notre Dame Basilica, completed in 1829 and resembling Westminster Abbey. The bell requires 12 men when it is tolled manually and can be heard for 15 miles. It is operated electrically now.

The pipe organ there, one of the largest in North America, has 4 keyboards, 84 stops, 30 pedals and 6,800 pipes (the tallest is 12 feet). Also look at the carved, gilded wood interior of the church. See the gifts from Louis XIV in the tiny museum next to the Chapel.

Visit the magnificent St. Joseph's Oratory (open daily 06:00–22:00), one of the world's largest ecclesiastical buildings, completed in 1974. It is a complex with escalators that includes a lower church which seats 1,000 and a 4,000-seat basilica. (Its spectacular cupola is a copy of the one at St. Peter's in Rome. The cupola is 506 feet above street level and, because this church is atop Mount Royal, it is the highest point in Montreal.)

See the 30 stained-glass windows (all with biblical scenes) in Erskine and American Church, open daily 09:00–16:30.

The colection of arms, costumes, prints, paintings, photographs, documents and books at the David M. Stewart Museum on Ile Ste. Helene, open Tuesday-Sunday 10:00-17:00. Some of the many exceptional exhibits here: a floor map of the Atlantic Ocean, a scale model of Montreal as it was in 1760, and a spectacular large-scale model of the 18th century 70-gun French ship Le Jupiter.

A collection of furniture, glass, textiles and ceramics from 1935 to the present, at the Chateau Dufresne/Montreal Museum of Decorative Arts, at 2929 Jeanne d'Arc Avenue, open Thursday-Sunday 12:00–17:00.

The colonial-era costumes, maps, guns, engravings, paintings and wood sculptures as well as objects from China, India and the West Indies at Chateau de Ramezay at 280 Notre-Dame Street, open Tuesday-Sunday 10:00–16:30. It is considered by some to be the most interesting museum in Montreal.

The 34 galleries (exhibiting 19th century French impressionists, 18th century British portraits, works of early and contemporary Canadian artists) in the Museum of Fine Arts, at 1379 Sherbrooke Street West, open daily except Monday 11:00–17:00.

An ethnographic representation of costumes, decorative and folk art, paintings, prints, drawings and photos pertaining to Canada's various Indian tribes, in McCord Museum, at 690 Sherbrooke Street West, open Wednesday-Sunday 11:00–17:00.

Examples of 17th and 18th century furniture, furnishings, religious art and secular art in San Gabriel House, at 2146 Favard Street, with guided tours Tuesday–Saturday 12:30 and 15:00. On Sunday at 13:30, 14:30 and 15:30.

The Sulpician Seminary, built in 1685, the oldest building in Montreal. The oldest wood clock in North America is exhibited there.

The interesting 60-minute audiovisual history of the city, at the Montreal History Center, 335 Place d'Youville. The Place des Arts complex of concert and theater halls. The vast underground shopping malls in the ultramodern center of the city, called Place Ville-Marie. Take the short trip to Mount Royal.

Ottawa

During July and August, 80-minute guided bus tours start at Confederation Square daily every half-hour from 11:00 to 17:00.

The Gothic-styled buildings on Parliament Hill are dominated by a 302-foot-high Peace Tower, which has a 53-bell carillon. Free guided tours of the complex are conducted every 20 minutes 08:30–16:30. Free guided tours of Parliament are offered 09:00–11:00 and 13:00–17:00. During Summer, a changing-of-the-guard ceremony can be seen daily at 10:00.

See the superb Canadian and European art (some of the latter dating back to the 13th century) at the National Gallery, open during Summer months Monday-Saturday 10:00–18:00, Sundays and holidays 10:00–14:00. The National Arts Center.

The Arboretum at the Central Experimental Farm. The Governor General's Residence. Hog's Back Falls, located in the city. The Royal Canadian Mint. The display of weapons and uniforms at the Canadian War Museum, open daily 10:00–17:00. The Indian Burial Grounds. The Centennial Cabin Museum. The Old Depot Museum.

The antique skis at the Canadian Ski Museum, open daily 11:00–16:00. The National Postal Museum at 365 Laurier Street sells first-day covers. The Currency Museum in the Bank of Canada at 245 Sparks Street is open daily except Monday.

The Museum of Science and Technology at 1867 St. Laurent Blvd. is open daily 10:00–20:00. See floral displays, hundreds of types of trees, and Clydesale horses pulling wagons at the 1200-acre experimental farm south of Carling Avenue, near Carlton University.

Take the 5½-mile cruise on the Rideau Canal. It operates 6 times a day (starting at 10:00) July through September. Board near the Conference Center on Confederation Square. In the winter, this 123-mile-long canal is one of the longest ice-skating rinks in the world.

Visit the food shops and stands at Byward Market, near Notre Dame Basilica.

Quebec City

Guided walking tours start from the lobby of the Chateau Frontenac Hotel, the first of 3 daily tours beginning at 09:30 (10:00 on Saturday and Sunday). Across the street from the entrance of the hotel, there is a 30-minute audiovisual recreation of the 6 sieges to which the city was subjected (Musee du Fort, at 10 Rue Ste.-Anne).

Nearby at (69 Rue Ste.-Anne, across from City Hall), Eskimo weaving and stone carving are sold at Aux Multiples.

Shop for handmade jewelry, wood sculptures, leather clothing and pottery in the Quartier Petit Champlain, an old section of town that is near the river. See the collection of antique furniture in Chevalier House, at Place Champlain

Stroll on the Plains of Abraham. See the changing of the guard every morning at 10:00, at the 37-acre Citadel. Take the 4-hour cruise on the St. Lawrence Seaway. A 3-week Winter Carnival, ends on the night of Mardi Gras.

Toronto

A major port. See: The astounding view from the top of Canadian National's Tower, the tallest (1,800 feet) free-standing structure in the world. City Hall.

The George R.Gardiner Museum of Ceramic Art displays 2,000 pieces ranging from pre-Columbian pottery to 18th century porcelain (Meissen, Worcester, etc.). Located at 111 Queen's Park, it is open daily except Monday 10:00–17:00.

Across the street from the Gardiner is the Royal Ontario Museum, second-largest museum in North America (after New York's Metropolitan). It has an outstanding Chinese collection (complete temple clay wall paintings, the only Ming tomb complex in the Western Hemisphere), several extraordinary dioramas showing 13 dinosaurs in dramatic movement, an exceptional collection of Egyptian mummies — and its "Mediterranean World," a chronological depiction of the beginnings of Judaism, Christianity and Islam, starting with a 2,040 B.C. Sumerian clay that records the sale of 4 sheep.

The Royal Ontario Museum opens daily at 10:00, closing at 18:00 Monday–Wednesday, Saturday and Sunday. It closes at 20:00 on Thursday and Friday. Exhibits on space, communication and other technologies at the Ontario Service Center, open daily 10:00–18:00. The Marine Museum of Upper Canada. Fort York. Casa Loma Castle. The 19th century MacKenzie House, home of Toronto's first mayor. McLaughlin Planetarium. Black Creek Pioneer Village.

The Ontario Place recreation complex, at the waterfront. The fine paintings at the Art Gallery of Ontario (Monet, Degas, Gainsborough, Renoir, Picasso), more than 100 sculptures and 500 prints by Henry Moore, and a cross-section of 17th-20th century Canadian art. It is open Tuesday–Sunday at 11:00, closing at 17:30 on Tuesday, Friday, Saturday and Sunday, and at 21:00 on Wednesday and Thursday.

The Hockey Museum. Ride the special train through the 710-acre Metro Zoo for a view of the 4,000 animals exhibited there. Take a one-hour tour (beginning 10:00 most days) of the gigantic Skydome baseball park.

Board a ferry behind the Harbour Castle Hilton, at the foot of Bay Street, for a 10-minute ride to the Toronto Islands, a small archipelago of 19th century resorts that are now public parks. The most popular is a 612-acre complex of amusement rides, bike paths, parks, beaches and lagooons.

Go on one of the boats that tour the harbor, departing from next to the Hilton Hotel. Some of these have dinner-dancing cruises.

Vancouver

See: The Zoo and the killer whales in 1,000-acre Stanley Park. The view while walking across Capilano Suspension Bridge. The exhibit of the history of British Columbia from the ice age to today, at the Centennial Museum. The Shakespearean Gardens. Nitobe Gardens. Chinatown. The bazaar of saris, spices and sweets, glass bangles and gold jewelry in Little India, at the end of Main Street.

On the waterfront near the 1100 block of Chestnut Street: the Vancouver Museum, the Maritime Museum and the shows presented in the MacMillan Planetarium. One of the world's finest collections of Northwest Coast Indian art in the Museum of Anthropology at the University of British Columbia.

Halifax - Montreal   2 + 27

These trains require reservation, are air-conditioned, carry sleeping cars, have ordinary coaches and a restaurant car, and start both journeys on Monday, Thursday and Saturday. Arrive day 2.

Dep. Halifax	14:00		Dep. Montreal (Cen.)	18:45
Dep. Truro	15:39		*Set watch forward 1 hour.*	
Dep. Moncton	18:43		Dep. Moncton	11:00
Set watch back 1 hour.			Dep. Truro	13:51
Arr. Montreal (Cen.)	08:15		Arr. Halifax	15:20

Moncton - Saint John   27

Both of these trains require reservation, are air-conditioned, and have both ordinary coaches and a restaurant car.

Dep. Moncton	18:43 (1)		Dep. Saint John	08:46 (2)
Arr. Saint John	20:27		Arr. Moncton	10:40

(1) Runs Monday, Thursday and Saturday. (2) Runs Tuesday, Friday and Sunday.

Montreal - Ottawa   20

All of these trains are air-conditioned and have buffet or light refreshments.

Dep. Montreal (Cen.)	06:55 (1)	10:40 (2)	14:40 (3)	17:45 (2)
Arr. Ottawa (Union)	08:59	12:39	16:42	19:47

Dep. Ottawa (Union)	06:55 (4)	08:00 (5)	10:00 (2)	14:40 (3)	17:30 (2)
Arr. Montreal (Cen.)	08:58	10:05	11:59	16:43	19:34

(1) Runs daily, except Sundays and holidays. (2) Runs daily. (3) Runs daily, except Saturday. (4) Runs Monday–Friday, except holidays. (5) Runs Saturday only.

RAIL ROUTES FROM TORONTO

Toronto - Brantford - Toronto   18

All of these trains are air-conditioned and have buffet or light refreshments.

Dep. Toronto (Union)	08:40 (1)	12:35 (1)	16:15 (1)	17:15 (2)	19:20 (1)
Arr. Brantford	09:52	13:46	17:22	18:24	20:33

Sights in **Brantford:** The home of Alexander Graham Bell, with the world's first telephone business office. The history of Brant County, from Paleo-Indian culture to the days of the Six Nations Indians and Canadian pioneers, in the Brant Historical Museum. The exhibit of Woodland Indian artifacts at the Wood and Indian Museum.

Dep. Brantford	07:28 (3)	09:00 (4)	09:58 (7)	12:52 (4)	14:19 (5+6)
Arr. Toronto (Union)	08:32	10:19	11:16	14:10	15:34

(1) Runs daily. (2) Runs daily, except Saturday. (3) Runs Monday–Friday, except holidays. (4) Runs daily, except Sundays and holidays. (5) Runs Monday, Friday and Sunday. (6) Plus other Brantford departures at 17:24 (1) and 21:12 (1), arriving Toronto 18:38 and 22:33. (7) RUns SUndays and holidays only.

Toronto - Montreal   23

All of these trains require reservation, are air-conditioned and have buffet, unless designated otherwise.

Dep. Toronto (Union)	07:10 (1)	10:00 (2)	12:00 (3)	17:00 (5+6)
Arr. Montreal (Cen.)	11:38	14:27	17:13	20:59

Dep. Montreal (Cen.)	06:15 (1)	10:00 (3)	12:15 (5)	17:00 (5+7)
Arr. Toronto (Union)	10:42	15:15	16:41	20:59

(1) Runs daily, except weekends and holidays. (2) Reservation *not* required. Runs daily, except Saturday. (3) Runs daily. (4) Runs daily, except Saturday. (5) Plus another departure from Toronto at 18:00 (3), arriving Montreal 22:56. (6) Plus another departure from Montreal at 18:00 (3), arriving Toronto 22:59.

Toronto - Ottawa 23

All of these trains are air-conditioned and have buffet.

Dep. Toronto (Union)	09:00 (1)	11:00 (2)	15:00 (7)	17:30 (4)
Arr. Ottawa (Union)	13:08	15:19	19:03	21:48

• • •

Dep. Ottawa (Union)	06:00 (3)	07:35 (5)	11:30 (2)	15:35 (6)
Arr. Toronto (Union)	10:06	11:49	15:42	19:44 (7+6)

(1) Reservation required. Runs daily, except Sundays and holidays. (2) Runs daily. (3) Runs Monday–Friday, except holidays. (4) Reservation required. Runs daily. (5) Reservation required. Runs Saturday only. (6) Plus another departure from Ottawa at 17:40 (4), arriving Toronto 21:42. (7) Runs daily except Tuesday and Saturday.

Toronto - Winnipeg - Saskatoon - Edmonton - Vancouver 1

The spectacular scenery of 3 mountain ranges (Rockies, Selkirks and Coast), many ancient glaciers, large lakes and waterfalls attracts many tourists to this route.

Both of these trains require reservation, are air-conditioned, carry sleeping cars, ordinary coaches, a domecar and a restaurant car. An Amtrak bus provides transfer between the Vancouver and Seattle railstations. See end of chapter.

Dep. Toronto (Union)	12:45 (1)	Dep. Vancouver	20:00 (5)
Set watch back one hour.		*Set watch forward one hour.*	
Arr. Winnipeg	17:30	Arr. Edmonton	20:10 (6)
Dep. Winnipeg	18:30 (2)	Dep. Edmonton	20:40
Arr. Saskatoon	02:05 (3)	*Set watch forward one hour.*	
Dep. Saskatoon	02:25	Arr. Saskatoon	02:50 (7)
Set watch back one hour.		Dep. Saskatoon	03:10
Arr. Edmonton	08:30	Arr. Winnipeg	12:45
Dep. Edmonton	09:00	Dep. Winnipeg	13:45
Set watch back one hour.		*Set watch forward one hour.*	
Arr. Vancouver	08:30 (4)	Arr. Toronto (Union)	20:50 (8)

(1) Runs Tuesday, Thursday and Saturday. (2) Day 2 from Toronto: Wednesday, Friday and Sunday. (3) Day 3 from Toronto: Thursday, Saturday and Monday. (4) Day 4 from Toronto: Friday, Sunday and Tuesday. (5) Runs Monday, Thursday and Saturday. (6) Day 2 from Vancouver: Tuesday, Friday and Sunday. (7) Day 3 from Vancouver: Wednesday, Saturday and Monday. (8) Day 4 from Vancouver: Thursday, Sunday and Tuesday.

NORTHERN CANADIAN RAIL ROUTES

In addition to train service in Nova Scotia, to be covered later in this section, there are 12 rail routes on the mainland extending north from Canada's transcontinental lines.

Sept Iles - Schefferville 24

Indians are charged lower fares on these trains.

Both of these trains have light refreshments.

Dep. Sept Iles	08:00 (1)		Dep. Schefferville	08:00 (2)
Arr. Schefferville	19:15		Arr. Sept Iles	19:15

(1) Runs Thursday only. (2) Runs Friday only.

Montreal - Quebec City 27

All of these trains are air-conditioned and have buffet, unless designated otherwise.

Dep. Montreal (Cen.)	07:00 (1)	08:20 (2)	13:20 (3)	16:00 (1)	18:00 (3)
Arr. Quebec (Palais)	09:42	11:07	16:09	18:50	20:55
		• • •			
Dep. Quebec (Palais)	06:35 (1)	08:00 (2)	10:20 (3)	14:00 (1)	17:35 (3)
Arr. Montreal (Cen.)	09:19	10:46	13:02	16:49	20:29

(1) Runs Monday-Friday, except holidays. (2) Runs Saturday only. Light refreshments. (3) Runs daily.

Montreal - Hervey - Jonquiere 22

These trains are air-conditioned and have light refreshments.

Dep. Montreal (Cen.)	14:20 (1)	Dep. Jonquiere	11:05 (2)	13:25 (3)
Dep. Hervey	17:30	Dep. Hervey	16:35	18:54
Arr. Jonquiere	23:10	Arr. Montreal (Cen.)	19:35	21:55

(1) Runs Monday, Wednesday and Friday. (2) Runs Tuesday and Thursday. (3) Runs Sunday only.

Montreal - Hervey - Senneterre - Taschereau - Cochrane 24

All of these trains are air-conditioned.

Dep. Montreal (Cent.)	20:00 (1+2)	20:00 (1+5)
Dep. Hervey	23:37	23:37
Arr. Senneterre	08:50 (3)	08:50 (3)
Change trains.		
Dep. Senneterre	09:45 (4)	09:05 (6)
Arr. Taschereau	11:40	11:26
Arr. Cochrane	-0-	15:15

• • •

Dep. Cochrane	11:45 (7)	-0-
Dep. Taschereau	15:55	20:50 (4)
Arr. Senneterre	17:55	22:50
Change trains.		
Dep. Senneterre	18:10 (1+7)	23:05 (1+4)
Dep. Hervey	03:02 (8)	07:57 (9)
Arr. Montreal (Cent.)	06:10	11:05

(1) Carries a sleeping car and a coach. Light refreshments. (2) Runs Monday and Wednesday. (3) Day 2. (4) Runs Tuesday and Thursday. (5) Runs Friday only. (6) Runs Saturday only. (7) Runs Sunday only. (8) Day 2. Runs Monday only. (9) Day 2. Runs Wednesday and Friday.

Toronto - North Bay - Cochrane - Moosonee
Ontario Northland Rly. Timetable

"Polar Bear Express" makes one-day roundtrips into the Canadian wilderness daily except Friday, from late June to early September, between Cochrane and **Moosonee**, a trading post since 1673. For 1994 prices and overnight hotel reservations, contact Ontario Northland Railway, 555 Oak Street E., North Bay, Ontario, Canada P1B 8L3. (705-472-4500)

It is very, very important to bring insect repellent.

All of these trains are air-conditioned.

Dep. Toronto (Union)	12:00 (1)		Dep. Moosonee	09:00 (4)	17:15 (2)
Dep. North Bay (C.N.)	16:50		Arr. Cochrane	14:30	21:20
Arr Cochrane	21:50		*Change trains.*		
Change trains.			Dep. Cochrane		08:50 (1)
Dep. Cochrane	08:30 (2)	10:10 (3)	Arr. North Bay (C.N.)		13:50
Arr. Moosonee	12:50	15:45	Arr. Toronto (Union)		18:35

(1) Reservation required. Runs daily except Saturday. Cafeteria-style take-out service car. (2) "Polar Bear Express." Reservation required. Operates late June to early September. Runs daily except Friday. Restaurant car. (3) Operates late June to early September. Runs Tuesday and Thursday. Has buffet. (4) Operates late June to early September. Runs Wednesday only. Cafeteria-style take out service car..

Sault Ste. Marie - Hearst   12

The marvelous scenery on the one-day (08:00–17:00) Agawa Canyon sightseeing excursion train operated by Algoma Central Railway. Fall foliage is particularly outstanding, attracting up to 1,500 people daily. About 86,000 passengers make the ride during the late May to mid-October operation. The views of the Montreal River from a 130-foot high and 1,550-foot long bridge and of hundreds of lakes are some of the interesting sights on this ride. Comments are broadcast on the train's public address system. Before making the return ride to Sault Ste. Marie, passengers have time to climb to lookout points above the canyon and walk into the canyon. Hot lunches are sold on the train. The Canadian meat pie and strawberry shortcake are favorites.

All of these trains are air-conditioned.

Dep. Sault Ste. Marie	09:00 (1)	09:30 (2)
Dep. Eton	12:59	13:50
Arr. Hearst	18:20	19:15
Dep. Hearst	08:00 (1)	08:15 (2)
Dep. Eton	12:59	13:50
Arr. Sault Ste. Marie	17:00	18:10

(1) Operates mid-October to mid-May. From Sault: Runs Friday, Saturday and Sunday. From Hearst: Runs Saturday, Sunday and Monday. From early January to late March, buffet is offered Saturday and Sunday from Sault to Eton and v.v. (2) Operates late May to mid-October. From Sault: Runs daily except Monday. From Hearst: Runs daily except Tuesday. buffet is offered Wednesday–Sunday from Sault to Eton and v.v.

Winnipeg - Hudson Bay - Churchill   8

This is a mind-boggling train trip, 1,055 miles from Winnipeg to the chilly, distant Church-ill. Check VIA Rail Canada for a possible escorted 6-day "Hudson Bay Explorer Tour," a package that provides 2 nights in Churchill and includes rail fare, berth, all meals, and a tour of the surrounding area plus a day trip to **Eskimo Point**, an Inuit community.

These trains require reservation, carry sleeping cars, coaches and a restaurant car, and are air-conditioned.

Dep. Winnipeg (C.N.)	21:55(1)		Dep. Churchill	21:00 (2)	
Dep. Dauphin	01:50	Day 2	Dep. Gillam	05:10	Day 2
Dep. Hudson Bay	06:40		Dep. Thompson	11:40	
Arr. The Pas	09:35		Arr. The Pas	19:05	
Dep. The Pas	10:50		Dep. The Pas	20:20	
Dep. Thompson	19:20		Dep. Hudson Bay	21:25	
Dep. Gillam	01:25	Day 3	Dep. Dauphin	04:20	Day 3
Arr. Churchill	08:20		Arr. Winnipeg (C.N.)	08:00	

(1) Runs Tuesday, Thursday and Sunday. (2) Runs, Tuesday, Thursday and Saturday.

Sights in **Churchill:** This is the only town in the world that is located on a polar bear mi-gratory route. They can be seen here during September and October. Seals can be viewed here May–June and white beluga whales from mid-June to mid-September.

The grain elevator in Churchill fills ships from all over the world. See the restored 18th century stone Fort Prince of Wales, built by the Hudson's Bay Company over a 40-year pe-riod. The Eskimo Museum. Indian (Inuit) carvings are sold in several craft stores here.

Extended daylight in late June and early July (20 hours long) brings a great number of bird species to this area. Over 125 species breed here.

Arrangements to tour outlying areas by van or small bus can be made after arriving in Churchill. Boat trips are offered for spotting whales. There are flights to **Eskimo Point**, an Inuit settlement, where visitors can eat caribou and seal blubber as well as buy crafts.

Sights in **The Pas**: See notes under "Winnipeg–Lynn Lake"
Sights in **Thompson**: The huge International Nickel Company mining complex.
Sights in **Flin Flon**: The beautiful scenery at **Beaver Lake**.

Hudson Bay - Prince Albert - Saskatoon - Regina   Bus

When going west across Canada and detouring north to Churchill, it is not necessary to re-turn to Winnipeg in order to rejoin the transcontinental line. One can return from Churchill to the cross-country train line on a different route than that taken to Churchill by changing to a bus at Hudson Bay and proceeding from there to Prince Albert, Saskatoon and Regina.

The train from Prince Albert to Saskatoon was replaced by bus in 1982.

When going east across Canada, the detour to Churchill can start at Regina, and one can return from Churchill by continuing from Hudson Bay on to Winnipeg, rather than returning to Regina.

93

Dep. Hudson Bay		06:00 (1)		
Arr. Prince Albert		10:55		
Change buses.				
Dep. Prince Albert	09:30	10:30	14:00	18:00
Arr. Saskatoon	11:35	12:35	15:50	19:55
Change buses. 103				
Dep. Saskatoon	08:00	13:30	17:30	20:00
Arr. Regina	11:10	16:30	20:35	22:55
		• • •		
Dep. Regina	07:00 (2)	13:30	17:30	19:30
Arr. Saskatoon	10:05	16:25	20:35	22:25
Change buses. 93				
Dep. Saskatoon	14:00	08:35	18:00	09:00
Arr. Prince Albert	15:50	10:20	20:05	10:55
Change buses.				
Dep. Prince Albert	20:15 (3)			
Arr. Hudson Bay	00:25			

(1) Runs Tuesday, Thursday, Friday and Saturday. Departs 06:30 on Wednesday. (2) Monday-Friday only except holidays. (3) Runs Tuesday and Thursday only.

Saskatoon - Winnipeg   1 + 6

Both of these trains require reservation, are air-conditioned and carry a sleeping car, domecar, coaches and a restaurant car.

Dep. Saskatoon	04:00 (1)		Dep. Winnipeg	18:30 (2)
Arr. Winnipeg	12:35		Arr. Saskatoon	03:05 (3)

(1) Runs Monday, Thursday and Saturday. (2) Runs Wednesday, Friday and Sunday. (3) Day 3.

Winnipeg - Hudson Bay - The Pas - Lynn Lake

Bring food with you on the rides from The Pas to Lynn Lake and v.v. These trains have *no* food service. The days in early April when we made the trip, the temperature was below zero Fahrenheit. The area north of Winnipeg was under 4 feet of snow.

8		11	
Dep. Winnipeg (C.N.)	21:55 (1+2)	Dep. Lynn Lake	07:30 (4)
Dep. Dauphin	01:50 (3)	Arr. The Pas	17:35
Dep. Hudson Bay	07:40 (3)	*Change trains.*	
Arr. The Pas	09:35 (3)	*8*	
Change trains.		Dep. The Pas	20:20 (1+5)
11		Dep. Hudson Bay	22:25
Dep. The Pas	11:00 (3)	Dep. Dauphin	04:20 (6)
Arr. Lynn Lake	21:15	Arr. Winnipeg (C.N.)	08:00

(1) Reservation required. Air-conditioned train. Carries a sleeping car and a restaurant car. (2) Runs Tuesday, Thursday and Sunday. (3) Runs Wednesday, Friday and Monday. Day 2 from Winnipeg. (4) Runs Tuesday, Thursday and Saturday. Requires staying overnight in The Pas before taking the train the next day to Hudson Bay. (5) Runs Wednesday, Friday and Sunday. Day 2 from Lynn Lake. (6) Runs Thursday, Saturday and Monday. Day 3 from Lynn Lake.

Sights in **The Pas:** The hand-carved pews and the Ten Commandments in the Cree Indian language. The Museum. The Cathedral of Our Lady of the Sacred Heart.

The Pas, and most of the land north of it, is a massive reservation for Indians, a few of whom trap for furs.

The train from The Pas to Lynn Lake will stop at any point to let passengers board or get off. On our ride, it stopped in a completely deserted area so that a very old Indian man whose house could be seen on a hill a mile away from the track could get off. As the train started, we could see him beginning his long walk from the track to his house, on the other side of a frozen lake.

Our train for the 233-mile ride from The Pass to Lynn Lake was 23 freight cars, 2 passenger cars and a caboose, hauled by 4 locomotives. Only a few of the seats were filled, mostly by Indians.

The track goes alongside more than 20 very large lakes after the departure from Cranberry Portage, and nearly all of this route is heavily forested. Much ore is transported out of here in open gondola freight cars.

Some cabins of fur trappers are only a few feet from the rail track.In Winter, you can also see the snowmobile paths leading from the train track into the forest, to trapper cabins located away from the rail line.

From October to May, while there is snow on the ground, tracks of moose, deer, lynx, foxes and rabbits can be seen for hundreds of miles, only a few feet from the railway track.

In June, July and August, the splendid fishing and wilderness camping in the **Lynn Lake** area attract many tourists. It is possible to camp and hike only a short distance from either the rail track or from the well-traveled highway running between Lynn Lake and **Pukatawagan**.

Edmonton - Jasper - Prince George - Prince Rupert   6

There is very beautiful scenery between **Burns Lake** and Prince Rupert.

All of these trains require reservation, carry air-conditioned sleeping cars and coaches, and have a restaurant car.

Dep. Edmonton	08:55 (1)	Dep. Prince Rupert	11:30 (3)
Arr. Jasper	15:30	Arr. Prince George	00:05 (4)
Change trains.		Dep. Prince George	00:35
Dep. Jasper	20:10 (1)	Arr. Jasper	09:00
Arr. Prince George	02:30 (2)	*Change trains*	
Dep. Prince George	03:00	Dep. Jasper	14:55
Arr. Prince Rupert	15:40	Arr. Edmonton	20:10

(1) Runs Monday, Thursday and Saturday. (2) Day 2 from Jasper. Runs Tuesday, Friday and Sunday. (3) Runs Tuesday, Friday and Sunday. (4) Day 2 from Prince Rupert. Runs Wednesday, Saturday and Monday.

Sights in **Prince Rupert**: This area has many fjords, mountains and islands. Prince Rupert, the world's third largest natural harbor, is on **Kaien Island**. The rail line here from Prince George required 10,000,000 pounds of dynamite.

See 10,000 years of history (a flourishing Tsimshian society lived here 4,000 years ago) exhibited at the Museum of Northern British Columbia. The totems and flower gardens in Service Park. Take a gondola ride to the top of Mt. Hays. Go on a sightseeing cruise around the harbor and to the **Charlotte Islands**, or a sightseeing flight on an amphibious airplane.

Vancouver - Whistler - Lillooet - Prince George   BC Timetable

This is one of the most scenic rail trips in Canada. The train travels north along the fjord-like coast of Howe Sound before climbing alongside the massive rock cliffs and rushing whitewater of the steep and heavily-timbered Cheakamus Canyon to **Alta Lake**.

After stopping at the resort village of **Whistler**, the route continues to **Pemberton**, where snow-capped mountains stand above the lush forests and farmland of the Pemberton Valley. From here, the track negotiates a narrow path. The waters of Anderson and Seton Lakes are on one side, towering rock walls on the other side. Then, the track drops down into the historic gold-rush town of **Lillooet** in the Fraser River Canyon.

In the Fall, this route offers red, yellow and green foliage. In the Spring, there is a profusion of flowering trees and shrubs. From Lillooet, the rail route heads north along Fraser Canyon and provides marvelous vistas while climbing toward the Cariboo Plateau, where the landscape is green forests and rolling ranchland.

"Cariboo Class" is deluxe service available for traveling to and from Prince George. It includes spacious seating and full meal service. Coach passengers may purchase light snacks to eat at their seat. Both "Cariboo Class" and coach seats requires advance reservation. Reservation is not required for coach seats between North Vancouver and Lilloet

Whistler and Lillooet are popular for a day-trip from North Vancouver. Getting off in Whistler allows 8 hours for golfing on a championship course, windsurfing on **Alta Lake**, hiking on good trails, or simply exploring the village.

Those wanting a longer train ride can go to Lillooet, stop there for 2 hours, leisurely tour the Museum's exhibits of relics from early prospecting days, re-board and be back in North Vancouver at day's end.

For information and reservations, write to: BC Rail Passenger Services, P.O. Box 8770, Vancouver, B.C., V6B 4X6, Canada. Or, phone (604) 984-5246

Or you can use the following schedule on your own.

Both of these trains are air-conditioned. Both require reservations.

Dep. North Vancouver	07:00	Dep. Prince George (BCR)	07:15
Arr. Whistler	09:34	Dep. Lillooet	15:20
Arr. Lillooet	12:35	Dep. Whistler	18:10
Arr. Prince George (BCR)	20:30	Arr. North Vancouver	20:35

THE ROUTES OF
THE "ROCKY MOUNTAINEER"

Great Canadian Railtour Company Ltd. operates 2-day train journeys over more than 600 miles of fantastic Canadian Rockies scenery late May to early October. In order to not miss any of the scenery, passengers travel in the company's privately owned railcars during daylight and stay overnight in Kamloops.

The company's passenger cars are fitted with reclining seats, tray tables, picture windows and a non-smoking environment. Smoking is permitted only in designated areas.

Breakfast and lunch both days (and a dinner on the eastbound Banff–Calgary ride) are served to passengers at their seats, with emphasis on such famous Canadian food as British Columbia salmon and Alberta beef.

The Vancouver–Kamloops (and v.v.) route goes through the beautiful Fraser Valley and along the Fraser and Thompson rivers and Kamloops Lake.

The Kamloops–Jasper (and v.v.) route goes across the rolling plateaus of the North Thompson River and offers views of the snowy peaks of the Monashee Mountains, Pyramid Falls cascading 300 feet down Mount Cheadle, the glaciers of the Albreda Icefield, the highest mountain in the Canadian Rockies (12,972-feet-high Mount Robson), and the sparkling waters of Moose Lake and Yellowhead Lake.

It is only 4 hours by bus or car from Jasper to Edmonton.

The Kamloops–Banff–Calgary (and v.v.) route has scenery of the ranchland of the South Thompson River Valley, shining Shuswap Lake, the towering peaks and glistening glaciers of Glacier National Park, the "Spiral Tunnels" that go through Cathedral Mountain and Mount Ogden, Yoho National Park, the green Bow River, and the "Stampede" city of Calgary.

The 2 eastbound routes:

Dep. Vancouver	08:00		Dep. Vancouver	08:00
Arr. Kamloops	17:05		Arr. Kamloops	17:05
Overnight in Kamloops.			*Overnight in Kamloops.*	
Dep. Kamloops	08:00		Dep. Kamloops	07:30
Set your watch			*Set your watch*	
forward one hour.			*forward one hour.*	
Arr. Jasper	17:55		Arr. Banff	18:45
			Arr. Calgary	21:05

The 2 westbound routes:

Dep. Calgary	07:00		Dep. Jasper	09:00
Dep. Banff	09:20		*Set your watch*	
Set your watch			*back one hour.*	
back one hour.			Arr. Kamloops	16:55
Arr. Kamloops	18:20		*Overnight in Kamloops.*	
Overnight in Kamloops.				
Dep. Kamloops	07:30		Dep. Kamloops	07:30
Arr. Vancouver	16:55		Arr. Vancouver	16:55

"Rocky Mountaineer" tour includes assigned train seating, breakfast and lunch both days, a light dinner eastbound Banff–Calgary, complimentary snacks and non-alcoholic beverages, one night of hotel accommodation (including room tax) in Kamloops, roundtrip bus transfers in Kamloops train–hotel and hotel–train, and an information package.

For 2 weeks in Spring and 2 weeks in Fall, the tours are available at a substantial discount from the prices of the 16-week "Regular Season." The dates of its 1995 "Value Season" (from only Vancouver to Banff and/or Calgary) are: May 22, 26 and 31; September 25 and 29; and October 4.

"Value Season" (from only Calgary or Banff to Vancouver) 1994 dates are: May 24 and 29; June 2; September 27; and October 2 and 6.

The 1995 "Regular Season" departure dates from Vancouver to Banff and/or Calgary and also from Vancouver to Jasper are: June 5, 9, 14, 19, 23 and 28; July 3, 7, 12, 17, 21, 26 and 31; August 4, 9, 14, 18, 23 and 28; and September 1, 6, 11, 15 and 20.

"Regular Season" dates from Calgary, Banff or Jasper to Vancouver are: June 7, 12, 16, 21, 26 and 30; July 5, 10, 14, 19, 24 and 28; August 2, 7, 11, 16, 21, 25 and 30; September 4, 8, 13, 18 and 22.

For prices, brochures and any information, contact Great Canadian Railtour Company Ltd., Dept. "E," Suite 104, 340 Brooksbank Ave., North Vancouver, B.C., Canada V7J 2C1. Telephone (U.S.A. and Canada, except Vancouver): (800) 665-7245. From Vancouver: (604) 984-3315. Fax: (604) 984-2883.

Halifax - Truro - Sydney   Bus   132

The route north from Halifax connects in North Sydney with the ferry service to Port aux Basques, Newfoundland. (Table 51)

Dep. Halifax	08:00	13:00	17:00
Dep. No. Sydney	-0-	18:35	23:00
Arr. Sydney	15:50	19:00	23:30

Sights in **Halifax**: Tours by double-decker buses and 2-hour cruises are available. Also free guided walking tours.

See the Old Town Clock that was installed in 1803 by the Duke of Kent (son of George III, and later the father of Queen Victoria). A harsh military leader, he severely punished soldiers under his rule who were late in starting a duty assignment by flogging and hanging. When his men protested that they could not know the time because they did not have watches, he gave them this 4-faced clock on Citadel Hill. It can be seen from everywhere in Halifax.

Visit the exhibits of marine objects from the eras of sail and steam, at the Maritime Museum on Water Street. It is a short walk from there to the restaurants and craft shops at Historic Properties, a compound of restored 18th century buildings on the waterfront.

See the formal Victorian gardens on Spring Garden Road, called Public Gardens.

Dep. Sydney	07:30	11:00	14:15	19:10 (1)
Dep. No. Sydney	07:55	-0-	-0-	-0-
Arr. Halifax	14:45	17:15	21:50	22:20

(1) Runs daily, except Saturday.

BUS SERVICE IN NEWFOUNDLAND

Here is the daily cross-island bus service, connecting with the arrival of the ferry from Nova Scotia, and its return trip.

Port aux Basques - St. John's   Bus   143

These buses have special facilities for disabled passengers.

Dep. Port aux Basques	08:00	Dep. St. John's	08:00
Dep. Gander Airport	17:25	Dep. Gander Airport	13:00
Arr. St. John's	22:05	Arr. Port aux Basques	22:05

SPECIAL CANADIAN TRAIN EXCURSIONS

North Vancouver - Squamish - North Vancouver   4

This is an easy one-day roundtrip (27 miles each way), featuring a steam locomotive tour of scenic Howe Sound. Scenery on this trip includes forests, waterfalls and the seacoast. **Squamish** is a logging town. Visitors can shop there for Indian arts and crafts and see the 1,000-foot cascade of **Shannon Falls**, logging and sports shows, musical performances and sidewalk markets. There is an optional tour by airplane of the nearby glacier and an optional bus tour of the area.

A combination train-and-boat one-day excursion has been operated since 1982 by Harbour Ferries, #1 North Foot of Denman Street, Vancouver B.C. V6G 2W9, Canada. Their phone is (800) 663-1500 or (604) 688-7246. Operates June through September, Wednesday–Sunday.

Passengers have the option of either going from Vancouver to Squamish by Royal Hudson Steam Train and returning to Vancouver by luxury ferry (10:00–16:30) or the reverse (09:30–16:00). This train has special facilities for disabled passengers.

For the do-it-yourself train-only roundtrip, a bus departs from the downtown Vancouver bus depot at 09:00, making several stops on the way to the excursion train (front of the Hudson Bay Department Store, front of The Royal Bank, etc.). Look for the bus that displays a sign reading "Train Connection."

Here are the schedules for the ordinary train service. Mid-June to mid-September: runs daily in both directions. Mid-September to mid-June: runs Monday, Tuesday, Thursday and Saturday North Vancouver to Squamish....Runs Tuesday, Wednesday, Friday and Sunday Squamish to North Vancouver.

| Dep. North Vancouver | 07:00 | | Dep. Squamish | 19:15 |
| Arr. Squamish | 08:22 | | Arr. North Vancouver | 20:35 |

Victoria - Courtenay - Victoria   3

Good views of Vancouver Island scenery as this line winds along sheer cliffs high above Finlayson Arm, en route to Malahat Summit. There are spectacular vistas from many high trestles before the train begins its descent along Shawnigan Lake, en route to **Nanaimo**.

The station 13 minutes before arriving **Courtenay** is **Union Bay.** Many prefer to get off the train there in order to have a more leisurely lunch than is possible when going all the way to Courtenay.

A 2-day circle-trip can be made by taking the bus ferry Vancouver-Victoria (with a night in Victoria), and then the next day the Victoria-Nanaimo train and the Nanaimo–Vancouver ferry.

| Dep. Victoria | 08:15 (1) | Dep. Courtenay | 13:15 (1) |
| Arr. Courtenay | 12:50 | Arr. Victoria | 17:45 |

(1) Runs Monday-Thursday only.

Toronto - Niagara Falls - Toronto   16

All of these trains are air-conditioned.

| Dep. Toronto (Union) | 09:30 (1) | 17:45 |
| Arr. Niagara Falls (Canada) | 11:25 | 19:38 |

· · ·

| Dep. Niagara Falls (Canada) | 06:35 (2) | 08:30 (3) | 17:15 (1) |
| Arr. Toronto (Union) | 08:25 | 10:21 | 19:14 |

(1) Buffet. (2) Runs Monday–Friday. (3) Runs Saturdays and Sundays.

INTERNATIONAL ROUTES
FROM CANADA

The gateways for travel from Canada to the United States are: Montreal (to Boston, New York and south along the eastern U.S. seaboard), Toronto (to Buffalo and on to New York City or Cleveland, or to Detroit and on to Chicago), and Vancouver (to Seattle).

Montreal - New York City   196 + 199

Both of these trains are air-conditioned and have a buffet car.

Dep. Montreal	10:25 (1)	Dep. New York	10:35 (2)
(Cen.)		(Penn)	
Arr. New York	20:20	Arr. Montreal	20:06
(Penn)			

(1) Via Albany. Runs daily. (2) Via Albany. Runs Sundays and holidays only. (3) Via Albany. Runs daily. (4) Via New Haven. Carries a sleeping car. (5) Day 2. (6) Plus another Montreal departure [Table 196] at 17:20 (4), arriving New York City 07:55 (5).

Toronto - Niagara Falls - Buffalo - New York (or Cleveland and Chicago)

Both of these trains are air-conditioned.

17

Dep. Toronto (Union)	09:30 (1)		
Dep Niagara Falls (Can.)	11:30		
Dep. Niagara Falls (U.S.A.)	13:00		
Arr. Buffalo (Depew)	13:47	Arr. Buffalo (Depew)	13:47
Arr. New York (Penn.)	21:33	*Change trains. 186*	
		Dep. Buffalo (Depew)	03:51 (2)
		Arr. Cleveland (Lakefront)	06:56
		Arr. Toledo	09:09
		Arr. Chicago (Union)	12:58

(1) Buffet. (2) Restaurant car.

Toronto - Windsor - Detroit   17

Take a taxi from Windsor to Detroit through the International Tunnel.

All of these trains are air-conditioned.

Dep. Toronto (Union)	08:40 (1)	12:35 (1)	16:15 (2)	17:15 (3)	19:20 (2)
Arr. Windsor	12:58	16:43	20:20	21:25	23:45

(1) Light refreshments daily. Buffet daily, except Saturday. (2) Runs daily. Buffet. (3) Runs Thursdays, Sundays and holidays. Buffet.

Vancouver - Seattle   Bus   580

In 1981, this train service was replaced by bus transportation for connection between the Montreal-Vancouver train and the Seattle-Los Angeles train.

Dep. Vancouver	05:15	07:15	10:00	12:00	13:00 (1)
Arr. Seattle	09:15	10:45	13:25	15:10	16:55

(1) Plus other Vancouver departures at 15:00,17:30 and 19:30, arriving Seattle 18:10, 20:40 and 23:00.

MEXICO

Children under 5 travel free when accompanied by a parent. Half-fare for children 5–11. Children 12 and over must pay full fare.

There are 4 classes of service: Star (exceptional first-class only), Special First-Class, first-class and second-class.

Mexico's passenger trains are operated by Ferrocarriles Nacionales de Mexico (NdeM).

Its routes along the U.S. border originate from Juarez (El Paso), Piedras Negras, Mexicali (Calexico), Nogales, Nuevo Laredo (Laredo), and Matamoros (Brownsville), all of these providing service to Mexico City. Other N de M gateways to Mexico City are Tampico, Veracruz, Coatzacoalos, Oaxaca, Uruapan, Durango, Manzanillo and Guadalajara.

All Mexican railway schedules use the same time as U.S. Central Standard Time (same as Chicago).

Several U.S. and Mexican tour operators offer escorted private train tours of Mexico. Check your travel agent for details. Because Mexican railways do not pay travel agents a commission, an agent who assists you in obtaining train reservations is entitled to a fee of 15% of the ticket price. *Advance reservations are advisable.*

Mexico City

Largest population of any city in the world: more than 20,000,000. Its altitude of 7,350 feet (2,240 meters) limits activity for many tourists. Cool and dry weather except during the May-September rainy season.

Railways link Mexico City with 5 Gulf of Mexico seaports (Matamoros, Tampico, Veracruz, Coatzacoalcos and Campeche) and 4 Pacific ports (Los Mochis, Mazatlan, Manzanillo and Ciudad Hidalgo).

Most museums here are open daily except Monday 10:00–17:00. See the Diego Rivera murals that depict the course of Mexican history from the time of the Aztecs to the 1917 Mexican Revolution, at the National Palace on the main square, Plaza Mayor (also called "Zocalo"). Also, dozens of lovely Rivera frescoes can be seen at the Ministry of Education (30 Avenida Brasil).

See the extraordinary Aztec treasures at Museo del Templo Mayor (Great Temple), at 1 Avenida Argentina.

A wealthy German immigrant acquired 9,000 craftworks and art from the 16th century: ceramics, timepieces, furniture, gold and silver objects, and textiles. The best of these are displayed at Museo Franz Mayer (45 Avenida Hidalgo).

The art, sculpture, movies and scale models of ancient cities at the National Museum of Anthropology and History in the 1,500-acre Chapultepec Park (open 10:00–18:00) are the major attractions. You will see the results of more than 15,000 discovery sites, including the 167-ton statue of Tlatloc, the Aztec rain god, and a 30-ton Aztec calendar stone.

All the major Indian tribes of Mexico Maya, Toltec, Olmec and Aztec are represented at this fabulous museum (jewelry, paintings, furniture, sculpture). Guided tours are conducted in many languages, including English.

Also see the Museum of Modern Art, open 11:00–19:00. The 16th century Basilica de Guadalupe, most sacred shrine in Mexico. The mariachi bands in Plaza de Garibaldi. The daily markets, Centro de Abastos and San Juan. Window-shop the displays of silver jewelry on Juarez and Madero Streets. The shops in Zona Rosa. The textiles at the Londres Street Market. Visit the Cathedral, oldest and largest church in Latin America. The National Pawnshop (Monte de Piedad). Palacio Nacional. The Palace of Fine Arts. The good collection of European paintings at the School of Fine Arts. Plaza Mexico, the largest bullfighting ring in the world. Jai Alai at Fronton Mexico. The almost 1,000-acre Bosque de Chapultepec.

There are several splendid one-day excursions from Mexico City. It is only 40 miles to the pre-Aztec pyramids at **Teotihuacan**. Take the short ride to **Cuernavaca** and the Popocatepetl and Ixtaccihuati national parks. Do not miss seeing the floating gardens at **Xochimilco**.

Unless indicated otherwise, Mexico City departure and arrival times are for its Buenavista railstation.

U.S. RAIL GATEWAYS TO MEXICO

Brownsville-Matamoros or Laredo-Nuevo Laredo to Monterrey and Mexico City   1023

Take a taxi from Brownsville, to Matamoros or from Laredo, to Nuevo Laredo.

All of these trains have air-conditioned Special First-Class coaches.

Dep. Matamoros	09:20 (1)	-0-	Dep. Mexico City	09:00(4)	18:00 (2)
Dep. Nuevo Laredo	-0-	18:55 (4)	Arrive Monterrey	02:20 (3+4)	08:10 (3)
Arr. Monterrey	16:00	23:20 (4)	*Change trains.*		
Change trains.			Dep. Monterrey	02:20 (4)	10:30 (1)
Dep. Monterrey	19:50 (2)	23:30 (4)	Arr. Nuevo Laredo	07:20	-0-
Arr. Mexico City	10:00 (3)	19:00 (3)	Arr. Matamoros	-0-	17:10

(1) Reservation required. Light refreshments. (2) Carries an air-conditioned first-class sleeping car and a restaurant car. (3) Day 2. (4) Reservation required. Direct train. No train change in Monterrey.

Sights in **Matamoros**: The cannon, walls and turrets of old Fort Mata, site of the Casa Mata Museum. The Cathedral. The leather, jewelry and souvenirs for sale in the city's 2 street markets. The handwork of Tamaulipas artisans on sale at the Arts and Crafts Center, near the International Bridge.

Sights in **Monterrey**: Founded in 1579. See the collection of rare books in Indian languages and more than 2,000 editions of Don Quixote in many languages at the regional museum in the 200-year-old El Obispado, originally a bishop's palace. The painting and sculpture gallery in the Casa de la Cultura arts center, formerly a railstation. Sunday bull-fights and Mexican-style rodeos. Sampling free cerveza at the Carta Blanca brewery. The 18th century Cathedral in Plaza Zaragosa, where band concerts are performed. El Obispado (the Bishop's Palace), once occupied by Pancho Villa.

Nuevo Laredo - Monterrey - San Luis Potosi - Mexico City
1023

Many package tours of Mexico (transportation, hotels, sightseeing, entertainment and meals) start and end in Laredo. Check your travel agent for details. Several connections can be made from Monterrey.

Both of these trains require reservation, carry an air-conditioned Special First-Class coach, and have light refreshments.

Dep. N. Laredo	18:55		Dep. Mexico City	09:00
Arr. Monterrey	23:30		Dep. S. L. Potosi	17:20
Dep. Monterrey	23:40		Arr. Monterrey	02:20
Dep. S. L. Potosi	10:15		Dep. Monterrey	02:30
Arr. Mexico City	19:00		Arr. N. Laredo	07:20

El Paso - Ciudad Juarez - Mexico City   1016

Passengers transferring from or to Amtrak in El Paso have to make their own provision for crossing the border. There is taxi service. At Chihuahua, there is a connection for taking the "Copper Canyon Ride" to Los Mochis. At Torreon, a feeder line runs to Durango. At Irapuato, there is a connection for Guadalajara and Guanajuato.

Dep. Ciudad Juarez	07:00 (1)	22:00 (3)	Dep. Mexico City	07:10 (1)	20:00 (3)
Arr. Chihuahua	11:50	03:15	Dep. Irapuato	15:40	02:00 (2)
Dep. Chihuahua	12:20	03:25	Dep. Zacatecas	00:00 (2)	09:30
Arr. Torreon	20:35	12:00	Arr. Torreon	08:05	17:10
Dep. Torreon	21:00	12:10	Dep. Torreon	08:40	17:20
Dep. Zacatecas	05:02 (2)	20:05	Arr. Chihuahua	17:05	01:20 (3)
Dep. Irapuato	14:20	03:10	Dep. Chihuahua	17:35	01:30
Arr. Mexico City	22:05	09:30	Arr. Ciudad Juarez	22:35 (4)	06:45

(1) Runs daily. Light refreshments. (2) Day 2. (3) Reservation required. Has an air-conditioned Special First-Class coach. Light refreshments. (4) Day 3.

Sights in **Ciudad Juarez:** The statues of Abraham Lincoln and Mexico's counterpart of him, Benito Juarez. Visit the Museum of Art and History in Juarez Cultural Center. Bullfights. Dog and thoroughbred horse racing.

Sights in **Chihuahua City**: Our favorite sight here is the museum at Quinta Gameros, an old private residence. Its decor and furnishings are extraordinary. Visit the dungeon of Miguel Hidalgo, Mexico's George Washington, at the beautiful Federal Palace. The colonial Cathedral, built from 1724 to 1826 because Indian wars interrupted its construction. Quinta Luz, Pancho Villa's home, now a museum about him and his exploits. The 18th century Chihuahua Aqueduct, completed in 1764. Some of its arches are 59 feet high.

The murals in Governor's Palace, depicting the history of Chihuahua. Plaza de la Constitucion. Tarahumara Indians in colorful costumes roaming the streets. Chihuahua dogs. Benito Juarez Palace. There is much hunting and fishing here.

Interesting side trips can be made to **Santa Eulalia,** oldest mining town in northern Mexico; **Aldama,** a picturesque town in the center of an important fruit producing area; **Camargo,** famed for its hot springs; and **La Boquilla Dam,** one of the largest artificial lakes in the world and a fisherman's paradise.

Sights in **Zacatecas**: It is over 8,000-feet-high here. See the images of St. Peter and St. Francis, made from hummingbird feathers, in the Church de Nuestra Senora Guadalupe, and the hundreds of paintings there as well as the Christ on the Cross made of corn-stalks and the porcelain Virgin Mary. The Church of Santo Domingo.

The Temple of San Augustin. The ancient aqueduct. The outstanding wrought-iron in Pension Tacuba. The thousands of carved figures and designs on the main facade of the marvelous Cathedral. You can visit the tremendous El Bote Silver Mine by obtaining a permit and guide at the Tourist Office. Also, it is only a 30-mile drive south to **La Quemada** to see the prehistoric **Chicomoztoc Ruins**.

El Paso - Ciudad Juarez - Chihuahua - Los Mochis

This is the Copper Canyon ride. It offers some of the most spectacular scenery in Mexico. Highest point of the journey is 8,071 feet at **Los Ojitos.**

For best views Chihuahua–Los Mochis, sit on the left side. Completed only in 1961, the rail line to Los Mochis crosses 39 very tall bridges and passes through 8½ miles of 86 tunnels (one is 4,134 feet long) as it crosses the Sierra Tarahuamara mountain range. The bridge over **Septentron River** is 335 feet high. At several points, the route is so rugged that the track must double back in a complete circle.

Scenery includes spectacular deserts, mountains, pine forests and semi-tropical landscape. The journey begins as the line leaves the plateau west of Chihuahua City and climbs into the Sierra Madres. The aborigine Tarahuamara Indians can be observed from Creel to Divisadero. They are the most primitive people in North America, many of them living in caves, some of which can be visited at Creel and at Divisadero.

Delays in the 13-hour journey occur several times a year. Breaking the trip by overnighting at Creel, Bahuichivo (not shown on Cook's timetable), Divisadero or El Fuerte is advisable.

In **Creel**, the Hotel Nuevo (near the railstation) or the picturesque Copper Canyon Lodge (a 30-minute ride by the lodge's bus) will arrange many different short tours by pick-up truck or station wagon. Within 6 miles, there are vast forests, swimming and fishing in mountain lakes, waterfalls and archaeological sites. Hotel tours go to **Cuzarare** (12 miles), **Norogachi** (48 miles), **Basihuare** (24 miles) and **Sisoguichi** (18 miles).

Halfway between Chihuahua and Los Mochis, the train comes into **Divisadero**. Meaning "look-out point," Divisadero stands on the rim of **Urique Canyon**. The train stops here for 20 minutes for viewing down 6,000 feet into the canyon. We recommend overnighting here at the comfortable Cabanas Divisadero, perched on the very rim of the Canyon.

Then the train proceeds into a mile-long tunnel, making a 360-degree turn inside the mountain so that when it emerges from the tunnel and passes a 400-foot waterfall it is heading back in the direction from which it entered the tunnel.

Sights in **Los Mochis**: Fields of safflower. The Botanical Garden. Fifteen miles away is the harbor of **Topolobampo**. Excellent deep-sea fishing there.

Take a bus or taxi from El Paso to Ciudad Juarez.

1016			
Dep. Ciudad Juarez	07:00 (1)	22:00 (2)	-0-
Arr. Chihuahua	11:50	03:15	-0-
Change trains. 1013			
Dep. Chihuahua	-0-	07:00 (3)	08:00 (1)
Dep. Creel	-0-	12:26	14:00
Dep. Divisadero	-0-	13:45	15:30
Dep. El Fuerte	-0-	19:16	21:42
Set your watch back one hour.			
Arr. Los Mochis	-0-	20:50 (4)	23:25 (4)

The Los Mochis departure times shown in Cook are confusing, because they are one hour later than the time used throughout the city. **It is 06:00 at your hotel in Los Mochis when the 07:00 train departs Los Mochis for Chihuahua!** One needs to leave one's Los Mochis hotel at 05:15 for the very long ride to the railstation so as not to miss the "07:00" departure!

Dep. Los Mochis	07:00 (3+4)	08:00 (1+4)	-0-
Set your watch forward one hour.			
Dep. El Fuerte	08:26(3)	09:40	-0-
Dep Divisadero	13:35	15:25	-0-
Dep. Creel	15:14	17:05	-0-
Arr. Chihuahua	20:50	23:25	-0-
Change trains. 1016			
Dep. Chihuahua	-0-	01:20 (2)	17:35 (1)
Arr. Ciudad Juarez	-0-	06:45	02235

(1) Runs daily. Light refreshments. (2) Reservation required. Has air-conditioned Special First-Class coaches. Light refreshments. (3) Reservation required. Star service. Air-conditioned train has only Special First-Class coaches. Restaurant car. (4) One hour earlier in the city of Los Mochis. Railstation is on Central time. Los Mochis is on Mountain time.

Tuscon - Nogales - Sufragio (Los Mochis) - Mazatlan - Guadalajara - Mexico City   1012

The Copper Canyon ride can be made Los Mochis–Chihuahua from this line between Sufragio and Mexico City. (Sufragio is a 25-mile drive from Los Mochis.)
  It is a 2-hour bus ride at frequent times from Tuscon to Nogales (Table 546).

These "Star Service" trains require a reservation, have air-conditioned Special First-Class and ordinary first-class coaches and light refreshments.

Dep. Nogales	15:30		Dep. Mexico City	20:30
Arr. Sufragio	02:15 Day 2		Dep. Guadalajara	09:30 Day 2
Dep. Mazatlan	08:15		Dep. Mazatlan	18:30
Arr. Guadalajara	19:00		Arr. Sufragio	00:45 Day 3
Arr. Mexico City	08:25 Day 3		Arr. Nogales	11:50

Sights in **Mazatlan:** A marvelous seashore resort. Ride a 3-wheel "pneumonia" past the hotels, boutiques and shopping centers that line the seaside Avenida de Mar. Prize billfish and marlin are caught here. Much hunting for wild boar, deer, rabbit, ducks, quail and pheasant in the nearby mountains.
Sights in **Guadalajara**: The 16th century Cathedral, surrounded by 4 plazas in the shape of a cross. The Cabanas Institute arts center and its marvelous Orozco murals, at the former Orphanage. Near there, the sculpture and fountains at the new Plaza Tapatia. Municipal Palace. The State Museum. The Library. Mercado Libertad, Mexico's largest public market. Casa de las Artesianas de Jalisco, a state-run arts and crafts exhibition and shop.

Mexico City - Guanajuato   1016 + 1030

This schedule requires staying overnight in Guanajuato in order to sightsee there.

These "Star Service" trains require reservation, are air-conditioned Special First-Class only, and have light refreshments.

Dep. Mexico City	20:00		Dep. Guanajuato	14:25
Dep. Irapuato	02:00		Dep. Silao	15:10
Dep. Silao	12:45		Arr. Irapuato	15:40
Arr. Guanajuato	13:25		Arr. Mexico City	21:15

Sights in **Guanajuato**: Many ornate 17th century churches that were endowed by the wealth of the richest silver mine in the world. Visit the former residence of the man who owned that mine. There is much late Renaissance architecture here.

The evolution of the career and the style of Diego Rivera is traced in nearly 100 paintings , lithographs and sketches exhibited in the house where Rivera spent his infancy, now a museum. Included are a watercolor of a Greek bust he painted when he was 12 and a caricature of John Foster Dulles.

See the ghoulish exhibit of mummified corpses at the Panteon Museum. An old underground aqueduct that is now used as a subterranean road. The Palace of the Governor.

THE CALIFORNIA GATEWAY

The California connection with rail travel to Mexico City begins by walking or driving from Calexico across the border to Mexicali and taking the short line from Mexicali to Benjamin Hill, where a connection can be made with the Nogales–Guadalajara line.

Mexicali - Sufragio - Mazatlan - Guadalajara - Mexico City

The Copper Canyon ride can be made Los Mochis–Chihuahua from this line to Mexico City. (Sufragio is a 25-mile drive from Los Mochis.)

The trains Benjamin Hill–Mexico City and v.v. are "Star Service," require a reservation and have air-conditioned Special First-Class and ordinary first-class coaches.

1007		*1026*	
Dep. Mexicali	09:00 (1)	Dep. Mexico City	20:30 (4)
Arr. Benjamin Hill	17:10	Arr. Guadalajara	08:15 (3)
Through cars switched here. 1012		*Change trains. 1012*	
Dep Benjamin Hill	17:45 (2)	Dep. Guadalajara	09:30 (2)
Arr. Sufragio	02:15 (3)	Dep. Mazatlan	18:30
Dep. Mazatlan	08:15	Arr. Sufragio	00:45 (5)
Arr. Guadalajara	19:30	Arr. Benjamin Hill	09:25
Change trains. 1026		*Through cars switched here. 1007*	
Dep Guadalajara	21:00 (4)	Dep. Benjamin Hill	11:45 (1)
Arr. Mexico City	08:25 (5)	Arr. Mexicali	17:55

(1) Light refreshments Mexicali–Benjamin Hill and v.v. (2) Light refreshments Benjamin Hill–Guadalajara and v.v. (3) Day 2. (4) Carries an air-conditioned first-class sleeping car, Special First-Class coach and dome car. The restaurant car is *not* air-conditioned. (5) Day 3.

Mazatlan - Tepic (San Blas) - Guadalajara 1012

It is a one-hour bus ride from Tepic to San Blas.

Dep. Mazatlan	04:35 (1)	08:15 (2)	Dep. Guadalajara	09:30 (2)	12:00 (1)
Dep. Tepic	10:25	13:30	Dep. Tepic	13:35	16:45
Arr. Guadalajara	17:55	19:00	Arr. Mazatlan	18:20	22:45

(1) Has only non-air-conditioned second-class coaches. Buffet. (2) Reservation required. "Star Service." Has an air-conditioned Special First-Class coach. Light refreshments.

Mexico City - Morelia - Patzcuaro - Uruapan 1035

Excellent Michoacan farm scenery is viewed on this ride.

Dep. Mexico City	21:00 (1)	Dep. Uruapan	18:10 (1)
Dep. Morelia	05:20	Dep. Patzcuaro	21:15
Dep. Patzcuaro	06:45	Dep. Morelia	22:40
Arr. Uruapan	09:00	Arr. Mexico City	07:30

(1) Reservation required. Has air-conditioned Special First-Class coach. Buffet.

Sights in **Morelia**: Many of the structures in this 16th century city date from the 17th century. Visit the twin-towered, 200-foot-high Cathedral built between 1640 and 1744, the tallest in Mexico. One of Mexico's most splendid, its high altar's tremendous silver font and the enormous gold crown on a crucified Christ are worth seeing.

The tourist office, 2 blocks west of the Cathedral, in the Palacio de Clavijero, on Nigromante, has information about city bus tours.

Visit the Morelos Museum. The arcade with 50 candy stalls. The city aqueduct's 250 arches. Cuauhtemoc Park. The carved flowers, gilded columns and painted statues in the Sanctuario del Guadalupe. The Conservatorio de las Rosas, a 17th century convent, the oldest musical school in North America. Next door to it, the dancing and art displays at Casa de la Cultura which houses a small museum of pre-colonial artifacts.

See the exhibits at the Museum of Michoacan, near the main plaza. The Cardenas mural in the Palace of Justice. Regional crafts at Casa de Artesianas. Another display of handcraft articles from various parts of this state copperware from **Vila Escalante**, stringed instruments from **Paracho**, lacquer trays and cups from **Uruapan** at the 16th century Convent of San Francisco. The 18th century aqueduct.

Sights in **Patzcuaro**: Many 16th century buildings around Plaza Grande, a large green park. See the 16th century church, La Compania. One block from it, craftsmen's studios and shops at House of 11 Patios.

Tarascan Indians bring lacquer, copper, wood and paper-mache items to the Friday market-day.

See the large mural in the Public Library, depicting this region from prehistoric times to the 1910 revolution. The museum of folk art at the site of the 16th century San Nicolas College, before it moved to Morelia. Satisfy your sweet tooth at Joaquinita's Chocolate Supremo.

The 14-mile-long **Lake Patzcuaro,** famous for tasty whitefish, is 2½ miles from the city center. A ferryboat goes to **Janitzio,** largest island on the lake, which has many restaurants specializing in fish and a gigantic statue of Jose Morelos. He was the hero of Mexican independence from France and was shot in 1815.

A good place to shop for pottery and straw items and to rest is at the ruins of **Tzintzuntzan,** capital of the Tarascan Empire, near the lake's eastern shore – a 7-mile drive from Patzcuaro.

Sights in **Uruapan**: It is one mile high here. Founded in 1540. Tjarascan Indians are native to this area. Their crafts, including outstanding lacquerware, are exhibited and sold at the Gutapara Museum, next to the crafts market and on the ground floor of the Hotel Mansion de Cupatitzio, a 16th century structure noted for its lovely patio. See the jungle foliage of Eduardo Ruiz National Park (called "Cupatitzio"), a garden of tropical plants, rustic walks and bubbling streams along both banks of the **Cupatitzio River**.

Tzararacua Falls is 7 miles south, along the river.

See the daily market that runs along Constitucion, starting at Calzada Benito Juarez, and ending at the plaza. The crafts market is one block before reaching the plaza. Excellent lacquerware there: wood chests, small boxes, trays. Try the crispy barbequed pork at the Antojitos food stalls.

ROUTES SOUTH OF MEXICO CITY

There are 4 principal train routes south from Mexico City: to Veracruz, Oaxaca, Merida and Ciudad Hidalgo.

Mexico City - Veracruz

The excellent tropical mountain scenery on this route, including **Orizaba Volcano** (Mexico's tallest), warrants taking this trip during daylight. It is necessary to bring your own food. Box lunches can be purchased on the lower level of Mexico City's Buenavista Railstation.

	1044	*1043*	*1043*
Dep. Mexico City	07:20 (1)	07:45 (2)	21:15 (3)
Arr. Veracruz	19:50	18:50	07:10

Sights in **Veracruz**: A very picturesque resort. See the excellent 17th century Palacio Municipal. Look for the silver-decorated tortoise-shell jewelry that is a specialty here. The beautiful Isla de Sacrificios beach. Take the bus marked "Ulua" to see the 16th century San Juan de Ulua Castle on **Gallega Island** (reached by a road).

	1044	*1043*	*1043*
Dep. Veracruz	07:20 (1)	08:00 (2)	21:30 (3)
Arr. Mexico City	19:55	18:55	07:40

(1) Takes the route **via Jalapa.** Light refreshments. (2) Takes the route **via Orizaba.** Second-class only. (3) Takes the route **via Orizaba.** Carries an air-conditioned first-class sleeping car, and Special First-Class coach and a domecar. Light refreshments. Reservations required.

Mexico City - Puebla - Oaxaca   1042

Both of these trains require reservation, are air-conditioned, and carry Special First-Class and ordinary first-class coaches and have light refreshments.

Dep. Mexico City	19:00	Dep. Oaxaca	19:00
Arr. Puebla	23:30	Arr. Puebla	04:05
Arr. Oaxaca	09:25	Arr. Mexico City	09:20

Sights in **Puebla**: The beautiful tiles at the Patio de los Azulejos. The great view of many snow-capped volcanoes from the top of Avenida Internacional, and a similar view from the Cathedral's bell-tower.

The marvelous onyx and marble statues, marble floors and gold leaf decor in the Cathedral. Nearby, Casa del Alfenique (Sugar Candy House). The outstanding museum of Mexican history near the forts of Guadalupe and Loreto. The sensational 16th century Talavera tiles in the Museo de Santa Rosa. The 17th century Church of San Cristobal.

The courtyard and tiled entrance at the Consejo de Justicia. The Cinco de Mayo civic center. The 16th century theater, oldest in the western hemisphere. The collection of Talavera pottery and Chinese porcelain in the Museo de Bello. The onyx and souvenir stores on Plaza Parian. The fascinating architecture, Indian statues in Santa Maria de Tonantzintla Church, and the excavated pyramid at nearby **Cholula.**

Sights in **Oaxaca**: Pronounced "wah–HAH–kah." The arcaded Zocalo Plaza, with the 16th century Cathedral built of pale green stone and, nearby, the fantastic gold leaf and the national museum in Santo Domingo Church. The Saturday Indian market. Do not miss seeing the sculpture and ironwork in the 17th century La Soledad Church. See the view from the monument to Juarez on Cerro de Fortin.

Shop for woolen zarapes, gold and silver jewelry, blankets made from cane, green and black pottery, embroidered blankets and clothing, rugs, etc. The Regional Museum has exhibits of Zapotec Indian treasures from the nearby Monte Alban tombs and Mixtec art from **Mitla**, another archaeological site on the outskirts of Oaxaca.

Mexico City - Palenque - Campeche - Merida 1047

Stopovers en route at Palenque and Campeche (to see Mayan ruins) can be arranged. Short excursions from Merida to Uxmal and Chichen–Itza are recommended. A first-class bus to Uxmal leaves Merida for this one-hour drive at 8:00, 9:00, 12:00 and 17:00. Departures from Uxmal for the ride back to Merida are at frequent times. Price in 1994 was 6000–7000 Pesos.

A bus for the 1½-hour drive to Chichen Itza departs Merida at 08:45, and departs Chichen Itza at 15:00 for the ride back to Merida. Price in 1994 was 14,000 Pesos.

A special tour bus to 5 archaeological zones (including Uxmal and Chichen Itza) departs Merida at 8:00, arriving back there at 17:00. Price in 1994 was 35 Pesos

Both of these trains have only ordinary second-class coach cars, and have light refreshments.

Dep. Mexico City	21:15		Dep. Merida	18:15
Dep. Coatzacoalcos	15:40 Day 2		Dep. Campeche	21:40
Dep. Palenque	22:49		Dep. Palenque	05:02 Day 2
Dep. Campeche	05:45 Day 3		Dep. Coatzacoalcos	11:30
Arr. Merida	09:35		Arr. Mexico City	07:40 Day 3

Sights in **Coatzacoalcos:** An important river and ocean port.

Sights in **Palenque**: Interesting Mayan ruins of stone buildings from the 7th and 8th centuries constructed without the aid of the wheel, metal tools, or beasts of burden are located only 5 miles from this lovely orchard village.

Palenque originally covered about 20 square miles. The area visited today is only slightly more than 30 acres, which the jungle would engulf within a month if it were not constantly cleared of growth.

One of the ruins, the pyramid-like Temple of the Inscriptions, was built into the side of a hill. Visitors can descend 65 feet below its entrance to the tomb of a Mayan ruler and see the 12½-foot long carved stone slab that once covered a sarcaphagous.

Or, visitors can climb up 69 steep and narrow steps to the top, 75 feet above the ground, to see pillars remaining from a temple. The pillars are decorated with bas-reliefs of priests holding up offerings to both the sun and to the god of maize (corn). Inside the portico, 3 enormous, carved stone panels have the hieroglyphics for which the temple is named (Temple of the Inscriptions) recording the ancestry and accession to the throne of the ruler who was interred inside it.

A palace complex covers about the area of a typical American block. It has underground passages that lead to ancient chambers, latrines and steam baths. The fireflies in this area are so large that a newspaper can be read by the light of a few captured ones.

Sights in **Campeche**: A fortified city, walled in the 17th century for protection from marauding pirates. See the white and vermillion painted wood altars in the 16th century San

Francisquito Church. The excellent museum. The rocky seacoast. The museums at the 18th century San Miquel Fort. About 25 miles by road, the Edzna pyramid.

Sights in **Merida:** It is great to sightsee here in a horse-drawn carriage (about $3.00 U.S. per hour). See the marvelous wrought-iron on the mansions on Paseo de Montejo. The entire history of Mexico in bas-relief at the massive Monument of the Flags. Casa Montejo, home of the man who founded this city in 1542. Exhibits of pre-Columbian Yucatan in the Museum of Archaeology.

The 16th century Cathedral, built from stones of Mayan ruins found on the site. Buy souvenirs at the tremendous public market (traditional Yucatan costumes, embroidered cotton smocks, huaraches, hammocks, mountains of fruit). Maps and advice can be obtained from the English-speaking employees of the Tourist Office on Zocalo Plaza. Take the short bus ride to Progreso Beach to swim and to eat fish, turtle and shrimp. Try the mild regional Yucatan cuisine.

Sights in **Uxmal**: Ruins of the perfectly-proportioned 11th century Mayan buildings that are decorated with intricate stone carvings. One week here might be adequate there is that much to see here.

Sights in **Chichen Itza**: The best-preserved Mayan City, spread over an area of 6 square miles, occupied from 1,000 B.C. to the 15th century A.D.

The structural features of El Castillo, the 75-foot high grand pyramid atop which is a large temple extending another 15 feet higher, have chronological elements that measure days of the year as well as the Spring and Fall equinoxes. For the Mayans, March 21 was considered the best day to plant corn and September 21 the best day to harvest it.

INTERNATIONAL CONNECTIONS
FROM MEXICO

All the schedules for rail travel between Mexico and the United States appear at the start of this section.

The only train connection from Mexico to Guatemala is very difficult, and we advise against attempting this trip until the conditions improve. There is no acceptable lodging in either primitive Ciudad Hidalgo or in equally primitive Tecun Uman, the Guatemalan city on the other side of the border. Furthermore, there is a 16-hour overnight layover and no place for tourists to stay. The final obstacle is that *passengers attempting to transfer from Ciudad Hidalgo to Tecun Uman must walk more than one mile* in great heat and mucho dust, and a substantial toll charge is exacted to cross the border bridge!

Mexico City - Tapachula - Ciudad Hidalgo - Guatemala City

1043			*1043*	
Dep. Mexico City	21:15 (1)		Dep. Tapachula	13:15 (5)
Arr. Veracruz	07:10 (2)		Arr. Ciudad Hidalgo	14:35
Change trains.			*Change trains.*	
Dep. Veracruz	21:00 (3)		*1150*	
Arr. Tapachula	19:25 (4)		Dep. Tecun Uman	06:00 (6)
Change trains.			Arr. Guatemala City	18:00

(1) Reservation required. Carries air-conditioned first-class sleeping cars and both Special First-Class and non-air-conditioned second-class coach cars. Dome-car. Light refreshments. (2) Day 2. (3) Has second-class coach cars. Light refreshments. (4) Day 3 from Mexico City. (5) Second-class only. (6) Runs frequently from 04:30 to 18:30.

Sights in **Veracruz:** See "Mexico City - Veracruz"
Sights in **Tapachula:** The extinct Taconah Volcano that towers above the city. Fifteen miles south is the *Puerto Madero* beach resort.

INFORMATION AND RESERVATIONS

Because few travel agents book Mexican train travel, you will find the following sources of information and reservations helpful. The name of the city from which a trip originates indicates the contact for reservations in the list below.

CHIHUAHUA
Chihuahua Pacific Railway
P.O. Box 46 Chihuahua, Chih., Mexico
TEL: 13-09-93

CIUDAD JUAREZ
National Railways of Mexico
P.O. Box 2200 El Paso, TX. 79951
TEL: 13-48-82

GUADALAJARA
Pacific Railroad Calle Tolsa No. 336
Guadalajara, Jal., Mexico
TEL: 12-51-86

MEXICALI
Sonora-Baja California Rly.
P.O. Box 231 Calexico, CA. 92231
TEL: 57-23-86 and 57-21-01

MEXICO CITY
National Railways of Mexico
Buenavista Station
06358 Mexico, D.F.
TEL: 547-5819, 547-3190 and 547-4114

NOGALES
Pacific Railroad Calle Internacional
No. 10 Nogales, Son., Mexico
TEL: 2-00-24

NUEVO LAREDO
National Railways of Mexico
Passenger Station Nuevo Laredo,
Tamps., Mexico
TEL: 2-80-97 and 2-01-34
or
P.O. Box 595 Laredo, TX. 78042

UNITED STATES OF AMERICA

Children under 2 travel free. Half-fare for children 2–15 in coach-class only, when accompanied by a person 18 or older. Children 12 and over must pay adult fares when traveling alone.

The classes of train service in the U.S.A. are: compartments convertible to various sleeping accomodations, Slumbercoach (a high-density sleeping car), Club (Parlor) car, Custom, and ordinary coach.

On some day trains, first-class service consists of reserved-seat club cars with 2 seats on one side of the aisle and one seat on the other side.

Night trains have variable first-class sleeping compartments. Most are complete with private wash and toilet facilities. All have doors that can be locked. All sleeping spaces must be reserved in advance.

Trains *east* of the Mississippi River feature roomettes for one person. The seat used during the day folds over at night, making room for a bed that is lowered from a recess in the wall. Ticket prices for roomettes and bedrooms include meals.

Bedrooms are available in 2 different daytime styles, one with a 2-person divan, the other with 2 chairs. At night, the porter makes up one upper bed and one lower bed. Each bed is 35 inches wide.

The Bedroom Suite results when the dividing partition between 2 adjoining bedrooms is removed. Accommodates up to 4 persons and has 2 wash basins and 2 toilets.

A Slumbercoach costs much less than other sleeping spaces. Rooms for one or 2 persons are available. Much smaller than other sleeper spaces. A double slumbercoach has one upper and one lower bed (each 24 inches wide) and private toilet and washbasin. Meals are *not* included in the Slumbercoach ticket price.

West of the Mississippi River, 2-level Superliner sleeping cars have deluxe, economy, family and special bedrooms. Deluxe sleeps 2 persons and has private wash, shower and toilet facilities. Economy accommodates one or 2 persons but *does not* have either private wash basin or toilet. Family bedroom sleeps 3 adults and 2 children. Special bedrooms with private wash basin and toilet are available for handicapped persons.

Coaches have 2 seats on each side of the aisle. These seats are adjustable to a semi-reclining position, similar to airplane reclining seats. Most long-distance trains have reserved-seat coaches with reclining seats and leg rests for overnight journeys.

All Amtrak trains are air-conditioned. Most long-distance trains carry a restaurant car. Some short-distance trains have a snack bar or lounge car with counter food service. Most Amtrak long-distance trains operating west of Chicago carry 2-level Superliner observation-lounge cars with large wrap-around windows for viewing the scenery.

Amtrak's fares are shown in its free publications, available at Amtrak or by writing to: Amtrak Distribution Center, P.O. Box 7717, Itasca, Ill. 60143, U.S.A.

Trains in the U.S.A. run through 4 time zones: Eastern, Central, Mountain and Pacific. There is a one-hour difference between each adjacent time zone. Summer schedules are in effect from the second Sunday of April to and including the last Saturday of October.

U.S.A. TRAIN FARES

All Aboard America coach fares can be used either for one-way or roundtrip travel. Prices are constantly fluxuating but as a point of reference, the May 11994-September 10, 1995 prices were $178 for a trip within one region of the U.S.A., $238 for 2 regions, and $278 for all 3 regions (transcontinental). Half-fare for children age 2–15. These fares have holiday blackouts, some restrictions, and "are in limited inventory."

Eastern Region: Atlantic Coast west to Chicago and New Orleans. Western Region: Pacific Coast east to El Paso, Wolf Point (Montana), Albuquerque or Denver. Central Region: everything between the 2 other regions.

The trip itinerary must be set at the time the All Aboard America fare is purchased. Sleeping accommodations are extra. The trip can start any day of the week but must be completed within 45 days. Stopover is allowed at 3 cities between origin and completion.

Sleeping Car Tickets The price for a first-class sleeping car ticket includes meals that may be selected from the restaurant car menu (salad, entree, and choice of coffee, tea or milk), a morning wake- up with a complimentary newspaper, and a stationery and information packet. Call 1-800-USA-RAIL for price information.

Senior Citizen and Handicapped Person Discount. A 15% discount off the lowest available roundtrip coach fare for those who prove they are age 62 or older. Those who offer certification from a physician, a government agency or an organization of handicapped are eligible for 25% discount off the regular one-way nondiscounted coach fare. Handicapped fare is not available to a passenger using the "All Aboard America" or the "$7 Return Fare." Not offered on many days in holiday periods.

Packaged Tours. Amtrak offers more than 400 different packaged tours (some escorted, some independent), that include transportation and, in some cases, hotels.

"Amtrak's America" travel planner and tour books can be obtained from travel agents or by writing to: Amtrak Distribution Center, P.O. Box 7717, Itasca, Ill. 60143, U.S.A.

Both National U.S.A. Rail Pass and Region U.S.A. Rail Pass are sold outside North America. Citizens and permanent residents of the U.S.A. and Canada are not eligible to buy them. These passes offer unlimited stopovers and either 15 or 30 days of unlimited coach travel on all Amtrak trains other than Metroliners and Auto Trains. Unlike passes in Europe which (except for Spain) do not require obtaining a ticket, these passes must be presented prior to boarding an Amtrak train in order to obtain the actual ticket that Amtrak requires.

High-Season fares are in effect May 30 to August 28, 1996. Children's prices apply to ages 2–15. Children under 2 not occupying a separate seat travel free.

Reservation should be made as much in advance of travel day as possible. Coach seats can be upgraded by paying an additional fee for reserved-seat club car or for sleeping car space. Travelers wanting more information or the prices for the regional passes listed below should write to: Amtrak International Sales, 60 Massachusetts Ave., N.E., Washington, D.C. 20002, U.S.A.

National U.S.A. Rail Pass. The 1996 adult high season prices are: $340 (U.S.) for 15 days, $425 for 30 days. Children: $170 and $212.50.

East Coast Pass. Travel in New England (except Maine), New Jersey, Maryland, Washington D.C., and eastern areas of New York State, Pennsylvania, Virginia, North Carolina, South Carolina, Georgia and Florida.

Eastern Region Pass. The area from Chicago and New Orleans to Atlantic Coast cities.

Western Region Pass. From the Pacific Coast as far east as Chicago and New Orleans.

Far Western Region Pass. Travel within Arizona, Colorado (west of and including Denver), Idaho, Oregon, Montana (west of and including Wolf Point), Nevada, New Mexico (west of and including Lamy), Utah, Washington and Wyoming.

West Coast Region Pass. California (west of and including Sacramento), Oregon (west of and including Portland), and Washington State (west of and including Seattle).

TRAVEL PLANNER

The 1996, free 90-page booklet features Amtrak's travel packages to 70 major destinations and includes a dozen escorted tours. It gives a complete explanation of Amtrak's routes, equipment and service.

A copy of both a domestic and an international edition of "Amtrak's America" in English are available at no charge from Amtrak's Distribution Center, P.O. Box 7717, Itasca, IL 60143, U.S.A.

Notes for sightseeing in 9 principal U.S. cities appear below.

Boston

The collection of Oriental and Egyptian art at the Museum of Fine Arts. The splendid Italian Renaissance paintings in the Isabella Stewart Gardner Museum. The many outstanding museums of science and industry at Harvard University. The elegant 19th century architecture of the Boston Public Library, which has many fine murals.

The New England Aquarium. Arnold Arboretum. The Massachusetts Institute of Technology. The Museum of Science and the Hayden Planetarium, both in Science Park. The Christian Science Mother Church. Take the Bay Cruise.

Many historic places are open to the public: Boston Massacre Site. Old South Church. Bunker Hill. The Tea Party Site. Boston Common. Haymarket Square. The Paul Revere House. The ship "Old Ironsides." Old South Meeting House. King's Chapel. Benjamin Franklin's birthplace.

Chicago

The Field Museum of Natural History. Shedd Aquarium, world's largest collection of sealife. Adler Planetarium. The collection of Near East art at Chicago University's Oriental Institute and, near it, a World War II submarine and the Apollo-8 spacecraft in the enormous Museum of Science and Industry. Lincoln Park Zoo. The Picasso statue at Civic Center Plaza. The Chagall mosaic at First National Bank Plaza. The Museum of Contemporary Art. The exhibit of impressionist art at the splendid Art Institute of Chicago. Sightseeing motorcoach tours leave from Union Station.

Los Angeles

You cannot depend on public transportation to sightsee in Los Angeles. To do so by taxi is extremely expensive. Car rental is the solution. See Olvera Street across from the 1939 railstation, which is an Art Moderne version of the white churches that Spanish missionaries built throughout California, replete with beautifully landscaped patios. This is where the city began.

See the incomparable Music Center complex of 3 outstanding theaters and the City Mall, leading from it to City Hall and the Civic Center of city, county, state of California and Federal buildings.

The marvelous Victorian interior of the 19th century Bradbury Building (elegant tile work and paneling, ornate cast-iron stairways, and open-cage elevators that rise from a marble floor), open daily except Sunday 10:00–17:00. The Coliseum, site of the 1932 Olympics and also where the 1984 ceremonies and many games were held. Near it, a splendid Natural History Museum.

Heading west on Wilshire Boulevard toward the Pacific Ocean, the Los Angeles County Museum of Art at 5905 Wilshire Blvd., open Tuesday-Friday 10:00–17:00, Saturday and Sunday 10:00-18:00, closed Monday. A 2-minute walk from it, the Page Museum of prehistoric mammals and birds at the La Brea Tar Pits. Nearby, Farmers' Market for the finest fruits, vegetables, meats and seafood in the world, also restaurants serving Mexican, Chinese, Italian and American food.

In the **Hollywood** area: The interesting forecourt at the Chinese Theater, with footprints and handprints of Hollywood's greatest stars from Mary Pickford to Sylvester Stallone. The major musical events at the Hollywood Bowl all Summer.

The many wealthy residential estates in **Beverly Hills, Bel Air, Westwood and Brentwood**. The Alcoa "Century City" complex, between Beverly Hills and Westwood. Window-shop the row of high-priced stores on Rodeo Drive in Beverly Hills. Visit the University of California at Los Angeles campus, in Westwood.

The expanse of great beaches on the Pacific Ocean shoreline, from **Santa Monica** north to **Malibu** and **Oxnard**, and south to **Newport Beach, Laguna Beach, La Jolla** and **San Diego**. The spectacular array of private yachts at both **Marina Del Rey** (near Los Angeles International Airport) and at **Newport Beach-Balboa**, a one-hour drive south of Los Angeles International Airport. Malibu has a priceless collection of paintings and sculptures at the J. Paul Getty Museum (17985 Pacific Coast Highway, Malibu 90265) open daily except Mondays and holidays 10:00-17:00. Reservations are mandatory.

Take the guided tours of both Universal Studios in **Universal City** and the National Broadcasting Company in **Burbank**.

Hearst's Castle in **San Simeon** is a 5-hour drive north by auto (or by Amtrak to **San Luis Obispo**) from Los Angeles. Disneyland, in **Anaheim**, is a one-hour drive south by auto, as is **San Pedro** which has the Queen Mary.

In **Pasadena**, 20 minutes by car from the Los Angeles Civic Center, there is more to see than can be done in a single day. See 18th century art (including Gainsborough's "Blue Boy") at the Huntington Library, Art Gallery and Botanical Garden (1151 Oxford Road, San Marino, adjacent to Pasadena), open daily except Monday 13:00–6:30. The Norton Simon Museum at 411 W. Colorado Blvd., open Thursday-Sunday 12:00–18:00, has a much larger and more diverse art collection than the Huntington.

The Pacific Asia Museum (46 No. Los Robles Ave.) is the only museum in Southern California specializing in Far Eastern art. It is open Wednesday-Sunday 12:00–17:00. Visit Gamble House (4 Westmoreland Place), a combination of an Alpine chalet and a Japanese temple, to see its Tiffany stained-glass door and original furnishings from 1908, the year it was built. Open Tuesday and Thursday 10:00–15:00 and every Sunday (except when a major holiday falls on a Sunday) 12:00–15:00.

Entry to the William Wrigley Italian Renaissance Mansion (391 So. Orange Grove Blvd.) is allowed late January to late September on Wednesdays. See other old mansions on Arroyo Terrace. A very wide collection of paintings from the early Renaissance, early tapestries, and modern art at the Norton Simon Museum of Art (411 W. Colorado Blvd.).

Free tours of the California Institute of Technology are guided by students Monday, Wednesday and Friday at 15:00, and on Tuesday and Thursday at 11:00, starting from the school's public relations office (315 So. Hill St.). Lasting 60–90 minutes, this tour visits many laboratories, including Cal Tech's world-famous seismology lab.

A collection of Indian artifacts is exhbited at the Southwest Museum (234 Mission Dr.), open Tuesday-Saturday 11:00–17:00, Sundays (except holidays) 13:00–17:00. Art from the Far East can be seen at the Pacific Asia Museum (46 No. Los Robles Ave.).

The Rose Bowl Stadium. The 165-acre Descanso Gardens, noted for its collection of 600 varieties of camellias, at the Los Angeles Arboretum (301 No. Baldwin Ave.) in nearby **Arcadia**, near Santa Anita Racetrack.

New York City

The Statue of Liberty. The United Nations complex. The view from the top of the Empire State Building. The New York Stock Exchange. The Rockefeller Center complex. The Metropolitan Museum of Art, greatest art museum in the United States. The Whitney Museum of American Art. The Solomon R. Guggenheim Museum. The American Museum of Natural History.

The International Center of Photography. Central Park, but never after dark. The Museum of the City of New York. The Cathedral of St. John the Divine(largest Protestant church in the world), far more interesting than St. Patrick's, but often neglected by tourists. The 10,000-pound bronze statue of the archangel Michael was placed on Peace Fountain there in 1985.

The exhibits and movies at the U.S.A.'s first capitol, at 26 Wall Street. The museum of Revolutionary War relics and Washington memorabilia at Fraunces Tavern. Guided tours at the Federal Reserve Bank. Chinatown. The Bronx Zoo and Botanical Garden.

Philadelphia

The Liberty Bell and Independence Hall, on Independence Square. Stroll down Elfreth's Alley, one of America's oldest streets, to the Betsy Ross House. Nearby, the grave of Benjamin Franklin. See the hundreds of fine portraits at The Historical Society of Pennsylvania.

The War Library and Museum. Rosenbach Museum. The Pennsylvania Academy of Fine Arts. The Academy of Natural Sciences. The Rodin Museum, largest collection of Rodin sculptures outside Paris. The Philadelphia Museum of Art. The 388-acre food industry park (stores, warehouses, processing plants) called Food Distribution Center. Performances of the Philadelphia Orchestra at the Academy of Music. The Civic Center Museum. The Franklin Institute of Science Museum. The University Museum.

San Francisco

Fisherman's Wharf. Watch them making chocolate at nearby Ghirardelli Square. The Maritime Museum. The Chinese Museum. The treasures for sale at Gump's store. Chinatown. North Beach. The Presidio. Golden Gate Bridge. The Arboretum and the spectacular exhibits of Far Eastern art at the de Young Memorial Museum, both in the 1,017-acre Golden Gate Park. Fleischacker Zoo, one of the world's best zoos. The pyramidal Transamerica Building. San Francisco Museum of Art. Nob Hill and the cable car ride from there, down California Street.

Seattle

A 90-second monorail ride starts from Fourth Avenue and Pine, ending at the 74-acre Seattle Center (an amusement park, Pacific Science Center, Modern Art Pavilion, Center House Food Bazaar) for a magnificent view of the city, Puget Sound and mountains from the observation deck of the 607-foot high tripod Space Needle tower.

The Aquarium at Waterfront Park. The marvelous seafood, fruits and vegetables in Pike's Farmers' Market, at the waterfront. The 200-acre Arboretum. A tour of Boeing's 747 assembly plant (phone 206-342-4801 for reservations and directions). The Seattle Art Museum. The more than 1,000,000 used books, for sale at Shorey Bookstore. The granite sculptures at Myrtle Edwards Park. The crafts in the specialty shops at Pioneer Square. Take the 2½-hour sightseeing cruise of Puget Sound, from Pier 51 (at 10:30 and 13:00). Or, go on the ferry-boat ride, starting at the foot of Marion Street.

Washington, D.C.

See the 1908 Beaux Arts Union Station, restored in 1988, open 24 hours. Many sightseeing tours leave from it.

Then visit the many great museums in the Smithsonian Institution complex: The exhibit of balloons, dirigibles, primitive propeller airplanes and on to the Apollo II space ship in the Air & Space wing. The several displays (dinosaurs, Hope Diamond and other gems, etc.) in the Natural History Museum. The numerous old machines and clothing in the Museum of History & Technology. The marvelous French Impressionist and Italian Renaissance paintings at the National Gallery of Art. The sculptures and mobiles in the circular Hirschorn Museum. The collection of art in the Freer Gallery.

Most of these museums are open 10:00–17:30.

See Congress in session. Tours of the House of Representatives and the Senate operate every 15 minutes from 09:00–15:45 daily, starting from the Rotunda. Walk up the 897 steps to the top of the 555-foot high Washington Monument obelisk, open 09:00–17:00 daily (also 20:00–24:00 in the Summer). The Reflecting Pool in West Potomac Park. The Jefferson Memorial, open 24 hours. The Lincoln Memorial, always open.

The National Zoo. The National Arboretum, with its large display of azaleas, daffodils and magnolias. The eternal-flame tomb of John F. Kennedy, the Greek Revival Arlington House, and the Tomb of the Unknowns, all in Arlington National Cemetery.

The largest collection of books, maps, newspapers, documents and manuscripts in the world, at the Library of Congress (guided tours Monday-Friday 09:00–16:00.)

See the art collections at Corcoran Gallery, Phillips Collection, the National Portrait Gallery and the National Collection of Fine Arts. Take a tour of Federal Bureau of Investigation, every 15 minutes (09:15–16:15, Monday-Friday) at 13th Street and Pennsylvania Avenue. There is a 25-minute tour of the Bureau of Engraving & Printing (where money is not printed as fast as it is spent) Monday-Friday 08:00–11:30 and 12:30–14:00.

Visit the White House for a 40-minute tour Tuesday-Saturday, 10:00–12:00. Tour the Supreme Court when the Court is not in session, Monday-Friday 09:00–16:30 and, when it is in session, 10:00–14:30. Take the short guided bus trip to Mt. Vernon.

AMTRAK RESERVATION and INFORMATION TELEPHONE NUMBER
1 (800) 872-7245

Amtrak will accept both sleeper and coach reservations up to 11 months in advance, Travelers need to make sleeping car reservations well in advance of travel date, because sleeping space is very limited. Coach travel in Summer should also be reserved well in advance. Although the phone number above is a 24-hour service, it may be easier to reach a reservation agent either early in the morning or late at night.

If a sleeping accommodation is cancelled less than 48 hours before departure time, the cancellation fee (depending on its price) is $10–$150.

For those who want to take daytime sightseeing tours and/or to travel only during the day and stay in hotels along the way at night, Amtrak's tour operator (open Monday–Friday 09:00–17:00 Central Time) will reserve sightseeing tours and/or rooms in those hotels in which Amtrak buys blocks of rooms. U.S.A. telephone: (800) 321-8684. Canadian telephone: (800) 321-9885.

TRANSCONTINENTAL RAIL ROUTES

There is a rail route from New York City to Chicago. From Chicago, there are 4 different train routes to the West Coast of the United States.

Another route to the West is from New York City, the long ride via New Orleans. There is also Miami-Los Angeles service.

NEW YORK ROUTES WEST

New York - Albany - Buffalo - Cleveland - Chicago 186

This route can also be started in Boston, by connecting in Albany. (See "Boston–Albany" below.)

These trains require reservation, run daily, are air-conditioned, and carry sleeping cars, slumbercoach, ordinary coach and a restaurant car.

Dep. New York (Penn.)	19:10		Dep. Chicago (Union)	19:15
Dep. Albany	22:23		*Set your watch forward one hour.*	
Dep. Buffalo (Depew)	03:51		Dep. Cleveland	03:01
Dep. Cleveland	07:06		Dep. Buffalo (Depew)	06:17
Set your watch back one hour.			Arr. Albany	11:17
Arr. Chicago (Union)	12:58		Arr. New York (Penn.)	14:49

Sights in **Cleveland**: Sea World. The Cleveland Museum of Art. Blossom Music Center. A cruise along the Lake Erie shore on the Goodtime Sightseeing Boat. Playhouse Square Theater Complex. The NASA Lewis Research Visitors Center. The Cleveland Health Education Museum.

Boston - Albany - Chicago   186

These trains require reservation, run daily, are air-conditioned, and carry sleeping cars, slumbercoach, ordinary coach and a restaurant car.

Dep. Boston (South)	16:20	Dep. Chicago (Union)	19:15
Arr. Albany	21:15	*Set your watch forward one hour.*	
Set your watch back one hour.		Dep. Albany	12:00
Arr. Chicago (Union)	12:58	Arr. Boston (South)	16:50

Detroit - Chicago   227

All of these trains run daily, are air-conditioned, have an ordinary coach and serve light refreshments, unless designated otherwise.

Dep. Detroit (Woodward Ave.)	06:47	10:00	17:13
Set your watch back one hour.			
Arr. Chicago (Union)	11:35	14:45	21:45

• • •

Dep. Chicago (Union)	07:00	14:05	18:15
Set your watch forward one hour.			
Arr. Detroit (Woodward Ave..)	13: 22	21:41	00:40

Sights in **Detroit**: Belle Isle. Cranbrook Educational Community. Greenfield Village & Henry Ford Museum. Renaissance Center. University Cultural Center. The Zoological Park.

New York - Pittsburgh - Chicago   185 + 225

This route can be started in Washington (see next timetable) with a connection in Pittsburgh. *These trains require reservations, are air-conditioned, and carry a sleeping car, a slumbercoach. an ordinary coach and a restaurant car.*

Dep. New York (Penn.)	12:45	Dep. Chicago (Union)	20:15
Dep. Philadelphia		*Set watch forward one hour.*	
(30th Street)	14:57(1)	Dep. Pittsburgh (Penn.)	07:40
Dep. Pittsburgh (Penn.)	23:02	Arr. Philadelphia	
Set your watch back one hour.		(30th Street)	15:29 (2)
Arr. Chicago (Union)	08:14	Arr. New York (Penn.)	17:50

(1) Stops only for passengers boarding train. (2) Stops only for passengers getting off train.

Sights in **Pittsburgh**: Gateway Clipper. Nationality Classrooms. Kennywood Park. Station Square. Carnegie Institute. Buhl Science Center. Duquesne Incline. Fort Pitt Blockhouse. Heinz Hall.

Washington - Pittsburgh - Chicago   220

These trains require reservation, are air-conditioned and carry a sleeping car, an ordinary coach and a restaurant car.

Dep. Washington (Union)	16:15		Dep. Chicago (Union)	18:25
Dep. Pittsburgh	23:52		*Set your watch forward one hour.*	
Set your watch back one hour.			Dep. Pittsburgh	05:10
Arr. Chicago (Union)	08:55		Arr. Washington (Union)	12:22

New York - New Orleans - Houston - Los Angeles

A long (3,417 miles) but interesting route from New York to the West Coast is via New Orleans, where there is a 20-hour layover on the trip West and more than 11 hours when going from Los Angeles to New York. Passengers were once allowed to occupy sleeping space on the train during each overnight stop, but now must make other provision.

A few miles west of **El Paso,** watch for "The Christ of the Rockies," a 27-foot high statue at the top of the 4,756-foot Sierra de Cristo Rey mountain.

Between Phoenix and Los Angeles, "Sunset Limited" rides at the lowest altitude of the Amtrak system: 231 feet (70 meters) *below* sea level, near Niland, California.

Sights in **Philadelphia:** see above.
Sights in **Baltimore**: The National Aquarium and its Marine Mammal Pavilion which features bottlenose dolphins. The view from the Observation Level of the World Trade Center. Ft. McHenry. The Maryland Science Center and Planetarium. The 18th century U.S. Frigate Constellation. The B & O Railroad Museum. Lexington Market. The Zoo.
Sights in **Washington**: see above.
Sights in **Atlanta**: Cyclorama and the Zoo, both in Grant Park. The Toy Museum. Fernbank Science Center. Swan House. Wren's Nest. Stone Mountain Park. White Water Parks.
Sights in **New Orleans**: Mardi Gras. Jazz on Bourbon Street and the Spanish-French architecture in the French Quarter. Visit the 1831 Hermann-Grima Historical House (820 St. Louis Street) and take a 20-minute guided tour of one of the earliest and best examples of early American architecture in the French Quarter. Its interior and garden have been restored authentically.

See Absinthe House. Audubon's Little House. Boat tours of the harbor. The view from the top of the 400-foot high International Trade Mart, at the foot of Canal Street.

Audubon Park and Zoo. The Cabrini Doll Museum. French Market. The Casta Hove

Museum. The Cathedral of St. Louis. The Museum of Art.

New Orleans is home base for the last 2 paddle-wheel steamboats: the 176-passenger "Delta Queen" and the 400-plus-passenger "Mississippi Queen" that offer cruises of 2-12 nights on the Mississippi, Ohio, Tennesse, Cumberland, Arkansas and Atchafalaya Rivers. Many of their special-event cruises (Kentucky Derby, Great Steamboat Race) are sold-out 6 to 12 months before departure. For a brochure, contact a travel agency or Delta Queen Steamboat Co., 30 Robin Street Wharf,New Orleans, LA 70130-1890. Telephone: (800) 543-1949.

Sights in **Houston**: The Astrodome. Johnson Space Center. Astroworld. The Museum of Natural Science. Hermann Park & Zoo. The downtown underground shopping center.
Sights in **Phoenix**: Desert Botanical Gardens. The Heard Museum. The Phoenix Art Museum. The Zoo. The Pueblo Museum and Indian Ruins. The Gila River Indian Arts and Crafts Center.

These trains require reservation, are air-conditioned and carry a sleeping car, an ordinary coach and a restaurant car. There is slumbercoach New York-Atlanta and v.v. The New Orleans–Los Angeles and v.v. portion also has special facilities for disabled passengers and an entertainment car.

190 + 223			193 + 244	
Dep. New York (Penn.)	13:42 (1)		Dep. Los Angeles	22:30 (5)
Dep. Philadelphia (30th St.)	15:31 (1+2)		*Set watch forward one hour.*	
Dep. Baltimore (Penn.)	17:09 (1+2)		Dep. Phoenix	07:08(6) Day 2
Dep. Washington(Union)	18:10 (1+2)		*Set watch forward one hour.*	
Arr. Atlanta (Peachtree St.)	08:30 (1) Day 2		Dep. El Paso	17:00
Dep. Atlanta (Peachtree St.)	08:45 (1)		Dep. San Antonio	
Set your watch back one hour.			(East Commercial St.)	06:10 (7) Day 3
Arr. New Orleans	19:28		Dep. Houston	10:55
Change trains.			Arr. New Orleans	19:35
193 + 244			*Change trains.*	
Dep. New Orleans	13:20 (3) Day 3		190 + 223	
Dep. Houston	21:40		Dep. New Orleans	07:05 (1) Day 4
Dep. San Antonio			*Set watch forward one hour.*	
(East Commercial St.)	02:55 (4) Day 4		Arr. Atlanta (Peachtree St.)	19:20
Dep. El Paso	13:45		Dep. Atlanta (Peachtree St.)	19:45 (1)
Set your watch back one hour.			Arr. Washington (Union)	09:33 (8) Day 5
Dep. Phoenix	21:40		Arr. Baltimore (Penn.)	10:50 (8)
Set your watch back one hour.			Arr. Philadelphia (30th St.)	12:27 (8)
Arr. Los Angeles	06:15 Day 5		Arr. New York (Penn.)	14:35

(1) Runs daily. (2) Stops only for passengers boarding. (3) Runs Monday, Wednesday and Saturday. Has special facilities for disabled passengers. (4) Runs Tuesday, Thursday and Sunday. (5) Runs Tuesday, Friday and Sunday. Has special facilities for disabled passengers. (6) Runs Wednesday, Saturday and Monday. (7) Runs Thursday, Sunday and Tuesday. (8) Stops only for passengers getting off.

CHICAGO ROUTES WEST

Here are the schedules for the 5 train services west from Chicago.

Chicago - Minneapolis - Spokane - Seattle (or Portland)
194 + 241

West of Minneapolis, the train passes waterfalls, dams, forests and Indian reservations.

These trains run daily, require reservation, are air-conditioned and carry sleeping cars, ordinary coaches, a restaurant car and an entertainment car, and have special facilities for disabled passengers.

From Spokane, one section goes to Portland, another section to Seattle.

Dep. Chicago (Union)	15:15		Dep. Portland	17:20 (4)	
Dep. Milwaukee	16:51 (1)		Dep. Seattle	17:00 (4)	
Dep. Minneapolis	23:59		Dep. Spokane	00:45	Day 2
Dep. Fargo	04:35	Day 2	*Set your watch forward one hour.*		
Set your watch back one hour.			Dep. Glacier Park	08:55 (2)	
Dep. Glacier Park	18:47 (2)		*Set your watch forward one hour.*		
Set your watch back one hour.			Dep. Fargo	02:45	Day 3
Arr. Spokane	02:10 (3) Day 3		Dep. Minneapolis	08:20	
Arr. Seattle	10:35 (3)		Arr. Milwaukee	14:35	
Arr. Portland	10:20 (3)		Arr. Chicago (Union)	16:20	

(1) Stops only for passengers boarding. (2) Stops in Glacier Park only from early May to mid-October. (3) From Spokane, one section goes to Portland, another section to Seattle. Buffet car Spokane–Portland. (4) One section starts in Portland, another section in Seattle. The 2 sections combine in Spokane. Buffet car Portland–Spokane

Chicago - Denver - Salt Lake City - Reno - Oakland - San Francisco   189 + 250

Many regard the Denver–Salt Lake City portion of this route, with marvelous views of the Rocky Mountains, to be the most scenic train ride in the U.S.A. The train reaches an altitude of 9,239 feet, the highest point of any rail line in the U.S.A., when going through the 6.2-mile-long Moffat Tunnel.

These trains run daily, require reservation, are air-conditioned and carry sleeping cars, ordinary coaches, a restaurant car and an entertainment car, and have special facilities for disabled passengers.

Dep. Chicago (Union)	15:05		Dep. San Francisco	09:35 (1)	
Dep. Omaha	23:59		Dep. Oakland	10:10	
Set your watch back one hour.			Dep. Reno	16:35	
Dep. Denver (Union)	09:10	Day 2	*Set watch forward one hour.*		
Dep. Salt Lake City	00:30		Dep. Salt Lake City	05:05	Day 2
Set your watch back one hour.			Dep. Denver	21:00	
Arr. Reno	09:36	Day 3	*Set watch forward one hour.*		
Arr. Oakland	16:15 (1)		Dep. Omaha	06:50	Day 3
Arr. San Francisco	17:15		Arr. Chicago (Union)	16:15	

(1) Bus service Oakland-San Francisco and v.v.

Sights in **Salt Lake City**: The temple and tabernacle of the Mormon Church, in 10-acre Temple Square, at the center of the city.

Visitors can attend recitals on the 11,000-pipe tabernacle organ in a building considered acoustically perfect since it is entirely wood, even to the wood nails that were used in its construction. Performances are offered Monday–Friday at 12:00; on Monday, Tuesday and Wednesday at 19:30; and on Saturday and Sunday at 16:00.

Every day except Sunday, more than 5,000 people of every faith use the Family History Library (35 North West Temple), containing statistics on more than one *billion* people who lived and died in 60 countries since 1538. It is open Monday 07:30–18:00, Tuesday-Friday 07:30–22:00, and Saturday 07:30–17:00.

Chicago - St. Louis - Dallas - San Antonio - Los Angeles
188 + 243

These trains require reservation, are air-conditioned, carry sleeping cars, ordinary coaches and have special facilities for disabled passengers.

These trains run daily Chicago-San Antonio (and v.v.) with a restaurant car. See footnotes for days of operation San Antonio–Los Angeles (and v.v.).

Dep. Chicago (Union)	17:45 (1)		Dep. Los Angeles	22:30 (3)	
Dep. St. Louis	00:15	Day 2	*Set watch forward one hour.*		
Dep. Dallas	14:49		Dep. Phoenix	07:08	Day 2
Dep. Fort Worth	16:32		*Set watch forward one hour.*		
Arr. San Antonio	23:40		Dep. El Paso	17:00	
Dep. San Antonio	02:55 (2)	Day 3	Arr. San Antonio	05:25 (4)	Day 3
Dep. El Paso	13:45		Dep. San Antonio	07:05	
Set your watch back one hour.			Dep. Fort Worth	14:30	
Dep. Phoenix	21:40		Dep. Dallas	16:05	
Set your watch back one hour.			Dep. St. Louis	07:35	Day 4
Arr. Los Angeles	06:15	Day 4	Arr. Chicago (Union)	13:35	

(1) Departures on Tuesday, Friday and Sunday continue on to Los Angeles, and have an entertainment car. (2) Departs San Antonio for Los Angeles on Thursday, Sunday and Tuesday. Carries an entertainment car and a restaurant car. (3) Departs Tuesday, Friday and Sunday for San Antonio and Chicago. Carries a restaurant and an entertainment car. (4) Arrive San Antonio Thursday, Sunday and Tuesday.

Chicago - Kansas City - Albuquerque - Los Angeles 187 + 248

At Flagstaff, there is bus service to the Grand Canyon. See last page of chapter.

These trains run daily, require reservation, are air-conditioned, carry sleeping cars, ordinary coaches, a restaurant car and an entertainment car, and have special facilities for disabled passengers.

Dep. Chicago (Union)	17:20		Dep. Los Angeles	21:15	
Dep. Kansas City	01:20	Day 2	*Set watch forward one hour.*		
Dep. Dodge City	07:19		Dep. Flagstaff	07:10	Day 2
Set your watch back one hour.			Dep. Albuquerque	13:40	
Dep. Albuquerque	17:10		*Set watch forward one hour.*		
Dep. Flagstaff	21:10		Dep. Dodge City	23:59	Day 3
Set your watch back one hour.			Dep. Kansas City	07:25	
Arr. Los Angeles	08:05	Day 3	Arr. Chicago (Union)	15:40	

Chicago - New Orleans 183

These trains run daily, require reservation, are air-conditioned, carry sleeping cars, ordinary coaches, a restaurant car and a domecar.

Dep. Chicago (Union)	19:50		Dep. New Orleans	14:40	
Dep. Memphis	06:27	Day 2	Dep. Memphis	22:28	
Arr. New Orleans	14:18		Arr. Chicago (Union)	09:03	Day 2

EASTERN SEABOARD TRAIN ROUTES

Boston - New York City - Philadelphia - Washington 202

Note: There are departures not listed here (see Cook's Table 213) from New York City to Washington at frequent times 05:20–21:40 and from Washington to New York City 05:45–22:10.

All of the trains listed below are air-conditioned and have light refreshments and ordinary coaches, unless designated otherwise.

Dep. Boston (South)	Arr. New York (Penn.)	Arr. Philadelphia (30th St.)	Arr. Washington (Union)
07:15	12:13	14:12	16:13
09:00	14:20	16:04	18:15
11:05	16:21	18:08	20:15
13:45	18:17	20:07	22:15
15:55	20:25	22:13	00:24
17:00(1)	21:10	23:07	01:10
17:40 (2)	22:24	00:10	02:27
21:35 (6)	03:16	05:24	07:55
-0-	07:34 (4)	09:15	10:59
-0-	08:56	10:50	12:50
-0-	09:17	11:14	13:15

Washington - Philadelphia - New York City - Boston 213

Dep. Washington (Union)	Dep. Philadelphia (30th St.)	Dep. New York (Penn.)	Arr. Boston (South)
07:35	09:31	11:30	16:29
09:35	11:31	13:35	18:49
11:35	13:29	15:29	20:27
13:35	15:39	17:44	22:47
15:35	17:31	19:25	00:30
17:00 (4)	18:35	20:15	-0-
22:10 (3)	00:31 (5)	03:15 (5)	08:39 (5)
-0-	07:35	09:31	14:33

(1) Runs Monday-Friday, except holidays. (2) Runs Saturdays, Sundays and holidays. (3) Carries sleeping cars. (4) Reservation required. Supplement charged. Runs Monday-Friday, except holidays. (5) Arrives 70 minutes later on Saturday and Sunday. (6) Runs daily except Friday and Saturday.

New York - Philadelphia - Washington - Miami

These trains run daily, require reservations, are air-conditioned, and carry sleeping cars, ordinary coaches and a buffet car.

	184
Dep. New York (Penn.)	10:42
Dep. Philadelphia (30th St.)	12:35 (1)
Dep. Washington (Union)	15:00 (1)
Arr. Miami	14:15 (2)

Sights in **Miami**: Metrozoo (12400 SW 152 St.), open daily 10:00–17:30. The nearly one square mile of orchids at Orchid Jungle (26715 SW 157 St.), open daily 08:30–17:30. Viscaya, a 50-room Italian Renaissance palace built in 1914 with a large formal garden (3251 S. Miami Ave.), open daily 09:30–16:30.

The collection of Oriental, American and European art in the Lowe Art Museum at the University of Miami in Coral Gables. The acquarium and performing dolphins at Seaquarium (4400 Rickenbacker Causeway), open 09:00–17:00. Nearby is Planet Ocean. Many uncaged tropical birds at Parrot Jungle (11000 SW 157 Ave.). The serpents and snakes at Serpentarium (12655 So. Dixie Hwy.).

"Little Havana," a 20-block section on Eighth Street. Monkey Jungle (14805 SW 157 Ave.). The 83 acres of tropical plants and trees from around the world in Fairchild Tropical Gardens (10901 Old Sutler Rd.), open 09:30–16:30.

	184
Dep. Miami	11:40
Arr. Washington (Union)	14:50 (2+3)
Arr. Philadelphia (30th St.)	17:55 (3)
Arr. New York (Penn.)	20:06

(1) Stops only for passengers boarding train. (2)Day 2. (3) Stops only to allow passengers to get off train.

WESTERN TRAIN ROUTES

Los Angeles - Las Vegas - Salt Lake City   191

"Desert Wind" eastbound connects in Salt Lake City with "Zephyr" heading east to Denver and Chicago. "Zephyr" westbound from Chicago and Denver connects in Salt Lake City with "Desert Wind" heading west to Las Vegas and Los Angeles.

These trains require reservations, are air-conditioned, carry sleeping cars, ordinary coaches, a restaurant car and an entertainment car, and have special facilities for disabled passengers.

Dep. Los Angeles	10:55		Dep. Salt Lake City	00:40
Arr. Las Vegas	17:45		*Set watch back one hour.*	
Set watch forward one hour.			Arr. Las Vegas	07:45
Arr. Salt Lake City	03:30 Day 2		Arr. Los Angeles	15:15

Sights in **Las Vegas**: Many gambling casinos. Nearby, **Boulder Dam** and **Lake Mead**.

Los Angeles - San Diego   253

Amtrak has a one-day independent tour package from Los Angeles to **San Diego** and return, which includes rail fare, transfers between the San Diego railstation and the exceptional San Diego Zoo (Balboa Park), admission to the Zoo, a 40-minute guided bus tour of the 128-acre wildlife facility, and a ride on the Zoo's aerial tram.

Other San Diego area attractions: Sea World, open daily 09:00–17:00. Old Town. Seaport Village. The large harbor. Four missions. Wild Animal Park. It is a 20-minute auto drive to Tijuana, across the border.

These trains have both a custom-class and an ordinary coach, are air-conditioned and have light refreshments.

Dep. Los Angeles	04:50 (1)	06:40	08:40	09:40 (2)	10:45	12:45
Arr. San Diego	08:00	09:37	11:35	12:40	13:35	15:33

Dep. Los Angeles	14:30	16:45	18:20 (1)	18:45 (2)	21:00	
Arr. San Diego	17:35	19:35	21:10	21:35	23:50	

• • •

Dep. San Diego	05:00 (1)	06:00 (10	08:30	10:30	12:30	14:30
Arr. Los Angeles	08:03	09:20	11:45	13:47	15:45	17:49

| Dep. San Diego | 16:30 | 17:45 (2) | 18:45 | 20:45 |
| Arr. Los Angeles | 19:50 | 20:30 | 21:40 | 23:52 |

(1) Runs Monday-Friday, except holidays. (2) runs Saturdays, Sundays and holidays.

Los Angeles - Oakland (San Francisco) - Portland - Seattle
192

A very scenic route: seacoast, forests, snow-capped mountains. On the northward route, views of the Cascade mountain range come into sight before reaching Portland, and the descent into the Willamet Valley is spectacular. The largest herd of llamas in Oregon often can be seen near Salem.

These trains run daily, carry sleeping cars, ordinary coaches, a restaurant car, an entertainment car, are air-conditioned and have special facilities for disabled passengers.

Dep. Los Angeles	09:50	Dep. Seattle	08:00	
Arr. Oakland	21:10 (1)	Arr. Portland	12:10	
Dep. Oakland	21:23	Dep. Portland	12:30	
Arr. Portland	15:25 Day 2	Arr. Oakland	06:25 (1) Day 2	
Dep. Portland	15:55	Dep. Oakland	07:55	
Arr. Seattle	20:10	Arr. Los Angeles	09:50	

(1) Bus service to/from San Francisco connects with arrival/departure.

Sights in **Portland**: The Oregon Historical Society's Museum (1230 SW Park Ave.), open Monday-Saturday 10:00–16:45. Nearby, the Portland Art Museum, open Tuesday-Sunday at 12:00. The Washington Park Zoo. Japanese Gardens. Washington Park International Rose Test Gardens. Western Forestry Center. The Oregon Museum of Science and Industry. Pittock Mansion. The Grotto at the Sanctuary of Our Sorrowful Mother

Portland - Seattle   264

These trains run daily, are air-conditioned, have an ordinary coach, and have special facilities for disabled passengers.

| Dep. Portland | 08:50 (1) | 14:40 (3) | 16:30 (2) |
| Arr. Seattle | 12:45 | 18:35 | 20:45 |

• • •

| Dep. Seattle | 07:30 (3) | 11:30 (3) | 17:10 (3) |
| Arr. Portland | 11:30 | 15:25 | 21:05 |

(1) Light refreshments. (2) Restaurant car. (3) Reservation required. Restaurant car.

Portland - Spokane   194

This is a spur off the Seattle-Spokane-Chicago route listed earlier. The train passes through the historic Columbia River Gorge, following the path of the Lewis and Clark expedition. Unfortunately, the best scenery is passed during night hours. The train unites in Spokane with the Seattle–Chicago service.

Both of these trains run daily, require reservation, are air-conditioned, carry sleeping cars, ordinary coaches and an entertainment car, have buffet service and have special facilities for disabled passengers.

Dep. Portland	17:20	Dep. Spokane	02:55
Arr. Spokane	00:45	Arr. Portland	10:20

Denver - Boise - Portland - Seattle   195

These trains run daily, are air-conditioned, carry sleeping cars, ordinary coaches and a restaurant car and have special facilities for disabled passengers.

Dep. Denver	09:45	Dep. Seattle	07:30
Dep. Boise	03:59	Dep. Portland	11:40
Set your watch back one hour.		*Set your watch forward one hour.*	
Arr. Portland	14:40	Dep. Boise	23:26
Arr. Seattle	18:35	Arr. Denver	18:05

Miami - New Orleans - Houston - Phoenix - Los Angeles   193

These trains require reservation, are air-conditioned, carry sleeping cars, ordinary coaches, an entertainment car and a restaurant car and have special facilities for disabled passengers.

Dep. Miami	12:30	Dep. Los Angeles	22:300
Set your watch back one hour.		*Set your watch forward one hour.*	
Arr. New Orleans	11:00 Day 2	Dep. Phoenix	07:08 day 2
Dep. New Orleans	13:20	*Set your watch forward one hour.*	
Dep. Houston	21:40	Dep. El Paso	17:00
Dep. San Antonio		Dep. San Antonio	
(East Commercial St.)	02:55 Day3	(East Commercial St.)	06:10 Day 3
Dep. El Paso	13:45	Dep. Houston	10:55
Set your watch back one hour.		Arr. New Orleans	19:35
Dep. Phoenix	21:40	Dep. New Orleans	22:40
Set your watch back one hour.		*Set your watch forward one hour.*	
Arr. Los Angeles	06:15 Day 4	Arr. Miami	22:50 Day 4

SCENIC RAIL TRIPS

The schedules for these 6 scenic train rides appear earlier in this section.

Denver - Salt Lake City (189 + 250) This route reaches a height of more than 9,000 feet and provides marvelous views of the Rocky Mountains.

Denver - Seattle (195) This route goes through 2 of the most scenic river valleys in North America: the Snake River Valley in southern Idaho and the Columbia River Valley through Oregon and Washington State.

Los Angeles - Seattle (192) Very fine views of the Pacific seacoast, forests and snow-capped mountains.

Raton Pass (187 + 248) Crossing the Colorado-New Mexico state line (Chicago-Albuquerque-Los Angeles route), the train goes over the 7,588-foot high Raton Pass.

Glacier National Park (194 + 241) Fifty-six miles of glaciers and soaring peaks can be seen as the Chicago-Fargo-Seattle route passes through Glacier National Park.

New York City - Albany (186) The train follows the beautiful Hudson River for 142 miles on this trip.

AlaskaPass Allows unlimited travel throughout Alaska on the trains, ferries and buses operated by Alaska Marine Highway and Alaska Railroad; in both Alaska and in Canada's Yukon Territory by the services of Alaskon Express Motorcoaches and the White Pass & Yukon Railroad; in the Yukon Territory by Greyhound Lines of Canada and Norline Coaches; and in Canada's British Columbia by the services of BC Ferries, BC Rail, Greyhound Lines of Canada, and Island Coach Lines.

Sold by travel agencies worldwide and AlaskaPass Inc. (P.O. Box 351, Vashon, WA 98070, U.S.A. The toll free telephone for both the U.S.A. and Canada: (800) 248-7598. Offered all year. Prices from May 15 to September 15, 1996: $499 (U.S.) for 8 days, $649 for 15 days, $769 for 22 days, and $899 for 30 days. Children age 3–11: $249, $335, $395 and $459.

AlaskaPass Flexible Offered all year. Prices from May 15 to September 15, 1996 for any 12 days within 21 days: $669 (U.S.) for adults, $345 for children age 3–11. For any 21 days within 45 days: $949 and $485.

TWO ALASKAN SCENIC RAILROADS

White Pass and Yukon Route

In the early 1980's, Skagway was practically a ghost town. Passengers from the few cruise ships that then stopped there a few hours were limited to wandering streets that were dismal in those days, haunting its "frontier" bars, and selecting cheap souvenirs before their ship weighed anchor.

The explosive revival of Skagway since 1983 has been matched by the increased volume of cruise ships calling at this port—over 240 ships carrying more than 150,000 passengers every year in the late 80's, compared to 30,000 passengers during 1973.

The U.S. National Park Service spent millions of dollars restoring several pioneer buildings, and the city paved many streets. Private businesses restored or built a dozen more 1898-style structures along Skagway's 7-block-long "Historic District."

The town became in the 1980's a living museum of the Klondike gold-rush that erupted one century earlier. Many artists migrated here and have transformed the town into "the Carmel of the North." Shops and galleries sell gold nugget jewelry, carved Alaskan ivory, jade sculptures, native wood carvings and much more.

The Klondike Highway connects Skagway with the Alaska Highway.

After gold was discovered in the Klondike Valley, early prospectors reached Skagway by ship and carried their outfits the 40-mile walk (mostly uphill) to **Lake Bennett**, proceeding from there by boat on the **Yukon River** to the gold field. It soon became impossible to provide the growing population in the Klondike with adequate supplies.

Construction of the famous narrow-gauge (36-inch) privately owned railroad began in May of 1898 and was one of the most difficult railroad projects ever engineered. Supplies had to be brought 1,000 miles on small coastal steamers from Seattle. There was no heavy construction equipment. Workers had only horses, shovels and black powder to cut through barriers of solid rock.

The track reached **White Pass** in February of 1899 and **Whitehorse** in July of 1900. This railroad had a colorful history as a major carrier for the enormous amount of construction material used to build the Alaska Highway during World War II, and supplying mines in the Yukon until its trains ceased running in 1982 when plunging world metal prices closed the major mines, the railroad's principal source of revenue.

Daily scheduled passenger service resumed in 1988, with trains operating late May through late September from Skagway to Fraser, British Columbia, on the Klondike Highway. At Fraser, the train connects with motorcoaches that go north to Whitehorse. Similarly, southbound travelers can go by bus from Whitehorse to Fraser and transfer there for the Fraser–Skagway train.

There are neither public eating nor lodging facilities in Fraser. Passengers wanting to stop there or to overnight at either Fraser or Lake Bennett must bring their own equipment: tents, sleeping bags, food, camp stove and water. Bennett is the stop for hiking the Chilkoot Trail.

Rivaling many of the most scenic train trips in Europe, the Skagway–Fraser route offers views of the original "trail of '98" Dead Horse Gulch (where 3,000 pack animals died while carrying prospector's supplies), Bridal Veil Falls, and Inspiration Point. Over 36,000 people rode the line when a limited excursion was operated in 1988. The railroad carried nearly twice that number during its first complete season, in 1989.

Another ride, particularly suited for cruise-ship passengers who have only part of a day ashore, is the short roundtrip Skagway–White Pass that features the most scenic portion of the Skagway–Fraser ride, going only to the summit of White Pass and then returning to Skagway.

Skagway - White Pass - Fraser - Bennett (Train) and Fraser - Whitehorse (Bus)
WP & YR Timetable

These trains operate mid-May to late September, run daily, and reservation is recommended for all of them. half-fare for children age 3–12. Children under 3 travel free.

Skagway - White Pass Roundtrip. The 1995 price was $72 (U.S.)
Skagway - Fraser One-way. The 1995 price was $62.
Skagway - White Pass - Fraser - Bennett The 1995 prices were: $72 for one-way and $119 for roundtrip (includes lunch).
Skagway - White Pass - Fraser - Whitehorse The 1995 prices for train-plus-bus were: $92 for one-way and $160 for roundtrip.

Dep. Skagway	08:10	08:45	08:55 (2)	12:45 (6)	13:15 (2)
Arr. White Pass	-0-	09:38	10:08	13:53	14:50
Arr. Fraser	10:00	-0-	-0-	14:35 (3)	-0-
Dep. Fraser	-0-	-0-	-0-	14:30 (3)	-0-
Arr. Bennett	-0-	-0-	-0-	15:15	-0-
Arr. Whitehorse	-0-	-0-	-0-	18:30	-0-
			• • •		
Dep Whitehorse	-0-	08:15 (4)	-0-	-0-	-0-
Dep. Bennett	11:10	-0-	-0-	-0-	-0-
Arr. Fraser	11:55	10:05 (5)	-0-	-0-	-0-
Dep. Fraser (Train)	12:00	10:20 (5)	-0-	16:30	-0-
Dep. White Pass	-0-	10:40 (6)	10:18 (2)	-0-	14:48 (2)
Arr. Skagway	13;35	11:55	11:45	18:15	16:15

(1) Skagway–Bennet roundtrip excursion. (2) Skagway–White Pass roundtrip excursion. (3) Change from train to bus in Fraser. (4) Bus. (5) Change from bus to train in Fraser. (6) Runs June 15-Sept. 22.

A few minutes after leaving Skagway, watch out the right-hand side of the train for the very small goldrush graveyard, only a few feet to the side of the track. The train climbs along the edge of mountains for an hour before reaching a plateau at the summit. This ascent of 2,885 feet is made in only 21 miles, with a grade of 4% at one point. During the ascent, there is a great view looking down at Skagway and up at the snow-topped mountains.

The final stretch, into Bennett, has excellent scenery, including many cold-blue indigo ponds and dwarfed pine trees. Other sights en route are the 100-ton granite Black Cross Rock, Bridal Veil Falls, Dead Horse Gulch (where 3,000 pack animals died while carrying the prospectors' supplies) and Beaver Lake.

Bennett was where more than 10,000 men built rafts and crude boats in 1898 to get themselves and their equipment up the Yukon River to the Klondike gold fields. Highest point on the complete Skagway–Whitehorse route is 2,916 feet, at Log Cabin, B.C.

For more information, contact White Pass & Yukon Route, P.O. Box 435, Skagway, Alaska 99840. Telephone from the U.S.A.: (800) 343-7373. Telephone from British Columbia, Yukon Territory, or Northwest Territories: (800) 478-7373. The telephone to call from other locations: (907) 983-2217. Fax: (907) 983-2734

ALASKA RAILROAD

Reservations are required at least 2 weeks in advance of travel date. Write: P.O. Box 107500, Anchorage, Alaska 99510, U.S.A. Telephone: (907) 265-2685 or (800) 544-0552.

Mt. McKinley (Denali National Park) Rail Route

Completed in 1923, the Alaska Railroad's 356-mile line from Fairbanks to Anchorage with Vistadome cars ranks among the world's most exotic train journeys. Fairbanks is only 160 miles south of the Arctic Circle, the northernmost rail terminal in the Western Hemisphere. In Summer, there are 20 hours of daylight every day here.

Also riding along with the Alaska Railroad passenger cars are private luxury domecars owned by Princess Cruises & Tours and by Gray Line of Alaska (owned by Holland America Line-Westours Inc.). Seating in these domecars is offered as part of cruise/tour packages to Alaska.

This railway, first surveyed in 1914, provides access to North America's highest mountain, Mt. McKinley (20,320 feet). Construction began in 1915. The temperature on this route ranges from 100(F) in Summer to -70 (F) in Winter.

The Fairbanks–Anchorage line affords many interesting travel possibilities: (1) an easy one-day roundtrip Anchorage–Talkeetna (site for viewing Mt. McKinley)–Anchorage, (2) an-other easy one-day roundtrip Fairbanks–Denali National Park–Fairbanks, (3) the complete ride from Fairbanks to Anchorage (and vice versa), and (4) the complete Fairbanks–Anchorage or Anchorage–Fairbanks ride with a stopover at the **Denali National Park** resort.

Inside the 3,030 square mile national park are 3 other prominent mountains: Mt. Foraker (17,000 feet), Mt. Hunter (14,960 feet) and Mt. Russell (11,500 feet). On some Summer days, Mt. McKinley and Mt. Foraker are clearly visible from Anchorage, more than 150 miles to the South.

Headquarters for park activities is the McKinley Park Station Hotel, built in 1972 and operated by a private firm, with accommodations for 275 guests. The hotel is open from late May to late September. A highway links the hotel with such points of interest as Sable Pass, Polychrome Pass, Caribou Pass, Toklat Creek, Igloo Creek, Camp Eilson, Wonder Lake, Camp Denali and Richardson Highway.

Hotel and Park Tour reservations can be made through ARA Denali Park Hotels: 825 W. 8th Ave., Suite 240, Anchorage, Alaska 99501, U.S.A. Telephone: (907) 276-7234.

Caribou, giant Alaska moose, 33 other mammals and 112 kinds of birds comprise the animal life in the park. There are grizzly bears and 200-pound mountain sheep to be seen there. Salmon and trout abound in the nearby lakes, streams and rivers.

The hotel offers 2 guided tours. One starts at 06:00, so as to have maximum opportunity to observe wildlife. For late sleepers, a second tour starts at 15:00.

Both the Park Station Hotel and other hotels just outside the Denali Park entrance provide free transportation from them to the train station and to the free shuttle bus, which runs through the park on an hourly basis.

Pack trips in and around the park are available.

Some of the interesting points along the route from Fairbanks to Anchorage are: **College**, where the northernmost institution of higher education in the world is located, the University of Alaska. **Dunbar**, from which trails lead to a goldmining district. (It is F 70 degrees below zero here in the Winter.) **Clear**, a military post. Mountain sheep, between **Healy** and **Denali National Park**. **Honolulu**, with many beaver dams, on the western side of the track. Hurricane Gulch, which the train crosses on a bridge that is 296 feet above the creek. From Mt. McKinley Station to Chulitna, there are (weather permitting) splendid views of Mt. McKinley, and then such views again from Curry to Nancy.

Fairbanks - Denali National Park - Anchorage   AR Timetable

One hundred thousand people ride this route every year.

Going south (from Fairbanks), for the best views sit on the left side until Denali Park, on the right side Denali Park-Anchorage. The reverse is advised when going north (from Anchorage). About 60 miles south of Fairbank, the train travels over the **Tanana River** on the 700-foot high Mears Memorial Bridge, one of the longest single-span bridges in the world. Before the completion of this bridge in 1923, passengers had to cross the river on a ferry.

Fifty miles after leaving the town of **Nenana,** passengers begin to view the 600-mile-long Alaska Range. Its peaks are snow-covered all year. The track clings to the side of cliffs as it goes along the Nenana River Canyon.

Most passengers overnight at **Denali National Park** in order to take a 7-hour narrated bus tour which affords glimpses of **Mount McKinley,** (tallest mountain in North America) and the area's wildlife (caribou, Dall sheep, grizzly bears, wolves, foxes, birds, etc.). For reservations at many of the hotels and lodges in the Denali area, use a travel agency or contact Denali Central Reservations & Travel, 2815 Second Avenue, Suite 400, Seattle, WA 98121, U.S.A. Telephone: (800) 827-2748. Fax: (206) 443-1979.

Moose are often spotted near **Honolulu Pass**, halfway between Fairbanks and Anchorage. The view is marvelous while crossing the 918-foot-long, 296-foot-high bridge over **Hurricane Gulch**: watefalls and a river in an immense glacial valley.

Approaching Anchorage, the train goes through the **Matanuska Valley,** where extraordinary vegeatables (70-pound cabbages, radishes the size of a baseball!) thrive in the 19 hours of daylight during Summer.

Mid-May to mid-September: runs daily and has a restaurant car in both directions. Mid-September to mid-May: runs only Saturday Anchorage–Fairbanks and runs only Sunday Fairbanks–Anchorage. These trains have a vistadome and private domecars all year.

Dep. Anchorage	08:30		Dep. Fairbanks	08:30
Arr. Denali Park	15:45		Dep. Denali Park	12:15
Arr. Fairbanks	20:30		Arr. Anchorage	20:30

PORTAGE - WHITTIER SHUTTLE

South of Anchorage, the town of Whittier was built during World War II to serve as a deepwater port for the military. The only ground access to Whittier is by rail.

Much of the 12-mile Portage-Whittier track is inside 2 long tunnels. The train passes popular Portage Glacier en route to Whittier, now serving as a port for cruise ships. Another use of the train is to board in Whittier dayboats which take passengers to both Columbia Glacier and College Fjord. The train carries passengers in gallery railcars and hauls vehicles on flatcars.

Portage - Whittier   AR Timetable

About 200,000 people take this 30-minute ride along the **Portage Glacier** every year.

Phone Alaska Railroads for times (907) 265-2685. *Late May to mid-September: runs daily, at least 4 roundtrips per day. Mid-September to late May: runs Wednesday, Friday, Saturday and Sunday, 2 roundtrips on each of those days. These trains carry vehicles.*

A sightseeing boat offers cruises on **Prince William Sound** from Whittier to **Valdez.** Scenery along the way includes **Columbia Glacier**, a spectacular colony of black-legged kittiwakes, whales, porpoises, sea otters and sea lions.

SEWARD ROUTE

This 114-mile ride from Anchorage to Seward has spectacular scenery, winding along the Saltwater Turnagain Arm and offering views of the only bore tides in North America (a con- tinuous wave that covers miles of mudflats as contrasted with waves that "break" with a crash and move up and down a beach as the tide changes).

Sighting American bald eagles and mountain goats is common during the first 60 miles of the route. After passing Portage, the train climbs through steep mountains, allowing vistas of river gorges and 3 large glaciers, also alpine meadows, waterfalls, moose and black bears. From Seward, a deepwater port founded in 1903, you can take a dayboat to **Kenali Fjords National Park** to view whales and puffins.

Anchorage - Seward   AR Timetable

Operates late May to early September. Runs daily. These trains have light refreshments.
      At Portage, the track climbs to high country, passes a few miles from Skookum Glacier, and then skirts the banks of the sparkling **Placer River**. There is a good chance to see moose grazing in the meadows near **Moose Pass**.

Dep. Anchorage	06:45		Dep. Seward	18:00
Arr. Seward	11:00		Arr. Anchorage	22:00

Anchorage

Alaska's largest city (240,000 population). Named for Captain Cook having anchored his ships here in 1778. See the National Park Service movies 12:15 and 14:30 at the NPS Information Center at 540 West Fifth Ave. Subjects covered in the film are park lands, Alaskan history and the northern environment (Canada and Alaska).
      Also see the traditional prospector's log cabin, which houses the Visitor Information Center at Fourth Ave. and "F" Street. The 139-foot high Sitka spruce flagpole at the City Hall. Many Eskimo, Aleut and Athabascan Indian artifacts at the Anchorage Museum of History and Art, 121 West Seventh Ave. The Oscar Anderson House. Eklutna Russian Orthodox Church. **Lake Hood,** one of the largest seaplane bases in the world. The Alaska Aviation Heritage Museum. Take a tour of the Crow Creek Gold Mine.
      There are good buys here in fox, mink, seal, beaver, muskrat, wolf and coyote furs. Also Eskimo carvings (scrimshaw) in whalebone, walrus ivory, jade and soapstone.

INTERNATIONAL ROUTES FROM
THE UNITED STATES

All of the schedules for train trips to Mexico appear earlier in this chapter, in the section on "Mexico"

The U.S. gateways for train trips to Canada are: Boston, New York, Detroit and Seattle.

Boston - New Haven - Montreal

These trains run daily, are air-conditioned and have ordinary coaches.

202
Dep. Boston (South)   09:00 (1)
Arr. New London   11:45
Change trains.
196
Dep. New Haven   14:04 (2)
Arr. Montreal (Cen.)   00:15

(1) Light refreshments. (2) Carries sleeping cars and a buffet car.

New York - Montreal   199

This train runs Sunday and holiday sonly, is air-conditioned, has ordinary coaches, and has buffet.

Dep. New York (Penn.)   10:35
Arr. Montreal (Central)   20:15

New York - Toronto   16

There is excellent Hudson River scenery for 142 miles after leaving New York City. For best views, sit on the left side of the train when going to Toronto, on the right side when going to New York City. The train crosses the gorge below Niagara Falls.

These trains run daily, are air-conditioned, have ordinary coaches and have buffet.

Dep. New York (Penn.)	07:15	Dep. Toronto	09:30
Dep. Niagara Falls (USA)	16:10	Dep. Niagara Falls (USA)	13:00
Arr. Toronto	19:14	Arr. New York (Penn.)	21:40

Detroit - Windsor - Toronto 16

Take a taxi from Detroit through the International Tunnel to Windsor.

These trains are air-conditioned, have a parlor car and ordinary coaches.

Dep. Windsor (Walkerville)	06:00 (1)	07:00 (2)	09:35 (1)	11:15 (3+5)
Arr. Toronto (Union)	10:12	11:11	14:03	15:29

(1) Runs daily, except Sunday and holidays. Buffet. (2) Runs Sundays and holidays only. Buffet. (3) Runs Monday, Friday and Sunday. Buffet Monday and Friday. Light refreshments on Sunday. (4) Runs daily. Light refreshments. Also has buffet daily, except Saturday. (5) Plus other departures from Windsor at 14:35 (4) and 18:15 (4), arriving Toronto 18:38 and 22:27.

Seattle - Vancouver Bus 880

In 1981, this train service was replaced by bus transportation between Amtrak's Seattle terminal and VIA Rail Canada's station in Vancouver, allowing for connection with the Vancouver–Toronto train.

Dep. Seattle	07:00	09:00	09:30	11:15	11:45	12:30	12:45 (1)
Arr. Vancouver	10:30	12:15	12:55	14:40	15:00	16:45	16:30

Dep. Vancouver	05:55	06:00	07:15	10:00	11:15	13:00	15:30 (2)
Arr. Seattle	09:15	09:45	10:45	13:25	15:10	16:30	19:15

(1) Plus other departures from Seattle at 15:00, 17:15, 19:00 and 20:30, arriving Vancouver 18:15, 20:45, 22:15 and 23:55. (2) Plus other departures from Vancouver at 17:30 and 19:30 arriving Seattle 21:00 and 23:00.

Here are the previously mentioned bus services between Flagstaff and the Grand Canyon. Summer service only.

Flagstaff - Grand Canyon Bus 540

Dep. Flagstaff	07:30	15:45
Arr. Grand Canyon	09:40	17:35

Dep. Grand Canyon	10:00	18:30
Arr. Flagstaff	11:45	20:20

SKUNK RAILWAY

This California route is one of the most popular steam train rides in the U.S.A.

Fort Bragg - Willits - Fort Bragg 267

Dep. Fort Bragg	09:20 (1)	13:40 (2)	
Arr. Willits	11:30	17:25	

• • •

Dep. Willits	09:10 (1+2)	13:20 (3)	13:30 (2)
Arr. Fort Bragg	12:40	15:30	15:50

(1) "Skunk" train. (2) Operates mid-June to early September. (3) Operates early January to mid-June and mid-September to late December.

CHAPTER 15

CENTRAL AMERICA and WEST INDIES

In Central America, a train scheduled to run on a certain day may actually leave a day later. Check all timetables at the local stations and tourist offices to be sure your train is running.

COSTA RICA

Children under 3 travel free. Half-fare for children 3–10. Children 11 and over must pay full fare.

There are no train connections from Costa Rica to adjacent countries. Until 1990, it was possible to travel by train in Costa Rica from the Caribbean (Limon) to the Pacific Ocean (Puntarenas). En route, the train passed through Cartago and San Jose, the country's capital.

Cartago

See the tiny (under 6 inches tall) statue of the legendary Indian Black Virgin, in the Basilica of Our Lady of the Angels. Pilgrims come from all over Central America to see La Negrita.This is the location where a primitive structure was built in 1715 on the place where the Virgin Mary is believed to have appeared to a peasant girl. The Sunday market is an interesting event. Take the short bus trip to see the crater of the **Mount Irazu Volcano**. Its eruption in 1723 destroyed the original town.

Limon

Millions of bunches of bananas are exported from this seaport every year. See the gardens in Vargas Park. It rains 300 days each year on the jungle and forest near the Caribbean coast.

San Jose

The capital of Costa Rica. See: The National Theater, with its statues, gold-decorated foyer and marble staircases. The excellent collection of pre-Columbian (as far back as 10,000 B.C.) ceramic and stone vases, figurines, tools and other antiques in the National Museum, open daily except Monday, 09:00–17:00. Thousands of pre-Columbian jade birds, ornaments, musical instruments and human figures at the Jade Museum (in the Insurance Building on Calle 17), open daily except Monday, 10:00–16:00. The National Liquor Factory, in Parque Espana. Frescoes of Costa Rican life in the Salon Dorado at the old La Sabana Airport, now an enormous park.

See the colored glassware and carved wood pieces sold at the government craft center, next to Soledad Church. One of the world's largest collections of insects, displayed at the University of Costa Rica. The leather goods for sale at Caballo Blanco on Moravia Church Plaza. There are all-day bus tours to the Monteverde Cloud Forest, a 4,000-acre biological reserve. Cool at its 4,500-foot altitude, the reserve has 2,000 species of plants and 320 of birds.

The 19th and 20th century paintings and sculptures in the Museum of Costa Rican Art, at the former International Airport Terminal. The food and curios at the indoor Central Market. The miles of broad white-sand beaches at Manuel Antonio Beach Park, a 4-hour drive. Take a bus trip to the volcanoes, Poas and Irazu.

CUBA

Children under 5 travel free. Half-fare for children 5–11. Children 12 and over must pay full fare.

The categories of Cuban trains are: Especial, Primera Especial, Primera and Segunda. Especial requires reservation, is air-conditioned and has reclining seats. Primera Especial is air-conditioned, with reclining seats. (Segunda is tantamount to fourth-class.)

The 4 rail trips from Habana are west to Pinar del Rio and Guane, a short trip east to Matanzas, and the route southeast to both Cienfuegos and to Santiago de Cuba.

Habana

This is the largest, most cosmopolitan and most beautiful city in the Caribbean.

See: El Morro Castle. The view from the tower of the city's oldest fort, La Fuerza. Marvelous gardens in Parque Central. Vermay paintings in El Templete on Plaza Carlos Manuel Cespedes. The patio at the former palace of the Captain's General, on the west side of the Plaza Cespedes.

The lovely interior of La Merced Church. The view from the east tower of the Cathedral. The National Museum in Palacio de Bellas Artes. The Botanical Gardens on Avenida Allende. The Museum of Natural Sciences, in the Capitol building. The Museum of the Revolution, in the Presidential Palace. The statues and mausoleums in the outstanding Colon Cemetery.

Ernest Hemingway's home, maintained as it was when he lived there in 1960. The art gallery, carnival rides, equestrian center and restaurants in the enormous Lenin Park. The tremendous monument to Jose Marti, a leader of the last century's revolution against Spain, in the Plaza of the Revolution, competing with the enormous picture on a government building of Che Guevara, who helped Fidel Castro overthrow Batista in this century.

Habana - Matanzas 1510

All of these trains are fourth-class only.

Dep. Habana (C.B.)	04:50	10:38	15:15	20:55	
Arr. Matanzas	07:54	13:42	18:19	23:53	

Dep. Matanzas	05:00	10:35	15:15		21:00
Arr. Habana (C.B.)	08:07	13:41	18:20	23:58	

Habana-Santiago de Cuba 1515

Dep. Habana (Central)	18:01 (1)
Arr. Santiago de Cuba	10:30

• • •

Dep. Santiago de Cuba	19:19 (1)
Arr. Habana (Central)	12:11

(1) Primera-Especial class only. Air-conditioned train. Reclining seats. Restaurant car. Alternate days only.

GUATEMALA

Children under 3 travel free. Half-fare for children 3–11. Children 12 and over must pay full fare.

It is possible to travel in Guatemala by train from the Caribbean (Puerto Barrios) to the Pacific Ocean (Tecun Uman).

Guatemala City

See Mayan treasures in the Archaeological Museum in La Aurora Park, open daily except Monday. A very large collection of Mayan figurines, masks and pottery at Popol Vuh Museum (9 Calle 3-62), open daily except Sunday. Museo Ixchel (4 Avenue 6-27) has a good exhibit of Indian textiles and clothing, open daily except Monday.

The murals, stained-glass and tiled patios and fountains in the National Palace, near Central Park. Next door is the Metropolitan Cathedral. The gold and mahogany altar at

Cerro del Carmen Church, and the splendid view of the city from the gardens there.

The marvelous assortment of fabrics at the Central Market. The Botanical Gardens. The Zoo. The National Museum of History and Fine Arts. A display of products made in Guatemala, at the Popular Arts and Handicrafts Center (10 Avenue and 11 Calle). The fish-shaped Templo de la Expiacion. These churches: La Merced, San Francisco, Santa Domingo, Las Capuchinas, and Santa Rosa.

The slide lecture on Mayan archaeology, every night at 19:00 Camino Real Hotel, 9 Calle 4-69.

Take a local bus to the western side of the city to see the Mayan ruins of Kaminal Juyu (Valley of Death). It is a short bus ride to see these nearby Indian villages: **Chinautla, San Pedro Sacatepequez** and **San Juan Sacatepequez**.

Visit nearby (28 miles) **Antigua** to see many colonial churches, plazas, fountains and walled palaces where 70,000 people lived before Antigua was destroyed by earthquake in the 18th century. One of the many giant volcanos here is still very active.

Visit nearby (90 miles) **Chichicastenango** for fabulous bargains in strawgoods, fabrics (tablecloths, napkins, etc.) and pottery at the extraordinary Thursday and Sunday markets.

Visit nearby (134 miles) **Quirigua** to see excellent remains of the Mayan Old Empire. Visit nearby 50-square-mile **Lake Atitlan** to see its beautiful setting amid mountains and volcanos. The lake's color changes constantly.

Guatemala City - Puerto Barrios   1151

This route goes through many banana plantations and dense jungles. Watch for 3 volcano cones, a short distance from Guatemala City. *The train to Puerto Barrios usually runs 2–6 hours late, and the return is often one day late.*

Dep. Guatemala City	07:15 (1)	Dep. Puerto Barrios	06:00 (2)
Dep. Rancho	11:30	Dep. Zacapa	13:20
Dep. Zacapa	13:50	Dep. Rancho	16:15
Arr. Puerto Barrios	21:35	Arr. Guatemala City	21:00

(1) Runs Tuesday, Thursday and Saturday. (2) Runs Wednesday, Friday and Sunday.

Sights in **Zacapa**: En route from Guatemala City, a stop is made here for dining at the railstation. This was the junction for the train service to and from El Salvador before 1989, when all passenger train service in El Salvador was suspended because of uprisings.

Sights in **Puerto Barrios:** Nearby beaches (Escabas and Santo Tomas de Castilla) are very popular.

Guatemala City - Esquintla - Mazatenango - Tecun Uman 1150

Dep. Guatemala City	07:00 (1)	Dep. Tecun Uman	06:00 (2)
Dep. Escuintla	09:49	Dep. Mazatenango	10:20
Dep. Mazatenango	14:10	Dep. Escuintla	14:45
Arr. Tecun Uman	18:55	Arr. Guatemala City	18:00

(1) Runs Saturday only. (2) Runs Sunday only.

Sights in **Escuintla**: Famous for fruits and medicinal baths. Nearby are giant sculptures in La Democracia (an archeological park) and the 13th century ruins at **Mixco Viejo**.

Sights in **Mazatenango**: The production of tropical fruits, coffee, sugar and cacao.

INTERNATIONAL ROUTE FROM GUATEMALA

This is the train connection from Guatemala to Mexico.

Guatemala City - Tecun Uman - Ciudad Hidalgo - Mexico City

1150

Dep. Guatemala City	07:00 (1)
Arr. Tecun Uman	18:55

It is possible, although very difficult, to travel by train from from Guatemala City into southern Mexico. The reasons we always advise against attempting this trip until conditions improve are:

There is no acceptable lodging in either primitive Tecun Uman or in equally primitive Cuidad Hidalgo, the 2 border cities where a transfer is necessary.

Further, there is an *overnight* interval of 14 hours between arriving in Tecun Uman and departing from Ciudad Hidalgo for Tapachula and on to Veracruz and Mexico City.

The final obstacle is that passengers attempting this transfer have to walk more than a mile in great heat and mucho dust from Tecun Uman to Ciudad Hidalgo, and pay a substantial toll charge to cross the border bridge.

1043

Dep. Ciudad Hidalgo	08:30 (2)
Arr. Tapachula	09:50
Change trains.	
Dep. Tapachula	07:30 (3)
Arr. Veracruz	06:00 (4)
Change trains.	
Dep. Veracruz	21:30 (5)
Arr. Mexico City	07:40 (6)

(1) Runs Saturday only. Second-class only. (2) Runs daily. Second-class only. (3) Runs daily. Light refreshments. (4) Day 2. (5) Reservation required. Runs daily. Air-conditioned train. Carries a sleeping car, a Primera Especial-class coach, and a domecar. Light refreshments. (6) Day 3 from Ciudad Hidalgo.

HONDURAS

Children under 3 travel free. Half-fare for children 3-11. Children 12 and over must pay full fare.

The country's rail lines serve banana plantations and 2 seaports.

Puerto Cortes

Honduras' main port. Very hot climate here. Take the bus ride to see the castle at **Omoa**.

San Pedro Sula

This is the gateway (by air or bus) for travel to Tegucigalpa. Terribly hot here. The population is cosmopolitan: North American, Irish, Cuban, Russian. Fabulous Mayan ruins are located at **Copan**, 112 miles by road from San Pedro Sula.

Tela

This seaport ships mountains of bananas. See United Fruit Company's experimental farm in nearby **Lancetilla**.

San Pedro Sula - La Ceiba - Tela - Baracoa - Puerto Cortes
1250

The run between La Ceiba and Tela is a very scenic 2-hour ride through banana plantations and jungle.

Dep. San Pedro Sula	N/A (1)		
Dep. La Ceiba	N/A		
Dep. Tela	N/A		
Arr. Baracoa	N/A		
Arr. Puerto Cortes	N/A		

• • •

Dep. Puerto Cortes	07:00	08:15 (2)	-0-
Dep. Baracoa	08:15	N/A (1)	-0-
Dep. Tela	10:30	-0-	14:00 (2)
Arr. La Ceiba	-0-	-0-	-0-
Arr. San Pedro Sula	-0-	10:30	17:00

(1) Time was not available in 1994. (2) Carries second-class and third-class coaches only.

PANAMA

Children under 5 travel free. Half-fare for children 5–14. Children 15 and over must pay full fare. A supplement is charged both children and adults for air-conditioned space.

There are no rail connections between Panama and adjacent countries.

A. T. Peters told us in 1985 that the statement by Cook about air-conditioning is inaccurate: "There is *no air-conditioning* in any car, and many seats are missing. Some of the remaining seats are damaged.

"Delays while waiting for the canal passage are 5 times longer than they were before Panama took over operating the railway. Trains often depart later than scheduled and arrive late even when they depart on time."

Panama City

Stroll down Paseo de las Bovedas and see the view from there of the Bay of Panama and the islands offshore (Flamenco, Naos and Perico). See the President's Palace, called

Palacio de las Garzas. The egrets there are worth the visit. The gold altar and famous organ in San Jose Church.

The view of the bay from the top of La Cresta. Inca and Spanish treasures in the National Museum. The monument dedicated to the Canal, at Plaza de Francia. Instituto Bolivar. The 17th century Cathedral, facing Plaza de la Independencia.

Panama City - Colon   1500

The train ride from the Pacific Ocean (Panama City) to the Caribbean (Colon). This has excellent views of ships passing through the Canal and of the jungle. From Panama City, sit on the right side for the best views. From Colon, sit on the left side.

Dep. Panama City	04:40 (1)	06:45 (1)	08:30 (2)	12:35 (2)	15:20 (1+3)
Arr. Colon	90 minutes later				

Sights in **Colon**: This is one of the world's busiest ports. See the statues on Paseo Centenario. The Cathedral. The Casino. Many nightclubs. Shop for English bone china, ivory, furniture and perfume on Front Street.

There are 3 good excursions from Colon: To Gatun Locks and the nearby jungle. To Fort San Lorenzo, at the mouth of the Chagres River. And a boat trip to the San Blas archipelago.

The old Spanish ruins at the city of **Portobello** are *not within walking distance of Colon, and the road to them is impassable after a heavy rain.*

Dep. Colon	04:40 (1)	06:40 (2)	06:55 (1)	10:45 (2)	15:35 (1+4)
Arr. Panama City	90 minutes later				

(1) Runs Monday–Friday, except holidays. (2) Runs Saturday only. (3) Plus other departures from Panama City at 17:40 (1) and 17:50 (2). (4) Plus other departures from Colon at 16:00 (2) and 17:25 (1).

Concepcion - Puerto Armuelles   1502

Dep. Concepcion	08:30	13:30	Dep. Puerto Armuelles	13:30
Arr. Puerto Armuelles	11:30	16:30	Arr. Concepcion	16:30

CHAPTER 16

SOUTH AMERICA

Winter in South America (south of Colombia and Venezuela) is from June 21 to September 20. Summer is from December 21 to March 20.

In South America, a train scheduled to run on a particular day may actually leave a day later. In planning trips based on information in this chapter, readers are advised to consider the fact that throughout Eastern Europe, Asia, Africa and Latin America, second-class space is usually primitive and almost always extremely crowded. It is best to reserve first-class space when traveling these areas by train.

Due to reductions in passenger train services in Columbia and Ecuador, *The Eurail Guide* no longer covers these countries.

ARGENTINA

Children under 3 travel free. Half-fare for children 3–11. Children 12 and over must pay full fare. The 3 classes of coach cars are: air-conditioned class, first-class and second-class.

There are 27,000 miles of rail service in Argentina, radiating out from Buenos Aires.

Due to major reductions in Argentinian rail service in 1993, there is no longer international rail services from Argentina to surrounding countries.

ARGENTINA'S TRAIN PASS

Argempass *Not* transferable. Unlimited first-class train travel. Sold only in Argentina, at railway booking offices. Can be upgraded for sleeping car accommodation by paying the supplemental charge for sleeper space. The validity period begins on the first day the pass is used (which must be within 30 days after it is issued) and ends at 24:00 on the final day.

The 1995 adult prices were: $148.77 (U.S.) for 30 days, $250.15 for 60 days, and $349.22 for 90 days. There is a 50% discount for children 3–12 years old.

There is a small charge for obtaining a refund before starting to use the pass. When a 60-day pass has been used any part of the first 30 days, it can be returned to the Argentine Railways for a refund that results in the passenger paying only for a 30-day pass.

TICKET DISCOUNTS

Children	50% for childern age 3-12.
Group	10%–25% for 10 to 25 or more persons.
Family	25% for mother, father and one or two children.
Youth	25% for persons under 30 years old.

| Senior | 25% for women 55 years of age or older, and for men 60 years of age or older. |
| Students | 25% |

Buenos Aires

This is an enormous city with a population of 11,000,000. A 3-hour bus tour costs only $7 (U.S) and is advisable before starting independent sightseeing.

The railstations here and the routes they serve are: Constitucion (southern), Lacroze (northeastern Paraguay), Once (western), Puente Alsina, Retiro (Chile and Bolivia), and Velez Sarsfield (northwestern).

Stroll the magnificent Avenida 9 Julio. See Colon Opera House. Visit the Museum of Modern Art. The statues, formal gardens and 2 lakes in Palermo Park...and the nearby Zoo (open daily except Monday 09:30-18:30) and Botanical Gardens (open daily 08:00-18:00) with more than 6,000 plant species. The excellent statues and paintings in the Cathedral. See and hear the inimitable tango in San Telmo, the oldest section of the city, where an antiques market takes place every Sunday.

Eva Peron's mausoleum, in Recoleta Cemetery. The collection of gaucho artifacts, silver and iron objects, musical instruments and tapestries in the Museo de Motivos de Jose Hernandez (Avenida de Libertador 2373). The tapestries and antiques at the Museum of Decorative Arts and the National Museum of Oriental Art (both at Ave. de Libertador 1902), open daily except Tuesday and Sunday 15:00-19:00.

Argentina's largest art collection, in the Museo de Bellas Artes (Ave. de Libertador 1473), open daily except Monday 13:30-19:30, on Saturday 09:00-19:30. The Natural Sciences Museum (Avenida Angel Gallardo 470). The outstanding collection of colonial silver in the Isaac Fernandez Blanco Museum of Spanish-American Art (Suipacha 1422), open daily 14:00–19:00. El Pilar Church (Junin 1904). The Municipal Museum. The Numismatic Museum at the Banco Central.

Buenos Aires - Rosario   2266

Both of these trains have light refreshments.

Dep. Buenos Aires (Retiro)	12:30 (1)		Dep. Rosario (Norte)	07:10 (2)
Arr. Rosario (Norte)	20:40		Arr. Buenos Aires (Retiro)	12:30

(1) Runs Monday, Wednesday and Friday. (2) Runs Tuesday, Thursday and Sunday.

Sights in **Rosario**: The Juan B. Castagnino Municipal Museum and the Provincial Historical Museum, both in Parque Independencia. The Cathedral (Calle 25 de Mayo). Stroll on Boulevard Orono. The Monument of The Flag, along the river bank.

Buenos Aires - Rosario - Tucuman (via La Banda) 2266

Both trains have light refreshments.

2Dep. B.A. (Retiro	12:30 (1)
Arr. Rosario (Norte)	20:40
Dep. Rosario (Norte)	20:50
Arr. Tucuman (GM)	12:30 Day 2

· · ·

Dep. Tucuman (GM)	16:00 (2)
Arr. Rosario (Norte)	07:00 Day 2
Dep. Rosario (Norte)	07:10
Arr. B.A. (Retiro)	12:30

(1) Runs Monday, Wednesday and Friday. (2) Runs Tuesday, Thursday and Sunday.

Buenos Aires - Rojas 2263

All of these trains are third-class only.

Dep. Buenos Aires (Lacroze)	19:05 (1)
Arr. Rojas	23:19

· · ·

Dep. Rojas	04:30 (2)	17:00 (3)
Arr. Buenos Aires (Lacroze)	08:45	21:22

(1)Runs Monday, Wednesday and Friday. (2) Runs Tuesday and Thursday only. (3) Runs Sunday.

Buenos Aires - Las Flores - Quequen Necochea 2272

These trains have air-conditioned coaches and light refreshments.

Dep. Buenos Aires (P. Con.)	20:30 (1)	Dep. Quequen Necochea	20:30 (3)
Dep. Las Flores	N/A (2)	Arr. Las Flores	N/A (2)
Arr. Quequen Necochea	06:25	Arr. Buenos Aires (P. Con.)	06:25

(1) Runs Thursday only. (2) Day 2. Time was not available in 1994. (3) Runs Tuesday only.

Buenos Aires - Santa Rosa 2273

Both of these trains have an air-conditioned coach and light refreshments.

Dep. Buenos Aires (Once)	20:00 (1)	Dep. Santa Rosa	21:45 (2)
Arr. Santa Rosa	07:48	Arr. Buenos Aires (Once)	09:30

(1) Runs Monday, Wednesday and Friday. (2) Runs Tuesday, Thursday and Sunday.

Buenos Aires - Bahia Blanca - San Carlos de Bariloche
2274 + 2281

Both of these trains have an air-conditioned coach and a restaurant car.

Dep. Buenos Aires (P. Con.)	22:00 (1)
Arr. Bahia Blanca (Sud)	09:20 (2)
Arr. San Carlos de Bariloche	10:00 (3)

* * *

Dep. San Carlos de Bariloche	22:20 (4)
Dep. Bahia Blanca (Sud)	21:45 (5)
Arr. Buenos Aires (P. Con.)	09:00 (6)

(1) Runs Wednesday and Sunday. (2) Day 2. (3) Day 2 from Bahia Blanca. (4) Runs Wednesday and Sunday. (5) Day 2 from San Carlos de Bariloche. (6) Day 2 from Bahia Blanca. Day 3 from San Carlos de Bariloche.

Sights in **Bahia Blanca:** The statues and lakes in Parque de Mayo. The Zoological Garden in Parque Independencia.

Sights in **San Carlos de Bariloche**: Developed as a recreation center at the beginning of the 20th century, this is the biggest ski area in South America (7 different chairlifts). Known internationally for its fashionable ski slpoes that operate June–September, the town (similar to an Alpine village) has a wide range of hotels. There is also much mountain climbing here.

You can't miss the chocolate shops that line the 200 block of Mitre Street including Del Turista, a chocolate supermarket.

See the collection of Indian artifacts in the Nahuel Huapi Museum. For scenic views, go on the cable car from Cerro Cathedral.

Many tours of Argentina's Lake District originate in Bariloche. Take the 35-mile ride, by auto, around **Lake Nahuel Huapi**. There is daily boat service to Isla Victoria in the center of the lake, where there is a forest of arraya'n trees. Found nowhere else in the world, these reddish-brown trees have heavily gnarled trunks that appear sinister.

The interesting lakes in the Bariloche area are: **Argentino, Nahuel Huapi, Correntoso, Espejo, Traful, Gutierrez, Mascardi, Futulafquen, Meliquina, Falkner, Villarino, Epulafquen** and **Tromen**. There is outstanding trout fishing in many of them.

Take the 35-mile ride by auto around Lake Nahuel Huapi.

Buenos Aires - La Plata   2265

Dep Buenos Aires (P. Con.)	Frequent times from 05:25 to 23:30
Arr. La Plata	1½ hours later

Sights in **La Plata**: Founded in 1882, its city plan was modelled on that of Washington D.C. Re-named Eva Peron by Juan Peron in 1952, it resumed its original name after he was overthrown in 1955.

Its museum has one of the most important paleontological and anthropological collections in South America. See the Gothic-style cathedral.

Dep. La Plata	Frequent times from 04:10 to 22:45
Arr. Buenos Aires (P. Con.)	1½ hours later

Buenos Aires - Mar del Plata   2280

All of these trains have an air-conditioned first-class coach, unless designated otherwise.

Dep. B.A. (P.Con.)	01:25	08:00	15:30 (1)	18:30 (2)	23:00 (1)
Arr. Mar del Plata	07:05	13:50	21:10	00:10	04:55

Sights in **Mar del Plata**: Five miles of attractive sandy beaches. A very large casino.

Dep. Mar del Plata	08:25	15:15 (1)	17:00	23:05 (3)	23:50 (1)
Arr. B.A. (P.Con.)	14:10	20:00	23:00	05:00	05:35

(1) Light refreshments. (2) Supplement charged. Runs Saturday only. Restautant car. (3) Runs Sunday only. Restaurant car.

THE LAKE DISTRICT BUS CONNECTION

San Carlos de Bariloche - Puerto Montt   2300

Puerto Montt is the Southernmost train station in the Western Hemisphere.

Here is the schedule for continuing on from Argentina's Lake District to Chile (and v.v.), a 7-hour bus trip.

Dep. San Carlos de Bariloche	N/A	Dep. Puerto Montt	N/A
Arr. Puerto Montt	N/A	Arr. San Carlos de Bariloche	N/A

Puerto Montt - Santiago   2430

Here is the schedule for continuing on from Argentina's Lake District to Chile (and v.v.).

Dep. Puerto Montt	10:00 (1)	16:30 (2)	Dep. Santiago (Ala.)	17:45 (2)	19:45 (1)
Arr. Santiago (Ala.)	09:45	12:50	Arr. Puerto Montt	14:05	18:30

(1) Second-class only. Restaurant car. (2) Carries a sleeping car, an air conditioned first-class coach and a restaurant car.

BOLIVIA

Children under 3 travel free. Half-fare for children 3–11. Children 12 and over pay full fare. All of Bolivia's scant 1,400 miles of railway are narrow-guage, one metre wide.

La Paz

This is the world's highest capital (11,735-foot altitude). See the collection of colonial and contemporary art at the National Art Museum, across from the Cathedral, in the Palace of the Condes do Arana, open Tuesday–Friday 09:30–12:00 and 14:30–18:30, Saturday 10:00–12:30. Next to the Art Museum is the Presidential Palace.

Two blocks away is the Ethnographic and Folklore Museum (916 Calle Ingavi), with exhibits of the culture of several Indian groups. It is open Monday–Friday 08:30–11:30 and 14:30–17:45. Then, it is a 3-block walk to Calle Jaen, on which many other museums are located. Among these are: The collection of native handicraft, furniture and art in Casa de Murillo, home of the hero of Bolivia's War of Independence… the collection of Inca and pre-Columbian gold and silver ornaments at Museo de Metales Preciosos… and the exhibit of local customs at Museo Costumbrista. All 3 museums are open Tuesday–Friday 09:30–12:00 and 14:30–18:30, Saturday and Sunday 10:00–12:30.

Window-shop on Calle Comercio. See the Central Food Market, largest one in South

America. Visit the House of Culture. Stroll Calle Sagarnaga, called "Street of the Indians" to examine the assortment of handicrafts sold there. The view of La Paz from Monticulo Park. See ancient Indian arts and crafts in The National Museum (Calle Don Bosco 93).

The baroque Spanish architecture of the 16th century Church of San Francisco. Next to it, the handicrafts (musical instruments, weavings) in a shop sponsored by the church, open Monday–Friday 10:00–13:00 and 14:30–19:00, only in the morning on Saturday and Sunday. On nearby Calle Linares, see the women who wear bowler hats while selling medicinal herbs. The 3rd–12th century stone monoliths and figures in Tiwanacu Prehistoric Park.

For $5, you can have a seat and beverages (snacks and meals are extra) at any one of several "penas" halls where Indian groups perform with native musical intruments. Penas are open Thursday–Saturday after 21:00. Several performances are offered each night.

Go to the **Tiahuanco** ruins, 49 miles from La Paz.

La Paz - Cochabamba   1900

All of these trains have first-class coaches, for which a supplement is charged.

Dep. La Paz	08:00 (1)	21:00 (2)	Dep. Cochabamba	08:00 (3)	20:30 (4)
Arr. Cochabamba	16:00	05:40	Arr. La Paz	16:40	05:48

(1) Runs Monday and Friday (2) Runs Friday only. (3) Runs Tuesday and Thursday. (4) Runs Sunday only.

Sights in **Cochabamba:** This is the most comfortable area in Bolivia, a mere 8,500 feet altitude. See: The former home of tin baron Simon Patino, now a museum. The several museums in the Palace of Culture. Colorful stalls in the Municipal Market.

La Paz - Potosi - Sucre   1902

This train ride over the Andes is both the highest meter-gauge track in the world (15,705 feet at El Condor, between Rio Mulato and Potosi), **and it is also the world's highest passenger train run on any gauge**.

Dep. La Paz	- 0 - (1)	-0-
Arr. Potosi	06:18 (2)	-0-
Dep. Potosi	07:20	07:30 (5)
Arr. Sucre	14:00	11:53
	• • •	
Dep. Sucre	17:00 (3)	18:50 (4)
Arr. Potosi	21:34	00:35 (2)
Dep. Potosi	21:54	-0-
Arr. La Paz	09:00	-0-

(1) Runs Saturday only. Buffet. (2) Day 2. (3) Runs Wednesday and Sunday. Has a first-class coach. (4) Second-class only. Runs Saturday only.

Sights in **Potosi**: In 1650, when its population was 160,000 (now only 90,000), this was one of the most important cities in the world. Many tourists find it difficult to acclimate to the thin air of its 15,000-foot altitude. Most stores and offices are closed 14:00–15:30.

See the silver and silk statue of Christ in San Francisco Cathedral. The silver altar in the 16th century San Lorenzo Church. Only 4 blocks away is the Mercado Artesiana, where exceptional handmade weavings, belts, antiques, silverware and ponchos are sold.

Half-day tours of the tin mine are offered weekdays at 09:00, starting at the headquarters of COMIBOL. The mine can be reached by taxi or by taking the 07:45 bus from Plaza 10 de Noviembre. After the tin mine tour, you can see the nearby ancient Inca hot springs.

Do not fail to visit the Royal House of Money, built in 1773, for a 2-hour tour of this enormous ancient mint near the Plaza 10 de Noviembre.

A guide there charges only 10 U.S. cents for a 3-hour tour that includes seeing 8-foot-high wood gears and wheels originally operated by slaves, a display of thousands of coins that were made here for Spain and for many Latin American countries (many custom-made for wealthy residents who used them for wedding souvenirs), numerous colonial paintings, and a collection of sculpture and exquisite furniture. Coins that were minted here several centuries ago and also elegant silverware made in this area can be purchased from small stands near the entrance to the market on Calle Oruro.

Sights in **Sucre:** This city is 10,300 feet high. The Tourist Office cannot arrange for English-speaking guides. Hire one at a travel agency to take you on a tour of the 17th century San Felipe Neri Church and to take you to the roof of that church for a view of numerous roofs made of ceramic blocks that are bonded by silver from the Potosi mines.

The Cathedral is famed for its statue of the Virgin, covered by a multimillion-dollar garment of gold, diamonds, emeralds and pearls that were donated by wealthy people from 1538 to 1825. See the desks, paintings and books inlaid with mother-of-pearl, at the museum next to the Cathedral. Visit the House of Liberty, where Bolivia was founded, the place where its constitution was completed, open 11:00–12:00 and 15:00–17:00.

See the weavings, colonial paintings and furniture, and archaeological objects at the University Museum (Calle Bolivar 698), open Monday-Friday 08:30–12:00 and 14:00–18:00, Saturday and Sunday 09:00–12:00. The marvelous 16th and 17th century architecture. The ancient University of San Francisco Xavier. The Palace of Justice. Guided tours of the Monastery of La Recoleta (in Spanish language) are conducted 10:00–12:00 and 14:00–17:00.

INTERNATIONAL ROUTES
FROM BOLIVIA

The route to Peru is via Cuzco

La Paz - Cuzco - Lima

1910 Bus		*Change to train.*	
Dep. La Paz	08:00 (1)	*1801*	
Arr. Puno	18:30	Dep. Huancavelica	N/A (4)
Change to train.		Arr. Huancayo	N/A (4)
1800		*Change trains.*	
Dep. Puno	07:00	*1802*	
Arr. Cuzco	17:00	Dep. Huancayo	N/A (4)
1820 Bus		Arr. Lima (Des.)	N/A
Dep. Cuzco	N/A (3)		
Arr. Huancavelica	N/A (3)		

(1) Runs daily. (2) Runs Monday, Thursday and Saturday. (3) Time has not been available since 1980. Direct Bus is available Cuzco–Lima: Depart Cuzco 08:00–Arrive Lima 03:00 on day 3. (4) Train service was temporarily suspended in 1992.

There are 2 rail routes from La Paz to Chile: southwest to Arica, and south to Antofagasta.

La Paz - Charana - Arica   1901

Marvelous Andean scenery while riding on an excellent train. Passengers are amazed by the elegant complimentary service of tea, sandwiches and cookies on individual silver trays. You travel on 30 miles of rack and pinion track during a portion of this 270-mile trip. The highest place on this route is 14,000 feet at **General Lagos**.

The unique housing units, each containing expensive apartments, buildings for middle-income workers, and a complete shopping center. The National Cathedral. Nearby, the 18 buildings that are each for a different government department. Planalto Palace, where the President's office is located. Alvorada Palace, residence of the President. Arcos Palace. The Metropolitan Cathedral. The 600-foot-long Gallery of States shopping mall, featuring handicrafts from each of Brazil's 22 states. Take the 50-mile drive around Paranoa.

The Museum. The Hall of Mirrors, scene of formal state receptions. The exquisite interior of Alvorada Palace. The National Theater.

Both of these trains charge a supplement and have first-class coaches and a restaurant car.

Dep. La Paz	07:00 (1)		Dep. Arica	09:30 (2)
Dep. Charana	11:17		Dep. Charana	15:35
Arr. Arica	22:30		Arr. La Paz	20:04

(1) Runs Monday and Friday. (2) Runs Tuesday and Saturday.

The best scenery is at the start of the trip, during the ascent from La Paz. The Chilean border is only 5 minutes from **Charana**, at **Visviri**, where the passport control procedure takes more than one hour. Many herds of llamas roam here. Because military installations are nearby, photo-taking is not permitted at the frontier area.

Seventy miles before reaching Arica, the track plunges from 11,000 feet to sea level. The scenery on this stretch is a jumble of brown lava rocks.

Santa Cruz - Sao Paulo - Rio de Janeiro

There is great jungle scenery on the Santa Cruz-Puerto Suarez portion of this train trip to Brazil.

1907

Dep. Santa Cruz	13:50 (1)	14:05 (3)	18:00 (4)	
Arr. Puerto Suarez	07:25 (2)	06:00 (2)	06:12 (2)	
Change trains. 2011				
Dep. Corumba	N/A (5)			
Arr. Bauru	N/A (5)	Day 2 from Corumba		
Change trains. 2015				
Dep. Bauru	23:55 (6)	04:49 (8)	06:41 (8)	12:42 (8)
Arr. Sao Paulo (Luz)	07:20 (7)	12:32	14:56	20:09
Change to a bus. 2130				
Dep. Sao Paulo (Luz)	Frequent times from 05:00 to 01:00			
Arr. Rio de Jan. (D.Ped.)	6 hours later			

(1) Runs Wednesday and Sunday. Has a first-class coach. Restaurant car. (2) Day 2 from Santa Cruz. It is 11km (7 miles) from Puerto Suarez to Corumba. (3) Runs Monday and Friday. (4) Sup- plement charged. Runs Tuesday and Saturday. Has a first-class coach. Buffet. (5) Information on this service has not been available since 1991. This trip was 33 hours in 1991, departing Corumba Monday, Wednesday and Friday at 07:00, arriving Bauru 16:00 on day 2. (6) Runs daily. Train is first-class only. Carries a sleeping car. Buffet. Reservation required. (7) Day 2 from Bauru. (8) Second-class only. Runs daily. Buffet.

Santa Cruz - Yacuiba - Pocitos - Salta

Another train route to Argentina.

1907			
Dep. Sta. Cruz	08:00 (1)	15:40 (2)	19:00 (3)
Arr. Yacuiba	17:49 (4)	06:42 (4)	07:54 (4)

2261	
Dep. Pocitos	N/A (5)
Arr. Salta	N/A

(1) Runs Thursday, Friday and Sunday. First-class only. Restaurant car. (2) Runs Wednesday and Sunday. Second-class only. (3) Runs Monday and Friday. Has a first-class coach. (4) It is 4km from Yacuiba to Pocitos. (5) The Pocito - Salta route was one of the many casualties of Argentina's 1993 reduction of passenger train service. (6) Runs Wednesday only. Has a first-class coach.

Sights In **Salta**: This city of 300,000 people is built on flat land at almost 4,000-foot altitude. Be sure to visit the many 18th century houses that are open to the public, including the Provincial Fine Arts Museum in the Arais House (on Calle Florida).

BRAZIL

Children under 3 travel free. Half-fare for children 3–9. Children 10 and over must pay full fare.

Nearly all (91%) of Brazil's 23,000 miles of rail lines are located within 300 miles of its shoreline on the Atlantic Ocean. Brazil employs 5 different rail gauges. However, most of its tracks are one metre.

Belo Horizonte

See the odd-shaped church at Pampulha, on the edge of the city. Palacio de Liberdade, in Praca de Liberdade. The City Museum. The collection of lamps, photographs, tools, maps and crystal in the Tassini Museum. The 2,000 varieties of trees in the Municipal Park gardens. The marble and glass Museum of Modern Art. The Governor's Palace. The enormous (110,000 seats) soccer stadium. The Fantastic rock shapes in the 22 million-year-old Lapinha Cavern.

Brasilia

See the tomb of Kubitschek, the former president of Brazil who campaigned in 1955 on the pledge to transform what had been until then an uninhabited and remote area into the the country's new capital, which Brasilia has been since 1960.

Walk a short distance from that monument to the Trelliswork Tower and take the elevator there to its 250-foot high observation deck for a panoramic view of the entire city.

Next, go to the National Cathedral and then to the Three Powers Plaza, at which a colorful flag-lowering ceremony highlighted by a military band and a parade by the honor guard takes place every Tuesday at sundown.

Also see the lovely water gardens at the Ministry of Foreign Affairs, the most beautiful structure in Brazil. Across from it, the Palacio de Justica. The blue glass Church of Dom Bosco. Great sculptures throughout the city. The view at night of the white marble federal buildings, sparkling in the glow of spotlights.

Rio de Janeiro

Perhaps the most beautiful city in the world. Take the funicular from Rua Cosme Velho 513 to see the incredible 100-foot-high 700-ton statue, Christ The Redeemer, at the 2400-foot-high top of Corcovado, and the view of the city from there. The ride starts at 513 Rua Cosme Velho every hour from 08:00–20:00. It is a short walk from the Cosme Velho station to the 5 marvelous colonial-style houses in the little square called Largo do Boticario.

Confeitaria Colombo, founded in 1884, is a double-tiered restaurant noted for both its food and decor. Diners are surrounded by gigantic ceiling-high mirrors mounted in hand-wrought Brazilian rosewood frames. There is a stained-glass skylight, and additional illumination is provided by light bulbs set in tulip-petal sconces.

Ride the cablecar from Praia Vermelha (in Botafogo) to the top of Sugar Loaf for the fine view of Rio's beaches from there. (Among the city's 16 marvelous beaches, the best-known are Ipanema, Copacabana and Sao Conrado.)

See the concrete and steel Candelaria Cathedral (styled after Mayan temples). Next to the Cathedral is a stop for the city's last streetcar. Ride it for a one-hour roundtrip on its route through the hilly Santa Teresa residential area.

Sao Bento Monastery. The Church of Penha. Gloria Church. The Museum of Modern Art on Avenida Presidente Vargas. The Museum of Fine Arts (Avenida Rio Branco 100). The Natural History Museum. The collection of movie theaters, called Cinelandia.

The photos, jewels and costumes of the great Brazilian entertainer of the 1930's, at the Carmen Miranda Museum. The collection of weaving, stone works, leather and ceramics in the Indian Museum (Rua das Palmeira).

Gems and precious stones at the Museum of Geology and Mineralogy (Avenida Pasteur 404). The Museum of Villa-Lobos (Rua da Imprensa 16). The Museum of the Republic (Rua do Catete 153) in the granite and rose-colored marble Catete Palace. The Museum of Sacred Arts. The Museum of Pictures and Sound. The Municipal Theater.

The enormous collection of flora at the Botanical Gardens (Rua Jardim Botanico), open 08:00–17:00. Founded in 1808, the gardens contain 135,000 plants and trees.

The National Library (Avenida Rio Branco). Fine colonial art in the Convent of Santa Antonio. The Church of Candelaria. Early phones, in the Telephone Museum (63 Rua Dois de Dezembro, Catete). The National Museum in the Quinta da Boa Vista Park at Sao Cristovao (with one of the world's best collections of birds, reptiles and insects) open daily except Monday 10:00–16:45. The nearby Zoo is open daily except Monday 09:00–16:00.

Take bus # 206 from Largo da Carioca to Silvestre. Visit Ipanema, Barra da Tijuca and Leblon beaches.

Salvador

Called "Bahia" by Brazilians. English-speaking guides are available at the Tourist Office at Praca da Se. To its left is the 18th century Archbishop's Palace. On the other side of the Tourist Office is the 18th century Holy House of Mary Church.

See the Sao Damaso Seminary. The absolutely beautiful Church of Sao Francisco Convent, filled with gold-leaf decorations. The picturesque market near Praca Cairu. Take the ride on the Lacerda elevator, from Praca Cairu to Praca Municipal to see the Government Palace and Municipal Library, and to window-shop on Rua Chile.

The 17th century furniture in Sao Bento Church. The Instituto Geografico e Historico. Sao Pedro Fort. The Zoo, in the Botanical Gardens at Ondina. The view from Ondina Hill. The 16th century Basilica Cathedral and the church of St. Peter of the Clerics, in the square of Terreiro de Jesus. The silver altar and the tiles in the Museum of Sacred Art in the 17th century Santa Teresa Church.

Do not miss seeing Largo do Pelourinho, on Alfredo de Brito Street. The 17th century Convent of the Desterro, most beautiful of all of Brazil's convents.

Dique, the 17th century artificial lake below the Tororo steps. The blue tiles inside University Rectory, en route to Lagoa do Abaete. The beach at Itaparica. The lofty coconut trees at Itapoa Beach. The forts of Santa Maria and Sao Diogo. Igreja da Graco, Salvador's first church. The stalls of fish, pork, beef and tropical fruits at the Agua de Meninos market.

The Fratelli Vita glassblowing factory. The fort of Mont Serrat and, nearby, Mont Serrat Church. The Cacao Institute, for a look at the processing of chocolate from seed to candy.

Sao Paulo

Largest city in Latin America. See the view while standing on the bridge that spans Avenida Anhangabau. The Municipal Theater, across from Praca Ramos de Azevedo. Instituto Butantan, South America's largest snake farm. Nearby, the collection of antique pottery and furniture in Casa do Bandeirante.

Stroll through huge, lake-dotted Ibirapuera Park, with its statues, Japanese Pavillion (an exact copy of Japan's Katura Palace), the various museums (Science, Aeronautics and Technical Arts) in the History Pavillion, contemporary art in the Pavillion Pereira, and the Planetarium. Visit Praca de la Republica. Walk along Praca do Patriarca, the Times Square of Brazil. Window-shop on Rua Augusta.

The Zoological Park (Avenida Miguel Estefeno), considered to be the world's largest. Nearby, the world-famed orchid collection (over 35,000 species). To visit the orchids and Zoo, take Bus # 546 from Praca da Liberdade or from Anhangabau.

There is an outstanding collection of Renoir, Lautrec, Rembrandt, Frans Hals, and many modern Brazilian painters, at the Art Museum (Avenida Paulista 1578). See the Sound and Image Museum (Avenida Europa 158). South America's largest cathedral, in Cathedral Plaza. Liberdade, the city's oriental district (rock gardens, herb stores and many restaurants).

The Museum of Brazilian Art (Rua Alagoas 903), with its collection of copies of all the statues and monuments in the buildings and parks of Brazil. The Museum of Sacred Art in Convento da Luz. The State Art Collection (Avenida Tiradentes 141).

The collection of Indian artifacts at Casa do Sertanista (Avenida Francisco Morato 2200).

If you want to learn to dance the samba, there are 44 samba schools here. Sao Paulo's annual Carnival features their students.

ROUTES IN NORTHERN BRAZIL

Sights in **Fortaleza**: The best lobsters in Brazil. The museum and shops in the Tourist Center. Excellent beaches. Good textiles are sold here, including exquisite handmade laces. Handicrafts from all over the Northeast area of Brazil are sold in the shopping mall at the old city prison on Rua Monsenhor Tabosa, also along the beachfront at night.

Fortaleza - Crato   2130 Bus

Dep. Fortaleza	10:00	19:45	21:00
Arr. Crato	9 hours later		

Recife - Caruaru   2130 Bus

Dep. Recife	Frequent times from 05:10 to 19:30
Arr. Caruaru	2 hours later

* * *

Dep. Caruaru	Frequent times from 05:00 to 19:30
Arr. Recife	2 hours later

Sights in **Recife**: Long, beautiful beaches. Many sugarcane plantations. Named for the reefs along its coastline. Called the "Venice of Brazil" because it is on three rivers.

Start walking at the 3-story, old prison on Rua Floriano Peixoto which has housed the state of Pernambuco's House of Culture since 1973. The displays there of this region's folk art include jewelry, ceramics, leatherwork, woodcuts and the handmade lacework for which this area is famous. Former cells have been converted into boutique shops and snack bars.

Then visit the 17th century, lavishly gilded Capela Dourada (with its gold carved altar) on Rua Imperador Pedro II, one of the most important examples of this area's religious art.

Go down cobblestoned alleys to the nearby 17th century square called Patio de Sao Pedro where the 18th century Baroque church, Sao Pedro dos Clerigos, is located. This square, with its small outdoor cafes, is a popular gathering place at sunset. Other churches to see are the 18th century Convento de Sao Francisco, Madre de Deus, and Conceicao dos Militares, and the 17th century Santo Antonio.

Everything from dried snakeskins to cassette tapes is sold at the crowded San Jose Market. Visit the Museum of Sugar and Alcohol. The oldest church in Brazil, the 16th century San Cosme e Damiao, is in nearby **Igaracu**.

Many of the town's best restaurants and small hotels are on the boulevard that runs along what is considered the finest beach in the area, at **Boa Viagem** (an island suburb, 10 miles south of Recife). It is a small version of Rio de Janeiro's Ipanema.

Many who visit Recife are attracted to the faithful reproduction of Jerusalem at **Nova Jerusalem**, 115 miles to the west.

Olinda, a seaport 5 miles north, is the arts and crafts capital of this region and has been called "the most idyllic place in Brazil." There are marvelous old mansions here, decorated with silver, gold and brilliant Portuguese ceramic tiles. It has a nice sand beach, and water sports are popular here (sailing, scuba diving, water skiing).

Don't fail to visit the display of colorful costumes, masks and musical instruments used in religious festivals at the Museum of Northeast Man, in the Casa Forte neighborhood. It also has anthropological and historical exhibits on this region's many centuries of sugarcane production.

See the view of Olinda from the hill called "Alto de Se," where a seminary is located. As you walk down winding roads from there, you come to the beautiful 16th century church of St. Francis and to the Museum of Sacred Arts, which has exhibits of both popular paintings and Baroque sculptures.

Also in Olinda, visit the Ribeira Market, originally an 18th century slave market and now a center for the exhibition and sale of folk arts and crafts.

Caruaru, Great leather, straw articles and pottery bargains at the Wednesday and Saturday markets.

Belo Horizonte - Itabira - Vitoria   2007

The Itabira -Vitoria (and v.v.) train has a buffet car.

Bus		Train	
Dep. Belo Horizonte	05:30	Dep. Vitoria (Nolasco)	07:20
Arr. Itabira	07:30 (1)	Arr. Itabira	18:20
Change to train.		*Change to bus.*	
Dep. Itabira	08:00	Dep. Itabira	18:50 (1)
Arr. Vitoria (Nolasco)	18:50	Arr. Belo Horizonte	21:30

(1) Estimated.

Sights in **Vitoria**: A beautiful seaport. Marvelous beaches.

Campo Grande - Ponte Pora 2017

Both of these trains have a restaurant car.

| Dep. Campo Grande | 09:20 (1) | Dep Ponte Pora | 07:50 (2) |
| Arr. Ponte Pora | 18:50 | Arr. Campo Grande | 17:30 |

(1) Runs Monday, Wednesday and Friday. (2) Runs Tuesday, Thursday and Saturday.

Porto Santana - Serra do Navio 2001

All of these trains are second-class only.

| Dep. Porto Santana (Macapa) | 07:01 (1) | 12:31 (2) | 20:31 (3) |
| Arr. Serra do Navio | 11:47 | 16:56 | 00:27 |

Dep. Serra do Navio	07:01 (4)	14:01 (1)	20:00 (2)
Arr. Porto Santana (Macapa)	12:25	19:25	00:15

(1) Runs Tuesday and Thursday. (2) Runs Friday only. (3) Runs Sunday only. (4) Runs Monday only.

Santos Ana Costa - Juquia 2000

Both of these trains are second-class only.

| Dep. Santos Ana Costa | 13:15 | Dep. Juquia | 06:00 |
| Arr. Juquia | 17:43 | Arr. Santos Ana Costa | 10:31 |

Sao Luis A. Guarda - Parauapebas 2005

Both of these trains have a buffet car.

| Dep. Sao Luis A. Guarda | 08:00 (1) | Dep Parauapebas | 08:00 (2) |
| Arr. Parauapebas | 20:20 | Arr. Sao Luis A. Guarda | 20:20 |

(1) Runs Monday, Wednesday and Friday. (2) Runs Tuesday, Thursday and Saturday.

ROUTES IN SOUTHERN BRAZIL

Curitiba - Foz do Iguacu   2130 (Bus)

Dep. Curitiba	13 times a day from 03:00 to 23:30
Arr. Foz do Iguacu	10 hours later

• • •

Dep. Foz do Iguacu	12 times a day from 06:30 to 21:30
Arr.Curitiba	10 hours later

Sao Paulo - Panorama   2015

All of these trains are second-class only.

Dep. Sao Paulo			Dep. Panorama	05:10 (1)	21:15 (1)
(Luz)	08:10 (1)	16:00 (2)	Arr. Sao Paulo		
Arr. Panorama	23:14	07:05	(Luz)	20:09	12:32

(1) Buffet. (2) Light refreshments.

Sao Paulo - Presidente Prudente   2016

All of these trains carry an air-conditioned first-class sleeping car and have a buffet car.

Dep. S. Paulo (B.F.)	16:57 (1)	Dep. Pres. Prudente	19:37 (1)
Arr. Pres. Prudente	09:36	Arr. S. Paulo (B.F.)	11:40

(1) Coach is second-class only.

Sao Paulo - Porto Alegre   Bus   2130

Dep. Sao Paulo	16:30	18:00
Arr. Porto Alegre	10:30	12:00

Sights in **Porto Alegre**: A marvelous modern seaport city, at the junction of 5 rivers. The environment here is very Germanic. See: Farroupilha Park. The Zoological Gardens. The Julio de Castilhos Museum. Rua dos Andradas, a strolling street.

Dep. Porto Alegre	14:00	23:00	20:30	22:00
Arr. Sao Paulo	08:00	17:00	14:30	16:00

(1) Supplement charged.

Santa Maria - Porto Alegre   2021

Both of these trains have a restaurant car.

Dep. Santa Maria	08:30 (1)	Dep. Porto Alegre (Pestana)	08:20 (2)
Arr. Porto Alegre (Pestana)	17:50	Arr. Santa Maria	19:30 (3)

(1) Runs Saturday only. (2) Runs Friday only. (3) Estimated.

BRAZIL'S MOST SCENIC RAIL TRIPS

Curitiba - Paranagua (originating in Sao Paulo)

This railroad was built in the 19th century to haul coffee and cotton from mountain plantations to the port of Paranagua. It takes 3-4 hours to travel this tortuous 70-mile route. One of the 3 trains that were in service in 1990 carried a modern, air-conditioned coach. One of the others, named Gralha Azul (Blue Chatterbox), is more desirable because its windows are open, allowing passengers to lean out and photograph waterfalls, villages and wildflowers.

On the spectacular ride from Curitiba to the coastal town of Paranagua, the train descends from 3,000 feet to sea level. Along the way, there is great mountain, canyon, waterfall and jungle scenery. A one-way ticket in recent years was $3.50.

As the schedules below indicate, a same-day roundtrip Curitiba-Paranagua-Curitiba is easy.

Bus 2130
Dep. Sao Paulo	Frequent times.	
Arr. Curitiba	6 hours later.	

Change to train. 2022
Dep. Curitiba	07:00 (1)	08:30 (1)
Arr. Paranagua	10:50	11:45

• • •

Dep. Paranagua	15:30 (1)	16:30 (1)
Arr. Curitiba	18:30	20:20

Change to bus. 2130
Dep. Curitiba	Frequent times.	
Arr. Sao Paulo	6 hours later.	

(1) Runs daily, except Tuesday and Thursday. Second class only.

Sights in **Curitiba**: This is Brazil's melting-pot: Italian, Polish, German, Slav, Japanese and Syrian settlers galore. See: The Cathedral, patterned after the one in Barcelona. The

Civic Center. The tropical fish collection at the Aquarium in Passeio Publico, a public park in the center of the city. The Coronel David Carneiro Museum. The Paranaense Museum, in the old city hall.

Trips to **Iguacu Falls** originate from here. It has been calculated that 500,000 gallons of water crash every second (30,000,000 gallons every minute!) over the 1½-mile long line of 275 separate waterfalls.

The roar can be be heard 5 miles away. The perpetual mist creates constant rainbows.

Because most of the falls are on the Argentine side, the best views are from the Brazilian side. There are hotels on both sides of the falls, and there are inexpensive airplane flights that circle the falls several times and also take passengers 12 miles below the falls to where the Iguacu and Upper Parana rivers meet…and also to Itaipu Dam – more than 620 feet high and about 7 miles long and to the 550-square-mile lake that was created by the dam.

These rivers form the borders of Brazil, Argentina and Paraguay in this area. Local bus and ferry services connect all of the tourist centers that surround the falls: Brazil (**Foz do Iguacu** and **Porto Meira**), Argentina (**Puerto Iguazu** and **Puerto Canoas**), Paraguay (**Puerto Strossner** and **Puerto Pointe France**).

Sights in **Paranagua**: Much of Brazil's coffee is shipped from this seaport. See: The Museum of Archaeology and Popular Art in the wonderful Colegio dos Jesuitas building. The fascinating market near the waterfront. The Church of Sao Benedito. The 17th century fountain. Nearby, the Nossa Senhora do Rocio shrine. Take the one-hour boat trip to see the 18th century Nossa Senhora dos Orazeres Prazeres fort. Shop here for crafts. Try the seafood.

Sao Paulo - Santos   2130 (Bus)

One of the rail wonders of the world was experienced before 1986 on the 50-mile trip from Sao Paulo to Santos. At 5 separate locations, the entire train was lifted by wire cables from one elevation to another until the train reached the top of the 2300-foot high Serra do Mar escarpment. Now this trip can be taken by bus.

Dep. Sao Paulo	Frequent times throughout 24 hours.
Arr. Santos	1 hour later.

Sights in **Santos**: A very popular holiday resort and Brazil's most active seaport. Many monuments in the various parks: Praca da Republica, Praca Rui Barbosa, Praca Jose Bonifacio. Night-life activities in the Gonzaga area.

Dep. Santos	Frequent times throughout 24 hours.
Arr. Sao Paulo	1 hour later.

INTERNATIONAL ROUTES
FROM BRAZIL

Rio de Janeiro - Buenos Aires   Bus 2130

Dep. Rio de Janeiro	13:30
Arr. Buenos Aires	07:30 Day 3

Rio de Janeiro - Santiago   Bus 2130

Dep. Rio de Janeiro	18:00 Monday, Wednesday and Friday.
Arr. Santiago	18:00 Day 4

Rio de Janeiro - Sao Paulo - Montevideo   2130 (Bus)

Dep. Rio de Janeiro	Frequent times			
Arr. Sao Paulo (Luz)	6 hours later			
Change buses				
Dep. Sao Paulo	16:30	18:00	14:00 (2)	22:30 (3)
Arr. Porto Alegre	10:30 (1)	12:00 (1)	08:00 (1)	16:30 (3)
Change buses.				
Dep. Porto Alegre	-0-	15:30	20:00	22:00 (5)
Arr. Montevideo	-0-	02:30 (4)	07:00 (4)	08:00 (4)

(1) Day 2 from Sao Paulo. (2) Supplement charged. (3) Direct bus. No bus change in Porto Alegre. (4) Day 2 from Porto Alegre. (5) Runs Monday, Wednesday and Saturday. (6) Day 3 from Sao Paulo.

Sao Paulo - Antofagasta

Although there is a Pocitos–Salta train that runs on Thursday only and arrives the next day, this train requires layingover in Salta for 5 nights to connect with the Salta–Antofagasta bus that runs only on Wednesday night. The most practical mode is to take the daily *bus* Pocitos–Salta. Depart Pocitos Tuesday and arrive Salta Wednesday morning.

For a stay of one night or more in Salta, depart Pocitos the appropriate number of days prior to the Wednesday Salta–Antofagasta bus trip.

1907

Arr. Santa Cruz from Sao Paulo	06:53 (1)	08:15 (4)	20:54 (6)	
(See preceding timetable.)				
Change trains. 1907				
Dep. Santa Cruz	08:00 (2)	10:40 (5)	17:00 (7)	18:00 (8)
Arr. Yacuiba	17:15 (3)	08:35 (3)	07:23 (3)	06:42 (3)
It is 4km (2.5 miles) to Pocitos.				
Change to a bus. 2300				
Dep. Pocitos	14:00 (9)	21:00 (9)	21:30 (9)	23:00 (9)
Arr. Salta	23:30	08:30	09:00	10:30
Change buses.				
Dep. Salta				16:00 (8)
Arr. Antofagasta				10:00 (10)

(1) Arrives Tuesday and Friday. Only the Friday arrival provides same-day connection with the Santa Cruz–Yacuiba train. (2) Supplement charged. First-class only. Restaurant car. Runs Thursday, Friday and Sunday. (3) Day 2 from Santa Cruz. (4) Arrives Wednesday and Saturday. Only the Wednesday arrival provides a same day connection with the Santa Cruz–Yacuiba train. (5) Runs Wednesday and Sunday. (6) Arrives Wednesday, Friday and Sunday. The Wednesday and Sunday arrivals require only a one-night layover in Santa Cruz, and the Friday arrival a 2-night layover. (7) Supplement charged. Runs Monday and Friday. (8) Runs Wednesday only. (9) Runs daily. (10) Day 2 from Salta.

CHILE

Children under 1m.20 tall travel free. Children 1m.20 and taller must pay full fare.

From September to March, first-class train tickets in Chile are difficult to obtain. It is advisable to reserve space far in advance of travel date through a prominent travel agency in Santiago or Antofagasta.

Train service runs from Antofagasta to Puerto Montt, on the shore of the Gulf of Ancud. Feeder lines branch off the main north-south line, eastward to great resorts at **Lake Villarrica**, **Lake Panguipulli**, **Lake Ranco**, **Lake Puyehul** and **Lake Llanquihue**. The Lake District is the area east of the rail line from **Temuco** to Puerto Montt. The connecting point is **Puerto Varas**.

The average width of Chile is a scant 120 miles, ranging from 312 miles at its widest to 56 miles at its narrowest..

Antofagasta

There are many beautiful beaches, parks and plazas in this city.

Arica

Founded 1570 on the site of a pre-Columbian community. Arica belonged to Peru until captured by Chile in 1897. An important transportation hub: Chile's northernmost seaport, an international airport, a rail terminal for trains from Peru and Bolivia, and located on the Pan-American highway.

Santiago

See the Presidential Palace. The view of the city from the terrace of Castillo Gonzalez on Santa Lucia Hill in the center of the city, site of its founding in 1541. A museum, chapel and fountains are on the top of this 226-foot-high hill.

The Popular Arts Museum in Castillo Hidalgo. The 19th century European furnishings and decorations in the Cousino Palace (Dieciocho 438), open daily except Monday 10:00–13:00.

The Cathedral, near Plaza de Armas, with its fine painting of The Last Supper. These churches: Santo Domingo, San Francisco (location of the Colonial Art Museum, open daily except Monday 10:00–13:00), San Augustin, La Merced, Santa Ana, Recoleta Dominica and Recoleta Franciscana.

The foods and souvenirs (saddles, baskets, ceramics, dolls, rugs) in the central market. The collection of both foreign and national art at the National Art Museum in Parque Forestal. The National Library and the Historical Museum, both in the same building at Alameda, between Miraflores and McIver streets.

The Natural History Museum and Modern Art Museum, both in the Quinta Normal. The exhibit of Indian textiles, pottery and funerary masks in the Chilean Museum of Pre-Columbian Art at Bandera 361, open daily except Monday 10:00–18:00.

Take the funicular to the top of San Cristobal Hill (and enjoy tastings at the Wine Museum there) for a spectacular view of Santiago, stopping on the ascent to see the Zoo that is about one-third of the way up.

Valparaiso

See the Beaux Arts Museum. Severin Public Library. The view from Miradero O'Higgins, in Alto del Puerto.

Take the 20-minute ride to the beaches at **Vina del Mar,** called "The Pearl of the Pacific" and "The Garden City." Also in Vina: The Academy and Museum of Fine Arts in the Quinta Vergara, the Naval History Museum, and the Municipal Casino.

Valparaiso - Santiago - Chillan - Cabrero - Concepcion

Marvelous scenery: fertile farms (first colonized by Germans in the early 19th century), snow-capped mountains, shimmering lakes, mile after mile of wildflowers, vineyards and pine forests.

The 3-hour train service Valparaiso–Santiago was replaced in 1987 by 1½-hour bus service after a fire destroyed most of the train cars.

2465 Bus

Dep. Valparaiso (Puerto)	Frequent times from 06:10 to 21:30			
Arr. Santiago (Mapocho)	2 hours later			

Change to train…and to Alameda station.
2430

Dep. Santiago (Alameda)	08:30 (1)	09:15 (2)	13:30 (1)	22:30 (3)
Arr. Chillan	13:32	14:58	18:33	N/A (4)
Arr. Concepcion	17:15	18:50	22:10	07:30

• • •

Dep. Concepcion	08:30 (1)	09:15 (2)	13:00 (1)	22:00 (3)
Dep. Chillan	12:01	12:58	16:32	N/A (4)
Arr. Santiago (Alameda)	17:20	18:40	21:45	07:10

Change to bus…and to Mapocho station
2465

Dep. Santiago (Mapocho)	Several times from 04:05 to 20:30			
Arr. Valparaiso (Puerto)	2 hours later			

(1) Has an air-conditioned "salon" car. Buffet car. (2) Second-class only. Light refreshments. (3) Carries a sleeping car, an air-conditioned "salon" car and a buffet car. (4) Did not stop in Chillan in 1993.

Sights in **Chillan**: The thermal hot springs here have attracted tourists for over 150 years. Skiing (June–October) became popular after a ski lift and hotel here were remodeled in 1984. The top of the chairlift is 8,200 feet above the resort. Of the 6 ski runs, the main slope has a vertical drop of 2,300 feet. A learner's slope drops only 98 feet over a 1,312-foot-long run.

The resort, Termas de Chillan, will pickup visitors at the railstation, airport and bus terminal by prior arrangement.

Crafts in wood, leather and iron, also pottery, ponchos and hats are made and sold here.

Sights in **Concepcion**: The Pedro del Rio Zanartu Museum. The view of the city from Cerro Amarillo. A lovely view from Cerro Caracol of valleys and **Bio-Bio**, Chile's largest river.

Arica - Santiago   Bus 2465

Rail passenger service for this 1,300-mile trip, basically a freight train with limited passenger accommodation, is considered to be so appalling that the state railway refuses to publish information about the journey. Should you still decide to got to Santiago, here is the schedule for the bus trip:

Dep. Arica	09:00 (1)	10:30	18:00	22:00
Arr. Santiago	16:30 (2)	18:00 (2)	01:30 (3)	05:30 (3)

• • •

Dep. Santiago	09:00 (1)	18:00
Arr. Arica	16:30 (2)	01:30 (3)

(1) Runs daily, except Wednesday. (2) Day 2. (3) Day 3.

Antofagasta - Santiago   Bus 2465

All arrivals are on Day 2.

Dep. Antofagasta	06:00	10:45	11:00	15:00	17:00 (1)	18:40 (4)
Arr. Santiago	03:30	08:15	08:30	12:30	14:30	16:10

• • •

Dep. Santiago	09:00 (2)	10:00 (3)	11:00	15:00	18:00	19:00
Arr. Antofagasta	06:30	07:30	08:30	12:30	15:30	16:30

(1) Runs daily except, Wednesday and Sunday. (2) Runs daily, except Wednesday. (3) Runs daily, except Sundays and holidays. (4) Plus other departures from Antofagasta at 19:00, 20:00 (2) and 21:30, arriving Santiago Day 2 at 16:30, 17:30 and 19:00.

Antofagasta - Arica   Bus 2465

Dep. Antofagasta	08:00 (1)	19:00	20:00	21:00
Arr. Arica	20:00	21:00	08:00	09:00

• • •

Dep. Arica	09:00 (2)	10:30	18:00	20:30	21:00	22:00
Arr. Antofagasta	21:00	22:30	06:00	08:30	09:00	10:00

(1) Runs daily, except Thursday. (2) Runs daily, except Wednesday.

Santiago - Puerto Montt   2430

Puerto Montt is the southernmost train terminal in the Western Hemisphere. In late 1990, the trains with sleeping cars had 2-passenger sleeping compartments that were clean, spacious and lined with mahogany—for which the price was $44 (U.S.).

Dep. Santiago (Ala.)	17:45 (1)	19:45 (2)	Dep. Puerto Montt	10:00 (2)	16:30 (1)
Arr. Puerto Montt	14:05	18:30	Arr. Santiago (Ala.)	09:45	12:50

(1) Carries a sleeping car, an air-conditioned "salon" car, and a restaurant car. (2) Second-class only. Restaurant car.

SPECIAL ONE-DAY ANDEAN SCENIC TRAIN TRIP

Valparaiso - Los Andes   2426

Here is an exciting one-day glimpse by train at the overwhelming Andes mountain range.

All of these trains are first-class only.

Dep. Valparaiso	08:45 (1)	18:45 (2)	19:15 (3)
Arr. Los Andes	11:45	21:45	22:15

• • •

Dep. Los Andes	08:15 (1)	12:00 (1)	19:05 (1)
Arr. Valparaiso	11:15	15:00	22:05

(1) Runs Saturdays, Sundays and holidays. (2) Runs Friday and Sunday. (3) Runs Sundays and holidays.

Santiago - Los Andes   Bus 2465

Since 1985, only bus service has been offered between Santiago and the Los Andes resort.

Dep. Santiago	09:00	Dep. Los Andes	15:00
Arr. Los Andes	11:00	Arr. Santiago	17:00

INTERNATIONAL ROUTES
FROM CHILE

Until 1980, there was transcontinental train service all the way, from Valparaiso to Buenos Aires. The Los Andes-Mendoza portion of that rail trip was the most exciting train ride in South America.

Valparaiso (Santiago) - Mendoza - Buenos Aires

Altitudes (in feet) En Route

Ascent		Descent	
Valparaiso	-0-	Tunnel Exit	10,452
Los Andes	2,669	Las Cuevas	10,331
San Pablo	3,174	Puente del Inca	8,915
Salto del Soldado	4,141	Punta de las Vacas	7,852
Rio Blanco	4,764	Zanjon Amarillo	7,236
Guardia Vieja	5,397	Rio Blanco	7,000
El Juncal	7,321	Uspallata	5,741
El Portillo	9,408	Guido	4,957
Caracoles (tunnel entrance)	10,420	Portrerillos	4,443
(The summit is 13,082.)		Cacheuta	4,080
		Blanco Encalda	3,502
		Paso de los Andes	3,069
		Mendoza	2,518

On the trans-Andean train ride that operated until 1980, there were great amounts of snow Los Andes–Mendoza from May to November. It was a steep descent from Portillo (a Winter sports resort) to Las Cuevas, another ski resort. Then, it was a rack railway from Las Cuevas to Puente del Inca. The ride from Puente del Inca to Mendoza was by narrow-gauge, through a scenic valley.

Since 1980, only bus service has been offered to Mendoza.

Valparaiso - Mendoza - Buenos Aires   2465 Bus

Dep. Valparaiso	07:00	07:45	08:00	08:30
Set your watch forward one hour.				
Arr. Mendoza	16:00	16:45	17:00	17:30

ROUTES TO BOLIVIA, BRAZIL AND PERU

There are 4 rail routes from Chile to Bolivia: Santiago-Mendoza and then Mendoza north to Tucuman and then on from there to either La Paz or Santa Cruz; Antofagasta–La Paz; and Arica–La Paz.

The one rail route from Chile to Brazil is from Antofagasta to Sao Paulo.

The bus ride to Peru is Santiago–Arica–Lima.

Mendoza - Tucuman

2465 Bus
Arr. Mendoza
Change buses.
2300

Dep. Mendoza	13:00	14:00 (1)	20:30	21:00
Arr. Tucuman	03:30	04:30	11:00	11:30

(1) Runs Monday and Friday.

Sights in **Tucuman:** At the Plaza Independencia, you'll see the Church of San Francisco, the Cathedral, the Government Palace and the Statue of Liberty. Nearby Tucuman is the beautiful Villa Nouges residential area.

Antofagasta - La Paz

Bus 2465		*Train 1900*	
Dep. Antofagasta	21:30	Dep. Calama	N/A
Arr. Calama	00:30 (1)	Arr. Oruro	00:05 (3)
Change to train.		*Change trains.*	
		Dep. Oruro	05:23(4)
		Arr. La Paz	09:40

(1) Day 2. (2) Runs Saturday only. Second-class only. (3) Arrivies Sunday. (4) Supplement charged. Runs Wednesady and Saturday only.

It is easy to understand why this train trip of 705 miles takes 36 hours. The first 18 miles out of Antofagasta, there is an ascent of 1,800 feet as the route crosses the **Atacama Desert**. In the next 211 miles, the train climbs to the summit of the Chilean section of the ride: 13,000 feet above sea level, at **Ascotan**.

There is generally a 3 to 4-hour wait at **Ollague** (the Chile-Bolivia border) while Bolivian customs officers go through the train to check passports and inspect baggage.

One of the most unusual sights on this trip occurs on the second day, just before reaching **Poopo**. Thousands of flamingos can be seen on a lake that is 12,000 feet above sea level.

Arica - Charana - La Paz   1901

There are 30 miles of rack and pinion track during this 270-mile rail trip. During the first 70 miles after departing Arica, the track climbs from sea level to 11,000 feet. The scenery on this stretch is a jumble of brown lava rocks. The highest place on this route is 14,000 feet, at **General Lagos**. The Bolivian border is only 5 minutes from Charana, at Visviri, where the passport control procedure takes more than one hour. Many herds of llamas roam here. Because military installations are nearby, photo-taking is not permitted at the frontier area.

The best scenery is during the last portion of the trip, on the 1,000-foot *descent* into the highest capital in the world. La Paz is nearly 12,000 feet above sea level. During the last 6 miles, a series of loops traveled very slowly, there is excellent scenery of 3 tremendous Andean peaks: Illampu (21,490 feet), Illimani (21,315 feet) and Huayna–Potosi (20,407 feet) if there are no clouds or fog.

Dep. Arica	09:30 (1)			Dep. La Paz	07:00 (5)	22:00 (6)
Arr. Charana	15:35 (1)			Arr. Charana	-0- (5)	05:55 (3)
Change trains.				*Change trains.*		
Dep. Charana	15:35	09:10 (4)		Dep. Charana	11:17	11:17 (7)
Arr. La Paz	20:04	18:40		Arr. Arica	22:30	18:00

(1) Runs Tuesday and Saturday. Direct train. No train change in Charana. Has first-class coaches. Restaurant car. (3) Arrives Wednesday. (4) Runs Wednesday only. Second-class only. (5) Runs Monday and Friday. Supplement charged. Direct train. No train change in Charana. Has first-class coaches. Restaurant car. (6) Runs Tuesday only. Second-class only.

Antofagasta - Salta - Yacuiba - Bauru - Sao Paulo

2465 Bus				*1907 Train*		
Dep. Antofagasta	15:00 (1)			Dep. Santa Cruz	13:30 (8)	18:00 (10)
Arr. Salta	09:00 (2)			Arr. P. Suarez	06:45 (9)	05:49 (9)
Change to train.				*It is 11km (7 miles) to Corumba.*		
2261						
Dep. Salta	N/A (3)			*Change trains.*		
Arr. Yacuiba	N/A (4)			*2011*		
Change trains.				Dep. Corumba	N/A (11)	N/A (11)
1907				Arr. Bauru	N/A (12)	N/A (12)
Dep. Yacuiba	16:00 (5)	21:00 (7)				
Arr. Santa Cruz	05:38 (6)	06:08 (6)				
Change trains.						

(1) Runs Wednesday and Saturday. (2) Day 2 from Antofagasta (Thursday and Sunday). (3) This route was among the casualties of Argentina's 1993 reduction of passenger train service. (4) Twenty hours after derparting Salta. (5) Supplement charged. Runs Thursday only. (6) Day 2 from Yacuiba. (7) First-class only. Supplement charged. Runs Thursday, Saturday and Sunday. Restaurant car. (8) Supplement charged. Runs Wednesday and Sunday. Restaurant car. (9) Day 2 from Santa Cruz. (10) Supplement charged. Runs Tuesday, Thursday and Saturday. Buffet. (11) The Campo Grande-Bauru portion of the Corumba-Bauru route was among the casualties of Brazil's 1993 reduction of passenger train service. (12) Day 2 from Corumba.

All of these trains run daily.

2015

Dep. Bauru	04:49 (1)	06:41 (1)	12:42 (1)	23:55 (2)
Arr. Sao Paulo (Luz)	12:32	14:56	20:09	07:20

(1) Second-class only. Buffet. (2) Carries a sleeping car. Coach is first-class only. Buffet.

PARAGUAY

Children under 3 travel free. Half-fare for children 3–9. Children 10 and over must pay full fare.

All of the locomotives here are steam, and most of them were built before 1914.

Paraguay's only rail routes are from Asuncion to Encarnacion and San Salvador to Abai. Its only passenger train service to an adjacent country is the extension from Encarnacion to Argentina.

Asuncion

The capital of Paraguay. Linked by rail (via Encarnacion) with Buenos Aires. Most of the sights can be seen by starting at the Customs House and going from it down Calle El Paraguayo Independiente. You will first come to Government Palace, styled after the Louvre in Paris.

Next, the Congressional Palace on Plaza Constitucion. During the legislature's April-December session, the public is allowed to observe the debates there. The 19th century Cathedral is on the same Plaza. Two blocks away, on Calle Chile, is the Pantheon of Heroes, the national shrine designed to emulate the Invalides in Paris.

See the Gran Hotel del Paraguay. The view of Asuncion from Parque Carlos Antonio Lopez. Window-shop on Calle Palma. Take a ride on one of the old trolleys, maintained for tourists as are those in San Francisco, CA.

It is a 45-minute train or bus ride to nearby **Trinidad,** where a Botanical Garden, a Museum of Natural History and a pathetic Zoo are located. Eighteen miles east by road is **Itaugua,** famous for the "spiderweb" lace made there, called *nanduti.*

Encarnacion

A busy port on the Alto Parana River. Posadas, on the Argentine side of the river, is a base for taking auto or airplane trips to see the **Iguazu Falls**, most spectacular from August to November. See notes about the falls under "Curitiba." Local bus and ferry services connect both of the tourist centers surrounding the falls: **Puerto Strossner** and **Foz de Iguacu**.

Asuncion - Foz do Iguaco   Bus 2250

Dep. Asuncion	00:15	02:00 (1)	07:00	11:00	12:00
Arr. Puerto Strossner	05:05	06:50	11:50	15:50	16:50
Arr. Foz do Iguacu	05:45	07:30	12:30	16:30	17:30

• • •

Dep. Foz do Iguacu	07:00	11:00	12:30	14:30	20:00 (1)
Dep. Puerto Strossner	07:40	11:40	13:10	15:10	20:40
Arr. Asuncion	12:30	16:30	18:00	20:00	01:30

(1) Supplement charged.

Asuncion - San Salvador - Encarnacion - Posadas - Buenos Aires

The 40-hour Asuncion-Buenos Aires trip is a very rough ride, 930 miles through dense brush and jungle. The inconveniences include hard wood seats, stifling heat, swarms of mosquitoes and much dust. The locomotive was built in 1912, and the train is said to be the oldest in South America.

At night, from Asuncion to Encarnacion, the station platforms at villages along the route are lined with people who enjoy watching the trains pass by while sitting at tables, eating and singing.

The Posadas-Buenos Aires route was one of the many casualties of Argentina's 1993 reduction of passenger train service.

2230			2260	
Dep. Asuncion	18:00	Friday	Dep. Posadas	N/A (1)
Dep. San Salvador	01:01	Saturday	Arr. Buenos Aires	
Arr. Encarnacion	09:30		(F. Lacroze)	N/A (2)
Arr. Posadas	12:00			
Change trains.				

(1) Service suspended since 1993. (2) Day 2 from Posadas.

PERU

Children under 4 travel free. Half-fare for children 4–11. Children 12 and over must pay full fare.

Many rail routes in Peru are at such high altitudes that several trains provide passengers with free oxygen. Details on trips follow a description of interesting sights in 6 cities which can be visited by train.

Buffet-Class is far superior to first and second-class cars, which are dominated by animals (on the seats, below them, and on overhead racks).

Demand for Buffet Class (which includes breakfast and lunch served to passengers at their seats) is limited and in great demand. Reservations can be made only from 09:00 to 11:00 on the morning prior to the trip day.

Arequipa

This is called "The White City" because it is built mostly of white volcanic rock. It lies at the foot of 19,200-foot high El Misti Volcano. See: the beautiful furniture in the 17th century Santa Cataline Convent, reflecting medieval architecture and life. The flowery Plaza de Armas. The colonial residences: Casa del Moral, Casa Ricketts and Casa Gibbs. Leatherwork is a specialty here. At an altitude of 7,500 feet, much lower than Cuzco, Arequipa has a splendid climate.

Cuzco

The oldest continually inhabited city in the Americas, dating from either the 10th or 11th century. November to March is the rainy season. This is the popular tourist spot in Peru the rest of the year. At 11,400 feet altitude, it is often cold here in what was once the capital of the Inca Empire. A tea made from leaves of the coca plant is usually helpful for relieving altitude sickness.

There are many Inca remains in this area. See: the famous stone of Twelve Angles, in the walls of the Palace of Inca Roca. Main Square, where Incas held their celebrations and ceremonies.

Stroll Callejon Loreto, a perfectly preserved Inca street. Visit the unusually quiet Indian market. The base of the ancient Temple of the Sun, now in the foundation of the Church of Santa Domingo. The gold and bejeweled pulpit, also the nearly 400 paintings from the Cuzco school, in the 17th century Cathedral. The House of the Chosen Women, now the Convent of Santa Catalina. Five colonial churchs are interesting: El Triunfo, La Merced, Santa Domingo, Jesuite, and Jesus and Maria.

Also see the excellent murals, carved altars and paintings in La Compania de Jesus, Cuzco's most beautiful church. The magnificent main altar in Belen de los Reyes Church, outside the city. The Inca stonework throughout the city's streets. The prominent colonial residences: La Casa de Garcilaso de la Vega Inca, La Casa de los Marqueses de Buenavista, La Casa de Diego Maldonado, and La Casa de Concha.

The museums: Art, Anthropological and Archaeological, Culture, Larco Herrera, and

Viceregal. Nearby is an ancient fort: Puca Pucara (the "red fort").

Take a taxi 12 miles to **Pisac**, an Inca complex so vast that it takes more than a week to explore it completely. The Sunday market there is an outstanding event.

En route to Pisac, stop one mile from Cuzco at the enormous Sacayhuaman (pronounced "sexy woman") with its 3 tremendous parallel walls. Some of its stones weigh an estimated 300 tons each and were placed without mortar so precisely that a knife blade cannot be wedged between them. Stand at the edge of the cliff there for a splendid view of Cuzco, below.

Also stop a few minutes at **Tambo Machay**, the Inca Baths. See the ruins of **Quenko**, **Tambomachay** and **Pucara**. The great excursion from Cuzco is the trip to Machu–Picchu, the large ancient Inca city-fortress.

Huancayo

Located where an Inca highway once existed, in a wide valley at 10,696 feet altitude. Sunday fairs is the event that attracts tourists here (herbs, fruits, embroidered skirts and petticoats, vegetables, furs, silver jewelry, gourds, etc.). This is the most famous market in Peru, attracting both Peruvian and Bolivian Indians.

Juliaca

Great woolen goods, leather items and alpaca knits are offered in the Sunday and Monday markets in the enormous Plaza Melgar.

Lima

Shopping for silver and gold jewelry, alpaca and llama furs, and colonial antiques is a key tourist activity in Lima.

See much fine 16th and 17th century colonial architecture. Torre Tagle Palace and these churches: Santa Domingo (one block west of Government Palace), La Merced (on Jiron de la Union, 2 blocks from Plaza de Armas), San Francisco (one block east of Government Palace), San Augustin (2 blocks from Plaza de Armas), and San Pedro (2 blocks east and one block south of Plaza de Armas).

The curved mahogany ceiling in the main hall at the Court of the Inquisition. The city's famous bullring. Plaza San Martin, a lovely park. The centuries-old, 15-minute ritual of Changing of the Guard at Government Palace, daily except Sunday at 13:00.

The Museum of Art (5,000 years of Peruvian culture) in the 1868 Exposition Palace on Paseo Colon. Pre-Hispanic relics (back to 500 B.C.) in the Museum of Anthropology and Archaeology, and the adjoining Museum of the Republic, both at Plaza Bolivar. The Museum of Peruvian Culture at 650 Alfonso Ugarte Ave.

Colonial paintings, furniture and costumes in the Museum of Vice-royalty in the Quinta de Presa mansion. The Museum of Italian Art on Paseo de la Republica. The gold and silver collection at the Rafael Larco Herrera Museum. The mosaic tiles at **La Punta**, along the beach. The Military Museum at Fort Felipe Real. Shop for alpaca fur coats and silver filigree.

The most ornately decorated colonial churches here are San Francisco and Santo Domingo. The cavernous cathedral is plainer than them, and disappointing. There is good surfing at the nearby **Herradura**, **Punta Hermosa** and **Ponta Rocas** suburbs.

See the fantastic gold and silver items in the Gold Museum at **Monterrico**, another suburb.

Puno (and Lake Titicaca)

It is cold and windy here, at 12,648 feet. The legend is that the Sun God created the first Inca king and his queen on the Island of the Sun in Lake Titicaca, on Peru's western border with Bolivia.

Today, 37-pound trout are the monarchs of a lake that is more than 2 miles above sea level, 35 miles wide and 95 miles long. There are many hydrofoil boat excursions to small "floating islands" of reeds, populated by Uru Indians.

Lima - Huancayo   1802 + PTO Timtable

Even in Peruvian Summer (January, February, March), the weather on this trip is very cold. Pickpockets and bag-slashers are a menace on this trip.

For an optimum experience, depart Lima on Saturday morning, spend that night in Huancayo, see the weekly Indian market there on Sunday (silver, llama wool blankets, hides, etc.), and return to Lima on Monday morning.

The Lima–La Oroya portion of this train journey is the highest standard gauge rail trip in the world (built in 1893 and reaching a height of 15,681 feet at **Calera**, the world's highest railstation) and carries a staff doctor. The descent to 10,696-foot high Huancayo becomes a relief ! The altitude is so debilitating that most passengers sleep or take oxygen inhalation.

WARNING! There are usually long lines for the tickets that cannot be purchased until the day of travel. Seating in the first-class buffet car requires reservation. Many passengers in the regular first-class and second-class coach cars have to stand. It is advisable to get tickets and reservations through a Peruvian travel agency in Lima. The 1995 adult prices were: $14 (U.S.) for Buffet Class and $12 for first-class. Children's fares were $8 and $6. A breakfast of sandwiches and coffee or tea is served in the first-class buffet car soon after departing Lima.

A breakfast of sandwiches and coffee or tea is served in the first-class buffet car soon after departing Lima.

Not shown in Cook's timetable, the first stop out of Lima is the former resort, **San Bartolome** (5,000 feet altitude). Fruit sellers go through the train there during the period that the locomotive is moved to the rear of the train so as to maneuver the first of 20 switchbacks that enable the train to zig-zag 2,000 feet up the mountain in 17 minutes.

At the early part of the trip is **Chosica**, a popular Winter resort. Then, the train goes through scenic valleys and passes by Indian farmhouses and rustic railstations where Indian women sell fruits and flowers. The track follows the **Rimac River** as it crosses 59 bridges, goes through 66 tunnels and makes 22 switchbacks. The "descent" into Huancayo is along small wheat farms.

At **Rio Blanco** (11,400 feet), the train doctor leaves the "downhill" Huancayo-Lima train to board the Lima-Huancayo train. Service of a tasty, hot lunch, then begins.

Cuzco to Machu-Picchu and Inca City　PTO timetable

One of the most popular train journeys in Peru is from Cuzco to Machu-Picchu, paralleling the turbulent **Urubamba River**. The 5,000-foot descent from Cuzco through the verdant jungle is considered by many as one of the most scenic rail trips in the world. The other attraction, of course, is seeing the incredible 15th century Inca ruins at **Machu Picchu**, an 8,000-foot high plateau surrounded by snow-covered mountains, unknown until discovered in the early 20th century by Hiram Bingham, a Yale University professor.

In his book "The Lost City of the Incas," Bingham wrote: "I know of no other place in the world that can compare to this sight."

Reserve a window seat on the left going to Machu Picchu, and on the right for the return ride (and be sure it is the seat that faces forward) overlooking the Urubama River. A cart comes through the train with coffee, tea, gingerale and cookies.

At a village called **Purchoi** (not shown on Cooks Timetable), large-kerneled sweet corn can be purchased. Watch in this area for coveys of green parrots. In the Urubama Valley, you will see hundreds of Inca-built terraces still being farmed. The train goes through dense jungles.

At some train stops, native women go through the train, selling tortillas. En route, the train goes through a fertile valley at **Ollantaytambo**.

The ruins, called **Inca City,** are open daily 06:30–17:00. It is estimated that 500-1,000 people lived here in about 250 houses made of rock and clay mortar.

The buses that provide transportation 5 miles from the **Puente Ruinas** railstation 1,000 feet up to Inca City have been inadequate for many years, and some tourists have to wait unsheltered as long as 2 hours (sometimes in heavy rain). In such frequent instances, visitors don't reach the ruins until noon and have only 90 minutes for exploring there — far too little time.

Because of this chronic problem, it is highly advisable to reserve at least 3 months in advance of arrival a room at the 25-room Machu-Pichu Pueblo Hotel, near the Puente Ruinas railstation. That way, the entire afternoon on arrival day can be used to visit the ruins, before returning to Cuzco the next day.

Reservations can be made the day before travel and are essential. A roundtrip in 1993 cost $69 (U.S.), including the 25-minute bus service for the 5-mile ascent from Puente Ruinas to Inca City, plus admission to the ruins.

Dep. Cuzco (S.Pedro)	06:00 (1)	12:45 (2)
Dep. Machu-Picchu	10:23	-0-
Arr. Puente Ruinas	10:30	16:00

•　•　•

Dep. Puente Ruinas	07:15 (1)	14:40 (2)	04:50 (1)
Dep. Machu-Picchu	07:30	14:50	- 0 -
Arr. Cuzco (S.Pedro)	13:40	21:25	09:00

(1) Has a parlor car and a first-class coach. (2) First-class only.

Juliaca - Arequipa 1804 + PTO Timetable

The train passes along many grain fields. Highest place on the route is 14,688-feet high **Crucero Alto**. After it, all water flows toward the Pacific Ocean.

Many tall mountains can be seen as well as grazing vicunas, sheep, llamas and alpacas. The train descends in 189 miles from Juliaca (12,500 feet) to Arequipa (7,500 feet).

All of these trains have a restaurant car or buffet.

| Dep. Juliaca | 20:50 (1) |
| Arr. Arequipa | 06:00 |

| Dep. Arequipa | 21:00 (2) |
| Arr. Juliaca | 06:55 |

(1) Runs Monday, Thursday and Saturday. (2) Runs Wednesday, Friday and Sunday.

INTERNATIONAL ROUTES
FROM PERU

Rail + Boat connection was available prior to 1985 from both Cuzco and Arequipa to Bolivia. Puno, on the shore of Lake Titicaca, is 12,648 feet high.

The extremely scenic Cuzco-Juliaca route along the heights of the Andes is close to the main, centuries-old Inca highway, which required a month by foot. At the Juliaca railstation, Indian women sell colorful knitted garments.

The train reaches an altitude of 14,000 feet at **La Raya** (not shown in Cook's timetable). After going downhill to the lush **Vilcanota River Valley**, it ascends to a bleak mesa and then plunges down the other side of the Andes to Puno.

A first-class roundtrip ticket in 1995 was only $34 (U.S.) for this 11-hour, 232-mile train trip.

Cuzco-Juliaca-Puno 1800	**Arequipa-Juliaca-Puno** 1804
Dep. Cuzco 07:00 (1)	Dep. Arequipa 21:00 (2)
Arr. Juliaca 16:40	Dep. Juliaca 06:55 (2)
Arr. Puno 18:00	Arr. Puno 08:00 (2)

(1) Runs Monday, Thursday and Saturday. (2) Runs Wednesday, Friday and Sunday.

URUGUAY

Almost all passenger train service in Uruguay was suspended in November, 1987. Children under 3 travel free. Half-fare for children 3–9. Children 10 and over must pay full fare.

Montevideo was the hub for Uruguay's 1,874 miles of rail service. The 4 lines from there went to Colonia, Mercedes, Rio Branco and Rivera. A branch off the line to Rivera led to Salto and Artigas.

Colonia

See the Municipal Museum. The Mansion of the Viceroy. The beautiful plaza. The Parochial Church.

Montevideo

Peak tourist season here is January and February. The major attraction is the city's big beaches. See the enormous marble Legislative Palace. The National Historical Museum (Rincom 437). Plaza Independencia and the nearby Natural History Museum (Buenos Aires 652). The large lake and National Fine Arts Museum in Rodo Park.

The Oceanography and Fish Museum (Rambla Republica de Chile 4215). The Zoo on Avenida de Rivera. The Military Museum (Montevideo Hill), and the view from there. The Pre-Columbian Museum (Mateo Vidal 3249). The collection of paintings and sculptures at the Joaquin Torres Garcia Museum (Constitujente 1467). The outstanding Rose Garden (850 varieties) and Municipal Museum of Fine Arts and History, both in El Prado Park. The Sunday morning flea market on Calle Tristen Narvaja, across from the University's statue of David.

The many fine statues in Batlle y Ordonez Park. The Cathedral, on Plaza Constitucion. Stroll down Avenida 18 de Julio. East of Plaza Zabala, see the Customs House, the Bolsa (Stock Exchange) and Banco de la Republica. Lunch at the stand-up bars (barbecued meats, fruits, soups, sandwiches, fish) at Mercado del Puerto, at the waterfront. Then walk to the breakwater at Punta Santa Teresa to see ships coming into port, or walk along the beaches bordered by Rio de Plata

The nearby **Punta del Este beach** resort, during the peak season (mid- December to mid-March). The Casa Pueblo Museum, featuring the work of Uruguayan painter Carlos Paez Vilaro, the Picasso of South America. Night life centers at the local gambling casino. Stroll Avenida Gorlero to see its antique shops, notable for American and European Art Nouveau items from the early years of this century. Take a boat to **Isla de Lobos** to see the seal colony there.

Rivera

See: Canapiru Dam. Plaza Internacional. Stroll the street which is the border with Brazil. On the other side of the street is the Brazilian city **Santta Ana do Livramento.**

Salto

See: Solari Park and don't miss the walkway along the Uruguay River.

INTERNATIONAL ROUTES
FROM URUGUAY

Montevideo - Buenos Aires   2211

Bus

Dep. Montevideo	03:15	04:30	06:15	07:30	09:15
Arr. Colonia	06:00	06:40	09:00	09:40	12:00
Change to hydrofoil.					
Dep. Colonia	06:20	07:00	09:20	10:00	12:20
Arr. Buenos Aires	One hour later				

Bus

Dep. Montevideo	11:00 (1)	13:15	14:00	16:15	17:00
Arr. Colonia	13:10	16:00	16:10	19:00	19:10
Change to hydrofoil.					
Dep. Colonia	13:30	16:20	16:30	19:20	19:30
Arr. Buenos Aires	One hour later				

(1) Runs Monday, Friday and Saturday.

Montevideo - Porto Alegre - Sao Paulo   Bus

2220

Dep. Montevideo	08:00 (1)	22:00	22:30
Arr. Porto Alegre	07:00	09:00	09:30
Change buses.			
2130			
Dep. Porto Alegre	14:00	20:30	22:00
Arr. Sao Paulo	08:00	14:30	16:00

(1) Runs Wednesday, Friday and Sunday.

VENEZUELA

Children under 3 travel free. Half-fare for children 3–11. Children 12 and over must pay full fare.

There is no train service between Venezuela and adjacent countries. The only rail service for which timetables are available is the 105-mile route from Puerto Cabello to Barquisimeto.

Puerto Cabello - Barquisimeto   1650

These trains run only Saturdays, Sundays and holidays.

Dep. Puerto Cabello	06:00	16:00
Arr. Barquisimeto	08:45	18:45

• • •

Dep. Barquisimeto	06:00	16:00
Arr. Puerto Cabello	08:45	18:45

Sights in **Puerto Cabello**: A heavily industrialized city.

Sights in **Barquisimeto**: A collecting point for sugar, cacao, cereals, coffee and cattle.

CHAPTER 17

EURAIL GUIDE ROUTE CHART

In view of the fact that there are over 100,000 miles of railroad lines in just the 17 Eurailpass countries, it would be impossible to list every conceivable trip one could make by train in Europe. We do provide you in this chapter a list of 734 trips that most people touring Europe might make, showing the travel time and one-way first-class fare for each.

The list of ticket prices enables our readers to (a) compute the cost of ordinary tickets for an itinerary and (b) compare that total cost with one or a combination of the train passes described in Eurail Guide.

We have condensed route descriptions by listing them only in alphabetical priority. For example, the first route is Alborg to Copenhagen. If you were looking for the trip from Copenhagen to Alborg, you would refer to the name that has alphabetical priority: Alborg. Similarly, the trip Rome-Paris will be found as Paris-Rome, etc.

The rates listed are first-class fares, in U.S. dollars. To compute second-class fares, figure 66% of the first-class fare shown. While this will not always be the exact second-class fare, it will be very close to it.

Also remember that European train fares, like the prices of all other European goods and services, are subject to change relative to the exchange rates for U.S. dollars and other non-European currencies.

On the other hand, once a Eurailpass, France Railpass, German Railpass, or any other train pass has been issued to you, you are protected from the devaluation of your currency increasing the cost of your train transportation — another hidden plus to having a pass.

All the fares listed in this chapter are subject to a seat reservation fee of $3 (U.S.) per person (if you want to be sure of having a seat). This is a charge whether traveling with a ticket or with Eurailpass. However, a Eurailpass holder does not have to pay this *supplement* when riding on some EuroCity or TGV trains (savings range from $3 to $8).

Keep in mind that on trips which involve both a Eurailpass country and also a country not covered by Eurailpass such as Vienna-Athens (via non-Eurailpas Yugoslavia), the passenger holding a Eurailpass has to purchase a ticket for the non-Eurailpass portion of that trip.

Note: Because Paris has 6 different railstations, we indicate in parenthesis the name of the Paris railstation at which a train is departing or arriving.

EURAIL GUIDE ROUTE CHART

1996 first-class train fares, *not* including seat reservation fee.

	Travel Time	Fare
ALBORG		
Copenhagen	6½	66.00
ALGECIRAS		
Cordoba	4½	33.00
Granada	5	31.00
Madrid	11½	79.00
Malaga	4	27.00
Seville	6	38.00
ALICANTE		
Valencia	2	21.00
ALKMAAR		
Amsterdam	½	11.00
AMSTERDAM		
Antwerp	2½	43.00
Basel (via Roosendaal)	9½	156.00
Berlin	8½	147.00
Bremen	4	94.00
Brussels	3½	53.00
Cologne (Koln)	3	59.00
Copenhagen (Kobenhavn)	13	232.00
Dusseldorf	2½	59.00
Frankfurt	6	132.00
Hamburg	6	126.00
Hannover	5½	98.00
Heidelberg	6½	147.00
Hoek Van Holland	2	27.00

Luxembourg (via Roosendaal)	5	87.00
Milan	15½	338.00
Munich (Munchen)	8½	251.00
Paris (Nord)	5½	113.00
Rome	21	412.00
Rotterdam	1	21.00
Salzburg	10	293.00
Utrecht	½	11.00
Vienna (Wien)		
(via Passau)	15	306.00
Wiesbaden	6	124.00
Zurich	11	273.00

ANDALSNES

Oslo	7	97.00

ANDERMATT

Brig	2	50.00
Chur	2½	45.00
Luzern	2	55.00
Zurich	2	71 .00

ANTWERP

Brussels	1	11.00
Paris (Nord)	3½	72.00
Rotterdam	1½	24.00

AOSTA

Milan	3½	27.00
Turin (Torino)	1½	18.00

ARHUS

Copenhagen (Kobenhavn)	4½	48.00

AROSA

Chur	1	16.00
Zurich	3	71.00

ASSISI

Florence (Firenze)	3	24.00
Rome	2½	24.00

ATHENS

Patras	3	37.00
Thessaloniki	9	74.00

AVIGNON

Barcelona	6½	79.00
Cannes	3	66.00
Carcassonne	2½	58.00
Geneva	3½	73.00
Lourdes	7	91.00
Lyon	1½	53.00
Marseille	1	35.00
Nice	4	71.00
Paris (Lyon)	3	114.00
Port Bou	4	64.00

BADEN-BADEN

Basel	2	45.00

BARCELONA

Bilboa	9½	77.00
Carcassonne	6	58.00
Geneva	9½	134.00
Genoa	13½	148.00
Lourdes	9	98.00
Lyon	7	111.00
Madrid	7	77.00
Marseille	6½	91.00
Nice	9	121.00
Paris (Austerlitz)	11½	165.00

Rome	20	209.00
Seville	13	103.00
Toulouse (Via Port Bou)	7	73.00
Valencia	4	40.00
Vigo	18¼	118.00
Zaragoza	3½	42.00

BARI
Bologna	7½	76.00
Brindisi	1½	16.00
Messina	9	76.00
Milan	10	106.00
Naples	4	39.00
Pescara	3½	36.00
Rome	6	65.00
Taranto	1½	16.00
Turin (Torino)	13	118.00
Venice	13	94.00

BASEL
Bern	1	40.00
Brig	3	93.00
Brussels	7	107.00
Bucharest (Partly covered by Eurailpass)	29	353.00
Budapest	16	234.00
Cologne (Koln)	5	147.00
Copenhagen (Kobenhavn)	13	367.00
Florence (Firenze)	10	161.00
Frankfurt	3	113.00
Geneva	3½	100.00
Genoa	9	140.00
Hamburg	6½	266.00
Hannover	5½	220.00
Heidelberg	2½	84.00
Innsbruck	6	99.00
Interlaken	2½	64.00
Lausanne	2½	67.00
Locarno	4½	110.00
Luxembourg	4	70.00
Luzern	1½	43.00

Milan	6	121.00
Montreux	3	85.00
Paris (Est)	5	75.00
Rome	13	195.00
Rotterdam (via Brussels)	8½	137.00
Salzburg	9	152.00
Strasbourg	1	33.00
Venice	10	152.00
Vienna (Wien)	12	184.00
Wiesbaden	3½	101.00
Zurich	1	50.00

BAYONNE

Madrid	6½	81.00
Paris	4½	134.00

BAYREUTH

Nurnberg	1	26.00

BERGEN

Bodo	26½	262.00
Flam	3½	56.00
Goteborg	12	192.00
Myrdal	2½	38.00
Oslo	7	115.00
Trondheim	14½	184.00
Voss	1½	26.00

BERLIN

Bremen	5	113.00
Brussels	10	210.00
Cologne (Koln)	7	161.00
Copenhagen (Kobenhavn)	12	155.00
Dusseldorf	5½	156.00
Frankfurt/Main (via Erfurt)	6	146.00
Hamburg	3	81.00
Hannover	3½	79.00
Leipzig	2	45.00
Luxembourg	11	227.00
Malmo	9½	114.00
Munich (Munchen) (via Leipzig)	9	186.00

Nurnburg	6	131.00
Oslo	19½	253.00
Paris (Nord)	11	262.00
Rotterdam	10	171.00
Stockholm	17	214.00
Vienna (Wien) (Sudbf.) via Prague	14	143.00

BERN

Brig	2	65.00
Geneva	2	71.00
Interlaken	1	34.00
Lausanne	1	43.00
Lugano	4½	106.00
Luzern	1½	45.00
Milan	4½	89.00
Montreux	3½	78.00
Paris (Lyon) via Verrieres	5	124.00
Zurich	1½	69.00

BILBAO

Hendaye	4¼	31.00
Madrid	6	61.00
Vigo	14½	84.00
Zaragoza	4½	38.00

BODEN

Haparanda	2	41.00
Narvik	7	102.00
Stockholm	16	144.00

BODO

Goteborg	24½	275.00
Oslo	19	213.00
Trondheim	11½	154.00

BOLOGNA

Florence (Firenze)	1½	12.00

Genoa	4½	36.00
Innsbruck	6½	56.00
Milan	2½	27.00
Naples	6½	76.00
Paris (Lyon)	10	212.00
Ravenna	1½	11.00
Rimini	1½	16.00
Rome	3¼	54.00
Turin (Torino)	4½	42.00
Venice	2	21.00
Verona	1½	16.00

BONN

Cologne (Koln)	½	10.00
Frankfurt (Main)	2	52.00
Koblenz	1	16.00

BORDEAUX

Geneva	10	128.00
Hendaye	2¼	51.00
Lourdes	3½	56.00
Lyon	7½	108.00
Marseille	5½	113.00
Nice	8	140.00
Paris (Austerlitz)	3	111.00
Toulouse	2	55.00
Tours	3	70.00

BREMEN

Budapest	19½	341.00
Cologne (Koln)	3	93.00
Copenhagen (Kobenhavn)	6½	139.00
Dusseldorf	3	82.00
Essen	2½	71.00
Frankfurt/Main	3¼	166.00
Hamburg	1	33.00
Hannover	1	42.00
Heidelberg	5½	182.00
Munich (Munchen)	6	229.00
Stuttgart	5	218.00

Vienna (Wien)	9	295.00
BRIG		
Chur	4½	102.00
Interlaken	1½	54.00
Lausanne	1½	61.00
Zermatt	1½	49.00
BRUGGE		
Brussels	1½	19.00
BRUSSELS		
Budapest	20½	328.00
Calais	3	50.00
Cologne (Koln)	2½	49.00
Copenhagen (Kobenhavn)	13	279.00
Frankfurt	5½	110.00
Ghent	½	13.00
Hamburg	8	173.00
Liege	1	19.00
Luxembourg	3	41.00
Munich (Munchen)	8½	243.00
Paris (Nord)	3	103.00
Rotterdam	2	34.00
Vienna (Wien) (via Nurnberg)	15	282.00
Zurich	13	160.00
BUCHS		
Innsbruck	3	31.00
Zurich	1½	52.00
BUDAPEST		
Cologne (Koln)	18	280.00
Frankfurt/Main	15½	220.00
Hamburg	18	358.00
Milan	16½	165.00
Munich (Munchen)	11	138.00
Paris (Est)		
via Munich	18	339.00
via Basel	25	325.00
Prague	9½	89.00

Rome	25	205.00
Sofia	13	117.00
Trieste	16	132.00
Venice	13	138.00
Vienna (Wien)	4	51.00
Zurich	18	206.00

CADIZ

Madrid	8	77.00
Seville	6	17.00

CALAIS

Paris (Nord)	3	96.00
Strasbourg	9½	104.00

CANNES

Florence	11	65.00
Geneva	8	114.00
Genoa	3	38.00
Lille	7	185.00
Lyon	5	94.00
Marseille	2	43.00
Milan	7½	53.00
Paris (Lyon)	6	141.00
Rome	13	99.00
San Remo	3	20.00

CARCASSONNE

Lourdes	3	56.00
Marseille	3¼	66.00
Nice	6	97.00
Paris (Austerlitz)	6	132.00
Port Bou	2½	39.00
Toulouse	1	25.00

CHAMONIX-MONT BLANC

Geneva	2½	43.00
Grenoble	2¼	53.00
Martigny (Second-class only)	3	28.00
Paris (Lyon)	8	139.00

CHARTRES
    Paris (Montparnasse)   1   23.00

CHERBOURG
    Paris (St. Lazare)   3½   74.00

CHUR
    St. Moritz   2½   54.00
    Zurich   1½   58.00

COLOGNE (KOLN)		
Copenhagen (Kobenhavn)	10	204.00
Dortmund	1	30.00
Dusseldorf	½	11.00
Essen	1	21.00
Frankfurt	2½	55.00
Hamburg	5	114.00
Hannover	3	76.00
Koblenz	1	23.00
Luxembourg (Via Koblenz)	4	63.00
Luzern	7½	190.00
Mainz	2	50.00
Mannheim	3	71.00
Milan	12	268.00
Munich (Munchen)	6	173.00
Paris (Nord)	6	101.00
Rotterdam	3½	74.00
Salzburg	8½	216.00
Stuttgart	4½	109.00
Vienna (Wien)	12	234.00
Wiesbaden	2	50.00
Zurich	7½	197.00

COIMBRA
    Lisbon   2½   20.00

COMO		
Lugano	½	15.00
Luzern	4	87.00
Milan	1	7.00
Venice	4	39.00
Zurich	4	96.00

COPENHAGEN (KOBENHAVN)

Frankfurt	10½	217.00
Fredrickshavn	7	55.00
Hamburg (via Puttgarden)	5	91.00
Helsinki (Partly by Ship)	23½	163.00
Hoek Van Holland	12	207.00
Kristiansand (Ship)	15½	100.00
Luxembourg (via Koln)	13½	296.00
Malmo (Hydrofoil)	½	27.00
(Not covered by Eurailpass.)		
Milan	20	468.00
Munich (Munchen) (via Berlin)	19	327.00
Narvik	31	184.00
Odense	3	39.00
Oslo	10½	160.00
Paris (Nord)	15	331.00
Rome	25	562.00
Rotterdam	14½	237.00
Stockholm (via Hassleholm)	8	140.00
Trondheim (via Goteborg)	19	266.00
Venice	22	439.00
Vienna (Wien)	19	278.00
Wiesbaden	9½	286.00

CORDOBA

Granada	3½	21.00
Madrid	5	38.00
Malaga	2½	17.00
Seville	2	12.00

DAVOS

St. Moritz	1½	39.00
Zurich	3	77.00

DIJON

Lausanne	3	56.00
Lyon	2	44.00
Paris	2	73.00
Strasbourg (via Belfort)	4	67.00

DORTMUND

Paris (Nord)	7	129.00

DUSSELDORF

Essen	½	11.00
Frankfurt/Main	3	72.00
Hamburg	4	116.00
Hannover	3	78.00
Munich (Munchen)	6½	184.00
Paris (Nord)	6	109.00

FLAM

Myrdal (2nd class fare)	1	19.00
Oslo	6½	101.00

FLORENCE (FIRENZE)

Geneva	10	147.00
Genoa	4	30.00
Innsbruck	8	62.00
Lausanne	9	152.00
Livorno	1½	16.00
Luzern	9	132.00
Marseille	12	100.00
Milan	3	39.00
Munich (Munchen)	10	101.00
Naples	5¼	65.00
Nice	11	57.00
Paris		
(Lyon) via Iselle	15	218.00
(Lyon) via Pisa	18	179.00
(Lyon) via Turin (Torino)	18	172.00
Perugia	2½	21.00
Pisa	1½	11.00
Ravenna	3	18.00
Rome	2½	39.00

Siena	2½	12.00
Turin (Torino)	6	54.00
Venice	3	33.00
Vienna (Wien)	13	116.00

FRANKFURT/MAIN

Hamburg	3½	174.00
Hannover	2½	134.00
Heidelberg	1	39.00
Innsbruck	6	181.00
Luxembourg	4½	78.00
Mainz	½	11.00
Mannheim	1	37.00
Nurnberg	2½	66.00
Paris (Est)	6½	135.00
Rotterdam	6	135.00
Salzburg	5	178.00
Stuttgart	1¼	64.00
Vienna (Wien)	9	174.00
Wiesbaden	½	12.00
Zurich	5	163.00

FREDRICKSHAVN

Hamburg	7½	116.00
Oslo (Ship) (Not covered by Eurailpass.)	10	90.00
Stockholm (Ship) (Not covered by Eurailpass.)	7½	98.00

GARMISCH-PARTENKIRCHEN

Innsbruck	1½	15.00
Munich (Munchen)	1½	29.00

GAVLE

Stockholm	2	44.00

GENEVA

Genoa		
via Milan	7½	103.00
via Turin (Torino)	7	72.00
Grenoble	2	38.00
Grindelwald	3½	104.00
Gstaad	2½	74.00
Interlaken (via Bern)	3	91.00
Lausanne	½	34.00
Locarno	4½	124.00
Lourdes	10	114.00
Luzern	3½	98.00
Lyon	2	38.00
Marseille (via Lyon)	5½	89.00
Milan	6	91.00
Montreux	1	44.00
Nice (via Lyon)	10½	118.00
Paris (Lyon)	3½	110.00
Rome	9¼	176.00
Turin (Torino)	6	64.00
Venice	8	142.00
Zurich	3	110.00

GENOA

Lausanne	7	99.00
Luzern	7½	111.00
Marseille	6½	73.00
Milan	2	21.00
Monaco-Monte Carlo	3	25.00
Munich (Munchen)	11½	112.00
Naples	8½	88.00
Nice	4	30.00
Paris (Lyon) (via Torino)	12	147.00
Pisa	2½	21.00
Rome	7	65.00
Salzburg	14	113.00
San Remo	2	18.00

Turin (Torino)	2½	21.00
Venice	7	48.00

GOTEBORG
Copenhagen (Kobenhavn)	4½	78.00
Hamburg	10	171.00
Helsingborg	3	59.00
Kalmar	5	82.00
Oslo	5	94.00
Stockholm	4½	98.00
Trondheim	21	174.00

GRANADA
Madrid	6½	52.00
Malaga	3	21.00
Seville	4½	31.00
Valencia	8	73.00

GRAZ
Vienna (Wien)	3½	36.00

GRENOBLE
Lyon	1¼	35.00
Marseille	4½	53.00

GRINDELWALD
Interlaken (Not covered by Eurailpass)	1	13.00
Zurich (Only partially covered by Eurailpass)	3½	98.00

HAMBURG
Hannover	1¼	60.00
Heidelberg	5	193.00
Helsinki (Partly by Ship)	33	243.00
Luxembourg	8½	191.00
Munich (Munchen)	6	247.00
Oslo	15½	253.00
Paris (Nord)	9½	225.00

Rotterdam	6½	131.00
Salzburg	10	286.00
Stockholm	13	225.00
Stuttgart	5¼	220.00
Vienna (Wien)	10	310.00

HANNOVER

Munich (Munchen)	4½	198.00
Paris (Nord)	9½	236.00
Rotterdam	5	103.00
Wurzburg	2	129.00

HAPARANDA

Helsinki	12	92.00

HEIDELBERG

Koblenz	2	50.00
Luzern	4½	123.00
Mainz	1	26.00
Munich (Munchen)	3½	98.00
Nurnberg	4	71.00
Paris (Est)	6	122.00
Rothenburg ("Castle Road" Bus)	3	64.00
Stuttgart	1	31.00
Wiesbaden	1½	29.00

HELSINKI

Kuopio	6	64.00
Oslo (Partly by Ship)	22	164.00
Oulu	7½	86.00
Stockholm (Ship)	12½	68.00
Turku	2¼	32.00

HENDAYE

Lisbon	17	101.00
Lourdes	2½	40.00
Madrid	10	69.00

Paris (Austerlitz)	5½	139.00
Zaragoza	4¼	36.00

HOEK VAN HOLLAND

Innsbruck	13	293.00
Munich (Munchen)	12	250.00
Rotterdam	½	8.00

INNSBRUCK

Kitzbuhel	1	19.00
Luzern	6	102.00
Milan	6½	56.00
Munich (Munchen)	4	44.00
Paris (Est)	11½	204.00
Rome	12	102.00
Salzburg	4	43.00
Venice	5	50.00
Verona	5	38.00
Vienna (Wien)	8	89.00
Zurich	5	85.00

INTERLAKEN

Lausanne	2	71.00
Luzern	2	33.00
Milan	5	79.00
Montreux	3	74.00
Paris (Lyon) via Verrieres	7½	154.00
Zurich	3	85.00

KARLSTAD

Oslo	3	64.00
Stockholm	3½	76.00

KLAGENFURT

Salzburg	4	40.00
Venice	4½	41.00
Vienna (Wein)	6	54.00

KLOSTERS
Zurich   2½   71.00

KOBLENZ

Luxembourg	2½	42.00
Munich (Munchen)	5½	149.00
Paris (via Reims)	7	115.00
Vienna (Wien)	10	209.00
Wiesbaden	1	26.00

KONSTANZ
Zurich   1   36.00

KRISTIANSAND

Oslo	5	93.00
Stavanger	3½	65.00

LAUSANNE

Locarno	4	106.00
Lugano	5½	119.00
Luzern	3	78.00
Milan	4½	87.00
Montreux	½	12.00
Paris (Lyon)	4	140.00
Rome	13¼	157.00
Venice	8½	123.00
Zurich	2½	91.00

LE HAVRE
Paris (St. Lazare)   2½   48.00

LIEGE

Luxembourg	3	29.00
Paris (Nord)	4	72.00

LINZ

Salzburg	2	24.00
Vienna (Wien)	2	32.00

LISBON

Madrid (Atocha)	9	68.00
Paris (Austerlitz)	25	229.00

Porto	4	28.00
Santiago de Compostela	9	51.00
Seville	12	57.00
Vigo	9	42.00

LIVORNO
Pisa	½	3.00
Rome	3	39.00

LOCARNO
Lugano	1	23.00
Luzern	3	77.00
Milan	1	42.00
Zurich	3½	84.00

LOURDES
Madrid	12	109.00
Paris (Austerlitz)	6½	143.00
Toulouse	2	41.00

LUGANO
Luzern	3	78.00
Milan	1½	20.00
Venice	6	51.00
Zurich	3½	85.00

LUXEMBOURG
Marseille	10	138.00
Metz	1	18.00
Munich (Munchen)	7	201.00
Nurnberg	7	150.00
Paris (Est)	4	85.00
Salzburg (via Strasbourg)	10	242.00
Strasbourg	3	47.00
Stuttgart (via Strasbourg)	6	95.00
Vienna (Wien)	13	250.00
Zurich	5	120.00

LUZERN
Milan	4½	92.00
Montreux	5½	90.00

Munich (Munchen)	6½	134.00
Paris (Est)	7½	134.00
Rigi	1½	47.00
Rome	12¼	166.00
Venice	8	123.00
Vienna (Wein)	13	173.00
Zurich	1	34.00

LYON
Marseille	3	67.00
Milan	4½	79.00
Nice	5	98.00
Paris (Lyon)	2	102.00
Strasbourg	5½	84.00
Turin (Torino)	4½	62.00
Tours	7	131.00

MADRID
Malaga	7	67.00
Pamplona	8½	48.00
Paris (Austerlitz)	13	197.00
Port Bou	10	90.00
Rome	34	280.00
San Sebastian	7	67.00
Santiago de Compostela	7½	71.00
Seville	5	61.00
Toledo	1¼	8.00
Valencia	4¼	44.00
Vigo	8	71.00
Zaragoza	3	36.00

MAINZ
Munich (Munchen)	4	124.00
Paris	6½	128.00

MALAGA
Seville	3½	25.00

MALMO

Stockholm	6	115.00

MARSEILLE

Milan	9½	88.00
Nice	2½	48.00
Paris (Lyon)	5	119.00
Port Bou	4½	72.00
Rome	15	134.00
Toulouse	4	79.00
Venice	17	123.00

MILAN

Montreux	4	78.00
Munich (Munchen)	8½	95.00
Naples	6¼	100.00
Nice	5	45.00
Padua	3	30.00
Paris (Est) via Chiasso	9	212.00
Paris (Lyon) via Vallorbe	7½	182.00
Rome	5¼	76.00
Stuttgart	9	163.00
Turin (Torino)	2	21.00
Trieste	6	54.00
Venice	3	33.00
Verona	1½	18.00
Vienna	15½	116.00
Zurich	4½	101.00

MONTREUX

Paris (Lyon)	4½	115.00
Zurich	3	98.00

MOSJOEN

Oslo	14	175.00

MUNICH (MUNCHEN)

Nurnberg	2	67.00
Oberammergau	2	27.00

Paris (Est)	8½	201.00
Rome	13¼	141.00
Rotterdam	11	247.00
Salzburg	2	42.00
Stuttgart	2	78.00
Venice (via Innsbruck)	9	86.00
Vienna (Wien)	6	93.00
Wiesbaden	4	139.00
Zurich	5	112.00

MYRDAL

Oslo	5½	86.00

NANCY

Paris (Est)	3	74.00

NAPLES

Nice	14	115.00
Paris (Lyon)		
via Rome-Florence	20¼	281.00
via Rome-Pisa	23½	232.00
Reggio Calabria	5½	59.00
Rome	2	27.00
Taranto	5	39.00
Turin (Torino)	10	106.00
Venice	8½	94.00
Vienna (Wien)	18¼	180.00

NARVIK

Oslo	33	204.00
Stockholm	22	161.00

NICE

Paris (Lyon)	7	144.00
Rome (via Pisa)	10	91.00
Turin (Torino)	6	42.00
Venice	10	80.00

OSLO

Stavanger	8½	141.00
Stockholm	6½	134.00
Trondheim	7	135.00
Voss	5½	97.00

PALERMO

Paris (Lyon)	32	268.00
Rome	13	112.00

PARIS

Port Bou (Austerlitz)	10½	146.00
Rheims (Est)	2	43.00
Rome (Lyon) via Pisa	15	208.00
Rouen (St. Laz.)	1¼	38.00
Salzburg (Est) (via Munich)	10	243.00
San Sebastian (Austerlitz)	7	130.00
Stockholm (Nord)	25	451.00
Strasbourg (Est)	4	93.00
Stuttgart (Est)	6	135.00
Toulouse (Austerlitz)	7	125.00
Tours (Aust.)	2	71.00
Trieste (Lyon)	14	229.00
Turin (Torino) - (Lyon)	6½	130.00
Venice (Lyon) via Vallorbe	12¼	218.00
Vienna (Wein) - (Est)	13½	275.00
Zurich (Est)	6	141.00

PERUGIA

Rome	3	27.00

PISA

Rome	3½	42.00
Siena	2½	16.00

PRAGUE

Rome	38¼	207.00
Vienna (Wein)	8	61.00
Warsaw	13	68.00

RATTVIK
Stockholm   3   68.00

RAVENNA
Rimini   1   7.00
Venice   3   24.00

RIMINI
Venice   3½   33.00

ROME
Siena   4½   33.00
Trieste   7   88.00
Turin (Torino)   7   82.00
Venice   5¼   71.00
Vienna (Wien)   19¼   156.00
Zurich   8¼   175.00

ROTTERDAM
Vienna (Wein)   19   309.00

SALZBURG
Trieste   7½   57.00
Venice   7½   63.00
Vienna (Wien)   4   51.00
Villach   3   32.00
Zurich   8½   124.00

STOCKHOLM
Trondheim   12½   155.00
Turku (ship)   12½   37.00
Uppsala   1   15.00

STUTTGART
Vienna (Wien)   7   171.00
Zurich   4   78.00

TRIESTE
Venice	2½	21.00
Vienna (Wien)	10	83.00

TURIN (Torino)
Venice	5	54.00

VENICE
Verona	2	16.00
Vienna (Wien)	10	89.00
Zurich	7	135.00

VIENNA (WIEN)
Zurich	12	156.00

INDEX OF CITIES, RESORTS
AND SCENIC PLACES

ORDER FORM European Rail Passes
Prices effective Jan. 1, 1996

EURAIL PASS (17 Countries) 1st Class

Days	❑ $522	2 Months	❑ $1,148
Days	❑ $678	3 Months	❑ $1,468
Month	❑ $838		

EURAIL FLEXIPASS – 1st Class

❑ Days in 2 Months	❑ $616
❑ Days in 2 Months	❑ $812

EURAIL SAVERPASS – 1st Class

❑ Days	❑ $452	1 Month	❑ $712
❑ Days	❑ $578		

*ʳice is per person / 3 people must travel together
all times. (Two people may travel between Oct.
st and March 31st)*

hildren 4 - 11 half fare – Children under 4 free

EURAIL YOUTHPASS* – 2nd Class

❑ Days	❑ $418	2 Months	❑ $798
Month	❑ $598		

EURAIL YOUTH FLEXIPASS* – 2nd

❑ Days in 2 Months	❑ $438
❑ Days in 2 Months	❑ $588

**Pass holder must be under age 26
on first day of use.*

EURAIL DRIVE PASS

here is an excellent Rail/Drive program that
ombines a Eurail Flexipass with Hertz or Avis
ent-a-Car. Call us for a brochure and prices.

EUROPASS (5 Countries)
France / Germany / Italy / Switz. / Spain

3 COUNTRIES EUROPASS – 1st Class

5 Days in 2 Months	❑ $316
6 Days in 2 Months	❑ $358
7 Days in 2 Months	❑ $400

4 COUNTRIES EUROPASS – 1st Class

8 Days in 2 Months	❑ $442
9 Days in 2 Months	❑ $484
10 Days in 2 Months	❑ $526

5 COUNTRIES EUROPASS – 1st Class

11 Days in 2 Months	❑ $568
12 Days in 2 Months	❑ $610
13 Days in 2 Months	❑ $652
14 Days in 2 Months	❑ $694
15 Days in 2 Months	❑ $736

*Note: You must specify the countries when ordering
and countries must border each other.*

Europass Youth available for ages up to 26 in 2nd
class at substantial discounts. Call us for prices.

EUROPASS ASSOCIATE COUNTRIES

These countries may be added to any EuroPass for a
flat charge per country. They expand the geographic
scope of the pass, not the duration.

❑ Austria $45	❑ Portugal $29
❑ Benelux $42	❑ Greece $90
(Belgium/Luxembourg/	*(Includes Brendisi-Patras*
Netherlands)	*Ferry HML/ADN-RT)*

SPECIAL EUROPASS BONUS
*Second adult receives half fare
discount on all Europasses*

For Travelers from North America

CALL TOLL FREE 1-800-367-7984 – ASK FOR DEPT. EW6

(Charge to Visa, Discover or MasterCard)

FORSYTH TRAVEL LIBRARY, INC.

9154 W. 57th, P.O. Box 2975 Dept. EW6 • Shawnee Mission, KS 66201-1375

*Forsyth Travel Library, Inc., is the leading agent in North America for the European and British
Railroads and distributor of the famous Thomas Cook European Timetable. Members: ASTA,
Better Business Bureau of Kansas City, MO and International Map Trades Association.
Free catalogs upon request listing all rail passes, timetables, Hostel Memberships, Maps, etc.
All prices shown are US Dollars.*

ORDER FORM European Rail Passes
Prices effective Jan. 1, 1996

AUSTRIA RAILPASS

Any 4 Days in 10 Days	❑ $165 1st Class
	❑ $111 2nd Class

BENELUX TOURPASS

Any 5 Days in 1 Month	❑ $217 *1st Class*
	❑ $155 *2nd Class*

FRANCE RAILPASS

	1st Class	2nd Class
3 Days in 1 Month	❑ $198	❑ $160
Add'l Rail Days (6 max)	❑ $30	❑ $30

Couples: Special Discounts. Call for Rates.

France offers a comprehensive series of Rail 'n Drive, Rail 'n Fly & Fly Rail 'n Drive passes. Ask for our free catalog and prices.

GERMAN RAILPASS – Adult

Validity	1st Class/Twin*	2nd Class/Twin*
5 Days in 1 Mo.	❑ $260/$390	❑ $178/$267
10 Days in 1 Mo.	❑ $410/$615	❑ $286/$429
15 Days in 1 Mo.	❑ $530/$795	❑ $386/$579

Twin: Total price for 2 adults traveling together. Call for German Rail youth Pass Prices.

GREEK FLEXIPASS

	1st Class-Adult	Child
3 Days in 1 Month	❑ $86	❑ $58
5 Days in 1 Month	❑ $120	❑ $85

PRAGUE EXCURSION PASS

From any Czech Republic border crossing to Prague and return First Class – within 7 days.

❑ $49 Adult	❑ $39 Youth	❑ $25 Child

SPAIN FLEXIPASS

	1st Class	2nd Class
Any 3 Days in 2 Months	❑ $180	❑ $144
Add'l Rail Days (7 Max)	❑ $40	❑ $32

(AVE & TALGO 200 require a supplement)

ITALIAN RAILPASS

Please add a $15 admin. fee to the cost of each Italian pass/non-refundable

	1st Class	2nd Class
8 Days	❑ $248	❑ $168
15 Days	❑ $312	❑ $208
21 Days	❑ $362	❑ $242
1 Month	❑ $436	❑ $290

ITALIAN FLEXI RAILCARD

Any 4 Days in 1 Month	❑ $194	❑ $132
Any 8 Days in 1 Month	❑ $284	❑ $184
Any 12 Days in 1 Month	❑ $356	❑ $238

ITALIAN KILOMETRIC TICKET

3,000 Kilometers in 20 Trips.

1st Class ❑ $264	2nd Class ❑ $156

SCANRAIL PASS

	1st Class	2nd Class
Any 5 Days in 15	❑ $222	❑ $176
Any 10 Days in 1 Month	❑ $346	❑ $278
21 Day - Continuous	❑ $400	❑ $320
1 Month - Continuous	❑ $504	❑ $404

Call for Youth and ScanRail 55+ Senior rates

SWISS PASS

Good on Swiss National Railroads, most private railroads, lake steamers, city transport, trams, etc.

	Adults		Couples/each	
	1st Cl.	2nd Cl.	1st Cl.	2nd Cl.
4 Days	❑ $264	❑ $176	❑ $198	❑ $132
8 Days	❑ $316	❑ $220	❑ $237	❑ $165
15 Days	❑ $368	❑ $265	❑ $276	❑ $192
1 Month	❑ $508	❑ $350	❑ $381	❑ $262

SWISS FLEXIPASS

Any 3 Days in 15 Days	❑ $264	❑ $176	❑ $198 ❑ $132

SWISS CARD

1 Month/1 Round Trip	❑ $142	❑ $116

(Couples Passes valid 5/1/96 - 10/31/96 only)

NOT SHOWN: Rail Passes for Hungary, Bulgaria, Portugal, Benelux, Holland, Norway, Finland & East Europe, Czech Republic. Call for 1996 Rates and Plans. We can also handle sleepers, ferry bookings, point-to-point tickets, groups, etc.

SHIPPING There is a $9.50 handling and priority shipping charge for all orders using 2nd Day/AIR UPS Rush service with overnight delivery is available for $25. RAIL/DRIVE Programs are available for most countries. Call for rates and free brochures.